ROUGH COUNTRY

ROUGH COUNTRY

How Texas Became America's Most Powerful Bible-Belt State

Robert Wuthnow

PRINCETON UNIVERSITY PRESS

Princeton and Oxford

Copyright © 2014 by Princeton University Press
Published by Princeton University Press, 41 William Street, Princeton, New Jersey 08540
In the United Kingdom: Princeton University Press, 6 Oxford Street, Woodstock, Oxfordshire OX20 1TW

press.princeton.edu

Library of Congress Cataloging-in-Publication Data

Wuthnow, Robert.
Rough country : how Texas became America's most powerful Bible-belt state / Robert Wuthnow.
pages   cm
Includes bibliographical references and index.
ISBN 978-0-691-15989-8 (hardcover : alk. paper) 1. Texas—Church history. I. Title.
BR555.T4W88 2014
277.64—dc23
2013025817

British Library Cataloging-in-Publication Data is available

This book has been composed in Minion Pro and Memphis

Printed on acid-free paper.

Printed in the United States of America

10 9 8 7 6 5 4 3 2 1

CONTENTS

Introduction   1

CHAPTER 1
In Rough Country   14
Bringing Order to the New Frontier

CHAPTER 2
For the Advance of Civilization   51
Institution Building and Moral Character

CHAPTER 3
With Liberty of Conscience   88
Defining the Separation of Church and State

CHAPTER 4
The Fundamentalist Belt   121
Coming to Terms with Science

CHAPTER 5
From Judge Lynch to Jim Crow   154
Celebrating Limited Inclusion

CHAPTER 6
A Load Too Heavy   196
Religion and the Debate over Government Relief

CHAPTER 7
Moving onto the National Stage   225
Everything Is Big

CHAPTER 8
Meanest, Dirtiest, Low-Down Stuff   269
The Politics of Tumult

CHAPTER 9
Power to the People   303
Framing the Issues, Taking Sides

CHAPTER 10
God Can Save Us   325
The Campaign for a Moral America

CHAPTER 11
In a Compassionate Way   369
Connecting Faith and Politics

CHAPTER 12
An Independent Lot   409
Religion and Grassroots Activism

CHAPTER 13
Afterword   448
Religion and the Politics of Identity

Acknowledgments   483

Notes   485

Selected Bibliography   593

Index   627

ROUGH COUNTRY

INTRODUCTION

O n Sunday, May 11, 1845, Nicholas and Anton Riedel, recent arrivals with
their family from Germany, penned a letter from their new home in
Texas. The journey had been long and filled with anticipation. But what
stood out more than anything else, now that they were here, was the freedom and
the fact that people were treated equally. "This is a free land," they wrote, "and
the poorest is regarded and respected as the richest. Here no one has priority."[1]

The previous day a group of nearly three hundred Baptist leaders gathered in
Augusta, Georgia. They too valued freedom. The central issue was freedom to
own slaves, against the wishes of their northern counterparts. To be of service
to the heathen and the destitute, they formed the Southern Baptist Convention.[2]

How does religion shape a nation? Is it through the private beliefs of individuals who quietly pursue their faith in small ways? Is it through convictions
that show up at work, through families, and perhaps at the voting booth? Does it
come about through high-profile clergy who organize powerful mass movements
and capture the attention of public officials? Or does religion matter much at all?
Perhaps nations are moved only by economic and political self-interest.

When these questions are asked of America, they elicit answers that reflect the
nation's distinctive religious history. Seekers of religious freedom settled America, the argument goes, and we became a nation in which competing denominations gave voice to different ethnic groups and races and the various nationalities
that constituted the population. America became a nation of Christians and Jews,
Protestants and Catholics, and numerous smaller traditions. Its religious heritage
gained expression in the First Amendment, in a commonsense understanding of
biblical morality, and in thousands of meeting halls and places of worship. More
recently the story includes chapters about the role of religious leaders in the civil
rights movement and in electoral politics and referenda about abortion, gay marriage, school prayer, intelligent design, and a host of related issues.[3]

But that story about America writ large fails to capture a huge portion of what
religion is actually about. Religion may be painted in broad brushstrokes as the
beliefs and practices of Christians and Jews, Protestants and Catholics, and other
traditions, but it is fundamentally experienced in specific locations. It happens

among families and in neighborhoods. People worship in congregations and share their convictions and doubts with friends, coworkers, and fellow believers. For this reason a valuable approach to the study of religion has emerged in recent years focusing on the lived practices of people in congregations and communities.[4]

Yet, as interesting as these microlevel studies are, they tell us little about the larger influences of religion beyond the family, neighborhood, or congregation. They show that a congregation encourages volunteer work, for example, or that women feel empowered from participating in the congregation, but beyond that the *implications* become murky. It may help to know that there are thousands of such congregations. And yet congregations are only part of the story.

The most neglected aspect of American religion occurs in the middle range at the level that bridges families and congregations with the nation. It was here that Alexis de Tocqueville saw the key to American democracy when he visited in the 1830s.[5] Families and congregations effectively combine and channel their interests through entities that are large enough to convey power and yet not so large as to be impersonally beyond reach. This is American federalism, or, more precisely, the multitiered layers of government that span from boroughs and townships upward through counties to states and congressional districts. Something similar characterizes American religion as well. Congregations join together in associations, dioceses, and presbyteries, and these form larger organizations called denominations.

These vertically and horizontally bridging organizations, though, are only part of what must be considered at the middle range. Religious practices interlace with local and regional traditions. The religious idioms through which faith is expressed are inflected by myths of origin, by prevailing understandings of race and ethnicity, and by stories of major events, such as civil conflicts and natural disasters. Bringing these into focus requires situating religion in a place that includes local communities but that also extends beyond them.

Religion functions at this intermediate level of social organization to infuse meaning about divine purposes into the particular circumstances in which people live, including the dangers they may face, the lines that divide or unite them, and their aspirations. The dangers include universals such as illness and death but also the local uncertainties of crop failures and unemployment or threats from hostile neighbors. Lines of division and unity stem from racial and ethnic identities, differences of wealth and occupation, and political partisanship. Aspirations include hopes for a more secure livelihood, safety, and the civic institutions necessary to ensure the lives and ambitions of a coming generation. Religious idioms and practices embed themselves in these wider circumstances of life.

It is this embedding in turn through which religion exercises its shaping influence. Religious idioms provide the language in which stories are told about heroes and villains, enemies and friends. These narratives influence racial and ethnic divisions and how to think about them. Religious organizations form that facilitate the continuing separation of races or their coming together. These organizations facilitate the creation and maintenance of additional institutions. By articulating with an expanding population with access to enlarged resources, the idioms and practices perpetuate themselves.

In sociological parlance, the lines of division that define and separate religious traditions, ethnic groups, and racial categories can be understood as symbolic boundaries—conceptual categories present in the public mind in ways that also shape who interacts with whom and on what basis.[6] Symbolic boundaries ebb and flow in political salience and meaning, with some constituting enduring inequalities, especially between races, while others, such as the language in which people classify themselves religiously, are often more fungible. Looking closely at a distinct geographic region over an extended period of time provides an opportunity to see how these changes occur.

I have selected instances in which the continuities and changes in categories defining the relationships among religion, race, and ethnicity can be observed in some detail. The relationships show that symbolic boundaries are influenced by the practices through which clergy and lay leaders build congregations and form alliances among those congregations—processes that demonstrate the extent to which religious leaders themselves occupy a precarious midlevel social position dependent on the approval, as it were, of authorities above and members of the local community under their charge. The relevant categories into which religious affinities are classified are in turn closely related to wider power arrangements and institutions.

This argument builds on the tradition of scholarship that emphasizes religion's role in human adaptation to the exigencies of daily life. In this understanding religion offers hope in the midst of routine hardships. It provides comfort and encouragement. For many, faith is a source of transcendence, an avenue for experiencing awe and for expressing reverence. Under widely varying circumstances, religion reinforces moral discipline and promotes cooperation. It is sometimes a source of empowerment that facilitates efforts to combat suffering and exploitation. In the process it may of course generate conflict and exacerbate bigotry.[7]

For generations of Americans who came as immigrants and carved a new life in small towns and on the open frontier, the idea of a rough country was a way of describing the exigencies of life. Rough country was terrain difficult to traverse, farmland yet to be improved, thickets needing to be cleared, and roads impassable from rain and mud. It was dangerous territory inhabited by villains and scoundrels, a place subject to the threat of ruffians. It was hardship, the grinding struggle for daily existence that stood in the way of a better life in which beauty, wonder, and creativity could more fully be expressed. To people proud of fine breeding it connoted an absence of good manners, a rough society in which roughnecks prevailed. It meant the rough treatment slaveholders inflicted on slaves. It often meant the prospect of dying in childbirth or from an incurable illness. Rough country was the equivalent of problems that are of major twenty-first-century concern such as cancer, addiction, pandemic influenza, and weapons of mass destruction.

Religion is often thought of as the vehicle through which the exigencies of life can be escaped, perhaps by anticipating release from the present veil of tears in a perfect life to come. That may be part of it, but it is not all that religion does. The comfort that religion seeks to provide also comes through the social solidarity it facilitates and through the rituals that draw people together as well as the acts of service it promotes. It may be evident in the lament of a bereaved loved one or, as we will see, in less expected places, such as a public hanging.

A second way in which religion shapes a community or a nation is in defining evil and identifying an appropriate means of resisting it. Symbolic boundaries are not just mental categories that divide the world into "us" and "them" for purposes of cognitive convenience. The "other" is often demonized as a group in league with evil forces. Evil may reside in the person of an ominous satanic force or in more tangible dangers, such as a marauding enemy, an alien regime, or a savage neighbor. Religious leaders may take it upon themselves to draw sharp boundaries between good and evil and to show what must be done to guard against evil. The mourners' bench is a place for such definitions to be driven home. So also may be the cry of outrage that leads to an act of vengeance.

Undergirding conventional definitions of respect is a third way in which religion influences its contexts. Whether one is rich or poor, one of the hallmarks of social status for the occupants of any social category is respect. Being a person of faith is often a means of being known as a respectable and respected member of the community. Being respected implies that a person can be trusted to behave responsibly whether in business or as a neighbor. Earning respect requires conforming to certain shared standards of morality and perhaps attempting to impose those standards on other members of the community.

And then religion addresses the exigencies of life not only through symbolic definitional endeavors but also through institution building. Congregations become the vehicles through which hospitals and orphanages are constructed. Religious leaders organize and staff schools that promote literacy and colleges that train nurses and social workers. Efforts are made to advance civilization in ways that render living in rough country less difficult. The process of institution building of course requires resources and usually brings religion into closer contact with the people who command these resources, especially public officials. The relationships between religious organizations and government agencies reflect continuing debates about who has the right to lay claim to public goods and for what purposes.

As an institution builder, religion's role has always gravitated between generating and controlling its own resources, on the one hand, and forging ties with and facilitating the growth of organizations in wider spheres, on the other hand. Religious leaders understandably encourage members to be faithful supporters of congregations, to adhere to particular doctrines and styles of worship, and to spend time at activities organized under religious auspices. In short, they want social networks to be centered in congregations. At the same time, religion's influence is limited if it only focuses on its own activities. Its influence increases to the extent that it bridges into such wider venues as education, health care, charitable service, and government as well as forming specialized organizations to promote particular moral agendas and policies. A recurrent tension exists between these two tendencies, encouraging religious leaders especially to stay within their own domain and yet repeatedly promoting wider social involvement as well.

In the United States these religious activities have been profoundly influenced by race. The nation's history of slavery resulted not only in a legacy of racial inequality and discrimination but also in racially segregated communities and institutions. Religious institutions evolved as predominantly segregated congregations and denominations with distinctive traditions and leadership styles. And yet there was typically mutual awareness and interaction. Comfort, evil, and respect were defined with racial connotations. Institution building ran in racially segregated channels and occasionally transcended them.

The particular case under investigation here provides an opportunity to examine over a period of approximately a century and a half how religious organizations developed in a context charged not only by racial and ethnic divisions but also by a long trajectory of new settlement and economic expansion. The process involves religion as a source of comfort and encouragement, a means of defining and resisting evil, a provision of respect, and a facilitator of institutions through which civilization was to be advanced. From slavery through Reconstruction, to a long history of lynching and Jim Crow segregation, and through mobilization for and against civil rights, race was a prominent influence. Racial separation was often perpetuated by religious organizations, only to be challenged repeatedly by wider connections established through benevolent associations, moral crusades, and new government initiatives. The result was a deeply religious part of America that has had an increasingly powerful influence on the nation.

Texas is America's most powerful Bible-Belt state. It is the most populous, resource-rich, and politically influential part of the nation in which theologically conservative Protestant churchgoing thrives. Twice as many Southern Baptists— the nation's largest and one of its most theologically and politically conservative denominations—live in Texas as in any other state. For many years the nation's largest Southern Baptist congregation was located in Dallas. Today Dallas and Houston are home to some of the nation's largest predominantly white, predominantly African American, and predominantly Hispanic megachurches. Several of these congregations claim to have more than twenty thousand members. In addition, Texas has long been a center of religious radio and television broadcasting and has attracted some of the most influential international ministries that send out preaching and advice videos as well as worship services and music around the globe.

As important as these religious organizations are, my interest in them stems less from their size and more from what we can learn from their history and location. American religion cannot be understood apart from considering its reciprocal relationship with race. The familiar observation that white and black churches evolved as and largely continue to be separate institutions does not go far enough. It also mattered that this institutional separation bred misunderstanding and indeed fear as well as inequality. American religion was profoundly shaped as well by the frontier experience, the westward movement grounded in the nation's sense of manifest destiny, and the dangers involved. National encounters and immigration have repeatedly altered the contours of American religion. These are the local and regional influences that require closer scrutiny.

Besides the sheer size and strength of the state's churches, Texas residents who are known for their personal faith or as leaders with interests influenced by religion have played a singularly important role in the nation's economic affairs and in politics. Entrepreneurs, oil moguls, and politicians with names such as Bass, Bush, Butt, Hunt, Johnson, LeTourneau, and Perry are among the state's and the nation's most influential figures, past and present. With more representatives in the U.S. Congress than any other state except California, and having been the home of several of the nation's most powerful senators and representatives, as well as of three recent U.S. presidents, Texas has been well positioned to exert its influence far beyond its own borders.

All this lends itself to Texans' long-held belief that their place in America is unique. It is the only state, Texans proudly proclaim, that has been under six flags. It is the only state ever to have declared its own independence as a separate republic. It is by far the largest state in sheer land area of any part of the United States between Mexico and Canada. More oil and gas have been supplied from here than from any other state. Even the climate is more varied than almost anywhere else in the country. In considering the role that religion and race have played, it would thus seem appropriate to treat Texas as if it were different from any other part of America.

However, that is not the perspective from which the material here is presented. Although it is true that much about Texas is distinctive to its own location and history, Texas also serves valuably as a place in which to examine the developments and cultural dynamics that have over the past century and a half decidedly shaped America. It lends itself especially well to examining the complex relationships that emerged and changed in the years immediately following the American Civil War among African Americans and white landowners and residents, and to understand those relationships as families moved from farms to cities, and in the context of a growing Hispanic population. Because of its large land area and varied climate, Texas took longer than any other state to be settled and to transform its basic institutions into the orderly system of governance and social control to which its leaders aspired. A focus on the activities of its communities and congregations evokes a larger story of how Americans confronted their fears of evil and how they struggled to overcome roughness as they perceived it in their midst.

The story I tell here is an interpretation of those complex singular developments that occurred in this particular part of our nation. It is a story that foregrounds the interaction of religion and race and how that interaction in turn at each period influenced what was to come later. These influences shifted from decade to decade. It would be unsatisfactory, for example, to argue that everything later stemmed from the fact that Texas was settled predominantly by southerners or that it joined the Confederacy. Nor would it be satisfactory to argue that a culture of violence shaped all that followed.

The argument is rather about a series of processes that happen in distinctive ways and yet illuminate aspects of the relationship between religion and society that are best seen at this intermediate level of social organization. One of these processes derives from the ordering, chaos-reducing, *nomizing* role that nearly all discussions of the relationship between religion and society have emphasized. A significant aspect of that ordering role is assisting communities as well as individuals in coming to terms with the exigencies of life, particularly death and the fear of death as well as bereavement and suffering. Although specific threats, such as death from a contagious disease, may be dealt with, there is also likely to be ambiguity and indeed spillover such that dangers are mapped onto one another and blended. The blending of danger from illness, frontier life, and racial differences is particularly powerful in its religious and cultural implications.

Another connection between religion and its social environment involves efforts to define and combat evil. Religion does this through theological arguments. Preaching and teaching informs the faithful about the presence of evil and tells how to avoid it. Sometimes the arguments identify people of other races and ethnicities as singularly dangerous. Religion also combats evil by building institutions. The hope of advancing a more civilized social order in newly settled places, for example, is pursued by founding places of worship, schools, and benevolent associations. Those efforts take place amid an awareness that evil exists outside of these institutions and continues to threaten them.

For its part, institution building creates heroes and villains about whom stories are told and who serve as positive or negative role models for future generations. Fallen soldiers, great leaders, cowboys, and wildcat oil drillers may be among the most familiar heroes and villains, but circuit riders, poorly educated frontier preachers, school teachers, and even victims of lynch mobs may be among them as well. These heroes and villains provide personified symbols of larger themes, such as the value of being a free spirit or of contributing to the development of one's community.

The interplay among specific religious beliefs and practices and these wider themes includes a prevailing tension between the roughness of lived experience, especially in new settlements on the open frontier, and aspirations for a more civilized society in which danger from violence and disease is reduced and moral behavior is rewarded. The interplay includes a recurring ambivalence especially among the white population about the roles that African Americans are expected to play, ranging from subservience to cooperation to self-improvement. A further interplay casts regional independence and personal autonomy against national identity and incorporation. The shifting definition of the region itself in relation to the United States, Mexico, the North, South, and Southwest emerges as a continuing theme.

Although the story of the place we call Texas could begin with Spanish explorers in the sixteenth century or with indigenous people considerably earlier, the narrative in which the state's influence as an emerging power in the American Bible Belt dominates begins much later. After the scattered settlements established there by Americans from other states in the 1820s, and following the victory at San Jacinto that led to independence in 1836, eastern Texas attracted a steady stream of settlers in the 1840s and 1850s. With statehood in 1846, the population reached 212,592 in 1850 and then climbed to 604,215 by the 1860s. Having been settled largely by residents from the Deep South and having relied heavily on slavery to develop its growing cotton industry, Texas joined the Confederacy and with the rest of the South experienced the Civil War and Reconstruction in ways that would long shape its self-perception. Especially during Reconstruction and in the years immediately following, a new relationship between blacks and whites, and between religion and politics, was formed that would influence much that was to come.

Three themes in particular become evident in these years. For the white population, religious involvement is not only a source of assurance about eternal salvation but also a reliable means of attaining and demonstrating respectability. That is especially true among families who are or who aspire to be regarded as members of the respected middle class. For the black population, religion is more clearly a means of dealing with insecurity and making sense of suffering. That is also true for those among the white population who have fewer resources. Neither theme is particularly surprising or by any means unique. Both are themes that have been evident before and that will remain in other locations. But on the emerging frontier and with the aftereffects of war far from settled, there is a third theme which is best expressed in the observation that nearly everything is rough: the land is rough, earning a living is rough, the people are rough, even the preachers are rough. What to make of this roughness, and how to overcome it, are the most basic questions of everyday life.

During the quarter century from around 1870 to 1895, the struggle to overcome roughness gains expression largely through efforts to define and restrain evil. Nearly every firsthand account during this period, whether from newspaper stories or from letters and diaries, speaks of troubling, violent, and even catastrophic events. Neighbors are killed, women are raped, bad weather destroys crops, and people die from typhoid and yellow fever. The word that appears again and again is outrage. Innocent citizens have been the victims of outrage

committed against them by Union soldiers or by federal agents during Reconstruction. Outrage has been committed against white women, reports declare, by
surly, dark-skinned bucks. Indian raids periodically effect outrage among settlers
on the new frontier. It is this sense of outrage, either as having happened to one's
family or neighbors or as an imminent threat, that stands always in the background as people seek ways to restrain evil through their beliefs, their efforts to
build churches, and their attempts to gain social control.

By the end of the nineteenth century, these efforts have achieved sufficient
success that a new kind of individualism is evident. This individualism is possible because of the social institutions that have been successfully established.
It differs from the ragged individualism usually associated with life on the open
plains or with the rugged cowboy spirit so often associated with the region. It is
of course resonant with the emphasis on personal salvation that has always been
central to American Protestant Christianity. But now it is more nearly the kind
of personal ethic that Alexis de Tocqueville argued was needed when he visited
America in the 1830s and hoped would become more pervasive as American
democracy progressed. He called it individualism rightly understood. It combined the pursuit of individual self-interest with an appropriate level of self-
restraint oriented toward the common good. It was, as many of Tocqueville's interpreters were to suggest in later years, an ethical commitment instilled in the
conscience of good citizens. However, what closer inspection of the evidence
shows is that it also required a framework of established and reliable institutions. Right-minded individualism depended on knowing that one's property
was protected by law, that one's children could better themselves by attending
local schools, and that there were opportunities to be pursued in business and
the professions. In religion, this is the social context in which personal piety
increasingly comes to focus on leading an orderly and productive life in the
present world.

As religious and civic institutions expanded, the emerging understanding
of individual responsibility necessarily posed questions about the relationships
among these institutions. In particular, there were questions about the appropriate role of clergy in relation to government, and about how best to ensure
individual liberty while maintaining a desired level of social order. The resources
available for working out the answers to these questions are invariably present in
the founding myths of a nation, or in the case of Texas, in its myths of origin as a
republic. The watchword was liberty: liberty of conscience, liberty from tyranny,
and liberty from religious authority. And yet it included respect for certain interpretations of that authority. It was significant that the region's dominant religion
was Baptist, and that Baptists could look to a tradition that called for strict separation of church and state. But it was also significant that the region could point
to a time when the Roman Catholic Church had prevailed under Mexican rule
and that a growing share of the population was Catholic. As the national strength
of the Democratic Party increasingly depended not only on the Protestant South

but also on the votes of Catholics in northern cities, these traditions required new thinking and redefinition.

Against the backdrop of anti-Catholicism and concerns about the shifting role of African Americans, Texas became the home of white fundamentalist preachers who fought evolution and modernist theology by inveighing against it from large urban pulpits and in the state legislature. Important as they were in founding and growing new congregations, they were more influential in pulling the large Baptist and Methodist denominations that dominated the state to the right. There was reason to believe that Texas was part of the fundamentalist belt even though the rubric did not quite fit the reality. Fundamentalism here was more politically active than in many parts of the country, and it was a significant force in the rise of premillennial dispensational theology.

By 1936, when Texas celebrated the centennial of its independence, America was in the throes of the Great Depression. Parts of Texas were suffering from the same drouth that resulted in the Dust Bowl and caused sharecroppers to emigrate to California, while other segments of the population were faring reasonably well because of the expanding oil industry. As was true in northern cities, the African American population was increasingly relocating from small towns and rural areas to urban locations. Dallas and Houston were well on their way toward becoming large cities. The understanding of how blacks and whites should interact was changing but also reflected earlier misgivings and racial prejudice, as well as notions about freedom of conscience and moral uplift. The legacy of lynching that had been present for so many years continued even more prominently in Texas than in many other locations. White church leaders quietly deplored the practice but said little in public. They preferred to think that separate black churches and schools were best for everyone. Jim Crow laws solidified and postponed for a later generation what would be needed to protest effectively against them.

Having been identified in the 1920s as part of the fundamentalist belt and then in the 1930s as a significant location of America's Bible Belt, Texas came increasingly to be linked in popular mythology and in reality to northern evangelical Protestants. After World War II these linkages intensified in conjunction with trade, population growth, and the nation's growing dependence on oil and gas. This was the context in which Texas abandoned its Reconstruction-born loyalty to the Democratic Party by voting for Dwight Eisenhower in 1952 and 1956 and setting the stage for the closely contested race in 1960 between Richard Nixon and John F. Kennedy, with Kennedy choosing Lyndon Baines Johnson as his running mate. With national influence already having risen, Texas came suddenly to the forefront with Kennedy's assassination in 1963 and LBJ's succession to the White House.

Other than Dr. Martin Luther King Jr., no person played a more pivotal role in the civil rights movement than LBJ. It fell to his leadership to pass the federal civil rights legislation that institutionalized much of what the movement had championed. It was his administration as well that evoked the considerable backlash between 1964 and 1968, first from those on the right who opposed the civil rights movement and the Great Society legislation, and then from those on the left who opposed the Vietnam War. New arguments about the nation's moral decline brought religion increasingly into partisan political debates. Through these dramatic and often conflicting developments, the changing configurations of race, religion, and regional politics could also be seen. Slowly a new awareness of their potential role in local and national affairs became apparent among white and black religious leaders alike.

Mobilization and division about how best to achieve racial integration grew in intensity with the black power movement at the end of the 1960s. The period is particularly instructive in illuminating the social factors facilitating and in-hibiting alliances among African American clergy through congregations and civil rights organizations with local and state public officials. Chicano activism emerged as well, bringing questions about possibilities of support and opposition from Catholic leaders to the forefront as never before.

At first blush the line separating the progressive politics of the civil rights movement from the conservative Reagan-era politics of the 1980s could not be more distinct. However, a closer look at what was taking place in Texas illumi-nates a connection that was generally overlooked but also important in many other locations. Religious leaders who had for decades argued for strict separa-tion of church and state, and indeed who knew the dangers locally of speaking too forthrightly about social and political issues, came increasingly to think dif-ferently about their role in public life. This was true of the few white clergy from theologically liberal denominations in the North that went south to participate directly in the civil rights movement. Less apparent was the fact that other clergy, including ones who were against the movement or indifferent to it, also decided that it was appropriate to speak out. White clergy who never would have imag-ined taking an active role in political events learned that it was possible and even desirable to do so. In Texas they also found role models in community activists working among farm laborers and with Hispanic immigrants. When concerns among conservative clergy about abortion, gender equality, and homosexuality moved to center stage, ideas about clergy activism were already in place.

Nowhere was the campaign for a moral America that took place in the 1970s and 1980s more seriously undertaken or with as far-reaching consequences as in Texas. The two Virginians who became the national symbols of moral conservatism—Jerry Falwell and Pat Robertson—came and went without ever exerting much influence beyond their own evangelistic empires. But the efforts in Texas that observers there at the time recognized contributed significantly, despite resistance, to the triumph of the more conservative faction within the Southern Baptist Convention and to Ronald Reagan's successful southern strat-egy for the presidency in 1980 and the eventual success of two presidents named George Bush. It mattered that Texas was a large state with significant electoral clout. It also mattered that white conservative Protestants were well organized and numerically dominant. Much of the mobilization that occurred among conservative religious leaders was connected through a growing perception that the federal government was an enemy and that conservatives were a political category with increasing potential to influence elections.

With all that has been written about the Religious Right and its role in opposing abortion and homosexuality, surprisingly little attention has been given to the connection between these efforts and fiscal conservatism.[8] And yet the argument that taxes were too high and that welfare spending should be reduced was a strong theme among the opponents of LBJ's Great Society legislation in the mid-1960s, and there was some evidence that it carried implicit, if not overt, connotations of continuing prejudice among white voters against African Americans. It was a theme Ronald Reagan honed in campaigning for Barry Goldwater in 1964 and that became particularly prominent in Reagan's campaign for the presidency in 1980. Texans prided themselves on fiscal conservatism, pointing especially to the fact that they had no state income tax and frequently arguing that private charity was better anyway than expensive public programs. George H. W. Bush raising taxes after promising not to was widely regarded as a reason for his defeat for reelection in 1992 against Bill Clinton, and fiscal conservatism was one of the appeals voiced loudly and frequently by Texan H. Ross Perot in his third-party bid in that campaign. All this served as background for the theme of compassionate conservatism that emerged in the late 1990s during the governorship of George W. Bush, and that became a feature of the Bush administration's national emphasis on faith-based community initiatives.

Another theme that became part of the Reagan legacy and carried through the two Bush administrations was the idea that small government is best. Although the scope and cost of federal government grew steadily under these administrations, the rhetoric was, as Reagan had said in his first inaugural address, that government is not the solution, government is the problem. By 2008, with war costs and federal debt spiraling, and Barack Obama becoming the nation's first African American president, the stage was set for libertarian champions of small government to reemerge under the banner of Tea Party activism. Among its advocates was conservative Texas governor Rick Perry, who on at least one occasion made headlines by suggesting that if things did not shape up in Washington, Texas might just secede. While the Tea Party's eventual role in national politics remained uncertain, its appeal again evoked questions that had been asked before. What is the relationship between faith and politics? Between conservative faith and conservative politics? Between race and faith?

Because these are recurring questions does not mean they should be asked each time in the same way. The relationship of race and politics has of course been examined again and again, usually with the results showing that white and black Americans hold different views of government and accordingly vote differently much of the time. How the Hispanic electorate behaves is of more recent interest and has proven to be less predictable. Religion's role in American politics has been monitored with growing interest since the rise of the Religious Right in the 1980s and has generally been expressed in evidence that white conservative evangelical Protestants and conservative Catholics vote Republican. Race enters the picture in treatments of religion mostly through discussions of black churches as historically separate institutions.

What I have tried to do here is to complicate the story by examining how the policies and social orientations of white conservative Christians were influenced, inadvertently, implicitly, or explicitly, by the presence of racial and ethnic divisions in their communities. This is not to suggest that racial and ethnic relations were always the decisive considerations, but to acknowledge that those relations could seldom be ignored. Nor was it the case that dominance and discrimination were always the prevailing motivations, although they certainly were at times. The evil that white settlers sought to restrain on the open frontier was stoked by fears of black insurrection and by violence committed by whites and blacks against each other. Outrage was a crime that carried racial and ethnic connotations. Lynching clearly did. Less obvious but equally important was the view that racially separate churches, each promoting individual moral uplift, were the best way to effect racial harmony. White Protestant leaders could safely refrain from becoming directly involved in politics because the dominant party was seldom challenged. Changing all that resulted in new roles for clergy. It also provoked new concerns about morality, welfare spending, and the size of government.

Texas is a location in which these complicated relationships among religion, race and ethnicity, and politics repeatedly came into sharp relief. But it is not unique. If Texas has a distinctive history, its history is thoroughly a part of America's story. If Texas is large, that is all the more reason to understand that it is inextricably entwined with the nation. Texas is one of the nation's centers of conservative religion. That does not imply that its political or economic influence can be understood only as an expression of its churches or that the Bible Belt functions differently there. It does imply that insight about America can be found within its borders and in the connections that transcend them.

The freedom that Nicholas and Anton Riedel cherished as Texas immigrants in 1845 was about religious liberty as well as economic and political opportunity. In their community the first worship services were held at an outdoor meeting on Good Friday. A Protestant church was founded that welcomed the faithful of all denominations, and soon afterward a Catholic church began as well. A visitor in 1854 found that many of the original settlers had moved on and been replaced by more recent immigrants who cultivated small farms, tended shops, raised large families, and attended the Protestant or Catholic church. But outside of town was a wealthy landlord who owned a hundred slaves. The visitor wondered if the community's commitment to freedom would prevail. "Will this spirit resist the progress of slavery westward," he wrote, "or must it be gradually lost as the community in which it now exists becomes familiar with slavery?"[9]

CHAPTER 1

IN ROUGH COUNTRY

Bringing Order to the New Frontier

They are men of real benevolence and great talent; but it does seem to me
circumstances have given a singular twist to their minds.

FREDERICK LAW OLMSTED, *A JOURNEY THROUGH TEXAS*

O n Tuesday, November 30, 1869, a well-respected businessman named
B. W. Loveland failed to show up for the 7:00 p.m. meeting of the Lone
Star Odd Fellows lodge of which he was a member. Loveland operated a
grocery store one block from Main Street in the heart of the city, only a few doors
from the present-day site of Christ Church Cathedral and the Magnolia Hotel in
downtown Houston. He was a quiet, unassuming man, a Confederate veteran
who attended lodge and church meetings faithfully. And that made his absence
puzzling. In fact, just that afternoon he had mentioned to a fellow member his
intention of being present at the meeting. When his store remained closed the
next day, a neighbor looked through the window and saw his body on the floor
near the cash register. Someone had crushed his skull with a fatal blow to the
back of his head.

Police determined that Loveland had been cutting a slice of bacon for a cus-
tomer when the murder occurred. In the street outside the front door, neighbors found an iron dray pin covered with blood. There was also evidence that
Loveland had been robbed. His living quarters behind the store had been rifled,
although it was impossible to know how much money may have been taken.
Investigators soon located a witness who claimed to have seen a black man in
the vicinity of the store with what appeared to be bloodstains on his pants. Other
witnesses claimed they had heard and seen nothing. There had been too much

noise, they said, because of the large crowd that was in town that day. It would be months before a version of the truth was established.[1]

The reason for the crowd was that Texas was in the midst of one of the most important and hotly contested elections in its history. In compliance with an act of the U.S. Congress and by proclamation of President Ulysses S. Grant, the election ran from November 30 through December 3. It was held to determine whether the state would ratify a new constitution that complied with the Reconstruction laws of Congress and thus be reincorporated into the United States as a state in good standing. With more than nine thousand residents, Houston was the third largest city in Texas, outsized only by San Antonio and Galveston, each with more than twelve thousand residents. Another eight thousand lived outside the city on farms and in small unincorporated towns in Harris County. The election, which had been well publicized and thoroughly debated in person by rival candidates and in editorials in rival newspapers, pitted Republican Edmund J. Davis in the gubernatorial race against fellow Republican Andrew Jackson Hamilton. Voters who flocked to the polls at the Harris County courthouse, located just three blocks from Loveland's store, were agitated not only by the turbulence of the race, but also by rumors of irregularities, intimidation, and tensions between blacks and whites.[2]

Although it was coincidental that the Loveland murder and the election happened at the same time, the two events illustrated a great deal about the troubled character of the period. Texas had been the seventh state to secede in support of the Confederacy and was now the last state to approve a constitution that would normalize relations with the rest of the country. The large majority of its population had emigrated from the Deep South, and nearly all its African American population had been slaves. Misgivings between blacks and whites, and between Texans and the government in Washington, ran deep. Texas had been an important resource for the Confederacy, and it would increasingly be a vital outlet for new settlers and entrepreneurs. Violence, hardship, and uncertainty were the inevitable realities of daily life. Besides plantation owners, former slaves, sharecroppers, traders, and homemakers, itinerant preachers and lay pastors played an important role in the new settlements. Religion's place would be well illustrated both in the election itself and in the outcome of the Loveland murder investigation. Two members of the clergy in particular, one a white Methodist preacher and the other a black Baptist pastor, would quietly show the complex results that could occur when race and religion mingled with politics.

A ROUGH PLACE

Four decades had passed since the first white settlers in any significant number had come to Texas as part of Stephen Austin's colony in 1825. In the intervening years Texas had been a part of Mexico and had become an independent republic in 1836 with victory at the Battle of San Jacinto under the leadership of General Sam Houston. It was annexed to the United States a decade later and subsequently attracted large numbers of settlers from the Deep South who embraced slavery. It seceded from the Union in 1861 and fought under the stars and bars of the Confederacy. Now that the war was over and slavery had been abolished, Texas was an open land, rich with natural resources and ripe for immigration, but it was also faced with the task of establishing a new government under the controversial laws of Reconstruction. Over the next half century it would become one of the most economically powerful states west of the Mississippi, rivaled only by California. Its ascent, which was slow at first and then increased to a crescendo by the turn of the new century, was facilitated by its size, location, and natural resources but could not be explained solely in terms of agricultural, industrial, and urban development. Faith, politics, and the uncertain oscillating tensions between its white and black populations and with its growing Hispanic population were to be crucial factors as well.

"The entire state was in an unsettled condition," a man traveling as a boy with his family through desolate stretches of Smith and Anderson Counties in eastern Texas in 1866 recalled some years later. "Strange and desperate men," veterans and renegades from the Civil War, roamed the countryside. Ruffians taking advantage of weak and uncertain law enforcement killed neighbors and raided military depots. Settlers feared being attacked by hostile Indians and learned to be wary of horse thieves and rattlesnakes. There were men like Henry Scroggins, a whiskey-drinking gambler who carried his weapons at the ready. Scroggins was said to have slit a man's throat on one occasion and suffered multiple wounds in a shoot-out on another. This was the Texas that would live in legends of the Wild West. And there were settlers like Till, known only by her first name, an ex-slave who now in freedom lived at the mercy of the white family who governed her every move, cooking and scrubbing and on sultry summer days hoeing potatoes and picking beans.[3]

After quadrupling in the 1850s, the state's population had stalled during the war but was expected to grow rapidly now that hostilities had ended. With nearly 170 million acres and fewer than 700,000 people, Texas was ripe for settlement. Much of the land was as undeveloped as it had been a decade earlier. During their journey through Texas from November 10, 1853, to May 26, 1854, Frederick Law Olmsted and his brother John Hull Olmsted saw territory that they occasionally described as rich, fertile, already productive and selling for a good price, or promising for the new immigrants who were arriving daily. But these areas were frequently located along rivers that flooded and were separated by desolate terrain in which it was easy to get lost and always difficult to travel. On their way from Trinity to Centreville in Leon County, the Olmsteds encountered grass that was coarse, reedy, and dry and became lost on a road that was "little better than a cow-track." Despite the fact that residents were eager to promote the state, the Olmsteds observed that conditions even on the established plantations were seldom as good as local accounts suggested. "One-third to one-half the cotton crop on some of these rich plantations had been cut off by the worm," they observed, and slaves suffered from dysentery and pneumonia.[4]

U.S. Army captain Randolph B. Marcy, who visited Texas the same year as the Olmsted brothers, wrote of country in parts of East Texas so rough with briars and scrub oaks that it was nearly impassable. Then west of present-day Fort Worth, he found a region he considered completely inhospitable. "For all purposes of human habitation—except it might be for a penal colony—those wilds are totally unfit," he concluded. "Destitute of soil, timber, water, game, and everything else that can sustain or make life tolerable, they must remain as they are, uninhabited and uninhabitable."[5]

Arriving from Chicago in 1856 with her husband and children, Amelia Barr had an impression of Texas that was more favorable than Captain Marcy's. "Texas was a new world," she wrote. "The flowery prairie rolled away magnificently to the far-off horizon, here and there jumping into hills, over which marched myriads of red cattle. Masses of wild honeysuckle scented the air for miles and miles, and a fresh odor of earth and clover, mixed with the perfume of wild flowers, was the joy we breathed." The best part, she thought, was simply the sweetness of the atmosphere. "It made us laugh, it made us sing, and I never heard on any other spot of earth such melodious fluting as the winds of Texas made all around us."[6]

But that same evening Barr found herself filled with melancholy, as if anticipating the danger and heartache that were to befall her a decade later. She had seen the hard conditions in which slaves and sharecroppers lived and witnessed women mourning the death of husbands and children. The sweet atmosphere of Texas included wild animals, dark underbrush, and disease. She dreamed that night of being in a "lonely desolate place."[7]

Abbé Emmanuel Domenech, a French-born Catholic priest who arrived in Texas in 1848 at the age of twenty-two and served in the Brownsville area until 1854, published an engaging narrative of his adventures four years later. A reader in England fascinated by Domenech's thorough and exceptionally candid account wrote in the *Eclectic Review*, "We can scarcely conceive how it is possible to live and be happy in a country where every man's hand seems to be raised against his neighbor; where the law is disregarded from the inefficiency of the central government to enforce its execution, where each member is the sentinel of his own safety, and where the shedding of blood, and even of life, is held to be a mere bagatelle." If that was not enough to deter anyone from settling in Texas, the reviewer observed, "The ceaseless presence of mosquitoes, flies, scorpions, heat, and drought must naturally drive us away from such inhospitable regions."[8]

It was not that settlers in Texas faced more extreme difficulties than pioneers did elsewhere. Texas was in this respect like the America that pioneers everywhere found as they moved west into the open frontier and, for that matter, not so different from the hard living that the nation required of most of its inhabitants. In some ways settlers in Texas had it easier, not having the fierce blizzards that pioneers in Minnesota and the Dakotas faced or the plagues of grasshoppers that destroyed whole sections of Kansas and Nebraska. It was more the sense that whatever was to be gained from the land would not be won easily. The first European explorers in the area that would become Texas had termed it a rough country because of its difficult terrain. Journeying up from Mexico across the buffalo plains, Coronado remarked on the barren expanse that lay in all directions and the hillocks and arroyos where it was impossible for horses to go.[9] Later on, settlers observed the area's considerable variation in soil conditions and rainfall, temperature, and geological formations. Parts of East Texas were overrun with impenetrable thickets while much of West Texas was treeless and dry. "I almost forgot what a tree looks like," Soloman Wiles wrote in a letter to a relative in Indiana. "As to the heat let me tell you that it is the next place to hell."[10] "No stranger seeing the land for the first time," writer Elmer Kelton observed of his boyhood home much later in the Texas sand hills, "would describe it as scenic." It was more "like the ugly child loved only by its mother."[11]

Illustrative of the rough terrain settlers encountered were the stories that circulated about a mysterious wild woman who lived in the densely wooded Navidad bottoms somewhere between Houston and Corpus Christi. One version held that there had also been a man but the man had died. Nobody had ever seen the woman, but she was reported to have entered houses while the occupants were sleeping and stolen food, medicine, and, on at least one occasion, several pigs. Some reports suggested she was Mexican, others that she had been driven from her home by Mexican soldiers, and still others that she somehow had connections in New York. A reward of four cows was offered for her capture. Several searchers located footprints. Another reported finding one of her nests. Yet another claimed to have lassoed her, but she magically escaped.[12]

The Wild Woman of Navidad was the best publicized but by no means the only such creature that stirred the public's imagination. Along the Red River a hunting party reported having encountered a creature they called the "monster of the forest," which stood six feet four inches and was covered with brownish hair four to six inches long. The monster attacked the men, badly injuring them, and stole their horses.[13] Other reports included the story of a wild man who lived on the flesh of stolen house cats and was briefly captured, only to escape into the hills, and a beautiful naked woman with long dark hair and clear blue eyes, who also ate cats and ran through the woods, leaping ten to fifteen feet at a time.[14] Tales of wild creatures illustrated both the allure and the dangers of living at the edges of civilization.

However productive the land would eventually become, the challenges facing settlers engaged in farming were immense.[15] By 1870 fewer than three million acres were improved farmland under cultivation or fenced for grazing. That was an increase of only 12 percent since 1860—considerably less than the rate of increase in most newly settled territory between the Mississippi and the Rockies—and constituted only 2 percent of the state's land, one of the smallest proportions anywhere, certainly in comparison with states to the east such as Kentucky, where a third of the land was improved, and Tennessee, where a quarter was, or even Iowa, which was being settled at the same time as Texas. Texas was nearly five times as large as Iowa, and much of Texas was in the western part of the state where rainfall was too sparse for farming. But even in East Texas, where settlers had been farming for a quarter of a century and had turned fertile land into rich cotton plantations, the percentages were low. Among the most productive of these areas, only 12 percent of the land was improved in Fayette, Grimes, Harrison, Panola, and Smith Counties, and only 11 percent in Austin and Rusk.[16]

At a time when manufacturing in Texas was virtually nonexistent, except for an occasional cotton or woolen mill, and when commerce was largely restricted to Galveston and a few other coastal towns, the key to Texas becoming a productive state was turning raw land into farms and transforming open country into improved land. The economic advantages to be gained were considerable. In Collin County, which boasted of having the richest soil anywhere in East Texas, for example, improved land was selling for five to fifteen dollars an acre in 1867, compared to only one to five dollars an acre for unimproved land. In neighboring Grayson County, improved land brought as much as twenty-five dollars an acre while unimproved land seldom sold for more than ten dollars an acre.[17] Eventually much more of the land would be improved. But it would take a long time. In 1910 two-thirds of all the land in Texas was in farms, but only a quarter of that was improved farmland.

The task of turning open country into improved farmland required arduous labor, work that in antebellum Texas had mostly been done by slaves. Because land was so plentiful, it mattered little if hillocks and thickets remained unimproved. A good slave, it was said, could clear and maintain twenty acres planted in cotton or corn. Getting the results to market, though, was another matter, especially if the crop had to be transported long distances over rough country roads that were often too narrow for anything other than pack mules. By 1860 only a few efforts to bring other means of transportation had begun. Nationwide a majority of the counties in twenty-two states had either rail or water transportation, and in twelve states 90 percent of the counties did. In only three states was the proportion of counties with rail or water transportation 20 percent or less. Texas was one of the three (the other two were Minnesota and Iowa). During the next decade most of the construction that resulted in completion of rail service across the nation in 1869 missed Texas. In 1870 Texas had only 511 miles of railroad, an increase of only 50 miles since 1860.[18]

Drouths, floods, weather-borne illnesses, inadequate sanitation, and sparse medical care added to the difficulties settlers faced. The great Galveston flood of 1900 that killed eight thousand people was only the worst in a succession of devastating storms along the Gulf. On September 18, 1842, a violent gale raged through Galveston, filling the streets with four feet of water, destroying two churches, and forcing most residents to evacuate.[19] Another storm hit

Galveston with hail the size of oranges as well as lightning that set the main hotel on fire.[20] The town lacked drainage and fresh water, a visitor wrote, observing pigs hunting snakes and cleaning garbage off the streets. It was a "hard-swearing, rough society," he observed, "where women were so scarce they had to marry in self-defense."[21]

Besides the recurrent coastal devastation from floods and hurricanes, inland streams became flooded and impassable at times and ran dry at others. To the north and west, tornadoes and dust storms were settlers' constant fears. A particularly violent storm swept through the Austin and San Antonio areas and to the east toward Houston in June 1854, leveling most of the corn for miles around and causing damage to many of the buildings. The next day on the road from Victoria to Hallettsville citizens found the lifeless bodies of two men who had been struck by lightning.[22] Two years later a massive tornado tore through Dallas County, demolishing two churches and numerous houses and killing nine people.[23]

On December 22, 1847, a young man named Philip Gildersleeve wrote a letter from Galveston to his father in Connecticut describing an event that would continue to be a common occurrence in Texas. "I have been very dangerously ill," he wrote. "For three days my life was despaired of which I was not aware of during my sickness." After four days and nights apparently running a high fever, he recovered.[24] Others were not so lucky. In 1849 a cholera epidemic swept through Galveston and along the Brazos and Rio Grande, killing five hundred in San Antonio. "The dead and the dying," an observer wrote, "were packed up in the open air unattended."[25] A year later, as temperatures rose above a hundred degrees, cholera again raged along the Brazos.[26]

Historians Robert W. Fogel and Stanley L. Engerman compiled data on 10,000 deaths that occurred in seven southern states in 1850, including 528 recorded in Texas. Of the 8,200 deaths for which a cause was given, more than half (4,296) occurred as a result of cholera and related illnesses, such as fever, pneumonia, consumption, and diarrhea, or similar diseases, such as typhoid fever, scarlet fever, congestive fever, and bilious fever. More than 300 died of worms, 130 women died in childbirth, and 31 people were listed as having been killed or murdered. Infanticide took the lives of eleven more. Three quarters of the persons who died did not reach their twenty-first birthdays. A third died at birth or in their first year of life. In Texas the median age of death for males was eleven years and for females seven years. That compared with twenty-one years and sixteen years, respectively, in neighboring Louisiana. The median age of death for African Americans in Texas was six, compared with twenty in Louisiana.[27]

Langston Goree, a wealthy physician and landowner from Alabama, brought his family and forty slaves to Texas in 1850, settling at Huntsville and purchasing property in the area. Following his death three years later, his wife, Sarah Kittrell Goree, whose father was a wealthy planter in North Carolina and whose brother was a physician in Texas, continued to manage the farm and send her children to college. Her son Robert Goree graduated from Baylor, took up farming, and began courting his sweetheart, Melissa Hayes, just as the war began. He enlisted in the Confederate army, rose to the rank of captain, and was involved in a number of skirmishes. At the Battle of Pleasant Hill, which incurred extensive casualties on both sides, he was taken prisoner. After he was released, he remained in service in Texas until the end of the war.

Melissa Hayes was seventeen in 1861 when she and Robert began their courtship. They were married in August 1864. Under the watchful medical care of her husband's uncle, she died sixteen months later, two days after giving birth. Her infant son also died. "She was noble, kind, generous and affectionate," a friend wrote, "and the constant practice of these virtues made her a universal favorite." By request, she and her son were buried in the same coffin near the grave of her father, "there to rest until the resurrection morn, then to rise as we trust to a glorious and blissful immortality."[28]

Fogel and Engerman's research demonstrated that deaths among women giving birth and among newborns were not the most common sources of mortality, but they were heartbreaking for the families involved. These causes of death, statistics showed, were also more frequent in rural and newly settled areas than in established urban places. In 1870, 4,810 deaths occurred nationwide from childbirth, abortion, and puerperal convulsions, about the same rate per total population as in 1850 and 1860. The rate in frontier areas ranged from 30 percent to 50 percent above average.[29]

Epidemics and communicable diseases continued to be the most common causes of death in the 1850s and 1860s. In 1852 cholera-related deaths were recorded in San Augustine, San Antonio, Rutersville, and several other locations; near Huntsville the entire slave population on one plantation perished from the disease.[30] The next year officials in Galveston and Houston placed their towns under quarantine following deaths in the area from yellow fever.[31] That summer more than five hundred deaths from yellow fever occurred in Galveston. Hundreds of deaths occurred again in 1854, 1858, and 1859. With frequent travelers from New Orleans, where ships were periodically under quarantine with limited effectiveness, Galveston experienced minor instances of yellow fever again in 1861, 1862, and 1864.

Nothing compared with the outbreak of yellow fever in 1867, which affected upward of eight thousand in Galveston and left more than eleven hundred dead, including most of the physicians and nurses and many of the family members who cared for the sick. Despite efforts at quarantine, the fever spread to Houston, Corpus Christi, Indianola, New Orleans, and other towns along the coast, and inland to Millican, Navasota, and La Grange, killing as many as 20 percent of the population in some of the towns. Churches, synagogues, Masonic lodges, and a charitable organization called the Howard Association sent aid to the families of victims.[32] With little knowledge of the disease's origins and no means of curing the afflicted, doctors, nurses, and volunteers could do little except ease the

suffering as people died. "There are but few of our citizens now able to do anything for the sick," a Millican resident wrote to the Howard Association. "We are
very much in want of some mustard, orange leaves, oil, ice, and tincture of iron."
Blankets and sheets were also in short supply. "Most of our patients who take the
fever at this place die."[33] In Galveston and surrounding towns, officials posted
names of orphans needing homes, adding assurances that the children were now
healthy. "The insidious working of the pestilence," a resident of Galveston wrote
when the epidemic finally waned, "was in our midst, and subject to its demands,
death was to stalk abroad in our streets, enter our every household, and its withering touch strike down the chosen victims, scatter the family circle and paralyze
the remaining mourners for life."[34]

Many of the yellow fever fatalities were young people in their twenties and
thirties who were newly arrived from Europe, Canada, and the northern United
States. On Friday, August 9, 1867, the Galveston sexton buried fourteen people,
thirteen of whom died from yellow fever. Their average age was twenty-five. The
next day twenty-one were buried, and the following day twenty-one more, with
an average age of 28. They were from Germany and Poland, Ireland and Wales,
Canada and England, Pennsylvania and Maryland, New Jersey and Illinois. One
was from Wisconsin. She was the sister of Reverend George W. Honey, a former
chaplain in the Union army, who stayed on as a carpetbagger. Reverend Honey,
his wife, and children all fell desperately ill from the fever, but none but Honey's
sister died. He was one of the two clergy who would play an important role in
Texas politics two years later.[35]

Amelia and Robert Barr had been living in Austin since their arrival in Texas
a decade earlier, but they moved to Galveston in 1867. On August 20 she had
a premonition of being visited by a frightening and mysterious spiritual force.
The next night her son Alexander took ill with yellow fever and was delirious
by the following morning. That day daughters Lilly and Mary also fell ill. As yet,
son Calvin and another daughter remained well. A day or two later the children
seemed to be recovering enough that the family had Sunday dinner together.
"It was a very happy day," she recalled. "I remember every hour of it. It was the
last day I was to spend with my husband and sons, but I knew it not. Surely, I
thought, God has heard my prayers, and we shall all be spared." The next day
she herself became delirious with the fever. When she regained consciousness
two days later, she learned that Alexander and Calvin had died. The next day her
husband died.[36]

"Oh, help me to live," she prayed, knowing that if she died she would leave her
three daughters with no mother in a strange land, without money, and without
any relative or friend to care for them. Her prayer was answered. A few weeks
later the epidemic in Galveston subsided. But in the middle of October a hurricane devastated the community. In 1868 Barr left Texas for good.[37]

When bad weather and illness were not at hand, there was the prevailing
awareness of distance that separated people from their loved ones and neighbors,

a grinding sense of the immensity of sky and land that could dwarf any sense of personal efficacy. Historian Robin W. Doughty thought the feeling of isolation may have been especially prevalent among European immigrants used to living in compact villages within a few miles of their birthplaces, but it could have been just as acute among emigrants from southern plantations and New England towns. Walking two hundred miles after entering the state before finding a home would surely have increased that sense of distance. It became all the more necessary, Doughty argued, to "tame the roughness" by clearing the bushes and brambles so that a kind of order could be imposed on the land.[38]

If personal efficacy was challenged among settlers who came voluntarily, that was much more the case for those brought as slaves. Betty Farrow, a slave who was moved to Texas from Virginia in 1857, recalled years later how frightened she and the others were. She couldn't remember how long the journey took but said it "'twas a long time and 'twarn't a celeb'ation towards the last." She thanked the Lord that none of the wagons tipped over. Texas was "an unsettled rough country," a writer who edited the narratives of Farrow and other ex-slaves remarked, "and their memories often vividly recalled both the harshness of the land and the cruelty of those who enslaved them."[39]

People who lived at the margins of civilization existed in daily fear of attacks from hostile Indians, outlaws, and renegades. Then as now, newspapers relished in reporting the details of vicious slayings in which whole families were destroyed. Settlers on the western frontier were especially vulnerable, but so were unsuspecting visitors in Galveston and Houston as well as farmers and townspeople in small communities. "Social matters are so unhealthy," a visitor in Galveston declared, "that nobody who cares for his life ventures out after dark." Men there, the writer said, "shoot and cut up each other on the least provocation" and "bowie knives and pistols are conspicuous ornaments."[40] That was in 1866 before things got worse. The next year the number of homicides committed statewide jumped from 142 to 331. Between January and June ten murders or attempted murders occurred in Galveston alone. As yellow fever spread north from Galveston past Houston and Huntsville, officials in Crockett posted notices that travelers from those places would be stopped and quarantined for forty days. But citizens also learned that the sheriff had just filled a resident with buckshot during a domestic quarrel, that an attempted rape had taken place, and that a murderer was on the loose.[41] On July 1, 1867, Major General Charles Griffin, charged with bringing law and order to Texas, wrote from Galveston that murder was "bold and unchecked" in large parts of the state, and that in these parts "the life of a white man is worth but little, the life of a freedman is worth nothing."[42] Six weeks later Griffin died of yellow fever.

Texas had experienced its share of disorder, deprivation, and violence during the war, although compared with other Confederate states the extent of destruction and number of actual casualties was relatively low. In all, nearly four thousand soldiers from Texas were estimated to have been killed in battle, died of

FIGURE 1. Young Texas, 1873, Bowie knife engraved with "For Reconstruction," illustrating the state's desire to rid itself of the federal government's Reconstruction programs. Photograph by A. W. Judd. Lawrence T. Jones Jones III Texas Photography Collection, Southern Methodist University, Central University Libraries, DeGolyer Library, Ag.2008.005.

wounds, or perished from disease. In comparison, more than fourteen thousand died from Virginia, fifteen thousand from Mississippi, seventeen thousand from South Carolina, and forty thousand from North Carolina.[43] But the casualties in these other states affected many Texans personally. Bitterness among white Texans was fueled as well by Reconstruction laws that enfranchised African Americans, required loyalty oaths, and in several instances imposed martial law. Law and order was, as Griffin suggested, difficult to maintain because of the vast territory involved and the prevailing racial and political tensions.

In 1868 the U.S. Congress ordered a special investigation of lawlessness and violence in Texas. The report concluded that 939 people had been killed in Texas between 1865 and 1868, including 429 African Americans, and that only 5 of the perpetrators had been convicted. Subsequent examination of the data indicated that whites had committed 373 of the African American murders and that African Americans had murdered 10 whites. The data further suggested that as many as a thousand nonfatal assaults by whites against blacks had occurred in these years, with the largest number of incidents occurring during elections and when politics were being discussed. After a temporary lull during the worst of the yellow fever epidemic, the violence increased again in 1868 as the Ku Klux Klan organized under the banner of *Sic semper tyrannis* and called for vengeance and blood. In one incident, the Klan lynched a black man and mutilated his body with knives, and in another it fired shots at a group of African Americans at a party, killing four outright and mortally wounding three others. In another, a crowd of more than a thousand attended a Klan rally followed by a night of threats and intimidation against freedmen and their families. In yet another, robed Klansmen went from farm to farm threatening death if families stayed in the county, stole the property of those who left, and killed at least seven of the men, including one whose wife was ordered to sit on his lap while he was shot in the head. Although it was impossible to assess the extent of under- or overreporting, the figures and related reports seemed to confirm that Texas was a troubled place.[44]

The violence was by no means limited to politically and racially motivated incidents. Shortly after midnight on January 12, 1869, twenty-one-year-old Leroy "Bud" Cotton entered a house of prostitution in Galveston run by Maggie Mitchell and shot Major John B. Lochman, a Confederate veteran who was the proprietor of a nearby saloon. Ms. Mitchell testified that she hid in a closet when the shooting began and then ran to rescue "a little child I had in my charge." Miss Frenchie, a second witness, testified that she saw Cotton fire his six-shooter into Lochman's lower abdomen. Cotton was arrested soon after and denied bail for fear of local citizens who threatened to lynch him. Newspapers editorialized that the incident showed the depths to which public morality had sunk. Cotton was sentenced to hang but prior to the execution consumed a lethal dose of morphine.[45]

ESTABLISHING A SOCIAL ORDER

When Alexis de Tocqueville made his famous tour of the United States in the 1830s, the parts of America he visited showed every indication of having developed the social institutions a functioning democratic society required. The principal institutions Tocqueville considered necessary were a system of local, state, and federal government that administered the processes of legislation, elections, and adjudication; families that safely supported one another, raised children, and functioned as domestic households; schools that effectively communicated common core values to the coming generation; and voluntary community organizations, such as churches and Masonic lodges, that bridged the connections among families and performed the necessary rituals accompanying births, deaths, and the desire for worship. All of that worked reasonably well in places like Pennsylvania and Ohio where the ratio of people to land was relatively high. Making them work in sparsely populated territories like Texas was more difficult. On his journey to New Orleans, Tocqueville also pondered the implications of slavery. He concluded that slavery could not survive but predicted that the task of ending it could challenge the fate of the Union itself. What the longer-range implications of racial division might be were more difficult for him to foresee.[46]

Sometime around 1870 a wagon drawn by a yoke of Texas longhorns arrived in a small town in southern Minnesota. A tired-looking woman held the reins, several children huddled behind her, and a small boy, a man, and a dog came up alongside. Sensing that they were emigrants returning from Texas, where he had lived for some years, a local alderman greeted them. "From Texas, I presume?" "Yes, sir." "Didn't you like the country?" "No, sir." "Didn't you like the climate?" "Oh, yes." "Did you have good health out there?" "Yes." "Wasn't the land good?" "Yes." "How about the crops?" "Oh, we made splendid crops." "Well, then, ma'am, what on earth is your objection to Texas?" "Why sir," she replied, "I couldn't stand the society in that rough country."[47]

The story was probably apocryphal. It nevertheless captured an impression that was long to be associated with Texas and indeed with much of the American Southwest. The area was populated, some said, by ruffians and outlaws, drunken cowboys and cattle rustlers, swindlers, hustlers, ill-mannered women, and prostitutes. It was also fraught with racial tensions rooted in the region's history of slavery, which made it an unpleasant place to live, especially for African Americans. Maybe the good guys wore white hats, but they were just as likely as the lesser sorts to be poorly educated, bigoted, and given to rude manners. A rough country could easily turn out rough people if corrective measures were not taken to restrain the worst aspects of human nature. The true challenge was ensuring that civilization would prevail.

That need was evident to Benjamin H. Rutherford, a visitor from Macon, Georgia, who crossed the Sabine River into Texas in May 1835, traveling to Nacogdoches and recording his observations as he went from there north to the Red River. Other than brackish water that was generally in short supply, the area held considerable promise for settlement and development, Rutherford observed. He found an abundance of turkey, deer, beaver, and buffalo and saw fine large cows that gave generous quantities of milk. The climate was particularly well suited for planting cotton. He nevertheless advised prospective settlers to think twice about coming to Texas because of the unappealing social conditions they would experience. Land speculators and swindlers were everywhere, and laws protecting life and property were poorly enforced. Most certainly, families would suffer. "There are obligations which men owe their families," he counseled, "which, if willfully neglected, will rise up in judgment against them in a future day, when it is too late to repent or to change." Bringing women and children to Texas was, in his view, about the same as murdering them. "If I were to see a man moving to that country, and did not warn him to stop, I should feel that I was at least guilty of a sin of omission in not telling him that he was about to do an act which I conscientiously believe would forever blast the prospects of his family in this life, and perhaps in that which is to come."[48]

That was sobering advice, which of course differed dramatically from the glowing accounts publicized in southern newspapers encouraging emigration to Texas. In retrospect it would be a long time before the area was able to boast of well-established social institutions. Rutherford's advice was not, however, only the view of a cynic who doubted the wisdom of anyone moving to the new frontier. A year before Rutherford's visit, Colonel Juan Almonte spent three months in Texas preparing a thorough statistical report of existing conditions. At Nacogdoches he found a population of 3,500, which made it one of the largest towns in the area, with another 500 people living nearby. But like Rutherford, he found deplorable legal uncertainties about contracts and property rights and only one school, which was poorly equipped. The settlers, he noted, exhibited crude customs that were "not compatible with the manners practiced by persons of good breeding."[49]

Perhaps that said more about Colonel Almonte than about the good citizens of Texas, but thirteen years later Reverend William Capers, a Methodist bishop from South Carolina who visited San Augustine in eastern Texas in December 1847 made a similar observation. The people he met there frequently referred to their environs as rough country. The women, Capers said, blamed dirty clothing, a badly kept house, and poor cooking—and the men, laziness—on living in a rough country. If aspiring immigrants considered more carefully the challenges they would face, he opined, the need for apologies would be reduced and the chances for civilization and good religion increased. "If the country is rough, who make it so? Is it not themselves? The country, indeed! The roughness is their own."[50]

Capers's negative assessment paled in comparison with those of some northerners who remained convinced that annexing Texas had been a fool's bargain that only strengthened slavery, created opportunities for land speculators, and incurred continuing expenditures for its defense.[51] In 1848 a correspondent for the *New York Tribune* wrote from the Rio Grande valley that Texas was "a miserable country" that was unlikely ever to produce much grain or cotton and was destined to be nothing but a source of turmoil and expense to the rest of the nation. It was populated, he wrote, by "semi-civilized Mexicans, a vicious conglomerate by interbreeding of the dregs of Spanish Europe, the wild Indian tribes, and the negroes, and worse than these the cut-throat renegade American and European whites, who are wont to congregate where population is sparse and where the prompt administration of wholesome laws is impracticable."[52]

How Texans viewed themselves, and how they hoped prospective immigrants to their state would view them, was of course much different. Any number of positive attributes were possible to emphasize, for instance, that Texas was a great place for rugged individualists to strike out on their own, gaining independence from the strictures of timeworn traditions. Appeals could have featured the remarkable possibilities in Texas for extending the highbrow culture of southern gentility. Or it could be argued, as some did, that it was possible in Texas to become fabulously wealthy by planting cotton or herding cattle. In reality, though, the traits Texans sought to portray to the world were similar to the ones that Tocqueville had identified as the essential ingredients of a well-functioning civil democracy.[53]

Nowhere were these traits more clearly described than in the *Texas Almanac*, which was published annually beginning in 1857 as a guide to Texas horticulture, weather, laws, industry, and accomplishments both for residents and for people in other states who might be thinking about emigrating. In early editions the most generous praise was evident in descriptions of heroes who had fought bravely to win independence from Mexico and who, like the women who accompanied them, were persons "of distinguished intellectual and moral worth" and were typically unstinting in their "charity and benevolence among the poor and needy."[54] Leaders were characterized not only as courageous but also as persons of spotless character who gave unsparingly to the benefit of their communities.

In subsequent editions of the almanac, these encomiums shifted more to ordinary people and the institutions they were establishing. In 1859 a writer observed of San Augustine that the town "has a good courthouse, with several churches, and some of the best high schools in the state."[55] "We have quite a number of good schools in the county, and the citizens manifest more than an ordinary interest in the education of their children," a correspondent from Robertson County wrote in 1860.[56] A year later in an essay about the management of sheep in Texas, a writer noted that "modern times" had arrived and the old days when men could tell tales about how tough life had been had "passed away."[57]

Descriptions of Texas as a place with fine, upstanding people and progressive institutions continued during and after the Civil War. Although war and Reconstruction slowed the pace of new settlements, writers in the *Texas Almanac* portrayed their communities in the best possible light. A correspondent from Dallas observed in 1867 "the people are industrious, moral, and religious, and take great interest in the establishment of good schools." "The county is tolerably well supplied with common schools in all the settlements," a writer from Brazoria noted. That was also true in Washington County, a writer from Brenham explained, where the "schools and colleges were wonderfully well maintained" and included several boarding schools, colleges, and training in law and medicine.[58] Nacogdoches, Shelby, and surrounding counties in East Texas, another writer explained, were all filling up with "intelligent and refined," "elevated people" who were "intelligent, moral, and law-abiding, with a proper ambition for the improvement of their country by the erection of churches, the establishment of schools, the building up and beautifying their towns, and the improvement of their homes."[59]

Schools, courthouses, civic organizations, improved farms, and businesses of all kinds were in fact being established in growing numbers. Yet the demographic evidence demonstrated that these institutions were being shaped by the distinctive characteristics of the territory and the requirements it necessitated of the people inhabiting it. In places where a population has been settled for a long time, for example, the number of men and women generally tends to be about even, which carries certain implications for social institutions, such as the fact that people can more easily find marriage partners and have families. But in frontier areas men usually outnumber women because of the dangers involved, the kind of work that needs to be done, and the simple fact that homes have not yet been built.

These patterns were clearly evident in the 1860 U.S. Census. In settled states such as New York and New Jersey, the number of men was about the same as the number of women. That was also true in southern states such as Georgia and South Carolina, where the number of adult white men and the number of adult white women were about the same. The greatest imbalance was in California, where adult white men outnumbered women three to one, largely because of the gold rush that brought thousands of single men to the state. Iowa, which had become a state in 1846 and was being settled largely by families, had 20 percent more adult white men than women. But Texas, which had become a state about the same time as Iowa, had 32 percent more adult white men than women. The imbalance was even greater in some of the more heavily populated areas, such as Galveston, with 46 percent more white adult men than women, and Houston, where white adult men outnumbered white adult women by 51 percent.[60]

An excess of men who in all likelihood are unmarried and do not have children confers certain advantages on newly inhabited places. Men without attachments provide the personnel for militias, cavalries, and cattle drives, as well as for shipping companies and railroad construction gangs where being on the move over long periods is necessary. They are more easily attracted to places that may be in danger of Indian raids or to farmland that has not yet been improved. Texas clearly had need for men of this kind who could herd cattle, serve as marshals, and withstand the risks of farming new land and operating new businesses. But an excess of men also carries certain disadvantages and, indeed, was one of the reasons that Stephen Austin had favored families over single men in 1825 and was an important factor in the preference for homesteading families that was to take place in much of the Middle West. Lacking family ties, single men without families more easily remain uninvolved in the community, drift from place to place, and may be regarded by the stable population as vagabonds. Not surprisingly, there was a strong negative correlation (−0.536) among Texas counties between the ratio of men to women and the ratio of young children to adults.[61] As much as anything else, children provided the incentive for men to settle down and farm or take regular jobs, and for communities to organize stable institutions such as schools and churches. There may have been other disadvantages as well, such as a greater likelihood of carousing, drunkenness, and prostitution. Texans worried about all these potential disadvantages. They worried about "ruffians," like the one from Kansas they hung for stealing slaves; they worried about drunks, like the one in Bastrop, who accidentally committed suicide; and they worried about prostitutes, like the ones who paraded the streets of Galveston.

They especially worried about the safety and education of children, and thus about the slow pace at which schools were being established. "Lack of education serves to make bad men," a San Antonio resident observed, "and bad men serve to make bad communities." A person unable to read and write was "a burden upon the body politic," incapable of rising above inherited ideas and fettered by custom. "The uneducated mind has within it no germ that can carry it above and away from contact with evil, but rather falls back upon instinct to guide and determine its moral and social code."[62] This was similar to the impression Texas made on Robert H. Williams, a Confederate soldier who arrived in 1862. "There the scum of the population rises to the surface," he wrote, "and there corruption and self-seeking are rife."[63]

Common school laws in 1854 and 1856 set aside funds to be allocated to counties based on the number of school-age children living in each county, and teachers were required to report the names of students. In 1859 the law was further amended, permitting county officials to pay up to ten cents a day toward the tuition of each student. Nevertheless, many eligible children remained unenrolled. In 1860 only 42 percent of white children in Texas ages six through sixteen were in school, which was one of the lowest proportions anywhere in the country, even compared with Iowa, where settlement was still under way but 72 percent of eligible children were in school, and Minnesota, where 53 percent were in school.[64] Although reports of progress in Texas frequently mentioned schools being available, it was often difficult for children to attend regularly, a problem that remained after the Civil War.

The state constitution that Texans approved in 1869 stipulated as a duty of the legislature making "suitable provisions for the support and maintenance of a system of public free schools, for the gratuitous instruction of all the inhabitants of this state between the ages of six and eighteen years." The constitution further established an elected position of state superintendent of public instruction and, following the pattern in other states, a system of school districts with local boards, certification of teachers, and public funds through land grants and taxes for the support of schools and teachers.[65]

The difficulties in implementing these expectations, though, were described in a widely circulated essay by Homer S. Thrall, a Methodist preacher from Ohio who as one of Texas's earliest settlers had sided with the South when his denomination split over slavery and was to gain renown as a leading journalist, educator, and historian. Acknowledging that free public schools were not only a good idea but also in keeping with "the whole tendency of public sentiment throughout the civilized world," Thrall listed four principal difficulties facing educators in Texas. First, the population was so scattered in parts of Texas "that it will be hard to collect children enough to organize a school." Second, sending a child of eight some distance to school might be possible, but it was neither safe nor proper for a six- or seven-year-old. Third, children in their late teens were needed at home to help with farmwork, and for that matter, many girls of that age already had "two or three children of their own." And above all, it would be exceedingly difficult, Thrall argued, to find teachers and board members qualified to "give the time and attention necessary to secure good school houses, well furnished; [and] to employ teachers and see that the children of the district are collected and properly taught."[66]

Thrall was confident that these difficulties could be overcome, or at least circumvented, and it was in fact the latter that prevailed. The plan for a statewide system of free public schools was implemented in 1871, which meant that information supplied in the 1870 U.S. Census was radically understated owing to a lack of systematic reporting from local officials. According to those data, Texas had only 548 schools, 706 teachers, and just over 23,000 students, which were the lowest rates when adjusted by total population of any state in the nation. In 1872 Texas officials obtained more accurate information, showing 1,924 schools, 2,299 teachers, and just over 84,000 students. Those numbers were markedly better.[67]

However, the rate of schools, teachers, and pupils in Texas, adjusted for total population, was still well below the national average. For schools, it was 51 percent of the national average; for teachers, 40 percent; and for pupils, 45 percent. Those figures resembled the rate in southern states, such as Alabama, Georgia, and Mississippi, and were far lower than in northern states that were undergoing rapid settlement, such as Iowa and Nebraska.[68] Part of the difficulty, as Thrall had foreseen, was attracting well-qualified teachers. With only a slightly larger population, for example, Iowa employed four times as many teachers as Texas. A further difficulty, as Thrall also suggested, was the sheer size of the territory to be covered, which, even when divided into twelve districts, required each supervisor to manage up to a dozen counties with anywhere from one to more than two dozen schools in widely scattered locations.

Of all the particular adaptations instituted in Texas, slavery was the one having the most enduring consequences. There were 58,000 slaves, constituting 27 percent of the total population in Texas in 1850, a number that climbed to 182,000 or 30 percent of the total population, in 1860. That was a smaller number and a smaller proportion than in Alabama, Georgia, Louisiana, Mississippi, and the Carolinas. It was nevertheless sufficiently large to be a determining factor in the state's decision to join the Confederacy. There were more than 21,000 slaveholders in 1860 scattered across 89 counties, with concentrations of at least 200 in 47 counties, and the top 10 counties were all located in the Northeast and East Central regions that had been populated earliest and were among the most

productive. Counties with higher percentages of slaves also had larger populations (correlation of 0.528) and higher total values of farms, farm equipment,
and farm products (correlation of 0.761). At an average assessed value of $625.64
per slave, slaves totaled almost $114 million in value statewide. In comparison,
horses and cattle, which were usually tallied in adjacent columns with slaves in
official reports, totaled $52 million, and land, farm equipment, and products to-
taled $174 million.[69]

Like many northerners who visited antebellum Texas, Olmsted was appalled
at seeing slavery firsthand, especially the beatings and misery as well as the auctions that separated families. He was surprised to see emigrants from Germany
who owned slaves and treated them as badly as emigrants from the Deep South.
What puzzled him most was slaveholders' belief that they were doing slaves a
favor by providing them with work and somehow exposing them to civilization.
"Unless they was whipped," a woman who previously thought of herself as an abolitionist told him, "they was good for nothing." The views whites held of slaves,
Olmsted observed, extended to their Mexican neighbors as well. Mexicans were
treated, he wrote, "not as heretics or heathen to be converted with flannel and
tracts, but rather as vermin, to be exterminated."[70]

At the end of his journey Olmsted wrote to Boston abolitionist Edward Everett Hale that "fighting free soilers" in Kansas were talking about "taking Western Texas next." Olmsted heartily supported the idea. "It can be done easily," he
wrote, and "when it is done the process of bringing the South to its senses will
be very rapidly accelerated. Be sure that once surrounded, slavery will retreat
upon itself and free soil will be advanced with a rapidity that will soon become
frightful." Were it possible "to encourage attention to Texas among the right sort
of man," he believed, slavery there would soon be in full retreat.[71]

And yet what Olmsted observed in Texas was but the local manifestation
of racial and ethnic understandings that were deeply rooted in all parts of the
United States and simply gained different expression under different conditions.
These understandings included the idea that races differed in native ability and
temperament and that racial superiority or inferiority was somehow divinely ordained. Olmsted, like Tocqueville before him, puzzled over the seeming impossibility of equal treatment ever being successfully instituted. One thing was sure,
Tocqueville had written: that as soon as African Americans "join the ranks of
free men; they will soon be indignant at being deprived of almost all the rights
of citizens."[72]

In the near term white Texans in the late 1860s confronted the fact that freedmen were no longer enslaved and had the right to vote, but like other white
southerners they found it difficult to imagine how this could work in practice.
Especially as white voters contemplated ratifying a new state constitution and
electing new state and local officials, the prospect of African Americans influencing the outcome was a topic of considerable debate. Some were cautiously
optimistic, arguing that freedom was far better for all concerned than slavery

and that African Americans were happier than before, more industrious, and showed a keen appetite for knowledge.[73] But others who feared the worst pledged to restrict black voting and instituted a series of codes that penalized, fined, and imprisoned blacks for the slightest transgression. "White men, prepare to vote; you know your duty to your country and to your God," one newspaper editorialized. "Down with freeniggerism—down with tyranny and oppression—speak like men; don't allow yourselves to be intimidated. Vote for a white man's government."[74]

Two aspects of the relationship between blacks and whites were immediately evident. One was that in the minds of white residents, African Americans were the symbolic manifestation of all that they themselves aspired not to be. To the extent that whites saw themselves as hard-working, industrious citizens who took responsibility for themselves and their communities, they perceived African Americans as precisely the opposite: lazy, irresponsible, and lacking in ambition. Slavery had been the necessary means of curbing that natural disinclination to work, which meant that in the absence of slavery nothing much of virtue could be expected. "The present crops are but about half an average," a writer near Brazoria observed in 1867, "owing entirely to the impossibility of getting the Negroes to work." They were working about a forth as hard, he said, as when they were slaves.[75] A writer near Huntsville was slightly more charitable. "Negroes seem to be quiet and inoffensive," he wrote, "but do not compare in industry and efficiency with former habits. They are, as a class, inclined to run into vagabondage."[76]

The other expectation that would shape religion and politics for years to come was that the races should be separate. Freedmen and their families were to live in separate areas and attend separate schools if they attended at all. In Thrall's discussion of the difficulties facing Texas schools, the provision of adequate schools for the children of freedmen was not one of particular concern. Someone during the constitutional convention, he noted, introduced a motion requiring white and black children to attend the same schools, but that idea was promptly voted down. "We are satisfied no friend of either race will ever renew it," he noted. "We have heard of no application of one race to be admitted to the schools of the other. We do not know why there should be any difficulty on that score in the future."[77] Whether schools that were separate could also be equal would of course be debated for decades, but at the time the extent to which inequality prevailed was abundantly clear. African Americans were nearly a third of the Texas population, but only 6 percent of the population currently in school, and 72 percent of the population that could not write.[78]

As violence and vigilantism spread, white Texans accused the federal government in Washington of indifference. In turn, Washington officials charged white Texans with instigating or at least tolerating a culture of rebellion. Reconstruction pitted Republicans against Democrats, conservative and moderate Republicans against radical Republicans, and whites against blacks. A "mobocracy" in which thugs and ruffians took the law into their own hands and became a law unto themselves seemed to be the direction in which events were heading. Some saw it as the inevitable consequence of the region's history of slavery, while others attributed it to years of war, carnage, and provisional government.[79]

Uncertain political conditions, vigilantism, and the recurring threat of disease, intermittent violence, and hardships of daily life inevitably led to questions about the human propensity for evil and the need for morality as well, and to thoughts about religion. A good society required good people who knew and respected the difference between right and wrong. It necessitated a language in which to express personal aspirations and grief, a language in which to make sense of injustice and to curb truculence and hate. Religion offered biblical precepts that aimed to reveal divine perfection and thus elevate the scale of humanity. As a writer in Dallas observed, the aim of these precepts is "to restrain and correct our evil propensities."[80]

IN GOD'S SERVICE

On Monday, April 12, 1852, nineteen-year-old Lizzie Scott, the daughter of wealthy plantation owners near Anderson, Texas, and engaged to be married in little over a month to Will Neblett, wrote in her diary, "Oh how often tho' it is sinful, do I earnestly desire death, as an end of grief, sorrow, and trouble and wish that the boon of life had never been bestowed on me. Oh God! We know not thy designs, and should not murmur. [O]h! Help my unbelief! I will I am determined by God's assistance to lead a better and a happier life, for I believe with some writer that our happiness is a sacred deposition, for which we must render an account at the final day."

Like other daughters of wealthy southerners (the Scotts owned sixty-five slaves), Lizzie's upbringing included exposure to religion not only through preaching services and revival meetings but also the female academies at which they studied the Bible and read Milton and Shakespeare. She mentioned attending church from time to time, but on this Monday she apparently had spent the previous day reading magazines and writing letters. Feeling despondent from saying "wicked and ungrateful words" to her mother and having mixed emotions about her impending marriage, her thoughts turned to religion. Including implicit references to phrases from Isaiah, Daniel, and Hebrews, she wrote of her failings and her desire to improve.

In daily life, perhaps especially for women, religion provided a language in which to express feelings about themselves, their worries, and fears. It offered encouragement as well, both in prompting a person to live a better life and in holding forth divine strength. "My heart needs purifying," Lizzie wrote. "Next Sunday I think I will join the Methodist church on probation. And see if that will aid me any in my reformation, it will do me no harm I know." She felt that she had "fallen from grace." She had "always felt doubtful concerning my religion" and was determined not "to be a hypocrite." Perhaps it was that desire to sincerely believe that kept her from carrying out her plan the next Sunday or the next. But eventually she did join and wrote repeatedly about going to church in subsequent years.[81]

As early as 1850 there were 339 churches in Texas. Nearly half were located in just five counties, all in the northeastern quadrant of the state. If they had been filled to capacity, they could have accommodated approximately 65,000 residents. That was about 30 percent of the total population. On average, one church was available for every 627 residents. Considering the fact that Texas had been a state for less than a decade, it was doing well in founding churches. The ratio of churches to population was as high as it was in well-established northern states like Massachusetts, New York, and Pennsylvania, and considerably better than in Iowa (where there was only one church for every 929 residents), but not yet up to the level in southern states where many of the settlers had previously lived, such as Alabama, Georgia, Kentucky, and Tennessee.[82]

Nearly all the churches were affiliated with southern denominations. With 173 churches, Methodists were by far the best-represented denomination and accounted for more than half of all the churches in Texas in 1850. Baptists came in second with 82 churches, and Presbyterians were a distant third with 46. The abundance of churches attested to what seemed to be a prevailing interest in religion. A correspondent wrote from Columbia, Texas, in November 1836 of a "decided preference to that which we term Evangelical religion," noting that "public sentiment leans towards the Bible."[83] Two years later a correspondent in New Orleans wrote glowingly of the work being done in Texas by itinerant Methodist preachers, of whom there were said to be as many as three hundred. "They are the pioneers of civilization," the writer observed. "They heed not danger however imminent; they stay not for luxuries; they care not to tread the carpeted hall or to seek learning or pleasure in cloister or saloon, but on, on they go, to the remotest verge of the globe."[84]

In Brownsville Abbé Domenech observed that the place seemed to be crawling with Methodists and ants, neither doing much in his view to civilize the frontier. "The greater part of the Methodist, Presbyterian, Baptist, and other ministers of Texas," he wrote, "are as ignorant as their disciples." He did find Episcopalians and Quakers to be better informed "and consequently more tolerant and less violent against the Catholics."[85]

Itinerant preachers and Protestant missionaries had been active since Texas gained independence in 1836 and in a few cases before when Roman Catholicism was still the official religion. Baptist preaching occurred at several locations from 1826 until 1833, when the first Baptist church was organized.[86] As early as 1831 Bibles in English and Spanish were being sent to Texas by various Bible societies. Within a few years, Bibles were being collected and distributed by local Bible societies as well, such as the one at San Augustine, founded in 1834, and one organized in Houston in 1838.[87] By 1840 Methodists, Baptists, Cumberland Presbyterians, and Episcopalians had founded churches in these and a few other towns and were attempting to start more by sponsoring preaching services in homes.[88]

The responses were mixed. On the one hand, families with long traditions of churchgoing were eager to participate. For example, an autobiographical account by a man born in Red River County in 1827 notes that his parents and grandparents were Methodists and by the time he was twenty he himself was engaged in frontier ministry. When a Methodist bishop and another pastor visited in 1849, he and his family hosted them and helped them make contacts throughout the community.[89] Another family with devout Methodist roots visited Mount Hope near Russell's Creek in Tyler County sometime in the early 1840s and was so impressed with the Methodist camp meeting taking place there that it decided to move to Texas. Only a few years earlier, a Methodist missionary near the same location had described it as a place of "darkness, ignorance, and superstition" where "profaneness, gaming, and intemperance" prevail.[90] Solidarity in the face of evil seems to have motivated the Cumberland Presbyterians near Nacogdoches who met in secret in 1834 to organize a church when it was illegal to do so and who received a candidate for ministry three years later, built a log structure that doubled as a meeting house and fort, and on several occasions defended it against Indian attacks.[91]

On the other hand, some Texas residents viewed church planting efforts less favorably. Another account from the early work of Cumberland Presbyterians featured an incident in which itinerant missionary Sumner Bacon was attacked by desperadoes who threatened to kill him during a preaching service, only to be rescued by a former ruffian who had been converted during a previous attempt on Bacon's life. One version of the story held that Bacon's rescuer was Jim Bowie.[92] At a different camp meeting, the preacher John B. Gough was accosted by twelve drunken ruffians, whom Gough was able to turn away with brilliant rhetoric. That story, printed in a popular elocution manual and repeated again and again in sermons and tracts, became part of Texas lore.[93]

The difficulties preachers faced stemmed not only from ruffians. Pastors had to cater enough to their congregations to attract steady attendance. More than a few failed in that endeavor and were forced to move on or find other work. Preachers came in for criticism because their sermons were boring or because they lived too comfortably. A notable example was Hiram Chamberlain, a Presbyterian in his fifties who had grown up in Vermont and traveled west as a missionary with his wife and family before settling in South Texas in 1850. A woman who eagerly awaited his arrival was soon disappointed by his monotonous sermons. He further alienated the congregation by raising funds to build a church, only to construct a house for his family instead. A decade later he was still there when Robert E. Lee visited his church, but his sermons apparently had not improved. Lee's companion, Major Samuel Heintzelman, described the pastor as "a good man, but not much of a preacher."[94]

A letter from a Texan named Charles W. Presler in 1847 to his family in Germany also gave a rare perspective on church meetings. "They say we have freedom of religion, and nobody will ask you of course what you believe. But you let them know you are atheist or of another religious group and you are living between Methodists or any other religious group, your property and life is in danger." He added, "I met an American from the Trinity River who was living between Methodists. They threatened to lynch him and set his house afire if he would not become Methodist. He left for the West." As if to underscore the point, Presler described a Methodist revival meeting he attended in Houston. "The preacher told them to join the Methodist church otherwise they will never go to heaven. Three ladies finally came out of the crowd and trumpets announced their new membership." No men joined, so the preacher told them how sad it would be for them to go to hell instead of to heaven with the ladies. "An old man finally went up to the altar. Another trumpet announcement. I left scared!"[95]

Plenty of anecdotal evidence suggested the presence of good-natured and yet serious competition between denominations, especially between dyed in the wool Baptists and Methodists. Olmstead reported the following conversation he and his brother had with an African American they met near Victoria who stood up firmly for his convictions. "I s'pose you've read de Bible, haint' you?" the man asked. "You've read about John de Baptis'?" When they said they had, the man quipped, "Well, you never read 'bout any *John de Methodis*'. He concluded, "I has de Bible on my side."[96]

Competition between denominations was clearly evident in the statements of religious leaders as well. A Methodist leader in 1839, for example, described new efforts by Catholics, Episcopalians, Presbyterians, and other sects as a reason Methodists should work harder in Texas. "I am unfeignedly glad of the interest taken by any evangelical sect in this unequaled field of Christian usefulness," he wrote, "but I am anxious the Methodist church should have the conviction that the field is peculiarly her own—that she is best capable of improving it—that therefore she bears its chief responsibility."[97]

But if competition between denominations was present, so was a sense that when religion was scarce creedal differences could be overlooked. In another fledgling town, Olmstead and his brother asked if there was a church and, when the answer was yes, inquired about which denomination. "Oh, none in particular," was the reply. "They let anybody preach that comes along."[98] That degree of cooperation was also evident in the fact that fifty of the congregations in 1850 were listed as union churches.

Whether competition, cooperation, or simply the sheer increase in population was responsible, the number of churches in Texas tripled to 1,070 by 1860. That was one church for every 584 residents, which, as it had in 1850, put Texas ahead of Massachusetts, New York, Illinois, Iowa, and a few other northern states and was now roughly on par with Alabama, Kentucky, Mississippi, and South Carolina among southern states. Total seating capacity of churches quadrupled over the same period, now providing space for up to 45 percent of the resident population. With 411 churches, Methodists were still the most numerous, and Baptists followed with 280.[99]

That a church had been organized did not mean it held services every week, as would be true later. Martha's Chapel Methodist Church near Huntsville, where the minister came once a month and preached on Sunday after staying with one family or another on Friday and Saturday nights, was fairly typical. Men sat on one side during the service and women and children on the other. When weather was good, families visited outside before and after services, and for rural families church was often the time to hear news and pick up mail.[100] These opportunities for socializing were especially cherished by women who lived on isolated farms with few close neighbors and whose husbands may have been away during the war or traveling on business. Lizzie Scott Neblett, for example, wrote in her diary of regret at not being able to visit with friends at church during her times of confinement. While her husband was serving in the Confederate army, she relied on the Methodist preacher to pick up mail and bring it to church each week. It was also from the preacher that she learned of recent casualties.[101]

On special occasions, revivals or protracted meetings that lasted for several days were held. "The men would build a big arbor and cover it with freshly-cut small tree branches," one participant recalled. "It was cool and comfortable, but the members' backs got tired, for very few of the benches had backrests. In those days when the preacher started, he had no certain time to stop."[102] Revivals were the occasion to mourn one's sins and declare in the presence of one's neighbors an intent to strive toward heavenly perfection. Protracted meetings were especially the seasons in which mothers and wives hoped their sons and husbands would give up drinking and pledge to guard against other temptations. General Sam Houston's wife, for example, was said to have been overjoyed when he decided to be baptized following a revival meeting in 1854.[103]

A man baptized the same evening as Houston wrote to his widowed mother, "I have enjoyed myself so much since I professed," noting a sense of tranquility he had never before experienced. "It is true," he acknowledged, "that occasionally my mind is disturbed by Satan whispering in my ear that I have been deceived, that it is nothing but excitement; but, thank God by prayer I am enabled to clear away all such feeling."[104] Believers must have taken religion with something less than absolute piety, though, judging from the frequent mention of dances, parties, and tavern escapades, as well as the fact that one prominent citizen named his favorite racehorse "Methodist Bull."[105]

Abbé Domenech noted that camp meetings served as places for young men and women to meet as well as for more devout aims, but he was especially impressed with the meetings' emotional fervor. "Women of a certain age get into melting moods, weep, and utter cries of anguish and repentance at the sight of their sins," he wrote. "Sometimes they imagine that the Holy Ghost descends upon them." The women preached "impelled by a desire of making their brethren sharers in their happiness."[106] It was from these meetings that churches grew.

Besides population, the demographic factors that affected the presence of churches were similar to the ones influencing the availability of schools. Taking account of differences in population, counties with balanced numbers of men and women had more churches per capita than counties in which men significantly outnumbered women. The same was true of counties that had higher birthrates. In short, churches took root where families did.[107]

In addition, and especially important for the future of religion in Texas, there were more churches per capita in counties with higher proportions of slaves than in counties with lower proportions of slaves.[108] Several factors were likely the reason. One was that these counties were generally settled sooner and thus had more time in which to establish churches. A second was that high-slavery counties were also more prosperous, which helped in covering the cost of building churches and supporting clergy. There was also some indication that white residents felt the need to be better organized when slaves were present and sometimes established churches for the enslaved population as a mechanism of social control.

Whatever the specific reasons, white churches—nearly three quarters of all churches in 1860—were located in the parts of Texas in which slavery was most prevalent. In subsequent years, with all that was to happen to change those relationships, the development of these churches as individual congregations and as denominations would be profoundly influenced by the continuing presence of racial differences. Some of the time these relationships would be guided by amity and at other times by animosity. The murder that occurred several years later in Houston would serve as a preview of the complexity of these relationships.

As was true nearly everywhere, the founding of new churches ground to a halt during the Civil War, and many of the more recent congregations that had organized just before the war struggled to stay in existence and were unable to erect buildings for several years after the war. The 1870 U.S. Census, in which the number of churches, like the number of schools, was undoubtedly underreported, showed that the total number of churches in Texas fell to 843, down from 1,035 in 1860; the number of Methodist congregations dropped from 411 to 352; and the number of Baptist congregations declined from 280 to 275.[109] With only one pastor for every 913 people, Texas was well behind Indiana, Kansas, Minnesota, Nebraska, and Ohio in clergy representation, which may have been due to the fact that many Baptist and Methodist congregations were served by lay preachers, and in any case was better than in Alabama, Georgia, Mississippi, and the Carolinas.[110]

Although local reports written in hopes of attracting immigrants touted the presence of churches, just as they did the availability of schools, clergy and lay leaders were hindered in organizing congregations in the late 1860s by weak growth in population and a lack of funds from southern denominations. Unlike churches in northern frontier areas, they generally lacked support from northern denominations as well, despite some efforts in this regard. At an 1865 meeting of bishops in Erie, Pennsylvania, for example, the northern Methodist Episcopal Church resolved to work toward unity with its southern counterpart and pledged "to send such ministry from time to time as shall be necessary to care for the people, irrespective of color, who shall place themselves under our charge, and to provide for such ministers as shall be received by our Annual Conference."[111] Congregationalists and Presbyterians in the North also passed resolutions to support church building or rebuilding and to send clergy to southern states. These efforts, however, proved meager and indeed were met with misgivings and resistance. Shortly after the meeting in Pennsylvania, for example, southern Methodist bishops met in Columbus, Georgia, and pledged in words that rang of bitterness to resist efforts at reunion with the northern branch. Northern Methodists, the bishops charged, had demeaned the South with invidious language about secession and schism while filling northern pulpits with perverted agitations that were unhealthful to personal piety and productive only of discord.[112] A resolution at a subsequent meeting in Palmyra, Missouri, stated, "the abolition of slavery has not destroyed all the differences that existed between the two bodies [because] the question upon which the church divided was not whether the institution of slavery was right or wrong, per se, but whether it was a legitimate subject for ecclesiastical legislation." The resolution further declared the southern bishops' opposition to any "political tests of church fellowship."[113]

At least one northern Methodist pastor had been murdered in Texas for preaching against slavery, and a minister across the border in Arkansas had been lynched in 1861 on suspicion of fomenting a slave rebellion.[114] As in other states, Texas clergy who supported slavery and states' rights generally expressed hope that war could be avoided and then vigorously supported the effort when war began.[115] In a sermon on May 12, 1861, in Marshall, Texas, for example, a pastor voiced hope that Christ would "save our country from impending ruin" and that brotherly feeling would prevail instead of war.[116] As hostilities began, another pastor warned that a "war of extermination is to be waged upon us" and counseled against underrating the resources and courage of the enemy.[117] Churches supported the war effort through preaching and in prayer, as well as organizing educational funds for the disabled and children of the deceased.[118] Congregations provided a language in which to express grief and a refuge for those who mourned. "While our country's cause is bleeding," a Baptist pastor near Pleasant Grove in Leon County wrote, "the mantle of widowhood is thrown around many a soldier's wife—sadness and gloom are manifest around the once peaceable and happy fireside, and disappointed hope pines away after listening in vain for the familiar footsteps, or looking for the lovely face of returning father, brother, husband, son or lover." The church, he hoped, was helping in a small way to "cheer the Christian in his pathway from earth to heaven."[119] Even as the tide turned against the Confederacy, pastors counseled courage in the face of oppression. At a meeting in 1864, for example, Texas Baptists called for "redoubled energies for the deliverance of our country from Yankee thralldom and oppression."[120] It was hardly surprising that Texas clergy were less than welcoming toward overtures from northern denominations when the war ended.[121]

THE LOVELAND MURDER

Few incidents illustrated the complex role of religion in Reconstruction Texas as clearly as the Loveland murder in 1869. As officers in Houston and Harris County investigated the murder of B. W. Loveland, the trail led to Jake Johnson, an African American whom witnesses said they had seen in the vicinity of Loveland's store and who the prosecution argued had planned and carried out the crime. A former slave, Johnson was tracked down some thirty miles away in an adjacent county where he worked as a wage laborer on a cotton plantation and with two accomplices was arrested and brought back to Houston to await trial.[122]

At the trial, which took place in April 1870, several curious aspects of the investigation emerged. One was that a defense attorney was not provided for Johnson until two months after his indictment by the grand jury. Another was that an alleged accomplice of Johnson, an African American named Doc Wheeler, died in jail before he could be tried and thus was unavailable to testify either for or against Johnson. The charges against a second alleged accomplice, Jules Mitchell, who became the key witness for the prosecution, were dropped when the prosecution persuaded Mitchell to testify against Johnson. Contrary to established court procedure, Mitchell was permitted to hear the prosecution's charges at the trial before being called to testify. The testimony of another witness, who claimed to have seen Wheeler and Mitchell counting Loveland's money, was dismissed on grounds that she was a prostitute.[123]

In view of these irregularities, the defense attorney appealed the case to the Texas Supreme Court. But instead of emphasizing these aspects of the lower court's handling of the case, the attorney chose to make it a test case for the larger uncertainties of Reconstruction law itself, of which there were many. One that was well known among defense attorneys was that it was sometimes difficult to know who among elected and appointed officials actually held authority. For example, in 1868 counsel for an African American in South Carolina threatened the sheriff with criminal proceedings if his client was hung, arguing that the sheriff was not the legal occupant of his position. That argument was discussed half seriously in Texas newspapers as a possible defense for a similar case in Houston. That case, which would have been familiar to Johnson's lawyer, resulted in the defendant, a freedman convicted of murder, being sentenced in March 1868 and, according to Texas law, hung several weeks later. It also resulted in an outpouring of public sentiment to the effect that, however appealing it may have been to challenge Reconstruction law, it was better for an execution to take place because that would surely be a deterrent to the crime and bloodshed that had become a public disgrace.[124]

Johnson's attorney probably knew that his chances of winning on appeal were at best slim but chose anyway to argue that the lower court that found Johnson guilty did not have the right to do so because the judge who presided at the trial had not been duly elected but had been appointed by a general of the U.S. Army who had no authority to do so. Or if he did, then the court had no authority to impanel a jury. And in any case, the crime had been committed in November, when the court appointed under Reconstruction had been in place, and that the trial had then been conducted the following April under a different court.

The argument made little sense on the surface, and if upheld, would have posed thorny jurisdictional questions with which nobody wished to deal. Not surprisingly, the high court upheld the ruling of the lower court. Having lost his appeal, Johnson appeared before the judge of the criminal court on Saturday, July 9, for sentencing. When asked if he had anything to say, Johnson asserted that two of the witnesses against him had sworn falsely and that he was not guilty of murdering Loveland. "My last words at the execution," he said, "will be that I had nothing to do with the killing of Mr. Loveland." The judge then sentenced him to be hung until dead and remanded him to jail until that time.[125]

The execution of Jake Johnson took place on August 5, 1870, at Hangman's Grove in the southwestern suburbs of Houston. This was the same location at which another African American convicted of murder had been hung two years earlier and was an event no doubt familiar to Johnson and the local African American population, many of whom had been present to witness the execution and to hear the man confess his crime and affirm his belief that God's angels would come for him, as well as to join with him in singing a farewell hymn.[126] Johnson's execution adhered to the same script, point for point. On the preceding afternoon, Johnson's friends and family as well as his spiritual adviser were admitted to the jail to be with him and to say their final good-byes. The next morning a crowd of freedmen and their families began arriving at the jail around eleven o'clock, and by noon at least a thousand people were estimated to have gathered. As Johnson was escorted from the jail to the gallows at Hangman's Grove, members of the crowd, on horseback and walking, accompanied the carriage in which he was riding. One observer reported, "It seemed as though the entire colored population of the county had turned out." Johnson then addressed the crowd for twenty minutes. Reversing his earlier claim that his last words would be to assert his innocence, he explained that his two alleged coconspirators had appeared in a dream urging him to confess, and that he now did confess that he had killed Loveland and had done so alone. He asked specifically that no harm be done to a third man whose name had come up during the trial. "Nobody else had anything to do with it," Johnson declared. He had made peace with God, he said, and was going home to Canaan's happy shore where someday he would be reunited with his loved ones. The executioner then bound Johnson's hands, put the death hood over Johnson's head, and tripped the trap door. Johnson struggled and suffered for several minutes and after a quarter of an hour was declared dead.[127]

The Loveland murder and execution of Jake Johnson brought into sharp relief the several key functions that religion played at the time, and indeed would continue to play in frontier settlements like Houston and across America for decades to come. For businessmen like Loveland, and for the large and growing majority of Americans who were, or who aspired to be, among the respected segment of the population known as the middle class, religion was a reliable marker of respectability. Whatever else it did, being known as a faithful church member set one apart from that other segment of the population that was seldom free from the suspicion of being unreliable and prone to worldly temptations. A bachelor in his mid-forties who ran a small grocery store on a back street near the center of town at the time he was killed, Loveland was neither a family man nor particularly successful. He could well have been the kind who visited brothels and spent time gambling. But the fact that he was white, operated a business, and was apparently free of accusations among his neighbors and customers of any wrongdoing earned him respect. So did the fact that he was a Confederate veteran who carried a wound in his leg and was a member of the Masons. It mattered, too, that he was a member of the Presbyterian Church, which was located in the same neighborhood as his store. News accounts of the tragedy typically mentioned these facts.

As much as for Loveland himself, religion's role as a mark of respectability was evident for Dr. M. M. Michau, a dentist who lived in the same building as Loveland and at one point in the investigation was seriously under consideration as having asked Johnson to commit the murder. More than anyone else, Michau knew of Loveland's affairs and had knowledge of how much money there may have been to steal. One report claimed that Michau possessed some of Loveland's money after the murder. Another held that Johnson identified him in conjunction with the crime, and yet another suggested that Michau behaved evasively when questioned. But Michau had several advantages. He was white, a dentist, and a Mason. He was also an "attentive member and local preacher of the Methodist church." Thus he was considered a "reputable citizen" who seemed trustworthy when he appeared in court. One observer described his demeanor positively as demonstrating a lack of excitement or alarm, while the same demeanor on the part of an accused African American suggested a "low order" of intellect and feeling.[128]

For Jake Johnson, being associated with a church, in his case one of the "colored Baptist" churches in Houston, also conveyed respectability, at least among the African American neighbors who knew him. That was an important role that African American clergy and congregations would increasingly play. It included an emphasis on moral uplift, education, sobriety, and community engagement. But in this particular instance the salient public function of faith for Johnson was as a vehicle of comfort and support. Although religion provided a way of siding with good rather than evil, the latter could never be entirely escaped, whether in the form of death from yellow fever or being accused of murder. At his execution Johnson asserted that he had asked and received God's forgiveness. His faith, Johnson said, ensured that he would see his family in heaven. He asked their prayers and encouraged them to live uprightly. He especially encouraged young men in the crowd to be wary of temptation. His spiritual adviser, whom Johnson asked to serve as his young daughter's guardian, read a hymn, which was sung by those assembled, and then as his final action Johnson knelt and prayed.[129]

The clergy performed the other role that religion played. It included such traditional pastoral duties as visiting the sick, burying the dead, and presiding at public events. For Jake Johnson, this role was played by his spiritual adviser, Reverend Sandy Parker, whose presence and prayers at the hanging added legitimacy to Johnson's confession and undoubtedly was of comfort to those gathered. In addition, clergy were the community leaders who sometimes were called on to hold office and to weigh in on controversial public issues. Although clergy shouldered these responsibilities from time to time, it was seldom their place to do so, and there were often costs to be paid.

Reverend Parker illustrated the public roles that African American clergy were often expected to play. He was the pastor of the "colored Baptist" church founded by freed slaves in 1865 as one of only two African American churches in Houston and the predecessor of Antioch Missionary Baptist Church, which has remained in operation over the years as one of the city's most important African American congregations.[130] Soon after its founding, the church hosted and assisted in organizing a "Loyal League," the purpose of which was to encourage voting for candidates and measures aimed at normalizing relations with the rest of the United States. At a meeting in March 1869, when plans were announced for a general election in the fall, the Loyal League voted to disband and hold open meetings under the name of the Republican Association of Houston. In June of that year, Parker was elected by the Republican Club of Harris County to serve as a delegate to the Republican State Convention. That fall he was elected as an alderman from Houston's predominantly African American third ward. Like many who served during Reconstruction, his tenure in office was short-lived. He was elected as part of the Republicans' victory in 1869, which many of the community's white voters roundly condemned as having been fraudulently won. After serving as an alderman in 1870, he was defeated and removed from the position in February 1871. Then in June 1871, as a new administration took over, he was brought before the court on the charge that he had let pigs wander in the street.[131]

If it was sometimes difficult for an African American pastor to thrive in public office, it was also risky for a white member of the clergy to seek office, especially during Reconstruction. The most notable case in point was that of Reverend George W. Honey, the Methodist pastor in Galveston whose family suffered from yellow fever in 1867 and whose sister died. Honey ran successfully in 1869 for the office of state treasurer. Although their experiences in politics were some-what different, Honey and Parker undoubtedly knew each other because both attended and spoke at a meeting of fewer than a hundred Republicans in 1867, both were present at the Republican State Convention in 1867 and again in 1869, and Honey campaigned frequently at African American churches. Honey was a former chair maker from Two Rivers in Manitowoc County, Wisconsin, who had served during the Civil War with the Fourth Wisconsin Cavalry as a chaplain, part of the time in Louisiana. When the war ended, his regiment was sent to Texas and Honey was transferred to the Freedman's Bureau. He then settled in Galveston where he worked for the American Missionary Association to orga-nize schools for freed slaves. He also served as presiding elder of the Methodist Episcopal Church (North), establishing four new churches in that role, and was appointed as district clerk of the Texas Supreme Court. On being nominated to run for the office of state treasurer, he at first declined on grounds that his pasto-ral work was more important but then changed his mind.[132]

During the election campaign, Honey was attacked by the opposition as an example of the worst kind of Reconstruction carpetbagger. A particularly vi-cious attack appeared three weeks before the election in *Pomeroy's Democrat*, a widely circulated partisan newspaper published in Chicago. The article alleged that Honey had signed on as a chaplain because he was afraid of combat and had recruited others to the chaplaincy with the same fears. It accused him of being sick whenever there was fighting, of outright desertion on one occasion, and of selling or consuming the food and clothing he was sent home to solicit on another occasion. Were that not enough, "his preaching never amounted to a row of pins," the article asserted. In one community, he stole a Bible, it said, and in others his standard tactic was to "talk about religion with the lady of the house, while his nigger robbed the hen-house in the backyard." By the end of the war, this hypocrite who had been poor as a church mouse a few years before, the article said, was able to move into a fine house in Galveston, work among "the colored people to good advantage," and become wealthy. Apparently referring to the African Americans with whom he was working, the writer concluded that Honey "induced a number of young women to go down South and teach the young gorillas, some of whom came back whole, and some did not."[133]

The ridicule did not end when Honey assumed office. Although the Republi-can newspaper in Houston continued to support him, both for his work in public office and as a presiding elder now of the Austin District, other papers had noth-ing good to say about him. "We fancy that the day is not far distant," a writer in Galveston declared in June 1870, "when the Reverend Treasurer will have to take up the melancholy spade and dismal hoe, or else have a call to preach the gospel at some cross roads in Wisconsin." A few months later he was again ridiculed when a railroad bill that the legislature passed over the governor's veto went missing. The one bright spot for his public reputation occurred when the young

FIGURE 2. Reverend George W. Honey, ca. 1865, wearing clergy garb and holding a Bible. Photograph by T. H. Carpenter, New Orleans, Louisiana. Civil War Collection, Wisconsin Historical Society, Madison.

son of a coworker at the Treasury Department fell into a cistern, and when the father jumped in to rescue the boy, Honey procured a rope and pole and succeeded in extricating father and son.[134]

Honey was also attacked physically. While he was speaking in April 1869 at a quarterly meeting of the African Methodist Episcopal Church in Columbia, Texas, a man who was not a member of the church entered the building brandishing a revolver, threatened Honey's life, and broke up the service.[135] Five years later Honey was attacked by members of the Ku Klux Klan while preaching in Belton, Texas, sometime after which he apparently decided to decamp for safer territory because he preached and performed at least one wedding in Rice County in central Kansas in 1876 and appears to have spent his later years on the East Coast. But by that time he had already been put out of office, charged in 1872 with inappropriate use of public funds.[136]

Parker and Honey were by no means the only clergy who served in public office during Reconstruction. Reverend Matthew Gaines, an African American pastor from Washington County was nominated on the Republican ticket in 1869 to run for state Senate from the sixteenth district, won a six-year term, and served from 1870 until 1874. It was seldom easy, though, for officials to escape criticism and ridicule from their opponents. When Gaines was nominated, for example, the local newspaper described him as "a decidedly black little imp of a negro." Not to be outdone, another newspaper reported a conversation in which the governor asked Gaines, "Whose nigger were you before the war?" And, the writer concluded, "the fact that [Gaines] was seven years ago a slave is proof almost as strong as Holy Writ that he is not fit to be a senator now." Two years later Gaines was indicted for bigamy, and in 1874 he was declared ineligible for further service.[137]

It was not that politics was such a contentious profession that people of faith necessarily found it difficult to participate. Besides Gaines, one other clergyman was a member of the state legislature in 1870, and besides him a majority identified as lay members with one denomination or another. Seventeen were Methodists, ten were Baptists, nine were Presbyterians, and seven were Episcopalians. But it was unnecessary to profess religion to be elected. One was deist, one was a spiritualist, four identified themselves merely as liberal, and twenty-eight said they had no religion.[138]

PUBLIC RELIGION AND SOCIAL ORDER

The danger evident in the lives of men and women who lived in rough, uncertain, and sometimes lawless places inevitably nurtures the view that religion serves importantly as a source of emotional support. In that capacity, religion communicates to the individual believer, as it did for Jake Johnson as he faced execution, that God is present amid hard times and that suffering in this life will be compensated with rest and reunion, even joy, in the life to come. These are more than vaguely felt beliefs or unspoken faith convictions. They exist in the lyrics of familiar hymns, such as the ones sung at Johnson's execution, and in the cadence of repeated prayers, in scripture verses memorized and in comforting words spoken and heard. All that may be evident, and yet it misses the vital role that religion also plays in sustaining the social order.

The value of considering religion in a time less settled than our own is that its place, perhaps more in potential than in realized manifestation, can be seen more clearly. Social order is instantiated in law, in the institutions of law enforcement, and in the regularities of economic, political, and family life that follow. These institutions are differentially effective, operating with greater or lesser degrees of effectiveness for the privileged and less privileged. In a society in which slavery is so recent that one race monopolizes economic and political power and another race toils as sharecroppers and domestic servants, these differences are abundantly apparent. Religion may play a comparatively small role in the development and maintenance of social order relative to that of other institutions. A rough country and a rough people come under greater control chiefly through the extension of cultivated land, roads and railways, new business ventures in small and large market towns, schools, honest elections, legal codes, and trustworthy public officials. Religion is nevertheless implicated in the day-to-day workings of all these other institutions. It does so principally in two ways: through the public idioms in which common cultural understandings are communicated, and through the public rituals in which the rudimentary elements of social solidarity are affirmed.

As an example of public idioms, consider two brief notices that appeared adjacent to each other in a Texas newspaper in 1869, the week immediately prior to the Loveland murder and the election to ratify the state constitution. The first references a newly installed safe at the First National Bank in Columbus, Ohio. The safe, the notice says, "resembles Paradise inasmuch as thieves do not break through them to steal." The second is a tongue-in-cheek remark that the paper's theater critic considers being at the theater each night "his religious duty" but has recently been disturbed in this effort by the current political campaign.[139] Neither is actually about religion, and both are sufficiently brief that they would hardly register in the mind of a casual reader. But that is the point. As recent research on religious language has demonstrated, it extends well beyond religious institutions themselves, even though it depends on those institutions to be produced, and it surfaces in odd, implicit, unremarkable ways during the course of everyday activities. Tacit religious idioms appear as references to God, angels, the devil; in profanity; and in oblique statements about heaven, hell, death, birth, salvation, and guilt. Here a passing reference to Paradise elevates the meaning of being able to secure one's possessions at a bank and at the same time gently reminds the reader that theft is an inevitable feature of human life. Similarly, the religious duty of attending the theater suggests that some duties, perhaps not this one, actually are to be taken quite seriously and leaves the reader to ponder whether theater or an election more nearly qualifies.

Religious idioms became part of public discourse in frontier Texas through preaching on Sundays and during revival meetings but also through biblical lessons, hymns, and poetry that young people may have studied in school, through family devotions, in the letters people exchanged with friends and relatives, and in conversations. Illness, grief, and visits to the bereaved were especially the occasions for sharing religious idioms. Deaths of parents, children, siblings, and neighbors were all too familiar. Over the course of a few months, Lizzie Neblett wrote in her diary of visits to the bedsides of dying neighbors, letters bearing news of dead relatives, memories of deceased childhood friends, and thoughts of her own death. Despite the doubts she sometimes expressed about religion, she took for granted that heaven existed.

Yet her letters and diary entries illustrate that religion was important not only for its promise of eternal life; it served equally as a language in which to articulate her thoughts about death. She felt close to her best childhood friend and her brother because she could envision them as persons in heaven. Heaven was a source of wisdom and of other blessings, such as the rain and the love she felt for her husband, but was also a barrier to her happiness and was sometimes lacking in mercy. Nevertheless, she repeated the doctrines she had been taught about God often enough to persuade herself that they were probably true. "I believe God to be all wise, merciful and good," she wrote, as she anticipated the possibility of her death giving birth. And on another occasion she wrote, "The constant cry of my soul is 'Lord save or I perish' and 'have mercy upon my soul.' "[140]

The role of religion as idiom and ritual is clearly evident in the details of Jake Johnson's execution. Although a public hanging is, as Michel Foucault argued about imprisonment and torture, an act that dramatizes the state's power over the individual body of the person who suffers and dies at the hand of the executioner, it is also an occasion for the community to come together. If it is the executioner who exhibits the ultimate power of the state, it is nevertheless the assembled community that interprets the meaning of the event. The community, moreover, does not make up that interpretation on the fly, as it were, but follows a script that is passed along from event to event and through this repetition reinforces the sense of those gathered that they are participating in something more enduring and powerful than their own fleeting existence. The strong expectation is that the person to be executed will attempt to heal the breach that has occurred in the social order by confessing guilt and appealing to the community and to God for forgiveness. That restored solidarity is symbolized by communal singing of a familiar hymn. It is facilitated by the presence of a person known as a member of the clergy and by the public utterance of familiar words about God, angels, heaven, and forgiveness.

In a racially divided society, these rituals necessarily have racial connotations as well. It is the fact that a black man is being executed that is important and that the assembled crowd, immediate relatives and friends, and the pastor are African American. The hymn is undoubtedly one that is familiar in the African American congregations to which some of those gathered belong. The executioner and his associates in law enforcement are, in this instance, undoubtedly white. The event is one of coming together and demonstrating both renewed solidarity and an affirmation of commitment to law and order, on the one hand, and, on the other hand, of racial difference between white and black and between those with power and those over whom power is exercised.

A public hanging is but one of the occasions in which religion's role in affirming the social order is evident. An execution is simply an event that occurs on a larger numeric scale and includes a more encompassing share of the community than, say, a small gathering at a church for a wedding or christening. It is in this respect similar to a revival meeting that draws a large number of people from various sectors of the community. Common to these various events, whether held within or outside of a local house of worship, or conducted under the authority or only with the assistance of a member of the clergy, is the fact that deeply felt and publicly displayed emotion contributes to the distinctive importance of the occasion. The solidarity that the community experiences and enacts is immediately special and subsequently memorable for this reason.

These acts of coming together and sacralizing them through the use of religious language appear again and again but in different ways from decade to decade as the social order changes. Public hangings in local communities continue from year to year to assert the desire for justice, if not revenge, and continue to reinforce racial differences. Over time they are also accompanied by vigilante lynchings and mob behavior, and they eventually are replaced by executions in the electric chair. Revival meetings recur from season to season and take on different meanings as small gatherings in the countryside give way to large meetings in cities. As these changes take place, the roles of clergy and their congregations also shift, especially in relation to state and national politics as travel and communication technology advance.

If public religion is most evident in the large gatherings that assemble at revival meetings, in congregations, and even at hangings, it is important to remember that public religion also finds expression in quieter settings, such as the interaction that takes place among a few people sitting together at a ball game or on a bus or standing in a hallway at work. What scholars refer to as lived religion occurs in these out-of-the-way places where an offhand remark generates new insights and opens new possibilities for interpretation.

A fitting example that further illustrates the hard character of American life in the years immediately following the Civil War took place at a county clerk's office in southern Indiana in 1867. Two African American men entered the office to procure a marriage license for one of them. When asked his fiancée's name, the man said "Mary," and when asked her surname he explained that she did not have one. After some consultation between the two men, he gave the name of the woman's recent master in the South. Noting that one of the bystanders who overheard the conversation was now laughing at him, he explained, "It can't be helped, sir; we come from de rough country."[141]

Whether he meant Texas or some other place in the South, it was clear that his reference was to slavery. "Thank the Lord," the person reporting the story added. "The man and woman are now one, joined together by the power of the law in a civilized land, and the daughter of the couple, should such be the issue, will never have to acknowledge the humiliation and shame of having come from the 'rough country.'"

CHAPTER 2

FOR THE ADVANCE OF CIVILIZATION

Institution Building and Moral Character

Forward, forward let us range,
Let the great world spin for ever down the ringing grooves of change.

ALFRED LORD TENNYSON, *LOCKSLEY HALL*

In 1866 Martha Ann Otey moved from Mississippi to Huntsville, Texas, where she became a teacher and assistant principal at the Andrew Female College. She was well educated, having graduated from Bascom Seminary at Grenada, Mississippi, and Sharon Female Academy near Canton, Mississippi, and she had previously taught school at Lexington, Mississippi. Her brother, James Hervey Otey, was also well educated and was currently serving as an Episcopal clergyman in Columbia, Tennessee. With her husband, Colonel Armistead George Otey, a lawyer who was widowed with two young sons, she had founded a private school for girls at Castillian Springs near Durant, Mississippi. In 1861 seventy girls from prominent southern families were enrolled as boarders at the school, but when the war started the school was requisitioned by the Confederate army as a hospital.

By the time Martha moved to Texas at age thirty-three, she was a widow. Her husband had died of cancer in 1863. One of her brothers had died of typhoid, and two had died as soldiers in the war. She had two children, Lillian, who at age eight was old enough to come with her to Texas, and George, who at age four was young enough that she left him behind with her parents in Mississippi. She also brought her twenty-two-year-old sister, Eliza "Tommie" Nolley, who joined her in teaching at the school. Martha and Tommie were typical of the women, many of them single or widowed, who came to Texas in the late 1860s and 1870s and who taught at, established, and administered schools. Inspired by faith and the desire to advance civilization, they worked alongside clergy, public officials, shopkeepers, and homemakers to build institutions that would shape character. "I think this state will fast fill with people from all parts of the South," Martha wrote on July 15, 1866. "It certainly presents greater facilities for the unbounded energies than any other."[1]

Andrew Female College had been founded in 1852 and chartered in 1853 by the Texas Conference of Methodist Churches. It was a four-year institution that offered young women a classical education and classes in a range of topics that included music, art, and embroidery.[2] Huntsville was an ideal location for an institution to educate young women from families who could afford tuition at a private school. It was the home of Sam Houston and other prominent persons, such as attorneys Henderson Yoakum and Anthony Martin Branch, as well as the Goree, Kittrell, and Hightower families, who owned plantations in the area. Methodist, Baptist, and Cumberland Presbyterian churches were organized there in the 1840s, and Disciples of Christ and Episcopal churches were founded in the early 1850s. Huntsville's educational institutions included the Huntsville Academy, chartered in 1846; Huntsville Male Institute, chartered in 1848; and Austin College, established in the early 1850s. Huntsville's best-known institution was the Texas State Penitentiary, which received its first convict in 1849 and became an important source of uniforms for the Confederate army during the Civil War. When she arrived in 1866, Martha had good reason to believe that Andrew Female College would not only provide a secure livelihood but also fulfill her aspirations as a teacher.

A year after Martha took up residence in Huntsville, a man who was later described only as a stranger arrived from Galveston. He may have been one of seven prisoners transferred to the state penitentiary at Huntsville from the county jail at Galveston. Their transfer by the Galveston sheriff and two deputies occurred the same day that Catherine Honey and twenty others in Galveston died of yellow fever. Although disinfectant had been used at the Galveston jail, yellow fever was present among the prisoners there at the time the seven were transferred to Huntsville.[3] The stranger in any case died of yellow fever, and soon there was an outbreak at the Huntsville penitentiary as well, where at least 40 inmates and 2 administrators were taken ill. Within a month the disease was spreading through the community like a forest fire out of control. Charity workers sent an appeal to neighboring towns for nurses and ice. By the end of September, the death toll had risen to 75. Three weeks later the number had climbed to 130, with 25 more from illnesses likely associated with the epidemic.[4] Among the dead were Reverend R. T. Heflin, president of Andrew Female College, and Dr. P. W. Kittrell, president of the school's board of trustees and uncle of Robert D. Goree.[5] This was the physician who cared for Melissa Hayes Goree and her infant son in 1865. Martha Otey devoted herself to helping the sick and dying. "Sickness in every family, save two or three," she wrote in her diary. "Those who are well, or thus far have escaped the fever, are worn down by fatigue. The few of us, thus situated, have had to nurse night and day, irrespective of sex and class." She added, "The wail of the orphan and widow is a daily occurrence." And to her mother in Mississippi, she wrote, "Tyranny and despotism feast upon the sorrow of a prostrate ruined people."[6]

A few days later, Reverend J. J. Cochran wrote to Martha's mother that Martha had died. "Mrs. Otey tried to do her duty in the sphere in which God placed her," he wrote. "About the last conversation she held on earth was with myself. She expressed a perfect resignation to the will of God; she died leaning on the strength of Christ; she requested me to be a friend to her sister, with which request I will of course comply." Brokenhearted, her sister wrote to a friend that she feared Martha's death would be impossible for their mother to bear. "I think constantly of my Mother's deep distress," she wrote. "I fear she cannot survive the shock. It is so terrible to me, and her affliction is certainly more intense. A mother, weeping for the loss of her eldest, I may say, best loved, child; her grief will be unutterable."[7]

Knowing that her death was near and that she would not be able to carry on her work as a teacher, Martha wrote a last message to her sister a few days before she died. In it she expressed a philosophy of life that combined her faith and her moral commitment to human improvement. She concluded with lines from the German poet Julius Sturm:

> Pain's furnace within me quivers,
> God's breath upon the dire doth blow,
> And all my heart in anguish shivers,
> And trembles at the fiery glow.
> And yet, I whisper: "As God will,"
> And in His hottest fire hold still.[8]

Tommie Nolley continued teaching at Andrew Female College, living at the home of Dr. Kittrell's widow. A year later Tommie married Robert Goree's brother Thomas J. Goree at the Methodist church in Huntsville. He was a Confederate veteran who had served as General James Longstreet's aide.[9]

On March 17, 1869, a visitor wrote in glowing terms about the progress evident in Huntsville. "The Austin and Andrew Female Colleges of this place are in a prosperous condition, having an able faculty and a great many students." At these schools, he "witnessed a determination on the part of students to successfully master their studies by bringing perseverance to bear in the scale of thought." Some attention was being paid to "the education of freemen," the penitentiary was flourishing, a new Episcopal church was being built, and the infantry company stationed there was composed of "fine looking and well behaved men." With its intellectual and moral resources, he was sure that Huntsville would raise up a "new generation of hardy, industrious people" who would steer the "car of progress."[10]

That was the hope, but women like Martha Otey and Tommie Nolley were more often islands of sanity in a sea of uncertainty and danger. On Wednesday, January 11, 1871, a melee broke out at the Walker County courthouse in

Huntsville that left the sheriff and a second law enforcement officer wounded and resulted in the escape of two men, both white, who with two accomplices were accused of having murdered an elderly African American man. A witness to the incident said that forty or fifty shots were fired. As the accused exited the courthouse, they were greeted with enthusiastic cheers from the crowd that had gathered, and twenty to thirty armed men assisted in their escape. Unable to persuade the sheriff to organize a posse, the judge wrote to the governor the next day asking for assistance. The governor replied that help would be sent and that whatever expense was incurred would be charged to the citizens of Huntsville. A month later the accused were still at large. A committee appointed by the state legislature arrived to investigate, and martial law was proclaimed. With the assistance of twelve state police and the militia from another county, twenty residents of Walker County were arrested and charged with abetting the escape. Eventually one of the escapees was captured, tried, and acquitted. The other escapee apparently was never located or brought to justice. Charges against one of the accused who had not escaped were dropped. The fourth accomplice was convicted, upon which he sued for false arrest and was pardoned by the governor. Nine months later he was arrested for aggravated assault and rape, convicted, and sentenced to two years in the state penitentiary. "Our district attorney," one grateful citizen wrote, "is very fair and reasonable but a terror to evildoers."[11]

The incident was widely discussed in rival newspapers as evidence that injustice had been done variously to the friends of the accused, the accused, those wounded, the murdered victim, or the law-abiding citizens of Huntsville. It illustrated the troubles that continued under Reconstruction but was one of the many difficulties those working toward a more civilized order confronted. Although the election held in 1869 resulted in Texas approving a new constitution and being reincorporated into the United States in good standing, the outcome left many Texans unhappy, and a more enduring constitution was not approved until 1876.[12] Governor Davis pledged that law and order would be restored, internal improvements made, and "Indian depredations" suppressed, but these promises proved difficult to fulfill.[13] While Jake Johnson was awaiting execution in Houston, a bill was introduced to the U.S. Senate proposing to divide Texas into three states, following earlier proposals that would have divided it into five, and scattered violence continued, including a shooting at Bastrop that left the city marshal and two African American women dead.[14]

Weary of the strife, a woman who described herself only as a "Huntsville lady" implored her fellow citizens to work toward something better. "Many of us were enthusiastic rebels during the war," she acknowledged, "and many of us lost dear ones in the terrible conflict." But now, she thought, women especially were sick of "everlasting endeavors to stir up ill blood on all possible occasions." It was difficult, she admitted, to get used to the idea of "the negroes voting, but then, after all, they must either be citizens and voters, or slaves." She saw the recent founding of a "school for colored children" as a sign of better things to come.[15]

FIGURE 3. Huntsville, Texas, 1870s, showing businesses in the center of town. George Fuermann "Texas and Houston Collection." Courtesy of Special Collections, University of Houston Libraries, Houston.

FORWARD, LET US RANGE

In a series of essays, including one under Tennyson's phrase "Forward, Let Us Range," the prominent Texas writer, editor, and publicist Willard Richardson outlined a vision for the advance of civilization that he considered sure to lie ahead. Richardson and his wife Louisa were well-educated Old South Episcopalians who taught school early in their careers, migrated to Texas, and took up residence in Galveston where he served starting in 1843 as editor of the *Galveston Tri-Weekly News*.[16] Richardson had been a proponent of slavery, states' rights, and secession, but now that the war was over he devoted himself to writing and to rebuilding the newspaper into what would eventually become the highly respected *Dallas Morning News*.[17] Like many scholars of his time, Richardson envisioned progress in the rising trajectory of "large and well-ordered societies" and took heart in the "greater impatience with evils" which he saw taking root with increasing insistence. With Walt Whitman and Herbert Spencer he saw progress stemming fundamentally from science and intellectual inquiry and from the material achievements evident in transcontinental rail transportation, greater efficiency in the means of production, and easier distribution of goods. It was possible even to imagine, he thought, "that there was something beautiful and useful in the late social condition of the South" with slavery having somehow served in its time and needing to pass away so that the greater humanizing and enriching of civilization could take place.[18]

As well as anything else at the time, Richardson's essays, which drew on years of reading and reflection and were now being written only a few years before his death, pointed compactly to the major issues requiring consideration as efforts to build a new progressive society moved forward. There were five in particular: first, identifying an appropriate mingling of intellectual inquiry and scientific investigation with strict adherence to high standards of moral conduct; second, determining the relationship of individual character to social institutions and the relative importance of each; third, moving past the recent hostilities and current political ordeal toward an established system of government and law; fourth, coming to terms intellectually and emotionally with the legacy of slavery and finding a new understanding of the relationships between blacks and whites; and fifth, clarifying the role of religion and religious education in relation to these other considerations.

The balance between intellectual inquiry and moral conduct was perhaps the easiest to contemplate for there was little concern that one might be inimical to the other. Grassroots discussions of Darwinism as a threat to moral decency were well in the future. Evolution meant possibilities for human improvement through better farming methods, settling the land, and increasing the population, as well as greater opportunities for charity and moral elevation.[19] The one caveat, Richardson believed, was always to remember that blessings fell on the just and unjust alike. A lack of material success, say, in the American South compared to the North, or for that matter among blacks compared to whites, thus should not be taken as an indication of moral depravity among the less successful, nor should efforts to improve the situation of people who were clearly behind be withheld on grounds that their deficits were caused by a lack of moral standards. This was an argument that white people who thought about it could relate to African Americans as well as to people living in India or China, though it may have been more difficult. It suggested that efforts to provide exposure to progressive ideas through education were an appropriate investment of time and energy.

The proper relation of individual moral character and social institutions, Richardson believed, was reciprocal, with each serving to enhance the other. There was, however, a growing awareness that social institutions had to be built and individuals appropriately situated within them for character to prevail. That understanding was in contrast with the idea that an open frontier like Texas was best subdued by rugged individualists who struck out on their own, performing heroic tasks by themselves as cowboys, soldiers, and pioneers. It was a manifestation of what Tocqueville had termed "self-interest rightly understood," but with the important proviso that right understanding was not only individual sentiment oriented toward the common good but the presence of social institutions that directly facilitated the common good.[20] Schools were the most obvious institutions in which character could be facilitated. Others included prisons and asylums, institutes to train teachers and doctors, and businesses in which to employ those with better training.

The concern for ending political upheaval and moving toward a stable system of government and law was felt most acutely during Reconstruction, and was thus partly resolved with the constitution of 1876 and subsequent legislation, but included larger and more enduring questions as well. The discussions leading initially to secession and continuing during Reconstruction posed questions especially about states' rights in relation to the federal government. It was reassuring amid seeming chaos that an underlying system of law existed in nature and could be worked toward in establishing government even by parties that disagreed with one another. Borrowing from Puritan leader Thomas Hooker, Richardson observed, for example, "That the seat of law is the bosom of God and her voice the harmony of the world is, when properly viewed, very full of comfort." If law was rooted in Supreme Goodness, then it was possible to assume "that evils of all kinds are subject to laws greater than themselves." Further, the reality of basic natural law implied that social order could be sustained and anarchy avoided without resort to strong central government. In an argument that might also have been drawn from Tocqueville, Richardson asserted that the kind of centralization existing under aristocratic rule in France or the anarchy that followed its overthrow could be avoided, even though new claims for equality between the races were being made. A "good and wise citizen," therefore, "will be very far from being a fanatic in favor of equality, or a worshipper of power in the government." On those grounds, a person could be in favor of restricting racial equality, keeping the power of the federal government in check, and looking to state and local government as well as voluntary organizations as the mainstays of civic order.[21]

Coming to terms with the legacy of slavery and establishing a new regime of white supremacy went hand in hand. Richardson's argument that there had been a kind of beauty in slavery—and that the antebellum regime had been a necessary phase preceding the current one—was an example. Anyone who had read Darwin's treatise might have noticed that the title prior to the sixth edition in 1872 included the phrase "the preservation of favoured races in the struggle for life."[22] One version of the argument that appeared occasionally in popular writing was that the black population of Texas, like its Native American population, would simply fail to survive now that slavery's protective embrace was gone. All to the good, this argument suggested, because hardworking white immigrants whose energy would ensure material progress would now populate Texas. "The black race came hither as the servant of the whites, did the service well, and prospered as it served," Richardson argued. "But just as that work was accomplished, and just as the South began to need an influx of a higher quality of labor than the blacks could supply, emancipation removed an insuperable obstacle out of the way of white immigration." Now that slavery had been put aside, "this immigration will develop industry at the South on a higher and more diversified scale than has before been known." The result, he was sure, would be "an immense accession to Southern wealth and power." And if in the process the black race did not become extinct, Richardson believed, blacks and especially whites would prosper because southern whites understood "the permanence of race distinctions" and imparted such "humanizing and refining influences to the black race that truly harmonious relationships could be expected.[23]

By most accounts, religion was expected to play an important supportive role in nearly all these efforts, especially in encouraging morality, and yet this role was never quite as prominent or straightforward as might later be assumed. On the one hand, the seeds of what would later be called fundamentalism were certainly evident in the kind of revival preaching that left listeners scared for the mortal destiny of their souls. Such preaching was widely practiced in the prevailing Baptist and Methodist congregations. On the other hand, the kind of skepticism that earlier resulted in preachers being run out of town now found quieter expression in arguments favoring reticence in favor of dogmatism. Richardson, who probably registered a view more common among his fellow Episcopalians than among Baptists and Methodists, argued that greater practical good would be served by treating with reticence the life to come that is always "behind the veil" of knowledge in the present world. Better to help people, he thought, than to convert them. "Missionaries come over our way ranting about hellfire and brimstone," a rough Rio Grandean told him, Richardson said, "and there is not a man on the Rio Grande who believes in either of them; if they would set about getting up schools and teaching our children, they could get the bottom dollar, with thanks into the bargain."[24]

REGULATING MORALITY

While it was possible to argue that a kind of divinely ingrained, commonsense morality was present in all humanity, at least in potential if not in reality, it was not at all taken for granted that flawed individuals would necessarily adhere to these moral standards. Writers, educators, and religious leaders thought civilized people would live according to such standards but doubted that uncivilized people would or could. Ideas about how best to advance civilization also varied. Some leaders favored home training and education. Others worried more about the need to curb rough living, intemperance, and violence.[25]

It was one thing to start academies and create a system of public free schools in the interest of bettering the coming generation. Schools reinforced commonsense morality as well as taught children to read and write. Schools also performed a kind of policing role by keeping children in places where they could do no harm except on occasion to an unsuspecting teacher. It was different to try regulating morality among adults through civic codes that levied harsh penalties. Many states tried with measured success to pass Sunday closing laws and to control drunkenness and prostitution. Texas tried with the support of clergy, women's organizations, and temperance societies to do all these things, albeit with limited success.

Regulating drunkenness had been of concern to law-abiding Texans from earliest days. Baptists, Methodists, and Cumberland Presbyterians all insisted on abstinence from alcohol, although seldom with complete effectiveness. At the mourners' bench during revival meetings, confessions of having imbibed or having succumbed to the temptation apparently were common.[26] By 1870 societies with names such as the Temperance Council, Friends of Temperance, Sons of Temperance, and Band of Hope had formed in Galveston, Houston, San Antonio, and elsewhere in scattered locations, and by 1871 a weekly newspaper was being published in Houston as the *Temperance Family Visitor* and local groups had formed a statewide federation affiliated with similar organizations in other states. The local societies usually drew warm support from clergy, who often served on leadership boards, lectured, and hosted meetings in church buildings. Tensions nevertheless appeared that sometimes illustrated residents' ambivalence toward temperance itself. Finding it unable to attract young people, one temperance society held dances, much to the dismay of clergy who considered dancing nearly as sinful as drinking. Another group that promised not to disclose members' names was unable to attract local Hard Shell Baptists for whom membership in secret societies was forbidden. Yet another temperance group risked disappointing pastors who favored total abstinence by recognizing that hard whiskey drinkers might only be able to cut back gradually. Sunday closing laws succeeded in shutting down saloons in some communities one day a week, but barkeepers occasionally found it profitable simply to incur the small fines levied for staying open. Clergy typically argued that the only sure cure for alcoholism was salvation in Christ. Yet one pastor reported that among a hundred converts he knew personally, not one had given up drinking.[27]

To those conceding that temperance was in principle wise, it could nevertheless be rankling to think that clergy were such killjoys as to be against dancing, attending the theater, reading fiction for enjoyment, and indeed engaging in amusements of any kind. "Religious teachers of many Christian denominations have, more or less, inculcated the idea that suffering, voluntarily incurred in this world, will in some sort be recompensed in the next," a Galveston resident complained. That view, he argued, was utterly mistaken. The Lord "has created this world as much for our enjoyment as He has heaven." A person could certainly engage in revelry from time to time without being considered evil.[28]

With voluntary abstinence seeming less effective than temperance societies hoped, attempts were made to impose a legal or constitutional ban on drinking.[29] That idea proved upsetting enough to saloon proprietors and their patrons that temperance meetings were widely ridiculed in newspapers and on several occasions broken up with guns. Opponents of prohibition included proprietors in Galveston and Houston, where saloons were common, town leaders along the Louisiana border who feared that patrons would simply do more business out of state, and counties in which large numbers of Roman Catholics and German immigrants lived. The 1876 constitution provided for prohibition to be decided by local option, thus acknowledging the regional, ethnic, and economic diversity by leaving it to each county whether to ban, license, or in some other way regulate alcohol. Local option elections were held over the following two years. In heavily Baptist and Methodist counties where alcohol was banned, druggists sold "spirituous liquors" for medicinal purposes, and "blind tigers" or "blind pigs" emerged in which proprietors legally charged patrons a quarter to view something as innocent as a pig or a dog and then provided a complimentary drink.[30]

Lacking the franchise, women who disapproved of drinking participated in temperance organizations in hopes of pressuring local officials to pass or more effectively enforce laws regulating alcohol. They also publicized their concerns in letters to friendly editors. "If there is a place in this state that is more cursed than another with intemperance, it is Austin," a woman who identified herself only as a "Republican lady" wrote. "The social glass ruins more young men than any other form of dissipation—in fact it is the key to all dissipation. They drink to be social, and by the time they have taken two or three glasses, their sensibilities are blunted and reason is perverted, and they do many things of which they are at first ashamed, but after a few repetitions they manifest a 'don't care' spirit, and in a few years die, that worst of all things, a drunkard."[31] The same writer acknowledged her inability to influence legislation. "If you hear of any one who is foolish enough to think that I could be of any assistance in putting through the legislature any measure," she wrote, "just tell them I cannot do it, as I am a temperance woman and opposed to smoking, and champagne and cigars are always required."[32]

With prohibition for the time being left to local voters to decide, mobilization at the state level of the kind that occurred in some northern states was unnecessary, and clergy could quietly speak their mind at temperance meetings without organizing large-scale rallies. Temperance sometimes took on larger meaning when rival political candidates accused one another of being drunks, on the one hand, or too strict about prohibition, on the other hand. White leaders understood that African Americans might be the deciding factor in local option elections and on occasion appealed directly to them. For example, at a meeting in Austin the Honorable William E. Dodge of New York addressed African Americans in the audience, encouraging them to vote on the side of law and order and public safety. By doing so, he said, they would contribute toward making "this county a prosperous, peaceable county, to which emigration will come, and you have it in your power to prevent intemperance from destroying yourselves."[33] Judging from local commentary, though, the more common view among white voters was that African Americans were so naïve and so driven by extreme emotions, either in favor of complete abstinence or easily drawn to drunkenness, that their votes were unreliable.[34]

The most serious effort in favor of prohibition occurred in 1887 when proponents succeeded in placing a constitutional amendment on the ballot to ban the manufacture, sale, and exchange of intoxicating liquors except for medicinal, mechanical, sacramental, and scientific purposes. Woman's Christian Temperance Union president Frances Willard had toured towns in East Texas with some success in 1882, but her visit also aroused skepticism because of northern temperance leaders' history as abolitionists and Willard's own embrace of women's suffrage as well as antipathy among southern church leaders toward social activism.[35] Prohibition nevertheless gained some support in Texas among Baptists and Methodists.[36] At a meeting of the Baptist General Convention of Texas in Waco during the summer of 1886, for example, a preliminary report on prohibition drew enthusiastic support. "I would live the balance of my natural life on corn cobs and stump water rather than back down on this question," one delegate proclaimed.[37] Dr. J. B. Cranfill, a Baptist layperson who practiced general medicine and edited an antisaloon paper, became one of the most vocal champions of the amendment, and on one occasion Reverend Dr. B. H. Carroll of the First Baptist Church in Waco took part in a public debate about prohibition.[38] At least one Baptist church in Dallas hosted a prohibition lecture by former Kansas legislator Reverend Calvin Reasoner of Kansas City, the response to which included criticism for bringing politics into a church but was otherwise generally favorable.[39] Leaders of the Democratic Party and advocates of prohibition themselves, though, were divided about how best to proceed, and even some who favored it were repulsed by what they saw as an "intemperate zeal for the promotion of a righteous cause."[40] Opponents of prohibition appealed to the legacy of Thomas Jefferson in defense of limited government, and even the advocates of prohibition conceded that a rationale other than religion was needed because, as one explained, "In this country the church is one thing and the state another."[41] In one community opposition to the measure ran so high that a prohibition speaker was saluted with a fusillade of rotten eggs so severely that he retreated under a bench after a failed attempt to flee through a window.[42]

County by county, the prohibition measure was approved by overwhelming majorities in 8 counties, where as many as two-thirds of the votes cast were favorable, and rejected by overwhelming majorities in 9 counties, where fewer than 5 percent of the votes cast were favorable. In all, 31 counties approved the measure by a bare majority while the remaining 151 counties in which votes were cast rejected it. Counties with higher proportions of Methodists and Baptists were more likely to approve, while counties with larger proportions of African Americans and Roman Catholics were more likely to disapprove.[43] Overall the amendment failed by more than 90,000 votes, leaving local option in effect. Over the next decade 53 of the state's counties used local option to become dry, and 79 others used it to become partly dry.[44]

FIGURE 4. Town Square, Honey Grove, Texas, ca. 1885, an example of new towns on the emerging frontier. Photograph by Frank B. Wolcott. Lawrence T. Jones III Texas Photography Collection, Southern Methodist University, Central University Libraries, DeGolyer Library.

In subsequent years social observers found it surprising that a state in which conservative religion seemed to prevail had failed to pass prohibition. In reality, though, Texas was sufficiently diverse culturally and ethnically and had a tradition of tolerance that ran against the idea of regulating morality through law. This tradition was well explained in answer to a letter in 1887 inquiring about the possibility of prohibition ever passing in Texas in which *Kansas City Times* editor John N. Edwards, who had spent time in Texas, replied that it was about as likely as finding cologne in a pigpen. Texas is "an exceedingly cosmopolitan state," he explained, "made so by its very immensity. Tolerance is indigenous there because of that exalted idea of person or individual freedom which finds its highest type and its most exalted expression in range, latitude, and boundlessness." Prohibition might be popular in Kansas, he wrote, but things were different in Texas. "When a man in Texas begins to prescribe certain fixed metes and bounds wherein his neighbor shall walk and conduct himself, he is either lassoed or scalped."[45]

Compared to temperance and prohibition, efforts to regulate prostitution were generally more agreeable to the public at large but met with some resistance as well. Ambivalence was especially evident in Galveston, where part of the population thought the town should be like New Orleans, taking a permissive stance toward the "social evil," while others felt strongly that evil should be outlawed. The differences were sometimes described as a Continental European approach, on the one side, which reflected Texas's French and Spanish traditions, and an Anglo-Saxon approach, on the other side, which honored the conservative Protestant traditions of the Old South and New England. Defenders of prostitution also argued that it was simply unreasonable to regulate natural male appetites. "Marriage in the average of cases takes place at about the age of twenty-four," a writer observed, "whereas puberty commences at the age of fourteen. For ten years, therefore, and that in the very flush of life, the sexual appetite is starved. This discrepancy between the marriage system and nature is one of the principal sources of prostitution."[46]

CHURCH EXPANSION

Besides laws curbing the worst offenses against public morality, the best alternative for keeping unruly behavior to a minimum, many residents apparently believed, was to start churches in which members voluntarily policed one another's behavior. In this, Texas was far more successful. After the fairly weak showing by religious organizations in the 1870 census, better times and better record keeping led to a substantially larger number of churches being reported in subsequent census data and in contemporaneous counts by denominational leaders. Methodists in 1878, for example, reported 503 churches with a total of 77,944 members. Cumberland Presbyterians tallied 400 congregations with 18,000 members. And there were 112 Roman Catholic churches and chapels with 104,000 baptized adults and children. Baptist statistics included only 174 church buildings with 17,203 members, but unofficial estimates ranged as high as 150,000, served by more than 500 local and traveling preachers.[47]

The 1880 U.S. Census collected no data on religious organizations but asked about the occupations of anyone employed over the age of fifteen, thus providing a rough estimate of the number of clergy in each state, not including lay preachers who may have listed some other primary occupation. Texans included 2,161 clergy, which amounted to 1 pastor for every 737 residents. That number was better than in any of the other states that had been in the Confederacy. For example, Virginia had only 1 pastor for every 860 residents; North Carolina, 1 for every 933 residents; and Alabama, 1 for every 1,039 residents. Among the more recently settled states, Kansas, with 1 pastor for every 594 residents, had the best ratio, followed by Nebraska, with 1 for every 608 residents, and Iowa, with 1 for every 658 residents. But it was clear that Texas was becoming one of the most religious states by this measure at least and was especially so were lay preachers also taken into account.[48]

Data collected in 1890 showed that Baptists and Methodists were running neck and neck in founding churches and attracting members. There were approximately 2,300 white Baptist congregations, with nearly 130,000 members. The Methodist Episcopal Church South included 1,700 congregations with

139,000 members. Among African Americans, Baptists were clearly in the lead with 1,300 congregations and 104,000 members, compared to fewer than 500 congregations and approximately 45,000 members among the several predominately African American Methodist denominations. Other than Baptists and Methodists, the only other denomination that included a large segment of the population was the Roman Catholic Church, with nearly 100,000 members, counting both adults and children.

Texas belied the notion that a religious market with countless small religious bodies thrives better than one with just a few leading competitors. Setting aside Catholics, the two largest denominations—Baptists and Methodists—accounted for nearly three-quarters of all Protestants in the state, and both were flourishing. Their dominance did not deter the efforts of smaller denominations, but those were mostly traditions already represented among the state's earliest settlers or distinctive to more recent immigrants. Examples included Disciples of Christ with 42,000 members, Cumberland Presbyterians with 22,000 members, and Ohio Synod Lutherans with 1,700 members. With Texas's large and expanding population, including growth in major towns such as Houston, Dallas, and San Antonio, some diversity among less prominent traditions was also becoming evident. Statewide there were eighteen Universalist churches, fifteen Seventh Day Adventist congregations, eleven synagogues, six Dunkard groups, five Christian Scientist organizations, and one Spiritualist church.

"Texas has been, and to some extent is yet, looked upon as rather an uncivilized country, in which wild cowboys and lawlessness reign supreme," a Lutheran pastor observed in 1897. "It was a rough country, some fifty years ago, it is true, but things have had ample time to undergo radical changes since then." He was encouraged that Swedes, Norwegians, and Germans could all find Lutheran churches in which to worship. Through "Christianity and its handmaid, general education," he wrote "social and political life everywhere is made better."[49]

As impressive as membership figures may have been, it was equally impressive to observe how active churches had been in erecting buildings and organizing members into associations and conferences. With total membership statewide of 670,000, there were enough buildings to seat 1.5 million, which meant plenty of space for new members and their families as well as for visitors. The total value of these buildings was estimated at approximately $8.6 million. Organizing members into associations was best illustrated among the Baptist churches, which were organized into more than seventy associations, each with a moderator, clerk, corresponding secretary, and treasurer. The Baptist associations worked especially well in providing some coordination, discipline, and support at the local level, usually for no more than twenty or thirty congregations, while giving each congregation and preacher considerable latitude in making decisions.

To the extent that competition with other denominations may have encouraged church growth, it was just as likely that preachers within each denomination competed to make their church and their association successful. Certainly there was wide variation in the size and resources of particular congregations, which not only reflected the opportunities available in different locations but also gave pastors an incentive to work hard in order to make their own congregation grow and to be selected for an opening at a larger one. For example, First Baptist Church in Dallas had grown to 700 members by 1895 and had a facility valued at $75,000, whereas the Cedar Hill Church, which was one of the Dallas area's oldest congregations, had only 92 members and a building valued at $1,250. Cedar Hill, though, was faring much better than nine nearby congregations, none of which had more than 60 members, and six of which did not have a regular pastor.[50]

Statewide the Baptist General Convention of Texas reported having 2,818 churches in 1895, or about 500 more than in the 1890 U.S. Census, with a total membership of 170,588, which, when adjusted for the 171 congregations that did not report, might have been closer to 182,000. Pastors' annual salaries averaged $545, but nearly half of all congregations did not have a pastor of their own.[51] First Baptist Church in Dallas was the second largest congregation in the state, exceeded only by First Baptist Church in Waco, with 885 members. Eighty-five congregations reported having at least 200 members. More than 650 congregations reported having fewer than 30 members. The median among all churches reporting membership was 50.[52]

The Baptist data underscored several conclusions. For one, there was considerable variation in size of congregations. Though unsurprising, this was an aspect of religion less evident in the county-level U.S. Census reports. Second, the number of churches and church members was probably larger than those included in census reports, or else there had been significant growth between 1890 and 1895. And third, the variation in size among congregations was an important clue to understanding why churches were so successful in attracting members. Just as denominational diversity enabled American religion to adapt to different preferences, variation in congregational size facilitated adaptation to different locations. As the U.S. population grew and expanded westward, religion advanced in sparsely populated locations where a mere handful of people could form a church and meet in homes with preaching provided on occasion by an itinerant pastor. It advanced in small towns where as few as fifty people could join forces and build a modest church. And it adapted in fledgling cities like Dallas and Waco where much larger congregations could flourish.

Baptists and Methodists were especially good at adapting to these various locations. While the two differed in style of church government and in understandings of the sacraments, both held revival meetings and employed itinerant clergy that facilitated the founding of congregations in places with sparse populations. Without pastors or buildings, these congregations were then organized into local and regional associations. In places with expanding populations, congregations developed through a process of selection that favored the communities with stronger growth. The Baptist figures are revealing in this regard. Of the congregations with the largest memberships, nearly all were in larger towns such as Dallas, Waco, Fort Worth, Austin, San Antonio, and Houston, and in towns in the northeast quadrant that had been settled early, such as Belton, Corsicana, Marshall, and Paris. Nearly all congregations with at least fifty members were located in or near incorporated towns. In contrast, the smallest congregations were less likely to be located in or near such towns. Small or large, congregations were also subject to the uncertainties of crop yields, population reversals, and the popularity or unpopularity of particular pastors. For example, the Baptist church at Anderson in Grimes County had grown to 153 members by 1876, but in 1880 its African American members withdrew to form their own congregation, leaving a membership of 85 which declined to 40 in 1885 and sank to a low of 26 before climbing back to 49 in 1909. Meanwhile the Baptist church at Navasota, ten miles from Anderson, grew to 250 members in no small part because of faster population growth and better rail service.[53]

In small congregations the fact that neighbors and relatives were intimately acquainted with one another was also an important aspect of church life. J. M. Dawson, who later earned distinction as a leader among Texas Baptists, recalled boyhood experiences in two Baptist churches in the 1890s that illustrated these social aspects of small congregations. The first was at Auburn, an unincorporated town of fewer than three hundred people in Ellis County. In this small community there were two grocery stores, two cotton gins, a post office, an elementary school, a Masonic lodge, and four churches. The Baptist church where Dawson's family attended had about thirty-five members. According to Dawson, it nevertheless "rated at the top of rural congregations in size of membership, stewardship, evangelism, and quality of worshipers." Following tradition, the men still sat on one side of the aisle and women and children on the other. The hymns were sung with gusto, he remembered, and the services were sometimes even livelier. "In revivals not infrequently a few women shouted, whirled in unrestrained emotion or sank into a trance which I fancied was death. Once during a solemn prayer for the wicked, a penitent man screamed so loudly I thought I would die from fright."[54]

The other church, which Dawson joined at age fourteen, was in Italy, an incorporated town of about four hundred people, also in Ellis County. The Baptist church here had about two hundred members. At first Dawson felt estranged and instead of listening to the sermons devoted himself to identifying oddities among the individual worshippers. "My unexpected conversion changed all that foolishness in a flash. On that day after Father had spoken to me about my eternal salvation, Brother Lloyd had expounded the Sunday school lesson, and Pastor W. R. Selvidge had preached; I knelt, confessed my sins, and humbly took Jesus Christ to be my Savior." He instantly felt better about his eternal salvation. But to his surprise, and illustrating how salvation mattered socially as well as spiritually, he also now felt powerfully that he belonged. No longer estranged, his conversion made him a member who was fully accepted by the community. "When I opened my eyes the congregation appeared transfigured. I loved everyone." The congregation then officially "voted me into the membership."[55]

The social benefits of church membership were not lost among church leaders. While eternal salvation was certainly the greatest benefit of religion, leaders argued explicitly for the moral betterment it offered as well. Without the moral uplift provided by religion, it was very likely that people would simply move away and a town would die, a pastor in Dallas explained. "No man wishes to raise his children without such restraining and beneficent influences. Men here settled for life would speedily make their exit. For want of customers trade would be practically suspended." The morals of the young, he said, "would be forever ruined, and life would be wholly insecure in a community bereft of its churches and its Sunday schools." Indeed, better churches were as important as, if not more than, better law enforcement. "The gospel of Christ throws around you a stronger and more efficient protection than can be given by law or by musket."[56]

UNDER THREAT OF OUTRAGE

With churches at nearly every crossroads, it was easy to imagine that Texas in the late 1880s had become a state populated by pious Christians who were seldom in danger from one another or their neighbors. Besides that, law enforcement was better and more towns had grown large enough to be incorporated and levy taxes for roads, schools, police, and other amenities. Texas nevertheless was still part of the expanding frontier, and, as this reference to law and musket suggests, the sense of civilization as an island of sanity with danger on all sides remained.

For African Americans intimidation by the Ku Klux Klan, lynching, and black codes that imposed severe penalties for the slightest infractions provided ample reason to believe that a religious congregation was one of the few available sanctuaries in a dangerous world. Even that was not always the case. Seventy miles west of Houston in the vicinity of Columbus, several towns were chartered in the late 1870s that reversed the usual process of starting a town first and then adding churches as civilizing agents. Here the towns of Rocky Chapel, Toland Chapel, and Hill's Chapel were founded because a church was already there. Because the churches were racially segregated, the towns followed suit. Hill's Chapel was African American, but the town was short-lived. When several of the cattle owned by white ranchers in the area went missing, a mob descended on Hill's Chapel, riddled one African American man with bullets, burned his house, and forced his terrified family and their neighbors to flee. Soon after, the mob returned and burned all the buildings in the town, including the church.[57]

Among white Texans, episodes publicizing villainous acts by African Americans served as palpable symbols of the danger threatening civilized people. Stories of outrage reminiscent of earlier atrocities committed by renegade Indians and undisciplined Union soldiers circulated. White women especially were said to be the victims or potential victims of outrage by black men. This fear was a recurring factor that had to be taken into account whenever white people discussed the good that churches and schools were doing for African Americans as well as the presumed limits of those efforts.

Stories of outrage followed a characteristic script. Usually the outrage happened at night and was against a white woman or girl who presumed she was safe in her own bedroom when a shadowy African American figure appeared at her window, stood by her bedside, touched her, or was seen trying to enter the house. The terrified woman then screamed and her father or husband ran in pursuit, only to be eluded by the furtive black man. In variations of the story, the woman or her husband shot at the intruder and missed, or the sheriff joined in the failed pursuit. On occasion the intruder was never identified or captured, while on other occasions someone in the community who appeared to match the description of the shadowy figure was identified, captured, and executed. There were instances in which the outrage was undoubtedly real and others in which it was only presumed to be real. In either case, the stories in which an outrage was described dramatized the tension not only between whites and blacks but also between the forces of good that civilized people hoped were on their side and the forces of evil that constantly posed threats against civilization.

One such outrage occurred in Paris, Texas, in 1888 when the pastor of the Methodist church was awakened at two o'clock in the morning by the screams of his cook. "Hastily going to the room occupied by her, and in which the cries were trying to be repeated as if stifled, he found that some black fiend had entered the room and attempted to commit an outrage on the woman." The fiend, however, escaped capture by jumping out the window.[58]

A similar episode took place in Waco in 1886 when a servant girl of German parentage reported that a black man entered her room through a window and crept to her bedside while she was asleep. "She was awakened by his touch and began to cry out for help, when he caught her by the throat and threatened to kill her unless she gratified him." The report continued, "After a scuffle she succeeded in freeing herself from his clutches and again cried out for assistance," whereupon the man fled. "The officers were informed of the fact and the matter kept quiet while the monster was being ferreted out." An African American barber in Waco was subsequently arrested.[59]

Three months later the citizens of Waco were terrified to read that another outrage had taken place in their community. This time a farmer's daughter was the victim. "The farmer says he was aroused last night by his daughter's cries, and, upon going to the room, was told by his horrified daughter that [an African American man] had entered the room and attempted a diabolical outrage upon her person."[60]

Before the year was over, four African Americans had been lynched in East Texas. Another had been disemboweled and left for dead but lived long enough to tell neighbors what happened. In West Texas Chinese railroad workers were tortured and robbed.[61] A few months later an African American youth in Marcos, Texas, was imprisoned for "attempted outrage," seized by a mob, and hanged.[62] Seemingly, lynching was the only possible solution. Later that year a young woman in Dallas was attacked in the city park by two African Americans who presumably found her buxom figure too appealing to resist. Lynching was too good for the perpetrators, residents said. A proper example would require burning them at the stake.[63]

That verdict became a reality five years later when an African American named Ed Coy who was accused of assaulting a white woman was captured near Texarkana. Seeing that the man was about to be hung, the crowd cried, "Burn him, burn him," to which officials replied that for the sake of women and children present the burning should at least be conducted outside of town. Having located a suitable space, the crowd poured several cans of kerosene oil over the man and asked the woman who had been assaulted if she might like to strike the match. She did, applying it to his clothes in two places and watching as the man shrieked in agony until he died. Six thousand citizens witnessed the event.[64]

When outrages were presumed to have been committed by an African American, the reports usually said so explicitly, but they did not do the same when the guilty party was assumed to be white, thereby leaving open the possibility that the person may have been black or at the least was a mysterious stranger whose characteristics were just as threatening. A particularly gruesome event that surely would have stoked fears among respectable law-abiding citizens occurred around the same time as the two in Waco and involved a German woman who was attacked by three assailants. "They went to this woman's house and made an attempt to outrage her. Her husband, who was sleeping in an adjoining room, hearing the noise and screams of his wife, went to her relief." After the husband was wounded, "the woman was beaten with a club and bit in several places about her arms and person, and they mutilated her breast, rendering it impossible for her to give nourishment to a suckling babe."[65]

Despite the harsh official or unofficial punishments delivered when assailants were caught, reports of outrage continued. In 1889 a white woman in Floresville reported that a black man had suddenly entered her bedroom only to be scared off by her dog, who would have done the man more damage had the dog's teeth not been old and badly worn.[66] The following year a reporter in Dallas located a woman who said a black man had awakened her and when she called to her husband the intruder dropped to the floor, crawled to the window, dove through, and escaped. The same reporter said a second outrage had occurred the same night in a different part of town when a black scoundrel was scared off by a woman's husband and two police officers who fired shots at the fleeing man but missed.[67] And so it went.

Shocked citizens could take solace in the fact that horrendous events like this did not occur often, and when they did the perpetrators could be found and summarily punished. Outrage was nevertheless a reminder that ultimately nobody was completely safe. It was thus incumbent on good citizens to do their best to strengthen the institutions upholding common decency. In the first instance, that involved proper law enforcement. Public officials should not, as one writer argued, turn their back on "outrages against good people."[68] In addition, the larger message was that moral character should somehow be strengthened and upheld. Honesty, integrity, and sobriety were sorely needed. Relationships across racial and ethnic lines were perhaps so fraught with danger that segregation was the only imaginable solution, and yet schools, churches, revival meetings, and civic organizations of all kinds could presumably reinforce a kind of moral density that would keep tendencies toward evil at bay.

How effective that might be, though, remained uncertain. A year and a half before the immolation at Texarkana witnessed by six thousand citizens, a hugely successful series of revival meetings had been held in Texarkana. Every night for a week and on Sunday afternoon, traveling evangelist Dixon Williams preached to a capacity crowd at the local opera house. Not even the presence of a circus that came through at the same time dampened the crowd's enthusiasm. With every seat filled and several hundred standing in the aisles and outside, the participants joined in singing "What a Friend We Have in Jesus" and "Yield Not to Temptation." Brother Dixon exhorted the men especially to bear in mind the gospel message that "whatsoever a man soweth that shall he also reap" whenever they considered the temptations of lust and licentiousness. At the end of each evening's service at least a hundred went forward seeking prayer and forgiveness. When it was over, Brother Dixon figured his efforts had "stirred the community on religious subjects" to a degree never before approximated.[69]

In the months following Dixon's revival, churches in Texarkana—Methodist, Baptist, Presbyterian, Christian, and Roman Catholic—were active as never before. Preaching, Sunday school classes, ladies' auxiliary gatherings for tea, musicals, and Christmas festivities were held with regularity. As news of the lynching of Ed Coy spread in national and international newspapers, writers wondered what could possibly have gone wrong in Texarkana. How was it possible for such a horrible event to have taken place almost in the shadow of local churches? "The noble women here," a resident of Texarkana wrote, "have organized charitable associations," and the town includes many "who lead the lives of consecrated Christians." He was confident that Texarkana could experience "steady, healthy growth," although he questioned whether that could happen while "being chained to the African."[70] Others expressed particular confidence in the churches and schools. Is the law "so futile and crime so diabolically strong," another writer asked, "that women are only safe when criminals are burned at the stake?" What was the answer? Better laws would not be enough, the writer argued. "The church and the school house" were a more effective source of humane and civilized behavior. "The churches and school houses have not failed in Texarkana. They have simply fallen short. They must be doubled, tripled, quadrupled. Nothing else will avail, but this surely will."[71]

WIDENING THE SCOPE OF INSTITUTIONS

Better churches and schoolhouses, along with better law enforcement and greater security in public affairs and in business, were widely regarded as the means of bringing about a more humane and civilized society. By the end of the nineteenth century, the place of religion in Texas could be understood only in part by considering the number of congregations that had been founded. Religion was only in the first instance a matter of churching the state. It was also an endeavor involving the creation of institutions spanning nearly every aspect of life, from schools and colleges to hospitals and publishing houses. Religion was in this respect becoming big business. At the same time, religious institutions were also taking their place amid a broader division of labor in which many of the tasks of social life were performed by organizations disconnected from or only loosely connected to religion. Thus as religion expanded, its scope was also circumscribed by the activities of these other organizations. Religion's activities occurred largely within its own realm, rather than through direct action in the political sphere, as would become the case later. Church leaders focused on preaching and teaching as the preferred ways of guiding the faithful and looked to schools, colleges, benevolent institutions, and even prisons to do their part in educating good citizens and maintaining law and order.

Like churches, the number of schools and teachers grew considerably during the last third of the nineteenth century. From approximately 2,000 in the early 1870s, the total number of schools rose to more than 7,000 by 1885 and the number of teachers increased from about 2,500 to 8,600.[72] At that date Texas was nevertheless widely regarded as having one of the poorest school systems anywhere, despite ample land and resources for the support of education. In 1888 state superintendent Oscar H. Cooper observed, "In many counties the value of the common jail exceeds that of all the school property." Rural schools were especially deficient. More than five thousand were housed temporarily in neighborhood churches and vacant barns. Municipalities were able to authorize bonds for school construction, but the law forbade counties from doing so. Overall, local taxes levied for schools were barely half the national average. Only feeble efforts were being made to promote secondary education. One view, Cooper noted, was that secondary education was in fact detrimental because children should be left to develop their natural talents on their own.[73]

In following years the number of schoolchildren and teachers steadily expanded. There were 226,000 children in school in 1880, representing 14 percent of the total population. That number grew to 545,000 in 1890, 706,000 in 1900, and 949,000 in 1910, in each year representing 24 percent of the total population.[74] Statewide, the number of certified teachers rose to 10,162 in 1891 and then climbed at a rate of approximately 500 a year to reach 21,277 in 1910, with women accounting for approximately 70 percent of all teachers compared with only a quarter in the 1870s.[75]

The huge differences in educational attainment and opportunities between white and black populations that had been present in the 1870s remained. In 1900, 94 percent of native-born adult white males were literate, but that was true of only 54 percent of black adult males. In urban areas with younger populations

FIGURE 5. Gathering cotton in Texas, ca. 1900, showing African American adults and children working as sharecroppers and day laborers. Keystone View Company. Lawrence T. Jones III Texas Photography Collection, Southern Methodist University, Central University Libraries, DeGolyer Library.

such as Dallas, Houston, and San Antonio, the rates among black adult males were generally higher, ranging from 65 to 75 percent, but in the earliest settled rural counties, such as Chambers and San Augustine, the rates were closer to 30 percent.[76] Forty-six percent of white children ages five through eighteen were enrolled in school, well below the national average of 58 percent, while among black children only 38 percent were in school.[77] Detailed statistics for the 1919–20 school year showed that 17 percent of the state's school-age children were African American, but only 5 percent of students enrolled in high school were

African American. Of the 150 public high schools for African Americans, only 34 offered four years of instruction.[78]

For those able to afford it, higher education was increasingly available under both public and denominational auspices. Baptists had founded Baylor University in Waco in 1845, and Baylor Female College, which eventually grew into the University of Mary Hardin–Baylor, started at the same time. St. Mary's University in San Antonio was founded by Society of Mary brothers and priests in 1852. Cumberland Presbyterians formed Trinity University in Tehuacana in 1869 from three small colleges that had failed during the Civil War. Texas Christian University was founded in Fort Worth as AdRan College in 1873 by Disciples of Christ leaders Addison and Randolph Clark. Also founded in 1873 was Wiley College, begun in Marshall by the Methodist Episcopal Church South as a black college. Southwestern University emerged in 1875 from four Methodist colleges, the oldest of which had been founded in 1840.

Among public institutions, Texas A&M University began in 1871 and held its first classes in 1876. The University of Texas at Austin came five years later in 1881. That year also saw the opening of Tillotson Collegiate and Normal Institute in Austin with support from the American Missionary Society as a college for African American students. To these, Polytechnic College, which became Texas Wesleyan University, was created in 1890 by the Methodist Church, and Hardin-Simmons University, founded as Abilene Baptist College, was added in 1891.

After the turn of the century new institutions appeared with increasing frequency. Samuel Huston College, one of the state's historically black colleges, opened in Austin in 1900. Texas Woman's University in Denton was created in 1901 by an act of the state legislature, Abilene Christian University was formed as the Childers Classical Institute in 1906 by the Churches of Christ, Southwestern Baptist Theological Seminary in Fort Worth was established in 1908, Wayland Baptist University held its first classes in Plainview in 1910, Southern Methodist University in Dallas was added in 1911, and Rice University in Houston was founded in 1912.[79] Statewide, the number of college students increased from 2,071 in 1900 to 7,159 in 1918, the number of college professors rose from 293 to 751, and the total income of colleges and universities jumped from $451,000 to $4.9 million.[80]

Whether this expansion would benefit denominational colleges or redound increasingly to public universities was unclear. On the one hand, ownership by church bodies, administration by trustee boards composed of clergy, mandatory Bible courses, and regulations governing the activities of students ensured that denominational schools would for the time being carry out their distinctive mission of religious education. On the other hand, educators predicted that higher education would increasingly be monopolized by state institutions with large budgets, leaving church colleges on the periphery as "adjuncts or feeders," almost in the role that preparatory schools had played in the past.[81] For their part, public universities might deviate sharply from the aims of religiously minded parents unless special efforts were made to minister to students in those contexts, and with that aim in mind religious organizations were founded at each of the state's universities. At the University of Texas, for example, the Young Men's Christian Association was one of the largest organizations on campus, with between four hundred and five hundred in attendance at weekly meetings. It encouraged students to devote their lives to Christ and tried to steer them from worldly temptations. "The majority of the students come from Christian homes," the leader observed, but on campus students were faced with new freedom. "Perfect liberty is the product of perfect law, and failure to realize this results sometimes in wrecked lives or selfish and indifferent ones," the leader hoped they would see.[82]

Benevolent institutions were another kind of organization that was becoming more common during the last years of the nineteenth century. They included hospitals, orphanages, permanent group homes for older and disabled people, asylums for insane people, day nurseries, dispensaries, and temporary homes for unwed mothers and their children. These organizations were particularly interesting as an expression of contemporary understandings of moral character and responsibility. They demonstrated an awareness that society bore some responsibility to care for those who were unable to care for themselves. Many were founded by religious groups or by private individuals motivated by their faith. Public institutions required support through taxes and from veterans' pensions. Some benevolent organizations, such as homes for unwed mothers, included efforts to instill moral values in those deemed by society to have fallen short of those standards. In relation to the wider society, benevolent institutions also served as the context in which roles were defined and facilitated that helped concerned citizens to act on their moral principles. They provided employment for doctors, nurses, wardens, caretakers, and others in the service professions. Some of the benevolent institutions relied on volunteers, and many depended on the work of church groups, ladies' auxiliaries, and other charitable organizations.

The United States government conducted an extensive investigation in 1904 to determine how many benevolent institutions there were, how many people they served, and how they were supported. The inquiry identified 4,207 benevolent institutions nationwide and determined that 2,004, or nearly half. had been founded during the previous fourteen years. On average about 140 new institutions were being founded annually, and there was some indication that the pace had quickened since the turn of the century. There were 1,493 hospitals, 1,075 orphanages and children's homes, 753 permanent homes for adults or adults and children, 449 temporary homes for adults and children, 166 day nurseries, 156 dispensaries, and 115 schools or homes for people who were deaf or blind. The report noted that many short-lived organizations would have served for a few years but would not have appeared in the overall figures. In all more than two million people had been assisted by these institutions in 1903 at a cost of more than $55 million. Religious groups operated 32 percent of the organizations, 56 percent were under private auspices, and 12 percent were public institutions. The study concluded that approximately 80 percent of the persons served by benevolent institutions of all kinds were helped through private charity. Hospitals and orphanages were particularly in the hands of private charity, while permanent homes for those who were disabled, deaf, or blind were more likely to be under public auspices.[83]

There were 76 benevolent institutions in Texas, operating at a cost of $600,000 in 1903 and serving approximately 28,000 people. Twenty-six of the organizations were under the auspices of religious groups, 36 were under private auspices, and 14 were public institutions. The oldest organizations were the Texas Blind Asylum, founded in 1856, and the Texas School for the Deaf, founded in 1857, both in Austin.[84] A few of the organizations had been founded shortly after the Civil War. For example, St. Mary's Infirmary in Galveston was founded by Sisters of the Sacred Heart in 1866, the Santa Rosa Infirmary in San Antonio began under the auspices of the Sisters of Charity in 1869, and the Houston Infirmary Sanitarium for railroad employees began in 1872. The majority dated from the 1890s and included municipal institutions such as Parkland Hospital in Dallas and the John Sealy Hospital in Galveston, private hospitals for railroad workers such as the St. Louis Southwestern Railway Hospital in Texarkana, and dispensaries and emergency clinics associated with medical schools such as the Free Dispensary of the Medical Department at Fort Worth University.[85] Nearly all the temporary homes for unwed mothers were under private auspices, such as the Anna B. Cunningham Mission Home operated by the Woman's Home Mission Society of the Methodist Episcopal Church South in Dallas for "erring girls" and the Texas Rest Cottage under the auspices of the International Apostolic Holiness Union in Pilot Point for "prostitutes and unfortunate women and their children."[86] The efforts of religious organizations were particularly evident among orphanages and permanent homes for older or disabled people as well. These included St. Matthew's Home for Aged Women in Dallas under sponsorship of St. Matthew's Episcopal Cathedral, Cumberland Rest sponsored by the Cumberland Presbyterian Church in Fort Worth, and the Juliette Fowler Orphans and Widows' Home in Grand Prairie sponsored by the Christian Church of Texas.[87]

The study found considerable variation among states in the number of benevolent institutions, persons assisted, and cost when standardized by size of population. Newer states west of the Mississippi generally had higher rates of benevolent institutions than older states, although Indiana and Ohio had the highest rates because of having established a system of organizations in each county under public auspices. Northern states had higher rates than southern states. Southern states were also particularly deficient in organizations under religious auspices, presumably because Roman Catholics and northern Protestant denominations were more likely to have started benevolent organizations than southern denominations, but perhaps also because of racial differences.

The rate of benevolent institutions in Texas reflected its location and historic association with the South. Although hospitals, orphanages, and permanent or temporary homes for persons in need were being established by the state, municipalities, colleges, private charities, and churches, Texas had relatively few such organizations relative to the size of its population. A comparison between Texas and Missouri was revealing in this regard. Both had populations of approximately three million in 1900, and the two shared similar histories in terms of founding dates and slavery. Compared with the 76 organizations present in Texas, there were 140 in Missouri. Missouri's benevolent organizations assisted twice as many people as Texas's and did so at twice the cost. Among all states, Texas ranked thirty-third in terms of the number of persons assisted per 100,000 population. It ranked thirty-ninth in terms of per capita expenditures for the support of benevolent institutions.[88]

The statistics on benevolent institutions in Texas suggested two emerging patterns. On the one hand, Texas was steadily creating new institutions that contributed to the overall density of organizations through which persons of goodwill could express their charitable values. Along with churches and schools, benevolent institutions contributed toward the advancement of civilization that civic leaders desired. On the other hand, the Texas pattern reflected a reluctance to devote public funds to benevolent activities and a preference for charitable work done by private organizations. Churches were certainly involved, but the efforts of Roman Catholics, Methodists, and other denominations were more evident in the statistics than the work of Baptists. There was perhaps evidence as well of the view that persons who needed assistance should help themselves or look to their families and congregations rather than depending on public assistance.

These patterns were evident in methods of dealing with convicted criminals as well. Institutions for confinement were handling larger numbers of inmates but procedures for minimizing cost to the public were also in place. Of particular interest was the state penitentiary at Huntsville. Its walls separating those inside from the townspeople outside offered tangible evidence of the contrast between good and evil. Here was the embodiment of wrongdoing amid a community that prided itself on educational academies, debutante balls, church services, and lodge meetings. From 1849 to 1940 a total of 95,500 prisoners were incarcerated at Huntsville. This number included a nine-year-old African American boy serving a five-year sentence for robbery and an eleven-year-old African American girl sentenced to three years for administering poison.[89] To reduce costs, convicts were leased to plantation owners in the area who paid the prison for the use of this labor. By 1900 the number of inmates had risen to the point that new calls were made to investigate ways to reduce the rising financial burden on the state.

MOLDING THE MORAL INDIVIDUAL

Clergy and others with deep religious convictions felt it necessary on occasion to become involved directly and publicly in political contests and controversies. Reverend Honey and Reverend Parker were two examples during Reconstruction.

As a lay Baptist leader, J. B. Cranfill did so for the cause of prohibition in the 1880s. But compared to the late twentieth century when religious leaders seemed intent on playing a major role in political campaigns and policy discussions, these earlier activities were relatively infrequent. Clergy and church people in southern states for the most part appeared reluctant to engage in social activism. The reticence stemmed from earlier misgivings about abolitionism among northern clergy and from the extent to which temperance activism was led by northern organizations, Republicans, and suffragists. It was perhaps a mark of southern gentility or of complacency. It was also related to the assumption that moral uplift was being advanced more effectively in other ways. It involved shaping the moral character of the individual person and was accomplished in the context of laws that punished the worst offenses and that largely maintained the status quo in terms of racial disparities but otherwise were deemed to be in the best interest of private individuals. Good behavior was to be taught rather than tightly regulated, and if regulation was required, as was sometimes considered to be the case with prohibition, it was to be decided locally.

The task of instilling good behavior in individuals fell in the first instance to families and then to the institutions most closely associated with families: congregations and schools. Congregations were loosely coordinated through denominational associations, and schools were administered according to standards established by the state, but both institutions were governed by strong conventions of local autonomy. The democratic ideal that Tocqueville had observed was instantiated in churches, schools, Masonic lodges, neighborhood gatherings, and benevolent institutions. None of these institutions functioned as smoothly as the democratic ideal suggested they should, certainly not for those with meager incomes and those who were routinely discriminated against because of their race. It was rather the expectation that progress could be advanced on the moral front as well as economically by creating an array of local institutions.

Compared to the kind of social organization involved in labor organizing or in mobilizing large-scale political movements, this emphasis on the moral character of individuals appeared to be wildly individualistic. It was easily interpreted as the kind of bootstrap individualism portrayed so vividly in the rags-to-riches writing of Horatio Alger or more clearly in Texas-sized stories of adventuresome cowboys. Neither was a good description of what was actually going on. The civilizing process in reality meant restraining the wild spaces in which cowboys and outlaws prevailed. It meant fencing the land, turning it into farms, erecting schools and churches, building courthouses, and creating a safe environment for families and businesses. This was the dream that settlers brought in the 1840s and now a half-century later was still being carried out. With a larger population, better transportation, a greater number of towns, and more schools and churches, it was possible to imagine that individuals could learn to do what was right not through personal fortitude alone but through the social institutions they were creating.

Religion undergirded moral behavior through biblical admonitions and promises of eternal reward for good behavior. But the idea that religion contributed to the civilizing process only by inculcating doctrinally defined beliefs was inaccurate. Belief mattered to the extent that it was woven into the fabric of daily life. A candid remark in a letter written by a teenager in Bonner, Texas, in 1897 illustrated the point as clearly as anything. The letter was part of a series published by the *Dallas Morning News* in which "cousins" discussed what was happening in their communities, the books they were reading, and what they were learning in school. "We have a beautiful country, good people, well taught schools, and good churches," Ollie Mae Rogers wrote. "But one thing is lacking—we cannot carry on a Sunday school. It never lasts longer than two or three months, then it breaks up." After a few lines about *David Copperfield* and several other books, she asked, "Have any of the cousins ever read the Bible through? Mamma told me if I would read it through by the time I was eighteen she would buy me a silk dress." This was the kind of bribe that devout parents might have used to good purpose, especially in the absence of a reliable Sunday school. But Ollie Mae did not succeed. "I started and read twenty-seven chapters and found so many words I could not pronounce [that] I gave it up. I often think of trying it again, but I am going to school now and have other fish to fry."[90]

School may have been a place for other fish, but in 1897 it was also where the Bible stories that children failed to navigate on their own were part of the daily routine. Besides church and Sunday school, this was the institutional context in which religious idioms about moral behavior were learned. Common practice included opening the school day with a story from the Bible followed by a prayer and perhaps a hymn. As another teenager explained, "We sing two religious songs every morning at school [and] read a chapter in the Bible."[91] Religious leaders had no need to work on behalf of particular lawmakers or legislation because the practice was seldom questioned, and when it was there was little doubt that it would be retained. That in fact happened in 1908 when plaintiffs in the small town of Corsicana, fifty miles south of Dallas, sought to prevent Bible reading, prayers, and hymn singing in the public school their children attended. In ruling against the plaintiffs, the Texas Supreme Court determined that the Bible was not a sectarian book but one from which all children learned the basic principles of morality on which civilization advanced. To deprive schoolchildren of the Bible, the justices wrote, "would be to starve the moral and spiritual natures of the many out of deference to the few."[92]

Coming years would provide ample occasion to examine the complexities of church and state relationships, but for now the consideration at issue was moral instruction. However it was accomplished, families, congregations, and schools had as a primary goal the inculcation of moral principles which in turn were grounded by consensus in religion. No clearer statement of this consensus was given than one by Leo N. Levi, a prominent attorney in Galveston where he served as president of Congregation B'nai Israel from 1887 to 1889 and was

actively involved in a number of other civic organizations. Few were as passionate about the importance of morality in community life as he was.[93] In his 1899
commencement address at the University of Texas, Levi articulated the close relationship he envisioned between personal morality and social institutions. On
the one hand, personal morality consisted of the pursuit on the part of the individual of peace, virtue, contentment, respect, and honor and the avoidance of
temptation, especially from the desire for wealth and power. On the other hand,
personal morality was of necessity facilitated by the context in which an individual was placed or chose to be placed, just as the flowering of a seed depended
on soil and water. Family loyalty was to be preferred over individualism. "The
home gives effectiveness to religion, tone to social life, stability to government
and nourishment to the arts. It engenders worship of God, devotion to country, love for our fellowmen and the self-uplifting to higher and better things not
otherwise obtainable." To that, he assumed, his audience would agree, and yet he
considered it necessary to counsel the young people graduating that day against
striking out on their own instead of settling down. "Nomads never progress far
in civilization." And in settling down it was crucial to consider the context, "the
moral and intellectual tone of its people" as indicated in such small matters as
home ownership and whether the court docket was crowded with divorce suits.
"Between the home and its social and political surroundings the most intimate
relations exist," he advised. "If society be debased or benighted, the moral and intellectual tone of its constituents will be affected thereby. Therefore, the uplifting
and betterment of your social environment is your right and duty."[94]

The reciprocal relationship between persons of virtue and their social and
political surroundings was grounded, Levi believed, in divine law. "Enlightenment without religion is a factitious and unstable support for morality," he asserted in another lecture. "It is safe to say that in the Decalogue is to be found a
comprehensive moral code; certainly so, if it be supplemented with the Mosaic
'thou shalt love thy neighbor as thyself.'" People might disagree about the origin
of those words, he conceded, but there was no doubt in his mind about their
validity. "Unless virtue is regarded as the mandate of God, its practice cannot be
widespread, persistent or enduring."[95]

Some of the clearest arguments about how specifically homes, schools, congregations, and benevolent institutions were to mold individual character occurred in discussions of the different responsibilities of women and men. The
lonesome cowboy and the heroic soldier might be fitting models of male virtue,
but women's responsibilities were to their family, especially to their children, and
to their communities and for this reason involved a direct connection between
the person and home and between the home and surrounding social institutions.
It was this special sense of responsibility that inspired women like Martha Otey
and Tommie Nolley to teach and to assist in the founding of female academies.
That vision remained evident at the end of the nineteenth century as writers
again addressed the question of coeducation.

"The culture to be derived from literature and language, from mathematics and the sciences, from history and philosophy is neither masculine nor feminine," George T. Winston, who was to become the first regular president of the University of Texas, argued in 1896. Knowledge of that kind made men and women better parents and citizens. It ennobled the soul. In addition, women were expected to perform special duties "connected with domestic and social life." These included rearing children, helping in the alleviation of sickness and poverty, promoting kindness, rescuing the fallen from vice, and contributing to the elevation of moral and aesthetic standards. These, Winston argued, were "higher, more sacred, and more difficult."[96]

With suffrage for women well in the future, the relevance of arguments like these was to elevate concerns about domestic life, children, charity, and gender in discussions about public morality. These concerns moderated emphasis on traditional masculine traits of adventuresome nonconformity with a focus on the charitable concerns for nurture and empathy that were traditionally associated with femininity. Although a sharp division of roles was taken for granted, the fact that both characteristics were considered suitable topics for public discussion and worthy of promotion through education was important. These were virtues to be pursued increasingly in service professions, such as medicine, nursing, and teaching. They were congruent with the ethic of service held dear in religious teachings even though women were seldom included in religious leadership roles.

The census of religious bodies conducted in 1916 confirmed, as anecdotal impressions had long suggested, that women were involved in significantly greater numbers than men. This was as true in Texas as it was in other parts of the nation. Fifty-eight percent of all church members in Texas were women. Among the largest predominately white denominations, women made up 59 percent of the Methodist Episcopal Church South, 59 percent of Churches of Christ, and 58 percent of Southern Baptists. In the predominantly black denominations, women constituted 64 percent of African Methodist Episcopal members, 61 percent of National Baptists, and 60 percent of Colored Methodist Episcopal members. The exceptions in which numbers of women and men were about equal were Roman Catholics, Jews, and Greek Orthodox.[97]

The 1916 figures also showed the extent to which religious organizations had grown. Since 1890 the total number of congregations had risen from 8,644 to 14,316, and the total number of members had climbed from 670,320 to 1,784,620. Contrary to impressions sometimes given in later reports, the growth in membership was not an indication that people were becoming more "churched," at least not in Texas. The growth in church membership was largely a reflection of growth in total population. Indeed, the proportion of population overall who were members decreased slightly from 43 percent in 1890 to 41 percent in 1916. However, there were several notable shifts in the relative trajectories of denominations. Catholics experienced the largest growth, multiplying fourfold.

FIGURE 6. Baptist Church with tabernacle, Killeen, Texas, 1900, typical of small rural churches founded in large numbers after 1870. Lawrence T. Jones III Texas Photography Collection, Southern Methodist University, Central University Libraries, DeGolyer Library.

Southern Baptists increased at a slightly faster pace than Methodists. And the largest growth among African American denominations was among Baptists. Overall the proportion of African Americans who were church members also increased, reaching nearly 50 percent by 1916.[98]

The other noticeable difference between 1890 and 1916 was in the number of church buildings, which more than doubled. By the latter date, 90 percent of congregations had buildings compared with less than two-thirds in 1890. Differences still separated some of the larger and more affluent congregations in cities from the many humble edifices in small towns and rural areas. And yet, having a permanent place in which to meet allowed congregations to grow and to host a wide variety of classes, church socials, and other activities.

Large urban congregations were particularly well suited to promote a wide range of social and cultural activities in addition to the usual round of preaching services and Sunday school lessons. Old-fashioned suppers organized by church women as fund-raisers for auxiliary missionary and relief programs, for example, became increasingly popular as events that typically included musical performances, recitations of poetry, and readings. Indicative of the changing expectations associated with gender roles among middle-class women, ladies' auxiliaries organized special programs for the wider community as well. For example, the ladies' aid society of the First Methodist Church in Dallas put on a performance in 1899 about busy men and pretty milkmaids that the local society columnist described as a "bright little operetta" that "contained an element of novelty and picturesqueness which was catchy and drew a packed house." Not to be outdone, women of the First Presbyterian Church put on a fashion show the same week that included beautiful costumes fashioned by artists as well as "a flash of diamonds and silver spangles" all in the name of missionary work.[99]

A more subtle change associated with the establishment of larger churches in urban areas such as Dallas and Houston was harder to gauge. It is the question of whether understandings of the self and perhaps of moral responsibility were changing as the scope and location of revival meetings shifted. Revival meetings in small towns and rural areas, like the one in the early 1890s described by J. M. Dawson, seldom included more than a hundred people and largely depended on group pressure from family members, neighbors, and fellow churchgoers. While the spiritual transformation that was expected to occur through prayer and by going forward to the mourners' bench was a matter of the heart, it was very much a product of the group who knew the individual intimately. This is one of the reasons Dawson felt closer to and more accepted by the group following his conversion.

In contrast, urban revivals consisted of mass meetings at which a traveling evangelist spoke to a large number of people who constituted an audience of strangers. These venues where large numbers of souls could be claimed for God in a single series of meetings were increasingly popular among prominent evangelists such as R. G. Pearson, Dixon Williams, and Sam Jones who toured the South in the 1890s.[100] Williams, for example, preached to a crowd of between four and five thousand on a single evening in Dallas in 1890, and Jones spoke to an audience of more than a thousand in Fort Worth the same month. Other than the possibility of being accompanied by a family member, the persons who attended were unlikely to know one another. Accounts of the meetings seldom mentioned anyone in the audience by name. Publicity instead focused on the presence of a large choir and the captivating cadence of the evangelist's preaching. As was true in smaller settings, heightened emotions were an important part of urban revivals. However, a person could go forward to pray privately with the preacher at the end of the service without anyone knowing what sins might be weighing on that person's heart. It was possible even to withhold the fact of having gone forward from one's neighbors or fellow church members the next day.

Whether conversion made any difference was thus in large measure up to the individual, which was uncertain at best, and for this reason increasingly involved the participation of congregations. Evangelists encouraged penitents to become involved in congregations. In turn, congregations attempted to reproduce the kind of small-group surveillance that had been present in rural communities. Increasingly congregations also taught that moral responsibility was learned and reinforced through the regular performance of specific roles. These included regular attendance at weekly church services, attendance at Sunday school, participation in men's and women's auxiliary groups, and having home Bible study and prayer sessions with one's family. In the absence of an intimate rural community in which strong social norms could be enforced through personal ties, well-prescribed roles that could be learned and performed in religious institutions became the ways in which moral responsibility was understood.

In a quite different way the opportunities that were becoming available to the privileged through higher education and employment in the professions posed possibilities of another shift in understandings of moral responsibility. In addition to behaving responsibility as a parent or in tending one's farm or business, it was now possible for those in the professions to enact deeds of kindness and perform civic duties more often through their work. What doctors, lawyers, clergy, and a few others had been trained to do was now available on a larger scale as the professions expanded. The professions represented a way to institutionalize certain understandings of virtue such that behavior was reinforced by the training and credentials associated with the job as well as by an internalized code of personal morality.

The time when large numbers were employed in the professions was well in the future. In 1910 the total labor force in Texas was slightly more than 1.5 million, but fewer than 56,000 or 3.6 percent of the labor force were employed in the professions. Compared with other states, Texas was nearly at the bottom, ranking thirty-seventh out of forty-eight. It was like the other southern states in this respect, all of which ranked low. In contrast, Iowa, with only half the labor force as Texas, employed almost as many people in the professions. California had a considerably higher proportion in the professions than did Texas. Even Idaho and Montana did.[101] Still, the opportunities were there, and with the founding of more hospitals, high schools and colleges, and charitable organizations, they were becoming better as time went on. Between 1910 and 1920 the total labor force in Texas grew by only 10 percent, but employment in the professions rose by 36 percent. In addition, nearly 300,000 people, or a sixth of the labor force, were employed in clerical occupations, public service, or trade.[102]

The Goree family into which Tommie Nolley married in 1868 following her sister's death the previous year provides an interesting illustration of the ways in which careers in the professions changed during the second half of the nineteenth century. As a settler arriving in Texas in 1850 with training as a physician, Dr. Langston Goree was rare and in his case at least earned more of his living as a slaveholder than from practicing medicine. Goree's son Thomas graduated from college and earned a law degree, setting him on a path that was unavailable to all but the offspring of the wealthiest families. But Thomas returned from fighting for the Confederacy to find "that there was very little money to be made in my profession" and after trying his hand at farming for a year was forced to concede that "on account of excessive rains and worms, [I] have not met with success." "I am poor," he confessed to Tommie Nolley's father, "and have very little to offer your daughter but an honest, loving heart, and a willing hand."[103] Following a failed effort as a merchant, he returned to Huntsville and in 1877 was appointed by Governor Richard B. Hubbard as superintendent of the state penitentiary, a position he held until 1891. His appointment illustrated the continuing importance of political patronage for the privileged few. It also illustrated the fact that such positions were becoming more plentiful as a result of the expansion of social institutions. The state penitentiary was an important example of this expansion.

Thomas Goree's brother Langston Jr. illustrated another way in which career opportunities in the professions were changing. After the Civil War Langston Jr. earned a degree in dentistry and opened a practice in Navasota, where immigration grew the population from less than a thousand in 1870 to nearly four thousand by 1900. With few dentists anywhere in the area, his practice expanded. His patronage "was not merely a local one, for the reputation that he had acquired for skill and dexterity brought patients from all the surrounding country to obtain the treatment that was not yet accessible near their country homes," a biographer wrote. "He became regarded as a master of his profession, and, not content with the knowledge which his early study had given, he kept his eyes open to the progress of the art and adopted every improvement that the advancement of dentistry introduced." In other words, he was a pioneer who illustrated the value of being at the forefront of an advancing profession. His son, Langston III, also practiced dentistry, starting in 1895. As a profession, dentistry was rapidly becoming institutionalized. In 1880 there were fewer than a hundred dentists in Texas. By 1910 there were more than eight hundred.[104]

These opportunities were largely restricted to men, but there were exceptions for women, especially in teaching, nursing, and on rare occasions other professions. An example was Minnie Fisher Cunningham, who like the Goree family also hailed from Huntsville. In 1902 at age eighteen she became the first woman to receive a pharmacy degree from the University of Texas Medical School at Galveston. She served as president of the Texas Equal Suffrage Association from 1911 to 1918, playing an important role in winning women the right to vote in Texas in 1918.[105]

For those fortunate enough to enter the professions, understandings of one's moral and ethical responsibilities depended on internalizing standards that were institutionalized in the training and certification process associated with the profession. A person practicing a profession was expected to adhere to a moral code that required honesty, integrity, and service to the community not only from the dictates of conscience but also because one's career depended on following the norms established and regulated by the profession. That was also true among career military officers, the numbers of which expanded during World War I, and to a certain extent among business owners and shopkeepers who increasingly were involved in civic organizations. It was a form of individualism that depended on conformity to institutionalized norms rather than the kind of individualism marked only by rugged self-determination.[106]

The other context that provides an interesting view of changing understandings of individual responsibility is the manner in which executions of persons convicted of serious crimes occurred. The execution of Jake Johnson in Houston in 1870, like many other executions during the 1870s and 1880s, was a public spectacle with the aim of serving as a cautionary morality tale for the assembled crowd. The person about to die was expected to confess to having done wrong and to beg for God's forgiveness. The person was expected to counsel the crowd to avoid evil and do good. The presence of a member of the clergy ensured that the connection with organized religion would be made and that a formal prayer would be included. Singing a hymn together reminded the crowd that the event was special in the same way that church was. Little attention was given to the privacy of the accused. The event was for the benefit of the public.

By the 1890s that understanding of public executions was beginning to change. Prison reform advocates argued that public hangings were inhumane. The accused, in these emerging understandings, was not simply a means through which the public was to be cautioned but was a person who had rights and indeed feelings that demanded respect. For the incarcerated, prison reform included greater attention to personal privacy, retraining, and rehabilitation. For those condemned to die, the execution was no longer required to be held in the community where the crime had been committed so that the crime could be avenged in that way. Nor was it required to be performed in public. It could be performed inside the prison walls and eventually in an electric chair in a closed room where only a few could watch. In the process, the implicit message about moral responsibility shifted. The public no longer could learn about moral responsibility by watching as a condemned person confessed and was hung. The public increasingly had to trust that moral responsibility was effectively institutionalized in the judicial system and among the officials charged with enforcing the law. That kind of moral responsibility required individuals to internalize expectations about right and wrong and then rely on social institutions to reinforce those expectations.

Calls for reform in the manner in which executions were conducted in Texas grew out of earlier concerns about overcrowding and the treatment of prisoners as well as security in communities like Huntsville where prisons were located. Periodic escapes from prison farms and by convicts on lease to neighboring farmers stoked public fear. A widely circulated story and drawing of a frightened, dark-skinned escapee being chased by bloodhounds stirred defensive reactions to critics from other states who deplored the treatment of convicts in Texas.[107] Discussions of prison reform drew wider attention in 1897 when it was noted that the incarcerated population statewide had grown to more than 7,500 and that Texas appeared to be lagging behind other states in both deterrence and rehabilitation. Criticism was directed especially at instances of brutal treatment of convicts on farms and in work camps. Attention shifted to the prison at Huntsville following a balanced but critical "insider" report in 1899 by a journalist about conditions there.[108]

Unlike the execution of Jake Johnson in 1870, executions at the end of the century were generally held within a prison or other confined area to prevent large crowds from attending for fear of the crowd becoming violent. The hanging of an African American at Kaufman, Texas, in March 1890, for example, took place in an enclosure to which only sixty-five people were admitted by ticket from a crowd of about two thousand.[109] In several other states, including New York where death by electrocution began in 1891, agitation from prison reform groups concerned about inhumane treatment of inmates resulted in executions by electric chair replacing hanging.[110] Proponents argued that electrocution induced death quicker and with less pain. Conducted in a closed room, electrocution also provided the accused greater privacy, with only a spiritual adviser and doctor present in the final moments preceding death.[111] That innovation was widely resisted in Texas on grounds that hangings should be done locally so that victims of crime could better feel that justice had been done and in hopes of more effectively deterring crime in the future. An electric chair, following lectures at town halls and churches about how it worked, was finally installed at the Huntsville prison in 1923, and the first death by electrocution occurred a few months later.[112]

During the half century before World War I, religion had increasingly become located among a larger establishment of social institutions that were in place to define and reinforce moral responsibility. As the population grew, opportunities to establish towns increased. And as towns grew, possibilities increased to build churches and schools and to provide the kinds of businesses and services that residents regarded as desirable features of a civilized society. By 1890 nearly 3,000 towns had been established. Nearly all were small; indeed, two-thirds were too small for population figures to be recorded at all, 723 had fewer than five hundred residents, 114 had between five hundred and a thousand, 69 had between a thousand and two thousand, and only 57 had two thousand or more. But 80 percent of all towns had a post office and 44 percent had a railroad stop. Among towns with at least five hundred people, 99 percent had a post office and 81 percent had a railroad stop.[113]

The larger institutional context in which churches functioned was evident in the kinds of businesses and services that townspeople established. With a population of only 1,500 in 1890, Huntsville, for example, had an opera house, a roller skating rink, a cotton gin and grist mill, a printing shop, a jewelry store, a Masonic hall, three drug stores, three restaurants, five clothing stores, and five church buildings. By 1910, with a population of only 2,000, these and additional businesses had grown to include two more churches, a city waterworks, a fire station, an electric light and power company, and a normal institute for teacher training. Hallettsville in Lavaca County, where wild woman sightings had occurred a few decades earlier, was smaller than Huntsville but showed a similar pattern of business and services. An opera house, a bookstore, a photography shop, an ice cream parlor, a Masonic hall, a Chinese laundry, a firehouse, a county jail, an electric light and power company, and three churches served its thousand residents in 1890. Two decades later Hallettsville had only thirteen hundred residents, but its local establishments included two additional churches, a farmers union, a city cemetery, a Jewish cemetery, a Wells Fargo express office, a boys school, a second county jail, and the Academy of the Sacred Heart.[114]

Expectations about individual conformity to standards of right and wrong emphasized the self and individual talents and behavior. It was decidedly the individual's responsibility to work hard, live right, and succeed or fail. That emphasis on individual responsibility was possible because the rugged frontier spirit in which isolated persons struck out on their own was less common than an understanding of selves who learned proper behavior in school and at home, in church, and through their jobs, household duties, and communities. Churches contributed to this understanding through preaching that recounted the biblical narratives in which appropriate personal behavior was revealed and by establishing Sunday schools, colleges, seminaries, and religious magazines as well as by encouraging temperance, marital fidelity, and an appreciation of quality literature and the arts. Church leaders trusted other institutions to perform their part in terms of education, law enforcement, and social welfare.

The irony of benevolent institutions is that they bridge the lines between rich and poor and the divisions separating races, providing well-intentioned and constructive social assistance, and at the same time dramatize and reinforce the moral significance of economic and racial inequality. Homes for unwed mothers and orphans demonstrate the worth of intact families while helping the disadvantaged. Insane asylums and hospitals care for the sick but also define wellness. Those who receive assistance are expected to uphold the moral norms of those providing it.

As civilization advanced, it provided not only the institutions for those with resources capable of creating these institutions a barrier against civil disorder but also a definition of what a morally respected citizen should be. Lacking the means to construct institutions or to participate fully in them, the disadvantaged could be blamed for their own moral failings. As Willard Richardson had suggested, this kind of civilization did not require becoming a fanatic for equality.

It was largely unnecessary for church leaders to take direct action in the political sphere. The role of clergy was to work for the benefit of churches and not to enter directly into the political realm. It made sense to argue that the basis of a good society was morally responsible individuals. As social institutions expanded to provide roles in which individuals could behave responsibly, the rough edges of living in a place that had been the frontier so recently could gradually be refined.

CHAPTER 3

WITH LIBERTY OF CONSCIENCE

Defining the Separation of Church and State

To discriminate against a thoroughly upright citizen because he belongs
to some particular church or because, like Abraham Lincoln, he has not
avowed his allegiance to any church, is an outrage against that liberty of
conscience which is one of the foundations of American life.

THEODORE ROOSEVELT, LETTER TO J. C. MARTIN, 1908

It is the natural and fundamental and indefeasible right of every human
being to worship God or not, according to the dictates of his conscience,
and, as long as he does not infringe upon the rights of others, he is to be
held accountable alone to God for all religious beliefs and practices.

GEORGE W. TRUETT, "BAPTISTS AND RELIGIOUS LIBERTY," 1920

By the 1920s the opportunity to practice one's faith with liberty of conscience was a theme expressed increasingly by Texas religious and political leaders. Emphasis on liberty of conscience implied freedom from any
monopoly over religion by government or of government by a religion. It also
favored the right and duty of the individual to make a decision about his or her
faith and to relate accordingly to God. In practice, liberty of conscience deterred
clergy and lay leaders from bringing their faith in an official or organized way
into the political arena. This was to be the dominant understanding of church
and state relationships that would prevail for most of the next half century before
it came to have a radically different meaning.

Because Baptists were such a powerful force in Texas religion, it was possible to imagine that strict separation of church and state basically derived from
Baptist teachings as far back as Roger Williams's first efforts in colonial New

England. With Anne Hutchison and a few others, Williams fled colonial Massachusetts to Rhode Island where he became a champion of religious freedom. That view in which individual conscience gained primacy over efforts to use the coercive powers of government to control public worship was certainly a factor in the thinking of prominent Texas Baptists, such as Reverend George W. Truett of Dallas, who championed religious liberty in a 1920 address delivered from the East Steps of the Capitol in Washington.[1]

Baptist doctrine emphasizing liberty of conscience was only one of the factors and perhaps not even the most important one reinforcing the tendency in Texas for religious leaders to steer clear of political entanglements. The legacy of Reconstruction remained an important consideration well into the twentieth century. Carpetbaggers like Reverend Honey and black preachers like Reverend Parker who became directly involved in public office were examples of an outside element that did not understand the proper place of white southern clergy. The role of clergy and respected laypeople of faith was to resist evil in their own lives and to work for the moral uplift of all individuals in their community. This was fundamentally a matter of repentance and conversion as practiced in old-time revival meetings. Revival religion was otherworldly, focusing on salvation from damnation in the life to come. At the same time it was this-worldly in emphasizing right living and the avoidance of evil behavior. Working for the advance of civilization was a second reason for religious leaders generally to avoid direct involvement in political life. The social institutions through which civilization was expected to advance were largely in the private sphere and were presumed to need only minimal government involvement to flourish. As these institutions developed, religious leaders could more reasonably assume that the dictates of personal conscience would produce good behavior. An additional source of emphasis on liberty of conscience was concern on the part of Baptists and Methodists about the possible influence of Roman Catholics. This concern became more important in the 1920s in conjunction with both local and national politics but was part of Texas lore from the time of independence from Mexico.

Liberty of conscience manifested itself in the activities of Texas clergy and on occasion in the statements of public officials in several distinct ways that were already apparent between 1870 and 1890 and became increasingly evident from the 1890s through the 1920s. Clergy continued the basic work of saving souls, preaching moral repentance, and holding worship services. They devoted themselves energetically to starting new churches and increasing the size of existing ones. These activities left little time and few resources for anything else. Baptists and Methodists fought on occasion among themselves, but the conflicts were generally over worship, doctrine, church finances, and church publications than about public policy or political campaigns. The conflicts were fierce enough to serve as cautionary tales for other clergy. Conformity to local and denominational customs was the order of the day. As the two dominant denominations, Baptists and Methodists could safely argue that freedom of conscience was the best policy knowing that the exercise thereof was of little danger to their own churches. Roman Catholics were to a significant extent geographically separate with the Rio Grande valley still the location in which they were most numerous. In Dallas, Houston, San Antonio, Galveston, and a few other towns where Catholics and Jews were present alongside Baptists and Methodists, liberty of conscience was an appeal that minority groups could also embrace in the name of religious pluralism.

An emphasis on individual conscience proved to be generally compatible with Texas-style progressive reforms. Church people and civic leaders could argue that moral uplift was best achieved through good preaching, good schools, a growing number of colleges and seminaries, and better social services at the local level. The national debate over prohibition that resulted in ratification of the Eighteenth Amendment, which became effective on January 16, 1920, included an interesting new interpretation of liberty of conscience being used on both sides of the debate. Advocates and opponents of prohibition both argued, albeit with different conclusions, that the rights and duties of the individual should be upheld. The most vocal appeals to liberty of conscience appeared during the 1928 presidential election, which found Texas Protestants feeling the need to speak directly in the political sphere against perceived threats from the Catholic Church to religious liberty.

LIBERTY OF CONSCIENCE IN TEXAS CIVIL RELIGION

In the *Social Contract* Jean Jacques Rousseau famously argued that a civil religion in which there is a minimalist understanding of God as the preserver of justice and beneficence could be an essential component of solidarity in an otherwise diverse and fragmented society.[2] Scholars have debated the extent to which the basic values of various nations include something that might be called a civil religion and whether it functions as Rousseau suggested. Sociologist Robert N. Bellah argued in a 1967 essay that America had indeed developed a powerful civil religion. The American version, according to Bellah, incorporates belief in a kind of deist God and associates this belief with its founding democratic principles.[3]

Whether states as well as nations can have a civil religion has seldom been considered in the scholarly literature, but the historical record demonstrates beyond doubt that Texas has a civil religion in much the same way that the United States does. This should not be particularly surprising for a state that was once under the sovereign rule of Mexico, achieved independence, and became a republic before it was ever a state. Like the United States, Texas has its martyrs, its heroes, and its founding figures. Davy Crockett, Jim Bowie, and Sam Houston hold prominence in the pantheon of Texas leaders just as George Washington, Benjamin Franklin, and Thomas Jefferson do for the nation. The founding of Texas also includes an explicit religious dimension. The struggle for Texas independence was especially in later renditions seen as a quest for religious freedom.

On March 2, 1836, delegates of the people of Texas met at Washington-on-the-Brazos and declared their independence from Mexico. Among the grievances they expressed toward the Mexican government, the declaration asserted that "It denies us the right of worshipping the Almighty according to the dictates of our own conscience, by the support of a National Religion, calculated to promote the temporal interest of its human functionaries, rather than the glory of the true and living God." The assertion was in reference to the fact that Protestant churches had been disallowed under Mexican rule.[4] Both in preceding weeks and in subsequent commentary, American writers defended the Texas quest for independence as a just and righteous cause. It was a struggle willed by the God of nature not only against tyranny and oppression but to overthrow the "power of a superstitious hierarchy."[5]

The successful thirteen-day siege by Mexican troops against the Alamo which ended on March 6, 1836, with the deaths of some two hundred Texans and two to three times that many Mexican soldiers solidified the Texans' resolve for independence and led to the Battle of San Jacinto on April 21 at which "Remember the Alamo!" became the rallying cry for victory. While initial reports focused on the courage and military tactics involved at the Alamo, subsequent accounts brought religious aspects more clearly into view. On the first anniversary of the battle at the Alamo a ceremony was held in which the ashes of the fallen heroes were collected and taken to the parish church at Bexar for burial. Speaking in Spanish, Colonel Juan N. Seguin of the Texas volunteers told the assembled dignitaries that "the genius of liberty is looking down from her lofty seat, smiling with approbation upon our procedures" in honor of the heroes who had cried "God and liberty, victory or death."[6]

On the fourth anniversary of the Battle of San Jacinto, Dr. R. F. Brenham, a leading figure who was to die three years later in efforts to further secure the boundaries of Texas against Mexico, explained the rise of Texas in language that stopped just short of referencing divine providence. "Texas presents to the view of the world another instance of emancipation from arbitrary thralldom to brighten the galaxy of existing nations and enlighten posterity in the value of political freedom," he said. "She has emerged from the darkness of despotism in which she was shrouded and now basks in the radiance of liberty." Just as America had gained liberty from British tyranny, so Texas had achieved freedom from the scourge of Mexico. It was as inevitable as the shining lights of heaven, he thought, that the "degenerate Mexican" had succumbed to the "proud, free and untrammeled soul of the *legitimate white man*."[7]

The following December, in a speech to the Austin Masonic Lodge on the anniversary of St. John the Evangelist, the Honorable David S. Kaufman expressed in even stronger terms the idea that God had ordained Texas to achieve greatness in ways that would never have been possible by the races who had previously inhabited it. "The tawny sons of the south-west vainly attempted to subdue the unconquerable spirit of freemen, but the presumptuous effort ended, as all others of a similar character will end, in the complete overthrow of the enemies of the Anglo-Saxon race!" It was no accident, he believed, that hardy pioneers were eradicating the wild buffalo and the savage Comanche. "Praises now ascend to the living God where the war whoop was wont to be heard foreboding a dreadful fate to helpless women and children."[8]

In 1841 an engraver in New Orleans retrieved a stone from the Alamo and created an obelisk-shaped monument on which he inscribed the names of the fallen. The inscription read, "To the God of the fearless and free is dedicated this Altar, made from the ruins of the Alamo." The monument was taken by wagon from San Antonio to Houston and was exhibited in Galveston in 1842 or 1843 but then was lost from view for eight or nine years before it was obtained by the State of Texas and relocated at the capital in Austin.[9]

A rendition featuring the role of God and of religion during the actual defense of the Alamo appeared in an 1847 story pieced together by a visiting army officer from North Carolina as if it were a blow-by-blow account from an eyewitness. As the story begins, the Texans are determined to provide "whatever resistance to the progress of the tyrant that God and their own energies should permit." As the battle continues, Sunday comes "but brings no rest to those whom God has created in his own image, yet endowed with such unhallowed passions." The storyteller then describes how the Mexican attackers betrayed the spirit of their own faith:

> Perhaps within the chapel of the Alamo, consecrated to the worship of the Almighty, and distinguished by the emblem of man's salvation which surmounts the dome, heads may be bowed in prayer to the God of battles for deliverance from their sanguinary foe; but that foe takes no heed of Sabbaths. Exclusive followers as they proclaim themselves of the true church, they doom to destruction the very temple they have erected for its worship and kissing the cross suspended from their necks, and planted before every camp, they point their guns upon the image of that Saviour they once made the tutelary deity of the Alamo.

With stars smiling in the firmament and the "repose of paradise" hovering above, the story ends as Crockett dies and the Alamo falls.[10]

Had that been all, the story would have been a tale of tragedy and defeat, but it was from the fallen that courage arose phoenixlike in the person of Sam Houston. Distraught at the news from the Alamo and subsequent setbacks, Houston experienced the darkest hours of his life, according to another writer, neither eating or sleeping for two days and then mustering his troops to succeed in victory at the Battle of San Jacinto. It was essential that Houston would win. "There was no longer a doubt in the mind of anyone who knew the position of affairs," the writer explained, "that the salvation of Texas, under God, had been thrown entirely upon Houston's arm."[11]

These accounts, especially the one about the fall of the Alamo, were reprinted in various versions as Texas and the nation commemorated its history.[12] The main points were that Texas was conceived in a struggle against tyranny that may have been evident in the Roman Catholic Church's monopoly of religion under Mexican rule, and that liberty was the opposite of tyranny. In addition the struggle may have been divinely sanctioned as a racial struggle in which white people of European ancestry triumphed over darker-skinned Mexicans and Indians. It was in any case a triumphant effort that brought about religious freedom. By implication, liberty of conscience was to be preserved and any intrusion into the affairs of religion by government was akin to tyranny.

Periodic tensions with Mexico continued to spark occasional denunciations of the tyranny there that contrasted so sharply with the freedom of religious expression Texas provided. Civil unrest in Mexico was said to be the result of government taxes supporting the Roman Catholic Church despite a popular desire for religious liberty. Mexican priests were accused of being licentious, vain, and intolerant. Unlike Catholics in Texas, the faithful in Mexico were said to be deprived of good teaching. In contrast, Texas could proudly assert that no preference should be given to any religious denomination or mode of worship and thus give religious liberty to all and at the same time refrain from mixing religion with politics. "Our clergy wisely abstain from the introduction of politics into the pulpit," one writer observed, "and confine themselves to preaching the Gospel."[13]

The idea that clergy should refrain from becoming involved in politics had precedent in another aspect of Texas civil religion that was somewhat more favorable toward its Mexican history. Writers advocating separation of church and state noted that the Mexican constitution of 1824 banned bishops and archbishops from holding office in the Congress of the Republic and that the constitution of Coahuila and Texas disallowed clergy in active service from participation in the legislature. Whether the same principle should have been applied when Texas gained independence from Mexico was illustrated in a story about William C. Crawford, a Methodist preacher from Georgia who was elected as a delegate to the convention in 1836 that declared the republic's independence. According to the story, "the Romish priesthood in Mexico was strongly condemned in Texas and a prejudice [existed] against all ministers of religion. A section was introduced into the Constitution disfranchising all preachers, and forever prohibiting them from occupying any office of profit or trust in the republic." Crawford argued that the measure was too strong and succeeded in modifying it so that preachers were excluded only from holding elected legislative or executive offices.[14] A decade later that clause was included in the state constitution of 1846 following two days of discussion in which prominent Baptist preacher and jurist R.E.B. Baylor argued for its inclusion.[15] It was deleted in the constitution adopted in 1876, which stated that no religious test should be required for holding public office but stipulated that officeholders were required to "acknowledge the existence of a Supreme Being." The 1876 constitution also protected "the rights of conscience in matters of religion," but the framers stopped short of adopting a resolution promising that "no citizen shall be hurt, molested, or restrained in his person, liberty, or estate, for his religious profession or sentiments, or for the absence on his part of any religious profession or sentiment, provided he does not disturb the public peace, infringe upon public morality, or obstruct others in their religious worship."[16]

When later generations of Texans thought about separation of church and state, it was thus possible to locate the idea in the legends of their own state and not simply in stories about the earlier and more distant founders of America. One of the more ardent defenders of church-state separation, for example, was Oscar Branch Colquitt, a lifelong Methodist who ran afoul of his pastor in Galveston for failing to support prohibition in 1911, served from 1911 to 1915 as governor, and in the early 1920s became an outspoken critic of the Ku Klux Klan. True to his southern roots, Colquitt affirmed his belief that "ours is a white man's government," but he resorted to the Texas constitution as well as to the Bible, John Wesley, and Roger Williams in arguing for religious liberty. The worst thing a person could do for God or the country, he said, was to destroy religious tolerance. If America was to be a light to other nations, it could only do so by upholding the torch of religious liberty.[17]

If liberty of conscience was emphasized in the Baptist and Methodist congregations that made up the lion's share of Texas churchgoers, the same sentiments were expressed in the traditions that attracted fewer adherents. In these traditions liberty of conscience meant freedom from the kind of governmental interference that could have been imposed had the dominant denominations chosen to do so. Freedom implied the opportunity to teach and believe in something that the majority did not share. At the same time it was possible for adherents of the various faiths to identify conscience as an emphasis about which there could be apparent agreement.

The leader of the Dallas Spiritualist Society met with members of the Texas legislature in 1912, for example, to seek their assistance in challenging what he understood to be a vagrancy law that classified all mediums, ministers, and members of spiritualist societies as vagrants. Spiritualism was a legally organized church that should enjoy the same rights as other religious organizations, he argued. "No one is forced to be a Spiritualist no more than he is a Methodist or anything else," he said, and for that reason a person "should have the right to be one if he desires to be without being arrested and fined as a vagrant."[18]

Minority religions that emphasized individual moral conscience were particularly favorable to the view that individuals should have the right to develop and express the dictates of their own conscience in different ways. Groups as different as holiness churches that sought the indwelling of the Holy Spirit and Quakers and Unitarians who believed in an innately implanted divine spark could agree on the importance of religious freedom. This was the kind of freedom, a Unitarian minister explained, that was most evident in the home where privacy prevailed and where mothers taught their children the basics of right and wrong without government intrusion.[19]

The view that adherents of minority religions were on the wrong path and needed to be converted was certainly present among leaders of the majority faiths. A story that probably illustrated how many well-meaning Christians thought about Jews occurred during World War I when Reverend J. Howard Williams, a Baptist chaplain who later became president of Southwestern Baptist Theological Seminary, met a Jewish soldier in a hospital in France. Williams "attempted to win the boy to the Lord" but the "boy rejected Christ." According to Williams's biographer, this encounter taught Williams "about doubt and despair in the human heart," a lesson that encouraged Williams in bringing people to the saving power of Jesus Christ.[20]

Believing in liberty of conscience was not popularly understood to mean that all religions were equally valid. It was, however, a belief capable of facilitating respect as well as mere tolerance. Respect was based both on the idea that individuals should be guided by their own conscience and on biblical teachings about setting one's own house in order before judging others. Pastors who argued that only Christians could be saved could thus assert in the same context that Christians should cleanse their hearts before judging others. In a sermon in Beaumont, for example, the pastor of a Disciples of Christ church related a story about Jews in Russia complaining about persecution only to be told by the czar that if they would "accept the Christian religion" it would stop. But, the pastor said, an apt retort would be, "If you so-called Christians would live according to your own religion it would settle the matter."[21]

Liberty of conscience could be interpreted as an argument not only for living up to the ideals of one's own faith but also for upholding the rights of others. In 1914 following an incident in which critics of President Woodrow Wilson accused him of religious favoritism, for example, the *Fort Worth Star Telegram* editorialized that right-thinking people including "Protestants, Catholics, Jews or what not" could "enjoy the full freedom of worship." Persons of "all creeds and without creeds," the writer argued, were intent on avoiding any union of church and state while uniting in the liberty of opinion that the nation's institutions assured.[22]

Respect was facilitated on occasion as well by gatherings at which representatives of various faiths were present to demonstrate that religious freedom was indeed a cherished ideal. World War I provided an occasion for such meetings as the nation sought to highlight its freedoms in contrast to other nations. For example, at a meeting in Dallas in 1916 Jews and Christians joined forces to celebrate America as the land of freedom. Leaders of both faiths complimented one another on being broad-minded and representing splendid ideals. People of many different beliefs and creeds, one of the Christian speakers explained, populated America, but it was a conglomeration capable of living together in unity.[23]

One of the more impressive applications of the principle of liberty of conscience toward members of a minority faith occurred in 1923. In response to rising expressions of anti-Semitism in Europe and following a series of Ku Klux Klan demonstrations that included anti-Semitic statements, Baptist leader J. B. Cranfill published a lengthy essay defending the civil and religious rights of Jews and praising Jews for their civic contributions. Jewish and Christian charitable organizations in Dallas, Cranfill argued, were greatly indebted to the generosity of leading Jewish citizens, such as Phillip Sanger, Alex Weisberg, and numerous others. "Of course, as a Christian I wish they were Christians," he conceded. But he was not surprised that they were not, given the selfishness, hatred, and ignorance of people professing to be Christians. It was the duty of Christians, he believed, both as Christians and as Americans to uphold the right of everyone "to worship God according to the dictates of their own consciences and to work out their destinies unabashed and unafraid and unawed by any who would deprive them of these inalienable rights." These were the rights of Jews, Gentiles, Catholics, Protestants, believers, and unbelievers alike. Everyone should be able to worship and order their affairs "according to the dictates of their own consciences."[24]

An important implication of Texas civil religion was that the proper role of religion in politics was more clearly to be exercised by laypeople than by clergy. Mexican despotism and the potential danger to religious freedom among God-fearing Protestants from the Roman Catholic hierarchy were important parts of the story. Citizens were supposed to freely exercise their right to worship according to the dictates of conscience. At the same time, conscience was widely considered to depend on belief of some kind in a Supreme Being and thus to warrant inclusion of Bible reading and prayer in public schools. This was also an argument that on occasion went further. For example, in 1923 the Board of Regents of the University of Texas adopted a resolution that "no infidel, atheist or agnostic be employed in any capacity in the University of Texas [and] while no sectarian qualification shall ever be required of persons now serving or who shall in future be elected or appointed to positions in this institution, no person who does not believe in God as the Supreme Being and the Ruler of the Universe shall hereafter be employed or at any time continue to be elected or appointed to any office or position of any character in this university."[25]

Unless understood as grounded in theism, liberty of conscience was an invitation to nonconformity as well as a paean of respect for the founding greatness of Texas. Freedom of religion could sit lightly enough on the shoulders of believers to invite novel interpretations of doctrine. It pertained in politics as well, where the Democratic Party enjoyed a virtual monopoly of power and yet was constrained by the view that government should refrain from dictating too closely what people thought or did. From time to time this was the message that interpreters drew from the Alamo and San Jacinto. If those who died gave their lives for freedom, it was necessary to leave room for a certain freedom of spirit. "I am at liberty to vote as my conscience and judgment dictate to be right,"

Davy Crockett had argued, "without the yoke of any party on me, or the driver at my heels, with his whip in hand, commanding me to go gee-wo-haw just at his pleasure."[26]

With precedent in the founding legends of the state to respect liberty of conscience as long as it was loosely grounded in theistic convictions, religious leaders at the end of the nineteenth century and in the early years of the twentieth century largely avoided taking public stands on public issues. They nevertheless worked in the private sphere to promote reforms and to continue with the task of advancing civilization. These activities sometimes resulted in legislative action as well, although those were the exceptions more than the rule. Apart from constitutional reasons, clergy had more than enough to do in their congregations and communities without becoming involved in politics.

THE PROGRESSIVE CHURCH

The Progressive Era that flourished from the 1890s to the 1920s is most easily remembered as a time of social activism in which forward-thinking reformers worked to curb ruthless business practices in banking and railroads and sought to overcome corruption in city governments. Activists championed the rights of women and worked to end the exploitation of child labor. Progressive legislation introduced child labor laws, a minimum wage, and government regulation of working conditions in factories. Big trusts were broken up and new appeals were voiced on behalf of the common person. As such, progressive activism mostly occurred in and was directed toward northern cities.

Activism though was also oriented toward ordinary men and women who lived in small towns and rural areas. It was an expression of the same desire to advance civilization that had been present in frontier communities as the nation's population moved west. Besides the prominent reformers and public officials who associated themselves with progressive causes, it was carried forward at the grass roots by clergy, teachers, and community leaders. At that level it sometimes meant voting for one candidate instead of another but more often focused on better sermons and Sunday school classes, school improvement, private charity, and occasional discussions of such topics as prison reform, care for the infirm or insane, and universal suffrage.

Religious leaders noting the rapid changes taking place in their communities felt it especially urgent to intensify and extend their efforts at winning souls and building churches. A Baptist leader, for example, described the period from about 1898 to 1905 as a time of exceptional challenges. "The growth of the population was not slow, not even steady," he wrote, "it was phenomenal." Whereas earlier immigration had been from southern states and included large numbers of Baptists, the new population "represented all shades and phases of thought, socially, politically, morally, religiously." New ideas were circulating that posed

FIGURE 7. Weaving cotton cloth at the Dallas Cotton Mills, ca. 1905, illustrating turn-of-the-
century growth of industry and urbanization. Keystone View Company. Lawrence T. Jones III
Texas Photography Collection, Southern Methodist University, Central University Libraries,
DeGolyer Library.

new challenges to traditional understandings of the gospel. "It was a wilderness
of thought, a seething caldron of sentiment," he said.[27]

Texas resembled other states in having huge differences between rural and
urban areas. In some ways these differences were even more pronounced because parts of West Texas and the Texas panhandle were still little more than
frontier settlements while towns such as Dallas, Fort Worth, Galveston, Houston, and Waco were becoming cities. In rural areas summer camp meetings with
families spending the week in tents and listening to sermons on rough-hewn
benches were still common while churches in the larger towns were meeting in
large auditoriums with electric lights and effective heating. With an 1890 population of 14,000, Waco, for example, had a fine Baptist church with four hundred
members who met in a building constructed at a cost of between $25,000 and
$30,000. Waco's new brick Catholic cathedral accommodated more than a thou-
sand parishioners. The Episcopal church, a correspondent wrote, was a "magnificent Gothic structure" that was "an ornament to the city and a monument to
the zeal, fidelity and energy of the Episcopal congregation." No less impressive

was the Presbyterian church, which was said to be "one of the most imposing structures in the state" and attended by "some of the best and most refined people of Waco." Those were just a few of the town's twenty congregations, which also included a Spiritualist organization, six African American churches, and a Jewish congregation.[28]

By 1890 the population of Dallas had grown to 38,000, making it the largest town in the state, and over the next twenty years its population shot up to more than 92,000. In 1890 there were already forty-four churches in Dallas as well as twenty-six smaller church societies.[29] Unlike the humble frame buildings in which churchgoers in the countryside met, members of the better-established churches in Dallas enjoyed padded pews, carpeted aisles, stained glass windows, and fellowship halls with modern appliances. One of the principal reasons to forbid tobacco chewing in church, members argued, was to prevent staining the fine carpets. Besides the congregations available to Protestants of nearly all denominations, Church of the Sacred Heart and St. Patrick's Church offered worship for Roman Catholics, the Ursuline Academy provided a boarding school for girls, and Temple Emanu-el served the city's Jewish community. The number of fine, well-attended congregations, a local journalist wrote, was a reflection of the "standing, development and progress" of the city as well as ample testimony that the people of Dallas were a "moral and religious people keeping step with the civilization and progress of the age in all things."[30]

Arguments that the more prosperous urban churches in Texas were as progressive as anywhere in the nation retained historic sectional sentiments about the distinctive cultural amenities of the South. When the Southern Baptist Convention met in Fort Worth in 1890, a participant acknowledged being unable to "refrain from feeling a pride in southern civilization, southern manhood, southern sobriety, southern intelligence and southern humanity." The speeches were eloquent, the business was conducted with efficient precision, and it was impressive to be in the midst of more than a thousand delegates representing every southern state. It was especially empowering to be in such a large gathering knowing that there were more than two million Southern Baptists nationwide, nearly four million children in Southern Baptist Sunday schools, hundreds of thousands of dollars being spent on publishing and missionaries, and new churches being organized in Africa, Brazil, China, Japan, and Mexico. As the assembled delegates sang "Rock of Ages" and considered God's handiwork across the prairie and beyond, this was the kind of confidence that filled their hearts.[31]

Reports from various agencies and corresponding secretaries in the 1890s showed Texas Baptists busily raising money to support and expand Baylor University and from there to train ministers and send out preachers to assist in organizing new churches. Lots were located and purchased on which to construct new churches and parsonages. Guest sermons were being given and visits by denominational leaders were being made to guide and encourage local pastors. Money was being raised to provide loans to fledgling congregations interested in building churches and purchasing church furniture, Bibles were being distributed, hundreds of thousands of pages of religious literature were being printed, and funds were being collected for domestic and foreign missionary efforts. An educational fund was being organized to assist members of African American churches. Orphanages were being supported and money was being raised to support indigent and retired pastors and missionaries.[32]

Better roads, better transportation and communication, more people, more money, and better-educated clergy contributed to these developments. The larger and more affluent urban congregations increasingly sought pastors who not only had seminary training but also held earned doctorates or law degrees. Dr. James William Lowber, who held a doctorate and a law degree as well as certificates from five universities, for example, became the pastor of the Central Christian Church in Austin in 1896, a congregation that was considered to have one of the handsomest and most commodious buildings in the state. With doctors, lawyers, and state legislators among its members, the congregation took pride in its new pastor's eloquent sermons and educational pedigree. Lowber represented the kind of progress to which the congregation aspired. Already a fellow of the Royal Geographical Society, he was elected to the American Association for the Advancement of Science in 1906 and the following year during a lecture tour across Europe was made a fellow of the Society of Antiquarians of Scotland. By 1913 he was credited with having added more than twelve thousand members to the Central Christian Church.[33]

Although few clergy could match Lowber's credentials, churches increasingly sought pastors with advanced degrees or with other marks of distinction in higher education and public service. Reverend Turner Ashby Wharton, for example, became the pastor in 1909 of the First Presbyterian Church in Sherman, a rapidly growing town of ten thousand in northeastern Texas. Wharton held degrees from the University of North Carolina and Union Theological Seminary in Richmond and an honorary doctorate and law degree. A decade later he served as moderator of the Presbyterian Synod of Texas.[34]

For pastors who did not have particularly compelling advanced degrees, eloquent speaking that facilitated successful fund-raising offered a promising path to denominational prestige. Among Methodists one of the more flamboyant examples was Hubert D. Knickerbocker, who ascended from smaller to larger pulpits and in 1913 gained wider acclaim by offering to raise $100,000 for Southern Methodist University. A biographer described him as a "fast-rising" preacher who was best known for his "spectacular ability to raise money and preach highly creative and spell-binding sermons." A favorite fund-raising tactic was the "cash on the barrel head" appeal, which began with Knickerbocker putting a cash portion of his salary on the top of a barrel, mentioning how meager his salary was (but failing to mention his substantial income from real estate investments), and calling on wealthy members by name to come forward with large donations. Another tactic was to stoke guilt among his congregation, calling them "dead

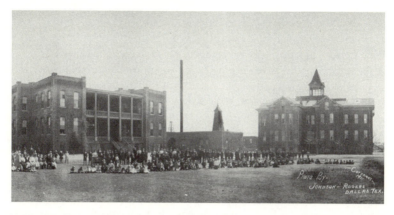

FIGURE 8. Buckner Orphans Home, Dallas, 1911, one of the important charitable institutions supported by Texas Baptists. Johnson & Rogers, Photographers. Library of Congress Prints and Photographs Division, Washington, DC.

Christians" for failing to be more generous, and graphically illustrating the point by having them file past a casket in which they saw themselves reflected in a strategically placed mirror.[35]

Among Baptists one of the most prominent fund-raisers of the era was Reverend Robert Cooke Buckner. He was the founder of the Buckner Orphans' Home in Dallas and played leading roles in the National Prison Reform Association and the National Society of Charities and Corrections as well as organizing the Dallas Humane Society.[36] Although rank-and-file Baptists seldom earned large incomes, there were a few exceptions. One was C. C. Slaughter, a devout Baptist who earned a fortune in the 1880s running cattle on some 260,000 acres in West Texas before turning his attention to the lucrative banking industry in Dallas. Through Buckner's cultivation, Slaughter donated more than $750,000 to various Baptist projects and organizations.[37]

With so much to do and at a time when it was uncommon except in a few of the largest churches to have secretaries and assistant pastors, clergy devoted themselves to the work of building up their own congregations, helping start new ones, and assisting with the activities of their denominations. This was the work to which they felt called and for which they were rewarded. From week to week there was little reason to think that government was doing anything to hinder church development or was an appropriate mechanism for furthering it. Whatever municipal leaders did to attract new people and to keep communities safe was also good for local churches. The one exception, which had bothered pastors for decades and was now becoming of greater concern, was competition on Sundays from businesses and secular amusements. Sunday-closing advocates argued that government regulation of business hours would enhance rather than restrict individual liberty or violate expectations about freedom of religion. Liberty, they argued, could be preserved only if the moral conscience of tomorrow's leaders was firmly established through the Sunday instruction of children, which was more easily accomplished without competition from secular activities.[38]

In the spirit of progressive reform, churches ventured increasingly beyond the usual tasks of preaching and moral instruction to consider questions about the incarcerated, insane, or disabled. Most of this work was done through the various religious, private, and public benevolent associations, although church leaders spoke occasionally at legislative meetings about the work of charitable organizations.[39] Church members were enlisted as volunteers and served on association boards. Meetings were held at churches to solicit charitable donations and to describe conditions and needs at asylums and prisons. Funds were raised to start additional hospitals, homes for orphans and indigent women, and night schools for uneducated workers.[40] At a single meeting in Fort Worth, Southern Baptists raised $15,000 to remove the debt from one of the denomination's orphanages and with a large pledge from Slaughter $125,000 toward construction of a memorial sanitarium in Dallas.[41]

Besides the work done by denominational agencies, new interdenominational efforts were also becoming increasingly important. One example was the Christian Endeavor Society, which began in 1881 in New England as a nondenominational evangelical ministry to youth and expanded to include some sixty-seven thousand local chapters with approximately four million members worldwide by 1906. By 1910 Endeavor membership in Texas was estimated at twelve thousand with activities that included youth programs in English and Spanish, a prison ministry, and an overseas educational fund.[42]

An additional way in which churches participated in progressive reform efforts was by hosting and helping to convene gatherings organized by community groups. The City Federation of Women's Clubs, for example, was a thriving organization in Dallas of approximately twelve hundred women from many of the community's prominent congregations. As part of its growing interest in prison reform, the group hosted Maud Ballington Booth, the founder of Volunteers for America and a leading advocate of prison reform, who came out from New York to give two well-attended public lectures. The evening lecture was given to an audience of between 2,500 and 3,000 people at the First Baptist Church following an invocation by Rev. Dr. Truett. Appealing to the crowd for funds to further the work, books to be donated to prisons, and volunteers to visit prisoners as well as organize homes for discharged prisoners, Booth emphasized the need to "help God" in giving prisoners the opportunity to become good citizens and earnest Christians. The key, she believed, lay in the human heart and depended on moral strength. "Do not wear your wishbone where your backbone ought to be," she said.[43]

Although the work of benevolent organizations was generally regarded as a worthy endeavor, there were also occasional expressions of concern that too much benevolence from public or private sources would encourage dissolute behavior. At an afternoon meeting at the First Methodist Church in Fort Worth, for instance, the assembled crowd pondered the increasing number of people who claimed to be insane and wondered if the state's generosity was attracting insane people from beyond its borders.[44]

Liberty of conscience reinforced the view that benevolence and social reform efforts should be directed especially toward the moral improvement of individuals. When properly understood and adhered to, biblical guidelines not only would keep individuals from evil but also would contribute toward personal success. Few were as well positioned to emphasize these principles to an appreciative audience as Truett in Dallas. For the achievement-oriented middle class who attended his church, it was possible to argue that the same principles were evident in the Bible as in business and the professions. Specifically, it was necessary to specialize not just in law or medicine but in particular branches of law and medicine in order to concentrate sufficiently to get ahead. This was the meaning of the biblical injunction against attempting to serve two masters, Truett believed. A successful person had to be careful about trying out too many things or joining too many organizations. It was also imperative to forget about past failures or accomplishments and instead press forward toward higher aspirations. If there was one thing to be learned from the Apostle Paul, Truett argued, it was that "we need to live strenuous lives and always be pressing forward."[45]

If liberty of conscience implied individual effort, it was an ideal that could also be employed against government programs or, for that matter, large-scale organizations in the private sector, such as labor unions and farmers associations. An interesting example occurred during a debate in the Texas legislature in 1909 over a controversial bill to increase government regulation of state banks in response to panics that had occurred in several preceding years. Opponents saw the proposal as an invitation to embark on the raging sea of socialism via a despotic regime with the support of an overreaching farmers union. With references to the Apostle Paul and Methodist preaching, one of the most vocal critics of the proposal argued, reasonable people should uphold "one gospel" as the "hope which stands for the only freedom which makes men truly free—the right to live without abiding under the shadow of governmental despotism, and to die without taking an enforced passage on some chartered ship to the havens of the blest."[46]

THE CHURCH AND PROHIBITION POLITICS

The issue that began significantly to redefine previous understandings of the relationship between religion and politics more than any other was prohibition. Following the state's decision in 1887 to regulate liquor consumption through local option programs instead of attempting to impose a statewide ban, church leaders worked to curb drinking largely in ways that conformed to popular

interpretations of the appropriate role of religion in politics. These interpretations emphasized liberty of conscience and thus freedom of religion from government intrusion. The civil religion gave religious freedom a special place in the
state's self-understanding of its history and included sentiments against Mexican
and Catholic control that fit well with Protestant ideas about denominational
pluralism. Clergy were generally to refrain from holding public office or using
the pulpit for explicitly partisan purposes. It was nevertheless appropriate in
these popular understandings to expect that public officials would believe in a
Supreme Being and that the free exercise of conscience depended on moral instruction and reinforcement from nonpartisan civic institutions.

In 1919 when Texas voted to approve a Prohibition amendment to the state
constitution similar to the one passed by the state legislature a year earlier ratifying the Eighteenth Amendment to the U.S. Constitution, it was nearly a foregone conclusion that the measure would pass. The more interesting aspects of the
struggle for prohibition occurred in 1911 when a statewide referendum narrowly
failed. How church leaders pressed for prohibition in that election and how they
emphasized new strategies in the wake of defeat provide the most revealing indications of the opportunities religious leaders took advantage of when working
for an issue that clearly was partisan and had political overtones. These were
not exactly the same as the ones that would be used at the end of the twentieth
century because social conditions were quite different by then, but they foreshad-
owed some of those methods and showed that it was possible for church leaders
to exercise considerable influence in a context that otherwise favored strict separation of church and state.

By 1911 it was widely known that church leaders were almost universally opposed to the unregulated sale and consumption of alcohol. Baptists and Methodists discouraged drinking among their members, as did many Presbyterians
and members of the Disciples of Christ. Episcopalian, Lutheran, and Catholic
churches used wine as part of the Eucharist and represented ethnic traditions in
which total abstinence was seldom featured, but there were leaders even in these
traditions who favored regulating the sale of alcoholic beverages. Church leaders
were sufficiently confident that a statewide bill could pass that they supported
putting it to voters. At the same time they knew that opposition was sufficiently
strong to require concerted effort from organized religion.

Analysis of county variations in the votes cast in 1911 shows that popular
interpretations at the time of why the bill nearly succeeded but ultimately failed
were largely correct. Saloon owners were more numerous and better organized
to oppose the measure in urban areas. In Dallas alone, for example, there were
more than 250 saloons in business when prohibition advocate Carry Nation visited in 1904 and received a mixed welcome.[47] Fifty-eight percent of the votes cast
there in 1911 were against prohibition, despite well-publicized efforts by church
leaders supporting it, including numerous news stories and editorials in the *Dallas Morning News*. Among the twelve largest cities statewide, Tyler and Wichita

Falls were the only two in which a majority of voters approved the measure. The county data show that ones in which a higher percentage of residents lived in "urban" areas, defined as incorporated towns of more than 2,500 residents, were significantly less likely than other counties to vote for prohibition. Taking those differences into account, counties with larger percentages of Mexican Americans were also less likely than other counties to favor prohibition. That was also true of counties with higher proportions of African Americans, although that difference was a statistical artifact of other factors. Not surprisingly, counties that were already dry by virtue of local option laws or in which some municipalities were dry tilted more toward the measure than "wet" counties. There was concern especially among those favoring prohibition that opponents were finding ways to encourage a large turnout and in retrospect may have even helped more residents to vote on their side than the number who were actually eligible. The *Dallas Morning News*, which was a strong supporter of prohibition, published a lengthy report following the election suggesting that the turnout was artificially high in some counties. New analysis of the data shows that, controlling for other variables, there was in fact a negative correlation between the turnout rate and voting for prohibition. Taking account of all these other contributing factors, the data also demonstrate that voting was related to counties' religious composition. Counties in which Catholics made up a larger share of total church membership were less likely than other counties to vote for prohibition. Counties in which Baptists and Methodists composed larger proportions of total Protestant membership were more likely than other counties to vote favorably.[48]

The role of Baptists and Methodists in shaping the outcome was attributable only in part to the quieter ways in which members were discouraged from consuming alcohol. As the two largest denominations among white Protestants in the state, both were well connected to national temperance organizations, both held statewide meetings at which clergy heard temperance speakers, both published widely distributed church magazines in which temperance messages were included, and both had prominent leaders who toured, lectured, and wrote on behalf of temperance. Even in small towns it was possible to read quotes about prohibition in local newspapers from Baptist and Methodist publications and for Baptist and Methodist churches to be the venues in which antisaloon lectures were given.[49]

Church leaders with long histories of opposition to the liquor trade found themselves having to navigate uncharted political terrain. A case in point was Reverend George C. Rankin, a Methodist who immigrated to Houston in 1892 from Tennessee following a brief period in Kansas City, Missouri. Having taught school and served in a number of southern pulpits, Rankin noted the immediate respect accorded him in his new location. "The very fact that the church vouches for his character and standing is sufficient to give him the right of way to their confidence and love the moment he enters upon his work among them," he wrote. He felt not only that he was accepted by the congregation but also "as an asset in the community" with influence that extended beyond the congregation and enabled him to be "a dominant factor in the forces that enter into the moral, the civic and the religious life of the people."[50] Before long Rankin cultivated the friendship of local business leaders, raised enough money to pay off the congregation's debt, hosted a well-attended revival meeting at the town's auditorium, and launched a personal crusade against gambling that led to grand jury appearances and the indictment of several offenders.

After four years in Houston, Rankin moved to Dallas where he became the pastor of the First Methodist Church, which was widely considered the best appointment in the conference. North Texas was "like coming into contact with another civilization," he wrote. An outspoken advocate of prohibition, he had campaigned for it in Tennessee and been dismayed by the prevalence of saloons in Kansas City. Houston he felt was also dominated by saloons. As in the rest of South Texas, there was a large element of foreigners who had no regard for the Sabbath, and many of them belonged to the "Roman Church," which "neither elevates nor leads them out of these ideas and usages," he observed. Dallas, with its "largely native" population, was a welcome contrast. "Protestant Christianity, the public schools and the English language have the right of way." Moral sentiment was strong, the saloons were perhaps abundant but had less influence than in Houston, and officeholders even in the city respected the rural vote.[51] Rankin continued his work on behalf of prohibition and played a prominent role in arguing for extended Sunday closing hours for saloons. In 1898 he became editor of the *Texas Christian Advocate*, which further extended his influence.

But in 1906 controversy involving Rankin developed during the reelection campaign of Senator Joseph W. Bailey, who in 1902 had physically assaulted Senator Albert Beveridge and was under charges of having illegally represented the Waters-Pierce Oil Company after the firm was expelled from Texas for violating antitrust laws.[52] Bailey was reelected, but controversy continued at widely attended meetings in Dallas and through well-publicized inquiries that included stories about incidents in Mississippi. Rankin was drawn into the scandal because he had known Bailey since at least 1887 and had enlisted his help in the effort for prohibition.[53] To Bailey's opponents, the association with Rankin was grist for arguing that preachers had better mind their own business. A good Methodist, critics charged, should stick to teaching common everyday honesty: "Is it possible that our Christian ministers have fallen so low in their ethical ideals, conceptions and teachings as to subscribe to the proposition that every unjailed rascal is a fit subject for the United States Senate?"[54]

The added difficulty church leaders faced was that supporting legislation prohibiting the liquor trade exposed them to the criticism that they were violating the separation of church and state. "They say all the Church wants is legislation," an Amarillo resident who opposed prohibition complained. "Well, that is the dangerous part of it to a man [who] wants his liberty or one who does not happen to belong to the Church that is in power. This is the history of Church rule.

They want to make it against the law to do anything the Church objects to." It struck him as odd that citizens could boast about their religious liberty and yet live in places where it was nearly mandatory to belong to a particular church. A state such as Kansas might get away with instituting prohibition, but surely that should not happen in a state that truly valued religious liberty. "I hope to never see the day that Texas will be Kansasized," he said.[55]

When the 1911 measure failed, the immediate response among some of the church leaders who had worked for it was to argue that a similar bill should be placed on the ballot again. As a Presbyterian leader explained, "More extensive and complete organization for another submission and another appeal to the voters of the state" would be the next step.[56] However, that plan was accompanied by strategies that reflected popular understandings of the appropriate ways for churches to influence public behavior. These strategies emphasized what had been least controversial to date, namely, appeals that associated prohibition with moral freedom of conscience on the part of individuals, strategies that were oriented toward local concerns, and efforts that could be described as nonpartisan and indeed as not involving direct participation by organized religion.

The appeal to free exercise of conscience was reflected in the language in which both state-level and national organizations identified themselves. Instead of emphasizing "prohibition," which on the surface connoted a lack of freedom, advocates for the Prohibition bill identified themselves as opponents of saloons, as was most explicitly evident in the title of the Anti-Saloon League, a national organization that included more than two hundred local chapters in Texas. Saloons were local establishments that were often regarded locally as places in which ruffians gathered. To oppose saloons was thus to be against something that ran against the grain of freely exercised moral conscience. Liquor clouded rather than enhanced personal judgment, opponents argued. Unlike schools and churches, saloons as community organizations were accused of offering nothing in the way of positive moral instruction. Increasingly opponents also portrayed saloons as large, impersonal organizations rather than small-town places in which friends and neighbors gathered. The liquor trade was portrayed as "liquor traffic," "the brewing interest," an "industry" run by northerners who lived in big cities, a conspiracy against civilization itself, or simply something that was "big" and "powerful" and under the control of interests that were outside the local community and hard to identify. Saloons "seek to dominate the politics and control the policy of the state," Baptist leader Dr. J. H. Gambrell, who headed the Texas Anti-Saloon League, explained, "and most of those who operate such saloons are foreigners who know little or nothing of the genius and fundamental principles of our government."[57]

Strategies that focused on local communities proved to be as attractive to Prohibitionists as attempting to revitalize a statewide referendum. Local option laws that had been in place for decades gave greater legitimacy to these efforts and provided entry points for more aggressive regulation. Laws that prohibited saloons from conducting business within a specified distance from a church or school could be extended to increase the distance or to call for stricter enforcement. Publicity could also be gained by staging strategic violations of these regulations and thus posing opportunities for meetings at which antisaloon arguments were made.

The two-hundred–plus liquor stores that operated in Dallas were subject to numerous constraints that had to be approved by only a majority of the board of city commissioners as well as state and county laws. These included state, county, and municipal fees totaling $750 a year, state and city taxes of approximately $125 a year, and a fine of between $500 and $1,000 and a mandatory jail term for anyone selling intoxicating liquor without a license. Any tax-paying citizen could file a complaint against any liquor dealer, in which case a hearing before the county judge was required. Establishments selling liquor were prohibited in any block in which a church or school was located and within three hundred feet thereof as well as in certain residential blocks except by approval of a majority of the residents. In 1909 additional statewide restrictions were approved preventing anyone from becoming a proprietor of a liquor-selling establishment who had lived in the city less than two years and who was employed by or represented some other person or corporation. Other regulations prevented taverns from masquerading as social clubs, prohibited gaming and loud music, and imposed nightly and Sunday closing laws.[58] In 1913 these regulations were stiffened requiring saloons to close at 9:30 instead of midnight, prohibiting the shipment of liquor into dry territories, and preventing liquor from being imported into dry territories from other states.

Strict as these regulations were, church leaders experimented with various ways of testing and extending them. A church in Fort Worth, for example, appealed unsuccessfully to the state attorney general to determine if holding Sunday evening worship services at a downtown theater could necessitate the closing of any saloons in the vicinity.[59] In another instance a liquor license was temporarily withheld while state officials investigated whether construction of a nearby church was in fact going forward or whether the lot was merely the location in which a church might be built at some indefinite time in the future.[60] In yet another case Salvation Army volunteers challenged a different set of ordinances that prohibited street meetings that blocked sidewalks or disrupted businesses as well as the solicitation of funds by religious organizations except at religious services. The volunteers violated these regulations by staging marches accompanied by tambourines through local saloons.[61]

Church leaders argued that their efforts on behalf of prohibition were nonpartisan because they were not supporting a particular candidate over another candidate. Although they sometimes argued for legislation to be passed, they also argued that their role was not to press for legislation but only to prick the conscience of believers about an important moral issue. Partisan politics, they argued, were divisive and governed by the personal interests of politicians, whereas speaking against the liquor traffic was merely the necessary expression of moral convictions with which any reasonable person could agree.[62] Leaders demonstrated that their efforts were not in violation of separation of church and state by showing that many different faiths were involved. Besides Baptists and Methodists, antisaloon committees were organized that included Presbyterian and Episcopal clergy. White clergy were joined in these efforts by black clergy who shared the stage at well-publicized meetings of the Texas Negroes' State-Wide Prohibition Association."[63] Occasional Roman Catholic clergy who spoke at community forums also accompanied Protestant leaders.[64]

As ostensibly nonpartisan and nonsectarian organizations such as the Anti-Saloon League and the Women's Christian Temperance Union became more widely organized, often through the efforts of clergy and lay members, church leaders were then able to argue that they were not directly supporting or opposing particular political candidates or legislation but merely lending their support to a separate nonpolitical and nonreligious civic organization. To support such organizations, it was possible to argue, was no more in violation of church and state than sponsoring a private orphanage or hospital.

Clergy who spoke most openly in favor of legislation against saloons employed some of the same discursive tactics that would become evident again decades later in discussions of hot-button issues such as abortion and evolution. Stopping short of arguing on scriptural grounds, pastors spoke about why they personally were opposed to liquor and why anyone, Christian or otherwise, could see that abstinence was the path to happiness and prosperity. They drew on arguments about better health, greater longevity, declining rates of insanity, and flourishing economic conditions in states with Prohibition. Lectures were given on Sunday afternoons and at evening services rather than during the appointed hour for worship on Sunday mornings. Children's choirs were enlisted to enhance the message at these events by singing "My Country Tis of Thee" and "Texas Going Dry."[65] Speakers were invited who held credentials as ordained pastors within their denominations but who could also represent themselves as something other than pulpit preachers. They spoke as officers of the Anti-Saloon League, as editors of church magazines, and as faculty at denominational colleges and seminaries.

The emphasis on local communities especially facilitated arguments comparing the contribution of saloons unfavorably with those of churches, schools, and benevolent associations. The saloon was a place that ordinary citizens could visualize, smell, and easily regard as a breeding ground for lawlessness. As a Methodist preacher explained, "No institution has a right to live that cannot give a valid reason for its being." Churches, schools, hospitals, and legitimate businesses all contributed to the community, he said, but the saloon alone did not. "It blights the home, robbing it of its peace and happiness; it is the enemy of the public school and robs the school of a multitude of bright pupils. It despises the church."[66] A Presbyterian pastor cast the argument in similar terms. Saloons currently had a right under civil law to exist, he argued, but even though they might have legal standing, they violated God's law, which called humans to stand on principles of "moral character" and to demonstrate benevolence toward their communities.[67]

When the Prohibition amendment to the state constitution appeared on the ballot in 1919, voters approved the measure by a 53 to 47 percent margin.[68] By that time approximately 80 percent of the state's population lived in counties or municipalities under Prohibition. The turnout was considerably lower than it had been in 1911. County by county, the best predictor of the 1919 results was how the county had voted in 1911. Predominantly Catholic counties were less likely than other counties to favor the amendment, while counties with large percentages of Baptists and Methodists were more favorable.[69] It was well understood that Texas was in support of prohibition even though only a few years earlier that had not quite been the case. "We kept the drive steadily in the local option section," Baptist leader Dr. Arthur. J. Barton observed, and saw "dozens of communities captured."[70] Much of the rhetoric about liberty of conscience remained in place. It was possible to claim that religion had not breached the wall of separation. It was rather that freedom of religion had made it possible for morally minded people to promote prohibition. A few years later that understanding would come into play again when the close connection between conservative religion and the Democratic Party fell into question.

DANGER FROM ROME?

The 1928 presidential campaign that pitted Al Smith as the Democratic candidate against Republican Herbert Hoover represented a new challenge for Texas church leaders of the kind not seen, and then only in a very different light, since Reconstruction. Although church leaders had debated about the respective strengths and weaknesses of Democratic candidates at the local and state level who were for or against prohibition, Smith's nomination elevated the discussion to the national stage. Even more important, it was the Democratic Party that now embraced a candidate who was Roman Catholic. The quandary for Protestant church leaders in Texas who had been able to follow the Democratic Party with few questions for half a century was now whether to stay loyal or to oppose Smith on grounds that he was Roman Catholic and probably against prohibition as well. Preachers who never would have spoken from the pulpit before about national politics decided their voice should be heard. They went against tradition in doing so, but in simplest terms their message contradicted the very act of voicing it. The message was that strict separation of church and state should be observed. Making that claim without seeming to violate it depended on emphasizing liberty of conscience.

Religion had emerged at least once before as a potentially divisive factor in presidential elections. In the 1908 election that pitted Republican William

Howard Taft against Democrat William Jennings Bryan, questions were raised about Taft's suitability as a candidate on grounds that he was a Unitarian who seemed not to attend any church and thus may have been an infidel. It was also rumored that his wife and brother were Roman Catholics. In a letter to President Theodore Roosevelt a voter named J. C. Martin who lived in Dayton, Ohio, demanded that Taft disclose his religious beliefs, and it was in response to Martin that Roosevelt wrote his reply about religious discrimination being an outrage against liberty of conscience. Martin doubted that the public would vote for Taft if they considered him to be in sympathy with Roman Catholics. Martin held that "if a man does not believe in God it would be a difficult thing for him to have a conscience." For these reasons Martin argued that Taft should not hesitate to let the world know what he in fact believed. Roosevelt felt a reply was inappropriate until after the election (in which Taft received 52 percent of the popular vote nationally and 66 percent of the electoral votes) and thus sent his letter to Martin shortly thereafter, asserting his strong belief that liberty of conscience in matters of religion was a foundational American principle.[71]

The leading newspapers in Texas carried stories from the national press about the controversy involving Taft's religion and printed at least one editorial asking if Taft was indeed an atheist. Mr. Bryan "was raised a Cumberland Presbyterian and his orthodoxy is so unquestioned as to make him a popular pulpit substitute for the regular minister in whatever town he may happen to spend a Sunday," the writer editorialized, but thus far nobody seemed to know whether Mr. Taft was religious at all.[72]

At a meeting in Dallas shortly after the election and in response to Roosevelt's letter, the Texas Holiness Association, an organization composed of theologically conservative Methodists and members who had left other denominations in favor of one that emphasized spiritual perfection and the indwelling of the Holy Spirit, passed a resolution denouncing the president elect for being a person who did not believe in Christ.[73] "We feel it is an insult to the principles of this government to elect as chief executive of this nation a man who denies the divinity of Christ," the leader of the association said, "a man who would call Jesus Christ an illegitimate child, and who thus thinking would have nothing but sneers and contempt for our churches." It was an insult to "the very vitals of our government."[74] A denunciation of this kind as an official act of any religious body was rare, but it was also notable that the holiness group waited until after the election to deliver its condemnation rather than making earlier statements that might have been interpreted as an attempt to influence the election. The leaders of other denominations apparently refrained from passing similar resolutions.

Although Texans who doubted Taft's religious credentials may have worried about the ramifications of his winning the election, there was little reason to have pondered the matter deeply as they went to the polls that November. Texas had voted Democratic in every presidential election since 1848, including twice before for Bryan in 1896 and 1900. Bryan had given lectures in Texas about prohibition and in 1907 purchased a ranch in the lower Rio Grande valley for a winter home.[75] It could be taken for granted that Texas would give Bryan a win again in 1908. The only question was by how much. Would Taft's religion give Bryan an even larger victory than in previous elections?

When the votes were tallied in 1908, Bryan's margin of victory in Texas was 74 percent compared to 22 percent for Taft. That 52-point spread was larger than the spread of 38 points Bryan received in 1896, larger than the 32-point margin he earned in 1900, and slightly larger than the 49-point spread between Democrat Alton Parker and Republican Theodore Roosevelt in 1904. On that basis it appeared that religion might have been a factor.

County comparisons also pointed to the effect of religious differences. There was a moderately strong positive correlation of 0.414 between the percentage of church members who were Catholic and the percentage of votes for Taft. Among Protestants there was a moderately strong negative correlation of −0.419 between the percentage of Protestants who were Southern Baptists and the percentage of votes for Taft and a weak negative correlation of −0.128 between the percentage of Protestants who were Methodists and the percentage of votes for Taft. In the fifteen counties in which Roman Catholics were a majority of the churchgoing population, Taft won 35 percent of the votes. In the fifteen counties in which at least 30 percent of Protestants were Southern Baptists, Taft received only 12 percent of the votes.[76]

Despite the state's emphasis on liberty of conscience, its Protestants had never been fully at ease with their Catholic brethren. In 1824 Stephen F. Austin wrote to a Protestant pastor who had been hoping to start churches in Texas that the Roman Catholic Church was the "exclusive religion" and that the law of the land must be obeyed. "If a Methodist or any other preacher except a Catholic was to go through this colony preaching, I should be compelled to imprison him. All the children in this country without exception must be baptized in the Roman Church and all marriages must be celebrated in that Church."[77] That ordinance was never strictly enforced, but after 1836 when religious freedom was achieved it served along with stories about the Alamo and Catholic oppression in Mexico as background for discussions about liberty of conscience.

The earliest Catholic missionary activities, which began with Spanish explorations in the sixteenth century and resulted in missions being established by the 1680s, were concentrated in the Rio Grande valley.[78] Independence and the decade in which Texas was a republic was a time for Catholics when "troubles followed troubles," as one recalled. Churches were left in ruins, and the few who adhered to the faith "were deprived of the instruction necessary to render its teachings intelligible to themselves or to enable them to transmit it to their children in its purity."[79] The work nevertheless continued to the point that the diocese of Galveston was organized in 1847 to supervise efforts throughout southern Texas.[80] Two years later the first Missionary Oblates arrived and established centers in Brownsville and Roma from which they traveled on horseback to conduct services throughout the lower Rio Grande valley.[81] In 1850 there were an estimated forty thousand Catholics in Texas, most of whom were in southern Texas.

Impressions of the Roman Catholic Church among white Protestants in Texas were influenced by the state's struggle for independence from Mexico and by the extent to which Catholic inhabitants of Mexican origin populated churches in southern and southwestern Texas. The 1870 census, for example, identified twenty-three thousand persons of Mexican birth living in Texas, of whom three-quarters were concentrated in just eight counties that included San Antonio but otherwise were located along the Rio Grande valley. Ten of the state's twenty-five Catholic parishes were in those counties. Eighty percent of the state's counties had no Catholic parishes.[82] Whatever may have been said about liberty of conscience, members of majority white Protestant churches knew that Catholics generally lived in other parts of the state and were likely to have hailed from different ethnic origins. Methodists could find denunciations of Romish superstition among the teachings of their tradition.[83] Baptists who looked to Roger Williams for inspiration may have discovered his fears of Catholic insurrection sufficient that he suggested they be required to wear distinctive clothing.[84]

By 1890, as a result of European immigration, the earlier geographic pattern was beginning to change. The Mexican-born population totaled 51,559, or just 2.3 percent of the state's population, and two-thirds of that number were still concentrated in San Antonio and along the Rio Grande valley. Statewide there were 189 Catholic churches, 263 parishes, and almost 100,000 members. Only 36 percent of the state's Catholics lived in the eight counties in which the Mexican-born population was most heavily concentrated. The Catholic population was becoming more widely dispersed, with at least a dozen Catholics living in at least half the state's counties. There was still considerable geographic concentration of the Catholic population, however. Twenty counties accounted for 72 percent of the total Catholic population. Two-thirds of the counties did not have a single Catholic church. San Antonio and Galveston were still the only towns of any size in which Catholics outnumbered Protestants.[85]

The census of religious bodies conducted in 1916 demonstrated that change in the size and location of the Catholic population had continued during the preceding quarter century. The total number of Catholics had quadrupled from 100,000 to 402,874. The historically Mexican American areas that included San Antonio and the Rio Grande Valley were still heavily Catholic. Overall the location of the Catholic population was still heavily skewed compared to that of the Protestant population, but the increase in numbers of members meant that at least a few Catholics were present in most predominantly Protestant areas. The Catholic population was increasingly located in the state's largest cities, which now included Dallas, El Paso, Fort Worth, Galveston, and Houston. Catholics were also more likely to be found even in less populated rural areas. Catholics were now absent in only a third of the state's counties.[86]

The changing religious demographics had three important implications: First, there were significantly more Catholics to be reckoned with by Protestant leaders and elected officials. Although there were still far more Protestants than Catholics, Catholics were now in a better position to organize churches, launch parochial schools, and weigh in on community matters than ever before. Second, the growing prominence of Catholics in the state's leading cities increased the likelihood of discussions of religion in those places having to be more mindful of the Catholic presence. And third, the wider geographic presence of Catholics even in smaller areas increased the likelihood that farm communities and rural school districts in which Protestantism had been taken for granted would from time to time be confronted with the necessity of taking Catholic views into account. All this was complicated by the fact that a significant number of Catholics were of Mexican American descent and were an economically disadvantaged population that was subject to recurring prejudice and discrimination.[87]

Although scholars of religion would later contend that competition among denominations was a decisive influence on the overall growth of religious membership, it was doubtful that local clergy spent much time thinking explicitly about those dynamics, especially when significant population growth provided ample opportunities for all denominations. There was little evidence particularly of Protestants seeking to convert Catholics or Catholics making converts of Protestants. However, it was increasingly possible that Protestant clergy might worry about the growing presence of Catholics in their communities when religion posed questions about electoral outcomes, as it did in 1928. Had they paid close attention to the local statistics, Southern Baptist clergy would have realized that they were outnumbered by Catholics in 65 of the 250 counties in which church membership was reported. Methodists would have been outnumbered by Catholics in 76 counties. And Catholics would have claimed more members than Southern Baptists and Methodists combined in 55 counties. Perhaps more to the point, Catholics and Protestants were concentrated in different parts of the state, despite the widening dispersion of both.

The 1928 presidential election was religiously complicated in a way that the 1908 campaign had not been because the Democratic candidate, Al Smith of New York, was Catholic. The quandary Texas Protestants who had nearly always voted Democratic faced was whether to remain loyal to their party despite concerns about Smith's religion or to be swayed enough by religious concerns to switch parties. The question was further complicated by the deeply held belief that liberty of conscience meant to some extent keeping religious issues out of politics.

How much to say specifically about Catholics depended partly on which audience Protestant leaders were addressing. Editors of the *Baptist Standard*, for example, published articles for their Baptist readership that condemned presumed efforts by the Catholic Church to take over the United States government and impose authoritarian religious teachings on the American population.[88] In wider contexts the message was less likely to mention Catholics specifically than to mention unnamed state churches that might be endangering religious freedom. At a meeting in Atlanta in 1924 attended largely but not exclusively by Southern Baptists, for example, Truett of Dallas declared the "spiritual adultery" of state churches that sought temporal power as being fundamentally at odds with Baptists' emphasis on religious liberty.[89]

The campaign for Prohibition had established a precedent, making it somewhat more acceptable for clergy to speak their minds about political issues. The Southern Baptist Convention at its meeting in Oklahoma City in 1912 passed a resolution condemning the Taft administration for cutting off federal funds to schools run by religious organizations for Indian children. The issue was thorny because the administration's decision was in response to criticisms of Catholic schools. Noting that Taft had recently sent a message welcoming a Catholic cardinal visiting the United States, a Baptist leader from Texas contended that the administration was merely upholding separation of church and state in the current matter. Others though took the opportunity to criticize not only the administration but also Catholics. "I am for the destruction of the Catholic Church," a proponent of the resolution argued. "Roman Catholics are endeavoring to transfer from Europe their power to this soil." He saw a terrible conflict ahead. "They came here to conquer for the Pope and we are here to win for Jesus Christ."[90]

A year later the Baptist General Convention of Texas issued a statement in Dallas that appeared to lean considerably more in the direction of liberty of conscience than toward criticism of Catholics. In conjunction with broader ecumenical efforts to forge greater unity among the nation's scattered Christian denominations, the statement declared Texas Baptists in support of these efforts. "We hold that all people who believe in Christ as their personal Savior are our brothers in the common salvation, whether they be in the Catholic communion or in a Protestant communion or in any other communion, or in no communion." The statement further emphasized readiness to cooperate with all fellow Christians and fellow citizens "whether Protestant or Catholic, whether Jew or Gentile, in every worthy effort for the moral and social uplift of humanity, as well as for the equal civil and religious rights of all men in all lands." The statement nevertheless made it clear that Baptists were unwilling to compromise the denomination's distinctive beliefs. "We steadfastly believe and hold that until one is born again, by the Spirit of God, into the Kingdom of Christ," it said, that person "is not a Scriptural subject for baptism and cannot of right become a member of Christ's church." In short, Catholics and any Protestants who practiced infant baptism were not true believers.[91]

Other developments showed that church leaders were experimenting with direct endorsements of political candidates. In 1920, with Prohibition having gone into effect, preachers who had been vocal proponents of the measure now argued that particular candidates should or should not be supported because of positions they had taken on the law. Cranfill, the Baptist leader who had championed prohibition for decades, for example, argued that the candidacy of a particular person he opposed was "an assault upon every sacred thing in our Christian civilization." It was beholden on pastors, Cranfill said, to be "political preachers." It was irresponsible, he believed, to remain silent "when the very life of civilization is menaced."[92] Another leader took a similar view, stating, "I am a preacher and I think as long as I obey the laws of the state I have as much right to speak my mind as any other law-abiding citizen."[93] Leaders in other denominations apparently shared these views as well. In the 1922 election that pitted ex-governor James E. Ferguson against Earle B. Mayfield in the race for United States Senate, for example, Ferguson claimed with some basis that Methodist clergy were preaching sermons endorsing Mayfield. At least one who campaigned aggressively for Mayfield was the flamboyant fund-raiser Knickerbocker. Mayfield for his part exhibited a letter from a Catholic priest claiming that Catholics would throw their support to Ferguson.[94]

The more important carryover from Prohibition to the 1928 campaign was that most of the rhetoric directed against Smith by Protestant leaders focused on concern that he might overturn Prohibition rather than on his being Catholic. One of the first and most influential church leaders to declare his opposition to Smith was Edwin D. Mouzon, a Methodist pastor who had held pulpits in Texas since 1889 and currently served as bishop with episcopal supervision over seventeen Methodist conferences, including Texas, most of the South, several in the West, and several in Latin America. More than a year before the election, Mouzon announced that southern Democrats were "emphatically dry" and thus should not support Smith, who was an "antiprohibitionist."[95] Soon after Mouzon's statement the Central Texas Methodist conference adopted a resolution that stopped short of condemning Smith by name but called for loyalty to God and country over party. At the same meeting a temperance committee report called on Methodists to "warn our political leaders that if they force on us as a candidate for office a man whose personal position or past record is out of harmony with [Prohibition] they do so at their party's peril." Southern Baptists expressed a similar warning.[96]

These moves set off a storm of controversy among diehard Democrats. One argument held that party loyalty was in principle nearly sacred while another contended that Democrats alone could ensure peace and prosperity. Appeals to liberty of conscience also came into play. "The question of prohibition and antiprohibition and church membership should not interfere," a Farmersville resident argued, "keep church and state separate."[97] A Cisco resident went further, arguing that preachers should stick to preaching the gospel "and not the fetish prohibition or any other false god." Preachers in politics reminded him of the last days in which the prophet Isaiah warned, "The leaders of this people cause them to err and they who are led of them shall be destroyed."[98]

But Smith's opponents, with strong backing from church leaders, persisted. On the national stage Senator James Thomas "Cotton Tom" Heflin of Alabama led the opposition with an eighty-minute tirade on the Senate floor in which he charged that Smith was "a wringing wet, a nullifier and a Roman Catholic," adding that "there is enough to defeat him without his being a Catholic but being a Catholic, that ends it."[99] In Dallas a few weeks later two hundred community leaders gathered to form the Dallas County Dry Democratic League as a step toward organizing a statewide effort to nominate a dry progressive Democrat instead of Smith.[100] During the spring, as party leaders debated ways of replacing, opposing, or supporting Smith without seeming to cave on Prohibition, the relationship between church and state came increasingly into question. At their national convention in Chattanooga, four thousand Southern Baptists endorsed a resolution to vote against any wet candidate for president. Texans who favored Smith argued that it was a violation of the constitutional clause against invoking a religious test for public office to vote against Smith solely because he was Catholic. Those who opposed Smith argued that it was an expression of their liberty of conscience to vote against him on grounds that he was not only wet but Catholic. All that separation of church and state implied, they said, was that if he were somehow elected, his religion should not prevent him from taking office. But if opposition was as strong as it seemed, that eventuality would never occur.[101]

As it happened, the Democratic National Convention met in Houston that June, thus intensifying local interest in the outcome and drawing national attention to Texas. With hotel space for twelve thousand and an auditorium accommodating five thousand, Houston was an attractive location for the convention. The location sent other signals as well. "Take a northern wet down into the home of the drys," a writer for the *Chicago Daily Tribune* quipped, "and make him acceptable to the kleagles in konklave, to the southern fundamentalists and to the most enthusiastic professors of prohibition."[102]

In a spirit of religious unity at the convention, Monsignor G. T. Walsh of Houston offered an opening prayer, which was followed by tributes to Vice President Thomas R. Marshall and standard-bearer William Jennings Bryan with singing of "Nearer My God to Thee" and "Rock of Ages." All was well until Senator Joseph Taylor Robinson of Arkansas, who had been an outspoken foe of Heflin's anti-Catholic bigotry, reminded the delegates of the constitutional guarantee that no religious test shall ever be required as a qualification for public office. Following a melee that required police wielding night sticks to break up, Smith's name was successfully placed in nomination to the apparent rejoicing of most concerned. Little else was said about religion except by Senator Alben W. Barkley of Kentucky, a Presbyterian, who asserted that he was "not ashamed to lift my feeble voice in behalf of the nomination of one who is not of my faith, but who has as much right to his as I have to mine."[103]

Across Texas and across America, religious bodies that had never considered breaching the separation of church and state to the point of endorsing or opposing specific candidates for public office now did so. Within a week of the Democratic National Convention the Central Texas Conference Epworth League at its summer assembly in Fort Worth passed a resolution put forward by three prominent Methodist pastors to oppose Smith and censure the Democratic Party for nominating him.[104] The same day in Austin the president of the Texas WCTU declared her opposition to Smith and pledged to convene meetings to widen the effort.[105] In San Antonio the Federated Protestant Women's Association followed suit. In Dallas Methodist Bishop John M. Moore announced that he would work to defeat Smith. "For forty years I have been a Methodist preacher and a voter [and] have declined to take any public part in political affairs because of my ministerial position," he explained. "Now, however, high moral interests are threatened." Specifically, Moore feared that Smith was a pawn of Tammany Hall who would work to repeal Prohibition. Tammany's control and its pledge to overturn the Eighteenth Amendment, Moore declared, was like slavery. "Southerners know about the overseer's lash driving slaves to do their master's will." Moore avoided saying anything about Smith being Catholic but noted that Methodists, Baptists, and Presbyterians, all with strong Scotch-Irish and Anglo-Saxon roots, were uniformly against Smith. "I am no political preacher, nor preacher politician," he said, "but I am a preacher deeply concerned for the moral and religious welfare of this country involved as it is in this campaign."[106]

Besides passing resolutions at religious assemblies and voicing their preferences as individuals, clergy became directly involved in political organizations. Moore's efforts, for example, included serving on the platform committee for the statewide Anti–Al Smith Democrats of Texas organization that formed in Dallas two weeks after Smith's nomination and in that capacity included in the platform a statement that "all the Evangelical bodies in the South through their accredited representatives served due advance notice" that they would not support wet Tammany candidates for election.[107] Similarly, the newly formed Tarrant County Democratic Vote-For-Hoover organization selected a Fort Worth Baptist pastor, Dr. C. D. Edwards, as its head. Edwards in turn pledged to secure the involvement of as many Methodist, Christian, and Baptist clergy as he could. "This issue is not religious, it is not one of Protestantism against Catholicism," he said. "We are realizing that it is to preserve our Eighteenth Amendment that we must again fight, shoulder to shoulder."[108]

Others were less cautious about emphasizing the religious issues involved and breaking with tradition by doing so from the pulpit during the Sunday morning worship hour rather than only at other times. Preaching on "The Religion of the Next President," Dallas Methodist Dr. Carl C. Gregory drew a clear contrast between Hoover and Smith. As a Quaker Hoover was known for his work on behalf of food relief during the war and followed a religion that stressed the "inner guidance of the conscience by the Holy Spirit." Smith's Catholicism, however, gave him pause, Gregory said. It was not that he or other Protestants were intolerant of Catholics. He had personally attended Catholic services. It was rather that "Catholics are 100 percent intolerant of Protestants and Catholic leaders refuse to join other ministers in civic righteousness movements." Smith's attitude toward

Prohibition was reason enough to oppose him, but that was not all. There was still the troubling matter of the papacy failing to understand true separation of church and state. "If the Pope would renounce his political ambitions I'd vote for a Catholic as soon as I would for a follower of any other faith," Gregory said. But "the Pope claims the right to crown and uncrown Princes and to direct the governments of the world."[109]

If Protestants were reluctant to support Smith because of his religion, the card that Democrats hoped would carry the day against Hoover was race. "As long as I am a white man, live among white people and respect the white womanhood of the Southland," a Smith supporter told a rally in Fort Worth, "I will never vote for Herbert Hoover, the advocate of racial social equality and the man who forced white girls working in his department to share with negro women the lavatories and comfort stations." The speaker was Democratic congressman Sam Rayburn. The rally was held at Fort Worth's First Baptist Church.[110]

How much religion mattered when voters went to the polls was impossible to assess precisely, but an indication that it probably made a difference was evident in county comparisons. Taking into account the possible effects of differences between urban and rural counties and differences in racial composition, there was a statistically significant positive relationship between the percentage of church members who were Catholics and the percentage of votes cast for Smith. And there was a statistically significant negative relationship between the percentage of Protestants who were Southern Baptists or Methodists and those voting for Smith. But there was also evidence supporting church leaders' claim that the issue was Prohibition rather than religion. In statistical models in which the percentages that voted for Prohibition in 1911 or in 1919 were taken into account, the effects of the Catholic and Baptist variables were no longer statistically significant.[111] Smith was defeated by twenty-six thousand votes.[112]

In retrospect the extent to which religion mixed with politics in the 1928 election was unprecedented in ways that anticipated similar developments a half-century later. Clergy who had never before endorsed or opposed candidates publicly did so. They discussed candidates from the pulpit and held office themselves in partisan organizations. Having been reluctant to speak against the Roman Catholic Church, Protestant leaders announced that they would not vote for a Catholic and were fearful of the pope's political intentions. Sentiments about religious inclusion and civic nonpartisanship that had been present a decade earlier in public discourse were no longer emphasized. Liberty of conscience came increasingly to mean freedom to defy pledges to the Democratic Party and freedom from the influences of organizations such as Tammany Hall. Separation of church and state in Protestant discourse implied doing what was necessary to check Catholic influences.

The concern about religion centered on Smith's candidacy for president but spilled into other races as well. In a complex and heated runoff campaign for a seat in the U.S. Senate, candidates solicited endorsements from clergy, gave campaign speeches at houses of worship, were introduced at rallies by clergy, and hurled charges about religious malfeasance at opponents. A Methodist pastor who endorsed one candidate, for example, claimed that the candidate's opponent was probably a Catholic sympathizer because the opponent's daughter attended a Catholic school. When it was discovered that the daughter did not attend a Catholic school because she did not exist, the preacher then charged that the opposing candidate was probably prejudiced against Catholics because rumor had it that the opponent had fired a secretary because she was Catholic.[113]

If much of that was new, it was nevertheless contingent on the particular circumstances in which church leaders found themselves. Had it not been for the extensive effort and organization that had gone into Prohibition between 1911 and 1919, it seems doubtful that clergy would have been quite as ready to enter the political arena as directly as they did. The possible repeal of Prohibition became the rallying cry more than anti-Catholic opinion. Democrats who bolted for Hoover were able to argue that Smith himself had paved the way by not supporting the Democratic Party's dry platform. The need to organize in opposition to the established party machinery led to calls for involvement by prominent clergy and administrators of church-related colleges, whereas little of that had been required when politics operated as usual.

On the heels of Prohibition, the vociferous opposition to Smith by Protestant leaders served notice to anyone who may have been watching that religion under the right conditions could be a powerful political force. It was not the case, however, that once religion had mingled with politics it would remain involved. By their own interpretation, religious leaders said it was necessary to become involved only when the nation was facing a supreme moral crisis. It had taken years for prohibition to be regarded as having that kind of serious moral implication. Other factors would have to fall into place for that to happen again.

CHAPTER 4

THE FUNDAMENTALIST BELT

Coming to Terms with Science

It is adequate, comprehensive, simple, concise—more than that, after
standing in its unique simplicity for centuries, often assailed by tentative
and immature science, it is today vindicated by the last word of the
latest science.

CYRUS I. SCOFIELD, "THE DIVINE BIBLE," 1905

It was a minor kerfuffle freighted with meaning. In 1930 Governor Dan
Moody of Texas responded to news of gangster-led violence in Chicago by
asserting that a few rangers from his state could clean up the mess in no time.
Incensed at the governor's audacity, the *Chicago Daily Tribune* editorialized that
Texas should try cleaning up its own act first, starting by ridding itself of bootleggers and lynch mobs. The state's greatest contribution to science was paralysis,
the paper said, and to public morality "the hypocrisy of the bottle nosed saint in
the garb of the Ku Klux." Texas was a "fundamentalist belt of primitives."[1]

Back in Texas the jibe was taken surprisingly well. Maybe they were the fundamentalist belt, but that was better than living in big cities in the North where
parochialism was so prevalent that people could hardly see beyond the suburbs.
At least the "back woods of Texas" was not a gangsters' paradise, Moody replied.[2]
Chicago was beginning to feel the blight of its lawlessness, while "the fundamentalist belt has managed to ride herd on its own criminals without the aid of the
federal government," an editor in Galveston observed.[3] What if H. L. Mencken
said they were part of the Bible Belt? Bibles were in fact selling in record numbers, others noted. These were merely the criticisms of wets that wanted Prohibition repealed, they said. Besides that, fundamentalism itself had come under
vicious attack only to have defended itself and found a receptive audience in a
huge state with millions of devout churchgoers.

121

In standard renderings fundamentalism was born in the waning years of the nineteenth century as a response not only to Darwin but also to the rise of cities and the influx of new immigrants as well as to highbrow intellectual currents that poorly educated people on farms and in small towns could not understand. It gained traction in northern states, causing basic rifts in northern denominations and in northern seminaries, while having little impact in the South where nearly everyone was too securely conservative to be much interested. But of course that account is too simple.

Despite the prevailing Protestant orthodoxy preached in its prominent Baptist and Methodist churches, Texas was a cauldron of theological controversy. By the early 1890s conflicts were making national headlines and quieter debates were occurring at denominational meetings about doctrinal interpretation. The long battle for Prohibition on which there was nearly universal consensus among Protestant leaders overshadowed the concerns that were increasingly being expressed about science, evolution, the content of textbooks in public schools, and what was being taught at colleges and seminaries. These discussions demonstrated that religion not only was becoming better institutionalized but was also a space in which divergent opinions could take root. Liberty of conscience posed perennial questions about how much religious freedom could be embraced and under whose authority.

Although fundamentalism was a reaction to the rising tide of modernity, an interpretation that views it only as that gets it wrong. Fundamentalism was as much an adaptation to new opportunities as it was resistance to new challenges. The ideas that grew in small revival meetings and large urban congregations and that forged new relationships across denominational lines and among Bible scholars in scattered locations across the country had two important implications that have to be understood as background to the conservative religious politics that were to emerge with such force a half century later. One was that church leaders developed ideas and organizations with which to challenge what they considered faulty in circles of education and learning. The other was that a more encompassing theology took hold that harnessed individual salvation and the struggle against evil with a cosmology grounded in its own version of science.

If the *Chicago Daily Tribune* was one of the first to identify Texas as a hotbed of fundamentalism, that perception surfaced again and again in subsequent years. Critics of Prohibition viewed the Lone Star state as an arid land that would resist repeal from every pulpit and pew. During the Depression Texas and Oklahoma were understood to be the source of fundamentalists migrating to Southern California. Progressive theologians identified it as the home of reactionary religious leaders. In the decades after World War II it came to be regarded as a bastion of McCarthyism and where a Catholic candidate for president had little chance of winning among dyed-in-the-wool conservative Protestants. Writers who grew up or lived there, such as sociologist C. Wright Mills and journalist Willie Morris, said it was overrun with fundamentalists.[4]

Their point was not that Texas was the only place conservative religion flourished. It was certainly possible to argue, as many did, that the entire South and perhaps much of the Midwest as well was America's Bible Belt. Fundamentalist roots could be traced to churches in Boston and Chicago, to colleges in Illinois and South Carolina, and to evangelists headquartered in North Carolina and Southern California. Nor was it that anyone believed Texas to be monolithically fundamentalist. It was just that fundamentalism seemed so firmly planted that its impact increased and steadily gained wider influence as the state itself became one of the nation's most powerful.

Consideration of what was happening in Texas religion in the 1920s enables a better understanding of how those perceptions about its embrace of fundamentalism began. Several possibilities are worth considering. One is that the perceptions were simply inaccurate. Texas was, after all, large and regionally and ethnically diverse. Its majority religions included Roman Catholics as well as Protestant denominations in which liberty of conscience was emphasized. The view that fundamentalists dominated Texas may have been based on little more than it being the home base of one of the nation's most flamboyant fundamentalist preachers.

A second possibility is that Texas was thoroughly conservative in matters of faith from the very start and fundamentalism, if anything, was merely a new label for what had always been present. In this view the reason Texas came to be associated with fundamentalism is simply that it was part of the South, settled by devout Protestant southerners who were that way before the Civil War and remained that way long afterward. There was thus nothing much to be explained apart from saying that the Bible Belt was located in the South.

A third possibility poses the somewhat more nuanced argument that Texas was indeed religiously conservative like the rest of the South but became more distinctly associated with fundamentalism only as an outpost of ideas imported from the North. Dallas especially was viewed in this interpretation as a kind of northern city with a southern heritage that northern fundamentalists found to their liking as they expanded in search of new territory.[5]

Each of these arguments is plausible enough to be taken seriously but ultimately leaves important questions unanswered. If the popular perception of Texas as a fundamentalist breeding ground is wrong except for the influence of one controversial preacher, the question remains of what else may have been going on to facilitate the enormous effort that went into promoting Prohibition and turning lifelong Democrats against Smith's candidacy. It leaves open the question of how a single fundamentalist preacher could have made as much of an impact as he did in the debates that developed about evolution. The argument that everything can be explained by locating Texas in the South fails to explain why Texas increasingly identified itself not with the South but with the Southwest, and, for that matter, why it came to be such an important influence in southern religious conservatism. Attributing this influence to northern connections acknowledges that there were such connections but falters in paying insufficient attention to what else was happening locally.

A better argument takes account of the cultural understandings that were deeply ingrained in Texas religion at the end of the nineteenth century and the new challenges it faced during the first decades of the twentieth century. The three cultural understandings that significantly shaped Texas religion in the nineteenth century were the need to restrain evil, the desire to advance civilization, and the ideal of sustaining liberty of conscience. Evil was both a theological premise and an existential reality. It existed in the memory of early struggles for survival in rough country and against the tyranny of northern aggression as well as the fear among white residents of slave insurrections. It continued in the realities of illness, death, and bereavement as well as the threat of lawlessness. The desire to advance civilization facilitated the founding and growth of schools and churches, colleges and seminaries, improved farms and businesses, and towns and benevolent associations. Church leaders were institution builders who developed a vast infrastructure of organizations through which to promote their understandings of a civilized culture grounded in religious faith. Liberty of conscience was conducive to a diverse entrepreneurial spirit among religious leaders but carried with it the challenge of maintaining denominational authority in the face of room for theological and ecclesiological innovation.

The new challenges that became increasingly important during the first decades of the twentieth century were the rapid expansion of population and economic resources and the emergence of new ideas that posed new threats to accepted religious doctrines. More people with more resources at their disposal required new and better churches and more effective means of promoting and coordinating these efforts. Enlarged resources, especially in urban areas such as Dallas and Fort Worth and through publishing, also created opportunities for rival organizations to emerge. The new ideas that posed challenges came especially from Darwinian arguments about human origins but also from expectations about better education and greater exposure to formal knowledge as well as for deeper biblical training for clergy and lay leaders.

Texas was by no means unique in these respects but included several distinctive social characteristics that facilitated the rising influence of fundamentalism and conservative biblical interpretations. The state's size, its population growth, and its expanding economic base, especially with the growth of the emerging oil industry and cattle trade, made it different from the Deep South and more like Southern California. In 1900 Texas already claimed more than $2 billion in real property, not counting the value of land, and ranked fifteenth among states nationally. By 1912 that figure had tripled and Texas ranked seventh nationally.[6] Over the next decade crude petroleum production in Texas shot up almost tenfold, putting the state behind only California and Oklahoma.[7] The large number of Baptists and Methodists both in absolute terms and relative to other denominations in Texas and coreligionists elsewhere in the South composed a well-organized block of institutions that made a large difference locally and nationally when events shifted their center of gravity to the right. By 1916 more Southern Baptists and more members of the Methodist Episcopal Church South lived in Texas than in any other state.[8] And over the next decade these denominations added more members in Texas than anywhere else. At the same time the emphasis in Texas on religious liberty, the localized and loosely coordinated governance structure of these denominations, and the abundance of new resources created opportunities to extend what was commonly known as a tradition of church infighting, especially among Baptists.

The perception that Texas was overwhelmingly fundamentalist was never completely true, but it was not without basis either. It was more accurate to say that religious leaders who believed in a conservative interpretation of the Bible represented an almost unchallenged understanding of theology in Dallas to a greater extent than would have been the case in Boston, Philadelphia, Chicago, or Los Angeles. It was increasingly accurate to say that conservative Baptists and Methodists along with members of several smaller denominations carried greater influence in their denominations than their counterparts did in any other state. How that happened became evident in the church controversies that escalated between the 1880s and 1920s, in the opposition church leaders mobilized against evolution, in conflict between fundamentalists and modernists, in the monitoring of what was taught in schools and seminaries, and in the rising popularity of biblical interpretations emphasizing dispensational theology.

CHURCH CONTROVERSIES

The growth that occurred in churches and among church-sponsored benevolent associations during the Progressive Era positioned these institutions to exercise continuing influence in the future. Liberty of conscience provided the cultural space in which congregations could grow. But it created opportunities for controversy as well. Besides differences rooted in theological interpretation, church leaders had larger enterprises to fight about and more resources with which to fight. They fought over the control of large-scale church publications that sometimes made money and more often lost it and required personal investments and loans. They squabbled about the control of large congregations and prominent benevolent associations. Conflicts about worship and doctrine gained publicity through denominational publications and in national media as the state itself gained prominence economically and politically. The conflicts occurred especially among Baptists, perhaps because pastors enjoyed greater autonomy than in most other denominations and perhaps because there were so many of them. Before fundamentalist-modernist controversies appeared, these earlier conflicts commanded the attention of denominational leaders, showed that denominational sanctions were sometimes necessary, and demonstrated that sanctions were not always effective.

Unlike Prohibition, few of these intradenominational conflicts involved churches' relationship with government. They were debated in the pages of church newspapers and at denominational meetings. Rarely did they involve litigation or intervention by public officials. This was in some ways fortunate because it upheld prevailing understandings of church-state separation. It nevertheless established precedents that would come into play when more serious divisions emerged surrounding fundamentalism. Having command of church publications, holding pulpits in large urban churches, being able to attract headlines, securing a platform at denominational meetings, and forging networks among like-minded leaders were the instruments needed to win.

Clergy were always dependent on the goodwill of their local constituents. A pastor's first obligation was to preach and teach, warning against evil, proclaiming the gospel, and shepherding the flock. The skepticism and downright disrespect that sometimes followed clergy in early frontier settlements continued to be part of the environment in which clergy worked decades later. An unpopular pastor could be summarily dismissed. The need to stay in good graces encouraged conformity to local norms. And yet those norms varied from place to place and could reinforce regional disputes. Church leaders who edited denominational publications and who ran benevolent institutions or taught at church colleges faced different pressures. They functioned in wider venues where the lines of authority were not always clearly drawn.

In 1874 a controversy arose between the editors of rival Baptist newspapers. The *Religious Messenger* was a fledgling publication edited by R. C. Buckner, the pastor who decades later would be one of the denomination's most effective fund-raisers on behalf of benevolent institutions and was already in charge of an orphanage as well as the newspaper. His rival was J. B. Link, editor of the *Baptist Herald* in Houston. Hoping to discourage Buckner, Link privately wrote letters threatening conflict and published items criticizing him for failing to emphasize Christ sufficiently. Three years later the tension escalated. Buckner's paper had become the more widely circulated *Texas Baptist*, published in Dallas, where Link was also now located in an appointment to the denomination's educational commission. Both sought and attained membership at the First Baptist Church of Dallas, but as accusations continued, factions coalesced and each faction claimed that the other should be excommunicated. When the Link faction seized control of the church building, the Buckner faction sought recourse from the denomination, which had no authority to intercede in congregational affairs except that several of the parties involved in the dispute held denominational offices. At its associational meeting the denomination's delegates voted that Buckner's membership should be reinstated. In defending the decision and the fairness of the procedures involved, the association's president urged that liberty of conscience be the ruling principle in any future disputes.

"Every Texan's heart and soul," he said, "should be as large and free as our un-bounded prairies."[9]

Three years after the Buckner-Link conflict was settled, tension surfaced in the same congregation, this time among three other prominent Baptist minis-ters. Reverend R. T. Hanks, pastor of the church, was on one side. Allied against him were Reverend S. A. Hayden, the *Texas Baptist*'s new editor, and Reverend A. J. Holt, secretary of the Mission Board of the Southern Baptist Convention. Trouble began when rumors circulated accusing Hanks of unseemly conduct with one of his female congregants—rumors traced to Hayden. After three years during which the tension worsened, the matter was brought before a council of fourteen prominent ministers. Both sides promised to bury their differences, but peace was short-lived. Each side charged that the other was lying and engaging in perfidious slander. Before a new council could be convened, Hayden and Holt procured an affidavit from a former resident of Dallas claiming she had seen Hanks with a married woman named Minnie Ferrin seated on his lap. Ferrin's husband, hearing the news, believed it to be false and instead of attacking Hanks tracked down Hayden and horsewhipped him while Hayden ran yelling for the police to intervene. The affair ended with Ferrin being tried at a packed court-house in which attorneys hurled epithets describing the pastors as black sheep, dogs, crows, and buzzards.[10]

Had the conflict been limited to slander and alleged infidelity it would have been serious enough, but it was part of a wider power struggle among Texas Bap-tists. Partisans interpreted it as a struggle for control of the denomination. Dis-gusted with Hayden's handling of the *Texas Baptist*, rivals founded an alternative newspaper called the *Baptist News* and within a few years enlisted Hanks as part owner and editor. During much of the subsequent decade the two newspapers took opposing sides on issue after issue.[11]

The issues reflected not only personality conflicts but also questions of biblical interpretation and church governance. A young pastor named Matthew Thomas Martin, who had formerly taught mathematics in Mississippi, preached a doc-trine that became known as Martinism in which believers were encouraged to seek positive assurance of salvation following baptism by being rebaptized. As the doctrine spread to the point of nearly founding a new denomination, the Texas Baptist leadership asked him to recant, which he chose not to do, depart-ing for Georgia only to return a year later and finding a new congregation, which was then put out of the Baptist association until the matter was resolved seven years later. Another doctrine emerged through the teaching of George Fortune, a traveling evangelist who taught that original sin did not exist and that the Bible was not fully inspired by God. Yet another conflict surfaced when Reverend B. H. Carroll, the state's most distinguished Baptist leader, took issue with the president of Southern Baptist Theological Seminary in Louisville for teaching that Bap-tists hailed from seventeenth-century English Puritans instead of directly from John the Baptist.[12] Were these controversies not enough, a movement developed among Southern Baptists favoring the holiness idea of a "second blessing" of the Holy Spirit as a means of spiritual assurance, and the Foreign Mission Board contended with a view espoused by one of the denomination's missionaries in China that missionaries should dress and behave as much like the indigenous population as possible.[13]

The Baptist infighting heightened by rival newspapers appeared to be on the verge of ending in 1906 when Reverend J. Frank Norris, a recent graduate of Southern Seminary, used the life insurance money from his father-in-law, who had recently died falling from the rear platform of a train, to purchase both the *Texas Baptist Herald*, still owned by Hayden, and the *Baptist Standard*, edited by longtime prohibition advocate Cranfill. Had Cranfill stayed on, the *Standard* might have taken a different direction, but he resigned to save the denomination embarrassment following an incident in which it was alleged that he held a pistol and meant to use it on Hayden en route to a meeting of the Southern Baptist Convention.[14] Norris, who as pastor of the Dallas McKinney Avenue Church had come under fire for comments about fellow pastors, selected J. B. Gambrell to edit the newly combined paper. But a year later Gambrell resigned, asserting that "the fact that men can traffic in papers as they do jackknives and use denominational papers for their personal ends" made it impossible for him to continue.[15] Norris persuaded J. M. Dawson, a rising leader who had hoped to purchase the paper himself and was to become one of the denomination's leading authorities on church-state relations, to take over the editorship. Dawson resigned the following year, leaving the paper to Norris, who sold it a year later to a consortium of investors that included Gambrell, Buckner, and Truett.[16]

Controversial as the paper was, the prominence Norris earned through his brief involvement in the state's leading Baptist publication helped secure him the pastorate in 1909 of the First Baptist Church in Fort Worth, where he continued to attract and produce conflict.[17] For an ambitious pastor like Norris, Fort Worth was a plum location. By the end of the 1880s the roughness of the frontier in what had heretofore been little more than a rural outpost was fading. As the population edged above twenty thousand, residents began thinking of their town as a city. The new eleven-hundred-seat First Baptist Church building, constructed in 1887 just a block from the Anheuser-Busch Brewing Company, was one of twenty-seven new projects that year.[18] Over the next decade progress slowed as a result of setbacks in the cattle trade and meat-packing industry as well as an overall decline in the number of businesses and value of manufacturing.[19] Population edged up only slightly, and public revenue was so meager that local officials eased restrictions on gambling and saloons and confined prostitution and "leg shows" to restricted areas rather than banning them completely.[20] As a county seat, railroad hub, and manufacturing center, the city was nevertheless well positioned for further development.

The new century brought renewed prosperity and rapid growth to Fort Worth. With the arrival of several new packing houses and with an expansion of railroad shipping, the number of livestock handled by the Fort Worth stockyards jumped fivefold between 1902 and 1904.[21] By 1907 Fort Worth had become the largest rail center in the region, with ninety-eight passenger trains daily and an annual total of more than eight hundred thousand freight cars. That year more than seven hundred building permits were issued. Between 1900 and 1910 the population shot up from 26,688 to 73,312. Religious work was being done by seventy-one different denominations with regular activities for 17,000 children and more than 20,000 adult members, including 6,500 Roman Catholics, 3,600 Baptists, 3,600 Methodists, and 1,000 Jews. Church buildings were estimated to be worth at least $650,000.[22]

Between 1910 and 1920 an influx of new manufacturing plants, oil companies, and military bases and rapid expansion of the cattle trade and rail shipping elevated Fort Worth's population to 106,482. In 1918 an estimated 5,000 new residents were arriving each month, and bank deposits showed the fourth largest increase of any city in the nation.[23] A visitor saw it as a wide-open boomtown with a profusion of worldly excess set against a pious campaign for sobriety. "No city ever presented a sharper contrast than Fort Worth," he wrote in the *New York Times*, "between her Main Street and hotel crowds of oil-mad speculators and promoters and the streets where the churches and dwellings are."[24] One of the city's most successful congregations was Norris's First Baptist Church. In 1919 the church constructed a new building with an auditorium for five thousand, one of the largest anywhere in the country.[25]

Norris was an energetic leader with unbounded aspirations and an appetite for controversy. His preaching attracted an enthusiastic audience, and as Fort Worth grew, First Baptist used its ample facilities in ways that would become the hallmark of American megachurches a half century later. The church hosted piano concerts, sponsored its own basketball team, and organized musical extravaganzas for the Christmas holidays. A woman who attended there as a girl and later became Norris's daughter-in-law recalled the music program as one of the church's most appealing assets. She loved John Phillip Sousa's marches, and it was there that she saw Sousa's band in person. There was nothing stuffy about the worship services either, reflecting a decision Norris made in 1911 to emphasize what he termed sensationalized preaching.[26] "I thought the whole thing was just a circus," she said. "I mean I couldn't believe what I was seeing and hearing."[27] And when he was not in residence, Norris was making a name for himself nationally by preaching at large churches in New York City and Los Angeles and headlining conferences of fundamentalists.[28]

Norris's preaching included messages about capital punishment, business leadership, prosperity, race relations, foreign missions, and urban problems as well as evangelism and Christian charity. "The existence of the church today depends upon the interest it takes in outside conditions," he declared, "in the sociological conditions and questions that are confronting rich and poor from different angles and which they must work out together."[29] Although opposed to suffrage for women, Norris promoted plans for a joint effort among Fort Worth's downtown churches to construct a six- or seven-story building as a residence for single working women.[30] His flair for showmanship ranged from selling peanuts on the train between Fort Worth and Dallas to raise money for youth activities, to organizing a parade of three thousand Baptist young people, to sending Sunday school children to canvass the city with messages about the need to shut down prostitution.[31] He participated in community wide debates about Sunday closing laws, made trips to Austin to speak for race track regulation, and organized meetings between business leaders and labor unions.[32]

In conjunction with the state's prohibition efforts, Norris made national headlines as the "saloon-fighting Baptist minister" from Texas.[33] He denied church membership to anyone owning property used for immoral purposes and called on commissioners to rid the city of saloons, gambling, and prostitution.[34] He received threatening letters, which supporters claimed were sent by opponents of his attacks on prostitution and gambling, but which forensic evidence suggested may have come from the church parsonage itself. In 1912 the church and parsonage were damaged by fire and Norris was charged with arson. Several indictments and a sensational monthlong trial ensued, with Norris being acquitted. Four years later a young member of Norris's church accidentally shot himself in the hand during a church service when the gun he was carrying discharged. An investigation of the incident uncovered a plot in which the man was supposed to have fired into the ceiling, leaving Norris to claim he had survived an assassination attempt.[35] In 1922 Norris resumed his interests in publishing by founding the *Fundamentalist*, which continued his attacks on what he perceived as liberalizing tendencies among mainstream Southern Baptists.

CONTENDING AGAINST EVOLUTION

Besides Norris's general discontent with the direction of Texas Baptists, an impetus for the *Fundamentalist* was his growing concern about the teaching of evolution. On January 5, 1922, *Baptist Standard* editor E. C. Routh wrote in no uncertain terms that evolution denies "the truth of the Scriptural account of the creation of man and of his fall." No reconciliation of biblical teaching and evolution was, in his view, possible.[36] Norris, however, charged that Baylor University, the denomination's flagship university, was teaching evolution. Routh denied the charge and defended Baylor in a subsequent essay in the *Baptist Standard*.[37] Norris retaliated by attacking the paper and the Baptist General Convention of Texas. A month later the Tarrant County Baptist Workers, whose territory included Fort Worth, adopted a resolution criticizing Norris for his stance against the denomination and describing his practices as unsound. Norris replied that the resolution was merely a distraction from the true problem, which was "the now confessed teaching of evolution at Baylor University."[38]

This was by no means the first time that southern church leaders had voiced concern about the rising tide of heretical beliefs in evolution. At its 1888 meeting in Baltimore, the general assembly of the southern Presbyterians went on record that humans had not evolved from lower animals and cautioned clergy against preaching otherwise.[39] A similar discussion occurred at an ecumenical Methodist meeting in Washington, DC, in 1891. Bishop Keene of the Methodist Episcopal Church South admonished the assembled clergy that higher criticism based on Darwinism threatened to create a "great fissure in the Methodist faith." His listeners, he advised, should go home and do their best to get rid of it. "If you can't get rid of the doctrine, get rid of the men and the institutions that teach it, no matter how dear they are to you. They will blow you up if you do not," he warned.[40] Evolution had become a theme among the evils traveling evangelists warned about at revival meetings as well. "There are fellows going with their hair parted in the middle saying they are infidels and talking about evolution," a preacher conducting a revival meeting at Belton, Texas, in 1893 intoned. You should "run them in their holes and twist them out like you would a rabbit," he suggested.[41]

The clearest line of attack on proponents of evolution was to suggest that intellectuals who believed it were simply out of touch with commonsense reality. An infidel with hair parted in the middle was an outsider who probably worked for an eastern university or newspaper. Intellectuals were portrayed as pretentious elites who believed too quickly that science was more valid than the Bible. At a meeting of Texas Baptist Sunday school teachers in Dallas in 1893, this was the prevailing message. Critics of the Bible, the keynote speaker argued, were claiming that miracles could not happen, that the creation story was wrong, and that the biblical stories were historically inaccurate, but closer study and newer discoveries were merely showing what "the author of the Bible always knew" and leaving the critics with nothing to say.[42]

The idea that humans had evolved from monkeys was the part of popular understandings of Darwinism that came in for the greatest ridicule. "We have tried our best to believe Darwin on evolution," a journalist in Austin quipped, because "so many men we see look like the descendants of monkeys, but we have too much respect for Adam to swallow evolution."[43] Students at Presbyterian-related Austin College in Sherman reported having actually found the missing link in the person of a fellow student whose "skull is very thick, very low in the arch and very prominent in the brows."[44] Even later, when the Scopes trial drew wider attention to the topic, there was a kind of dismissive attitude toward the idea that scientists might know something worth understanding about the origins of life. As the editor of an East Texas newspaper proclaimed, "We don't know anything about evolution and cherish no hope of ever learning anything about it."[45]

More serious critics of evolution argued that the Bible was a better way to understand human existence not because humans evolving from monkeys was laughable or even because the Bible claimed divine authority but on empirical grounds. The case for believing the Bible was not, as would later become more common, because the biblical story was about spiritual truth whereas science was about nature. It was rather that the Bible and science could be evaluated on the same grounds, with the result being that the Bible had facts on its side. A common argument was that science had been unable to identify the missing link between lower animals and humans, whereas archeological discoveries were increasingly finding evidence in support of the Bible. This was the basis on which Reverend C. L. Seasholes of the First Baptist Church in Dallas disputed evolution. "Evolution has never found the missing link between monkey and man," he argued, leading the "unscientific skeptic" to argue that humans must have originated by chance. But archeology was demonstrating, he believed, that humans originated as the Bible said in the Garden of Eden, which was probably located at the North Pole at a time when the climate was warmer there, and then migrated to other continents.[46]

Seasholes's views were controversial enough that Waco editor William Cowper Brann, who took a dim view of Baptists anyway, declared him not "overly bright," and in 1897 Seasholes decamped to Philadelphia when the Dallas congregation asked him to resign.[47] Another defender of the Bible against evolution was Pastor Charles T. Russell of Pennsylvania, whose followers founded the Jehovah's Witnesses movement following his death during a speaking tour in Texas in 1916.[48] In 1879 Russell began publishing a monthly religious journal, and by 1903 his syndicated sermons were appearing in as many as four thousand newspapers. In 1904 he preached to large audiences in Dallas, Sherman, and San Antonio, and Texas newspapers began publishing his sermons and advertising his books. Russell held that the Darwinian theory of evolution was attractive to people who looked around and saw progress but on closer inspection was tenable only to the "superficial reasoner." Believing that history showed the first humans to have existed only about four thousand years ago, Russell argued that the notion of upward evolution over that time span was belied by the existence of the pyramids and the great thinking of Socrates, Confucius, and other early scholars.[49]

In mainstream pulpits and at pastors' conferences, speakers defended the Bible against what they described as the attacks of scientists by arguing that science itself was incomplete, was perhaps itself evolving, or was producing facts not yet fully understood or digested as only trained philosophers and theologians could. Some conceded that the six days of creation described in the Bible might have been of unspecified duration, while others insisted these were ordinary twenty-four-hour days. One certainty was that the Bible would stand. Taking the side of evolutionists was tantamount to having no faith.[50]

It was not the case, however, that evolution was without defenders. At the University of Texas, where instructors were expected to believe in God, faculty chair Leslie Waggoner declared in 1890 that "if the theory of evolution prove to be true, we will teach it though the pope declare it heresy."[51] Evolution was

intriguing enough that small religious bodies outside the mainstream denominations also entertained novel ideas of how it might inform their understandings of spirituality. Theosophists, spiritualists, free thinkers, and Unitarians—all
present in Dallas and a few other Texas locations—actively experimented with
these ideas. Proponents argued that science was on the verge of discovering new
levels of consciousness that could be harnessed for material and spiritual improvement.[52] Variants included ideas about the discovery of higher forces, spirit
worlds, a fourth dimension, new physical laws, and keys to immortality. At the
First Spiritualist Church in Dallas, Reverend R. C. Travers argued that evolution
was dissipating the "narrow views of theists," unlocking the "secrets of nature,"
and revealing the "rhythm of cosmic art." The next phase of human evolution, he
believed, would come through electro molecular changes in the brain that would
enhance the transmission of sensory information.[53] At a meeting in Waco, an
eclectic gathering of theosophists contemplated the relationships among Darwinism, the law of karma, and reincarnation.[54] The Dallas Free Thinkers Society
took a more down-to-earth view, arguing that the scientific era was replacing the
primitive doctrines of the past.[55] That was also true at the First Unitarian Church
of Dallas, which regarded religion more favorably than did the free thinkers but
emphasized that humans were "children of the universe" who were not morally
depraved but evolving in dignity and understanding.[56] These interpretations associated evolution with humanity being on an upward trajectory—a view rooted
in Progressive Era optimism that fundamentalists would increasingly dispute.

　　Religious leaders who placed credence in evolution also considered ways in
which the idea could be reconciled with biblical theology. In Austin Reverend
Lowber's credentials as a scientist as well as his role in the church gave him a
platform from which to speak about Darwinism. Lowber's view was that evolution was simply "God's method of creating the first [humans]," and that method
"was still a miracle." Christ himself, Lowber believed, was an evolutionist who
understood nature and taught that God is in nature as well as transcending it.[57]
Another defender of evolution was Reverend Martin, the former math teacher
who became controversial for his views about assurance of salvation. Before a
full house at the Central Christian Church in Dallas in 1892, Martin argued that
science and the Bible were entirely compatible. The apparent conflict was rooted
in misunderstanding. "God pity the preacher who is as ignorant of science as is
the average scientist of the Bible," he said. Creation occurred in ages rather than
days, he believed, with basic laws of order, repulsion, and attraction operating
in each.[58]

　　For those who did not embrace Darwin's theory of the origins of human life,
it was still possible to find some value in the idea of social evolution—what became known in academic circles as social Darwinism. Focusing on social change
rather than evolution of species, social Darwinism drew an analogy between
biological organisms and societies. Just as organisms became more complex and
better adapted to their environments, the argument went, so did societies as they

developed from primitive to modern forms. The idea gained credence among Progressive Era reformers who saw improvement coming from the institutions and activities in which they were involved. It fit well with long-standing notions about the advance of civilization in overcoming the rough life of the open frontier. Better medicine, better hospitals, and better schools were making progress, it was argued, because this was how societies evolved. "Evolution is the law of life," a University of Texas education professor declared at a meeting of the Texas Federation of Women's Clubs in Houston. This was the basic principle of the universe, even of humankind, which, he tactfully noted, was "created a little lower than the angels." And now it was primarily the schools that would ensure the continuing physical, spiritual, and moral "advancement of our race."[59]

Among the few who were college educated, trained in the professions, teaching at colleges or universities, or conversant with the latest intellectual trends through women's clubs and reading groups, the idea that progress was a scientific law must have been reassuring. In 1903 the *Dallas Morning News* published a full-page article that surely would have intrigued these educated readers about recent fossil discoveries, under the heading "Walked about in America Fifty Million Years Ago," illustrated with a drawing of an eighty-foot "brontosaur" towering against the superimposed outline of a cowboy on horseback.[60] But for the average person in the pew, who even in 1940 still had only a ninth-grade education, it would have been easy to assume that evolution was an idea adhered to by people in other places who were quite unlike himself or herself.[61]

As long as evolution was an external threat, the preferred response in churches was to hunker down, proclaim the gospel, preach from the Bible, and strengthen Sunday schools to promote better understanding of the Bible. However, internal rifts were emerging that could be more threatening than any danger from outside. This possibility began appearing in news items and at denominational meetings in discussions about preachers and teachers having to be removed from positions in places that could easily have been closer to home. News came in 1901, for example, that a natural sciences instructor at a small Methodist college in Salina, Kansas, had been charged with heresy and ousted for believing in evolution.[62] And only two years earlier members of the Northern Baptist Convention learned that A. H. Strong, president of their seminary in Rochester, New York, fully accepted the theory of evolution and thought it should be applied to the interpretation of scripture.[63]

For Texas Baptists the threat posed by evolution became a rallying cry for stronger and more closely governed institutions. In 1905 Baylor University's theological department dean, Dr. Carroll, called for the department to expand into a "complete school of divinity, teaching all the courses and conferring all the degrees of a regular first-class theological seminary." Carroll worried that Texas was attracting pastors from other states "trained in schools loose in doctrine." These pastors would erode the denomination's fundamental doctrines and plant seeds leading to confusion and trouble. Most worrisome was the fact that "many preachers nowadays have become disciples of the old heathen evolution theory and have been carried away with the teachings of the radical wing of the higher critics." It would be impossible to counter these dangerous trends as long as pastors' training was deficient.[64]

There was nothing specifically Texan about these arguments other than the fact that Baptist leaders especially and Methodists to an extent knew that theirs were the dominant faiths, and that the sheer number of believers as well as the growing population and resources of Texas made it a kind of beacon to the world. Regional pride continued to matter, in arguing both that Texas churches needed to be strengthened against threats from the North and that they needed to become more like evangelical Christians who benefited from well-supplied seminaries and churches in those states.[65] As was true in other places, it was possible to argue with a high degree of conviction that old-time beliefs and practices were being preserved in Texas against an onslaught of novel doctrines stemming from scientists, northern cities, and infidels.

The fact that Texas was growing and becoming better educated gave church leaders added confidence that they were not simply fighting a rearguard action but were on the winning side of history. They had believed for a long time that they were in the vanguard of civilization, bringing law and order to a land of savagery and evil. Churches were now larger and better staffed than ever before. Benevolent associations were expanding. Rich Christians had more wealth to bestow on these projects. The battle for Prohibition was being won. A growing number of church members were living stable, middle-class lives, coming out for public lectures, and sending their children through high school and sometimes even to college. The way to combat evolution was not to ignore it or ridicule it but to outmaneuver it with better churches, stronger church colleges and seminaries, and clearer biblical knowledge. In his last sermon at Dallas's First Methodist Church in 1906, Bishop Moore captured the prevailing sentiment well. The "thinking [person's] relation to the world, to truth, to self and to others is properly realized and understood only through the mind of Christ," he asserted. Theories advanced by ungodly scholars such as David Hume, Thomas Huxley, and Charles Darwin were destined to fail in attempting to demonstrate that God had made the world and then deserted it. No creed could satisfy, he believed, unless it was based on Christ.[66]

Church leaders voiced all the reasons that would be repeated in later debates for why the Bible was right and evolution was wrong. They were convinced that scientific claims were as yet unproven. They believed that geological discoveries and closer examination of the historical record were demonstrating the accuracy of the Bible. Some considered it possible that a kind of theistic evolution would emerge in which evolution was understood as God's means of creation. A few, anticipating later arguments about intelligent design, said it was simply impossible to view the marvelous handiwork of nature without believing that a divine mind was behind it all. And if nothing else, it was possible to argue when violence occurred and when church attendance flagged that the reason was a kind of materialistic hedonism emanating from the spread of Darwinism.[67]

The possibility of biblical religion winning against evolution on these grounds was well illustrated in 1907 when a standing-room-only crowd of more than five thousand packed the civic auditorium in Dallas to hear a lecture by William Jennings Bryan. With Judge N. Webb Finley presiding, an invocation given by Dr. Truett of the First Baptist Church, and an introduction by U.S. senator Charles A. Culberson, Bryan rose to prolonged applause from the crowd and declared himself there to present the simple truths of the Christian religion. He believed in the biblical account of creation, he said, and would continue to do so. "If a man desires to believe that his ancestors were monkeys, let him do so," he said, "but he can't connect me with his family tree without more evidence than has yet been adduced." The truth was, "the scientist knows a great deal, but he does not know all about creation." There were many things scientists did not understand even about something as simple as a watermelon, he quipped. "Until a scientist can explain the laws of the watermelon let him not essay to suggest what God would or would not do."[68]

FUNDAMENTALISTS AND MODERNISTS

The warm reception Bryan received in Dallas that summer—only the Unitarian pastor tried to formulate a rebuttal—suggested that Texas, like much of the rest of the country, was in solid agreement that evolution was contrary to the Bible. But a large tent uniting all Christians in common warfare against Darwinism was impossible to maintain, even in Texas. The idea that well-educated, thoughtful people guided by highly trained clergy could play the winning hand was less than persuasive to the many churchgoers who had little schooling and went to churches pastored by licensed preachers without much training.

Since the early 1890s church leaders who opposed evolution voiced broader concerns about liberalism, or what they called modernism, as well. They often referred to higher criticism, a method of examining the biblical texts in the light of historical evidence and other texts to identify inconsistencies and alternative meanings. In focusing on the contexts in which the biblical texts had been written, higher criticism challenged the idea that scripture should be taken literally as verbatim, error-free divine revelation. In the nineteenth century higher criticism was associated especially with German biblical scholars such as Friedrich Schleiermacher and Ludwig Feuerbach, but it had also attracted interest among theologians in England and the United States. The reaction against higher criticism that became known as fundamentalism affirmed basic Christian doctrines such as the divinity of Jesus and the historical reality of miracles described in the Bible. Fundamentalism emerged in scattered locations and established a loose network of relationships among leaders through such activities as the Niagara

Bible Conference, which met regularly in Ontario between 1876 and 1897, the teaching of faculty at Princeton Theological Seminary in New Jersey, and a series of twelve volumes called *The Fundamentals* published in 1910 with funding from California philanthropists Milton and Lyman Stewart, whose fortune came from the rapidly expanding oil industry.[69]

Between 1900 and 1910 Texas church members heard sermons emphasizing the "fundamentals" of Christianity, such as the necessity of believing in the Virgin Birth and divine inspiration of the Bible, but these arguments were seldom linked to the fundamentalist movement. One of the few direct connections occurred in 1909 when Dr. Francis L. Patton, a lackluster former president of Princeton University whom a faculty colleague had described as a "wonderfully poor administrator" and who now headed Princeton Theological Seminary, journeyed to Dallas to deliver a series of lectures at the First Presbyterian Church.[70] Patton had gained publicity early in his career for bringing heresy charges against a fellow pastor in Chicago and was known for his denunciations of liberal theology and his emphasis on biblical inerrancy as well as his interest in prophecy.[71] His lectures in Dallas addressed the "Fundamentals of Christianity."

Among Texas church leaders themselves, division that would become more pronounced a few years later was beginning to stir. If Patton's defense of Christian fundamentals found a receptive audience among some Presbyterians, others were more inclined to seek reconciliation between theology and new intellectual developments. At Dallas's Central Presbyterian Church, for example, Reverend J. Frank Smith urged members to embrace reason. "To discount the wisdom of political economists, the physicians, the great religious teachers of mankind, the scientists who have thought through life's intricacies," he explained, "is to mock the work of the human and divine for a thousand generations." In his view God's revelation extended beyond the Bible.[72]

Disagreements about biblical interpretation sparked wider debates because denominational associations had the authority to bring charges against pastors who might be suspected of espousing heretical views. A case of this kind occurred among Presbyterians in 1905 when the Presbytery of Fort Worth installed the Reverend William Caldwell from Baltimore only to have the Synod of Texas at Austin receive and endorse a complaint that Caldwell's theology was errant. Caldwell was then asked to supply written answers to 112 questions, and the resulting seventeen-page document was read aloud at the meeting of the state-wide assembly a year later. The questions ranged from whether divine election was conditional or unconditional, to whether Caldwell believed in the "substitutionary penal sufferings of Christ," to whether he felt that any part of the first five books of the Bible included myth, allegory, or parable. Despite agreement that Caldwell's answers were largely satisfactory, the synod's pastors continued to debate whether proper procedures had been used and whether the hearing had been conducted in the spirit of fraternal goodwill or was an expression of ultraorthodoxy.[73]

Another controversy between competing interpretations of the Bible flared in 1910 when Texas Christian University president Dr. Clinton B. Lockhart told the Fort Worth Pastor's Association that the story of Jonah in the belly of a whale for three days was more likely to have been fiction than fact.[74] Lockhart made no mention of higher criticism and indeed argued that understanding the ways in which people in biblical times thought and wrote helped in appreciating the divine revelation of the Bible. But Lockhart's views drew immediate reactions. A churchgoer who found herself quite offended asked, "Are the schools in beloved Texas, the home of orthodoxy and conservative thought, to drift in a class with the Northern schools?"[75] A few days later the Tarrant County Baptist Workers passed a resolution in response to Lockhart affirming their own belief in the Bible as wholly inspired by God.[76]

Norris, who had already been preaching about "modern infidelity" a few months earlier, escalated the controversy by charging that Lockhart was not alone in his heretical views but that they were shared by many who taught at Baptist schools in other parts of the country. Especially to blame, he said, were theology professors at the University of Chicago who "strut around like peacocks and echo the weird doctrines of Voltaire and Ingersoll." Norris's criticism was simply the latest expression of long-standing concerns among conservative Baptists about the University of Chicago. In the 1890s when the university's president, William Rainey Harper, had come under attack for embracing higher criticism, *Texas Baptist Standard* editor Cranfill interviewed Harper, showing that he not only found value in some aspects of higher criticism but also believed in the Darwinian theory of evolution.[77] Texas, in contrast, Cranfill observed, was soil in which higher criticism and other heretical microbes could not take root.[78] Norris, though, was concerned that what had happened in Chicago was now happening in Texas. Noting that John D. Rockefeller had funded the University of Chicago and that Baylor University might be in line for Rockefeller money, Norris expressed hope that "Texas Baptist schools wouldn't fall under the spell of this baptized infidelity."[79] With Baptist institutions themselves coming under suspicion, Southwestern Theological Seminary president Carroll preached a series of sermons declaring his belief in the verbal inspiration of the Bible. "The preacher or professor who does not believe in the integrity of the Bible should resign at once," he asserted. "Higher criticism or the infidelity of the schools is the boldest kind of atheism. It is a crime for a so-called Christian school to attack the inspiration of the scriptures. It makes my soul sick to see the schools rejuvenating an old, worn out paganism and palm it off under the label 'science.'"[80]

Besides rejecting higher criticism, fundamentalists departed from modernists in asserting that the direction of human evolution—by which they meant social change—was down rather than up. This argument ran counter to the progressive spirit of the era that saw advances in civilization. For some it may have resonated with southern nostalgia for an earlier time and the pessimism associated with what came to be known as the myth of the lost cause.[81] It may have appealed to church members whose hopes for better times were not being realized.[82] It clearly stemmed from biblical understandings of sin and an awareness of the continuing reality of evil. But it was not limited to those who believed in the biblical story of the fall and humanity's inevitable descent toward divine judgment. An interesting and much discussed view of society's decline appeared in a 1913 book titled *Social Environment and Moral Progress* by Alfred Russel Wallace.[83] Wallace was a British naturalist known for having proposed a theory of evolution similar to Darwin's and for being a prominent defender of Darwin. Wallace was also drawn to unconventional ideas that included spiritualism, phrenology, hypnotism, and mesmerism. His 1913 book, published in the year of his death at age ninety, argued that society had produced material progress over the centuries but had also generated a social system that was the worst the world has ever seen. His criticisms echoed those of social reformers of the era who criticized extremes of wealth and poverty, urban crowding, exploitation of women and children, and corruption in business and politics. As a respected natural scientist, his arguments carried special weight, especially in separating natural and material evolution from what he saw as no accompanying improvement in human intellect and character. Biblical fundamentalists could hardly claim him as one of their own, but his argument that society was going downhill and that evil and immorality were pervasive was similar to theirs.

During and after the First World War it became more common to emphasize the German origin of ideas about higher criticism and thus to portray them as alien to patriotic Americans. At a revival meeting in Fort Worth in 1918, popular evangelist Billy Sunday, who had honed his anti-European rhetoric to a fine art, told the crowd that mud and filth were filling liberal pulpits as a result of German theology. "From Germany came every phase of modern doubt," he declared. Liberalism that denies the authority of the Bible and that leads to dead churches was now a threat from within America as well, Sunday contended. In a kind of populist appeal to the ordinary men and women who flocked to his meetings, Sunday announced that the person who "preaches humanitarianism, progress, culture, sociology, and leaves out Christ [is] the devil's pastor."[84]

In 1920 Norris hosted a weeklong conference on "Christian fundamentals" that included meetings at his church, the First Methodist Church, and the Chamber of Commerce auditorium. The conference brought together the most prominent leaders of the international fundamentalist movement. A. C. Dixon came from London where he pastored the large Spurgeon Tabernacle. A. B. Winchester arrived from Toronto. Henry Ostrom represented the Moody Bible Institute in Chicago. W. Leon Tucker from New York edited a fundamentalist journal called the *Wonderful Word*. And W. B. Riley was pastor of the First Baptist Church in Minneapolis, Minnesota.[85]

Dixon returned to Texas in 1921 where he participated in another Bible conference, featuring most of the previous year's cast at Norris's church in Fort Worth, and delivered a well-attended lecture at the Jefferson Theater on the

"Menace of Evolution." Dixon had become one of Darwin's leading critics by arguing not only that evolution was contrary to scripture but also that Darwin's theory was both inaccurate and dangerous. The fallacies, which Dixon traced to a misreading of Plato and Malthus, probably had little impact on the audience, but the danger he saw from alien ideas was all too familiar so recently after the Great War and the Bolshevik revolution. Through its emphasis on survival of the fittest, Dixon argued, evolution encouraged autocratic rule and oppression of the weak by the strong. It was sad enough that Germany had embraced Darwinism, he said, but England and France had succumbed as well. "The religious liberal leaders of England and France, realizing that their rationalistic theories and their books based upon them are in danger, are reasserting with nervous haste their destructive teachings," he declared.[86]

MONITORING TEXTBOOKS AND TEACHERS

Critics of higher criticism and evolution repeatedly expressed concerns, such as the ones Norris and Carroll voiced in 1910, about what was being taught in colleges and seminaries. In 1913 these concerns gravitated to the public schools as well. Opposition centered on a statement in a physical geography textbook that "the origin of man is unknown, although scientists generally agree that he has developed, by the process of evolution, from some high form of animal." Among those leading the opposition against further use of the book in Texas schools was Reverend Hanks, the combatant in the Hanks-Hawley feud of the 1880s who was now pasturing a church in Abilene. Hanks and his allies charged that children from good Christian homes where the Bible was taught would now lose their faith if their teachers taught that humans descended from lower animals. Or if teachers went against the textbook, students would lose confidence in the value of education. Drawing from *The Fundamentals*, which were now circulating widely among conservative clergy, Hanks argued that Darwin himself was a poor scientist and that evolution was an unproven theory. The best scientists, he was sure, would reject it.[87] Texas parents had a choice. Either they could choose to believe a book whose author of dubious credentials lived in Ithaca, New York, or they could believe the divine word of God. Surely it made no sense to favor the "high-sounding verbiage of sacrilegious science and pseudo-philosophy" over the Bible. Parents should complain to the state board of education until the textbook was replaced.[88]

It probably did not help that one of the few religious leaders to rise publicly in defense of the textbook was the pastor of Dallas's First Unitarian Church, Dr. W. L. Smith. Banning it, Smith said, was to suppress science and discredit the intelligence of Texas citizens, a plea that reasonable citizens probably could have accepted. But Smith went further, mentioning the names of scholars and church leaders in New York and Chicago who accepted higher criticism. If conservative

Texans thought modernism was flourishing in northern seminaries, here then was proof.[89] Over the next several months at statewide meetings, Presbyterians, Baptists, and Free Methodists went on record deploring the teaching of ideas in Texas schools that would discredit the Bible, and for its part the state school board promised to correct any such infidelities.

A more serious controversy arose in 1921 when Hanks again took the state board of education to task over textbooks allegedly contradicting the book of Genesis.[90] In the intervening years Baptist leaders had consistently affirmed their belief in a literal interpretation of the Bible. Clergy in other traditions who may have disagreed said so less publicly. And relationships among fundamentalist leaders strengthened through meetings in Los Angeles and New York, through lecture tours such as one conducted in Fort Worth in 1917 by California Bible lecturer and author Dr. R. A. Torrey and the Billy Sunday revival meetings in 1918, and the fundamentalist conferences hosted by Norris in 1920 and 1921. With Darwinism and higher criticism in the background, these events emphasized the authenticity of the Bible, the factual reality of the resurrection, and the necessity of vigilance against doubt and infidelity.[91]

Little was different from the earlier textbook controversies except that the passage of Prohibition had both emboldened and complicated the manner in which church leaders expressed concerns. On the one hand, clergy who sided with Hanks entertained thoughts of asking the state legislature to act on their behalf and proposed adding criticism of the motion picture industry and the state's newspapers. On the other hand, some of the earlier infighting reappeared as clergy called for less extreme measures, encouraged more cautious wording of resolutions, or seemed content to focus on the enforcement of Prohibition rather than tackling additional issues.[92]

The debate about how best to curb infidelity deepened in February 1922 when the Kentucky legislature, spurred by Baptist minister John W. Porter of Lexington, considered a bill barring any school or college receiving tax funds from teaching "any theory of evolution that derives man from the brute or any other form of life."[93] Northern newspapers predictably criticized the bill, but so did southern newspapers. The *Savannah News*, for example, noted the time when Kentuckians could drink whiskey if they pleased and no lawmaker could tell them what their religious beliefs should be. Perhaps carpetbaggers were running this new crusade, critics argued. With opposition among Kentuckians themselves, the bill in several versions failed to be enacted.[94]

The possibility that Texas might adopt antievolution legislation prompted a flurry of commentary about what should and should not be taught in schools. A few free thinkers took the opportunity to propose that not only Darwin but other controversial writers—Tom Paine, for example—should be included. Clergy who had already gone on record against evolution found the occasion ripe for reaffirming the value of biblical faith. Prohibition leader Cranfill, for example, worried about the hearts and minds of little children being poisoned by misguided

teaching in the public schools. "Heaven knows that we have enough sorrow, distrust, agony, tragedy and tears in the world without adding to the sum of earth's
discouragements and doubts," he said.[95] Following a spirited plea from Cranfill
to redouble its efforts against textbook heresies, the Baptist General Convention
of Texas at its December 1921 meeting unanimously reaffirmed its statement of
doctrinal faith.[96]

Hanks supplemented his earlier antievolution arguments by framing the issue
in terms of separation of church and state. If the constitution forbids teaching
religion in state schools, he argued, it was equally impermissible to teach anything contrary to religion. The theory of evolution, he argued, "contradicts the
fundamentals of the Christian religion," so teaching it is unfair.[97] Norris took up
the fight as well, including an appearance before the state legislature in which he
argued that the teaching of evolution in public schools should be outlawed on
grounds similar to those suggested by Hanks. Not only did it violate separation
of church and state, he believed, it also promoted alien ideas that undermined
morality. "Evolution was made in Germany," he said, and was "like poison gas of
the German armies."[98] Compelling as these arguments may have been to fellow
conservatives, they ran into much the same resistance as in Kentucky. The Texas
legislature was not persuaded.

The challenges directed at textbooks and teaching came home to roost in 1921
when Norris called for an inquiry into suspected heresy at Baylor. The same infidelity to scripture he had warned of in northern colleges and seminaries was
now afflicting the schools of his own denomination, he charged. Baylor's biology
professors were soft on evolution, he believed, and there were faculty whom he
suspected of thinking that parts of the Bible were allegorical rather than literal
references to historical facts. As for himself, he believed firmly that humans "did
not evolve from a monkey or any other species of organism or animal," and he
could cite chapter and verse from the Bible showing that God intended it as the
only and final word of God.[99]

Finding an appropriate response was awkward, to say the least. At its 1921
meeting, the Baptist General Convention sought ways to deny that anything heretical was being taught at Baylor without seeming to whitewash the allegations.
While individual leaders rose in defense of Baylor and spoke against infighting,
the delegates voted that the best strategy was to appoint a committee to conduct
a thorough investigation of Baylor and the other colleges sponsored by the denomination. How exactly to find the right balance between Baptists' tradition
of religious liberty and the need to guard against heresy was underscored in the
remarks of Dr. L. R. Scarborough, head of the Southwestern Baptist Theological
Seminary in Fort Worth. Cooperation to protect against heresy, he argued, should
not impair the doctrine of freedom of speech. "But when you employ freedom of
speech in the wrong direction it becomes license instead of liberty." Scarborough
was equally at pains to find the best way to think about criticism. "The most
dangerous man of today is the man with the critical mind," he said, referring to

Bolshevism as an example and probably inviting his listeners to hear an implicit reference to higher criticism and the teaching of evolution. Yet in a deft turn of meaning, he cautioned, "While we are getting after some of our teachers let's not subscribe to this wave of criticism." The doctrine of total depravity was the easiest doctrine to live up to, he observed to the crowd's amusement.[100]

In his commencement address on June 16, 1922, Baylor president Dr. Samuel P. Brooks praised the university's students, faculty, and alumni for their support of Prohibition and faithfulness to the Bible. Then, without mentioning Norris by name, he offered a strong defense of intellectual freedom. He counseled simply to ignore the prophets of despair who ignorantly attack science. "They set up monkeys as the fathers of scientists and make monkeys out of themselves," he accused.[101] That fall in a chapel address he made more of a point of condemning Darwinian evolution of any sort and affirming that any infidelity from the Bible would not be tolerated for a minute. At the same time he articulated a vision of the religious landscape that clearly set Norris's fundamentalism to the theological right of where he wanted Baylor to be. On the one hand were "literalistic religionists who insist upon an absolutely literal interpretation of all scripture, refusing to reckon with or accept the results of scientific research and investigation." On the other hand were the "materialistic philosophers who rely entirely upon scientific investigation for their conclusions, discarding the Bible as a revelation from God." Baylor and its teachers, he said, reject materialistic philosophies and "reverently look to God's Book as the source of all spiritual authority [and teach] a spiritual religion based on redemption by grace through faith in God's Son as revealed in His inspired Word." He did not say explicitly that Baylor rejected biblical literalists. It was sufficient from his characterization of literalistic religionists that he did not side with them.[102]

The investigating committee sided with Brooks and the denomination's leaders. "In no single instance have we found a teacher who accepted as a fact the Darwinian theory or in any way taught it as such," it concluded. The report noted the importance of avoiding the kind of factionalism that had divided northern Baptists and underscored its finding that nothing was being taught in any of the Texas Baptist schools that would undermine the faith of any student.[103] Separate from the report, Baptist General Convention leaders directed criticisms at Norris over several matters concerning his congregation, finances, and publications. Norris responded angrily that the denomination had become overly institutionalized and that he had no intention of doing what any prelate ordered him to do.[104]

In circling the wagons against Norris, the Baptist leadership solidly affirmed their own support of theological conservatism, an affirmation that was formalized in 1925 in the Southern Baptist Convention's Confession of Faith. The Bible was true, infallible, and divinely inspired. Jesus was the divine son of God who came to earth, died, and was resurrected. By stating that Darwinian theory was not taught as fact, Texas Baptists left open some wiggle room for entertaining it as theory or as conjecture, but that was done in the spirit of open-mindedness and not as a declaration of anything other than the biblical story of human origins.[105]

Whether they sided with Norris or with the Southern Baptist leadership, observers seemed to believe that there was more agreement than disagreement in Texas about basic Christian doctrines. Writing in the *Mexia Daily News*, editor A. Garland Adair expressed a typical view in noting that modernism may have spread in Europe but was largely "ineffective in gaining much attention on this side of the Atlantic." Maybe the controversy was just another attempt by the "Reds" to undermine America, he speculated. "Large service to America and to Christianity may be done by all who help to restate the old facts and unchanged truths in terms that will make them vivid and vital to others," he urged.[106]

But of course that was hardly the end of it, even in Texas. The Scopes trial in Dayton, Tennessee, in 1925 drew national attention to questions about teaching evolution in public schools. As if in prelude to that event, Norris's six-thousand-member church was continuing to attract attention locally and nationally as a center of fundamentalist preaching. In late 1922, after declaring his antipathy toward the Baptist General Convention of Texas, Norris participated in a gathering of several thousand Baptist Fundamentalists in Chicago and the following year pled his case for an antievolution law before the Texas legislature. Methodists who had been relatively more interested in Prohibition than in evolution joined the fray at a statewide meeting in December 1922 when speakers stressed the importance of taking a literal interpretation of the Bible and attacked instructors at several Methodist colleges they claimed were teaching higher criticism, evolution, and other heresies.[107] The following May, during a meeting of the World's Christian Fundamentalist Conference attended by three thousand delegates at Norris's church in Fort Worth, a mock trial was held in which students from the state's Methodist colleges testified against professors they said were teaching evolution.[108] Two weeks later delegates attending the annual meetings of the Southern Baptist Convention went on record adhering to Christian doctrine as taught in the Bible and protesting against "the unwarranted procedure of some so-called scientists."[109] That summer, as the University of Tennessee dismissed four faculty for allegedly teaching evolution, the gubernatorial race in Texas brought out candidates at farm picnics and Fourth of July celebrations who called for more preaching of an old-time religion. In Fort Worth a young Episcopal rector who had become known as the "fighting parson" for taking the liberal side against Norris and fundamentalism fell out of favor with his own bishop, who charged him with heresy for denying the validity of the Virgin Birth.[110] The following year the southern branch of the Presbyterian Church at a meeting in San Antonio denounced Darwinism as clergy from the denomination assisted in founding a new fundamentalist seminary in Dallas.[111] The Cumberland Presbyterian Church followed suit at its statewide meeting in Austin, declaring itself "squarely, fixedly and unmovably against these infidelic theories [that are] poisoning the minds of the rising generation."[112]

Agitation against alleged supporters of evolution cropped up in scattered places over the next few years. One of the most drastic incidents occurred in May 1929 when the trustees of Des Moines University, a Baptist institution known for its embrace of fundamentalism in Iowa, fired its president along with most of the faculty and shut down the campus over allegations of modernism fueled with innuendo about an alleged affair between the president and a woman who served as secretary of the trustee board. Students took up sides, pelted the administration building with eggs, and rioted until police were called to quell the demonstration and a court order reopened the campus.[113] Nothing quite that extreme occurred in Texas. In 1925, as the Scopes trial drew national attention to religious conservatism, Norris was forging wider connections with fundamentalist leaders in New York and California, Baptists and Methodists as well as several other groups again went on record in opposition to evolution, and the state board of education removed all references to evolution from textbooks used in public schools.[114] So thorough were the revisions that even the word in contexts having nothing to do with Darwinian theory was replaced with "development," and no mention was made of humans having lived in an uncivilized time.[115] On May 12, 1926, the Southern Baptist Convention meeting in Houston again resolved to reject every theory teaching that "man originated in or came by way of a lower animal ancestry."[116] But just as Norris's leadership of Texas fundamentalism seemed to be unchallenged, events proved otherwise.

On July 17, 1926, Norris was arraigned for killing a wealthy Fort Worth lumberman in the pastor's study at the First Baptist Church in the aftermath of a sermon in which Norris accused the mayor, who was a friend of the lumberman, of leading a young woman astray. After a trial that drew national attention, Norris was acquitted on grounds of self-defense, but if he had been viewed as controversial before, he was even more so now.[117] That spring Norris had attempted unsuccessfully to spark a showdown at the national convention of Northern Baptists over the modernism he said was taking over the denomination, but his efforts fell short of causing a split.[118] Baptists and other groups in Texas did, however, continue to denounce the teaching of evolution. In 1929 agitation again emerged from several clergy groups to introduce an antievolution bill to the Texas legislature. After much discussion and several alternative bills, the measure was again defeated, partly through clergy voicing opposition on grounds of keeping government separate from religion.[119] To carry on the antievolution effort as well as to promote cooperation among conservative clergy, pastors organized the Fundamentalist Baptist Preachers' Conference of Dallas with plans to become a statewide organization devoted to a "more faithful practice of Bible teachings."[120]

For the broader development of American fundamentalism, Norris's contribution was certainly colorful but was also significant. By building up the First Baptist Church of Fort Worth to one of the largest congregations in the country, he created a venue in which to promote fundamentalism locally and to bring Texas into a continuing relationship with fundamentalist leaders from other parts of the nation. His activism against evolution and his willingness to challenge the Texas Baptist establishment pushed the leaders of that establishment to the right—not into the fundamentalist camp itself but close in terms of firmly upholding fundamental Christian beliefs and distancing themselves from anything that smacked of modernism. If Texas played only a bit part in the early development of fundamentalism, it had become by the time of the Scopes trial in 1925 a powerful actor in the further promotion of conservative white Protestant religion. That influence rested in the fact that Texas had a large and rapidly growing population, was rich in agricultural and mineral resources, and was dominated religiously by Baptists, Methodists, Presbyterians, members of the Christian Church, and a few other denominations that shared basic doctrinal beliefs. Its influence could not be understood in those terms alone, however.

PROMOTING DISPENSATIONAL THEOLOGY

Through an unusual set of circumstances, Texas became the venue in which one of the most powerful theological developments that would shape conservative Protestantism in the twentieth century took root. Dispensational theology held that a close reading of the Bible proved that God had organized history into several distinct eras or dispensations in which different aspects of divine revelation governed human affairs. The current dispensation was variously understood to have begun with the first coming of Christ, with Christ's resurrection, or at Pentecost and would end with Christ's return, which would be preceded by a time of tribulation and followed by the establishment of Christ's kingdom on earth. This understanding was known as premillennialism because it argued that Christ's second coming to earth would precede Christ's thousand-year reign that was predicted in the Bible. It contrasted with the prevailing nineteenth-century doctrine of postmillennialism which anticipated Christ's physical return coming at the end of a thousand years of work toward improvement and redemption by the church. Premillennialism offered a pessimistic view of current events in which affairs were becoming worse rather than better. It encouraged believers to see current evils such as hardship brought on by natural disasters and violence from lawlessness and war as signs that Christ's return was imminent.[121]

Dispensational theology emerged in scattered teachings and Adventist movements in the antebellum North as well as in Great Britain and then drew increasing interest in the 1870s and 1880s.[122] Partly in response to Darwin and more generally in conjunction with the rising influence of science, technology, and industry, dispensational scholarship focused on decoding numbers and prophecies presumably hidden in the Bible that would show exactly when Christ's return among other events would occur. In extreme interpretations it encouraged believers to separate themselves from the world and wait in eager anticipation of Christ's return.[123] But dispensational theology was not, as later treatments often assumed, only or primarily about prophetic predictions. It was also an attempt, as it were, to outmaneuver higher criticism of the Bible through closer examination of the biblical text itself in light of favorable archaeological and historical discoveries. If much of popular fundamentalism focused on rejecting higher criticism, dispensational theology was fundamentalism's best hope of deploying scholarly and scientific inquiry into defending the biblical account.

Texas's role in the promotion of dispensational theology came about through the work of Reverend C. I. Scofield, an unconventional northerner from Michigan who had fought for the Confederacy, worked as a lawyer and served in the Republican-led state legislature in Kansas, married and divorced a Roman Catholic, become ordained as a Congregationalist minister, and then settled in Dallas in 1883.[124] Scofield's interest in dispensational theology began shortly after his conversion to evangelical Christianity in the late 1870s through the influence of James H. Brookes, a Presbyterian pastor in St. Louis. His interest deepened from attending a meeting of the Niagara Bible Conference in 1888, the same year in which he published a pamphlet, "Rightly Dividing the Word of Truth," outlining his own views of dispensational premillennialism. Like Norris, Scofield was a dynamic preacher, building his small Congregational Church from fewer than twenty members when he arrived to five hundred in 1895.[125] Also like Norris, Scofield maintained close ties with like-minded religious leaders outside of Texas, having worked briefly with evangelist Dwight L. Moody in St. Louis, befriending missionary Hudson Taylor at the Niagara Bible Conference, and superintending home mission activities in Louisiana. In 1895 Scofield moved to Massachusetts, where he occupied a Congregational pulpit until 1903 when he returned to Dallas.

Scofield studiously avoided the intradenominational politics and personal rivalries that characterized Norris and many other fundamentalist leaders.[126] Also in contrast to Norris, Scofield's influence had little to do with his congregation, to which he devoted minimal effort after his return in 1903, or in meeting with state legislators or challenging the leadership of a large denomination. From the start his role as a Congregational minister gave him almost complete autonomy within a denomination that was relatively weak in Texas. That autonomy increased in 1908 during his absence when the First Congregational Church in Dallas withdrew from the Lone Star Association of Congregational Churches and became an independent church. The reason was to protest the action of another church in the association, the First Congregational Church of Texarkana, for reordaining Reverend F. E. Maddox after Maddox had been tried for heresy and suspended by the Presbyterian Church he was pastoring.[127]

Scofield's influence came through his writing, lectures, appearances at Bible conferences, and especially his work in producing the Scofield Reference Bible to which he devoted himself almost full time with the help of a team of scholars from 1903 to 1909. Scofield's preaching invited his audiences to turn repeatedly in their Bibles from verse to verse, not only in familiar New Testament texts but also in otherwise obscure Old Testament passages from which he drew detailed inferences about what was to happen before and after Jesus came again. It followed from his view of scripture that a Bible filled with annotations and cross-references was more authoritative than any scholarly theory only loosely connected to the biblical text. The Scofield Bible gained almost immediate acclaim among fundamentalists as the most definitive statement of premillennial dispensationalism. It went through an extensive revision in 1917 and by the end of World War II was said to have sold more than two million copies.

Scofield's project was one of many that had been inspired by calls over the past two decades for better understanding of the Bible. Russell's work that led to the subsequent founding of the Jehovah's Witnesses, for example, included extensive study of biblical prophecy in relation to historical events and previous theological predictions about end times and the second coming of Christ. The success of his *Food for Thinking Christians* in 1881, with circulation of one and a half million copies, encouraged him to launch a massive series of scriptural studies under the title of *Millennial Dawn*, which included six volumes published between 1886 and 1904 and a seventh published posthumously in 1917.[128] Another example was the thirteen-volume *New Schaff-Herzog Encyclopedia of Religious Knowledge*, published from 1908 to 1914 under the editorship of New York University professor of church history Samuel Macauley Jackson.[129] Scofield's, however, was unique in placing his commentary within a bound volume of the Bible itself rather than as a separate volume or series of volumes. The Scofield Bible could be used in any denomination. It was placed in pews of local congregations, given to adults at revival meetings and to children as a reward for attending Sunday school, and used as a handy reference by pastors and Sunday school teachers.

Although Scofield was ordained and called himself a doctor of divinity he had no formal training in a theological seminary or divinity school. That lack combined with the fact that many of his interpretations of the meaning of particular dates and events in the Bible were dubious opened his work to criticism from better-trained theologians. Scholars schooled in Calvinism and Reformation theology who favored postmillennialism or who viewed biblical prophecy in figural terms were especially critical of the Scofield Bible. As one critic observed, "Its theory of the Bible is crude and false, its use of the Bible is mechanical, arbitrary, and violent, and the consequence of its theory is the sacrifice of what is highest in Christianity to the lower levels of an earlier faith."[130] Such criticisms were offset to some extent, though, by the fact that Scofield had assembled a team of scholars who favored dispensationalism to assist in the work and included the names of some of the most prominent evangelical preachers of his time in the acknowledgments, which helped give the Scofield Bible legitimacy.

Its grassroots appeal perhaps reflected the period in which it was produced as well. Pastors who believed that evolution was wrong but who felt that better scholarship was on God's side could take heart in Scofield's assertion that the Bible was being "vindicated by the last word of the latest science."[131] As a Methodist pastor

in Dallas observed, "The comments are so obvious in meaning and so conservative in statement that little question can be raised concerning their helpfulness."[132]
For church members with little schooling who knew they were being left behind
as better training in high school and college became available, Scofield's notes
made it possible to regain a sense of having an authoritative understanding of
the Bible at their fingertips. To the vast majority of Americans who labored on
hardscrabble farms and in factories, it was easier to imagine that the trajectory of
history was down or at best faltering rather than up. Daily news about violence
and unrest was a reality. "The nineteenth century, in which most of us here present lived, was the bloodiest of all the centuries of history," Scofield observed in
an address given in Dallas in 1908, "and the twentieth has made a start which
promises to surpass it."[133] Postmillennial optimism may have made sense during
the Progressive Era, but the turmoil and slaughter the world incurred during the
Great War and the economic uncertainty that followed soon after made the more
pessimistic outlook of premillennial theology more plausible.

The spread of dispensational ideas was furthered through the founding of
Bible institutes, seminaries, and fundamentalist churches and through conferences and publications. Scofield himself traveled extensively, assisted in the
founding of two Bible institutes, and preached sermons that were widely reproduced in newspapers and church magazines. Although his interpretations of biblical prophecy attracted particular interest, he provided practical advice through
his expository preaching as well, typically with a kind of authoritative voice that
reflected his belief in having discerned the deepest meanings of the Bible. Consistent with teachings in Baptist, Methodist, and holiness theology, he emphasized
the possibility of not only an escape from sin but also a more joyous existence
through acceptance of Christ. In prophetic terms humanity was under divine
condemnation, but in practical terms the born-again Christian could experience
an abundant life. He preached on such topics as stewardship, work, marriage, and
parenting, as well as how to live as a happy, prosperous Christian. His interest in
these topics and that of his audiences belied the notion that premillennial Christians withdrew their attention from the present world to eagerly await the return
of Christ. A better understanding is that dispensational theology connected the
small details of daily Christian life with a story about the larger movement of
human and cosmic events—or as Scofield put it, a harmonization of the facts of
being with the facts of the universe.[134] Salvation continued to point toward eternal life in heaven but now provided a way to understand and participate in the
unfolding of a larger drama as well.

Although Scofield's work in itself had a national and international impact,
Texas contributed to that impact in several important ways. The Evangelical
Theological College that conservative scholars organized in Dallas in 1924 as
a nondenominational school and in 1926, through a gift from the widow of a
wealthy cattleman, purchased a colonnaded mansion built by one of the city's
first millionaires was from the start oriented toward premillennial theology.[135]

Besides Scofield's history with Dallas, Reverend William M. Anderson Jr., pastor of the city's First Presbyterian Church, played a critical role in organizing and generating local support for the effort.[136] Under the leadership of Lewis Sperry Chafer, who had been associated with Scofield in Massachusetts and became the interim pastor of Scofield's Dallas congregation when Scofield died in 1921, the school grew into Dallas Theological Seminary, added a doctoral program in 1926, produced numerous books by Chafer and others on dispensationalism, and trained many of the leaders who would carry on the movement after World War II. Chafer was well acquainted with Norris but saw the need for a seminary that was distinct from the kind of hot-button fundamentalism that Norris represented. The new seminary, Chafer hoped, would be more intellectually rigorous than any other seminary in the South and at the same time would not be narrowly identified with the divisiveness that characterized fundamentalism. That vision enabled the institution to become one of the nation's most important training centers for dispensational theology and a key link between Texas and evangelical leaders in the North.[137]

In addition, Texas played an important role in spreading dispensational theology through Norris's church in Fort Worth and his connections in wider fundamentalist circles. Norris had come to embrace dispensational ideas through his contacts with Scofield, Riley, and others and eventually developed a theology of his own that identified three dispensations rather than the seven that Scofield taught.[138] Norris had never lacked in self-confidence anyway, and his interest in dispensational theology "seems to have fed his ego," one of his biographers has argued, because it gave him access to special biblical wisdom that nonfundamentalists and ordinary scholars did not have.[139] In 1931 Norris's First Baptist Church, now with a membership of twelve thousand, launched the Premillennium Baptist Missionary Fellowship, which became the predecessor of the World Baptist, Bible Baptist, Southwide Baptist, and Independent Baptist Fellowships.[140] And through Norris and fellow Texas Baptist fundamentalist Earl Anderson, a variant of dispensational fundamentalism took root in Texas that was more prone to social and political activism than was true of many other fundamentalists.

Within a few years Texas was the home of a few churches that had withdrawn from or been founded separately from the Southern Baptist Convention, advertised themselves under the banner of fundamentalism, and embraced dispensational theology. In Abilene a small fundamentalist church founded by a Simmons University student grew to four thousand by 1931.[141] On a smaller scale the Fundamentalist Baptist Church in San Antonio began meeting in a building vacated by a Presbyterian church in 1929 and by 1931 was a flourishing operation sponsoring lectures around the state on premillennial prophecy.[142] The Calvary Baptist Church in Denton began advertising with the titles of its sermons that it was a fundamentalist church and in 1931, with a membership of six hundred, reorganized as the Fundamentalist Baptist Church.[143] Meetings were being held in other locations as well. In Weatherford, for example, the pastor of the Fundamentalist

Baptist Church distinguished himself from mainstream Baptists by wearing overalls while delivering his sermons.[144] In Big Spring members of a new congregation called themselves fundamentalists while they deliberated on what the proper name of their church should be.[145] Without a separate fundamentalist church, Lubbock's residents organized an interdenominational Scofield Bible Class and hosted a well-attended revival by a fundamentalist preacher from Denver who spoke about "The World Depression in the Light of Bible Prophecy."[146]

Although premillennial dispensationalists typically eschewed direct political involvement, Norris was a notable exception, as was his colleague Anderson, a Baptist pastor who with Norris's help launched a large fundamentalist church in Dallas. Norris's involvement in benevolent associations and charitable activities began with his arrival in Fort Worth, and his engagement in political activities included his efforts on behalf of Prohibition and antievolution legislation. Like Norris, Anderson had been an outspoken critic of doctrinal infidelity and between 1925 and 1929 became increasingly active in promoting antievolution legislation.[147] Both had personal contact with the police and the judicial system, Norris through the charges against him for arson and murder, and Anderson for violating a court injunction and having to spend time in jail during the construction of his new $50,000 tabernacle in Dallas.[148] In 1930 Norris and Anderson campaigned actively for the gubernatorial nomination of former U.S. senator Earle B. Mayfield. Besides speaking in his own church and from other pulpits, Norris became one of the first preachers to use a hookup of radio stations to broadcast his views across the state.[149] Anderson led another campaign to persuade the state board of education to ban a textbook, this time on early European history, which he alleged not only taught evolution but also contained pro-Catholic tendencies.[150] When that effort failed, Anderson organized the Public School Protective League and toured the state calling on voters to help rid the schools of heretical teaching.[151] Norris continued until his death in 1952 to address domestic and international political topics through his preaching, radio broadcasts, weekly newspaper, and public appearances.

Norris, Anderson, and the few others who held forth in the name of fundamentalism would hardly have stirred much attention outside of Texas had it not been for the wider impact of conservative church leaders in textbook controversies, debates about evolution, conflicts within denominations and at seminaries over biblical interpretation, the role of religion in the 1928 presidential campaign, and continuing questions about the retention and enforcement or repeal of the Eighteenth Amendment. From the standpoint of fundamentalist leaders, the world was increasingly under the authority of Satan, with only an embattled remnant of true believers keeping faith with the Bible. Progressive leaders who had favored the insights provided by higher criticism, saw it quite differently. In their view, something akin to fundamentalism—"snarling and scrambling for political mastery," as one observer noted—was the dominant thrust in American religion, threatening religious freedom itself.[152]

As an organized movement fundamentalism would experience hard times like nearly everyone else during the 1930s. Displaced sharecroppers and unemployed day laborers found meaning and perhaps comfort in the eschatological scenarios of premillennialist preachers, but sparse offerings made it harder for fundamentalist leaders to attend national conferences and start new Bible institutes. That was true in Texas as well, where drouth and sinking cotton prices pared earnings on farms and in small towns to the bone. Parts of the Texas economy that were associated with the expanding oil and gas industry experienced continuing growth, however, which eased the difficulties faced by the leaders of fundamentalist churches. Under Chafer's leadership, Dallas Theological Seminary steadily expanded its curriculum and the geographic scope of its appeal.[153] Norris's church in Fort Worth and his radio ministry regularly reached thousands of like-minded believers. The seeds planted in the 1920s also led to a new generation of fundamentalist leaders. In 1921 a student at Baylor University with ambitions he felt could not be realized in Texas headed north to study at the University of Chicago, where modernism was the reigning view, only to find himself captivated by a speech at a Chicago church about the Bible and its enemies by William Jennings Bryan. Feeling called to preach, the young man returned to Texas, took seminary classes in Fort Worth, and began holding revival meetings around the state. Norris became his mentor, booking speaking engagements for him at fundamentalist conferences and airing his sermons on radio broadcasts. The protégé's prominence as pastor of a rapidly growing fundamentalist church in Dallas increased year by year, leading to a break with Norris in 1936. He was John R. Rice, the influential preacher, author, publisher, and radio minister whose biweekly publication *The Sword of the Lord* grew over the next decade into the most widely circulated fundamentalist magazine in the country and whose two hundred books were said to have circulated in more than sixty million copies by the time of his death in 1980.[154]

When the *Chicago Daily Tribune* identified Texas as part of the fundamentalist belt, there was no reason to consider it a special breeding ground for religious conservatism more than other parts of the South or Midwest. That was also true in subsequent years when others identified Texas as a place in which fundamentalism prevailed. They might have mentioned Tennessee, with its legacy of the Scopes trial, or Kansas, as the most enthusiastic supporter of Prohibition, or Los Angeles, Chicago, and Philadelphia, where fundamentalist Bible institutes were located. There was nevertheless truth in viewing Texas as a state favorable to theologically conservative ideas and well positioned to have greater influence in the future. Norris was not alone in organizing fundamentalist meetings and connecting them with fundamentalists around the country. When mainstream Texas Baptists and Methodists distanced themselves from ultrafundamentalist biblical literalists, they did so by repudiating higher criticism and affirming their allegiance to basic biblical fundamentals. Both groups were large and well organized, with growing memberships and influence beyond Texas itself. Having

always prided itself on its size, Texas was rapidly becoming one of the most populous and richest states, with opportunities especially in Dallas and Fort Worth for
huge congregations and influential seminaries to flourish. These resources were
largely in the hands of white Protestants. But Texas had yet to come to terms with
its legacy of slavery and racial discrimination. That challenge would significantly
shape its role as a Bible-Belt state as well.

CHAPTER 5

FROM JUDGE LYNCH TO JIM CROW

Celebrating Limited Inclusion

In singular and fine sense the slave became master, the bondservant
became free, and the meek not only inherited the earth, but made the
heritage a thing of questing for eternal youth, of fruitful labor, of joy and
music, of the free spirit and the ministering hand.

W.E.B. DUBOIS, *WHAT THE NEGRO HAS DONE FOR THE
UNITED STATES AND TEXAS,* 1936

On Friday June 19, 1936, the prominent Dallas pastor Reverend Dr.
George Washington Truett greeted one of the largest gatherings ever
assembled for worship in that city. The well-dressed crowd that day included fellow pastors, business leaders, and dignitaries from as far away as Kansas City and St. Louis, churchwomen, students, housewives, domestic servants,
day laborers, and sharecroppers. Nearly all were African American.[1]

Truett spoke briefly, offering a warm Texas welcome, and then introduced
the main speaker, Reverend Dr. Lacey Kirk Williams. Truett, who was white,
headed Dallas's massive First Baptist Church, where he had served since 1897,
steadily growing its membership to more than seven thousand, making it the
largest Southern Baptist congregation in the United States. Williams, an African
American, was known to the local audience from having pastored congregations
in Dallas and Fort Worth and now headed the twelve-thousand-member Olivet
Baptist Church in Chicago, the nation's largest African American congregation.
Truett was president of the Baptist World Alliance, an international organization devoted to the promotion of fellowship and cooperation among Baptists
throughout the world, and had just returned from a well-publicized round-the-
world tour with his wife on behalf of that organization. Williams was the alliance's vice president.

The occasion was the Texas Centennial Exposition, which a few days earlier had hosted President Franklin Roosevelt speaking to a crowd of fifty thousand at the newly named Cotton Bowl. Celebrating the anniversary of Texas's independence from Mexico in 1836, the exposition included more than fifty buildings, cost an estimated $25 million, and by the time it ended in November attracted more than ten million visitors. It was a remarkable achievement for a state and for a nation mired in the Great Depression. The special event that brought Williams to town and Truett to the stage on June 19 was the commemoration of the state's abolition of slavery on that day in 1865. Besides Williams's lecture, the day's activities included music by a three-thousand-member African American choir, dedication of a "Negro Life and Culture" building, a track meet in the Cotton Bowl, an African American beauty contest to select the Cleopatra of the fair, a boxing match, a "Little Harlem" concession area, and a concert by "his hi-de-highness of hi-de-ho," Cab Calloway.[2]

By almost any indication, the Texas Centennial Exposition signaled the hope that a New South was being born, led by the nation's most powerful southern state, in which the legacy of slavery, the Civil War, Reconstruction, lynching, and Jim Crow laws were being relegated to the past. Organized at such cost in the midst of the Great Depression, the event was nothing short of spectacular. The buildings that remain more than three quarters of a century later are considered among the finest examples of art deco architecture anywhere. With more than a quarter of a million people living in Dallas and another 165,000 living nearby in Fort Worth, the Dallas–Fort Worth metropolitan area had become one of the largest anywhere in the South, rivaled only by New Orleans. The exposition's organizers boasted that theirs was the only exposition with a "Negro Life and Culture" exhibit. Texas, it appeared, was leading the nation into a new era of prosperity, with racial harmony included for good measure. The joint appearance of two of the nation's most influential clergy signaled that religion was meant to have a place in the new era.

Anyone paying closer attention to the Texas Centennial Exposition, especially from the "colored" side of the racial barrier that divided the state, would have recognized immediately that real life was quite different from the sanguine image presented by the celebration. African Americans attending Roosevelt's speech at the Cotton Bowl were seated in a segregated area near the rodeo pens. Restrooms in the hall featuring African American culture were segregated. Newspaper accounts repeated racial slurs in describing the exposition's African American events and patrons. Only a few months earlier two African American teenagers had been murdered by a lynch mob.

How was it possible for Texans—and indeed for much of the country—to imagine that race relations had become so accommodating for all concerned in 1936? Was it the result of a kind of dual consciousness in which people knew deep down that the situation left much to be desired but on the surface wanted to put on a good appearance for anyone who might be watching—and they hoped the world was watching and thinking well of Texas? Or was it that the Centennial Exposition celebrated significant changes that had taken place over the past century and even over the past half century—changes that nearly everyone regarded as about the best anyone could hope for, but which also reflected the fact that race relations still had a long way to go?

The most revealing answers came from the African American side. In the pamphlet W.E.B. DuBois was commissioned to write for the exposition and of which some fifty thousand copies were distributed free to the exposition's attendees, the accomplishments of the state's African Americans were presented in bold detail.[3] Under slavery they had enriched the state by clearing land and tending cotton. As sharecroppers after the Civil War, former slaves continued to develop the state's agriculture. Schools and churches for African Americans were founded by the thousands, and some progress had been made in launching colleges as well. African Americans who visited the exposition testified that they were impressed with its portrayal of their race's accomplishments. At the same time they were keenly aware of the segregated facilities and noted how the exhibition hall for their accomplishments was set off to the side and largely shielded from view by a row of trees.

All the ways in which white religious leaders had been involved in the major developments of the state to that point had been deeply inflected by the fact that Texas also had a large and growing African American population. White religious leaders who privately deplored lynching seldom raised a voice against it. Many of them were willing to support the Ku Klux Klan because it favored Prohibition and catered to white Protestants' fears of Roman Catholics and African Americans. They wondered whether African Americans were sufficiently on their side in advocating for Prohibition, and they restricted African American voting through the poll tax and intimidation. Fundamentalists appealed almost exclusively to white audiences. At the same time African American leaders developed a parallel set of institutions in their own communities, sometimes with the assistance of white churches and community leaders. African American churches especially became the venues in which leadership could be cultivated and racial uplift could be encouraged. It would take an unusual network of activists under these circumstances to promote interracial cooperation and advocate against lynching.

AN EXPOSITION IN BLACK AND WHITE

Rituals lift to public consciousness what is only dimly realized in ordinary life about the power of society and how it is organized.[4] That holds true in small ways when communities gather to honor their heroes and bury their dead. It happens in much larger ways when nations commemorate their independence or the cessation of a great war. For Texas, the 1936 exposition was an opportunity to take pride in all that it had accomplished and to showcase its accomplishments to the nation. A place of any size and national significance knew the importance of organizing a celebratory event that would boost its image and draw thousands of visitors. The best example was the World's Columbian Exposition, which drew twenty-seven million visitors from more than forty nations to Chicago in 1893 in commemoration of the four hundredth anniversary of Christopher Columbus's arrival in the New World. Others included the Louisiana Purchase Exposition held in St. Louis in 1904 and San Francisco's Panama-Pacific International Exposition in 1915. Although the Texas exposition was modeled on these and included similar exhibits and artistic performances, its focus was decidedly less national or international. The date featured its independence as a republic rather than its later annexation by the United States. The occasion permitted the heroes of the Alamo and the Battle of San Jacinto to be honored yet again, and the stories of which Texas civil religion was composed to be retold. It was also a forward-looking event that emphasized the state's recent economic and demographic growth, cities, and plans for the future.

Dallas was hardly the most logical place for a celebration of the state's history. San Antonio would have been a better place to remember the Alamo. Houston and Galveston had been settled earlier and played a larger role in the state's history. Austin was the state capital. Leaders from Goliad and Gonzales thought their towns should have been considered. Even Huntsville, as the home of Sam Houston, could have laid claim to being the best site for a historical event. Dallas's promoters knew this and used their economic muscle to win the argument about where the exposition should be located. As the state's second largest city, it was able to pledge the most money in local contributions, provide the most spacious grounds and accommodations, and highlight the state's rising national prominence.

Dallas was not only one of the largest and fastest-growing cities in the region. It was also the location of a well-organized business community capable of spearheading the effort required to host a major exposition. By the end of the nineteenth century, Dallas was an important rail center for shipping between the Gulf Coast and northern cities. It was the world's leading inland cotton market as well as the most important hub in the region for farm machinery and agricultural supplies.[5] In 1905 area businessmen organized the 150,000 Club with the goal of increasing the city's population to 150,000 over the next five years, during which time a major program of urban renovation and annexation was undertaken. In 1909 nearly 800,000 miles of new railroad was constructed statewide, and the following year more than a million miles were added, much of it providing new connections with lines passing through Dallas.[6] By 1920 the city was the location of a Federal Reserve Bank and a Ford assembly plant. The 1920s also saw the 400-member Dallas Chamber of Commerce increasingly engaged in promoting the idea of a "Magic Circle of Texas," an area served by a network of farm-to-market roads and rail lines with Dallas at the center that included more than

40 percent of the state's population, farms, and businesses.[7] Community leaders boasted of its cultural institutions as well. Besides Southern Methodist University, which grew to more than 2,000 students by 1925, Dallas was the location of Baylor University's medical and dental schools, 9 other colleges and preparatory schools, 5 business colleges, 5 high schools and 43 elementary schools, 160 churches, a symphony orchestra, and numerous music and drama associations.[8]

As near as anyone could recall, the first fair in Dallas had been held in 1859 when the town's population was about 2,000.[9] With the arrival of rail service in 1873, the town's population began to increase, and attendance at the annual fair climbed to 30,000 by 1877. After a hiatus of nearly a decade, the fair resumed in 1886 with horse racing and hot air balloon rides among its featured attractions and became a state fair and exposition a year later. Seeing its economic and public relations value, boosters steadily enlarged the fair and advertised it more widely in each successive year.[10] By 1930 total attendance topped 675,000.[11]

The idea for a centennial exposition appears to have been considered as early as 1923, about the time that Reverend Norris was attacking Southern Baptists and fundamentalists were lobbying to eradicate heretical teachings about evolution from the state's textbooks. Business leaders from around the state at a meeting of the Advertising Clubs of Texas in Corsicana thought a major celebration marking the Texas centennial could be a significant way of attracting visitors, immigrants, and new business. The Dallas Chamber of Commerce picked up the idea and with the mayor's support persuaded residents to approve a $3.5 million bond package for improvements to the state fair grounds and other expenses related to the exposition.[12]

Had they known that the exposition would be held amid the Great Depression, voters might have been less eager to approve the bond package, but the investment turned out to be a good one. With skin in the game, as it were, residents and business owners pitched in to help advertise the event. Dallas also received $3 million in additional funds from the state and federal governments. Some of the Wild West atmosphere associated with the Texas frontier was retained, but the exposition's organizers were mostly intent on showcasing Dallas as a modern city rivaling the largest urban centers anywhere in the country. Visitors were invited to arrive by automobile, train, and airplane and to see in Dallas's new thoroughfares and shopping districts that it was a place where money could be made and success could be achieved. As one of the exposition's brochures proclaimed, visitors would discover the "industrial and economic rise of an empire in the Southwest."[13]

Locating Texas in the Southwest rather than the South was an explicit aim of the exposition's organizers. Anticipating later associations with the Sun Belt, the state was presented as a sunny place with warm winters and a mild climate. The state was rich in oil exploration and cattle shipping, and although cotton farming was emphasized, that was done without reference to the plantations and slaves who had pioneered in growing cotton. The Mexican American population received attention mostly as part of a long-ago history of Spanish exploration and missions.

The most southern aspect of the exposition was the presence of daily religious services, usually conducted by Southern Baptists and with music by the combined choirs of Baptist churches. Besides Truett the lineup included a former president of the Southern Baptist Convention from Shreveport and the current president of Baylor University. But in keeping with the exposition's larger regional aims, leaders were also invited from some of the northern denominations, such as a former head of the Northern Baptist Convention who traveled in by train from St. Louis.[14] At a separate event organized by the Dallas Council of Churches on the eve of the exposition, leaders of more than a dozen local religious organizations expressed faith that the city could flourish spiritually in the months ahead as well as commercially.[15] In his sermon on June 11, flanked by numerous Baptist leaders and other dignitaries from around the state, Truett likened the greatness of Texas to the greatness of America. The "inalienable right to worship God, or not, and always according to the dictates of his own conscience," he said, was the most cherished ideal of all.[16]

The fact that nearly a million African Americans lived in Texas, including more than fifty thousand in Dallas County, meant that the exposition could hardly focus only on the white population. But it was easier to deemphasize racial differences in Dallas than it would have been in counties to the east where a third or more of the population was African American or even in Galveston where close to a quarter were.[17] Having a diverse population that could perform gospel spirituals and host Cab Calloway could even be viewed as a positive indication that Dallas was a cosmopolitan city just as much as Chicago and Philadelphia were.

Dallas's black leaders greeted the idea that something special for African Americans would be included at the exposition with enthusiasm. In June 1935 as plans emerged to construct a building celebrating African American achievements, a group of black business and community leaders pledged to help raise $50,000 toward the effort.[18] In late December the Federal Fine Arts Commission approved designs for the building, and two months later the U.S. Congress approved a plan that included a contribution from the federal government of $50,000 to pay for the building.[19] That spring Sam W. Houston of Huntsville, a prominent educator whose father had been one of General Sam Houston's slaves and had remained with him as a personal bodyguard after emancipation, was chosen to chair an advisory committee and head up public relations for the exposition's African American activities.[20] Houston's family background as well as his personal vigor and leadership experience served him well in this new capacity. Black newspapers around the country, such as the Kansas City *Plaindealer*, the Wichita *Negro Star*, and the *Atlanta Daily World*, publicized plans for the event.[21] An editorial in the *Dallas Morning News* noted that it was expected to attract visitors and probably improve interracial relations but observed that segregated accommodations would be required and expressed hope that organizers would bear in mind that Texas "never had a large slave population."[22] That hope was largely realized through exhibits that traced African Americans' role in Texas only since emancipation.[23]

The Dallas Morning News had long been the state's newspaper of record and one of the city's most distinguished assets. It publicized plans for the exposition months in advance, advertised each day's events, and sold thousands of copies to the exposition's visitors. Its coverage included descriptions of the activities of greatest interest to African Americans as well as those of more general interest, such as the exposition's opening parade and Roosevelt's visit. But the paper's predominantly white readership was also treated to the kind of dismissive ridicule of African Americans that characterized the period. "Mandy wasn't there when Dallas sat down to cold supper Friday night for with Rastus, and thousands of care-free members of her race she was busy putting in a glorious Juneteenth at the magic Texas Centennial Exposition," the story of the Juneteenth celebration began. It described the African Americans attending the event as "dusky country merrymakers who had deserted catfish streams" and as spectators with "rolling eyes and flashing white teeth." "Black faces deep into slices of watermelon" stormed the exposition, and "dusky belles disporting neat curves" in tight bathing suits "danced before an audience of rolling eyes." Giving the "swarm" credit for having "stayed clear of the law's long arm," the story praised the "Negro spirituals" the event included but noted that the usual "strip shows" had been shut down for the day, apparently to prevent an outrage of illicit passions.[24]

As far as local coverage conveyed, African American visitors were thoroughly pleased with their experiences at the exposition. It fell to reporters covering the exposition for black newspapers elsewhere to register a different side. One concern was the thick row of cedar trees that essentially hid the "Negro Life" building from the rest of the grounds. Another was signs printed in large letters over the lavatories "For Colored Men" and "For Colored Women," which were at best odd since no toilets were provided for white patrons. Yet another was that segregated bus transportation to and from the fairgrounds was inadequate. The strip shows being closed probably would not have resulted in complaints had it not been for officials stating on the record "niggers had no business seeing nude white women." The *Dallas Morning News's* racial slurs did not go unnoticed, either; nor did the fact that visitors were charged exaggerated prices for food and amusements.[25]

An African American visiting the exposition from Texarkana walked blocks in torrid weather with his nine-year-old companion after being told by a white bus driver that no colored people could ride. When they finally spotted a drinking fountain along the way, they were faced with a "For Whites Only" sign. At the magnificent General Electric building the gentleman at the door told them no people of color were allowed to enter except on June 19. "By this time it began to dawn upon me," the visitor wrote, "that I was not particularly wanted in that section of Dallas at that time." On his way back to Texarkana he mused about the taxes he had to pay to support the exposition. "In the last 100 years, Texas has made wonderful progress," he thought. But that progress originated in "cotton fields dominated by Negro labor and Negro suffering." Take that away and Texas would still be "wilderness."[26]

The misunderstanding and prejudice evident at the exposition reflected a larger reality. The "special trains" put into service to bring African Americans from other cities for the exposition were special because African Americans were not allowed to ride in regular accommodations.[27] Streetcar conductors had the authority by law to change where African Americans could be seated in order to accommodate white passengers. It was unclear if that authority included the right to beat someone who refused.[28] When African Americans complained about Jim Crow segregation on the city's buses, white leaders denied that segregation dis-criminates on the basis of race or color. "It merely separates the races in the in-terests of harmony," they said.[29] If orderly behavior at the exposition was notable, news that two African Americans had been killed and twenty-six others injured was merely the "usual quota of casualties" for a Juneteenth celebration in Dallas.[30]

Not that black residents were considered by their white counterparts as a source only of trouble. White residents found them ridiculously amusing as well. Two "young negro bucks" were overheard watching the motorcade on the open-ing day of the exposition, a society columnist reported. "Theah he is," exclaimed one. "Right theah in the car whut says 'Governor.'" Asked by his companion who he meant, he replied, "Roosevelt, of course, fellow! Don't you know who's Gover-nuh?" To which the other responded, "Go back home, country boy. Everybody knows Marse Cullen F. Thomas am the Governuh of Texas."[31]

FDR's visit was one event that blacks and whites could equally applaud, even if they did so from separate sections of the Cotton Bowl. Eighty-eight percent of Texans had voted for Roosevelt in the 1932 election, and when voters went to the polls in 1936 that margin fell only to 87 percent. Still, white voters in Texas and across the South found it puzzling that with such strong support Roosevelt felt it necessary to curry favor with African Americans. That was distressing enough to a group of dissident Texas Democrats led by a former Dallas prohibition advo-cate to form an organization called the Southern Committee to Uphold the Con-stitution. After distributing literature throughout the South attacking Roosevelt on the "Negro question" and circulating photographs of Eleanor Roosevelt in the company of black escorts in an effort to damage the administration, the leaders were summarily read out of the party.[32] But the Texas delegation was less than pleased when the Democratic National Convention, meeting in June just after Roosevelt's visit to Dallas, invited an African American pastor to offer a prayer. This political wooing, they figured, must have been to court northern African Americans. Back in Texas the fuss seemed strange. "Republicans don't want them and the Democrats won't have them." Hardly any African Americans paid their poll taxes anyway, white critics charged.[33]

As the exposition came to an end that December, its organizers concluded that the effort had been a great success. Certainly it had been an effective means of advertising Texas to the world, they thought, and it had portrayed the state as a rising power. Of course eastern newspapers found the event lacking in cultural sophistication. As a writer for the *Washington Post* observed, the plum-colored pants and purple shirts were a bit much, and the heroes of San Jacinto would hardly have been honored by "imported gold diggers and champagne wastrels."[34] But such faults notwithstanding, all agreed that Texas had done itself proud.

There were indications that the exposition had accomplished some of its objectives toward improving race relations as well. More than four hundred thousand people toured the "Negro Life" exhibits. African American visitors who experienced discrimination and prejudice while attending saw examples of the progress that had been made since emancipation. Some of the white visitors found those accomplishments eye-opening as well. An example reported by an employee at the information desk of the "Hall of Negro Life" described a white woman from Corsicana who advanced a few feet into the hall and stood transfixed looking about her. "No, no, niggers did not do this," the woman exclaimed shaking her head. Another white woman was more gracious. "You are way ahead of white folk and there's no telling where you will go," she remarked. Said another, "Well, I'm just surprised and shocked. Why, if you were to give Negroes an equal chance, they would surpass white people."[35]

EXTRACTING VENGEANCE

The most startling contrast between the amicable race relations the Texas exposition sought to portray and the circumstances of real life was in the continuing recurrence of vengeance executed under the rule of what was euphemistically termed Judge Lynch. On Thursday, June 18, the day before the Juneteenth celebration in Dallas, a frenzied mob of three hundred at El Campo, a small town seventy-five miles southwest of Houston, attempted to capture and lynch five African American men and four African American women suspected of killing a deputy sheriff. Although no charges had yet been filed, law officers secretly removed the African Americans from the area for safekeeping while the mob searched from jail to jail and torched the building where the killing had occurred.[36]

Seven months earlier at Columbus, a town of two thousand some forty miles north of El Campo, Bennie Mitchell and Ernest Collins, ages fifteen and sixteen, were less fortunate. On November 12, 1935, a masked lynch mob seized them from the sheriff's custody and hanged them. The boys were said to be guilty of murdering a white girl and could not be executed legally because they were underage. The "citizens who meted out justice to the ravishing murderers," the county judge explained, were justified in taking the law into their own hands. I consider their "action an expression of the will of the people," he said. When the will of the people of Texas is expressed "with a handkerchief over its face," the *New York Times* editorialized, "that does not look much like a proud and sovereign will."[37]

A Tuskegee Institute investigation showed that eighteen African Americans and two whites were lynched in 1935. Thirteen were in the hands of the law at the time they were murdered. In addition, fifty-three attempted lynchings were thwarted.[38] The Southern Baptist Convention at its national meeting in 1936 expressed embarrassment that so many lynchings were in the South. "We Southern people," the Baptists observed, "rejoice that a larger percentage of our population professes Christianity and holds church membership than is true in any other section" and thus feel shamed "that mob violence holds larger away in our midst than in any other section."[39]

As Dallas boosters made final preparations for the Texas Centennial Exposition, proudly announcing that African American progress would be included, federal antilynching legislation was going nowhere in the U.S. Congress. A bill supported by the National Association for the Advancement of Colored People and proposed by Senators Edward P. Costigan of Colorado and Robert F. Wagner of New York that would have provided federal assistance in lynching cases similar to that provided in interstate kidnapping cases had been successfully filibustered under the leadership of Senator Tom Connally of Texas.[40] A new resolution proposed by Senators Frederick Van Nuys of Indiana, Arthur Capper of Kansas, and Charles L. McNary of Oregon to launch a senatorial investigation of the 1935 lynchings was being held up in the appropriations committee where a request for $7,500 to conduct the investigation was blocked. The committee chair, James F. Brynes of South Carolina, refused to call a meeting to consider the request.

In the House an antilynching measure first introduced by Representative Leonidas C. Dyer of Missouri in 1918 had been repeatedly filibustered and buried in the judiciary committee chaired by Hatton W. Sumners of Texas.[41] "As long as I am chairman of the committee I will never permit an antilynching bill to be reported out," Sumners declared. Sumners had risen to prominence through the support of Dallas's business leaders and in 1936 was serving his twenty-fourth year in Congress.[42] During the exposition his campaign championed his bid for reelection by touting his success in securing three million dollars from the federal government for the exposition and a government exhibit valued at an additional fifteen million dollars. His efforts had brought more than twenty-five federal agencies to Dallas, creating several thousand new jobs. Most of all, his campaign emphasized, he had "led the fight against the Dyer Anti-Lynching Bill."[43]

Neither Connally nor Sumners considered his opposition to antilynching legislation in any way indicating that they endorsed lynching or favored violence toward African Americans. Both framed the issue in constitutional terms as interference from the federal government in matters appropriately delegated to the states. There was even fear that federal intervention might stir racial animosity and provoke an increase in lynching. Nor were there religious considerations that might have persuaded them to oppose the antilynching bills. Sumners was a lifelong Methodist who attended the Munger Place Methodist Church in Dallas when he was not in the nation's capital. He was a progressive Protestant known for being tightfisted about personal and public spending but generous in supporting the YMCA, Southern Methodist University, and various charitable organizations.[44] Connally had joined his wife's Methodist church soon after they were married and early in his career had on one occasion unsuccessfully defended an African American accused of murder. During the heated 1928 senatorial race, when his opponent accused him of religious prejudice, he asserted that his staff included Catholics and Jews as well as Protestants.[45] "I go to church," he wrote in a letter that circulated in Texas pulpits in 1930, "to do reverence to the Deity and to the gentle Christ, and to receive spiritual and intellectual inspiration from sermons by preachers of moral character and mental attainments. I attend church to lend my aid to the commendable campaign which the church is making for the uplift and improvement of mankind."[46] That better law enforcement at the local level could handle the problem was also the view taken by religious leaders when they considered the issue, as the Southern Baptist Convention did in 1927, concluding with satisfaction that such violence "has almost disappeared."[47] Uplift, improvement, moral character, and law and order—these were the virtues that progressive religious leaders espoused. With little contact between white clergy and African American leaders, it was hard for religious convictions to impel concerted action to bring lynching to an end.

Over the years Texas followed the rest of the South in the frequency with which lynchings were carried out. Between 1882 and 1968, 493 persons were killed in Texas by lynch mobs. Of this number, 352 were African American and 141 were white Anglo or Hispanic. Only the numbers in Georgia and Mississippi exceeded the number killed in Texas. The worst decade was the 1890s, when 110 persons were lynched. The number fell to 90 in the following decade and then rose slightly to 93 during the 1910s. After that a significant reduction occurred with 47 lynchings in the 1920s, 12 in the 1930s, and 2 each in the 1940s and 1950s.[48]

Viewed this way, Texas was showing improvement in efforts to curb lynching by the time of the centennial exposition. However, in relation to the rest of the South, Texas was lagging behind. Data for ten other southern states in which a total of 2,805 lynchings occurred between 1882 and 1930 show that only 23 percent occurred between 1910 and 1930, whereas 40 percent of the lynchings in Texas happened in those decades.[49]

Not surprisingly, lynchings were heavily concentrated in East Texas, where the African American population was largest. The highest number of lynchings occurred in Grimes and Harrison Counties, where African Americans made up 46 percent and 64 percent of the population, respectively, in 1910. In eight counties in which blacks were a majority of the population, an average of ten persons per county were lynched between the 1880s and 1930s. That number compared with four per county in the forty-two counties in which blacks were between a quarter and half the total population, and approximately two per county in the forty-nine counties in which blacks were between 5 percent and a quarter of the population. Still, it was also the case that lynchings were fairly widely dispersed. In all, lynchings occurred in ninety-eight different counties, or approximately 40 percent of the state's counties. Forty-six people were lynched in counties in which less than 5 percent of the population was African American.[50]

It might have been presumed that the brutality involved would have deterred citizens in which a lynching had taken place from engaging in a similar activity a second time. But there were numerous instances in which lynching occurred in the same community on more than one occasion. Lynchings occurred in Harrison County on thirteen different occasions between 1897 and 1919. Ten different incidents took place in Grimes County between 1890 and 1920. Indeed, in the counties that had at least one lynching, more than half had more than one. Texarkana in Bowie County was an example. Although the lynching that occurred there in 1892 received wide publicity and condemnation, the community became the location of another lynching in 1922. As an African American was being transported by car on a misdemeanor charge, four masked men fired at the deputy sheriff who was driving, stopped the car, and seized the prisoner. Four hours later the dead body was found riddled with bullets on a country road.[51] Eager to distance itself from the event, the local Ku Klux Klan offered a reward for the killers, but a few nights later masked men in several cars fired shots into the home of the deputy sheriff.[52]

The relationship between lynchings and religion was complicated. On the one hand, the prevailing view among white clergy and church members who regarded themselves as good, law-abiding citizens was undoubtedly one that included shock, horror, and quiet expressions of disgust and disapproval. Lynching was in this view something that unruly mobs did only under extreme circumstances, such as when the authorities failed to act. On the other hand, lynchings reflected biblical assertions about extracting vengeance. They occurred in the context of real and imagined stories of white women being "outraged" by black predators and could easily be regarded as evidence that the world was filled with evildoers who were of constant danger to fine, upstanding churchgoers.

That lynching was carried out not only by mobs of drunken enraged marginal citizens who did not respect law and order was evident on May 15, 1916, when photographer Fred Gildersleeve captured the local gentry on film in Waco as they watched eighteen-year-old Jesse Washington being burned to death. Nearly all the men were sporting straw hats, and many wore jackets and ties. Had it not been a Monday, the crowd might have been coming from church. Years later the prominent Baptist preacher and writer J. M. Dawson, who was serving in Waco at the time, recalled seeing the mob "drag the terror-stricken Negro youth to the city hall square [and] toss him into the flames." Dawson saw them "heap the faggots about his tortured body" and watched as they "tied a rope around it to be hitched to the horn of a saddle for a so-called man to race with it hurtling on the ground to a creek bed in the country."[53]

None of the clergy in Waco spoke against the lynching, even though they claimed privately to have deplored it. When it was determined that the murdered man was probably innocent, a pastor told Dawson, "This must be despicable in the sight of God."[54] But Dawson concluded that the pastor said nothing publicly for fear of losing his job. The Presbyterian pastor later claimed that his church "lifted up its voice in protest" despite being advised that doing so would injure his reputation and the church.[55] If the Presbyterians lifted their voice, though, it was apparently too quiet to have had much of a local impact. For his part, Dawson "swore then on the altar of God I would henceforth forever fight lynching."[56] But it was years before lynching ended.

Had it not been for Gildersleeve's pictures and an account by a young suffragist named Elisabeth Freeman, the Waco lynching might have been forgotten entirely. But Freeman wrote up the incident and NAACP publications director DuBois printed it as a special eight-page supplement in *The Crisis*. The story described the fine businesses of Waco and noted that the town hosted thirty-nine white churches and twenty-four African American churches as well as Baylor University and several smaller academies and training schools. When Freeman asked the local judge what she should write, he said "the best thing was to forget it." The ex-mayor told her that "the better thinking men and women of Waco were not in it." She replied, "But some of your better men were down there. The whole thing savors so rotten because the better men have not tried to protest against it. Your churches have not said a word."[57]

Between 1918 and 1927, a total of 57 Texans became victims of lynching. Two were white, one was Hispanic, and all the rest were African American. Nationwide, 454 persons were lynched in this period. In *Rope and Faggot: A Biography of Judge Lynch*, NAACP writer Walter White observed that even though the number was lower than during the previous decade, the brutality involved was worse. Of the victims, 42 were burned alive, the bodies of 16 were burned after death, and 8 were beaten to death or cut to pieces. Three women were pregnant at the time they were lynched.[58]

RACIAL UPLIFT

Whatever they thought should be done about lynching, leaders on both sides of the racial divide recognized that racial tensions were a prevailing feature of social life. Hardly anyone believed it was possible for blacks and whites to interact as equals. The question was what if anything could or should be done. Schools, churches, and public facilities were segregated, but did that mean the races should go their separate ways or that one should help the other? Did white

Americans and perhaps especially white Christians have a responsibility to help erase racial inequality?

The joint appearance at the Texas exposition of the pastor of the nation's largest African American congregation with the pastor of the largest white Baptist congregation reflected one of the deeper realities of Texas religion and indeed of American religion more generally. Churches were racially segregated, but efforts were also being made to bridge that separation. "We work," a white Baptist leader responsible for outreach to African American churches observed in 1936, "in different groups, circles, or organizations," but "we ought to move as a common fellowship in a common cause." Understanding that white people had scant knowledge of African Americans, he nevertheless thought Baptists of both races could somehow find ways to cooperate. "What could we not do, as one mighty host of people of the common Baptist faith?"[59]

The growth of separate black congregations and denominations dated principally from the early 1870s when Reconstruction provided sufficient opportunities for autonomous leadership and African American church members took advantage of those opportunities. A separate state convention of African American Baptists called the Baptist Missionary and Educational Convention of Texas organized in 1874 and grew to more than a hundred thousand members over the next two decades. The African Methodist Episcopal Church formed a conference in 1875 and counted more than twenty thousand members by 1890. A Colored Methodist Episcopal Church organized around the same time, as well as the smaller African Methodist Episcopal Zion denomination. A few black Presbyterian, Cumberland Presbyterian, and Episcopal congregations also formed in the 1880s and 1890s. Catholic leaders organized black churches and schools at Galveston, San Antonio, and several other locations.[60]

Of the predominantly black churches, the ones that flourished most were Baptist. When Texas celebrated its centennial, more than 388,000 African Americans belonged to black Baptist churches. That number was larger than the membership of the predominately white Southern Baptists or the predominantly white southern Methodists. It accounted for approximately 90 percent of the membership of all black denominations statewide. The next largest was the Colored Methodist Episcopal Church with fewer than 32,000 members.[61]

The success of black Baptist churches reflected growth through natural increase among the families living in Texas and already attending those churches during Reconstruction. It stemmed from African American immigrants who were attending Baptist churches in other states. Baptist churches were also governed in ways that rewarded entrepreneurial leadership. A lay leader could become a preacher without having gone to seminary and had almost complete freedom in starting a new church, building its membership, and staying for an indefinite time. In addition, black Baptist leaders formed cooperative associations among local congregations, held regional conferences, and supported the founding of new churches, colleges, and seminaries.[62]

But if separate black churches were successful at attracting members, there were sharp differences from white churches not only in worship styles but also in the economic resources available to their ministries. The average black Baptist church was smaller by about fifty members than the average white Baptist church. The church buildings in which black Baptists worshipped cost on average only a quarter the amount of the buildings in which white Baptists worshipped. And the annual budget of a typical black Baptist church was only a third that of a typical white Baptist church. The resources with which other black denominations functioned were even smaller. Colored Methodist Episcopal congregations, for example, averaged half the size of white Methodist Episcopal congregations and worshipped in buildings averaging a sixth the cost.[63] As educational credentials for clergy became more important, there were also concerns that few African American pastors had more than rudimentary common school training.[64]

With approximately equal memberships and as two of the largest denominations in the state, white Baptists and black Baptists could hardly ignore one another. What the relationship should be, other than remaining separate, was seldom clear. With greater resources, white leaders considered whether they should help black churches or whether it was better to encourage autonomy. Black leaders faced questions about how to balance autonomy and opportunities for closer cooperation. Just as white Baptists did, black Baptists formed ladies' auxiliaries, organized their own associations, held statewide and national conventions, and trained Sunday school teachers.[65] By the start of World War I, black Baptists in Texas had organized an orphans home, a rescue mission for wayward girls, and industrial training schools in Houston and Fort Worth. Foreign mission work began in 1880 and by the 1930s was active in Liberia, Nigeria, and South Africa. A Sunday school publishing board formed in 1896, and a building to house the national operation was dedicated in Nashville at a cost of a million dollars in 1926. Other activities included a home mission board, a national training school for women and girls, a young people's organization, and a benefit board to assist retired clergy. Denomination-to-denomination cooperation with the Southern Baptist Convention occurred in several of these activities, most notably through the board of education organized in 1893 and the home mission board organized in 1895.[66] In 1915 the Southern Baptist Convention pledged $50,000 toward the establishment of a theological seminary for African Americans. The seminary opened in Nashville under control of the National Baptist Convention in 1924.[67]

As white religious leaders founded orphanages, hospitals, and other charitable institutions for the white population, they assisted in founding similar organizations for African Americans. One such organization was the Dickson Colored Orphanage, which opened in 1901 at Gilmore under the leadership of Dr. W. L. Dickson and in cooperation with R. C. Buckner, the Baptist leader who raised funds and helped organize a number of benevolent associations. Over the next decade the Dickson orphanage served more than eleven hundred children,

FIGURE 9. Orphans picking cotton, 1913, near Waxahachie, Texas. The boys were among the children at the Baptist Orphanage supported by the Baptist General Convention of Texas. Photograph by Lewis Wickes Hine. Library of Congress Prints and Photographs Division, Washington, DC.

providing them with industrial training, and placing them in "good Christian homes." In appealing for continuing support, Dickson emphasized the races' economic interdependence as well as the religious affinity between white and black Christians. African Americans, he said, had been true to their white friends, were equally opposed to scalawags and bums, and were Christians who "purely believe in the doctrine of one Lord, one faith and one baptism."[68]

An indication of the relative scale of white Baptists' involvement in African American activities is evident in annual reports of the Woman's Missionary Union, the arm of the Baptist General Convention of Texas to which local women's missionary societies reported. In 1930, 702 societies reported their activities, 546 had distributed food baskets and trays, and 362 had aided outside charities, but only 84 had done "work for Negroes." Among the additional 150 young women's associations, only 4 listed "work for Negroes."[69] The following year, despite financial difficulties from the Depression, the number of local societies increased modestly to 755, but the number of groups reporting "work for Negroes" grew only to 107. The largest change was in the total number of conversions reported, which climbed from 1,588 in 1930 to 2,349 in 1931.[70]

For the most part, white Baptist leaders in Texas presented themselves as beneficent supporters of black Baptist churches who in turn they described as friendly fellow believers. The Baptist General Convention of Texas routinely appropriated small amounts to assist the work of black Baptist associations. It was not uncommon for white preachers and seminary professors, for example, to speak at gatherings of African American clergy and at meetings of organizations such as black Baptist missionary and educational associations and the black Baptist Young People's Union Chautauqua. *Baptist Standard* editor J. H. Gambrell, who frequently spoke at these meetings, expressed a typical view in declaring that "the Negroes never had a better friend than this writer."[71] Friendship nevertheless meant extending a hand downward rather than in horizontal equal partnership. "Social equality between the races will never be tolerated in the South," Gambrell believed. And to the extent that racial tensions did exist, they were to be overcome with each side living closer to the Lord. "Eliminate politics and white and Negro politicians from the [Negro] problem," Gambrell observed, "and its solution will be found in righteousness."[72]

But eliminating politics was not the solution Baptist leaders always embraced. In 1909 the Fort Worth Baptist pastors association went on record unanimously endorsing a proposed law making it a felony for whites and blacks to marry.[73] The law added to a series of Jim Crow statutes that forbade sexual intercourse and cohabitation between blacks and whites, prohibited white males from entering the homes of black women, and allowed restaurants and public transportation companies to refuse service to African Americans.[74] That year ten lynchings occurred in Texas, more than in any states except Georgia and Mississippi.[75] Church leaders were duly concerned but felt little could be done. Years later a member of the First Methodist Church in Dallas recalled one of the incidents. The mob attacked an African American on trial for rape, pulled him from the courtroom, killed him, and hung his body from a light pole not far from the church. "Most people now think the victim," she said, "was innocent."[76]

What black religious leaders felt privately about their white counterparts or expressed quietly to their congregations was seldom recorded, but at public gatherings the message was one of encouragement for good behavior.[77] Clamoring for equal rights was no substitute for hard work. "The most miserable man on earth is the Negro who is always complaining and fussing with God because God made him black," Negro Baptist president Dr. L. L. Campbell told the state convention of his denomination in a 1914 address. The ideal was to be a good tenant. Communities with good tenants were less likely to have their chicken houses invaded and their hog pens molested. "Don't be so particular about your rights," he counseled. "I thank God that the Negro has always had sense enough to live in peace with his white neighbor."[78]

Living peaceably with white neighbors meant black pastors attending to their own churches, preaching, ministering to the sick, and encouraging the faithful. It frequently extended beyond the church itself to community-wide activities such as organizing farmers associations and promoting technical training schools.[79]

Just as among white believers, it involved revival meetings, such as the ones Reverend J. Gordon McPherson, the "Black Billy Sunday," conducted from Chicago to Texas and across the South, preaching the gospel, it was said, with a punch that made "hypocrites in the amen corners whine."[80] Living peaceably included participating as representatives of their race at meetings of white denominations. It also included public affirmations of support for policies of special interest to white churches. For example, during the 1911 campaign for prohibition, black clergy responded to a request for support by declaring, "We stand today on this question just where we stand each day in the year around in keeping with the word of God, and our church laws against the use of liquor by those composing our churches, and since we do not want the public to wonder about our position, we do most emphatically declare that we favor prohibition."[81]

For white southerners, providing assistance to black churches was a way of carrying the "white man's burden," an understanding that evolved with progressive ideas about racial uplift. It was a view that fit well with social Darwinism at the same time that fundamentalists were taking issue with Darwinian views of human evolution.[82] An earlier view espoused by defenders of the Bible emphasized the story of Noah, whose sons after the flood included Ham, who was black, cursed, and destined to struggle. As more detailed defenses against evolution emerged, the Ham story was elaborated with ideas supposedly drawn from philology and the history of human migration. C. L. Seasholes's argument about the Garden of Eden being at the North Pole, for example, included the notion that the three sons of Noah were named for the parts of the world they would occupy: Shem meant the nations of the East, Japheth meant the nations of the West, and Ham was another word for blackness, which referred to the nations of Africa.[83]

To the extent that evolution could be interpreted as a struggle in which the fittest survived, the triumph of Caucasians and especially of Anglo Saxons was something that white defenders of the Bible were increasingly able to regard as both biblical and empirical fact. Various articulations of this argument were already appearing by the early 1890s. In 1897, as part of Tennessee's centennial celebration, a prominent Texan was invited to speak in recognition of the many families in Tennessee with relatives in the Lone Star state. The lecture was delivered by Joe H. Eagle, an aspiring twenty-seven year-old lawyer from Houston who had previously taught and served as a school superintendent and would later own a realty company and be elected to the United States House of Representatives.[84] Eagle's remarks focused on four fundamental beliefs uniting all southerners: liberty, fraternity, progress, and Anglo-Saxon supremacy. It was plainly evident, he argued, that in each area social evolution in the sense of improvement toward greater realization of southern ideals could be seen. "Side by side the two races work [and] share alike the rewards of labor, the negro's capacity alone being the limit of his exertion and power." Progress might be taking place among the inferior race, but "the negro can never rule in the south." The reason could be found in the basic principles of evolution.

> The time has not come when [the negro] can stand the equal, morally and intellectu-
> ally, of the Anglo-Saxon race, the strongest race in history; and it is a maxim old and
> true as human history that the strong shall rule the weak. The evolution of men in the
> progress of the race is based upon that eternal law. It is the one hope of the progress
> of mankind. Emerging from the night of darkness, the race has come to the faint
> light that ushers in the glorious day of its own full growth.[85]

The distinct relationship of the superior and inferior race was the white man's burden, Eagle believed. "Especially do our conditions at the south demand [attention] to the logic of evolution where two races touch, alien in instinct, history, capacity; and here must the intelligence, the strength and the virtue of the white race lend its light to making clear the way down which the negro race shall travel through the long night of its ignorance and weakness to the breaking of the day."[86]

At a well-attended meeting of African American pastors in conjunction with the state fair at Dallas three years later, Booker T. Washington took up the theme of race and evolution. His theme was similar to Eagle's in acknowledging that African American progress had far to go, but the emphasis was more clearly on self-help. With a reminder that the responsibility of white Americans toward African Americans was a "sacred obligation," Washington counseled his African American audience that recognition and political inclusion would come "through no process of artificial forcing, but through the natural law of evolution." It was necessary, he believed, to pay the price, working up gradually and naturally toward civilization. Religion and morality would remain the foundation but would be elevated by education and industry.[87]

Two years later Washington used the same words in addressing a crowd of prominent African Americans in Houston. It was again the "natural law of evolution" that underlay African American progress. Washington emphasized, as he did in all of his work, the value of better education and especially of industrial training. White responsibility was to help but more importantly not to condemn or stand in the way. For African Americans the Christian gospel, he urged, was to turn the other cheek, rendering kindness in response to injustice. "You may call this cowardice," he said, but "if so, it is the kind of cowardice that Christ taught and practiced, and it is the kind of cowardice that in the long run will win our cause."[88]

White religious leaders agreed that African Americans were making progress but used rather different language from Washington's. At the Baptist General Convention of Texas meeting in 1906, the association's Committee on Negro Population reported that African Americans had "high animal propensities" and a superstitious nature that reflected their proximity to the jungle. As African Americans progressed, the committee predicted, they would seek equality to which whites would understandably resist because "never before was the Saxon more determined to dominate." The best solution for keeping blacks in their place, the committee recommended, was to make allies of black pastors.[89] There was no questioning that whites were the superior race, but for white Christians that also implied a kind of paternalistic responsibility. As one pastor observed, "degenerate and immoral" blacks were "a trust committed to us [whites] by God."[90] It was on these terms that African American religious leaders learned to relate to their white counterparts. As an African American women's missionary leader put it in appealing for help to a gathering of white women, "What will it profit you if you spend a million to save souls and let a race that is next to your door go unsaved. I appeal to you for a race that is rough and uncouth but whose souls must be saved."[91]

In 1910 the Juneteenth address in Houston was delivered by Washington's secretary, Emmett J. Scott, a Houston native who was serving on a government commission to investigate conditions in Liberia and who would go on to write an important book about African Americans' role as soldiers in World War I. Like Washington, Scott emphasized the value of better educational opportunities, especially through industrial and technical schools, and the need for "cordial support and help and encouragement of southern white" people. He regarded these as the resources needed for social and moral uplift. He also appealed to the common faith shared by blacks and whites. "In the working out of the intricate problems of self-government," he said, "may all the people of the south, white and black, receive from the God of men and nations a new baptism of faith, may they under his guidance rise superior to the past with its misunderstandings which so long have retarded the progress of both races."[92]

History would prove Washington and Scott correct in believing that education was a key ingredient in racial uplift. It was also correct that progress was slow and would remain so. It would indeed take a new baptism of faith for the racial divisions grounded in the old baptism to be uprooted. That was especially apparent in the 1920s when racist organizations gained new prominence and as white supremacy and mob violence continued.

FIGHTING THE KU KLUX KLAN

A factor in southern politics during Reconstruction, the Ku Klux Klan emerged with new vitality and on a national scale in the early 1920s. In addition to its previous emphasis on white supremacy, it drew on a rising tide of nativism responding to immigration as well as to the Americanism fueled by World War I. At well-attended rallies, Klan leaders argued variously that Anglo Saxon purity was being compromised by foreign languages and customs, that lawlessness and immorality were on the rise as a result of the war and urban growth, and that Bolsheviks, communists, and the Japanese were drawing African Americans into

Fifth Column activities. In Texas Klan activity reached a crescendo in the 1922 Democratic primary campaign for the U.S. Senate between ex-governor James E. Ferguson and former state senator and railroad commissioner Earle B. Mayfield. Ferguson was a controversial figure who had opposed Prohibition during his tenure as governor, was indicted for misapplication of public funds, and was removed from office in 1917.[93] Mayfield gained the support of religious leaders who favored Prohibition. He also attracted Klan leaders who organized large rallies on his behalf. With an estimated 100,000 to 150,000 members, the Klan helped Mayfield win the election and secured control of city governments in Dallas, Fort Worth, and Wichita Falls as well as a majority of the state's House of Representatives. Nationwide, Klan membership grew to an estimated four million by 1925. Its influence in Texas continued through the 1928 presidential campaign, but on a much-reduced scale.[94]

On April 2, 1921, an African American named Alexander Johnson, who worked as a bellhop at a Dallas hotel, was seized from his home after midnight by fifteen masked Klan members who took him to a remote spot, threatened to hang him until they evoked a forced confession about insulting a white woman, flogged him, and burned a KKK on his forehead with silver nitrate. To ensure that the incident terrorized the African American community, the Klan notified reporters that something interesting was going to happen, blindfolded them, and took them to witness the violence being perpetrated on Johnson.[95] When the incident was publicized, the Dallas sheriff announced that no investigation would be conducted. "The men who attacked [Johnson] were good citizens," he declared. "I am satisfied with their treatment of him. He no doubt deserved it." A local judge agreed. "Maybe it will be a lesson," he said.[96] Several weeks later, apparently feeling that the lesson was insufficient, Klan members nailed thousands of red and white posters to telegraph poles and advertising boards proclaiming, "Lawbreakers to reform or leave town."[97]

Over the next six months, Klan threats and violence spread across the state. In San Antonio *La Prensa* reported Klan intimidation of the city's Mexican American population. Responding to Klan pressure, white shopkeepers in South Texas towns posted signs stating "No Mexicans Allowed." In an incident similar to the one in Dallas, an African American bellboy in Marshall was seized and mutilated. Hotels in Texarkana received warnings to "get rid of all" African American porters. An African American in Belton was kidnapped, flogged, and returned with a placard on his back, "Whipped by the Ku Klux Klan." Near the county courthouse in Austin, Klan members posted signs stating that the Klan adhered to "the tenets of the Christian religion" and thus felt it necessary to warn against miscegenation, half-breeds, pimps, bootleggers, agitators, and lewd women. "One hundred per cent Americanism must prevail," the signs declared. Residents of an African American neighborhood in Fort Worth received Klan letters warning them to leave town or be horsewhipped, tarred, and feathered.[98]

By early fall, threatening placards were being posted in African American neighborhoods and large Klan parades were being held in smaller towns, such as Bastrop, Groesbeck, Mexia, and Nacogdoches, often to cheers from hundreds of white residents. On October 11, 1921, witnesses at a hearing in Washington, DC, convened by the U.S. House of Representatives testified that Texas towns were almost completely under Klan control. Another witness, though, said that was just fine. In tough towns where "no school girl or lady is safe," he said, it took only one "visit" from the Klan to make the town "almost a Sunday school class."[99]

The Klan posed an interesting difficulty for community leaders who opposed its tactics and believed that what it was doing was wrong and yet were reluctant to go very far in condemning the underlying sentiments on which Klan activism was based. The challenge was to find a specific language in which to levy condemnation while embracing assumptions about racial differences that were as yet seldom questioned. An interesting example occurred on the evening of Tuesday April 4, 1922, when five thousand residents gathered in and around the Dallas City Hall to organize the Dallas County Citizens League in opposition to the Klan. Among the speakers were former governor O. B. Colquitt and Baptist prohibition advocate Cranfill. Colquitt appealed to the crowd's sense of history. The Klan was like the lawless radicals who had menaced good citizens during the state's founding decades, he argued. If there was fear, perhaps from racial mixing, though it was unnecessary to mention that by name, it was the constitution rather than hooded intimidation that would ensure "that our liberty remains unpolluted." Cranfill used his credentials as a religious leader to strike an inclusive note, arguing that as a Baptist he would "give every drop of my blood to protect the liberties of all Catholics here" and declaring that some of his friends were Klan members. He deplored Klan violence but conceded that he too was a white supremacist. "I am for white supremacy," he said, "but I want that white supremacy to be really white. We are a superior race, let us do it by deeds of charity and kindness and we will have no trouble with the Negro."[100]

Opposition to the Klan was complicated by religion. Protestants who belonged to or otherwise favored the Klan considered the organization an ally in promoting Prohibition and protecting their communities against Catholics. Under the banner of protecting state government from Catholic influence, a Baptist pastor from Georgia explained to a packed auditorium in Fort Worth that the Klan was their best hope. More than sixty masked Klan members and an Episcopal rector who declared his membership in the organization joined the pastor on stage.[101] In the Mayfield-Ferguson contest, prominent clergy such as Hubert Knickerbocker of Wichita Falls and A. C. Parker of Dallas supported Mayfield because Ferguson was against Prohibition, but in the process they also defended the Klan. For its part, the Klan sought to identify itself with religious pluralism by inviting Protestant, Catholic, and Jewish clergy to join, but it also cultivated religious divisions, emphasizing distinctions between Catholics and Protestants and noting that Catholic leaders favored Ferguson.[102] At a well-attended meeting in Waco in

1922, for example, an office-seeker who openly favored the Klan argued that he was not anti-Catholic but considered the Catholic Church a menace and believed the Klan, in contrast, was "bringing more boys directly and more girls indirectly into Protestant churches than any other organization in the world."[103]

Robed Klan members frequently entered churches during Sunday morning or evening worship services and either silently put an offering in the collection plate or made a brief statement from the pulpit, sometimes earning the pastor's endorsement in reply. In one incident worshippers attending an evening service at the Birdville Baptist Church were greeted by four Klansmen who complimented the pastor on his fine work in the neighborhood and gave him a bouquet, after which the pastor declared, "I am, both as a citizen and a minister of the gospel, a friend of the Klan and I stand for everything that it stands for without any reservations."[104] At a Christian Church in Fort Worth, a $50 donation to the congregation's poor relief fund was followed by an appeal by the pastor to support the Klan in its efforts to promote Americanism, better homes, better citizens, better public officers, and better law enforcement."[105]

Pastors who supported the Klan did not have to mention white supremacy specifically to convey ideas with racial implications. "Stemming the tide of lawlessness and immorality" was an argument that could refer to troubles caused by blacks and whites alike but was most likely to resonate with white audiences' concerns about African Americans.[106] This argument denied that the Klan itself might be engaged in lawlessness. Law-abiding church members could in good conscience be members of the Klan. Nativist appeals carried similar implications. Protecting Anglo-Saxon culture implied keeping it pure of both African American and foreign influences. "The Knights of the Ku Klux Klan is an institution God founded in the Southland of America and called out by God to do the work the church hasn't done," a Presbyterian pastor from West Virginia explained to a large crowd in Dallas. "When the Ku Klux Klan gets the right kind of men in office," he said, "there will be no more newspapers published in this country except pure Anglo Saxon unadulterated English."[107]

An informal estimate suggested that half the clergy in Texas supported the Klan in 1922. Those who opposed it seldom did so on grounds that it was a racist organization with a history of particular intimidation against African Americans. Opponents characteristically conceded that law enforcement needed to be improved and that patriotism promoted by the Klan was laudable. Their criticism stressed the Klan's illegal activities that were sometimes directed against innocent victims. Reverend William N. Ainsworth, a bishop of the Methodist Episcopal Church South in Texas, expressed the idea well in asserting that "hearsay, whim, caprice" and prejudice had wreaked "vengeance upon innocent people again and again." It was his strong view that civilization rests on law and that "unauthorized bands of men" who took the law into their own hands were uncivilized no matter how laudable the principles they claimed to defend were.[108]

There was a practical concern as well. As the Klan's influence increased, religious leaders saw it as a potential threat to their own authority. Ainsworth, for example, observed that Klan rituals were beginning to interfere with church customs in performing funeral services, and he warned that taking charitable gifts from the Klan would further compromise the church's authority. "It will not be long before masked men will assume to dictate to the pulpit what it shall preach," he cautioned, "and threaten to run men from their pulpits who refuse to do their way."[109]

What black pastors thought of the Klan was not hard to imagine, although fear of intimidation made quiet condemnation more likely than open opposition. One of the few who publicly supported the Klan was Reverend McPherson, the evangelist known as the Black Billy Sunday. Cautioning audiences that they had nothing to fear as long as they were law abiding, he praised the Klan for its role in upholding law and order.[110] In other churches Klan visits sometimes ensured that a similar message came through. At an African American revival in Wichita Falls, twenty-five robed and hooded representatives showed up to emphasize that "good black men" have nothing to fear from the Klan.[111] A similar event occurred at an African American church in Vernon where a band of hooded visitors emphasized the importance of keeping the races separate.[112] The message at a predominantly African American Catholic Church in Beaumont was more pointed: the Klan threatened to dynamite the church and its school and tar and feather the pastor.[113]

STIFLING THE BLACK VOTE

The ambivalence white Texans exhibited toward African Americans—celebrating black progress on the one hand and condoning the Ku Klux Klan on the other hand—manifested itself less ambiguously when it came to voting. White residents did everything they could to disfranchise African Americans. That was as true in 1936 as it had been thirty years earlier, and it would be another three decades before much changed. It was fine to talk about progress as long as that did not mean equality as enfranchised citizens.

Other than raw intimidation, the weapon of choice in stifling the black vote was the poll tax. The Florida legislature implemented one in 1889, Mississippi and Tennessee followed a year later, and over the next decade similar measures became law in Arkansas, South Carolina, Louisiana, North Carolina, Alabama, and Virginia.[114] By popular referendum in which two-thirds of the electorate voted favorably, Texas put the poll tax into effect in 1902. The tax was a payment of $1.50 to $1.75 that any eligible male age twenty-one and over had to pay and show proof of having paid in order to actually vote. Nothing explicit about it discriminated against African Americans. The tax simply made it less likely that anyone earning a subsistence income would vote. Even though in retrospect the amount seemed small, it was at the time equal to as much as a week's income for a poor family—even more in years when subsistence farmers suffered crop failures.[115] It was the equivalent a century later of asking a poor family to pay a fee to vote of about $500. No sooner had the poll tax gone into effect than the voter turnout rate in Texas—as it did across the South—plummeted.[116]

Public discussions at the time it was established acknowledged that its intent was to deter African American voting but usually argued that its main purpose was to reduce fraud and help the schools. On the surface, the fraud reduction argument resembled arguments in colonial America about limiting the franchise to property owners. They presumably were stable patriotic citizens who had more of a stake in electoral outcomes than their less established neighbors. "We are only doing what the people of Connecticut and other New England states did years ago," Senator Joseph W. Bailey of Texas explained, while acknowledging, "The white people of the south propose to rule themselves and not to be ruled by their former servants."[117] But if showing a paid poll tax receipt was meant to reduce fraud, it left open the door for a wealthy employer or landowner to pay the poll tax for poor neighbors who promised to vote for a particular candidate.[118] Helping the schools was the more popular argument because two-thirds of the poll tax revenue went toward funding public schools.[119] Otherwise schools would be unable to function, the argument went. Despite the fine schools Texas promised prospective immigrants in the 1870s, and despite the ample public lands the state had available to pay for better schools, per capita spending on education in Texas was still far below the national average and not much better than in the rest of the South. Southern resistance to state and local property taxes that stemmed from antebellum reluctance to pay taxes on property when property included slaves was one of the principal reasons that revenue to pay for education was unavailable.[120]

As soon as the poll tax went into effect, observers noticed that relatively few African Americans were paying it. Besides the obvious fact that people with meager incomes might find it hard to pay, white leaders gave three reasons when the matter came up for discussion: African Americans were so lazy they probably just never got around to it, they may have meant to pay it but were generally forgetful or irresponsible, and they were not patriotic enough to pay it. When framed charitably, the first two were explained on grounds that African Americans simply were not yet ready for the franchise any more than a child might be.[121] The other reason may actually have included some truth, not in terms of patriotism as such but in recognizing that the poll tax was of less value to someone whose vote counted for little anyway in actually shaping an election's results.

Critics of the poll tax, from its inception until it was eventually declared unconstitutional in federal elections in 1964 and in state elections two years later, argued that it was indeed meant to discriminate and served that purpose well.[122] At the time it was difficult to tell for sure if that was the case and if it was, to what extent. The turnout rate in the 1904 presidential election was lower than in

1900, but that could have been caused by any number of factors, including the possibility that the candidates were different and the contest may have generated less interest. Exactly how much the vote was being suppressed was impossible to determine in the absence of records showing how many people of different races and income groups went to the polls.

However, a rough estimate can be made by comparing the turnout in the 1900 presidential election before the poll tax went into effect with the turnout in the 1904 presidential election after the tax went into effect, and for each election comparing counties with larger or smaller percentages of African Americans and larger or smaller percentages of illiterate white males—the other relevant item recorded in the 1900 U.S. Census. In 1900 the correlation between percent African American and voter turnout was −0.242, meaning that turnout in counties with higher proportions of African Americans was already lower than in other counties before the poll tax went into effect. But that negative correlation increased to −0.341 in 1904, suggesting that the poll tax did have an additional suppressive effect. In 1900 there was not a statistically significant correlation between percent white male illiteracy and voter turnout, but in 1904 there was a significant negative relationship of −0.265, again suggesting the suppressive effect of the poll tax.

Another way of estimating the effects produces similar results. Overall the contest in 1900 between Bryan and McKinley produced almost 424,000 voters, whereas the election four years later between Alton Parker and Theodore Roosevelt generated a significantly lower turnout of only 234,000 voters. But taking that difference into account by controlling for the earlier turnout, the percent of African Americans and the percent of illiterate white males both had an additional negative impact on the 1904 turnout. The relationship between race and turnout was particularly notable. In counties with all white or nearly all white populations, turnout in 1904 was only about 10 percentage points lower in 1904 than in 1900, whereas in counties with populations that were at least 20 percent African American, the turnout rate fell from 63 percent in 1900 to 39 percent in 1904.[123]

In the 1910 gubernatorial election a partly similar pattern was evident. The county-level correlation between the percentage of eligible voters actually voting and the percentage of eligible voters who were African American was −0.386. Unlike in the earlier election, however, there was not a significant relationship between voter turnout and the percent of illiterate white males. The 1911 election, in which the principal issue was the referendum about prohibition, provided a further exception to the previous pattern. In that campaign African American clergy worked closely with white church leaders in organizing a statewide black prohibition association and encouraging African Americans to pay the poll tax. Clergy argued that prohibition would "lessen the occasion for race riots and the perpetration of crimes against innocent womanhood, which are often the source of lynchings" and would "build up the negro race morally, educationally and religiously." To avoid accusations of fraud, prohibition advocates further argued

that African Americans should not allow anyone to pay the poll tax for them.
"When the election day comes, go to the polls like a patriotic citizen and vote
for our country, our homes and our God."[124] Counties with higher percentages
of illiterate white males of voting age had lower percentages paying the poll tax
and a lower turnout rate. But neither was affected by the percentage of African
American males of voting age. The increase in total votes cast in 1911 over the
number cast in 1910 was in fact positively correlated with the percentage of eligible African Americans.[125]

In addition to whatever suppressive effects the poll tax may have had, African
Americans were effectively disfranchised by the practice in Texas and throughout the South of holding primaries in which only whites were permitted to vote.
When primary elections replaced closed conventions as the vehicle for selecting
candidates, the practice of limiting primaries to white voters was formalized in
legislation passed in 1903 and revised in 1911.[126] Then in 1921 an African American in El Paso who had been denied the right to vote in a Democratic primary
sued the state, and in 1924 a series of appeals reached the U.S. Supreme Court,
which dismissed the complaint because it pertained only to an election now long
in the past.[127] Meanwhile Texas passed legislation in 1923 barring African Americans from participating in any primary election. The NAACP brought suit against
this legislation and in 1927 won a unanimous decision from the U.S. Supreme
Court. Justice Oliver Wendell Holmes wrote, "It seems to us hard to imagine a
more direct and obvious infringement of the Fourteenth Amendment."[128] African
American newspapers around the country hailed the NAACP's victory and predicted that African Americans would now swarm to the polls in large numbers.
Texas, however, passed a new law that said in effect that if states could not legally
bar African Americans from voting in primaries, the Democratic Party could.[129]
The Texas legislators reasoned that primaries were actually activities organized
by political parties rather than by the state, and that no court could tell a political
party what it could or could not do. Under this new procedure, the Texas Democratic Party barred African Americans from voting in primaries until 1944, when
the procedure was finally ruled unconstitutional.

Although the various laws under which white primaries were held underwent
revision as a result of legal challenges themselves, several other considerations
were involved as well. One was the fear among white voters that African Americans sympathized with Republicans, as they had done during Reconstruction,
and that if permitted to vote in primary elections would opt for the Democratic
candidate least likely to win against a Republican in the general election. This was
a minor consideration because Democratic candidates generally won by margins of 75–80 percent in statewide elections. However, in the 1900 gubernatorial contest the Democratic candidate won by only 67 percent, and in 1920 the
margin fell to 60 percent, hitting a low of 59 percent in 1924, which was enough
to stir some fears about the possible effect of an enfranchised black electorate.[130]
In eastern parts of the state with large African American populations, candidates

in local elections were also at risk.[131] More to the point were uncertainties in the primary elections themselves owing to closely contested elections among Democratic contenders. During the 1920s, runoff elections occurred in 1920 and again in 1924 and 1926.[132] The desire among white citizens to protect white primaries was also fueled by fears driven by the war, talk of Bolshevik conspiracies among African Americans, and the resurgence of the Ku Klux Klan.

African American clergy and women's groups in black churches encouraged church members to pay the poll tax and vote in general elections.[133] But white religious leaders played a minimal role in public debates about the poll tax and white primaries. On the one hand, this was not surprising in view of the general sense among religious leaders that church and state should be separate. On the other hand, the fact that clergy became as involved as they did in Prohibition, in championing or opposing candidates in primary elections because of concerns about Prohibition or its repeal, and in debating Smith's religious qualifications in 1928 would have made it possible for religious leaders to become more involved in discussions about the poll tax and white primaries than they did. Had religious leaders been as intent on helping African Americans improve, as they often said they were, they might have considered equality at the polls an important issue as well.

On one issue having to do with primary and general elections religious leaders did become involved. In 1915 an amendment to the Texas constitution was proposed that would have allowed men traveling on business to vote at a location other than in their hometown or county. The idea was roundly condemned by religious leaders who were promoting prohibition and dry local option laws as well as by public officials. They opposed the measure on grounds that it would open the door to fraud and political corruption and "readmit the negro into politics."[134]

Although there may have been little reason to think African Americans could significantly influence elections in Texas, white leaders worried that African Americans were having undue influence in national politics. That concern surfaced less often as something that Texans could do anything about than as a kind of rhetorical plea for white voters to do the right thing. Clergy who represented majority white religious organizations were not above making such arguments. During the 1928 campaign against Smith, leaders in Texas branded him not only as a person who consumed large quantities of liquor and followed the pope but also as someone who could not be trusted because of Tammany Hall and its treacherous behind-the-scenes influence over various categories of dark-skinned Americans. The two groups at issue were southern Europeans and African Americans. "Tammany wants its brothers and sisters of Southern Europe to gain admittance to this country," Trinity University's Dr. John Harmon Burma declared at an anti-Smith rally in Dallas, adding, "The ignorant negro, it appears, is to be the instrument of Tammany nationally, as ignorant foreigners have served for Tammany in New York."[135]

Apart from direct involvement from clergy, religion did play an indirect role in maintaining the poll tax and white primaries. It did so partly by diverting attention from the disfranchisement of African Americans. The main diversion was Prohibition. In working for Prohibition, clergy and lay groups such as the WCTU focused on candidates who supported it and increasingly on the added support that would come from women's suffrage, but they saw little reason to help African Americans vote. Although Prohibition encouraged clergy to speak about politics, it also generated enough controversy that some clergy may have been deterred from speaking. The 1924 gubernatorial election was especially contentious in this regard.[136] A more direct deterrent to clergy saying much on behalf of African American enfranchisement was the Klan's influence in 1922. Knowing that some prominent clergy were Klan leaders themselves, and knowing that many church members were Klan followers, clergy arguing in favor of African American enfranchisement would have felt themselves at risk.[137]

Religion may also have figured implicitly in arguments favoring white primaries. Proponents of white primaries argued that the Democratic Party was like any other nongovernmental organization in having the right to choose its own leaders. It was no different, proponents said, from a religious body such as the Baptist denomination or the Methodists—an analogy meant to inspire confidence and lead away from thoughts about machine politics and the pursuit of self-interest. In an engaging essay educator and journalist Clarence Ousley argued that the primary system should encourage public service in the same way as a church. "The members of a church choose deacons or stewards who represent the membership in the execution of church policies," he observed, explaining that these leaders then act on behalf of the membership "under recognized rules of trust" rather than for personal ambition.[138] Political parties were no different, he thought, also serving their members. What did not have to be stated explicitly was that the religious organizations in mind were segregated white organizations.

ANTILYNCHING ADVOCACY

On May 13, 1907, the second triennial convention of Southern Congregationalists, meeting at the Central Congregational Church in Dallas, devoted the day to discussing the "Negro problem." Since 1890, 169 persons had been lynched in Texas. All but twelve were African American. Over the next three decades, 183 more lynchings would occur in Texas. No mention was made of this aspect of the "Negro problem" at the Congregationalists' meeting.[139]

Yet by 1936 the number of lynchings had fallen dramatically, failing to exceed two in any year during the preceding decade. Public opinion appeared increasingly to have turned from blood lust to abhorrence. A strong grassroots movement against mob violence had somehow taken root at least sufficiently to result in more frequent public condemnations as well as some actual ameliorative proposals. Across the South, the movement enlisted support in more than a thousand counties and in nearly three thousand towns.[140]

What had happened? For someone who might have found lynching abhor-
rent, the circumstances for doing something about it were not at all encouraging.
If the state's elected officials in Washington were any indication, the possibility of mobilizing efforts for better legislation through the political process was
slim. African Americans were largely disfranchised. Schools and civic organizations were segregated. Churches were nearly always separated into houses of
worship that kept whites and blacks from ever worshipping with one another.
White churches seemed intent on tackling racial problems in quieter ways than
addressing lynching.

The Congregationalists' meeting was forward looking in addressing racial issues at all and yet reflected common assumptions about these issues. Leaders
from several southern denominations spoke that day. One emphasized "what
the Negro has done for himself." Another blamed well-meaning northerners for
sowing seeds of racial discord. A preacher from Austin observed, "The effects
of twenty centuries of jungle life yield slowly to the grace of God." It fell to the
only African American speaker to mention the need for interracial cooperation.
He alluded to lynching as well but did not refer to it directly. Arguing that any
crime committed by a black person should be punished, he noted that the person
should be "punished according to law."[141]

Although church groups continued from time to time to invite guest speakers
to discuss race relations, a decade passed before any sustained advocacy for interracial cooperation and against lynching developed. Those efforts benefited from
the goodwill of pastors and church members but emerged largely without the
direct involvement of denominations and congregations. At a time when Texas
was increasingly positioning itself as part of the American Southwest and attracting immigrants and businesses from the North, it was through its traditional ties
to the South that a network of leadership was organized.

One of the key organizations through which this leadership network developed was the Southern Sociological Congress, which received funding from liberal Nashville Methodist railroad and banking heiress Anna Russell Cole and
held annual conferences from 1912 to 1920 in southern cities, including a 1915
meeting in Houston.[142] At its inaugural conference in Nashville, convened by
Tennessee governor Ben W. Hooper, more than seven hundred delegates met to
consider practical ways of improving "social, civic, and economic conditions in
the South." The "race question" was one of a long list of topics discussed, ranging
from prison reform and care for the feeble-minded, to alcoholism and vice, to
marriage and divorce, to child labor and school attendance, to closer cooperation
between churches and social agencies. The meeting's speakers and officers included scholars, social workers, heads of benevolent associations, public officials,
and clergy. University of Texas law professor C. S. Potts was an elected member
of the organization's executive committee.[143]

Several of the lectures at the 1912 meeting touched on the question of how
to deter lynching. Vanderbilt sociology professor G. W. Dyer, for example,

mentioned it in passing in a larger discussion of crime, and Wilbur F. Crafts, a pastor from Washington, DC, praised the South for its condemnation of lynching.[144] The following year at the congress's meeting in Atlanta, YMCA leader W. D. Weatherford from Nashville drew a more specific connection between lynching and the church's potential for leadership in combating it. Talking about it was not enough, he said. A "great crusade" should be launched against this "horrible cancer that eats at the heart of our civilization." It was high time for white churches to awaken to this responsibility, he felt, because only the church could truly cultivate human respect and an appreciation for the sacredness of all persons.[145]

Hope that the churches would indeed lead a great crusade against lynching may have been inspired at the same meeting by Dr. Arthur J. Barton, Anti-Saloon League director and civic righteousness committee chair of the Baptist General Convention of Texas, who spoke at length about the special responsibility of white church members of means. "Our millions have come to us largely through the negro's toil," he confessed, adding that it was thus incumbent to recognize that debt. Yet Barton's lecture conveyed indications that a church-led crusade against lynching was unlikely. Detailing his antebellum southern lineage, Barton distinguished "first-class white folk" like himself and his audience who held "genuine affection for the negroes" from "white trash." By implication, only the latter were responsible when "the mob spirit is aroused" and someone's "body is riddled with bullets or he is burned in the city square." For the most part, law officers and judges were doing their job, Barton believed, and white taxpayers were contributing millions toward "negro education." The church's role was to preach the Christian gospel, help the weak, encourage the "negro ministry," and "visit the negro congregations and preach to them."[146]

This view of the churches' role was widely shared among progressive church leaders. In recognition of stark racial inequality, the special role of the church was to encourage uplift among African Americans through charitable giving and support of African American churches and schools. The church's more general contribution was to preach the gospel and thus encourage good citizenship, kindness, and respect for law and order. These ideas were by no means incompatible with condemning mob violence; if anything, it was merely taken for granted that lynching was not something civilized, first-class white folk would condone. Specific arguments against lynching followed accordingly.

Opponents of lynching attacked it on grounds that would appeal to better-educated members of the white middle class intent on distancing themselves from the lower class and identifying themselves with up-to-date, civilized ways of life. A speaker at one of the Southern Sociological Congress meetings, for example, argued that "something closely akin to the methods of Judge Lynch" may have been useful in frontier communities to prevent anarchy but was no longer appropriate in modern communities with better laws and an organized government. The only reason it continued, he said, was that "self-seeking politicians" were misleading a "certain class of voters."[147] Newspaper accounts in which the barbarity perpetrated on victims of mob violence was described in gruesome detail facilitated the argument that this was not the kind of behavior that people claiming to be civilized should condone.

Antilynching advocates further argued that mob violence did not deter crime. Lacking systematic evidence about crime, speakers at community gatherings relied on anecdotes about assaults and robberies appearing to increase rather than decrease following particular instances of lynching. Whether those anecdotes were convincing was hard to say, but they reinforced the prevailing idea that law and order was preferable to a culture of sporadic violence. A related argument against lynching was that it neither upheld the honor of white women nor protected them from assault. Although accounts of lynchings frequently claimed that the person lynched had assaulted a white woman, it was harder to infer if deep-seated ideas of southern chivalry were at work or whether a raw thirst for vengeance was operative. It helped that white southern women became increasingly vocal in opposing lynching. It also helped as evidence was collected showing that only a small fraction of lynchings actually involved alleged crimes against women.

Less common than may have been expected were arguments about innocent victims being lynched or lynchings occurring as a result of racial prejudice and discrimination. White audiences were apparently more likely to be moved by arguments that lynching was, if anything, harmful to their own interests. News of mob violence in a community, antilynching advocates said, could dampen business and deter immigration. It could signal that local sheriffs and judges were not in charge and possibly encourage voters to remove them from office. In the worst scenarios, unchecked violence could result in intervention from the state, higher courts, northern do-gooders, or even the federal government.

Specific efforts to organize a concerted campaign against lynching in Texas emerged around the same time as the Southern Sociological Congress and enlisted leaders from similar kinds of institutions, including colleges, benevolent associations, and civic groups. The 1915 meeting in Houston, which focused on health, was presided over by Baylor president Samuel P. Brooks. Its organizing committee made a special appeal to pastors in the city to publicize the event and invite church members to participate. A few months after the meeting, Brooks enlisted Southwestern University president Charles M. Bishop to organize an antilynching conference in Waco. Bishop expressed hope that college presidents across the state would join in launching a campaign against lynching. It was an obligation to society, he argued, and "to the cause of Christianity to do some effective thing to stop this growth of general outlawry." He felt it important too to do something to combat the contemptible "self-righteous attitude and ignorance" of northern writers critical of the South.[148] Within a few days of the meeting, five hundred students joined the effort.[149] Besides their own leadership, the college presidents at the meeting saw the Southern Sociological Congress as an additional vehicle for combating mob violence.[150] At its meeting the following year, Bishop presented a detailed critique to the congress of lynching's causes, consequences, and possible remedies. He thought the pulpit would eventually utter its voice when attention had been fully called to the matter, but he regarded schools, colleges, and independent organizations as the most effective short-term solutions.[151]

With suffrage bills pending before the state legislature, suffrage leaders played a visible role at the 1915 Southern Sociological Congress meeting as well. Houston principal of schools and suffragist Helena Holley argued that women's suffrage would be an important step toward improving public health in general, while other delegates noted the role that improved suffrage for African Americans could play.[152] That connection continued several years later as suffragists became involved in the antilynching campaign. Immediate proposals to curb mob violence included better efforts to post critical editorials in newspapers, a law requiring automatic removal from office of any sheriff who failed to guard prisoners from mob violence, and the possibility of holding towns in which mob violence occurred responsible for damages.

A development that would lead in a small way to further mobilization occurred in 1916 when Robert E. Vinson, who for the past fourteen years had taught at and then served as president of Austin Theological Seminary, was appointed as president of the University of Texas. Vinson was a Presbyterian minister who believed that universities bore a special responsibility to shape public opinion on major social issues of the day. Born in South Carolina, he graduated from Union Theological Seminary in Richmond, preached in West Virginia, and studied briefly at the University of Chicago under William Rainey Harper. With relatives who taught mathematics, practiced law, and served as missionaries, he was clearly among the "first class" of white folk, and he was well toward the modern side of any modernist-fundamentalist debates.[153] In 1917 he successfully fought off an attempt by Governor Ferguson to fire him and most of the University of Texas faculty, continuing as president until 1923 when he departed to head Case Western Reserve University in Ohio.[154] Vinson served as founding chair of the Texas Commission on Inter-Racial Cooperation, a branch of the multistate Commission on Inter-Racial Cooperation begun in 1919, and in that capacity convened a meeting that created a women's association to spearhead a new campaign against lynching.[155]

The women in charge of the antilynching campaign included Sallie Hanna, Mrs. J. S. Turner, and Jessie Daniel Ames. Hanna and Turner had previously made joint appearances at Federated Council of Church Women meetings in Dallas speaking against lynching and in favor of better railroad accommodations for African Americans.[156] Hanna was a Presbyterian, was active in the WCTU and League of Women Voters, and was currently serving as national YWCA vice president.[157] Ames was the widow of Roger Post Ames, a U.S. army surgeon who worked with Walter Reed in 1900 and 1901 searching for the causes of yellow fever and who died in 1914 carrying on Reed's work in Guatemala.[158] A graduate of Southwestern University, she lived in Georgetown where she raised her three children and helped her mother operate a successful telephone company.[159] While in college she had joined the Methodist church and through her involvement in Methodist women's groups became interested in suffrage. Inspired by suffragist Minnie Fisher Cunningham, she organized a local women's suffrage group in 1916, became increasingly involved in the suffrage movement, and served in 1919 as treasurer of the Texas State Suffrage League and in the same year as president of the newly organized Texas League of Women Voters. These activities solidified her relationship to a network of reform-minded women and men and put her in increasing demand as an advocate for social reform. She lectured frequently at churches and at church meetings.[160]

FIGURE 10. Jessie Daniel Ames, ca. 1919, president of the Texas League of Women Voters from 1919 to 1924. Williamson County Historical Commission. Reproduced with permission from the Methodist Collections at Drew University, Madison, NJ.

By the time the Texas Commission on Inter-Racial Cooperation came into being, the need for its work had been heightened by racial conflict in Texas and in other states. In 1917 a series of minor conflicts in Houston between city police and African American military police at Camp Logan escalated into an armed riot that left seventeen dead.[161] That year mob violence involving labor and racial conflict also developed in Chicago and East St. Louis as well as at a ship plant in Newport News, Virginia. A yearlong investigation of the Houston riot resulted in nineteen executions. In 1919 rioting broke out in Longview, Texas, resulting in hundreds of shots being fired and five African American houses being burned.[162] The Longview episode was one of more than two dozen riots during the so-called Red Summer of 1919, the worst of which occurred in Chicago.[163] Shortly after the Longview riot, NAACP national secretary John Shillady, who had come to Texas to investigate, was attacked and beaten by assailants who included a constable and the county judge.[164] Between 1915 and 1918 the NAACP had succeeded in attracting more than seven thousand members in Texas and starting thirty-one branch offices. But after the Shillady beating, official and unofficial intimidation made it difficult for these offices to continue.[165] The Texas secretary of state routinely turned down all requests for charters from other organizations suspected of promoting racial equality as well. Such organizations were deemed "contrary to the real interest of citizens of Texas as a whole."[166]

The multistate Commission on Inter-Racial Cooperation emerged partly in response to these events. As a southern organization it sought to avoid the sectional animosity stirred by the NAACP and other northern groups. Its stated aims included research, scholarship, and uplift rather than racial equality. Another such organization was the University Commission on Southern Race Questions composed of delegates from eleven southern institutions, including the University of Texas's School of Education dean William S. Sutton.[167] The university group conducted research on race relations, convened conferences, and worked toward more generous funding for black schools and colleges.[168] Both organizations sought to combat mob violence and promote law and civilization. The interracial group strategically cultivated not only educators but also suffragists as well as white and African American clergy and community leaders.[169] The network in which Ames played an increasingly central role was typical.

Like many other suffragists, Ames became involved in a number of social reform causes and organizations.[170] In 1920 she took an active part in the debate about which gubernatorial candidates were better suited to the causes of suffrage and prohibition and was a delegate to the Democratic National Convention.[171] In 1921, through the League of Women Voters, she advocated for a minimum wage and prison reform, cooperating with members of the National Catholic Welfare Council on these activities. Through Vinson and at the urging of her sister's husband, J. C. Hardy, who taught at Southwestern University and was a member of the Texas Commission on Inter-Racial Cooperation, she helped initiate and rapidly became a leader of the women's movement against lynching. Unlike progressive religious and community organizations that emphasized racial uplift, this organization specifically included in its mission statement a plea for racial justice. "Recognizing the universal existence of prejudice among people of different races, and deploring its existence and its consequent unjust results," the mission statement explained, "we therefore are resolved that the Negro should have a hearing in his own behalf, and further resolve that we shall not be content simply with being kindly disposed to the race but that our good will shall reach to the effort to secure for its members justice in all things and opportunities for living the best life." It continued, "We desire for the Negro, as for all men, personal and racial justice in private life and in the courts of the land."[172]

As one of its last acts, the Southern Sociological Congress presented an urgent plea to a national conference of governors in 1919 to prevent lynching.[173] A Tuskegee Institute investigation the following year nevertheless showed that sixty-one lynchings took place nationwide of which ten occurred in Texas, the largest number for any state.[174] By 1922 new efforts across the South led by the Commission on Inter-Racial Cooperation produced more than seven hundred local chapters in thirteen states and a widening interest in the prevention of lynching. The Texas commission expanded its membership, appointed new committees to supervise a wider range of activities, and hosted a meeting at which African American pastors and scholars from around the state emphasized the need for better cooperation and greater vigilance in preventing mob violence.[175]

Up to this point several northern church bodies had condemned the racial violence that continued in scattered locations while southern churches generally ignored it.[176] But in 1923 both the Southern Baptist Convention and the Southern Methodist Board of Missions passed resolutions on the issue. "Mob violence," the Baptist resolution asserted, "defies all law, despises every principle and function of government, and tramples into the dust every human right." The Methodist board asserted its "sorrow over the crime of brutal murder by mobs so frequently occurring throughout our beloved land, not only because of the unrighteousness of such deeds and the defiance of the law, but also because of the reflection upon our Christianity in the eyes of pagan people."[177] Whether the resolutions intended to condemn lynching, black violence against whites, or both remained unclear.

That year the Texas Commission on Inter-Racial Cooperation wrote congratulatory letters to officials in counties where lynchings had not occurred, lobbied for better railroad service, organized an interracial health awareness week, proposed a school for delinquent African American girls, and placed on record demands for interracial activities and greater racial inclusion at the Dallas state fair. Besides Ames, the meeting included presentations by the new presidents of Southwestern University and the University of Texas as well as the presidents of Texas A&M and Southern Methodist University.[178]

Over the next few years, Ames became increasingly active on a number of fronts, attending the Democratic National Convention again in 1924, serving on the Texas Committee on Prisons and Prison Labor in 1925, and heading the efforts of the Texas WCTU in 1928 to promote dry resolutions at the county, state, and national levels. But her activities increasingly focused on interracial cooperation. In 1925 she was a speaker at the annual meeting in Atlanta of the Southern Interracial Commission. She wrote letters encouraging newspapers to play a more active role in bringing the problem of lynching to public awareness. Churches, colleges, and civic groups provided her with an increasing number of venues in which to lecture about race relations. These included a lecture on the relationship of churches to racial justice at a symposium sponsored by the Civic Federation of Dallas and staffed by Southern Methodist University faculty in 1924 and a lecture the following year on interracial cooperation at a Presbyterian church in Dallas. [179] In addition, she lectured on racial discrimination to churchwomen at annual meetings of the YWCA and was a featured speaker at a number of Baptist, Presbyterian, and Methodist statewide meetings of women's missionary societies as well as meetings at black churches. When plans for a "Negro Hospital" in Houston were drawn up, Ames was invited to speak to the organizing committee on behalf of the Texas Commission on Inter-Racial Cooperation. "Mrs. Ames is a very able and well informed woman," the committee chair wrote to his colleagues, "and I am sure her experience and views with reference to the hospital, its management, etc., will be helpful."[180]

In 1929 Ames moved to Atlanta where she headed the women's committee for the entire Southern Interracial Commission, traveling widely including numerous trips to Texas. She worked closely with her sister, Lulu Daniel Hardy, now widowed, who taught at Gulf Park College in Mississippi and presided over the Mississippi Federation of Women's Clubs. In 1932 at a Baptist church in Dallas in cooperation with a former president of the YWCA, a WCTU leader, and a number of other church women Ames helped organize the Texas Association of Women for the Prevention of Lynching, an organization that soon grew to include some four thousand women statewide.[181] Over the next few years individual pastors, pastors associations, and church assemblies began to speak openly against lynching. Their work found an advocate in President Roosevelt as well. Lynch law, Roosevelt told a meeting of the Federal Council of Churches of Christ in 1933, "is murder and a deliberate and definite disobedience of the commandment, 'Thou shalt not kill.' "[182] No longer should church leaders be content with mere "preachings" against this vile form of murder, the president cautioned. Leaders should recognize that a collective effort involving government "in accord with the social teachings of Christianity" would be necessary.[183] Six months later the Association of Southern Women for the Prevention of Lynching under Ames's direction had branches in thirteen states and a registered membership of twenty-two thousand.[184]

In Texas the interracial commission's work increasingly focused on literacy, education, and assistance for low-income families. Through meetings at church buildings and seminaries and with invocations delivered by clergy, a symbolic connection with religion was retained even though much of the work was being directed at other institutions. Federal relief programs under the administration's New Deal policies made it possible for the commission to focus on legislation aimed at putting farm tenants on the road toward farm ownership and for consideration to be given to racial aspects of the National Labor Relations Board. In 1937 the organization turned its attention to legislation aimed at securing state funds to assist African Americans become doctors, dentists, and lawyers. Ames traveled from Atlanta to Dallas to participate in the effort. Hanna continued to be involved in the commission as well as in the YWCA. Interracial cooperation and goodwill also became topics for discussion at teachers' conferences, in gatherings of clubwomen, on campuses, and at church meetings. The meaning of interracial cooperation continued to focus on black-white relationships, but with war clouds on the horizon it included discussion of attitudes toward Jews as well as relationships with Americans of Japanese and Chinese descent.[185]

By 1938 Ames was convinced that the battle against lynching needed to move on, shifting focus toward other forms of racial discrimination and disfranchisement. "The rich white people of the south keep the poor white people so busy hating Negroes that they cannot get up themselves," she said. "Disfranchisement of the Negroes in the south has contributed more to its economic retardation than any one single force."[186] She thought that ending disfranchisement would be the only way to promote better relationships between blacks and whites. But if disfranchisement was far from being abolished, so was prejudice and discrimination. When the commission invited an African American leader to speak in Dallas that spring, a community group called the Sons of Confederate Veterans organized protests on a sufficient scale to force removal of the event from the white YWCA building to the black YWCA and require police protection.[187]

THE FACES OF SOCIAL REFORM

The relationships between religion and race evident by the mid-1930s illuminate differences in the ways in which social reform was being organized. Variants that represent broad contrasts include progressive reforms that emphasized racial uplift, conservative reforms that emphasized doctrinal purity, and public advocacy that emphasized racial justice. Although there is reason to think that white leaders who were involved in these various efforts held racial beliefs that reflected common cultural understandings of the time, it is also reasonable to assume that these leaders were well meaning and understood that African Americans remained disadvantaged. Although the traces of activism are more readily available among white leaders, it is also the case that the manner in which reform efforts were organized fundamentally included the work of African American leaders as well.

Progressive reforms in this period are clearly illustrated by the joint appearance of pastors Truett and Williams at the Texas Centennial Exposition. Truett was a local icon who not only headed the largest church in Dallas but was also called upon for ceremonial functions, such as hosting meetings, offering invocations at community events, and serving on the boards of community organizations. That was undoubtedly a role Williams played in Chicago as well at least for the African American population. Progressive Era reforms over the past quarter century and longer had worked to organize public and private benevolent associations including orphanages and hospitals, to improve conditions in prisons, and to support schools and colleges. With involvement from religious leaders, these activities enlisted the goodwill and resources of businesses and government. Racial considerations were involved in programs to create separate institutions such as schools and orphanages as well as sponsoring some activities in which black and white leaders were jointly involved. The Baptist World Alliance in which Truett and Williams served was one such organization. For religious leaders it was essential to remain in the good graces of their denominations and the members who went to church and paid the bills. The progressive philosophy that focused on racial uplift as part of the broader advance of civilization was basically an optimistic worldview. Believing in this worldview rested on real and symbolic evidence that progress was in fact occurring. The 1936 exposition was a celebration of such progress and a prediction that it would continue.

Conservative reforms were best illustrated by fundamentalist leaders such as Norris and Anderson and by dispensationalist scholars such as Scofield and Chafer. Although later critics easily regarded fundamentalism as a throwback to simpler times, it was better understood as a genuine reform effort that not only opposed the ideas of progressives but also attempted to develop new organizations that pointed in a different direction. Large congregations such as Norris's in Fort Worth, small independent Bible churches, conferences attended by fundamentalist leaders, and new colleges and seminaries were examples. These organizations were almost exclusively white and did little compared with progressive reformers to assist or work together with black leaders. Without explicitly articulating racist ideas, it was possible to work within a white population because of the racial separation that already existed in religion and the Jim Crow practices that maintained segregation. Like progressive reformers, conservative leaders depended on support from grassroots church members. Although Norris and Anderson and a few other conservative leaders engaged lawmakers with appeals about teaching and textbooks, their activities were directed mainly toward the church itself. Their effectiveness was measured in activities that either drew members into their own churches or pulled denominations in their direction. While progressive ideas required proof of progress, conservative ideas were more easily reinforced by evidence that the world was overrun with evil.

Public advocacy was illustrated by networks of activists who worked for Prohibition, women's suffrage, racial justice, and better enforcement of laws against lynching. The involvement of Ames and a few other leaders in all these activities illustrates the networks and experience that led from one to the others. Outspoken as she was, it was the social location of the organizations in which Ames participated that facilitated their unique role in reform advocacy. Suffragists were less beholden to political party machinery than their male counterparts, more critical of that machinery, and more closely aligned in bringing religion, prohibition, and larger social reforms together. In a 1928 letter Ames saw all these as the unique contribution of women's suffrage. "It has aided to destroy machine politics," she wrote, and it has stressed "fitness for office" over party alignments and been a "powerful influence" for penal reform, better treatment of the insane, prohibition, and child labor laws.[188]

Social class mattered in terms of having the cultural capital with which to craft public lectures and newspaper editorials as well as to mingle with people of sufficient means to attain advanced degrees, travel, and devote their time to civic organizations. Speaking as a member of the "first class" of white folk conferred authority on what one said. Enlisting college presidents and faculty conferred further prestige. Networks that focused on educational improvement, research, public health, and condemning mob violence had the added advantage of being able to circumvent whatever the mass population might think. Unlike public officials who depended on the electorate to stay in office, and unlike referenda such as Prohibition, few of the issues with which racial advocacy organizations were concerned at the time required approval by a majority of the public.

The sharpest contrast with the other kinds of reform in terms of religion is that few of these activists were employed as clergy with obligations toward church members or denominational leaders. That autonomy provided greater freedom to experiment with new ideas that sometimes worked and sometimes did not, as well as to voice criticisms of established institutions. The personal autonomy of individual leaders was further realized in the founding of independent organizations such as the WCTU, YWCA, League of Women Voters, NAACP, and Southern Sociological Congress. These independent organizations drew on the networks and institutional resources of churches, women's clubs, and civic associations, but they were not formally or informally constrained by understandings about separation of church and state in the way that religious organizations were. Some of these organizations, while formally under the auspices of their denominations, also enjoyed partial autonomy. A reason Methodist women may have found it easier to become involved in racial advocacy was that their missionary associations had greater financial and administrative autonomy from the denomination than Baptist missionary associations did.[189] Unlike religious leaders who founded churches and progressive reformers who organized orphanages and hospitals, these advocates were not institution builders. For that reason they were freer to travel, to show up at meetings to give lectures or confer symbolic support, and to shift from issue to issue. That was also a weakness. Other than lifting their voice for various reforms, they were able to accomplish little on their own unless other leaders, such as clergy, journalists, teachers, social workers, and elected officials, took up the cause. The continuing appeal of their efforts depended less on recurrent evidence of progress or the lack thereof, but on finding welcoming forums in which to advocate for basic principles.

Understanding the differences in social organization of these kinds of social reform puts into perspective the different uses of religious idioms. None of the three depended exclusively on religious arguments. Progressive ideas reflected broader intellectual arguments about civilization as well as the concrete reality of improvements in agriculture, industry, and civic life. Conservative ideas extended beyond prophetic biblical arguments to the lived realities of lawlessness, immorality, and death. Public advocacy drew from nonreligious as well as religious ideas about justice and equality. Explicit religious language played a more prominent role in the former two than in public advocacy. Progressive leaders depended on religious arguments to demonstrate that what they favored was legitimate in terms of prevailing denominational teachings and grassroots understandings in congregations. Conservative leaders were especially intent on demonstrating that their biblical interpretations were correct and that what was taught in seminaries and preached in churches reflected those interpretations. In contrast, the presence of religious language in the work of public advocates

such as Ames is less notable. While identifying organizations and issues as ones
nominally associated with Christianity, it was more common for these leaders to
draw on the implicit legitimacy of religious organizations by speaking at church
meetings and using church auditoriums as venues. Nevertheless, the evangelical
zeal in which leaders sometimes imbibed in Methodist missionary societies and
at YWCA meetings provided a template for campaigning against lynching. "The
'false chivalry' of lynching cast women as Christ-like symbols of racial purity,"
Ames biographer Jacquelyn Dowd Hall observes, "and translated every sign of
black self-assertion into a metaphor for rape." Reversing this logic so that white
lynch mobs became the fornicators and powerless black women were the victims
was a key part of the antilynching crusade's rhetorical success.[190]

The differences in social organization among these kinds of reform shed light
on what each was able to accomplish and not accomplish. The contrast between
the racial progress highlighted at the Dallas exposition and the realities of Jim
Crow segregation that African Americans attending the exposition experienced
points to the fact that progressive reformers found it useful to argue that things
were better than they were in reality. The exposition was a celebration staged to
show what had been accomplished on various fronts and thus to shield from view
the difficulties that remained. That was not without value. In showing what had
been done, the exposition suggested that those efforts were not in vain and that
more could be accomplished in the future. For whites and especially for African
Americans, the exhibits featuring "Negro progress" offered hope of better things
to come. The conservative reformers made few claims to being interested in racial
reconciliation or uplift. White fundamentalists did implicitly believe that black
churches should preach the same message of individual repentance and salvation as white churches. By going their separate ways, white and black churches
developed leadership and organizations that ensured the strength of their congregations and denominations. Public advocacy on behalf of interracial cooperation was forward-looking in ways that anticipated the later civil rights movement
but in the short term even in the eyes of its leaders accomplished only modest
measurable results. Although goals such as the prevention of lynching were quite
specific, it was difficult to know if lower numbers were the result of advocacy
itself or of a more general change in public opinion. Other goals were admittedly
diffuse, ranging from better schools and public health to more amicable interpersonal relations. Difficulties in attaining them stemmed, as one historian has
noted, from the amorphous nature of geographically scattered organizations that
were only loosely coordinated.[191] Compared to the legislative successes gained for
Prohibition and women's suffrage, the gains for racial justice were small. Advocacy nevertheless provided a voice for racial justice and for greater cooperation.

As the Great Depression deepened, social reforms of these various kinds became inestimably more difficult than they had been during the more prosperous
preceding decades. Economic recovery on a national scale required intervention
from the federal government. In Texas it helped that the Democratic Party was

solidly behind Roosevelt, but convictions about states' rights and local autonomy also ran deep. As the nation mobilized for the possibility of another world war, religious leaders in a state so dominated by the political party in power raised their voices less often to condemn war than to argue that it was necessary. In race relations the rule of Judge Lynch diminished, but Jim Crow continued. During and immediately after the war, as new leaders contemplated the possibilities for further social reforms, segregation was the reality that could not be avoided.

CHAPTER 6

A LOAD TOO HEAVY

Religion and the Debate over Government Relief

It has been suggested—mostly by preachers, I am sorry to say—that it
would be a load too heavy for the church to carry.

REVEREND THOMAS B. HUFF, SOUTH HARWOOD CHURCH OF CHRIST, DALLAS, 1939

For a nation that prided itself on individual initiative and freedom from
federal government intervention, the Great Depression presented a
significant challenge not only in sheer economic terms but also in self-
understanding. Was it possible for individuals, families, churches, and local community organizations to provide sufficient relief for the hungry and unemployed?
Or was it necessary to turn to the government for help?

During the 1930s religious leaders and public officials debated all sides of
this question. Feeding the hungry, clothing the naked, and dealing mercifully
with the poor and downtrodden were clearly mandated in the scriptures that
most Americans claimed to believe. Equally mandated were biblical injunctions specifying an appropriate role for government in the care of its citizens.
Religious leaders in the past had worked with local officials to organize emergency relief programs as well as institutions to care for orphans and widows,
blind people, veterans, and insane people. But a nation governed by constitutional separation of church and state restricted the extent to which the two
were supposed to interact in furthering common projects. Religious leaders
did not want to shoulder greater responsibilities for public welfare than they
reasonably could bear, but they also feared government intrusion. They were
not alone in these concerns. Social workers, the heads of private charities, business leaders, and state and local government officials had their own views about
how much or how little the federal government should become involved in
their affairs.

In later years it would be easy to look back on the New Deal era and assume that the great needs during the Depression to which the Roosevelt administration's programs were addressed fundamentally changed people's minds about the federal government's role. That assumption would be even easier to make for a state like Texas that was already strongly Democratic and that voted overwhelmingly on three occasions for FDR. But if Texas was that favorable to the federal welfare system, it becomes puzzling to understand how the same state became so antagonistic to big government a half century later. The story would necessarily be one of stark discontinuity. The truth, however, is more complex. Although Texas benefited from and supported the New Deal, it did so with considerable misgiving. Indeed, the story is particularly revealing because it shows the extent to which grassroots resistance to government intrusion existed even in such an unlikely political context. One of the principal reasons for this resistance was religion, especially religion that emphasized individual self-sufficiency and was with relatively few exceptions staunchly in favor of a clear separation of church and state. That meant concern not only about government intrusion into the affairs of religion but also about it staying out of the lives of religious people. Besides religious organizations themselves, strong private charity agencies existed as well. The religious and charitable organizations were unable to deal with the social needs that increased so dramatically during the Depression, but they played a strong hand in stating how social welfare should be understood. Those inclinations were to surface again with strong political implications at the end of the twentieth century.

Texas clergy in the 1930s were still influenced by the legacy of the Confederacy and Reconstruction in which the federal government was regarded as an enemy rather than as a friend. Separation of church and state held that government involvement in activities usually administered by religious organizations was asking for trouble. The churches had done their part in founding and maintaining benevolent associations. But now the needs of destitute citizens were greater than ever before. For religious organizations to shoulder the responsibility through private charity might indeed, as some argued, be a load too heavy.

Through the New Deal, the Roosevelt administration offered assistance to states and local communities. Unlike Republican-dominated states in the Midwest, Texas was run by Democrats who generally trusted FDR and had ready access to New Deal funds. But should the leaders of churches and private charities embrace this funding? Was that a bargain with the devil? And for that matter, the administration itself understood that government dollars would go further if supplemented by private charity.

The questions were complicated by race and ethnicity. Although they were a minority of the population, African Americans and Hispanics were in greater need of assistance than most of the white Anglo population. White leaders worried that African Americans and Hispanics on the public dole could upset the balance of power enjoyed by the white majority. Could Jim Crow laws and white primaries offset that danger? Or was it necessary for white churches and benevolent associations to provide more assistance across racial and ethnic lines?

How these questions were resolved would have important implications well after the 1930s. As the nation prepared for war, state and local leaders who generally favored the Democratic Party and the assistance they were receiving from the federal government found it harder to criticize the buildup leading to war than was often true in other locations. And yet criticisms were voiced. By the end of the war, Texas also found itself with new leaders with closer ties to the federal government and more favorable attitudes toward racial equality. The tension between these attitudes and more traditional views toward government and race would move to center stage during the civil rights movement.

HARD TIMES

The Great Depression comes into sharpest relief for later generations of Americans through grainy black-and-white motion pictures of men in breadlines along some otherwise deserted downtown street in New York City or Chicago. Or it is captured in sepia-toned photographs of dust clouds billowing across the Kansas plains. It is vividly commemorated in the era's two most successful fictional portrayals, *The Grapes of Wrath* and *The Wizard of Oz*. But those images apply to Texas as well. Unemployment spread across Dallas and Houston while rural areas suffered from dry weather and crop failures. Families who had done well during the 1920s and who expected to see their children enjoying the fruits of their labor faced a new reality in the 1930s. The difficulties initially seemed like only the temporary downturns the economy had experienced before but increasingly appeared as if they would never end.

Mae Knox Burton's parents were typical. Her father served in World War I, returned home to a small farm sixty miles north of Dallas near Sherman, and married his sweetheart in 1926. Times were good, but instead of replacing the weather-beaten farmhouse with a better one, her parents took out a loan to purchase additional land. When the Depression came, the crops no longer brought in enough cash to cover expenses. "Even butter and eggs could not be sold," Burton remembered. The well went dry, forcing the family to carry water in buckets from a spring half a mile away. Somehow they managed to be among the fortunate few who did not lose their farm. Burton's most vivid childhood memories were of hoboes coming to the back door asking for food.[1]

Ma Springer was less fortunate. At age sixty-five she and her two unmarried daughters were scraping by on a farm near Sherman when wild dogs attacked their milk cows, killing all but one. The three women tore the tin roof off their barn, fashioned a makeshift house on a wagon, and, with two horses pulling it and their meager belongings, set off for Colorado where they hoped a cousin could help them find work. Along the way they borrowed gunnysacks to keep warm on cold nights and begged food from townspeople. It took three months to get to Colorado. They did find temporary work, but when that ran out they returned to Texas and repeated the journey two years later.[2]

Officially the farm population was expected to be able to fend for itself. Suffragist Minnie Fisher Cunningham, now with the Texas A&M extension service, surveyed farmers and farm leaders in a hundred Texas counties and determined that there were twenty-five million cans and jars of meat, vegetables, and fruits on their shelves—more than enough to last the winter. But that was in 1931 when nearly everyone thought the Depression would be short-lived.[3]

Although no part of the state escaped, West Texas was hit especially hard. A map produced by the U.S. Soil Erosion Service in 1935 showed areas of moderate or serious wind erosion damage that stretched from Odessa up through Lubbock and the Texas panhandle, across western Oklahoma and Kansas, and on through Nebraska and the Dakotas into Canada.[4] Data collected by the U.S. Department of Agriculture showed that crops failed on more than 80 percent of the land that had been planted in 1934 in nine Texas counties. In eighteen other counties at least 50 percent of the cropland failed to produce. Statewide, crop failures affected nearly 6.5 million acres, up from only 1.8 million in 1929.[5]

Bill Godfrey was a boy in Dickens County during the Depression. His family owned a farm and ran a Ford dealership on the side. "We were in debt for our land," he recalled. "Cattle were $15.00 a head, but we mortgaged ours. Cotton, if it rained, was five cents a pound, not worth gathering. Sand blew until we could not see the sun at noon." Several of the cows starved to death. Older ones had to be shot. Children picked cotton to earn a few pennies a day. School started six weeks late because families were delinquent paying their taxes.[6]

The principal reason for failed crops was drouth. Almost everyone who lived in arid parts of the state experienced the dust storms that blew in from the north and west and blackened the sky. Howard McCarley, who went on to earn a PhD degree and become a biology professor, recalled sitting in a second-story classroom as a child and seeing reddish clouds of sand and grit blowing in from the west. The dust coated everything and created a noticeable odor. "My mother used old towels, rags and pieces of newspaper to block gaps around the windows and doors," he remembered.[7]

On March 30, 1935, Alex Peterson was making his inaugural run as a rural mail carrier in West Texas when a billowing black cloud engulfed his car. Dallas residents knew from radio broadcasts that a massive dust storm was sweeping in from Kansas and across the Oklahoma panhandle. But Peterson and his neighbors had no warning. Bringing the vehicle to a halt, he found himself stranded by a huge mass of tumbleweeds that completely blocked the road. The storm came up so quickly that women in the area were unable to snatch partially dry clothes from the line or gather up baby chicks. A tractor buried up to its exhaust pipe remained undisturbed for more than a year.[8]

The dust storms were aggravated by the fact that more of the state was being tilled for crops than ever before. Midland County in West Texas was typical. In 1909 fewer than 7,000 acres were under cultivation, but by 1929 that number had risen to more than 47,000.[9] Cotton, which required less moisture than wheat and corn, was the state's most important cash crop. The price farmers received for cotton dropped from nearly twenty-five cents a pound during World War I to an average of nine cents a pound from 1931 to 1935 and remained below that level at the end of the decade. The per acre yield fluctuated from year to year depending on weather, but there was an overall reduction in the number of acres farmers planted of nearly 50 percent from the late 1920s until 1939. As a result, the total annual value of cotton production statewide fell from more than $400 million in the early 1920s to less than $125 million in 1939. Over the same period the total annual value of cottonseed fell from $480 million to $149 million.[10]

In the Rio Grande valley drouth and declining wages were particularly devastating to the large number of Mexican Americans and Mexican immigrants who worked as farm laborers. The average wage per hundred pounds of cotton picked fell from $1.21 in 1928 to only $0.44 in 1931, far below the amount needed to live.[11] Deportation raids and voluntary repatriation to Mexico began in 1928 and escalated over the next three years. Nationwide an estimated 138,000 Mexicans were repatriated in 1931, up from 70,000 in 1930, after which the number fell to 77,000 in 1932 and declined steadily to 8,000 in 1937.[12] At least half the numbers repatriated in 1931 were in Texas.[13] A U.S. Bureau of Labor Statistics report indicated that communities in the Southwest had "aided" repatriation to relieve charity burdens and attributed the departures not only to lack of jobs but also to "attraction of home ties" and "the belief that they can providentially obtain assistance from their relatives or others."[14] Those who stayed and did find work were typically employed as migrant laborers. "They find themselves welcomed at the start of each crop season and hounded out of the community two days after the last acre has been harvested," a study concluded. They were typically "ostracized from community activities, without club, lodge, church or home ties," and their children faced ridicule and discrimination at school if they were able to attend at all.[15]

Townspeople in Dallas, Houston, San Antonio, and some of the smaller communities fared better than country people as long as they were able to keep their jobs. By 1929 Dallas was reveling in population growth and banks were flourishing. Rich people could board a flight at the new airport and be in Los Angeles or New York by the next day. At first it seemed that the city might escape the Depression. The 1930 census showed fewer than six thousand unemployed, but by the end of the year more than eighteen thousand residents were out of work. In Houston an estimated twenty-nine thousand were jobless.[16] In San Antonio, where laborers who were fortunate enough to find work received as little as fifty cents a day, five thousand jobless men demonstrated in hopes of rallying public assistance.[17] The situation was similar in El Paso, where five thousand heads of families were said to be jobless.[18] Unemployment worsened through 1933 before there was much improvement. Times were better in 1935, and business in Dallas improved sharply during the centennial exposition in 1936, only to decline again to the point that mob violence and labor unrest broke out in 1937 and again in 1938.[19] Data collected in 1937 showed that more than 229,000 Texans were registered as unemployed, or approximately 9 percent of the labor force. Fifteen thousand were unemployed in the Dallas area, and 17,000 were unemployed in Houston and Harris County.[20] Families made do by tightening their belts and finding creative ways to pay the bills. One woman recalled how "mama worked as a live-in maid in the city" while the rest of the family lived at the grandparents' in a smaller town.[21] Others remembered peddling newspapers before school and picking cotton to supplement their family's income.

Church budgets and opportunities for new ministries declined significantly during the Depression. Baptists and small independent churches that relied on lay leaders and the services of preachers who earned their livings in other ways were somewhat better positioned to withstand the downturn than churches fully dependent on salaried clergy. Jimmy Allen, who later became president of the Southern Baptist Convention, recalled his parents moving from Detroit to Texas in hopes of finding work, and his father preaching while working as a door-to-door salesman. The family lost their life savings in 1933 when the banks failed. Allen's father continued to sell insurance part-time, his mother worked at a café, and by canvassing the neighborhood they were able to start a small church.[22] Other pastors recalled raising their own chickens, living on black-eyed peas, church women paying the congregation's bills by selling eggs, and being paid in produce or milk.[23]

Data from Methodist churches showed the extent to which belt tightening was occurring statewide. Between 1929 and 1933 annual receipts of the Central Texas conference fell from $1,682,000 to $687,335. Receipts of the North Texas conference declined from $1,419,000 to $730,000; in the Northwest Texas conference, from $1,320,000 to $591,000; in the Texas conference, from $1,877,000 to $1,053,000; and in the West Texas conference, from $1,276,000 to $629,000. Overall the receipts in 1933 totaled only 48 percent of the receipts in 1929. The decline in conference receipts resulted in closure of three of the state's Methodist colleges and reduced the denomination's ability to start new churches or staff existing congregations. Presbyterians and Catholics experienced similar difficulties.[24]

Southern Baptist leaders who had proudly announced annual gains on all fronts during the 1920s were now confronted with mixed reports. Although baptisms, youth work, and total membership continued to grow as the population expanded, church finances registered losses. In 1931 contributions toward the support of local church work in Texas totaled $4.7 million, by far the largest amount for Southern Baptists in any state, but were down by $900,000 from the 1929 figure. The decline was partly offset by a lower cost of living but in adjusted

FIGURE 11. Texas oil field, 1930s, showing impact on the land and makeshift housing for workers. Reproduced with permission from the Permian Basin Petroleum Museum, Library and Hall
of Fame, Midland, TX. University of North Texas Libraries, The Portal to Texas History.

dollars still represented a 6 percent reduction.[25] Subsequent figures reported for
the Southern Baptist Convention as a whole showed that per member giving for
the support of local church work fell to a low of $4.70 in 1933, down from $8.41
in 1929, representing a cost-of-living adjusted decline of 26 percent. In 1935 per
capita giving on an adjusted basis was still 25 percent below the 1929 figure, after
which steady increases brought the adjusted decline in 1939 to only 9 percent
below the 1929 figure.[26]

Despite the general downturn, there were considerable differences from congregation to congregation. African American congregations continued to meet in
more modest buildings and operated on significantly smaller budgets than white
congregations. The First Baptist Church in Waco managed to sustain its annual
mission giving only by reducing the pastor's salary.[27] Fundamentalist Frank Norris carried on an extensive radio ministry and took in enough money to com-
mute regularly by airplane between his congregation in Fort Worth and one in
Detroit. Baptists in Lubbock were able to move into a new building. Five new
church buildings were dedicated in Amarillo. But in a small town near Amarillo,
the women's auxiliary struggled to collect $125 during the year for payments on
the pastor's manse.[28] In later years church members fondly recalled potluck din-
ners, church picnics, Bible quizzes, and favorite Sunday school teachers. There
was little evidence, though, that hard times pushed people measurably closer to
God. If they prayed fervently for better crops or to avoid losing their job, they
undoubtedly wondered at times if their prayers were heard.

The one bright spot on the larger horizon was that oil discoveries were opening new opportunities for the unemployed. Near Henderson in Rusk County,
oil was discovered on October 3, 1930, in what was for a time considered the

FIGURE 12. Presbyterian Church in Kilgore, Texas, 1939. With oil wells on its property, it was reputed to be one of the richest churches in the world. Photograph © Russell Lee. U.S. Farm Security Administration—Office of War Information Photograph Collection. Library of Congress Prints and Photographs Division, Washington, DC.

largest oil field in the world. Within a few months population in the area swelled from two thousand to more than ten thousand. The discovery not only sparked the local economy but also created opportunities for preachers to hold revival meetings and launch new churches.[29] With rising income and eager to attract new residents, the members of a Church of Christ congregation in Longview invested in a new English Gothic–style building at a cost of $18,000. An African American Baptist church benefited directly when drilling on its property struck oil.

But news that jobs might be available sometimes created as many problems as it solved. With thousands of job seekers flocking to these communities, housing was in short supply, crime and fear of crime increased, and the demand for jobs generally exceeded the number of jobs available. In February 1931 members of a small rural church near Kilgore became the unsuspecting victims of an oil boom when they arrived for Sunday worship services one morning only to find the church occupied by drifters seeking work as roustabouts for the drilling company. Fearing, probably with good reason, that the drifters had left behind a healthy population of lice, the congregants abandoned the building until it could be deloused. In the meantime Texas rangers took over the building for a headquarters, rounded up idlers from local dives and domino halls, and brought them to the church for fingerprinting before arresting dozens and suggesting in no uncertain terms that others leave.[30]

WHAT SHOULD BE DONE?

Everyone recognized that the economy was in the doldrums, but nobody knew how long the downturn would last or how severe it would become. There were wildly differing opinions about what was wrong, and these views influenced what people thought needed to be done. Some of the arguments identified specific problems that could be fixed, while others pointed to long-term social changes or to vaguely defined problems for which there was no obvious solution. With churches in nearly every community and with pastors regularly mounting the pulpit to express their observations, it was not surprising that religion was among the topics to which people referred in making sense of what should be done.

Sixty-eight percent of the Texas population in 1920 lived on farms or in small rural communities of fewer than 2,500 residents. The 1930 census showed that this proportion had slipped to 59 percent. Knowledgeable observers identified the shift from farms to towns as one of the reasons for the current economic slump. If people were leaving the farms, the argument went, it was probably because of drouth, poor crops, and weak markets for farm products. If they were moving to town in large numbers, that was probably the reason unemployment was rising. Although the exact extent of rural to urban migration during the 1930s could have only been estimated, the 1940 census bore out what observers suspected. The rural population had shrunk further to only 55 percent. The percentages of course did not mean that the rural population was actually shrinking; it was declining only in relation to the urban population. In raw numbers, the rural population of Texas grew from 3.1 million in 1920 to 3.4 million in 1930 and to 3.5 million in 1940.[31] Still, the urban population was growing faster.

What might be driving the shift from farms to towns was a matter of further debate. It was obvious enough that farmers gave up when crop failures and low prices made it impossible for them to continue or in scattered instances when tornadoes or floods destroyed their homes. By the end of the 1920s there was already concern, though, that mechanization in the form of steam-powered and gasoline-powered tractors was pushing small farmers off the land who could not afford the new equipment and making it possible for prosperous farmers to cultivate more land with fewer people. As the depression continued, observers argued that tenant farmers especially were leaving because they could no longer earn a living on the land.

The mechanization argument was reinforced by the fact that during the 1929 season Texas farmers used 37,348 tractors, up from only 16,780 a decade earlier, and by 1939 that number grew to 98,918. That was still only one tractor for every four farms, but it did suggest that some farmers were probably replacing human labor with machines and thus contributing to the problem of unemployment. Although farming with tractors required humans to operate and repair the machines, it was understood that fewer humans were needed than when fields were being cultivated by horse-drawn equipment. And the number of horses statewide fell from almost a million in 1919 to about 638,000 in 1939. The agricultural data also supported the idea that tenants were leaving farms. From 1919 to 1934 the overall number of farms in Texas actually increased, rising from 434,000 to 501,000 before shrinking to 418,000 in 1939. The number of farms operated by tenants, in contrast, peaked in 1929 at approximately 300,000 and then fell steadily during the 1930s to 204,000 in 1939.[32]

Tenant farmers not only were more precarious economically but were also a subservient stratum in the community who were expected to show deference to their superiors. Bill C. Malone grew up in a tenant farm family in the 1930s near Galena, eighty miles east of Dallas. "Tenants and other poor farmers paid deference to their 'betters' with respectful words and a tip of the hat," he recalled. "People always knew who ranked above and below them."[33] To fall even from that stratum into the uprooted and unemployed was an inestimable disgrace that risked being regarded by one's neighbors as morally contemptible.

Tenant farmers forced off their land by hard times became legendary in *The Grapes of Wrath*. South of Dallas near Coolidge, a community leader observed in 1934 that "the ranks of relief organizations are full of farmer tenants and farm laborers who have no land to work and can't get a job as laborers."[34] Bill Godfrey remembered a different side of the story. With failing crops on mortgaged land and no money to pay either the taxes or the mortgage, Godfrey's father asked the tenant renting the land to move. Instead the tenant moved his children and their families onto Godfrey's land and refused to leave even when the sheriff served an eviction notice. "In the middle of the afternoon," Godfrey recalled, "Dad came to the house, his face rigid and pale. He went straight to the closet for his revolver, cleaned it carefully, and loaded it. 'I don't want to kill that farmer or any of his sons. But they're drunk and bragging all over town that they're going to kill me.'" No shots were fired, but Godfrey remembered his father praying more earnestly that evening for God's protection.[35]

At first farmers held meetings at community buildings and churches, invoked God's blessings, and listened as agriculture specialists and Chamber of Commerce leaders offered suggestions about more efficient production and better marketing. As prices continued to decline, they listened more intently to arguments about the need to limit production. In May 1933 the Agricultural Adjustment Act, which provided farmers subsidies for letting a portion of their land lie fallow, became law. A month later farmers around the state began plowing up a third of the acres they had planted to cotton that spring. Government checks began arriving in their mailboxes in August. The program nevertheless remained controversial not only because farmers were unused to being told by the federal

government what they could and could not do but also because it was unclear
that the subsidies compensated sufficiently for lost revenue from smaller crops.
In 1935 Texas farm leaders claiming to represent thousands of dirt farmers who
were bitterly opposed to the Agricultural Adjustment Act trekked to Washington
to express their concerns. In 1936 the U.S. Supreme Court ruled the act unconstitutional, and a revised program went into effect two years later.

The difficulties that farming communities experienced in the 1930s were
particularly acute for African American farmers. The shift from slavery to
sharecropping had left African American farmers with small farms, often on
less productive terrain, and unable to accumulate sufficient cash to purchase
land of their own. In 1929 the average farm operated by African Americans in
Texas consisted of only 52 acres compared with an average of 294 acres among
white farmers. Things got worse during the 1930s. The number of farms operated by African Americans fell 39 percent while the number operated by whites
declined by only 11 percent. The overall acreage farmed by African Americans
declined 32 percent, compared with only 4 percent among whites. The value of
farm land and buildings fell 60 percent for African American farmers, compared
with 33 percent for white farmers. As the decade ended, the African Americans
who remained operated farms of only 57 acres, compared with white farms averaging 317 acres. The value of farm land and buildings averaged only $1,361
per farm for African Americans, compared with $6,261 per farm among white
farmers.[36]

A study conducted by the U.S. Department of Agriculture revealed further
differences between white and African American farm families. The study did
not include Texas but secured comparable responses from more than six hundred randomly selected respondents in four other southern states. The median
years of school completed was seven among white male heads of households but
only four among black male heads of households. Thirty-two percent of white
families had a radio, but only 4 percent of African American families did. White
families received an average of a hundred dollars in the past year from government farm subsidies; black families, twenty dollars. The white families on average
contributed thirteen dollars a year to the support of their churches; the black
families contributed five.[37]

In 1931 Herbert Hoover appointed African American educator, religious
leader, and businesswoman Nannie H. Burroughs to chair a committee on Negro
housing. Burroughs firmly believed that farms provided a more promising future
for African Americans than cities did. "If the laboring class of Negroes cannot
make it on the soil in the country," she declared, "they certainly cannot make it
on the pavement in the city."[38] Some white landowners agreed, pressuring African American tenants to stay on the land. But as the Depression continued, farming on small acreage at depressed prices became less and less viable.

With diminishing resources, African American sharecroppers looked to the
Southern Tenant Farmers Union to press the federal government for programs

that would protect their right to bargain with landowners over threats of expulsion, rent hikes, and disadvantageous contracts. "Tenant farmers, sharecroppers and farm laborers are being swept from farms," an African American farm woman named Mollie Robinson explained at one of the meetings. "Families which formerly worked the farms are being supplanted by tractors and machinery."[39] Black churches frequently served as venues for sharecropper meetings. Clergy often experienced intimidation for their role in these meetings. An incident that was widely publicized in Texas occurred in Tennessee in January 1936 when a pastor involved in sharecropper organizing was dragged from his church and threatened with lynching by a mob of landowners wielding blackjacks and clubs. Men, women, and children at the meeting were clubbed as well.[40]

In South Texas, where Mexican American farm laborers were suffering, clergy became involved on occasion in similarly controversial activities. Near Crystal City, where immigration from Mexico multiplied the population sevenfold during the 1920s, Father Charles Taylor led an effort in 1930 and 1931 among farm laborers to form a union. At a time when epithets such as "dirty Mexican dogs" were common and discrimination took the form, as it was said later, of Jim Crow with a sombrero, an activity like this was doubly controversial. The church's role was understood to be one of evangelization, not social reform. The union dealt directly with farmers instead of labor contractors, called for a minimum wage, and opposed child labor. In other communities priests and nuns occasionally opened schools, trained social workers, and organized employment agencies.[41]

It was under these conditions of suffering and impoverishment that new healing ministries that were to become a mainstay of Pentecostal churches flourished as well. In South Texas under the leadership of Brother Francisco Olazábal, Mexican Americans were drawn to healing services and revival meetings that differed from traditional Catholic worship, drew support from Anglo leaders in Assemblies of God and Church of God churches, and were also condemned by writers who thought the meetings included Aztec rituals and jungle dances. Following Olazábal's death in 1937 in an automobile accident, healing ministries and services of spirit baptism continued to be popular among Mexican Americans throughout the region.[42]

Religious leaders more commonly addressed the farmers' and farm laborers' problems in ways long familiar. Churches in rural communities did what they had always done to assist members who lost homes or who were in obvious need of food and clothing. They baked casseroles, made quilts, and quietly supplied emergency assistance through pastors' and deacons' discretionary funds. They kept small rural churches open and encouraged members to give generously to denominational programs distributing food and clothing to the needy.[43] They also bemoaned the social changes they associated with mechanization, urbanization, and the decline of rural life. A few saw the apocalypse approaching in these changes. More considered it necessary to warn against drinking and other vices and to buttress the moral upbringing of children.

One of the more colorful leaders of the period was Reverend Edgar Eskridge, pastor of the First Baptist Church in the small town of Orange thirty miles east of Beaumont. Eskridge was a strapping figure who loved horses, cowboy boots, and guns and wore a ten-gallon hat. Increasingly troubled by violence and what he regarded as declining morals in the area, Eskridge became a self-appointed crusader against lawlessness, preached vehemently from the pulpit, conducted raids on local liquor establishments, and claimed to be the recipient of threatening letters for his efforts. In 1935 he was arrested for impersonating a law officer, held briefly, and released. The next day he shot and killed the police chief on a downtown street, fled the scene, and when apprehended was found to have a small armory in the trunk of his car.[44] During the trial he recalled having led a mob on one occasion that lynched an African American.[45] The prosecution asked for the death penalty, but defense attorneys succeeded in securing a five-year sentence for him at the state prison in Huntsville.[46]

Texas leaders who favored Prohibition were quick to argue that repealing it was not the way to spark the economy. In 1933, as voters contemplated and then on November 24 approved the Twenty-first Amendment to repeal Prohibition, the Roosevelt administration came under withering attack from Prohibition advocates. "Our mothers and fathers taught us that when times are strenuous we must work harder and save more," a United Forces for Prohibition speaker declared. "Now we have a prophet in the White House who counsels us to work less, stay drunk and spend all our money. Gamblers will tell you that the term new deal means that the sucker has been drawn in a bit and the marked cards are being brought into play."[47] Although Prohibition continued to be widely discussed in 1934, voters ratified a repeal of the state dry law in 1935. The issue surfaced again during the 1936 presidential campaign and in 1938, but it ceased to be the front-burner issue it had been earlier.

Wholesale condemnations of the social arrangements underlying the hardship people were experiencing were rare but by no means absent. One such critic was James H. "Cyclone" Davis, a colorful East Texas county judge who gained notoriety as a Populist organizer and served in the U.S. House of Representatives from 1915 to 1917.[48] In his late seventies when the Depression started, Davis vehemently denounced the social injustices that had concerned him as a populist and which he now identified as the underlying source of poverty and unemployment. "In the 109th Psalm when David wanted to punish his enemies he prayed that the extortioner might get hold of them," he observed. "The extortioners have got the common herd in this country and have had hold of them fifty years. Hence, we have millionaires and mendicants, bread lines and busted banks, purse proud plutocrats and poverty-stricken farmers, all because our statesmen will not regulate commerce so as to establish justice and domestic tranquility."[49] Davis considered the problem a failure of political nerve but also one of moral decay. "When moral codes and moral creed shall have given way to lush and greed," he wrote, "I see our land in sad dismay."[50]

A few religious leaders took the occasion to criticize the social arrangements they considered having contributed to the Depression as well. One such critic was Dallas Central Congregational Church pastor Grover L. Diehl. In a Labor Day sermon at the church in 1933, Diehl criticized laissez-faire economic theory for having encouraged injustice and individual greed. "Conditions in this country are a challenge to the followers of Christ, who fed the multitudes and condemned men who robbed the widows," he asserted. Government regulation of business, he believed, would prevent profiteering and curb injustice while maintaining sufficient room for rugged entrepreneurial individualism.[51]

At the opposite end of the theological spectrum, fundamentalists argued that hard times were the result of divine punishment. People were turning away from God, they said, living in sin, drinking, committing adultery, and being seduced into false beliefs by teachers indoctrinating children with ideas about evolution. "We have sinned, forgotten God, broken his commandments," a believer in Britton, Texas, observed. The only way out was repentance.[52] A Baptist pastor in San Antonio reminded his congregation that in the days of Malachi there was a great depression with much suffering, all caused by backsliding and the failure of God's people to pay their tithe.[53] Some saw parallels between edicts from the White House and tyranny depicted in the Bible. The end times were at hand. "There are just two powers, one of God and one of Satan," the pastor of the fundamentalist Church of the Living God in Cisco observed, "and the latter seems to be in the supremacy." He thought Congress should call for a national day of fasting and prayer. It had worked miracles before, he said, noting that a day of fasting and prayer on May 30, 1918, resulted in an allied victory over the Germans the following day.[54] The Bible, a Baptist pastor in Dallas explained, taught that drouth was divine punishment for people's backsliding and was meant to "turn them again to God."[55]

Dispensationalists who expected the imminent return of Christ drew sharp contrasts between that glorious reign and the present veil of tears. The "Improved Uniform International Sunday School Lesson" published weekly by Moody Bible Institute in Chicago and used widely in Texas churches and nationally featured lessons about the messianic kingdom ruled by Christ in which God's enemies would be scattered, righteousness would prevail, and justice and equity would be meted out. "It will be a prosperous reign," the lessons promised. "There will be no depression at that time."[56]

Fundamentalists were not the only ones deploring immorality and calling for repentance in response to the nation's economic woes. Acknowledging the hardship nearly everyone was experiencing, church leaders emphasized the deeper spiritual malaise they also felt had overtaken the nation. The Social Service Commission of the Southern Baptist Convention, which had been on the front lines of the denomination's efforts to deal with changing social conditions, reported in 1935 that the nation's supreme need was "to return to God in humble confession of sin." Industrial and economic recovery might occur, the commission observed, but a "nation-wide revival of pure evangelical religion" was more important. Rampant change and confusion could be dealt with only through individual personal regeneration.[57] The sense that basic moral foundations were crumbling was evident in other circles as well. Meeting in Dallas in October 1939, the North Texas Conference of Methodists burst repeatedly in shouts of "amen" as speakers encouraged the assembled pastors to sweep away the filth of nudity, gambling, and liquor that was wrecking the national character. Motion pictures, stage plays, and novels that might have been regarded as valuable social criticism—and would later be viewed that way—were considered differently. "Books like *Grapes of Wrath* are filled with mire and filth," one of the speakers explained.[58]

As it had in the past, religion provided a language not only of eschatological hope but also in which to express the heartaches of everyday life. "Mama found her consolation in religion," Bill Malone said. She went regularly to the Tin Top Pentecostal Church, found her salvation there, and in the simple cadence of scripture and hymns dispelled her loneliness and gave voice to her frustrations.[59] For others biblical language provided the idioms in which to describe a parched land, a wilderness of human distress. There was soul erosion as well as soil erosion, people said. They longed for green pastures. A 1932 version of the Twenty-Third Psalm that circulated widely in Texas communities expressed the heartaches in these words:

> Depression is my shepherd; I am in want.
> He maketh me to lie down on park benches;
>   He leadeth me beside the still factories.
> He restoreth the bread lines; He leadeth me in
>   the paths of destruction for his party's sake.
> Yea, though I walk through the Valley of Unemployment,
>   I fear every evil; for thou art with me;
>   the politicians and profiteers they frighten me.
> Thou preparest a reduction in mine salary before
>   me in the presence of mine creditors;
>   Thou anointest mine income with taxes;
>   My expenses runneth over.
> Surely unemployment and poverty will follow me all my days;
>   and I shall dwell in a mortgaged house forever.[60]

If biblical verse was good for lamenting hard times, religion helped on occasion to see the lighter side of life as well. Amarillo journalist and newspaper editor Henry Ansley, who died in an automobile accident at the age of thirty six, published an essay only a few months before his death entitled "I Like the Depression" in which he joked about having a healthier diet and more time to relax. "Three years ago, I never had time to go to church," he wrote. "I played golf all day Sunday and besides I was so darned smart there wasn't a preacher in West Texas who could tell me anything. Now I go to church regularly, never miss a Sunday." He added that if the Depression kept on, "I will be going to prayer meeting before long."[61]

PRIVATE CHARITY

Hard times, drouth, sagging markets, and even bank foreclosures had happened before. People of faith might interpret them as acts of God, as trials to strengthen their faith, or as a sign of the end times. The obvious response besides praying for help was to provide temporary relief to persons in need. In later years scholars would dismiss these voluntary relief efforts as misguided, ill informed, and naïve compared to the government programs effected through the New Deal. Other writers would voice criticisms of what they regarded as an expensive and ineffective welfare state by looking back to a time when neighbors simply helped one another through small acts of kindness. Neither view, however, adequately captured the fact that private charity had become well organized during the Progressive Era and, while unable to meet the challenges of the Depression alone, was a complex and evolving array of activities that adapted as well as it could to the changing times.[62]

Prior to the Depression religious organizations were already playing an important role in helping the hungry, homeless, and jobless. Many of these efforts dated to the 1890s when faltering economic conditions and progressive idealism prompted civic-minded clergy and lay leaders to create organizations to help the needy. These included efforts that continued under religious auspices, such as the Saint Paul Sanitarium, which opened in 1898 through the work of the Sisters of Charity of Saint Vincent de Paul. Other efforts, such as a campaign in 1896 by Methodist leader Virginia Johnson, led to nonsectarian organizations that received funding from local taxes as well as from private donors. An organization of this kind that was to play an important role during the Depression was United Charities, which began in Dallas in 1896 and took the place of short-term charitable efforts such as a clothing drive and charity circus the year before.[63] By 1915 the organization had been instrumental in a number of initiatives that ranged from an infant welfare association to a free kindergarten to a homeless shelter and that year came under closer coordination through a new municipal welfare department. Other organizations that were active in charity work by World War I included the Salvation Army, YMCA, YWCA, Red Cross, Jewish charities, and various ethnic associations.[64] Urban growth in the 1920s sparked additional charity and relief efforts. The Baptist Gospel Mission, founded in downtown Dallas in 1926, for example, held religious services daily, housed more than five thousand homeless men during its first three years, and served more than sixty thousand free meals.[65]

With the financial collapse in 1929, conditions worsened for the jobless and homeless as Texas also experienced its coldest winter in three decades. Service organizations faced rising demand at the same time that donations diminished. In Dallas relief work was organized by the Citizens' Emergency Relief Bureau with the support of voluntary donations to United Charities as well as public funds. In Houston relief efforts were organized by the Houston Community Chest, which required applicants for assistance to register with the city's unemployment bureau. Transients and persons living in Houston less than a month were required to work for meals and lodging, earning scrip exchangeable for food and shelter at a rate of twenty-five cents an hour.[66] City and county employees agreed to donate 1 percent of their salaries to assist in the effort.[67] Several dozen indigent families were said to be proudly working their way back to economic independence by planting gardens on untilled tracts near the city.[68] In both cities, churches and other religious organizations as well as civic clubs assisted in soliciting donations and providing volunteers.

The South Harwood Church of Christ in Dallas illustrated how even a small congregation could assist. The tiny church that could seat a crowd of no more than a hundred sitting on homemade plank benches was the spiritual home of white working-class families who decided they should follow the gospel message of caring for the poor. Two of its members were social workers who kept the congregation apprised of needs in the community. A shipping clerk headed up the relief effort, which included clothing, groceries, and medicine for families in need. Pastor Huff was confident that if all the churches in Dallas did their share, every needy family could be helped. But he was right in recognizing that there was also resistance.[69] Pastors worried that church members would not give or would quit attending if too much pressure was applied. Additional misgivings stemmed from concerns about relief itself and what it implied about self-sufficiency.

The question that was to be asked repeatedly was how to provide relief without encouraging perpetual dependence among the recipients. "When you become a charity worker in a retail way by buying a meal or giving a dime to a beggar, you are always confronted with the [question], was that a needy cause?" a spokesperson for United Charities in Dallas observed. It was consoling to think that no harm was being done, he acknowledged, but that was not sufficient when charity work was being done on a large scale. "We must have investigation, not alone to guard against exploitation by those not really in need," he argued, "but to ascertain such facts as will enable us to eliminate the cause."[70]

Charitable organizations publicized stories about destitute families who were receiving help. One such story described a migrant farmworker family not far from Dallas. The mother died in the cotton fields. As winter set in, the father, with three older sons and four younger children, sought refuge in a deserted house. Two of the children did not have shoes or stockings, and the family had

FIGURE 13. African American preacher, 1939, San Antonio, Texas, reading the Bible during door-to-door evangelism. Photograph © Russell Lee. U.S. Farm Security Administration—Office of War Information Photograph Collection. Library of Congress Prints and Photographs Division, Washington, DC.

nothing to eat. Volunteers rescued the family, placed the younger children in a boarding home, and got one who was ill to the hospital. The father and older boys insisted on shifting for themselves. "A true case like that makes us realize how close comparative ease and comfort is to destitution and deprivation," the story concluded.[71]

But stories of appreciative recipients who insisted on being as self-sufficient as they could were matched by cautionary tales. These stories reminded donors and volunteers that the poor could not be trusted. A man who came seeking help from a service organization in Dallas illustrated the point. It turned out that over a seven-year period he "received help from practically every church and social agency" in the city.[72] The main point of the story was that private charity needed to be handled by experts who could make proper inquiries of supplicants coming for help and judiciously decide between the shiftless and those willing to shift for themselves. In this instance it was United Charities staff who were capable of making the appropriate decisions and not the unsuspecting pastors of local churches. It was also clear that people were out there posing as beggars who truly did not deserve help.

As the numbers who were jobless, homeless, and hungry increased, it became harder for private charity to keep up, not only because of financial difficulties but also because of how private charity was organized. United Charities took pride in working closely with the families it served, knowing them and their individual needs, and providing them with professional assistance from trained social workers. "Their records are on file by name, assumed name, address, former address and the times at which they are helped and by whom," an announcement explained. "All this information is kept for the use of hospitals, churches, clinics, nurseries, Salvation Army, United Charities."[73] In conjunction with the public welfare board, United Charities operated a social service exchange to further monitor who was asking for and receiving what kinds of help. This program was of considerable value in ensuring that swindlers who might come to residents' homes selling candy or New Testaments or asking for handouts could be limited. It provided a way for churches to coordinate giving and volunteering. But it sometimes pitted centralized professional efforts against the decentralized volunteer efforts of congregations. And it was not well designed to address the needs of transients or of the vastly rising numbers of unemployed.

In December 1930 United Charities in Dallas announced that it would henceforth deal only with needy families without able-bodied heads, and the city welfare board would be responsible for helping families with an able-bodied person who was unable to find work. In addition, these able-bodied persons would be required to earn the assistance they and their families received by cleaning alleys, clearing vacant lots, improving parks, and performing other public service activities. The following month the welfare bureau reported that it had fed 107 Mexican families, 1,161 African American families, and 1,026 white families; there was a special soup kitchen for African Americans feeding 150 persons a day.[74]

But by the middle of 1931 people were being turned away, the amount of assistance available per family was reduced, and the Red Cross was having to solicit additional help from citizens in providing emergency food and clothing. Stories circulated of families having survived the winter on meat from turtles and skunks. In Lubbock the Salvation Army was feeding fourteen hundred people, and United Charities was providing emergency relief to more than a thousand.[75] The Negro Interdenominational Ministers' Alliance in Dallas, which included seven of the city's prominent African American pastors, pledged to step up its efforts to help the needy and jobless, as did the Jewish Social Service Bureau and the Society of Saint Vincent de Paul.[76] Downtown congregations solicited in-kind donations of flour from local mills and produce from members' gardens. Not to be outdone, the Good Sinners' Recreation Club initiated a relief program for Mexican Americans, gave out blankets and bread, and made plans for a community garden. The Dallas pastors association announced a plan to organize churches and enlist their help more systematically in working with United Charities. "These trained workers in charity, both in denominational and nondenominational service, can apply your money more intelligently than you can yourself, because they know hundreds of cases by name and history for months and even years back," the association argued.[77]

Besides dealing with increased needs, private charities faced two concerns. One was that other programs, such as schools and educational activities that came under the heading of character development and in the 1920s had received upward of 80 percent of the funding solicited through United Charities, were having to be dramatically reduced. "That the hungry must be fed, the naked clothed and the homeless housed admits of no argument," observed a pastor who served on the United Charities board. But he was concerned that "more intangible benefits such as character development and educational projects are not so readily endorsed by the public" despite these being the true sources of "sound economically independent citizenship."[78] The other concern was that by 1931 some governors and legislators in other states were already calling for assistance through a program of federal government loans. A program of this kind was deeply undesirable, the *Dallas Morning News* editorialized, because it would "promptly dry up private and local governmental contributions and almost surely result in extensive grafting and in political log-rolling."[79]

A report compiled by the Russell Sage Foundation showed that in 1931 community chests in two hundred cities nationwide raised more than $67 million. Seventy-one percent came from tax funds and 19 percent from private contributions. The amount raised in Dallas on a per capita basis was 49 cents, well above the 15 cents per capita in San Antonio, but well below the amount raised in most New England and North Atlantic cities.[80] In 1932 United Charities in Dallas operated at a deficit as its overall case load doubled compared with the previous year; that winter the organization received as many requests for help each month as it had during the entire winter in 1929. In Galveston, where United Charities was operating at a deficit, board member Rabbi Henry Cohen appealed for donations as a way to halt the moral decline of the city. "Our churches seem to be well-filled, but of what service is prayer and praise if our fellow-kind starves?" he asked.[81] Beaumont, where most of the funds for charitable relief came from county taxes, drastically reduced its relief budget. "There are too many people just looking for a chance to get something for nothing," one of the county commissioners explained.[82] The Red Cross was again called on to provide emergency food and clothing. Squatters from farms and from other states were living in tent communities. Agitation was forming among unemployed workers. Hunters organized rabbit-killing drives to supply meat to the homeless and jobless.[83] That fall when voters went to the polls, Roosevelt received 57 percent of the popular vote nationally to 40 percent for Hoover. In Texas Roosevelt won by an overwhelming 88 percent to 11 percent margin.

GOVERNMENT PROGRAMS

Although they thought private charity could go a long way toward solving the problems associated with the Depression, Texas leaders looked to local, state, and federal government programs for assistance from the start. Initially leaders expected construction projects to be the solution for unemployment. In 1930 leaders sought federal assistance through the Bureau of Public Roads, which promised ten million dollars for highway construction if the state would match those funds. Over the next year a six-million-dollar irrigation project was begun in Maverick County, and a federal building costing nearly half a million dollars was begun in Wichita Falls.[84] Other projects included a federal prison, improvements of the intercoastal waterway along the Sabine River, and half-million-dollar construction projects at Fort Sam Houston and Randolph Field in San Antonio.[85] The Wichita Falls federal building proved beneficial not only to the wider community but particularly to the trustees of the First Methodist Church, who received $125,000 for the land on which the building was constructed.[86]

By late 1934, despite vociferous opposition from the National Association of Manufacturers, who accused the federal government of imposing Soviet-style opposition, new projects were being funded to directly provide jobs in sectors beyond construction. One of the chief projects in which Texas participated was the opening or reopening of twenty-eight plants for the production of clothing and mattresses from surplus cotton. The plan aimed not only to create jobs and use surplus cotton but also to provide clothing and mattresses at prices the unemployed could afford. Plants employing between fifteen and twenty-five workers, most of whom were women, were opened in Austin, Beaumont, Dallas, El Paso, Houston, Huntsville, Lubbock, and twenty other Texas towns.[87] Officials estimated that $20 million of the $500 million allocated nationally by the federal government for civil works projects was being spent in Texas.[88] Construction projects organized through the Civil Works Administration, though, were barely making a dent in the overall situation.[89] The Federal Emergency Relief Administration reported that eighteen million persons were on relief nationally, an increase of nearly five million over the previous year, and social workers predicted that few of this number would be self-supporting any time soon. [90] The peak of the relief load in Texas occurred in January 1935 when 278,000 cases involving 1,251,000 persons were on the rolls.[91]

That January when the Texas legislature met to vote on measures that would allow the state to benefit from federal assistance, T. J. Holbrook, a prominent Democratic senator from Galveston, bitterly assailed the proposals for more than an hour. Property rights and indeed personal liberty were at stake, Holbrook charged. These were socialistic programs that would lead to a dictatorship like the ones in Europe. The New Deal would mean hordes of federal agents swarming all over the state, he warned. These were the criticisms being voiced in other states by prominent Republicans. But in the Texas legislature they were not widely shared. The bills passed with Holbrook's as the only opposing vote.[92]

Drouthstricken areas of Texas were now eligible for assistance from federal programs offering temporary work on highway construction projects, assistance for purchasing feed for cattle and seed for forage crops, and soil conservation projects. The government would purchase livestock that farmers could no longer afford to feed and would purchase bales of cotton. Plans were also discussed to resettle abandoned farms. Other federal programs established transient camps for temporary workers, made housing loans available, forestalled bank closures, and provided student loans. On August 14, 1935, Roosevelt signed the Social Security Act with provisions for unemployment compensation, old-age insurance, public health services, and aid to families with dependent children. When Roosevelt toured Texas the following June, more than a million people turned out to see him. He received 87 percent of the popular vote that fall.

Pastors and lay church leaders had mixed views of the government programs instituted by the Roosevelt administration. On the one hand, they wanted government to help the needy because that role was too heavy for the churches to bear alone. "As I see it," a lay Baptist leader in Dallas explained, "Christian churches were not established for the purpose of supporting the indigent and unemployed." The church's main task, he reasoned, was to minister to spiritual rather than temporal needs. Churches were already giving generously to programs for orphans and widows. "To expect the churches to shoulder the tremendous task of supporting the unemployed and the indigent of our country is unthinkable," he said. "This task is a governmental affair."[93] Others praised the New Deal's emphasis on brotherhood and equality. "The brotherhood of man is now supreme," an Episcopal bishop explained. "Never again shall the dividends of the rich be made the blood money of the poor."[94] It was perhaps sweet music to some ears as well that church modernization and improvement projects could be subsidized through loans from the Federal Housing Administration.

On the other hand, clergy worried about government gaining influence over people's lives. "Many millions are trusting in no God other than the government's bread basket," a Dallas pastor told the general assembly of the Cumberland Presbyterian Church in June 1935.[95] President C. C. Selecman of Southern Methodist University expressed a similar view, noting the tendency of government "to take over most of the former social functions of the church."[96] That was the message at the 1939 gathering of Methodists as well in which the *Grapes of Wrath* was denounced. "There has been set up what is called a planned economy," one of the speakers observed. "What the individual needs today isn't planned economy, but a planned regeneration."[97]

Lifelong Democrats had found themselves at odds with the national party often enough to be critical of the New Deal. Clergy who fought for Prohibition in 1919 and opposed Al Smith in 1928 felt betrayed when Prohibition was repealed. As the Depression continued, they saw little to be pleased about in government programs. "Like the prodigal son," Baptist leader J. B. Cranfill mused in 1939, "the new deal has wasted its substance in riotous living." There was no possibility, he thought, that any benefit would come from the "billions wasted" by the administration on the "idiocies" of its various programs.[98] The worst part, Cranfill argued, was not only that the government had wasted in his estimation more than fifteen billion dollars, but also that the individual initiative so vital to American freedom and prosperity was being undermined. "Many lazy, thriftless men who have become wards of the government will never willingly work again," he believed. "Individual initiative has in a great degree disappeared. From diapers to doughnuts the new deal wastrels are seeking to prescribe for the American people the new manner of life, which is to bleed the government in every possible way for personal gain."[99]

Clergy were especially concerned about the rising influence of government when they likened this increase to the spread of communism. That concern was on the mind of the Dallas pastor as he warned about dependence on government. With "communism gaining ground," he said, "we need to dig again the old well of Christian patriotism."[100] It might even be good to endure economic hardship if that experience strengthened Americans' spiritual resolve. A similar theme emerged at a meeting of the National Council of Catholic Women in Galveston in 1936. A bishop from Amarillo observed that the National Recovery Act was generally sound despite flaws, but a bishop from Natchez, Mississippi, warned that powerful forces were tearing people from God, promoting materialism and communism, and teaching atheism in the schools.[101]

Besides arguing that spiritual conviction and old-fashioned morality were the true answers to the nation's problems, clergy who opposed government expansion perceived it as a real threat to their own institutions. They feared that social security provisions could undermine their own pension programs and open the door for federal taxes on churches. They worried that government welfare programs would undermine the role of congregations and church-run benevolent associations in serving the needy. They especially wondered if federal aid for education would threaten church-run schools and colleges. Meeting in Oklahoma City in May 1939, the Southern Baptist Convention denounced an $855 million proposal by the Roosevelt administration to provide federal funds for education. The most worrisome aspect of the proposal, the Baptists said, was its potential to violate separation of church and state, by which they meant supporting Catholic schools. The proposal would have also provided funds to Baptist schools, but opponents argued that any such dealings with the federal government would be tantamount to the church selling its birthright.[102]

The American Protestant Hospital Association at its 1938 convention in Dallas expressed similar concerns. Fearing that the White House was promoting socialized medicine, the association strongly condemned any proposal for government aid that would include compulsory health insurance. It encouraged representatives from each state to establish special committees to expand voluntary health insurance plans and to promote Protestant hospitals. A letter was read from the president of the Catholic Hospital Association, meeting concurrently in St. Louis, stating similar concerns about socialized medicine. Roosevelt's program was "very dangerous to the existence of voluntary hospitals, the Protestant leader observed. "If the government builds 500 hospitals, it will sap away the work of [our] institutions."[103]

Having developed their own means of helping one another and having resisted government interference before, Latter-Day Saints leaders took an even stronger

stand, urging members to refuse any government aid. Willful waste makes woe-
ful want, Elder Charles Rowan of the Texas Mission counseled in 1935. "Rugged
individualism of the pioneers of the church is the one sure way to success."[104] To
supplement individualism, Mormon families fasted two meals each month and
in turn donated fifty cents toward the church's relief fund.[105]

The Social Security Act generated little concern initially but by 1939 stirred
criticism from religious leaders who worried that a proposal to include clergy
and other religious workers in the plan would constitute undue intrusion of
government in church business. When it became clearer that religious workers
would receive benefits as well as paying into the plan, Catholic leaders ceased
criticizing the proposal and endorsed it, but Southern Baptists worried all the
more that separation of church and state was being violated. Meeting in Baltimore in 1940, church leaders asserted their general support for Social Security
but stated strong opposition to any amendment to the law that would mandate
participation by religious workers. Such an amendment, they said, would put to
the test "one of the cardinal tenets of our Baptist fold . . . namely, the separation of
church and state . . . for which Baptists have always stood and which constitutes
one of the main bulwarks of religious freedom and personal liberty."[106]

Although Southern Baptists' concern about Social Security stemmed most
clearly from the denomination's historic stance toward strict separation of
church and state, a related consideration derived from the denomination's relief
and annuity program that provided pensions for its retired clergy. The fund was
administered in Dallas, where state law exempted it from regulation by either
the state insurance or state banking department. Its treasurer, Orville Groner,
who filled the position three years after graduating from Toby's Business College
in Waco in 1915, was the brother of Frank S. Groner, the executive secretary of
the Baptist General Convention of Texas. With assets of only $106,000 in 1918,
the fund grew to $4.8 million by the end of 1939, of which $3.3 million reflected
earnings—a fact that the board proudly observed constituted spectacular growth
despite the Depression.[107] The fund was heavily invested in Texas Corporation
railroad bonds as well as in a diversified portfolio of treasury bonds, mortgages
and real estate, and stock. For anyone who may have been weighing the merits of
government-run programs, the fund's success served as an argument for private
investments.

Opposition to rising government influence stemmed from sources that may
have been heard at church meetings, but that reflected a more general view that
individuals and businesses should be left alone. This sentiment was certainly
shared by the oil and gas industry, whose leaders strongly resisted government
regulation of drilling and government control of fuel prices. At statewide hearings oil company executives repeatedly derided the federal government not only
as a specific hindrance to their own activities but also as a general impediment
to freedom and progress. As one leader summed up the prevailing view: "The
federal government has never made a success of anything it has tried to run."[108]

The oil and gas industry was not alone in voicing concern about government regulation. The Texas grain dealers association expressed worries that government controls on crops would dampen profits. Bank officials went on record in opposition to federally financed mortgage loans. Rio Grande valley grapefruit shippers challenged the Agricultural Administration Act's constitutionality. The state's insurance agents met to discuss ways to prevent government agencies from cutting into their business. Although these were not religious organizations, it was not uncommon for leaders who were good church members living in heavily churched communities to invoke divine blessings on their proceedings. Clergy shared rosters with bank presidents and Chamber of Commerce heads, meetings began with invocations and hymns, and on special occasions church choirs added lyrical reminders of God's presence.

For African American clergy an infusion of federal government funds generated hope that conditions would improve for struggling low-income families. Federal projects providing jobs in construction and federal housing loans were especially welcome. However, the local administration of these projects and loan programs left much to be desired. The NAACP received numerous complaints of discrimination against African Americans in the distribution of relief assistance. White administrators made it difficult for African Americans to qualify, and jurisdictional disputes clogged the process of distributing funds.[109] A study by the National Urban League in 1936 showed that 50 percent of Austin's African American population had annual family incomes of less than $500, but a significantly lower percentage were receiving government relief assistance.[110] It did not help that the Social Security Act excluded domestic workers, many of whom were African American women. In Dallas the local housing authority confiscated a large number of African American homes in order to construct a new project and promised only to help the displaced families find houses for sale in white neighborhoods. Increasing racial tension in the affected neighborhoods ensued. By 1940 effigies were being burned, street fights were occurring with increasing frequency, and white vigilantes were bombing African American houses. Black pastors threatened to seek help from the U.S. Department of Justice if measures were not taken to halt the violence. City officials responded by removing the African American families who had recently been moved into white neighborhoods and by promising to reestablish clear lines of segregation.[111]

MOBILIZING FOR WAR

Southern church leaders may have worried about the federal government becoming too involved in the affairs of local communities, but when it came to Roosevelt's efforts to mobilize the nation to defend itself and then to mobilize against totalitarianism in Europe, they were among his most enthusiastic supporters.

Truett of Dallas was still president of the Baptist World Alliance when it held its sixth international congress in Atlanta in July 1939. Dr. L. K. Williams, who had addressed the Texas Centennial Exposition with Truett in Dallas in 1936, was there as head of the National Baptist Convention. Both leaders received enthusiastic applause when they greeted the assembled crowd of thirty thousand. But the strongest applause came during a message read by general secretary Dr. J. H. Rushbrooke of London from Roosevelt. "Institutions of free government are challenged," the message stated, leaving no question that this was happening in Europe. And in view of that threat, Roosevelt explained, Baptists had a special role to fulfill. "As inheritors of the noble tradition of Roger Williams, their place must ever be among those who uphold freedom of conscience" and work to ensure that "justice may be maintained and extended among men and nations."[112]

Roosevelt was careful to acknowledge that religious sentiments ran against going to war while arguing that freedom should be defended at any cost. In a radio address to the nation a few weeks after his message to the Baptist assembly, he expressed hope that the United States could keep out of the war that was taking place in Europe even as the details he described of the aggression there suggested that this hope might be impossible to sustain. "Most of us regardless of what church we belong to believe in the spirit of the New Testament," he said, "a great teaching which opposes itself to the use of force, of armed force, or marching armies and falling bombs." Americans understandably wanted peace, he observed, but that desire had to be balanced against the preservation of national safety, which might include acting elsewhere to prevent war from coming to America.[113]

Through much of the buildup toward World War II, Texas church leaders had in fact embraced peace efforts more publicly than war preparations. The large urban churches that routinely served as venues for public lectures by visiting speakers hosted numerous events under the banner of peace. In 1936 clergy and lay volunteers from Dallas churches and Southern Methodist University organized the Emergency Peace Campaign to solicit funds and sponsor meetings on behalf of world peace. The following February suffragist, social worker, and author Maude Royden from Oxford included a lecture at the First Baptist Church in Dallas on a thirty-seven-city tour of the United States in which she appealed for legislative measures requiring the nation to remain permanently neutral except in cases of invasion. The Dallas Emergency Peace Campaign, now chaired by the pastor of the First Methodist Church, sponsored the event.[114] Royden condemned Hitler's dictatorship but, in an appeal aimed at listeners who knew what living through the Great Depression was like, observed that the German people were suffering from poverty induced by the terms under which the previous war had been settled.[115] Her lecture was well attended but also sparked criticism. Was it wise to trumpet pacifism when the world was clearly heading for war, critics asked? Of course everyone preferred peace, they said, but the president was making every effort to prepare defensive armaments. Patriotic Americans should support the president.

In 1940 Dallas churches were still publicly proclaiming the need for peace, although with less confidence that America's entry into the European conflict could be avoided. In early September, following an appeal for peace by Roosevelt, the city's leading pastors devoted Sunday services to the topic of world peace. All the downtown Catholic churches included prayers for peace and special sermons. Presbyterians, Lutherans, Episcopalians, Methodists, Baptists, and Christian Scientists each at their own services heard the president's proclamation read from the pulpit and listened as pastors stressed the need for Christian love among nations. With aerial bombing spreading across Europe, the prayers were not that war itself could be prevented but that peace could be restored. It was notable, too, that patriotic hymns were sung with considerable fervor and that reading the president's proclamation was as much about rallying around the president as it was about peace.[116]

One of the few prominent pastors to vocally oppose preparations being made for U.S. military involvement in the months prior to Pearl Harbor was Earl Anderson, the former ally of Frank Norris who had broken with the fundamentalist leader. Anderson opposed the lend-lease bill and legislation permitting U.S. Navy convoys, argued for a negotiated peace, and hoped to host an "America First" lecture by Charles A. Lindbergh or Senator Burton K. Wheeler. Anderson found himself increasingly on the defensive, though, and by May 1941 he was acknowledging the obvious fact that if the war became America's war, then it would be necessary to fight.[117] At a clergy forum that summer, he was the only speaker to caution against what he saw as American aggression. The Baptist, Catholic, Lutheran, and Methodist speakers expressed confidence in the president and argued that his judgment deserved their full support.[118]

Patriotism was now encouraged more than ever before. A newly formed American Home Defense League staged patriotic parades, pledged itself ready to assist public officials in maintaining law and order, and investigated reports of alleged un-American activities. Legislators called for an investigation and general housecleaning of alleged communistic and Nazi activities at the University of Texas following publication of an essay in the student newspaper ridiculing the military. "They'll tell you how we have had a personal message from God informing us that He is on our side," the essay accused, adding that military leaders would say it made God smile when someone was killed. Organizations and population groups that may have been suspected of subversive activities during World War I or in conjunction with fears about communism faded from public view.[119]

The state's Mexican American population especially felt the need to demonstrate their loyalty to the United States.[120] Borrowing a page from Wisconsin, where the German-ancestry population felt a similar need, Mexican American organizations in Texas held special Citizens' Day ceremonies backed by Catholic and Protestant clergy, veterans organizations, civic associations, and the schools. "Little has been said of the duties of the citizens towards the government and it is our intention to emphasize these duties," the organizer of a Citizens' Day event in Brownsville in September 1939 explained. The event, he believed, would be a positive step toward "combating all 'isms' and subversive movements" that might be gaining ground. It would demonstrate "that there will be no room for any other ideal than Americanism."[121]

UNITY AMID CONFLICT

The national unity that World War II evoked was real in the sense that northerners and southerners, blacks and whites, Hispanics and Anglos, Catholics and Protestants, and Jews and Christians uniformly supported the war effort. An external enemy had that kind of effect on the nation's consciousness. Yet there were continuing divisions that would reappear and become contentious again when the war ended. Texans who were lifelong Democrats would continue to support Roosevelt's vice president when Roosevelt died but like many Democrats would find themselves dissatisfied with Truman's administration and attracted by the Republican candidacy of Dwight Eisenhower in 1952.[122]

How the military contributed to racial integration and how the NAACP worked to ensure that integration continued after the war would take further shape in the Supreme Court's 1954 ruling against school segregation in *Brown v. Board of Education of Topeka* and in the federal government's intervention in Little Rock in 1956. A legacy of the New Deal in Texas was the rising influence of public officials with strong ties to the federal government and to progressive voters.

The racial divisions that had long separated white and black church members continued but were softened by the leadership of clergy on both sides who favored racial reconciliation. Fundamentalists such as Norris opposed the more inclusive style of leaders and organizations such as the Baptist World Alliance. The potential influence of progressive clergy was limited as well by lingering suspicion of northern organizations such as the Federal Council of Churches that seemed too eager to embrace causes that worried southern clergy.

Always at stake were concerns about morality, whether in voicing opposition to dancing and motion pictures or in continuing the fight against the liquor industry. Mobilizing against abortion was still decades in the future, but anyone paying close attention might have anticipated that conflict over an issue having to do with sex and gender was certainly on the horizon. In 1931 at a meeting in North Carolina, the southern branch of the Presbyterian Church severed ties with the Federal Council of Churches. The grievance was the council's approval of birth control.[123] On this issue at least, southern Presbyterians and Catholics agreed. *Commonweal*, the lay Catholic weekly, declared the council's move an unconditional surrender to secularism.[124]

A new fissure that would have important implications in the years to come had also emerged. In Texas politics a line was now evident between two kinds of Democratic leaders. On the one hand were public officials whose electability depended on local ties and long-standing loyalties to the established machinery of local and state politics. The New Deal had been good to them, but their constituents in business, the churches, and local communities were concerned about federal intervention in local affairs. On the other hand was a new breed of officeholders whose fortunes were closely tied to the New Deal and to the federal government. They were successful enough in their own right and were well connected in their communities, but they also had wider relationships and interests. One example was Clifford Jones, a West Texas ranch owner who served as three-state regional director of the Public Works Administration, helped organize the Texas Centennial Exposition, built the Episcopal church his family worshipped at in his home community, and became the head of Texas Tech University in 1939.[125] Another of the new breed leaders gained a footing in politics directing the New Deal's youth employment program in Texas and ran successfully for a seat in Congress in 1937. His name was Lyndon Johnson.

CHAPTER 7

MOVING ONTO THE NATIONAL STAGE

Everything Is Big

Bigness in anything human—or in any divine enterprise entrusted to human fallibility—runs to machinery, to overlordship, to caucusing, committeeizing, compromise and watering down the gospel to a modicum of commonplace doctrine and maximum of statistics, reports and spinning wheels.

LYNN LANDRUM, "THINKING OUT LOUD," 1954

We've been reading a great deal about Texas in the last few days, and we have some Texans on the platform that are on our team. . . . Everything in Texas is big.

REV. DR. BILLY GRAHAM, NEW YORK CITY, 1957

I build machinery, almost any kind of machinery as long as it is big, and powerful, and can move around to do things no other machine could do before. Some people think I'm all mixed up—that you can't serve the Lord and business, too, but that's just the point. God needs businessmen as partners.

R. G. LETOURNEAU, *MOVER OF MEN AND MOUNTAINS*, 1960

The assassination of President Kennedy in Dallas on November 22, 1963, and Lyndon Johnson's succession to the White House put Texas in the national spotlight as never before. However, the state was already gaining greater attention in national affairs. Whatever else observers thought about it, they agreed that it was big. Texas was not only a large state that covered hundreds of thousands of square miles and had a colorful history. It was an increasingly important player in shaping American culture. Since the 1940s journalists had been describing it as a paradise for adventuresome commercial entrepreneurs, brimming in new wealth and power. In the 1950s Speaker of the House Sam Rayburn from Texas was said to be the most powerful person in Washington. Presidential hopefuls were making mandatory visits to meet with Texas oil barons. Fashion critics were trooping to extravagant celebrations at Neiman Marcus in Dallas and Houston. When locals appeared on television, there seemed to be an endless parade of cowboy hats and bolo neckties. There was also the Bible-Belt conservatism that pundits had been noting since the 1930s and that survey data now documented.

A Gallup Poll in 1962 showed 40 percent of the nation having attended worship services in the past week, but that number in Texas was 57 percent.[1] A 1964 survey found that 48 percent of American adults believed the Bible was "God's word and all it says is true," but the figure in Texas was 63 percent.[2] To the extent that religion influenced how people lived and how they thought about social issues, as it had during Prohibition and as it would increasingly in the 1970s and 1980s, what Texans did and believed religiously mattered. That was all the more evident because of the state's growing population and its rising economic and political clout. With twenty-five electoral votes, Texas was well positioned to be a decisive factor in any future election.

But Texas was still a relative newcomer in terms of economic and political power. The Depression had been hard on the state's economy. The steady population growth Texas had experienced during the preceding half century ground nearly to a halt in the 1930s. Although the state did not lose population like Oklahoma and the upper Great Plains, natural increase barely exceeded outmigration, resulting in net growth of only 1 percent a year. California grew twice as fast, giving it nearly a half million more people in 1940 than Texas did, despite having had a smaller population in 1930. The rest of the Southwest (Arizona, Nevada, and New Mexico) grew at a significantly faster pace, and Florida grew at three times the rate of Texas. Even North Carolina and Louisiana grew faster.[3]

The factor that significantly affected states' economies and demography in the 1940s was military spending.[4] A state as large as Texas and strategically located along the Gulf Coast and midway between the Atlantic and Pacific was well placed to be the recipient of a huge federal investment in military-related spending. It enjoyed a favorable position politically as well, not only because of its long Democratic tradition and overwhelming support for FDR, but also because one of the most influential public servants in Washington was from Texas. Rayburn had represented his district in Congress ever since 1913 prior to serving as Speaker of the House from 1940 to 1947.

Texas did benefit significantly from military installations and contracts. By 1945 the state was home to sixty-five army airfields, thirty-five army forts and camps, seven naval stations, and more than sixty prisoner-of-war camps. An estimated 1.5 million people received military training in Texas.[5] Between June

1940 and September 1945, the federal government spent $3.7 billion in Texas on major war supply contracts for combat equipment, $2.2 billion on other war supply contracts, and $1.2 billion on industrial war facilities contracts. Many of these projects brought personnel to Texas who stayed. The projects also left valuable infrastructure that businesses, colleges, and other institutions capitalized on after the war.

Yet in absolute terms or on a per capita basis, federal military contracts in Texas during World War II were relatively small. More than twice as much was spent in California, New York, Michigan, and Ohio, and as much or almost as much was spent in Connecticut, Illinois, Massachusetts, and Pennsylvania. On a per capita basis, federal spending on military contracts was higher in twenty other states than in Texas. The reason was that military production depended on industry and thus was located most heavily in industrial states. But on a per capita basis, spending was higher even in Kansas, which was not a state known for its industry.[6]

Although Dallas, Fort Worth, Houston, and San Antonio had become large population centers, much of Texas in the 1940s was still predominantly rural. In 1940 a majority of the population (55 percent) still lived on farms or in towns of less than 2,500 people. By the end of the decade, as mechanization spread and the size of farms increased, that proportion fell to 37 percent. Agriculture nevertheless remained the backbone of the state's economy. In 1949 the value of farm products totaled $1.7 billion, more than in any other state. Living in rural areas meant both a different source of income from urban areas and a different way of life. In 1940 only 20 percent of Texas farms had running water and only 18 percent had electric lighting, whereas these amenities had been present in cities for a generation or more. By 1950 most farms had electricity, but less than a quarter had telephone service.[7] Rural families' incomes fluctuated wildly from year to year depending on weather and crop prices, and communities struggled to consolidate and upgrade schools, while cities dealt with congestion and continuing debates about residential segregation.

The upshot of these patterns was that Texas was a state of extreme inequalities. In 1950 median yearly income for adult males age twenty-one and over was $2,250 for white Anglos, $1,250 for Mexican Americans, and $1,050 for African Americans. By 1960 median incomes across the state rose by 47 percent in inflation-adjusted dollars, but incomes among Mexican Americans and African Americans remained at about half the level of incomes among white Anglos. These differences, plus the fact that average incomes were higher in cities than on farms, resulted in marked geographical differences as well. In twenty-seven counties, including the ones in which Dallas, Fort Worth, Houston, and Lubbock were located, fewer than one family in five earned less than $3,000 in 1960, whereas in sixteen counties, most of which were located in the lower Rio Grande valley or in East Texas along the Sabine River, more than three-fifths of the families earned less than $3,000.[8]

Scattered across the state also were the few fortunate Texans who had done very well for themselves. Two percent of the population earned at least four times the median income, and 1 percent earned upward of eight to ten times the median amount. These included oil tycoon H. L. Hunt, whose fortune in 1957 was estimated at $400 million to $700 million, and Houston architect and developer Wyatt C. Hedrick, whose father-in-law Ross S. Sterling earned a fortune as the organizer of the Humble Oil Company. Although the New Deal was usually regarded as a leveling influence in American life, it was a source of enormous wealth for a few as well. One beneficiary was developer and publisher Jesse Holman Jones, whose good fortune of having invested in Humble Oil earned him enough prominence to be appointed in 1933 by President Roosevelt as chair of the Reconstruction Finance Corporation. In that capacity Jones was said to be one of the most powerful men in America. His death in 1956 left the *Houston Chronicle* in the hands of his nephew John T. Jones, who became one of Lyndon Johnson's strongest supporters for the presidency in 1964.[9]

More than anything else, oil had become the source of wealth and influence in Texas. New fields, additional wells, and soaring demand for fuel from the automobile industry, aviation, agriculture, and the military resulted in unprecedented expansion. In the 1920s Texas lagged well behind California, Oklahoma, and Pennsylvania in mineral production, but that changed with the discovery of oil in the Longview area in 1930 and further development in West Texas around Midland. By 1932 only Pennsylvania exceeded Texas, and in 1935 Texas rose to first place. In 1948 the value of mineral production in Texas was twice that of any other state. By 1959 Texas was producing more than $4.2 billion annually in petroleum and natural gas, accounting for almost half of all such production in the entire nation.[10] Nearly six thousand companies were directly involved and employed more than 136,000 workers.

The petroleum industry contributed to further inequalities based on landownership, location, race, and ethnicity. Income from leases and jobs resulted in a significant positive correlation (0.499) at the county level between total receipts from mineral industries and median family income. In addition, surplus that far exceeded contributions to local landowners and employees was concentrated among the few who held principal shares in the drilling and production companies.[11] Entrepreneurs such as Hunt and Sterling who got in on the ground floor were only a few of the ones to strike it rich. Another was Sid W. Richardson, who became an independent oil producer in Fort Worth in 1919, purchased leases in large numbers in the 1930s, and at the time of his death in 1959 was said to be worth as much as $800 million. Yet another was Clinton Williams Murchison, the oil and gas developer who partnered with Richardson in the 1920s and in 1945 formed the Delhi Oil Corporation, which became one of the largest independent oil companies in the United States.

Success in the oil industry required government involvement to authorize leases, charter companies, protect property rights, create easements for roads and pipelines, build roads and pipelines, and channel military contracts. But for the most part the industry reinforced prevailing sentiments against government intrusion. To that end the industry's leaders cultivated ties with public officials who saw things their way. Richardson, for example, paid cordial visits to Roosevelt and Truman, kept them apprised of the industry's interests, carried on a close personal friendship with Dwight Eisenhower starting in 1941, and played a role in persuading Eisenhower to run for president in 1952.

These were among the economic, demographic, and political contexts in which religion emerged from World War II and contributed to the further shaping of race relations, faith convictions, and power. Churches benefited from the population growth driven by the postwar baby boom as well as from prosperous economic conditions. In many ways the late 1940s and 1950s were a time of calm serenity in which religious leaders could focus on church growth and family formation. That was certainly an image that made sense to later observers who viewed the period from the perspective of the more turbulent civil rights era that followed. And yet these were years of remarkable developments in religion, politics, and business—years of inequality, discrimination, and conflict. These as well as new discussions about the separation of church and state set the stage for the civil rights movement and shaped the response to it.

SHIFTING PATTERNS OF RELIGION

Baptists had always been strong in Texas, but by the early 1950s their numeric strength reached new heights. A privately funded study completed in 1952 provided better data than ever before on the location and membership of America's denominations and religious traditions. The number of Southern Baptists in Texas totaled nearly 1.4 million. That was more than twice the number of Southern Baptists in any other state. Much of the reason for this numeric superiority was that Texas had the largest population of any southern state. But Southern Baptists had managed to grow at a significantly higher rate than the general population. Since 1926, when the last credible figures on religious bodies had been attained by the U.S. Census, the population of Texas had grown 44 percent, but Southern Baptist membership increased by 194 percent. Texas was not unique in this regard. In the fifteen southern and border states where they were most heavily concentrated, the rate of increase in Southern Baptist membership exceeded the rate of population growth in every instance. However, the extent to which membership growth outdistanced population increase in Texas was among the highest. In raw numbers, more than 900,000 members were added in Texas in little more than a generation, nearly three times as many as in any other state.[12]

Methodists in the past had kept pace with Southern Baptists, starting churches in similar locations and attracting similar numbers of members, but by 1952 Methodists had fallen significantly behind. Compared to the nearly 1.4 million

Texans who were Southern Baptists, the number of Methodists totaled slightly less than 638,000. As was true among Southern Baptists, that number put Texas in the lead among all states in total Methodist membership. But the margin was much smaller for Methodists than for Southern Baptists. Several other states had nearly as many Methodists as Texas did. And unlike Southern Baptists, Methodist growth since 1926 was just barely larger than the increase in general population. In fact, the ratio of Methodist growth to population growth was smaller than in twenty-seven other states.

The extent to which Southern Baptists dominated Texas demography in 1952 could also be seen clearly in county-level comparisons. In a fifth of the state's counties, Southern Baptists outnumbered all other Protestants by two to one. In two-thirds of the counties, Southern Baptists accounted for at least half of all Protestants. Methodists, in contrast, were a majority of Protestants in only two counties. And they outnumbered Southern Baptists in only a dozen counties.

Numerous as they were, Southern Baptists and Methodists were not the only denominations that found Texas a fertile place to grow churches. Denominations that had come early were still a significant minority presence. African American Baptists numbered at least three hundred thousand. Disciples of Christ and Episcopalians each had more than a hundred thousand members, as did Presbyterians if the northern and southern branches were combined, and the same was true if the various Lutheran denominations were considered together. Newer groups that had mostly come into their own since World War I were beginning to make a showing as well. Assemblies of God claimed more than 75,000 members, Nazarenes numbered almost 14,000, Foursquare Gospel churches included about 2,500, and there were a few Churches of God and Pentecostal Holiness congregations.[13]

Following an initial ministry in Houston earlier in the century, Pentecostalism's inroads in Texas were largely among white, working-class families, although by the 1930s leaders of the predominantly African American Churches of God in Christ had founded several congregations in Texas, and other Pentecostal leaders were starting African American congregations. Pentecostal fellowships were spawned by traveling revivalists and by converts migrating to Texas from the South and from Southern California, and by entrepreneurial lay preachers inspired by experiences of divine healing and spiritual renewal.[14]

But if all the other predominantly white Protestant denominations, not counting Methodists, had decided to join forces, they still would have had fewer congregations than Southern Baptists, and their combined membership would have been less than half the number of Southern Baptists. That also did not take account of the fact that Texas included about as many Roman Catholics as Southern Baptists, as well as at least fifty thousand Jews. The relationships between Protestants and Catholics and between Christians and Jews were to become even more important than they had been in the past, but these relationships would be shaped by Southern Baptists' exceptional growth.

Why were Southern Baptists so much more successful than Methodists? Studies that have attempted to provide a general explanation for church growth have emphasized something called religious economies, which point to the idea that religious organizations compete with one another in the same way that businesses do.[15] According to this interpretation, Baptists and Methodists did better at competing for members during the nineteenth century than Congregationalists, Episcopalians, and Presbyterians by deploying such strategies as moving westward with the frontier, organizing themselves into small fellowships, utilizing itinerant clergy, and engaging aggressively in evangelism. That seems to have been true in Texas as well as in other parts of the country. But it does not explain why Baptists were doing so much better than Methodists by the middle of the twentieth century.

Part of the difference may have been demography. An explanation that seems to have explained later differences in membership trends reasonably well can be extended to the earlier period by considering differences in birthrates.[16] In 1940 birthrates in southern states were slightly above the national average, and that continued to be the case in 1950.[17] If higher birthrates meant that adults focused more of their attention on child rearing and thus tried to inculcate basic religious values, that could have contributed to the strength of a denomination that was predominantly located in the South. Of course that would have been true in Texas for Methodists as well as for Baptists.[18]

A better explanation stems from factors internal to the denominations themselves. Although the Depression imposed hardship on both denominations, Southern Baptists weathered the difficulties better than southern Methodists. From 1929 through 1937, the total number of Southern Baptist congregations nationwide increased by 834 while the number of southern Methodist congregations decreased by 249. Both denominations grew in membership, but Southern Baptists gained nearly 825,000 members, or an increase of 22 percent, while southern Methodists gained 228,000 members, or an increase of just 9 percent. In both denominations the number of clergy declined, but the number of Southern Baptist clergy had been growing in the 1920s while the number of southern Methodist clergy had been stagnant, such that by 1929 Southern Baptists had almost as many pastors as congregations while Methodists had only half as many clergy as congregations. Southern Baptists required fewer educational credentials than Methodists, and more of the Baptist clergy supported themselves with other jobs in addition to preaching. That difference, combined with lower congregational expenses overall, made it somewhat less difficult for Southern Baptists than for Methodists to withstand the Depression.[19]

In the 1920s progressive Southern Baptists such as Truett in Dallas developed closer ties with northern Baptists through the Baptist World Alliance, but there was little inclination to merge with northern Baptists, especially in view of conservatives' and fundamentalists' concerns about the influence of modernism in northern Baptist seminaries. In contrast, Methodists began serious discussions in the late 1920s about merging the southern and northern branches. These discussions came to fruition at a meeting in Kansas City, Missouri, over a three-week period in April 1939 when a union was enacted among the Methodist Protestant Church, Methodist Episcopal Church, and Methodist Episcopal Church South. As a final step before the meeting in Kansas City, Bishop John M. Moore convened a gathering in San Antonio in January 1939 to work out differences between the two branches concerning missionary activities and support. The meeting was hailed as a success, and the prospect of a larger, united denomination inspired hope that the church would be more effective at home and abroad in a world increasingly dominated by imperialism and on the verge of another global war.[20]

At a practical level, the plan was a response to the Depression as well, giving the administrators of Methodist colleges, schools, and mission boards hope that new resources would now be available. On the surface, the northern branch with nearly 4.4 million members and 24,000 congregations was significantly stronger than the southern branch with 2.8 million members and only 16,000 congregations.[21] But in some ways the northern branch had the most to gain. Concentrated as it was in the Midwest, where population was declining as a result of the Depression, the northern branch had lost as many members in the 1930s as the southern branch had gained. In any event, leaders on both sides proudly observed that theirs was now the largest denomination in America.

The chief unresolved issue was race. On the one hand, union was regarded by all who favored it as a major accomplishment in finally putting the Civil War and the legacy of slavery in the past. On the other hand, the African Methodist Episcopal and African Methodist Episcopal Zion denominations were not included, which meant a continuation of the racial segregation that characterized much of American Protestantism. In addition, the presence of some African Americans and a more inclusive attitude in the northern branch still did not sit well with some of the southern leaders.[22]

As the merger went into effect, Bishop James Henry Straughn was named general superintendent charged with the task of implementing it. Straughn was congenial and well liked but was also the right choice because he was from the small Methodist Protestant denomination and thus could be viewed as impartial with respect to the main northern and southern Methodist Episcopal branches. But several ministers from his own denomination voted against the merger and refused to leave their pastorates until a court ruling forced them to do so. Bishop Collins Denny of the Methodist Episcopal Church South conference in Richmond voiced disapproval of the merger as well. "To become a part of this new church is to accept substantially everything against which the fathers of my church protested; is to deny substantially everything which they maintained. This I cannot do," he declared. "I must keep faith with the dead, as well as the living, for it was from those mighty dead I received a trust which I vowed to defend."[23] The most serious holdout was the South Carolina conference, which not only voted against the union but also filed a lawsuit to challenge its validity. Grassroots resistance also emerged through a group calling itself the Laymen's Organization for Preservation of the Southern Methodist Church.[24]

Over the next several years, individual congregations quietly petitioned to cease being Methodists and shifted their official ties to various other denominations.[25] In instances where separate congregations from the two branches joined to form one congregation, holdouts drifted away or purchased the empty building to form an independent church. Families who were disgruntled shifted their membership to other churches where relatives and neighbors attended, which in the South generally meant a Baptist congregation. Others who initially went along with the merger became increasingly worried at news that further steps might be made to include African American denominations or to forge an alliance involving other white Protestant denominations. None of these problems reflected dissent among the majority of Methodists, but there was just enough dissatisfaction to gnaw around the edges.

If that was not enough to cause worries, Methodist growth compared to Baptist increases was hampered by the denomination's governing structure and financial picture and perhaps by its theology as well. The centralized polity of the denomination kept doctrinal disagreements under control, just as the Southern Baptist Convention did, and the hierarchy collected and distributed resources that helped keep struggling congregations in business. But centralization that included rotating clergy from place to place every few years did not facilitate the entrepreneurialism that went with being able to build up a congregation and benefit as it grew. Faithful Methodists paid an apportionment that went for the support of centrally administered activities, such as mission boards and colleges, but when more of those were in the North rather than closer to home, southern Methodists had less incentive to give generously. By the early 1950s conservative church leaders were also wondering if southern theological traditions were being swept aside by liberals trained in northern seminaries. That concern took wing in 1950 when the *Reader's Digest* published a widely read article titled "Methodism's Pink Fringe" in which it accused an organization called the Methodist Federation for Social Action of lacking patriotism and quoted the U.S. House of Representatives Committee on Un-American Activities as regarding the federation as a tool of the Communist Party. Southern Methodist leaders, including Bishop William C. Martin of Texas, found themselves on the defensive and quickly distanced themselves from the federation by arguing that the northern branch had started it.[26]

The effect of these various circumstances was clearly evident by the early 1950s. From 1940 until 1953, the total number of Methodist churches nationally declined by 2,359 as a result of consolidation and closures, while the total number of Southern Baptist churches increased by 4,463. With the postwar baby boom, both denominations grew, but Methodist membership increased by only 24 percent while Southern Baptist membership soared by 59 percent. Moreover, these trends were to continue. In 1962 Southern Baptist membership for the first time exceeded Methodist membership.[27]

In 1957 one of the first national surveys in which it was possible to distinguish Baptists and Methodists suggested another possible difference. Among white Baptists reared in the South, only 9 percent had any education beyond high school, whereas among white Methodists reared in the South, 33 percent did.[28] Polls conducted in Texas in 1960 found a similar pattern. Twenty-one percent of white Baptists in Texas had some college education, while among white Methodists in Texas 38 percent did.[29] Educational differences would be seen in subsequent studies as well and were one of the factors that would increasingly distinguish Baptists and Methodists on a wide range of theological, social, and political issues.

For Southern Baptist leaders, the South was still their primary focus of reference, even though new congregations were increasingly being initiated in the North, and Texas was well situated to be the denomination's most influential conference. In 1952, for example, the *Baptist Standard*, which was published in Dallas, circulated to 262,931 households, while the second most widely distributed paper, published in Greenville, South Carolina, had a circulation of only 85,534. Baylor University had property and endowment assets of more than $15 million, while the University of Richmond was in second place with only $7 million. Women's missionary societies in Texas raised more than half a million dollars that year, while their second-place counterparts in Georgia raised only a quarter of that amount. Texas Baptists contributed more than twice as much that year as Baptists in any other state to the denomination's home mission and foreign mission outreach. The relief and annuity account, which was still located and managed in Dallas, having dedicated a new $193,000 building there for its headquarters in 1941, now totaled more than $26 million.[30] In 1949 the Baptist General Convention of Texas reported "some denominations have experienced marked recessions in various phases of their work" but noted that "for years we have been majoring on and achieving, in comparison with others, unusual results in the field of evangelism." By 1953 the convention reported that fifty thousand souls were being baptized annually. In the interim, its central budget had nearly quadrupled, and its endowment was significantly enhanced through the generous giving of wealthy philanthropists.[31]

The point was not that Texas's numbers and wealth were moving the Southern Baptist Convention in a new direction. Baptists ensured that no location gained the upper hand by electing leaders and appointing boards reflecting the wider geographic diversity of the denomination. And for that matter five of every six Southern Baptists did not live in Texas. If anything, it was more that Southern Baptists held a strong place in Texas and were well placed to influence its affairs. One indication of what that influence might be was from an informal survey of the denomination's pastors in 1952. Ninety-seven percent said they believed that all Christians should be baptized and that baptism should be done by immersion under the authority of the church. Only 5 percent said they invited members of other denominations to share in observing the Lord's Supper.[32] Another indication of how the denomination was faring in Texas could be seen in comparisons among the state's counties. Southern Baptists were good at staying in familiar locations and even better at facilitating growth. Between 1926 and 1952 the denomination held its own and even increased its membership in counties with declining population or where the population was stable. And it was doing especially well in places where the population was growing, such as Dallas and Houston and the oil-rich areas around Longview and Midland. In counties where population doubled, Southern Baptist membership multiplied fivefold.

Texas Methodists, in contrast, were part of a national denomination in which two-thirds of the membership lived outside of the South and for the most part had no reason to embrace distinctive southern traditions. Well before the 1939 merger, Texas Methodists had been exploring closer ties with the northern branch. Southern Methodist University president Robert S. Hyer had proposed as early as 1910 that a plan for unification be prepared, and Texas bishop Moore, whose education included a Yale doctorate, drew up the plan.[33] William C. Martin, who became the Dallas–Fort Worth area bishop in 1948, also had connections outside of the South, previously serving the Kansas-Nebraska region from offices in Topeka and subsequently presiding over the National Council of Churches in 1953 to 1954 and the World Council of Churches from 1954 to 1961. As part of a national denomination, Texas Methodist leaders were also increasingly named to the boards overseeing national missions, educational programs, and church policies.

A 1964 survey provided some additional comparisons between Baptists and Methodists. Unlike the 1957 study that was less representative, the 1964 data showed that educational differences between the two groups among white southerners existed but were relatively small. Seventeen percent of white Southern Baptists living in the South were college graduates compared with 22 percent of white southern Methodists. Only 49 percent of the former lived in rural areas, while 64 percent of the latter did. Members of both denominations overwhelmingly said they believed in God, but Baptists were more solidly committed than Methodists to the kind of exclusive Christianity that was typically associated with fundamentalism and evangelical interpretations of the Bible. When asked if "a person who doesn't accept Jesus can be saved," 84 percent of white Southern Baptists in the South said no, compared with 62 percent of white southern Methodists.[34]

That emphasis on the necessity of believing in Jesus was certainly a cardinal teaching of Southern Baptists and was very likely a reason for an exceptionally high rate of active church participation. In the survey only 17 percent of white Southern Baptists in the South said they attended church services only several times a year or less, whereas 33 percent of white southern Methodists attended that infrequently.[35]

Extensive participation in their congregations had mixed implications for involvement in other kinds of organizations. Although the notion that Americans were joiners was borne out in the fact that people who went to church were also more likely to be members of other organizations, this was less true of Baptists than of Methodists. Fifty-six percent of white Southern Baptists in the South said they belonged to at least one club or organization such as a union, lodge, church group, political organization, or social club, whereas that was true among 67 percent of white southern Methodists. The sharpest differences were in organizations that the researchers classified as fraternal orders or school fraternities and sororities. Only 23 percent of the white Southern Baptists belonged to one of these, compared with 45 percent of white southern Methodists.[36]

If Baptists and Methodists were becoming more clearly differentiated in these ways, they and other denominations nevertheless faced common challenges. Unlike the 1930s when scraping together enough funds to survive was the principal challenge, the task as World War II ended was to build new churches fast enough to accommodate the population explosion taking place in cities and suburbs and near military bases and oil fields. By 1950 the churches had to build nurseries and new educational wings to handle the baby boom as well. Prosperity, generous loans, ample building supplies, and eager real estate developers facilitated the process. So did visionary church leaders who anticipated that newer, larger, and more commodious buildings would attract members. A Methodist leader speaking at a pastors' conference at Southern Methodist University in 1949 said his denomination nationally planned to open a new church every day during the next four years.[37]

National figures showed that contracts totaling $336.3 million were awarded to construct religious buildings in 1950. That was a tenfold increase since 1945 and was more than during the entire decade from 1931 to 1940.[38] Texas was experiencing a major building boom, with contracts for construction of all kinds exceeding $1 billion in 1950, which put it in third place among states, exceeded only by New York and Pennsylvania. More than twelve thousand new homes went up that year in Dallas, nearly the same number in Houston, seven thousand in Fort Worth, and six thousand in San Antonio.[39]

In oil-rich Houston, new church construction boomed almost immediately when war-induced building material scarcities ended. By 1947 Dallas and Fort Worth were following suit, with Baptists, Methodists, and Catholics all planning new buildings in the hundred thousand to three hundred thousand dollar range.[40] Over the next five years, church construction in Dallas alone included a hundred new projects totaling $15 million. Baptists accounted for nearly half the new projects.[41] In rural areas new churches were being constructed as well, although at considerably lower cost. In the small town of Tuscola, twenty miles south of Abilene, Baptists who had been meeting in the same small building since 1919 completed a new church in 1948 at a cost of only $25,000, doing much of the work themselves.[42] Meanwhile, Methodists in Abilene planned a structure for a new congregation there at a cost of $300,000.[43]

INNOVATIONS IN MINISTRY

Besides church expansion, the postwar period was marked by innovations in ministry that were to take on increasing significance in coming decades. These included greater use of radio, specialized parachurch ministries, larger evangelistic crusades, and experiments with religious television. Religious radio had been available on a small scale to listeners in Texas even before World War I. In 1922 the First Baptist Church in Dallas began broadcasting through "wireless telephony" and was pleased to report that listeners as far away as the Catalina Islands were hearing Truett's sermons. As the "radiomania epidemic" spread, other pastors began airing sermons but also worried that believers would opt for jazz from Kansas City or opera from Chicago.[44] Within two years, broadcasts were emanating from Norris's Baptist Tabernacle in Fort Worth.

In the 1930s a new 75,000-watt station at Villa Acuña, Mexico, opposite Del Rio, Texas, opened opportunities for broadcasters who wished to escape supervision by U.S. authorities. One who took advantage of the new facility was controversial Kansas doctor J. R. Brinkley, who proffered a goat gland concoction as an enhancement to male virility. Another was fundamentalist Gerald Winrod, who broadcast pro-Nazi propaganda and ran unsuccessfully for public office in 1938.[45] The station was powerful enough to transmit religious broadcasts, as Brinkley proudly proclaimed, "from the wind-kissed waves of the Atlantic to the placid billows of the Pacific—from the balmy banks of the Rio Grande to the Canadian's frozen land." Although the Mexican government shut it down in 1939, the station reopened a few years later, provided an outlet for Corpus Christi Pentecostal faith healer Reverend Asa A. Allen in the late 1940s and 1950s, and in the 1960s served as a broadcasting location for popular DJ Wolfman Jack.[46]

Throughout the 1930s radio brought comfort and inspiration as well as news and weather to Depression-ridden families through the Baptist Hour, gospel music, and sermons by local preachers. In 1937 Texas audiences began listening to radio evangelist Charles E. Fuller, whose *Old Fashioned Revival Hour* immediately gained popularity. When Fuller preached at the Scofield Memorial Church in 1940. more than four thousand people flocked to the event. By the mid-1940s church leaders determined that the cost of programming on AM stations was increasing to the point that FM broadcasting would be more efficient in the future. A station capable of broadcasting over a seventy-five-mile radius could be built or purchased for as little as $11,000 while larger stations might cost up to $40,000. By 1949, thirty-nine FM stations were in operation in Texas, including several owned and operated by Baptists from which preaching and gospel music aired.[47]

The growth of radio brought into being an organization that would later, through the combined efforts of radio, television, and large congregations, play an important role in national politics. Born at a gathering in Columbus, Ohio, on April 12, 1944, it brought together a small group of gospel broadcasters. Not surprisingly, many of the founders, including its first president, William Ward Ayer, were from large media markets such as New York and Los Angeles. But the group's other principal organizer and founding secretary was Texas fundamentalist Dale Crowley.[48] As a student at Baylor, Crowley had been expelled after accusing the school of teaching heresy. Like fellow fundamentalist Frank Norris, Crowley earned the dubious distinction of being arrested for murder. The incident involved the shooting of the church janitor in 1933 and Crowley's eventual acquittal. It occurred as part of what became known as the Jonesboro church wars in Jonesboro, Arkansas, when competing factions over a two-year period struggled to control the Jonesboro Baptist Church. Recently arrived from Denton, Texas, Crowley and revivalist Harvey Parnell fought over whose theology was most fundamentalist, drew crowds of up to five thousand people, and required the intervention of National Guard troops and the courts.[49] "Dallas has had her taste of rowing in the church house," the *Dallas Morning News* editorialized, but the writer hoped the city enjoyed a greater spirit of tolerance than in Jonesboro. "Losing religion in the church is not always so difficult as it ought to be," the writer observed.[50]

Crowley left Jonesboro soon after his acquittal, toured as an evangelist preaching about the second coming of Christ, supported the conservative Baptist Layman's Fellowship, and founded the Back to the Bible Crusaders of America radio ministry, which grew into a popular broadcast that included Bible quiz programs in which U.S. senators and representatives participated.[51] Years later a history professor pondered the Jonesboro church war and wondered if it had any significance except as a lesson in local eccentricity.[52] Crowley's role in specialized ministries certainly did extend further. The organization he helped found in 1944, the National Religious Broadcasters Association, became a deal maker in the religious wars of the 1980s.

Other specialized parachurch ministries prior to World War II, such as missionary auxiliaries, youth groups, and evangelistic crusades, mostly functioned through local congregations. Apart from the YMCA and YWCA, which were truly independent and increasingly received funding through community chest drives, these organizations were "parachurch" only to the extent that they were facilitated by denominational agencies and extended beyond the usual preaching and teaching activities of congregations. In the 1940s that changed. Nondenominational groups that targeted particular segments of the population, such as high school age youth or college students, increasingly organized specialized ministries. These organizations had been attempted with some success earlier in the century, especially on college campuses where volunteers formed missionary and evangelistic teams. But now with the experience of chaplaincies during the war and easier communication and travel, these ministries expanded. They focused especially on evangelism and were an outgrowth of the various evangelical, fundamentalist, and dispensationalist efforts of the 1920s and 1930s. Like those organizations, they bridged regions of the country, crossed denominational lines, and trained leaders who went on to lead conservative Protestant congregations.

A parachurch organization that achieved considerable success in Texas and nationwide was Youth for Christ, organized on a small scale in 1940 by evangelical leader Jack Wyrtzen in New York and then on a larger scale in 1944 by Chicago Baptist Torrey Johnson. In March 1944 Youth for Christ launched meetings at several Methodist churches in Dallas.[53] Although Youth for Christ was nondenominational, it canvassed neighborhoods for prospective churchgoers, enlisted youth who otherwise may not have attended church, encouraged them to join a church, and thus was apparently well received by Methodist pastors. Baptist leaders in Texas the following year took a different position. Viewing the movement as a threat to their own work, they denounced it for being interdenominational, declared that Baptists should remain true to their own "strict religious convictions," and set out to raise $6 million to expand their own youth programs. A pastor in West Texas charged that Youth for Christ was trying to organize a youth center in his town where dancing would occur, and he feared that "hard drinking" would undoubtedly happen nearby.[54]

Despite this rebuff, Youth for Christ prevailed. In 1946 it enlisted Harlin J. Roper, pastor of Scofield Memorial Church in Dallas, as one of its traveling conference speakers and arranged for local events in tandem with Dallas Theological Seminary. Youth for Christ leaders brought in guest speakers from Chicago and New Orleans, included lectures by gospel radio broadcasters, held meetings at Christian and Methodist churches, worked with the Salvation Army, organized groups in high schools, and sponsored community events that included choir music and tap-dancing performances as entertainment. Under the enlarged rubric of Youth for Christ International, its speakers included evangelists from other countries, and its fund-raising efforts extended to appeals to help launch overseas chapters. It drew audiences through talks by prominent college athletes, held Bible quizzes, showed films, and hosted college choir performances. One of the films featured the threat of annihilation from atomic weapons. Another emphasized the biblical story of creation. One of the singing groups in 1948 was from Bob Jones University, the fundamentalist college in South Carolina.

Shortly after the event at which the Bob Jones singers performed, a front-page story appeared in the *Southwest Advocate*, the official publication of the Methodist Church in Texas, criticizing Youth for Christ. The story disclosed that the Association of Christian Educators of Greater Dallas had conducted an investigation of the movement and concluded that its successes were worrisome. The movement was wooing young people away from the churches, the report said. It was attracting more young people than even the best congregational youth programs. Some of the critics charged that the movement was using "jazzed up" gospel music. Others argued that it was promoting fundamentalism.[55]

The criticisms did little to deter Youth for Christ from continuing its work. By 1950 Baptist clergy were appearing as speakers for the movement, and events were being held in Baptist churches as well as in high schools and community buildings. That June, a musical ensemble from Bob Jones University again performed in Texas. But by then another Youth for Christ leader was gaining even more attention.

Billy Graham had become Youth for Christ's first full-time worker in 1944 and was touring the country speaking at rallies and serving as its vice president from his home in North Carolina. In 1947 Graham preached in Dallas as part of a Youth for Christ team that included its president Torrey Johnson and youth evangelist Cliff Barrows, who had met Graham at a rally in 1945 and would continue as song leader for the evangelist's crusades over the next half century.[56] When Texans thought about Billy Graham in 1945, they probably had in mind the welterweight boxer by that name whose bouts were receiving more attention, but the other Graham was quietly gaining the confidence of church leaders.

Graham had been raised in the Associate Reformed Presbyterian Church, which was a strong conservative denomination in North Carolina, briefly attended what was then Bob Jones College in 1936, and graduated from Wheaton College near Chicago in 1943. Texas Baptists' skepticism toward Youth for Christ included Graham. In September 1950 *Baptist Standard* editor David M. Gardner criticized Graham on grounds of working too easily across denominational lines. "If Billy Graham has ever been vitally connected with Southern Baptists, we have not heard of it," Gardner wrote. "He would like to have Baptist support, but he is not supporting fundamental gospel principles for which Baptists stand."[57]

However, other Baptists were already warming to Graham. In 1949 an evangelistic crusade in Los Angeles drew national attention and led to the founding of the Billy Graham Evangelistic Association with headquarters in Minneapolis. In January 1950 Graham missed being a keynote speaker at a Baptist General Convention of Texas evangelism conference because a flight to Dallas was grounded in Minneapolis.[58] In early 1951 Graham conducted a successful monthlong series of revival meetings in Fort Worth.[59] J. Howard Williams, executive secretary of the Texas Baptist convention from 1946 to 1953, was said to have been the one who invited Graham to conduct evangelistic campaigns in Texas and encouraged him to win the support of local pastors by making the local congregation more important to his crusades.[60]

In 1953 Graham returned to Texas for an evangelistic crusade at the Cotton Bowl in Dallas. Some sixty thousand people showed up, a crowd so impressive that Graham referred to it again and again in subsequent meetings and enlisted several who participated for future events.[61] During the crusade Graham became a member of Dallas's First Baptist Church, now pastored by W. A. Criswell, who had succeeded Truett in 1944 and was already one of the Southern Baptist Convention's most prominent leaders.[62] Graham's membership at the Dallas church continued for the next half century, and Criswell remained an influential friend and supporter of Graham over the years. Graham also cultivated ties with a twenty-five-year-old Texan named Howard E. Butt Jr., who became another lifelong friend and supporter. Butt was the vice president of HEB Food Stores, a Texas chain of grocery stores begun by his grandmother in 1905. Shepherded since 1919 by his father into a flourishing enterprise of fifty-eight supermarkets, the chain would grow into a $250 million corporation by 1971.[63] Butt's father was a tradition-minded Baptist deacon who refused to sell beer or wine in his stores. In 1933 he established the H. E. Butt Foundation, one of the earliest independent philanthropies in Texas and a generous donor to religious and charitable organizations over the years.[64] Howard Jr. served on the board of the Billy Graham Evangelistic Association and through the family foundation played an increasing role in evangelical lay ministries and church renewal.[65]

Graham had yet another connection with Texas Baptists that illustrated an even more complex relationship among the churches and new emerging parachurch ministries. In 1939 a natural-born American citizen named Reiji Hoshizaki who was of Japanese ancestry and had recently finished high school in California moved to the Dallas area to work on a chicken farm. Hoshizaki had been raised Buddhist but was converted to Christianity shortly after arriving in Dallas and hoped to become a preacher. His parents were interned at a camp in Arizona during the war, lost everything, and in 1944 moved to Chicago to start over. While visiting them, Hoshizaki, who was now a student at Baylor, attended a Youth for Christ rally. Graham was the preacher.[66]

Inspired by Graham's message, Hoshizaki returned to Baylor, attended several Youth for Christ rallies in California, and hoped to engage in youth revival work just at the time that Texas Baptists decided they should organize such work themselves rather than cooperating with Youth for Christ. Hoshizaki and several other students planned a youth revival meeting in Waco, thinking at first that Youth for Christ speakers from Chicago would be featured, but they soon decided to work on their own. The weeklong revival proved to be a success and encouraged the students to plan a larger one the following year in Houston. One of the organizers that year was Howard Butt Jr.[67] With encouragement from Texas Baptist executive secretary Williams and Texas Baptist student ministries director W. F. Howard, the organizers, under the general directorship of Butt, held dozens of revivals over the next five years in cities across the South, from Atlanta to Fort Worth and as far away as Honolulu.[68] It was Butt's involvement in these crusades that caught Graham's attention, prompting him to term Butt "America's greatest young preacher."[69]

In conjunction with parachurch organizations and radio programming, television was the other new development that would play an important role in evangelistic ministries. Through its radio commission, the Southern Baptist Convention made plans at the end of World War II to cover the entire world with a network of international shortwave stations and to produce motion pictures to showcase church work and train ministers. These efforts put church leaders in contact with broadcasters and film producers who saw television as the next technological breakthrough. "This new method of broadcasting with picture as well as sound is hailed by big business and by leadership in the radio field as the most effective medium of mass communication discovered down to date," a 1947 report stated. "In a matter of months, Southern Baptists must face the opportunity of this new open door for the propagation of the gospel."[70]

By the end of 1947 only seven television stations were in operation anywhere in the United States. The first station in Texas began operating in Fort Worth on September 27, 1948, and by 1950 six stations were in operation, three of which were in the Dallas and Fort Worth market, two in San Antonio, and one in Houston.[71] During his Fort Worth revival in 1951, Graham preached twice at Criswell's church in Dallas, with both events televised locally to viewers as well as broadcast nationally by radio.[72] In 1952 Criswell was quoted as saying that television was a "gift from God" for spreading the gospel.[73] Services from his church as well as from the East Dallas Christian Church and the First Methodist Church of Dallas were being televised regularly. That year more than 290,000 Texas households purchased televisions, more than twice the number the previous year.[74] By 1953 the number of television stations in Texas had grown to ten, and two years later the number climbed to twenty-nine.[75] A statewide poll conducted in 1954 showed that 51 percent of white Anglos, 44 percent of Hispanics, and 20 percent of African Americans owned a television set.[76] The era of large-scale television ministries was still well in the future, but the groundwork had been laid.

Television was destined to become such a visible feature of the relationship between religion and power in the 1980s that writers would emphasize its importance again and again. But there was another innovation in ministry that also had a profound impact. From the unlikely location of Longview, Texas, it consolidated the success of industrialist R. G. LeTourneau and demonstrated the possibilities for wealth to be combined with evangelistic outreach in ways that shaped not only the spread but also the content of those ministries. It brought Texas-sized religion into public prominence in new ways and played a role in the work of both Youth for Christ and Billy Graham. Most of all, it presaged what was to become known as the gospel of prosperity.[77]

In 1944, when *Life* magazine devoted its first pictorial feature to LeTourneau and his spectacular machines, the industrialist had not yet established himself in Texas or reached the pinnacle of his success.[78] However, he was well on his way toward being one of the nation's best-known Christian business leaders. Having dropped out of school at age fourteen, the young man whose family was from Minnesota and who would soon make his home in California turned his adolescent fascination with cars and trucks toward learning electrical and mechanical engineering as well experimenting with new machinery. Like entrepreneurs who earned fortunes apart from the highly competitive business of automobile production itself or the risky world of drilling for oil but in lucrative auxiliary markets such as tires and batteries, LeTourneau specialized in building the equipment used in constructing the roads on which automobiles would travel, clearing forests, erecting bridges, and assisting in the creation of drilling projects and oil refineries. These were good businesses to be in during the 1920s, but difficult to sustain in the 1930s. However, by then LeTourneau was adept in producing large-scale earth-moving equipment and was well positioned to win government contracts. He was one of the contractors who gained valuable experience from the Boulder Dam project in Nevada between 1931 and 1936 and was manufacturing machines used in reclamation projects and clearing land for military installations. During World War II LeTourneau specialized in producing large-bore artillery shells and was said to have received over 50 percent of the government's military contracts for heavy earth-moving machines.[79]

LeTourneau had come early through his family's membership in Plymouth Brethren congregations to embrace a theologically conservative biblical faith that included an emphasis on missionary zeal and evangelistic outreach. In 1936, at the nadir of the Depression, he set aside the unprecedented sum of thirteen million dollars to create the LeTourneau Foundation for the support of evangelistic and charitable projects.[80] In doing so he was following the example of an earlier generation of philanthropists, such as Arthur Tappan, John Wanamaker, and J. Howard Pew, who used their wealth to support religious activities. He differed from them in not being located on the East Coast and taking a more active personal role in ministerial outreach. By 1939 he was touring the country speaking at churches and at conferences convened by the Christian Business Men's Association and the Association of Businessmen's Evangelistic Clubs.[81] As the nation moved reluctantly toward war, he argued that "a right heart attitude toward God" and a return to "spiritual values" were sorely needed to heal the emerging tensions.[82] But he was also deeply critical of Christian pacifists, whom he regarded as Christian sissies.[83] Notwithstanding the fact that his business owed much to government contracts, he presented himself as a rags-to-riches success story whose rise depended mostly on gutsy faith and hard work.

In 1946, with postwar construction booming, LeTourneau decided to establish a new manufacturing plant in Longview, Texas, where the nation's largest oil business was thriving and where rapid population growth was stimulating huge demand for new houses, roads, and businesses. On an advance visit LeTourneau's attorney, Clifton Brannon, determined that both the economic and legal environment were such that the company's headquarters should be moved there as well.[84] As LeTourneau and his wife flew in, they spotted a large, abandoned army hospital and housing complex, which they were able to secure at minimal cost. It provided space for a new technical training institute that was to expand into a college and eventually into LeTourneau University.[85]

LeTourneau's religious activities included contributing critical financial support to the emerging Youth for Christ movement, speaking at Baptist churches and interdenominational evangelistic meetings, helping Brannon launch an evangelistic ministry of his own, building and operating a radio station for religious broadcasts, purchasing a nineteen-hundred-acre ranch as a school for orphaned and delinquent boys, and publishing a newsletter about Christian leadership and philanthropy that made its way into church leaflet supplements and stories in Christian magazines.[86] As cold war defense contracts with steep tax write-offs expanded, LeTourneau spent more of his evangelistic time in the nation's capital, where business contacts could be cultivated and diversified into new lines of heavy equipment, shipping, and aircraft. Pictures of gigantic machines towering over Lilliputian individuals conveyed the message that things were indeed big in Texas, and that large aspirations could literally move mountains. By the early 1950s LeTourneau had become personally acquainted with evangelical leaders such as National Association of Evangelicals board member Carl F. H. Henry, the heads of evangelical colleges and seminaries, evangelical politicians such as Frank Carlson from Kansas and Mark Hatfield from Oregon, and Billy Graham. As Graham conducted his 1953 revival crusade in Dallas, LeTourneau constructed a freestanding aluminum dome capable of seating twelve thousand people and shipped it to London for Graham's next crusade.

In 1953 LeTourneau sold the earth-moving equipment branch of his corporation to Westinghouse for $31 million and invested most of the proceeds in developing innovative platforms for offshore oil drilling operations.[87] With an increasing share of his business in other countries and involving sales to foreign companies, LeTourneau's religious activities expanded overseas as well. One of his projects involved the purchase and outfitting of a World War II supply ship with building materials and donated food and clothing. Sending it to a leased half-million acre plantation in Liberia, he hoped to inspire economic development that would include Christian converts and large construction projects.[88] Another project involved earthmovers and tree-crushers to clear a million acres of "waste land" in Peru, where he planned to create a similar outpost of evangelical Christian civilization.[89] These endeavors presaged what was to become a permanent and expanding relationship between Texas-based ministries and international evangelistic mission and outreach organizations.

Until his death in 1969 at the age of eighty, LeTourneau exemplified a biblical Christianity that could be interpreted as a kind of prosperity gospel. Pastors challenged their congregations to give generously by noting how LeTourneau reversed the traditional understanding of contributing a tithe to God, donating 90 percent and keeping only 10 percent for himself. Whether LeTourneau actually did that, and whether it was easier for someone who earned millions, was not the issue as much as the message of supporting the church beyond all reasonable expectations. When critics spoke against him for his union-busting business practices and sometimes for his support of Youth for Christ, writers came to his defense, arguing that labor disputes were best resolved by everyone examining their hearts and joining in Christian fellowship.[90] Ripley's *Believe It or Not* suggested that his business flourished when he gave more of his money to God.[91] In his public appearances and in his autobiography, LeTourneau claimed that God was his business partner and implied that the business flourished because God wanted it to prosper. "By accepting God as your partner," he wrote, "no limit can be placed on what can be achieved."[92]

Although his claim of partnering with God put LeTourneau in the spotlight, his message was neither typical nor unique. About the only generalization that could be made of his wealthy contemporaries is that enormous personal fortunes were a kind of wild card in Texas religion and politics. Apart from massive individual wealth, the best way to mobilize sufficient resources to build major institutions was through the small donations of thousands of churchgoers, which could fund a Baptist institution such as Baylor University, or through tax dollars, which could support an institution like the University of Texas. But personal fortunes could be used, as LeTourneau did, to start a nondenominational institute and support evangelical ministries. Or they could be used as multimillionaire oil executive Hugh Roy Cullen did. Cullen's mother was a devout Baptist and his wife was an Episcopalian, but Cullen's fortune of some $160 million went to support hospitals and to create the University of Houston.[93]

LeTourneau's view that piety and success somehow went together was part of a larger emphasis already becoming evident in the 1950s. It drew from the nation's sense that victory in the recent war was connected with being right with God. The idea that God favored some more than others was part of America's self-understanding in the emerging cold war with Russia. Its roots could also be found in new ideas about mental health and the rising popularity of psychology. The most vocal proponent of this version of faith-based self-help psychology was Dr. Norman Vincent Peale, the noted pastor of Marble Collegiate Church in New York City and best-selling author of *The Power of Positive Thinking*. Peale's columns appeared regularly in the *Dallas Morning News*, and his radio programs aired throughout Texas as well as across much of the nation.[94] "Why not accept God as a partner?" Peale advised, pointing frequently to examples of indigent Americans who earned fortunes by merging with God.[95]

As important as these ideas were to be in future years when clergy launched huge congregations by preaching that God and prosperity went hand in hand, LeTourneau's impact was probably greater in terms of the organizational arrangements he popularized. He showed, as earlier philanthropists had, that private wealth could launch and sustain new evangelistic ministries that were free of governance by elected clergy boards and capable of crossing denominational lines. His foundation illustrated a mechanism that other families of wealth would use and to which religious leaders would increasingly turn for financial support. Parachurch ministries such as Youth for Christ, Young Life, Campus Crusade for Christ, Navigators, and Inter-Varsity Christian Fellowship would increasingly cultivate wealthy business leaders and encourage high school and college students to emulate these leaders. LeTourneau's college demonstrated that institutions of higher learning could still be established, as some had been in the nineteenth century, with a clear evangelical Christian

FIGURE 14. R. G. and Evelyn LeTourneau, 1954, with reconditioned World War II bomber purchased to travel to international missionary fields and production facilities. Photograph © Herman's Studio and Camera Center. Longview Public Library, Longview, TX. University of North Texas Libraries, The Portal to Texas History.

identity without denominational ties and with a unique combination of specialized technical training and biblical instruction. His was one of the first corporations to employ its own chaplains.[96] And his were among the more innovative efforts to engage directly in faith-inspired overseas economic development projects.

The common aspect of these and other new parachurch ministries was their capacity to reach beyond local congregations and to connect people in ways that transcended denominational organizations. Most were conservative in theological orientation and evangelistic in outreach. They supplemented but did not replace the activities of evangelical denominations. Southern Baptists especially made full use of the new methods not only by holding youth revivals and televising worship services but also by purchasing stations and holding special training seminars to equip pastors in the use of new technology. The day was coming when a single preacher could reach a huge audience through television and attract members to a suburban megachurch from miles away. But that development—what ethicist Gibson Winter would term *The Suburban Captivity of the Churches*—first depended on the growth of a new suburban population. And that in turn was part of a larger and continuing pattern of racial separation.[97]

WHITE FLIGHT AND SEGREGATION

Church expansion and the new construction of housing projects and shopping districts driven by postwar population growth and middle-class incomes conformed to and reinforced the racial, ethnic, and geographic inequalities that characterized Texas communities. Although commuting to religious services by automobile had become so common by 1950 that Dallas briefly considered passing an ordinance requiring any plan for new church construction to include an ample parking lot, the idea of the neighborhood church that people could attend easily and in which their children could participate with friends from school was still the norm. An additional expectation that church growth planners would later embrace more explicitly was that houses of worship should be consistent with the lifestyles of their members. God might not respect the rich any more than the poor, but it was somehow demeaning, they believed, for God to occupy a building less spacious and less architecturally pleasing than the community's homes, banks, and boutiques.

The unspoken norm that a church building should be pleasing to God was reinforced by the assumption that it should be pleasing to its neighbors as well. Rigid zoning laws stipulating how and where churches could be built had not yet been instituted, but a suit filed in the Oak Cliff section of Dallas in 1945 illustrated how much property values mattered. When the Victory Assembly of God congregation planned a new structure in the area, neighbors argued that the "cheap building" would greatly decrease their homes' value. The court ruled that it could not dictate how much or how little should be spent, but the case showed that incongruities between church values and local property values could stir conflict.[98]

One might have assumed that racial segregation among churches was carried forward simply by inertia, but that was not quite the case. The chance to start new congregations and build new churches could have been an opportunity to rethink race relations and to put in practice ideas about interracial cooperation. Instead, congregations' decisions mostly reinforced racial separation.

Much of the new church construction in Dallas, Fort Worth, and Houston was in predominantly white suburbs where large housing developments were attracting young, middle-class families. Capital improvements and repairs on older, established downtown churches were closer to African American neighborhoods but at congregations attended almost exclusively by white members. In formerly white neighborhoods that were becoming African American, a recurring response by white churches was to sell their property to a black church and move to a new location in a white suburb. That was a pattern noted especially in South Dallas, where several neighborhoods south of Second Avenue were more than 90 percent African American, and where some formerly white neighborhoods north of Second Avenue were at least 40 percent African American. "We have no hard feelings," the pastor of a white church leaving the area explained. He thought it would be a good idea if all two dozen white churches in the area relocated. It would show "how the churches in this area are meeting the difficulties that are involved by encroachment of the Negroes," he said.[99]

Church groups were drawn into the larger discussion about segregation as well. In 1948 fourteen bishops of the African Methodist Episcopal Church pledged their support of President Truman's civil rights program, which aimed to enact legislation abolishing the poll tax, ending segregation in transportation, and providing fair employment.[100] The Federal Council of Churches expressed support as well.[101] In Texas opinion was divided about how much or how little churches should be involved in civil rights issues. *Dallas Morning News* columnist Lynn Landrum, a Methodist who had been an outspoken critic of the Ku Klux Klan and was known for taking controversial positions on social issues, argued that segregation and fair housing for African Americans could be reconciled. Noting that the Texas Council of Church Women endorsed Truman's plan, he considered the endorsement less telling than the fact that nearly all Texans worshipped in segregated meeting halls. "Church groups which vaguely preach racial brotherhood and the wiping out of color lines produce tensions and increase tensions which already exist," he warned.[102]

Apparently agreeing with Landrum, several local church women's groups resigned from the state organization, and the council's president, a Presbyterian whose husband was president of the American Bankers Insurance Company, immediately backpedaled, explaining that the council had meant only to suggest that Truman's plan deserved further study.[103] Still unsatisfied, critics of the council declared that nothing could be worse than ending segregation, and that churches had no business arguing otherwise. "I cannot believe that this state of affairs is desired by a majority of our southern church women, regardless of their denomination," an incensed critic observed. "If this is really the aim and intent of the modern church, then I for one will never again set foot in a church or assist in any way in foisting such degradation on the land that has been the home of my people since 1625, my beloved Dixie."[104]

But others saw the matter differently. Attorney Robert L. Ivy, for example, considered it ludicrous to defend segregation any longer. "No one suggests that the doors of a person's home be opened to any but those he desires to let in as his friends," he argued, "but it is terrible hypocrisy to profess to be a Christian and then close the doors of your church to certain men, and to profess to believe in democracy and close the doors of your schools and business houses to people with dark skins, no matter what their qualifications."[105]

Former national YMCA director Sherwood Eddy inadvertently added fuel to the fire by delivering a lecture at Dallas's First Methodist Church while the church women's controversy was still brewing. Eddy declared that most people in the world did not believe in segregation. His point was that two-thirds of the world's population disbelieved in white supremacy because they were not white.

But in suggesting that, for all its faults, Russian communism's doctrine of racial equality appealed to these people, he managed to imply that embracing racial equality might be related to embracing communism. At least that was how some regarded the matter and would continue to do so as both issues became even more controversial over the next few years.[106] It did not help that Reverend William Fraser, a pastor at Norris's fundamentalist church in Fort Worth, had recently accused the president of the Southern Baptist Convention at a meeting in Amarillo of favoring an alliance with communist Russia.[107]

Two weeks after Eddy's lecture, Texas Baptist General Convention executive secretary J. Howard Williams at the organization's annual meeting charged that President Truman's intentions about equal rights might be right, but his methods were wrong. "You can't force a moral code or cloak on the people," Williams said. The only way to achieve human rights was "through the hearts of men," he believed, and the way to accomplish that was by increasing Sunday school attendance. That was also the best way to uphold American democracy.[108]

The following week, when the generally progressive Baptist World Alliance held its national meeting in Houston, the organization's president, C. Oscar Johnson of St. Louis, also distanced himself from Truman's civil rights plan and defended the organization against criticism on other grounds. The race problem could never be solved, Johnson noted having said to Truman, "if you force an issue." African Americans were certainly welcome at his own church, Johnson said, but none had chosen to join. He thought "rushing to racial amity" would only delay progress. Nor was he in any way promoting union between southern and northern Baptists, he said.[109]

In May 1948 Southern Baptist Convention delegates met in Memphis in what was expected to include a conference swirling in debate about civil rights. Meeting in Boston two weeks earlier, the General Conference of the Methodist Church approved a strongly worded resolution asserting that "the principle of racial discrimination is in clear violation of the Christian belief in the Fatherhood of God, the brotherhood of man, and the kingdom of God—the proclamation of which in word and life is our gospel. We therefore have no choice but to denote it as un-Christian and to renounce it as evil. This we do without equivocation." Describing the manifestations of racial discrimination from slavery to condescension and declaring the need to root it from both the denomination and society, the resolution proposed a series of concrete steps going forward that stipulated greater inclusion of "colored personnel" in church positions, equality of church accommodations, and scrutiny of policies in church-related schools and hospitals. Without mentioning Truman's civil rights program by name, the resolution pledged that Methodists individually and collectively would "stand for equality of political franchise and of economic and educational opportunities for all races."[110]

The Baptists' deliberations contrasted sharply with the Methodists' resolution. The issue that threatened to disrupt the gathering more than civil rights was whether fundamentalist Norris would be seated as a delegate. As the meeting got under way, Norris advertised in the Memphis newspaper that he planned to confront the gathering with various criticisms involving its views toward Catholics and communists and would seek to be seated as a delegate even though he was not a member of the Southern Baptist Convention. Intent on avoiding further controversy, the gathering included him and turned its attention to the more pressing matters of evangelism and church policies. But when the Social Service Commission presented its report on race relations, it announced that no recommendation would be made beyond that of the previous year in which the convention affirmed the fundamental principles of its Baptist faith. Those principles had been framed in general terms about promoting interracial goodwill and "ordering our racial attitudes and actions in accordance with Christian truth and Christian love." The convention pledged itself to a "long range program of education" that would deal with the race question and bring Christian doctrines to bear on racial attitudes.[111] Delegates were left to decide for themselves what that might mean.

With Southern Baptists avoiding a definitive stand one way or the other, voters across the South agreed to disagree about how much to support Truman's candidacy in the 1948 presidential election. Those who opposed Truman's views on civil rights and favored the continuation of strict segregation organized the States' Rights Democratic or Dixiecrat Party and ran South Carolina governor J. Strom Thurmond as their nominee. Truman spent three days campaigning in Texas, where crowds who hailed him as a man of the people received him enthusiastically. Republicans believed in a trickle-down policy, he warned. "Take care of the big boys and some of the money will trickle down to the little fellow."[112] Truman reminded voters that Speaker Rayburn in the House and Senate candidate Lyndon Johnson were in his corner, as was Baptist leader Pat Neff, who as Baylor University president had bestowed an honorary degree on the president a year before. Governor Beauford Jestor, who only a few months earlier had criticized Truman's civil rights program, also came around.[113] Nowhere was Truman's effort to garner support from Texas leaders clearer than on Sunday, September 26, when he and Jester attended worship services at the First Baptist Church in San Antonio. Here was a denomination, a reporter for the New York Times observed, that "wields real power in Texas politics."[114]

Thurmond's showing in Texas was modest compared to the overwhelming victories he achieved in Alabama, Mississippi, and South Carolina. He nevertheless received 113,776 votes, or 9 percent of the ballots cast in Texas. County comparisons show that the strongest predictor of the predominantly white votes cast for Thurmond was the percentage of counties' residents who were African American (a correlation of 0.781). In counties where at least 20 percent of the population was African American, Thurmond averaged 16 percent of the votes casts, compared with only 5 percent in counties with smaller proportions of

FIGURE 15. The fundamentalist preacher Reverend J. Frank Norris, 1941, addressing the Texas legislature on February 17, 1941. Photograph by Neal Douglass. Austin History Center, Austin Public Library. University of North Texas Libraries, The Portal to Texas History.

African Americans. That pattern was not surprising since white voters living in the vicinity of African Americans were more intent on preserving segregation than voters living where race was less of an issue. But religion mattered as well. Controlling for differences in counties' racial composition, counties in which a higher proportion of Protestants were Southern Baptists were significantly more likely to have voted for Thurmond than counties with lower percentages of Southern Baptists (a standardized regression coefficient of 0.141, significant beyond the 0.001 level). There was no relationship between voting for Thurmond and the proportion of Protestants who were Methodist.[115]

Although Thurmond's support was strongest in relatively rural East Texas counties where slavery had been practiced, there was sufficient Dixiecrat sentiment in urban areas to garner more than ten thousand votes in Dallas County

FIGURE 16. Lyndon Johnson, 1948, campaigning for U.S. Senate in Jefferson County, Texas. Photograph by James Everett. University of North Texas Libraries, The Portal to Texas History.

and nearly twenty thousand votes in Harris County, where most of the voters lived in Houston. During the 1940s the African American population in Dallas County increased from 61,000 to nearly 83,000 and in Harris County from 104,000 to more than 149,000. Neither increase represented an overall rise in the percentage of residents who were African American, but they did result in tensions about housing and segregated neighborhoods.

The racial conflicts that began in conjunction with housing relocation programs in 1940 continued sporadically over the next decade. An analysis of Dallas in 1949 likened the city's African American population to toothpaste in a tube being squeezed until either the cap flew off or the sides began leaking. The report showed that 86 percent of the city's African Americans in 1940 were living in substandard housing, and that nine years later the number of housing units had increased by only 10 percent, resulting in thousands of families having to share quarters with other families. White landowners refused to sell property for low-income housing developments, and on at least a half dozen occasions white protestors had prevented African American housing from being built adjacent to white neighborhoods. The report found similar problems in other southern cities but noted that Houston had made somewhat greater progress than Dallas in initiating public housing projects.[116]

The study's conclusions were reinforced by results obtained in the 1950 census. Seventy-one percent of Dallas's African American population lived in just 8 of the city's 104 census tracts, and in these 8 tracts 74 percent of the residents were African American. Crowding was evident in the fact that population density in the 8 predominantly African American tracts was 11,318 persons per square mile compared with only 5,504 in the remaining tracts. Much the same pattern was evident in Houston, where 68 percent of the African American population lived in 13 of the city's 117 census tracts, and 79 percent of the residents in those 13 tracts were African American. Density in the predominantly African American tracts averaged 9,322 persons per square mile compared with 4,266 in the remaining tracts.[117]

In both cities the African American population was already geographically concentrated in 1940, and population density in those neighborhoods was already higher than in white neighborhoods. As the population expanded, it affected black and white neighborhoods differently. With limited possibilities for additional housing in already predominantly black neighborhoods, the additional black population moved into a few adjacent lower-income white neighborhoods, as indicated by the addition of one predominantly black census tract between 1940 and 1950 in Dallas and five in Houston. These were the neighborhoods in which conflicts between whites and blacks over property values and segregation were most likely to occur. Most of the additional white population was in suburbs, which were located at increasing distances from the center city and from black neighborhoods, as indicated by the addition of thirty-nine new, predominantly white census tracts in Dallas and sixty-two in Houston. In these tracts where lots and home sizes were generally larger, population density was lower in 1950 than it had been in 1940 by about 25 percent in Dallas and 46 percent in Houston.[118]

Residents on both sides of the issue invoked moral as well as economic arguments. At a hearing in 1949, Sallie Hanna, whose work on behalf of interracial cooperation had begun in the 1920s and who was now vice president of the United Council of Church Women, supported the builder who wanted to construct a large apartment complex for African Americans in South Dallas. "We are now insisting that Negroes live in terribly congested areas," she observed. "We ought to hang our heads in shame. Nothing has opened up for them until now but bitter, bitter opposition." But white residents who objected to the proposal were equally adamant. "We plead with you with prayers on our lips," said one, "to think of the white folks first."[119]

In 1951 conflict over housing erupted into violence on several occasions in Dallas as the homes of African Americans who had moved into white neighborhoods were firebombed. The Dallas Chamber of Commerce interracial committee called unsuccessfully for a grand jury to be convened to investigate the bombings. The Dallas Council of Negro Organizations convened meetings at area black churches to raise funds for the victimized families and to call for a return to law and order. African American pastors were extensively involved in these meetings.[120] White clergy were notably silent.

Besides conflicts over housing, segregation in other venues was coming increasingly under scrutiny as well. Billy Graham's appearance at the Cotton Bowl in 1953 was to a segregated audience, just as Roosevelt's had been in 1936. But white primaries had been ruled unconstitutional in 1944, and during the late 1940s the NAACP brought numerous cases to the courts involving segregation.[121] In 1950 the U.S. Supreme Court ruled that the University of Texas should enroll Heman Marion Sweatt in its law school on grounds that the Negro law school established by the University of Houston would not be equivalent to the school provided for whites. One of the briefs filed on behalf of the plaintiff was by the Federal Council of Churches, which declared "segregation in the matter of a place to live means the ghetto" and "segregation in matters of the mind and spirit means second class citizenship."[122] Texas attorney general Price Daniel criticized the council's involvement. Texas Methodists, Episcopalians, and Presbyterians, he charged, disagreed with the council's view, and for that matter most of the denominations represented by the council had separate congregations for whites and blacks in southern states. The reason for segregation, he argued, was "the right of a state or a church to offer the same education or worship in separate schools or separate churches if the segregated system would better preserve the peace, welfare, opportunities and happiness of a majority of races."[123] In the same session the high court declared segregated classrooms at the University of Oklahoma and segregation in railroad dining cars to be unconstitutional. Setting the stage for continuing conflict, Attorney General Daniel determined that the University of Texas ruling should be interpreted narrowly and not regarded as an indictment against segregation in public schools.[124]

On May 17, 1954, the U.S. Supreme Court ruled in *Brown v. Board of Education of Topeka* that separate public schools for black and white students were unconstitutional. Texas was one of seventeen states that required school segregation. A statewide poll in November asked Texans what they considered the most serious problems facing their state. By far the most frequently mentioned problem was race relations, including segregation. Among white respondents who mentioned any problem, 46 percent mentioned race relations, as did 49 percent of African American respondents. When asked what they would do in view of the Court's decision were they a member of their school board, white residents overwhelmingly said they would either resist or move ahead slowly. Twenty-three percent said they would "keep the races separate even if I have to disobey the law." Thirty percent thought it best to "find a way to keep the races separate by getting around the law." Thirty-six percent agreed it made sense to "begin mixing the races gradually starting where there is least opposition." And only 10 percent said they would "obey the law even if I have to let all races go to the same schools immediately." African Americans were significantly more favorable toward integration. Thirty-three percent favored gradual integration, and 36 percent wanted immediate integration. Hispanics were the most favorable toward integration. Forty-eight percent favored gradual integration, and 33 percent wanted immediate integration.[125]

THOSE RASCALS IN WASHINGTON

When seventy-year-old W. R. Baxter, an East Texas print shop operator, told a reporter he wanted to turn the rascals in Washington "out to pasture," he might have been talking about the U.S. Supreme Court. Texans were truly dismayed at the Court's decision in 1954. But Baxter's remark was in 1952 and referred to Washington bureaucrats he feared had "grown fat on graft and corruption."[126] That fall Baxter was one of more than a million voters who gave Dwight Eisenhower a 53 percent to 47 percent win over Adlai Stevenson, the first Republican victory in Texas since 1928. It was in some ways a shocking victory because Stevenson won in nearly every other southern state. In Texas 63 percent of eligible voters were Democrats while only 6 percent were Republicans. But Eisenhower polled more than eight in ten of the 26 percent who were independents and garnered nearly four in ten among Democrats.[127]

In other ways, of course, Eisenhower's victory was no surprise at all. Not only was he the popular war hero who had led the Allied forces to victory; he was running against an administration whose record was so unpopular that many in Truman's own party were dissatisfied. If that were not enough, Eisenhower had been born in Denison, Texas, and although his family moved to Kansas when he was two, Texans could legitimately regard him as a native son. Eisenhower's friendship with Sid Richardson gave him an edge with members of the business community. And whether they were millionaires like Richardson or shop owners like Baxter, many of the state's residents were weary of New Deal policies and wanted an end to what they saw as handouts to undeserving recipients. Sixty-one percent of white voters with average or above-average incomes opted for Eisenhower, compared with only 44 percent of white voters with low incomes.[128]

Eisenhower's success among Texas Democrats, some observers argued at the time, represented an element of score settling against Truman for his efforts on behalf of civil rights. Distrust of Washington rascals stemmed partly from deep-seated resentment against federal intervention in state affairs. It was tempting to throw the rascals out when they started meddling in local affairs, especially ones involving race relations. County comparisons, though, show that locations in which Thurmond won larger percentages of the vote in 1948 actually tilted more toward Stevenson in 1952 than toward Eisenhower (correlation of 0.161, significant at the 0.01 level). Ike did best in West and South Texas, where he received 54 percent of the vote, and poorest in East Texas, with only 44 percent of the vote.[129] And in 1954 his supporters were slightly more favorable toward school desegregation than Stevenson's were.[130]

But Eisenhower's victory demonstrated that new considerations were becoming important. Democratic strength in Texas remained nearly invincible. The governor, lieutenant governor, attorney general, comptroller, treasurer, and land commissioner were all Democrats. That had been true since 1874 and would remain so until 1978. Democrats occupied all 31 seats in the state Senate and all but 1 of the 150 seats in the state House. In the U.S. Congress someone other than a Democrat had won no more than one seat at a time since 1876. And yet personal fortunes were the wild card in politics, just as in religion. Richardson worked not only to persuade Eisenhower to run but also to ensure support for him from fellow oil barons. Hugh Roy Cullen had thrown his support in 1948 to Thurmond and now was one of Ike's strongest supporters.[131] One of Ike's few preelection campaign promises favored the restoration of tidelands oil drilling control to the state and continuation of an oil depletion tax allowance.[132] Columnist Drew Pearson reported that Wendell Willkie's error in 1940 was alienating the Texas oil interests. "The good Lord put all this oil in the ground, then someone comes along who hasn't been a success at doing anything else, and takes it out of the ground," Willkie had remarked. "The minute he does that, he considers himself an expert on everything from politics to petticoats." Truman had alienated them as well by threatening federal regulation of tidelands drilling. Richardson and Cullen, Pearson said, made sure Eisenhower would not make the same mistakes.[133]

Two years into his presidency, though, Eisenhower's supporters were less than satisfied. Cullen was upset with the administration's foreign policy, charging that communists were running it.[134] Others were unhappy that Ike had named former California governor Earl Warren to the Supreme Court, especially in view of the Warren court's decision in *Brown v. Board of Education*. Desegregation remained the unresolved issue for citizens and community leaders alike. "The churches are passing lovely resolutions and doing nothing about it," NAACP chief counsel Thurgood Marshall charged. "They could clean up this whole thing in five minutes."[135]

Because segregated schools were now unconstitutional, the question at hand was how quickly to implement desegregation or how much to resist it. Religious leaders were drawn into the debate on both sides. On the one hand, the Texas Council of Churches went on record in 1955 in support of the Supreme Court's decision. With representatives from nearly all the state's major Protestant denominations except Southern Baptists, the council called on Christians "to face the implications of this issue with all honesty and integrity rather than with attempted evasion."[136] United Church Women of Texas the following year took a similar position, asking its 575,000 members to oppose discrimination through their congregations and by asking the state legislature to do the same.[137] As leaders in southern states discussed a little-known policy called interposition, by which they could block federal implementation of desegregation, the Texas council again declared its support of integration.[138] College student groups, including the Baptist Student Union at the University of Texas, opened themselves to members of all races.[139] Individuals joined the effort as well by writing letters to newspapers. "Segregation is wrong!" observed a student at Southwestern Baptist Seminary who was offended by religious leaders who claimed otherwise. "It is wrong in the eyes of God, and God is greater than any terrestrial power."[140]

On the other hand, religious leaders who opposed desegregation spoke vehemently against it, developed a repertoire of new and old arguments as they did so, and found allies among public officials. A recurring theme was that Washington should mind its own business and let local communities and states do as they wished. As local decisions that would escalate a few weeks later in the conflict at Little Rock Central High School came under scrutiny, the *Dallas Morning News* published an editorial criticizing clergy for supporting desegregation. The reasoning was couched in long-standing arguments against clergy engaging in politics. The issue was less about separation of church and state and more about clergy staying within their appropriate domain. "Clergymen have been sometimes more vocal about brotherhood by act of Congress and decree of the Supreme Court than they have been about brotherhood by the way of the Heavenly Father and Creator of us all," the editorial declared. If there was to be integration, the writer argued, it would be better if "churchly leaders had signed fewer petitions to Congress and had shown us more about such matters in the fellowship of the church."[141]

Although the criticism was directed toward religious leaders who favored desegregation, it spoke to the reality of clergy doing little to promote integration within their own congregations, let alone in wider venues. "I'm for the Negro. I'm the best friend they've got," fundamentalist Baptist leader Norris declared in a radio address from his church in Fort Worth. But he continued, "Now let me stop here and say that civil rights—that means that Negroes will be equal with the white people in every respect—well, God didn't make them that way. It's hard to go against God's laws." Norris was troubled by the "big Negro vote" even though "some mighty good friends of mine" were of that race. "I like them," he said. "But I am not in favor of them coming into my home and sitting down with my family."[142]

Former Norris protégé Earl Anderson, still at the helm of Dallas's Munger Place Baptist Church, explained in a *Time* magazine interview why it was unChristian to invite African Americans into white churches. Two of his arguments were decades old: it was unbiblical, he thought, for races to mix, and it was better for both races to have their own churches. But another argument was newer and would be used again and again by critics of desegregation. It reflected the nation's cold war fears about communism. "An aim of Communism," Anderson declared, "is to 'mongrelize the human race.'"[143]

In Abilene Anderson's view was echoed by the pastor of an independent fundamentalist church affiliated with the Baptist Bible Fellowship. He too felt that communists were behind the integration movement. They were working to integrate all religions and all governments into one, a move that was directly contrary to scripture that, in his view, did not argue for "brotherhood" at all. He feared the devil was working to interbreed the races in a way that would also result in stamping out the Jews, contrary to scriptural prophecies about the role Jews were to play in the end times.[144]

W. A. Criswell, whose pastorate of Dallas's eleven-thousand-member First Baptist Church made him one of the most prominent Southern Baptists in the country, argued that segregation should be upheld both in schools and in churches. Criswell offered several arguments in defense of his position on segregation. It was customary, and to change it would stir up trouble, he believed. Like Anderson, he thought religious groups fared better when people "stick to their own kind." He feared that desegregation would lead to miscegenation. It especially bothered him that outsiders were calling for change. "We built our lives according to deep intimacies that are dear and precious to us," he said. "We don't want to be forced by laws or statutes to cross into those intimate things where we don't want to go."

For Criswell the line in the sand was not only between the deep intimacies of local life, on the one hand, and federal laws, on the other hand. It was also between conservative, God-fearing pastors like him and religious leaders whose beliefs could not be trusted. "Let them integrate," he said, adding with derision, "let them sit up there in their dirty shirts and make all their fine speeches. But they are all a bunch of infidels."[145]

"Some people manage to get muddled on all sorts of things without actually being infidels," columnist Landrum quipped the next day, noting his own failure to put on a clean shirt that morning.[146] Reached for comment, Billy Graham said, "My pastor and I have never seen eye to eye on the race question." Graham did not amplify or withdraw his membership from Criswell's church but explained in an essay later that year that his crusades were no longer segregated and that he felt the "weight of scripture" was to treat everyone with "neighbor-love" regardless of race.[147] Baptist leaders in Texas mostly said nothing, although one thought it unwise for pastors to criticize other pastors, and another felt it would just take a long time for religious leaders to think through the problem of desegregation.[148] Feeling that his remarks were being misinterpreted, Criswell explained several weeks later at a meeting in Oklahoma City that the infidels he had in mind were "Communists and racial agitators." He was certainly opposed to the federal government coming in and imposing laws on people. "We don't want to be in church with colored people," he declared. "Ducks live only with other ducks."[149]

Criswell's remarks prompted people who otherwise would probably have kept their views to themselves to air them in letters to their newspapers. Many of the writers took Criswell's side. "Thank God for Dr. W. A. Criswell," a Longview resident wrote, grateful for the preacher's efforts to keep schools segregated. "I'm proud to be a Southerner," the writer added. "'Dixie' sounds sweeter every time I hear it played."[150] A member of the Texas Citizens' Council in Dallas said she "prayed that all true preachers of the gospel of Christ would, in no uncertain terms, expose the apostasy of the liberal ministers, who are advocating racial integration."[151] "Many thousand people of the south are of the same opinion and have been waiting for a Christian leader of any denomination to present our views," a woman in Dallas observed. "Dr. Criswell speaks for the majority of Southern Baptist church members," said another. Every Christian should take "a firm stand for God and His people, whom He created and segregated, and they should remain that way," declared another.[152] When Baptists across the region met that summer in Little Rock, desegregation was on everyone's mind. Preachers who supported racial integration were "cowards, pussyfooters, and apostles of Satan," Texas Baptist Institute dean Albert Garner told the crowd. "Some of the larger Protestant denominations," he explained, "have joined hands with communists and nudist colonies, free thinkers and infidels in encouraging a standard of farmyard ethics and animal morals for the youth of our nation." To forestall that, he encouraged the group to pass a resolution supporting segregation.[153] That fall the Baptist Missionary Association of Texas affirmed the prevailing sentiment. "Most of our members feel that the policy of segregation of the races should remain in force," the association's president explained.[154]

Meanwhile Criswell suffered a minor setback when delegates to the Southern Baptist Convention's annual meeting narrowly elected a pastor from Kansas City as the organization's vice present instead of Criswell.[155] But in Dallas, Criswell announced a plan that heralded similar efforts in cities across the South. If public schools were to be integrated, as events in Little Rock suggested they would be, then he would simply open a segregated school of his own. Denying that the plan was to avoid integration, he declared that the idea was to have a Baptist school. "The school would be just like our church," he explained. "Our church is segregated." With its five-million-dollar plant in downtown Dallas, the church already had classrooms and equipment to spare. "In my opinion integration will greatly multiply private schools," he predicted.[156]

Eisenhower won in Texas that fall by about the same margin as four years earlier. But Democratic leaders who had defected or remained on the sidelines in 1952 rallied around Stevenson. Using the theme of throwing the rascals out that had worked for Eisenhower, they called on Texas Democrats to rid the nation of Eisenhower's rascals. They disliked Vice President Richard Nixon, fearing he was intent on succeeding Eisenhower in 1960. They secured a promise from Stevenson that he would honor the state's rights to the oil-rich tidelands. And they argued that Stevenson would go slower on desegregation than Eisenhower and avoid the use of force.[157]

Former attorney general Price Daniel, who had been elected to the U.S. Senate in 1952 and was running what would be a successful campaign for governor in 1956, was one of the state's strongest advocates for control of tidelands rights and against desegregation. At an enthusiastic rally in Dallas, Criswell opened with prayer and then turned the platform over to Daniel, a fellow Baptist. "Texans do not want a man in their governor's office who is tied hand and foot by the radical left-wingers whose entire philosophy is based upon a system of government where everything is centralized and controlled in Washington," Daniel declared. "They do not want a man who will sit back and let the federal government do as it pleases." He promised, "I will do everything in my power to preserve the local control of our schools."[158]

THE PRESSURE OF CLERICALISM

In 1959, at a statewide meeting in Corpus Christi, the Baptist General Convention of Texas passed a resolution condemning racial prejudice in the strongest terms to date. Baptists have an "imperative from God to act and speak redemptively now," the resolution stated. The "un-Christian indignities of the caste system long imposed on Negroes in this land are foreign to the spirit and teachings of our Lord," it declared.[159] Since 1956 Houston had become the focus of national attention when a lawsuit was filed against the school board following an incident in which an African American girl was refused admission to an all-white school after being intimidated by white students wielding knives. As local officials worked on a plan for gradual integration over an unspecified number of years, an interfaith panel of Protestant, Catholic, and Jewish clergy published a statement calling for peaceful engagement in the process. Defying court-mandated desegregation, the clergy said, would encourage "other dangerous elements in our society to follow the same destructive procedure" and lead to anarchy.[160] With only a hundred school districts statewide having instituted racial integration, the Texas Council of Churches in 1957 called on congregations to exert pressure in local school board elections and to urge the courts to uphold desegregation.[161] The following year Caesar Clark, pastor of the Good Street Baptist Church in Dallas and former NAACP state president, and another African American pastor ran for board of education seats but were defeated by a wide margin.[162] "Everything is big in Texas," quipped a writer for the Baltimore *Afro-American*, except plans for desegregation.[163]

In October 1959 former president Truman came to Dallas and preached a sermon that praised Texas for its proud history of independence and freedom, touched on a number of national and international topics, and gently reminded his listeners of the story of the Good Samaritan. "It means to treat your neighbor as you yourself would like to be treated," he declared. "It makes no difference whether he is of another race or another creed or another color."[164] Color may have been uppermost in mind, but creed was becoming increasingly controversial as well.

At the same meeting in which they condemned a racial caste system, Baptist delegates approved a resolution accusing the Roman Catholic Church of being "an ambitious political system aspiring to be a state." While the resolution cautiously acknowledged that "no person's religious affiliation per se should rule out his candidacy" and noted that "theoretically, a Roman Catholic has as much right to be elected to public office as anyone else," it went on to say that the Catholic

Church "rejects as a 'shibboleth of doctrinaire secularism' the American doctrine of separation of church and state." It concluded, "There is a practical question as to whether a Catholic office holder would be able to resist the pressure of clericalism."[165] The statement reflected growing concern that a Catholic might indeed become an officeholder, perhaps at the highest level. "Baptists believe a Catholic has as much right as any person to seek an elective office," the *Baptist Standard* editorialized, but "they have the right to oppose his election when they have reason to believe that it would ultimately lead to the loss of the freedom they have purchased at such a great price."[166]

By the early 1950s Catholics in Texas numbered approximately 1.4 million, which put them slightly ahead of Southern Baptists as the largest denomination in the state, although Catholics counted children and Baptists did not. Catholic concentration was still highest in the Rio Grande valley, accounting for upward of 90 percent of all church members in eight counties and 80 percent in eleven others. Three-quarters of the church members in El Paso were Catholic, and approximately two-thirds were in San Antonio and Galveston. But Catholics were also well represented in the state's largest urban areas. In Harris County, where Houston is located, 158,000 residents were Catholic, and in Dallas County more than 36,000 were.[167]

Backed by a 1939 papal encyclical declaring equality among all baptized members of the Church and with a strongly worded 1951 pastoral letter by the archbishop of New Orleans condemning segregation as un-American, Catholic leaders in Texas issued statements in 1954 opposing segregation in public schools and stating that segregation would not be practiced in Catholic schools.[168] San Antonio archbishop Robert E. Lucey, the state's highest-ranking Catholic leader, joined with leading Methodist, Presbyterian, Christian Church, Episcopal, and Jewish clergy in endorsing the Court's decision in *Brown v. Board of Education*.[169]

An inquiry conducted by the Associated Press in September 1954 found African American children attending Catholic schools with white children in San Antonio, El Paso, Austin, Fort Worth, and several other towns.[170] A report from the archdiocese that winter, though, showed the numbers were small. Fewer than fifty African Americans were among the twenty-five thousand students enrolled in Catholic schools.[171] Priests in communities where no African Americans were attending Catholic schools explained that no requests had been received, that requests had been turned down because the school was already full or because the children were not Catholic, or that no African Americans lived in the area.[172]

As attempts proceeded on other fronts to block desegregation, Catholic leaders continued to speak against these efforts. In 1957 when the Texas legislature entertained a bill to ban NAACP members from public employment, Archbishop Lucey accused them of hypocrisy and stupidity and suggested they should resign if they could not get over their "hatred against colored citizens." One legislator responded that the bishop lacked knowledge of the problem. Another declared, "I never pay attention to crackpots."[173]

An effort to gauge opinion around the state through qualitative interviews found white residents in East Texas "boiling mad" about desegregation, while those in West Texas were relatively unconcerned. Strong support for desegregation in the Rio Grande valley and around San Antonio appeared attributable both to Catholic leaders and to the Hispanic population's own experience with discrimination.[174] A case that went to the U.S. Supreme Court from Texas in 1954 charged that all-white Anglo juries were systematically discriminating against Mexican Americans.[175] Another lawsuit was brought on behalf of Hispanic parents whose children were placed in segregated schools.[176] In 1955 El Paso became one of the first school districts in the state to ban segregation, but a Hispanic resident who grew up there recalled years later that the community was extremely segregated well into the 1960s. The parks, the theater, and even the cemeteries were segregated. With local government dominated by white Anglos, he said, "none of the streets in the part of town where the Mexican and black families lived were paved or had sidewalks."[177]

In rural communities migrant farmworkers from Mexico who drove down wages for resident laborers complicated the situation. On the one hand, migrant workers had few rights, which led to low wages, long hours, and exploitation. As one laborer observed to a church volunteer, "We live like animals."[178] On the other hand, resident laborers wanted laws passed to restrict migrant workers—a cause in which Archbishop Lucey joined them without success. In 1957 Hector Garcia, founder of the American GI Forum in Corpus Christi, summarized the situation. "Throughout the nation generally we are rated as second-class citizens, in Texas as third-class."[179] A Texas poll in 1957 showed 82 percent of Hispanics favoring immediate or gradual school integration, compared with an average of 47 percent for the state and only 34 percent among white residents in East Texas.[180] That fall state senator Henry Gonzalez of San Antonio was credited with preventing the passage of several strong prosegregation measures by East Texas legislators.[181]

While segregation and desegregation were being debated locally, the question of public funds for parochial schools and the possibility of a Catholic running for the nation's highest office were generating additional discussions among religious leaders. The Southern Baptists' concerns in 1959 about Catholic officeholders and the pressures of clericalism were preceded in 1957 at the Baptists' annual conference when one of the speakers condemned the "mounting Roman Catholic pressure for government subsidies to their schools."[182] The speaker was Glen L. Archer, executive director of Protestants and Other Americans United for Separation of Church and State. Founded in 1948, Americans United had come into being to oppose what it regarded as efforts by the Catholic Church to gain unfair support from the federal government. At issue was Truman's appointment of an ambassador to the Vatican, and more significantly the U.S. Supreme Court's five-to-four ruling in *Everson v. Board of Education* that public tax receipts could be used for pupils' transportation to Catholic parochial as well as public schools.

Southern Baptists' efforts to uphold separation of church and state were led by J. M. Dawson, the pastor who in 1916 had witnessed the lynching of Jesse Washington in Waco. After editing the influential *Baptist Standard* from 1943 to 1946, Dawson became the first full-time director of the Baptist Joint Committee on Public Affairs, serving in that capacity until 1953. From 1945 through 1947 he participated in efforts encouraging the United Nations to promote international religious freedom, including a petition drive that elicited a hundred thousand signatures from local Baptists. From his office in the nation's capital, Dawson argued that Southern Baptists should make vigorous pronouncements on social and governmental issues. Speaking to the Negro National Baptist Convention in Houston in 1948, he denounced the *Everson* decision.[183] At the Southern Baptist Convention's annual meeting in 1949, he urged the body to notify Catholics that Baptists "do not intend to exchange our free American life for totalitarian dictatorship from the Vatican."[184] Two years later he charged that Truman's appointment of an ambassador to the Vatican was "disruptive of national unity" and "perhaps a frantic bid for holding machine-ridden big cities in the approaching hot presidential race."[185] Over the following year he traveled widely, speaking against the appointment under the auspices of Protestants and Other Americans United for Separation of Church and State, serving as the organization's secretary.

Advocacy for separation of church and state was firmly grounded in Baptists' emphasis on liberty of conscience. Nevertheless, Southern Baptists' involvement in Protestants and Other Americans United was not without controversy. Besides Dawson and Southern Baptist Convention president Louie Newton from Atlanta, Americans United's principal organizers were northern leaders from church boards and seminaries from which fundamentalists and conservative Southern Baptists had distanced themselves for decades.[186] Newton was already being attacked by fundamentalist Norris for being soft on communism. When Americans United formed, a Baptist pastor in Dallas attacked the group as yet another example of communistic philosophy infiltrating American Protestantism. This philosophy, he declared, "Has been taught in sociological studies in the majority of Protestant colleges and universities and in theological seminaries for the last quarter of a century." It was alien, contrary to the profit motive that inspired capitalism, and un-Christian, he said. This new group, he feared, was simply diverting attention from the real enemy by crying wolf. "The wolf is not in Rome. The wolf is in Moscow."[187]

The *Everson* decision presented another complication. An ambassador to Rome gave legitimacy to the Vatican, which in Dawson's view was the appropriate focus of concern and not ordinary Americans who happened to be Catholics. *Everson* was more about ordinary Catholics who simply wanted their children to have transportation to school. There were Protestants who sent their children to private schools as well. That had always been true in Texas and, if Criswell's prediction was correct, would increasingly be so among white Protestants in the wake of public school desegregation. Opposing public support for transportation to Catholic schools could hardly be done without denying it to Protestant schools as well. Columnist

Landrum anticipated the problem as soon as Americans United announced its op-position. "If we are going to haul parochial scholars to one school in a public school bus," he wrote, "then we ought to haul all parochial scholars in such a bus."[188]

By the late 1950s Americans United was arguing that it represented Jewish and Catholic as well as Protestant concerns. However, its focus remained on po-tential violations of church and state separation by the Catholic hierarchy. Still of concern were the appointment of an American ambassador to the Vatican and the use of public funds for Catholic schools. In anticipation of the next presiden-tial election, the organization also called for any candidate who was Catholic to take a clear position on these critical issues.[189] On February 22, 1959, during an appearance on *Face the Nation*, Senator John F. Kennedy of Massachusetts was asked if he thought a Catholic candidate could be elected president. "I should think that probably if a Catholic became a candidate that this matter of his views on the question of the first amendment—separation of church and state—would become a matter of public discussion," Kennedy replied. "And it's quite proper that it should. Whether it would mean his defeat, I don't know."[190]

In Texas the question was again the one that voters had confronted in 1928. In a state where Democrats nearly always won, would a Catholic running on the Democratic ticket prevail? Or would the state's Protestant leaders persuade vot-ers that a Catholic president was a bad idea? The difference was that in 1928 the fear of Prohibition being repealed was a central consideration. The other differ-ence was that Texas had gone Republican in 1952 and again in 1956. Republicans were better organized than ever before. Civil rights were hotly contested. Oil barons were the wild card. But at the grass roots, religion seemed destined to play a more visible role than ever before.

A statewide poll in May 1960, when it was still unclear who the contend-ers might be, suggested that Kennedy's chances were slim. Among Catholics a bare majority (51 percent) thought a Catholic candidate could win, while among Methodists only 21 percent did, and among Baptists the proportion was only 18 percent. Were the race to be between Nixon and Johnson, the native son was favored by more than two to one among Catholics and Protestants alike. But if it were between Nixon and Kennedy, the survey predicted a dead heat, with Catholics opting for Kennedy by a wide margin and Baptists and Methodists significantly favoring Nixon.[191]

The story of Kennedy's narrow 44,000-vote win in Texas has generally empha-sized his selection of a running mate and his speech on September 12, 1960, to the Greater Houston Ministerial Association. Johnson provided the eastern sena-tor with a home-team advantage, and the Houston speech clarified Kennedy's position on the critical issue of church and state separation. But there were other threads in the story illustrating the changes that were taking place in Texas reli-gion and foreshadowing events to come.

One thread can be traced to a fateful Thanksgiving Day in 1950 in the small town of Bells northeast of Dallas near the Oklahoma border when a Methodist minister went out back to burn dry grass and failed to anticipate a wind that would reignite the fire, spreading it within minutes and burning his beloved church to the ground. Needing twenty-five thousand dollars to rebuild and having only fifteen thousand from insurance and the congregation, he devised an inventive plan to raise the balance. He would ask ten thousand people if they would each contribute one dollar, which he also determined would stretch for a mile if the bills were taped end to end. On May 6, 1951, the reverend's mile of dollars, now complete, was strung out along the highway. *Life* magazine learned of the story and published a large photo of the happy pastor swathed to his ears in dollar bills. Baxton Bryant was on his way to becoming a national figure.[192]

A year later Bryant relocated to a Methodist church in suburban Dallas, where he again made headlines, this time leading a group of aroused prohibitionists intent on keeping beer from being sold in their community.[193] Like other Methodist pastors, Bryant moved every two or three years, serving at a church in Gainesville and then in 1958 moving to the Elmwood Methodist Church in the Oak Cliff suburb of Dallas. With Eisenhower in office, Bryant made no secret of being a loyal Democrat. In 1948 Bryant had met Truman when Truman was visiting Rayburn's home in Bonham, some eighteen miles from Bryant's congregation in Bells. When Truman visited Dallas on October 18, 1959, it was at Bryant's invitation. Following Bryant's introduction, Truman delivered his sermon at the Elmwood Methodist Church. Rayburn and Senator Ralph W. Yarborough joined Truman and Bryant on the platform.[194] As journalists inquired further into the visit, Bryant reported that he and a group of young people from the church had recently stopped at Truman's library in Missouri on the way back from a trip to the nation's capital that included twenty minutes with Kennedy. "I am sure Senator Kennedy will remember the 38 young Texans who sang for him in his office 'The Eyes of Texas Are upon You,'" Bryant observed.[195]

Truman's sermon at Bryant's church and Bryant's comments about visiting with Kennedy occurred just prior to the Baptist General Convention of Texas meeting at which the state's Baptists were warned about the pressures of clericalism on any Catholic who might be a candidate for public office. Over the next six months Bryant defended himself against critics who charged that he should not be using the church for political meetings and at a meeting of the North Texas Methodist Conference was one of the leaders who defended Methodist leaders against accusations of being too liberal on social issues and in league with communists. At the state's Democratic meeting in June, Bryant also emerged as a leader, and talk surfaced that he might be a candidate for a seat in Congress. A few days after Kennedy's nomination at the Democratic National Convention, Bryant spoke at a meeting in Dallas in which he argued that Kennedy would uphold "the strictest separation of church and state that we have seen in decades."[196]

By the end of the summer, though, it appeared that Bryant's view was in the minority. On Friday, September 9, at the Miller Road Baptist Church in Garland, an organization of clergy called the Dallas County Christians United for a Free

America discussed strategies for working quietly within their churches for Nixon and against Kennedy without stirring reactions among the community's Catholics. "You know the dangers involved in electing a Roman Catholic to the presidency," a letter formulated by the group stated. "Many of our people who have only heard the cry 'religious bigotry' need to be informed as to the real reasons for opposing the election of a loyal subject of the Vatican state to the highest office of our land." Bryant publicly criticized the group, charging that it was urging clergy to get their people out for Nixon.[197]

Kennedy's speech to the Greater Houston Ministerial Association occurred the following Monday. In what was to be one of the most important and memorable speeches of the campaign, Kennedy addressed the question of his religion at length. "I believe in an America where the separation of church and state is absolute," he declared, "where no Catholic prelate would tell the President (should he be Catholic) how to act, and no Protestant minister would tell his parishioners for whom to vote." He stated his belief that church schools should not be granted public funds and that no public official should accept instructions on public policy from the pope. Referencing Jefferson's plea for religious freedom, he expressed hope that "Catholics, Protestants and Jews, at both the lay and pastoral level, will refrain from those attitudes of disdain and division which have so often marred their works in the past, and promote instead the American ideal of brotherhood."[198]

Informal interviews with clergy around the state who had viewed the speech on television or in person predictably drew mixed responses. Bryant's enthusiasm was shared by most of the Methodist, Presbyterian, and Jewish clergy who were reached for comment. Criswell, who had been outspokenly against Kennedy, was said to remain unconvinced, as was true among most of the Baptists interviewed. *Baptist Standard* editor E. S. James, who had warned readers over the past five years about the dangers of the Roman hierarchy, said Kennedy had made "a splendid statement about his personal individualism" but doubted that "the church will allow him to act individually."[199]

As the election drew closer, preachers who opposed Kennedy on religious grounds warned specifically against voting for him. The most notable example was Criswell, who preached a sermon to his now twelve-thousand-member congregation arguing that a victory for Kennedy would lead to the Vatican destroying religious freedom in America. More than a hundred thousand copies of Criswell's sermon were printed and distributed. Because the sermon was distributed anonymously in violation of federal election laws, an investigation ensued. The investigation revealed that a member of Criswell's church, oil millionaire H. L. Hunt, funded the project.[200]

The other thread that illustrates the complex religious environment in which the 1960 presidential election took place is the role played by Baptist pastor Luther Holcomb. In 1952 while Bryant was raising money to build a new church, Holcomb's small Lakewood Baptist Church in Dallas was struggling with a

similar issue, hoping to sell its current property in order to complete a new facility a few blocks away.[201] Like Bryant, Holcomb had interests in community
leadership activities that extended beyond the congregation. One was serving
on the Community Chest board. Another was the Dallas Housing Authority
Board. Yet another was speaking at Brotherhood Week events. Brotherhood
Week was sponsored by the National Conference of Christians and Jews (NCCJ)
and included such prominent Texans as Braniff International Airways president
Tom Braniff, St. Mary's University president Louis J. Blume, and Rabbi Hyman
Schachtel of Temple Emanuel in Houston. The NCCJ worked to combat racial
hatred as well as to promote greater understanding among religious traditions.[202]
"I like to think of America as being great enough to be the greatest Jewish nation
on earth, the greatest Catholic nation on earth, and the greatest Protestant nation
on earth," Holcomb told an audience in Lubbock in 1954.[203] By that date he had
also given invocations at meetings of the state legislature in Austin, met Lyndon
Johnson and Governor Daniel, spent several months in Korea as a chaplain, met
Vice President Nixon, and given an opening prayer in the U.S. Senate.

Holcomb exemplified the diversity that existed among Texas Baptists but
also the growing opportunities that came from working beyond denominational
lines. He attended annual meetings of the Southern Baptist Convention and delivered addresses at the meetings. His father was the head of the Southern Baptist
Foundation in Nashville. And on several occasions Holcomb hosted lectures by
the *Baptist Standard* editor who was warning against Catholic clericalism. At the
same time, Holcomb spoke at meetings of Hadassah, shared the platform with
NAACP leader Roy Wilkins as a speaker at an NAACP rally, made additional
international trips on behalf of the air force chaplaincy service, and served on
numerous civic committees.[204] In 1958 Holcomb left the Lakewood pastorate to
become full-time executive secretary of the Greater Dallas Council of Churches.
In this new capacity, his closest associates became the pastors of Methodist, Presbyterian, and Episcopal congregations.[205]

As the 1960 presidential election took shape, Holcomb was careful not to
overstep the expectations of his position in the interdenominational council.
When Lady Bird Johnson came to Dallas to celebrate LBJ Day, Holcomb was on
hand to welcome her and to preside at the festivities, but his role was largely ceremonial. Unlike Bryant, he did not appear at rallies or offer statements after the
Democratic National Convention picked Kennedy and Johnson as its standard-
bearers. However, he was a signatory in a widely publicized statement that appeared the day before Kennedy's address in Houston. The statement, signed by
a hundred clergy from across the nation, including Methodist bishop William
C. Martin of Dallas and Archbishop Lucey of San Antonio, vehemently opposed
voting on the basis of a candidate's faith or excluding a candidate from public office on grounds of religion.[206]

On the eve of the election, Holcomb's name also appeared in newspaper advertisements among a long list of Kennedy and Johnson supporters. Holcomb

and several of the others listed objected, saying their permission had not been asked. Bryant, now serving as a Democratic spokesperson, said the error was regrettable but had served a good purpose. "At our conventions and other functions," he said, Kennedy could see that "certain fence-straddlers are his friends."[207]

To anyone searching for historical continuities, the concerns felt by Baptists and by many other Protestants about having a Catholic for president were the most obvious links with the past. Liberty of conscience and separation of church and state were cherished ideals. And in many respects, Kennedy's speech in Houston reinforced those ideals. Another form of continuity was evident in the resistance to ending racial segregation. But these continuities were being expressed in a context marked by profound social change. Southern Baptists were more numerous relative to other denominations than ever before. However, the influence of conservative religion was starting to be exercised through parachurch groups and interdenominational ministries as well as by congregations. Leading Methodists, Presbyterians, Episcopalians, and a few other groups were leaning in a different direction on racial issues from that of many of the most vocal Baptist leaders. At the same time there was a diversity of views among leaders of all denominations. Common ground was being explored in new ways among Protestants and Catholics and between Christians and Jews. Elections could be decided by powerbrokers and by independent voters. The 1960 election demonstrated that the unexpected could happen.

Kennedy had visited Texas twice during the 1960 campaign. In early 1963 he toured the Manned Spacecraft Center in Houston. Hearing of Kennedy's interest in visiting again that year, Governor John Connally asked Holcomb to organize a meeting to arrange the visit. To avoid tensions within the planning group, the trip was billed as a nonpartisan affair except for a fund-raiser in Austin.[208] When plans were announced, Bryant and other liberal Democratic leaders were eager for Kennedy to spend additional time in Dallas. A lunch was planned for Dallas business leaders, but Bryant suggested an appearance at the airport as well. "From the invitation list so far in Dallas," Bryant complained in a wire to the White House, "one would think Nixon won and was coming to greet his dedicated workers."[209]

When Kennedy arrived at the Dallas airport, Connally and Holcomb were there to welcome him. "Governor Connally introduced me to the President," Holcomb recalled, "saying 'Mr. President, this is Luther Holcomb. He is going to offer the invocation at the luncheon today.'" Holcomb thought the president's facial expression tried to convey acceptance of him as a Protestant. "He looked at me with a warm smile and about the invocation he said 'Make it a good one.'" Holcomb was in the fifth car of the motorcade entering Dealey Plaza when gunshots rang out.[210]

CHAPTER 8

MEANEST, DIRTIEST, LOW-DOWN STUFF

━━━━━━━━━━━━━━━━━━━━━━━━━━━━━━━━━━━━

The Politics of Tumult

Just the meanest, dirtiest, low-down stuff that I've ever heard. Ought to
go to jail for it. It's just inhuman!

LYNDON JOHNSON, WHITE HOUSE TAPES, 1964

Johnson's frustration in making this remark to running mate Hubert Humphrey at the conclusion of the 1964 election was palpable. Since mid-October
the campaign against the Democratic presidential ticket by challenger Barry
Goldwater had become increasingly vicious. The Citizens for Goldwater organization had produced a thirty-minute film accusing the president of drinking and
driving, running a corrupt administration, and leading the nation to moral ruin.
In Johnson's home state of Texas, rumors circulated that Johnson's henchmen
had prevented the film from being broadcast. Humphrey had been dispatched to
shore up the administration's image by speaking about the importance of public
morality. Johnson had now returned to the LBJ Ranch in Texas, where he was
receiving telephone updates from his staff while awaiting the election results.
He was tired and his voice was hoarse. "Hubert, I wish you would see what these
sons-of-bitches have done!" Johnson exclaimed. "They bought four full-page ads
in most papers; some of them just got twelve pages, some sixteen. Four full pages
in this state, and it's all integrity, and morality, and Baker, and Jenkins, and Billy
Sol Estes."

In southern cities, fliers and radio spots were warning African Americans
against voting at all. "If he's ever had a traffic ticket, if he's ever been under suspicion, if he's ever been speeding, if he's ever had an over-parking ticket, if he ever
hasn't paid his taxes on time, if he's ever been discharged from employment,"
Johnson observed, an African American voter was being told "that he'll have
to report right away to the sheriff, and that these things will have to be settled

before they can clear his record to vote." "God!" Humphrey replied. "They put those out in all southern cities," Johnson continued, "just the meanest, dirtiest, low-down stuff that I've ever heard. Ought to go to jail for it. It's just inhuman!" "Well," Humphrey added, "they were doing it out in the Mexican areas, the same thing in California."[1]

The significance of Johnson's exchange with Humphrey lies not only in what it says about the 1964 campaign but also in what it reveals about the early 1960s and how developments in that era connected with the rise of the Religious Right in the 1980s. Johnson's landslide victory that fall, winning in all but six states and earning 90 percent of the electoral college votes, obscures the extent to which the nation was divided. The civil rights movement had been gaining momentum across the South with protests organized by the Southern Christian Leadership Conference in Alabama, Mississippi, and Georgia. But it was also stirring white resistance from leaders such as Alabama governor George Wallace. The U.S. Supreme Court had ruled in February 1962 that segregated transportation facilities were unconstitutional, and in June 1963 Kennedy had proposed wide-ranging but controversial civil rights legislation to Congress. Elected by the slimmest margin in any presidential contest since 1880, his administration was marked by tension over civil rights as well as the botched Bay of Pigs invasion of Cuba in 1961 and the Cuban missile crisis in 1962. In Texas Kennedy's narrow win in 1960 was followed by a divisive primary contest in 1962 and the closest governor's race since Reconstruction. If the 1964 campaign seemed mean, there was reason to believe that the meanness reflected something more than partisan chicanery.

But recalling the political tensions of the early 1960s also provides perspective on the turmoil that escalated later in the decade and extended into the 1970s. By 1980 a new era of Republican ascendancy had dawned. Ronald Reagan won all the formerly Democratic states in the South except for Jimmy Carter's home state of Georgia. Running mate George Bush cast Texas in a new light from the Johnson era. Evangelical Protestants were more engaged in politics than ever before. Television preachers such as Jerry Falwell and Pat Robertson were among its most visible leaders. The question that these developments sparked was whether they represented something fundamentally new or were rooted in the past.

What was new was easiest to see. Reagan's success in the South contrasted sharply with Johnson's and Carter's victories and with the Democratic Party's seldom rivaled hold over the region since the Civil War. Falwell's and Robertson's political activism reflected the power of religious television and contrasted sharply with earlier fundamentalists' such as Bob Jones and Carl F. H. Henry, who counseled keeping the faithful separate from such engagements. The fervor surrounding religious groups' antiabortion activism was easily traced to the controversial 1973 U.S. Supreme Court decision in Roe v. Wade. The continuities were harder to grasp. They required understanding the extent to which American religious traditions emphasized engagement with their communities, acknowledgement of grassroots concerns about intrusion by the federal government in local affairs, and recognition of differences of opinion within political parties and religious denominations. These continuities reflected local concerns and varied accordingly.

Texas is a particularly interesting location in which to consider both the continuities and discontinuities. It was part of the Democratic South, the state that Kennedy had to win in order to become president in 1960, and the state from which Johnson succeeded to the presidency in 1963, and yet it would be a strong ally of Reagan and the home of two subsequent Republican presidents. It was a bastion of Southern Baptist influences and yet was rife with religious disagreements. It was the location of tense relationships between Protestants and Catholics and between Anglos and Hispanics as well as conflicts over racial segregation and civil rights.

In the early 1960s Texas voters faced an array of issues as diverse as anywhere in the nation. Potential for division existed along partisan, racial, ethnic, educational, religious, and geographic lines. Republicans had gained strength and Democrats were divided among liberals, moderates, and conservatives. Groups bearing the label of arch- or ultraconservative were in play, and religious disagreements ranged across and within denominations. Independent religious organizations were increasingly active. Questions about crime and violence, communism, and civil rights dominated headlines. The civil rights movement was far from having achieved its goals but had made sufficient progress that new opportunities were available for leadership in schools, government, and civic organizations. Mobilization around social issues was diverse but was also becoming aligned in ways that would lead to the polarization that became known in the 1980s as the culture wars.

The 1960s are widely regarded as a time of national upheaval and transition. Through a wide-angle lens, the nation's changes revolved around the civil rights movement and the Vietnam War, both deeply controversial and amplified by television, by young people coming of age, and by shifts in sexual practices and understandings of gender. Close-up snapshots focus on locations where the upheaval was most evident, such as the University of California campus at Berkeley where the free speech movement blossomed, or Birmingham and Selma where the most contentious civil rights demonstrations took place. From such inquiries it is possible to understand in broad terms the new religious, racial, and cultural alignments that changed America. But neither the broad overview nor the close-up scrutiny of conflicts provides a satisfactory understanding of the processes through which change took shape. These processes were experienced differently in different parts of the country and were marked by debates over civil rights and Vietnam, but they were inflected through local institutions and given local interpretations.

Texas experienced its share of tension over school desegregation and fair housing but was different enough from the Deep South that civil rights controversies were sometimes overshadowed by other issues, especially by concerns about declining morality. The 1964 election may have been mean and dirty, but it also showcased questions about morality that brought religion into the political sphere. Morality was the language in which citizens expressed concern that something they did not quite understand was terribly wrong. The Goldwater film that Johnson considered reprehensible was one of several examples that showed how morality was regarded. Crime and violence, sex and gender, communism, and the Vietnam War became the focus of competing moral claims. Racial, religious, and political demarcations shifted, resulting in new, crosscutting alignments. Elections were closer than they generally had been in the past and were contested within as well as between parties. For religious leaders, speaking about social issues presented risks even though it seemed more imperative than ever to address these issues.

SOMETHING IS WRONG

Johnson considered the 1964 campaign mean and dirty because Republicans tried to suppress African American and Hispanic voting and because they attacked him personally. Charges that he was power hungry and morally deficient were low blows to a man who saw himself as a steward of the public trust—a person who held backyard barbeques for his friends and who went regularly to church whether he was at home in Texas or in Washington. Johnson hailed from devout Texas Baptists, joined the Disciples of Christ as a teenager, and over the years came to regard himself as an open-minded leader working for the common moral good.[2] Goldwater's supporters felt equally beleaguered. Here was a person who prided himself on being a churchgoer but was now accused of being an extremist connected to radical right-wing organizations such as the John Birch Society and ready to launch a nuclear conflagration at the least provocation.[3] The nastiness could be interpreted as acts of desperation, especially on Goldwater's side where polls showed there was little chance of winning, but also on Johnson's where his approval ratings were sinking month by month. Memories remained of how close the 1960 election had been and the role television had played in contrasting Nixon and Kennedy. Televised advertising played an even greater role in 1964.[4]

But meanness in the campaign occurred in the context of public anxiety about the moral unraveling of America itself. If Goldwater referenced morality in campaign speeches, so did Johnson. On September 5, 1964, Johnson met with speechwriter Bill Moyers—ordained as a Baptist minister—to plan the fall kickoff event scheduled two days later in Detroit. "Let's get a little of this Holy Roller populist stuff," Johnson suggested. "A land where every child can have training to fit his abilities. A home to protect him from the elements. A church to kneel in. And throw at least two biblical quotations in . . . that every one of them has heard. . . . These auto mechanics. It's what you Baptists just pour to them all the time!"[5]

FIGURE 17. Lyndon Johnson, 1964, signing an autograph on November 3. Photograph by Neal Douglass. Austin History Center, Austin Public Library. University of North Texas Libraries, The Portal to Texas History.

The "daisy commercial," showing a little girl picking daisy petals while an ominous voice in the background counted down toward a nuclear explosion, which appears as a mushroom cloud in the girl's eyes, became the most memorable part of Johnson's September 7 opening drive. Moyers did not exactly include the Holy Roller biblical quotations that Johnson wanted. But the hint of godly morality was there. "I want all the ages of man to yield him their promise," Johnson said to the crowd in Cadillac Square, "the child will find all knowledge open to him; the growing boy will shape his spirit in a house of God and his ways in the house of his family." Johnson expressed hope that the boy at the end of his journey would have lived the kind of life that led people to say, "There on this earth as in the eyes of God walks my brother." Commenting on the speech, columnist James Reston observed, "the old biblical cadences came together with wonderful effect."[6]

Over the next eight weeks, both candidates reminded audiences of the moral laxness they sensed pervading the country. Johnson saw it as a breakdown of law and order and, conversely, as a need for greater commitment to moral principles. In a speech given at the Mormon Tabernacle in Salt Lake City, he quoted from a hymn about moving toward eternal perfection and away from reckless eternal damnation, pledging his commitment to moral responsibility toward God and one another. "We are all God's children," he declared, "and the true morality of private life is the true morality of a free society: the Golden Rule, do unto others as you would have others do unto you."[7] Goldwater made morality an even more frequent refrain. He ran ads stating that Americans knew in their heart that he was right about the nation's "moral crisis" and declaring the need for leaders with moral courage. His "profound faith in God," he said, was the foundation of "deep personal honesty" and integrity.[8]

Morality was one of those campaign themes—like freedom and patriotism— that could be linked to any number of concerns. It came up in discussions of law and order, sexual promiscuity, child rearing, and religion. For some, it was still a way of talking about the liquor industry. It did not have to point to anything specific at all. When life is orderly and standards of right and wrong generate general agreement, the moral order seems intact. When it is uncertain what the rules are, or when the rules that should be upheld are not, anxiety sets in about moral decay. "The American people generally have a feeling that 'something is wrong,'" columnist Eric Sevareid observed in a thoughtful analysis of the 1964 campaign. "There are many different feelings among many different American groups that make up the general malaise," he added. Perhaps it was symptomatic of Americans' sense that life was somehow spinning out of control. Perhaps the typical American individual felt small against the bigness of government or the sprawl of large cities. It surely did not help that communism seemed to be spreading or to know that nuclear explosions could annihilate the planet.[9]

Free-floating angst of this kind crystallizes around specific events that can be defined as evidence that something larger, deeper, and more fundamentally to be feared is truly wrong. The relevant events can be as small and localized as a death in the family or a lost job. They occur on a larger scale as well, taking form in discussions of death rates and unemployment trends and public scandals. Power resides in the ability to define the meaning of these events. Moral scandals in the midst of a presidential campaign can have particularly powerful implications. One such scandal occurred at the height of the 1964 campaign.

On Wednesday evening, October 7, 1964, Walter Jenkins and his wife attended a party together in the nation's capital, departing around seven o'clock, she to attend another meeting and him to catch up on some work at the office. At 8:35 that evening Jenkins was arrested. He was forty-six at the time, a Baptist from Texas who had become a Catholic and fathered six children. This was the Jenkins LBJ referred to in his conversation with Humphrey a few weeks later. The Johnsons and Jenkinses had known each other back in Texas. Their children played together, and the families saw each other at picnics and community gatherings. Jenkins had worked for Johnson since 1939 and was one of Johnson's most trusted acquaintances, now serving as his principal administrative assistant. The arrest occurred at the YMCA three blocks from the White House. Jenkins and another man were arrested in a basement men's room by the Washington police morals squad and charged with being disorderly by making "indecent gestures."

The arrest remained unnoticed for a week until journalists received an anonymous tip that it might be worth checking the police blotter for the evening of October 7. Two hours after the news broke, the White House announced that Jenkins had resigned. Amid the flurry of reporting that followed, it was revealed that Jenkins had been arrested once before at the same location on a similar charge, that he had now been taken to a hospital suffering from fatigue and a nervous breakdown, and that the FBI was investigating to determine whether Jenkins might have been a victim of blackmail leading to a breach of national security.[10]

Coverage of the incident reflected the period in which it occurred. Although later accounts speculated that oral sex may have been involved, the terms considered appropriate for public discussion at the time included "pervert," "sexual deviate," and "morals charge." There was little doubt that Jenkins had been caught in a homosexual encounter. The men's room in which the arrest took place had become sufficiently familiar to the police as the location of such encounters that surveillance through a peephole led to the arrest.

Predictably, the Goldwater campaign connected the incident to the claims Goldwater had already been making about moral decay. "Nothing is more clear from history than the moral decay of a people begins at the top," he had observed at an appearance in Wheaton, Illinois, on October 3. "It seeps down from the highest offices into all walks of life. And what do we see today in those unlighted highest offices? We see the shadow of scandal cast across the White House itself."[11] Campaigning in Texas a few days before the Jenkins scandal became public, Goldwater criticized Johnson for failing to answer questions about morality in government arising from several earlier scandals and called on him to "return a sense of morality to government."[12] It fell to surrogates to make the direct connections. Former vice president Nixon and Goldwater's running mate William E. Miller called immediately for Johnson to explain how it was possible for a key presidential aide to be arrested on a morals charge.[13]

Texas newspapers featured the story in bold headlines, typically with coverage from national wire services. Although shorter stories sometimes spared readers the more lurid details of the arrest, the fact that a close confidant of the president had been arrested and had subsequently resigned over a morals charge was a common feature of the coverage. During the next two weeks leading up to the election, Texas newspapers carried essays by national syndicated columnists criticizing or defending Johnson against accusations associated with the Jenkins case. Goldwater ran ads stating that "Americans everywhere are indignant about the moral decay in Washington and nobody should accept corruption in positions of public trust as a way of life." Some of the papers endorsed Goldwater, while others endorsed Johnson. A typical endorsement for Goldwater was the one in the *Pampa Daily News*, a conservative paper that regularly advertised its belief that freedom is a gift from God. "Americans must come to the realization that even our mighty edifice of freedom cannot withstand continued assaults by empty and alienated men who are drunk with the nectar of their endless promises of effortless bounties for all," the editor wrote. Adjacent to the editorial the paper carried an essay from the *Chicago Tribune* about the Jenkins affair. "The case of Walter Jenkins involves issues of public morality, White House ethics, and official discretion," it declared. "These are the things that Barry Goldwater has been bringing before the American people. In your heart you know he was right all along."[14]

The most notable aspect of the Jenkins story was the quandary it posed for clergy. On the one hand, clergy were clearly on record for being concerned about moral decay and wanting to uphold morality. It was doubtful that many at the time considered homosexual encounters anything but moral perversion. And clergy had been outspoken in expressing their political views during the 1960 campaign. It would have seemed obvious that clergy should now speak again. On the other hand, it may have seemed that preaching quietly about godly behavior rather than making wider public pronouncements was sufficient, especially when political operatives and journalists were themselves making the connection between morality and the election.

Whatever the reasons, religious leaders issued surprisingly few formal statements about the Jenkins case. One exception was the American Council of Christian Churches, which under the direction of New Jersey fundamentalist Carl McIntire passed a strongly worded resolution at its annual convention. "The presence of such iniquity at the highest level not only shames our faces," the resolution stated, "but it must be fully exposed so that the consequences of it may be dealt with by the American people."[15] The statement concluded, "Immorality of this nature deserves the strongest condemnation." In contrast, the five thousand Texas Baptists who met in Corpus Christi for their annual convention just prior to the election opted to steer clear of political issues.[16]

The dilemma religious leaders faced over the Jenkins case was further revealed by the response from several of the nation's most prominent clergy. Republican leaders had been courting Billy Graham in hopes of eliciting a statement, if not directly endorsing Goldwater, at least embracing the candidate's arguments about the need to combat moral decay. The possibility was not out of the question. Graham's crusades in the early 1960s typically included arguments about moral decline, and on several occasions Graham had given hints of who he thought had presidential potential. At a crusade in Boston only a few days before the Jenkins incident, Graham warned that immorality was "rampant throughout the nation."[17] Reports indicated that some fifty to sixty thousand telegrams to Graham in the days prior to the 1964 election ran fifty to one in favor of requests that he endorse Goldwater.[18] But Graham's ties to Texas were strong and he was a friend of Johnson.

On October 20, 1964, Graham phoned the White House, telling Johnson he was praying for him and was sure he had the election wrapped up big. Graham then got to the point of his call. "You know when Jesus dealt with people with moral problems, like dear Walter had—and I said to Bill [Moyers] I wanted to send my love and sympathy to him—he always dealt tenderly, always. This was the way he handled it, and that's the way I feel about it. I know the weaknesses of men and the Bible says we're all sinners and we're all involved one way or another. I just hope if you have any contact with him you'll give him my love and understanding." Johnson thanked Graham, said this would mean more than anything to Walter, and invited Graham to come down for dinner on Saturday evening.[19]

The other response from religious leaders further illustrated the complexities involved in linking religion and morality to politics. On October 30, 1964, thirty prominent Protestant, Roman Catholic, and Jewish clergy issued a statement about the Jenkins case. John C. Bennett, president of Union Theological Seminary in New York City, organized the effort. Among the signers were Reinhold Niebuhr, Paul Tillich, Thomas Merton, and Abraham Heschel. These were four of the most prominent religious leaders in the world. Niebuhr, Bennett's colleague at Union Theological Seminary, was one of the chief proponents of neo-orthodox theology, regularly toured the country lecturing, was the author of more than a dozen books including the widely read *Moral Man and Immoral Society*, and was said to be a key source of theological inspiration for Dr. Martin Luther King Jr. Tillich, also at Union, had been writing influential books about theology for nearly four decades and was similarly said to be an inspiration for King. Merton was the Trappist monk whose *Seven Storey Mountain* in 1948 put him at the forefront of work in the Catholic mystical tradition and who would die tragically in Bangkok in 1968 after becoming an outspoken critic of the Vietnam War. Abraham Heschel was a professor at the Jewish Theological Seminary of America in New York, the author of numerous books, and widely regarded as one of the most influential Jewish leaders in the United States. The statement they signed condemned any use of the Jenkins case in the national political campaign. "We desire to make a public protest against the way 'morality' is being used as a weapon in this campaign," they declared, adding, "Nothing that has been discovered justifies the smears of the kind that are now so frequently repeated."[20]

At face value, it was unusual for the clergy involved to issue a declaration so readily interpreted as an endorsement of one candidate over another. But at another level the statement signaled the extent to which morality was being contested in ways that could have a political influence. The statement went on to explain that to these theologians, the larger moral issues warranting consideration dealt with civil rights, injustice, and peace in the world. There was implicit agreement that morality was deeply relevant to political discussions, only disagreement about how morality should be defined.

A TIME FOR CHOOSING

Although the Jenkins incident received wide publicity, its impact on the election was muted by the fact that the story was overshadowed by events on the world stage, especially China's explosion of a nuclear bomb and the fall of Soviet premier Nikita Khrushchev, both occurring in the same week. In a curious way, it was the Goldwater film that Johnson complained about to Humphrey—a film that was never televised—that illustrated most clearly the range of anxieties associated with the discussion of morality during the 1964 election. The film, titled *Choice*, was intended to complement a televised speech by Ronald Reagan called "A Time for Choosing."[21] Reagan was Goldwater's campaign director in California and had been giving stump speeches on Goldwater's behalf once or twice a day for more than a month. The speech was delivered well, was rebroadcast several times on national television, and was regarded as a major factor in Reagan's rise to national prominence as a conservative leader.[22] It also played a pivotal role in shaping the views of two aspiring leaders who would play important roles in Texas and national politics: future House majority leader Dick Armey and future representative Ron Paul. The speech focused on errant government policies, ridiculing Washington bureaucrats for failed and expensive government welfare programs initiated by Kennedy and Johnson. In contrast, *Choice* used graphic newsreel footage combined with staged depictions of events to portray the moral upheaval facing American society.

Ostensibly the film was produced and financed by Mothers for Moral America, a loose-knit, grassroots movement that started in Nashville in mid-September 1964 and within a month had chapters in thirty-seven states. In reality the film was conceived at a meeting of Citizens for Goldwater-Miller strategists in Beverly Hills. The strategists discussed three possible themes—the threat of nuclear war, the high cost of living, and moral issues—and settled on the third as the best way to generate anger among viewers. The moral issues to be emphasized included juvenile delinquency, crime, violence, immorality in government, influence peddling, narcotics, and pornography. The plan was to remind people of the moral crisis, "bring it down to them and make their stomachs tighten," and then focus the anger on Johnson.[23]

The film opened with a black Lincoln careening violently along a country road. Resembling the president's limousine, the vehicle was meant to symbolize Johnson, wildly driving the nation toward ruin. At one point the driver throws an empty beer can into the ditch. Subsequent scenes shift from young people frenetically dancing themselves into moral abandon amid a din of raucous music, violent clashes between civil rights demonstrators and police, street riots and looting in black ghettos, a topless dancer at a strip club, and a series of magazines and book covers portraying pornographic content. Alternating between these scenes of moral chaos are clips of neatly dressed white children reciting the Pledge of Allegiance, pioneers courageously crossing the plains in covered wagons, stately national monuments, and the text of the U.S. Constitution. Quoting scripture, the narrator intones, "And I will say to my soul, thou has much goods laid up for many years. Take thy rest. Eat, drink, make good cheer. But God said to him, 'Thou fool. This night do they require thy soul of thee.' This night is here. Now. Two Americas and you, you alone, stand in between them. Which do you really want?" The film ends with actor John Wayne, a rifle on the wall behind him, calling on Americans to vote.[24]

Prepublicity for the film generated considerable criticism and led to speculation that the most lurid scenes would be edited out or censored. After viewing it at a private screening in Philadelphia, Goldwater ordered the film not to be shown and all prints of it returned. "I'm not going to be made out a racist," he told his staff. "You can't show it." The scenes of ghetto rioting, he was sure, would backfire and do nothing but stir up trouble.[25] Nevertheless, Mothers for Moral America sold two hundred copies to local groups and distributed more than three million copies of a brochure in Illinois and Texas emphasizing similar connections between Johnson and immorality. Had the film been televised, it undoubtedly would have been condemned both for its racism and for its depictions of nudity and pornography.

All the same, the film was largely a compilation of scenes that the American public was already viewing regularly on the evening news. Its message that something was wrong in America would have been readily understood. The staid America of the pioneers and the Eisenhower era was being displaced by tumult. White middle-class suburbs and quiet small towns were being supplanted by violent African American ghettoes. Those who shared Kennedy's dream of American greatness were now feeling threatened by his successor. As one of the film's originators explained, "This guy, Johnson, by an act of God, moves in and has not only allowed all this immoral stuff to start, he has literally destroyed all the work that Kennedy had started to accomplish."[26]

MORAL DECAY

Seen only as a lesson in political rhetoric, the 1964 election can be viewed as a low point in which strategists, if not the candidates themselves, resorted to fearmongering and personal attacks to win votes. But that perspective misses the larger cultural context in which these appeals were made. To grasp this wider context requires considering the important role that religious institutions played in defining what morality meant and why it seemed to be so terribly at risk. Religious leaders may have felt conflicted about speaking too openly in the closing days of a presidential election. However, they had for some time been paying attention to what they regarded as devastating moral decay, and they would continue to do so well after the contest between Goldwater and Johnson ended.

A case in point occurred in June 1965 when the Southern Baptist Convention held its annual conference in Dallas. "We find ourselves in the midst of a moral revolution of unprecedented proportions," the delegates declared. The statement was in the context of a resolution condemning obscenity in radio, television, movies, and literature. The delegates went on to deplore violence, illicit sex, and the debasement of elementary moral values. They called for a new commitment to moral development that would combat the rising scourge of materialism, gambling, price fixing, cheating, and moral relativism. "Eat, drink, and be merry for tomorrow you may die" seemed to be the motto by which modern Americans were living. The gathering's presidential address hit on almost the same themes as the repudiated Goldwater film. "We are faced with the social and moral decay of society," the speaker declared, "the 'sex revolution,' rising crime rates, the criminal exploitation of our citizenship by the liquor industry." The race issue had devolved into marches in the street and pickets at the gate. No longer was there an orderly environment in which moral and spiritual ideals could grow. The delegates, he argued in implied reference to the Johnson administration's social programs, should seriously ponder the question, " 'How can we create a great society out of a morally sick society?' Legislation can structure the economics, but only the church can produce the moral foundations for that great society. God's mandate to twentieth-century America is 'behave or be damned.' "[27]

Anyone reading Texas newspapers in these years would have known that morality was a topic of particular interest. The *Dallas Morning News* published 4,561 articles between 1960 and 1964 containing the words "moral," "morals," or "morality." That was up from 3,774 the previous five years and 3,447 the five years before that. Over the next five years, the number increased to 5,360.[28] One of the most frequent references to these topics was the syndicated weekly column by Norman Vincent Peale. Criticized for his public opposition to Kennedy in 1960, Peale now steered clear of political endorsements and encouraged local pastors to do the same. But he repeatedly addressed what he regarded as the moral deterioration of American culture, typically relating stories from readers and from people who had come to him for counseling to drive home the point. One anecdote was about a college student who was expelled for plagiarism. Another was the story of a medical student who got his girlfriend pregnant. The new attitude, Peale wrote, seemed to be "to heck with old restrictions and decencies and morals." He thought religious leaders were largely to blame for focusing too much on large social issues such as racism and war and not enough on basic personal morality.[29]

"Moral decay has been discussed by thousands of speakers, not all of them in church pulpits," the editor of the *Corpus Christi Caller-Times* observed. Every national magazine carried stories about the breakdown of moral fiber, he wrote. Polls showed that the public believed standards of honesty and moral decency were in disarray. "Western nations are going through a period of severe moral change," the editor concluded. "This is not hard to account for when one considers the sociological earthquakes this generation has suffered. The hope now . . . is that from this period of change there will emerge a new commitment to standards that undergird our civilization."[30]

The possibility that churches and church leaders were themselves to blame for the apparent decline in morality was widely entertained.[31] For the first time, church membership statistics, such as they were, seemed to indicate that a slightly smaller percentage of the American population were members than had been true a few years earlier, and weekly attendance at religious services seemed to have peaked as well. It would be 1966 before *Time* magazine ran as its cover story the question, "Is God dead?" But theologians were already positing that secularization was happening in the United States just as it had in Europe. Perhaps the evangelical zeal that had driven itinerant pastors and circuit riders to found churches as the frontier pushed westward was waning. Perhaps the parishes and temples to which immigrants had flocked to preserve their ethnic identity were now less important to the children and grandchildren of these immigrants. Americans were getting used to the material comforts of middle-class life and were spending more time at work, watching television, and participating in other community organizations. Niebuhr, true to his conviction that instances of personal indiscretion such as the Jenkins case should not detract from larger issues, thought that perhaps the churches were declining precisely because they had focused too much on such matters. "Perhaps the churches themselves have been superficial," he wrote, "preoccupied with trivia, rather than squaring up to universal religious demands in crucial situations, such as the race issue."[32]

But what may have seemed trivial remained important in local churches. As pastors in Texas considered the implications of the civil rights movement, they turned repeatedly to the language of morality. Workshops, conferences, and sermons emphasized morality as the legitimate focus of church teachings. Unlike social policy that was more appropriately dealt with in the political domain and through legislation, morality was regarded as the church's business. If there was moral confusion, it was all the more incumbent on the churches to evangelize and to teach morality, whatever that might mean.

One of the more notable aspects of the concern about moral decline was the extent to which crime and violence were mentioned as evidence that morality was indeed in jeopardy.[33] Dallas residents sometimes derided Houston by calling it the murder capital of America, but they worried about violence in their own community as well. Available statewide statistics showed that some kinds of crime were indeed on the rise. Between 1959 and 1963 the number of rapes in Texas per 100,000 population increased by 8 percent, as did the number of aggravated assaults, while the number of robberies grew 15 percent, burglaries increased by 23 percent, and larceny climbed 38 percent. Only the murder rate and number of auto thefts did not increase. In several of the categories—murder, rape, aggravated assaults, and burglaries—the rate in Texas was also significantly higher than the national average.[34]

But concerns about crime can be driven as much by a general feeling that something is wrong as by statistics. It was not hard for Texans to associate a subliminal angst of this kind with crime in the aftermath of Kennedy's assassination in Dallas. An East Coast writer who had lived in Texas captured the complex reaction in observing that the local atmosphere was one of pathological hatred and smoldering xenophobia and at the same time a painful awareness of being a kind of barren steppeland governed by a continuing frontier code of violence.[35]

Although commentators distinguished the assassination from anything else about the state in which it occurred, writers did not hesitate to say that crime was *soaring* or rising at an *alarming* rate and that it was a *formidable* problem because of its *magnitude* and the *multiplicity* of things that needed to be done. To be sure, analysts said, there were contributing factors such as urbanization and uncertain economic conditions. But somehow the moral climate seemed to be deteriorating and respect for law and order was declining. Indeed, conditions were such, some mental health professionals warned, that the potential for more assassinations needed to be considered. Murder could spring from some hidden frustration a child experienced at home or in school. Violence in the streets could be the result of a disturbed home environment. Parents who already had plenty to be anxious about needed to be aware of these latent dangers.[36]

On Monday, August 1, 1966, these warnings seemed to come true. Charles J. Whitman, a twenty-five-year-old former marine who was currently a student at the University of Texas in Austin, climbed to the twenty-eighth-floor observation deck of the university's administration building and from there engaged in a shooting spree that left sixteen people dead and thirty-two others wounded. "Shortly before the tower's clock struck noon," a local journalist wrote, "the first shot rang out. For the next hour and twenty minutes, the lazy summer campus was turned into a hellish battleground of death, dying and wounded."[37] It was considered the worst massacre carried out by a single gunman in the nation's history. An autopsy revealed a brain tumor the size of a pecan that pathologists said could have resulted in intense headaches and contributed to the killings. But observers wondered about the incident's larger implications. Was this an instance of someone pushing too hard to succeed in college? Was it further evidence of something badly wrong with the culture itself? "Every night the television programs stress homicide," Texas senator Ralph W. Yarborough observed. "Murder, sudden and quick, is piped into every home for viewing as entertainment. Every day our newspapers headline how many people were killed in Vietnam until 'kill-ratio' has become a common term in the language."[38] In Washington, Johnson expressed hope that gun-control legislation pending since Kennedy's assassination would now be passed.

If crime and violence were not enough to suggest that the country was suffering from moral decay, the problems parents identified in relating to the younger generation provoked additional concerns. By the 1960s the children who constituted the postwar baby boom were teenagers. Nationally there were four million more teens ages thirteen through seventeen in 1960 than there had been in 1950. In Texas this age-group grew from 605,000 to 832,000, an increase of 38 percent during the 1950s, and then climbed another 38 percent during the 1960s.[39]

This was the setting in which religious leaders identified a widening generation gap in personal morality. Young people seemed to be growing up without firm standards of right and wrong. College students especially seemed to be at risk of losing whatever moral standards they had learned growing up. "When people of my age were young," Peale observed, "the advantage we had morally was we knew right from wrong, even though we did not always act right." Nowadays, he thought, young people were exposed only to a wide gray area of moral relativism. In the breach they were being guided too much by promiscuity in movies and on television and were easily seduced by the sexual revolution.[40]

Historian Will Durant, in his seventies at the time, took a widely publicized position similar to Peale's. Much of the blame, he thought, lay in the hypocrisy to which young people were exposed. "We have pretended to a moral core favoring pre-marital continence," he wrote, "while we have surrounded the young with every stimulus to sex [and] given them the example of seeking sexual excitement in a hundred forms and ten thousand places of entertainment."[41] Billy Graham's crusades identified a broad moral catastrophe occurring in America along many fronts but usually mentioned sexual immorality as one indication of the problems that turning to Christ could solve. The present generation, he declared, "has been schooled in violence, sex and mischief [and] led into lawlessness." The problem, he thought, stemmed largely from increasingly graphic depictions of sexual activity. "No one can doubt that movies are dirtier than ever," he said. "Even magazines and billboards magnify sex out of all proportion."[42]

Stung by incidents of vandalism and juvenile delinquency, local leaders joined the call for moral renewal. Texas was truly part of the national culture in ways it had never been in earlier decades, its youth exposed to the same promiscuity and violence on television and in the movies as youth everywhere, and its newspapers filled with columns by nationally respected writers and preachers. And yet it was local parents and pastors and community officials who felt that something constructive must be done.[43] One of the more interesting efforts was organized in La Marque, a rapidly growing, racially mixed town of about thirteen thousand—future senator Kay Bailey Hutchison's hometown—in Galveston County. La Marque suffered no lack of churches but was troubled by the prospect of juvenile delinquency. Not content to leave the problem solely in the hands of clergy, more than a hundred of the community's businesses joined forces to support youth organizations, solicit letters from parents, and publish essays in the local newspaper promoting godliness, morality, and family values. "The home that rears its children in the fear and admonition of the Lord is not greatly in danger of being affected with delinquency," one of the essays advised. "Children must be led to know and revere God. They must be encouraged to honor parents, cherish the home, and value their church."[44]

Pastors undoubtedly applauded such efforts to promote godliness and deter juvenile delinquency. A scheme put forward by oilmen Richardson and Murchison to combat delinquency was considerably less well received. Neither man's family was personally affected as far as anyone knew by unruly offspring. Murchison's son earned top grades at the Lawrenceville School in New Jersey and studied mathematics at MIT before returning to oversee the family fortune; Richardson was a bachelor who had no children. Nor was either particularly motivated by religion, although Richardson kept on sufficiently good terms with the churched community that Billy Graham came out to conduct the funeral when he died. The plan they came up with was to start a national organization called Boys Incorporated that would support local centers for indigent boys who might otherwise turn to crime. The idea might also go some way, observers remarked, toward redeeming the public image of Texas oilmen as rough-hewn, hard-drinking, self-interested money-grubbers. The controversial part involved raising the money through a racetrack where the oilmen and their wealthy friends could enjoy betting on the ponies while doing their good-hearted, tax-exempt philanthropic work. After church groups blocked an attempt to purchase a racetrack in Detroit, the project shifted to the Del Mar Turf Club in Southern California. Church groups again protested the idea of charitable revenue stemming from gambling, but the plan succeeded for more than a decade until a lawsuit by the Internal Revenue Service persuaded the principals to shut it down.[45]

It was far less controversial for pastors and community leaders simply to speak against youthful immorality and to deplore premarital sex and promiscuity in the movies. What churches should advise, if anything, about contraception and family planning was more ambiguous. Anecdotes suggested that the sexual promiscuity depicted in the Goldwater film was rampant on the nation's campuses. Stories of drunken parties and an anything-goes attitude toward sex suggested that the younger generation had lost its moorings. The few studies that investigated the situation in greater detail indicated that promiscuity was far from rampant.[46] And yet birth control was becoming more openly discussed, and the pill was available in many areas for married women; speculation suggested that it would soon become available for unmarried women as well. The Vatican studied the issue of birth control, deciding in 1965 that contraception was not to be practiced by Catholics, but by that time many married Catholic women were already using the pill. A study in Corpus Christi that year found some two thousand Catholic women receiving birth control advice from Planned Parenthood's four clinics, which in turn were supported through federal grants under Johnson's antipoverty program.[47]

Feminism and gender equality were not yet the hot-button issues they would become by the end of the decade. Women's groups, however, remained an active feature of congregational life, working on missionary and social outreach activities and occasionally sponsoring interracial gatherings. Anticipating some of the more conservative women's organizations that formed a few years later, a loose confederation of Women for Constitutional Government held meetings in 1963 in an effort to mobilize women who felt indignant about the direction America was heading. Among the issues they hoped to spark indignation toward were communism and the federal government's role in pushing integration. Former general Edwin Walker was the featured speaker at one of the group's events in

Texas.[48] Dallas, a Democratic leader said noting the group's activities, was becoming the "nut capital of the world."[49] It did not help matters when Walker announced plans to tour the country with archconservative Tulsa radio preacher Billy James Hargis in a campaign to rid the nation's churches of communist infiltrators.[50] As the tour proceeded, it was picketed in Kansas and Ohio and denounced by the NAACP, but back in Texas the team became increasingly pronounced in their anticommunism, criticism of Kennedy, and support for Goldwater. When United Nations ambassador Adlai Stevenson spoke in Dallas a few days before Kennedy's fatal visit, members of the indignant women's group who supported Walker picketed the event and heckled Stevenson during his speech.[51]

Although church groups mobilized on occasion for what they regarded as higher moral standards on television and in movies, the issue that generated the most pointed concern was what could or could not take place in public schools. On June 25, 1962, the Supreme Court in *Engel v. Vitale* ruled that state officials could not compose an official state prayer and require it to be recited in public schools even if the prayer was denominationally neutral and pupils who did not wish to participate were permitted to remain silent or be excused from the room.[52] The ruling drew widespread criticism from pastors and lawmakers who were already skeptical of the Court and who vowed immediately to work for a constitutional amendment circumventing the decision. Specific responses ranged from denying that school prayer had ever hurt anyone to declaring that the nation would soon fall victim to a Marxist revolution.[53] Meanwhile, school administrators in Texas as in other states experimented with ways to continue time-honored practices while abiding by a strict interpretation of the ruling. One method was to have student groups propose prayers in place of an official prayer, another was to offer a prayer in the moments immediately preceding the official start of the school day, and yet another was to offer devotionals showcasing "moral and spiritual" values instead of religion. It was imperative to prevent irreligion from becoming the established religion, a pastor in Brazosport explained, because that would lead to further juvenile delinquency, a rising crime rate, and "moral delinquency in many areas of our national life."[54] Apart from the Court's ruling about school prayer, questions were also being raised about the content of textbooks.

One of the most vocal sources of concern about textbooks came from a conservative organization called Texans for America. Precedent for special-purpose groups of this kind could be found in the antisaloon groups of the 1920s and the antilynching effort mobilized by Jessie Daniel Ames in the 1930s. But Texans for America had less in the way of direct support from any religious groups and in fact evoked opposition from some religious leaders. It reflected divisions that were becoming more evident within and between the two major political parties. It also showed the emerging possibilities for small networks of activists to gain publicity and support for specific issues.

Texans for America was led by J. Evetts Haley, a rancher from Canyon, Texas, a few miles south of Amarillo. Haley had attempted to organize a group of Texas

Democrats against Roosevelt in 1936 and ran for governor in 1956 as an opponent of school desegregation. Attired in cowboy hat and boots and with the
distinction of being a trustee of the national Cowboy Hall of Fame, Haley campaigned vigorously on a states' rights platform against the "immoral and destructive" power of the federal government but scored fewer than 6 percent of
the votes cast in the Democratic primary that year. The campaign nevertheless
forged a small network among like-minded archconservatives with Haley at the
center. Raised as a Methodist, he believed earlier in life that faith should be a
matter of private conviction but came increasingly to argue that religion should
play a direct role in government. Having focused on communism and concerns
about the rising influence of the federal government and the Supreme Court, his
attention shifted in 1960 toward the state textbook committee.

Textbook content and state educational policies had sparked controversy
periodically since World War II. In 1953 the annual convention of the Texas
Congress of Parents and Teachers became the focus of an effort by conservative
women from Houston to overturn what they saw as a liberal agenda among the
organization's leadership. The effort received backing from local chapters of Minute Women of the United States of America, a grassroots movement concerned
about communism, inflation, foreign aid, and perceived threats to women's roles
and the family.[55] A more sustained effort to bring conservative principles more
clearly to bear on textbooks and educational policy was led by Mel and Norma
Gabler, active members of the First Baptist Church in the small East Texas town
of Hawkins. The Gablers founded an organization called Educational Research
Analysts to challenge what they saw as inaccuracies in the state's textbooks and
toured the state making speeches calling attention to the need for greater emphasis on "moral values, love of country and love of home and family."[56]

Between 1960 and 1962 Haley lobbied successfully to have several textbooks
barred from approval by the state board of education, sought unsuccessfully to
have The Grapes of Wrath banned, and argued that his efforts were aimed at preserving the Christian ethic against socialistic teachings. In 1964 he wrote a critical biography of Johnson in which he described the president as a vindictive "evil
genius" driven by "monumental egotism." The book sold seven million copies.
Haley's network included Dallas anticommunist radio and television commentator Dan Smoot and General Walker, whom Haley supported for Texas governor
in 1962. When Haley's wife died in 1958, former Norris protégé Earl Anderson
conducted the funeral. The John Birch Society distributed Haley's biography of
Johnson. At some of the textbook hearings, Baptist clergy joined Haley's effort
to combat "the communist conspiracy to lower the morals of our youth," but
the book against Johnson was too much. Baptist bookstores removed it from
their shelves. Haley's effort to bring religion into state politics was vehemently
opposed by Baptist leader Dawson, the long-time champion of church and state
separation now in his eighties, who vividly recalled fundamentalists' efforts to
shape politics in the 1920s.[57]

COMMUNISM

The thread connecting Smoot, Haley, and Walker with Hargis and the indignant women's group was concern about the spread of communism—yet another way of thinking about what was wrong morally, spiritually, and politically with America and the world. The related tie connecting them was that they all held membership in or received support from the John Birch Society. Founded in 1958 by entrepreneur Robert Welch Jr. and named for a Baptist missionary killed by communists in China in 1945, the group was headquartered in Indianapolis but consisted of a loose network of business leaders, several of whom were from Texas. One was oil multimillionaire H. L. Hunt. Another was Fred Koch, a former student at Rice whose fortune also derived from the oil industry and who had witnessed communism firsthand while working in Russia during the 1930s.[58]

The John Birch Society was one of several groups that critics at the time pegged as radical right-wing, ultraconservative organizations. Hargis had his own organization, Christian Crusade Ministries, which included daily and weekly radio broadcasts aired on stations across the nation, a monthly newspaper, and a television series. Another was Fred Schwarz, whose Christian Anti-Communism Crusade publicized itself through books, newsletters, and speaking tours. Schwarz addressed a joint session of the Texas legislature in 1959 and cultivated ties with members of the Dallas Freedom Forum, a conservative group that hosted Schwarz on several occasions along with other anticommunist speakers and introduced several of his books into the Dallas high school curriculum.[59] Without explicitly endorsing Goldwater, Schwarz's organization ran large newspaper advertisements in Texas during the 1964 campaign warning that attacks on Goldwater were inspired by communists aiming to confuse and demoralize the public.[60] Yet another organization was a fledgling network of Christian Citizen groups organized by multimillionaire real estate developer and Southern Baptist lay leader Gerri von Frellick. The von Frellick group in Texas distinguished itself from the Hargis and Schwarz organizations by appealing to moderate conservatives and refraining from taking partisan stands on particular issues, but it insisted that members believe in Christ and sought to train them to become political candidates. By seeking specifically to enlist clergy in political activities, the von Frellick group nevertheless evoked a statement from the director of the Baptist General Convention of Texas Christian Life Commission cautioning clergy against compromising church-state separation.[61]

Judging from surveys, none of these organizations attracted more than a small percentage of the public. But coming on the heels of the political witch hunts conducted in the 1950s by Senator Joseph McCarthy and having ties with wealthy backers, these organizations suggested to critics that something worrisome might be happening on the far political right that could grow. Radio audiences in Texas could listen each Saturday evening for two hours to Hunt's conservative *Life Line* broadcasts, which combined anticommunist themes with hymns and religious appeals, and then stay tuned for another hour and a half of Hargis's Christian Crusade.[62] Hargis also made personal visits to Texas, speaking at churches, holding rallies, and giving interviews. "I have seen the whole anti-communist fight take on a wholly religious nature," he explained on one of his visits. "The fight against those forces that would tend to communize our country has taken on a holy aspect." He thought conservatives should recapture America's pulpits and considered Goldwater the best person to combat communism in politics.[63]

Fears of communist expansion were prompted by world events as much as by right-wing activist organizations. Russia's successful launch of Sputnik in 1957, Castro's victory in Cuba in 1959, and the escalating nuclear arms race stoked citizens' concerns. Americans worried not only about nuclear warfare but also about the possibility of godless communists infiltrating the nation's schools and churches. It was not difficult to draw a connection between this possibility and the wider concerns about moral decay. Running for governor in 1962, John Connally made the connection one of his central arguments. "The great threat we face is a communist challenge to our political, economic, moral and spiritual institutions," he explained in his standard stump speeches.[64] During a weeklong visit sponsored by the Dallas Freedom Forum, Ronald Reagan struck at the same themes, warning an enthusiastic audience of five thousand against the danger of creeping communism and arguing that welfare programs were destroying American freedom.[65]

Whatever they may have thought of Connally and Reagan, voters did not have to look far to imagine that they were right. FBI chief J. Edgar Hoover, who claimed to have details of communists' secret activities in the bureau's files, published essays repeatedly making the connection. His columns routinely appeared in Texas newspapers, as they did elsewhere, but there was also a more intimate connection between Hoover and Texas. Like Murchison and Richardson, Hoover loved horse races and fine dining. For twenty years he spent monthlong visits as their guest in Southern California, and in 1958 his best-selling anticommunist book, *Masters of Deceit*, was published by Henry Holt, a company Murchison owned. Christians, Hoover declared, wanted to follow the Apostle Paul in becoming new creatures in Christ, but "communist morality, of course, is rooted in total rejection of a belief in God and in the values of the Christian moral code."[66]

In 1964 public concerns about communist expansion were only beginning to focus on Vietnam. The state's casualties included forty-four-year-old master sergeant Chester Ovnand from Copperas Cove, who had been killed in Vietnam by small arms fire on July 8, 1959, and twenty-two-year-old air force second lieutenant Glenn Matteson from Dallas, who was killed in Laos on March 23, 1961. But thus far the number of casualties was relatively small. Thirteen from Texas died in 1963, and eighteen died in 1964. As far as military action was concerned, the most significant impact on the state was defense contracts. In 1964 Texas received nearly $1.8 billion in defense contracts, second only to California.[67]

The escalation leading to Johnson's decision not to seek reelection in 1968 was vividly evident in the number of casualties, rising to 115 from Texas in 1965, 366 in 1966, 670 in 1967, and reaching a peak of 1,009 in 1968. By the end of 1968, approximately 623,000 troops from across the nation were serving in Southeast Asia, and military expenditures there were costing American taxpayers more than $73 million a day.[68] In 1965 only 28 percent of the public nationally disapproved of Johnson's handling of the situation in Vietnam. By February 1968 that proportion rose to 54 percent.[69] But whatever they thought about Vietnam, widespread concern about communism at home as well as abroad remained. In a Harris Survey that summer, 56 percent of the public said communists were a major cause of the breakdown of law and order in the United States, another 26 percent thought communists were a minor cause, and only 9 percent thought communists were not to blame.[70]

CIVIL RIGHTS

Choice and Goldwater's reaction in pulling the film illustrated how readily discussions of moral decay spilled into accusations and counteraccusations about race and civil rights. On the one hand, the view expressed by Niebuhr, Tillich, Merton, Heschel, and others was that racial inequality and discrimination were the central moral issues at stake. On the other hand, moral language was used to condemn civil rights demonstrations and even to suggest that civil rights legislation was misguided. After all, critics said, it was impossible to legislate morality.

Although attitudes were changing, resistance to school integration, fair housing, and interracial contact in general remained widespread. A survey in 1964 found southern whites overwhelmingly opposed to anything suggesting greater equality between whites and African Americans. Eighty-two percent thought "a restaurant owner should not have to serve Negroes if he doesn't want to." Seventy-nine percent said there should be "laws against marriages between Negroes and whites." Seventy-six percent said they "would not like my child to go to school with a lot of Negroes." A majority (55 percent) agreed that "generally speaking, Negroes are lazy and don't like to work hard."[71]

The survey also revealed interesting differences between members of the South's two dominant religious denominations. Whereas 41 percent of white Methodists in the South thought "white children and Negro children should go to the same schools" rather than to "separate but equal schools," the comparable proportion among white Baptists in the South was only 13 percent. Sixty percent of white southern Methodists thought "Negroes are as intelligent as white people," but only 46 percent of white southern Baptists agreed. And while 52 percent of white southern Methodists agreed that "Negroes are lazy," that proportion rose to 64 percent among white southern Baptists.[72]

A Texas Poll did not ask about religion but showed the extent to which Texans remained ambivalent about racial integration. Sixty-three percent of white Anglos thought the Johnson administration was pushing integration too fast. Sixty-two percent said they would not want Negroes using the same swimming pools as whites, 44 percent did not want their children going to the same schools as Negroes, and 38 percent preferred attending racially separate churches. Among African Americans with school-age children, only half said their children had ever attended school with white children. Hispanics felt better about the pace of integration than white Anglos did, but 35 percent thought it was too fast. Thirty-five percent also preferred not sending their children to the same schools as African Americans, and 30 percent felt that way about attending the same churches.[73]

The racial composition of Texas had been changing as a result of significant in-migration among whites and significant out-migration among African Americans, putting the state in the curiously ambiguous position that provided the background for Johnson's conversation with Humphrey. On the one hand, Texas included more African Americans (more than 1.2 million) than any southern state—and indeed than any state in the country except New York. On the other hand, the proportion of residents who were African American (12.4 percent) was the lowest of any southern state and only slightly higher than the national average.[74] This ambiguity meant that white Texas politicians like Johnson could hardly ignore its African American population, and yet it was tempting to do so when the white population constituted such a large majority. Racial politics were further complicated by the fact that more than a third of the state's African American population lived in Dallas and Houston and most of the rest lived in East Texas, while West Texas was predominantly white.

Another important change from earlier decades was that fewer of the state's population hailed from other parts of the South. Only 8 percent had been born in other southern states. Nearly three-quarters were native Texans. Eleven percent had been born in other countries. That did not mean the ancestral affinities between Texas and the Confederacy were absent, but it did imply that those connections were not as distinct as they once were.[75]

Discussions of racial and ethnic equality and of civil rights were also beginning to take into account greater consideration of the state's population of Hispanic origin, which totaled more than 1.5 million in 1960, or approximately one person in six. That was the largest number of any state and the highest proportion of any state except Arizona. Nearly all the Hispanic-origin residents of Texas were of Mexican ancestry, and upward of 95 percent were Catholic, although by the early 1960s Texas Baptists had succeeded in founding some four hundred Hispanic congregations, with approximately 33,000 members.[76] The number of Texas residents actually born in Mexico totaled 655,000, only slightly below the number of California residents born in Mexico and the largest percentage of any state except Arizona. More than half the Mexican-born population of Texas lived in just five counties, with the largest concentrations in the vicinity of San

Antonio, El Paso, and Houston. Two-thirds of the state's counties included no residents of Mexican birth.[77]

Large differences in socioeconomic status continued to separate the state's white Anglo population from African Americans and Hispanics. Median family income in 1960 among white non-Hispanics was $5,500, the highest of any southern state and only slightly below the national average. Median family income for African Americans was only $2,650 and for Hispanics $3,050. Forty-eight percent of white non-Hispanic adults age twenty-one and over had completed high school, compared with 24 percent of African Americans and only 14 percent of Hispanics. The figure for African Americans was the highest of any southern state but well below that of other large states such as California, Illinois, and New York. The figure for Hispanics was the lowest of any state.[78]

Protestant religious leaders regarded civil rights and race almost exclusively as questions about the relationships between blacks and whites. African American clergy continued to combat the poll tax at the same time that they sought to encourage voters to pay it. Clergy-led groups formed to support liberal Democratic candidates and found themselves at odds with groups supporting moderate candidates.[79] Although, judging from the survey evidence, white Methodists across the South were less eager to maintain racial separation than white Baptists, there were differences of opinion within both denominations. At a meeting in 1964, Dallas Methodists found themselves on all sides of questions about civil disobedience, laws pertaining to public morals, and how best to be relevant to issues of community concern.[80] With declining membership, the denomination's leaders were torn between focusing on social issues and rededicating themselves to evangelism and moral renewal. The Southern Baptist Convention was divided between theological moderates and theological conservatives who differed not only about church priorities and biblical interpretation but also about segregation. Moderates thought segregation should be discouraged through gradual and peaceful means, while conservatives were more likely to say it should be retained.

In 1963 the Southern Baptist Convention elected as its president conservative Houston pastor K. Owen White, whose 3,600-member congregation did not include a single African American. When an African American applied for membership that year, his application was denied. White issued a statement saying that the decision was "in the best interests of the Lord's work" and when asked for clarification stated, "We would rather not enlarge on it at all."[81] As word of the decision spread, civil rights groups attempted unsuccessfully to seek membership for two more African Americans. Following the third attempt, White announced that the congregation was adopting a new policy. Instead of rejecting African American applicants outright, the new policy would involve meetings at which they would be questioned.[82]

Prompted by the Houston affair, the Baptist General Convention of Texas conducted a survey among its four thousand pastors, to which about a third responded. Sixty-three percent said they had no "official policy" regarding race with respect to membership, but five of every six of these pastors said they would permit African Americans to attend if any chose to do so. Substantially fewer—about 20 percent of the pastors who responded—said they would permit an African American to become a member of their church. The report nevertheless considered it encouraging that congregations were beginning to think more about the issue, albeit as quietly as possible in most cases. A related study canvassing the denomination's fourteen thousand congregations nationwide found that 90 percent were segregated.[83]

The differences of opinion led some in the churches to take strong positions. Segregation still found support in earlier claims about divine order. "That racial segregation is an evil of some sort to be overcome by education and personal contact," a San Antonio resident observed, was simply wrongheaded. Humans were endowed by their creator with a hereditary instinct to maintain racial separation. For clergy to deny this fact was "obviously an illustration of hypocritical stupidity."[84] In contrast, the Baptist General Convention of Texas Christian Life Commission, under new leadership, won approval in 1963 for a pointed statement calling on Baptists "to assume a constructive role in the struggle to achieve a higher level of justice for all men, regardless of race." Prompted by recent violence in Birmingham, Alabama, the statement also expressed grief over those who "died violently this year because of the vicious behavior of hate-filled men."[85]

Yet another response among religious leaders was to seek middle ground. Billy Graham. during a revival crusade in Texas in 1963, for example, affirmed his view that racial integration was proper and expressed optimism that gains were being made, but he also took the occasion to criticize proponents of integration. "There is a great deal of hypocrisy about this race business," he observed. "I know a man who pushes integration all the time. I was invited to play golf on a very exclusive course and someone pointed out this man's home, which was on the golf course. I asked are there Negroes nearby? I was told that there were no Negroes nearby nor were Jews allowed on the course. Here was a man who wanted integration but for other people."[86]

As the civil rights movement challenged racial discrimination, groups in Texas mobilized similar efforts directed at reducing ethnic discrimination against Hispanics. "They say there is no discrimination, but we have only to look around us to know the truth," community leader José Angel Gutiérrez declared to a crowd of between fifteen hundred and three thousand Mexican Americans in Crystal City in 1963. "We look at the schools . . . the houses we live in . . . the few opportunities . . . the dirt in the streets . . . and we know."[87] The community, located seventy-five miles from the Mexican border, was composed largely of farmworkers who spent half the year in Texas and the remaining months following the crops as far north as Washington state or Wisconsin.

Gutiérrez, who went on to become an attorney and a professor at the University of Texas at Arlington, had grown up in Crystal City, graduating high school in 1962 and struggling to make sense of the ethnic stratification that divided the community. "I thought in white. I even imagined that God was white, an Anglo," he recalled. "And to make matters worse, the baby Jesus figure I saw at the Sacred Heart Catholic Church did look like an Anglo baby." As an altar boy, Gutiérrez held the little statues of angels and realized they all looked like Anglos. So what was he? "Not Anglo, not Mexican, but what?"[88]

Catholic services were among the few occasions in which Anglos and Mexican Americans were permitted to gather in the same place. Baptists, Methodists, and Pentecostal groups in Crystal City generally held services only for Mexican Americans or for Anglos. It was illegal for Mexican Americans to join the country club or service clubs such as the Lions Club or Chamber of Commerce. Mexican American children went to separate schools, where they were often held back for lack of English language skills, and they were barred from joining Anglo organizations such as Boy Scouts and Girl Scouts.[89]

Besides discrimination and inadequate schools, the issue of greatest concern among Mexican Americans in the Rio Grande valley was the ability to organize a farmworkers union to protect laborers against nonunion braceros and other migrant workers from Mexico. Landowners and moderate Democratic leaders, including Governor Connally, resisted the efforts, while organizers received assistance from the AFL-CIO and from local groups such as the Political Association of Spanish-Speaking Organizations.[90]

With little having been gained by these efforts, farmworkers went on strike on June 1, 1966, demanding a minimum wage of $1.25 an hour instead of the current minimum of $0.85. Bishop Humberto Medeiros and Father Phillip Byron pledged their support.[91] However, four priests who assisted the striking workers the following year did so in violation of orders from Archbishop Lucey. Two were arrested, and all four were suspended by the archbishop, which meant that they could not administer the sacraments, say mass, or take confessions. In support of the priests, parishioners staged protest demonstrations and denounced church leaders.[92]

The archbishop had generally been considered by priests and residents in the San Antonio area as a progressive voice because of his order in 1953 for Catholic schools to integrate and his support of greater equality for Mexican Americans since then. But by the middle of the 1960s his leadership was being challenged by priests and lay leaders who felt he was not pressing fast enough on civil rights. Following the incident in 1967, 68 of the 448 priests in the archdiocese called for Lucey's resignation.[93]

A study involving interviews with 30 of the priests calling for the archbishop's resignation suggested several conclusions that extended beyond the Rio Grande valley. One was that the priests were younger and influenced by the Second Vatican Council reforms that encouraged greater involvement in ecumenical efforts. A second suggested that the priests were somewhat irreverent toward authority in the same way that students participating in campus protests were. The third was that they were the minority who had spoken out but probably reflected wider disagreements among priests who had remained silent. One thing was clear: both the demands for civil rights in the Rio Grande valley and the divisions within the Catholic Church would continue.

SHIFTING ALIGNMENTS

Apart from the specific issues that were generating discussion, such as civil rights and morality, the 1960s witnessed important shifts in the alignments that had previously characterized the relationships between religion and politics. Although Democrats dominated state politics, the party was divided between liberals and conservatives and between those who generally favored what they saw happening in Washington and those who did not. Runoffs had been required in the primaries for governor in 1954 and 1956 and were needed again in 1962 and 1968. In the general election Republican challenger Jack Cox received almost 46 percent of the votes in 1962, the highest proportion for any Republican candidate since Edmund J. Davis's victory in 1869. After winning both seats in the U.S. Senate in every election since 1877, Democrats lost one of those seats to Republican John Tower in 1962. Eisenhower's victories in 1952 and 1956 represented the first Republican wins in Texas for presidential contenders since 1928, and Nixon received more than 48 percent of Texas votes in 1960.

Although significant regional differences in voting patterns remained, nearly every part of the state had become one in which both parties were represented by the early 1960s. In the race for governor between Cox and Connally in 1962, for example, Cox received fewer than 20 percent of the vote in only ten counties, and Connally won at least a third of the votes in all but three counties. Goldwater's campaign two years later was less successful overall but won at least 20 percent of the vote in all but twenty of the counties. However, continuities from election to election suggested that preferences for one party or the other were coming to be institutionalized. County by county, one of the best predictors of how well a Republican candidate would do in the 1960s was how successful Eisenhower had been in 1952. That was evident in correlation coefficients between the percentage voting for Eisenhower in each county in 1952 and the percentages voting for Republican candidates in subsequent elections: for Eisenhower in 1956 (0.823), for Tower in 1960 (0.808), for Nixon in 1960 (0.786), for George H. W. Bush in his unsuccessful U.S. Senate campaign in 1964 (0.693), for Goldwater in 1964 (0.639), and for Nixon in 1968 (0.823). This was one meaning of alignment. Although individual voters may have shifted from one party to the other, party preferences at the county level were fairly stable from year to year.[94]

Alignment could also be thought of as the relationship between counties' voting and local religious patterns. As the state's largest denomination, Southern Baptists had traditionally lent their support at the polls to Democratic candidates. That pattern was still evident in the 1950s. Despite Eisenhower's popularity as a military hero and his image as a product of the Bible Belt, counties in which higher proportions of total Protestant membership were Southern Baptists were significantly less likely to vote for him than counties with lower proportions of Southern Baptists. In 1952 the correlation was −0.468 and in 1956 it was −0.514. Those were the coefficients from regression models in which additional factors such as race, income, and farm population were taken into account. But the coefficients for elections during the 1960s were weaker: for Tower in 1960 (−0.431), for Nixon in 1960 (−0.386), for Bush in 1964 (−0.312), and for Goldwater in 1964 (−0.317). Only for Nixon in 1968 was the coefficient again strong (−0.504), but that was partly because Southern Baptist counties opted moderately for segregationist George Wallace (0.147). It had also been the case that Haley's bid in 1956 on a segregationist platform had received moderately elevated support in counties with larger proportions of Southern Baptists (0.158). In short, counties with higher proportions of Southern Baptists could still be counted on to tilt toward Democratic candidates, but that traditional alignment was weakening.

To the extent that any alignment was present between voting and counties' representation of the state's other large denominations—Catholics and Methodists—this alignment was weaker and less consistent than it was for Southern Baptists. Counties in which Catholics made up a larger share of total church membership tilted slightly against Eisenhower in 1952 and slightly for him in 1956, but neither correlation coefficient was statistically significant. They leaned away from Tower in 1960 (−0.292), away from Nixon in 1960 (−0.416), away from Goldwater in 1964 (−0.305), and slightly away from Nixon in 1968 (−0.213) but more strongly away from Wallace in 1968 (−0.413). Counties in which Methodists made up a larger share of total Protestant members tilted only slightly away from Republican candidates (−0.135 on average) and were neutral with respect to Goldwater in 1964.

Among the reasons that the religious composition of counties was not more strongly aligned with partisan voting in the 1960s were the effects of other distinguishing factors. With the poll tax still in effect until 1966, voting in racially mixed counties generally reflected the preferences of white voters and for that reason usually tilted slightly away from Republican candidates in counties with higher proportions of African Americans. However, that pattern was changing. In 1956 Eisenhower did as well in counties with higher proportions of African Americans as in counties with lower proportions. That was also true for Goldwater in 1964 and undoubtedly reflected the fact that Goldwater's criticism of the 1964 Civil Rights Act attracted some of the votes that otherwise would have gone to Johnson.

The more notable changes were in the relationships between economic factors and voting patterns. Over the decades Democrats had generally done well in rural farming counties, but by the 1960s the role of farming had become less significant, and farmers' views were shaped as much by administration farm policies as by party loyalties. In 1956 counties with higher proportions of population living on farms were less likely than other counties to vote for Eisenhower, whose farm policies were widely criticized, while in 1960, 1964, and 1968 voting was weakly or insignificantly related to counties' farm populations. In contrast, Republicans were consistently doing better in counties in which more of the population enjoyed middle-class incomes. The correlations with the percentage of counties' population whose family incomes in 1959 were at least $10,000 were, for Eisenhower in 1952 (0.343), for Eisenhower in 1956 (0.163), for Tower in 1960 (0.309), for Nixon in 1960 (0.306), for Bush in 1964 (0.512), for Goldwater in 1964 (0.472), and for Nixon in 1968 (0.466).[95]

Taking account of these differences in family incomes, counties with more oil revenue voted differently from other counties in only a few of the elections. Not surprisingly, they tilted slightly in 1964 toward Bush, whose connections with the oil industry were well-known, and for Goldwater, whom Bush supported. For less evident reasons, counties with more oil revenue also leaned slightly toward Edwin Walker in 1962 and George Wallace in 1968. Oil wealth nevertheless remained an important factor in Texas politics. During the 1960s gross revenue from oil and gas production climbed another 25 to 30 percent, reaching nearly six billion dollars by the end of the decade. How the wealth would be spent and whether it would be devoted to supporting one political candidate over another depended both on policies toward the industry and on personalities. After supporting Johnson in the Democratic primary in 1960 and working against Kennedy in the general election, multimillionaire Hunt continued to fund articles and radio broadcasts critical of the Kennedy administration. The criticisms were so well-known that the FBI advised Hunt and his family to lie low and helped them leave town when Kennedy was assassinated for fear that retaliation would be directed against them. The Warren Commission investigating the assassination interviewed Hunt and his sons on suspicion they may have been involved but found nothing to confirm this suspicion. Rumors circulated briefly that Hunt wanted Billy Graham to run for president in 1964, but Hunt denied it. Hunt did lend his support to Goldwater but claimed not to have given the candidate financial help. With Johnson in office, Hunt turned his energies toward founding a political education institute that would identify and train conservative Republicans.[96]

In other hands, oil wealth supported different political interests as well as religious, educational, and charitable institutions. Richardson's death in 1959, for example, benefited Democrat Connally, who served as co-executor of the estate with Richardson's nephew Perry Bass. Bequests from Richardson benefited Baylor, Hardin-Simmons, Texas Christian, Rice, and several other universities. Murchison, like Richardson, had backed Eisenhower over Stevenson in the early 1950s, but by the 1960s Murchison's interests focused on the Dallas Cowboys, which he owned. Fellow oilman and football fan John W. Mecom was a friend and donor to Johnson. LeTourneau's interests continued to focus on business and religion rather than politics, although the company entered into a major equipment contract in the middle 1950s with the Zapata Offshore Company, the president of which was George H. W. Bush.[97]

By 1968 the pattern most evident to political strategists was that Texas was a state that Republicans could win. Although Humphrey edged out Nixon that fall, his victory represented a margin of fewer than 40,000 votes and owed much to Wallace receiving nearly 600,000 votes. As a larger share of Texas voters moved solidly into the middle class, Republicans could expect to do even better in the future. That expectation proved to be true in 1972 when Nixon won by a landslide.

For religious leaders, the implications were different. It made even more sense than it had in the past to keep religion separate from politics. When everyone in the congregation was a Democrat, a pastor might inadvertently let slip from the pulpit a comment about politics with few repercussions. But when half the congregation might be Republicans, a comment of that sort was risky. It was risky even if all the members were Democrats because they were likely to be divided between liberals and conservatives and about the Vietnam War or civil rights. It was a good time to focus on evangelism and worship and to talk about morality without venturing too far into social and political topics.

FINDING A NEW VOICE

Critics of religion in the 1960s noted that clergy activists occasionally made headlines at civil rights demonstrations or in campus protests, but that clergy for the most part were quiet about these issues. Critics charged that the clergy were silent shepherds and were spending most of their time promoting complacency in comfortable suburban congregations. There was plenty of evidence suggesting that the criticisms were well placed. But if that was the case, it became all the more puzzling a few years later to understand how clergy with conservative views on social issues suddenly became mobilized. The only plausible explanation, it seemed, was that conservative clergy had become incensed about abortion, government threats to their lucrative television ministries, and a few other issues. Another, less obvious factor, though, was also involved.

The 1960s made it risky for clergy in quiet suburban congregations to speak too forthrightly about controversial social issues, but the period also created new opportunities for clergy to speak their minds in other venues. These opportunities took shape in civil rights organizations and as new possibilities for African Americans and Hispanics to run for elected office. Additional opportunities appeared on college campuses and in campus chaplaincies. Congregational autonomy in some denominations and insulation for clergy and lay leaders to serve in religious orders and in special ministries opened opportunities as well. Perhaps ironically, these clergy who in many instances found ways to advocate for progressive causes provided a template for those who followed a decade later to speak more openly on behalf of conservative issues.

Luther Holcomb's move from a Baptist pulpit into the directorship of the Greater Dallas Council of Churches was an example of the freedom and visibility clergy sometimes gained outside of a traditional congregational ministry. Following his meeting with Kennedy the day the president was killed, Holcomb helped the city mourn and then in May 1964 accepted a position in the Johnson administration as a member of the new Equal Employment Opportunity Commission. Regarding the position almost as if it were a chaplaincy job, Holcomb rose to serve as vice chairman of the commission and played a major role in promoting workplace integration.[98]

Other than the Dallas Council of Churches, the most important group representing the city's churches was the Dallas Pastors Association. As Holcomb departed, Methodist minister Zan Holmes was named to head the pastors group, becoming the first African American to hold the position. In this capacity Holmes was called on frequently to speak at interracial meetings and to serve as a buffer between white and black congregations. In late 1964 he helped form the Dallas County Council of Organizations for Political Action to conduct a poll-tax drive and run African American candidates for public office. Over the next two years the group also pressed for greater representation in city- and county-appointed offices. In 1968, now occupying Holcomb's previous position as head of the Dallas Council of Churches, Holmes ran successfully for the state legislature. Unlike Holcomb, Holmes did not leave the ministry for good but returned to the pastorate, becoming the leader of St. Luke's Community United Methodist Church in downtown Dallas and playing an influential role in forging relationships with social activist groups and the city's music and arts organizations.[99]

Baxton Bryant illustrated yet another career path. Following his role during the 1960 Democratic campaign in defending Kennedy against criticism from other pastors, he emerged as a leader of the liberal loyalist wing of the party in Texas. With interests increasingly outside of the pastorate, he took a leave of absence from the Elmwood Methodist Church to serve as a deputy state director for the Treasury Department. In 1962 he ran for the state legislature but was narrowly defeated in the primary by a conservative Democrat. It was in the aftermath of this loss and the continuing feud between liberals and moderates that Bryant wired the White House asking if Kennedy could schedule an additional meeting in Dallas on November 22, 1963. In 1964 Bryant ran unsuccessfully again for office, this time for a seat in the U.S. House of Representatives. Like other candidates that year, he stressed morality, defining racial equality as the moral issue of greatest concern.[100]

Foiled in his bid for elected office, Bryant was without a job, but not without connections. One connection was with Will D. Campbell, a white civil rights activist sent by the National Council of Churches to work in Tennessee. Campbell had visited Luther Holcomb in Dallas in 1962 and had found Holcomb helpful in contacting James Meredith during the struggle for integration at the University of Mississippi. It may have been through Holcomb that Campbell also met Bryant. Campbell called Bryant "Booger Red" because of his red hair and considered him a bit of a wild man but invited him to come and help with the work in Tennessee. Bryant agreed and moved to Nashville, where he became director of the Tennessee Council on Human Relations and took an increasingly active role in civil rights demonstrations, including the sanitation workers strike that brought Dr. King to Memphis in 1968.[101]

The loose connections that put leaders such as Holcomb, Campbell, and Bryant in contact with one another became more intentional about extending across racial lines as a result of the civil rights movement. Personal ties such as the ones forged in the 1930s through the Baptist World Alliance and the Southern Interracial Commission evolved into nationally prominent organizations such as the Southern Christian Leadership Conference (SCLC) that King organized in 1957 and more localized efforts guided by pastors associations and church councils. One of Holcomb's associates in the Dallas Council of Churches was Dr. E. C. Estell Sr., pastor of an African American Baptist congregation. Following a meeting of Johnson's interracial committee in Washington in August 1964, Estell and Holcomb issued a joint statement in Dallas calling on civil rights groups to scale back sit-ins and demonstrations and focus on legal recourse against discrimination through the Civil Rights Act. That fall Holcomb and Estell spoke at "Johnson for President" meetings. During the summer Estell had also been a delegate to the state Democratic convention and traveled to Pittsburgh as one of fifteen thousand delegates attending the National Sunday School and Baptist Training Union Congress, of which he was vice president.[102]

The featured speaker at the Pittsburgh convention was William Lawson, a young African American Baptist minister from Houston. Lawson was the head of a biracial group advocating nonviolent civil rights activism in Houston. In June 1964 Campbell came over from Nashville to meet with the group and strategize about the future of civil rights activism. Lawson had been the director of the student ministry sponsored by the Baptist General Convention of Texas at predominantly black Texas Southern University in Houston. When a group of students inspired by the 1960 sit-ins in Greensboro, North Carolina, approached him about organizing a similar effort in Houston, Lawson took the position of the Southern Baptist Christian Life Commission in arguing against organizing civil rights demonstrations. The students organized sit-ins anyway, and the biracial committee that Lawson headed grew out of that effort. In June 1962 Lawson became the pastor of the Wheeler Avenue Baptist Church near the TSU campus and in 1963 opened the church as a base of operations for further protests against segregation. In May 1964 Lawson succeeded in securing a visit to the TSU campus from Dr. King. A year later, as Houston officials dragged their feet in implementing school integration, Lawson formed an organization called People for the Upgrading of the Schools in Houston (PUSH) and threatened to call a boycott if action were not taken. Ninety percent of the African American students in Houston participated in the boycott, and more than two thousand persons participated in a downtown demonstration. It was another five years before speedier desegregation efforts were instituted by orders of a federal judge. "We desegregated," a student at one of the schools recalled, "but we never integrated."[103]

In the interim, protest demonstrations at several locations in Houston led to a clash on May 16 and 17, 1967, between TSU students and police that resulted in the shooting death of policeman Louis Kuba. According to a witness, the incident began when police attempted to arrest a TSU student who resisted the attempt. A few minutes later approximately five hundred police armed with rifles, machine guns, and shotguns arrived and were ordered to charge the dormitories and to shoot as they charged. The witness was Reverend

FIGURE 18. Barbara Jordan, 1976, giving the keynote address on July 12 at the Democratic National Convention in New York City. U.S. News & World Report Magazine Photograph Collection. Library of Congress Prints and Photographs Division, Washington, DC.

Lawson. "Police kept shooting through windows despite instructions to shoot high," he said. "They continued to shoot even when students inside begged to be allowed to bring out [a wounded student] shot through a wall while he lay on his belly."[104]

Five months after the TSU riot, Dr. King launched a nationwide "Stars for Freedom" fund-raising effort headed by singer Harry Belafonte for the benefit of the Southern Christian Leadership Conference. Lawson was named as co-coordinator of the effort in Houston. The other co-coordinator was Barbara Jordan. Jordan had been part of the school desegregation boycott Lawson organized in 1965 and was now serving in the Texas legislature, the first African American woman elected to that body. In 1972 she was elected to the U.S. House of Representatives, where she served until 1979. A Baptist preacher's daughter, Jordan illustrated a different relationship to the church from Lawson, King, and many other civil rights leaders. Although she made speaking appearances at churches, she did not on the whole find her religious upbringing and subsequent relationship to the churches personally nurturing. "I do not recall any message of joy or love or happiness generated out of this experience," she recalled. "It was a confining, restricting mandate. I did not feel free to do anything other than what was presented to me as the way one must proceed; that whatever you do in this life has to be in preparation for that other life. So on balance, my church relationship was, without doubt, a very imprisoning kind of experience."[105]

TURNING POINTS

In retrospect, 1968 would appear as a turning point or perhaps as a series of turning points, bringing to fruition the changes that had been taking place for more than a decade in the struggle for civil rights. Theologians and social scientists began writing about a new breed of clergy who were socially active, engaged in the pressing issues of the day, speaking out, and taking a more active role in the nation's moral and political life. Anecdotes pointed to freedom fighters in the South and pioneers in efforts to bring about gender equality. Studies showed that there were in fact people in pulpits and pews who seemed eager to help bring about social change.

There may have been a brief time in the early weeks of 1968 when optimists could imagine that the corner had been turned in promoting racial equality and that leaders were speaking more openly about social issues. Those who worried about moral decay could take heart in the fact that morality was at least being discussed. The meanness that Johnson had witnessed during the 1964 campaign was perhaps softening. But whatever optimism may have been felt did not last long. With the nation deeply divided about the Vietnam War, Johnson announced on March 31 that he would not seek reelection. On April 4 Dr. King was assassinated in Memphis. Robert F. Kennedy's brief run for the Democratic nomination was cut short on June 5 when he was assassinated.

However much they may have felt that religious faith should play a more active role in the life of the nation, clergy and lay members knew implicitly that this was not a good time to say much about how one felt on the most controversial issues of the day. A study of clergy in California concluded that churches were a sleeping giant with a huge reservoir of moral authority—and that the giant was likely to remain asleep. For all the talk of new breed clergy, the pulpits were places in which the silent majority mostly found solace that things were going to remain the same. California was probably not that much different in this respect from Texas. More than a hundred of the clergy surveyed were Southern Baptists. Only 10 percent of the Southern Baptists said they were in favor of clergy helping migratory farmworkers organize. Fewer than that—8 percent—had written to a public official about fair housing. Only 1 percent of the Southern Baptists had organized a social action committee within their congregation around some social issue. And only 1 percent had attended a protest meeting about the Vietnam War.[106]

When people were unsure of what position to take on social issues, or when they were sure but knew that the issues were deeply controversial, it was difficult to speak openly. It was not as dangerous in Texas for clergy to get involved in politics as it had been during Reconstruction. But it almost was. To do so and stay in the good graces of one's congregation required enormous diplomacy. Otherwise it was better to find some other platform from which to speak. Holcomb's platform was the Equal Employment Opportunity Commission. Bryant's became the Tennessee Council on Human Relations. For Lawson it helped being across the street from a university at a congregation that was essentially composed of students and faculty. Jordan's platform was elected office. This was not to say that other pastors were uninvolved in pressing for social change. Some were, and over the next several years they would play a more important role in organizing civil rights and antiwar demonstrations. But the extent of clergy activism should not be exaggerated. In the 1960s it was easier to talk about morality than to engage in political action.

The delicacy with which church leaders addressed social issues was evident even in the pastorate of W. A. Criswell, whose huge Baptist church in Dallas gave him the platform from which to say anything he wanted, but which in reality was also an institution with implied constraints. In May 1968 word came that he was likely to be elected president of the Southern Baptist Convention at its next meeting. Criswell had preached in no uncertain terms against desegregation in the 1950s, but by 1968 that stance was far less tenable, a point the Southern Baptist Convention's public relations secretary made clear in a private message to Criswell and in public statements. Criswell knew what had to be done and how to accomplish it. Before doing anything that might generate much of a backlash, he called a meeting of his deacons and finance committee to make sure they were on board. Then he tentatively let it be known that he wanted his church to be an open congregation. After hinting several times that he would not oppose someone who might want to join his church if they happened to be African American, he declared himself against segregation.[107]

If it appeared to some that everything they had known and believed in the 1950s was now turned on its head at the end of the 1960s, it was true that much had in fact changed. And yet religion was neither the leader that some hoped it would be nor the laggard that it often seemed. Congregations were caught up in the changes of the 1960s, neither definitively leading nor lagging, but inescapably a part of the process, tumultuous as it was.

CHAPTER 9

POWER TO THE PEOPLE

Framing the Issues, Taking Sides

It is imperative that the organized clergy become more involved in social and political advances if good government is to be achieved and maintained.

INTERDENOMINATIONAL MINISTERIAL ALLIANCE, DALLAS, 1965

We are not here to bathe in the victories of yesterday, but to gird our loins in a struggle for survival.

REVEREND DR. JOSEPH E. LOWREY, DALLAS, 1972

Hundreds of protesters squared off against heavily armed riot police in the largest civil rights demonstration in Dallas history. The date was Saturday, October 21, 1972. The march began that morning in South Dallas, gathering momentum for five miles along Harwood Street as it approached Corinth, where police hoped it would end, and then proceeded another mile to City Hall Plaza. Along the way marchers sang "We Shall Overcome," raised clenched fists, and shouted "Black power." From the steps of city hall, Southern Christian Leadership Conference head Reverend Ralph Abernathy urged the crowd to defend itself against violence and discrimination. "We've got to organize this black community and get out and take political power. Get rid of the Uncle Toms who sell out the black community for a pat on the back," he said to shouts of "Right on" and "Power to the people." "I oppose with all the power within me any type of senseless and useless violence."[1]

The senseless violence on everyone's mind was the killing of twenty-three-year-old James Charles Brown, whose wagon-drawn coffin officials had turned back at the corner of Harwood and Corinth. Police had shot Brown on October

13, the second African American killed by police in two days. Twelve hours after Abernathy's address, officers wounded yet another African American man. In all, Dallas police killed nine African Americans that year and wounded eleven others.[2]

The shootings temporarily unified what had otherwise become a severely factionalized effort to solidify the gains accomplished thus far on behalf of civil rights. Abernathy's mention of Uncle Toms was an oblique reference to the divisions among civil rights leaders themselves. Black clergy held differing views of how best to confront continuing racial discrimination. These differences merged with tensions between local and national leaders and among competing national organizations. They were compounded by the separate interests of Hispanics and white Anglos and by conflicting views about campus demonstrations, women's liberation, and the Vietnam War.

Religious groups were drawn into these conflicts, often reluctantly just as they had been in the 1960s, only now it was becoming clearer that two sides were taking shape and that what could and could not be said on each side was better understood. On the one hand, groups were organizing around particular social and political issues, energized by the urgency of effecting change in an environment that offered opportunities for empowerment and at the same time created uncertainty about what could be achieved. On the other hand, groups distrustful of those activist organizations were hardly resting quietly on the sidelines. They too were taking advantage of new opportunities, focusing on evangelism, church growth, and inventive ministry styles. While the more politically engaged activist groups made headlines, the broader landscape could not be understood without paying attention to these quieter developments as well.

The story was one of difference and division, but by no means understandable as stark polarization. What pundits would later refer to as a culture war was still well in the future. With opportunities to exercise power now more available than in the past, activist religious and community leaders vied with one another over the most workable short- and long-term strategies. Dissatisfaction over the Vietnam War and with both political parties prompted alternative movements and coalitions. Remnants of the far right that had supported Goldwater in 1964 stayed active. The youth culture produced new religious movements that largely eschewed political involvement. There was also the great silent majority that Nixon saw as his most reliable constituency. Many of them were faithful churchgoers who hoped for moral renewal and were fairly certain about where it could be found.

Religious leaders who engaged directly in social activism knew they were taking risks in doing so. African American and Mexican American leaders played important roles in efforts to oppose police brutality and challenge discriminatory practices in labor, schools, and government. Clergy and lay leaders played roles in campus antiwar activism as well. On all these fronts, empowerment posed questions about how best to achieve it and what to do with it once it was attained. Diverse as it was, the leadership of these activities established a precedent for continuing involvement by clergy and others of faith in social and political activism.

A FRAGILE UNITY

The unity expressed in the October 21, 1972, demonstration reflected not only the sense among South Dallas residents of being under siege by the police but also the efforts of local SCLC field coordinator Reverend Peter Johnson. Like Luther Holcomb and Baxton Bryant, Johnson held a position that provided greater opportunities for social activism than was the case for many congregation-based clergy. Johnson had come to Dallas from Atlanta in 1969 and in the interim had worked to organize community welfare programs and voting drives and to build a coalition that included Hispanics and lower-income white Anglos as well as African Americans. Under Johnson's leadership, the city's African Americans had threatened demonstrations to disrupt the Cotton Bowl Festival parade and staged two marches through downtown Dallas, one memorializing Dr. King and the other protesting the repression of poor people and to commemorate the deaths of students at Kent State University in Ohio and at Jackson State University in Mississippi. These demonstrations had led to a campaign against hunger and a boycott aimed at pressuring local Safeway stores to hire more African Americans and Hispanics. In March 1971 Johnson drew national attention to the campaign against hunger by staging a hunger strike. It was his invitation that brought Abernathy to speak in 1972 from the steps of city hall.[3]

But the demonstration that day illustrated some of the tensions among the various groups involved as well. In small ways the uncertainty as to whether the march would end at Harwood and Corinth or extend to city hall and the fact that Abernathy arrived half an hour later than expected reflected some of the difficulties in coordinating the event. The clenched fists and calls for black power registered wider disagreements within the civil rights movement. It was unclear whether the demonstration would be a one-time event or whether the momentum would be sustained.

A partial answer came on Monday evening, October 23, in response to the shooting that occurred on Sunday. A smaller march led to city hall, where demonstrators chanted "Power to the people" and "Soul power" and applauded as speakers condemned the "white racist police" and promised to continue protesting until "these walls come tumbling down like Jericho." The demonstration was organized by SCLC coordinators George Holland of Dallas and Reverend James Owens of Atlanta but was convened at Mount Olive Lutheran Church, a white congregation whose pastor, Mark Herbener, served as director of Dallas Community Action and president of the South Dallas Coordinating Council, both of which had been involved for several years in racial justice and poverty issues.[4]

Holland held a news conference the next morning, organized another protest march that evening, and hosted a meeting at Herbener's church later in the week to plan future events. Holland had been working with the SCLC in Dallas since 1969 as director of its Operation Breadbasket program. He had been active in the Safeway boycott and now became the most vocal organizer of efforts to combat police violence. Garbed in faded blue jeans and matching denim jacket, he was younger than most of the other leaders and more inclined toward confrontation. Over the next several weeks, as a hearing exonerated police officers involved in the shootings, Holland organized a rally at the Crossroads Community Center that prompted another demonstration at city hall, organized a boycott of a shopping complex, and staged a sit-in that disrupted a meeting of the city council.[5]

Holland was convinced that aggressive confrontation was necessary to bring an end to racial injustice. "The conditions in South Dallas between blacks and police are now as grave and as tense as they can get without some type of explosion," he told a reporter in late November. "The string is drawn tight." But others, including local NAACP leaders, were less convinced. "The black community doesn't want to tell SCLC not to speak out," a South Dallas business owner said, "but they're just not sure whether to follow them or not." Over the next six months, the Dallas SCLC experienced a dramatic decline in financial support, lost its charter, amassed debts, and was unable to pay its franchise taxes and salaries. In July 1973 Holland announced that the chapter was planning to suspend operations.[6]

The city's most influential African American clergy organization was the Dallas Interdenominational Ministerial Alliance. Representing some two hundred congregations, it was led by Reverend S. M. Wright, the founding pastor of People's Baptist Church located in the same neighborhood as Herbener's Mount Olive Lutheran Church. Ministerial alliances had become popular in the 1920s in conjunction with Progressive Era social activism and by the 1950s were present in communities across the state. By spanning denominational lines, the alliances facilitated communication, forged coalitions that protected clergy to some extent from criticism within their own congregations, and promoted engagement with community issues. By focusing on local activities, the alliances usually avoided complaints about violating the separation of church and state. It was the Dallas alliance that stepped up efforts in 1931 to help the needy and jobless, pledged its support for the continuation of Prohibition in 1933, and helped organize meetings about housing-related violence in 1951. For many years Luther Holcomb's associate Dr. E. C. Estell presided over the alliance and promoted its growth. Unlike the SCLC's more confrontational approach to police violence, the alliance's response in 1972 was to issue a statement calling on the police chief and city council to investigate the shootings. "We are concerned about having a community that is free of crime," Reverend Wright explained, "but we are also concerned about any overzealousness on the part of any law enforcement officers because this can be detrimental to the peace and security of the citizenry we have worked so hard in the past 50 years to secure."[7]

FIGURE 19. Clark and Wright, 1962, showing Dr. Caesar Clark and Reverend S. M. Wright with John Connally during his campaign for governor. Photograph © Marion Butts. Marion Butts Collection, Dallas History and Archives, Dallas Public Library.

The differences between Wright's group and the SCLC were not new. In an interview many years later, Reverend Johnson recalled talking with Dr. King shortly after the SCLC leader's visit in the early 1960s when black clergy in Dallas asked their parishioners not to attend his public appearances. "It always affected him that black people boycotted him," Johnson recalled. "He was really hurt; he was visibly shaken by it." Subsequent visits by King in 1966 drew mixed responses as well. Johnson remembered King's advisers at the time describing Wright and his fellow pastors as "mere pawns of white city leaders who rewarded them with access and small favors in exchange for keeping the black community in its place." During the Safeway boycott in 1970, Johnson found himself and Wright on different sides. While Johnson was picketing, Wright was encouraging residents to cross the picket lines. Johnson had no doubt who Abernathy had in mind in 1972 when he mentioned Uncle Toms. "Ralph Abernathy despised the black preachers here," Johnson said. "He thought they were the biggest Uncle Toms."

The ministerial alliance's supporters did not deny that the organization worked with the Dallas establishment. With congregations that relied on peaceful relations with their neighbors and that hoped to stay in business for a long time, it made sense to cultivate the connections clergy had with elected officials.

In 1959 the alliance backed Reverend Caesar Clark of the Good Street Baptist Church for a post on the Dallas Board of Education. In 1962 Wright supported Connally's bid for governor and in 1964 spearheaded LBJ's election campaign in Dallas's black community. That fall the alliance also endorsed Dallas mayor Earle Cabell as a candidate for the U.S. House of Representatives and Senator Ralph Yarborough's bid for reelection. On occasion the alliance lent its name to calls put forward by the NAACP to curb segregation, and in 1966 it pressed for equal hiring in city and county government jobs. A minor breach occurred around the same time, however, when Wright personally endorsed several conservative Democratic candidates against the wishes of other members of the alliance. Besides their involvement in electoral politics, Wright and other leaders of the alliance routinely spoke at and hosted community events, such as teachers' conferences, special days of prayer, and screenings of religious films. A longtime member of Wright's church who became a Democratic precinct chair said her pastor "was always trying to help his people out, but he had to deal with the whites to get things done." In her view, that did not mean he was on the white establishment's side.[8]

Disagreements about candidates and strategies increased as the 1960s came to an end. Black leaders held mixed views of Nixon's presidency and of Connally's ties with Nixon. Despite their earlier skepticism of King, it was difficult to do anything but honor King after his assassination, and yet the current leadership of SCLC was coming under increasing criticism. The clergy alliance was openly critical of black-power advocates such as James Forman and Stokely Carmichael, but in focusing on quieter, incremental measures it found itself in new territory, as it did in 1969, for example, in endorsing an amendment to the state constitution to prevent cuts in assistance to the needy—which conservative pastor Criswell of Dallas's First Baptist Church also supported. By 1970 the alliance and SCLC leaders such as Johnson and Holland were taking notably different approaches to hunger assistance, boycotts, and protest demonstrations.[9]

The wider political and religious context surrounding the 1972 demonstration could be gauged at several levels. The SCLC held its national convention in Dallas that year in August. It was at this meeting that Reverend Lowrey called on the thousand delegates present to work harder as the organization struggled for its very survival. Some of the delegates were unhappy with Abernathy's increasing involvement in international peace efforts, feeling that these activities were detracting from the movement's emphasis on civil rights. At the same time, gains were slowly being made in electoral politics, with more than eight hundred African Americans holding office in southern states, sixty-one of whom were in Texas, including state senator Barbara Jordan, who spoke at the convention. The Great Society welfare programs instituted during the Johnson administration provided assistance in lower-income communities but gave white leaders a weapon to threaten residents who might be tempted to vote for the wrong candidates. Another convention speaker was Angela Davis, the controversial

California activist who had appeared on the FBI's "ten most wanted" fugitive list in 1970 in conjunction with a shooting there and had been acquitted after spending eighteen months in jail. Abernathy publicly endorsed George McGovern in the presidential contest that fall. When the National Baptist Convention—the largest African American denomination—met in Fort Worth around the same time, though, its fifteen thousand delegates were divided about supporting Mc-Govern or Nixon. Observers thought the differences in views about the future of civil rights were even more significant. Leaders who favored a politics of cooperation between whites and blacks were at odds with leaders who favored black separatism.[10]

Toward the end of the decade, with some of these differences having abated, representatives from the NAACP's national office in New York City came out to reorganize its three Dallas chapters—branches that often took different approaches to local issues—by merging them into one. Reverend Wright and the Interdenominational Ministerial Alliance were still being criticized. In conjunction with the NAACP reorganization, critics accused the alliance of using its influence to perpetuate the city's "entrenched black establishment at the expense of an enthusiastic young leadership" that was seeking a greater role in the NAACP. Meanwhile, the alliance helped establish a Dallas chapter of Reverend Jesse Jackson's Operation PUSH (People United to Save Humanity), hosting him at a meeting in 1976, and a former branch president of the NAACP worked to reopen the defunct chapter of the Southern Christian Leadership Conference.[11]

CHICANO ACTIVISM

On Saturday, July 11, 1970, in the South Texas town of Mathis—a small community between Corpus Christi and San Antonio—thirty-one-year-old Fred Logan was killed by a bullet shot at point-blank range into his heart. The shooter was Erich Bauch, the deputy sheriff. On the surface the incident had nothing to do with racial and ethnic conflict. Logan had ridden his motorcycle to a local restaurant that evening, gotten himself too drunk to ride home, and pulled out his gun while standing in the parking lot, firing several shots into the air. That prompted someone to call the law. Bauch, who had only recently returned from sick leave following surgery, answered the call. Bauch took Logan's gun from him, put him in the back seat of the patrol car, and drove off. En route Logan got the door unlocked and started to open it, Bauch stopped the car, both men got out, and the two men struggled. Bauch fired a warning shot, Logan renewed the struggle, and Bauch fired the fatal shot. Unfortunate as it was, the incident was a matter of someone forcibly resisting arrest and paying the consequences.

But other details about the event provide insight into the tensions present in South Texas at the time. Logan wore his hair long, had a beard and sideburns, and was known locally as a hippie, or, precisely, as "the hippie doctor." He was an osteopath who had grown up in Corpus Christi, become a militant liberal in his political views, and devoted himself to helping the Mexican Americans—the Chicanos—who made up two-thirds of the local population. At Logan's clinic, farmworkers and others with little or no money could receive treatment for a pittance or free. "He used to ask if you had enough to pay him and still buy medicine," a young Chicano said. "If you didn't, he would say, 'just forget me and buy the medicine.' Sometimes he would even loan you four or five dollars for the medicine."[12]

In a community with a long history of discrimination against Mexican Americans and where calls for Chicano power were now being voiced, Logan had been the rare Anglo who deviated from tradition. "I've heard Anglos say of Logan, 'We ought to kill that S.O.B.,'" the mayor, who was Anglo, reported. The ethnically mixed town council passed a resolution stating that the death "suggests the possibility of a political murder." It poured rain the day of the funeral. More than a thousand of the town's Mexican Americans stood in the rain to mourn their beloved doctor.[13]

Some of the mourners that day wore brown berets. They were members of the Mexican American Youth Organization (MAYO), a Chicano power movement founded at St. Mary's University in San Antonio in 1967. One of the founders was Willie Velásquez, a graduate of Central Catholic High School in San Antonio and St. Mary's University. Velásquez played a key role in the 1966 labor dispute in which farmworkers with leadership from the National Farm Workers' Association boycotted melon fields during harvest to demand a minimum wage of $1.25 an hour. The Starr County Strike, as it became known, included a large, well-publicized march to the state capital in July 1966, continuing the following year when several picketers were beaten, and gaining the support of the Texas Council of Churches as well as attention from civil rights organizations. Another MAYO founder was José Angel Gutiérrez from Crystal City.[14]

Religion played a different role in Chicano activism from the role it played in African American civil rights organizing. The principal difference was the leadership structure of the relevant denominations. Segregation and local autonomy in Baptist congregations resulted in African American pastors becoming leaders in their communities, whereas Catholic parishes were ethnically mixed and with few exceptions administered by Anglo bishops and priests. One exception was Reverend Antonio Gonzalez, who served as the representative for Spanish-speaking affairs in the Houston diocese and was one of the organizers of the 1966 farmworkers march to Austin. During the march Gonzalez wore a Star of David in recognition of the Houston Jewish Community Council's support of the event and was joined by Baptist pastor James Navarro of Houston, Methodist pastor Don Post of San Antonio, and Father Sherrill Smith, who had recently participated in the civil rights march in Selma, Alabama. To show their conviction that faith was on their side, the marchers carried a Christian flag and a large picture of Our Lady of Guadalupe. The priests and the religious connection they symbolized emboldened the strikers, historian Brian D. Behnken observes in his

FIGURE 20. Marchers participate in a rally organized by MAYO. 1969. Hershorn Photographic Collection. Dolph Briscoe Center for American History, University of Texas at Austin.

definitive study of civil rights activism in Texas, and "played an important role by blunting criticisms that the protest was anarchic or communistic."[15]

In San Antonio Archbishop Lucey preached a passionate sermon in which he endorsed the marchers' cause. "May God be with you as you march to Austin," he said, "May your reception there be in complete harmony with your dignity as human beings, American citizens and children of God."[16] Another supporter was Humberto Medeiros, a priest born in the Azores who arrived in South Texas from Massachusetts in 1966 and as bishop of the Brownsville diocese consistently supported the Chicano community by working for reconciliation between farmworkers and landowners.[17] He too was on hand to bless the 1966 march and during the four years he spent in South Texas worked to bridge the gap separating Anglo and Chicano Catholics and to cultivate relationships with representatives of non-Catholic organizations such as the Texas Council of Churches and the American Jewish Committee.[18]

In addition to the efforts of Gonzalez, Medeiros, and a few others, Chicano activism was furthered indirectly by the Church through its provision of Catholic education, as in the case of Velásquez, starting in elementary school and continuing through college. "By the mid-sixties, some post–World War II barrio 'baby boomers' were graduating from Catholic high schools and entering local Catholic colleges and universities," a study of Chicano activism in San Antonio observed. "These first-generation college students would constitute an important pool of leaders and supporters for the emerging Chicano movement."[19]

Besides the farmworkers' strike, Chicano activism was spurred by the 1966 election in which Tower's victory over Democratic candidate Waggoner Carr for a seat in the U.S. Senate was thought to have been facilitated by Mexican American voters who felt Carr had been unsupportive of the strike. In 1967 the Brownsville diocese under Medeiro's leadership organized a campaign to increase the number of Mexican Americans registered to vote. During the 1968 election, Gonzalez made a surprise endorsement of Carr, now a gubernatorial candidate in the Democratic primary, arguing that Carr was more supportive of farmworkers' interests than Preston Smith, the eventual winner. Frustrated in gaining a greater role in the Democratic Party, Velásquez and other Chicano leaders organized a statewide conference in San Antonio and founded El Movimiento Social de La Raza Unida, which evolved into the Raza Unida Party in 1970.[20]

San Antonio journalist Robert Berrellez, writing in 1968, observed divisions in the emerging Chicano power movement around degrees of militancy, specific aims, and interest in cooperating with Anglos and African Americans. However, the principal sources of disagreement, Berrellez found, were the diverse range of issues and needs involved. Federal funds opened opportunities but also initiated competition for resources. The needs of greatest concern to Chicanos in Texas were not necessarily the same as those of Chicanos in California or New Mexico, and further differences existed between farmworkers and urban residents.[21]

The disagreements Berrellez noted in 1968 were evident in April 1969 when 250 people gathered in Austin for a statewide meeting organized by MAYO. "To effect meaningful social change, we must be prepared to use any means necessary to accomplish our goal," Gutiérrez told the assembly. "Words alone will not resolve conflict, but the threat of force and words can and do work wonders." But as Gutiérrez advocated a more aggressive challenge to "gringo power," other leaders expressed different views. A speaker representing the Progressive Labor Party argued that Chicanos and Anglos should combine forces around labor issues, while a San Antonio lawmaker called for working within the electoral system to replace officials with ones more sympathetic to Mexican American interests. Speaking at the same time in Kingsville where students were protesting, state representative Carlos Truan condemned the tactic of boycotting classes and called on MAYO to leave the matter in the hands of local authorities.[22]

The one issue that spanned the various differences was education. Among states with large Mexican American populations, Texas continued to lag in educational attainment for residents of Spanish-speaking origin. Statewide statistics indicated that 52 percent of the Spanish-surnamed population was functionally illiterate, meaning not having completed four years of schooling. And among the same population group age twenty five and over, 20 percent did not have more than one year of schooling.

To challenge existing discrimination in public schools, Mexican American parents, students, and community leaders organized meetings and staged protests. In October 1969 Mexican American high school students in Abilene boycotted classes to call attention to discriminatory treatment in education and employment. In a subsequent lawsuit involving six of the students, the Mexican American Legal Defense Fund in San Antonio assisted with the defense.[23] Two months after the Abilene boycott, seventeen hundred Mexican American high school students in Crystal City boycotted classes to protest the school board's refusal to consider requests for bilingual education and an increase in the number of Mexican American teachers and counselors.[24]

The following spring, under Gutiérrez's leadership, Raza Unida successfully ran two candidates for Crystal City's school board and won two city council seats in nearby Cotulla. That fall, state and federal courts denied Raza Unida a place on the official ballot. Calling the denial a problem of "harassment, intimidation, and outright fraud," Gutiérrez and the party conducted a write-in campaign but failed to win any of the local races.[25] The 1970 election cycle nevertheless witnessed an expansion of activities by Raza Unida, MAYO, and other Chicano organizations.

In April 1970 the League of United Latin American Citizens sponsored a rally in Houston to which both Republican and Democratic candidates were invited. Among those attending were future president George H. W. Bush and future vice presidential candidate Lloyd Bentsen. As Bush was about to speak, chants of "Viva" came from the audience. Bush turned the microphone over to Gregory Salazar, a leader of MAYO. "We will say to the gringo political establishment that the Chicano is tired of token Chicano leadership in the Democratic and Republican parties," Salazar said. Neither of the candidates was quite ready to agree. Bush responded that the Nixon administration was trying to extend policy positions to Mexican Americans. Bentsen took a different tack, arguing that "a disease of ultra-liberalism in the problems of narcotics, crime and a permissive society [was] trying to substitute a government of men for a government of law."[26] Three months later Senator Walter Mondale, serving as chair of the Senate Committee on Equal Educational Opportunity, visited San Antonio where he met with students, parents, and residents. Mondale's attitude was more sympathetic. "Discrimination and repression of minority groups," he declared, "is severe and blatantly open. This ranges from police brutality to insults, to economic sanctions such as firing of parents of black and Chicano students who were protesting discrimination."[27]

Between then and the 1972 election, Chicano organizing advanced on a number of fronts. In San Antonio MAYO president Carlos Guerra, speaking on behalf of Raza Unida, called for the Nixon administration to launch a federal investigation into the death of prominent Mexican American journalist Rubén Salazar, killed during a demonstration in Los Angeles when a tear gas projectile slammed into his head.[28] At Texas A&I University in Kingsville, MAYO and the university's chapter of the Political Association of Spanish-Speaking Organizations hosted conferences and training sessions. In San Antonio priests established PADRES as an organization to promote greater understanding of Mexican American culture. Students at the University of Texas El Paso organized the Movimiento Estudiantil

Chicano de Aztlán to press for student rights. In January 1971 an appeals court ruled in favor of the Upholsterers Union, the membership of which was 90 percent Mexican American, which had gone on strike in 1968.[29] And in July 1971 Mexican Americans in San Antonio marched and picketed city hall to protest police harassment of the Chicano population.[30] On a wider front, Chicano organizations were forging closer connections between Texas and California and across the Southwest, registering voters, pressing for bilingual education, and challenging prejudice in the media. Early in 1970 Stanford University sociologist Thomas Martinez, in cooperation with the Mexican American Anti-Defamation Committee, secured an end to offensive television commercials featuring the Frito Bandito.

Leaders of the several organizations working in each community in the late 1960s had proposed possibilities for closer cooperation between Mexican Americans and African Americans. When the Southern Christian Leadership Conference held its national meeting in Dallas in 1972, Ralph Abernathy introduced Ramsey Muñiz, the twenty-nine-year-old Waco attorney running as Raza Unida's gubernatorial nominee, and strongly encouraged the delegates to vote for Muñiz.[31] That fall Raza Unida placed forty-nine candidates on the ballot but did so with sparse resources for statewide contests, which meant that Abernathy's endorsement was an especially welcome boost. Muñiz turned in a respectable showing as a third-party candidate, winning 214,149 of the nearly three million votes cast.[32] But cementing closer relationships between African American and Chicano organizations proved difficult. It was hard enough to agree on strategies within each population.

In September 1972 Raza Unida held a convention in El Paso that drew fifteen hundred participants from twenty states and attracted national attention. Gutiérrez presided over the convention and was elected as the party's national chair. Among the many resolutions the convention debated, ranging from protesting the Vietnam War to calling for Puerto Rican independence, one that illustrated the party's difficulties in securing consensus was whether to endorse McGovern for president, make no endorsement, or run a third-party candidate. California farmworkers' leader Cesar Chavez did not attend the meeting, which reduced its appeal and left the leadership to Gutiérrez representing Texas, Corky Gonzales from Denver, and Reies Lopez Tijerina of New Mexico. A decision was reached to endorse no candidate, but the three leaders disagreed among themselves whether this was a good result.[33]

Raza Unida ran Muñiz as its candidate for governor again in 1974, but Muñiz won approximately twenty thousand fewer votes than he did in 1972. Analysts noted that it was difficult for the party to identify common ground between the state's rural and urban Chicano constituents and to focus on issues sufficiently broad and at the same time different enough from the Democratic Party to score victories except in local elections. In 1976 Raza Unida experienced even less success at the polls and by 1978 was essentially ineffective as a third party. The period nevertheless saw continuing activism emphasizing Chicano identity and focusing on farmworkers, schools, and college administration. In 1973 the likelihood of continuing support from religious leaders was signaled by Archbishop James Peter Davis of Santa Fe, who joined a march to Austin on behalf of Chicano workers, and by San Antonio archbishop Francis J. Furey's involvement in boycotts by the Texas Farm Workers Union. In 1979 Patrick Fernandez Flores, the first archbishop of Mexican American origin, succeeded Furey.[34]

CAMPUS UNREST

By 1970 nearly 440,000 students were enrolled in Texas colleges and universities, up from only 186,000 in 1960.[35] Of the 123 public and private institutions of higher education statewide, 25 had come into existence during the 1960s, and almost all of the rest had undergone enormous expansion. The University of Texas at Austin had more than 30,000 students, 21,000 were enrolled at Texas Tech in Lubbock, 14,000 at Texas A&M, 11,000 at the University of Texas El Paso, 7,000 at Texas Southern University, and 10,000 at Texas State University in San Marcos, the alma mater of Lyndon Johnson. In anticipation of additional demand, a $21 million contract was awarded for expansion of the Richardson campus of the University of Texas at Dallas, and plans were unveiled for new University of Texas campuses in Tyler and Odessa and a new branch campus of East Texas State University at Texarkana. With only 6,500 students, Baylor remained small by comparison to the public institutions but was implementing plans to expand to more than 8,000 over the next four years.

The civil rights demonstration that Reverend Lawson witnessed at Texas Southern in 1967 had been followed by student rallies and protests at other locations in Texas, including a mass demonstration in San Antonio in April 1969. Lawson's charge that police rather than students had been responsible for the 1967 violence had been circulated widely in a special report by the Student Nonviolent Coordinating Committee (SNCC), the black-power organization several members of which had been implicated in the incident. SNCC became active in the 1969 demonstration in San Antonio sparked by the killing of an African American named Bobby Joe Phillips by police. The most prominent African American civil rights leader in San Antonio at the time was Reverend Claude William Black Jr., pastor of the Mount Zion First Baptist Church. Like Reverend Wright in Dallas, Black had been involved in civil rights activities for several decades and was known mostly for achieving success against discrimination by working as a mediator between the black community and white public officials. One of his favorite stories, he said in an interview, was about a bull that stood bravely on the tracks hoping to intimidate a freight train. "He had a lot of courage," Black observed, "but his judgment was poor." But by the late 1960s Black had become seriously troubled by police brutality. He supported SNCC's efforts in 1969, hosted a forum for SNCC leaders at the church, helped organize the demonstration, and played a mediating role between SNCC and city hall.[36]

While SNCC's efforts focused on black power, other student organizations mobilized on behalf of free speech and against the Vietnam War. Students for a Democratic Society (SDS), which had been organized in 1960 at the University of Michigan, hosted events at the University of Texas in Austin that grew to about five hundred students by 1968. The following year SDS held its national council meeting in Austin, a gathering mostly distinguished by the factionalism that led to the formation of the Revolutionary Youth Movement, which later became the radical Weather Underground Organization. To send a strong signal that unrest on Texas campuses would not be tolerated, the legislature passed a bill in March 1969 stating that any participation in disruptive campus activities, such as seizing control of a building or preventing other students from attending classes, would bring fines up to $200 and jail terms up to six months.[37]

A month later plans began to be made on the East Coast for a coordinated nationwide effort to protest the Vietnam War. LBJ's decision not to seek reelection in 1968 and Nixon's victory had raised hopes that hostilities in Southeast Asia could be brought to an end. Nixon outlined a plan of Vietnamization that would reduce American involvement and leave the fighting to the South Vietnamese. New peace talks began in January 1969 shortly after Nixon's inauguration. The withdrawal of American troops began the following July but was accompanied by an expansion of bombing into Laos and Cambodia. The nationwide protest took the form of a moratorium on October 15, during which students on campuses across the country, with participation from community leaders and residents, staged marches, boycotted classes, and held teach-ins about the war. By that date some forty-five thousand Americans had been killed in the war and nearly half a million troops were still deployed in the region. The moratorium was believed to be the largest demonstration in U.S. history, with an estimated two million participants. A quarter of a million people participated in the protest in Washington, DC, and nearly that many did in San Francisco.

In Texas the largest demonstration took place in Austin, where five thousand participants marched from the university to the state capitol and as many as ten thousand were estimated to have boycotted classes or taken part in some other way. Speeches focused on stopping the bombing and ending the war, although a small protest focusing on black power organized by the Black Panther Party occurred the same day. In Houston an estimated twenty-five hundred people gathered in Hermann Park for a rally organized by the Rice University Forum Committee. Barbara Jordan addressed the crowd, emphasizing that America could not afford an extended continuation of the war. In Dallas approximately fifteen hundred demonstrators participated in a day of speeches and rock band music. Smaller antiwar demonstrations took place on campuses in San Antonio, Fort Worth, Lubbock, and at several other locations without incident, except at North Texas State in Denton where a hundred protestors clashed with police, resulting in ten arrests. A rally in Austin several weeks later drew a crowd of approximately a thousand.[38]

The following spring student protests focused on the continuing American bombing of Cambodia. On May 4, 1970, the deaths of four students and wounding of nine others by National Guard troops at Kent State University in Ohio prompted further unrest on campuses across the nation. One estimate revealed that at least 270 campuses shut down classes in response to the event. Another report found strikes and protests at more than 330 campuses. Texas campuses mostly carried on business as usual, although some students at the University of Texas in Austin marched peacefully from campus to the capitol building, and students at Texas Tech briefly impeded the morning ritual of raising the American flag.[39]

Whatever hopes students had that Nixon would quickly bring an end to the war were not yet realized as the 1972 election approached. Besides Raza Unida, other groups were organizing as independent parties or seeking to influence the Democratic Party's nominating process. In November 1971 more than seven hundred delegates gathered in Dallas in an attempt to forge a national coalition from such diverse local and regional groups as the Peace and Freedom Party, New Reform Party, New World Party, Vermont Liberty Union, and Kentucky People's Party.[40] The following spring students on campuses nationwide again staged protests as the administration stepped up the bombing of Hanoi and Haiphong. At the University of Texas in Austin, protestors targeted Sid W. Richardson Hall—part of the campus's $18 million LBJ library—breaking windows and spraying graffiti such as "LBJ War Criminal" on walls. Witnesses said helmeted police armed with guns and mace charged the crowd and injured several of the students.[41]

Campus chaplains and clergy serving congregations near campuses participated in the antiwar movement by counseling students facing the draft and by joining demonstrations. One of the most visible participants was Rabbi Irwin Goldenberg from Dallas's Temple Emanu-El, who helped organize the 1969 moratorium and gave speeches at antiwar events. Another was Rabbi Moshe Cahana of Congregation Brith Shalam, who played a similar role in Houston. When school administrators suspended several high school students in Dallas for wearing black armbands to protest the war, two Methodist pastors and one Unitarian minister joined the American Civil Liberties Union's defense of the students. In addition, Clergy and Laity Concerned, a group that had organized against ballistic missile testing, helped sponsor antiwar events in Dallas, and a clergy group held peace vigils in Houston.[42]

But religious leaders also took cautious stands as they sometimes had toward civil rights demonstrations, arguing for peaceful reconciliation as opposed to militant protests. A few days after the Texas legislature stiffened laws against campus violence, for example, Reverend Holmes spoke at the Methodist Church in Austin to an audience that included many of the legislators. Holmes noted that

God is "concerned" about student unrest, poverty, and other problems but called on the church to bridge the divide separating people on these issues.[43]

One of the most outspoken critics of the antiwar movement was W. A. Criswell of the First Baptist Church in Dallas. Criswell's views reflected the strong anti-communist sentiments he had embraced for years and that had joined him in common cause with multimillionaire H. L. Hunt. Criswell saw communism as the world's greatest threat to America, and his sermons frequently portrayed it as the enemy against which fundamentalist Christians especially were waging mortal combat. One of his most extended diatribes occurred the Sunday fol-lowing Kennedy's assassination in 1963, which Criswell attributed to "red com-munism"; he then proceeded to trace the history of communism from Marx and Engels' *Communist Manifesto* in 1848 to the takeover of Russia and the growth of communism in China, its role in World War II, its spread in Vietnam, and the infiltrators that Hoover's FBI was fighting to expose. As president of the eleven-million-member Southern Baptist Convention, Criswell vehemently denounced the 1969 antiwar moratorium. "These traitors are marching up and down the streets and making blasphemous speeches," he told a gathering of Baptists in Atlanta. "We must draw a line on communism somewhere," he declared. To his assembled congregation in Dallas and fifty-thousand-member radio and televi-sion audience, he elaborated that the peace rallies were just a step toward com-munists seizing power in America. Now was the most critical hour the nation had ever faced. America was becoming a place of filth and debauchery. "Anybody can sweep us away, destroy us, come into our country, infiltrate us, leave us in shreds. That's why we need to preach and to teach the Word and the will of God; you cannot stand without the Lord."[44]

The debauchery Criswell had in mind was as much the sexual revolution on the nation's campuses as the peace marchers he so thoroughly distrusted. Campus clergy and student ministry associations were increasingly confronting these issues as well. An example was the Clergy Consultation Service on Prob-lem Pregnancies near the North Texas State campus in Denton. The procedure was that women seeking counseling were required to bring a note from their gy-necologist or obstetrician certifying that they were pregnant and indicating the length in weeks of their pregnancy. Two of the center's staff available for confi-dential counseling were members of the clergy. The counseling process involved describing to the woman four options, including getting married and having the child, having the child and giving it up for adoption, having the baby and rais-ing it as an unmarried mother, or terminating the pregnancy. After discussion and due consideration, the woman then was asked to make a decision. Most of the women, according to the pastors, opted for an abortion. If the woman was under eighteen, parental consent for an abortion was required. Otherwise the woman was given a booklet describing various abortion procedures and referred to a clinic in New Mexico, California, or New York, where abortion was legal. "Before I became pregnant, I was very liberal—anyone who wants one ought

FIGURE 21. First Baptist Church of Dallas, established in 1872, pastored by W. A. Criswell from 1944 to 2002, showing the central building in the church's multiblock location. In 2010 the congregation pledged $115 million to rebuild and reshape the historic church. Photograph by First Baptist Church. Courtesy of the Southern Baptist Historical Library and Archive, Nashville, TN.

to have it," one of the women who opted for an abortion following a visit to the center explained. "I don't have any moral hang-ups. I've been thinking of the practical aspects."[45]

Permissive sexual attitudes, antiwar protests, and other developments among college students were profoundly disturbing to many clergy and community leaders. "Campus unrest and street demonstrations make us reappraise old values and ideas," a full-page advertisement in the *Galveston Daily News* declared in June 1972. The otherwise forward-looking essay, noting that the little red school house was being replaced by new ideas in science and education, went on to suggest, however, that readers overwhelmed by these developments should seek solace in God. "God's love is for you. Your church is where you find out about it. Try it next Sunday. It will help you grasp an old idea, even if it is a new one for you." The advertisement was paid for by the local Ford dealer, the Shell service station, and more than thirty other businesses. Criswell's language about young people involved in the sexual revolution was more pointed. "Their lives are promiscuous like alley cats," he said.[46]

SAVING SOULS

Although turmoil surrounding race, ethnicity, gender, sexuality, and politics significantly affected the religion landscape, it is important to remember that the early 1970s were years in which religious organizations worked aggressively to ensure their continuing strength, especially among the coming generation. A national study of entering college freshmen found that 28 percent said they discussed religion "frequently," but observers debated whether that was a lot or whether religion was declining. In hopes of keeping at least that much interest in religion alive, leaders poured money into supporting campus ministries. Campus Crusade for Christ had chapters on most of the campuses in Texas, and in June 1972 the groups organized a massive conference that brought seventy-five thousand college and high school students, laypersons, and pastors to Dallas for practical training in personal evangelism, an inspirational message from Billy Graham, and gospel music by Johnny Cash and Kris Kristoferson. Reverend Wright brought special greetings to the several thousand African American students who participated.[47] Catholics, Jews, Presbyterians, the United Church of Christ, Episcopalians, Methodists, and Lutherans had ministries on most of the larger campuses, where campus clergy were supported by denominations or local congregations and in many instances by teaching Bible courses and classes in Christian ethics as part of the regular university curriculum. Baptist Student Union ministries expanded as well, aiming, as one staff member explained, to "help the student share his faith on the campus and in the normal facets of his life."[48]

The 4.7 million Southern Baptists in Texas also continued to be active in promoting evangelism on other fronts. The denomination's Woman's Missionary Union set annual goals of a million dollars or more in pledge drives to support foreign missionaries. Baptist men's groups under the direction of a lawyer turned evangelist who had worked in Billy Graham crusades sought to enlist men and boys for overseas missionary work as well.[49] Although most of these efforts remained divided along racial lines, one of the innovations resulting from the civil rights movement was that pastors associations that included both blacks and whites organized citywide revival meetings. A well-attended evangelistic meeting in Galveston organized by the Baptist Ministers' Association was one example.

Another innovation was that small denominations, independent churches, Bible institutes, and nondenominational ministries were playing a more active role than ever before in promoting evangelism. During the 1950s and 1960s, numerous institutes and independent seminaries were founded to train lay ministers, missionaries, and evangelists. Examples included the Sunset International Bible Institute founded by the Churches of Christ in Lubbock to train Spanish-speaking preachers, a Baptist Bible institute in the Rio Grande valley for Hispanic converts, the independent Texas Bible College in Houston, South Houston Bible Institute, and the Christ for the Nations Institute in Dallas. Congregations associated with the Bible Baptist Fellowship International had grown among fundamentalists. Assemblies of God churches had become more numerous, as had Pentecostal Holiness congregations. Faith-healer Kathryn Kuhlman's services appeared weekly on television and from time to time attracted busloads of spiritual seekers from across Texas to special events. Healing evangelist Oral Roberts was drawing students from Texas to his new university in Tulsa, Oklahoma, and his weekly television and radio programs were being aired on five hundred stations nationwide. Viewers in Texas were also receiving regular telecasts from Rex Humbard's Cathedral of Tomorrow, a five-thousand-member church near Akron, Ohio, that was airing services to more than 350 stations across the nation. Humbard was reportedly receiving $80,000 a week from dedicated fans, enough to cover the broadcasting costs with plenty left over for a private jet, restaurant, two shopping centers, and several commercial buildings. Eschewing controversial social issues, Humbard's folksy sermons emphasized the prevalence of sin and the world's desperate need for salvation.[50]

The churches' emphasis on evangelism was welcome news to conservative Christian pastors and parents hoping to see their congregations and offspring flourishing in godly ways. The response was less enthusiastic among the state's Jewish leaders, who saw the efforts as unwelcome attempts at proselytization. The anticommunist movements led by Hargis and Schwarz included enough fundamentalist xenophobia to raise concerns about faith-inspired anti-Semitism. A study funded by the Anti-Defamation League of B'nai B'rith suggested a possible link between conservative evangelical beliefs and anti-Semitism, at least if those beliefs emphasized the view that Jews had rejected Christ and were currently unsaved. Now that Campus Crusade and Southern Baptists were prominently promoting evangelism, the worries among Jewish leaders increased. As Union of American Hebrew Congregations president Maurice Eisendrath observed, such efforts "could damage the carefully cultivated roots of Christian-Jewish relations" and "subject young Jewish people and adults to repeated harassment and attempts at coercion."[51]

A QUICKENING RELIGIOUS PULSE

The period from around 1968 to 1972 is often viewed as the watershed moment when America became divided between people who were fundamentally conservative in their political and religious views and people who were basically liberal in their thinking about these issues. Quibbles can be raised about the extent of this division and whether it pertained to a large range of issues or only a few, and whether most Americans after all hewed to the middle or did not much care one way or the other. But the question remains of why such an alignment on one side or another of several rather different issues emerged at all.

By 1972 it was evident that leaders and lay members of the Southern Baptist Convention were shifting loyalties from the Democratic Party toward the Republican Party. African American leaders may have differed among themselves about black power and the pace of civil rights but mostly supported the Democratic Party. It was less clear who would lead the Democratic Party and whether Roman Catholics, including the growing number of Hispanic Catholics, would be Democrats or Republicans. This was true nationally and was especially the case in Texas. The point was not that some other dramatically different outcome could have developed, but that these alignments depended on particular issues and the ways in which they were framed.

Demonstrations about black and Chicano power and protests against the Vietnam War emphasized freedom of speech, communicated criticism of existing power structures, and focused on the empowerment of marginalized constituencies. These emphases were consistent with the appeals that black clergy and other supporters of the civil rights movement had made with growing urgency since the 1950s. They resonated with concerns voiced on the nation's rapidly growing campuses about academic freedom and free expression as well as calls for the democratization of higher education. Among a young activist segment of the Catholic leadership, they reflected the church's efforts at laicization and inclusiveness as expressed in the Second Vatican Council and its emphasis on social justice and service to the poor; by the end of the decade, the teachings known as liberation theology gave a further expression to this focus on social justice for the oppressed and underprivileged.

On the other side of the emerging cultural divide, civil rights activism in the form of demonstrations, strikes, and protest marches was roundly condemned by leaders who argued that law and order needed to be upheld, that faith in existing power structures was warranted, and that agitation was likely to undermine patriotism and somehow assist America's enemies. In quiet neighborhoods, Nixon's silent majority flew American flags during the protests to show their disagreement with the demonstrators. Texas Republicans such as Tower and Bush supported the Nixon administration's efforts in Vietnam. Democratic leaders in Texas were generally hawkish toward the war during the Johnson administration and now found themselves divided between moderates who still supported the war and liberals who opposed it. Religious leaders with few exceptions took the position that although peace was desirable, protest demonstrations were not the way to attain it. Questions about feminism, the ordination of women as clergy, homosexuality, and abortion were beginning to mobilize religious leaders who felt that liberalization of long-held norms on these topics was fundamentally unbiblical.[52]

For all the upheaval and uncertainty about public issues, religion at the grass roots remained remarkably strong. Its strength resided in the fact that it was so well institutionalized—solidly grounded in local congregations and in the habits of community life, not to mention in well-staffed seminaries and smoothly organized denominational structures. To an even greater degree, its strength inhered in a roll-up-your-sleeves attitude that encouraged adaptation. With the civil rights movement far from having accomplished all its aims and with the war in Southeast Asia still unresolved, congregations focused on what they had always done best. They held regular worship services, conducted weddings and funerals, and trained the young. It was this last activity that posed the greatest challenges and offered the greatest opportunities because it was the one on which congregations' futures depended. Clergy and lay leaders knew they had to stay relevant in order to secure the commitment of the coming generation.

Interviews conducted in Lubbock in 1972 offered an illuminating picture of how the community's congregations were adapting. Lubbock had been one of the fastest-growing towns in the country during the 1940s and by 1960 had a population of more than 128,000. In 1970 community leaders boasted that Lubbock was the largest all-dry city in the United States—which made it an unlikely site for a Woodstock-inspired rock concert that spring, which promoters hoped would draw a crowd of thirty thousand until cold wind and rain dwindled attendance to less than a tenth that number. As evidence that times were indeed changing, citizens voted two years later to permit liquor by the drink. The interviews ranged across denominations, including Baptists and Methodists, Presbyterians and Catholics, Churches of Christ and Unitarians, and members of several other traditions. Denominational and theological differences hardly came up. There was keen awareness that times were changing. Lubbock had lost its frontier spirit and developed a "settler type" of religion, one of the interviewees said. He meant that settler religion acts like a police chief telling people what the law allows and what it does not allow. That needed to change, he felt, because there were new frontiers of body, mind, and soul to be explored. Others said there was less interest, especially among the younger generation, in denominational lines and greater emphasis on interpersonal relationships. People had been put into stained-glass boxes, a pastor said, but what they wanted was other people knowing their names. There needed to be more emphasis on service and on making the conscience of the church felt in the community. They saw a quickening of the religious pulse, as one put it. But for that to continue, it would be necessary to work harder and to entertain new ideas.[53]

The writer Gail Caldwell was a student at Texas Tech in Lubbock from 1968 to 1970. Compared with her straitlaced Amarillo upbringing, the campus culture at Texas Tech was liberating. She met champion barrel-racers, protested the killings at Kent State, and got arrested for possession of marijuana. But the town lived up to its image of quiet, churchgoing, white middle-class Protestants, she felt, who hoped black people and Chicanos would stay away. If the community was forward looking, its intentions in these respects escaped her. West Texas was still the Bible Belt, she wrote, a place where grain reports and church billboards competed for attention and where the angular wheat fields and blank vistas were oppressively predictable. She decamped for Austin, entranced by the community's hip institutions—progressive law offices, farmworkers' strike supporters, antiwar organizations, vegetarian restaurants, and food co-ops. She was delighted, she wrote, to "leap from academic familiarity into the rough country of my new life."[54]

In 1998 Mark Herbener, the Dallas civil rights activist, came out to Lubbock to help the members of Slaton's Grace Lutheran Church celebrate its seventy-fifth anniversary. For the past ten years he had been serving as bishop of the Northern Texas–Northern Louisiana Synod of the Evangelical Lutheran Church in America. He was still proud of his role in the civil rights demonstrations of the early 1970s—and still displeased with Reverend Wright for not supporting them more. Wright had gone on to become the president of the National Missionary Baptist Convention of America and was a vice chairman for the Billy Graham Crusade of the Southwest.[55] His death in 1994 left the pastorate of People's Missionary Baptist Church in Dallas to his son. In 1995 Governor George W. Bush renamed a stretch of Highway 175 the S. M. Wright Freeway.

CHAPTER 10

GOD CAN SAVE US

━━━━━━━━━━━━━━━━

The Campaign for a Moral America

To me, humanism—and as I say, that is a nice academic word for atheism—humanism, like a floodtide, is coming in to destroy our homes, destroy our young people, destroy our school system, destroy our government.

W. A. CRISWELL, FIRST BAPTIST CHURCH, DALLAS, 1980

If Dallas is the buckle on the Bible Belt, First Baptist Church is a big old ruby in the center of that buckle.

STEVE BLOW, CORPUS CHRISTI, 1976

On Friday evening, August 22, 1980, Ronald Reagan spoke to an enthusiastic crowd of seventeen thousand evangelical leaders and laypeople at Reunion Arena in Dallas. Criswell opened the two-day conference the previous day, challenging the audience to fight humanism and homosexuality and calling on them to renew their faith in the "God who can save us." Television preacher Jerry Falwell flew in from Virginia to appear on stage with Reagan and shake his hand. Reagan told the audience, "I know you can't endorse me. But I want you to know that I endorse you." That fall Reagan won 51 percent of the popular vote nationwide, beating President Jimmy Carter by nearly 10 percent. In Texas Reagan's margin of victory was 14 percent. It was the largest win by a Republican presidential candidate in the state's history. A statewide poll showed that 84 percent of conservative Protestants voted for Reagan.[1]

More than any other single event, Reagan's enthusiastic reception by conservative religious leaders at the National Affairs Briefing in Dallas put observers on notice that something they were calling the New Christian Right or simply the Religious Right was a potentially powerful new force in American politics. Most of the leaders who greeted Reagan with thunderous cheers and thankful amens were Baptists. And yet it was Reagan rather than fellow Baptist Carter who sparked their support.

The rise of the Religious Right has been examined from all angles, and several key factors have been identified. It clearly depended on leadership. The most visible leaders were Falwell, whose Moral Majority rallies at state capitals had been gaining attention in the late 1970s, and fellow televangelist Pat Robertson, whose popular *700 Club* television program included discussions of social and moral topics. Both were canny entrepreneurs who knew how to attract media attention, and there were conservative political operatives eager to enlist their support. There were unifying issues as well, such as opposition to abortion, homosexuality, and promiscuity, and the more general sense that religion was under siege by secularity and humanism. And there were lingering divisions within Protestant denominations and among Catholics over such issues as social activism, the legacies of the civil rights movement and the Vietnam War, communism, gender equality, the ordination of women, and theology.[2]

Each of these factors, as it happens, fits neatly with what is known about the impetus of social conditions more generally in the mobilization of large-scale social and political movements. Theories of resource mobilization emphasize the nuts and bolts that must be present for any significant movement to get started and gain traction. Falwell's and Robertson's television ministries were bringing in millions of dollars and reaching large segments of the population in ways never before enjoyed by local pastors, denominational heads, or even the most charismatic traveling evangelists. It mattered that they knew how to make headlines, and ironically it helped that Carter's born-again Baptist faith put discussions of evangelical religion in the national spotlight. Quieter, behind-the-scenes resources helped as well. For instance, it mattered that political operatives knew how to exploit the mailing lists of television ministries and that these ministries developed networks among local pastors.

The unifying issues of the Religious Right correspond with other strands of social movement interpretation. On the one hand, the old "whose ox is gored" interpretation suggests that movements mobilize when people feel threatened. Such threats may well have been felt by conservative churchgoers who feared that homosexuality and promiscuity were undermining their values. Falwell and Robertson emphasized not only these wider cultural threats but also the more specific possibility that God's work could be impeded by unfavorable Federal Communications Commission regulations or court decisions about taxes and separation of church and state. To white residents who may have been less than eager to embrace racial integration, the federal government probably evoked additional concerns that all was not as well as it could be. On the other hand, an equally plausible interpretation suggests that social movements develop when people realize they have enough clout to make a difference. In short, activism stems from entitlement, just as it did in the civil rights movement for African Americans, but now among a predominantly white constituency of conservative Christians who realized that one of their own was in the White House, that other candidates were courting their vote, and that their numbers were in fact large and growing.

The role of divisiveness within religious organizations draws attention to the wider organizational environment in which social movements develop. Well-institutionalized organizations, such as schools and hospitals, political parties, and religious denominations, for the most part maintain the status quo, encourage incremental social reforms, and discourage upstart movements from forming. When the authority of these established organizations erodes or is challenged, opportunities for new leaders with new ideas emerge. In the 1960s and 1970s opportunities of this kind were present in nearly all the major religious organizations. Clergy and laity mobilized to support or oppose civil rights and the Vietnam War. They fought or promoted denominational mergers, ecumenical councils, innovations in worship, and new independent ministries. Special-purpose groups organized within denominations and across denominational lines to mobilize concerned members. These groups developed coalitions and articulated positions on many of the issues that gained wider attention in the Religious Right. The new identities that emerged retained denominational labels but increasingly involved categories that cut across these traditional lines. A person of faith might still be a Baptist, but it also mattered that one was a conservative Baptist rather than a moderate or liberal Baptist.

General arguments about social conditions in which the Religious Right took root nevertheless leave unanswered questions about the processes involved. One such question pertains to resources that get mobilized. How do leaders come to realize that these are indeed resources that can be deployed for some new endeavor? And related to that is whether the resources are depleted in being mobilized or whether it is actually mobilization that creates them. Similarly, the unifying issues need to be queried more closely to see if they have been brewing for a while, are new or newly salient, and whether some played a more unifying role than others? By the same token, the place of division within established organizations is not satisfactorily understood without addressing questions about the specific opportunities, constraints, role models, and coalitions involved, and in this instance the shifting understandings of religion's relationship to politics.

Although the Religious Right played a national role in the 1980 presidential election and continued to be of national interest throughout the 1980s and beyond, the processes through which it developed were local as well as regional and national. They varied from state to state, and they reflected local and regional differences in the strength of religious traditions, changes in the demographic composition of these traditions, political rivalries, and influences stemming from racial and ethnic factors. Texas is a particularly interesting location in which to observe these processes, not only because of its political clout and the strength of its Southern Baptist churches, but also because of its divisions between Democrats and Republicans, its Catholic population, and the changing relationships among white Anglos, African Americans, and Hispanics.

BROTHER ROLOFF AND RADIO EVANGELISM

The person who played one of the most influential roles in bringing conservative religion into a combative relationship with politics in Texas is seldom mentioned in standard histories of the Religious Right. Reverend Lester Roloff, a Baptist who grew up on a farm near Dawson, Texas, became one of the state's most prominent radio evangelists. As he liked to explain, he was a sickly child who on one occasion felt himself so near death that he prayed, "Lord, if you let me wake up in the morning, I'll be a preacher." The opportunity came in 1932 when the eighteen-year-old Roloff preached his first sermon as a freshman at Baylor. Soon he was conducting revival meetings in the area, causing people to shout and weep, declaring that they were born again, and in one town chasing the bootlegger away and shutting down the gambling hall.[3]

During World War II, Roloff moved to Corpus Christi where the community was filled with navy recruits, pastored the Park Avenue Baptist Church, and in 1944 began the daily broadcasts of a radio program called the *Family Altar*. The program aired on station KWBU, owned by the Baptist General Convention of Texas, and could be heard in twenty-two states. The venture proved so successful that Roloff abandoned his congregation, formed Roloff Evangelistic Ministries, and devoted his energy full-time to radio preaching and in-person tent revivals that drew huge crowds.

Roloff thrived on controversy, condemning whisky drinkers and communists and causing public disturbances with loudspeakers from his "gospel van" and tent meetings. In 1945 he argued at a meeting of the Baptist General Convention of Texas that Baylor should not award Truman an honorary degree because of the president's rough language. By 1955 his criticisms of fellow Baptists, who he claimed were no longer preaching the true gospel, grew to the point that the Baptist General Convention of Texas banned him from broadcasting on KWBU and he was no longer welcome in most Baptist pulpits. As a result, his ministry grew. Brother Roloff's *Family Altar* was heard on hundreds of stations nationwide, and he was piloting his own airplane to conduct revivals across the country.

Radio, of course, had long been the medium through which charismatic preachers were able to extend their ministries. Truett's broadcasts from the First Baptist Church in Dallas in the 1920s, Norris's from Fort Worth a few years later, and Winrod's from near Del Rio in the 1930s were early examples. With few regulations governing what could be said on the air, radio preachers were largely on their honor to keep religion separate from politics. Truett for the most part did, while Norris and Winrod did not. Broadcasts that aired as worship services from

local congregations and through the Baptist General Convention of Texas generally adhered more closely to the expectations governing these organizations than
did broadcasts from independents such as the Roloff Evangelistic Ministries.

For every radio preacher who made it big, there were dozens who launched
smaller ministries. One was the Reverend Donald Skelton of Dallas, whose Victory New Testament Fellowship included a radio ministry and who attracted
small audiences when he spoke in person at independent fundamentalist
churches. Another was Church of Christ pastor Landon Saunders, whose Herald
of Truth religious programs aired from Abilene. Others included Seventh Day
Adventist pastor Bob Thrower—the Hour of Prophecy evangelist from Corpus
Christi—and Allen Ehlers's Faith Mission International in Del Rio. There were
also Spanish-language ministries, such as Reverend Juan Valenzuela's evangelistic radio programs from San Antonio.

Broadcasting's potential to create lucrative empires was most evident in the
ministry of another radio evangelist with Texas ties, Herbert W. Armstrong, a
former Quaker whose broadcasts began in 1933 from a small station in Eugene,
Oregon, and evolved into a national ministry featuring apocalyptic prophetic
messages. Headquartered in Pasadena, California, Armstrong's Worldwide
Church of God ministries grew to include television broadcasts on nearly four
hundred stations as well as international radio and publishing and were earning
between $35 and $40 million annually by the late 1970s. The church claimed
some eighty-five thousand members nationwide who were expected to give as
much as 30 percent of their wages to support the ministry's far-flung activities.
In the early 1950s an East Texas resident named Buck Hammer donated a small
parcel of land to the ministry, with the result that thousands of members started
making annual pilgrimages to the area for a weeklong Feast of Tabernacles. In the
mid-1960s Armstrong purchased more than four thousand acres about a hundred miles east of Dallas near Big Sandy and constructed Ambassador College, a
campus for Christian young people interested in clean living and willing to work
for the institution at least twenty hours a week in addition to their studies. Several years later when a breach occurred between Armstrong and his son Garner
Ted Armstrong, the younger leader founded the Church of God International
nearby.[4] In 1977, when flagging donations led the senior Armstrong to consider
selling the Big Sandy campus, Roloff offered to buy it for $10 million.[5]

Roloff's radio and revival ministry had grown steadily during the 1950s and
1960s. In the late 1950s he held revival meetings in tents, school auditoriums,
and municipal buildings, and many of his public appearances were still at local
churches, often in independent congregations or at Baptist meetings convened
by fundamentalist pastors. He sometimes linked faith in Christ with worldly
success, appearing at Rotary International meetings and preaching to business leaders. But these appeals proved less effective than framing himself as an
old-fashioned preacher bringing a simple message of repentance and hope. In
1959 his supporters in Corpus Christi constructed an air-conditioned worship

facility for his ministry with ample parking and seats for sixteen hundred.[6] By the mid-1960s he was appearing in larger venues, such as the Scofield Memorial Church in Dallas, and across the nation on radio stations featuring Hunt's *Life Line* broadcasts, McIntire's fundamentalist sermons, and Fuller's *Old-Fashioned Revival Hour*. Over the next few years his radio ministry expanded to include television broadcasts and he was conducting well-attended evangelistic services in Arizona, Florida, Illinois, Iowa, Kansas, New Mexico, and Virginia as well as in towns across Texas. Half-page newspaper advertisements described him as "one of the greatest preachers in America."[7] Nothing yet signaled the celebrity he would attain in the 1970s.

Broadcasters' conflicts with government in those years most often resulted from questions raised by the Federal Communications Commission (FCC). For example, in 1972 the FCC challenged fundamentalist McIntire's broadcasts and "March for Victory" rallies on grounds that his messages were too partisan to qualify for public airtime reserved for religious programming—prompting a supporter in Texas to warn of the "danger in the heavy hand of political government." The following year state and federal authorities charged that Ohio broadcaster Rex Humbard's $12 million a year ministry was being financed in part by selling unregistered securities through unlicensed brokers.[8] But Roloff's ministry faced a different challenge.

As his ministry expanded, Roloff discovered that listeners were eager to support programs that not only saved souls but also rescued men from alcoholism and led wayward boys and girls back to the straight-and-narrow. By 1967 the ministry was supporting the City of Refuge farm home for alcoholics, the Good Samaritan Rescue Mission, the Lighthouse Home for delinquent boys, and another home for girls. The Rebekah Home for Girls drew especially favorable responses as several of the girls participated in a singing group at Roloff's revival meetings and in 1970 appeared with Roloff on Phil Donahue's popular television program. In most respects, the homes reflected the same social service commitment that had led to the founding of denominational orphanages and hospitals earlier in the century and were similar in purpose to the Salvation Army's rescue missions and evangelist David Wilkerson's "Teen Challenge" program for delinquent youth in New York City that gained national acclaim through Wilkerson's 1962 best-seller *The Cross and the Switchblade*. The one difference was that Roloff refused mandatory state licensing of the homes.

The issue came to a head in 1973 when sixteen of the girls and their parents charged Roloff with physically abusing the girls. Roloff acknowledged that the girls had received corporal punishment but declared that the spankings were no worse than his daddy had given him as a boy and were in fact consistent with scriptural teachings about sparing the rod and spoiling the child. Alumnae of the home came to Roloff's defense, testifying that the girls were rebellious troublemakers and deserved what they got.[9] At first Roloff agreed with a court order requiring him to obtain licenses from the state welfare department for his homes for troubled children. But in 1974 the Texas Supreme Court ruled that he did not have to comply with the lower court. The incident drew wider attention when hearings before the state legislature raised questions about potential church and state conflicts, licensing of other child-care activities, and the role of state and local welfare offices in monitoring social services.

Instead of quietly acceding to the state's request to secure a license, Roloff staged a public rally at the state capital at which some of the once-wayward girls sang and gave their testimonies. He was then fined and sentenced to five days in jail for contempt of court, only to have the decision reversed by the Texas Supreme Court. The notoriety immediately drew invitations for Roloff and his Honey Bee Quartet to speak and sing at church gatherings. Lawmakers contemplating measures to tighten the regulation of child-care facilities were deluged with messages from Roloff's supporters complaining that any such laws would infringe on their religious liberties. Referring to his revival meetings as "liberty rallies," Roloff argued that he was waging a "battle for religious liberty and freedom and for separation of church and state for which our forefathers [came] to this new world to enjoy."[10]

To Roloff and the many who supported him, the phrase "liberty of conscience" that had for so many years held special meaning for Texas believers came increasingly to mean that government should not interfere with religion, not that religious leaders should avoid politics. Keeping religion out of politics was an argument Protestants used against Catholics and against fellow preachers who might be viewed locally as being on the wrong side of the issues. It put preachers at risk if they ventured too far into partisan politics, as illustrated by figures such as Reverend Honey and Baxton Bryant. But it had not deterred preachers from arguing for dry laws, speaking against Al Smith, working with public officials to organize orphanages, preaching against JFK, participating in farmworkers' strikes, meeting with municipal officials about housing discrimination, and helping to organize civil rights demonstrations. Still, it was easier to defend making statements about public policies when those policies appeared to be infringing on religious freedom. Liberty of conscience meant freedom to run church-related hospitals and colleges without government inference, to hold tax-free real estate, to preach on radio and television, and to provide homes for juvenile delinquents without state licensing.

The controversy over Roloff's programs continued through the end of the decade. In 1976 he was again sentenced to jail for several days on charges of contempt of court. Angry citizens compared the state's intervention with that of the federal government desegregating the schools. In Georgia and Alabama, community groups organized "freedom rallies" to hear Roloff speak about his persecution from the government. Fundamentalists in Texas introduced a "Brother Roloff Bill" to exempt religious child-care centers from state licensing requirements, only to have the bill narrowly defeated. A district judge declared a mistrial in a $4.7 million damage suit against Roloff brought by a youth paralyzed from the waist down in a diving accident at Roloff's home for boys. Critics accused Roloff of possibly having kidnapped some of the youth at his homes, and allegations of physical abuse continued.

Roloff stood his ground, threatening to die or spend his life in jail to keep the government from interfering with his religious freedom. "The license from the state has to do with controlling my spiritual liberty," he argued. "I believe the Lord reserves the right to give that license to me." He objected not only to the principle of licensing but also to state regulations about sex education, social workers having high school diplomas, food safety and nutritional standards, and the placement of babies born at the homes. His ministry continued to grow, and his cause drew wider and wider attention. In 1978 a rally in Dallas on his behalf was estimated to have attracted ten thousand participants. That fall the case became an issue in the gubernatorial race between Republican Bill Clements and Democrat John Hill. Roloff used his pulpit and broadcasts to campaign against Hill and took credit for swaying as many as a quarter of a million votes for Clements. As attorney general, Hill had led the drive to force Roloff to obtain state licenses. Roloff associates sent out letters a few weeks before the election charging that Hill would "signal the bureaucrats to move in for the kill." The Sunday before the election, Roloff's supporters distributed forty-five thousand brochures at churches stating that Clements believed in "parental rights," "salvation by grace," and "a free church without government controls."[11]

This was the moment at which Roloff felt he could raise the $10 million to purchase Ambassador College. His stand for religious liberty was attracting favorable comments and bringing in donations from supporters across the country. Over the next eighteen months, bills to stiffen child-care protection and to exempt Roloff's homes continued under consideration in Austin, and a grand jury continued to investigate charges of abuse. As the National Affairs Briefing convened in Dallas, another former resident of the Rebekah Home for Girls came forward with testimony of whippings and painful memories of force-fed Christianity.[12]

It all ended for Roloff on November 2, 1982, when his single-engine Cessna crashed in a thunderstorm, killing him and the four young women traveling with him. Fundamentalist leader Bob Jones Jr. of Bob Jones University eulogized Roloff as a man of God who "stood in the gap" and bore the brunt of the battle. "He knew what it was to be lied about and slandered and opposed by the wrong kinds of preachers and the wrong kinds of public officials," Jones declared. Inspired by Roloff, other pastors announced their intention of following his example. "Texas can't be our boss. God is our boss," a pastor near Fort Worth argued in 1986, defending his decision to refuse state licensing of a Baptist boys home. "Texans will pay if they oppress God's people. They'll pay dearly. God knows how to do that through different types of tragedies." Roloff's homes remained open and continued to be charged periodically by former residents with allegations of physical abuse. In the 1990s, as Texas lawmakers considered new measures to encourage greater involvement of faith-based organizations in social service provision, a plan was approved to permit faith-based children's homes to be accredited by a private agency rather than the state. "What a blessing it is," Roloff's successor observed. "Our God hears and answers our prayers."[13]

GOD'S ANGRY MAN

When rumor spread in 1977 that Armstrong hoped to shed Ambassador College from his holdings, the other Texas evangelist who tried to buy it was James Robison. "God's angry man," as sociologist William Martin aptly described him, Robison was destined to play a role in mobilizing the Religious Right similar to Roloff's, only more directly.[14] Whether he planned it that way or simply discovered it as he went along, Roloff found that mobilizing the faithful is more effective when conflict with the government is involved than when it is not, and when that conflict extends over a period of years. Not by chance did supporters come to liken his ordeal with the struggle at the Alamo when martyrs for freedom bravely stood against an alien tyranny. A religious leader could hardly be accused of breaching the separation of church and state if it was the state infringing on religious freedom. Robison found the same to be true.

In 1964 twenty-one-year-old Austin native Robison conducted wildly successful revival services in Baptist churches at several locations across the South, including one at a large church in Shreveport and another in Houston. Robison was soon touted as the next Billy Graham and was being invited to preach special revival campaigns at dozens of churches. By 1966 he had his own advance man at work lining up weeklong Billy Graham–style crusades for Christ organized in cooperation with local churches spanning a number of Protestant denominations and complete with music by a large choir and personal counseling. His most successful crusade that summer was in Lockhart, where crowds of about a thousand filled the high school football stadium night after night to hear the dynamic young evangelist. With West Texas soloist John McKay offering music and giving his testimony about finding God, the revivals were tailor-made for Texas audiences.

The following spring Robison formed the James Robison Evangelistic Crusade Association to expand the work, again on the model of Graham's organization. Baptist churches in Baytown, Big Spring, Freeport, Kerrville, Lubbock, Midland, and San Antonio, among others, placed advertisements in local newspapers encouraging the community to turn out for the young man who was being used by God more than any person other than Graham himself. Tanned, tall, and rugged, Robison's good looks resembled those of actor James Garner. Like Graham, Robison held a worn Bible in his hand while preaching, quoted scripture for memory, and called on audiences to repent. Soon Robison's half-hour syndicated television program *Get Together* was also attracting a growing audience, but in-person revival meetings were still the mainstay of his ministry. Besides invitations to speak at churches, he was holding citywide crusades in municipal auditoriums and preaching to students and teachers at assemblies in high school gymnasiums. At a weeklong crusade in Garland in 1970, some forty thousand persons—mostly young people—filled the stadium night after night. By 1974 Robison claimed to have conducted more than 350 crusades in some thirty states and preached in person to six million people.[15]

Robison's fundamentalism, strict belief in biblical inerrancy, and success in soul winning drew particular praise from the state's most influential Baptist. Criswell declared that Robison was "a new star in the galaxy of God's flaming, shining lights who point men to Christ" and noted that his "evangelistic crusades are becoming nothing short of Pentecostal in their power and in their outreach." Some years later Criswell would accuse Robison of becoming too Pentecostal, deviating from what Criswell believed to be the true interpretation of scripture by encouraging believers to speak in tongues and practice exorcisms. But for now, Criswell saw only the need to extend his blessing to the young evangelist. "We rejoice that in our day and in our generation we have lived to see so marvelously blessed a young man," he said. "May God keep him in strength and in increasing power through the unfolding years that lie ahead."[16]

With headquarters at Hurst near Fort Worth, Robison devoted an increasing share of his time after 1975 to the television ministry while enlarging the variety of in-person meetings conducted by his staff. In addition to old-fashioned preaching services, meetings included special concerts of religious music and meetings with topics oriented toward youth. Among others, singer Johnny Cash performed on behalf of the organization, and husband and wife team Billy and Winky Foote toured for the ministry, preaching, singing, putting on magic shows, and hosting fun nights at churches for children and teenagers. The ministry's outreach was further assisted by the work of Mike Huckabee, the young media assistant who would later serve as governor of Arkansas and run for president in 2008.

But Robison's most notable success was the conversion of Fort Worth celebrity T. Cullen Davis, a multimillionaire oil equipment dealer who found Christ after being charged in two sensational murder trials. In 1976 a shooting spree occurred at his mansion, and Davis was accused of killing his twelve-year-old stepdaughter. Eventually acquitted, he was also accused and then found innocent of trying to buy the death of a judge hearing a divorce case. Davis abandoned his playboy lifestyle and through the guidance of Robison declared himself a born-again Christian who henceforth would commit himself to combating the decadent humanism that he felt was destroying society and was surely the source of his own difficulties. That commitment reportedly stemmed from Davis reading the Bible four or five hours a day over a period of months, giving up alcohol, and becoming increasingly distraught about the teaching of evolution and humanism in public schools. One evening Davis and Robison reportedly took the multimillionaire's million-dollar collection of gold, silver, jade, and ivory objects, which Davis decided were pagan idols, and smashed them with hammers in the parking area outside Davis's mansion.[17]

Robison's trouble with the FCC began in 1977 when the evangelist's television program, seen weekly in some seventy cities, was canceled by its home station WFAA in Dallas because of Robison's attacks on homosexuals and *Playboy* magazine publisher Hugh Hefner. The cancellation occurred according to the station's interpretation of FCC rules because mentioning any specific person by name required advance notification of that individual. The Agape Metropolitan Community Church of Fort Worth, which ministered to homosexuals and had not been mentioned specifically, demanded equal time and filled the time slot with a program of its own.[18]

The brouhaha appeared to be over when Robison apologized and WFAA reinstated his program. But the station manager acknowledged having received phone calls and letters by the "bucketsful" in support of Robison. Although preachers and conservative churchgoers had been railing against sexual promiscuity for years, homosexuality had recently become a front-burner topic through a campaign in Florida led by singer Anita Bryant. A former Miss Oklahoma from Tulsa, Bryant was well-known for her appearances on television, had sung during the graveside services for Lyndon Johnson in 1973, and was regarded by many in Texas almost as if she were a hometown girl. When Miami passed an ordinance banning discrimination against homosexuals, Bryant formed a campaign called Save Our Children that challenged the ordinance and succeeded in its repeal.[19] A survey conducted a few months prior to the Florida campaign showed the nation almost evenly divided on a question about homosexuals teaching in public schools, with 54 percent saying they should be allowed to teach and 46 percent saying they should not. But among white evangelical Protestants in the South, only 29 percent said they should be allowed to teach while 71 percent said they should not.[20] According to a report given by WFAA, many of the calls and letters in support of Robison mentioned Bryant and asked why the FCC did not cancel programs criticizing her by name.[21]

Like Roloff, Robison benefited from the encounter with government. In 1978 prominent Baptist preachers appeared at his rallies and Texas Baptists scheduled one of its statewide events such that his would immediately follow. With $4 million in operating revenue, Robison planned a prime-time television blitz that would air in 225 markets at an estimated cost of $20 million. Huckabee, now serving as spokesperson for the organization, declared, "Money is really no object."[22] But before the blitz could be arranged, Robison again found himself in trouble with FCC regulations. WFAA once more canceled his program because of incendiary remarks against homosexuality. Robison replied that he had attacked no individual or organization by name, yet the station held that it had received a complaint from the Dallas Gay Caucus and had determined that the gay community had indeed been attacked.[23]

In further responding, Robison drew a distinction that had been successfully made in the past and would become a central argument of the Religious Right. The station argued that such matters as homosexuality should be dealt with on news and public affairs shows rather than on religious programs. Robison in turn argued that the issue was not political but moral. "Many people treat it as a political issue," he acknowledged. But it is a "moral issue," a "biblical issue," and as such he felt "that as a preacher I have the privilege as well as the responsibility to preach what the Bible said."[24]

The distinction maneuvered the station into a corner. The station's management agreed that Robison had a right to talk about moral issues, including adultery, murder, and rape, but drew the line on talking against homosexuality. Huckabee replied, "Does that mean if we talk about the evils of alcohol that the owner of Joe's Bar would get equal time?" He asked, "If we talk about the evils of adultery, would a wife-swapping club qualify for equal time?" The idea seemed so ludicrous that Robison's attorneys suggested a lawsuit against the station might be in order.[25] Outraged viewers saw the station's position as an affront not only to Robison but also to God. "It is time that Christians took a stand on issues such as this," a pair of offended viewers declared, "and let the world know we are going to unite and fight."[26] In reply, the Religion and Life Committee of the Dallas Gay Political Caucus declared that it too had scripture on its side. Robison had defamed the gay community, the committee said, by portraying it in terms of the most bizarre activities of an unrepresentative group. "The Bible warns us against false prophets and wolves in sheep's clothing," it said.[27]

Almost immediately Robison found he had powerful allies. Eddie Chiles, a Fort Worth oil baron and owner of the Texas Rangers, was an ardent defender of Americanism and free enterprise who offered a regular radio commentary that began, "I'm Eddie Chiles and I'm mad as hell." Usually he was mad about something the government was doing, such as raising taxes or regulating oil drilling. Chiles made his private airplane available to Robison and Huckabee for a trip to Houston, explaining that Robison's fight for the First Amendment was his fight, too. In Houston, Robison and Huckabee met with attorney Richard (Racehorse) Haynes, who agreed to serve as counsel. Haynes was the attorney who successfully defended Cullen Davis in the murder case and controversial divorce hearing. Huckabee, seeing the impending suit as an opportunity that "God engineered" for the "cause of Christianity," announced that it would not be directed toward WFAA but against the federal government itself.[28]

Baptist leaders from Texas and beyond rallied to Robison's support as well. The *Baptist Standard* editorialized that the FCC ruling was an infringement on freedom of the pulpit. Robison warned that the attack on him was like an atom bomb that could explode to the devastation of all religious programming. Haynes secured the assistance of a top communications lawyer to develop the case. Dallas Cowboys coach Tom Landry agreed to serve as honorary chair of Robison's "National Call to Arms" committee to raise $15 million for broadcasts about the nation's moral problems. Criswell and more than eight hundred Baptist ministers from around the state and several other states met to organize a "Freedom of Speech" rally at the Dallas Convention Center. "We're going to take them to the mat," Haynes told the gathering, referring to the FCC. "They say we have to be fair," Criswell observed, "yet we see hours and hours and hours of filth, violence and sexual immorality on our television daily. But when a man speaks up and says what God says about an issue, they say he is not fair."[29]

Although homosexuality had been the precipitating issue, the planners wanted the "Freedom of Speech" rally to focus on the larger and more encompassing issue of freedom to preach over the airwaves about religion and morality. To this end, they decided against inviting Anita Bryant, ostensibly to avoid security problems but also to avoid clouding the issues—a wise decision in retrospect that gave added impetus to the Religious Right. Freedom of speech was the framing device that permitted the movement to attract supporters such as Chiles who disliked government regulations whether they had to do with religion or not. The idea resonated especially with Baptists' perennial emphasis on liberty of conscience. And it was an umbrella under which the broad range of moral concerns that had stirred Goldwater and Hunt in the 1960s and that were still of central concern to Criswell could receive attention. On Tuesday, June 5, 1979, with Haynes, Criswell, and Falwell seated on the platform, Robison defended his right to preach the Bible as he saw fit to an appreciative audience of more than ten thousand.[30]

THAT BIG OLD RUBY

Robison's stand against the FCC played an important role as preparation for the National Affairs Briefing that brought Reagan to Dallas in 1980. Robison himself was the event's chief planner and by his own account personally invited Reagan and suggested the "I endorse you" remark.[31] Criswell's support, though, was more than incidental. The "big old ruby" adorning the Dallas Bible Belt buckle, as journalist Steve Blow described Criswell's First Baptist Church, was the center not only of Baptist power in Texas but of Texas power itself. While the rise of the Republican Party in Texas could probably be understood without reference to Criswell's church, the connection that developed between Republicans and conservative Protestants in Texas requires close consideration of the church's role.

Standard treatments of the Religious Right place heavy emphasis on public opinion. One rendition starts at the bottom and argues that conservative southern Protestants were fed up with Democratic policies that favored civil rights. Having voted twice in recent elections for fellow southerners and having been disappointed in both Johnson and Carter, they were ready by 1980 to join the GOP. All it took was prompting from Falwell, Robertson, and a few others to see that Republican candidates were closer to true biblical morality than Democrats.

The other version starts at the top, giving Reagan and his advisers most of the credit for crafting language appealing to the moral sentiments of conservative white southerners without seeming to be overtly racist.

The two arguments are not mutually exclusive and yet in combination miss an important aspect of the process through which the Republican Party gained power and was assisted by the Religious Right. Although social movements are sometimes powerful enough to swing general elections toward one party or the other, imagining that they have done so—and making claims to that effect—can readily exaggerate their influence. That may especially be the case when an election is otherwise not close. A social movement more reasonably may exercise influence in closely contested local elections and primaries. In 1980 the Republican Party in Texas already had considerable strength dating to the Eisenhower and Nixon administrations and evident even among Goldwater's supporters in 1964 and the party's growing appeal among the middle class. The Religious Right's role in Texas was less in shifting votes from Carter to Reagan in the general election than helping in small, symbolic ways with Reagan's contest against George H. W. Bush in the Republican primary. How that marginal effect occurred is best illustrated among the state's Southern Baptists and with particular reference to Criswell.

In 1980 there were approximately sixteen thousand religious congregations in Texas, with a total of nearly 7.8 million adherents. That was by far the largest number of congregations in any state and more adherents than in any state other than California and New York. In many ways Texas resembled the rest of the United States in being the home of diverse religious traditions. A study of religious membership in 1980 showed 2.3 million Catholics living in Texas, 932,000 Methodists, nearly 196,000 Presbyterians, 174,000 Episcopalians, 144,000 Lutherans, and 30,000 Jews. However, the state's history as a bastion of Southern Baptist strength remained undiminished. There were nearly four thousand Southern Baptist congregations, with a total of nearly 2.7 million adherents. That was more than double the number of adherents in Georgia or North Carolina, the other states with the largest numbers of Southern Baptists. In addition, there were another million evangelical Protestant in Texas who belonged to small, independent, fundamentalist, Assemblies of God, Brethren, Church of God, Churches of Christ, Holiness, and Pentecostal congregations and who differed from Southern Baptists on matters of doctrine but generally held similarly conservative views on social, moral, and political issues.

Baptists' tradition of local congregational autonomy meant that no single individual or body could dictate exactly what clergy preached or what members were expected to believe. The considerable agreement on basic teachings about personal salvation, soul winning, and adherence to the Bible stemmed from common training of clergy in the denomination's seminaries and Bible institutes as well as statements of faith for ordination and membership. Congregational autonomy also made the denomination agile, just as it had been throughout the state's history. Small congregations adapted well to sparsely populated farming communities. They adapted equally well to rapidly growing suburban communities with large populations. Indeed, they adapted especially well to these communities because a pastor who preached effectively, worked hard at canvassing the neighborhood for newcomers, and was reasonably good at fund-raising could benefit from a growing congregation with an increasing financial base that could support a better salary for the pastor and a larger staff.

County comparisons in 1980 show that Southern Baptists had churches in 98 percent of the state's counties and made up at least 40 percent of all Protestants in 87 percent of the counties. Historic patterns were still evident in the fact that Southern Baptists made up slightly larger proportions of the Protestant population in counties with lower median incomes and slower population growth. Southern Baptists nevertheless accounted for at least half of all Protestants in counties with above-average median incomes, higher than average population growth, and larger than average urban populations.[32]

The largest Southern Baptist congregation in Texas was still Criswell's First Baptist Church in Dallas. Officially the congregation included 21,793 members in 1980. This compared with a median of only 288 members for Southern Baptist congregations statewide. Membership never meant that everyone faithfully attended. But First Baptist's 3,500 seats were generally filled to capacity at least twice on Sunday mornings. More than 3,000 attended Sunday school classes, and as many as 50,000 tuned to the church's radio and television broadcasts.[33]

Criswell was uniquely influential in Dallas and in Southern Baptist circles nationwide. Serving at First Baptist since 1944, he had consolidated power within the congregation by surrounding himself with loyalists who were themselves influential in banking, oil, and real estate as well as with staff and associate pastors who commanded authority in the denomination. In a state that took pride in being big and in a city that liked to call itself "Big D," being the president of the nation's largest Protestant denomination—as Criswell was from 1968 to 1970—and being able to speak as head of the denomination's largest congregation mattered.

Dr. Joel Gregory, who joined Criswell's staff in the early 1990s, mused that the First Baptist Church of Dallas held a place in Southern Baptists' minds similar to Canterbury for Anglicans, Salt Lake City for Mormons, and Rome for Catholics. For aspiring preachers, he wrote, Criswell's church evoked "something in the spiritual realm akin to sexual lust in the fleshly realm."[34] Of course few would have put it quite that way. It was rather that Criswell's success seemed clearly to be a manifestation of God's mission being accomplished on earth.

By the early 1970s Criswell's political views were well-known. He was firmly opposed to big government, and he was a Republican. On government, one of his most characteristic remarks was in a 1976 sermon when he observed, "More and more the government is seizing the daily lives of the people." Big government connoted the Soviet-style totalitarianism to which he had been firmly opposed throughout the Cold War, and it was something that liberals were wittingly or unwittingly condoning. As he explained, "I can easily understand the acceptance and expansion of the Red Russian Empire in the nations of the world by an immediate and patent reason. It lies in the left-winger, in the socialist, in the welfare-stater, in the liberal, in the fellow traveler. The only thing that a liberal is against in America, or any of the nations of the world, is the conservative who believes in work and in paying his debts and living within his budget." What was wrong about communism was, in his view, what he also associated with domestic policies helping the poor. He may have shifted his mind about civil rights, but it still was part of his thinking that welfare policies were somehow giving African Americans too much power. "They're making black cities out of our great cities," he said, noting that Atlanta was "virtually all black now" and that white residents were fleeing Dallas by the thousands. He blamed school integration—another reason to distrust big government. "The parents ought to have the choice—not the government and least of all the courts," he observed.[35]

Holding Kennedy and Johnson responsible for school integration and the welfare state, Criswell saw Republicans rather than Democrats as the better choice. During the 1976 campaign between Carter and Ford, Criswell repeatedly took jabs at Carter. On October 10 Ford attended worship services at Criswell's church. In comments to the crowd before turning to the biblical text of the morning, Criswell criticized Carter for an interview in *Playboy* magazine in which Carter acknowledged having had adulterous thoughts. After the service Criswell endorsed Ford while standing on the steps of the huge church, and Ford graciously accepted the endorsement. The story of Criswell's endorsement and a photo of Ford and Criswell at the church circulated in national newspapers and in most of the small newspapers serving communities in Texas. Over the next three weeks, journalists followed Criswell to see if he had more to say about the election, editors considered the endorsement's potential impact, and readers wrote letters expressing heated views about it. A Texas Baptist would have had to be severely isolated from the media to have avoided knowing about Criswell's endorsement. Some attributed the endorsement simply to Criswell's concerns about Carter's *Playboy* interview, while others thought it stemmed from Carter somehow being too sympathetic toward the charismatic movement they felt was threatening Baptists. There was general agreement that an endorsement from someone as powerful as Criswell was important.

It was of course by no means the first time Texas preachers had found ways to show their pleasure or displeasure with public officials. However, such a public display of support on the eve of a national election was so blatant that even Criswell came under attack from fellow Baptists for having crossed the invisible line separating church and state. In North Carolina Wake Forest University president James Ralph Scales and Sanford business leader George McCotter countered by forming a group calling itself Baptist Laymen for Carter. At a Baptist conference in Little Rock, several pastors called a press conference denouncing Criswell's endorsement. The Dallas Pastors Association condemned Criswell for making political comments from the pulpit. And Baptist General Convention of

Texas president James G. Harris said he personally did not endorse candidates. The criticism seemed only to embolden Criswell, who repeated his attacks on Carter. "My land," Criswell told a reporter, "I just expressed an opinion. If we can't state an opinion, we have lost our democracy."[36]

Criswell's endorsement fueled speculation in the press that religion was already playing too much of a role in politics because of Carter's self-professed born-again evangelical faith. Arthur Schlesinger Jr., for example, charged that a person's religion or lack thereof should be private and "should stay out of politics." But in a move that would later give them reason for pause, liberal church leaders came out in favor of mixing religion and politics. New York's Union Theological Seminary president Donald Shriver, for example, defended Carter, arguing, "Biblical faith includes both dimensions, the personal and the social." With Dr. Martin Luther King Jr., Reinhold Niebuhr, and many other pastors and theologians having spoken on social and political issues, Shriver thought it beyond debate that a presidential candidate should be free to voice religious convictions. "It's almost as if a politician merely mentions the name of God, it's some kind of heresy," Shriver observed. "Many people are interested in knowing the religious convictions of national leaders. It's a basic, motivating influence."[37]

Carter's victory tamped down Criswell's criticisms, causing him even to declare that Carter was a fine Christian who deserved everyone's prayers. But Criswell's concerns about big government continued. Shortly after the 1976 election Criswell was the keynote speaker in Del City, Oklahoma, at the annual meeting of the Baptist General Convention of Oklahoma. The Oklahoma convention had experienced a twenty-five percent increase in baptisms over the past ten years and the Del City church with some 3,500 members was the largest one in the state. Criswell told the crowd that evil forces were trying to seduce America into secularism and materialism. The convention also discussed the perceived threat against conservative Baptists from the federal government. "Government should not be allowed to investigate the financial records of churches or of religious organizations because of their activity in carrying out their concept of the mission of the church," a leader of the Oklahoma conference declared, "even if that mission means activity to influence legislation and the formation of public policy."[38]

By 1979 Criswell's influence seemed unbounded. At age seventy he was in good health, worked out at the YMCA every day, routinely made headlines, and pastored what journalists usually described as the largest congregation in America, if not in the world. The church was not only large in numbers; it was also where the rich and famous showed they were devout Christians by holding membership and donating generously. Hunt's wife gave $800,000 to purchase the old downtown YMCA building for use as the new Criswell Center for Biblical Studies. Mary Crowley, wealthy founder and president of Home Interiors and Gifts, gave the church $750,000, and members matched it in one evening to cover the cost of the new Mary Crowley Building. The total value of Criswell's church property in downtown Dallas was $18 million on the books, and leaders said in reality it was closer to $25 million. As a person of deep faith, Criswell naturally gave God the credit for the ministry's success. But nothing was left to chance. In 1979 the congregation with great fanfare accepted its twenty thousandth member. That member just happened to be Dallas Cowboys place kicker Rafael Septien. And at the same service commentator Paul Harvey became member number 20,001.[39]

In 1980 Criswell's influence became especially evident in what sociologist D. Michael Lindsay has termed convening power. Lindsay's argument in examining a later generation of evangelical pastors, business executives, and government leaders is that their influence is easily underestimated if only the extent of their wealth or even the frequency with which they are featured in the media is considered. Their behind-the-scenes influence, Lindsay suggests, is typically expressed in being able to convene meetings by calling in personal favors and cultivating networks to whom only a few have access.[40] "Opportunity hoarding" is the less charitable term sociologist Charles Tilly invented to describe the same phenomenon. It operates, Tilley wrote, "when members of a categorically bounded network acquire access to a resource that is valuable, renewable, subject to monopoly, supportive of network activities, and enhanced by the network's modus operandi."[41] Examples might include racially segregated country clubs with membership fees only the superwealthy can afford or high-priced study retreats for the wealthiest board members of an Ivy League university.

Convening power uses social capital to get the right people together and to exclude others. Reagan's trip to Dallas for the National Affairs Briefing in 1980 included a private reception at the Hyatt Regency. The host was Criswell's wealthy church member and faithful donor Mary Crowley. A majority of the select group were also members of the First Baptist Church. They included oil baron Clint Murchison and his wife, Cullen Davis and his wife, and Eddie Chiles and his wife. Associate pastor Dr. Paige Patterson and his wife were there. A guest not from Criswell's church was Dr. B. Clayton Bell, Billy Graham's brother-in-law who pastored the metroplex's large, upscale Highland Park Presbyterian Church and who had officiated at the weddings of H. L. Hunt's granddaughters Ellen Finley Hunt and Elizabeth Bunker Hunt. Their parents, Mr. and Mrs. Nelson Bunker Hunt, who had recently spearheaded a $60 million Campus Crusade for Christ fundraising campaign, were among the guests at the Reagan reception. Another guest was Judge Paul Pressler of Houston, one of the most outspoken supporters of the fundamentalist wing in the Southern Baptist Convention. Criswell presented Reagan with a Bible and told him to use it for the swearing-in ceremony in January.[42]

BAPTIST BATTLES

It is impossible to fully appreciate Criswell's role and that of other religious leaders in 1980 apart from the battle for control of the Southern Baptist Convention that was occurring in the late 1970s. The skirmishes that had erupted periodically from the 1890s through the 1950s in which fundamentalists accused fellow Southern Baptists as well as pastors and seminary professors from other denominations of heresy returned on a wider scale than ever before. The conflict pitted fundamentalists who believed that the Bible should be interpreted as liter-ally inspired and free of historical and scientific errors against moderates willing to embrace at least some room for variation in human interpretation and the historical record. Why the controversy erupted when it did can be traced to sev-eral dynamics within the denomination and the wider society. Southern Baptist pastors of course disagreed with one another during the civil rights movement about the pace of change and what the denomination's position should be. In those years, younger and better-educated pastors and lay leaders increasingly sided with the denomination's Christian Life Commission that favored more progressive steps toward integration against the wishes of older and more con-servative gradualists. In the 1960s Southern Baptists took differing views of the policies toward women's ordination that were dividing other denominations and were being discussed in some Southern Baptist congregations. Personalities and struggles for the control of seminaries and colleges mattered. There were also concerns that fundamentalists inspired by high-profile leaders such as Falwell were leaving the denomination and joining independent Baptist fellowships.

Sociologist Nancy Tatom Ammerman, who conducted an extensive study of the conflict, including results from a survey of Southern Baptist pastors and laity, found that socioeconomic factors and location also made a difference. Moder-ates tended to be better-educated, middle-class members with above-average incomes, and they lived in cities and suburbs where they attended large Baptist congregations. The fundamentalists included both middle-class and working-class members, but they were more likely to have grown up on farms or in lower-income families, and they were more likely to attend rural churches or small urban congregations. There was a kind of "us versus them" mentality among the fundamentalists, as one pastor explained, an outsider mindset that pitted believ-ers against the world and especially against those who went to college and got an education.[43]

In 1979 the conflict took on additional importance when Criswell's associ-ate pastor, Patterson, and Judge Pressler mounted a highly publicized six-month campaign to ensure that the next SBC president would be a fundamentalist. Pat-terson was a graduate of Hardin-Simmons University in Abilene and New Or-leans Seminary, a well-known polemicist and preacher, and the son of a promi-nent pastor who had been chief executive of the Baptist General Convention of Texas. In 1970 the younger Patterson became the president of Criswell College, the Bible institute that Criswell founded with the help of several wealthy donors to promote premillennial and dispensationalist theological training. Pressler was a Southern Baptist lay leader whose hackles had been raised in 1961 by a professor at Midwestern Baptist Theological Seminary in Kansas City who pub-lished a book on Genesis that Pressler thought deviated from biblical truth about creation. Surprised that the professor was not immediately rebuked, Pressler wrote later that he was "absolutely appalled by the way that was handled and that let me know there was liberalism" in the denomination. To Pressler's dismay, he discovered that the books students were reading at Baylor were also "just liberal garbage." That discovery prompted him to enlist Patterson in hopes of turning the denomination around.[44]

Patterson argued that the administrators and faculty at the denomination's six theological seminaries and several of its colleges were straying from the denomination's 1963 statement of faith that affirmed the infallibility of scripture. Stung by the accusations, the six seminary heads came to Dallas and met personally with Criswell and Patterson. Following the meeting, the group announced that the seminary presidents denied any preferences for liberal interpretations of the Bible and were firmly in support of teaching and preaching biblical infallibility. Three weeks later in Houston at the denomination's annual conference, the nearly twelve thousand delegates approved Patterson's handpicked candidate, Dr. Adrian Rogers, a Memphis pastor committed to biblical inerrancy.[45]

Rogers's election is credited as the major step in what became known as the conservative resurgence within the Southern Baptist Convention. Over the next decade fundamentalists won every election for the denomination's highest office and successfully appointed likeminded leaders to key positions on denominational boards and at seminaries and colleges. The longer-term impact reinforced the denomination's support of conservative social and political as well as theological issues. Its near-term impact was conservative mobilization across the South and especially in Texas. To ensure success for their side, Patterson and Pressler canvassed Texas and persuaded a large number of conservatives to attend the denominational conference in Houston, including as many as several hundred who did so without having been properly elected as delegates from their congregations. When Rogers expressed uncertainty about allowing himself to be nominated, Patterson was on hand to persuade him that the presidency was God's will.[46]

Despite Patterson and Pressler's role in mobilizing the conservative resurgence, Ammerman's study found that pastors from Texas and neighboring states were not substantially more likely than pastors from elsewhere in the South to identify themselves as conservatives. Her survey, conducted in 1985, nevertheless showed how decisively the denomination's pastors tilted toward conservatism. Among all Southern Baptist pastors surveyed, only 19 percent said they were moderates or moderate conservatives, while 49 percent said they were conservatives and 33 percent said they were fundamentalists. Among pastors in Texas and neighboring states, only 15 percent were moderates, 47 percent were conservatives, and 38 percent were fundamentalists.[47]

The conservative resurgence among Southern Baptists places Criswell and the First Baptist Church of Dallas in a larger perspective. Although Patterson's role was obvious and direct, that was only part of the story. There were plenty of pastors in Texas and across the South who identified themselves as fundamentalists and conservatives. But few of them had the kind of credentials that gave them much in the way of cultural capital beyond their own congregations. In Ammerman's study only 33 percent of self-identified fundamentalist pastors had a college degree, let alone any training beyond college, and although higher education was more common among pastors who said they were fundamentalist conservatives, only a third of that group had postbaccalaureate degrees.[48] That contrasted sharply with Criswell and the leadership at First Baptist.

The simplest way to describe Criswell's influence is that many pastors and laity espoused fundamentalism, but Criswell made it respectable. He did so in several ways. As pastor and preacher, he demonstrated that a fundamentalist who interpreted the Bible literally could also be well read, conversant with literature, and capable of holding his own in any circle of well-educated people. From working with him in what was seldom an easy relationship, Dr. Gregory observed that in Criswell "the right-wing of American Christianity had a genuine Ph.D. who could quote Shakespeare and Browning by the mile from memory as well as he could the Apostle Paul." As a person, Criswell demonstrated not only a photographic memory and keen intellect in sermons but also a taste for travel, music, art, and antiques, including a collection that would have shocked many of his members had they known its extent and true value. And as leader of a congregation that included expensive downtown real estate and everything from ministries for the homeless to its own bowling alley and skating rink, Criswell showed without necessarily preaching about success that faith and worldly success were by no means incompatible. Having a deacon board of distinguished Dallas attorneys, bankers, and oil executives spread the same message. So did one of the church's most popular Sunday school teachers, the nationally acclaimed motivational speaker Zig Ziglar.[49]

How much the prestige, power, and educational credentials on display at Criswell's church mattered can be understood in relation to wider changes taking place among evangelicals in the 1970s. As the number of younger Americans going to college climbed from approximately seven million in 1970 to more than twelve million in 1980, the proportion of evangelicals who were college-educated increased as well. By 1980, four in ten Southern Baptists nationwide had some training beyond high school.[50] That was well below the proportion in other large denominations, but it accentuated the status differences within the denomination. On the one hand, skepticism persisted toward the well-educated elite who were considered a corrosive influence on tradition-minded people. A commonly held view among conservatives, for example, was that the best and brightest went off to seminaries in New York and Boston, got "swept off their feet," and came home too proud to sit in clapboard churches singing "Are you washed in the blood of the lamb?"[51] Against such temptations, it was good that a preacher as intellectually sophisticated as Criswell could write a book called *Why I Preach That the Bible Is Literally True.*[52] On the other hand, the kind of status anxiety

implied in criticisms of the educated elite suggested that fundamentalists themselves yearned for greater respect. No longer was it quite enough for a country
boy to start preaching as a teenager. An earned degree was better than an honorary title. It was reassuring to hear a pastor like Criswell conjugating Greek verbs
from the pulpit.

AN EQUAL ROLE FOR WOMEN

Against the backdrop of conservative preachers arguing about immorality and
government intrusion on their ministries, shifting arguments about gender roles
and the empowerment of women became an additional source of contestation.
By 1970 more than three million women nationwide were enrolled as students
in colleges and universities, and while the ratio of men to women was still 3:2 at
these institutions, almost three times as many women were going to college that
year than a decade earlier. In Texas 30 percent of women in their twenties had at
least some college training in 1970 compared with 40 percent of men. Women
were also increasingly involved in the paid labor force. While the proportion
of single women nationwide who were employed (about half) was the same as
in 1950, the proportion of married women who were employed rose from only
25 percent in 1950 to 41 percent in 1970.[53] In Texas nearly half (48 percent) of
women between the ages of eighteen and sixty-five were in the labor force.[54] Outside of work and family, women's involvement in public life continued to include
participation in churches and clubs, civic associations, advocacy organizations,
and service activities. As women entered the labor force, secured positions in
professional occupations such as law and medicine, and became more active in
advocacy organizations, they were increasingly exposed to instances of gender
discrimination, received lower salaries than men for similar work, and faced
mixed signals about what opportunities should be open to women and which
ones conformed best to expectations about gender roles.

In 1972 the U.S. Congress approved wording of a constitutional amendment
that, if ratified, would prohibit discrimination on the basis of sex. Ratification
of the Equal Rights Amendment (ERA) required approval by thirty-eight states
before March 22, 1979. Following failed attempts in the Texas legislature during
the 1960s to secure passage of laws prohibiting sex discrimination, the Texas
legislature ratified the federal amendment in March 1972, and voters approved
by 4-to-1 a state constitutional equal rights amendment eight months later.[55] By
1976 thirty-four states had ratified the amendment, which made the issue all the
more salient in the remaining states as well as in several states where ratification
was in danger of being rescinded.

The wide margin by which the state amendment had been approved in 1972
suggested that the matter of equal rights for women might have been settled
at that point in Texas. However, the federal amendment generated increasing

debate. In 1974 Maine and Montana became the thirty-first and thirty-second
states to vote for ratification, giving proponents hope that six more would soon
follow suit. But in Tennessee lawmakers debated rescinding their state's approval
following worries that the ERA would cause women to be drafted and sent to battle even if they were pregnant. Soon after, Florida legislators narrowly defeated a
step toward ratification in their state. In response, the National Organization of
Women and the League of Women Voters ramped up efforts to secure passage in
other states, and President Ford declared August 26, 1974, as Women's Equality
Day, urging Americans across the nation to work for final ratification of the ERA.
Between then and the 1976 presidential election, the ERA became a front-burner
issue nearly everywhere. Lawmakers in North Dakota approved it, but Tennessee
voted for rescission. In March 1975 Indiana and South Carolina defeated efforts
for ratification. In April efforts to advance ratification failed in Illinois, Florida,
and Missouri. The same outcome occurred that summer in Louisiana and the
following March in Arizona.

The ERA mobilized women as well as men on both sides of the issue. Whether
to vote in a state referendum to ratify it and whether to push for or against rescission solidified what was otherwise a complex issue on which many different
perspectives could have been taken into a forced choice. A person was either for
the ERA or against it. The fact that women played leadership roles in opposing it
as well as in favoring it illustrated two important aspects of the debate. Women's
involvement in civic activities and the fact that many were well educated and
held leadership positions in their communities meant that they were prepared
to engage with the debate about ERA ratification, whether that meant organizing
local events for speakers, serving as journalists and columnists for local newspapers, forming grassroots groups to get out the vote, or simply writing letters and
signing petitions. The other aspect was that the debate drew and reinforced a new
symbolic distinction transecting the larger gendered categories of male and female. The distinction was most clearly expressed in the term feminist. A woman
was no longer simply a woman, wife, mother, or homemaker, but a feminist or
antifeminist. Both sides argued that theirs reflected the best understanding of
biological differences between men and women, the truest way of protecting
the special roles and rights of women, and the clearest ideas about equality and
inequality.

Religion was an important part of the debate for several reasons. For those
who took the Bible seriously and who regularly heard sermons based on scripture as well as having grown up learning Bible stories, religion was a source of authoritative wisdom about gender roles. It included narratives about women who
faithfully served their husbands as well as texts explaining that women should be
submissive members of their households. It included other stories about strong
women with direct relationships to God as well as scripture injunctions about
gender equality, social justice, and helping people who were disadvantaged. In
congregations, women participated in Bible study groups, taught Sunday school

classes, and sometimes served on church boards. In addition, the question of whether women should be ordained as lay leaders and preachers was being widely debated and voted on in many of the major Protestant denominations, while among Catholics after the Second Vatican Council new ideas were being discussed about ways of empowering women laity as well as men while stopping short of altering traditional teachings about male celibacy as the necessary qualification for priesthood. Alternative understandings of gender equality were thus a matter of public discussion within religious circles at the same time that these discussions were becoming politically salient in relation to the question of ratifying the ERA.

Several denominations, including Congregationalists, Disciples of Christ, and Universalists, had permitted women to be ordained since the nineteenth century, but questions about ordination had never been debated as broadly or in as many denominations simultaneously as in the decade and a half prior to the controversy surrounding the ERA. Through wide-ranging discussions and changes in denominational rules, the Methodist Church and the northern branch of the Presbyterian Church voted to permit women to be ordained in 1956. Those decisions were followed in 1960 by the African Methodist Episcopal Church and in 1964 by the southern branch of Presbyterians. Then in 1970 the American Lutheran Church and Lutheran Church in America followed suit. The Episcopal Church did so in 1976, and the Reformed Church in America made the change in 1979. Meanwhile, seven smaller denominations also undertook rule revisions about women's ordination. The changes generated almost as much discussion and controversy as women's suffrage had in earlier decades. Biblical interpretation was necessarily involved as clergy and lay leaders reexamined the meaning of scriptural teachings about gender both inside and beyond the church itself. Politicking occurred at church conventions and included the various perspectives of parish pastors, missionaries, women's groups, and college faculty. Once the decision was made to allow women to be ordained, congregations faced questions about whom to hire and in what capacity. Many of the denominations, seminaries, and church-related colleges also wrestled with questions about gender-inclusive language in lectionaries, hymnbooks, and Bible translations. Studies showed that differences of opinion were still well in evidence in the 1980s, and that these differences typically fell along lines of age, education, region, and theological orientation.[56]

The first ordination of a woman to the ministry in the Southern Baptist Convention occurred in 1964, but the woman, Addie Davis of Durham, North Carolina, moved north after failing to find a pulpit anywhere in the South. A decade later only fifteen Southern Baptist women had been ordained, and nearly all of them went into nonparish work, such as college chaplaincies and counseling. The most public endorsement of the Equal Rights Amendment came at a meeting of the denomination's Woman's Missionary Union in San Antonio in October 1976 when the group's president expressed support of the measure and called on Baptist women to use their power to bring about social change. The denomination's male leaders were not in total agreement about women's roles in the church, but in the survey Ammerman conducted in 1986 only 2 percent of the respondents said their congregation had ordained a woman. Sixty-nine percent said they did not favor the Equal Rights Amendment.[57] At Criswell's church in Dallas, members undoubtedly held varying opinions about the ERA, but the church's official stance on gender equality was clear. Women were not allowed to preach or to serve as deacons. The one notable exception was Mrs. Criswell, who held considerable behind-the-scenes power and taught a popular Sunday school class. The policy that permitted her to do so was that she was nominally under the authority of her husband. Criswell himself felt that women's place was in the home and that if women ever chose something other than that God-intended role, society was in mortal danger.[58]

Opinion polls conducted among the general public showed that attitudes toward gender issues were complex. In a nationally representative survey conducted in 1976, for example, 66 percent of the women interviewed agreed that "many qualified women can't get good jobs [while] men with the same skills have much less trouble." Fifty-two percent of the women surveyed agreed that to overcome discrimination, "women must work together to change laws and customs that are unfair to all women." But on another question, 78 percent of the women said the "best way to handle problems of discrimination is for each woman to make sure she gets the best training possible for what she wants to do," while only 22 percent said "only if women organize and work together can anything really be done about discrimination." When asked directly about the Equal Rights Amendment, 67 percent of the women said they approved of it. Views of the "women's liberation movement," though, were more evenly divided, with 51 percent of the women saying its influence was about right, 17 percent saying its influence was too little, and 32 percent saying its influence was too much.[59]

The responses to these questions varied by age, race, and region; by political party affiliation; by whether a woman was currently working; and by whether she had graduated from college. But taking account of these differences, the strongest influences were religious participation and ideology. The odds of favoring the Equal Rights Amendment were about a quarter lower among women who attended religious services weekly than among women who attended less often. And these odds were further reduced by more than half among women who said they felt close to "conservatives."[60]

How the ERA generated discussions that made these differences more politically salient at the local level was illustrated in numerous events during the 1970s. For example, a prominent women's club in Corsicana whose leaders had long been involved in service activities for the community organized a meeting in April 1975 to discuss the ERA. The speaker was a well-educated man whose credentials included coming from "two well-known [local] families." In his remarks, which were also carried in a report by the women's editor of the *Corsicana*

Daily Sun, he assured the crowd that he fully believed that women were equal to men and should receive equal pay for equal work. He was also certain, however, that men "are more muscular, more agile and daring than their consorts," and that a woman's place was that of "lover, mother, and keeper of the hearth." The Equal Rights Amendment, he declared, was "hogwash," a violation of everything he had been taught and everything he revered. The amendment struck at the very heart of family life, in his view. If it were passed, women would be responsible for the financial support of their families, divorced women would no longer be entitled to child support, and children would be packed off to day-care centers like they were under Hitler's regime.[61]

Advocacy organizations to promote the ERA or to oppose it mobilized constituents, forged connections with national associations, and elevated leaders to public prominence in ways that symbolized what each side stood for and sharpened the differences in public perceptions. On the pro-ERA side, the Texas Women's Political Caucus was founded in 1971 under the leadership of Dallas attorney Hermine Dalkowitz Tobolowsky and played a key role in the state's ratification process in 1972. Other prominent leaders with positions in the professions, government, or business included attorney Gretchen Raatz, Chicana businesswoman Olga Soliz, African American state representative Eddie Bernice Johnson, state board of education member Jane Wells, El Paso county clerk Alicia Chacon, San Antonio mayor Lila Cockrell, assistant attorney general Martha Smiley, and state representative Sarah Weddington. Organizations that supported the ERA ranged from local groups, such as the Dallas nonprofit planning organization Women for Change, led by feminist Beverly Myres, to statewide organizations, such as the Texas Nurses Association and Tejanos for Political Action, to chapters of national associations, such as the American Bar Association, Association of American University Women, National Organization for Women, and the National Federation of Business and Professional Women's Clubs. More than a dozen religious organizations, including Church Women United, the National United Methodist Women's Caucus, and the Presbyterian General Assembly, also supported the ERA.

Organizations that formed in opposition to the ERA in Texas included American Women Are Richly Endowed (AWARE), Committee to Restore Women's Rights, Concerned Citizens for Feminine Freedom, Humanitarians Opposed to Degrading Our Girls (HOTDOG), Happiness of Womanhood (HOW), Stop Taking Our Privileges (STOP), and Women Who Want to Be Women (WWWW). Local parent-teacher organizations, women's clubs, and churches sometimes voiced opposition, as did the Church of Jesus Christ of Latter-day Saints and the Archdiocesan Council of Catholic Women. The WWWW, under the direction of founder Lottie Beth Hobbs, was one of the most active anti-ERA organizations in Texas. A lay leader, church secretary, and Bible teacher in the evangelical Churches of Christ denomination, Hobbs gained a following in the 1960s by authoring a series of Bible study guides and devotional books oriented toward women readers on topics such as *Mary and Martha*, *Your Best Friend*, and *Victory over Trials*. Disturbed by the Equal Rights Amendment, she prepared a flyer titled "Ladies! Have You Heard?" which the printer who worked on her books dressed up in pink and made ten thousand copies of, which she then distributed on church literature tables and got reprinted in small-town newspapers. The flyer wove warnings about threats to wives and children from disgruntled militant feminists with biblical statements about God calling women to a beautiful and exalted place at home.[62] The flyer's success facilitated the founding of the WWWW, which she described as an association of "fundamental Bible-believing people, people who believe in the family as the building block for a stable society." The group's principles included belief in the Bible, opposition to secular humanist philosophy, and conviction that husbands should be family heads and providers with wives serving as full-time homemakers.[63]

By late fall 1974 it was evident that efforts would be made when the Texas legislature convened in January to persuade it to rescind the state's 1972 ratification of the ERA. That possibility propelled groups on both sides to mobilize petition drives, hold public meetings, and stage demonstrations. Organizations such as the Texas Women's Political Caucus that had worked for ratification were joined by new groups, such as the Dallas Committee of Texans for the ERA, and gained support from established organizations, such as the League of Women Voters and Texas Conference of Churches, in lobbying to fend off rescission. On the other side, WWWW members demonstrated against the ERA wearing army uniforms, hard hats, and football uniforms to illustrate the roles women would be expected to play if the ERA became national law.[64] They persuaded Representative Bill Hilliard, a conservative Democratic insurance executive from Fort Worth, to introduce a rescission bill. Hilliard was an active member of the Sagamore Hill Baptist Church, where he served as superintendent of the Sunday school.[65] The Sagamore Hill church was an evangelistic-minded congregation the associate pastor of which in the early 1970s was Jack Graham, who later became the head pastor of Plano's eleven-thousand-member Prestonwood Baptist Church and served two terms as president of the Southern Baptist Convention.[66] "I want the state to take care of its own," Hilliard declared, "and leave the federal government out of Texas' business."[67]

A study conducted by two political scientists at the University of Houston among 154 women who appeared at the Texas capital on April 14, 1975, to advocate rescission found that nearly all the women were white, middle-aged, and middle to upper-middle class. The majority had attended college, but two-thirds had grown up in small towns or rural areas, and three-quarters were housewives. Nearly all were church members, and two-thirds were fundamentalists. Like Hobbs, many were members of the Churches of Christ. Ninety-one percent agreed that "the federal government is taking away our basic freedoms," and 88 percent agreed that the nation had moved "dangerously close to socialism."[68]

The conservative activism that spring, columnist Richard Morehead observed, was a potentially powerful force in the state's politics that contrasted sharply with the more familiar liberal mobilization that had occurred in relation to the Vietnam War and civil rights. The presidential candidate most likely to benefit from this activism, Morehead predicted, was Reagan, whose radio broadcasts and newspaper columns were well-known in Texas and who was coming to a fundraiser in Dallas a few months later. Already there was a conservative Republican caucus that would indeed turn in a strong showing for Reagan and at the Republican National Convention in Kansas City the following year lead an unsuccessful effort on the platform committee to oppose ratification of the ERA.[69]

Meanwhile, both sides of the ERA forged stronger network ties between local and national organizations and increased the topic's political salience. At the thousand-member National Women's Political Caucus convention in Boston in July 1975, Texas women in leadership roles included Liz Carpenter, former press secretary for Lady Bird Johnson and vice president of the international public relations firm Hill & Knowlton, TWPC cofounder Jane Wells, and outgoing national chair Frances Sissy Farenthold. On the other side, Hobbs was working to turn the WWWW into a national network and was aligning the organization more closely with Phyllis Schlafly's Stop ERA movement and Eagle Forum, in which Hobbs would later serve as vice president. Schlafly was a well-educated, conservative Catholic Republican who had written seven books, penned numerous newspaper columns, and become the most visible leader on the national stage opposing the ERA. She considered feminism a threat to homes, husbands, families, and children and blamed women's liberation for the rising divorce rate. She also considered the struggle one of protecting states' rights against the federal government. In a speech to the Public Affairs Luncheon Club of Dallas on March 15, 1976, she argued that pro-ERA groups were "trying to cram the Equal Rights Amendment down our throats with federal money." "It's all a grab for power at the federal level," she declared. "They're trying to take the last remaining jurisdiction from the states."[70]

Whether mobilization for or against the ERA affected voter turnout in 1976 was difficult to determine. Certainly both sides hoped that it did. A study comparing turnout among women and men found that turnout was 4.9 percent higher among men than among women in 1964 but was only 0.8 percent higher in 1976. However, the change appeared to be entirely attributable to women's increasing participation in the labor force. Comparisons of turnout among men and women taking account of whether they were employed or not showed almost identical rates between men and women within employment categories in both elections.[71]

More relevant than turnout differences between men and women, though, were the differences between conservatives and moderates or liberals. Among all white southerners, 85 percent of conservative women voted in 1976 compared with only 58 percent of nonconservative women, and among men, 88 percent of the former voted compared with only 63 percent of the latter. The importance of these differences was further evidenced by the fact that in national data several constituencies that generally favored the ERA—those with college educations, African Americans, and employed persons—had higher than average turnout rates while southerners had lower than average turnout rates, but these influences were countered by higher than average turnout rates among Republicans, weekly churchgoers, and conservatives. Indeed, when all these factors were taken into account, the odds of having voted in 1976 were three and a half times as high among conservatives as among nonconservatives.[72]

Further indication of the salience of the Equal Rights Amendment was evident in a 1978 CBS Election Day Survey in which voters were asked if the ERA had made a difference in how they voted. The national data showed that almost 40 percent of voters said it had mattered, although it was unclear from the raw results just how it may have mattered. More telling results were evident when the responses of southern Republican women voters were examined in relation to who they hoped would win the presidency in 1980. Among those who said the ERA mattered, 57 percent hoped Reagan would win, compared to only 37 percent among those who said the ERA had not mattered.[73]

Through 1976 most of the efforts for and against the ERA in Texas had been locally organized and focused on state more than on national policies, with the latter shaping opinion mostly through news reports and the 1976 presidential election. On November 18, 1977, Texas became the center of national attention because of two simultaneous conventions that opened that day in Houston. At the Albert Thomas Convention Center some ten thousand delegates and supporters from across the nation gathered for the International Women's Year National Women's Conference at which Betty Friedan, Barbara Jordan, and other noted leaders spoke, while across town at the Astro Arena some twenty thousand women convened at a Pro-Family Rally under the leadership of Hobbs and with Phyllis Schlafly as one of its keynote speakers. "Women's libbers, follow Jesus Christ and your husband and your pastor, repent," one of the signs at the Astro Arena read. Although Schlafly's earlier efforts on behalf of Goldwater and against communism in the 1960s had garnered some interest and financial support from H. L. Hunt and her newsletter was well-known to Hobbs and other anti-ERA leaders, her Stop ERA network had been preoccupied mostly in other states where more active legislation was pending. Schlafly regarded the Houston conference as the decisive turning point that spelled doom for the ERA partly because of the enormous enthusiasm generated by the profamily event but even more so because of what happened at the other conference, where abortion rights and lesbian rights had been embraced more publicly than ever before. The feminist movement, Schlafly declared, "has sealed its own doom by deliberately hanging around its own neck the albatross of abortion, lesbianism, pornography and federal control."[74]

As the March 1979 deadline approached, ERA advocates successfully petitioned Congress for an extension until June 30, 1982. Efforts focused on securing ratification in Illinois, Florida, North Carolina, Missouri, and Oklahoma, but none of these efforts succeeded. Meanwhile, Kentucky and South Dakota rescinded their previous ERA votes. Pro-ERA leaders stuck to their guns, as political scientist Jane Mansbridge showed in her brilliant requiem, *Why We Lost the ERA*, not acceding to the criticisms opponents levied against the movement, but arguing that the amendment would indeed bring about much needed significant change.[75] The shifting tide that resulted in defeat not only mobilized conservative women but also reduced the prospects for moderate Republicans who had supported the ERA, especially if they were also defenders of abortion rights.

Like the civil rights movement, Chicano activism, and previous efforts to alter the social position and power of different parts of society, the ERA ratification efforts showed that symbolic boundaries dividing "us" and "them" do not simply emerge full-blown from human propensities for categorization or from institutional arrangements. Symbolic boundaries are the result of contestation involving the strategic deployment of catch phrases and labels that inflect the categories with meaning. The labels that serve conveniently as shorthand signifiers in news stories, polls, and political campaigns convey ideas about values that are implicitly respected or that are said to be deserving of respect. The claim is not only a call for recognition but also an implicit understanding of why recognition is merited.

Leaders play important roles in mobilizing support through speeches and statements to the media, and they formulate policies that sometimes result in effective legislation or the blockage of legislation. But leaders also dramatize the symbolic meanings and perceptions associated with particular "us" and "them" categories. On the pro-ERA side, the most prominent leaders in Texas symbolized the new possibilities for career advancement in the professions, government, and business that women could achieve and the struggles against discrimination that these achievements so frequently required. The personal and organizational networks involved were of value not only as social ties but also in further demonstrating that the ERA was a legitimate endeavor accorded with respect from national organizations with credentials in the professions, government, and business. Leaders were keenly aware of the symbolic importance of demonstrating their commitment to inclusiveness and of cultivating larger constituencies by including Chicana and African American women as well as women of white Anglo descent and by transcending the political lines separating Democrats and moderate Republicans. They knew the ERA held less appeal among homemakers than it did for workingwomen, but they sought to overcome that disadvantage through meetings in rural areas and by cultivating support from labor unions.

Both sides explicitly cultivated religion in ways that dramatized different connections between religious identities and the ERA. The pro-ERA side drew connections with the more liberal and moderate Protestant denominations that had been more supportive of racial integration and had shifted toward

ordaining women clergy. Few of the most prominent leaders in Texas identified themselves primarily through a connection with religious organizations,
but varying personal affinities were present. Tobolowsky was Jewish, taught
and sang in the choir at Temple Beth-El in San Antonio, and kept active relations over the years with Jewish organizations; Smiley was a graduate of Baylor
University where she had served as student body president; Weddington was
the daughter of a Methodist minister and grew up playing the church organ
and giving Sunday devotionals; and Myres was an elected elder in her Presbyterian church and served as a commissioner to the Presbyterian General Assembly.[76] The anti-ERA side's religious connections were evident in Hilliard's
Baptist membership and especially through Hobbs's appearances at churches
and frequent references to biblical teachings. Hobbs argued that the ERA was a
moral issue that churches should address because its humanist agenda clashed
fundamentally with Christianity.

As the debate about the ERA took root, opponents gained ground by increasingly arguing that they were the profamily side of the debate and suggesting by
implication that ERA supporters were antifamily. Opposition to the ERA was
thus publicly described as something other than what its demographic correlates
may have suggested. It was presented, not as the position of a constituency that
was older, less well educated, and unsupportive of gender equality; it was rather
that part of the population that believed in the virtues of strong families. That
definition resonated especially well with married heterosexual couples who either had children or hoped to have them, and it played well among active church
members whose congregations generally encouraged marriage and provided
family-centered programs for married adults and children. By implication, the
"other" who supported the ERA were men who got their girlfriends pregnant and
failed to stay around to parent their children, unwed mothers who deviated from
patterns of ideal two-parent families, women who valued family life so little that
they aborted their fetuses, married or single women who valued a career more
than motherhood, and homosexuals.

How difficult it was for ERA supporters to counter the impression of being
antifamily was evident in 1977 when delegates met in Houston. Press releases
emphasized that many of the women at the conference were good wives and
mothers. Editorials favoring the resolution encouraged readers to consider the
fact that all the ERA did was ban discrimination on the basis of sex and not to be
swayed by emotionally charged language about it being antifamily. But some of
the newspapers that carried these articles and editorials also published a political
cartoon that spoke eloquently. The cartoon depicted a woman wearing an ERA
button struggling desperately to stay afloat in a tempestuous sea, surely destined
to drown because of four huge boulders roped to her neck and pulling her down.
The boulders were labeled government child support, gay rights, abortion issue,
and feminists' demands.[77] Opponents' success in casting the ERA as an antifamily amendment associated with radical feminism, homosexuality, and abortion

was evident in public opinion. The proportion of women favoring the ERA declined from 67 percent in 1976 to 48 percent in 1978 and rose modestly only to 53 percent in 1980. In 1980, 32 percent said they disapproved of it, up from 16 percent in 1976.[78]

ROE V. WADE AND BEYOND

Like the ERA, abortion generated discussions about rights, freedom, and whether the federal government was friend or foe. Abortion became one of the defining culture war issues of the 1980s and was hotly contested by religious leaders. But well before the U.S. Supreme Court's 1973 decision in *Roe v. Wade*, abortion evoked sharply differing public interpretations. In one view, abortionists and the clientele they served connoted moral debauchery similar to that of drug users, adulterers, and communists. A well-publicized 1964 case in Dallas, for example, accused the male defendant not only of having attempted to perform an abortion but also of adultery, molestation, lewdness, drunken driving, and several other unnamed immoral acts.[79] The Walter Jenkins incident and accusations of moral decline that critics of the Johnson administration voiced that fall included allegations that Washington cronies were running call girl and abortion rackets.[80] But other discussions considered it unfortunate that women were dying because professionally performed abortions were unavailable. One estimate suggested that nationwide more than a million illegal abortions were being performed every year, and that at least five thousand women annually died as a result.[81] Responding to the tragedy of thalidomide-induced birth defects and considering the more general issue of dramatically rising population growth, community organizations sponsored symposia to discuss the possible legalization of abortion.[82] As the sexual revolution took hold, the story line in motion pictures and novels wrestled with teen pregnancy, failed contraception, and ethical questions surrounding abortion. Health officials in Dallas estimated that for every four births, there was at least one abortion.[83]

Steps toward legalizing abortion under carefully defined special circumstances were proposed during the 1960s with little avail. In 1966 forty-one states, including Texas, permitted therapeutic abortions only if necessary to save the life of the mother. Discussions about the possibility of easing restrictions were initiated by the Texas Medical Association, which saw the need to include consideration of impaired physical and psychological health of the mother, birth defects, and pregnancy from forcible rape or incest.[84] The health policy discussions broached ethical questions as well, such as whether it was more desirable to perform an abortion or force a rape victim to continue an unwanted pregnancy. These questions connected with larger cultural debates. One was the debate in theological circles prompted by the concept of situational ethics, which suggested that absolute moral standards should be compromised by reasoned consideration of utilitarian assessments having to do with personal happiness.[85] The other was the one Goldwater, evangelist Billy Graham, and countless others had been voicing about the moral decline of American culture. Easy access to abortion was one more indication that the nation was sliding down a path of sexual permissiveness toward moral oblivion.

As the Texas legislature in 1967 considered a bill easing restrictions on abortion, Catholic Charities director Reverend John A. Matzner published an editorial in *The Texas Catholic* condemning the measure. Matzner argued that the issue was not about compassionate concern for the mother or well-being of the baby, but about the rights of an unborn infant. An unborn infant with a grave physical or mental defect, he argued, had just as much right to be born as a healthy infant. To compromise that right, he said, would be to violate God's law according to Catholic doctrine "that human life is sacred and that the direct killing of an unborn defenseless child is still murder, no matter how much rationalization to the contrary is prevalent."[86]

Matzner's editorial sparked interest in what other religious leaders' views might be. From New York news arrived that Cardinal Frances Spellman and other leading American Catholic officials strongly opposed all "attacks upon the lives of unborn children," while in England the Archbishop of Canterbury reportedly thought Anglican teachings could accommodate further easing of restrictions.[87] In Texas citizens weighed in with views that abortion was morally wrong and destructive of civilization, on the one hand, and morally imperative, on the other hand. For the time being, testimony before the Texas legislature came from the medical community. The terms of debate focused on the extent to which mental health considerations should be included, whether rape cases were being given sufficient attention, and what risks the proposed legislation might create for doctors.[88] As the debate continued, and as similar legislation was being proposed in Colorado, Oklahoma, and several other states, public interest increased. In September 1967 an international conference on abortion drew additional attention to the issue. Then in October the Texas Supreme Court brought further interest to the issue by ruling that an unborn child has rights.[89]

In 1968 the Texas Medical Association and the Texas legislature continued to search for consensus about an appropriate revision of laws regulating abortion. At its national conference in May, the United Methodist Church passed a resolution favoring laws permitting abortion when birth would endanger the mother, when a child would be born grossly deformed, or when pregnancy resulted from rape or incest. But as the presidential campaign that fall focused attention on economic policies and the costs associated with public welfare, commentators drew a new issue into the abortion debate. They argued that abortion was mainly a problem because so many women were getting pregnant out of wedlock, which in turn was said to be an indication of loose morality. Who exactly was at fault remained unclear, but the implication was that welfare mothers with illegitimate children, single mothers failing to instill proper morals in their sons and daughters, and rising interest in abortion were all somehow part of the same problem.[90]

As the Texas legislature convened in January 1969, a new bill to ease restrictions on abortion was introduced. Citing polls that the vast majority of Protestant and Jewish women and upward of two-thirds of Catholic women favored such legislation, the bill's sponsors were surprised when a large number of cards and letters arrived with opposition outpacing support twenty to one.[91] Two months later the bill was dead. The chief opponent was seventy-eight year-old Archbishop Lucey of San Antonio. Any legislator who voted for the bill, the archbishop declared, should be charged with murder.[92]

More than anything else to date, the bill's defeat galvanized efforts to condemn or support the liberalization of Texas abortion laws. The bill's chief sponsor, Representative James H. Clark Jr. of Dallas, denounced the Catholic Church's hypocrisy in opposing the bill but doing little to care for grossly deformed children with serious birth defects or to help families strapped with devastating medical expenses. The *Dallas Morning News* published a series of articles examining the medical, theological, and legal aspects of the debate. Conservative Catholics, Protestants, and Jews wrote letters to the editor and to Clark arguing that God would punish Texas if the bill passed and suggesting that killing the elderly would be next. "Continue to push this diabolical kind of murder," one letter to Clark declared, "and you have no guarantee that you will not die a helpless, demented old man on your own dung heap." Other Catholic leaders took the same position as Archbishop Lucey. That view held that human life starts at conception and the person's soul is present at that point. In consequence, abortion not only was murder but was particularly heinous because it was inflicted against the most innocent and defenseless of all humans. Those who disagreed sought counterarguments suggesting that it was impossible to know exactly when human life began.[93]

In retrospect, the two sides that would continue arguing about abortion well into the next century were already defined at this juncture. Those who were opposed insisted that any abortion constituted murder and thus should be impermissible by any standard, moral or legal. They claimed to have both God and science on their side, giving certainty in value as well as in fact. The other side held that neither God not science was quite that clear, meaning that a kind of consequentialist reasoning should prevail in which legislation should be passed that reduced the likelihood of doctors being charged with criminal penalties, mothers dying, or infants living with terrible suffering. In face of the opposition's claims, the supporters of liberalized legislation opted for freedom of choice. As one supporter argued, "There is nothing in the proposed law changes that require that an abortion be done on anyone or in any hospital that does not wish to do so."[94]

As Texas lawmakers pondered what steps to take next, some fifty bills in more than two dozen states were proposed, and eleven states approved laws permitting abortions under particular circumstances. Religious bodies gingerly put forth

statements as well, with groups ranging from the Union of American Hebrew Congregations to the United Presbyterian Church in the USA expressing approval of less restrictive access. Other religious organizations formed networks of clergy and counselors from whom women could seek advice if they were considering having an abortion. The Baptist General Convention of Texas did not immediately side with those who opposed less restrictive access to abortion. Its Christian Life Commission submitted a report suggesting that meaningful changes to the state's abortion laws had been delayed too long. "This delay ignores the expressed need for change from a majority of lay and medical groups including a special Texas Medical Association committee to study abortion laws," the report stated. On the related issue of illegitimacy, the report also expressed support for increased ceilings on welfare support and argued that welfare payments do not necessarily contribute to illegitimacy among the state's low-income people.[95]

With prospects for legislation on the issue in Texas apparently dead, a Dallas married couple and an unmarried pregnant woman filed suit in federal court on Tuesday, March 3, 1970, arguing that Texas abortion law deprived women of the fundamental right "to choose whether to bear children." The suit further argued that state laws infringed on the plaintiffs' right to secure adequate and private medical advice and in the case of the unmarried woman to receive a safe abortion under the care of a competent licensed physician. The woman denied that her life was endangered by the pregnancy, claiming only that she was a victim of economic hardship and social stigma. Because of the stigma, she identified herself as Jane Roe. The defendant was Dallas County district attorney Henry Wade.[96]

When the U.S. Supreme Court ruled in favor of the plaintiffs on January 22, 1973, *Roe v. Wade* became the source of one of the nation's most enduring controversies. Norma L. McCorvey, a.k.a. Jane Doe, gave birth long before the case was decided. Sarah Weddington at age twenty-seven became the youngest attorney ever to argue a successful case before the high court. Besides her continuing involvement in the ERA ratification movement, Weddington served three terms in the Texas House of Representatives. In religion and politics, the two sides whose positions in 1969 had still been difficult to sort into well-organized factions became the pro-life movement and the pro-choice movement. As the decade proceeded, the two not only became better organized and more sharply differentiated; they also solidified the meanings of conservative and liberal and elevated the importance of those distinctions in churches and in electoral politics.

In the months following *Roe v. Wade*, church groups lined up on one side or the other of the issue. In San Antonio Lucey's successor, Archbishop Francis James Furey, denounced the decision as tragic and called for an immediate end to the killing of unborn children.[97] Local and statewide right-to-life committees formed with leadership and local meetings in Protestant as well as in Catholic churches. The National Council of Catholic Bishops declared that passage of a constitutional amendment against abortion should be one of the nation's highest political priorities. Among Southern Baptists, the executive director of the Baptist Joint Committee on Public Affairs expressed opposition to the idea of a constitutional amendment against abortion while an organization of clergy and laity called Baptists for Life sent a delegate to Washington to testify in favor of the proposed amendment.[98] Meeting in Dallas that year, the Southern Baptist Convention elected as its president a conservative pastor from Lubbock, instructed the denomination's Christian Life Commission to publish materials on both sides of the abortion issue, voted against several proposals to combat gender discrimination and increase the number of women serving on church boards, but stopped short of passing a resolution against abortion.[99] The American Lutheran Church at its annual national convention heard sharply differing views about the virtues of the Supreme Court's decision and the dangers of abortion on demand.

Besides church groups and right-to-life chapters, service organizations were also drawn into the debate. The pro-life side was represented by homes for unwed mothers, orphanages, and new alternative pregnancy counseling, and adoption centers. The pro-choice side included hotlines and walk-in centers that dealt with drug abuse and family problems and that now provided referrals for abortion and counseling. Planned Parenthood clinics became a particular focal point of controversy. In business since the early 1940s as sources of birth control and family-planning information, these centers by the 1960s had become increasingly associated with discussions of teen pregnancy, out-of-wedlock births, and questions about poverty and rising public welfare costs. After *Roe v. Wade*, news media routinely advertised Planned Parenthood clinics as sources of information about sex, abortion, and venereal disease, which held negative connotations among a significant share of the public and in some publications were further connected with stories of addiction, promiscuity, slum life, and urban violence.

The *Roe* decision prompted negative reactions toward the federal government similar to the "us" and "them" tensions fundamentalist preachers saw in threats from the Federal Communications Commission and court rulings against school prayer. Pro-life groups reinforced the distinction between local activists and the federal government by organizing annual pilgrimages to Washington each year on the anniversary of *Roe*. In addition, bills were proposed to exert local power against the Court's decision. In 1975, for example, a court case in Orange County, Texas, opened the door for local nonprofit, publicly affiliated hospitals to bar abortions except when medically necessary. Two years later the Texas legislature enacted a bill that granted medical personnel and private hospitals the right not to participate in abortions.

Pro-life advocates differed from pro-choice supporters in ways that resembled results comparing the two sides on the Equal Rights Amendment. The sides differed in level of educational attainment and especially in terms of being homemakers or employed in the paid labor force. However, the abortion debate helped legitimate the argument that well-educated, reasonable, intelligent people could be socially and morally conservative, just as Criswell did in symbolizing respectable upscale support for theological fundamentalism. To opponents of abortion, it made sense that their side was the more logical position even though the other side might be represented by physicians and persons with high positions in the federal government. A backer from Texas who felt Republicans should include an antiabortion plank in its 1976 platform amply illustrated this view. "The unborn baby is just as much a human being as you or me. How can anyone say that one minute before birth a baby is any less a human being than one minute after, or one minute before six months pregnancy than one minute after six months?" In the writer's view, it was no less murder for a doctor to abort an unborn baby than to kill someone's living children, even though the parent might consent. "What is most disturbing," the writer continued, "is that there are people who think with such twisted logic and are responsible for making and enforcing the laws of this country. These people must be denied or removed from such positions before we find our country traveling down the same road as Nazi Germany."[100]

In 1976 the *Dallas Morning News* carried nearly 400 stories mentioning abortion, and smaller local and regional newspapers across the state mentioned the topic in more than 2,600 articles, more than twice the number in 1975. Much of the coverage focused on the Texas Republican delegation's plans to press for an antiabortion plank at the Republican National Convention and Reagan's stronger stance against abortion than Ford's and Carter's. In the process, the idea of conservatism itself became a more salient category than it had been since the 1964 campaign. Conservatism included lingering concerns about racial integration as well as specific points separating conservatives from moderate Republicans and Democrats. As a delegate from El Paso explained, "We would like to see a strengthening for the conservatives who want to get this country on some kind of an intelligent basis, instead of spending ourselves into oblivion." Conservatives were, in his understanding, the "idealistic wing" of the party who wanted it to be a party of principles that stood against "abortion, busing, and [turning over] the Panama Canal."[101]

Over the next three years, the abortion debate focused on state and national legislation having to do with questions such as Medicaid coverage and counseling requirements and was carried out by special interest organizations such as Texas Right for Life and Texas Pro Life, on one side, and the Texas Abortion Rights Action League and Texas Family Planning Association, on the other. Religious leaders expressed personal views on the various decisions, but on the whole they seemed willing to let the matter be pressed by lawmakers and in the courts. Polls nevertheless suggested that religious affiliations mattered. A national survey in 1978, for example, showed that 50 percent of mainline Protestants (such as Episcopalians, Methodists, and Presbyterians) considered abortion acceptable if a married woman wanted to have no more children, whereas only 32 percent of Catholics and 25 percent of evangelical Protestants (such as Southern Baptists) agreed.[102]

ELECTING RONALD REAGAN

Seventeen hundred people crowded the Houston Civic Auditorium the evening of Wednesday, April 23, 1980, to hear the sixth and final debate among the Republican presidential candidates. Early contenders had included Congressman John Anderson of Illinois, Senator Howard Baker of Tennessee, Bush from Texas, former Texas governor Connally, Congressman Phil Crane of Illinois, Senator Bob Dole of Kansas, businessman Ben Fernandez of California, Reagan from California, and former Minnesota governor Harold Stassen of Pennsylvania. The two candidates still in the race on April 23 were Bush and Reagan. The Houston venue gave Bush a hometown advantage. Although he was trailing badly in delegates won thus far, he was fresh from an upset victory in the Pennsylvania primary, and there was a fighting chance that he could take the contest all the way to the Republican convention in Detroit. That plan required a good showing at the debate in Houston and momentum to be gained from a win in his home state primary on May 3.

Reagan's success in winning the Republican nomination that summer and his victory that fall in the general election fueled continuing discussions about the role that the Religious Right may have played. The question gains traction when Reagan's decisive victories across the Bible Belt and in the South against a self-proclaimed born-again evangelical southern incumbent are considered. It acquires further credence in view of the National Affairs Briefing in Dallas and the outspoken support Reagan received from Robison, Criswell, Falwell, and others. The contest in Texas permits the question to be considered where the Religious Right's impact can be assessed most clearly. By the general election, many pundits considered it almost a foregone conclusion that Reagan would win, but the primary contest between Bush and Reagan was harder to predict.[103]

The path to the Houston debate began years earlier for both candidates. Having been the first Republican to win a congressional seat from the seventh district, in which Houston was located, Bush was reelected in 1968 and became known as a staunch conservative supporter of the Nixon administration. After losing in the 1970 senatorial race to Democrat Lloyd Bentsen, Bush served as ambassador to the United Nations for two years, chaired the Republican National Committee for a term, was an envoy to China, and spent a year as director of the Central Intelligence Agency. Reagan's time in public office began in 1966 when he ran successfully for governor of California after making a name for himself by campaigning for Goldwater in 1964. As a contender in the 1976 Republican primary against Ford, Reagan campaigned successfully in Texas for a victory that observers suggested encouraged his entry into the campaign four years later.[104]

The differing roles that religion would play in the Bush and Reagan campaigns were evident in the two candidates' opening campaign announcements. Bush announced his candidacy on May 1, 1979, in a brief, thousand-word statement that reflected his all-business approach to the campaign and that some observers saw as a reflection of his restrained personal style as well. Reagan's formal announcement came six months later on November 13, 1979, in a style honed through his years in Hollywood and as governor of California.

Bush's announcement made no mention of religion, focusing instead on inflation, taxes, the budget deficit, and foreign policy. Implicitly it signaled that Bush was a moderate, middle-of-the-road Republican who hoped to appeal to independents and conservative Democrats as well as to Republicans and who might be counted on to implement selected progressive policies such as greater opportunities for women in the labor force and a middle way between untrammeled individualism and social welfare programs. The Republicans he named as role models were Abraham Lincoln, Teddy Roosevelt, and Dwight Eisenhower.[105]

Reagan's announcement—a thirty-seven-hundred-word speech delivered on television with inimitable poise from a comfortable wood-paneled study—struck analysts as emphasizing the same themes they had heard in his 1964 "Time for Choosing" speech for Goldwater. Reagan hammered, as Bush did, at the need for lower taxes, only more emphatically by identifying federal welfare policies as the chief culprit. Deriding the "arrogance of a federal establishment," he championed states' rights, called for more domestic oil and gas production, and argued for strength against the Soviet Union. Unlike Bush, he mentioned religion directly. Seeking to unleash the nation's great strength by removing governmental roadblocks, he said, was something he would do "with God's help." The speech was devoid of arguments against abortion and homosexuality that religious conservatives might have been eager to hear. But Reagan asserted that the nation hungered for a "spiritual revival," pledged that "government cannot be clergyman," and concluded by referencing John Winthrop's sermon to the pilgrims in 1630 promising God that New England would be a city on a hill for the eyes of all people to behold.[106]

The Houston debate focused on foreign policy toward the Soviet Union and Iran and on economic issues involving questions about federal spending, inflation, and gasoline prices. Both candidates argued for tax cuts, but Bush favored a modest proposal of limited tax reductions and spending cuts that would balance the budget while Reagan argued for more extreme measures that he was certain would stimulate the economy despite Bush's criticism that these policies would hike inflation and worsen the federal deficit. Both agreed that President Carter was ineffective in ending the hostage crisis in Iran, and both argued that military action was probably necessary.[107] Polls conducted nationally and in Texas showed that these were indeed the issues uppermost on voters' minds.

That religion may have played a role in the Texas Republican primary is suggested by the results of county-level comparisons. Multiple regression analysis shows that counties in which larger proportions of total Protestant membership were composed of evangelical Protestants were significantly more likely to vote for Reagan than for Bush, controlling for a number of other factors including the proportion who were African American, Hispanic, poor, urban, and college educated. On average, for every 5 percent of Protestants who were evangelical, Reagan won an additional 1 percent of the vote. With a victory of fewer than eighteen thousand votes—a margin of only 3.4 percent—this much of an effect from religion could have been the decisive difference, especially because other factors such as the percentage of the population who were college educated benefited Bush.[108]

The possibility that religion played less of a role than the statistical results suggest is plausible as well. For example, the relevant variables for the two most populous counties in the state suggest that the Houston area in Harris County was nearly indistinguishable from Dallas County in many respects: nearly two-thirds of Protestants in both counties belonged to evangelical denominations, nearly half of Protestants in both counties were Southern Baptists, a fifth of the population in both counties was African American, one person in ten was below the poverty line, and nearly one adult in four was college educated. Reagan beat Bush by 1 percent of the vote in Dallas, but Bush's hometown advantage gave him a 26-point win over Reagan in Houston.

Other factors must be considered as well, especially that of Governor Bill Clements. Clements's relationships with Bush and Reagan were complicated enough that his support could have gone to either candidate. As fellow leaders in the Texas oil industry, Bush and Clements had led rival companies but at one point had also been partners in a venture in Kuwait. In 1964 Clements recruited Bush to run for the Senate against Yarborough, and Clements served as Bush's statewide finance chair in that campaign. Both held positions under the Nixon and Ford administrations, and Clements's 1978 campaign for governor included support from Bush. But Clements was ideologically closer to Reagan than to Bush. In 1976 Clements and his wife Rita, a state Republican chairperson, supported Reagan's bid against Ford, and in 1978 Reagan campaigned on behalf of Clements. The campaign seized on Carter's unpopularity and focused on curbing federal government expenditures, reducing taxes, and helping the oil and gas industry, as well as opposing the Equal Rights Amendment and abortion. During the 1980 Republican primary, Clements officially remained neutral, but his neutrality was interpreted by some of the state's leading Republicans as a lack of support for Bush. That interpretation seemed to be confirmed at the Republican National Convention when rumors spread that Clements was working to get Ford on the ticket as vice president instead of Bush. When Reagan selected Bush, Clements voiced approval, but of Reagan as much as of Bush. As the fall campaign got under way, Clements donated to Reagan's campaign and loaned Reagan a farm in Virginia adjacent to the home of John Warner and Elizabeth Taylor, which Reagan used as his East Coast headquarters for preparing his debates with Carter.[109]

An Episcopalian, Clements had no particular religious affinity with evangelical Protestants, famously declaring on one occasion when asked if he was born again, "No thanks, once was enough." The bond between Clements and Reagan was better described as small-government fiscal conservatism. Clements's closest allies fell into that category as well. In the 1978 campaign Clements's state campaign chair was George W. Strake Jr., the son of one of the state's wealthiest oilmen. A devout Catholic whose father had been a leading philanthropist of Catholic institutions in Texas, Strake was a graduate of the University of Notre Dame and Harvard Business School. He was an alternate delegate in 1976 when the Texas Republicans pledged their support to Reagan, became Clements's secretary of state from 1979 to 1981, and with Nelson Bunker Hunt and Phyllis Schlafly became active in the conservative Council for National Policy.[110]

Another ally of Clements who supported Reagan was Eddie Chiles, the conservative radio commentator whose "mad as hell" broadcasts aired in fourteen states by the late 1970s. Other than helping Robison, Chiles was more interested in defending free enterprise than in promoting religion. He did, however, gain the attention of popular evangelical writer Keith Miller, who in 1981 coauthored *With No Fear of Failure* with Houston waste management millionaire Tom J. Fatjo, which featured Chiles, Norman Vincent Peale, and Billy Graham as self-help role models.

Through Clements and fellow Dallas oilman Ashley Priddy, along with Houston journalist and conservative political activist Clymer Wright and Dallas Republican Women's Clubs leader Barbara Staff, a statewide network of supporters formed who had favored Reagan in 1976 and who were eager to see him win the nomination in 1980. In Dallas alone, more than two hundred contributors donated more than $125,000 to Reagan's primary campaign committee. Many of the contributors listed their occupations as oil and gas producers, petroleum engineers, geologists, oil investors, stock brokers, and real estate owners.[111]

Reagan held other advantages over Bush as well. Having campaigned for Goldwater in 1964, and having served as governor of California from 1966 to 1975, Reagan was a national figure in the Republican Party. As the state's early favorite for the presidential bid in 1976, he campaigned in Texas three times that year and received extensive media coverage. In Clements's 1978 campaign, Reagan lectured to enthusiastic crowds in Dallas, Houston, Austin, and San Antonio, demonstrating his capacity to raise funds and hinting that he might consider becoming a presidential candidate in 1979. Reagan repeatedly drew applause with arguments against the federal bureaucracy, high taxes, and welfare spending, and in favor of states' rights.[112]

Reagan's edge in the primary contest was thus a combination of several factors. It included not only the evangelical religious tilt evident in county comparisons but also the support of several leaders associated with conservative churches. Barbara Staff, for example, was active in Criswell's church, as were several others who contributed to the Reagan primary campaign. At the same time, the small-government fiscal conservatism that attracted contributions and votes was hardly limited to the Religious Right.[113]

PUBLIC RELIGION REDEFINED

The wider significance of the Religious Right outside of Texas and even beyond the political dynamics of the 1970s and early 1980s remains a matter of scholarly investigation. But one of the conclusions about which there is general agreement is that religion in the United States somehow became more public as a result. It shifted from being as focused on private belief and personal morality to being more about politics and the collective affairs of the nation. That shift can be interpreted as a reversal of long-term secularizing processes in which religion became less and less central to the functioning of major social institutions. Or it can be regarded as something ephemeral. Regardless of the specific interpretation, the question of how exactly this apparent reinsertion of religion into the public sphere happened is worth considering.

Among the various processes involved, one that deserves further consideration is the redefinition of some parts of the religious community from being essentially about solace to being more about empowerment and indeed the legitimate claimants of respect. In simplest terms, this is a redefinition of religion's personal as well as its ceremonial roles in the community from one that speaks to the downtrodden and gives special comfort when things go badly toward one that argues in effect that the underprivileged have new opportunities to gain power and respect. Religion played this role in the civil rights movement for African Americans, and it served similarly in parts of the Chicano power movement. It did so not only by offering idioms of empowerment and resources in the form of venues for meetings and leaders to organize those meetings; its role involved leaders who personally linked religious meanings with public political activities. In the same way, leaders of the Religious Right did that for believers who for the most part were white Protestants and Catholics with conservative religious and political views.

There is no evidence that leaders such as Roloff, Robison, Criswell, or Falwell contemplated the activities of the Southern Christian Leadership Conference or Raza Unida and gleaned ideas for engaging in political activism. The point is not about emulation but similarities of opportunity and strategy. The Religious Right came at a time when many of the white American population had moved squarely into the middle class and were restive about government intrusion, which they saw as unnecessary to their own well-being or as a threat because of school integration, fair housing and employment laws, and regulations of the environment and workplace. The civil rights movement, sexual revolution, urbanization, rising levels of education, increasing inclusion of women in the paid labor force, and new understandings of gender roles contributed to the awareness as well. The connection with religion was that the most conservative fundamentalist Protestant and traditional Catholic groups embraced beliefs and practices that were sometimes understood by their detractors as backwater ideas.

Fundamentalist and traditional teachings could provide otherworldly comfort and thus appeal to the marginalized but were out of step with the aspirations of forward-thinking people. The Religious Right challenged that view.

The best way to show that a marginalized group has more clout than anyone may have realized is to take on something or somebody with power. Roloff and Robison did that by challenging the power of the government to regulate what they were doing. Neither was well educated, and both spoke of the same old-fashioned sin and salvation that revivalists had featured in the nineteenth century. The difference was that converts could now imagine themselves as a population not only embattled, as they always had been by the forces of secularity and apostasy, but standing firmly enough to have power.

Criswell demonstrated that fundamentalism was powerful in a different way. With educational credentials, personal brilliance, and an extraordinary gift for retaining knowledge and speaking about it, he personified the idea that someone could be a fundamentalist and be respected at the same time. The result depended not only on personal talents but also on the reality of First Baptist Church. It commanded five blocks of high-end property in downtown Dallas, was regarded as the nation's largest church whether that was literally true or not, and counted as members some of the wealthiest persons in the state. Whether someone attended there, was a Southern Baptist in a community quite different from Dallas, or was a believer who held similarly conservative views, it was now possible to be proud as a fundamentalist, traditionalist, or evangelical.

Although the term evangelical became more prominent on the national stage after Carter's election in 1976, it is notable that in Texas and throughout much of the South, this was not the label that gained the greatest popular salience. Nor was it quite the case, as scholars would later argue, that evangelicals were distinguished from fundamentalists by virtue of better education and more active engagement in social and political affairs. That may have been the distinction characteristic of fundamentalist Bob Jones as opposed to Jerry Falwell, but Falwell still called himself a fundamentalist and so did Criswell. The more salient category among church leaders and journalists in Texas was conservative. Being a conservative implied that a person was on the fundamentalist side of Southern Baptist politics and against the ERA and abortion on social issues. It also meant that one was for Reagan, Clements, and other fiscal conservatives in electoral politics.[114]

As a symbolic boundary, conservatism in effect drew a line between white churchgoers and black churchgoers who generally held similar religious beliefs and opinions about moral issues but who voted for different political candidates and aligned themselves with different political parties. White conservatives in 1980 were seldom overtly racist in the way that earlier generations were. Indeed, like Criswell and other conservative Southern Baptist leaders, they were on record as being in favor of racial equality and participating in congregations that did not overtly exclude African Americans. Racial inclusiveness was evident even at the Pro-Family conference in Houston and at the National Affairs Briefing in Dallas, where a few black leaders were among those in visible roles.[115] It was just that most conservatives were white and attended white churches. The outsiders about whom they expressed concern were not explicitly African American or Hispanic, only liberals whose voting ranks happened to include larger numbers of African Americans and Hispanics and poor people who aroused conservative sentiments about promiscuity, abortion, and the costs associated with public welfare. White conservatives were able to attend middle-class churches that reinforced respectability through good preaching and high moral standards.

It was possible not only to feel that one's faith convictions were respectable. It was also possible to be a Republican. However deeply tied to the Democratic Party one's ancestral family may have been, a conservative person of faith knew that Republicans were now the ones who offered respect. They conferred respect by demonstrating that a person could be a reasonably well-educated member of the middle class who was making it on one's own without a government handout and held firmly to a set of moral principles. Little wonder, then, that the crowd at Reunion Arena applauded wildly when Reagan said, "I want you to know that I endorse you."

CHAPTER 11

IN A COMPASSIONATE WAY

Connecting Faith and Politics

This is America: the Knights of Columbus, the Grange, Hadassah, the
Disabled American Veterans, the Order of AHEPA, the Business and
Professional Women of America, the union hall, the Bible study group,
LULAC, "Holy Name"—a brilliant diversity spread like stars, like a
thousand points of light in a broad and peaceful sky.

GEORGE H. W. BUSH, REPUBLICAN NATIONAL CONVENTION, AUGUST 18, 1988

Government welfare programs need to be fought not because they are too
expensive—although, clearly, much money is wasted—but because they
are inevitably too stingy in what is really important, treating people as
people and not animals.

MARVIN OLASKY, *THE TRAGEDY OF AMERICAN COMPASSION*, 1992

We're moving people from welfare to lives of independence, and it's been
a very successful policy. I mean, people want to be independent. They
don't want to be dependent on Government, but it must be done in a
compassionate way.

GEORGE W. BUSH, JUNE 21, 2004

By the time Vice President George Herbert Walker Bush ran for the nation's highest office in 1988, the lines separating liberals and conservatives
and Democrats and Republicans were as clearly drawn as they had been
at any time since 1964. This was as true in Texas as it was nationally. Republicans had moved sufficiently to the right that fiscal conservatism with respect to
public welfare and opposition to abortion had become signature issues, while

Democrats took pride in championing the needs of the poor and the rights of minorities and women. The division within religion that emerged in the 1970s was equally apparent, with fundamentalists and other born-again believers increasingly active in politics on the right while liberal clergy and people on the margins of established religion found common cause on the other side of most issues. It was evident that televangelist Pat Robertson's bid for the Republican presidential nomination and the wide visibility of Jerry Falwell's Moral Majority signaled a new or intensified level of political involvement on the part of conservative Christians. The further involvement of the Religious Right seemed evident four years later when Pat Buchanan's run in the 1992 Republican presidential primary race brought the idea of a culture war into popular awareness. The line from W. A. Criswell and James Robison to Paige Patterson and Judge Pressler and from Ronald Reagan's moral conservatism to the wars over abortion and homosexuality that continued into the twenty-first century seemed direct and unbroken.

At least that is the story that has emerged from the two most common paths that journalistic and scholarly investigations into the culture wars have taken. One path has emphasized the Religious Right, focusing on its roots, ideology, organization, and rising cultural influence. This line of investigation stems from the literature on social movements, a tradition of inquiry rich with insights about movement leadership, the grievances that motivate people to join, the strategic framing of issues, and the mobilization of resources to achieve movement objectives. Studies of the Religious Right have illuminated the central roles played by Falwell and Robertson, religious television, antiabortion organizations such as Operation Rescue, the denominational clout of conservative megachurches, the growth of membership in these congregations, and the social networks that drew activists into participating in rallies and contributing money. These inquiries have also spawned investigations of countermovements on the left, such as pro-choice organizations, gay and lesbian organizations, environmentalist groups, and the sanctuary movement.[1]

The other line of inquiry has focused on public opinion. Based largely in the analysis of national survey data, this approach has examined the extent to which individuals that belong to different denominations or who espouse different views of the Bible also then differ when asked questions about abortion, homosexuality, and political party preferences. Related studies have examined changes in public opinion over time to see if attitudes have shifted to the right or left or become more polarized. The ensuing debate in the scholarly literature has centered on the question of whether public opinion is actually divided into distinct camps and whether that division has widened and embraced a larger number of issues. One side in the debate perceives a fundamental division of worldviews in which basic convictions about absolute moral values are pitted against relativistic situational ethics. Another side suggests that few Americans have strongly held beliefs one way or the other, and that truly divisive issues are rather limited, hyped by the media, and largely ignored by people in the muddled middle who make up their minds on the spur of the moment when queried by pollsters.[2]

As generative as these approaches have been, they illustrate the extent to which an important social phenomenon can be defined by the starting perspectives from which observers ask their questions. The Religious Right and public opinion inquiries essentially depict the culture wars as a kind of battle being waged on flat terrain. When perceived as a social movement, the Religious Right is a kind of army that musters its troops, trains and organizes them into units, and then marches them into conflict with an opposing army on the other side. Public opinion studies monitor the surrounding villages, as it were, to see if attitudes favor one of the combatants more than the other and to determine if anyone is willing to join the fray or if most of the public is apathetic.[3]

In both perspectives, the question of continuity or discontinuity is central. A social movement comes from somewhere, and usually close investigation can find relevant antecedents. It also progresses over time, adapting to changing circumstances if it hopes to survive. Public opinion similarly ebbs and flows, requiring comparisons with past survey results and invoking questions that can only be answered by interviewing the same people over a period of several years. The research suggests that there have been some changes in the leaders involved and among the issues people regard as most salient but on the whole point to continuity. The Religious Right in this perspective has shown remarkable resilience in training new leaders and in keeping religious conservatives mobilized to fight continuing battles against abortion and homosexuality. Public opinion is at least divided on some important issues, such as religious belief and attitudes toward abortion, and there appear to be demographic and institutional mechanisms reinforcing polarization.

However, there are important parts of the story that prove difficult to incorporate when the narrative about culture wars is recounted in these ways. Not enough attention is given to the fact that Bush was the moderate of the Reagan-Bush team and that Robertson and Buchanan both failed in their bids for the nomination. The story of straight-line succession minimizes the role of debates about public welfare and taxes and the Clinton administration's part in bringing about the most significant changes in the welfare system since Johnson's Great Society legislation. It misses the fact that one of the issues that most sharply divided religious conservatives and religious liberals was their view of government spending for public welfare.[4] Most significantly, a more complicated story is required to make sense of Republicans' own ambivalence toward the Religious Right and how the efforts to advance centrist ideas about volunteerism, compassion, and faith-based social services were refracted through the divisions separating conservatives and liberals.

Mapping a more complex story that takes account of these political dynamics requires shifting perspective from the flatland imagery of warring armies to a terrain in which multiple interests and a more diverse population of relevant constituencies come into view. The social movement approach to the Religious Right focuses too much attention on the claims and interests of movement activists. Important as those may be, they cannot be understood without also considering the roles of political candidates, political parties, and the stakes involved in political campaigns. Public opinion that is defined by national opinion surveys necessarily features the attitudes of the majority but says little about the roles played by racial and ethnic identities and perspectives. While it may be the case, for example, that the Religious Right in the 1980s and 1990s was largely a movement among white, religiously active Protestants and Catholics, the question of its relation to African Americans and Hispanics and its implications for policies that differentially affected minority populations and social classes also needs to be addressed.[5]

In the late 1980s Texas became more important in American politics and thus of greater interest as a location in which to examine the complex connections among faith and politics than ever before. Already a key state in electoral politics because of its population size and having come onto the national stage during the Johnson administration and through Reagan's campaigning there in 1976 and 1980, it was now the home state in 1988 of the Republicans' candidate for president and the Democrats' candidate for vice president. Two years later its gubernatorial race between Ann Richards and Clayton Williams was one of the most expensive, bitterly fought, and nationally watched of any campaign in the country. In 1992 it again became a key battleground in the presidential contest. And in 1994 the victory of its Republican candidate for governor, George W. Bush, set in motion policies that became central to Bush's presidential administration during the first eight years of the twenty-first century.

As important as these political developments were, Texas also provides a rich context in which to observe the connections among religion, race, and politics. It was still the home of the nation's largest conservative Protestant denomination and an important part of the battleground in which fundamentalists and moderates vied for control of the Southern Baptist Convention. The state was still sufficiently indebted to its southern legacy that racial issues were seldom far from the surface. It was also the state in which one of the largest and fastest-growing Hispanic populations was becoming a significant factor in state and national politics.

The critical factor in the complex relations among politics, religion, and race from the late 1980s through the 1990s was the Republican Party's quest to establish itself not only as a party of the rich or as one that could win occasionally with a candidate as popular as Reagan but also as a party capable of securing votes from a large share of middle- and lower-income voters. The most important aspect of this strategy had little to do with religion, focusing instead on policies of fiscal conservatism that included reducing social services and avoiding tax increases while maintaining a strong defense budget. With little hope of attracting black voters, Republican strategists appealed to white voters by emphasizing issues of interest to religious conservatives and by arguing for voluntary services administered by churches. If they were going to be the party of no tax increases and sharp cutbacks on social services, they could at least soften the charge of being heartless by promoting compassion. These appeals, strategists hoped, would also make some inroads among Hispanic voters. In this perspective, the relationship of faith-based community-service initiatives to the culture wars comes more clearly into view.

A THOUSAND POINTS OF LIGHT

Bush's acceptance speech at the 1988 Republican National Convention emphasized his service and accomplishments during the Reagan administration as well as his optimism about the future of America. It recalled his start in Texas forty years earlier, living in a little shotgun house and then a duplex, raising six children, going to high school football games on Friday evenings, and attending neighborhood barbecues. The line about a thousand points of light could easily have been missed, misunderstood, or forgotten had it not become a signature aspect of Bush's presidency through the Points of Light charitable service initiative and a forerunner of the faith-based compassionate conservatism that would gain widespread attention during the presidency of his son.[6]

It was not surprising that something about America's voluntary associations was part of the speech. The principal writer of the speech was Peggy Noonan, the thirty-year-old conservative Catholic Republican who had served as a speechwriter and special assistant to Reagan. In numerous speeches Reagan had emphasized a kind of Tocquevillean faith in the power of local churches, clubs, volunteer organizations, and neighborhood associations to uphold democracy and sustain American values. In neoconservative language, these were mediating structures through which individual citizens aggregated and discussed their ideas, channeled them upward to elected local and state officials, and in turn gained protection from centralized government. For Reagan, an emphasis on local associations went hand in hand with criticisms of big government.[7]

Bush's view was similar, although he emphasized that government had an important role to play and highlighted his own record in government service. "A thousand points of light," Noonan observed, "became Bush's shorthand way of referring to the network of helping organizations throughout the country." Associations connoted old-fashioned common sense, individualism, and the kind of grassroots gatherings that gave people warm feelings about their friends and neighbors. Associations typified Americans' can-do spirit of self-help, neighbors working together to solve their own problems, and local communities being at liberty to do as they wished, whether that meant getting tough on crime or protecting the right of children to say voluntary prayers in school.[8]

Associations were also the way to acknowledge the increasingly important diversity of the electorate. "We are a nation of communities, of thousands and tens of thousands of ethnic, religious, social, business, labor union, neighborhood, regional and other organizations," Bush said, "all of them varied, voluntary and unique." The examples he named illustrated the point. Knights of Columbus were Catholic, Hadassah was Jewish, Bible study groups were characteristically Protestant, and the Order of AHEPA was a Hellenic Greek-American fraternal organization that often met in Greek Orthodox churches—the religious tradition of Bush's opponent. Business and professional associations, unions, and the Grange pointed to different sectors of the labor force. LULAC—the League of United Latin American Citizens—signaled the growing importance of Hispanic voters. Founded in 1929, it was the oldest Hispanic civil rights organization and had long been active in South Texas as well as in California. The only major population group not referenced with the examples given was African Americans.[9]

Bush's call for a "kinder and gentler" nation amplified the meanings implicit in the references to community associations. The phrase resonated with the quieter style of leadership expressed in his personal demeanor and manner of speaking. It contrasted with Reagan's sharper and often more combative rhetorical style and suggested an interest in moving past the bitter partisan divisions of the past decade. It most specifically was a call for Americans to pursue their "better angels" by engaging in public and private acts of kindness. "Prosperity with a purpose means taking your idealism and making it concrete by certain acts of goodness," he said. Citing his wife Barbara's work in literacy education, he mentioned helping children learn to read and showing them love in the process. "Some would say it's soft and insufficiently tough to care about these things," he observed. "But where is it written that we must act as if we do not care, as if we are not moved?"[10]

Words acquire specific meaning within particular contexts, perhaps especially so when crafted as political campaign rhetoric. By mid-August the 1988 presidential campaign was already being described as one of the bitterest and nastiest in recent history. Although Massachusetts governor Michael Dukakis would win only nine states and secure only 21 percent of the electoral college votes, Bush's eventual lopsided victory was nothing to be taken for granted during the campaign itself. Dukakis was known as a hard campaigner with a strong record in Massachusetts and potential for appealing to working-class voters in populous northeastern and upper midwestern states. He also spoke Spanish, which gave him an edge in campaigning among Hispanic voters in Texas and California. If that were not enough, his running mate, Lloyd Bentsen, was a conservative Democrat from Texas who had beaten Bush in the 1970 race for U.S. Senate. Against those odds, it was uncertain whether Bush could even win his home state. His deficits compared with Reagan were obvious. He lacked Reagan's charisma and rhetorical flair. In contrast with Reagan's macho cowboy persona, Bush's critics easily characterized him as a wimp.

The other significant deficit was Bush's elite background. Having grown up in a rich East Coast family, attended an Ivy League university, and then become a wealthy Texas oilman posed difficulties in appealing to ordinary, working-class voters. "My parents were prosperous; their children were lucky," he acknowledged in his acceptance speech. He lacked Reagan's ability to speak in the language of small-town and rural America. On the campaign trail, Bush sounded more like a government bureaucrat than a cowboy. Dukakis repeatedly described him as being out of touch with common men and women. Besides that, Democrats accused the Reagan administration of having done more to help the rich than the poor and portrayed Democratic leaders as having been the better friend of working Americans. Even in historically Republican states, there were lingering concerns about "country club Republicans" that catered to big business interests instead of serving the common person.

The top issue in the 1988 election was government spending, including the rising federal budget deficit, and thus the question of whether taxes would have to be raised or some other means of getting government spending under control could be found. Apart from the fact that the defense budget had grown, the rising expenditures were clearly associated with social welfare programs, including Medicare and Medicaid, Social Security, food stamps, and assistance for low-income families with children. Under Johnson's Great Society program, these expenditures rose dramatically and became of sufficient public concern that they were one of the issues that contributed to Reagan's victory in 1980. Reagan avoided deep cuts in social programs but did so by increasing the federal deficit. In 1988 both parties emphasized fiscal conservatism, but Democrats emphasized maintaining social programs to a greater extent than Republicans did. The quandary for Republicans was finding a way to cut or at least hold the line on social programs without appearing so heartless that even self-sufficient working-class voters as well as the poor would vote Democratic.

The problem was especially evident in a state like Texas where a large number of electoral college votes were at stake and where Democrats' traditional strength still produced victories in local and statewide contests and remained solid among black and Hispanic voters because of Johnson's efforts on behalf of civil rights and social welfare programs. Democrats' down-ticket strength was clearly evident in the state legislature where Democrats occupied 25 of the 31 state Senate seats and 94 of the 150 House seats.[11] Discussions of wealth and poverty were accentuated in Texas because of a slump in the oil industry and by concerns about the state's regressive tax policies. A study conducted by Citizens for Tax Justice, a Washington-based tax research and lobbying group, found that Texas sales taxes were one of the most regressive revenue systems in the nation, absorbing more than 7 percent of poor families' incomes while taking only 1.5 percent from the wealthiest.[12]

If Texas was taxing the poor at high rates, it was also doing little to provide public assistance. A study conducted by the state Senate's Interim Committee on Welfare found that per capita welfare benefits were lower in Texas than in every other state except Alabama, Mississippi, and Tennessee. Average monthly benefits in Texas were $141, compared to a national average of $310. In addition, Texas laws prevented two-parent families from receiving benefits, which meant that women headed 95 percent of welfare families and, as critics argued, probably deterred some single parents from marrying. Besides that, Texas provided no public-funded job-training programs and offered little support for older people.[13]

But as calls for better funding of welfare programs through state taxes came from liberal Democrats, Republicans and conservative Democrats noted that Texas taxpayers were already supporting welfare programs to the tune of a billion dollars in food stamps and $400 million in welfare payments. Critics of these expenditures argued that the government programs were inefficient and ineffective. The poor, critics charged, were being given handouts that discouraged them from working. Welfare, an angry resident wrote to the *Kerrville Daily Times*, is "a cancer on our society." There were families in Texas, he said, that had "never worked a day" in the past half century. "The Department of Human Resources doesn't want the free loaders to work because they will lose their plush jobs."[14]

At the national level, the 1988 Family Support Act passed by the Reagan administration emphasized lowering welfare costs by putting mothers who were welfare recipients to work, thus significantly altering the Depression-era legislation that sought to aid mothers with dependent children by helping them stay out of the labor force. In an effort to curb Texas welfare expenditures, Republican governor Bill Clements expanded the Board of Human Services and appointed a Houston oil executive and several other Republicans to give it a new "philosophical" outlook. Among the reforms the governor hoped to initiate were making it harder for poor people to stay on welfare and shifting a greater part of welfare assistance to volunteer organizations.[15]

Welfare programs were of greatest personal benefit to low-income families, a disproportionate number of whom were African American and Hispanic. Data collected in the 1990 decennial census would show that median family income among white non-Hispanics was approximately $35,400, whereas it was only $21,200 among Hispanics and $21,500 among African Americans. The differences were also evident in the proportion of each with median family incomes under $25,000: 34 percent among white non-Hispanics, 57 percent among Hispanics, and 55 percent among African Americans. At the other end of the income distribution, 32 percent of white non-Hispanics had median family incomes over $50,000, while only 12 percent of Hispanics and 17 percent of African Americans did.[16]

Race and income were potentially important in the 1988 presidential election for two reasons. First, the proportion of the population that typically voted Democratic was increasing. In 1970 the state's population of 11.2 million had been 69.6 percent white non-Hispanic, 17.7 percent Hispanic, and 12.5 percent black. Over the next two decades, total population grew to almost 17 million, but by far the most rapid increase occurred among the Hispanic population as a re-sult of relaxed immigration laws after 1965 and natural increase owing to a high proportion of younger adults. By 1990 the Hispanic population would exceed 4.3 million, twice the size of the black population, and the overall composition of the state's population would be 60.6 percent white non-Hispanic, 25.5 percent Hispanic, and 11.9 percent black.[17] Second, Republicans might be able to appeal to the third of the white non-Hispanic population with incomes over $50,000 by cutting social programs and promising to keep taxes low, but the 34 percent of white non-Hispanics with incomes under $25,000 might depend on some of these programs as well and be less than pleased about voting for a rich oil man who sounded like a country club Republican.

If Republicans entertained little hope of appealing to black voters, the strategy to win enough votes to carry the state had to rely on other tactics. It could help, for example, if the black vote could be suppressed, but that was risky in view of the monitoring that had gone into effect since Johnson's outrage over those tactics in 1964. The Hispanic vote was trickier because suppressing it might help Republicans, or finding ways to attract Hispanic voters might help them more. Upscale, white non-Hispanics were a safe bet, especially if fiscal conservatism could be emphasized enough. That left white, lower-income non-Hispanics as a particularly important constituency.

Campaigns are run much like military operations, with tactics hinging on what worked in the last war as well as assessments of current strengths and weak-nesses. Reagan had won reelection by a wide margin in Texas in 1984, receiving more than 3.4 million votes to Mondale's 1.9 million and winning in 90 percent of the state's counties as well as in nearly every demographic category. The excep-tions were among black voters, only 8 percent of whom voted for Reagan, and Hispanics, 35 percent of whom voted for Reagan—a proportion that Republican strategists nevertheless considered encouraging. However, there were soft spots among white voters that could spell trouble for future Republican office-seekers less popular than Reagan. The most obvious soft spot was among low-income, white non-Hispanic voters. More than 40 percent of the votes cast by this group went to Mondale, compared with only 20 percent of the votes by white non-Hispanics with family incomes over $50,000.

The factor suggested by the 1984 results that could possibly reduce the dif-ference was religion. Reagan won more than 80 percent of the white born-again vote. And the proportion of white voters who said they were born again rose to almost 40 percent among those with incomes under $25,000, compared to only 28 percent among those with incomes over $50,000.[18] It was not hard to under-stand why Reagan did well among born-again Christians. Fewer than 10 percent of white voters said a member of the clergy had directly influenced their vote, but among this number two-thirds said the influence had been toward voting for Reagan. In addition, a large majority of white, born-again voters said they were political conservatives. Reagan's endorsement of conservative clergy at the briefing in Dallas in 1980 and his subsequent efforts to talk about God and associate himself with issues born-again Christians cared about had not gone unnoticed or unappreciated.[19]

The 1986 gubernatorial race between Republican Bill Clements and Democrat Mark White essentially replicated the pattern in the 1984 presidential contest. Black and Hispanic voters opted for the Democratic contender by margins of 5 to 1, while white voters gave Clements only a small but effective victory. Clements's margin among low-income, white voters was barely above 50 percent but rose to nearly two-thirds among those with incomes over $50,000. Religion again produced interesting results. Clements's widest margin was among white, self-identified fundamentalist and evangelical Christians, 72 percent of whom gave him their votes. The results suggested that Clements's support over the years on issues such as freedom from government interference in religion and opposition to abortion mattered to conservative Christians.[20] Another poll in 1986 found that upward of 80 percent of white, born-again Christians approved of Reagan's handling of his job as president. The only group even more favorable to Reagan was people deriving income from the oil and gas industry. They were better positioned economically than evangelicals to make a difference in politics. But evangelicals—who outnumbered them ten to one—held the numeric advantage in influencing elections.[21]

To the extent that religion mattered in Bush's 1988 bid for the presidency, its influence had to be considered in relation to questions about fiscal conservatism, social class, race, and ethnicity. Lee Atwater, the South Carolina political consultant who had helped Reagan win solid victories throughout the South in 1980, ran the campaign. Atwater's strategy was revealed in a 1981 interview published much later in which he explained, "You start out in 1954 by saying, 'Nigger, nigger, nigger.' By 1968 you can't say 'nigger'—that hurts you. Backfires. So you say stuff like forced busing, states' rights and all that stuff." But by the 1980s that language was also becoming unacceptable. "You're getting so abstract now [that] you're talking about cutting taxes, and all these things you're talking about are totally economic things and a byproduct of them is [that] blacks get hurt worse than whites. And subconsciously maybe that is part of it," Atwater acknowledged. "I'm not saying that. But I'm saying that if it is getting that abstract, and that coded, that we are doing away with the racial problem one way or the other. You follow me—because obviously sitting around saying, 'We want to cut this,' is much more abstract than even the busing thing, and a hell of a lot more abstract than 'Nigger, nigger.'"[22]

With nearly a quarter century having passed since the landmark civil rights legislation enacted under the Johnson administration, Atwater was correct in arguing that it was unacceptable in mainstream political campaigns to engage explicitly in racially prejudiced language. Race nevertheless remained an important part of the cultural and political landscape. A national poll in August 1988 found that 53 percent of whites and 68 percent of blacks thought American society overall was racist. The poll also found that 42 percent of whites and 69 percent of blacks thought blacks and other minorities did not have the same opportunities as whites.[23] Democrats' advocacy for civil rights, equal employment opportunity, and social welfare programs since the 1960s meant that the black vote nearly always went to Democratic candidates in general elections. If Republicans had little chance of winning converts, and if it was difficult to discourage black turnout, the remaining option was to play on fears that might prevent white voters from opting for Democrats. Those fears might be stoked most easily among lower-income white voters who worried that blacks and Hispanics were taking their jobs or inciting crime in their neighborhoods.

During the 1986 gubernatorial election, an example of explicit efforts to stoke racial fears in Texas occurred when the Ku Klux Klan decided to run its grand dragon, a Houston printer named Charles Lee, as a write-in candidate for governor. Campaigning by bus in South Texas, Lee argued that Democrats and Republicans alike were knuckling under to minority interests. White workers, he said, were being deprived of employment by black workers receiving preferential treatment and by illegal immigrants from Mexico. "In many parts of Texas, whites can't get jobs if they can't speak Spanish," he complained. The state's Democratic governor, Lee added, was wasting money on schools that would educate better if they were segregated and doing too little to combat crime inflicted on white people by members of minority races.[24]

Race became directly involved in the 1988 presidential contest when the Bush campaign focused on Willie Horton Jr., an African American convicted of murder who escaped during a Massachusetts prison furlough, stabbed a white Maryland man, and raped the man's fiancée. The Dukakis campaign accused the Bush campaign of evoking racial prejudice by emphasizing Willie Horton. National polls conducted in October 1988 showed that between a quarter and a third of registered voters knew who Willie Horton was, and when told, about a quarter thought the public's reaction was stronger because the criminal was black and the victims were white. Another survey found that 42 percent of likely voters said the commercial about Willie Horton had been effective as far as they were concerned.[25]

As the November election drew near, the Dukakis campaign also filed a complaint with the U.S. Justice Department, arguing that the Republicans were using scare tactics to suppress Hispanic voting in the Rio Grande valley. Concerns about voter suppression and low turnout among Hispanics were reinforced by the results of research conducted by the Southwest Voter Research Institute, founded in 1984 with offices in San Antonio by former MAYO and Raza Unida activist William C. Velásquez. The results showed that only 29 percent of Latino voters in Texas had voted in 1978, compared with 49 percent of non-Latino voters; that the respective turnout in 1982 was 38 percent compared with 51 percent; and in 1986, 29 percent versus 50 percent.[26] The complaint in 1988 arose over Spanish-language television and radio advertising warning Hispanics in what were described as ominous "Big Brother" tones that election officials were watching for voter fraud and checking papers to deport anyone found to be in the country illegally. Future New Mexico governor Bill Richardson, campaigning on behalf of Dukakis, counseled Hispanic voters to turn out in larger than expected numbers and called on Bush to emphasize "kinder and gentler" rhetoric.[27]

A Texas poll conducted in July 1988 suggested that turnout probably would be low among Hispanics and perhaps among African Americans as well. The poll also confirmed the preference among minority voters for the Democratic candidate. Twenty-nine percent of Hispanics planning to vote said they would probably vote for Bush—a lower proportion than for Reagan in 1984—as did only 21 percent of black voters. In comparison, 54 percent of white non-Hispanic voters in the poll said they expected to vote for Bush. The effect of social class was also evident. Only 24 percent of white non-Hispanics with incomes below $25,000 were for Bush, compared with 59 percent of those with incomes over $50,000. When asked their political party preference, 40 percent of those with incomes below $25,000 said they were Democrats, while only 25 percent of those with incomes over $50,000 did. Although the Bush campaign in Texas under the direction of George W. Bush attempted to reach voters in small towns and rural areas, the poll also suggested that Dukakis was likely to fare better among white voters in those parts of the state, whereas Bush enjoyed more of an advantage in Dallas, Fort Worth, and Houston.[28]

As had been the case in 1984 and 1986, religion appeared to be the additional factor that could influence the election. In the July 1988 poll, 35 percent of white Protestants outside of the major metropolitan areas said they were fundamentalists, compared with only 24 percent in the metropolitan areas. Among those with no college training, 34 percent were fundamentalists, compared with only 21 percent among those with college degrees. And fundamentalism ranged from 36 percent in the lowest income bracket to 23 percent in the highest. Sixty-two percent of the fundamentalists said they planned to vote for Bush. Although a majority of Hispanic and non-Hispanic Catholics said they planned to vote for Dukakis, it was also conceivable that Bush could pick up a few additional votes among religious conservatives in those groups.[29]

Both campaigns promised to come up with ways of helping low-income voters, especially in small towns and rural areas, while also appealing to upscale constituencies. Bush suggested worker-retraining programs and tax breaks to create rural enterprise zones. His plans to reduce the federal deficit without raising taxes included curtailing government involvement in health care and more efficient administration of Medicare and Medicaid. He favored expansion of the space program that was of such importance to the Houston area and argued that the oil industry was being hurt by too much talk about acid rain and government regulation of environmental standards. He favored tax incentives to promote domestic oil drilling. He thought it was a good idea for Americans to be fluent in English but favored bilingual education and opposed making English the official language. Dukakis told voters that Bush was insensitive to the pain in rural America, and he pledged to help the working poor and to bring government spending under control. It was reassuring, a supporter in Kerrville explained, that Democrats from FDR to LBJ had supported Social Security, Medicare, subsidized housing, union rights, and the minimum wage; she worried that Republicans would eradicate those programs.[30] Bentsen's positions were appealing as well. Besides attracting white voters upset by civil rights legislation, he favored business and national defense, just as Bush did, opposed gun control, considered the campus unrest of the 1960s deplorable, and was said to be lukewarm on the Equal Rights Amendment. That left abortion as one of the principal differences and thus posed possibilities for appealing to conservative Protestants and Catholics. Bush's position, as expressed carefully in his acceptance speech, was that he favored adoption rather than abortion, which left antiabortion groups worried about the strength of his convictions. But they were sure that Dukakis and Bentsen were against restricting access to abortions.[31]

A narrative that features only the Religious Right's success in mobilizing support for Pat Robertson's bid for the Republican presidential nomination in 1988 gets the story wrong. It was true that Robertson's broadcasting empire was expanding, and fellow Religious Right leaders such as Jerry Falwell and Jimmy Swaggart were attracting large followings as well. But Robertson's early success as second-place finisher in Iowa was not sustained. By the time he withdrew, he carried only four states while Bush carried forty-one. In Texas Robertson received only 155,000 of the nearly three million votes cast in the Republican primary. While supporters praised his courage in focusing the campaign on pornography and sexual immorality as well as government waste, critics even within the religious community saw him as a fringe candidate with shaky theological ideas. The state's Republican leaders saw him less as an ally and more as a divisive element who appealed mostly to the members of charismatic churches. Declaring that his prayers were the reason a hurricane diverted its course away from the Virginia coast did not help his cause with the mainstream media—who dubbed this the Wacko Factor—or, for that matter, with Baptists. As one study showed, only 28 percent of evangelical Baptist preachers named him their first choice for president. Most preferred Bush.[32]

The outcome of the 1988 election held varying implications for the parties involved. For Democrats the lesson to be taken from Dukakis's defeat was that liberalism had probably run its course and that moderate positions closer to Republicans' held better promise for the future. Republicans also saw that centrism could be a winning strategy. Indeed, the Texas media was already speculating that Bush's son, who had been stumping the state on behalf of his father, could run successfully for governor against any of the Democrats' more liberal candidates. The unanswered question for centrist Republicans was whether being against abortion was the only way to attract religiously conservative voters or whether something like the "points of light" idea could be compelling.

It held potential because caring and voluntary service were values embraced by the community, but whether it would matter much in elections was an untested idea. The constituency on the far right was the one least satisfied with the outcome. They doubted that the president-elect would do much to further their cause against abortion and homosexuality. On the national stage, Robertson's bid suggested that an independent candidacy might be plausible in the future, but probably not by someone representing the Religious Right. Falwell disbanded the Moral Majority and devoted his attention to developing Liberty University. Swaggart was caught up in a sex scandal. Antiabortion groups and Religious Right supporters would have to stay organized and work harder in state and local elections. One lesson that bode well for this effort was the presence of a small but dedicated network of conservative activists within the Republican Party.[33]

ELECTING ANN RICHARDS

Observers nationally viewed the 1990 gubernatorial election in Texas as the most critical test anywhere of how Republicans and Democrats might fare in the presidential race two years later. In the Democratic primary state treasurer Ann Richards defeated Attorney General Jim Mattox of Dallas and former governor Mark White of Houston to win the nomination. On the Republican side, businessman Clayton Williams secured the nomination running against Railroad Commissioner Kent Hance, attorney Tom Luce, and former secretary of state Jack Rains. The general election contest between "Claytie and the Lady," as journalists dubbed it, pitted rivals representing not only their respective parties but also the two visions of America that had come into conflict since the 1970s.

On the liberal side, Richards had drawn national attention addressing the 1988 Democratic National Convention in what she characterized as a real Texas accent, quipping, "Poor George, he can't help it. He was born with a silver foot in his mouth." Richards was born in Lakeland, grew up in Waco, graduated from Baylor, taught school, worked for *Roe v. Wade* attorney Sarah Weddington, championed the Equal Rights Amendment, and defended abortion rights. As the first woman to run for governor in her own right (Ma Ferguson having run on her husband's coattails in 1924), Richards personified the possibilities for women to play a more prominent role in public life. Pundits said she was the most liberal of any Democratic candidate for governor in the United States. But she was also known as a fiscal conservative who reined in government spending and opposed unfunded federal mandates. "If you can't fill the till, don't pass the bill" was one of her most-quoted statements.[34]

In contrast, Williams represented the kind of self-made wealth that featured prominently in Texans' mythology about their state and that middle-class Texans could imagine attaining in smaller measure. A multimillionaire oilman from Midland, Williams adopted the persona of a West Texas cowboy wildcatter made good. Although he portrayed himself as a rough-hewn, self-made man, his background suggested otherwise. His grandfather, Oscar Waldo Williams, was a Harvard-educated lawyer who served as a judge in West Texas. His father, Clayton Wheat Williams, had a college degree in electrical engineering, entered the oil business in the 1920s as an engineer and geologist, and earned enough to purchase more than twenty thousand acres of West Texas ranch land.[35] In the 1990 contest, Williams ran a good-ole-boy campaign that he hoped would appeal to Democrats in rural and small-town Texas as well as to upscale voters in urban precincts, spending as much as $7 million of his own money on television advertising. Leading in polls by as much as 20 points, he made a gaff that lost him the race, comparing rape to bad weather: "As long as it's inevitable, you might as well lie back and enjoy it."[36]

Years later, when Williams's net worth was estimated at close to a billion dollars, he was still ridiculed for his gaffs, his failed bid for the governorship, messing with strong Texas women, and simply being one of the dimmest bulbs in the chandelier. During the 2008 presidential campaign, John McCain's staff canceled a fundraiser at Williams's home upon remembering Williams's infelicitous remark about rape. During the 2012 Republican presidential primary, critics in Texas of candidate Rick Santorum accused him of committing sexist "Claytisms." Williams said he regretted the remark but took pride in having broadened the base of Texas Republicanism beyond the country club crowd. "I made it OK for Bubba to vote Republican," he told a reporter in 2011.[37]

The 1990 contest dramatized at least three of the political fault lines being debated in the wider culture: One was the shifting meaning of conservatism and liberalism. Were these to be categories defined largely by social issues or in other terms? A second was the line between government and the private sector. How much should government do, what should it regulate, and where was the line separating its intervention in private life? The third was between the interests of the white non-Hispanic majority population and minority groups, particularly the growing population of Hispanics, as well as African Americans. How did these interests differ, and were they to be defined in racial and ethnic terms or in the more abstract coded language that Atwater described?

At the end of the 1980s the labels conservative and liberal were still very much in use as categories with which to classify political and religious leaders and their constituencies. Political conservatives defined themselves, much as they had in the 1960s, as defenders of individual liberty, traditional morality, and strong national defense. They opposed big government, disliked bureaucracy, and feared that liberals were turning the country over to communists. Liberals in politics defined themselves as proponents of equality, civil rights, and social justice and worried that conservatives were old-fashioned, self-interested, and probably racist. While the labels were commonly used interchangeably with Republican and Democrat, it was as possible as ever to identify candidates within each party as relatively more conservative or liberal. The terms were reinforced by columnists who opined under one heading or the other.

The political labels mapped loosely onto the comparable division in religion. Theological conservatives defined themselves as defenders of literal biblical truth, while liberals took issue with the view that scripture could be regarded as verbally inspired by God without room for error in human interpretation. Among Southern Baptists, where fundamentalists had won all the top offices since 1979 and purged the denomination's colleges, seminaries, and boards of anyone they considered to be deviating from a belief in biblical inerrancy, the denomination's 1988 convention in San Antonio found the two sides as well mobilized and as bitterly opposed as ever. Having been outgunned at the start, liberals were increasingly organized into special interest groups as well. On the conservative side, the muscle exercised in church elections also flexed itself on social and political issues. When Martin Scorsese's *The Last Temptation of Christ* challenged orthodox renditions of Jesus's life, for example, religious conservatives turned out in droves to protest the film. The prize of greatest interest to both sides in Texas was Baylor University. As conservatives took over more of the university's trustee board, the institution's president and tenured faculty announced plans to seek court action to preserve the university's academic freedom.[38]

Although the categories of conservative and liberal remained politically and religiously salient, it was less clear at the end of the decade than it had been earlier what they meant. *Galveston Daily News* editor Dolph Tillotson observed, for example, that conservatism generally meant being against big government and in favor of less government spending; yet Reagan, who was the most conservative president in half a century, ran up a huge government deficit. Richard Viguerie and Howard Phillips, the conservative operatives who worked with Jerry Falwell to launch the Moral Majority, felt Reagan's conservatism had been a huge disappointment on both foreign policy and domestic issues. Reagan's failure to win approval for conservative Supreme Court nominees Robert Bork and Douglas Ginsberg was especially disappointing to antiabortion constituents hoping for *Roe v. Wade* to be overturned. Fiscal conservatives like Tillotson also thought the Religious Right had gone too far in pressing socially conservative issues. "I don't know whether to laugh, holler or weep when I watch the following people on TV," Tillotson wrote, "Jim and Tammy Bakker, Oral Roberts, Jimmy Swaggart. How can people be so gullible as to take that hogwash seriously?"[39]

The race between Richards and Williams further illustrated that conservatism and liberalism were categories subject to shifting definitions. Statewide and national polls showed that voters identified themselves in about equal proportions as conservatives, liberals, or moderates, and that moderates divided between those leaning right or left. Fiscal conservatism could be reduced to slogans such as "no new taxes" and fiscal liberalism to maintaining Medicaid and Social Security benefits. But the lines could also be blurred by subtler arguments about state and federal spending, deficits and balanced budgets, sales taxes, and funding for schools and infrastructure. Religious conservatives and religious liberals were deeply critical of one another, and yet it was sometimes unclear how that mattered in politics and whether preachers like Robertson and Swaggart mostly embarrassed Republican leaders. In the Texas gubernatorial race, both candidates were Methodists, and neither criticized the other's religious beliefs.

Abortion perhaps held greatest promise as a wedge issue separating conservatives and liberals, but its political potential also remained uncertain. As recently as 1988, the Texas Coalition for Life claimed to represent only about 200,000 members, and yet antiabortion sentiment was an important factor that year in Beau Boulter's victory over Houston businessman Wes Gilbreath in the Republican primary for U.S. Senate. Activists who organized themselves in Catholic and Protestant churches across the state routinely staged protests at women's health clinics in Dallas, Houston, and Austin.[40] In the state legislature, less than a third of the legislators in either chamber were considered to be clear advocates of abortion rights. Supporters of abortion rights nevertheless were well represented by the Texas Civil Liberties Union, Texas National Council of Jewish Women, Texas Family Planning Association, Texas Women's Political Caucus, and Texas National Organization for Women. Both sides were prepared to mobilize in 1990 as the possibility of new legislation to restrict access to abortion loomed. Richards clearly had the support of abortion rights groups, while Williams opposed abortion except in cases of rape and incest or to save the life of the woman.[41]

When politically salient categories become blurred, they can cease to be important, but the opposite in which symbolism and rhetoric takes on added significance can also be the result. That was evident in the contested meanings of public and private. On the one hand, the distinction still held its historic meanings among Texans who proudly cherished liberty of conscience and especially freedom from interference by the federal government. An oil executive like Williams symbolized the industry's long fight to rid itself of government regulation. On the other hand, the distinction was open for new consideration in two ways. One was the possibility of public-private cooperation in social service provision represented in Bush's points-of-light metaphor. Already the proposal was generating debate about how much each side should do. The other new consideration was symbolized in Richards's candidacy. In stereotypic traditional gendered understandings, women symbolized the protected domestic space of private life while maleness connoted the more bruising, abrasive public sphere. The distinction in reality had never been quite that clear and was certainly less so since the 1960s as a result of changes in the composition of the labor force and in understandings of gender. But the gubernatorial contest now opened the field for additional debate. Williams's attacks on Richards's personal life as a divorced mother and recovering alcoholic posed new questions about what was appropriate or inappropriate in a political campaign. Whether abortion, questions about public education and social service, and about civility itself were better addressed by women or by men also came squarely to the front. The best training for men seeking public office, pundits on the liberal side suggested, was probably motherhood.[42]

The separation of voters along racial and ethnic lines was also blurred and contested. To the extent that Williams could be successful in attracting the Bubba vote, as he put it, Republicans might now be in a position to claim not only the white upper-middle class but also the white working class, leaving Democrats with African Americans and Hispanics. But the growing number of Hispanic voters posed the possibility that Republicans might also need to be more attentive to the political potential of this segment of the population. There was perhaps potential in the fact that nearly all the state's Hispanics were Catholic, and the Catholic Church was strongly opposed to abortion.

In the months preceding the 1990 election, one of the state's most dramatic confrontations over abortion took place in South Texas. Corpus Christi native Rex Moses, a thirty-five-year-old financial consultant, converted to Catholicism in 1988 and began organizing antiabortion protests in connection with the state chapter of Operation Rescue. "I began to see that legalized abortion was not just an attack on unborn babies," he said. "It was an attack on the church, on every Christian's willingness to love his neighbor." By 1989, seeing the symbolic importance of focusing on Corpus Christi—literally, the body of Christ—Moses concentrated his antiabortion efforts on his hometown. Willie Z. Terry, pastor of the predominantly black True Faith Baptist Church, joined the cause, founding Freedmen for Life and arguing that abortion was as evil as slavery had been. The sheriff lent support by decorating his office with posters of crushed fetuses, and a local real estate developer provided Moses with finances. The community's most visible Hispanic leader, Bishop Rene Gracida, made national headlines by publicly excommunicating two of the diocese's Hispanic abortion providers.[43]

An exit poll in November 1990 showed that 88 percent of African American voters and 71 percent of Hispanic voters opted for Richards, while only 36 percent of white non-Hispanic voters did. Those results suggested that Republicans could pretty well forget appealing to black voters but kept the prospect of making inroads among Hispanic voters alive. Williams fared especially well among wealthier white Anglos, winning 72 percent of the votes among those with incomes of $100,000 or more, while Richards won a majority of the white Anglo vote among those in the lowest income category. It was evident, though, that Republicans could win a substantial minority of the low-income, white non-Hispanic vote.

Religion's impact was most notable in strengthening the Republican margin. Among white voters who identified themselves as evangelicals or fundamentalists, only 15 percent voted for Richards while 79 percent voted for Williams. Abortion proved to be one of the strongest factors differentiating votes for the two candidates. Among white Anglos who thought abortion should not be legal in any circumstances, 81 percent voted for Williams compared with 62 percent who said it should be legal in some circumstances, and only 38 percent among those who wanted it to be legal in all circumstances. The possibility that opposition to abortion might help Republicans among black and Hispanic voters was evident from the poll as well. Overall, black and Hispanic voters were somewhat *more* likely to oppose abortion than white Anglo voters. Approximately a quarter of black and Hispanic voters thought abortion should not be legal in any circumstances, compared with only 11 percent of white Anglo voters, and conversely, only about a quarter of black and Hispanic voters said abortion should be legal in all circumstances, compared with 36 percent of white Anglo voters. On another question, 45 percent of Hispanics said abortion should be against the law except in cases of rape or incest—9 percent more than among white Anglos. Williams won nearly a third of the votes among blacks and Hispanics who opposed abortion under some or all circumstances but garnered less than a tenth of the votes of blacks and Hispanics who thought abortion should be legal under all circumstances.[44]

COMPASSIONATE CONSERVATISM

As questions about public welfare continued to arouse controversy, the bright spot in an otherwise gloomy discussion was that Americans were still rising to the occasion when needs arose by doing good deeds through volunteer organizations. Local and national news media routinely ran stories about courageous acts of altruism and quiet but effective modes of community assistance. When tornadoes ripped through several towns in West Texas, it was the local Rotary club that extended a helping hand to the victims. If school budgets were stretched thin, parent-teacher organizations notably stepped into the gap. The Special Olympics drew volunteers. Soup kitchens and homeless shelters were helping indigent families. Stories like these countered the image critics of American culture had been voicing about the society being narcissistic, individualistic, and obsessed by greed and self-interest. On the political front, the narratives implicitly contradicted the view that welfare cuts were being driven by a tight-fisted lack of concern for the needy. Volunteering and charitable giving suggested that Americans who deplored welfare expenditures were not mean-spirited after all.

By the early 1990s, the debate about welfare and the role of volunteers had widened. On one side, new evidence from a study by Independent Sector in Washington showed that many Americans were engaged in supporting volunteer organizations with time and money but the overall amount given was declining, perhaps by as much as 20 percent from the previous year. Private charity was certainly important, the report suggested, but should not be considered a substitute for government-funded programs.[45] Writers and policy makers on the left increasingly absorbed the theme of compassion as an argument for strengthening social programs. At a symposium in Texas, compassion was also linked to the need to move past white racism still evident against blacks and Hispanics.

On the other side, critics of welfare spending argued that compassion was fine but needed to be practiced judiciously. Associating compassion with government programs, they said, could encourage welfare chiselers to feel even more than they already did that handouts were something they deserved. Compassion was better if provided through voluntary groups. A new argument suggested that it was even more effective when given by religious organizations.

The contrast in how religion was perceived could be seen clearly in two of the arguments that surfaced in Texas. At the symposium in which white racism was emphasized, religion was cast largely as a villain. Recalling the region's history of discrimination against blacks and Hispanics, the participants observed that the church had eventually played a constructive role in combating segregation during the civil rights movement but for the most part had reinforced the status quo. "All during this time, Christianity had a presence in the area," one of the participants declared, "but the lives of Mexicans, Mexican Americans and Blacks as second-class citizens continued." If things were to change, compassion would have to be cast in new ways that depended less on good intentions and more on laws and programs. The alternative view was expressed most clearly by Marvin Olasky, a University of Texas professor who argued that religion provided the best hope for charitable activities that actually worked. To back these claims, Olasky had gone undercover, posing as a homeless person seeking help at a shelter, where he observed that the assistance given seemed impersonal and devoid of spiritual meaning. That kind of assistance, he charged, was a "war on God." In contrast, he suggested that church-based programs could provide spiritual healing that would be effective in freeing people from poverty, addictions, and hopelessness. Some exceptional African American churches, he said, were providing exactly this kind of help.[46]

Although race seldom entered the discussion quite this explicitly, racial controversies remained an important part of the context in which welfare and volunteering were being considered. The riots in Los Angeles following the Rodney King beating in 1991 drew wide attention in racially divided Texas communities. Editorials and letters to local newspapers variously argued that the incident showed how much was still needed to overcome racism or suggested that white people were more civilized than black people. In Texas City African American leader Lynn Ray Ellison, who would later become the town's mayor, traced the rich history of black philanthropy and black church-supported self-help organizations in an effort to combat the view that African Americans were simply dependent on government welfare. "When African Americans receive certain things from the government," he observed, "it is not a gift or a hand-out, but things they need, things they would not have needed if the letters of the Declaration of Independence and the Constitution of the United States had been applied fairly and equally to all at the beginning."[47] In racially and ethnically mixed school districts, residents argued about the racial prejudices of teachers and board members. An African American board member in one district came under such criticism from white parents that the town's clergy alliance felt compelled to come to her defense. "Many a time I would get up in the morning and find a white foot or a blond head sticking out from the covers in the den or living room. All colors of kids have played in our backyard and spent time in our home," she said. "If I was a racist this would never have happened."[48] In another district, a white teacher lost her job after assigning racially charged readings from Mark Twain and William Faulkner, and in yet another community parents were divided about students reading Toni Morrison's *Beloved*.[49]

But the public language in which citizens argued about public policy had shifted since the civil rights movement. Although white residents may have had in mind that the poor people receiving welfare were black and Hispanic, the arguments against welfare were more often framed in moral than in racial or ethnic terms. The moral outrage that masked racial concerns added vehemence that would have been hard to understand had the arguments been only about tax rates. Welfare payments became handouts to immoral welfare chiselers who were lazy, unwilling to find work, refusing to get married, and having too many children. Public officials who considered this arrangement fair were in reality taking money from upstanding people who lived by moral principles and giving it to the morally undeserving. Wasn't it wrong, a pastor in Lockhart argued, to associate compassion with people on welfare instead of with people "living by the dignity of their own means?"[50]

As the Clinton administration proposed overhauling the healthcare system, these arguments about welfare shaped the public's reaction against it. Liberals were confiscating honestly acquired earnings in the name of compassion. The program was socialized medicine and indicated the socialistic direction in which the administration was headed. Some of the arguments against it even took a theological turn. "The Bible encourages us to voluntarily give some of our profits to those in need, in contrast to socialism, which forces us to participate in redistribution of the wealth," a Texas Republican talk show host explained. In his view, trying to help the poor through government programs just because the people happened to be Christian should not fool people. The better way was for people to work hard for what they got instead of expecting the government "to fluff up your pillows."[51]

It was not that the liberal side went undefended. The *Texas Observer*, founded in Austin in 1954, provided an outlet for muckraking journalism that frequently challenged conservative ideas concerning working people, poverty, and welfare. The *Observer*'s principal supporter was Bernard Rapoport, a Waco insurance executive whose parents were Russian Jewish immigrants and whose fortune went mostly to support nonprofit organizations, scholarships, and Democratic candidates. One of the *Observer*'s writers in the 1970s was Molly Ivins, daughter of a Houston oil and gas executive and educated at Smith College and Columbia University School of Journalism. Ivins's columns began appearing in the *Washington Post* and the *New York Times*, and by the early 1990s she was covering state

and national news for the *Fort Worth Star Telegram*. Ivins seldom passed an opportunity to chide conservatives over their lack of support for programs aimed at
helping the disadvantaged. When Newt Gingrich became the leading opponent
of the Clinton health reforms, Ivins wrote sarcastically, "I've thought Gingrich
had an unusual sensitivity about the problems of seriously ill people ever since I
learned that he gave divorce papers to his first wife while she was in the hospital
for cancer treatment."[52]

This was the context in which the 1994 gubernatorial race between incumbent Ann Richards and challenger George W. Bush took place. Richards's work
in the 1970s with Sarah Weddington and on behalf of the Equal Rights Amendment had burnished her credentials as a liberal Democrat. As governor, Richards
had focused on revitalizing the state's economic infrastructure and advocating
for prison reform, gun control, and equitable school financing.[53] Bush's visibility
stemmed from his role as state campaign manager for his father in 1988 and,
more recently, as managing general partner of the Texas Rangers baseball team.
In 1994 Richards ran on a platform emphasizing her experience, national reputation, efforts in securing defense contracts, and fighting crime. The campaign
described her as a fiscal conservative who had tightened the state budget, rooted
out waste, and held the line on taxes. Bush ran on his leadership experience
in business and willingness to fight harder against crime and high taxes. The
campaign criticized Richards on grounds that she favored taxpayer funding of
abortion, teaching about contraception in public schools, and benefits for homosexual partners of government employees. It also accused her administration of
expanding government regulations and relying on government welfare programs
to solve social problems. Both candidates attracted donations from all fifty states
and ran aggressive television campaigns. Although Richards outspent Bush on
advertising by about 25 percent, Bush secured a 53 percent to 46 percent victory,
carrying 188 of the state's 254 counties.

Exit poll results showed that several factors contributed to Bush's victory.
Richards won 85 percent of the black vote and 71 percent of the Hispanic vote,
but Bush received 62 percent of the white Anglo vote. Among all voters, Richards received nearly two-thirds of the votes cast by people in the lowest income
category, while Bush received almost two-thirds of the votes in the highest income category. Among white voters, Richards also did better among low-income
voters while Bush scored large victories among higher-income voters. Unsurprisingly, Richards drew large majorities among Democrats and self-identified
political liberals, while Bush attracted upward of 80 percent of Republicans and
self-identified political conservatives. With conservatives outnumbering liberals
by more than two to one, Bush had the clear advantage. Bush also fared better
among independents than Richards did.[54]

Asked what issues influenced their decision, Bush voters indicated that Bush's
campaign slogan "time for change" was an important factor, suggesting that the
anti-incumbent sentiment resulting in huge victories for Republicans in U.S.

congressional races was also at work. Richards voters were especially influenced by her experience and views about education, while Bush voters were more likely to have been swayed by concerns about abortion, crime, and taxes. Although the Richards campaign repeatedly accused the Bush campaign of lying about her record and distorting the facts about crime, twice as many voters overall thought Richards's advertising included unfair attacks than did so about Bush's advertising.

The exit results showed that religion was an important factor among white voters. Among Jews only 12 percent voted for Bush, while among Catholics 54 percent did, and that proportion rose to 66 percent among Protestants. Among white voters who considered themselves part of the Religious Right, 81 percent voted for Bush, and among those who described their religion as "born-again Christian or fundamentalist," 83 percent did. One-third of white Protestants and "other Christians" considered themselves born-again Christians or fundamentalists.

White conservative Protestants voting for Republicans had become an established pattern in Texas politics since Reagan's victory in 1980. Eighty percent of white, born-again Texans had voted for Reagan again in 1984. They were less persuaded about Bush in 1988 but gave him a 54 to 37 percent margin over Dukakis. In 1992 Bush again won a majority of the white, born-again electorate in Texas, receiving 57 percent of the vote compared with 27 percent for Perot and only 16 percent for Clinton. Their vote in 1994 was thus a continuation of previous voting but also reflected greater consensus than in recent elections. The other characteristic of white, born-again voters was that they were largely middle class. Only 32 percent had family incomes below $30,000 in 1992, barely higher than the 29 percent among all white voters, compared with 39 percent of Hispanic voters and 52 percent of black voters.[55]

The Republican "Revolution of '94" that included a net increase of fifty-four seats in the U.S. House of Representatives and eight seats in the U.S. Senate set the stage for the 1995 Personal Responsibility and Work Opportunity Act, which dramatically reformed the nation's welfare policies. The legislation included a "Charitable Choice" provision that aimed to place religious organizations on a level playing field with government and nonreligious service agencies in receiving government funds. Welfare reform and Charitable Choice resonated with growing public opinion that three decades of Great Society war-on-poverty programs had produced unsatisfactory results. Spending $350 billion annually on poverty programs, the nation seemed no closer to ending poverty. Indeed, critics charged, poverty programs were helping government bureaucrats more than the poor. In language reminiscent of the points-of-light metaphor, critics called for smaller local programs that combined voluntary assistance with government funds to give a more caring, personal, compassionate face to charitable service. "We're already spending the money, without much by way of results to show for it," *Washington Post* columnist William Raspberry observed. "Why not figure out how to spend some of it through organizations that, though demonstrably successful, are suffering for want of funding?"[56]

Research in the early 1990s demonstrated that voluntary charitable service in the United States was huge and that religion and religiously motivated individuals were an important part of these efforts. A national study of congregations conducted in 1992 by Independent Sector found that many congregations were involved directly in their communities or indirectly through their denominations in social service activities such as day care programs, soup kitchens, homeless shelters, and tutoring activities. Nearly all of the religious leaders surveyed considered tax-exemption and protection of First Amendment freedom of religion essential to their organizations' activities.[57] At that time few local congregations were receiving financial assistance for social service activities through government grants, but large, faith-based organizations such as Catholic Social Services, Lutheran Social Services, Salvation Army, and World Vision were participating in government programs distributing food and international humanitarian relief assistance. Other research showed that active involvement in congregations forged social networks and reinforced beliefs about altruism and compassion that translated into giving and volunteering not only to members' congregations but also to community-service organizations.[58]

That was certainly true in Texas, where churches had long been involved in charitable service activities. In one of the oldest communities in East Texas, for example, the Southern Baptist church had become known as the country club congregation, even though no country club existed anywhere near, because all its 250 members were white, and most were prominent in business and the professions. Recognizing that they were more privileged than many in the community, church members took pride in providing meals to children from low-income families and working with Habitat for Humanity to refurbish derelict housing. It was good, one of the leaders said, for country club church people to get their hands dirty, especially by working with African Americans and Hispanics who "may not have the best long-term feelings historically about white churches."[59] An elderly woman who attended a Methodist church in suburban Houston expressed the idea of faith and compassion going hand in hand particularly well. "If we dare to put our feet on the path that [Jesus] makes for us," she said, "we have to be open to the needs of all of those around us and not just their spiritual needs but also their physical needs."[60]

At large, urban churches, a wide variety of community services were typically included in the congregations' activities. At the Cathedral of Guadalupe in downtown Dallas, for example, staff and lay members taught literacy and English as a second language to new immigrants, worked with community arts organizations, and helped sponsor a food bank, a recreation center for neighborhood youth, and a program for people with disabilities. Similarly, the Brentwood Baptist Church in suburban Houston—a Southern Baptist congregation that had integrated in 1970 and by the early 1990s grown to a five-thousand-member, predominantly African American church with twelve buildings on a hundred-acre campus—devoted about $500,000 annually to various food pantries, tutoring programs, AIDS ministries, and job-training programs.[61] On a more modest scale, even small churches with dwindling memberships were providing similar services. At a small Baptist church in West Texas with only sixty members in a community that was predominantly Hispanic, for instance, the pastor and a few of the churchwomen were trying to transcend racial and ethnic barriers by helping the needy cover their medical and utility bills, provide a Vacation Bible School each summer for children, and help sponsor the local Thrift Store.[62] A statewide survey a few years later found nearly a quarter of all regular-attending church members involved in some kind of volunteer activities for human service.[63]

The state's charitable organizations were beginning to pioneer new efforts in international humanitarian and relief efforts as well. A prominent example was the Buckner Foundation, which originated in the orphanage that Reverend R. C. Buckner founded in the nineteenth century and expanded in the first years of the twentieth century through private philanthropy. By 2010 its assets would total more than $330 million, making it one of the largest charitable organizations in any state. In the early 1990s its board decided to expend a portion of these assets on orphanages and other humanitarian programs in other countries. Although it was still an evangelistic Christian ministry under the supervision of the Baptist General Convention of Texas, it was also poised to work more closely with U.S. government agencies and to implement programs receiving government grants as well as donations from individuals and congregations.[64]

Governor Bush embraced the idea of religious organizations working in partnership with state and local government to carry out social service activities. One of the first steps was creating a task force to examine the work already being done by faith-based programs and to identify ways in which to reinforce this work. By early 1997 the task force came up with a plan that called for churches and other private charities to assist directly in child-care, rehabilitation, substance-abuse, and work-training programs as part of the state's welfare-to-work initiative. Under the plan, voluntary charitable programs would not only supplement government welfare, as they had done over the past century, but receive government funding. In addition, welfare recipients would receive vouchers to be used in seeking help from these faith-based and other private programs. Backers considered it the most aggressive response to Charitable Choice of any state in the nation.[65] The key difficulty was making sure these programs did not violate the constitutional separation of church and state. The practical difficulty was ensuring that the various religious organizations were treated equitably. For example, the Texas Workforce Commission that was to oversee the program included twenty-eight regional advisory boards that by statute were to include a majority of private representation. Church leaders insisted that if their organizations were to be involved, clergy should be included on the boards, but it was unclear how they would be chosen and which denominations and traditions would be included. When the new laws went into effect, one of the provisions reflected Lester Roloff's long struggle against government interference in church-run programs: it provided for private rather than state accreditation and licensing of religiously run child-care programs.[66]

The Texas Association of Christian Childcare Agencies (TACCA) was established in 1998 as the new accrediting agency through which faith-based programs could apply. Its record was mixed. On the one hand, its process was much quicker than the Texas Department of Protective and Regulatory Services, as the directors of a center called A Place for Grace west of Fort Worth discovered after lengthy wrangling with the state agency and one in Kansas. The TACCA approved the center's plan to provide clients religious instruction and to refuse service to anyone unwilling to participate. On the other hand, the TACCA accredited the existing Roloff homes despite recent charges of physical abuse at one of the homes. In addition, fewer of the faith-based agencies in the state than expected took advantage of the TACCA accrediting option. When the legislature declined to renew the statute for private accreditation in 2001, only seven of more than two thousand religiously affiliated agencies had used the TACCA.[67]

Teen Challenge—the program for delinquent youth begun by evangelist David Wilkerson in New York City in the 1960s—was the one that Bush considered exemplary of the good work that faith could accomplish. By the early 1990s, Teen Challenge included a network of 150 centers nationwide, 5 of which were in Texas, including one in San Antonio that had run into trouble with the Texas Commission on Alcohol and Drug Abuse for failing to hire licensed drug counselors. Teen Challenge centers focused on drug rehabilitation, claiming exceptionally high rates of success based on testimonials from converted ex–drug users that resulted in teen addicts in the program turning over their life to Jesus and drawing strength from their newfound faith. The model was similar to Alcoholic Anonymous's reliance on a higher power but explicitly emphasized finding salvation through faith in Jesus. It resonated with Bush's own recovery from heavy drinking and, in any case, appeared to be an efficient way of addressing the state's long-standing concerns about juvenile delinquency, drugs, and alcoholism. "Teen Challenge should view itself as a pioneer in how Texas approaches faith-based programs," Bush observed in a 1995 interview.[68]

Another of the activities to which faith-based ideas were directed was crime. Bush's campaign against Richards had challenged her record on crime, arguing that violent crime under her administration had increased by as much as 30 percent. Richards argued that the overall crime index had actually declined during her time in office. Both arguments were correct, but crime, the overcrowding of jails, and the cost of maintaining jails and prisons remained topics of public concern.[69] The new faith-based programs included a bill encouraging law enforcement agencies to rely on faith-based programs to help lawbreakers to change their lives and reenter society. This idea was particularly appealing because it offered to lower the cost of maintaining prisons. As one local official observed,

"Maybe it will change the hearts of the people and relieve the uncontrollable burden of trying to help."[70]

The model for faith-based prisoner rehabilitation was convicted Watergate felon Charles "Chuck" Colson's Prison Fellowship, founded in 1976 after Colson had spent seven months in prison and become a born-again Christian. Prison Fellowship's InnerChange Freedom Initiative included a program at a prison near Houston that Bush considered effective by "changing one life at a time." Like Teen Challenge, InnerChange included an intensive program of Bible study through which prisoners learned that God could change their hearts. Visiting the prison in 1999, Olasky noted that recidivism among the program's graduates was only 17 percent compared with 60 percent of released inmates nationwide.[71]

In the foreword to Olasky's book entitled *Compassionate Conservatism*, Bush echoed the theme Reagan had emphasized about big government generating an immense bureaucracy that destroyed personal initiative and hurt rather than helped the poor. "Government can do certain things very well," Bush wrote, "but it cannot put hope in our hearts or a sense of purpose in our lives. That requires churches and synagogues and mosques and charities. A truly compassionate government is one that rallies these armies of compassion and provides an environment in which they can thrive."[72]

During the 2000 presidential campaign between Bush and Vice President Al Gore, both candidates spoke favorably about faith-based charitable service activities, although Bush said more about it and associated the idea more openly with his personal faith than Gore did. A national study in late August and early September found widespread support for "allowing religious organizations to apply, along with other organizations, for government funding to provide social services such as job training or drug treatment counseling to people who need them." Among white non-Hispanics, 66 percent favored the idea, and among black and Hispanic voters, nearly 90 percent did. Seventy-one percent of white non-Hispanics who said they were born again and attended church regularly favored the idea, compared with only 52 percent of white non-Hispanics who did not attend church.[73] The potential for faith-based programs to reach across racial and ethnic lines was illustrated at the Republican National Convention when Bush was introduced by African American pastor Kirbyjon Caldwell. Reverend Caldwell was a former investment banker who headed the eleven-thousand-member Windsor Village United Methodist Church in Houston, a racially mixed evangelical congregation actively involved in numerous community charity projects, including a food bank, tutoring program for children, a shelter for abused children, and a job-training program for low-income families. Bush had made contact with Caldwell in 1996 and drew inspiration from the church's service activities for his emphasis on faith-based programs.[74]

As one of his administration's first policy initiatives, Bush announced a plan to greatly expand and more aggressively implement a program of faith-based charitable service initiatives. Under the rubric of "rallying the armies of compassion," the new program established through executive orders a White House Office of Faith-Based and Community Initiatives and instructed five cabinet-level departments to establish Centers for Faith-Based and Community Initiatives. The executive orders were drafted by fellow Texan Don R. Willett, who had chaired the Texas task force on faith-based initiatives and several years later would fight to protect the Ten Commandments monument on the state capitol grounds and keep the phrase "under God" in the Pledge of Allegiance.[75] The nation's religious groups, Bush observed, were filled with quiet heroes who "lift people's lives in ways that are beyond government's know-how, usually on shoestring budgets, and they heal our nation's ills one heart and one act of kindness at a time." The plan called for eliminating federal barriers to faith-based service organizations receiving government grants, greater reliance on private giving to meet community needs, and stronger support within government agencies for programs that drew on faith-based charitable activities.[76]

FAITH AND POLITICS

The language in which questions about government funding for faith-based initiatives were discussed in the 1990s differed from the debates about church and state that had surfaced during the 1960 presidential election and even those in the 1970s prompted by Lester Roloff and James Robison. Although Southern Baptists were still the largest denomination in Texas, parts of the state were becoming some of the most religiously diverse locations anywhere in America. Annual surveys conducted in the Houston metropolitan area, for example, showed that only 4 percent of adult residents identified themselves as something other than Protestant, Catholic, or Jewish between 1990 and 1996, but in surveys conducted from 1997 to 2000, that proportion jumped to 12 percent, or approximately 300,000, among the total adult population.[77] When researchers led by sociologists Helen Rose Ebaugh and Janet Saltzman Chafetz surveyed Houston religious organizations in 1997, they found that recent immigrants had established nearly 800 congregations, including Buddhist meditation centers, Hindu temples, Muslim mosques, and Jain and Zoroastrian worship centers as well as dozens of Hispanic, Korean, Vietnamese, Chinese, and multiethnic Christian ministries.[78] Immigrants from predominantly Muslim countries had been particularly drawn by the state's oil- and petroleum-refining industries. The decennial census in 2000 showed more than 55,000 residents of Texas from Arab countries, with another 21,000 from Iran. Estimates from census surveys between 2006 and 2010 showed a total from these countries exceeding 100,000. Data collected as part of a national study in 2010 identified 102 synagogues in Texas, 36 mosques, 18 Hindu temples, and 40 Buddhist temples or meditation centers.[79]

That religious diversity had to be acknowledged was evident in Bush's mention of synagogues and mosques as well as churches in the foreword to Olasky's book. The language in "rallying the armies of compassion" underscored the same theme, noting that faith-based organizations were to be encouraged "whether run by Methodists, Muslims, Mormons, or good people of no faith at all."[80] Unsurprisingly, the potential political payoff of acknowledging religious diversity was not lost on political operatives. In an essay for the conservative Texas Public Policy Foundation, Americans for Tax Reform president Grover G. Norquist, who had become one of the most powerful advocates for fiscal conservatism, argued that Muslims had probably been the key to Bush's narrow victory in Florida in November 2000 and were an emerging "naturally conservative faith-based community" that Republicans should cultivate. To that end, Norquist had already been busy, serving on the founding board of directors of the Islamic Institute, which was interested in developing libertarian economic ideas from the Qur'an. With Norquist's help, the institute's president, Khaled Saffuri, brought a group of national Muslim leaders to meet with Bush in Austin prior to the 2000 election, secured a promise from Republican legislators to ease restrictions on Muslim immigration, and solicited endorsements for Bush from other Muslim organizations. Norquist considered these developments the positive background for Bush's remarks after the September 11, 2001, attacks to quell anti-Muslim sentiment. Norquist anticipated an "ecumenical right" consisting of evangelical Protestants, conservative Catholics, Orthodox Jews, and Muslims working in common cause against abortion and to combat the welfare state, the secular left, and higher taxes.[81]

Norquist may have been right about evangelical Protestants and other groups sharing conservative political ideas, but theological differences remained strong. In 1999 former Criswell Center for Biblical Studies president and fundamentalist leader Dr. Paige Patterson, now serving as president of the Southern Baptist Convention, received a letter from a coalition of sixty Jewish groups asking the denomination to stop supporting deceptive tactics to convert Jews. Efforts had been made following Southern Baptist Dr. Bailey Smith's remark at the 1980 National Affairs Briefing in Dallas that "God Almighty does not hear the prayer of a Jew" to achieve greater understanding of Jews among Southern Baptists, but tensions remained.[82] The controversy in 1999 arose amid protests in Houston led by Hindus over Southern Baptists' efforts to convert them from the "hopeless darkness" of their faith. The denomination's fundamentalist leaders organized similar campaigns to convert Muslims, Buddhists, and Jews. These were evangelistic efforts "to simply tell people about Jesus Christ," a Southern Baptist pastor in Houston explained, but he conceded that they were sometimes regarded as being judgmental.[83]

John Hanson was an oil company executive who attended a Southern Baptist congregation on the outskirts of Houston. He did not mind appearing judgmental. When asked about Hindus and Muslims, he replied, "Ooh! It makes me sick to think of what they're doing and what their beliefs are." In his view, they needed to learn the "real truth about who God is." Above all, that meant finding Jesus and developing a personal relationship with Jesus. "Unless people have that," he said, "I don't believe their life in eternity may be spent with him." Mr. Hanson was also fairly sure that Mormons were unsaved. One of his friends was Mormon, he said, and the man "really missed the boat" because he did not believe that Jesus was the savior of the world.[84]

The protests in Houston proved short-lived, but a national study a few years later found that as many as 30 percent of the American public believed that only Christians can go to heaven, and that among these "Christian exclusivists" there were strong misgivings about Muslims, Hindus, and Buddhists coming to America as immigrants. The study further showed that in cities where mosques, temples, and meditation centers were often located only a few blocks from a church, there was little contact and few efforts to bridge faith communities. The typical pattern was like people standing together in an elevator pretending to be alone. As a Hindu leader in Houston whose temple was right across the street from a Baptist church observed, "Maybe they feel that everyone who is not Christian is something they don't want to know about." He figured the lack of contact was because of Christians feeling frightened and regarding Hindus as "someone diseased." A Buddhist leader's experience in Houston was similar. Nobody paid his group much attention. He thought church people were just busy with their own activities. "Texas is quite a conservative state," he said.[85]

This was the context in which faith-based initiatives were introduced. There was enough diversity that the rhetoric required mentioning non-Christian groups even though Christians still composed at least 80 percent of the nation's religiously involved population. The idea that Bush, Olasky, and other advocates of faith-based initiatives had in mind was that the various religious groups could all become involved in their own way. Former president Jimmy Carter emphasized the same theme in calling on Catholics and Jews and Muslims and Baptists to embrace community service. "Imagine what would happen if the 145 million members of faith groups in the United States served just their immediate neighborhoods to ensure that every person went to bed adequately fed, every pregnant woman had prenatal care and every little child was immunized," he said.[86] At the local level, people were also increasingly aware of the diversity in their own communities. As the owner of a restaurant in San Antonio put it, "We've got so many different churches and different beliefs. Everybody believes that what they believe is best. I don't see why you have to criticize one to the other." Or in the words of a space scientist who attended one of the Hindu temples in Houston, "You can be a good Hindu or good Christian or good Muslim. To me the labels don't matter that much."[87]

As an accommodation to religious diversity, *faith* more often became the preferred language in which discussions about religion receiving public funding and otherwise connecting with the political sphere were framed. When the small town of Center Point northwest of San Antonio launched an experimental program in 1995 to teach values and morality to public middle school students, "faith" was at the top of the list, followed by responsibility, compassion, work, and self-discipline.[88] The idea appealed not only to conservatives and Republicans but also to some moderates and Democrats. When President Clinton observed that students need not leave their faith at the schoolhouse door, a Democrat in the small town of Clute on the Gulf Coast southwest of Galveston declared that the president was right. Schoolchildren could pray silently, if they wished, say grace before lunch, wear religious items, and study religious art and history. It was wrong, the journalist wrote, for religious conservatives to politicize the issue by calling for a constitutional amendment forcing mandated prayer.[89]

Faith was language that conveniently transcended denominational barriers while at the same time retained the distinctive connotations of particular traditions. At a clergy forum in Texas City, both ideas were evident. People were less interested in adhering to the teachings of particular denominations, one of the pastors explained, than in seeking spiritual depth. The church was not an institution, another suggested, but people of faith coming together to worship God. The idea was not to follow some canned theological prescription but to deepen one's faith and to be "faith-guided" in making decisions. Nondenominational and new ecumenical ministries were growing, the pastors agreed. Yet they also spoke of the differences separating evangelical and mainline congregations.[90] In other contexts, people of faith were attending rallies sponsored by Promise Keepers, the interdenominational men's organization that encouraged participants to be better husbands and fathers, and Women's Aglow groups that helped women gain personal strength through fellowship and prayer. Sunday school classes focused on faith enlightenment and faith enrichment. Bible studies went under the rubric Women of Faith and Men of Faith, and clergy sometimes referred to their congregations as factories of faith. Nationwide some 40 percent of the adult public claimed membership in small groups that met regularly for prayer, study, camaraderie, and service. Many of the groups had religious connections, but few were exclusive to a particular denomination.[91]

This was not the kind of faith, necessarily, that the authors of *Habits of the Heart*, the best-selling study of American individualism in the 1980s, had identified as "Sheilaism"—spirituality rooted only in oneself.[92] However, it did emphasize personal opinion, individual belief, and even faith in one's own spiritual path enough to temper some of the abrasiveness that otherwise characterized the differences among religious traditions. A woman in East Texas who had grown up in Peru illustrated the point especially well in asserting, "I believe in God big time," and then explaining that she had attended services at Catholic, Baptist, and various other churches but basically regarded faith as a "silent relationship between me and God."[93] Or as a woman in South Texas observed in describing her great aunt Irma, the elderly woman was a devout Catholic who exhibited faith in the church, but also a deep *"faith in her own faith."*[94] It was the kind of language that was especially good at conveying a dual meaning—faith in Christ to fellow Christians and at the same time openness to diversity. "I don't talk about a particular faith," Bush observed at a meeting in Houston hosted by Reverend Caldwell. "I believe the Lord can work through many faiths, whether it be the Christian faith, Jewish faith, Muslim faith, Hindu faith. When I speak of faith, I speak of all faiths."[95]

The possibility that religious conservatives, moderates, and liberals as well as Jews, Muslims, and Hindus might overcome their differences by coming together in small groups, emphasizing faith as a personal journey, attending churches where narrative expository preaching steered clear of controversial issues, and engaging in community-service activities sponsored by faith-based organizations, though, was only partly realized. The attacks on September 11, 2001, drew the nation together in a spirit of patriotic zeal that included Democrats and Republicans as well as liberals and conservatives. But the fault lines that separated conservatives and liberals and that pitted the two against one another in local and national elections continued. The more inclusive points-of-light metaphor had now become compassionate *conservatism*.

The difficulty of bringing religion as directly into the political sphere as the faith-based initiatives did was that funds provided by the taxpaying public posed hard questions about the equitable management and distribution of those funds. The task force Bush created to launch the initiative in Texas was sparse on religious diversity. Sixteen of the seventeen members were Christian, and among that number the majority were theologically conservative Protestants and Catholics. The one non-Christian was a Jewish layperson. Muslims and Hindus were not represented. Nor were Protestants and Catholics who favored strict separation of church and state and were skeptical of government-funded faith-based programs. Thirteen of the members worked directly for faith-based service organizations. Critics said the board members stood to benefit from their own recommendations, too often framed their arguments in distinctly Christian language, and failed to consider the views of religious leaders opposed to government involvement in faith-based social services. Providing funds to evangelical Christian programs such as the Roloff homes and Teen Challenge posed the possibility that funds could go to some other religion such as one of the existing polygamist groups of Mormon fundamentalists in West Texas or have been given to the Branch Davidian group near Waco that came under violent siege by the U.S. Bureau of Alcohol, Tobacco and Firearms in 1993.[96] As a member of the state legislature observed, Texans might have gotten used to the idea of some groups receiving government aid, but if it was a Muslim group, "I don't believe that would be very well accepted."[97]

Church leaders who were heavily involved in community-service activities worried that taking government money would not only bring government intrusion but also diminish the spirit of voluntarism and benevolence they considered essential to the church's mission. The pastor of a predominantly African American congregation in inner-city Dallas whose members were staffing assistance programs for the homeless, adult literacy education, and tutoring efforts expressed these reservations in explaining why he strongly opposed taking government funds. "My personal belief as a pastor," he said, "is that when you receive government monies to do ministries instead of receiving the tithes and offerings to do ministry that the Bible describes that you give the government the authority to tell you what you can and cannot preach." He thought the "stewardship principle in the Bible" required funding church programs through offerings and not through the government. Keeping free of the government also gave his congregation practical advantages in criticizing government policies. For instance, the congregation was part of a community network of African American churches that advocated against school closings in poor neighborhoods and criticized the state's policies on immigration.[98]

Pastors' views, though, were complex. Although some were outspokenly in favor of or against congregations receiving government funding, the larger climate of opinion was shaped both by the culture wars and by religious leaders' sense of being beleaguered by an anti-religious culture driven by secular humanism. A Methodist pastor in Dallas captured the resulting ambivalence well in observing, on the one hand, that it was difficult to work with some ministers on the right who wanted to create "over-simplified litmus tests" about everything, while, on the other hand, noting that pastors could hardly propose anything without critics on the secular left jumping all over them for being moralistic. "One of the things that gets very tiresome is when you're a church," he said, and "it's immediately assumed that you're the designated stick-in-the mud."[99] The views of lay leaders involved in service organizations were similarly complex. A leader in the Hispanic community in El Paso, for instance, was deeply influenced by the service ethic of her Catholic faith, appreciated the church's role in serving the poor, received most of the funds for the service organization she ran from private foundations, and had mixed feelings on social issues and about religion and government.[100]

A second difficulty in bringing government and religion together in these ways was that the results of faith-based programs now came under closer public scrutiny. Olasky's argument that faith-based prison ministries and drug rehabilitation programs were more successful than efforts run by government agencies was a claim that could be tested in empirical research. But as studies were conducted, they produced mixed results. Recidivism rates were affected by which inmates opted into the faith-based programs and how much special attention of any kind they were given. Teen Challenge selected a relatively small proportion of the juvenile population at risk and devoted larger sums of money and time per case than public programs did. Detailed results from a large study of low-income residents in Pennsylvania showed greater satisfaction with private agencies than with the public welfare bureau but did not show differences in satisfaction between recipients of services from religious and nonreligious private agencies. The study also showed that services received from private agencies were shorter-term and dealt with less serious needs than services provided through public welfare.[101]

There were also questions both in Texas and nationally that faith-based initiatives were being promoted as a way of appealing to religiously conservative voters and that religiously conservative organizations would reap the greatest benefit, perhaps even in violation of strict separation of church and state. Research addressing these questions also produced mixed results. In a national study of religious congregations, sociologist Mark Chaves found that about a third of the leaders of these congregations in 1998 were open to receiving government funds for faith-based social service activities, but that the leaders of theologically conservative congregations were more hesitant about the idea than were leaders of theologically liberal and moderate congregations. The study did find, however, that leaders of African American congregations were particularly open to receiving government funds. Other research found that in qualitative interviews clergy frequently expressed misgivings about the potential bureaucratic entanglements in drawing on government support, and those that did were careful to avoid using public funds for the purely religious parts of their ministries. However, evidence that public funds were being used to promote born-again religious convictions in several of the prison programs resulted in lawsuits being brought by watchdog groups.[102]

Research from national studies following the 2000 presidential election provided the clearest indication of which constituents favored faith-based organizations over government agencies as service providers. The most favorable constituency was white voters who identified themselves with the Religious Right. In one study respondents nationally were about evenly divided when asked if religious organizations, nonreligious community-based groups, or government agencies did the best job providing treatment for drug and alcohol addiction, but supporters of the "Christian conservative movement" opted for religious organizations two-to-one over government agencies. They also strongly favored religious organizations over government agencies for counseling and educating prisoners, feeding the homeless, and counseling teens about pregnancy.[103]

The fact that they preferred faith-based service provision to government programs did not mean that voters necessarily wanted their taxes to pay for these faith-based activities. As spokespersons for the new federal program discovered, it was one thing to argue that religious groups were doing quite a lot to help the needy, but harder to sell the idea that these groups should then become the recipients of government funding. Two-thirds of the public still favored the idea of allowing religious organizations to apply for government funding, but only a fifth strongly favored it, suggesting that much of the support was probably associated with the level-playing-field argument advanced under Charitable Choice, rather than the more aggressive promotion Bush advocated. Religious conservatives were twice as likely as the general public to say they strongly favored religious organizations applying for government funds. In addition, religious conservatives were particularly critical of public welfare programs, and although they thought more should be done to help the poor, they thought the problems stemmed mostly from poor people's own failures and from shortcomings among poor families. They also favored church people and their pastors becoming more actively involved in politics. Seventy-two percent of Christian conservative movement supporters, for example, thought churches and other houses of worship should *not* keep out of politics.[104]

Who the various constituencies in Texas preferred in the 2000 election was evident in exit polls. Bush captured nearly all the votes among the state's Republicans in the primary election. Eighty-seven percent of Hispanic Republicans and 88 percent of non-Hispanic Republicans voted for Bush (too few African Americans voted in the Republican primary to be included in the exit poll), and among Religious Right supporters the proportion for Bush rose to 91 percent. When asked if Bush had become more conservative than when he was elected governor, 55 percent of Religious Right supporters said he had. In the general election, Bush received 43 percent of the Hispanic vote, 73 percent of the white non-Hispanic vote, and 6 percent of the black vote. Among white non-Hispanic supporters of the Religious Right, Bush received 82 percent of the vote. Bush's support among Hispanic voters was higher than it had been in 1994 or for his father in 1988 and 1992 or for Williams in 1990. Among white non-Hispanics, those with high incomes voted overwhelmingly for Bush, but Bush also won a majority among those with low incomes, and at both ends of the spectrum Religious Right supporters voted in higher proportions for Bush than those who did not support the Religious Right.[105]

As favorite son, Bush's victory in Texas was never in doubt, but in the popular vote nationwide which Bush lost by less than half of 1 percent to Vice President Al Gore, the Religious Right's support was a contributing factor among three of the constituencies with whom Republican candidates traditionally had difficulty. Among white non-Hispanics earning less than $30,000, only 40 percent of non–Religious Right supporters voted for Bush, but 70 percent of their counterparts who supported the Religious Right did. Among black voters earning less than $30,000, only 3 percent of non–Religious Right supporters voted for Bush, but 11 percent of these low-income black voters who supported the Religious Right did. And among Hispanics, it was not low-income voters but those earning more than $50,000 among whom 45 percent of Religious Right supporters voted for Bush compared with 40 percent of non–Religious Right supporters.[106]

If Texas was becoming more diverse ethnically and religiously, conservative Christians' influence remained strong. Data collected in 2000 from denominational leaders showed that there were 3.5 million Southern Baptists in Texas. That was more Southern Baptists than in Georgia and North Carolina combined—the two other states with the highest number—and more than five times as many as in California. Another 1.5 million Texans belonged to other evangelical Protestant denominations, the largest of which were the Churches of Christ, Assemblies of God, Missionary Baptists, and Independent Charismatic Churches. The combined number of conservative Protestants in that study was three times the number of Texans belonging to other Protestant denominations variously described as mainline, moderate, or liberal. A statewide study conducted in 2004 found similar results based on a detailed classification of denominational preferences among adults. Among the state's Protestants, 70 percent belonged to evangelical or conservative denominations, while only 30 percent belonged to moderate or liberal denominations.[107]

Besides having been dominant from the start, conservative Protestantism's current strength reflected the fact that it had adapted well to the state's shift from small, rural communities to large, upscale suburban neighborhoods. Criswell's church in downtown Dallas attracted middle-class members from the suburbs and still considered itself the largest Southern Baptist congregation anywhere in the state, but other middle-class evangelical congregations had grown into megachurches as well. Prestonwood Southern Baptist Church in the North Dallas suburbs, for example, now had fourteen thousand members, two dozen pastors, over a hundred paid employees, and its own orchestra. The church provided a rich repertoire of programs that included classes for all age-groups, concerts, and occasional national telecasts. Although 90 percent of its members were white, it prided itself on being racially inclusive and supported service ministries in low-income neighborhoods.[108] Other conservative megachurches included the Fellowship Southern Baptist Church in Grapevine with more than twenty thousand members, Lake Pointe Southern Baptist Church in Rockwall with ten thousand members, and the nondenominational Gateway Church in Southlake with eleven thousand members.

A study of Dallas churches in the early 1980s showed that they were already adapting well to the sprawling, upscale suburban locations of the city's population. New churches like Prestonwood Baptist were purchasing large plots of land near major highways, and many were downplaying denominational identities, catering instead to mobile families with weak ties in several denominations and interested mostly in good preaching, inspiring music, and Sunday school classes for all ages.[109] Statewide, several of the new nondenominational churches were poised to grow into powerful ministries attracting tens of thousands of faithful members, preaching a gospel of redemption and prosperity, and launching radio, television, and video programs reaching far corners of the globe.

Former Oral Roberts employee and pop singer Kenneth Copeland developed his charismatic preaching ministry into a network of publishing and broadcasting employing some five hundred people at its headquarters near Fort Worth and reaching audiences in more than a hundred countries drawn to messages of inspiration and expectations of divine prosperity. Reverend John Hagee's Cornerstone Church in San Antonio, founded in 1975, constructed a new five-thousand-seat auditorium (which W. A. Criswell helped dedicate) in 1980 and grew into a nineteen-thousand-member congregation with radio and television programs reaching audiences on five continents. Lakewood Church in suburban Houston, founded in 1959 by Southern Baptist minister John Osteen, became a nondenominational charismatic congregation of five thousand by the late 1970s and then under the leadership of Osteen's son Joel mushroomed into a ministry by the turn of the century with some thirty thousand weekly attendees and weekly television viewers in more than a hundred countries. By the turn of the century, the state's other widely acclaimed church was Reverend T. D. Jakes's Potter's House Christian Fellowship in Dallas, a racially mixed congregation of more than twenty thousand members with some four hundred employees and ministries ranging from programs for teen mothers and abused women to assistance for the homeless, substance abusers, and ex-offenders.[110]

A national study conducted by the Hartford Institute found nearly two hundred congregations in Texas with at least fifteen hundred members—more churches of that size than in any other state. Thirty-four of the congregations had more than five thousand members. Nearly all the largest churches were Southern Baptist, independent Baptist, charismatic, or nondenominational evangelical congregations. Their size, budgets, and staff put them in a strong position to operate child-care programs, food banks, and other ministries for the needy through faith-based organizations funded entirely from private donations or in cooperation with government agencies.[111]

Large or small, conservative or progressive, congregations were actually doing quite a lot on their own to provide the kinds of social services that compassionate conservatives envisioned. A striking example was a ministry called First Contact, which began in Huntsville in 2002, where the state prison and local church and community leaders had experienced a tenuous relationship with one another for the past century and a half. In recent years the incarceration rate in Texas had become one of the highest in the nation, which meant not only that the prison population itself had grown but also that its impact on the community was greater than ever before. Nearly thirty thousand ex-offenders were being released through the Huntsville facility annually. Their needs were enormous, ranging from short-term accommodations for families arriving to meet them to longer-term issues such as finding jobs and securing social and emotional support. First Contact mobilized the members of local churches to assist in providing this support for ex-offenders and their families. It required cooperation from the Texas Division of Criminal Justice and secured financial support from the Baptist General Convention of Texas and private donors but did not necessitate government funding. Several years later a parallel ministry was implemented for females being released from a facility at Gatesville.[112]

The irony of compassionate conservatism was that programs like First Contact were capable of generating enthusiastic support from congregations across the theological spectrum and succeeding without requiring public funding or competing with other programs that were supported through public funds. Yet the rhetoric of compassionate conservatism emphasized private charity as an alternative to public welfare to such an extent that it played best among churchgoers who were antagonistic toward big government, held conservative views on social issues, and saw Republicans as their allies. Of course not all members of conservative Protestant denominations voted Republican or held conservative views on social and political issues. But the majority leaned heavily in that direction—enough so that in 2004 when President Bush ran for reelection against John Kerry, Bush adviser Karl Rove made a point of appealing especially to white conservative Protestants. Exit polls showed that among white evangelical Protestants in Texas who attended church regularly, 82 percent thought abortion should be illegal in most or all cases, 83 percent were Republican, 96 percent were opposed to gay marriage, and 100 percent defined themselves as political conservatives. Nationwide the results were similar. Eighty-nine percent of white evangelical Protestants who attended church regularly thought abortion should be illegal in all or most cases, 80 percent were Republican, 99 percent opposed gay marriage, and 100 percent said they were political conservatives. On some of these issues, Catholics who held similar views augmented conservative Protestants' strength. Among white non-Hispanic Catholics in Texas, for example, 58 percent thought abortion should be illegal in all or most cases, and 79 percent were against gay marriage.[113]

The 2004 results also suggested that the difficulties Republicans may have experienced among low-income, white voters in earlier elections were a thing of the past, thanks in large measure to conservative Protestants. Among white voters earning less than $30,000 in 2004, Kerry won 51 percent among those who were not conservative Protestants, but Bush won 88 percent among those who were conservative Protestants. The national results among low-income voters were similar. Kerry won 60 percent of the votes among those who were not white conservative Protestants, but Bush won 87 percent among those who were.

LINES OF DEMARCATION

Tracing the relation of religion, race, and ethnicity to elections and political issues in Texas from the late 1980s through the early years of the twenty-first century sheds additional light on a narrative about the Religious Right that usually focuses on Jerry Falwell, Pat Robertson, and antiabortion groups such as Operation Rescue. Pro-life and antigay activism was certainly important as litmus tests pushing religiously conservative voters toward Republican candidates. The Religious Right's political influence was strongest in the South, where Southern Baptists, Bible Baptists, and other conservative Protestant congregations were present in large numbers. However, relations between the Religious Right and mainstream Republican leaders were seldom simple and straightforward. Government spending, taxes, and federal deficits were as much on voters' minds as questions about moral and religious issues. Bringing those concerns into the picture helps to broaden the story. Doing so pays closer attention to the role of income inequality, race and ethnicity, and faith-based initiatives.

Atwater's acknowledgment that fiscal considerations became the key to Republicans' southern strategy and that these abstract coded discussions had racial ramifications illuminates an important aspect of American politics in the 1980s and 1990s. Although Reagan's personal charisma appealed broadly to white, lower-income as well as upper-income voters, Bush's elite background and wealth sharpened popular perceptions that Republicans were the party of the rich. Curbing government expenditures on public welfare contributed further to the possibility that Democrats could portray Republicans as heartless elitists disinterested in the problems of working-class voters. Promoting the work of private charities that were serving the needy was something that any kindhearted American could support and was a way of demonstrating genuine concern for the poor. Clayton Williams's efforts to attract the Bubba vote achieved some success but suggested that good-ole-boy rhetoric alone was probably not sufficient.

Discussions of government funding for faith-based social service programs developed in the 1990s with broad support from Democrats and Republicans and with wide appeal among various religious, racial, and ethnic constituencies. Conservative Protestants who regarded Republicans as allies in combating abortion and homosexuality were particularly interested in promoting faith-based programs, whether privately or through government policies that offered to level the playing field for religious organizations to compete with public and nonreligious organizations. Texas experimented with faith-based policies that would serve as a template for national policies under the Bush administration. Along with opposition to abortion and homosexuality, the language of compassionate conservatism defined faith-based service programs as part of conservative Republicans' appeal to religiously conservative voters. Although critics assailed the initiative as an avenue through which religious conservatives would gain special access to government funds, there was little evidence to support that criticism. The better interpretation was that contention between conservatives and liberals shaped how the initiative was perceived. If it put a kinder and gentler face on fiscal conservatism, it opened possibilities for religious organizations across the theological spectrum to play a somewhat enlarged role in social service provision and posed new questions about the benefits and dangers of religion mingling with government in these ways.

The lines of demarcation that were politically salient by the 2000 and 2004 presidential elections located African Americans and a majority of Hispanics in Democratic territory while conservative white non-Hispanic voters were largely in Republican territory. Democratic candidates could still win low-income, white non-Hispanics who were not part of the Religious Right, but low-income, white non-Hispanics who identified with the Religious Right were solidly on the Republican side. The Religious Right included conservative Catholics as well as Protestants and appealed to a small minority of African Americans and Hispanics as well.

It is a truism that elections are never won or lost by the votes of a single constituency. The demarcations among various racial, religious, and income groups nevertheless identified categories about which candidates and their campaign advisers could make reasonably reliable predictions. When voters were faced with hard decisions about taxes, government deficits, welfare spending, war, and a struggling economy, the possibility of candidates winning close elections with appeals to religiously and racially defined constituencies became all the more significant.

That did not mean, however, that religious leaders were always willing to play along with political strategists or that they were happy about the policies that resulted. The prophetic aspect of religion still came through in concerns about the culture's impact on believers' priorities. "Christianity is more nearly expressed by a certain kind of moral, pietistic, individualistic lifestyle than it is by being concerned as a Christian businessperson about the whole struggle of welfare recipients and their plight or the good of the community," Reverend Larry James of the Greater Dallas Community of Churches explained when asked about the city's faith communities. "Our values are shaped by American capitalism and the American marketplace," he added. "That impinges upon faith much more than faith impinges upon our values."[114]

CHAPTER 12

AN INDEPENDENT LOT

Religion and Grassroots Activism

We've got a great union. There's absolutely no reason to dissolve it. But if
Washington continues to thumb their nose at the American people, who
knows what may come of that. But Texas is a very unique place and a
pretty independent lot to boot.

GOVERNOR RICK PERRY, APRIL 15, 2009, AUSTIN TEA PARTY RALLY

My God, you are on the East Coast and you are in an Ivy League school
and I can't even imagine what the conversations are there about America
and its place in the world. I don't know what good it serves to convince
young people how bad America has been throughout the course of its
history.

EAST TEXAS COMMUNITY LEADER, JULY 21, 2011

While Republicans and Democrats jockeyed in gubernatorial and presidential races, religious organizations at the grass roots were mostly tending to business as usual. Pastors were preaching Sunday services, presiding at weddings, and burying the dead. It might be encouraging to hear office-seekers speaking of faith-based compassion, but the daily concerns of the churchgoing public centered more on families and personal life than on politics. The exceptions were community activists who cared about the ways in which moral principles they held dear were or were not being upheld.

The twenty-first century marked a turning point in Texas politics and religion. Republicans could count on winning in nearly any national election and in an increasing number of local elections. The contests were less between Republicans and Democrats than between moderate and conservative Republicans.

The state's largest Protestant denomination was still Southern Baptist, but its members remained divided between moderates and conservatives, and local autonomy increasingly meant pastors of mega-sized congregations influencing both the denomination and local communities. Denominational identities were less important than informal alliances among the leaders of conservative evangelical congregations who regarded themselves as the true adherents of biblical doctrine, on the one hand, and similar networks among progressive faith communities that emphasized inclusivity, on the other hand. Leaders of African American congregations could be found at both ends of the theological spectrum, as could the growing number of Hispanic Catholics and Hispanic Protestants.

In these respects, Texas was much like the vast swathes of Middle America that appeared as red states on election maps. The difference was that Texas was larger and economically more powerful than any other predictable bastion of Republican strength. Nearly all its forty-plus billionaires were Republicans who gave generously to conservative causes. International crises that drove up gasoline prices for the average consumer fed the wealth of the state's oil and natural gas producers. There were so many schools that textbook companies that failed to satisfy the state board of education did so at their peril. Political consultants who knew the secrets of getting a president reelected even during an increasingly unpopular war could be counted on when fund-raising was needed for other conservative candidates.

Religion had become so closely aligned with political divisions that some national studies suggested a growing number of younger Americans were simply becoming nonreligious—or at least unaffiliated—because of disgust with the apparent politicization of religion. That was probably true in Austin and Dallas or in Houston and San Antonio as much as it was in Philadelphia or Seattle. However, the Texas Sun Belt was still the Bible Belt. Pastors and community leaders described it that way whether they thought that was a good thing or a source of embarrassment. The Old South customs and the Midwest traditions of flocking to houses of worship for inspiration and fellowship remained strong. Texas was by far the most populous state in which a majority of the public could still be found in places of worship most weekends and where nearly everyone thought religion was important.[1]

Liberty of conscience defined the boundary between religion and politics about as tenuously as it ever had. It riled religious leaders to think the government was inhibiting their rights, but they differed about how much religion itself should inform discussions of public policy. The point on which there was general agreement was that religion's influence should appropriately influence views of morality. God might not be a Republican or Democrat but did care about moral behavior. For some that meant family values and standards of sexual conduct. For others it meant fair treatment and respect for individual rights. Where the line was drawn between high priorities and less important issues was seldom clear.

Activist leaders took a different view of what mattered than did most of the public. By the turn of the new century, activist organizations that had emerged to champion causes as different as support of or opposition to civil rights, the Equal Rights Amendment, and abortion had proliferated and matured. In a geographically large, populous, ethnically and racially diverse state in which legislative and executive decisions carried enormous weight, activist groups formed to advocate for or against tax proposals, water rights, environmental protection, the minimum wage, textbook content, abortion, gay marriage, immigration, and numerous other topics. As they had in the past, religious leaders who would never have dreamed of participating directly in politics could play a role in these activist organizations because the organizations were ostensibly nonpartisan.

How activism could mobilize among believers who basically thought the world was spiraling out of control until Jesus returned was always an enigma. The premillennial dispensational theology Scofield and Norris had taught was still prevalent. But it had never held that believers should simply sit back and wait for the end. The reigning idea was rather that things were getting worse—so bad in fact that nothing was sure except faith in Christ—and yet believers were called by God to do what they could to combat evil. No longer associated chiefly with persons of a different race, evil was ever-present in moral decline and threats to religion, the family, and traditions considered basic to American democracy.

After the 9/11 attacks, terrorism and war stoked grassroots fears, as did the threat of pandemic influenza, talk of climate change, and fears among some residents about the long-term consequences of immigration. Although these were concerns easily aroused by 24/7 cable news and talk radio, people who were already disposed to believe that evil was escalating to apocalyptic levels anticipated in graphic terms the devastation the world might face. Time itself seemed to acquire a different meaning as present woes replicated biblical episodes of radical destruction and the future was foreshortened into an urgent struggle to set things right before it was too late.[2]

A young woman who had recently graduated from one of the conservative Christian colleges in Dallas and who was a member of the Potter's House megachurch typified the responses of many conservative Christians when asked to discuss current events. On the one hand, she was confident that God was ultimately in charge, but on the other hand, she had vivid imagery in mind from the Old Testament and the Book of Revelation about massive fires, plagues, and wholesale slaughter. She could imagine something happening again that would result in "millions of dead bodies," so many that there would be "bodies on top of bodies," and on such a scale that the "masses of corpses" could not be buried and would have to be burned. The chances of such events occurring, moreover, were increased by the fact that on a day-to-day basis morals were getting worse and people were failing to follow God. And yet she insisted that these problems made her determined rather than depressed. She felt it incumbent to be aware of what was happening, warn others, and show compassion when she could. "It's just like with Noah's ark," she said. "The flood is coming. Be prepared. Do what you can do as [God has] enabled you to do."[3]

The lines separating conservatives and liberals or the distinctions that define cultural boundaries between racial and ethnic groups are never the mental categories that exist merely because of humans' need for cognitive order. Social networks and organizations that in turn collect and mobilize resources to define the world in particular ways reinforce such categories. At the grass roots, religious congregations are not in business primarily to defend or oppose conservative, moderate, or progressive politics or to maintain racial and ethnic boundaries. The processes through which these cultural distinctions are reinforced include the inadvertent consequences of separation, location, and rhetoric as well as more direct engagement in public discussions.

In 1989 the U.S. Supreme Court in *Webster v. Reproductive Health Services* upheld a Missouri law that restricted the use of state funds and the manner in which facilities and personnel could participate in performing abortions and providing counseling about abortions. The result of that decision was to shift the efforts of antiabortion groups from merely hoping to overturn *Roe v. Wade* toward protests and lobbying aimed at influencing state legislators and law enforcement officers. With tangible if incremental results in sight, antiabortion activists mobilized greater support from conservative church members and religious leaders. At the same time, questions about domestic partner benefits and same-sex civil unions generated opposition from religious groups that regarded homosexuality as sin and that considered it important to preserve traditional definitions of marriage.

Complicating these discussions were questions about the rising influence of immigrants, the cultural impact of greater ethnic and religious diversity, and what should be done to minimize or accommodate these influences. One question was whether the same standards of fair treatment and equality that had been fought for during the civil rights movement should now be extended to new groups, and if so, in what form. Another question was whether religious groups should work harder to preserve the distinctive Christian principles of the past and on which in many views the nation had been founded.

Why the conservative side of these issues seemed so often to be ascendant, though, could not be understood apart from the impact of continuing concerns about taxes and government expenditures. If Texas usually came in second to California on aggregate population and economic statistics, it was a matter of pride in Texas to be the state that most effectively embraced principles of fiscal conservatism. Few religious leaders would have argued that low taxes and small government were matters of biblical morality. Yet the ones who felt that Republicans strongly represented God's will on abortion and homosexuality seemed to feel that Republicans were also correct in wanting to keep the government from infringing on their economic freedom.

Keeping government from growing was never easy or entirely successful, even in Texas. It nevertheless played well with middle-class voters to think that public services should be kept at a minimum and that Washington was truly a danger if it fell into the hands of Democrats. The Tea Party movement gave new expression to that sentiment. For a brief time it appeared strong enough to elevate another born-again governor from the state to national prominence.

ABORTION

Nationwide the abortion rate fell from a peak of 29.3 in 1981 to 19.4 per thousand women aged fifteen to forty-four in 2005. While race, ethnicity, and social class were seldom discussed explicitly in publicity posted by antiabortion groups, statistics demonstrated that these demographic characteristics were important factors. Although white non-Hispanic women still represented 72 percent of the child-bearing-age population, these women accounted for only 36 percent of abortions. African American women comprised 14 percent of this age-group but accounted for 30 percent of abortions. Hispanic women made up the remaining 14 percent of this age-group but accounted for 25 percent of the abortions. The abortion rate per thousand women was 13 among white non-Hispanics, 33 among Hispanics, and 49 among African Americans. Abortion rates were also higher among unmarried women and women with incomes at or below the federal poverty level.[4]

Abortions in Texas resembled the national pattern but with one significant exception. White non-Hispanic women accounted for 42 percent of abortions but were 53 percent of the women statewide age fifteen through forty-four. African American women made up 12 percent of this age-group but accounted for 21 percent of the abortions. Hispanic women were 34 percent of the age-group but accounted for 37 percent of the abortions. The Texas pattern differed from the national one primarily with respect to Hispanic women, who in Texas accounted for about the same proportion of abortions as they did of the childbearing population. As a proportion of pregnancies, the relatively low rate of abortions among Hispanic women was also evident. Fewer than 14 percent of pregnancies among Hispanic women resulted in abortions compared to approximately 16 percent among white non-Hispanic women and nearly 28 percent among African American women.[5]

Antiabortion activists in Texas secured passage of legislation that went into effect on January 1, 2004, requiring a twenty-four-hour waiting period before a woman could have an abortion. The law also required that women be given state-printed information about fetal development and the possible risks of having an abortion, although the law mandated only that the information be offered rather than that women be forced to receive it or listen to a summary of it. A subsequent health regulation also required a woman seeking an abortion to provide identification with proof of her age and that the information be kept on file.[6] Other measures made it significantly more difficult for a woman to have an abortion in Texas than in neighboring Louisiana or New Mexico. Amniocentesis to determine the presence of fetal abnormalities was generally not performed until after the sixteenth week of pregnancy, but a woman seeking an abortion at that time was required to check into an ambulatory surgical center for the procedure—centers that were unavailable in many communities. Texas also approved a prenatal protection bill that critics regarded as a backdoor attempt to establish personhood for unviable fetuses.[7]

Activist organizations converged in their opposition to abortion from a number of different directions. Texas Right to Life was one of the oldest organizations, having formed in opposition to *Roe v. Wade* in 1973 through the efforts of various parish right-to-life committees in the late 1960s and citywide organizations in Corpus Christi, El Paso, Galveston, Houston, San Antonio, and several other locations. Texans United for Life and the Texans for Life Coalition had similar roots, both starting in the late 1970s. A later organization was the Texas Alliance for Life, which formed in Austin in the late 1990s specifically to press for legislation but also developed a range of programs that included Life Walk fund-raisers, silent auctions, prayer rallies, and participation in special Catholic masses calling on government officials to oppose abortion. A rather different organization was the Texas Justice Foundation, a public interest law group founded in San Antonio in 1993 by St. Mary's University law professor Allan Parker Jr. One of the group's first acts was suing the state on behalf of three low-income Hispanic families who wanted the state to pay private school tuition because of inadequate instruction in public schools. Over the next decade, while continuing its interests in school voucher programs, the group tackled questions ranging from school prayer to phonics instruction and turned its attention increasingly toward cases involving abortion. These groups were joined by the Texas Eagle Forum and by Texas members of Operation Rescue.[8]

The abortion rights side was represented by several organizations, including the Women's Health and Family Planning Association of Texas, which began in 1977 to promote equal access to reproductive health services and over the years worked to increase funding for family planning and health clinics. The organization also promoted sex education and teen pregnancy prevention. Another organization was the Texas Abortion and Reproductive Rights Action League, established in Austin in 1978 as a political action committee to defend women's access to abortion. Other groups that advocated for abortion rights included state chapters of the National Abortion Rights Action League, the National Organization of Women, and affiliates of Planned Parenthood. Concerned that opposition to abortion and support for conservative Republican agendas were identifying the state's religious leaders, moderate and progressive religious leaders formed the Texas Faith Network as an alternative.[9]

Opposition to abortion was strengthened by George Bush's victory over Ann Richards in 1994 and by Bush's promise to require parental consent and promote abstinence and adoption. On the national front, moderate Republicans considered dropping the antiabortion plank from the party's platform for the 1996 election, but conservative leaders vying for the nomination, including Texas Senator Phil Gramm, embraced retaining the plank and called for a constitutional amendment prohibiting abortion. Bob Dole's candidacy was strengthened, despite accusations of being a weaker opponent of abortion than conservatives wished, by a visit to Texas that included an appearance at Prestonwood Baptist Church in North Dallas where the pastor praised him for his "stand for the beliefs that we hold so dear as Christians and Americans."[10] At the 1996 Republican National Convention, a solid majority of the Texas delegation (which included the head of the Texas Christian Coalition) was outspokenly against abortion. The most notable exception was Senator Kay Bailey Hutchison, who briefly became the target of antiabortion leaders.[11] Three years later, antiabortion groups debated whether Bush's position was sufficiently clear to warrant their endorsement. The Dallas-based Republican National Coalition for Life, organized by Phyllis Schlafly, thought Bush barely qualified, while the National Right to Life Committee and the Christian Coalition said he met their standards.[12]

Efforts to restrict abortion continued with Lieutenant Governor Rick Perry's assumption of the governorship when Bush resigned to become president in 2000. Perry's position on abortion was that it should be illegal except in cases of rape and incest or to save the life of the mother. Opponents made increasing use of converts, such as former abortion provider Carol Everett of Dallas, who spoke at meetings about switching sides and opening a pregnancy counseling center after inviting Jesus Christ into her life. In her book *Blood Money*, Everett argued that abortion providers were raking in millions of dollars in ill-gotten gains.[13] Another symbolic victory was that Norma McCorvey, the plaintiff in *Roe v. Wade*, converted to Catholicism, joined Operation Rescue in 1995, and in 2003 with the assistance of the Texas Justice Foundation filed a motion asking the Supreme Court to overturn the *Roe* decision on grounds that scientific evidence now demonstrated the negative effects of abortion. A study of Texas adults in 2004 asked respondents whether "a pregnant woman should be able to obtain a legal abortion for any reason whatsoever if she chooses not to have the baby." Described in this fashion, unrestricted abortion-on-demand generated strong resistance. Fifty-four percent of white non-Hispanics, 64 percent of Hispanics, and 51 percent of African Americans said they disagreed with the statement.[14]

With public opinion on their side, antiabortion groups worked to further restrict women's reproductive rights. Among the restrictions sought or effected were efforts to ban late-term abortions even in cases involving the life of the mother, requiring a woman seeking an abortion to view an ultrasound image of the fetus, cutting off state and federal funds to clinics providing abortions, and discouraging private companies from providing insurance coverage for abortions. A study in January 2007 showed that Texas was one of the most restrictive states in the nation with respect to laws regulating access to contraception and abortion. It was more restrictive even than Oklahoma, Kansas, or Georgia and contrasted most sharply with California, which had the least restrictive laws.[15] As greater attention to the issue increased, the dangers faced by abortion providers also increased. At the Women's Health Center in Austin in April 2007, violence was narrowly averted when investigators discovered that a package left at the clinic was a deadly explosive device.[16]

Although the various groups opposing or promoting abortion rights were nonprofit entities, these and related organizations had become well institutionalized. Texas Right to Life reported an operating budget in 2007 of more than a million dollars. The Texas Justice Foundation's annual budget was more than $400,000. With income of slightly more than $100,000, the Texas Abortion and Reproductive Rights Action League was relatively small, but other organizations that provided reproductive health services were relatively large. Planned Parenthood of San Antonio, for example, received approximately a million dollars from contributions and grants plus another two million dollars from service revenue.[17]

Data from a representative statewide study of 1,003 adults conducted in May 2007 showed that public opinion toward abortion was divided, but a majority thought it should be illegal in all cases or legal only in exceptional cases. The proportions who thought it should never be permitted or permitted only in cases of rape or incest ranged from 50 percent among African Americans to 57 percent among white non-Hispanics to 67 percent among Hispanics. Nearly half of those sampled said they attended religious services every week. Among these respondents, 54 percent of African Americans, 72 percent of white non-Hispanics, and 75 percent of Hispanics opposed abortion.[18]

The study demonstrated that abortion was an important wedge issue as well. Overall, respondents were about evenly divided between Republicans and Democrats, and when independents were asked which way they leaned, they also divided about equally between the two parties. But among those who opposed abortion, Republicans outnumbered Democrats nearly two to one. Among all the respondents, about equal proportions said they would probably cast their vote in 2008 for the Democratic presidential candidate as for the Republican candidate. But among abortion opponents, the Republican nominee would enjoy a significant advantage of at least 12 percentage points. When asked who they hoped would be the Republican nominee, Texans favoring abortion rights named New York mayor Rudy Guiliani as the top choice, while Arizona senator John McCain was the preferred choice among those opposed to abortion. If abortion could serve as a wedge issue, its potential nevertheless appeared to be restricted to white non-Hispanics. Among these respondents, opponents of abortion were nearly five times more likely to say they would vote for whoever the Republican nominee was in 2008 than for the Democratic nominee. Hispanics and African Americans who opposed abortion, however, still overwhelmingly favored whoever the Democratic nominee would be. The reason, as one African American church leader explained, was that "there's a lot more to morality" than abortion, such as feeding the hungry and caring for the poor.[19]

Antiabortion activists continued to press on multiple fronts to mobilize public opinion and to achieve legislative and judicial victories. In press releases and at rallies and in legislative hearings, two arguments in particular gained increasing expression. The first, evoked through testimony from women who regretted having had an abortion, was that restricted access was necessary to protect women from making bad decisions that would damage their physical or emotional health. The second invoked religion. Although antiabortion activists from the start had argued that abortion was wrong on religious grounds, the argument now being emphasized drew on concerns about religious freedom and was perhaps reinforced by the notion implicit in faith-based initiatives that government should be more receptive to the interests of religious groups. If that was true, then it made sense to argue that religious organizations should not be compelled to provide health insurance that included abortion or that religiously motivated citizens should pay taxes to support social service programs that included abortion. Organizations such as the Texas Justice Foundation and spinoffs such as Operation Outcry and Prayer Surge drew on both arguments in calling on religious groups to pray and send donations in support of efforts to restrict abortion.[20]

Seeking reelection in 2009, Governor Perry received endorsements from the state's major antiabortion groups. Perry expressed particular appreciation to Texas Justice Foundation founder Parker Jr. for his group's endorsement and support. Had it not been for Parker and groups like his, Perry declared, "Our conservative values could have been compromised by left-wing litigation and our state's pro-life culture swept away by misguided legislation." Perry added, "Texas is one of the strongest states for protecting the child in the womb, and conservatives can be bold in speaking out for the values that unite us."[21] On May 24, 2011, with Parker by his side, Perry signed into law a bill requiring a woman to have a sonogram before deciding to have an abortion. "Every life lost to abortion is a tragedy we all must work together to prevent," Perry observed.[22]

One of the more outspoken leaders in the antiabortion effort was Bishop Edmond Carmody of the Corpus Christi diocese, which spanned eleven counties in South Texas. In 1999 Bishop Carmody instituted pastoral guidelines for the diocese that prohibited anyone in favor of abortion rights from holding church positions or speaking at church facilities. The intent was to encourage Catholics who favored abortion rights toward a "reconsideration of their pro-choice positions and be brought to a real conversion of heart so that they may accept wholeheartedly the truth of Christ as taught by the church." During the gubernatorial primaries in 2002, Carmody enforced the guidelines by prohibiting Democratic candidate Tony Sanchez from speaking at church facilities. Sanchez, who considered himself a devout Catholic and attended Mass a couple of times a week, said he personally felt abortion was wrong but did not think the government should impose itself in the matter.[23]

Bishop Raymundo J. Peña, who was the longest-serving active Hispanic bishop in the United States when he retired from heading the Brownsville diocese in 2009, was another leader in the efforts against abortion. Peña had been a prominent leader in Corpus Christi for nearly two decades and then in San Antonio and El Paso for another two decades. Although Peña believed abortion should be curbed primarily through legislation, he also worked diligently to impress hearts and minds about the evil committed when an abortion was performed. "Laws would not bring abortion to an end," he observed. "It entails a conversion of minds and hearts to seeing every child conceived in its mother's womb as a precious gift of God to the world, to be cherished, nurtured and protected." To that end Peña considered it important to bring about a "moral revolution" that emphasized chastity, marital intimacy, and spirituality. Shortly before he retired, Peña organized a campaign involving some sixty thousand predominantly Hispanic Catholics in the Rio Grande valley who opposed the Obama administration's Freedom of Choice measure, which they feared would require Catholic hospitals to perform abortions.[24]

In North Texas the most concerted antiabortion efforts were organized by the Catholic Pro-Life Committee of North Texas, founded in 1993 by Dallas Bishop Charles Grahmann and actively continued by his successor Bishop Kevin Farrell. By 2007 the organization was staffed by seven full-time employees and more than two dozen part-time or full-time volunteers and had an operating budget of $900,000. The group sponsored "sidewalk counseling" sessions in vigils at North Texas women's health clinics, claiming to have persuaded some three thousand women to have their babies and counting another two thousand as "hopeful turnaways." The group also supported several pregnancy clinics, a speakers bureau, and a Spanish-language outreach program. In 2011 Bishop Farrell and Bishop Kevin W. Vann of Fort Worth led approximately ten thousand demonstrators in Dallas who participated in a Culture of Life march to end abortions. In 2012 the bishops sent pastoral letters to parishioners calling them to resist the federal government's intrusion on their religious liberty by forcing Catholic employers to offer employees health coverage that included abortion-inducing drugs and contraception.[25]

Protestant pastors became active in the antiabortion movement as well. A prominent leader was Pastor Stephen Broden, founder of the nondenominational inner-city Fair Park Bible Fellowship in Dallas. Broden had been associated with James Robison's television ministry, studied and taught at Dallas Baptist University, and was one of the organizers of the National Black Pro-Life Coalition. In numerous personal, radio, and television appearances, Broden argued that abortion was a violation of the constitutional rights of the unborn child and represented a fundamental threat to the black community. "The practice of abortion," he declared, "is a genocidal plot to decimate the demography of our community." With members from his church, he staged regular protests at a local abortion clinic and participated in rallies against *Roe v. Wade* in the nation's capital. In

2010 Broden formed a new national organization called Life Always that targeted black neighborhoods through billboards and other media to challenge what he termed the "monolithic monotone of the abortion industry.[26]

The Baptist General Convention of Texas's efforts in the early 1970s to adopt a middle-of-the-road position that upheld the sanctity of life while preserving the rights of the mother gradually shifted. Bob Holbrook, a pastor in the small town of Halletsville between Houston and San Antonio, recalled that his opposition to abortion received little support from the Southern Baptist Convention in 1976, but with the help of a few other pastors, lay leaders, and concerned Catholics a grassroots movement took shape. From those efforts Southern Baptists for Life began in 1984. In 1988 the denomination's opposition to abortion gained a strong advocate when Richard Land, a Princeton- and Oxford-educated supporter of the Religious Right who had taught theology and church history at Criswell College in Dallas since 1975, was appointed as president of the Southern Baptist Convention's Ethics and Religious Liberty Commission. Land had been hosting a syndicated weekly radio program and spoke frequently about traditional family values and politics. During the tenure of Governor Clements, Land served as the governor's senior adviser on church and state issues and antiabortion legislation. Land regarded the unborn child as a person deserving the same legal protection as all Americans and over the years used his position to issue numerous statements in national media about the sanctity of life. In 2004 Land strongly supported Bush's reelection, noting that abortion had become a unifying factor between conservative Southern Baptists and Catholics. "There's a fault line running through American religions," he told *Washington Post* reporter Hanna Rosin. "And that fault line is running not between denominations but through them."[27]

Pastors who did not become frontline activists found quieter ways to oppose abortion or to support alternatives to it. At a four-thousand-member Southern Baptist congregation in East Texas, for example, Reverend John Blakely believed plainly that abortion is taking a life, and even though he had never personally picketed an abortion clinic, he felt it important to address the issue. His church sponsors an adoption and foster-care ministry and hosts a support group for women who may have had an abortion. Once a year his congregation and a nearby Catholic parish co-organize a sanctity-of-life rally. He says this is an activity in which the two churches have worked hand-in-hand for at least twenty years. In West Texas Dr. Fred Martin also holds strong views about abortion. At his two-thousand-member Southern Baptist church, he feels impelled to preach clearly that abortion is wrong. Increasingly he draws on science to argue about the completeness of a baby in the womb. He feels the baby has a right to independence and freedom. In his community, opposition to abortion has also drawn Baptists and Catholics together. A practical consequence of that convergence was a merger between the local Baptist and Catholic hospitals.[28]

With pastors speaking forthrightly against abortion, it was hardly surprising that Republican candidates who strongly opposed abortion fared better than

Democratic candidates who did not. In the counties where Blakely's and Martin's churches were located, 69 percent of the votes in 2008 went for McCain, while only 29 percent went for Obama. Although views about abortion had these political connotations, pastors regard the topic as a moral issue rather than as a political one and thus do not feel they are violating the separation of church and state by preaching about it. In interviews pastors repeatedly took the view that abortion was so clearly wrong in scripture that preaching against it was required. Were it a matter of personal opinion, they said, they would feel differently, but it was unthinkable to avoid talking about something that was biblical. And if that meant supporting one political candidate or party rather than the other, so be it. They might not endorse a specific candidate from the pulpit, but word got around anyway. Nor was abortion a sectarian issue, in their view, because Protestants and Catholics alike felt strongly about it. It was possible even for pastors to distance themselves from the more aggressive activities of right-to-life organizations while lending their support in less controversial ways such as preaching and staffing pregnancy counseling centers. Pastor Blakely says his congregation's adoption and postabortion support ministries would continue even if *Roe v. Wade* were overturned. Pastor Martin says right-to-life groups have become so hateful and extreme that he is reluctant to identify with any of them. He would never explicitly endorse a Republican candidate. Separation of church and state, he says, is a fundamental Baptist principle.[29]

HOMOSEXUALITY

Like abortion, homosexuality generated strong reactions from religious groups and prompted activists to organize on one side or the other of the issue. Over the years Texas had its share of incidents in which homosexuality moved to the forefront of public discussion. The Walter Jenkins incident in 1964 was of course one example. The fact that Jenkins was from Texas and worked as a senior aide for President Johnson drew local interest to the case. Although Billy Graham expressed sympathy to Johnson about the incident, his remarks were in private and contrasted to Graham's preaching against homosexuality as a symptom of national moral decay.[30]

Another high-profile incident was the murder of Texas Christian University dean John Lord in 1949. Eighteen-year-old Arthur Clayton Hester, who was convicted and sentenced to sixty years in prison for bludgeoning the victim to death, initially testified that Lord promised to lend him the family car in return for engaging in an "unnatural" homosexual act. Hester later repudiated his testimony, stating "Dr. Lord was no homosexual as I testified to and not at any time did he ever have an unnatural sexual relation with me or conduct himself in any manner that would lead me to believe he was a homosexual."[31]

Yet another well-publicized incident involving alleged homosexuality was the 1957 murder of Thomas Crawford, a thirty-six-year-old clerk in San Antonio. According to a friend of the accused, Army Sergeant Lyle Workman, who was stationed at Fort Sam Houston at the time, Workman said he killed Crawford because Crawford was a homosexual. "It's the old Army game," Workman told his friend, "when you meet a queer, knock him off."[32]

Publicity about such incidents played against a background that regarded homosexuality as the behavior of men who might appear to be normal but were shadowy individuals who led double lives and caused trouble for innocent victims.[33] To be attacked by a homosexual was bad enough, but blackmail and extortion could follow. In the worst-case scenario, homosexuals were not quite human. In 1956 when El Paso police arrested a homosexual, *El Paso Herald-Post* editor Edward M. Pooley editorialized, "They arrested a homosexual and they put it in a special cell. They didn't toss it into the tank with the hopheads." He worried that the police had given "it" special treatment.[34] Although the offenders were nearly always white men, they acquired a role in media accounts similar to the ones black men accused of sexual crimes had been assigned in the past. Homosexuals in these depictions were dangerous sexual deviants driven by passions they could not control.

In the 1960s homosexuality carried the connotations of lust, immorality, and deviance with which it was associated in previous years, but it took on several additional meanings as well. Homosexuals were characters in lurid books and stage plays appreciated by highbrow audiences but offensive to the common person. They were as un-American as communists. "Is homosexuality here to stay in high places as in high class books and plays?" conservative columnist Holmes Alexander asked. "My prudish typewriter declines to go into detail. But it doesn't take much memory to recall the defectors who have gone past the Iron Curtain, the cults and cells which are periodically discovered."[35] As the decade progressed, homosexuality became a topic folded into wider discussions about youth and the sexual revolution. Although a significant aspect of these discussions included hand-wringing and condemnation of sexual permissiveness, a process of medicalization also took hold. As doctors, psychiatrists, and researchers weighed in, advice columns and books portrayed homosexuality as a choice or disposition that required tolerance and understanding however unfortunate the choice may have been. "Homosexuals are not the monsters people once imagined them to be," one advice column observed. "The homosexual way of life is furtive, hazardous and lonely."[36]

A national study in 1973 found that only 49 percent of the public thought a homosexual should be allowed to teach school, and even fewer (45 percent) thought a book written by a homosexual should be allowed in the public library.[37] Another national study found that 63 percent of the public considered homosexuals harmful to American society. An informal study of school administrators in Texas a few years later concluded that in most districts a known homosexual would be fired.[38] It was possible nevertheless to find essays in general readership media that emphasized the plight of homosexuals, the discrimination they faced, and the work of organizations seeking to protect gay rights. In 1971, for example, the *San Antonio Express* published a full-page article by New York writer Merle Miller describing what it was like to be gay and detailing the work of the Gay Liberation Front, American Civil Liberties Union, and several other organizations concerned with gay rights.[39] In West Texas, Abilene journalist Jim Conley interviewed members of the local gay community about the discrimination and misunderstanding they experienced. Conley's interviews with community leaders, though, revealed a different story. According to community leaders, homosexuals in West Texas were treated well and would be as long as they kept their activities to themselves. The clergy Conley talked to said they definitely regarded homosexuality as a sin but said they tried to love the sinners anyway.[40]

Religious leaders' attitudes toward homosexuality became increasingly polarized in the 1980s as denominations and local congregations discussed whether homosexuals should be welcomed into membership and permitted to hold office as clergy. In 1982 the Baptist General Convention of Texas passed a resolution stating that the "homosexual lifestyle is not normal or acceptable in God's sight and is indeed called sin." The organization affirmed that statement in 1996, elaborating that all sexual relations except between husband and wife were contrary to God's purposes and in conflict with the Bible. Two years later the organization took action against a congregation that had ordained a homosexual as deacon by expelling the congregation from membership.[41] The state's second largest Protestant denomination equivocated. In 1971 a Methodist pastor in San Antonio was stripped of his credentials after declaring he was gay, but in 1982 a gay lay member was appointed to a conference board.[42] Presbyterian and Lutheran churches officially prohibited gays and lesbians from being ordained, although a few violations occurred. Explicit support for gay rights initially took shape through campus groups and nonreligious organizations, such as the Texas Gay Task Force, but included some connections with local congregations, such as the First Unitarian Church of Dallas which cosponsored conferences on gay rights in 1979 and 1980. Besides forging symbolic links between religion and gay rights, these events also provided occasions for discussing theological understandings of homosexuality. For example, at a Texas Gay Task Force conference in 1983, a featured speaker was the head of Evangelicals Concerned, a national organization providing support to gays and lesbians.[43]

One of the more significant developments connecting religion and homosexuality was the formation of the Metropolitan Community Church (MCC). Founded in 1966 in Los Angeles, the MCC grew slowly but developed local groups of gay and lesbians who met for worship and prayer. In Galveston, where the gay community was more public and better organized than in most Texas locations, an MCC ministry began holding services informally in 1971, but interest ebbed to the point that a congregation was not officially organized until several decades later. A more successful MCC ministry began in Dallas in 1970, called its first pastor a year later, and by 1976 had a membership of nearly 400. Renamed in 1990, the Cathedral of Hope had a membership of 1,900 people, regular attendance of 1,700 people, dozens of small groups, a television ministry, and mailing list of 30,000. It was the largest gay and lesbian church in the United States.[44]

Division among religious constituencies over gay and lesbian issues extended into discussions involving local, state, and national politics. An example occurred in 1982 when an antigay organization called Austin Citizens for Decency proposed an ordinance giving property owners the right to refuse to rent to people on grounds of sexual orientation. The proposal evoked opposition from a counterorganization calling itself Citizens for a United Austin, which enlisted the American Civil Liberties Union on its side and circulated a statement signed by fifty local clergy who argued that such discrimination was contrary to Judeo-Christian beliefs. The proposal was defeated but drew public attention to whether the state's law prohibiting sodomy should be strengthened to include sexual orientation or be repealed.[45]

Over the next two decades controversies erupted over allegations that homosexuality was being promoted in sex education classes and through prohomosexual books in local libraries or because of advertising campaigns. In Houston billboards advertised antigay themes and promoted a large conference on the dangers of homosexuality sponsored by James Dobson's conservative national organization Focus on the Family. The effort was organized by a Galveston resident, Joe Cline, who operated the Lighthouse Freedom Ministry, which claimed the capacity to turn gay people straight through the power of Jesus.[46] In 1996 controversy surfaced in Dallas when the Dallas Theater Center hosted award-winning playwright Tony Kushner's *Angels in America*, which included a nude actor and focused on gay men, AIDS, and conservative politics. The event drew denunciations from some of the city's church members and clergy but also demonstrated the diversity of views present in the area about religion and controversial social issues. As Dallas Theater Center director Richard Hamburger observed, "The churches are often much more progressive than we give them credit for." The small minority of extremely vocal antihomosexual groups, he thought, were only part of the story. Others looked to their religious groups "to broaden out and help other people whether they're poor, hungry, gay, or have AIDS."[47] These differences were evident again when the leadership of Criswell's First Baptist Church refused to host a performance for the American Choral Directors' Association by the city's nationally acclaimed Turtle Creek Chorale, a large gay men's chorus, but the event was held without problems at the First Methodist Church.[48]

When the Defense of Marriage Act, which restricted marriage to heterosexual couples, came before the U.S. Congress in 1996, Texas legislators lauded the measure. Congresswoman Sheila Jackson Lee was one of the few from any state who did not vote yea. In South Texas conservative representative Steve Stockman, who was strongly in favor of the bill, argued that marriage is "defined in our deepest moral and religious convictions" and should not succumb to special interest groups at odds with the nation's "sacred values."[49] A pastor in his district expressed what appeared to be a widespread view, observing simply that God created Adam and Eve, not Adam and Steve. Another constituent suggested, "These [gay] people should either go back to the closet or be put to sleep."[50]

Questions about gay rights and same-sex unions continued in discussions surrounding the next election cycles. In 2000 controversies surfaced about homosexuality in the Boy Scouts, in state elections in Vermont and Oregon, and about Bush's initial reluctance to meet with the gay Log Cabin Republicans. In 2004 referenda to place amendments against same-sex marriage were successful in eleven states and according to some accounts contributed to Bush's reelection by increasing turnout among conservative Republicans.[51] In 2005 a referendum to amend the Texas constitution to limit marriage only to the union of one man and one woman was approved by 76 percent of the voters.[52]

Data from a representative survey of more than thirteen hundred Texas adults the following year suggest why the state amendment passed by a large margin even though opinions about gay rights were more evenly divided. One was that white non-Hispanics were more likely than other groups to oppose gay marriage *and* more likely to have voted. In the 2006 study, 54 percent of white non-Hispanics said they favored a constitutional ban on gay marriage while only 45 percent and 39 percent of African Americans and Hispanics did, respectively. The turnout rate in the 2005 referendum was only 18 percent. In most of the heavily Hispanic counties in the Rio Grande valley, the turnout ranged between 6 and 7 percent. A second factor was that Republicans and born-again Christians who typically voted in high proportions were particularly opposed to gay marriage.[53]

The 2006 survey provided additional information suggesting that attitudes toward gay marriage were beginning to shift. Eighty-nine percent of Texans polled said they knew someone who was gay. Four percent said they themselves were gay, 20 percent said the gay person they knew was a member of their family, 28 percent identified the person as a close friend, and 48 percent said the person was a coworker or some other acquaintance. Unsurprisingly, among those who were themselves gay, nearly everyone opposed a constitutional ban on gay marriage. Among those who knew nobody who was gay or who knew someone only casually or among one's extended family, only a minority opposed a constitutional ban on gay marriage. In contrast, a solid majority of those who had a close friend who was gay opposed a constitutional ban on gay marriage.

Subsequent studies in 2009 and 2010 showed that Texans remained divided about gay marriage, but nearly a third of the public thought it should be legalized, and two-thirds were at least supportive of civil unions. Like the rest of the public, clergy held varying opinions, ranging from strongly opposing gay marriage to rethinking exactly what marriage was meant to be. "If you stand at the top of the stairs and scream at the top of your lungs that homosexuality is wrong," an evangelical pastor in East Texas observed, "it's going to be difficult [for any-one] to hear anything other than judgment." He was struggling to uphold the church's traditional understanding of marriage while acknowledging the mean-ing of marriage in legal and governmental terms. Other clergy who considered homosexuality morally wrong had come to the view that gay people should be included in their congregations. As a Baptist pastor in Waco explained, "I would characterize my views as welcoming but not affirming." The religious argument favoring gay marriage was also being articulated. As a woman in South Texas put it, "As I understand the God of the New Testament, we are loved by Him and nothing can separate us from Him, nothing." In her view, God created the genetic makeup that determined sexual orientation, and "gay people have as much right to [marriage] as anyone else." In 2009, against opposition from antigay groups and religious conservatives, Houston became the largest city in the United States to elect an openly gay mayor. By the end of the decade, Metropolitan Commu-nity Church congregations had been established in Austin, Corpus Christi, El Paso, Galveston, Houston, San Antonio, and Waco. In addition, more than two hundred congregations across the state, including several that withdrew from the Baptist General Convention of Texas, declared themselves inclusive and welcom-ing in terms of membership for gays and lesbians.[54]

One of the congregations that withdrew from the Baptist General Convention of Texas was the University Baptist Church in Austin. The process illustrated how context—being in a university community—and history—having opposed racial discrimination—mattered. Founded in 1908, the church ministered from the start to University of Texas faculty and students. In 1948 it voted to end seg-regated seating, and it was at the forefront of the civil rights movement in the 1950s and 1960s. In the 1970s it was one of the few Baptist churches anywhere in the South to ordain women as deacons. Having taken positions in favor of equal rights in the past, it voted in the 1990s to ordain a gay member as a deacon. When conservative leaders in the Baptist General Convention of Texas proposed that the congregation be "distanced" (a somewhat less assertive word than "dis-fellowshipped"), the congregation voted to withdraw from the convention and align itself with the American Baptist Convention, which in the area was pre-dominantly African American. The congregation lost members and contribu-tions as a result, but an elderly deacon who had been in the church in 1948 when it voted against segregation stood up and reminded the congregation of what he had said then, "We may die because we've done this, but I can't think of any better way of dying than by being Christian."[55]

In less overt ways pastors and lay leaders in other congregations were attempt-ing to think creatively about gay rights and related issues. One approach was to be a "welcoming" church with respect to gays and lesbians while continu-ing to argue that homosexuality was wrong. A second approach was to affirm same-sex civil unions and domestic partner arrangements while denying that homosexuals should marry. Yet another was to argue that gay marriage should be embraced. Some of the pastors who took these positions were Baptists whose congregations remained affiliated with the Southern Baptist Convention but who disagreed with the denomination's conservative leadership. In their view, liberty of conscience meant freedom to address controversial social issues in innovative ways. "We talk a lot about the separation of church and state," a pastor in Houston explained. "But honestly, the autonomy of the local church is what helps me every day."[56]

As support for gay rights grew in various locations, opposition became more vociferous. In Amarillo the idea that Houston could embrace an openly gay woman for mayor was sufficient evidence to Pastor David Grisham Jr. that America was rapidly descending into perdition. Grisham's small band of volunteers wearing black T-shirts with "Death finds us all, find Jesus first" emblazoned in large white letters was already calling on gays and abortion providers to repent, targeting a local swingers' club, and holding prayer vigils outside the Unitarian Universalist Church, where it claimed a coven of witches was worshipping. In 2009 the group announced that it was the "Army of God," would take action as the "Special Forces of spiritual warfare," initiated a citywide blitz under the rubric Repent Amarillo to root out demons, and encouraged believers everywhere to boycott gay-friendly Houston. On the anniversary of the 9/11 attacks, Grisham attempted to burn a Qur'an in the Amarillo city park, only to be foiled by a local skateboarder who swooped in at the last moment to save the kerosene-doused book.[57]

But if conservative activists were expanding into topics beyond homosexuality and abortion, progressive activists were increasingly mobilized as well. Besides supporting gay rights, University Baptist Church in Austin, for example, founded the Texas Freedom Network (TFN) in the late 1990s to combat the Religious Right's recurring efforts to remove teaching about evolution from the state's textbooks or to include arguments about creationism and intelligent design. Over the next decade, the TFN grew into an organization with some sixty thousand members statewide and a staff of ten people at its headquarters in Austin. It lobbied members of the state board of education and worked closely with three hundred to five hundred progressive clergy around the state to encourage voter turnout.[58]

Although it was a nondenominational organization that attracted support from progressive leaders, TFN's central message was rooted in the state's historic emphasis on liberty of conscience. As Deputy Director Ryan Valentine explained, the organization's philosophy was consistent with Baptists' insistence on strict separation of church and state. A lifelong Baptist himself, he felt it important to challenge religious conservatives who wanted to bring their ideology into the state legislature. "Strangely enough," he said, "the importance of separation of church and state was one of the things I was told growing up in my conservative Baptist background." Being "outspoken for religious liberty," he felt, was important not just to defend Baptists but also to defend other minority faiths and to combat intolerance toward African Americans, Hispanics, women, and gays and lesbians.[59]

To some observers, it seemed that homosexuality and abortion had dominated discussions of religion and politics to the point that other important moral issues were being ignored. As Barry Hankins, a professor of church-state studies at Baylor, put it, "The abortion issue got religious conservatives in politics [and then into] other human-life issues such as stem-cell research and same-sex marriage." These issues seemed more pressing, he supposed, because actual life was being taken, making it harder to give the same sense of urgency to issues of human suffering such as poverty and homelessness.[60] And yet life was also at stake in these circumstances, and especially in the struggles facing low-wage and undocumented immigrants.

IMMIGRATION

On June 8, 1998, as temperatures in South Texas soared above 90 degrees, Felipe and Pablo Bravo struggled through the brush in Kenedy County on their way from Mexico toward Houston, where they hoped to find work. As Pablo collapsed from dehydration, the coyote (smuggler) leading the group abandoned the pair. Desperate to save his brother, who was now seized with convulsions, Felipe ran a half mile to the highway where he tried without success to flag down a motorist for help. By the time a border patrol agent found them, Pablo was dead.[61]

Kenedy County was one of the busiest paths through which undocumented immigrants passed on their way from Reynosa or Matamores to find work in Corpus Christi, San Antonio, and Houston. It was also the location of the nation's largest privately owned ranch, the 825,000-acre King Ranch, established in 1847 on scrubland so rough that only weather-hardened range cattle could survive. Spanish explorers had named it El Desierto de los Muertos—the Desert of the Dead. By the end of the twentieth century, only 1 percent of the unforgiving land was under cultivation, and fewer than five hundred people lived in the entire county. In 1998 the area was the focal point of Operation Rio Grande, which brought in 260 new border patrol agents who in one three-month stretch intercepted more than a thousand illegal immigrants.[62]

Pablo was the first of more than four dozen illegal immigrants to die from heat-related causes in South Texas that summer. The deaths in July included a twelve-year-old boy and a man in his twenties with no identification and only ten dollars in his pocket. In August border patrol agents found a man whose friends had tried in vain to save him by building a shelter of weeds before going off in search of water. A few days later a forty-nine-year-old woman died from searing heat as her son searched in vain for help. By October the weather was better, but rattlesnakes and copperheads presented continuing dangers that rumor said could be avoided only by sleeping between the Union Pacific railroad tracks. It was that belief, authorities concluded, that led to six men being killed instantly by the early morning freight train from Houston to Brownsville.[63]

Border patrol agents did what they could to deter the illegal migration northward. But the complexity of the situation was illustrated in March 2000 when Armando Leal, an undocumented immigrant concealed in the brush, was run over by a border patrol vehicle, sustaining major injuries to his back and a crushed pelvis. Five days earlier Victor Manuel, another undocumented immigrant, was struck by another border patrol vehicle and seriously injured. Angered by the incidents as well as by border patrol vehicles frequently damaging the terrain and starting fires, the trustee board in charge of the land on which the incidents occurred canceled its agreement permitting access to the border patrol. "It was pretty rough," a spokesman said, explaining the board's concern about the humanitarian issues involved.[64]

The incident was one of many over a ten-year period in which federal authorities, the border patrol, and the FBI were involved in disputes with local authorities, ranch owners, clergy, and immigrant advocacy groups. At issue were questions about trade and bilateral law enforcement agreements with Mexico as well as border security, labor, and human rights. The larger context included the region's adjustment to a large-scale shift in ethnic composition.

Between 1980 and 2000, the total population of Texas grew from 14.2 million to 20.8 million, an increase of 46 percent, but the foreign-born population rose from 856,213 to 2.9 million, an increase of 238 percent. By the turn of the century, foreign-born residents made up nearly 14 percent of the state's population, up from only 6 percent two decades earlier. Sixty-five percent of the foreign-born population was from Mexico. Another 10 percent was from other Central and South American countries.[65]

With approximately 6.7 million or 32 percent of the state's population identifying as Hispanic or Latino, it was incumbent on office seekers to pay increasing attention to this constituency. Over the next decade, the state's non-Hispanic population would grow by only 10 percent while the Hispanic population would increase 42 percent, bringing it to 38 percent of the total population. With African Americans making up nearly 12 percent of the population and Asians another 4 percent, white non-Hispanics would comprise only 45 percent of the population by 2010.[66]

A study of Texas Hispanics in 2006 found, as other surveys did, that a large majority opposed abortion except to save the life of the woman and that gay marriage evoked disapproval twice as often as approval. Nearly half the Hispanics studied said they were born-again or spirit-filled Christians or involved in the charismatic movement. Nearly two-thirds said they attended worship services every week, and twice as many said they were political conservatives as identified themselves as political liberals. Yet, when asked their political preference, four times as many identified themselves as Democrats as said they were Republicans. In 2008 Obama won nearly two-thirds of the Hispanic vote in Texas.[67]

Research showed that Texas Hispanics were far more concerned about economic issues, education, employment, and immigration policies than they were about abortion or homosexuality. The issue mentioned most often in the 2006 study as the most serious problem facing the country was the economy. The problem mentioned second most often was illegal immigration. The vast majority favored immediate legalization or some kind of guest worker program leading to eventual legalization. A study found that immigration was high on the list of concerns among the general public in Texas as well. Two-thirds said illegal immigration was an important issue in their vote for U.S. senator that year.[68] Estimates placed the number of undocumented immigrants living in the state at 1.45 to 1.85 million and totaling as much as 9 percent of the labor force.[69]

The least controversial way to help immigrants—the method that compassionate conservatives and progressives alike could embrace—was to provide private charitable assistance such as emergency shelter and relief and helping immigrants gain citizenship. An example in the North Texas town of McKinney was Reverend Alex Camacho, a Baptist pastor whose congregation was half composed of recent immigrants and who directed a nonprofit immigrant services organization helping undocumented workers maneuver the maze of government regulations to become citizens and find work. Another example was a nonprofit organization called Opening Doors, initiated in Denton by members of the Trinity Presbyterian Church through a grant from the denomination to assist immigrants with legal counseling. On a significantly larger scale, Catholic Charities, Catholic Family Services, Catholic Immigration Services, and the Catholic Office of Hispanic Ministry provided a similar range of assistance to immigrants throughout the state.[70]

There was general agreement as well that churches should minister to the spiritual needs of new immigrants, providing opportunities for worship, engaging in family assistance and evangelism, training clergy, and initiating Spanish-language ministries or founding new churches. Although opportunities for worship were limited by language barriers and a shortage of Spanish-speaking priests, the Catholic Church included a growing number of Hispanic clergy and several Hispanic bishops and was encouraging more Spanish-language services. In the El Paso diocese, for example, where a majority of the nearly half a million faithful were Hispanic, Bishop Armando Ochoa promoted a ministry of inclusion called "the many faces in God's house" that aimed to embrace different languages, races, and nationalities and promote reconciliation among them. On a smaller scale, Protestant churches also saw opportunities for new ministries. The Hispanic Baptist Convention of Texas, for example, announced plans in 2003 to help start at least four hundred Hispanic churches throughout the United States and baptize at least ten thousand new Hispanic Christians. The plan noted the need for better-trained Spanish-speaking clergy as well as the implicit opportunities to reach immigrants whose Catholic roots may have been weakened as part of their transition to the United States.[71]

It was harder for church leaders to agree about assistance for undocumented workers. The Vatican annually commemorated World Day of Migrants and Refugees by calling on governments everywhere to embrace human dignity for migrants and enact policies to reunite families while counseling immigrants to respect the laws of their new countries. In Matamoros priests from both sides of the Rio Grande commemorated the day each year by erecting a large cross and holding an outdoor mass at which they promised assistance to immigrants on their way to the United States. In San Antonio Archbishop José Gomez said restrictive immigration policies that violated his religion might force him to break the law. In Brownsville Bishop Peña became one of the state's outspoken critics of U.S. immigration policies, denouncing the construction of a wall along the border and condemning harsh deportation measures that separated families. Peña distinguished between government policies upholding the rule of law and church practices that he argued should be governed by the rule of love. "The immigrant who comes seeking a better life personifies in himself or herself every one of the afflictions to which Jesus alluded in the last judgment narrative," he explained. He urged parishioners to write to their senators and representatives insisting on comprehensive immigration reform. He felt the church should also minister to the needs of all immigrants regardless of their legal status. "If the undocumented knock on our door or meet us on the street and ask for help," he counseled, "we will generously address their need, lovingly. Their legal status cannot deter us, since in God's eyes, no one is illegal."[72]

Progressive Protestant groups shared Bishop Peña's views. In April 2006 Protestant and Catholic leaders working cooperatively through a multiethnic ecumenical organization called Dallas Area Interfaith spearheaded the MegaMarch Immigration Rally that police estimated drew between 350,000 and 500,000 participants—the largest rally in the state's history—in a show of solidarity for immigrant rights.[73] When the United Methodist Church held its national conference in Fort Worth in 2008, the assembled delegates went on record in favor of comprehensive immigration reform that would facilitate legalization for currently undocumented workers. A smaller group led by Bishop Minerva Carcano staged a rally calling for open borders and more humane treatment of immigrants. "Everybody here," African American pastor Tyrone Gordon told the group, "came from somewhere else. Some came on immigrant ships, some came on slave ships, but we're all in the same boat now. And we're either going to sink or swim together."[74] At a meeting in Houston six months later, United Methodist bishop Janice Riggle Huie and Roman Catholic cardinal Daniel DiNardo jointly declared that legalization of undocumented workers already in the country should be granted and that job-site raids should end.[75]

Conservative leaders took a more cautious stance. Reverend Land of the Southern Baptist Convention, for example, argued that the Bible in Romans 13:1–7 showed clearly that citizens should uphold the government in its God-given duty to oppose bad conduct, which he said included protecting national security and

FIGURE 22. MegaMarch rally, 2006, in Dallas on April 9, showing a few of the 350,000 participants who marched in support of immigrant rights. Photograph © Claudia A. De La Garza.

deciding who can cross borders.[76] The Family Research Council, which had focused on opposing abortion and homosexuality, took the unusual step in 2006 of
hosting a national conference of conservative leaders on immigration. The meeting aired different sides of the topic but did not generate agreement. Some of the
leaders thought it best to remain silent while others considered it important to
speak strongly for border security. "As the United States Senate continues debate
on an immigration reform bill," Christian Coalition president Roberta Combs
declared, "the American people are backed up by the Bible in their demands that
America's national boundaries are to be respected. The left wing in this nation is
thoroughly wrong when they argue that because Christ showed compassion to
all of God's children, Christians should ignore violations of the law by aliens."[77]

The issue was complex enough that opinion at the grass roots was divided. In
the El Paso area, for example, where more than a hundred thousand illegal immigrants were arrested in 2006, Bishop Ochoa encouraged parishioners to advocate
for the human rights of immigrants whether they were crossing legally or illegally,
but when journalist Ramon Bracamontes talked to lay leaders, many thought the
bishop was placing too much emphasis on mercy and not enough on justice,
while others considered it inappropriate for the church to be talking about political issues at all.[78] A national study in 2006 asked people whether they favored
a proposal being considered in the U.S. House of Representatives emphasizing
"stricter enforcement and deportations of undocumented aliens" or a Senate proposal to "open a path to citizenship for current illegal immigrants." Seventy-one
percent of white non-Hispanics, 56 percent of African Americans, and 40 percent of Hispanics favored the House proposal. In Texas the results were similar.

The House proposal received support from 74 percent of white non-Hispanics, 65 percent of African Americans, and 44 percent of Hispanics. Among white non-Hispanics who said they were born-again Christians, the proportion favoring stricter enforcement rose to 84 percent, but even among white non-Hispanics who were not born again 68 percent opted for the House proposal.[79]

The role of religion in advocacy for immigrant rights was a confounding factor in the otherwise straightforward narrative about conservative religion going hand in hand with conservative politics. Bishop Peña's role as a vehement opponent of abortion and a strong advocate for immigrant rights was a particularly interesting case in point. As a priest in Peña's diocese observed during the 2008 presidential election, "The voter faces a dilemma," adding, "I do not like [Obama's] stance on abortion, but all the issues at stake are serious." He thought Obama probably was the least of the two morally flawed options available.[80] The antiabortion side found support among conservative Protestants and in the views of conservative Republican candidates for public office, while the immigrant-rights side forged common bonds with progressive Protestant and secular groups and more often with Democratic than with Republican candidates. The church's opposition to abortion was one of the reasons that abortion rates were relatively low among Hispanics and a source of support for Republican candidates among a minority of Hispanic voters. The church's advocacy for immigration reform was consistent with Democratic voting among a majority of the Hispanic population and with pressure even on the part of some Republican officeholders for a balanced immigration policy that provided for legalization as well as border security.

If there was a single thread that wove together opposition to abortion or homosexuality and support for immigrant rights, it was the view that policies emanating from the nation's capital were wrong. Whether it was couched in states' rights language of the Old South, in memories of Texas's struggle for independence, or in grassroots populism, the idea was that Washington was either in the hands of liberals who did not appreciate the values of ordinary people or ruled by bureaucrats who could not be trusted. This was an odd sentiment for Texans to espouse when one of their own occupied the White House. And yet this was not the first time that a president held office who postured himself as a Washington outsider whose roots were somewhere on the open frontier. It was reminiscent of LBJ in the 1960s and Reagan in the 1980s. It emerged again with a vengeance as Texas Republicans reacted to the policies of the Obama administration.

TAXES AND GOVERNMENT

Governor Perry's remark in 2009 about Texans being an "independent lot" drew national attention. Here was a governor, pundits supposed, who was just crazy enough to think that secession might be a good idea. Hadn't Texas

learned anything from the Civil War? Or perhaps Texas was so large and powerful that it could in fact secede. Neither interpretation made much sense. But
the remark was significant for two reasons that would become clearer over the
next several years than at the time: there was animosity toward the federal government that could easily be stoked by a whole variety of concerns, including
taxes and healthcare proposals; and there was a connection between all that
and religion.

The one thing in which Texas Republicans took exceptional pride was keeping
taxes low. From 1992 through 2012, state and local taxes in Texas averaged only
15.8 percent of the state's gross domestic product (GDP) and in only three years
exceeded 17 percent. State and local taxes in California—the state Texas leaders
most often used for comparative purposes—were more than a quarter higher, averaging 20.2 percent of state GDP and sinking below 18 percent only twice. The
rate for state and local taxes in Texas was also significantly lower than the rate for
federal taxes, which averaged 20.5 percent of national GDP over the same period
and rose to 25.2 percent in 2009 as a result of the Great Recession.[81]

Taxes in Texas not only were relatively low; they were also among the most
regressive in the nation, meaning that they fell more heavily on the poor than on
the rich. A report conducted by the Institute on Taxation and Economic Policy in
2009 found that Texas, Tennessee, South Dakota, Florida, and Washington had
the most regressive tax systems in the country. Texas was by far the most populous of these states. The study showed that the poorest 20 percent of the population in Texas paid 12.2 percent of their income in state and local taxes while the
wealthiest 1 percent paid only 3.3 percent. A study two years later by the Center
for Public Policy Priorities found similar disparities. The poorest quintile paid
14.6 percent of household income in state and local taxes while the richest quintile paid 3.6 percent. The contrast with California was again striking. In California the poorest and richest quintiles paid almost the same percentage of annual
income in state and local taxes.[82]

The principal reason Texas taxes were low and regressive was the absence of a
state income tax. Texas was one of only five states that had no income tax. Income
taxes are generally progressive, taxing higher incomes at higher rates than lower
incomes. With no income tax, Texas relied more heavily for revenue on state and
local sales taxes. The state sales tax rate was 6.25 percent, and state law permitted
localities to impose up to 2 percent in additional sales taxes. Sales taxes are regressive, even when purchases of food are exempt, because poor families spend a
larger share of their disposable income on necessities than wealthier families do.

The other way in which Texas kept taxes low was to spend relatively little on
welfare for the poor. In 2012, for example, Texas spent only 0.83 percent of state
GDP on state and local expenditures for welfare—the lowest of any state in the
nation. The average for all states was 1.74 percent, or twice the Texas rate. In
California it was 2.2 percent of state GDP. The amounts Texas spent on pensions
and health care were also well below the national average.

It mattered of course that Texas was the nation's largest petroleum producer, producing some $70 to $75 billion annually in oil and natural gas. That amount contributed nearly a billion dollars to the state budget each year but constituted only about half of 1 percent of total state revenue. It was also regressive, comprising a higher proportion of household income for low-income families than for high-income families. Petroleum infused the culture, though, as much as it affected the economy. In interviews even during the Great Recession, middle-class Texans talked with pride about oil discoveries providing well-paying jobs for everyone, not to mention royalties on leases for those fortunate enough to own land. It was almost as if the free market and God's blessings went hand in hand.[83]

In these ways Texas was a good place to live if a person was wealthy or even for people with above-average incomes, but less good for families that were poor or on welfare. That did not mean wealthy people flocked to Texas. California, with its attractive natural ambience, motion picture industry, and Silicon Valley venture capitalists, had four times as many top wealth holders as Texas. But Texas had more than a hundred thousand individuals who fell into this category and collectively held nearly a half trillion dollars in assets.[84] A comparative study conducted in 2011 also showed that Texas had the largest percentage of its population falling either below the poverty line or making more than $200,000 a year, relative to other states. The study suggested that inequality in Texas had been increasing as well, as measured by a GINI index coefficient of 0.47 compared to 0.42 in 1990 and 0.37 in 1970.[85]

One of the clearest assessments of how Americans felt about taxes was provided by a large national study conducted in 2008 among a representative national sample of more than thirty thousand respondents. The study asked, "If your state were to have a budget deficit this year it would have to raise taxes on income or sales or cut spending, such as on education, health care, welfare, and road construction. What would you prefer more, raising taxes or cutting spending?" Respondents were asked to pick a number between 0 and 100 where lower numbers meant tax increases and higher numbers indicated a preference for spending cuts. The question was well conceived because it focused on state rather than federal taxes and spending, avoided the complicating issue of defense spending, and allowed respondents to indicate a mixture of preferences for tax increases or spending cuts. Unsurprisingly, tax increases were far less popular than spending cuts (nationally, only 21 percent selected numbers less than 50, indicating a preference for tax increases, while 61 percent selected numbers between 51 and 100, indicating a preference for spending cuts). Nor was there a significant correlation overall between the responses and residence in states with more regressive or less regressive tax rates. However, the responses did vary significantly by race. Nationwide, 62 percent of white non-Hispanics favored spending cuts compared with 54 percent of Hispanics and 46 percent of African Americans. In Texas the differences were even more pronounced. Sixty-six percent of white non-Hispanics favored spending cuts compared with 54 percent of Hispanics

FIGURE 23. Tea Party rally, 2009, in Austin on April 15, showing a few of the five thousand who gathered to protest taxes and government spending. Photograph © Rita Quinn of Knots and Tots Photography, Austin, TX.

and 38 percent of African Americans. In ordinary least squares regression models both nationally and in Texas, race was the most significant variable affecting preferences for tax increases or spending cuts, taking account of gender, marital status, employment status, immigrant status, union membership, and age.[86]

Taxes were never less popular than in 2009 when Perry spoke to reporters at the Tea Party rally in Austin on April 15. The state comptroller was predicting that state revenue would drop by about $9 billion because of the recession, raising worries that tax rates would have to increase. The federal deficit, already more than $400 billion in 2008, was expected to quadruple by the end of the year. The rally in Austin was one of seventy across the state, timed to coincide with citizens filing their state and federal tax returns. The Tea Party movement had been gaining steam ever since the 2008 presidential election. Participants were especially angry at the Obama administration for bailing out Wall Street, raising the federal deficit, and proposing a costly universal healthcare plan. The protesters in Austin carried signs with phrases that read "No more bailouts," "Shut down D.C.," "Socialism kills," "Stop spending my grandkids' money," "No taxation without liberation," "Chains you can believe in," and "Hussein Obama: Keep the change."[87]

Over the Fourth of July weekend that summer, Tea Party rallies were held in towns and cities nationwide. One of the largest took place at the Southfork Ranch near Dallas, where the television series bearing the city's name had filmed from 1978 to 1991. An estimated fifty thousand people gathered on the grounds to hear speeches decrying the federal government. Some in attendance wore T-shirts that read "Texas Independence," and some were affiliated with the Texas Nationalist Movement, an extremist organization that advocated secession from the United States. The event's organizers, though, hoped to mainstream the movement by appealing mostly to middle-class taxpayers and attracting money from deep-pocket donors. The central themes were anti-Washington, anti–big government, and anti–government spending, although illegal immigration was also one of the complaints. Besides the Southfork event, rallies were held in Austin, Corpus Christi, Kerrville, Liberty City, Longview, Lufkin, Nacogdoches, Odessa, Wichita Falls, and numerous smaller towns.[88]

The Tea Party was a loosely connected collection of local groups that clustered under an all-purpose umbrella provided by the media. They pursued somewhat similar but often ill-defined objectives. Insofar as there was agreement, the groups' core values included limited government and fiscal conservatism. In Texas there were more than three dozen groups, ranging from local county and municipal organizations, such as the Irving Tea Party and Tyler Tea Party, to regional groups attempting to represent the whole state or part of the state, to various alliances and networks. While most included "Tea Party" in their name, others used terms such as 9/12, patriots, and grassroots. There was a sense, perhaps reasonably grounded, that Texas was taking the lead in the movement. That sense was reinforced by the fact that well-funded organizations such as Americans for Prosperity, Young Americans for Liberty, and the Texas Public Policy Foundation were offering encouragement. In a large national study, 48 percent of white non-Hispanic Texans said their views of the Tea Party were positive. Only in Georgia, Alabama, and Louisiana were the proportions higher.[89]

A study of Texas voters in 2010 found that 33 percent claimed to be in some way involved in the Tea Party movement. That included 42 percent of the white non-Hispanic population (9 points higher than in a comparable national survey), but only 6 percent of African Americans and 21 percent of Hispanics were involved. Among those who said they were involved in the Tea Party movement, an overwhelming 97 percent said they strongly disapproved of Barack Obama. This was an unprecedented disapproval number among any constituency but hardly surprising. At Tea Party rallies, Obama took the brunt of most of the ire. As one placard read, "See what happens when you give a junior senator a credit card!" Or as another sign declared, "I didn't vote for this Obamanation."[90]

There was no particular reason that religion should have been a factor in concerns about taxes or in support for the Tea Party.[91] Unlike abortion and homosexuality, which Bible believers could argue were unbiblical, paying taxes fell under the heading of "rendering unto Caesar" what was Caesar's. But in the large 2008 national study, weekly churchgoers, respondents who said they were born-again Christians, and respondents who belonged to evangelical denominations were significantly more likely than other respondents (controlling for race and a number of other characteristics) to favor spending cuts rather than tax increases. That was also true when only Texas respondents were considered. A clue as to why this might be the case was evident in the data as well. When political party affiliation and attitudes toward abortion and homosexuality were included in the models, nearly all the relationship between religious conservatism and fiscal conservatism disappeared. In short, religious conservatives were in contexts where the Republican Party and antiabortion and antigay sentiments prevailed, and it was in those contexts where exposure to fiscal conservatism also occurred.[92]

A woman who attended a large conservative Protestant church on the outskirts of Dallas illustrated how context mattered in shaping opinions. The congregation was theologically and politically conservative. The pastor routinely preached against abortion and homosexuality. She had strong views on these issues and could articulate them without hesitation. She believed that God created each person and that human personhood began at conception. She enacted her beliefs by volunteering at a crisis pregnancy center the church supported. She was equally clear that homosexuality was unbiblical and that gay parenting was damaging children. She was less clear on questions about taxes and fiscal policies, stating that these were beyond her grasp and finding it harder to articulate views about what kinds of tax were more or less fair. The bottom line, she thought, was that the government should handle its finances like a family did, meaning that it should cut spending instead of going into debt. She figured Republicans generally upheld these kinds of family values more than Democrats did. She found President Obama scary but respected President George W. Bush because of his family values.[93]

This constellation of ideas came together among supporters of the Tea Party. In national data, the odds of expressing positive views toward the Tea Party were two and a half times greater among born-again Christians than among other respondents even when controlling for race, gender, marital status, income, and age. And most of the difference in support was attributable to the facts that born-again Christians were strongly opposed to abortion and gay marriage.[94] In the 2010 Texas poll a similar pattern was evident. The Texas poll also demonstrated that the state's white non-Hispanic churchgoers clearly did not like Obama. Of those who attended church at least once a week, 79 percent strongly disapproved of Obama, another 5 percent somewhat disapproved, and only 13 percent approved.[95] They may have disapproved of him because he was raising the federal deficit, or simply because he was a Democrat, or even because he was black or they thought he was a Muslim.[96] The polls did not say. Interviews were more revealing.

What linked the Tea Party, views about taxes, opinions of the president, and religion was a conviction that the federal government, particularly under the Obama administration, stood in contradiction to the moral and spiritual values of conservative Christians. "I'm just a simple pastor," the minister at a small evangelical church in North Texas explained, apologizing for his lack of "smarts," but it seemed to him that the "principles of scripture" on which the nation was founded were totally at odds with what was currently happening in Washington.

Things had gotten "so far out of control," he said, that "I don't know if we can ever get back." It riled him that the president appointed the Supreme Court and that the justices held so much power. He was especially concerned about government spending. "Realistically, where is all this money going? Has there been any program that has benefited us in any way?" He liked what he had heard at the Tea Party rallies he attended. He felt it was good that the Tea Party was stirring things up.[97]

In other comments people expressed the view that Washington was so distant and that the federal government had grown so powerful that its leaders no longer stood for the values of common people. A community leader in East Texas thought people in his community generally felt that "we can take care of ourselves" if the federal government would just stay out of things. A school administrator in North Texas who did not personally support the Tea Party nevertheless felt it reflected the local sense that government was almost out of control and that politicians were no longer working for the common good or the common person. A pastor in West Texas thought it was mostly the federal debt that bothered people in his community. Most of the local leaders, he said, were small business owners. "In our area, debt is a four letter word," he explained. "There's a feeling that small businesses have to live within their means. If you don't have the money, you don't spend it." It was terribly frustrating, he thought, to know that the government was spending money it didn't have.[98]

These sentiments were reinforced by the organizations that assisted in sponsoring Tea Party rallies and spreading the word about them. The American Family Association (AFA) headed by Reverend Donald E. Wildmon in Mississippi carried information about Tea Party rallies on its website and through broadcasts on the two hundred radio stations it owned and operated nationwide. Focusing on evangelical gospel outreach and fighting indecency in the media and homosexuality, the AFA turned its attention in 2009 to promoting Tea Party rallies in more than a thousand towns and cities. More directly involved was Grassroots America, organized in Tyler in 2009 to promote conservative activism and government watchdog efforts aimed at restoring the nation's founding principles. Grassroots America explicitly combined appeals to social conservatives interested in traditional family values with ideals of individual freedom, personal responsibility, and small government. At a Grassroots America rally in Fort Worth, Pastor Broden of the Fair Park Bible Fellowship Church in Dallas told the group that America's founding Judeo-Christian ethic was fundamentally threatened by the current tyranny of an unjust government. In his view, godless socialists in the nation's capital were attempting to rob Americans of their God-given inalienable rights. "We can vote them out or we can impeach them out," he declared to enthusiastic applause. He considered government tax policies and regulations part of the moral decline the nation was experiencing and thought it important for churches to speak clearly on these issues. Americans needed to become more aware of "what is happening in Washington, D.C.," he said, especially the universal healthcare proposal which represented a "disconnect" between Washington and the grass roots.[99]

Building on its initial successes among churchgoers, Grassroots America began organizing "God and Country" meetings specifically for clergy and conservative church members. These events bridged the Tea Party's antigovernment and antitax agendas with the concerns of Christians who felt the government was promoting policies destructive of traditional family values, such as abortion rights and homosexuality. The goals included defending Christian moral values, informing Christian leaders about their legal rights, and encouraging conservative Christians to vote. Besides Pastor Broden, speakers included local Tea Party organizers and clergy and high-profile leaders such as Kelly Shackelford of the Liberty Institute and Dr. Rick Scarborough of Vision America. The Liberty Institute, headquartered in the Dallas suburb of Plano, was a national network of attorneys dedicated to defending and promoting religious liberty. Vision America, headquartered in Nacogdoches in East Texas, was a national ministry that grew from Scarborough's leadership at the First Baptist Church of Pearland in suburban Houston. Vision America's aim was to promote voting and active civic involvement among Bible-believing Christians.[100]

FreedomWorks, organized by former Texas House Majority Leader Dick Armey in 2003, was also centrally involved in grassroots activism. An early admirer of Goldwater and Reagan, Armey was a free-market Republican with a PhD degree in economics and an affinity for the ideas of Milton Freedman and Ludwig von Mises. Armey was also an evangelical Christian who attended an independent Bible church, considered himself a "values voter," defended the rights of Christian home-schoolers, and was frequently courted by social conservatives but with whom he sometimes sparred. In a 2005 interview he told sociologist D. Michael Lindsay about a contentious meeting in 1998 with evangelical leaders Charles Colson, James Dobson, and Gary Bauer. Armey had grown weary of these leaders' criticisms. "All you want to do is come up whining and complaining about the failures we've experienced and you ought to mind your own business," Armey recalled telling them. "In effect they're saying, you know, 'Look at me, I'm bigger than the Lord. I put you where you are, and I can take you out.' Who do they think they are?"[101] In organizing FreedomWorks chapters, training sessions, and rallies, Armey retained the conviction that Christian conservatives should avoid imposing their version of righteousness on the nation through the power of government. He nevertheless regarded freedom as a God-given gift that was being threatened by big government and hoped that devout Christians would be champions in the cause of freedom. In *Give Us Liberty: A Tea Party Manifesto*, coauthored with FreedomWorks cofounder Matt Kibbe, Armey described the Tea Party as a movement in defense of faith as well as family and country. "By reducing the size of the welfare state," he argued, "we increase the importance of the works of Christian charities and our church communities. By reducing the tax burden on families, we make it easier for

Christian households to tithe or for young mothers to stay home to raise their children."[102]

Studies of why people get involved in movements like the Tea Party point to a variety of reasons, ranging from being influenced by a speech or book like *Give Us Liberty* to joining because a close friend has persuaded them or they have experienced some personal grievance. All of these may be present among clergy, but pastors are already community leaders with organizations to run and thus may be influenced by other considerations as well. An interesting case in point was Fred Davis, a fundamentalist preacher who began pastoring a small Church of Christ near the Oklahoma line in the early 1980s and by 2010 was making headlines as an outspoken leader of the local Tea Party movement. Davis described several factors that facilitated his involvement: First, a deeply held theological conviction that the Bible had actually been written by God, word for word, and was meant to be taken seriously as the basis for Christians' lives as individuals and as a distinct people trying to follow the word of God. A second influence was that Davis, like many conservative clergy of his generation, had come of age just as the culture wars were dividing people of faith into conservative and liberal camps. In his case he began arguing with his otherwise relatively conservative professors in seminary, claiming that they were not being faithful to the Bible and were not speaking forcefully enough about abortion and homosexuality.

Davis's involvement in Tea Party activities reflected another local dynamic. His own congregation had failed to grow, and it was becoming difficult to attract people to any of the old-time revival meetings that had sparked interest in the past. He was aware that moral and political issues were on people's minds, though, and he was convinced from scripture that America was heading downhill the way so many stories in the Old Testament described the children of Israel. "God would warn them," he said, " 'You had better stay faithful to the principles or you're going to lose the land I gave you.'" Davis decided to hold a series of meetings about Christians and the U.S. Constitution. The principal message, he said, was that "the concept of a limited government and the concept of freedom are based on concepts that go back to God." These seminars were well attended, not only by his own members but by people from local Baptist, conservative Methodist, and Pentecostal churches. Inspired by the turnout, he turned next to talking more about limited government and holding public debates with people he regarded as secular humanists. He also turned his attention toward preaching against Islam, even to the point of attracting pickets and worrying members of his congregation that he was going too far and might be putting himself in danger.

Although Davis became more actively involved in the Tea Party than most of the clergy in North Texas, he encouraged people who came to his meetings to challenge their own pastors to become more involved. His success in attracting audiences from other denominations was facilitated by the fact that his own denomination gave him considerable latitude in what he said and did. He believed that distinctive denominational traditions about baptism and church music were important but considered it more important to enlist conservative Christians across denominations in common cause. At the same time, he felt called to criticize other Christians as well as Muslims and Jews because they either did not know Christ or were part of America's slide away from a biblical understanding of God and country. "Whether it be a Muslim, a Jew, an atheist, or a Hindu or Buddhist, it doesn't make any difference," he said. "All of them need the salvation of Christ."[103]

The Tea Party movement captured the attention of national media, but at the grass roots it was by no means the only connection between conservative religion and politics. There were plenty of Republicans who felt Tea Party advocates were too extreme and yet agreed that Washington was broken and conservative social principles needed to be reinforced. The pastor of a thriving West Texas Baptist congregation put it well when he remarked that the Tea Party had some good ideas "and yet they attract so many nuts that they ruin the fruitcake." He wished right-wingers were less ignorant than they often seemed to be. The pastor of a small rural church in West Texas held similar views. "Oh gag," she said when asked about the Tea Party. "It's just horrifying," she said. "It's deeply concerning to me." One of the state's most influential pastors also expressed reservations. He found it necessary to separate political from spiritual issues because "I have some very active Tea Party people in my church who want me, because I take a stand on abortion and same-sex marriage, they want me to take a stand on every issue." He considered it important to remind them that there was no biblical position on some of their issues. "I think that there are Christians who get more riled up about higher taxes than they do abortion," he said, "and I think that is one of the reasons that our influence has been diluted so much."[104]

A preacher in a smaller West Texas town was more generous toward the Tea Party. He felt it usefully challenged elected officials who went to Washington and got swallowed up by the system. He nevertheless believed strongly in separation of church and state, valued religious pluralism, and thought the best way to combat the moral chaos he perceived was through spiritual renewal. The pastor of an upscale church in one of the state's largest cities thought it was important to view the Tea Party movement from a historical perspective. He thought the civil rights movement had shown the value of churches becoming involved in politics and that Jerry Falwell's Moral Majority had followed suit, challenging evangelical Christians to become similarly involved. But now in the twenty-first century Christians were searching for new ways to exert their prophetic voice, he said, while respecting the more diverse society in which they lived. He saw the Tea Party as an expression of real disenchantment with government but hoped that less divisive moderate approaches would prevail. It bothered him that Governor Perry seemed to have moved so far in the direction of the Tea Party.[105]

But Perry's supporters were confident he would make an ideal candidate, especially in contrast to President Obama, who seemed in their view to be an outsider with no understanding or appreciation of true American values. As one Perry supporter explained, "He is a Christian, a rock star politician—the real deal." Perry understood that all Americans wanted or needed was "freedom, freedom, freedom." The only problem might be that he used too much hairspray.[106]

When Perry announced his candidacy for the Republican nomination for president, the connections among fiscal conservatism, social conservatism, and Bible-Belt religious beliefs were clearly on display. On August 6, 2011, with several dozen "freedom from religion" protesters outside, some thirty thousand people gathered at Reliant Stadium in Houston to hear the governor call for spiritual renewal. "Father," Perry prayed, "Our heart breaks for America. We see discord at home. We see fear in the marketplace. We see anger in the halls of government, and as a nation we have forgotten who made us, who protects us, who blesses us, and for that we cry out for your forgiveness." Afterward a woman who drove two hundred miles to attend the event told a reporter, "I believe that God has prepared Rick Perry for such a time as this." She added, "I believe he will be our next president."[107]

One of Perry's strongest backers was James R. Leininger, a San Antonio physician whose investments in venture capital and technology firms earned a fortune in the 1990s. Leininger was a founder of the conservative Texas Public Policy Foundation, a major funder of antiabortion groups, and an advocate of school vouchers and teaching creationism in public schools. Having donated nearly $250,000 to Perry's gubernatorial campaigns, Leininger organized a retreat to enlist other Christian conservatives in Perry's bid for the presidential nomination. At the meeting Perry assured the leaders attending, including James Dobson of Focus on the Family and Tony Perkins of the Family Research Council, that he solidly supported their views on social issues. A few days later Southern Baptist leader Richard Land wrote that Perry was a man of genuine faith who would be even more overtly Christian about his faith than George W. Bush had been. "Does America want to be more like [Perry's] pro-business, pro-growth Texas?" Land asked. "If the answer is 'yes,' Perry is the 'down to his bone marrow' Texan who is eager to lead them in that direction."[108]

Although Perry's candidacy faltered owing to his poor performance in the Republican primary debates, the religiously grounded antipathy toward the federal government under a Democratic administration continued. Uncertain about the depth of former Massachusetts governor Mitt Romney's commitment to socially conservative values and harboring misgivings about his Mormon identity, evangelical leaders from across the country convened in Texas a second time—on this occasion at the ranch of Southern Baptist lay leader Judge Paul Pressler—and endorsed Rick Santorum.[109] Only later did they get behind Romney, and by that time there were new concerns among religious conservatives about what was happening in Washington.[110] The administration was once again violating believers' religious liberty, critics argued. The war that had begun when prayer was abolished from public schools and when abortion was legalized was now being waged by government mandates asking religious organizations to pay for contraception even if that violated their religious principles. One of the chief critics of the Obama administration was Texas solicitor general Ted Cruz, the Tea Party favorite for the Republican nomination for a seat in the U.S. Senate.

The issue that brought questions of religious liberty onto the national stage in 2012 was whether Catholic institutions would be required under the new national healthcare law to provide insurance for employees covering birth control if the religious principles on which those institutions were founded regarded birth control as morally wrong. That was a significant question in Texas, where Catholic institutions were among the state's largest hospitals and social service organizations and where institutions run by conservative Protestants might find similar grounds for objecting to the national mandates. Although the Obama administration attempted to work out a compromise that would honor religious objections, forty-three Catholic dioceses, schools, and service agencies filed lawsuits challenging the administration's health insurance policies. The lawsuits followed a ruling three weeks earlier by a federal appeals judge temporarily blocking Texas from withholding government funding from Planned Parenthood. "President Obama, in my judgment, is the most radical President we have ever seen," Cruz told a reporter. "He is a true believer committed to growing the size and power and spending of the federal government." The good news, he explained in a subsequent interview, was that the reaction to the Obama administration was inspiring "a new generation of leaders in the Republican party who stand and fight for liberty and for the Constitution."[111]

The election to replace retiring Republican senator Kay Bailey Hutchinson pitted Cruz against Lieutenant Governor David Dewhurst in the Republican primary. The contest turned on which candidate could more effectively showcase conservative credentials. Both had held statewide office, both spoke Spanish (Dewhurst more fluently than Cruz, even though Cruz was of Cuban heritage), and both were conservative Christians. Dewhurst had played a pivotal role in supporting the legislature's passage of a bill that required women seeking an abortion to have a sonogram. His supporters included Governor Perry, Texas Right to Life, Texas Alliance for Life, the president of Texans for Life Coalition, and Scarborough of Vision America. "His Christian faith and values have never wavered," Scarborough said, adding that under Dewhurst's leadership "Texas has done more than any other state in the nation to advance traditional values through legislation that protects life, family and religious expression."[112] Cruz was a Princeton graduate who studied under conservative constitutional law professor Robert George and campaigned for Bush in 2000, attracted by Bush's compassionate conservatism. Cruz took credit along with Don Willett for defending the state's right to display the Ten Commandments monument on the state capitol grounds as well as other "religious freedom" causes such as school prayer and including "under God" in the Pledge of Allegiance. He won endorsements from the Tea Party Express, Family Research Council, Focus on the Family, FreedomWorks,

2008 vice presidential candidate Sarah Palin, and 2012 presidential candidate Senator Rick Santorum. A statewide survey conducted shortly before the primary showed Cruz the clear favorite among Tea Party supporters, with Dewhurst holding a substantial lead among other Republicans.[113]

The contest between Cruz and Dewhurst—with Cruz winning by a 14-point margin and then earning a 16-point victory in the general election—was indicative of how conservative the state's dominant party had become. Since 1980 Republican candidates for president had won every election in Texas, and two had been from Texas. Both U.S. senators from Texas had been Republicans since 1992. The state's congressional delegation in the House grew from only four Republicans in 1981 to twenty-three in 2012, and two had served as House majority leader. Ann Richards's defeat in 1994 put the governorship in Republican hands. Republicans held solid majorities in the state legislature as well.

Whether Texas had done more than any other state to advance traditional values, as Scarborough claimed, was hard to prove. If it had paved the way for Reagan's comeback in 1980 and groomed two of his successors for the White House, there were plenty of additional factors involved in all those victories besides traditional values. What was more clearly the case was that Texas had done well at preserving tradition within its own borders. The rough country that had once been barely inhabitable had become the home of large cities and sprawling suburbs. The population, like the rest of America, had been diverse from the start, composed of immigrants seeking new freedom and opportunities, and it had become even more diverse at the end of the twentieth century. In all this, there was a kind of stability rooted in the simple faith of plain people and in strong convictions about liberty of conscience. The pact that drove individuals to seek God in their own ways did not prevent them from bonding together in meeting houses or from forming charitable organizations. These same traditions, though, made it difficult to reach beyond racial and ethnic lines and to fully consider the implications of government policies that benefited the rich more than the poor.

It was never possible to regard Texas as a microcosm of America—or indeed in any way of being small. There was nevertheless a great deal about the trajectory of Texas that parallels the history of America. The traditions rooted in the largely European Protestant and Catholic practices of the nation's first years were forced to adapt again and again. The process was never one of mere accommodation to a more secular ethos. It has rather been characterized by the tensions involved in forming and defending religious organizations, extending them into new territories, and running to the constitutional limits placed on their relations to the state while testing and seeking to redefine those boundaries. Different nationalities have come together in a kind of melting pot of ecumenism. Transcending racial and ethnic differences has been harder.

This has been the story of America, not just of Texas. Populous and powerful as Texas always has been, it makes no sense to argue that Texas has somehow hijacked the American agenda. No state is ever that influential. Texas is better imagined as a case study in which much that characterizes all of America—albeit refracted differently in each locale—can be seen. Texas was shaped by slavery and by Reconstruction and over the years, with about the same proportion of African Americans as the rest of the nation, instituted polices that restricted African Americans from voting and attaining equitable schooling, housing, and jobs. Sharing a border with Mexico, Texas faced questions about immigrant labor, citizenship for migrant workers, and relationships between Hispanics and Anglos earlier and to a greater extent than the rest of the nation. The state's Bible-Belt traditions shared much that was present in other parts of the country, and these traditions influenced how people thought about race relations, wealth and poverty, and politics.

The central question of interest to scholars of society—why is inequality as durable as it is?—finds an answer when close consideration is given to a case study like this one. Over the century and a half in which white non-Hispanics as a group attained greater privileges than African Americans or Hispanics did, the decisive factor was exclusion from political power. Exclusion from the capacity to shape electoral outcomes and to determine state and local policies occurred initially through slavery, then from reactions to federal Reconstruction policies, and in subsequent decades from white primaries and the poll tax. When these practices finally became illegal, white non-Hispanic voters shifted in large numbers from the Democratic Party to the Republican Party, which essentially advocated fiscal conservatism that minimized expenditures on programs disproportionately of value to the poor. The effect was that racial and ethnic minorities who favored Democratic candidates were again excluded in large measure from exercising political influence.

Religion was seldom a determining factor in any of these policies but contributed to all of them. Segregated churches kept races apart and retained most of the assets of privileged congregations for their own members. Arguments about evil associated danger with outsiders of different races, and ideas about the advancement of civilization focused efforts on individual achievements rather than on wider societal characteristics. As exclusion shifted in emphasis toward fiscal conservatism, those ideas were reinforced in religious contexts in which freedom of religion, antigovernment views, and a focus on abortion and homosexuality dominated. These issues were not defined in racial terms but were supported in highest proportions by conservative white non-Hispanic churchgoers and had political consequences that inadvertently perpetuated inequality by promoting regressive tax policies and discouraging social safety net programs benefiting the poor.

To say only that racial and ethnic groups are religiously divided and apart, or to argue that they need to do a better job of coming together, offers little insight into the complex relationships inevitably involved. When clergy and lay leaders talk about their congregations, there is little reason to doubt that good work is being done to bridge racial and ethnic differences. Congregations large and small host food pantries, hold mixed-race Bible studies in prisons, send youth to Mexico on short-term mission trips, and provide counseling to new immigrants. In the wake of Hurricane Katrina, churches hundreds of miles from the Gulf Coast opened their doors and provided food and shelter to refugees.[114] Historically all-white denominations, recognizing that times had changed, elected members of racial minorities to top leadership positions and launched ministries geared toward racial and ethnic inclusion. All of that was beneficial. But when resources and opportunities are as unequal across racial and ethnic groups as they have been and continue to be, the programs of religious organizations are inevitably shaped by—and in turn influence—the varying economic and political interests involved. The difficulty for religious constituencies that have access to power and that seek to use power to promote their values is that the inadvertent consequences for groups with less power can easily go unrecognized. The issue is not one of good or bad intentions but of perspective. While religious organizations in Texas and elsewhere have made commendable progress in moving past racist ideology and denouncing segregation, many of them have done less well in understanding and addressing the wider societal impact of teachings that bear indirectly on racial inequality. As an African American pastor in Houston observed in talking about conservative Christians' attitudes toward abortion, "So many people who are pro-life are also anti-welfare" and thus fail to "champion issues of the poor and the oppressed."[115]

If any single culprit can be identified, it is the belief held by many religious leaders that what they do and say has no political consequences—or should have consequences only for particular issues such as abortion and homosexuality. Liberty of conscience and ideas about separation of church and state provide healthy cultural and constitutional protections against religion exercising governmental power or government using its power to promote or inhibit religion. But religion always has political implications, especially when it is as much a part of local communities as it has been in Bible-Belt America. These implications are not just a recent phenomenon attributable to some reversal of earlier understandings of church-state separation. Any time religious groups have tried to advance civilization through schooling and charitable efforts, as we have seen, and any time religious leaders promote arguments about who is morally upright and who is endangering the moral community, the impact of religious programs and ideas on political decisions and electoral outcomes is going to be felt. If religious leaders and public officials join hands in promoting private charitable activities, they also need to understand how those proposals may affect elections and how that in turn affects inequality.

The extent to which conservative religion has contributed to Republican politics in recent years poses the question of whether all of that may be coming to an end in places like Texas where the white non-Hispanic population is no longer the majority. Preferences among African Americans and Hispanics for Democratic candidates, observers suggest, will surely trump the religious conservatism of white non-Hispanics. And yet, as political strategists also note, it is important not to underestimate Democrats' capacity to seize defeat from the hands of victory. In states that have been Republican far longer than Texas, Republican primaries have been the venues in which moderates and conservatives have fought about taxes and social programs and in which the winners have done enough to attain power. Tea Party challenges to established Republican officials are only the latest example. However short- or long-lived these challenges may be, antigovernment sentiments are always ripe for exploitation. If the past is any indication, preachers will be available to reinforce these sentiments.

CHAPTER 13

AFTERWORD

━━━━━━━━━

Religion and the Politics of Identity

In these closing pages I want to reflect on what the particularities of religious history in the one location we have been considering may have to offer for thinking about similar questions in other contexts. To do this, we will need to shift to a more speculative mode that ventures beyond what can be established from the empirical evidence and focuses on the concepts and theoretical arguments that may be suggested by some of the developments we have considered.

I mentioned at the outset that there are certain opportunities for thinking about religion's relationships with its social context by focusing on a region large enough to include important denominational, institutional, and political structures but small enough to see the local, personal, and group processes that are often obscured in studies that aim to describe an entire society as large and complex as the United States. In focusing on events in Texas from Reconstruction to the early twenty-first century, we have been able to consider how religion was shaped by the legacy of slavery and by early settlers' adaptation to the harsh realities of frontier life and then to consider religion's role in the establishment of churches, schools, colleges, and social welfare organizations, and its changing relationships to partisan politics, the state, and the federal government. And we have been able to examine some of the ways in which denominational politics, social movements for racial and ethnic empowerment, and arguments about public morality have taken shape.

Against these contours and with evidence that can be drawn from other studies, we are able to look again at some of the main arguments in the social science literature about religion. In particular we can ask, what may be missing, and how can the existing theoretical approaches be modified? My focus here will be the literature in sociological studies of religion. This is a literature with a rich history that includes the insights of some of the discipline's central founding figures in the nineteenth century and that has continued to inspire a great deal of scholarly interest and research. It is unparalleled in posing important questions about the mutual influences between religion and society and in suggesting the conceptual tools needed to address these questions. At the same time, it is a literature that has usefully undergone significant revisions as new ideas and research results have appeared. In that spirit, we may again find it useful to consider this literature's main arguments, asking especially what needs to be included in order to grasp the complex relationships of religion to changing cultural and institutional configurations involving racial, ethnic, and political identities.

Sociological theorizing about religion rests on the assumption that religion is inextricably interwoven with social structures and processes that influence it and are sometimes influenced in return. Early foundational contributions from Weber and Durkheim as well as more recent writing on practice, ritual, symbolic boundaries, and environmental niches have argued for the value of examining religion through the lens of concepts that also pertain to other domains of social activity rather than insisting that religion is unique. But there is little agreement about what the relevant structures, processes, and influences are or about how best to conceptualize these relationships. Much of the discussion has been guided by an assumption that parsimony is the hallmark of good theory, which in consequence has produced insights but at the same time resulted in unfortunate squabbles over nonmutually exclusive claims and missed opportunities to consider the complex relationships among social structures and processes. Consideration of the actual details of almost any significant social phenomena suggests the need to consider these complex relationships. Certainly that is the case in thinking about the changing intersections among religion, race, ethnicity, and power.

I begin by briefly reviewing the two standard approaches to religion that are often regarded as the most widely discussed alternative perspectives on the relationship between religion and society—secularization theory and rational choice theory—for the purpose of showing the key assumptions about the qualities of good theory underlying both and the attendant limitations that resulted, as well as several of the most informed attempts to overcome these limitations. To that end I highlight a number of the points in the previous chapters and in other studies at which interesting empirical observations emerge that cannot be adequately understood from either of the conventional perspectives. Next I discuss how practice theory and an emphasis on lived religion have valuably focused attention on the intricacies of religious practice both outside and inside of religious institutions at the micro level of individual and small-group behavior and yet have failed to provide strong linkages with the macrolevel social structures and processes that interested scholars in earlier studies. In a third section I draw on studies of race and ethnicity to emphasize how the concept of symbolic boundaries serves as a useful way of thinking about religious categories and identities. I argue that the potential richness of this concept has been hindered by an impoverished theory of symbolism associated with an inadequate perspective on the nuances of meaning, narrative, and ritual. In a following section I outline the processes through which the identities defined by symbolic boundaries change over time along several dimensions including size, salience, closure, and status, and I suggest how to bring in consideration of the influences on these processes of political arrangements, demographic factors, and social institutions. Finally I suggest applications of this multilevel perspective to the analysis of religious actors' strategies of institution building, the dynamics of church and state relations, connections of religion to racial and ethnic politics, and the restructuring of religion. My argument is that one-dimensional, single-variable theories that largely point to linear developments in religion over time are usefully replaced by a multilevel process approach that illuminates more of the complexity about religion as it intersects with other aspects of society and undergoes significant change.

TWO THEORETICAL PERSPECTIVES

Recent efforts to identify dominant strands in sociological theorizing about religion have suggested fruitfully that much of the work produced through at least the 1960s and perhaps into the early 1980s was guided by assumptions drawn from Marx, Weber, Durkheim, and other contributors who emphasized secularization. In admittedly simplistic accounts of this perspective, the main empirical implication was that religion gradually diminished in social significance as societies developed and modernized. The contrasting perspective that emerged during the 1980s and 1990s argued that religion was better conceived of as goal-oriented behavior pursued by rational actors who exploited opportunities to achieve assurance of salvation and other supernatural rewards within spaces defined as religious economies by the presence of free-market competition. In this perspective, religion was expected to flourish rather than decline as societies became more open, pluralistic, and competitive. Secularization theory and rational choice theory were in these respects alternative perspectives that identified quite different long-term societal mechanisms and predicted nearly opposing scenarios about the development and future of religion. Proponents of rational choice theory posed strong criticisms of secularization theory, and some revisions of secularization theory were made as a result. However, critics have also pointed out certain commonalities in both perspectives. To understand their contributions and limitations, we need to revisit briefly the main arguments of both approaches.

Secularization theory is best understood in relation to the insights guiding nineteenth-century social thought about the impact of social differentiation. As societies developed from small, geographically concentrated, homogeneous tribal units to large, geographically dispersed, heterogeneous national units, their central sustaining social functions became more sharply differentiated, just as the parts of a biological organism did through the course of similar evolutionary processes. The maternal spiritual leader who also tended animals and conducted healing ceremonies, for example, evolved into separate roles conducted within specialized institutional settings devoted to spiritual practice, commercial agriculture and mechanized food processing, and medicine. The process of institutional differentiation suggested that religion had once been an integral aspect of traditional societies but in modern contexts exercised less authority over such distinct realms as commerce, law, government, and medicine. Constitutional separation of church and state in the United States in contrast with earlier systems of divine monarchy in Europe served as a case in point. To the extent that secularization was involved, the point was not that religion ceased to be important within its own restricted domain but that its wider societal authority was diminished.[1]

More specific arguments about secularization were derived from the work of theorists who identified crucial underlying developments in the transition from traditional to modern societies. Marx's emphasis on the rise of industrial capitalism associated the decline of religion with its gradual inability to provide solace in the face of capitalist-induced alienation and the eventual shedding of false consciousness in the proletariat's struggle for collective control of the means of production. Durkheim's argument about the shift from mechanical to organic solidarity included ideas about the decreasing effectiveness of religious rituals among physically copresent worshippers for sustaining social cohesion against the centripetal forces operating in complex societies with rising emphasis on the cult of individuality. Tönnies's description of *gemeinschaft* in small rural communities with intimate relationships among people and deep connections with the physical space in which they lived suggested that *gesellschaft* relations in larger urban places were characterized by utilitarian contracts fundamentally incommensurate with traditional religious values. Weber's interest in rationalization as the central process involved in modernization included arguments about the displacement of absolute values, the disenchantment of cognitive outlooks, and the settling of an iron cage on the shoulders of people whose ancestors had found ultimate meaning in religious faith.[2]

Were secularization theory applied to our case study of religion and social change over the past century and a half in Texas, the key insights could be illustrated by the following. Under Mexican rule, religion played a central role in legitimating central government power but became less important once Texas achieved independence, and less so again when incorporation into the United States brought constitutional separation of church and state. During the antebellum period, slaveholders founded churches that legitimated their traditional authority and taught slaves obedience to that authority, but merchants and independent farmers practicing a more rational form of capitalist trade and agriculture had less need for religion. The half-century after Reconstruction was characterized by the growth of industry and cities in which people were less dependent on the whims of nature, better educated, and better able to apply rational principles of organization to their work and family lives. Religion did not wither as a result, but churches taught a more rational form of belief, and a worldview that had once been enchanted with otherworldly ideas became increasingly disenchanted. The differences between white and black churches were attributable to the African American population having fewer of these modernizing advantages and thus retaining a more enchanted worldview that emphasized emotion and otherworldly solace. The twentieth century brought growth in secular universities, for-profit business, nonprofit social service organizations funded by private charity and government, and government agencies that expanded at both the state and federal levels. Religion accommodated these trends by supporting some parallel institutions of its own, such as church-related colleges and service organizations, but mostly by focusing greater attention on private life through such activities as Sunday school classes for children, women's auxiliaries, and pastoral counseling. As secularity advanced, some religious organizations also tried to resist it by espousing fundamentalist teachings, criticizing immorality and secular humanism, and forming movements to promote godliness and traditional family values.

Secularization theory thus illuminates some aspects of the story but leaves an impression that religion's influence declined to a more significant extent than was actually the case. It implies that residents under Mexican rule and during the antebellum period were more devout than many of them seem to have been. It underplays the continuing importance of agriculture and the rural population relative to commerce and cities. It fails to say much about the relationships between white and black residents or between Anglos and Hispanics and Protestants and Catholics. How the relationships between church and state continued to require negotiation is unexplained. Why churches grew as they did, and how that growth continued to affect the state's public life, seem especially to be contradicted by a story in which the dominant motif is religion's decline.

Rational choice theory is a perspective that aims to provide a better account than secularization theory of the continuing vitality of religious practices and organizations under certain conditions characteristic of modern societies. This theoretical perspective that, as sociologist of religion Christopher P. Scheitle observes, "has generated the most recent discussion and research in the past twenty years" draws inspiration from economics and includes as a central argument the view that religion flourishes under free-market conditions. In traditional societies with small homogeneous populations, markets are likely to be underdeveloped or controlled by the state, resulting in religion also lacking in diversity, freedom, and competition. In larger heterogeneous settings with free markets, religious diversity is likely to be present, resulting in greater competition and thus in more effective efforts to provide spiritual products that appeal to a diverse population. A key difference with secularization theory is rational choice theory's interpretation of separation of church and state as a beneficial development for religion. Freed from state control, religion is able to develop in multiple ways that include organizations for minority populations. A further difference is with secularization theory's interpretation of small conservative sects as essentially traditional organizations that become secularized as members become middle class. In rational choice theory small, conservative sects grow and flourish because they provide more distinctive rewards for their members and institute strict moral practices that exclude free riders from becoming burdensome to the group.[3]

Rational choice theory would identify several key aspects of religion and social change in Texas as being consistent with its main emphases. Mexico's rule that only the Catholic religion could be practiced restricted the growth of religion that occurred under independence and statehood when a free market for religion became available and church leaders of many different denominations arrived, working hard to beat their competitors in founding the most attractive congregations. Slavery impeded that competition until after the Civil War when black churches started flourishing under the same free-market system. Methodists and Baptists fared better in competing for white and black adherents alike than did Presbyterians, Episcopalians, and a few other denominations by virtue of emphasizing the immeasurable reward of otherworldly salvation attainable at the relatively low cost of appearing occasionally at the mourners' bench. In addition, moral strictness on such specific doctrines as temperance helped these denominations grow by cultivating ascetic habits and setting their members apart from their neighbors. As denominational competition increased during the twentieth century, Baptists did a better job of imposing strict rules than Methodists did, resulting in greater growth among the former than among the latter. The late twentieth century saw religion flourishing more than ever before because the de facto establishment of Baptists and Catholics as lazy monopolies was breaking down, creating room for everything from upstart fundamentalist sects to new religious movements to new immigrant congregations.

A story of growth fits much of the evidence better than a story of decline. Yet its emphasis on competition among religious organizations as the force propelling growth is too simple. It does little better than the other approach in focusing attention on the relationships between blacks and whites or in specifying the conditions giving rise to competition among leaders within the same denomination or the reasons behind incidents of particular competition between Protestants and Catholics. The effects of population growth, changes in the economy, distance, and how people coped with the difficulties of daily existence have no place in the story. Nor is much attention given to the relationships among churches and secular competitors or to religious entities' responses to political issues.

The appeal of both approaches lies in the fact that they do focus attention on a number of important aspects of religious development and do so in a way that organizes this information under the relatively parsimonious rubrics of differentiation-induced decline, on the one hand, and competition-induced growth, on the other hand. As simple explanations of long-term processes, one can hardly do better. These long-term processes start with societies located somewhere in the distant mists of time when ritually blessed tribal chiefs and divinely appointed monarchs ruled and move forward to the present when secular government bureaus are much more complicated but religious organizations flourish in great diversity, helping people meet enduring spiritual desires and sometimes mingling in the public sphere as well. They provide grand historical narratives, but to their credit they are also testable, up to a point, even in providing alternative hypotheses about what changes to expect and why.

Continuing interest in secularization and rational choice theories of religion is attributable to the fact that they provide alternative hypotheses about aspects of religion for which there is empirical evidence. Although secularization theory is more appropriately focused on long-term social change involving centuries and millennia, it has also provided a useful starting point for thinking about trends identified through public opinion surveys in church attendance or beliefs about the Bible over a few years. Secularization theory has proven useful in research examining such accommodations to secular culture as the blending of therapeutic ideas with religion or for explaining resistance to secularity through the embrace of fundamentalist teachings. Rational choice theory has also been of value in empirical studies. It has generated hypotheses, for example, about how religious organizations deal with free-rider problems and whether church membership truly increases when denominational competition is significant.

But an abundance of empirical research in recent years has led researchers to propose two lines of criticism against the secularization and rational choice theories. The first has basically suggested that the theories remain helpful in terms of arguments about institutional differentiation but need to be refined to take account of evidence that otherwise does not fit. An example is the argument advanced by José Casanova in *Public Religions in the Modern World* that "deprivatization" needs to be introduced as a concept along with privatization in order to make sense of processes through which religion once again becomes more active in the political arena.[4] Not only are there instances of reaction against secularization, the argument goes, but secularization itself occurs in fits and spurts that require greater contextual specification, and modern religion involves connections and tensions with the state as well as separation from it. Another example is the argument that free-market competition among religious organizations may encourage religious activity but at the same time may alter beliefs and practices in ways that might be thought of as forms of secularization.[5] The other line of criticism has been evident in studies suggesting that neither of the two main theoretical approaches fully addresses many of the most interesting aspects of religion. These criticisms stress that too much of the research guided by the two main theories has focused on behavior within religious institutions or that it has been overly concerned with statistical generalizations drawn from the numeric evidence attainable from religious

organizations or in surveys of public opinion. As Courtney Bender argues in
The New Metaphysicals, greater attention should be paid to "things in their
entanglements."[6]

THE PRACTICE APPROACH TO LIVED RELIGION

Practice theory has emerged as an alternative to secularization theory and rational choice theory. Practices are sequences of activities in which individuals
or collective social units engage over time in the pursuit of goals that are usually
intentionally sought after and that involve learned skills, habits, predispositions,
and interpretations that reflect the tacit social agreements and contexts in which
they occur. Examples include playing the piano, constructing a stone fence, writing a term paper, doing volunteer work at a homeless shelter, starting a business,
or cooking dinner. In each case the word *practice* is used in ordinary parlance
because the skill involved is learned through practice and because the particular way in which the activity is pursued reflects what has been learned and the
style, meanings, and habits involved. A goal is evident in each practice, but unlike in rational choice theory, the analysis does not assume that rationality is the
dominant mechanism for understanding how goals are pursued. The assumption
is rather that action is guided by previous experiences, by what is familiar and
comfortable, and by circumstances that produce contingencies and shape not
only the activities involved but the goals that are pursued. Practices take place
within institutional domains, such as business organizations, government bureaus, schools, families, and churches. But practices also are interlaced with other
practices and in ways that transcend institutions. For example, the manner in
which a person practices dieting may spill over to the habits that person exhibits
in conducting a business meeting.

Like secularization theory and rational choice theory, practice theory has developed in studies of religion from several different strands in which somewhat
different assumptions and emphases appear. One source is the literature on ethical practices, a second is the literature on social practices, and a third is the literature on lived religion. The ethical practices literature emphasizes intentional
sequences of activities through which mastery is attained and from which lessons
about moral virtues such as patience, courage, and cooperation are derived. For
example, playing soccer may be analyzed as a practice that teaches children the
value of teamwork, the importance of hard work, and the need for fortitude in
the face of defeat. The social practices literature focuses on routines in which
people engage that occur over time in patterned ways and thus reflect and reinforce social norms. An example would be the ways in which college students
meet one another for coffee and routinely talk about certain topics that they consider nonthreatening and at the same time exhibit their opinions about current
events. The lived religion literature implicitly regards activities as social practices

and distinguishes itself by focusing on activities more than on doctrine or belief and stipulates that these activities may occur outside as well as inside of religious institutions. For instance, a soccer player fingering an amulet or throwing a kiss at the sky after scoring a goal may be exhibiting a lived religious practice, as might a person practicing yoga with the expectation of securing spiritual as well as physical benefits.[7]

Practice theory relaxes the assumptions in secularization theory and rational choice theory about dominant master trends in religion. A practice such as participating in a yoga class rather than attending a preaching service may be influenced by secularity, but the point of examining this practice is to understand it rather than inferring something about larger trends. Practice theory similarly identifies activities that may be part of a competitive market of spiritual goods and services, as a yoga class might be, but does not argue that these can be understood by looking only at competition or at a supply-demand-pricing mechanism. For these reasons, practice theory is better regarded as a perspective than as a theory in which certain empirical predictions are made. It has proven attractive as a way to focus attention on the less predictable, messier, complex aspects of religion, including its variation and diversity, how it is inflected through the lens of gender differences and power arrangements, its meanings, and how practitioners talk about it. Examples include studies of prayer and meditation, healing, communes, bedside behavior in hospitals, self-help groups, spiritual practices associated with food and dieting, street festivals, tattoos and body piercings, and ethnic music.

In our case study, practice theory is illustrated by the roles we saw being played by religion and spirituality in public hangings and lynchings. Rituals of that kind convey complex meanings and follow scripts implicitly understood and conformed to by those who participate. They are influenced by religious organizations but occur outside of religious institutions. Other examples that illustrate the perspective provided by practice theory include the spiritual meanings that find their way into the deathbed accounts of people afflicted with yellow fever, the ways in which African Americans responded to the Texas centennial celebration, and how a Chicano leader's discomfort with church activities filtered into the meanings of political activism.

Although practice theory does not pertain only to the practices of individuals, most studies identified with this approach have focused on the microlevel behavior of individuals and small groups. The richness of descriptive material at this level has thus far made it difficult to connect observations at the micro level with ideas about larger, macrolevel social structures and processes. This is not to say that such observations are absent. The most common way in which they are brought in, however, is by suggesting that microlevel behavior reflects larger social and cultural arrangements. For example, a study of women's devotional practices in an evangelical religious organization might argue that the women are in a small way responding to larger cultural changes in the definition of gender role expectations. Less work to date has been done toward identifying specific relationships between microlevel practices and macro structures and processes.

MULTILEVEL THEORY

Multilevel theory is a movement within the social sciences to identify clusters of variables that in combination provide the conceptual tools necessary for describing and explaining complex social processes. Interest in multilevel theory has been driven by the realization that social processes typically involve contingencies, unique historical circumstances, constraints, and decisions that cannot readily be understood by single variables, no matter how theoretically rich or deductively logical those variables may be. Multilevel theory seeks especially to draw together insights from investigations of the micro practices of individuals and small networks in local situations with concepts illuminating the larger power arrangements, resources, and cultural influences in which those practices are situated.[8]

In his critique of theories of linear purposive action, for example, Alejandro Portes argued for a theoretical perspective attentive to "social processes, awareness of their concealed and unintended manifestations, and sustained efforts to understand the participants' own reactions to their situation." A multilevel approach of this kind, Portes suggested, would eschew the idea of grand empirical generalizations and focus greater attention on the complexity of social processes and the contextual contingencies involved.[9] Similarly, Charles Tilly proposed that the enduring inequalities that characterize social life in many settings but that also vary in duration and intensity must be examined through the lens of several jointly operating processes, including the imposition of cultural categories, the unequal distribution of rewards, networks of social exclusion, and instances of adaptation and emulation.[10] In another area of inquiry, Andreas Wimmer has developed a multilevel process theory for examining the making and unmaking of ethnic boundaries. Wimmer's approach identifies several of the possible ways in which ethnic boundaries may change in response to shifting configurations of power, institutions, and social networks.[11]

Interest in multilevel theory represents a shift in assumptions about what constitutes good theory, specifically away from older views in which theory was judged to be good if it adhered to standards of parsimony by explaining as much about human behavior with as few variables as possible. Among the reasons for this shift is the fact that results from quantitative research in which alternative variables were pitted against one another often produced differing conclusions depending on sites and populations under consideration, while total variation explained suggested ample room for additional variables. In both quantitative and qualitative studies, generalizations drawn from parsimonious theories have proven to be limited to particular times and places, such that contextual factors and contingent relationships needed to be taken into account. Multilevel approaches have been of particular interest in efforts to draw comparisons among different societies and across time periods.

Secularization theory and rational choice theory in studies of religion have been criticized in ways that suggest the need to move toward multilevel approaches. Although secularization theory posits a simple mechanism of religious decline rooted in institutional differentiation, comparative studies have argued that additional structural factors need to be taken into account to explain rates and timing of institutional differentiation and their effects on religion. These have included such factors as the differing relative power of landed elites and merchants in creating spaces within state structures for rival religious groups to mobilize and differing ethnic and regional factors in explaining opportunities for independent religious movements to emerge in posttotalitarian settings. Rational choice theory similarly is subject to criticisms oriented toward economistic arguments in other settings that suggest the importance of differentiating kinds of markets and market niches rather than assuming only that markets are uniformly free. State structures are particularly important in explaining why new markets may become available, for example, through colonization or territorial conquest and thus why certain religious organizations may be able to compete in those markets. Greater consideration of cultural factors is also indicated, for example, in understanding why heightened religious competition as a result of Muslim immigration into non-Muslim societies may have quite different consequences from an influx of Christian immigrants into a predominantly Christian society.

Practice theory has in effect focused on microlevel processes to such an extent that the influence of macro structures has remained undertheorized. For example, a study of street festivals and household gender relations in an immigrant community may offer rich insights into the immediate practices involved but leave unanswered the question of how that immigrant community assimilated over several generations and what the effects on religion may have been of women entering the labor force and children attaining higher levels of education than their parents. Similarly, a study of hybrid mixtures of several alternative religious and spiritual practices among upscale middle-class residents of a culturally rich metropolitan area may leave unexamined questions about the ethnic backgrounds of these practitioners, changing expectations about marriage and child rearing, and state-influenced economic conditions underlying selective geographic mobility.[12]

Multilevel theories that have been proposed in several substantive areas of investigation such as inequality and ethnicity appear to be especially promising for studies of religion. Religious practices have been shown to be influenced by differences in social status and to be associated with ethnic and linguistic differences. These contexts in turn are shaped by state structures and power arrangements. At the micro level, social networks, leadership, and the size and diversity of groups are also important considerations. The most suggestive multilevel approaches have started by considering the symbolic boundaries that identify and demarcate categories of people and then including the power arrangements and institutions that influence changes in the relative position of those categories. In the context of religion, I suggest that these variables provide a useful way of thinking about the changing relationships among religious groupings and their relationships with racial and ethnic categories, social classes, and the state.

SYMBOLIC BOUNDARIES

Symbolic boundaries are cognitive categories that delineate patterns of social behavior. Racial and ethnic categories that map distinctions in friendship networks are examples. The role of conceptual categories is understood to be rooted in basic cognitive processes that organize complex information signals into recognizable schemas. Facial recognition that organizes information about the shape and position of eyes, ears, cheeks, hairlines, and chins into a pattern understood as a human face is an example. Other examples include categories that divide people into male and female, young and old, related and unrelated, near and far, and similar or different. The composition and relative salience of these categories is understood to be culturally constructed even though there may be evolutionary neuropsychological predispositions favoring the human use of cognitive schemas and the use of certain phylogenetic markers in constructing them. For example, gradations in skin color are acknowledged in some societies but lumped into broad categories of black and white in others. Similarly, the most salient categories defining immigrants in a highly diverse metropolitan community may designate national origin, such as Taiwanese, Cambodian, and Vietnamese, while in others a broader category such as Asian American may be more salient.[13]

The potential value of thinking about symbolic boundaries in the context of religion is evident in the extent to which varying categories are used in discussions of religion. These range from broad categories such as Protestant, Catholic, and Jewish to more refined denominational designations such as Baptist and Methodist among Protestants or Orthodox and Reformed in Judaism. Just as with ethnicity, the categories are culturally constructed and contextually contingent. Notable examples include the development of such categories as Judeo-Christian, religions of the book, theistic and nontheistic religions, and fundamentalist or evangelical. The concept of religion itself is a constructed category that developed with varying success by Westerners attempting to find ways of describing practices in China under the rubric of Confucianism or in India under the term Hinduism as concepts parallel to Christianity, Judaism, and Islam. In the United States shifts in categories and their salience are evident in terms such as Baptist, fundamentalist Baptist, conservative Baptist, moderate Baptist, evangelical Protestant, and born-again Christian, heretic, Methodist, Lutheran, mainline Protestant, and liberal Christian or nonreligious.[14]

Although the importance of labels and categories pertaining to denominations and theological orientations is well established in studies of religion, the usefulness of thinking about these distinctions as symbolic boundaries is twofold. First, the more abstract concept of symbolic boundaries invites attention to the multiple and overlapping or crosscutting categories that include but are not limited to religion. For example, racial, ethnic, geographic, socioeconomic, and political demarcations come into play with religious distinctions and thus invite questions about which of these singly or in combination are more salient in various contexts. Why Hispanic Catholic or conservative Protestant become salient social distinctions would be among the questions that might be asked. Second, symbolic boundaries specify one particularly important dimension of social classification processes and thus facilitate asking questions about the possible influence of other social factors on these processes. For example, when Methodists are regarded as a denomination, studies variously focus on matters of belief, church doctrine, patterns of attendance, leadership, history, and governance, all of which may be important but the most salient of which may remain unspecified. Conceptualized as a symbolic boundary, Methodist refers specifically to the role that the term plays in schemas of cultural classification and to whether this classification results in such behavior as social networks being more interconnected among fellow Methodists than with members of other denominations. The rules and practices that establish Methodism as a salient cultural category in one context but diminish this salience in another context can thus be specifically examined.

In other studies symbolic boundaries have been of greatest relevance to inquiries about inclusion or exclusion and the attendant inequalities of status and access to resources. For example, the symbolic boundary distinguishing whites and blacks under apartheid in South Africa was a legal distinction that also protected white people's access to economic resources and political power and shaped patterns of residence and employment on both sides of the divide. The South African example illustrates the importance of questions about the salience of symbolic boundaries and how they are maintained. The racial categories involved were institutionalized at the micro level in patterns of individual thought and in social network behavior, and at the macro level in laws, power arrangements, and economic conditions. The processes involved depend on the symbolic boundary that lumps people into social categories on the basis of skin color and include exploitation, exclusionary social networks, and restricted access to potentially disruptive knowledge, such as ideas about mechanized technology or the intricacies of legal argumentation. In addition, the inequality involved depends on people getting used to familiar arrangements and regarding them as legitimate or at least as unchangeable and convenient.

It is the cultural processes through which symbolic boundaries are created, maintained, or changed that have remained undertheorized. Symbolic boundaries are not merely cognitive categories that serve as mental maps for dividing reality into distinguishable units, such as animal and plant or light and dark. Nor are symbolic boundaries only mental distinctions that happen to become implicitly important because people associate differently with persons in one category than with those in a different category. Those perspectives offer a flat, one-dimensional view of human cognition that belies the richness and the complexity of discourse, rhetorical devices, narratives, and behavioral gestures. Apartheid's cultural reality existed not only in a schema of racial classification but also in particular ways of talking about "us" and "them" and in narratives explaining why the differences existed and should be maintained as well as in arguments about moral worth and in differences of mannerisms, speech, posture, and gait.[15]

Practice theory suggests at least five ways in which the concept of symbolic boundaries can be enriched beyond the one-dimensional understanding implicit in arguments about cognitive classification. These ideas stem from the work of anthropologist Mary Douglas, who emphasized the importance of ritual violations of symbolic boundaries in arguments that extended Durkheim's writing about ritual and the sacred, and from the recent contributions of cognitive scientists who observe that domain violations and juxtapositions are an important way in which cognitive schemas are emphasized and preserved. In work on lived religion, writers have also been attentive in helpful ways to the role of discourse. Bringing these various insights together suggests the following.[16]

The salience and social significance of symbolic boundaries will be increased by dramatic violations of those boundaries. The key here is that some activity, idea, or person has to cross or threaten to cross an otherwise inviolate symbolic boundary, and that the importance of this crossing is amplified by it occurring publicly. From the perspective of the dominant group, the perceived crossing involves a boundary that has protected its privileged status. Examples of acts perceived as violations of racial boundaries include interracial marriage and a member of a subordinate racial group gaining wealth or holding political office. From the standpoint of the disadvantaged group, a boundary violation may be regarded as a potential threat because of retaliation from the dominant group. In previous chapters some of the boundary violations we encountered involved a black pastor holding elected office, a northern Republican winning an election, an ex-slave allegedly killing a well-respected white shopkeeper, and an African American youth allegedly brutalizing a white woman. In each instance the violation was public and became discussed publicly as an indication that goodness and law and order were being threatened by evil and chaos.

A specific person, group, or organization that comes to be regarded as representative of one of the categories involved often dramatizes the meaning and visibility of symbolic boundaries. In *Communities of Discourse* I termed these individuals figural actors.[17] In contests over the maintenance or redrawing of symbolic boundaries, they serve as heroes, villains, exemplary leaders, enemies of the people, and exemplars of inclusion or exclusion. Roland Barthes in *Mythologies*, for example, notes the symbolic significance of a photo slowing a French soldier of African origin saluting the tricolor, thus suggesting, "France is a great Empire [and] that all her sons, without any color discrimination faithfully serve under her flag."[18] In Texas lore Sam Houston was a figural actor symbolizing independence from Mexico. As another example, radio evangelist Lester Roloff became a figural actor dramatizing the apparently threatened boundary protecting the free exercise of religion from intrusion by the state.

Symbolic boundaries pertaining to social categories may be reinforced, clarified, defined, or dramatized through acts associated with the physical bodies of human individuals, such as feeding, reproduction, confinement, and abuse. As Mary Douglas suggested, the corporal bodies that define each person's existence as a distinct human individual provide readily available metaphors with which to talk about social identities and perceived threats to the integrity of those identities.[19] "The spectacle of the scaffold," as Michel Foucault termed it, was a compelling occasion for the symbolism of bodies and social boundaries to be enacted.[20] It served often in this way in nineteenth-century Texas. In addition, the white community's public discourse about threats to white women from black men and the periodic torture and burning to death of a black man vividly associated physical bodies with racial boundaries. The Religious Right's efforts to oppose abortion and the Equal Rights Amendment identified the control of women's bodies and how those bodies should be used, adorned, and protected as symptomatic of wider boundaries separating conservatives and liberals.

Narratives and collective rituals that provide occasions for the telling, retelling, and refinement of stories about figural actors, bodies, and threatening events explain why symbolic boundaries exist, how people so defined should behave, and why the categories are or are not legitimate. The version of Texas civil religion that associated the Alamo with liberty of conscience and white manifest destiny against dark-skinned Mexicans is an example. The annual Juneteenth events in which African Americans remembered the state's history of slavery and the eventual emancipation of slaves are another example. Stories of frontier life, hardship, danger, and the trope of living in a rough country dramatized the boundary not only between civilized and uncivilized territory but also between good manners and uncouth behavior, morality and immorality, respect and a lack of respect, and godliness and evil.[21]

Symbolic boundaries exist within fields of multiple categories the relative salience and correspondence of which can obscure, heighten, or render invisible the presence of particular boundaries. The 1960s and 1970s were an interesting period in this regard because the boundaries being contested included ones defining the distinctions between whites and blacks, Anglos and Hispanics, young and old, feminists and nonfeminists, and Republicans and Democrats. The intensity of the so-called culture wars that grew out of those debates could perhaps be explained partly in terms of the extent to which several of these boundaries corresponded with each other. The division between the black power movement and the Chicano power movement is an illustration of boundaries maintaining the distinct identities of parallel efforts. The salience of a conservative versus liberal boundary increased in the late 1970s and 1980s as the theological division within churches mapped onto the discussion of social issues and gained wider public importance in electoral contests between Republicans and Democrats and between conservative and moderate Republicans. The salience of this boundary as one separating conservatives from liberals was perhaps a factor in reducing the public perception that this was also a boundary with racial connotations.

DEMOGRAPHY, POWER ARRANGEMENTS, AND INSTITUTIONS

To make sense of the social factors that shape the relations among groups defined by symbolic boundaries—and to examine how the boundaries in turn influence these social factors—the contention of multilevel theory is that these factors should be specified rather than bunched too readily under single rubrics such as differentiation or religious economies that potentially obscure important variations in different contexts. Research on related topics, such as racial and ethnic boundaries, has shown the value especially of bringing demography, power arrangements, and the institutional environment into the picture. How each of these relates to the symbolic boundaries defining religious constituencies can be illustrated with a few examples.

Demographic factors include the size of populations, their geographic distribution, and relative rates of growth and decline. In the processes through which modern nation states have been built, religious as well as racial and ethnic boundaries have frequently been shaped by the ways in which national boundaries included or excluded populations. Cases in point would include the territorial consolidation of modern Germany in the nineteenth century, which brought formerly separate Catholic and Protestant states together in ways that required greater interaction; the secession of the Confederacy, which reinforced the lines already drawn in the United States between southern and northern denominations; and the reduction of Soviet influence in Eastern Europe at the end of the cold war, giving opportunities for ethnic and religious differences to reassert themselves in the Ukraine, Poland, and other parts of that region. Although the salience of religious and ethnic boundaries is often reduced as the nation-building process effects national laws and generates constitutional equality among individuals, instances can also be found of the process retaining the salience of those boundaries emphasizing group rights and recognizing differences in economic arrangements. The emphasis on individual rights featured in E. P. Thompson's *Making of the English Working Class* provided an example of how Methodism could spread under conditions of increasing uniformity in the legal treatment of individuals, while Michael Hechter's *Internal Colonialism* showed the conditions under which more distinct ethnic and religious identities were retained in the Celtic fringe areas of Wales, Scotland, and Ireland.[22]

The significance of how a population is distributed within a politically defined unit has been illustrated in several ways in the material we have examined in previous chapters. Had Texas been brought into the United States according to the plan briefly considered of dividing it into five states, the chances are high that the racial, ethnic, and religious composition of the five states would have influenced local laws and social networks in diverse ways, whereas the one-state solution gave the slaveholding East Texas region greater influence in shaping the entire state, while reducing the potential impact of the Hispanic population in Southwest Texas. Had Sam Houston persuaded Texas to refrain from joining the Confederacy, the period of rapid settlement after the Civil War would likely have included far fewer Southern Baptists and more of the diverse religious denominations that were prominent in the North. By the end of the nineteenth century, the large territory and resources that resulted in huge population increases and a wider distribution of this population across the state became a factor in the state being able to downplay its southern identity and describe itself to potential newcomers as part of the American Southwest. An interesting example of population size and distribution heightening the salience of racial boundaries was the conflict in the 1950s when housing shortages and high population density in the black neighborhoods of Dallas and Houston resulted in violence inflicted by whites as blacks attempted to move into predominantly white neighborhoods.

Religious boundaries intersect with demography in several important ways. First, the prospect or reality of significant population growth through natural increase, immigration and settlement, or the political conquest or opening of new territory presents opportunities that religious organizations are likely to attempt to exploit, albeit in distinct ways that reduce the competition among them by catering to different niches of the population under consideration. For example, the spread of religion in nineteenth-century America involved Methodists utilizing a relatively centralized administrative structure to amass funds from eastern churches and send them to the newly opened frontier, where circuit riders went from place to place organizing new churches. In the same period, Baptists with a decentralized administrative structure emphasizing local autonomy drew to a greater extent from local lay leaders who started preaching with relatively little training or coordination. In contrast, Catholics' better-trained celibate priests built churches and schools in more geographically concentrated locations, and the Catholic population grew significantly through immigration into ethnic enclaves and from natural increase. Presbyterians and Congregationalists targeted a smaller but wealthier niche by emphasizing advanced training for clergy and upscale churches in towns and cities. All these variations in national strategy were evident in the churching of Texas.

Another way in which demography and religious developments are shaped is through the persistence of salient racial boundaries. One interpretation of the

racial segregation of American religion is that racism among white churchgoers resulted in separate black churches being founded and developing different
worship styles that persisted in setting them apart from their white brethren. A
related interpretation is that white and black church members actually shared
many of the same beliefs, but that these beliefs did not explicitly address racial
prejudice, and thus segregated churches continued. While both those interpretations tell some of the story, another factor also warrants consideration. Once
racially separate churches were founded, as they were in Texas by 1860, subsequent efforts to organize ministries that crossed racial lines faced structural
barriers that destined most of these efforts to fail or to succeed only in limited
ways despite the good intentions of those involved. Despite the fact that meetings during Reconstruction, for example, brought white and black clergy such
as George Honey and Sandy Parker together in common political efforts, these
efforts were short-lived and did little to bridge the boundaries that white southerners erected to inhibit blacks from voting, holding office, or living in racially
integrated neighborhoods. An interesting example at the start of the twentieth
century was the effort by Charles Parham to move his racially mixed Pentecostal
ministry from Topeka to Houston or Galveston, only to find that racial boundaries in Texas presented such obstacles that Los Angeles proved to be a more conducive environment in which the new ministry could grow. The later examples of
Luther Holcomb and Baxton Bryant in working across racial lines for civil rights
illustrate the pressures that worked against such leaders remaining in congregational ministries. In the 1970s, when many of the state's white churches no longer
argued on theological or pragmatic principle for racial segregation, declarations
of being racially inclusive were probably facilitated by the fact that residential
segregation reduced the likelihood of blacks actually attending white churches.

Power arrangements refer to the unequal distribution of legal, coercive, and
economic resources that influence the explicit and implicit decision-making
processes through which further opportunities to attain and maintain resources
occur. Examples include the national state's authority to tax its domestic population, mobilize an army, and secure its borders against invaders and unwanted immigrants; state and local governments' capacity to define who is eligible to vote,
how crimes are to be punished, and what beverages may be purchased; and un-
elected elites who own land and capital to shape elections, define the conditions
under which the laboring population works, and control the boards of voluntary
community organizations. Power arrangements matter to religious organizations
because of laws and regulations that bear on religious practices as well as the
influence of prominent lay members over church policies and the administrative
structures through which decisions about congregations, seminaries, and other
church-related institutions are made.

Power is usually concentrated most formally and officially in state structures,
but these structures are not unitary or consistently legitimate, which means that
differences among particular state agencies and changes in the relative power of

these agencies must be taken into account in understanding the strategies used by and affecting the constituencies within particular symbolically bounded categories. Opportunity structures that increase the chances of a realignment among or redefinition of symbolic boundaries include the rise or decline in political, economic, and organizational resources associated with the relevant symbolic categories and the relative parity of these resources. Political processes may reinforce the salience and social significance of symbolic boundaries by creating winner-take-all contests that encourage mobilization among the constituents of one or more of the categories identified by the symbolic boundaries. This reinforcement is likely to be more important if such contests occur with periodic regularity.

Power arrangements within religious organizations are illustrated by the differences between the more centrally coordinated Methodist Church and the more locally autonomous authority structure of the Southern Baptist Convention. The former promoted efforts to reunite the northern and southern branches of Methodism in the 1930s and resulted in subsequent departures among members who disliked the implications. The latter facilitated somewhat greater flexibility for the denomination to initiate churches in diverse urban and rural contexts and probably inhibited the spread of some of the fundamentalist endeavors being promoted by particular pastors. The tradition of local autonomy ironically proved to be an advantage in the late 1970s when Patterson, Pressler, and other fundamentalist leaders realized that seizing control of the denomination's central hierarchy was actually a way to gain greater power than anyone had imagined. Another example of power arrangements mattering was the use by suffragists of women's groups in churches to forge the network to lobby against lynching. Yet another was the use of church networks by opponents of the Equal Rights Amendment to secure its defeat.

The relation of parish clergy to power arrangements in their denominations and among local constituents appears to be a particularly interesting topic for further investigation. David Zaret in *The Heavenly Contract: Ideology and Organization in Pre-Revolutionary Puritanism* emphasized the importance of this precarious middle-level position of local clergy in his study of Puritan history in which pastors increasingly found themselves caught between pressures from below for a more inclusive view of salvation and pressures from the church hierarchy above to uphold an exclusivist view grounded in Calvinist teachings about predestination.[23] Some of what we have seen in the Texas material suggests that local congregational autonomy put Baptist clergy especially at the mercy of local constituents who wanted results and did not appreciate preaching that criticized local traditions with respect to labor practices, family relationships, and race. Whereas a Methodist pastor who ran afoul of local traditions could be relocated—and indeed expected to be relocated in any case—by the presiding elder, a Baptist preacher either found some other employment or hoped to relocate on his own. For a Baptist pastor to succeed within the denomination, having

been able to stay in one location for a long time and having grown the congregation to a sizable enterprise was the surest way to gain election to a national office.
The alternative for power beyond one's local congregation, as perhaps best illustrated by Norris and Scofield, was to cultivate extended networks through travel,
publishing, radio, and other media.

The imprint of external power arrangements at the state and national levels
on religion can be illustrated with several examples from previous chapters. The
sense of having been wrongfully violated by federal troops during the Civil War
and by northern laws and carpetbaggers during Reconstruction carried through
repeatedly in religious as well as political arguments favoring local autonomy and
resisting ideas from the federal government, eastern cities, and northern seminaries. Whatever else may have been distasteful about these ideas, they could be
argued against because they violated a local boundary that had been breached
once before. At the same time, liberty of conscience legitimated local autonomy
to the extent that temperance was mostly resolved through local option laws even
though prominent Baptist leaders were generally as opposed to saloons and the
consumption of alcoholic beverages as prohibitionists were in other states. The
division that emerged in the late 1930s and during World War II between Democratic leaders beholden to local networks and Democratic leaders with ties to
the national administration in Washington provides an interesting illustration
of shifts in political arrangements opening possibilities for clergy to challenge
existing racial boundaries in new ways. The relative parity between Republicans
and Democrats and the divisions within both parties between 1960 and 1980
created opportunities for leaders in white, black, and Hispanic congregations to
exercise greater influence and for the symbolic boundaries defining their various
constituencies to be contested in new ways.

The institutional environment refers to the fact that symbolic boundaries are
shaped not only by cognitive classification schemes or demography and power
arrangements but also by the extent to which relevant populations are socially organized in terms of neighborhoods, schools, businesses, and community-service
agencies. It matters not only that a population is divided by racial and ethnic
boundaries but also that the various racial and ethnic subpopulations are organized in these ways. For religiously defined populations, it matters similarly if
congregations are being founded in places largely devoid of schools, township
governments, town councils, sheriffs, courthouses, improved farms, railroads,
post offices, and hardware stores compared to places where all those are present.

In previous chapters we saw a number of specific instances in which the presence or absence of a well-organized environment mattered significantly to the
conduct of religion. In the earliest decades when few organizations were present, religious leaders drew sharp distinctions between the security both in this
world and the next to be found among the faithful and the evil that surrounded
civilization on all sides and periodically endangered civilized people in the form
of disease, incursions from Mexico, and slave insurrections. As towns developed,

religious leaders focused greater attention on corruption from within, such as from saloons, drunks, prostitutes, thieves, and rapists. Religious leaders also worked with local officials, merchants, and landowners to police their communities, and these efforts periodically included vigilantism in the form of lynchings and Klan rallies. An important development by the end of the nineteenth century was that the kind of individualism-rightly-understood that Tocqueville had envisioned and that was embraced locally in the idea of liberty of conscience was becoming increasingly possible through a more densely organized array of local institutions. Through schools especially, but also through social welfare organizations and progressive prison reform efforts, it was increasingly possible to believe that individuals could lead morally upstanding civic lives because there were institutions in place to instill these practices, to support them, and to control those who deviated. This heightened confidence in the moral possibilities of individuals gave religious leaders hope that churches and Sunday schools could shape a progressive society and that the black population could pull itself up through the same efforts as the white population. That sense of moral uplift was challenged repeatedly during the Great Depression and by racial conflicts but persisted as one of the important ways of defining the boundary between political and religious constituencies later in the century.

One of the more interesting connections between religion and its institutional environment is the shaping of philanthropic endeavors. Most of the examples we have encountered consisted of efforts by clergy and community leaders to enlist philanthropy in the creation of organizations deemed to be of benefit to the local community and beyond. Although many of these organizations favored the white majority population and represented philanthropy from white donors, many of them crossed racial lines as well. Examples include private academies, schools for African American children, hospitals, orphanages, and chaplaincies. Denominational leaders founded church-related colleges and seminaries, and by the end of the nineteenth century private charity was heavily involved in orphanages, hunger relief, and ministries to alcoholics and unwed mothers. In Dallas, Houston, and other cities where population was increasing rapidly, textile, meat processing, and expanding manufacturing and retail industry created a demand for a stable, law-abiding, disciplined, semiskilled workforce. As those developments continued through World War II and in the 1950s and 1960s, private philanthropy facilitated the growth of churches and schools, and these efforts sometimes crossed racial lines and were part of the gradual movement toward racial integration and the development of a racially mixed middle and working class. While private philanthropy sometimes reinforced racial boundaries as well, the long-term direction seems to have been influenced by the fact that a residentially stable, skilled workforce was beneficial to the relevant parties involved.[24]

The contrasting cases appear to be associated mainly with the enormous wealth a few individuals derived from the petroleum industry. Their philanthropic efforts were quite different from the other pattern. From the most notable examples, it appears that less of this philanthropy was channeled into religious denominations and denominational organizations and more of it was given to hospitals, medical schools, and elite colleges. Examples also point to wealth being spent on lavish lifestyles and entertainment, including investments in the development of horse racing and professional sports. The religiously oriented philanthropy included support of independent parachurch ministries and prominent individual preachers. Better evidence would be required than is generally available about the disposition of private wealth, but an interesting line of investigation would be to see if there is a connection between these kinds of philanthropy and the institutional setting in which it occurred. For example, the oil industry was known for its transient labor force, dictated by the uncertainties of drilling. For the few who earned fortunes, the self-perceptions evident in stories suggest an emphasis on risk-taking, going against the grain, standing apart from society, and being the beneficiaries of fate.[25]

In his writing about the relation between religious ideas and the social strata that carried them, Weber argued that belief in fate as typified in legends of warrior heroes was quite different from the more rational ascetic belief in divine salvation evident in modern Christianity. The person who believed in divine salvation, Weber argued, was driven either by the conviction that good works needed to outweigh evil deeds or by the uncertainty that one was truly among the elect. In either case, the ethical imperative was to work hard, lead a disciplined life, live simply, and accumulate resources that could be gainfully invested or devoted to beneficent causes. The ascetic entrepreneur so driven was an individualist who stood alone before God but lived in a way that contributed materially and in an orderly manner to the collective good. The person who believed in fate, in contrast, was for Weber epitomized by the warrior hero who was also an individualist but whose courage and heroism set him apart from the rank-and-file soldier. The warrior hero was a risk-taker who sometimes was quite religiously devout, although usually in a way that deviated from the ordinary teachings of clergy, and believed that the gods must be smiling on his courageous exploits. Unlike the ascetic guided by a belief in divine salvation, these fatalists lived extravagantly as if there were no tomorrow, prided themselves on their exploits, rewarded themselves accordingly, and looked for new battles in which to demonstrate their prowess. Whether Weber would have noted similarities in the orientations of Texas oil barons would be interesting to know.[26]

STRATEGIES OF INSTITUTION BUILDING

The literature on symbolic boundaries has recognized that moral arguments through which one group claims superiority over another group are often an important part of the cultural work involved. But groups do not only brandish moral swords at one another. They also invest in institutions to advance what are regarded as sources of moral worth among their own constituents. And these institutions sometimes then dramatize the moral worth of insiders over against the moral turpitude of outsiders, while in other cases the danger perceived among outsiders prompts efforts to develop institutions that apply the same moral standards to those constituents. From the standpoint of a dominant group, it may be reassuring to see that outsiders are developing their own institutions and adopting the same moral standards.

Moral worth is variously defined in different circumstances, but studies examining its role in constituting symbolic boundaries in various contexts suggest that some of the most common criteria are honesty, integrity, hard work, self-sufficiency, loyalty and responsibility toward family members, and obedience to laws and community norms. Although religion is not the only source of these moral criteria, it is frequently regarded in the United States as an important means of promoting them and of adding gravity to them through biblical narratives and the disciplining functions of congregations. Religious teachings and practices add to moral injunctions the idea that the behavior expected is pleasing to God while deviations are marks of sinfulness and moral depravity.[27]

Religion's role in promoting moral standards is acknowledged in each of the theoretical perspectives traditionally informing the sociological study of religion. Secularization theory observes that religious organizations may lose their ability to shape moral norms as other institutions such as secular schools and the mass media become more influential. Rational choice theory posits that religious organizations compete with one another to define and promote conformity to particular moral norms. Practice theory emphasizes the learning of moral behavior that occurs through the experience of participating individually or collectively in such practices as prayer, the study of religious texts, or serving the poor.

An emphasis on symbolic boundaries brings in the added consideration of moral norms being the basis through which groups define the worth of their members over against that of other groups. The boundaries separating religious, racial, ethnic, and political constituencies are one of the factors motivating institution building to promote moral norms and shaping how resources are invested in the institution-building process. Although congregations are typically the first and most immediate institutions through which religious groups instill moral norms among their members, it is important to recognize that other religiously sponsored organizations also contribute in these ways. Among these other organizations, private church-related schools, church-related colleges, seminaries, orphanages, homes for unwed mothers, ministries to juvenile delinquents, prison ministries, and special advocacy organizations focusing on temperance or chastity or parenting may all be considered.

The Texas case has provided illustrations of these various religiously inspired institution-building projects. For the majority white population, most of these projects consisted of efforts to adapt to the hardships of frontier life by constructing organizations to facilitate the moral behavior of their own families and to protect themselves against the perceived threat of outsiders regarded as less civilized, including thieves, hooligans, roughnecks, Native Americans, and African Americans. Settlers founding private academies patterned after the ones they had experienced in other southern states illustrated the role of organizational templates. The manner in which symbolic boundaries may be dramatized by moral institutions was illustrated in the founding by white inhabitants during and after Reconstruction of some private academies for African Americans whose involvement was considered as evidence that at least some African Americans could conform to the same norms of civilized behavior as whites. Schools and churches founded by black leaders offered similar evidence.

Multilevel theory draws attention to the linkages between microlevel and macrolevel processes in the institution-building process. At the micro level, clergy worked with local leaders such as plantation owners, confederate veterans, sheriffs, and other officeholders to organize and staff academies, schools, clinics, and hospitals. Through these local efforts, clergy and lay leaders on occasion developed wider networks that led to the funding of denominationally sponsored colleges, seminaries, and welfare programs. At the macro level, the moral claims associated with ideas about the advancement of civilization were facilitated by the growth of towns, economic improvements, and political arrangements that protected property and assured the continuation of privileges for the white population.

DYNAMICS OF CHURCH AND STATE RELATIONS

Religious organizations' institution-building activities engage with state structures in two ways. The first occurs through the resources the state can provide toward facilitating these activities. For example, the state can levy taxes for the support of church-related schools, provide tax exemptions that encourage voluntary donations to churches, send out the cavalry to punish marauders interrupting worship services, organize flood relief and public health programs to keep churchgoing families alive, pass laws that prevent upstart cults from spreading, subsidize church-related prison reform efforts, quash demonstrations, and intimidate abortion providers. The second relation to state structures follows from the first and involves conflicts between religious organizations and nonreligious organizations over questions of taxation, compulsory school attendance, qualifications for public office, and voting. The two processes were inevitably linked because the state resources that benefited religious organizations at one moment were likely to engender conflict at another. As Reinhard Bendix observed in *Nation-Building and Citizenship*, the extension of individual rights in Western Europe and the United States during the eighteenth and nineteenth centuries included the right to freedom of association, which facilitated the work of religious organizations and indeed promoted faith-based moral arguments about the appropriate qualifications for individual citizenship but then in favoring the individual rights of national citizenship sparked conflict between clergy and government officials over questions of public schooling and equality for minority groups.[28]

Secularization theories have emphasized the conflicts that arise between religious organizations and the state more than the resources provided by the state. The conflicts in these interpretations appear for the most part to be resolved in favor of the state, which gradually becomes more powerful at the expense of religion or promotes modernity by restricting religion's influence in matters of business and government. In other variants, the state promotes science and technology, imposes compulsory public education, and passes laws that push religion out of public life and into the private voluntary sphere of personal behavior. Rational choice theory is generally silent about religion's relations to the state other than to posit that separation of church and state is good for religion. However, some empirical attention has been given to the possibility that some states may provide resources that are beneficial to religious organizations. Practice theory has been interested in power relations and the subversion of these relations at the micro level of personal behavior more than at the macro level.[29]

The Texas case illustrates the importance of recognizing that church and state relations involve cultural and institutional boundaries that frequently come together and provide occasions for boundary-dramatizing negotiations and conflict. The evidence at this level also suggests the importance of taking into account differences among the various state structures, including conflicts between political parties and between local or state and federal agencies. We have seen instances of religious leaders siding with one political party over another or taking positions favoring one or another faction within the same political party as well as instances involving appeals to federal or state authority. The arguments associated with liberty of conscience have been particularly interesting because at times these arguments discouraged clergy from engaging directly in political activities while at other times political engagement was legitimated by arguments about defending liberty of conscience. Although church and state relations became matters of explicit discussion on several occasions, such as the 1928 election involving Smith and the 1960 election involving Kennedy, the times of silence on these relations also seem instructive. For example, white clergy remained politically uninvolved much of the time with respect to questions about the poll tax and lynching.

An argument in the literature on symbolic boundaries suggests that church and state relations not only are matters of constitutional interpretation but also are occasions for dramatizing the power of each and the values favored by the contestants. This interpretation suggests that perceptions of threat and public ways to amplify those perceptions are sometimes more important than actual threats. For example, the likelihood of Smith being elected in 1928 and bringing about Vatican control of America seems to have been far less than the rhetoric that Protestant leaders devoted to talking about the threat. The extended conflicts with government involving the Roloff and Robison ministries in the 1970s illustrate another way in which the drama involved may have had larger repercussions than the particular issues that sparked conflict.

RELIGION IN RACIAL AND ETHNIC POLITICS

The considerable interest that researchers have devoted to the relationships between religion and race in the United States has emphasized the role of black and white religious leaders in the civil rights movement and the extent to which religious congregations remain racially segregated. Research on religion and ethnicity has identified the ethnic bases of religious divisions—for example, between German American Lutherans and Swedish American Lutherans—and the apparent decline in significance of these divisions through assimilation and denominational mergers. Additional interest in ethnicity and religion has been raised in recent decades by the growth of new immigrant populations and by greater attention to cross-national comparisons. These processes are not sufficiently examined through the lenses of secularization theory, rational choice theory, or practice theory. Multilevel process theory draws closer attention to the ebb and flow in salience of multiple religious, racial, and ethnic categories and to the strategies that religious actors mobilize in efforts to weaken, reinforce, or invert these categories.

Our examination of religion and race in Texas has illustrated a number of ways in which the two have intersected. Although racial segregation characterized much of the state's religious history, the federal government was an exogenous resource that came significantly into the picture at several points to complicate this relationship. Reconstruction created opportunities for white preachers from the North and black preachers from Texas to secure positions temporarily in public office that transcended the constraints otherwise present in their relation to local constituents. Federal antilynching legislation in the 1930s was perceived as an external threat to local autonomy, but suffragist mobilization provided Texas women with ways to organize church-based networks to pressure local law enforcement officers to combat lynching. Johnson's ties to the Roosevelt administration subsequently shifted power arrangements within the Democratic Party in ways that reduced the influence of local leaders and created opportunities for clergy to play a more active role in government-based civil rights efforts. As black clergy gained positions in local and state government, fissures developed between their gradualist emphases and the more confrontational strategies of black power leaders. As white conservative Protestants became supporters of socially and fiscally conservative Republican candidates, a new line of division between white and black churches developed despite segregation having been officially denounced.

In a state where differences between Anglos and Hispanics were potentially as important as those between whites and blacks, it is interesting to consider why the former were not as politically or religiously salient during much of the state's history. One possible reason is that black and white relationships were dominant in East Texas, where settlements and churches were established earlier, while Anglo and Hispanic relationships were more geographically localized along the Texas and Mexico border. At the same time, from the standpoint of symbolic boundaries, border crossings between the two countries carried particular significance. In early decades, the threat of Mexican incursions heightened negative valences, while subsequent border crossings implied transient labor that did not require full incorporation. The more salient boundary separating blacks and whites reinforced a tendency among middle-class Hispanics to emphasize an identity of whiteness.[30]

The larger influx of immigrants that began in the 1960s challenged taken-for-granted boundaries defined by religion and ethnicity. One important development was the emergence of Hispanic as a more clearly defined category in place of the various labels that had been used to describe Mexicans, Mexican Americans, braceros, Spanish speakers, Latin people, and Chicanos. Another was an extension of religious divisions within the religiously involved Anglo population between those for whom theological exclusivity reinforced anti-immigrant sentiments and those for whom theological inclusivity encouraged acceptance of immigrants. The differences in attitudes among Christian exclusivists and Christian inclusivists pertained to views toward Muslims, Hindus, and Buddhists as well.[31]

In broader historical comparative contexts, the question of religion's role in maintaining or challenging racial and ethnic inequality is of continuing importance as a topic of inquiry. Moving beyond arguments drawn from secularization theory and rational choice theory is possible by paying closer attention to the resources that religious actors may be able to mobilize. Larger and better-organized memberships as in the case of black Protestant or Hispanic Catholic congregations are one such resource. The extent to which local clergy are beholden to members, to superiors in the ecclesiastical hierarchy, or to external elites is an important consideration. For example, campus clergy and faculty in church-related colleges may be insulated from the pressures of congregational pastorates and empowered through connections with community leaders outside their own denominations.[32]

RELIGIOUS RESTRUCTURING

A final topic illustrating the potential usefulness of multilevel theory is religious restructuring. Interest in restructuring has focused on two rather different meanings of the term. In the first, restructuring means a change in the relative size of populations associated with particular religious traditions such as denominations or families of denominations. Examples include growth in the absolute numbers or percentage of a society affiliated with the Catholic Church relative to Protestants, an increase in the Muslim population relative to non-Muslim traditions, growth in the percentages of a society who claim to be nonreligious relative to those who hold a religious affiliation, and growth in the membership of evangelical Protestant denominations relative to that of mainline Protestant denominations. In the second meaning, restructuring refers to changes in the cultural, social, or political salience of the various categories in which religious traditions and practices are classified. In *The Restructuring of American Religion*, for example, I argued that the significance of denominational identities, such as Presbyterian and Methodist, was diminishing relative to a classification scheme loosely consisting of religious conservatives, moderates, and liberals.[33] Other examples might be the emerging cultural significance of categories such as traditional Catholic, Hispanic Catholic, Neo-Pagan, and spiritual seeker.

Either kind of restructuring poses a challenge to standard theories emphasizing secularization and rational choice. Change in the relative size of religious traditions is somewhat easier to address through these standard approaches if one assumes that change occurs through secularizing processes that affect one group more than others, or if it is regarded as a function of competition-induced rational choice. However, questions about the timing, exogenous influence, and consequences remain to be considered. The other kind of restructuring that involves the emergence of new classification schemes poses these questions as well. The advantages of a multilevel approach can be illustrated by revisiting the argument that conservative religious organizations will grow and perhaps gain salience as a cultural category because of processes inherent in religious market competition.

Posited by economist Laurence R. Iannaccone in "Why Strict Churches Are Strong," this argument suggested that denominations with moral tenets that make it difficult for just anyone to become a member unless they are truly committed have favorable effects for the organization because other, less committed potential members are deterred from getting involved and making claims on the group's scarce resources. In support of this argument, Iannaccone showed that denominations that experts judged to be morally strict, such as Southern Baptists, Assemblies of God, and Mormons, experienced higher levels of participation in the 1970s and 1980s than denominations considered to be less strict, such as Methodists, Presbyterians, and Lutherans.[34] The two main criticisms that have been advanced against this argument are that, first, it is unclear how it might apply in other instances because of difficulties in deciding what counts as strictness, and second, the conditions under which free riding might or might not be an issue also need to be better specified.[35] For example, in the all-too-typical case of large church buildings with unoccupied seating during worship services, a few nonpaying members filling those seats would constitute little drain on the organization's resources; indeed, the church might welcome these visitors in the hope that any short-term cost might translate into long-term paying membership.

Apart from these criticisms, an alternative explanation for differences in denominational growth patterns was advanced by Michael Hout, Andrew Greeley, and Melissa J. Wilde in "The Demographic Imperative in Religious Change in the United States," in which they argued that at least three-quarters of the variation could be explained by the fact that the conservative denominations in question during this period included more members from lower socioeconomic strata who had more children and had them when the parents were younger, meaning that denominational growth occurred mostly through natural increase.[36]

If we assume, though, that Iannaccone was onto something in suggesting that strictness matters, then one possible problem with the argument can perhaps be readily resolved, but another remains. The possibly resolvable problem is that family size is not entirely exogenous to what happens in churches. A strict church could arguably provide programs and teachings that encourage members to have children sooner and more often, and it could selectively attract members who already had more children and somehow implicitly discourage free riders who essentially were not contributing to the church by having fewer children. Furthermore, as Hout and his coauthors acknowledge, strictness may be the reason some denominations retain their members' offspring better than others do. If strictness does matter in these ways, we are still left with the question of what exactly it is and when it is most likely to be important in keeping free riders at bay.

A starting point should be evident in Iannaccone's argument about why strictness is potentially important. Unlike arguments in an earlier view that grew from the work of Weber and Ernst Troeltsch, Iannaccone's view is not that strictness is essentially a form of moral discipline that encourages an ascetic lifestyle and thus facilitates upward mobility and resource accumulation. Instead strictness separates the faithful from the rest of the population. In short, it is a symbolic boundary. The distinction between "us" and "them" is a culturally constructed category that has behavioral consequences. Two implications follow then from what we have suggested about symbolic boundaries. They are dialogically constructed and ritually dramatized through actions and reactions among groups that fall on both sides of the boundary. And their content and salience reflect strategies that are conditioned by particular demographic, political, and institutional arrangements.

In *American Evangelicalism: Embattled and Thriving*, Christian Smith provided information that supports the argument that strictness is usefully conceived of as a constructed symbolic boundary. Comparing self-defined fundamentalist and evangelical Protestants, Smith showed that the fundamentalists were not doing as well as evangelicals in terms of activities that might suggest growth or strength even though Iannaccone's argument would have suggested that fundamentalists should be doing better. The evangelicals were outperforming fundamentalists, Smith's data suggested, because they were constructing distinctions between themselves and the rest of society that facilitated their sense of being a beleaguered subculture without actually requiring them to be very different from other people in terms of education, careers, and family lifestyles. Indeed, a fundamentalist strategy of separation from society would involve less boundary-dramatizing activity than evangelicals' more active engagement with society. It was their sense of being embattled that helped them to thrive. This was an "us" and "them" distinction that reflected the symbolic differences that mattered in the early 1990s, such as views about abortion and homosexuality, rather than the ones that may have been more important in the 1960s and early 1970s, such as abstinence from alcohol and disapproval of divorce, and the symbolic boundaries had gravitated such that greater variation in attitudes toward the Bible and toward women's ordination could be embraced by those who considered themselves evangelicals. In addition, the newer symbolic boundaries were shaped by larger social developments and not simply by what a denomination's internal policies might be. For example, evangelicals in the early 1990s were better educated, more regionally dispersed, and more likely to live in suburbs and cities and work in the professions than had been the case a generation earlier.[37]

By enabling these other contextual factors to be included, a multilevel approach also suggests the continuing relevance of the demographic variables emphasized by Hout and his coauthors. If only strictness is considered on grounds that parsimonious theories are always best, then the argument fails to illuminate the period immediately following Iannaccone's article because in the 1990s and the decade following the earlier high growth rates among conservative denominations such as Southern Baptists and Assemblies of God diminished almost to nothing despite the fact that these denominations remained as strict as before, if not more so. The difference was that earlier demographic growth associated with the post–World War II baby boom and larger family size among working-class families had now shifted such that overall demographic growth was slower and there were smaller differentials based on socioeconomic status. Instead, demographic growth was mostly fueled by immigration, and to the extent that conservative Protestant denominations were growing, an important aspect of this growth was in attracting members among new immigrant populations.

Another emendation of rational choice theory is suggested by the observation that strictness implies something about social network ties or their absence. On one reading, strictness is mostly an argument about comparative advantages or disadvantages in a competitive religious market. In that interpretation, the most important implication is that strict religious organizations will be stronger, holding other things constant, and thus will grow faster or at higher rates than less strict organizations. That reading, however, fails to include one of the most interesting aspects of rational choice theory as posited in other contexts, namely, its emphasis on social capital. In *Foundations of Social Theory*, James S. Coleman developed an expansive treatment of the possible ramifications of rational choice for sociological questions and in this volume included an important chapter on social capital. Recognizing that rational choice theory is less about competitive markets and more about the bases on which social exchange takes place, Coleman argued that social exchange is facilitated by the trust and familiarity that develops in densely connected social networks that endure over time. Two of Coleman's examples featured religion. One was the New York wholesale diamond business, which Coleman suggested depended on high levels of trust reinforced by the religious and ethnic networks among the predominantly Jewish merchants involved. The other example was Catholic schools, which Coleman argued produced high rates of completion compared with public schools partly because of the religious connections that linked parents and students, parents with other parents, and parents with teachers and priests. In both instances there was a symbolic boundary based on religion that not only defined "us" and "them" categories but also encouraged dense in-group social networks.[38]

Considerable attention has been given to the role of social capital in studies of religion over the past two decades. The results demonstrate that symbolic boundaries having to do with religion do in fact include differences in patterns of social relationships. Homophily appears in social networks to some extent such that Catholics are more likely to include fellow Catholics among their networks of close friends than non-Catholics are and similar patterns are evident among Jews. That strictness matters is evident in results showing that conservative Protestants, for example, are more likely to have friends among fellow conservative Protestants and to do volunteer work that benefits their congregation to a greater extent than is the case among members of mainline Protestant denominations. These studies also suggest that more frequent participation in congregations influences the extent of a person's social capital by facilitating larger or denser social networks and in some cases by including network ties that bridge across other boundaries, such as racial and social class divisions.[39]

Bringing social networks more clearly into the picture has provided an additional way to think about religious restructuring beyond the fact that some organizations may grow more than others in a competitive market. The key insight is that social networks may be homophilous with respect to religious categories but are seldom completely so. Catholics are unlikely to associate only with fellow Catholics, Jews only with fellow Jews, or conservative Protestants only with other conservative Protestants. Other things being equal, heterophilous relationships are likely to be more common when there are more opportunities for such relationships to happen. A diverse religious environment, therefore, should be viewed not only as a market in which religious competition occurs but as a space in which religiously diverse social networks are possible. And if they do, several possibilities may follow. Familiarity may breed contempt or at least sharpens the competitive desire to outdo the other in ways that rational choice theory suggests. It may result in tolerance or acceptance or even in mutual understanding such that the competitive spirit diminishes. Tolerance may result in a relativistic least-common-denominator attitude of the kind that might be indicative of secularization. Or diverse network ties may be the occasion for proselytization and conversion.

Research on social networks shaped by race, ethnicity, proximity, and religion suggests that any of these outcomes is possible. Although homophily is particularly shaped by racial boundaries, these patterns are complicated by other factors, such as differences in social class or tendencies for students to comingle based on extracurricular activities or other divisions such as national origin or neighborhood.[40] For religious restructuring, the most readily imagined possibility is that increased opportunities for heterophilous relationships may lead to a weakening of traditional boundaries separating and perhaps being the cause of conflict among religious traditions. For example, in *American Grace* Robert D. Putnam and David E. Campbell argue that the increasing chances of having an Aunt Susan who is an atheist, a Muslim, or gay are reason to believe that intolerance toward atheists, Muslims, and gays will diminish over time.[41] I suggested in *The Restructuring of American Religion* that the significance of traditional distinctions between Presbyterians and Methodists or Lutherans and Episcopalians might be diminishing for similar reasons, especially as members of different denominations intermarried or moved to new neighborhoods and selected congregations based on proximity and neighborly recommendations.

An equally plausible result is that social networks can reinforce new social boundaries. In an interesting study Delia Baldassarri has shown that issue polarization on a topic such as abortion can develop and become more divisive if a few social relationships at an initial time correspond to this division and if other factors forge continuing relationships along those lines.[42] In religious settings, special-purpose groups organized around single issues, such as campus ministry, lay leadership, church doctrine, funding decisions, women's ordination, and abortion, may have been the impetus for new networks that then grew to the point that they transcended denominational boundaries. The development of e-mail, the Internet, and social networking websites has arguably made it easier for virtual networks to develop that cross existing social boundaries and facilitate mobilization around such topics as gay rights, tax reduction proposals, and recalls of elected officials.

The fact that social networks may be the mechanism through which symbolic boundaries are redefined should not obscure the larger point about the multiple influences through which these boundaries are shaped. The importance of symbolic boundaries is perhaps most evident in relation to questions about competition in religious markets. In the interest of generating empirical tests of the effect of competition on membership growth, affiliation, attendance, conversion, and other aspects of religion, it made sense for researchers to focus on denominations and to create measures of potential competition based on the extent of diversity among denominations in particular locations, such as counties, states, or nations. Doing so nevertheless introduces the tacit assumption that all denominational categories are equally significant and that the relevant consideration is only the distribution of a population across these categories. This assumption implies that competition is assumed to be greater if the population is equally distributed among ten denominations than if it is distributed among five, whereas in reality the competition may be most severe if only two denominations are present. Further, it does not take account of substantive differences in the salience of boundaries, such as the sharp tension that might exist after a split within a denomination compared with the relative lack of competition that may exist between two denominations that share the same style of worship and differ only in historic origins. Nor is sufficient consideration given to the possibility that differences within a denomination may be as salient as between denominations or that the most significant form of competition may not be with other religious organizations but with secular organizations.

In *Red State Religion* I found that competition was an important factor in the changes that religion in Kansas experienced over the century and a half following the territory's settlement in the 1850s, but not in ways involving straightforward, diversity-induced, free-market competition. The political, demographic, and economic factors making a religious market possible in the first place needed to be considered. These factors included the federal government's role in pacifying and relocating the territory's indigenous Native American population and constituting the territory into geographically surveyed quarter sections, townships, and counties; and the population growth immediately following the American Civil War in a predominantly agricultural-based economy that provided incentives for large numbers of settlers to relocate into the territory. The incentive to start new churches was driven as much by competition among towns to attract settlers as it was by competition among denominations. Indeed, the former was such that leaders and members of different denominations often cooperated with one another in founding new congregations. The most significant competition among religious traditions was between Methodists and Catholics, both with bishops who planned new churches and supplied them with itinerant preachers. However, the salience of this competition was minimized by geographic separation and the formation of separate educational institutions but flared periodically because of partisan political campaigns and debates about the funding of public education. Although there were upstart sects variously promoting holiness, spiritualism, atheism, vegetarianism, and apocalyptic visions, Methodists and Catholics as the two dominant traditions effectively combated these groups and promoted moderate individualistic piety and centrist civic engagement.[43]

The comparable developments in Texas over roughly the same period illustrate different effects on religion of an environment structured by different political, demographic, and institutional factors. Local congregational autonomy among Baptists created opportunities for more intradenominational competition and the periodic emergence of competition within the denomination between fundamentalists and moderates. Racial and ethnic divisions were more important, but the political divisions that separated Protestants and Catholics in Kansas were less salient in Texas, and with the exception of the 1928 presidential election, friction between the two was reduced by a relatively high degree of geographic separation.

The restructuring in the 1970s and 1980s that resulted in the categories of religious conservative and religious liberal becoming more salient provides an interesting example of multilevel social factors at work. In my earlier work at the national level, I argued that the rising salience of this distinction was empirically evident in the results of a national survey showing that a large majority of the American public was able to classify their personal beliefs and practices along a conservative-to-liberal continuum and that there were strong negative perceptions of liberals by conservatives and of conservatives by liberals. Conservatives and liberals were also distinguished from each other by separate social relationships and distinctly different attitudes on social and political issues. At the national level, the social, demographic, and political factors reinforcing the rising salience of this distinction included cross-denominational marriage and geographic mobility that reduced the salience of existing denominational boundaries, special-interest organizations making political claims, age-graded differences in educational attainment, partisan political divisions, and the promulgation of these labels through the national media.

However, the evidence from Kansas and Texas shows that additional factors must be considered in local contexts. In Kansas the most important developments included the appearance and rapid growth after World War II of Southern Baptist congregations in the state and the role of *Roe v. Wade* in shifting Catholics and Southern Baptists from earlier Democratic Party supporters into the Republic Party. In addition, the relatively small population of the state and the increasing concentration of population in cities and suburbs facilitated the growth of a handful of megachurches with sufficient resources to exert a disproportionate role in conservative politics. The Texas case contrasts with the national and Kansas developments. Unlike at the national level, where declining denominational boundaries were particularly important, the similar decline in Texas occurred mostly among other mainline denominations such as Presbyterians and Methodists but not among Southern Baptists, where, if anything, denominational identity became more important. The distinction between conservatives and liberals in fact became more salient because of the conflict within the Southern Baptist Convention.

Texas illuminates another aspect of the rising salience of conservative Protestantism. The empirical literature has variously operationalized what was considered to be the most important aspect of this development as a distinction involving denominations classified as evangelical Protestants, church members who self-identified as evangelicals, or church members who believed in a literal interpretation of the Bible or considered themselves born again. Although classifications in survey data are sufficiently crude that these labels often produced similar results, closer attention to the actual salience of the various categories at the time when their salience was increasing suggests that some were more applicable than others. The shift between the 1890s and 1960s from fundamentalist to evangelical is a development that pertained especially to northern denominations and was most evident in the rise of the National Association of Evangelicals. This development occurred in Texas as well through the multistate networks forged among Norris, Scofield, and northern evangelicals and through such parachurch organizations as Youth for Christ, Campus Crusade for Christ, and the Billy Graham Evangelistic Association. However, Norris, Roloff, Robison, and Criswell continued to use the term fundamentalist more than the term evangelical even though they were more actively engaged in social and political affairs than many northern fundamentalists were. Evangelical was less salient as a fine-grained distinguishing term in Texas because it embraced nearly all Southern Baptists and many in southern branches of Methodist, Presbyterian, and Episcopal congregations. Conservative became the more meaningful label defining differences from moderates or liberals because of the conflict within the Southern Baptist Convention. It was the term that mapped most closely with the division within the Republic Party of significance to Texas voters in the 1976 and 1980 elections as Reagan became the symbolic expression of that stance within the party.

The larger point is that close attention to the particular social circumstances in which religious developments occur necessitates moving beyond the expectation of earlier social science theorizing in which single dominant concepts were posited. Multilevel theory implies the need to identify a cluster of concepts that orient research and at the same time enable different combinations of structures and processes to be viewed in different contexts. I have suggested that an emphasis on the symbolic boundaries that inform popular thinking about religious classifications and that influence social relationships is one such approach. Symbolic boundaries function at the micro level of lived religious practice among individuals and groups and at the macro level of relationships among religious traditions and between religion and other institutions. The salience of these demarcations can be examined through the conflicts that occur and in the ways in which individuals and organizations define themselves in relation to one another. As we have seen here, the classifications that define religious activities are powerfully influenced by leaders who become the figural representatives of groups and ideas and by the racial, ethnic, and political categories with which these activities are associated.

ACKNOWLEDGMENTS

I am indebted to faculty and fellow graduate students at the University of California Berkeley whose ideas many years ago were formative in shaping my interests in the topics addressed here, especially Richard Apostle, Robert Bellah, Albert Black, Jualynne Dodson, Troy Duster, Charles Glock, Gertrude Selznick, and Neil Smelser, and more recently to colleagues at Princeton whose work has been of particular inspiration, including Wallace Best, Mitch Duneier, Tom Espenshade, Patricia Fernandez Kelly, Eddie Glaude, Angel Harris, Doug Massey, Sara McLanahan, Devah Pager, Nell Painter, Alejandro Portes, Al Raboteau, Val Smith, Howard Taylor, Eddie Telles, Marta Tienda, Melvin Tumin, Walter Wallace, and Cornel West. At the Center for the Study of Religion, the Women and Religion in the African Diaspora Project, directed by Marie Griffith and Barbara Savage, provided valuable opportunities to delve further into the literature on religion and race and to learn from the work of Anthea Butler, Deidre Crumbley, Marla Frederick, Cheryl Townsend Gilkes, and Carolyn Rouse, among others. Interaction with Michael Lindsay, Debbie Sharpe Smith, Joseph Smith, and Mary Smith, among others, proved beneficial for gaining perspective on the region under consideration.

The research was facilitated by the fact that Texas has a proud history and has sought to preserve this history through the work of the Texas State Historical Association, the *Southwestern Historical Quarterly*, the Portal to Texas History at the University of North Texas, the various archives of the University of Texas system and Baylor University, and numerous other books and essays. I made extensive use of census and other statistical information available as electronic data files from the Inter-University Consortium for Political and Social Research at the University of Michigan, the Association for Religion Data Archives, the Roper Center for Public Opinion Research, and Social Explorer. Beginning in the mid-1990s, several research assistants and I conducted in-depth, semistructured interviews and continued to do so through 2012, collecting information from more than two hundred pastors, church members, and community leaders who gave generously of their time. Sylvia Kundrats, Paul Martin, Christi Martone, Peter Mundey, Karen Myers, Steve Myers, Steve Offutt, Natalie Searl, and Libby Smith assisted me in this process.

The research received generous support from Princeton University through the Office of the Provost, the University Center for Human Values, and the Woodrow School of International and Public Affairs. Chandler Davidson, Darren Dochuk, Helen Rose Ebaugh, John Evans, John Giggie, William Martin, and Will Schultz provided valuable comments and suggestions on earlier drafts of the chapters. Donna Defrancisco and Anita Kline provided administrative support, and Jay Barnes magically kept the computers and websites from crashing. Through what turned out to be a rather long process of research and writing, my family provided moral support and much needed diversions.

NOTES

INTRODUCTION

1. Nicholas and Anton Riedel, letter dated May 11, 1845, from New Braunfels, Texas, quoted in "Our Culture and Heritage," New Braunfels, Texas, http://www.nbjumin.com. Nicholas Riedel was one of two sons and four daughters of Anton Riedel, born in 1791 in Stephanhausen, Germany, and Francisca Hombach, born in 1798 in Hallgarten, Germany, and married in Germany in 1827. The German settlement of New Braunfels is described in Judith Lynn Dykes-Hoffmann, "On the Edge of the Balcones Escarpment: The Urban and Cultural Development of New Braunfels and San Marcos, Texas, 1845–1880" (PhD diss., University of Texas at Austin, 2003); Jefferson Morgenthaler, *The German Settlement of the Texas Hill Country* (Seattle: Mockingbird Books, 2011); and Rudolph L. Biesele, "Early Times in New Braunfels and Comal County," *Southwestern Historical Quarterly* 50 (1946), 75–92.

2. Robert A. Baker, "Southern Baptist Beginnings," Baptist History and Heritage Society (1979), http://www.baptisthistory.org.; H. Leon McBeth, *The Baptist Heritage: Four Centuries of Baptist Witness* (Nashville, TN: Broadman Press, 1987), 413.

3. On arguments about American religious exceptionalism, see Robert Wuthnow, "Religion," in *Understanding America: The Anatomy of an Exceptional Nation*, ed. Peter H. Schuck and James Q. Wilson (New York: Public Affairs, 2008), 275–308.

4. Robert Orsi, "Everyday Miracles: The Study of Lived Religion," in *Lived Religion in America: Toward a History of Practice*, ed. David D. Hall (Princeton, NJ: Princeton University Press, 1997), 3–21; R. Marie Griffith, *God's Daughters: Evangelical Women and the Power of Submission* (Berkeley: University of California Press, 1997).

5. Alexis de Tocqueville, *Democracy in America*, ed. J. P. Mayer, trans. George Lawrence (New York: Harper & Row, 1966, originally published in 1838).

6. Relevant theoretical discussions of symbolic boundaries include Michèle Lamont and Virag Molnár, "The Study of Boundaries in the Social Sciences," *Annual Review of Sociology* 28 (2002), 167–95; and Andreas Wimmer, "The Making and Unmaking of Ethnic Boundaries: A Multi-Level Process Theory," *American Journal of Sociology* 113 (2008), 970–1022.

7. Scholarship in which the various adaptive functions of religion are emphasized ranges widely, from Talcott Parsons, *The Social System* (New York: Free Press, 1951), and Clifford Geertz, *The Interpretation of Cultures* (New York: Basic Books, 1973), 3–30, to Edward O.

Wilson, *On Human Nature* (Cambridge, MA: Harvard University Press, 2004); also of value is Peter L. Berger, "Some Second Thoughts on Substantive versus Functional Definitions of Religion," *Journal for the Scientific Study of Religion* 13 (1974), 125–33, and Michael Stausberg, ed., *Contemporary Theories of Religion: A Critical Companion* (New York: Routledge, 2009).

8. One exception is Matthew Avery Sutton, "Was FDR the Antichrist? The Birth of Fundamentalist Antiliberalism in a Global Age," *Journal of American History* 98 (March 2012), 1052–74.

9. Frederick Law Olmsted, *A Journey through Texas or a Saddle-Trip on the Southwestern Frontier*, introduction by Witold Rybczynski (Lincoln: University of Nebraska Press, 2004, originally published in 1857), 179; additional information about the introduction of slavery in the New Braunfels area is included in Myra Lee Adams Goff, "The Dark History of Meriwether's Millrace," *Around the Sophienburg*, September 6, 2011, http://sophienburg.com.

CHAPTER 1
IN ROUGH COUNTRY

1. Initial details of the Loveland murder were included in untitled reports from the December 2, 1869, editions of the *Houston Times* and *Houston Telegraph* and reprinted in "Our Houston Correspondence," *Galveston Tri-Weekly News*, December 3, 1869. A retrospective account was published as "The Gallows," *Houston Telegraph*, August 12, 1870, and reprinted in the *New York Herald*, August 30, 1870.

2. "The Texas Election," *New York Times*, January 24, 1870; "City Population History from 1850 to 2000," *Texas Almanac* (2011), http://www.texasalmanac.com; "Portraits of Texas Governors," *Texas State Library and Archives Commission*, http://www.tsl.state.tx.us.

3. James Britton Cranfill, *Dr. J. B. Cranfill's Chronicle: A Story of Life in Texas* (New York: Fleming H. Revell, 1916), 22.

4. Olmsted, *A Journey through Texas*, 93, 244.

5. William B. Parker, *Notes Taken during the Expedition Commanded by Capt. R. B. Marcy, U.S.A., through Unexplored Texas, in the Summer and Fall of 1854* (Philadelphia: Hayes & Zell, 1856), 173.

6. Amelia Barr, *All the Days of My Life: An Autobiography* (New York: D. Appleton, 1913), 182–83.

7. Ibid., 184.

8. Anonymous, "Domenech's Missionary Adventures," *Eclectic Review* 4 (1858), 164–76, quotation on p. 164; Abbé Emmanuel Domenech, *Missionary Adventures in Texas and Mexico: A Personal Narrative of Six Years' Sojourn in Those Regions* (London: Longman, 1858).

9. George Parker Winship, *The Journey of Coronado, 1540–1542, from the City of Mexico to the Grand Canon of the Colorado and the Buffalo Plains of Texas, Kansas, and Nebraska* (New York: A. S. Barnes, 1904), 31, 78, 86, and 226.

10. Letter from Soloman Wiles to David Wiles, Brasses St. Iago, September 18, 1846; Fred Smoot, Collection of Les Royal Provenance, 1998, http://www.americawriteshome.us.

11. Elmer Kelton, *Sandhills Boy: The Winding Trail of a Texas Writer* (New York: Tom Dougherty Associates, 2007), 2.

12. "A Wild Woman," *New York Daily Tribune*, March 19, 1849; "The Wild Woman of the Navidad," *New York Tribune*, February 4, 1850.

13. "The Wild Man Again," *New York Daily Tribune*, April 12, 1856.

14. "Capture of a Wild Man in Missouri," *New York Daily Times*, March 27, 1857; "The Wild Woman of Texas," *Saturday Evening Post*, April 18, 1868; "A Wild Woman," *New York Daily Tribune*, July 27, 1869. Although reprinted in New York newspapers, these accounts were from local newspapers in Texas and Louisiana.

15. Details of farm practices can be found in C. Allen Jones, *Texas Roots: Agriculture and Rural Life before the Civil War* (College Station: Texas A&M University Press, 2005).

16. U.S. Census, 1860 and 1870, electronic data files, courtesy of http://www .socialexplorer.com.

17. *The Texas Almanac for 1867 with Statistics, Descriptive and Biographical Sketches, etc., Relating to Texas* (1867), 91, 112.

18. U.S. Census, 1860, electronic data file. The counties in Texas with water transportation were located on the Gulf of Mexico or along the Sabine River and Red River. There was no rail service in 1850, but by 1860 service was centered between Galveston and Houston, with lines running west of Houston into Fort Bend, Wharton, and Colorado Counties, and east through Liberty and Jefferson Counties. Oliver Jensen, *The American Heritage History of Railroads in America* (New York: American Heritage, 1975); and S. G. Reed, *A History of the Texas Railroads* (Houston: St. Clair, 1941), 15, 29.

19. "Interesting from Texas," *Augusta Chronicle*, October 3, 1842; "From Texas," *Baltimore Sun*, October 6, 1842.

20. "From Texas," *Baltimore Sun*, April 22, 1851.

21. Quoted in David G. McComb, *Galveston: A History* (Austin: University of Texas Press, 1986), 68.

22. "Texas," *Wooster Republican* (Ohio), June 29, 1854.

23. "Texas Items—Terrible Hurricane," *New York Herald*, May 26, 1856.

24. Philip Gildersleeve to Sylvester Gildersleeve, from Galveston, Texas, December 22, 1847, http://www.americawriteshome.us.

25. "Cholera in Texas," *Boston Evening Transcript*, May 31, 1849; "Ravages of Cholera," *Daily Ohio Statesman* (Columbus), April 19, 1849.

26. "Cholera in Texas," *Baltimore Sun*, August 23, 1850.

27. Electronic data file compiled by Robert W. Fogel and Stanley L. Engerman, *Mortality in the South, 1850* (Ann Arbor: Inter-University Consortium for Political and Social Research, 1976). Among white women in Texas ages 20 through 49 in 1850, 11.75 percent of deaths (47 out of 400) were the result of childbirth (cholera and unspecified fever, which accounted for 47 and 89 deaths, respectively, were the most common causes; U.S. Bureau of the Census, *Mortality Statistics of the Seventh Census of the United States, 1850* (Washington, DC: A.O.P. Nicholson, 1855), 274; see also Sally G. McMillen, *Motherhood in the Old South: Pregnancy, Childbirth, and Infant Rearing* (Baton Rouge: Louisiana State University Press,

1990); and Judith Walzer Leavitt, *Brought to Bed: Childbearing in America, 1750–1950* (New York: Oxford University Press, 1986).

28. "Obituary," *Houston Telegraph*, December 1, 1865; a brief biography of Captain Robert D. Goree is included in B. B. Paddock, *History and Biographical Record of North and West Texas*, vol. 1 (Chicago: Lewis, 1906), 455–56 (Paddock inaccurately states that Goree and Hayes were married in 1863 and that Hayes was his second wife). A brief account of the Battle of Pleasant Hill is included in Art Leatherwood, "Red River Campaign," *Handbook of Texas Online*, http://www.tshaonline.org/handbook/online; additional information is given in John D. Winters, *The Civil War in Louisiana* (Baton Rouge: Louisiana State University Press, 1963), and Alvin M. Josephy, *The Civil War in the American West* (New York: Knopf, 1991). A reference to the courtship of Robert Goree and Melissa Hayes appears in an 1861 letter from Thomas J. Goree to Robert in Thomas J. Cutrer, ed., *Longstreet's Aide: The Civil War Letters of Major Thomas J. Goree* (Charlottesville: University Press of Virginia, 1995), 63.

29. American Public Health Association, *Public Health Reports and Papers* (New York: Hurd and Houghton, 1875), 131.

30. "The Cholera in Texas," *Middletown Constitution* (Connecticut), April 21, 1852; "Cholera in Texas," *Baltimore Sun*, June 25, 1852.

31. "Yellow Fever Quarantine Regulations," *New York Weekly Herald*, September 3, 1853.

32. American Public Health Association, *Public Health Reports and Papers*, 439; "Ravages of the Yellow Fever in Louisiana and Texas," *Baltimore Sun*, September 19, 1867; statistics on yellow fever deaths in Galveston are from Homer S. Thrall, "Yellow Fever Epidemics," in *The People's Illustrated Almanac: Texas Hand-Book and Immigrant's Guide for 1880* (St. Louis: N. D. Thompson, 1880), 201. Livingston Lindsay to Governor Elisha Marshall Pease, October 9, 1867, describes the extent of deaths at La Grange; in Records of Elisha Marshall Pease, Texas Office of the Governor, Archives and Information Services Division, Texas State Library and Archives Commission, http://www.tsl.state.tx.us/governors. The Howard Association is described in Alwyn Barr, "The Other Texas: Charities and Community in the Lone Star State," *Southwestern Historical Quarterly* 97 (1993), 1–10.

33. "Wednesday Morning," *Flake's Bulletin* (Galveston), September 28, 1867.

34. "A Sad Party," *Flake's Bulletin*, September 18, 1867; additional details are included in T. A. McParlin, "Report of the Epidemic of Yellow Fever in New Orleans during 1867," War Department, Surgeon General's Office, *Report on Epidemic Cholera and Yellow Fever in the Army of the United States during the Year 1867* (Washington, DC: Government Printing Office, 1868), 108–12.

35. "Local Intelligence," *Flake's Bulletin*, August 14, 1867. The Wisconsin death was listed as Cora Ella Honey, age 38, but was undoubtedly Catherine Honey, the sister of George W. Honey, who was age 38 and was from Manitowoc County, Wisconsin, and for whom no other record exists after 1867. The likelihood of the reported name being inaccurate is reinforced by a note from the editor of *Flake's Bulletin* the previous day, August 13, 1867, stating, "Our city sexton is not skillful in either orthography or penmanship. His written names of the dead sometimes bear but a faint resemblance to the cognomens by which the living were recognized."

36. Barr, *All the Days of My Life*, 277.

37. Ibid., 283.

38. Robin W. Doughty, "Settlement and Environmental Change in Texas, 1820–1900," *Southwestern Historical Quarterly* 89 (1986), 423–42, quotation on p. 429.

39. Andrew Waters, *I was Born in Slavery: Personal Accounts of Slavery in Texas* (Winston-Salem, NC: John F. Blair, 2003), xii.

40. "Texas," *Semi-Weekly Telegraph* (Salt Lake City), April 2, 1866.

41. "Texas Items," *Flake's Bulletin*, September 21, 1867.

42. Major General Charles Griffin to Major General O. O. Howard, Galveston, July 1, 1867; reprinted in *Flake's Bulletin*, August 13, 1867.

43. William F. Fox, *Regimental Losses in the American Civil War, 1861–1865* (New York: Albany, 1889), http://www.perseus.tufts.edu. Union deaths from all causes including battle and disease were highest among soldiers from New York (46,534), Ohio (35,475), Illinois (34,834), Pennsylvania (33,183), and Indiana (26,672).

44. *Report of Special Committee on Lawlessness and Violence in Texas*, U.S. Senate, July 20, 1868; *Communication from Governor Pease of Texas Relative to the Troubles in That State*, U.S. House of Representatives, May 11, 1868; Barry A. Crouch, "A Spirit of Lawlessness: White Violence; Texas Blacks, 1865–1868," *Journal of Social History* 18 (1984), 217–32; Gregg Cantrell, "Racial Violence and Reconstruction Politics in Texas, 1867–1868," *Southwestern Historical Quarterly* 93 (1990), 333–55; Randolph B. Campbell, *A Southern Community in Crisis: Harrison County, Texas, 1850–1880* (Austin: Texas State Historical Association, 1983); "Official Statement," *Flake's Bulletin*, June 18, 1868; "Texas Items," *Flake's Bulletin*, May 8, 1868; "Crime in Texas," *Tri-Weekly Republican* (Austin), May 28, 1868.

45. "The Inquest on the Body of Major Lochman," *Flake's Bulletin,* January 16, 1870; "Leroy Cotton, *Flake's Bulletin*, April 9, 1870.

46. Alexis de Tocqueville, *Democracy in America* (New York: Harper & Row, 1966), 363.

47. Quoted in W. W. Hall, *Hall's Journal of Health* (New York: Russell Brothers, 1873), 285.

48. Benjamin H. Rutherford, "Emigration to Texas," reprinted from the *Macon Messenger* in the *Daily National Intelligencer* (Washington, DC), August 21, 1835.

49. Juan N. Almonte and C. E. Castaneda, "Statistical Report on Texas [1835]," *Southwestern Historical Quarterly* 28 (1925), 177–222; quotation on p. 211.

50. William Capers, "Itinerancy," *Democratic Telegraph and Texas Register* (Houston), December 4, 1847; reprinted in *Texas Presbyterian* 1 (February 26, 1848), 1.

51. The debate over the annexation of Texas is examined in considerable detail in Andreas V. Reichstein, *Rise of the Lone Star: The Making of Texas* (College Station: Texas A&M University Press, 1989). For an illuminating discussion at the time, see Alexander H. Everett, "A Letter on the Texas Question," *Democratic Review*, September 1844, http://www.archive.org.

52. "Our New Frontiers—Horrible Outrages—Texas," *New York Daily Tribune*, September 13, 1848.

53. In her fictional reconstruction of the letters and dialog of a German family newly arrived in Texas in 1847, writer Marj Gurasich expresses this sentiment: " 'I will not live like a heathen,' Mama declared for one and all to hear. 'We do not need to be uncivilized, just because we go to an uncivilized country.' " Marj Gurasich, *Letters to Oma: A Young German Girl's Account of Her First Years in Texas, 1847* (Fort Worth: Texas Christian University Press, 1989), 4.

54. A. Somerville, "Memoir of General Sidney Sherman," *Texas Almanac* (1858), 113–16, quotation on p. 114.

55. John Nicholson, "San Augustine," *Texas Almanac* (1859), 181.

56. "Robertson County," *Texas Almanac* (1860), 180.

57. Henry S. Randall, "Summer and Winter Management of Sheep in Texas," *Texas Almanac* (1861), 152–66, quotation on p. 162.

58. *Texas Almanac* (1867), 82, 97, 170.

59. "The Railroads of Texas, with Glimpses of the Country through Which They Pass," *Texas Almanac* (1868), 118–45, quotations on pp. 119 and 133.

60. U.S. Census, 1860, electronic data file, courtesy of the Inter-University Consortium for Political and Social Research, University of Michigan.

61. U.S. Census, 1860, electronic data file; the correlation refers to the relationship between the gender ratio in each county (of white males age fifteen and over to white females age fifteen and over) and the ratio of white children under age five to the number of white adults age fifteen and over in each county.

62. "Education," *San Antonio Express*, June 16, 1870.

63. Robert H. Williams, *With the Border Ruffians: Memories of the Far West, 1852–1868*, ed. E. W. Williams (London: John Murray, 1907), 229.

64. Estimated from the 1860 U.S. Census, 1 percent Public Use Microsample, electronic data file, courtesy of Steven J. Ruggles, Trend Alexander, Katie Genadek, Ronald Goeken, Matthew B. Schroeder, and Matthew Sobeck, *Integrated Public Use Microdata Series, Version 5.0* (Minneapolis: University of Minnesota, 2010).

65. *Constitution of the State of Texas* (Austin: Daily Republican Office, 1869), article 9, Public Schools.

66. Homer S. Thrall, "Education in Texas," *Texas Almanac for 1870 and Emigrant's Guide to Texas* (1870), 83–87, quotations on pp. 85 and 86.

67. "Report of Public Free Schools, State of Texas, for May 1872," *Texas Almanac* (1873), 23–24; U.S. Census, 1870, electronic data file, summarizing results at the state level from *Statistics of the Population of the United States* (Washington, DC: Government Printing Office, 1870), table 12, courtesy of the Inter-University Consortium for Political and Social Research, University of Michigan.

68. U.S. Census, 1870, and school data for Texas from *Texas Almanac*, 1873; the comparison mentioned represents the number of schools and teachers per 10,000 total population and the number of pupils per 1,000 population for each state, divided by the comparable rates for the United States. For example, the number of schools per 10,000 population in Texas was 19 and in the United States as a whole 37, meaning that the rate for Texas was 0.51 that of the rate for the United States. The comparable rate for George was 0.43, for Mississippi 0.51, Alabama 0.81, Minnesota 1.51. Iowa 1.71, and Nebraska 1.76. The rates for teachers ranged from 0.37 for Georgia and Mississippi and 0.40 for Texas to 1.37 for Iowa; and for pupils, from 0.28 and 0.30 in Georgia and Mississippi to 0.45 for Texas, to 0.97 for Iowa and 1.30 for Minnesota. The data reported in Texas for 1872 did not make possible a separate breakdown by race.

69. U.S. Census, 1860, electronic data file. For examples of statistics reporting "Negroes" alongside horses and cattle, see *Texas Almanac* (1858), 45–48, and (1863), 42–44.

70. Olmsted, *Journey through Texas*, 249, 245.

71. Letter from Frederick Law Olmsted to Edward Everett Hale, January 10, 1859, Kansas Memory Collection, Kansas State Historical Society, Topeka.

72. Tocqueville, *Democracy in America*, 360.

73. For example, "Freedom and Slavery Contrasted," *San Antonio Express*, September 12, 1867.

74. From the *Texas Vidette*, reprinted in *Flake's Bulletin*, May 30, 1868. On restrictive codes, see Barry A. Crouch, "'All the Vile Passions': The Texas Black Code of 1866," *Southwestern Historical Quarterly* 97 (1993), 12–34.

75. M. S. Munson, "Brazoria County," *Texas Almanac* (1867), 82–83.

76. F. Charles Hume, "Walker County," *Texas Almanac* (1867), 169–70.

77. Thrall, "Education in Texas," 83–84.

78. U.S. Census, 1870, electronic data file, courtesy of http://www.socialexplorer.com. Texas was similar to other southern states in this respect; for example, African Americans were 53 percent of the population in Georgia but only 14 percent of those in school, and 84 percent of those who could not write.

79. An insightful essay among a number that sought to sort out the various issues in conjunction with the presidential election of 1868 was "Mobs, Riots, Lynch Law, and Vigilance Committees," *Austin Republican*, October 20, 1868.

80. "Believe God," *Dallas Herald*, March 20, 1869.

81. Erika L. Murr, ed., *A Rebel Wife in Texas: The Diary and Letters of Elizabeth Scott Neblett, 1852-1864* (Baton Rouge: Louisiana State University Press, 2001), 34–35. Elizabeth Scott Neblett's diary and letters are also discussed in Drew Gilpin Faust, *Mothers of Invention: Women of the Slaveholding South in the American Civil War* (Chapel Hill: University of North Carolina Press, 1996), 47–48, 64–70, 124–26, 132, 139–40, and 248–49.

82. U.S. Census, 1850, electronic data file; the average number of residents per church in selected southern states was 561 in Alabama, 580 in Arkansas, 478 in Georgia, 532 in Kentucky, 597 in Mississippi, 486 in North Carolina, 566 in South Carolina, and 495 in Tennessee. On the influence of southern origins, see Homer L. Kerr, "Migration into Texas, 1860–1880," *Southwestern Historical Quarterly* 70 (October 1966), 184–216.

83. "Respect for Religion in Texas," *Cincinnati Journal*, April 1, 1837.

84. "Methodism in Texas," reprinted from the *New Orleans Picayune* in *Atkinson's Saturday Evening Post*, August 25, 1838; a report a year later suggested that Methodists in Texas included about 550 members at organized churches and as many as a thousand members total, "Spread of Methodism in Texas," *Baltimore Sun*, September 21, 1839; statistics collected in 1840 showed 1,623 white and 230 black Methodists in Texas, the largest concentrations being in San Augustine and Nacogdoches, served by 18 ordained preachers, "Methodist Church in Texas," *New York Spectator*, February 27, 1841.

85. Domenech, *Missionary Adventures*, 136–37.

86. "Domestic," *New York Observer and Chronicle*, August 17, 1854.

87. H. Bailey Carroll, "Texas Collection," *Southwestern Historical Quarterly* 50 (1946), 269–303.

88. Dubose Murphy, "Early Days of the Protestant Episcopal Church in Texas," *Southwestern Historical Quarterly* 34 (1931), 293–316.

89. R. L. Jones and Andrew Davis, "Folk Life in Early Texas: The Autobiography of Andrew Davis," *Southwestern Historical Quarterly* 43 (1939), 158–75.

90. David Rudd Hamerly, *Family Ancestry: Describing the Early Days of Our Country and the Pioneers Who Settled Tyler County, Texas* (2001), http://www.hamcomm.com.

91. *History of Rock Springs Church, Nacogdoches County, Texas* (1975), http://www.cumberland.org.

92. Benjamin Wilburn McDonnold, *History of the Cumberland Presbyterian Church* (Nashville, TN: Board of Publication of Cumberland Presbyterian Church, 1888), 264–65; Richard Beard, *Brief Biographical Sketches of Some of the Early Ministers of the Cumberland Presbyterian Church* (Nashville, TN: Cumberland Presbyterian Board of Publication, 1874), 377.

93. Guy Steeley, *The Modern Elocutionist or Popular Speaker: A Manual of Instruction on Cultivation of the Voice, Gesticulation, Expression, Posing, Etc.* (Chicago: Thompson & Thomas, 1900), 215–18; P. T. Winskill, *The Temperance Movement and Its Workers: A Record of Social, Moral, Religious, and Political Progress*, vol. 3 (London: Blackie & Son, 1892), 51–53. Attacks at camp meetings in other states include one recorded by Frederick Douglass in Indiana in 1843, discussed in Connie A. Miller Sr., *Frederick Douglass: American Hero and International Icon of the Nineteenth Century* (New York: Xlibris, 2008), 92; also of interest are Louis Fairchild, *The Lonesome Plains: Death and Revival on an American Frontier* (College Station: Texas A&M University Press, 2002), 138, who asserts that "camp meetings were dogged by disorder—immorality, rowdiness, and brawling," and Dickson D. Bruce Jr., *And They All Sang Hallelujah: Plain-Folk Camp-Meeting Religion, 1800–1845* (Knoxville: University of Tennessee Press, 1981).

94. Domenech, *Missionary Adventures*, 134, gives an account of Hiram Chamberlin's difficulties; the woman quoted is from Helen Chapman, *The News from Brownsville: Helen Chapman's Letters from the Texas Military Frontier, 1848–1852*, ed. Caleb Coker (Denton: Texas State Historical Association, 1992), 175; the other quote is from Samuel Peter Heintzelman, *Fifty Miles and a Fight: Major Samuel Peter Heintzelman's Journal of Texas and the Cortina War*, ed. Jerry Thompson (Denton: Texas State Historical Association, 1998), 203.

95. "Translation of 1847 Letter by Charles W. Presler from Texas to His Family in Germany," *Family Footsteps* (Comal County Genealogy Society, Comal, Texas), March 1986, 2–8, and June 1986, 83–94; http://www.ccgstexas.org.

96. Olmsted, *Journey through Texas*, 77.

97. A. Stevens, "Texas Mission," *Western Christian Advocate*, August 23, 1839.

98. Olmsted, *Journey through Texas*, 85.

99. Taking account of county differences in population, there was a strong correlation between the two. Where there were more Methodist churches, there were also more Baptist churches. With county-level data from the 1860 U.S. Census and taking account of total population per county, the standardized ordinary least squares regression coefficient for the

relationship of Baptist churches to Methodist churches was 0.583 and the relationship of Baptist accommodations (seating capacity) to Methodist accommodations was 0.512, both significant beyond the 0.001 level of probability.

100. Elizabeth Oliphint, "Martha's Chapel Methodist Church," in *Huntsville and Walker County, Texas: A Bicentennial History*, ed. D'Anne McAdams Crews (Huntsville, TX: Sam Houston State University Press, 1976), 335–41, based on the writer's account of stories from her grandparents who attended the church in the 1850s.

101. Murr, *A Rebel Wife in Texas*, 64, 133, 137.

102. J. J. Head, Lola Winters Head, and Lucy Alice Bruce Stewart, "The Black Jack Methodist Church, Cemetery, and School," in *Huntsville and Walker County, Texas: A Bicentennial History*, 435–38, quotation on pp. 436–37.

103. Langston James Goree V, ed., *The Thomas Jewett Goree Letters*, vol. 1: *The Civil War Correspondence* (Bryan, TX: Family History Foundation, 1981), 14.

104. Ibid.

105. Opal McAdams Samuel, "The Walker County Community of McAdams, Texas," in *Huntsville and Walker County, Texas: A Bicentennial History*, 391–92.

106. Domenech, *Missionary Adventures*, 138.

107. U.S. Census, 1860, electronic data file; with Texas counties as the unit of analysis and controlling for the number of white adults age fifteen and over, the standardized ordinary least squares regression coefficient for the effect of a higher male to female ratio on the number of churches is –0.301.

108. Ibid.; with Texas counties as the unit of analysis and controlling for total population, the standardized ordinary least squares regression coefficient for percentage of population that were slaves on number of churches is 0.153, significant at the 0.05 level.

109. U.S. Census, 1870, electronic data file for states and counties.

110. Ibid., 1 percent Public Use Microsample, electronic data file.

111. "Action of the Bishops," *Houston Telegraph*, July 14, 1865.

112. J. O. Andrew, R. Paine, and G. F. Pierce, "Address of the Southern Methodist Bishops," August 17, 1865, Columbus, Georgia, reprinted in *Houston Telegraph*, September 4, 1865.

113. Quoted in "Editorial," *Houston Telegraph*, September 7, 1865.

114. "The Murdered Methodist Clergyman," *Daily Citizen and News* (Lowell, Mass.), September 7, 1860; "Attempted Insurrection," *Clarksville Standard* (Texas), June 8, 1861.

115. An extensive treatment of clergy perspectives is found in Harry S. Stout, *Upon the Altar of the Nation: A Moral History of the Civil War* (New York: Penguin, 2006).

116. T. B. Wilson, "A Sermon," May 12, 1861, reprinted in *Dallas Herald*, June 12, 1861.

117. "Sermon," *Dallas Herald*, August 21, 1861.

118. "Education of Disabled Soldiers and the Children of Deceased Soldiers," *Houston Telegraph*, January 27, 1864.

119. "Letter from John Clabaugh," *Houston Telegraph*, October 16, 1863.

120. Quoted in Paul Harvey, "'Yankee Faith' and Southern Redemption: White Southern Baptist Ministers, 1850–1890," in *Religion and the American Civil War*, ed. Randall M. Miller, Harry S. Stout, and Charles Reagan Wilson (New York: Oxford University Press, 1998), 167–86, quotation on p. 173.

121. By 1871 northern Methodists nevertheless felt that inroads were being made, with eighteen preachers and nearly eight thousand members in Texas; "The M. E. Church in Texas," *Christian Advocate*, January 5, 1871.

122. "Texas Items," *Flake's Bulletin*, December 22, 1869; "The Houston Murder," *Galveston Tri-Weekly News*, December 17, 1869; "Letter from Houston," *Galveston Tri-Weekly News*, December 20, 1869.

123. "The Gallows," *Houston Telegraph*, August 12, 1870. The most complete account of the case is reported in E. M. Wheelock, *Reports of Cases Argued and Decided in the Supreme Court of the State of Texas*, vol. 33 (Austin: Tracy, Siemering, 1872), 570–83.

124. "Capital Punishment in Texas," *Flake's Bulletin*, April 3, 1868.

125. "Too Many Hangmen," *Flake's Bulletin*, February 16, 1868; "Sam Johnson," *Flake's Bulletin*, March 4, 1868; "The Death Penalty," *Flake's Bulletin*, July 9, 1870.

126. "The Execution," *Houston Transcript*, April 4, 1868.

127. "The Execution," *Flake's Bulletin*, August 10, 1870; "Execution of Jake Johnson for the Murder of B. W. Loveland," *Houston Telegraph*, August 10, 1870;

128. "The Loveland Assassination Horror," *Houston Union*, February 24, 1870; additional exonerating detail, including the fact that Michau sold Bibles, is included in "The Case of Dr. M. M. Michau, Charged with the Assassination of B. W. Loveland," *Houston Union*, February 26, 1870.

129. "Execution of Jake Johnson," *Houston Telegraph*, August 10, 1870.

130. W. H. Logan, "Progress of Negro Churches in Houston since Emancipation or the Civil War," in *Red Book of Houston: A Compendium of Social, Professional, Religious, Educational and Industrial Interests of Houston's Colored Population* (Houston: Sotex, 1915), 21–23. The neighborhood context of the church is briefly described in Cary D. Wintz, "The Emergence of a Black Neighborhood: Houston's Fourth Ward, 1865–1915," in *Urban Texas: Politics and Development*, ed. Char Miller and Heywood T. Sanders (College Station: Texas A&M University Press, 1990), 97–100.

131. "Loyal League of Harris County," *Houston Union*, March 5, 1869; "Texas Items," *Flake's Bulletin*, June 9, 1869. *Proceedings of the City Council*, Houston, Texas, January 5, 1870, September 8, 1870, and December 29, 1870, show Parker as alderman of the third ward and in that capacity as a member of the Committee on Streets and Bridges. *Proceedings*, February 9, 1871, notes that Parker is removed and lists A. C. Rogers as third ward alderman. On the pigs in the street charge, see "Recorder's Court," *Houston Union*, June 9, 1871.

132. Federal Census of 1860, Manitowoc County, Wisconsin, p. 257. Information about the chair-making business in Two Rivers founded by George Honey's father, who was killed in 1868, is presented in Arthur H. Lohman, "Early Days in Two Rivers, Wisconsin, 1848–1900," *Manitowoc County Historical Society Occupational Monograph 50* (1983), 1–12, reprinted from an essay originally written in 1909, in which Lohman states that George W. Honey currently holds a government position in Washington, DC; courtesy of the Manitowoc County Historical Society. Other evidence, though, indicates that he died May 5, 1906. Material from the Wisconsin Veterans Museum in Madison, Wisconsin, indicates that the Fourth Cavalry in which Honey served was positioned in Louisiana from 1862 through 1865, when it was transferred to the Rio Grande area in Texas, and was disbanded in Milwaukee on June 14,

1866. Delegates including Honey from Galveston and Parker from Houston are listed in "The Convention at Houston," *Flake's Bulletin*, July 20, 1867. Statements by Honey and Parker are included in "Radical Republican Meeting," *Flake's Bulletin*, October 19, 1867. A speech given by Honey at the "colored Baptist" church in Galveston is described in "Local News," *Flake's Bulletin*, November 24, 1869; another account is given in "Republican Nominations at Galveston," *Houston Union*, November 24, 1869. Honey's campaign appearances are also mentioned in "Political Items from *Houston Union*," *San Antonio Express*, November 19, 1869. Additional biographical information is included in untitled articles in *Flake's Bulletin*, March 31, 1869; and *Houston Union*, June 30, 1869. Minutes of the meeting attended by Parker and at which Honey served as secretary and declined nomination for state treasurer are in "Republican State Convention: Official Proceedings," *Houston Union*, June 9, 1869. In Harris County, Honey received 1,412 votes, giving him a 61 percent majority; "Election Returns," *Houston Union*, December 9, 1869. He also polled especially well in Galveston County; "Returns from Galveston County," *Flake's Bulletin*, December 8, 1869.

133. "The Tale of a Chaplain," *Pomeroy's Democrat* (Chicago), November 10, 1869; references to the accusations in *Pomeroy's Democrat* appeared in the campaign rhetoric of Honey's opponents and in newspapers opposed to the Radical Republican ticket, for example, *Brenham Banner*, December 1, 1869. Historians now remember Honey as one of several northern carpetbaggers to hold public office in Texas during Reconstruction; see James Alex Baggett, "Origins of Early Texas Republican Party Leadership," *Journal of Southern History* 40 (1974), 441–54; Carl H. Moneyhon, *Republicanism in Reconstruction Texas* (Austin: University of Texas Press, 1980); Moneyhon, "Carpetbaggers," *Handbook of Texas Online*, http://www .tshaonline.org; Randolph B. Campbell, "Grass Roots Reconstruction: The Personnel of County Government in Texas, 1865–1876," *Journal of Southern History* 58 (1992), 99–116; Campbell, "Carpetbagger Rule in Reconstruction Texas: An Enduring Myth," *Southwestern Historical Quarterly* 97 (1994), 587–96; and Campbell, *Grass Roots Reconstruction in Texas, 1865–1880* (Baton Rouge: Louisiana State University Press, 1998).

134. "Hon. Geo. W. Honey," *Houston Daily Union*, December 20, 1870; "Editorial Paragraphs," *Flake's Bulletin*, June 9, 1870; "Letter from Austin," *Galveston Tri-Weekly News*, September 7, 1870; "Dangerous Accident," *Houston Daily Union*, September 7, 1870.

135. "Northern Papers Please Copy," *Flake's Bulletin*, May 1, 1869.

136. "Phillip Nickel," in *A Biographical History of Central Kansas*, vol. 2 (Chicago: Lewis, 1902), 1074, courtesy of Allen County Public Library, Fort Wayne, Indiana; and "Marriage Licenses," http://skyways.lib.ks.us. Details of the circumstances surrounding Honey's dismissal from office and subsequent reinstatement are in A. C. Freeman, ed., *The American Decisions Containing the Cases of General Value and Authority Decided in the Courts of the Several States*, vol. 83 (San Francisco: Bancroft-Whitney, 1887), 376–77; James R. Norvell, "The Reconstruction Courts of Texas, 1867–1873," *Southwestern Historical Quarterly* 62 (1958), 141–63; and William C. Nunn, *Texas Under the Carpetbaggers* (Austin: University of Texas Press, 1962). In 1875 Honey was listed in the Business Directory for Bastrop County compiled from the *Bastrop Advertiser* as the proprietor in Austin of Raymond House.

137. Baggett, "Origins of Early Texas Republican Party Leadership"; *Brenham Banner*, reprinted in "Texas Items," *Galveston Tri-Weekly News*, October 15, 1869; "General A. J.

Hamilton," *Flake's Bulletin*, March 2, 1870; "Latest News," *Dallas Weekly Herald*, March 28, 1874. Among white clergy from the North, an instructive example was Reverend Joseph C. Hartzell, a Methodist pastor in New Orleans with whom Honey was acquainted and corresponded. Hartzell avoided the maelstrom of Reconstruction politics by refraining from running for elected office himself, but he observed that several lay members of his congregation had done so only to find themselves wrongly accused of various misdeeds and irregularities; see Anne C. Loveland, "The 'Southern Work' of Reverend Joseph C. Hartzell, Pastor of Ames Church in New Orleans, 1870–1873," *Louisiana History* 16 (1975), 391–407. Other examples are given in Ralph E. Morrow, *Northern Methodism and Reconstruction* (East Lansing: Michigan State University Press, 1956). At the 1867 Republican Convention in Houston, another African American pastor, identified only as Brother J. Campbell from Houston, was present and delivered a prayer on the second day of the meeting. "Brother Campbell is very illiterate, but a shrewd colored preacher," the correspondent wrote. "His running comments showed more than ordinary penetration, and although exceedingly funny, were entirely free from any element of the ridiculous." Later in the proceedings an exchange between Campbell and Governor Pease occurs in which Pease states that "Every man who is assaulted must resist, being careful not to assault anybody else," and Campbell asks, "'Spose they draws the big revolver?" The correspondent then observes that "The Governor was floored, and Brother C's question still waits an answer." "The Convention at Houston," *Flake's Bulletin*, July 10, 1867.

138. "House of Representatives," *Dallas Weekly Herald*, June 25, 1870.

139. "Local News," *Flake's Bulletin*, November 24, 1869.

140. Murr, *Rebel Wife in Texas*, 65, 114.

141. "The Rough Country," *Philadelphia Inquirer*, August 28, 1867, reprinted from the *Indianapolis Journal*.

CHAPTER 2
FOR THE ADVANCE OF CIVILIZATION

1. Martha Ann Nolley Otey Papers, Mississippi Department of Archives and History, Jackson, Mississippi, 1866; Barbara J. Rozek, *Come to Texas: Attracting Immigrants, 1865–1915* (College Station: Texas A&M University Press, 2003), 99; Henri Gerard Noordberg, "The Yellow Fever Epidemic of 1867 at Huntsville," in *Huntsville and Walker County, Texas: A Bicentennial History*, ed. D'Anne McAdams Crews (Huntsville, TX: Sam Houston State University Press, 1976), 209–33.

2. "Andrew Female College," *Handbook of Texas Online*, http://www.tshaonline.org/handbook/online.

3. "Local Intelligence," *Flake's Bulletin*, August 14, 1867. "Sheriff Dierks, accompanied by deputies W. Corbett, Henry Painter and Barnes Nugent, left this morning for Huntsville in charge of the following prisoners, who are sentenced for the terms affixed to their names: Charles Oneil, 3 years; James Burns, 4 years; John Curby, 2 years; James McCanna, 3 years; Michael Matterson, 2 years and 6 months; John Clark, 3 years; Charles Smith, colored, 2 years." And in another item: "Two of the prisoners in the jail, John Holland, sentenced for

nine years, and a man named Pratt for three years have the fever. The whole jail is being white-washed and purified."

4. Noordberg, "The Yellow Fever Epidemic," 231; George Robinson, "Huntsville's Great Yellow Fever Epidemic of 1867," in *Huntsville and Walker County, Texas*, 237–47; "The Epidemic," *Flake's Bulletin*, September 22, 1867; "The Fever at Huntsville," *Flake's Bulletin*, September 9, 1867; "Yellow Fever at Huntsville," *Dallas Weekly Herald*, October 12, 1867.

5. Macum Phelan, *A History of the Expansion of Methodism in Texas, 1867 to 1902* (Dallas: Mathis, Van Nort, 1937), 6.

6. Noordberg, "Yellow Fever Epidemic," 221, 225.

7. Ibid., 229–30.

8. Ibid. Otey's notes indicate that she may have translated Sturm's verse, which had been published in 1854, from a French version, although an English translation had been published as "I Hold Still," *The Advent Review and Sabbath Herald* 7 (December 4, 1855), 1. The translation was included in Mary Wilder Tileston, *Hymns of Comfort* (Boston: Roberts Brothers, 1877), 222; it was incorporated at some point into the Methodist hymnal, was printed in the *New York Times*, June 11, 1898, under the title of "God's Anvil," and was quoted frequently by Charles H. Spurgeon, to whom it was sometimes attributed.

9. John W. Thomason Jr., "Huntsville," in *Huntsville and Walker County, Texas*, 5–15.

10. "Letter from Huntsville," *Houston Union*, March 17, 1869.

11. The quote is from an anonymous letter from Huntsville to the *Houston Daily Union*, December 8, 1871; details of the Huntsville troubles were reported in "Trouble at Huntsville," *Houston Daily Union*, January 16, 1871; "The Huntsville Riot," *Houston Daily Union*, January 24, 1871; "The Huntsville Difficulty," *Galveston Tri-Weekly News*, January 25, 1871; "Communication from Governor Davis," *Houston Daily Union*, February 16, 1871; "Complete Official History of the Troubles in Hill and Walker Counties," *Houston Daily Union*, February 16, 1871; "The Huntsville Assassins," *Houston Daily Union*, February 1, 1871; "Letter from Judge Burnett," *Houston Daily Union*, February 16, 1871; "Committee of the Legislature," *Houston Daily Union*, February 17, 1871; "From Huntsville," *Galveston Tri-Weekly News*, March 1, 1871; "The Huntsville Affair Once More," *Galveston Tri-Weekly News*, March 8, 1871; "From Huntsville," *Galveston Tri-Weekly News*, March 17, 1871.

12. For an interesting view of the "military despotism" that many Texans considered as having been imposed during Reconstruction, see John Henry Brown, *History of Dallas County, Texas: From 1837 to 1887* (Dallas: Milligan, Cornett & Farnham, 1887), 104.

13. "Letter from Governor Edmund J. Davis to President U. S. Grant," February 24, 1870, published as "The Situation in Texas," *New York Times*, March 14, 1870; and "Message of Gov. Davis to the New Legislature," *New York Times*, May 8, 1870; "Texas News and Views," *Houston Daily Union*, March 12, 1870. An engaging firsthand account of conditions in West Texas is given in "Narrative of the First Trip from San Antonio, Texas, to El Paso, Mexico," *Appleton's Journal of Literature, Science and Art* 4 (December 17, 1870), 738

14. "The Proposed Partition of Texas," *Chicago Tribune*, March 17, 1870; the proposal was introduced by Senator Jacob M. Howard of Michigan; "Texas Items," *Galveston Tri-Weekly News*, March 14, 1870.

15. "Letter from a Huntsville Lady," *Houston Daily Union*, April 10, 1871.

16. A brief biographical sketch and photograph of Louisa Blanche Murrell Richardson is included in Elizabeth Brooks, *Prominent Women of Texas* (Akron, OH: Werner, 1896), 47–48.

17. A. Ray Stephens, "Letter from the Texas Secession Convention, 1861: Willard Richardson to George Ware Fulton," *Southwestern Historical Quarterly* 65 (1962), 394–96; Randolph Lewis, "Richardson, Willard," *Handbook of Texas Online*, http://www.tshaonline.org/handbook/online; Marilyn M. Sibley, *Lone Stars and State Gazettes: Texas Newspapers before the Civil War* (College Station: Texas A&M University Press, 1983).

18. Willard Richardson, "Forward, Let Us Range," *Galveston Tri-Weekly News*, August 16, 1869.

19. Willard Richardson, "Morality and Something Else," *Galveston Tri-Weekly News*, July 12, 1869.

20. Alexis de Tocqueville, *Democracy in America* (New York: Harper & Row, 1966), 525.

21. Willard Richardson, "Our Ordeal," *Galveston Tri-Weekly News*, May 9, 1870; further discussion of views similar to Richardson's is given in Billy D. Ledbetter, "White Texans' Attitudes toward the Political Equality of Negroes, 1865–1870," *Phylon* 40 (1979), 253–63.

22. Charles Darwin, *On the Origin of Species by Means of Natural Selection, or the Preservation of Favoured Races in the Struggle for Life* (London: John Murray, 1859).

23. Willard Richardson, "The Race Question," *Galveston Tri-Weekly*, March 28, 1870.

24. Willard Richardson, "Behind the Veil," *Galveston Tri-Weekly News*, August 27, 1869 (the correction of the typographical error that appeared in the title of this essay is mine); a similar expression of religious tolerance appeared in "Political Intolerance—Clannishness and Prejudice," *Houston Daily Union*, July 15, 1969, in which an anonymous writer asked, "If my neighbor happens to be a Catholic and I a Protestant, is that a reason we should not agree upon other questions?"

25. A thorough treatment of religious understandings of commonsense morality, including a discussion of how race complicated these understandings, is presented in Mark A. Noll, *America's God: From Jonathan Edwards to Abraham Lincoln* (New York: Oxford University Press, 2002).

26. Letter from James Burke to E. C. Delavan, July 20, 1840; letter from E. Richardson to E. C. Delavan, July 30, 1840, reprinted in *Journal of the American Temperance Union* 4 (1840), 156–57; "Reasons for a General Law for the Suppression of Intemperance," *Journal of the American Temperance Union* 4 (1840), 29.

27. "Drunkenness Incurable," *Houston Daily Union*, July 2, 1869; "Brother John on Dancing," *Flake's Bulletin*, March 23, 1870; "Whirlagig Methodists," *Flake's Bulletin*, May 8, 1870; "Unappreciated Merit," *Houston Daily Union*, January 6, 1871; "Temperance Family Visitor," *Galveston Tri-Weekly News*, January 9, 1871; "Selling Liquor on Sunday," *Houston Daily Union*, May 4, 1871; "Temperance Reform," *San Antonio Express*, June 23, 1871; "Houston County," *Galveston Weekly News*, March 26, 1877. Although mostly devoted to prohibition efforts in the 1880s, some background that emphasizes ambivalence toward temperance in the 1870s is included in James D. Ivy, *No Saloon in the Valley: The Southern Strategy of Texas Prohibitionists in the 1880s* (Waco, TX: Baylor University Press, 2003), 1–18.

28. "Public Amusements and Religion," *Galveston Tri-Weekly News*, April 26, 1871; and a related discussion about dancing, "Worldly Amusements," *Flake's Bulletin*, July 13, 1870.

29. For example, a bill was introduced to the legislature in 1873 with the support of numerous temperance councils for passage of a stringent liquor law; "Telegraphic from Austin," *Galveston Tri-Weekly News*, March 7, 1873.

30. Letter from Clarence Ousley to Governor Oscar B. Colquitt, September 19, 1910, Texas Office of the Governor, Archives and Information Services Division, Texas State Library and Archives Commission. In response to local option, six drugstores, one with a ten-pin alley, opened almost immediately in Greenville, Hunt County; "Local Option," *Dallas Weekly Herald*, October 27, 1877. An interesting later discussion of blind tigers appears in "The Druggist's License," *Dallas Morning News*, June 10, 1897.

31. "Letter from Austin," *Houston Daily Union*, February 16, 1871.

32. "Our Lady Correspondent," *Houston Daily Union*, February 28, 1871.

33. W. E. Dodge, "On Temperance," *Galveston Weekly News*, March 12, 1877.

34. "The State Capital," *Galveston Weekly News*, March 7, 1877; "Local Option Elections," *Galveston Weekly News*, March 19, 1877; "Negroes Elevated over Foreigners," *Galveston Tri-Weekly News*, March 8, 1872; "Ghosts in the Third Ward," *Houston Daily Union*, April 21, 1871. Black voting and the primary issues under consideration in 1876 are discussed in Patrick G. Williams, "Of Rutabagas and Redeemers: Rethinking the Texas Constitution of 1876," *Southwestern Historical Quarterly* 106 (2002), 230–53.

35. James D. Ivy, "'The Lone Star State Surrenders to a Lone Woman': Frances Willard's Forgotten 1882 Texas Temperance Tour," *Southwestern Historical Quarterly* 102 (1998), 44–61.

36. For example, W. D. Jackson of Waco, who was nominated by prohibitionists for state treasurer, was described as a leading member of the Methodist Episcopal Church; "The Texas Prohibitionists," *Atlanta Constitution*, September 14, 1886.

37. "The Big Baptist Meeting," *Dallas Morning News*, July 2, 1886.

38. Cranfill edited the Waco *Advance* in 1886 and 1887; he was ordained as a Baptist minister in 1890 and in 1892 was the Prohibition Party's nominee for vice president; Travis L. Summerlin, "Cranfill, James Britton Buchanan Boone," *Texas Handbook Online*, http://www.tshaonline.org; J. B. Cranfill, *Dr. J. B. Cranfill's Chronicle: A Story of Life in Texas* (New York: Fleming H. Revell, 1916); a reference to the debate in which B. H. Carroll took part appears in his obituary, "Pioneer Minister of Waco Is Dead," *Waco Times Herald*, November 11, 1914.

39. "Prohibition Meeting," *Dallas Morning News*, March 1, 1887; in a letter critical of Reasoner, Judge Barnett Gibbs of Dallas complained that "a Kansas preacher opened the campaign in a Dallas church in behalf of the prohibitionists of the state [and] that the speech was political, although delivered in the church and interspersed with prayer and the singing of hymns, and that this was a new character of campaigning in the South," "Hon. Barnett Gibbs to Rev. Calvin Reasoner," *Dallas Morning News*, March 23, 1887. The text of an antiprohibition lecture by Gibbs is printed in "Mr. Gibbs on Prohibition," *Dallas Morning News*, March 20, 1887.

40. Vincent W. Grubbs, *Practical Prohibition* (Greenville, TX: T. C. Johnson, 1887), 378; "The Divided Prohibitionists," *Dallas Morning News*, September 26, 1886; "Prohibition in Texas," *New York Tribune*, July 30, 1887.

41. "Gibbs Answered: Speech of Hon. W. Poindexter," *Dallas Herald*, June 4, 1887; "Speech of Hon. R. Q. Mills," *Dallas Morning News*, May 29, 1887.

42. "The Prohibition Campaign," *Dallas Morning News*, July 29, 1887.

43. Results from ordinary least squares regression analysis for the number of yes votes in the 182 counties in which votes were cast in 1887, controlling for estimated total population in 1887 (based on a linear interpolation from 1880 and 1890 census data) and total votes cast: standardized regression coefficients for estimated black population in 1887, −0.150, significant at the 0.001 level; Catholic membership, −0.103, significant at the 0.001 level; white Baptist membership, 0.088, significant at the 0.06 level; and white Methodist membership, 0.245, significant at the 0.001 level. When Baptist and Methodist memberships were entered separately in models to test for collinearity, both remained significant, with the Methodist coefficient of 0.283 stronger than the Baptist coefficient of 0.178. Variables tested that were not significant included urban population (in places of 2,500 or more), number of towns per county, and number of incorporated towns per county. Value of real estate per county was negatively related to voting for the amendment, but this effect was not significant in models including the urban population variable. The prohibition vote per county was coded from *The Cyclopedia of Temperance and Prohibition* (New York: Funk and Wagnalls, 1891), 113; other variables are from U.S. Census, 1880 and 1890, electronic data files.

44. K. Austin Kerr, "Prohibition," *Texas Handbook Online*, http://www.tshaonline.org; and on subsequent efforts, Lewis L. Gould, *Progressives and Prohibitionists: Texas Democrats in the Wilson Era* (Austin: University of Texas Press, 1973); Larry Jerome Watson, "Evangelical Protestants and the Prohibition Movement in Texas, 1887–1919" (PhD diss., Texas A&M University, 1993), notes several factors contributing to the failure of the 1887 prohibition amendment, including divisions among Baptists and Methodists about the appropriateness of government regulation.

45. John N. Edwards, *Biography, Memoirs, Reminiscences and Recollections* (Kansas City, MO: Jennie Edwards, 1889), 87.

46. "The Social Evil," *Circular* 6 (August 23, 1869), 183. Studies of the history of prostitution in Texas include David C. Humphrey, "Prostitution in Texas," *Texas Handbook Online* (2004), http://www.tshaonline.org; David C. Humphrey, "Prostitution and Public Policy in Austin, Texas, 1870–1915," *Southwestern Historical Quarterly* 86 (1983), 473–516; Anne M. Butler, *Daughters of Joy, Sisters of Misery: Prostitutes in the American West, 1865–90* (Urbana: University of Illinois Press, 1985); and David G. McComb, *Spare Time in Texas: Recreation and History in the Lone Star State* (Austin: University of Texas Press, 2008).

47. Homer S. Thrall, "The Baptists of Texas and Other Religious Faiths," in *The People's Illustrated Almanac: Texas Hand-Book and Immigrant's Guide for 1880* (St. Louis: N. D. Thompson, 1880), 79–82.

48. U.S. Census, 1880, electronic data files for population from http://www.socialexplorer.com, and for occupations by state from the Inter-University Consortium for Political and Social Research; approximately 900 clergy had been recorded in the 1870 census, or 1 for every 913 residents. The number of residents per clergyperson in 1880 in other southern states ranged from 825 in Kentucky and 830 in Tennessee, to 854 in Arkansas and 855 in South Carolina, to 868 in Mississippi, 883 in Georgia, and 1,103 in Louisiana.

49. "Texas Letter," *Augustana Journal* 5 (August 2, 1897), 6, from a pastor in Austin identified only by the initials G. A. D.

50. James Milton Carroll, *Texas Baptist Statistics, 1895* (Dallas: Baptist General Convention of Texas, Texas Baptist Historical Committee, 1985).

51. Ibid., 98.

52. These figures are drawn from my analysis of an electronic data file created from the statistics compiled in 1985 by Carroll.

53. Irene Taylor Allen, *Saga of Anderson: The Proud Story of a Historic Texas Community* (New York: Greenwich, 1957), 101–6.

54. J. M. Dawson, *A Thousand Months to Remember: An Autobiography* (Waco: Baylor University Press, 1964), 23. Details about population and church membership are from Rand McNally maps and Carroll, *Texas Baptist Statistics.*

55. Dawson, *A Thousand Months to Remember*, 33.

56. "A Sermon to Business Men," *Dallas Morning News*, March 11, 1889.

57. Bill Stein, *Consider the Lily: The Ungilded History of Colorado County, Texas* (Columbus, TX: Nesbitt Memorial Library, 1999), http://www.library.columbustexas.net/history /part9.htm.

58. "Attempted Outrage," *Dallas Morning News*, June 8, 1888.

59. "Dastardly Outrage," *Dallas Morning News*, March 27, 1886.

60. "Attempted Outrage," *Dallas Morning News*, July 6, 1886.

61. "A Negro Butchered," *Atlanta Constitution*, December 9, 1886; "Hung Up by Their Queues," *Atlanta Constitution*, December 1, 1886.

62. "Domestic," *Daily Inter Ocean* (Chicago), March 5, 1887.

63. "The Outrage at the Park," *Dallas Morning News*, October 4, 1887; "A Couple More Arrests," *Dallas Herald*, October 22, 1887.

64. "Texas 'Leading Citizens' Horrible Deed," *Pall Mall Gazette* (London), February 22, 1892; "Horrible Lynching of a Negro," *Daily Inter Ocean* (Chicago), February 21, 1892. Texarkana on both sides of the state line had a population of just over 6,000 at the time; Bowie County had a population of approximately 20,000.

65. "An Outrage," *Dallas Morning News*, March 19, 1886.

66. "Attempted Outrage," *Dallas Morning News*, June 2, 1889.

67. "Still another Outrage," *Dallas Herald*, June 28, 1890.

68. "San Antonio Outrage," *Dallas Herald*, June 11, 1887.

69. "Evangelist Dixon," *Dallas Morning News*, September 30, 1890.

70. "Texarkana," *St. Louis Republic*, March 3, 1892.

71. "Help for Texarkana," *St. Louis Republic*, February 23, 1892.

72. Frederick Eby, *Education in Texas* (Austin: University of Texas Bulletin, 1918), 927–28.

73. Oscar H. Cooper, *Sixth Biennial Report of the Superintendent of Public Instruction for the scholastic Years Ending August 31, 1887, and July 1, 1888* (Austin: Texas Department of Education, 1888), 21–18, quotation on p. 22.

74. *Historical and Statistical Data as to Education in Texas* (Austin: Texas Department of Education, 1921), 199.

75. Ibid., 198; Eby, *Education in Texas*, 931.

76. U.S. Census, 1900, Texas counties, electronic data file.

77. U.S. Census, 1900, Public Use Microsample, electronic data file.

78. *Historical and Statistical Data as to Education in Texas*, 83, 205–9.

79. Brief histories of these and other colleges and universities are available at *Texas Handbook Online*, http://www.tshaonline.org.

80. U.S. Census, *Statistical Abstract* (Washington, DC: Government Printing Office, 1901), 431–34; and *Statistical Abstract* (Washington, DC: Government Printing Office, 1920), 126–28; for other colleges, including ones that did not survive, a useful source is J. J. Lane, *History of Education in Texas* (Washington, DC: Government Printing Office, 1903).

81. Quoted in Lane, *History of Education in Texas*, 325.

82. Charles Chamberlain McNeill, "Young Men's Christian Association," *University of Texas Record* 9 (1909), 104–5.

83. John Koren, *Benevolent Institutions* (Washington, DC: Government Printing Office, 1904), 9–54.

84. Ibid., 304.

85. Ibid., 210.

86. Ibid., 292.

87. Ibid., 260.

88. Ibid., 15, 18.

89. William E. Stone, C. Calvin McAdams, and Johanna Kollert, "Early Prisoners of the Texas Department of Corrections," in *Huntsville and Walker County, Texas*, 187–88; and Don Reid Jr., "The Texas State Prison Has Been in Huntsville a Long Time," in ibid., 191–97.

90. Ollie Mae Rogers, "The Cozy Corner," *Dallas Morning News*, January 10, 1897.

91. Mary West, "The Cozy Corner," *Dallas Morning News*, January 26, 1896; she was from Honey Grove. The Cozy Corner was edited by suffragist Sara Isadore Sutherland Callaway, who grew up in Michigan and Ohio, published two children's books in 1890, and in 1893 joined the *Dallas Morning News* as society editor. Although many of the letters published from children such as the two quoted here appear to have been written by children, some very likely were not. For example, a letter from Albert C. Adams (*Dallas Morning News*, May 24, 1896) discussed how "Adam and Eve sinned and were expelled from the Garden of Eden," how "Ham because he was disrespectful to his father was turned black," and "the wonderful miracles Christ performed" as well as his "death and glorious resurrection," and ended, "I am not quite 9 years old."

92. Quoted in William Seneca Sutton, "The Significance of Christian Education in the Twentieth Century," *University of Texas Record* 9 (1909), 263–76, quotation on p. 274; Sutton's essay was the text of his commencement address at Texas Christian University.

93. Henry Cohen, "Introduction and Biography," in *Memorial Volume: Leo N. Levi*, ed. John Hay and Joseph Hirsh (Chicago: Hamburger Printing, 1905), 12–15.

94. Leo N. Levi, "The Successful Life," *University of Texas Record* 1 (1899), 191–202, quotations on pp. 196–98.

95. Levi, "Let Woman Witness," in *Memorial Volume*, 134–41, quotation on p. 135.

96. George T. Winston, "The Education of Women in the University of Texas," *University of Texas Record* 1 (1898), 1–10, quotation on p. 8.

97. U.S. Census Bureau, *Religious Bodies, 1916: Part I: Summary and General Tables* (Washington, DC: Government Printing Office, 1919), table 62, p. 224.

98. Data from the 1890 U.S. Census indicated that 31 percent of the African American population in Texas were members of predominantly African American denominations, while the 1916 Religious Bodies data showed that 49.9 percent were; there was, however, considerable change in the denominations from which data were collected, suggesting that the figures reported were not entirely comparable. The valuable in-depth examination of institutional growth among African American churches in the Mississippi delta area from Reconstruction to World War I in John M. Giggie, *After Redemption: Jim Crow and the Transformation of African American Religion in the Delta, 1875–1915* (New York: Oxford University Press, 2008), describes the role of clergy, lay leaders, and related social factors such as the growth of newspapers and railroads that undoubtedly were taking place in East Texas as well.

99. "Doings of Gay Society, the Closing Days of Repentance in Dallas," *Dallas Morning News*, April 29, 1889.

100. Mary Bowen Pearson, ed., *Evangelistic Sermons by the Rev. R. G. Pearson* (Richmond, VA: Richmond Press, 1915); "The Evangelist Pearson," *Charlotte News* (North Carolina), January 10, 1889; "Evangelist Williams," *Dallas Morning News*, March 17, 1890; "Evangelist Williams," *Dallas Morning News*, March 18, 1890; "The Stingy Brother," *Dallas Morning News*, March 26, 1890; "Sam Jones Aftermath," *Dallas Morning News*, April 7, 1890.

101. U.S. Census, 1910, electronic data file for states, courtesy of the Inter-University Consortium for Political and Social Research.

102. U.S. Census, 1920, electronic data file for states.

103. Quoted in Cutrer, *Longstreet's Aide*, 11.

104. Frank W. Johnson, *A History of Texas and Texans*, vol. 4 (Chicago: American Historical Society, 1914), 2000; 1880 and 1910 U.S. Censuses, Public Use Microsamples, electronic data files; courtesy of Steven Ruggles, J. Trent Alexander, Katie Genadek, Ronald Goeken, Matthew B. Schroeder, and Matthew Sobek, *Integrated Public Use Microdata Series, Version 5.0* (Minneapolis: University of Minnesota, 2010).

105. Crews, *Huntsville and Walker County, Texas*, 300; in 1928 she ran unsuccessfully for the U.S. Senate, receiving support from Franklin Roosevelt and the daughter of Woodrow Wilson, "Wilson's Daughter Aids Campaign of Mrs. Cunningham," *Dallas Morning News*, July 20, 1928.

106. The role of institutions in shaping understandings of the self and of individual responsibility in the professions has been emphasized in John W. Meyer, "The Effects of Education as an Institution," *American Journal of Sociology* 86 (1977), 340–63; Meyer, "Self and Life Course: Institutionalization and Its Effects," in *Institutional Structure: Constituting State, Society, and the Individual*, ed. George M. Thomas, John W. Meyer, Francisco O. Ramirez, and John Boli (Newbury Park, CA: Sage, 1987), 242–60; Randall Collins, *The Credential Society: A Historical Sociology of Education and Stratification* (New York: Academic Press, 1979); and with emphasis on the state as a source of understandings of individuality in Reinhard Bendix, *Nation-Building and Citizenship* (New York: Wiley, 1964). On the professions, see especially Eliot Freidson, *Professionalism: The Third Logic* (Chicago: University of Chicago Press, 2001); and Magali Sarfatti Larson, *The Rise of Professionalism: A Sociological Analysis* (Berkeley: University of California Press, 1977).

107. "Texas Is Maligned," *Dallas Morning News*, April 15, 1895; "Bloodhounds Guard Texas Convicts," *Idaho Register* (Idaho Falls), December 25, 1896.

108. "Prison Reform in Texas," *Dallas Morning News*, December 19, 1897; "Observations in the Penitentiary," *Dallas Morning News*, May 28, 1899. Over the next decade advocacy for more humane treatment, on the one hand, and for harsher punishment and better security, on the other hand, continued with revelations about a plot to blow up the Huntsville prison, various escapes, and allegations of abuse on prison farms; "Plot at Huntsville," *Dallas Morning News*, September 10, 1903; "The Texas Prison Probe," *Daily Picayune* (New Orleans), July 23, 1909; "Whole Case Hinges on Process of Law," *Dallas Morning News*, January 28, 1911.

109. "King Martin Hanged," *Dallas Morning News*, March 17, 1900.

110. "Two Pay Penalty in Electric Chair," *Dallas Morning News*, September 1, 1922.

111. "Death Chair Being Installed in Prison," *Dallas Morning News*, July 23, 1923.

112. On discussions in the state legislature and the desire to hold executions locally, see "House Finally Passes Electrocution Bill," *Dallas Morning News*, March 9, 1923; "Electrocution Is Urged by Thomas," *Dallas Morning News,* April 18, 1923; and on details of electrocution, "Tommie Curry Dies in Electric Chair," *Dallas Morning News*, April 18, 1924. Huntsville penitentiary commissioner H. L. McKnight exhibited a miniature of the electric chair and explained how it works at public meetings including at least one at Baptist church, "Miniature Electric Chair Shown at Nacogdoches," *Dallas Morning News*, July 9, 1924.

113. Data for the number of towns, population in 1890, post offices, and railroad stops are from an electronic data file I created from information included in *The New 11 14 Atlas of the World* (Chicago: Rand McNally, 1895), and from online information from the Mardos Memorial Library of Online Books and Maps posted by Pam Rietsch at http://www.livgenmi.com.

114. Information for business and service establishments in Huntsville and Hallettsville is from Digital Sanborn Maps, 1891 and 1912, courtesy of Firestone Library, Princeton University.

CHAPTER 3
WITH LIBERTY OF CONSCIENCE

1. George W. Truett, "Baptists and Religious Liberty," May 16, 1920, http://www.biblebelievers.com.

2. Jean Jacques Rousseau, *The Social Contract and Discourse on the Origin and Foundation of Inequality among Mankind*, ed. Lester G. Crocker (New York: Washington Square Press, 1967), 136–47.

3. "Civil Religion in America," reprinted in Robert N. Bellah, *Beyond Belief: Essays on Religion in a Post-Traditional World* (New York: Harper & Row, 1970), 168–89; and elaborated in Bellah, *The Broken Covenant: American Civil Religion in Time of Trial* (New York: Seabury Press, 1975).

4. "The Declaration of Independence, March 2, 1836," *Telegraph and Texas Register* (Austin), March 12, 1836.

5. An anonymous writer in the *New Orleans Bulletin*, as quoted in the *New Hampshire Gazette* (Portsmouth), May 10, 1836; other comments are included in an untitled essay in the *Houston Telegraph*, September 27, 1836, and in James W. Robinson, "The General Council of the Provisional Government of Texas to the People of Mexico," *Telegraph and Texas Register*, January 2, 1836.

6. "Speech of Colonel Juan N. Seguin," *Houston Telegraph*, March 28, 1837.

7. "Dr. R. F. Brenham's Address," *Austin City Gazette*, May 13, 1840, italics in the original.

8. David S. Kaufman, "Address to the Austin Masonic Lodge," *Austin City Gazette*, January 13, 1841. Kaufman was a Princeton graduate from Pennsylvania who moved to Nacogdoches, Texas, in 1837, served as a member of the Texas House of Representatives from 1838 to 1843, and was a U.S. congressman from 1846 to 1851; Natalie Ornish, "Kaufman, David Spangler," *Handbook of Texas Online*, http://www.tshaonline.org.

9. The inscription is quoted in an article from the *New Orleans Picayune*, December 2, 1843, and reprinted in the *Boston Evening Transcript*, December 15, 1843; a subsequent reference describing the monument's location at the Texas State House appears in "The Heroes of the Alamo," *Charleston Mercury* (South Carolina), November 9, 1859; a chronology of what could be pieced together from other sources about the monument is found in C. W. Raines, "The Alamo Monument," *Quarterly of the Texas State Historical Association* 6 (1903), 300–310.

10. "The Defense of the Alamo in 1836," *Mississippi Free Trader* (Natchez), August 18, 1847; also included as "The Defense of the Alamo in 1836," *Littell's Living Age* 11 (1846), 175–77.

11. "Sam Houston and His Republic," *Kalamazoo Gazette*, September 10, 1847; reprinted from Charles Edwards Lester, *Sam Houston and His Republic* (New York: Burgess, Stringer, 1846), 79.

12. Examples include "Notes from My Knapsack," *Putnam's Monthly* 3 (February 1854), 170–80; "The Fall of the Alamo," *Daily Alta California* (San Francisco), October 4, 1857; William Ross Hartpence, *History of the Fifty-First Indiana Veteran Volunteer Infantry* (Cincinnati: Robert Clarke, 1894), 344–46. A rather different account that deals with the events and decisions involved is given in Sam Houston, "Campaign of 1836 and Its Termination in the Battle of San Jacinto," Speech to the United States Senate, February 28, 1859, reprinted in *Texas Almanac* (1860), 18–35.

13. "Evangelical Religion in Texas," *New York Observer and Chronicle*, September 18, 1856; on the contrast with Mexico of particular interest are "Yucatan," *The Civilian and Galveston Gazette*, December 9, 1843; "How to Conquer Mexico," *Red Lander* (San Augustine, Texas), July 31, 1847; and "What Shall Be Done with Mexico?" *Texas Union* (San Augustine, Texas), November 13, 1847. Despite negative views toward Roman Catholics in Mexico, Democratic Party leaders in Texas argued on principle against the Know Nothing Party, for example, "The Canvass," *Texas State Gazette* (Austin), June 23, 1855.

14. Homer S. Thrall, *History of Methodism in Texas* (Houston: E. H. Cushing, 1872), 27.

15. Many accounts of Baylor's career are available, for example, B. F. Riley, *History of the Baptists in Texas* (Dallas: B. F. Riley, 1907).

506

16. Article 1, sections 4 and 6, *Constitution of the State of Texas Adopted by the Constitutional Convention Begun and Held at the City of Austin on the Sixth Day of September 1875* (Austin: State of Texas, 1877), 2; Texas Constitutional Convention, *Journal of the Constitutional Convention of the State of Texas* (Galveston: News Office, 1875), 118.

17. "Why Colquitt Is Not Klansman," *Dallas Morning News*, March 5, 1922; on Galveston Methodist Church issue, see "Colquitt Defies Church," *New York Times*, May 29, 1911.

18. "Spiritualist Asks Fair Play," *Dallas Morning News*, December 8, 1912.

19. Reverend George Gilmour, "Religion and Our Mothers," *Dallas Morning News*, May 13, 1912.

20. Charles P. Johnson, "The Youth and Young Man," in *J. Howard Williams: Prophet of God and Friend of Man*, ed. H. C. Brown Jr. and Charles P. Johnson (San Antonio: Naylor, 1963), 1–7, quotation on p. 7.

21. Rev. A. E. Ewell as quoted in "Jesus' Interpretation of Second Command Was Pastor's Subject," *Daily Enterprise* (Beaumont), February 6, 1911.

22. "A Vexatious Scarecrow," *Fort Worth Star Telegram*, February 22, 1914.

23. Rev. John G. Slayter, pastor of the East Dallas Christian Church, as quoted in "Urges Preparedness to Maintain Our Ideals," *Dallas Morning News*, January 26, 1916.

24. J. B. Cranfill, "Jewish Citizenship Worthy of Praise," *Dallas Morning News*, October 30, 1923.

25. Quoted in Irving Louis Horowitz, *C. Wright Mills: An American Utopia* (New York: Free Press, 1983), 16, who argues that the University of Texas provided a stimulating intellectual environment for Mills in the 1930s but was an uncomfortable setting as well because of its "legacy of a rural South [and] an anti-Darwinian intellectual environment dominated by religious fundamentalism." A sympathetic view of the regents' action is given in W. S. Red, "On Austin College and Religious Liberty," *Dallas Morning News*, November 1, 1923, who argues that infidels live as laws unto themselves, whereas "liberty is living according to rightful authority [as understood by] those who believe in God as a Supreme Being and Ruler of the Universe."

26. Quoted in "A Bit of History Repeating Itself," *Dallas Morning News*, September 21, 1892; from David Crockett, *A Narrative of the Life of David Crockett of the State of Tennessee* (Philadelphia: Cary, Hart, 1834), 210.

27. Riley, *History of the Baptists of Texas*, 405.

28. "Churches of Waco and McLennan County," in *The Immigrant's Guide to Waco and McClennan County, Texas* (Waco: Waco Immigration Society, 1884), 32.

29. According to the Dallas city directory as reported in "State Focus of Religion," *Dallas Morning News*, January 27, 1890.

30. "The Churches of Dallas," *Dallas Morning News*, December 19 and 26, 1886.

31. "Baptists' Convention," *Dallas Morning News*, May 10, 1890.

32. Examples of these activities are included in "Texas Baptist Affairs," *Christian Index* 61 (April 5, 1883), 4; and "Texas," *Christian Index* 79 (February 23, 1899), 5.

33. Frank W. Johnson, *A History of Texas and Texans*, vol. 3 (Chicago: American Historical Society, 1914), 1789.

34. Brian Hart, "Wharton, Turner Ashby," *Handbook of Texas Online*, http://www.tshaonline.org; other examples included Reverend William M. Anderson of Dallas, Reverend

Robert Hill of Dallas, Reverend F. E. Fincher of Houston, and Reverend Arthur F. Bishop of Austin, all with doctoral degrees.

35. First United Methodist Church, *Church at the Crossroads: A History of First United Methodist Church Dallas* (Dallas: UMR Communications, 1997), 84–85; "Mr. Knickerbocker Has Undertaken Big Task," *Dallas Morning News*, January 17, 1913.

36. A brief account of his work is given in "Buckner, Friend of Orphans," *Fort Worth Star Telegram*, April 9, 1919; his work is described in detail in Karen O'Dell Bullock, "The Life and Contributions of Robert Cooke Buckner: Progenitor of Organized Social Christianity among Texas Baptists, 1860–1919" (PhD diss., Southwestern Baptist Theological Seminary, 1991).

37. David J. Murrah, *C. C. Slaughter: Rancher, Banker, Baptist* (Austin: University of Texas Press, 1981).

38. An example of these arguments occurs in discussions at Belton, as reported in "The State Press," *Dallas Morning News*, February 8, 1889. Dallas clergy periodically campaigned against Sunday theatrical performances, for example, "Texas News in Brief," *Daily Picayune*, December 1, 1907.

39. Bullock, *Life and Contributions of Robert Cooke Buckner*, 192.

40. An example of children's homes and night schools was the work initiated in Dallas at St. Matthew's Cathedral by Episcopal rector Hudson Stuck, David Bean, *Breaking the Trail: Hudson Stuck of Texas and Alaska* (Athens: Ohio University Press, 1988).

41. "Morning Session of Baptists," *Dallas Morning News*, November 14, 1908; Bullock, *Life and Contributions of Robert Cooke Buckner*, 178–79; the sanitarium, which became Baylor Hospital, opened as " modern, scientific institution where the sick may get the benefit of the highest medical and hospital advantages" as opposed to being a boarding house for the sick, "People and Places: Gazetteer of Hamilton, County, Texas," http://freepages.genealogy .rootsweb.ancestry.com/_gazetter2000; see also photos at http://media.baylorhealth.com.

42. "Endeavorers Hear Reports of Work," *Dallas Morning News*, June 10, 1910; letter from Christian Endeavor Secretary Charles Cotty to Senator Robert E. Cofer, August 5, 1910, printed in *Journal of the Senate of Texas: Third and Fourth Called Sessions of the Thirty-First Legislature* (Austin: Von Boeckmann-Jones, 1910), 70–71.

43. "Pleads for Justice to Convicted Men," *Dallas Morning News*, February 14, 1913; and Maud Ballington Booth, *After Prison—What?* (New York: Fleming H. Revell, 1903), 58, in which she wrote, "Christian life must be an earnest warfare of watchful struggle in which every faculty of the man is sincerely engaged," and included numerous examples of Christian charity and conversion.

44. "Insane Increase Is Over 400 Per Cent," *Fort Worth Star Telegram*, January 25, 1909.

45. "Sermon by Rev. George Truett," *Dallas Morning News*, January 3, 1910.

46. E. G. Senter, "Remarks by Senator Senter on Bank Guaranty Bills," *Journal of the Senate of Texas: First Called Session of the Thirty-First Legislature* (Austin: Von Boeckmann-Jones, 1909), 227–44, quotation on p. 241. Insight into Senter's religious views is to be found in a lengthy letter about prohibition, "Mr. Senter Answers Dr. Cranfill's Letter," *Dallas Morning News*, February 23, 1908, in which Senter states, "My mother was a shouting Methodist and with a zeal that thrilled and burned until her white hairs were laid away in the grave she taught as only may be taught in the life of a Christian woman the living religion of a

living Christ. From her and from the itinerant ministers whose devout and stern gospel was preached in the country churches which I attended in childhood came the ideas of religion which I could no more shake off than I could cast away physical form and feature."

47. First United Methodist Church, *Church at the Crossroads*, 101.

48. Ordinary least squares regression analysis of county variations in the 1911 prohibition vote yielded the following results for the percentage voting *against* the measure; Model 1: standardized regression coefficients of 0.164, 0.409, and 0.439 for percent of population in urban areas of 2,500 or more in 2010, percent African American, and percent Mexican American, all significant at or beyond the 0.01 level of probability; Model 2: 0.238, 0.068, 0.599, and 0.559, for the previous three variables plus the voter turnout rate in 1911, all significant at or beyond the 0.01 level of probability except for percent African American, which was not significant; Model 3: 0.131, 0.026, 0.370, 0.437, and −0.430, for the previous variables plus dry on local option in 1910, all significant at the 0.01 level except for African American; Model 4: 0.038, 0.057, 0.296, 0.267, −0.328, 0.230, −0.127, and −0.095 for the preceding variables plus percent Roman Catholic in 1906, percent Southern Baptist in 1906, and percent Southern Methodist in 1906, with percent Catholic significant at the 0.001 level and percent Baptist and Methodist significant at the 0.05 level; in a final model that did not include the dry local option variable, the coefficients for the religion variables were 0.292, −0.227, and −0.174, respectively. The adjusted R square for Model 4 was 0.616. Population density per square mile was significant in zero-order correlations but not when percent urban was included in models. Mexican American was defined as the percentage of total population in each county in 1910 who were born in Mexico or whose mother and/or father was not native born and was not born in any of the European counties listed in the data (this measure yielded a total number similar to that provided for the state in the 1910 1 percent Public Use Microsample data). Voter turnout was measured as the total vote cast in 1911 divided by the total number of eligible white male voters in 1910. The dry on local option measure was coded from data included in the *Dallas Morning News*, July 13, 1911, and coded as "2" if the county was dry, "1" if the county was partly dry, and "0" if the county was wet. Percent Roman Catholic was the number of Roman Catholics (adults and baptized children) divided by the total church membership as recorded in the 1906 Census of Religious Bodies. Percent Methodist was the number of members of the Methodist Episcopal Church South divided by the total number of Protestant members. Percent Southern Baptist as previously noted was estimated by adjusting the number reported, which included both white and black Baptists, with data from the 1916 Census of Religious Bodies and then dividing by the total number of Protestant members.

49. For an example of a Sunday evening sermon at a Baptist church about prohibition, see "Preaches Sermon on the Saloonkeeper," *Dallas Morning News*, March 6, 1911.

50. George C. Rankin, *The Story of My Life: More than a Half Century as I Have Lived It and Seen It Lived* (Dallas: Press of the Home and State, 1912), 320.

51. Ibid., 335.

52. Sam Hanna Acheson, *Joe Bailey: The Last Democrat* (New York: Macmillan, 1932).

53. William A. Cocke, *The Bailey Controversy in Texas with Lessons from the Political Life-Story of a Fallen Idol* (San Antonio: Cocke, 1908), 83, 107.

54. Ibid., 108; "Severe on Bailey," *Dallas Morning News*, December 14, 1906.

55. "Saloon Not Real Issue," *Dallas Morning News*, April 22, 1911.

56. Rev. G. W. Eichelberger quoted in "To Work for Resubmission," *Dallas Morning News*, September 19, 1911.

57. "Baptist Resolution on Liquor Traffic," *Dallas Morning News*, November 28, 1913; see also "Dr. Gambrell Writes on Power of Saloon," *Dallas Morning News*, May 21, 1911. Gambrell became professor of Christian ethics and pastoral theology at Southwestern Baptist Theological Seminary in 1912 and had previously served as editor of the *Baptist Standard*; Eugene Coke Routh, *The Life Story of Dr. J. B. Gambrell* (Dallas: Baptist Book Store, 1929).

58. "Over Two Hundred Saloons in City," *Dallas Morning News*, October 1, 1911.

59. "Church Will Not Seek Injunction against Saloon," *Fort Worth Star Telegram*, September 13, 1911.

60. "Saloon Permit Delayed," *Dallas Morning News*, July 7, 1911; this was a case in Columbus in Colorado County.

61. "Salvation Army Defies Ban Placed on Saloon Soliciting," *Fort Worth Star Telegram*, June 3, 1913.

62. See, for example, "Anti-Saloon League Will Meet in Waco," *Dallas Morning News*, January 4, 1915, in which the state convention of the Anti-Saloon League of Texas was described by its leaders as being held at the First Baptist Church in Waco.

63. "Negro Prohibitionists Issue Statement," *Daily Enterprise* (Beaumont), January 1, 1911.

64. "Father Murphy Speaks to Crowd in Keith Park," *Beaumont Journal*, May 26, 1911.

65. Examples can be found in "Methodist Pastor Tells Why He Is Opposed to Liquor Traffic," *Daily Enterprise*, March 13, 1911.

66. Rev. J. W. Moore quoted in ibid.

67. "Saloon Business Is Lawful, Says Pastor," *Dallas Morning News*, March 22, 1915.

68. "Complete Election Returns on Constitutional Amendments," *Dallas Morning News*, June 15, 1919.

69. Whereas more than 467,000 voted in 1911, fewer than 298,000 did in 1919; controlling for percent urban in 1910, percent black in 1910, percent Mexican American in 1910, and turnout in 1911, the relationship between percentage voting for Prohibition in 1911 and percentage voting for Prohibition in 1919 was 0.855; not controlling for the 1911 vote, the effect of percent Catholic in 1916 was −0.269, percent Southern Baptist in 1916 was 0.218, and percent Methodist in 1916 was 0.207, all significant at or beyond the 0.01 level of probability. These results at the county level are from an electronic data file I created from the results reported in the *Dallas Morning News*, June 15, 1919.

70. "Dr. Barton Resigns Place with Anti-Saloon League," *Dallas Morning News*, August 31, 1918; Barton had served as superintendent of the Anti-Saloon League of Texas.

71. Martin's letter, additional correspondence, and Martin's lengthy reply to Roosevelt were published in Texas after the election in "Explains Inquiry on Taft's Religion," *Dallas Morning News*, December 21, 1908.

72. "Is Taft an Atheist?" *Fort Worth Star Telegram*, August 1, 1908.

73. "Texas Association Clashes with President over Taft," *Fort Worth Star Telegram*, November 9, 1908.

74. "Taft's Election Is an Insult," *Fort Worth Star Telegram*, November 11, 1908.

75. "Bryan Will Farm Rio Grande Soil," *Fort Worth Star-Telegram*, June 19, 1910.

76. These results are from an analysis of the Pearson correlation coefficients for 222 Texas counties in which votes were cast in the 1908 presidential election and with religion data from the 1906 U.S. Census of Religious Bodies. The religious bodies data recorded the number of Roman Catholics as reported by church officials, which included all baptized adults and children in each county. The Methodist figures are for members of the Methodist Episcopal Church South. The Baptist data reported in 1906 combined the membership of white Southern Baptist congregations with that of black National Baptist congregations. To derive an estimate of the white Southern Baptist membership, the ratio of the two denominations that were reported separately in the 1916 data was used to adjust the 1906 data. The resulting estimate for total white Southern Baptists was 236,000, which corresponded well with the figure of 220,000 reported by the denomination in 1899. In interpreting county-level comparisons, caution is required because of the potential for ecological fallacies; for instance, the fact that Catholic counties voted for Taft does not necessarily mean that it was Catholics in those counties who did so.

77. Quoted in "Important from Texas," *Fincastle Mirror* (Virginia), October 29, 1824.

78. Carlos E. Castaneda, "Earliest Catholic Activities in Texas," *Catholic Historical Review* 17 (1931), 278–95.

79. A.A. Lambing, "Scenes from the Texas Mission of Half a Century Ago," *American Catholic Historical Researches* 3 (1887), 2–12, quotations on p. 2.

80. James Talmadge Moore, *Through Fire and Flood: The Catholic Church in Frontier Texas, 1836–1900* (College Station: Texas A&M University Press, 1992); Franklin C. Williams Jr., *Lone Star Bishops: The Roman Catholic Hierarchy in Texas* (Waco, TX: Texian Press, 1997). Jay P. Dolan and Gilberto Hinojosa, *Mexican Americans and the Catholic Church, 1900–1965* (Notre Dame, IN: University of Notre Dame Press, 1994), 21, observe that selecting Galveston as the seat of the diocese instead of San Antonio where a large population of Mexican American Catholics lived was an indication of the church's pattern of treating Mexican Americans as second-class citizens.

81. Linda Simpson, "Churches and Missionaries," *TXGenWeb Project*, http://www.txgenwebproject.

82. U.S. Census, 1870, electronic data file.

83. Thomas Coke and Francis Asbury, *The Doctrines and Discipline of the Methodist Episcopal Church in America with Explanatory Notes* (Philadelphia: Henry Tuckness, 1798), 18–21.

84. Edmund S. Morgan, *Roger Williams: The Church and the State* (New York: Norton, 1967), 137.

85. U.S. Census, 1890, electronic data file; a measure of skewness, which estimates the extent to which a distribution deviates from a normal curve, provides a statistical indication of how the Mexican-born and Catholic population compared with other ethnic and religious groups. In 1890 the skewness coefficient for the distribution among Texas counties was 1.836 for total population, 2.086 for white population, and 1.775 for African American population, but 5.843 for Mexican American population; for Catholics it was 4.639, which compared with 1.715 for Southern Baptists and 1.837 for white Methodists.

86. U.S. Census of Religious Bodies, 1916, electronic data file; the skewness coefficient for the distribution of the Catholic population across counties was 6.533 in 1916, compared with 2.58 among Southern Baptists and 2.781 among white Methodists.

87. In 1910 the total population of Texas was 3.9 million, of whom 3.2 million were white and 690,000 were black. The Mexican-born population had increased to 124,238. In addition there were 89,244 native-born Texans whose parents were foreign born but not included in any of the European countries about which questions were asked. That these parents were likely to have been from Mexico is indicated by the very high correlation (0.939) at the county level between numbers of Mexican-born residents and numbers of native-born residents with foreign parents from "other" countries. In addition to those born in Mexico, there were among the native born approximately 104,000 whose mother, father, or both mother and father had been born in Mexico, meaning that about 6 percent of the Texas population was either born in Mexico or of Mexican ancestry. That compared to 18 percent of the population that was black, leaving approximately 76 percent of the population as white Anglo. There were thirteen counties in which persons of Mexican ancestry made up at least 40 percent of the population.

88. Presnall H. Wood, "History of the Texas *Baptist Standard*, 1888–1959" (PhD diss., Southwestern Baptist Theological Seminary, 1964), 237.

89. "Church-State Pact Decried by Truett," *Dallas Morning News*, May 19, 1924.

90. "Southern Baptists Score Taft's Action," *Dallas Morning News*, May 21, 1912.

91. "Defines Attitude upon Church Union," *Dallas Morning News*, November 23, 1913.

92. "Dr. J. B. Cranfill's Chronicle," *Dallas Morning News*, August 15, 1920.

93. "The State Press," *Dallas Morning News*, August 14, 1920.

94. "More Charges Are Made by Ferguson," *Dallas Morning News*, August 10, 1922; "Knickerbocker Praises Klan in Speech for Mayfield," *Fort Worth Star Telegram*, August 16, 1922.

95. "Bishop Mouzon Will Not Vote for Smith," *Dallas Morning News*, July 27, 1927.

96. "Church Groups Put Dry Law before Party," *Christian Science Monitor*, November 26, 1927.

97. J. W. Neathery, "Thinks Smith Will Win for Democrats," *Dallas Morning News*, December 7, 1927.

98. Isaiah 9.16 quoted in W. H. Kittrell Sr., "Ministers Forget to 'Preach the Gospel,'" *Dallas Morning News*, December 7, 1927.

99. "Heflin Dares His Colleagues to Rebuke Him," *Dallas Morning News*, January 24, 1928.

100. "Dry Dems Open War on Smith," *Dallas Morning News*, March 5, 1928.

101. "About 'Religious Test' Clause in Constitution," *Dallas Morning News*, May 23, 1928; "Letters from Readers," *Dallas Morning News*, June 8, 1928.

102. "The Democrats to Texas," *Chicago Daily Tribune*, January 14, 1928.

103. "Robinson's Reference to Religion Starts Fists Flying in Convention," *Dallas Morning News*, June 28, 1928.

104. "Resolution against Nominee," *Dallas Morning News*, July 4, 1928.

105. "W.C.T.U." Fights Smith," *Dallas Morning News*, July 4, 1928.

106. "Bishop Moore Says He Will Oppose Smith," *Dallas Morning News*, July 13, 1928; "'Solid South' Is Organizing Against Smith," *Christian Science Monitor*, July 9, 1928.

107. "Anti–Al Smith Group Makes Campaign Plan, *Dallas Morning News*, July 18, 1928.

108. "Smith Foes Organize in Fort Worth," *Dallas Morning News*, July 14, 1928.

109. "Three Objections to Smith Told in Sermon," *Dallas Morning News*, July 16, 1928.

110. Quoted in Norman D. Brown, *Hood, Bonnet, and the Little Brown Jug: Texas Politics, 1921–1928* (College Station: Texas A&M University Press, 1984), 412.

111. In ordinary least squares regression models for the percent of voters in 1928 who voted for Al Smith in Texas counties in which the percent of population in 1920 living in towns of 2,500 or more and the percent of 1920 population that was African American were controlled, the standardized coefficient for percent of total church members that was Catholic in 1926 was 0.227 (significant at or beyond the 0.001 level of probability); for percent of total Protestants who were Southern Baptist in 1926, −0.147 (significant at the 0.05 level); and for percent of total Protestants who were Methodists, −0.119 (significant at the .06 level). With percent voting for Prohibition in 1911 in the model, the coefficient for Catholics was 0.014 (not significant); for Baptists, was −0.081 (not significant); and for Methodists, −0.177 (significant at the 0.01 level).

112. William F. Ogburn and Nell Snow Talbot, "A Measurement of the Factors in the Presidential Election of 1928," *Social Forces* 8 (1929), 175–83, examining zero order correlations for counties in eight states in the north and west concluded similarly that Prohibition and religion were factors and that the former was probably a more direct factor than the latter.

113. Milt Saul, "Connally Says 'Want to Nail' False Charges," *Dallas Morning News*, August 18, 1928. The Methodist pastor was J. W. Hunt of Abilene, who favored Earle B. Mayfield against Tom Connally; Mayfield drew strong support from Protestant clergy because of his support of Prohibition; Connally had joined his wife's Methodist church soon after they were married.

CHAPTER 4
THE FUNDAMENTALIST BELT

1. "Oh, Yeah," *Chicago Daily Tribune*, November 21, 1930.

2. "Gov. Moody Evens Score in Hot Reply to Chicago Paper on Texas and Chicago Thugs," *Mexia Weekly Herald*, November 28, 1930.

3. "A Few Kind Words from Hoodlumtown," *Galveston Daily News*, November 23, 1930.

4. Willie Morris, *North Toward Home* (New York: Vintage Books, 2000), and especially Morris, "A Word in Defense of Texas," *New York Times*, April 5, 1964; on Mills, see Irving Louis Horowitz, *C. Wright Mills: An American Utopian* (New York: Simon and Schuster, 1985), 16.

5. A useful discussion of the general historiography of southern fundamentalism is found in Helen Lee Turner, "Fundamentalism in the Southern Baptist Convention: The Crystallization of a Millennialist Vision" (PhD diss., University of Virginia, Charlottesville, 1990).

6. U.S. Bureau of the Census, *Statistical Abstract* (Washington, DC: Government Printing Office, 1931), 298.

7. Ibid., 802.

8. U.S. Censuses of Religious Bodies, 1916 and 1926, electronic data files; the number of Southern Baptists grew from 354,313 in 1916 to 465,274 in 1926, and the number of southern Methodists from 316,812 to 380,444.

9. Rufus C. Burleson quoted in "Dissensions at Dallas," *Galveston Weekly News*, March 4, 1880.

10. "Texas Church Scandal," *St. Louis Post Dispatch*, May 26, 1889.

11. Joseph E. Early Jr., *A Texas Baptist Power Struggle: The Hayden Controversy* (Denton: University of North Texas Press, 2005), 51–53.

12. Ibid., 54–55.

13. J. B. Cranfill, "Religious Intelligence: New Things among Southern Baptists," *The Independent* 49 (December 16, 1897), 15. Cranfill edited the *Texas Baptist Standard* and noted that Martinism was being promulgated by a rival newspaper.

14. J. M. Dawson, *A Thousand Months to Remember* (Waco, TX: Baylor University Press, 1964), 94–95.

15. J. B. Gambrell, "The Growing of a Great Religious Paper," *Baptist Standard* (April 25, 1907), 1.

16. Presnall H. Wood, "History of the Texas *Baptist Standard*, 1888–1959 (PhD diss., Southwestern Baptist Theological Seminary, 1964), 97–140; "Texas Baptist Standard," *Galveston Daily News*, November 5, 1909.

17. "Dr. Norris to Accept First Baptist's Call," *Fort Worth Star Telegram*, October 9, 1909.

18. Sanborn Maps, 1885 and 1889.

19. Oliver Knight, *Fort Worth: Outpost on the Trinity* (Fort Worth: Texas Christian University Press, 1990).

20. Harold W. Rich, "Beyond Outpost: Fort Worth, 1880–1918" (PhD. diss., Texas Christian University, 2006), 141–42.

21. Robert Harris Tallbert, *Cowtown-Metropolis: Case Study of a City's Growth and Structure* (Fort Worth: Leo Potishman Foundation, Texas Christian University, Texas Christian University Special Collections, 1956), 125.

22. "What the Churches Have Done in 1911," *Fort Worth Star Telegram*, December 10, 1911.

23. Rich, "Beyond Outpost," 265–66.

24. Charles A. Selden, "Prosperity and Progress in the Opulent Southwest," *New York Times*, February 1, 1920.

25. Karen O'Dell Bullock, "First Baptist Church, Fort Worth," *Handbook of Texas Online*, http://www.tshaonline.org.

26. David R. Stokes, *The Shooting Salvationist: J. Frank Norris and the Murder Trial That Captivated America* (New York: Steerforth Press, 2011), 32.

27. "Oral Memoirs of Martha Lucille Norris," interview conducted by Ellen Kuniyuki Brown, August 7, 1997; courtesy of Baylor University Institute for Oral History.

28. Norris's visits to Los Angeles and continuing role in Southern California are discussed in Darren Dochuk, *From Bible Belt to Sunbelt: Plain-Folk Religion, Grassroots Politics, and the Rise of Evangelical Conservatism* (New York: Norton, 2011), 45–47.

29. "Five Hundred Join One Church in Year," *Fort Worth Star Telegram*, August 21, 1911.

30. "Home for Working Women, Church Plan," *Fort Worth Star Telegram*, February 27, 1911.

31. "Sunday School in Tent," *Fort Worth Star Telegram*, May 20, 2011; "Preacher to Sell Peanuts," *Abilene Daily Reporter*, June 11, 1911.

32. "Dr. Norris Buys Best a New Hat," *Fort Worth Star Telegram*, October 29, 1911; "Church Asks Unions Reason for Coldness," *Fort Worth Star Telegram*, September 10, 1911.

33. "Preacher Is Indicted," *New York Times*, March 3, 1912.

34. Rich, "Beyond Outpost," 223; "Church Will Not Seek Injunction against Saloon," *Fort Worth Star Telegram*, September 13, 1911.

35. Rich, "Beyond Outpost," 224–25.

36. E. C. Routh, "Editorial: Concerning Evolution," *Baptist Standard* (January 5, 1922), 8.

37. E. C. Routh, "Baylor University and Pastor Norris," *Baptist Standard* (February 23, 1922), 1.

38. "Norris Denies Board Passes on Members; Cites Church's Beliefs," *Fort Worth Star Telegram*, September 15, 1922.

39. "The Anti-Evolutionists," *Galveston Daily News*, June 9, 1888; "Southern Presbyterians," *Galveston Daily News*, May 27, 1888.

40. "Methodists in Session," *Dallas Morning News*, October 22, 1891.

41. "The Belton Revival," *Dallas Morning News*, July 21 1893.

42. "The Closing Meeting," *Dallas Morning News*, June 27, 1893.

43. "The State Press," *Dallas Morning News*, October 3, 1893.

44. "Local Geological Survey," *The Chromascope* 17 (1916), 175.

45. Quoted on p. 47 in Patsy Ledbetter, "Defense of the Faith: J. Frank Norris and Texas Fundamentalism, 1920–1929," *Arizona and the West* 15 (1973), 45–62. See also Constance Areson Clark, "Evolution for John Doe: Pictures, the Public, and the Scopes Trial Debate," *Journal of American History* 87 (March 2001), 1275–1303.

46. C. L. Seasholes, "The Origin of Man," *Dallas Morning News*, January 25, 1894; Seasholes's authority for the Garden of Eden having been at the North Pole was a book by the first president of Boston University, William Fairfield Warren, *Paradise Found: The Cradle of the Human Race at the North Pole* (Boston: Mifflin, 1885); the wider history of this idea is discussed in Brook Wilensky-Lanford, *Paradise Lust: Searching for the Garden of Eden* (New York: Grove Press, 2011).

47. William Cowper Brann, *The Complete Works of Brann, the Iconoclast* (New York: Brann, 1919), 95.

48. M. James Penton, *Apocalypse Delayed: The Story of Jehovah's Witnesses* (Toronto: University of Toronto Press, 1997).

49. Charles T. Russell, "The Day of the Lord," *Dallas Morning News*, November 6, 1904.

50. For example, "Large Audience Hears Discussion by Dr. William Caldwell," *Fort Worth Star Telegram*, August 16, 1909.

51. "Affairs at Austin," *Dallas Morning News*, September 30, 1890.

52. Christopher G. White, *Unsettled Minds: Psychology and the American Search for Spiritual Assurance, 1830–1940* (Berkeley: University of California Press, 2009).

53. "The Rhythm of Cosmic Art," *Dallas Morning News*, July 19, 1897.

54. "Daily Budget from Waco," *Dallas Morning News*, July 13, 1987.

55. "Dallas Free Thinkers," *Dallas Morning News*, February 3, 1896.

56. "Dallas' New Church," *Dallas Morning News*, November 5, 1901.

57. "Lowber on Darwin," *Dallas Morning News*, January 8, 1894.

58. "Science and the Bible," *Dallas Morning News*, May 9, 1892.

59. W. S. Sutton, "How the School Affects Character," *Dallas Morning News*, December 19, 1904.

60. "Walked about in America Fifty Million Years Ago," *Dallas Morning News*, October 18, 1903.

61. U.S. Census, 1940 Public Use Microsample, electronic data file, courtesy of the University of Minnesota, for persons of all races age twenty-one and over; Texas ranked twenty-sixth, with educational attainment comparable to that in Illinois, New York, and Connecticut.

62. "Statement of Dr. Tubbs," *Dallas Morning News*, June 12, 1901.

63. "The New Bible," *Fort Worth Morning Register*, November 14, 1899.

64. "School of Theology," *Dallas Morning News*, September 3, 1905.

65. Edward J. Larson, *Summer for the Gods: The Scopes Trial and America's Continuing Debate over Science and Religion* (New York: Basic Books, 1997), 221.

66. "Dr. Moore's Sermon," *Dallas Morning News*, July 16, 1906.

67. On intelligent design, a good example is "Evolution and the Life Power," *Century Path* 13 (February 6, 1910), 7; and on hedonism, an example is a sermon preached by Reverend J. B. French of the Broadway Presbyterian Church in Fort Worth following the killing of a policeman, "Sermon by Dr. French," *Dallas Morning News*, August 16, 1909.

68. "Immense Crowd at Lecture," *Dallas Morning News*, June 24, 1907.

69. On the history of fundamentalism, see especially George M. Marsden, *Fundamentalism and American Culture: The Shaping of Twentieth-Century Evangelicalism, 1870–1925* (New York: Oxford University Press, 1980); and Ernest R. Sandeen, *The Roots of Fundamentalism* (Chicago: University of Chicago Press, 1970).

70. "Francis L. Patton," Presidents of Princeton University" (September 2005), http://www.princeton.edu; "Princeton Professor to Give Five Lectures," *Dallas Morning News*, November 28, 1909.

71. "Dr. Patton Resigns as Seminary Head," *New York Times*, May 6, 1913.

72. "Sermon on Divine Guidance," *Dallas Morning News*, July 26, 1909.

73. J. R. Jacobs, "Orthodoxy and the 'Caldwell Case,'" *Christian Observer* 94 (February 7, 1906), 6.

74. "Did Whale Really Swallow Jonah?" *Fort Worth Star Telegram*, December 5, 1910.

75. "Woman Answers Lockhart," *Fort Worth Star Telegram*, December 11, 1910.

76. "Baptist Workers Answer Lockhart," *Fort Worth Star Telegram*, December 21, 1910.

77. J. B. Cranfill, "An Interview with Dr. Harper," *Christian Observer* 84 (February 5, 1896), 16; among northern Baptists the controversy over Harper's views also resulted in the withholding of funds supporting the university by some local associations.

78. J. B. Cranfill, "The Lone Star State," *The Independent* 49 (July 15, 1897), 5.

79. "Infidelity Taught by Chicago," *Fort Worth Star Telegram*, December 19, 1910.

80. "Sermon on the Bible," *Dallas Morning News*, January 2, 1911; "School Infidelity Is Carroll's Subject," *Fort Worth Star Telegram*, December 23, 1910.

81. Rollin Gustav Osterweis, *The Myth of the Lost Cause, 1865–1900* (Hamden, CT: Archon Books, 1973); Gary W. Gallagher and Alan T. Nolan, eds., *The Myth of the Lost Cause and Civil War History* (Bloomington: Indiana University Press, 2000); and on the possible connection between lost-cause thinking and premillennialism, Pamela Elwyn Thomas Colbenson, "Millennial Thought among Southern Evangelicals, 1830–1885" (PhD diss., Georgia State University, Atlanta, 1980).

82. That argument, with particular emphasis on the rural South, was put forward in Stewart G. Cole, *The History of Fundamentalism* (Hamden, CT: Archon Books, 1931), but has been criticized for placing too much emphasis on social conditions and too little on theological arguments as well as underestimating the attraction of fundamentalism in urban centers.

83. Alfred Russel Wallace, *Social Environment and Moral Progress* (New York: Cassell, 1913).

84. Billy Sunday, "Christ Calls the Christian the Same as He Calls Sinner," *Fort Worth Star Telegram*, December 28, 1918.

85. "Fundamentals of Christianity to Be Debated Here," *Fort Worth Star Telegram*, February 8, 1920.

86. A. C. Dixon, "The Menace of Evolution," *Dallas Morning News*, April 30, 1921.

87. "Teaching of So-Called Evolution Opposed," *Dallas Morning News*, March 15, 1914.

88. "Objects to Textbook," *Dallas Morning News*, October 19, 1913;

89. "Minister Voices Protest," *Dallas Morning News*, November 5, 1913.

90. "Baptists Will Insist Textbooks Square with Genesis," *Fort Worth Star Telegram*, December 5, 1921.

91. On Torrey, see "Circumstantial Evidence Is Proof of Resurrection," *Fort Worth Star Telegram*, October 10, 1917.

92. "Baptists Will Insist Textbooks Square with Genesis"; for example, J. B. Cranfill called for less extreme measures than Hanks did.

93. Lowell H. Harrison and James C. Klotter, *A New History of Kentucky* (Lexington: University Press of Kentucky, 1997), 346; Alonzo W. Fortune, "The Kentucky Campaign against the Teaching of Evolution," *Journal of Religion* 2 (1922), 225–35.

94. "Outlawing Darwin from Kentucky," *Fort Worth Star Telegram*, February 14, 1922; "Evolution Bill Is Defeated in Kentucky House," *Fort Worth Star Telegram*, March 10, 1922.

95. "The Books Used in Our Schools," *Dallas Morning News*, December 14, 1921.

96. "Appointment of Committee on Heresy Is Baptist Task," *Fort Worth Star Telegram*, December 2, 1921.

97. "Teaching of Evolution," *Dallas Morning News*, February 18, 1922.

98. Barry Hankins, *God's Rascal: J. Frank Norris and the Beginnings of Southern Fundamentalism* (Lexington: University Press of Kentucky, 1996), 40.

99. "Norris Denies Board Passes on Members."

100. "Appointment of Committee on Heresy Is Baptist Task."

101. "Degrees Awarded Baylor Graduates," *Dallas Morning News*, June 17, 1922.

102. "Darwinism Is Not Taught as Fact in Baylor University Declares President Brooks," *Fort Worth Star Telegram*, October 22, 1922.

103. "Darwinian Theory Is Not Accepted," *Dallas Morning News*, September 13, 1922.

104. "Appreciates Advertising by Baptist Brethren, Norris says; Repeats His Charges," *Fort Worth Star Telegram*, September 24, 1922. The institutionalization to which Norris pointed was evident both in the Baptist General Convention of Texas and in the broader Southern Baptist Convention in greater centralization and coordination of publications, the founding and support of benevolent associations and seminaries, a sharper separation from northern Baptists following the Fortress Monroe Comity agreement of 1894, and the formation of the Southern Baptist Convention Executive Committee in 1917; on social changes leading to greater centralization among denominations, see especially Ben Primer, *Protestants and American Business Methods* (Ann Arbor, MI: UMI Research Press, 1979). Norris's church was ousted from the Baptist General Convention of Texas in 1924, and the congregation's request for reinstatement was denied in 1925.

105. The 1925 Southern Baptist Confession of Faith did not include a specific clause about evolution despite efforts to add one; Turner, *Fundamentalism in the Southern Baptist Convention*, 128.

106. "For Mexia, I Will," *Mexia Daily News*, May 18, 1924.

107. "Methodists Urge Absolute Faith," *Dallas Morning News*, December 30, 1922.

108. "Methodist Schools Placed on Trial," *Dallas Morning News*, May 2, 1923.

109. "To Adhere to Religion as Taught in Bible," *Associated Press* (Kansas City, Missouri), May 16, 1923.

110. "Texas Rector, Center of Heresy Dispute," *Boston Daily Globe*, December 23, 1923; "Rector Says Bishop Will Push Charge," *Baltimore Sun*, January 1, 1924.

111. "Church Denounces Organic Evolution," *Dallas Morning News*, May 22, 1924; "Nondenominational Seminary Planned," *Dallas Morning News*, May 18, 1924.

112. Quoted in Ledbetter, "Defense of the Faith," 56.

113. "Des Moines U. Is Opened by Court Order," *Abilene Morning News*, May 14, 1929.

114. S. J. Holmes, "Proposed Laws against the Teaching of Evolution," *Bulletin of the American Association of University Professors* 13 (1927), 549–54.

115. "No Evolution for Texas," *Literary Digest*, August 14, 1926.

116. Blewett Lee, "An Establishment of Religion," *Virginia Law Review* 14 (1927), 100–111; quotation on p. 102.

117. Stokes, *The Shooting Salvationist*, 135–50; Philip Kinsley, "Norris Tells His Story amid His Sobs," *Chicago Daily Tribune*, January 22, 1927.

118. "Fundamentalism Fight Is Planned at Baptist Meet," *Atlanta Constitution*, May 24, 1926; "Evolution Fight Expected Today," *Atlanta Constitution*, May 28, 1926.

119. "Ministers Write a Letter to Austin," *Dallas Morning News*, January 22, 1929; "Baptist Preachers Take Stand in Favor of Antievolution Bill," *Dallas Morning News*, January 22, 1929.

120. "Fundamentalist Preachers Form City Conference," *Dallas Morning News*, March 12, 1929.

121. Charles C. Ryrie, *Dispensationalism* (Chicago: Moody Publishers, 2007).

122. Larry V. Crutchfield, *The Origins of Dispensationalism: The Darby Factor* (Washington, DC: University Press of America, 1991); Mark A. Noll, *The Old Religion in a New World: The History of North American Christianity* (Grand Rapids, MI: Eerdmans, 2002).

123. Paul S. Boyer, *When Time Shall Be No More: Prophecy Belief in Modern American Culture* (Cambridge, MA: Harvard University Press, 1992).

124. Charles G. Trumbull, *The Life Story of C. I. Scofield* (New York: Oxford University Press, 1920).

125. "Dr. Scofield's Resignation," *Dallas Morning News*, November 19, 1895.

126. George W. Dollar, *A History of Fundamentalism in America* (Greenville, SC: Bob Jones University Press, 1973), 359.

127. "Congregational Church Withdraws Fellowship," *Dallas Morning News*, December 3, 1908.

128. Penton, *Apocalypse Delayed*, 13–46.

129. Samuel Macauley Jackson, ed., *The New Schaff-Herzog Encyclopedia of Religious Knowledge*, 13 vols. (New York: Funk and Wagnalls, 1908–14).

130. Harris Franklin Rall, "Premillennialism and the Bible," *The Biblical World* 53 (1919), 459–69, quotation on p. 459, referring to premillennialism and not only to Scofield.

131. Scofield, "The Divine Bible."

132. "Pays High Compliment to Dr. Scofield's Work," *Dallas Morning News*, May 3, 1909.

133. "Address by Dr. Scofield," *Dallas Morning News*, January 20, 1908.

134. C. I. Scofield, "The Harmonious Life," *Dallas Morning News*, March 12, 1905.

135. "Nondenominational Seminary Planned."

136. B. Dwain Waldrep, "Lewis Sperry Chafer and the Development of Interdenominational Fundamentalism in the South, 1900–1950" (PhD diss., Auburn University, 2001), 81–82.

137. John D. Hannah, *An Uncommon Union: Dallas Theological Seminary and American Evangelicalism* (Grand Rapids, MI: Zondervan, 2009), 77–95.

138. Hankins, *God's Rascal*, 75–76.

139. Ibid., 89.

140. Bullock, "First Baptist Church, Fort Worth."

141. "Jeffers Heard by Large Crowd Here," *Denton Record-Chronicle*, November 19, 1931.

142. "Spotlights," *San Antonio Light*, March 6, 1929.

143. "Calvary Baptist Church," *Denton Record-Chronicle*, October 19, 1929; "161 Additions from Revival by Fundamentalists," *Denton Record-Chronicle*, December 21, 1931.

144. "Church News," *Wellington Leader*, May 26, 1932.

145. "Special Service Set," *Big Spring Herald*, November 27, 1931.

146. "Revival Will Be at Rex Theater," *Avalanche Journal* (Lubbock), October 18, 1931.

147. "Attack Made on Evolution," *Dallas Morning News*, February 18, 1929; "Fundamentalist Again Takes Up War against Certain School Books," *Dallas Morning News*, October 16, 1930.

148. "Plans Move to Free Jailed Texas Pastor," *New York Times*, July 9, 1928; "Dallas Women Halt Tabernacle Work," *New York Times*, July 8, 1928.

149. "Voters Will Have Inning Saturday, Campaign Was Hot," *Corsicana Daily Sun*, July 25, 1930. Mayfield had garnered support in 1922 both from the Ku Klux Klan and from some

clergy, including Norris, because of his favoring of Prohibition; David M. Chalmers, *Hooded Americanism: The History of the Ku Klux Klan* (Durham, NC: Duke University Press, 1981), 43); David A. Horowitz, "Introduction: Setting the Context," in *Inside the Klavern: The Secret History of a Ku Klux Klan of the 1920s*, ed. David A. Horowitz (Carbondale: Southern Illinois University Press, 1999), 1–15.

150. "Refuse Bar History," *Corsicana Daily Sun*, May 18, 1930.

151. "Public School League to Hold State Rally," *Dallas Morning News*, June 24, 1930; "Fundamentalist Again Takes Up War against Certain School Books," *Dallas Morning News*, October 16, 1930.

152. Herbert Asbury, "Is Protestantism Declining?" *Forum* 79 (February 1928), 181; other examples of progressive concerns about the potential political and cultural impact of fundamentalism include Albert C. Dieffenbach, "Religious Liberty—the Great American Illusion," *The Independent* 118 (January 8, 1927), 36; and "Dissension Shakes the Churches," *Current Opinion*, February 1, 1924.

153. Hannah, *An Uncommon Union*, 104–14, 124–25.

154. Andrew Himes, *The Sword of the Lord: The Roots of Fundamentalism in an American Family* (Seattle: Chiara Press, 2011).

CHAPTER 5
FROM JUDGE LYNCH TO JIM CROW

1. "Negroes Stage Big Juneteenth at Centennial," *Dallas Morning News*, June 20, 1936.

2. "Colored Gentry to Celebrate June 19 with Cab Calloway," *Dallas Morning News*, June 16, 1936.

3. W.E.B. DuBois, *What the Negro Has Done for the United States and Texas* (Washington, DC: Government Printing Office, 1936); courtesy of the Eugene C. Barker Texas History Center of the University of Texas Library, Austin, Texas.

4. Sociologists will of course recognize this as the theme of Émile Durkheim, *Elementary Forms of the Religious Life* (New York: Free Press, 1915).

5. "Cotton Gin and Farm Machinery Made Here," *Dallas Morning News*, January 1, 1910.

6. "Dallas' Railroad Business Increases," *Dallas Morning News*, January 1, 1910.

7. "Fast Express Service Afforded to Dallas Merchants," *Dallas Morning News*, January 30, 1927; Thomas A. Hill-Aiello, "Dallas, Cotton and the Transatlantic Economy, 1885–1956" (PhD diss., University of Texas, Arlington, 2006), 303–5.

8. "Cultural Life of Dallas Has Made Tremendous Strides in Forty Years," *Dallas Morning News*, October 1, 1925.

9. Laura K. Bennett, "Rural and Urban Boosterism in Texas, 1880s–1930s" (Master's thesis, University of Texas, Arlington, 2008), 35; with information drawn from George Kessler, *A City Plan for Dallas* (Dallas: Report of Park Board, 1913).

10. "Dallas State Fair," *Dallas Morning News*, May 5, 1886; "Texas State Fair," *Dallas Morning News*, October 10, 1886; "The Coming State Fair," *Dallas Morning News*, April 17, 1887.

11. "Gates Closed until 1931 on Largest Fair," *Dallas Morning News*, October 27, 1930.

12. Bennett, *Rural and Urban Boosterism*, 38.

13. "Texas a Great State a Great Exposition," Santa Fe Railroad Brochure, Centennial Exposition collection, Dallas Historical Society, G. B. Dealey Library archives, Box 19, as quoted in ibid., 40.

14. "Baptists Arrange Centennial Plans," *Dallas Morning News*, May 8, 1936.

15. "Noted Churchmen Plead for Strong, Religious Dallas," *Dallas Morning News*, June 5, 1936.

16. "Liberty Called Crowning Gem for Humanity," *Dallas Morning News*, June 12, 1936.

17. U.S. Census, 1930, electronic data file; 15 percent of the total population of Texas was African American, as was 15 percent of the population of Dallas County, compared with 30 percent or more in thirty-two counties located in eastern Texas and 23 percent in Galveston county; among African Americans age ten and over the literacy rate was also higher in Dallas County than in these other counties.

18. "F.D.R. Will Attend Texas Centennial," *Dallas Morning News*, June 22, 1935.

19. "Texans to Ask Roosevelt to Extend Visit," *Dallas Morning News*, December 21, 1935; "Bill on Centennial Signed, New Type Building Projected," *Dallas Morning News*, February 13, 1936.

20. "Texas Centennial Exposition," *Plaindealer* (Kansas City, KS), April 10, 1936; "Sam Houston, Texas Character, Colorful," *Capital Plaindealer* (Topeka, KS), September 20, 1936.

21. For example, Lucille Bosh, "Dallas Mayor Boosts Centennial Exposition," *Atlanta Daily World*, February 27, 1936; and "Famous Bands to Play in Texas," *Plaindealer*, April 17, 1936.

22. "Texas and the Negro," *Dallas Morning News*, February 25, 1936.

23. David W. Kellum, "Race Praised on Progress at Exposition," *Chicago Defender* (June 27, 1936).

24. "Negroes Stage Big Juneteenth at Centennial."

25. "Race Jim Crowed at Texas Centennial," *Chicago Defender*, June 27, 1936; C. T. Medford, "Being Nice," *New York Amsterdam News*, June 27, 1936.

26. U. G. Goree, "Charges Prejudice Rules at Texas Centennial," *Pittsburgh Courier*, June 27, 1936.

27. "Negroes to Throng Fair in Observing Juneteenth Rites," *Dallas Morning News*, June 18, 1936.

28. "Jim Crow Law," *Dallas Morning News*, June 25, 1936.

29. "'Jim Crow' Law Is Impartial," *Dallas Morning News*, June 16, 1936.

30. "2 Negroes Killed, Twenty-Six Cut in Juneteenth Fights," *Dallas Morning News*, June 20, 1936.

31. "Not the Sheriff, Neither," *Dallas Morning News*, June 9, 1936.

32. "Foes of Roosevelt Attack First Lady in Negro Pictures," *Dallas Morning News*, April 16, 1936; "Kirby's Ouster from Party," *Dallas Morning News*, April 26, 1936.

33. "Texans Unruffled at Flurry Caused by Negro's Prayer," *Dallas Morning News*, June 26, 1936.

34. Jeffrey Paul, "Texas Centennial," *Washington Post*, August 18, 1936.

35. Roscoe Dunjee, "Texas Centennial Reveals Ignorance of Whites with Reference to Negro Ability," *New York Amsterdam News*, December 12, 1936.

36. "South Texas Mob Fails in Effort to Lynch Blacks," *Dallas Morning News*, June 19, 1936.

37. "Texas Senator Quizzed in Double Lynching," *Negro Star* (Wichita, KS), November 29, 1935; "Glorying in Their Shame," *New York Times*, November 15, 1935.

38. Archives of the Tuskegee Institute, Tuskegee University, Tuskegee, AL.

39. Southern Baptist Convention, *Annual of the Southern Baptist Convention* (St. Louis, 1936), 26.

40. "Texas Senator Quizzed in Double Lynching," Christopher Waldrep, *African Americans Confront Lynching: Strategies of Resistance from the Civil War to the Civil Rights Era* (Lanham, MD: Rowman & Littlefield, 2009), 75–86; Connally later reminisced that if the advocates of the antilynching bills "had been serious, they could have defeated us," Tom Connally, *My Name Is Tom Connally* (New York: Crowell, 1954), 172.

41. "Filibuster Delays Anti-Lynching Bill," *New York Times*, January 5, 1922; "Sumners Attacks Anti-Lynching Bill," *Dallas Morning News*, December 10, 1921.

42. Mary Catherine Monroe, "A Day in July: Hatton W. Sumners and the Court Reorganization Plan of 1937" (Master's thesis, University of Texas, Arlington, 1973).

43. "Negroes Urged to Write to Congressmen to Urge Anti Lynching Passage," *Kansas American* (Topeka), March 28, 1936; "Hatton W. Sumners for Congress (Political Advertisement)," *Dallas Morning News*, July 3, 1936.

44. Monroe, *A Day in July*.

45. "Connally Says 'Want to Nail' False Charges," *Dallas Morning News*, August 18, 1928.

46. "Why Five Men Go to Church," *Dallas Morning News*, May 5, 1930; Connally, *My Name Is Tom Connally*, 72.

47. "Baptist Meet Hears Report on Gambling," *Dallas Morning News*, May 8, 1927.

48. There are no exact statistics on lynchings; for a discussion of data limitations, see Lisa D. Cook, "Converging to a National Lynching Database: Recent Developments" (Department of Economics Working Paper, Michigan State University, East Lansing, 2011). The total numbers by state are from Tuskegee Institute archives as summarized at http://www.electricprint .com; data on years and locations are compiled from reports in Texas newspapers; David L. Chapman, "Lynching in Texas" (M.A. thesis, Texas Tech University, 1973); Ralph Ginzburg, *100 Years of Lynchings* (Baltimore: Black Classic Press, 1996); *The Lynching Calendar*, http:// www.autopsis.org; and *A Partial Listing of Negroes Lynched in the United States since 1859*, http://ccharity.com.

49. Electronic data file courtesy of Elizabeth Hines and Eliza Steelwater, Historical American Lynching Data Collection Project (Project HAL); see also Eliza Steelwater, *The Hangman's Knot: Lynching, Legal Execution and America's Struggle with the Death Penalty* (Boulder, CO: Westview Press, 2003); Steward Tolnay and E. M. Beck, *A Festival of Violence: An Analysis of Southern Lynchings, 1882–1930* (Urbana: University of Illinois Press, 1995); Stewart E. Tolnay, Glenn Deane, and E. M. Beck, "Vicarious Violence: Spatial Effects on Southern Lynchings, 1890–1919," *American Journal of Sociology* 102 (1996), 788–815.

50. These figures are based on the lynching of 390 persons for whom the county location could be determined.

51. "Lynching of Negro near Texarkana Condemned," *Dallas Morning News*, February 21, 1922.

52. "Volley Is Fired into Home of Deputy Sheriff," *Fort Worth Star Telegram*, February 15, 1922.

53. J. M. Dawson, *A Thousand Months to Remember: An Autobiography* (Waco, TX: Baylor University Press, 1964), 165.

54. Ibid.

55. Patricia Bernstein, *The First Waco Horror: The Lynching of Jesse Washington and the Rise of the NAACP* (College Station: Texas A&M University Press, 2005), 146; Bernstein's thorough inquiry tracked down the names of a number of the Waco residents who participated in the lynching, which did include some of the tougher elements of the community, but she concludes, "Although the better element of Waco may not have participated physically in the dirty work of the lynching, they watched and approved and made no effort to thwart the mob" (158).

56. Dawson, *A Thousand Months to Remember*, 165; Bernstein, *The First Waco Horror*, 122, notes that in a 1971 interview Dawson blamed the event on "the poorest classes" and said the general view was to "let the issue drop."

57. W.E.B. DuBois, "The Waco Horror," *The Crisis* 12 (1916), 1–8, quotations on p. 8; additional discussion of the context in which the Waco lynching and similar incidents occurred is given in William D. Carrigan, *The Making of a Lynching Culture: Violence and Vigilantism in Central Texas, 1836–1916* (Urbana: University of Illinois Press, 2004).

58. Walter White, *Rope and Faggot: A Biography of Judge Lynch* (Notre Dame, IN: University of Notre Dame Press, 2002), 20–21; although more speculative, White's observations originally published in 1929 (40–53) about the possible relationship between Christian traditions and lynching are of interest in this context

59. Charles T. Alexander quoted in Joseph E. Early Jr., *A Texas Baptist History Sourcebook: A Companion to McBeth's Texas Baptists* (Denton: University of North Texas Press, 2004), 288.

60. Alwyn Barr, *Black Texans: A History of Negroes in Texas, 1528–1995* (Norman: University of Oklahoma Press, 1996), 107.

61. U.S. Census Bureau, *Religious Bodies, 1936*, vol. 1 (Washington, DC: Government Printing Office, 1936), 144–49.

62. LeRoy Fitts, *A History of Black Baptists* (Nashville, TN: Boardman Press, 1985).

63. U.S. Census Bureau, *Religious Bodies, 1936*.

64. "Baptists Want No Alliances with Other Denominations," *Daily Enterprise* (Beaumont), May 14, 1910.

65. Evelyn Brooks Higginbotham, *Righteous Discontent: The Women's Movement in the Black Baptist Church* (Cambridge, MA: Harvard University Press, 1993).

66. U.S. Census Bureau, *Religious Bodies, 1936*, vol. 2 (Washington, DC: Government Printing Office, 1941), 152–55.

67. "The Southern Baptist Commission on the American Baptist Seminary Records," Southern Baptist Historical Library and Archives, Nashville, TN, 1968.

68. "Dickson Colored Orphanage," *Dallas Morning News*, January 7, 1911; "Support for Negro Orphanage Appealed for by President," *Dallas Morning News*, February 3, 1919; Dickson continued as director until 1929 when the orphanage was deeded to the state.

69. *Proceedings of the Woman's Missionary Union* (Dallas: Baptist General Convention of Texas, 1930), 50–51.

70. *Proceedings of the Woman's Missionary Union* (Dallas: Baptist General Convention of Texas, 1931), 66.

71. Presnall H. Wood, "History of the Texas Baptist Standard, 1888–1959" (PhD diss., Southwestern Baptist Theological Seminary, 1964), 103.

72. J. H. Gambrell, "The Negro Problem," *Baptist Standard* (June 13, 1907), 4.

73. "Baptist Pastors' Meeting," *Dallas Morning News*, February 9, 1909.

74. John W. Storey, *Texas Baptist Leadership and Social Christianity, 1900–1980* (College Station: Texas A&M University Press, 2000), 92.

75. "Contemporary Thought," *Dallas Morning News*, January 20, 1910.

76. Unidentified author quoted in First United Methodist Church, *Church at the Crossroads: A History of First United Methodist Church Dallas* (Dallas: UMR Communications, 1997), 104.

77. Kevin K. Gaines, *Uplifting the Race: Black Leadership, Politics, and Culture in the Twentieth Century* (Chapel Hill: University of North Carolina Press, 1996), xiv.

78. "What Is the Matter with the Colored Baptist of Texas," *Capital Plaindealer* (Topeka, KS), September 4, 1914.

79. An example of a farmers association led by the pastor of an African Methodist Episcopal Church is given in "To Organize an N.F.& I. Association," *Clerburne Morning Review*, April 16, 1911. See also Charles Postel, *The Populist Vision* (New York: Oxford University Press, 2007), 173–203.

80. "Rev. J. Gordon McPherson," *Broad Axe* (Chicago), July 5, 1919.

81. "Communication from Negro Ministers," *Beaumont Journal*, June 26, 1911.

82. Eric D. Anderson, "Black Responses to Darwinism, 1859–1915," in *Disseminating Darwin: The Role of Place, Race, Religion, and Gender*, ed. Ronald L. Numbers (Madison: University of Wisconsin Press, 2001), 247–66.

83. C. L. Seasholes, "The Origin of Man," *Dallas Morning News*, January 25, 1894.

84. "Eagle, Joe Henry," *Biographical Directory of the United States Congress*, http://bioguide.congress.gov.

85. Joe H. Eagle, "Texas Day Oration," *Dallas Morning News*, June 24, 1897; Eagle's views about southern progress are also expressed in Joe H. Eagle, "John H. Kirby—An Appreciation," *Manufacturers Record* 61 (February 22, 1912), 126–28.

86. Ibid.

87. "For a Better Life," *Dallas Morning News*, October 9, 1900.

88. Booker T. Washington, "The Negro's Opportunity," *Dallas Morning News*, January 2, 1903.

89. Baptist General Convention of Texas, *Proceedings*, 1906, 88–89; see also Storey, *Texas Baptist Leadership*, 94–95.

90. Quoted in Storey, *Texas Baptist Leadership*, 96.

91. "Baptist Women Hold 'Jubilate Service,'" *Dallas Morning News*, November 19, 1913.

92. "A Negro Educator on Emancipation: Emmett J. Scott Delivered Speech at Houston," *Beaumont Enterprise*, June 21, 1910.

93. Norman D. Brown, *Hood, Bonnet, and Little Brown Jug: Texas Politics, 1921-1928* (College Station: Texas A&M University Press, 1984).

94. Christopher Long, "Ku Klux Klan," *Handbook of Texas Online*, http://www .tshaonline.org; Edward Ranson, *The American Mid-Term Elections of 1922: An Unexpected Shift in Political Power* (New York: Edwin Mellen Press, 2007), 81–83; David M. Chalmers, *Hooded Americanism: The History of the Ku Klux Klan* (Durham, NC: Duke University Press, 1981), 39–48.

95. "Dallas Negro Lashed," *Fort Worth Star Telegram*, April 2, 1921.

96. "No Investigation to Follow Raid of Ku Klux Klan," *Fort Worth Star Telegram*, April 3, 1921.

97. "Ku Klux Klan Post Dallas with Warning," *Fort Worth Star Telegram*, May 23, 1921.

98. "Los Ku Klux Amenazan A Un Medico Negro," *La Prensa* (San Antonio), May 26, 1921; "Think Marshall Negro Bell Boy Was Mutilated," *Dallas Morning News*, July 23, 1921; "Hotels Warned to Fire Negro Porters," *Fort Worth Star Telegram*, August 5, 1921; "Masked Men Flog Negro at Belton," *Fort Worth Star Telegram*, June 17, 1921; "Signs at Austin Announce Klan Organizes There," *Fort Worth Star Telegram*, June 26, 1921; see also Benjamin H. Johnson, "The Cosmic Race in Texas: Racial Fusion, White Supremacy, and Civil Rights Politics," *Journal of American History* 98 (September 2011), 404–19.

99. U.S. House of Representatives, *The Ku Klux Klan: Hearings before the Committee on Rules* (Washington, DC: Government Printing Office, 1921), 6.

100. "5,000 Attend Anti-Klan Mass Meeting," *Dallas Morning News*, April 5, 1922.

101. "65 Robed Knights Sit on Platform as Ridley Speaks, Audience Cheers," *Fort Worth Star Telegram*, August 14, 1921.

102. "The News Is Criticized and Klan Given Praise at Mayfield Meeting," *Dallas Morning News*, August 16, 1922.

103. "Henry Tells Audience He Is Proud to Be Listed as Member of Ku Klux Klan," *Fort Worth Star Telegram*, April 9, 1922.

104. "Pastor Praises Ku Klux Klan; Raps Its Critics," *Fort Worth Star Telegram*, April 10, 1922.

105. "Minister Lauds Ku Klux Klan in Sermon," *Fort Worth Star Telegram*, February 6, 1922.

106. "Pastor at Kaufman Uses Ku Klux Klan as Subject," *Dallas Morning News*, March 7, 1922.

107. "Says God Founded the Ku Klux Klan," *Dallas Morning News*, August 1, 1923.

108. "Ku Klux Klan Is Menace to Society," *Dallas Morning News*, March 5, 1922.

109. Ibid.

110. "Klan Lauded by Negro Evangelist," *Fort Worth Star Telegram*, November 17, 1922.

111. "Visit Negro Church," *Fort Worth Star Telegram*, September 4, 1922.

112. "Negro Church at Vernon Visited by Ku Klux Klan," *Dallas Morning News*, February 28, 1922.

113. "Threaten Destruction of Negro Church," *Fort Worth Star Telegram*, March 22, 1922.

114. Frank B. Williams Jr., "The Poll Tax as a Suffrage Requirement in the South, 1870–1901," *Journal of Southern History* 18 (1952), 469–96.

115. Kyle G. Wilkison, *Yeomen, Sharecroppers, and Socialists: Plain Folk Protest in Texas, 1870–1914* (College Station: Texas A&M University Press, 2008), 70

116. Jerold G. Rusk, *A Statistical History of the American Electorate* (Washington, DC: Congressional Quarterly Press, 2001), and chart for Texas at http://www.utexas.edu. In the 1896 presidential election, turnout in Texas was 86.6 percent, or slightly higher than the national rate of 79.7 percent. It fell to 60.3 percent in 1900, compared with a national rate of 73.6, and then sunk to 29.2 percent in 1904 compared with a national rate of 65.4 percent. The low rate in Texas closely mirrored that of the South in general in those years.

117. "Only Way for the South," *Chicago Daily Tribune*, February 15, 1903; on fears of African American voters being corrupted, see also Paul E. Isaac, "Municipal Reform in Beaumont, Texas, 1902–1909," *Southwestern Historical Quarterly* 78 (1975), 409–30.

118. "Poll Tax Law a Rank Failure," *St. Louis Post Dispatch*, February 22, 1903.

119. Donald S. Strong, "The Poll Tax: The Case of Texas," *American Political Science Review* 38 (1944), 693–709.

120. Katherine S. Newman and Rourke L. O'Brien, *Taxing the Poor: Doing Damage to the Truly Disadvantaged* (Berkeley: University of California Press, 2011), 9–16.

121. Yancey Lewis, "Some Aspects of the Negro Question and Its Relation to Official Duty," *Dallas Morning News*, August 8, 1905.

122. William M. Brewer, "The Poll Tax and Poll Taxers," *Journal of Negro History* 29 (1944), 260–99.

123. These figures are based on county-level statistics for Texas counties from the 1900 U.S. Census and for county-level total votes cast for president in 1900 and 1904. Turnout is calculated by dividing the number of votes cast by the total number of males age twenty-one and over in each county. Percent African American is the percent of males age twenty-one and over who were recorded in the census as being African American. Percent illiterate white male is the percent of native born white males age twenty-one and over who were recorded in the census as being illiterate.

124. "Negroes Issue an Address," *Dallas Morning News*, January 1, 1911.

125. Electronic data files for 1910 U.S. Census and 1910 and 1911 elections at the county level; in ordinary least squares multiple regression models with percent of eligible persons voting in 1910 as the dependent variable, the standardized regression coefficient for percent of males age 21 and over who were African American was −0.386, significant beyond the 0.001 level, and for percent of eligible voters who were white and illiterate −0.01, not significant; for the 1911 turnout rate, the coefficient for percent African American was not significant and the coefficient for percent white illiterate was −0.243, significant beyond the 0.001 level.

126. "Purpose of Terrell Law Is Explained," *Dallas Morning News*, March 11, 1928.

127. "White Primary Case in Texas Is Decided by Supreme Court," *Dallas Morning News*, October 21, 1924.

128. Quoted in "NAACP Wins White Primary Case by Unanimous Decision of Supreme Court," *Broad Axe* (Chicago), March 12, 1927.

129. "Dallas Given Next Meeting of Democrats," *Dallas Morning News*, June 12, 1928; "No Legislation Needed on Primary Votes," *Dallas Morning News*, March 14, 1927; "The White Primary Is Held to Be Legal," *Dallas Morning News*, July 26, 1928.

130. The proportion of votes cast in the general election for the Democratic candidate for governor was 68 percent in 1900, 75 percent in 1092, 74 percent in 1904, 81 percent in 1906, 73 percent in 1908, 80 percent in 1910, 78 percent in 1912, 82 percent in 1914, 80 percent in 1916, 84 percent in 1918, 60 percent in 1920, 82 percent in 1922, 49 percent in 1924, 88 percent in 1926, and 82 percent in 1928, based on information provided in the electronic data file for United States Historical Election Returns, 1824–1968, courtesy of the Inter-University Consortium for Political and Social Research, University of Michigan.

131. Alwyn Barr, *Black Texans: A History of African Americans in Texas, 1828–1995* (Norman: University of Oklahoma Press, 1996), 77.

132. Alexander Heard and Donald S. Strong, *Southern Primary and General Election Data, 1920–1949* (Ann Arbor, MI: Inter-University Consortium for Political and Social Research, 1991), electronic data file; in 1920 the runoff was between Bailey and Neff; in 1924, between Robertson and Ferguson; and in 1926, Ferguson and Moody.

133. "Payment of Polls Passes 14,000 Mark," *Fort Worth Star Telegram*, January 29, 1917; statistical analysis of county data suggests only limited support for the possibility of positive relationships between the proportion of residents who were church members and the percentage who voted; turnout in 1904 was positively associated with total church membership in 1906 (the nearest year in which data were available) as a percentage of total population in 1900, but the relationships was not statistically significant for turnout in 1900, 1910, or 1911; percent Catholic was negatively associated with turnout in each year, perhaps indicating lower turnout among the state's Mexican American population.

134. "Voters to Vote while Away from Home," *Dallas Morning News*, July 1, 1915.

135. "Anti-Al Smith Group Makes Campaign Plan," *Dallas Morning News*, July 18, 1928.

136. "Bailey Criticizes Party Enemies," *Dallas Morning News*, October 19, 1924.

137. "Klansmen Parade Streets Unmasked after Election," *Dallas Morning News*, July 23, 1922.

138. Clarence Ousley, "Party Nominations Affect the Public," *Dallas Morning News*, August 30, 1918.

139. "Negro Problem," *Dallas Morning News*, May 14, 1907.

140. Jacquelyn Dowd Hall, *Revolt against Chivalry: Jessie Daniel Ames and the Women's Campaign against Lynching* (New York: Columbia University Press, 1979), 180.

141. "Negro Problem."

142. Edward T. James, Janet Wilson James, and Paul S. Boyer, *Notable American Women: A Biographical Dictionary* (Cambridge, MA: Radcliffe College, 1971), 358–59.

143. L. L. Bernard, "Southern Sociological Congress," *American Journal of Sociology* 18 (1912), 258–59.

144. G. W. Dyer, "The Purpose of Imprisonment," in *The Call of the New South: Addresses Delivered at the Southern Sociological Congress* (Nashville, TN: Southern Sociological Congress, 1913), 87–91; Wilbur F. Crafts, "The Potential Resources of the South for Leadership in Social Service," in ibid, 311–21.

145. W. D. Weatherford, "How to Enlist the Welfare Agencies of the South for Improvement of Conditions among the Negroes," in *The Human Way: Addresses on Race Problems at*

the Southern Sociological Congress, ed. James E. McCulloch (Nashville, TN: Southern Socio-logical Congress, 1913), 8–18, quotation on p. 8.

146. Arthur J. Barton, "The White Man's Task in the Uplift of the Negro," in *The Human Way*, 118–36, quotations on pp. 119, 125, 130, and 135.

147. William O. Scroggs, "Mob Violence—An Enemy of Both Races," in *Democracy in Earnest*, ed. James E. McCulloch (Washington, DC: Southern Sociological Congress, 1918), 185–90, quotations on p. 186.

148. "Anti-Mob Law Meeting," *Dallas Morning News*, October 19, 1915.

149. "Anti-Mob Association Formed by Students," *Fort Worth Star Telegram*, October 31, 1915.

150. "College Presidents Oppose Mob Violence," *Dallas Morning News*, October 26, 1915.

151. Charles M. Bishop, "The Causes, Consequences, and Cure of Mob Violence," in *Democracy in Earnest: Southern Sociological Congress, 1916–1918*, ed. James E. McCulloch (Washington, DC: Southern Sociological Congress, 1918), 191–200.

152. Helena Holley, "What Woman Suffrage Will Do toward the Conservation of Public Health," in *The New Chivalry—Health*, ed. James E. McCulloch (Washington, DC: Southern Sociological Congress, 1915), 307–13.

153. Francis White Johnson, *A History of Texas and Texans*, vol. 4 (Chicago: American Historical Society, 1914), 1862; Teresa Palomo Acosta, "In Memoriam: Robert Ernest Vinson," Documents of the General Faculty, University of Texas, Austin, 2001, http://www.utexas.edu/faculty/council.

154. The conflict with Ferguson and Vinson's support from the board of regents is described in Richard A. Holland, "George W. Brackenridge, George W. Littlefield, and the Shadow of the Past," in *The Texas Book: Profiles, History, and Reminiscences of the University*, ed. Richard A. Holland (Austin: University of Texas Press, 2006), 85–104; Vinson's own account is given in Robert E. Vinson, "The University Crosses the Bar," *Southwestern Historical Quarterly* 43 (1940), 281–94; his views about the university's responsibility to address social issues are described in Vinson, "Academic Freedom and Social Responsibility," in *Educational Problems in College and University*, ed. John Lewis Brumm (Ann Arbor: University of Michigan, 1921), 93–102; and on the relationship of churches to higher education in Vinson, "The Place of the Church in Education," *Union Seminary Review* 25 (1914), 178–92.

155. The role that religious convictions and networks played in the broader commission is shown in Charles Kirk Pilkington, "The Trials of Brotherhood: The Founding of the Commission on Interracial Cooperation," *Georgia Historical Quarterly* 69 (1985), 55–80; "Interracial Meeting Set for Dallas," *Dallas Morning News*, November 22, 1939.

156. "Welfare of Negro Race Is Subject of Church Women," *Dallas Morning News*, November 13, 1920.

157. Debbie Mauldin Cottrell, "Hanna, Sallie Little," *Handbook of Texas Online*, http://www.tshaonline.org.

158. Roger Post Ames was awarded the Walter Reed medal posthumously in 1929 for his participation in the yellow fever investigation in Cuba in 1900 and 1901.

159. Cora R. Jones, "Eve Up to Date," *Times Picayune*, February 7, 1927.

160. The definitive award-winning biography of Ames is Hall, *Revolt Against Chivalry*.

161. "Negro Soldiers Are Ordered Moved from Texas," *Montgomery Advertiser* (Alabama), August 25, 1917; "Echoes of the Race Riot at Fort Logan, Houston, Texas," *Broad Axe* (Chicago), September 1, 1917.

162. "Texas Race Riot," *Columbus Enquirer* (Georgia), July 12, 1919; "Negroes Wound 4 White Men in Clash at Longview over Slur at Young Woman," *Fort Worth Star Telegram*, July 11, 1919.

163. William M. Tuttle Jr., *Race Riot: Chicago in the Red Summer of 1919* (Champaign: University of Illinois Press, 1970); Cameron McWhirter, *Red Summer: the Summer of 1919 and the Awakening of Black America* (New York: Henry Holt, 2011).

164. "Shillady Tells of Attack Made on Him at Capital," *Dallas Morning News*, August 23, 1919; "Judge Thrashes Man Organizing Negroes," *Dallas Morning News*, August 23, 1919.

165. Melvin J. Banks, "The Pursuit of Equality: The Movement for First Class Citizenship among Negroes in Texas, 1920–1950" (PhD diss., Syracuse University, 1962); official intimidation included a telegram from Governor William P. Hobby to NAACP national chair Mary White Ovington stating that the association's representatives and propaganda should stay out of Texas; "Uplift Society Is Rebuffed by Hobby," *Dallas Morning News*, August 24, 1919. NAACP membership figures in Texas are given in "Attack on Shillady Bitterly Denounced," *Dallas Morning News*, August 30, 1919.

166. "Social Equality Is Aim of Negro Society in Texas," *Fort Worth Star Telegram*, August 29, 1919.

167. "To Assist in Adjustment on Race Relationship in South," *Augusta Chronicle* (Georgia), October 29, 1917; "Larger Educational Fund for Negroes," *Savannah Tribune*, September 7, 1918.

168. "University Race Commission Recommends to White College Students Study Facts Concerning Progress Negroes," *Negro Year Book* 6 (1922), 11; C. G. Woodson, "Negro Life and History in Our Schools," *Journal of Negro History* 4 (1919), 273–80.

169. Pilkington, "The Trials of Brotherhood."

170. The wider context of these activities is described in Anne Firor Scott, "After Suffrage: Southern Women in the Twenties," *Journal of Southern History* 30 (1964), 298–318.

171. Mark Stanley, "Booze, Boomtowns, and Burning Crosses: The Turbulent Governorship of Pat M. Neff of Texas, 1921–1925" (Master's thesis, University of North Texas, 2005).

172. "Lynching Condemned by Texas Women," *Broad Axe* (Chicago), April 15, 1922.

173. James E. McCulloch, *Distinguished Service Citizenship: Southern Sociological Congress, Knoxville, Tennessee, 1919* (Washington, DC: Southern Sociological Congress, 1919).

174. "Texas Led in 1920 Lynchings Over Country," *Fort Worth Star Telegram*, December 31, 1920.

175. "Negroes Address Inter-Race Body," *Dallas Morning News*, March 23, 1922.

176. Jan Voogd, *Race Riots and Resistance: The Red Summer of 1919* (New York: Peter Lang, 2008), 150–54.

177. "Growing Sentiment against Mob Action," *Journal of Social Forces* 1 (1923), 589.

178. "Better Facilities Asked for Negroes," *Dallas Morning News*, May 19, 1923; "The Negro Has His Week," *Dallas Morning News*, March 28, 1923.

179. "Mobs Forestalled," *Dallas Morning News*, November 7, 1925.

180. "Negro Church Women Hold Meeting in Waco," *Dallas Morning News*, June 17, 1925; "Stricter Enforcement of Dry Laws Urged by Missionary Speakers," *Dallas Morning News*, April 28, 1926; "Church Group Will Examine Life Problems," *Dallas Morning News*, February 18, 1929; "Race Problems Up for Study," *Dallas Morning News*, October 20, 1930; "Rebukes Dealt Negro as Issue of Politicians," *Dallas Morning News*, November 8, 1930; letter from W. W. Moore to the Advisory Committee regarding the Houston Negro Hospital, January 24, 1929, Joseph S. Cullinan Papers, 1895–1939, courtesy of Special Collections, University of Houston Libraries.

181. "Texas Women Plan Antilynching Work," *Dallas Morning News*, January 6, 1932.

182. "A Governor Rebuked," *Plaindealer* (Cleveland), December 8, 1933.

183. "Roosevelt Opens Fire on Lynching," *Plaindealer* (Cleveland), December 7, 1933.

184. "Seventeen Texas Sheriffs to Help Avert Lynchings," *Dallas Morning News*, December 9, 1934.

185. "Interracial Cooperation," *Dallas Morning News*, November 20, 1936; "Racial Commission Seeks to Aid Negro Higher Education," *Dallas Morning News*, September 9, 1937; "Texas Urged to Give Negro More Rights," *Dallas Morning News*, December 3, 1938.

186. "What Is Wrong about It All?" *Negro Star* (Wichita), November 18, 1938.

187. "Intolerance in Dallas," *Dallas Morning News*, May 2, 1938.

188. Jessie Daniel Ames, "Aftermath," Texas State Library and Archives Commission, 1928; http://www.tsl.state.tx.us.

189. Hall, *Revolt Against Chivalry*, 213.

190. Jacquelyn Dowd Hall, "Second Thoughts: On Writing a Feminist Biography," *Feminist Studies* 13 (1987), 19–37, quotation on p. 22.

191. Pilkington, "Trials of Brotherhood," 78.

CHAPTER 6
A LOAD TOO HEAVY

1. Mae Knox Burton, "Farmhouse Memories," in *Texas Millennium Book: The Way Things Used to Be*, ed. Jerry B. Lincecum and Peggy A. Redshaw (Sherman, TX: Austin College, 1999), 83–90, quotation on p. 83.

2. Jed Stockton, "Tin Wagon Keeps Depression Memories Alive," in *Telling Our Stories: Grayson County Reminiscences, the First 150 Years, 1846–1996*, ed. Jerry B. Lincecum (Sherman, TX: Austin College, 1996), 92–95.

3. "Relief Body Gets Encouraging News in Texas Reports," *Dallas Morning News*, October 22, 1931.

4. R. L. Duffus, "Dust Storms Bring Home Our Land Problems," *New York Times*, March 31, 1935.

5. U.S. Department of Agriculture, county-level data reported in 1930 and 1935, electronic data file, where the percentage of acres affected by crop failure is the number of acres listed for crop failure divided by the sum of these acres plus the number of acres of

crop land harvested (i.e., excludes cropland left fallow); Myron P. Gutmann, *Great Plains Population and Environment Data: Agricultural Data, 1870–1997* (Ann Arbor, MI: Inter-University Consortium for Political and Social Research, 2002). The counties with 80 percent or more of the cropland having failed were Andrews, Borden, Dallam, Deaf Smith, Edwards, Hartley, Moore, Oldham, and Sutton Counties, and the ones with at least 50 percent failure were Cochran, Cottle, Crosby, Dawson, Dickens, Gaines, Garza, Hockley, Hutchinson, Kent, Kinney, Lubbock, Lynn, Potter, Randall, Real, Sherman, and Uvalde Counties.

6. William Fike Godfrey, "By the Grace of God," in *A History of Dickens County: Ranches and Rolling Plains*, ed. Fred Arrington (Dickens, TX: Nortex Offset Publications, 1971), 344–51, quotation on p. 348; digital version on Portal to Texas History, http://texashistory.unt.edu.

7. Howard McCarley, "Dust Bowl Days," in *Texas Millennium Book*, 133–35, quotation on p. 134.

8. Deaf Smith Historical Society, *The Land and Its People, 1876–1981* (Deaf Smith County, TX: Deaf Smith County Historical Society, 1982), 35; "Dense Dust Storm Is on Its Way to Dallas," *Dallas Morning News* March 31, 1935.

9. E. H. Templin and J. A. Kerr, *Soil Survey of Midland County, Texas* (Washington, DC: U.S. Department of Agriculture, Bureau of Chemistry and Soils, 1933).

10. U.S. Census Bureau, *Statistical Abstract* (Washington, DC: Government Printing Office, 1940), 717.

11. Robert R. McKay, "Mexican Americans and Repatriation," *Handbook of Texas Online*, http://www.tshaonline.org.

12. Abraham Hoffman, "Mexican Repatriation Statistics: Some Suggested Alternatives to Carey McWilliams," *Western Historical Quarterly* 3 (1972), 391–404.

13. U.S. Bureau of Labor Statistics, *Handbook of Labor Statistics* (Washington, DC: Government Printing Office, 1936), 257, 269; reports annual figures not classified by country of origin or destination for all immigrant aliens admitted and emigrant aliens departed; for the United States in 1931 immigration exceeded emigration 97,139 to 61,882, but in Texas immigration was only 1,799 compared to emigration of 7,891; in 1931 the respective figures for Texas were 1,246 and 11,668; in 1933, 1,153 and 5,037; and in 1934, 1,116 and 2,795. The report indicated that the total number of Mexican emigrants leaving the United States between July 1, 1930, and June 30, 1932, was 61,398, but it acknowledged that data were incomplete.

14. Ibid., 269.

15. Quoted in J. L. Pope, "What Bible Says about Feeding the Hungry," *Dallas Morning News*, July 12, 1939; National Child Labor Committee, *Child Labor Facts* (New York: Herald-Nathan Press, 1938).

16. "6,050,000 Unemployed in U.S. in January, Lamont Announces," *Springfield Republican* (MA), March 21, 1931.

17. "Five Thousand Jobless Plan March at San Antonio," *Dallas Morning News*, April 3, 1930.

18. "El Paso Jobless Stage Rush on U.S. Bureau," *Dallas Morning News*, December 14, 1930.

19. Writers' Program of the Work Projects Administration in the City of Dallas, *The WPA Dallas Guide and History* (Dallas: Dallas Public Library and the University of North Texas Press, 1992), 96–98.

20. U.S. Census, 1940, electronic data file, county-level figures for registered unemployed in 1937 divided by the number of males and females age fourteen and over who were in the labor force.

21. Virginia R. Waller, "Girl in the Middle," in *Texas Millennium Book*, 141–45, quotation on p. 141.

22. Larry McSwain, *Loving Beyond Your Theology: The Life and Ministry of Jimmy Raymond Allen* (Atlanta: Mercer University Press, 2010), 38–39.

23. Mary Jacobs, "Another Depression Era? Methodists Recall Church's Role in 1930s Survival," *UM Portal*, November 10, 2008, http://www.umportal.org. A 1935 Southern Baptist report was largely upbeat but noted that a large number of congregations in rural Texas were unable to pay full time preachers or hold regular weekly services; J. M. Dawson, *A Century with Texas Baptists* (Nashville, TN: Broadman Press, 1947), 93–94.

24. "Texas Methodists Cope with Economic Depression August 1933," *Texas Methodist History*, August 20, 2011, http://txmethhistory.blogspot.com. The 1936 census of religious bodies obtained information from only 67 percent as many Methodist churches in Texas as in 1926, and from only 56 percent as many Southern Baptist churches, making comparisons of membership between the two time periods far from exact, but economic conditions were generally better in 1936 than they were in 1933, and that change was reflected in average expenditures per congregation, which were 82 percent of the 1926 figure among Methodists, 81 percent among Southern Baptists, 100 percent among African American Baptists, 76 percent among Presbyterians, and 75 percent among Roman Catholics. When adjusted for cost of living (which was 78 percent as high in 1936 as in 1926), this suggested relative stability; the overall economic situation did not significantly improve, however, until 1940.

25. Southern Baptist Convention, *Annual of the Southern Baptist Convention* (Nashville, TN: Southern Baptist Convention, 1932), 427.

26. Southern Baptist Convention, *Annual of the Southern Baptist Convention* (Nashville, TN: Southern Baptist Convention, 1940), 429–30; the cost-of-living adjustments are my calculations based on figures from the American Institute for Economic Research, http://www.aier.org.

27. Alan J. Lefever, "Recalling the Vision: A Brief History of First Baptist Church, Waco, Texas," *First Baptist Waco*, 2008, http://www.fbcwaco.org.

28. Hutchinson County Historical Commission, *History of Hutchinson County, Texas: 104 Years, 1876–1980* (Dallas: Taylor, 1980), 431.

29. Edward J. Robinson, *Show Us How You Do It: Marshall Keeble and the Rise of Black Churches of Christ in the United States, 1914–1968* (Tuscaloosa: University of Alabama Press, 2008), 63–64, includes a description of the work of African American preachers Marshall Keeble and R. N. Hogan in the Longview and Tyler areas.

30. Gene Cooper, "Ranger Raids Continued in New Oil Field," *Dallas Morning News*, March 4, 1931.

31. U.S. Census, county-level data for 1920, 1930, and 1940, electronic data files.

32. U.S. Department of Agriculture, county-level data for 1920, 1925, 1930, 1935, and 1940, electronic data files.

33. Bill C. Malone, "'Sing Me Back Home': Growing Up in the South and Writing the History of Its Music," in *Shapers of Southern History: Autobiographical Reflections*, ed. John B. Boles (Athens: University of Georgia Press, 2004), 91–113, quotation on p. 93.

34. W. M. Crichard, "Tenants Being Displaced," *Dallas Morning News*, May 28, 1934.

35. Godfrey, "By the Grace of God," 348.

36. U.S. Department of Agriculture, county-level data for 1930 and 1940, electronic data files.

37. U.S. Department of Agriculture, *Study of Consumer Purchases in the United States, 1935–36* (Ann Arbor, MI: Inter-University Consortium for Political and Social Research, 1999), electronic data file.

38. Nannie H. Burroughs, "Nearly All of the Educated Negroes Are Looking for Ready-Made Jobs," *Wyandotte Echo* (Kansas City, KS), August 14, 1931.

39. "Delegation Goes to Washington," *Negro Star* (Wichita, KS), February 2, 1940.

40. "Farm Union Demands Aid," *El Heraldo de Brownsville*, January 19, 1936.

41. James T. Moore, *Acts of Faith: The Catholic Church in Texas, 1900–1950* (College Station: Texas A&M University Press, 2002), 126–27; Roberto R. Trevino, "Facing Jim Crow: Catholic Sisters and the 'Mexican Problem' in Texas," *Western Historical Quarterly* 34 (2003), 139–64; John Rechy, "Jim Crow Wears a Sombrero," *The Nation* 10 (1950), 210–13; Neil Foley, *The White Scourge: Mexicans, Blacks, and Poor Whites in Texas Cotton Culture* (Berkeley: University of California Press, 1997).

42. Arlene M. Sánchez Walsh, *Latino Pentecostal Identity: Evangelical Faith, Self and Society* (New York: Columbia University Press, 2003), 24–48.

43. "Methodists Told Church Can Help End Depression," *Dallas Morning News*, November 13, 1931.

44. "Orange Chief of Police Shot to Death and Preacher Who Baptized Him Held," *Dallas Morning News*, May 30, 1935.

45. "Pastor-Slayer Recalls He Once Led Lynchers," *Dallas Morning News*, May 31, 1935.

46. "Eskridge Sentenced to 5-Year Prison Term," *Dallas Morning News*, June 18, 1936.

47. "Prohibition Speaker Attacks Roosevelt Recovery Program," *Dallas Morning News*, August 15, 1933.

48. Cyclone Davis, *Memoir* (Sherman, TX: Courier Press, 1935).

49. J. H. Cyclone Davis, "Concentrated Wealth Causing Hard Times," *Dallas Morning News*, March 3, 1930.

50. Davis, *Memoir,* 45; quoted in Donald W. Whisenhunt, "The Bard in the Depression: Texas Style," *Journal of Popular Culture* 2 (1968), 370–86, quotation on p. 372.

51. "Federal Control Declared Ending Individual Greed," *Dallas Morning News*, September 4, 1933.

52. "National Repentance Day," *Dallas Morning News*, July 17, 1934.

53. D. B. South, "The Heavenly Father's Chastening," *San Antonio Light*, October 18, 1931.

54. W. H. Kittrell, "Should Proclaim Day of Fasting and Prayer," *Dallas Morning News*, May 17, 1932.

55. Reverend H. H. Hargrove of Hillcrest Baptist Church, quoted in "Prevailing Drouth Compared to One in Biblical Time as Punishment for Sinfulness," *Dallas Morning News*, August 6, 1934.

56. "The Christian and World Peace," *Brookshire Times*, November 4, 1932.

57. Southern Baptist Convention, *Annual of the Southern Baptist Convention*, 1935, 60.

58. "Sweep Away Filth, Methodists Asked," *Dallas Morning News*, October 27, 1939.

59. Malone, "Sing Me Back Home," 98–99; and on similar experiences in other southern communities, see Wayne Flynt, "Religion and the Blues: Evangelicalism, Poor Whites, and the Great Depression," *Journal of Southern History* 71 (2005), 3–38.

60. "1932 Psalm," *Weatherford Democrat*, June 10, 1932; see also David G. McComb, *Texas: A Modern History* (Austin: University of Texas Press, 1989), 141.

61. Henry Ansley, "I Like the Depression," *Grand Prairie Texan*, April 29, 1932. Ansley died on August 13, 1932, and his obituary was published in the *Happy Herald* (Swisher County, TX), August 18, 1932; an account of how he came to write the essay, which circulated widely, appears in "Henry Ansley Missed from WTCC Meeting," *Big Spring Daily Herald*, May 7, 1933.

62. Lizabeth Cohen, *Making a New Deal: Industrial Workers in Chicago, 1919–1939* (Cambridge: Cambridge University Press, 1990), 213–49.

63. "Dallas Unselfish from Early Days, Aids Its Indigent," *Dallas Morning News*, October 1, 1935.

64. The founding and early activities of these organizations are discussed in Elizabeth York Enstam, *Women and the Creation of Urban Life: Dallas, Texas, 1843–1920* (College Station: Texas A&M University Press, 1998) 107–10; Patricia Evridge Hill, *Dallas: The Making of a Modern City* (Austin: University of Texas Press, 1996), 93–95; and Hollace Ava Weiner, *Jewish Stars in Texas: Rabbis and Their Work* (College Station: Texas A&M University Press, 1999), 44.

65. "Jobless Eat Turkey at Baptist Gospel Mission," *Dallas Morning News*, December 26, 1929.

66. "Dallas Reports Success in Task of Placing Jobless," *Dallas Morning News*, October 8, 1931.

67. "Relief Body Gets Encouraging News."

68. "Community Farming in Shadow of Skyscrapers Is Houston's Answer to Help for Unemployed," *Dallas Morning News*, April 2, 1932.

69. "Fighting Talk on Religion's Relief Responsibility."

70. "Rehabilitation Seen as Great Charities Task," *Dallas Morning News*, February 26, 1932.

71. "Leaders Cite Cases of Aid," *Dallas Morning News*, November 19, 1929.

72. Ibid.

73. "A Child at the Door," *Dallas Morning News*, January 16, 1931.

74. "Relief Agencies Get Many Calls," *Dallas Morning News*, February 28, 1931.

75. "Chest's Funds Still Paid to Special Units," *Avalanche Journal* (Lubbock, TX), June 7, 1931.

76. "Organize to Help Jobless," *Dallas Morning News*, October 29, 1930.

77. "Together for Charity," *Dallas Morning News*, June 11, 1931.

78. Reverend Max Strang of the Central Congregational Church in Dallas, as quoted in "Urges Intelligent Child Welfare," *Dallas Morning News*, August 12, 1931.

79. "National Need," *Dallas Morning News*, August 15, 1931.

80. "Dallas Spends But 49 Cents Each in Charity Work," *Dallas Morning News*, January 23, 1932.

81. Quoted in "Appeal for Contributions to Meet Greater Demands Made by Head of Charities," *Galveston Daily News*, July 17, 1932.

82. "County Charity Budget for 1932 Reduced to $50,000 as Commission Seeks Economy," *Port Arthur News*, January 7, 1932.

83. "Rabbits for Poor of City Assured," *Lubbock Morning Avalanche*, January 17, 1931.

84. "Plans of Texas to Aid Jobless Told Committee," *Dallas Morning News*, October 15, 1931.

85. "Vast Construction Plan Approved by War Department," *Dallas Morning News*, September 14, 1932.

86. "Accept Wichita Falls Federal Building Site," *Dallas Morning News*, November 6, 1930.

87. "Relief Agency Opening Many New Factories," *Dallas Morning News*, September 7, 1934.

88. "Relief Works Slash Causes Protest Flood," *Dallas Morning News*, January 20, 1934.

89. Bureau of Labor Statistics, *Handbook of Labor Statistics*, 143; as of April 1935 only 2,452 workers in Texas were employed in construction, of whom 835 were in Dallas, 133 in El Paso, 1,151 in Houston, and 333 in San Antonio.

90. "Many on Relief Rolls Expected Never to Leave," *Dallas Morning News*, June 14, 1934; Thomas F. Pettigrew, *The Sociology of Race Relations: Reflection and Reform* (New York: Simon and Schuster, 1980), 95.

91. "Peak of 278,000 on Relief Rolls," *Dallas Morning News*, December 21, 1936.

92. "Caustic Assault on New Deal Made by Texas Senator," *Dallas Morning News*, January 24, 1935.

93. John H. Cullom, "Function of Churches," *Dallas Morning News*, July 12, 1939; Cullom was a member of the Gaston Avenue Baptist Church, served as chair of the board for the Buckner Orphan Home, and was district clerk from 1920 to 1926 and Dallas County tax collector from 1926 to 1932.

94. "Reviving Hearts Promised Persons through Religion," *Dallas Morning News*, March 11, 1935.

95. "U.S. Bread Basket Is Called Sole God of Many Millions," *Dallas Morning News*, June 19, 1935.

96. "Trends in Religion," *Dallas Morning News*, June 23, 1935.

97. "Sweep Away Filth, Methodists Asked."

98. "J. B. Cranfill, "They're in Clover Now," *Dallas Morning News*, June 9, 1940.

99. J. B. Cranfill, "Roosevelt on Balancing Budgets in 1932," *Dallas Morning News*, April 20, 1938.

100. "U.S. Bread Basket Is Called Sole God of Many Millions."

101. "New Deal's Laws Praised in Talks at Catholic Meet," *Dallas Morning News*, October 21, 1936.

102. "Baptists Rap Federal Funds for Education," *Dallas Morning News*, May 20, 1939.

103. "Socialization of Medicine Coming, Hospital Men Told," *Dallas Morning News*, September 25, 1938.

104. "Refuse Federal Aid, Church Told," *Dallas Morning News*, January 3, 1935.

105. "Etex Mormons Take Care of Their Own," *Dallas Morning News*, May 8, 1938; "Mixing Religion and Relief," *Galveston Daily News*, July 5, 1936.

106. Southern Baptist Convention, *Annual of the Southern Baptist Convention*, 1940, 391.

107. Ibid., 392–403; "Orville Groner Dies," *Baptist Press*, January 4, 1954.

108. "Demand for Federal Control Draws Sharp Replies at Hearing," *Dallas Morning News*, May 18, 1938.

109. Christie L. Bourgeois, "Stepping over Lines: Lyndon Johnson, Black Texans, and the National Youth Administration," *Southwestern Historical Quarterly* 91 (1987), 149–72; "Drought Relief Discrimination Given to the Head of Red Cross," *Capital Plaindealer* (Topeka, KS), March 13, 1931.

110. "Relief High in Urban Sites FDR Told," *Capital Plaindealer* (Topeka, KS), January 17, 1937.

111. "City Develops Plans to Settle Racial Row," *Dallas Morning News*, October 11, 1940; "White Rally Sifts Issues in Race Ills," *Dallas Morning News*, October 23, 1940; Lynn Landrum, "Thinking Out Loud," *Dallas Morning News*, October 6, 1940; "Three Way Inquiry of Bombings Asked by Negro Chamber," *Dallas Morning News*, September 18, 1940; "Housing Battle Still Seethes in Dallas," *Negro Star* (Wichita, KS), December 20, 1940.

112. "World Baptists Open Their Sixth International Congress," *El Heraldo de Brownsville*, July 23, 1939.

113. "Text of Roosevelt's Neutrality Address," *El Heraldo de Brownsville*, September 4, 1939.

114. "Noted Woman to Emphasize Peace Benefit," *Dallas Morning News*, February 22, 1937.

115. "Passionate Plea for Peace Made by Maude Royden," *Dallas Morning News*, February 24, 1937.

116. "Churches Join Prayer for Peace," *Dallas Morning News*, September 9, 1940.

117. "Peace Rally Is Patriotic, Pastor Says," *Dallas Morning News*, May 24, 1941; "America First Group in Dallas Goes on Radio," *Dallas Morning News*, September 14, 1941.

118. "Reds Choice of Two Evils, Say Pastors," *Dallas Morning News*, August 23, 1941.

119. William M. Thornton, "Housecleaning at University Asked Because of Sarcastic Utterances on War and Peace," *Dallas Morning News*, June 20, 1940.

120. Thomas A. Guglielmo, "Fighting for Caucasian Rights: Mexicans, Mexican Americans, and the Transnational Struggle for Civil Rights in World War II Texas," *Journal of American History*, 92 (March 2006), 1212–37.

121. "Citizenship Ceremonies Will Be Planned Here," *El Heraldo de Brownsville*, September 14, 1939.

122. Andrew Preston, *Sword of the Spirit, Shield of Faith: Religion in American War and Diplomacy* (New York: Anchor Books, 2012), 365–83.

123. "Southern Group Will Sever Relations with Federal Council," *Dallas Morning News*, June 2, 1931; "Religion: Federal Council Scotched," *Time*, June 15, 1931.

124. "Birth Control Again," *Dallas Morning News*, April 7, 1931.

125. "Able Executive Made Head of Texas Tech," *Dallas Morning News*, January 1, 1939.

CHAPTER 7
MOVING ONTO THE NATIONAL STAGE

1. Gallup Organization, *Gallup Poll 1962–0659: Politics/Religion/Stock* (Storrs, CT: Roper Center for Public Opinion Research, 1962), electronic data file, survey conducted May 31 through June 5, 1962, with face-to-face interviews among 3,236 nationally representative adults.

2. Political Behavior Program, Survey Research Center, *American National Election Study, 1964* (Ann Arbor, MI: Inter-University Consortium for Political and Social Research, 1999), electronic data file, survey conducted among 1,834 nationally representative adult respondents; the alternative possible responses to the Bible question were that "the Bible was written by men inspired by God but it contains some human errors," "the Bible is a good book because it was written by wise men but God had nothing to do with it," and "the Bible was written by men who lived so long ago that it is worth very little today."

3. U.S. Census, County Data, 1944, electronic data file.

4. Bruce J. Schulman, *From Cotton Belt to Sunbelt: Federal Policy, Economic Development, and the Transformation of the South, 1938–1980* (Durham, NC: Duke University Press, 1994), 135–73.

5. Texas Historical Commission, *Texas in World War II*, http://www.thc.state.tx.us.

6. U.S. Census, County Data, 1947, electronic data file.

7. U.S. Census, County Data, 1947 and 1952, electronic data files.

8. U.S. Census, County Data, 1952 and 1962, 1 percent Public Use Microsamples 1950 and 1960, electronic data files.

9. Jones was a born-again Christian who helped fund John Brown College in Arkansas, as noted by Bethany Moreton, *To Serve God and Wal-Mart: The Making of Christian Free Enterprise* (Cambridge, MA: Harvard University Press, 2009), 32–33.

10. U.S. Census Bureau, *Statistical Abstract of the United States, 1962* (Washington, DC: Government Printing Office, 1962), 715.

11. U.S. Census, County Data, 1962, electronic data file, zero-order Pearson correlation among the 209 Texas counties in which any mineral industry receipts were reported in 1959; the largest receipts in that year were in the West Texas Permian Basin; in the six counties with the highest revenue, total receipts exceeded the total combined income of all families in those counties by more than $700 million.

12. National Council of Churches, *Churches and Church Membership in the United States: An Enumeration and Analysis by Counties, States and Regions* (New York: National Council of Churches, 1956), electronic data file for states and counties, 1952; courtesy of the Association of Religion Data Archives, http://www.thearda.com; Leon Edgar Truesdell and Timothy

Francis Murphy, *Religious Bodies, 1926* (Washington, DC: U.S. Government Printing Office, 1929), electronic data file courtesy of the Inter-University Consortium for Political and Social Research.

13. In the absence of data from the 1952 study, the estimate for African American Baptists is from adjusting the 1926 figure for population growth and from the number of African Americans in the 1960 Texas polls who indicated their religion as Baptist.

14. Grant Wacker, *Heaven Below: Early Pentecostals and American Culture* (Cambridge, MA: Harvard University Press, 2001), 119–23, 179–85.

15. Roger Finke and Rodney Stark, *The Churching of America, 1776–2005: Winners and Losers in Our Religious Economy* (New Brunswick, NJ: Rutgers University Press, 2005).

16. Michael Hout, Andrew Greeley, and Melissa J. Wilde, "The Demographic Imperative in Religious Change in the United States," *American Journal of Sociology* 107 (2001), 468–500.

17. U.S. Census, 1940 and 1950, counties and states, electronic data files. In 1940 the proportion of the total population who were children under the age of five averaged 11.3 percent for the fifteen southern and border states in which Southern Baptists were concentrated, compared to 9.6 percent in the other states; in 1950, the respective figures were 11.7 percent and 10.9 percent.

18. This assertion assumes that birthrates were the same among Baptists and Methodists in Texas; data are not available, but differences noted a few years later in education levels suggest that there may have been some differences in birthrates as well.

19. These data are from tabulations provided by the Association of Religion Data Archives, http://www.thearda.com, as compiled from various Federal Council of Churches statistics.

20. "Give Argument for Unifying of Methodists," *Dallas Morning News*, January 4, 1939.

21. Ibid.

22. On African American church leaders' concerns, see "Enter Epochal Merger Conference," *Plaindealer* (Kansas City, KS), April 28, 1939.

23. "Bishop Refuses to Acknowledge Methodist Union," *Times Picayune* (New Orleans), May 1, 1939.

24. Richard Nokes, "Methodist Test Due," *Oregonian* (Portland), January 10, 1940; "Bishop Moore Minimized Merger Fight," *Dallas Morning News*, April 19, 1939.

25. "Methodists Buck Merger," *Augusta Chronicle* (GA), April 17, 1941; and as Darren Dochuk, *From Bible Belt to Sunbelt: Plain-Folk Religion, Grassroots Politics, and the Rise of Evangelical Conservatism* (New York: Norton, 2011), 44, notes, another important development was the formation in 1946 in Memphis of the Evangelical Methodist Church led by Methodist preacher James Henry Hamblen from Abilene, Texas.

26. "Bishop Raps Body's Use of 'Methodist,'" *Dallas Morning News*, February 4, 1950.

27. Association of Religion Data Archives, http://www.thearda.com.

28. Gerald Gurin, Joseph Veroff, and Sheila Feld, *Americans View Their Mental Health* (Ann Arbor, MI: Inter-University Consortium for Political and Social Research, 1957), electronic data file; results based on 292 white Baptists raised in southern and border states and 125 white Methodists raised in southern and border states; 44 percent and 25 percent, respectively, had no schooling beyond eighth grade.

29. Belden Associates, *The Texas Poll: Business/Presidential Election* (Storrs, CT: Roper Center for Public Opinion Research, 1960), electronic data files; the polls were conducted in face-to-face interviews during February and May 1960 among representative samples of the adult population including 999 and 1,000 respondents, respectively; combing the respondents yields 588 white, non-Hispanic Baptists and 341 white, non-Hispanic Methodists, which are the numbers on which the percentages having graduated college or finished part of college are based.

30. Southern Baptist Convention, *Annual of the Southern Baptist Convention* (Nashville, TN: Southern Baptist Convention, 1953); "New Baptist Building Seen as Conservation," *Dallas Morning News*, July 17, 1941.

31. Joseph E. Early, *A Texas Baptist History Sourcebook: A Companion to McBeth's Texas Baptists* (Denton: University of North Texas Press, 2004), 311.

32. Ibid., 449–50.

33. "John Moore, Methodist Bishop Dies," *Dallas Morning News*, July 31, 1948.

34. National Opinion Research Center, *Anti-Semitism in the United States* (Ann Arbor, MI: Inter-University Consortium for Political and Social Research, 1964), electronic data file; exact wording of the questions is included in Gertrude J. Selznick and Stephen Steinberg, *The Tenacity of Prejudice: Anti-Semitism in Contemporary America* (New York: Harper & Row, 1969).

35. National Opinion Research Center, *Anti-Semitism in the United States*; 17 percent of white Southern Baptists in the South said they attended worship services several times a week, compared with 11 percent of white southern Methodists.

36. Ibid.; unlike many smaller theologically conservative denominations, Southern Baptists did not forbid membership in secret societies, and a number of prominent Southern Baptists, including Baylor and Truett, held membership in freemasonry organizations; however, conservative pastors sometimes counseled against involvement in other organizations that might detract from church involvement by the early 1980s formal concerns about offensive and idolatrous practices in freemasonry were being expressed at Southern Baptist Convention meetings; James Dotson, "New Publication on Freemasonry Available from SBC's North American Mission Board," *Baptist Press*, June 9, 2000; www.bpnews.net; *A Closer Look at Freemasonry*, www.southcarolinaconservative.com.

37. Alva Hutchinson quoted in "Methodists Set as Goal Church a Day," *Dallas Morning News*, June 28, 1949.

38. U.S. Census Bureau, *Statistical Abstract of the United States, 1952* (Washington, DC: Government Printing Office, 1952), 728.

39. Ibid., 729, 732–34.

40. "Durwood Fleming Preaches First Sermon at St. Luke's," *Texas Methodist History*, November 10, 2007, http://txmethhistory.blogspot.com; "Arlington First Baptist Church Opens New $225,00 Building," *Dallas Morning News*, April 17, 1947; "Grace Temple Baptist Church to Build $125,000 Brick Home," *Dallas Morning News*, March 23, 1947; "Lakewood Church Donated New Site," *Dallas Morning News*, March 2, 1947; "Park Cities Church Reports Growth," *Dallas Morning News*, January 13, 1947; "St. Cecelia's Catholic Church to Construct $150,000 Building," *Dallas Morning News*, June 11, 1947.

41. Stewart Doss, "Tremendous Building Program under Way by Religious Groups," *Dallas Morning News*, October 11, 1953.

42. "Tuscola Baptists Get New Church," *Abilene Reporter News*, November 9, 1948.

43. "McM Ex to Head St. Paul Church," *Abilene Reporter News*, May 29, 1950.

44. "Total of $184,254 Given to Church," *Dallas Morning News*, January 2, 1922; "Radiomania Epidemic Spreads Rapidly over Dallas and State of Texas," *Dallas Morning News*, January 22, 1922.

45. Winrod's broadcasts through 1947 are described in letters included in the Reverend Dr. Gerald B. Winrod Papers, Wichita State University Libraries, Special Collections and University Archives.

46. Brinkley quoted in David Parmer, *A Tribute to Dr. John R. Brinkley*, radio transcript, February 2, 1936, courtesy of Kansas Memory Collection, Kansas State Historical Society, Topeka; Robert Wuthnow, *Red State Religion: Faith and Politics in America's Heartland* (Princeton, NJ: Princeton University Press, 2012), 164; "Wolfman Jack's Old Station Howling Once Again," *Dallas Times Herald*, January 2, 1983; Gene Fowler and Bill Crawford, *Border Radio: Quacks, Yodelers, Pitchmen, Psychics, and Other Amazing Broadcasters of the American Airwaves* (Austin: University of Texas Press, 2002).

47. Early, *A Texas Baptist History Sourcebook*, 338–40.

48. Bill Ellis, "World's Largest Christian Broadcasting Convention in Texas," *Assist News Service*, March 2, 2006, http://www.assistnews.net; Ayer was pastor of Calvary Baptist Church in New York City and in 1947 was named third after Cardinal Francis Spellman and Eleanor Roosevelt among the city's most influential citizens.

49. Guy Lancaster, "Jonesboro Church Wars," *Encyclopedia of Arkansas History and Culture* (2007), http://www.encyclopediaofarkansas.net; Dusty Jordan, "Baptists Bring War to Jonesboro," *Craighead County Historical Quarterly* 21 (1983), 1–9; "Pastor Arrested for Street Fight," *Trenton Sunday Times* (New Jersey), February 19, 1933; "Tabernacle Door Locked Pending Action by Court," *Times-Picayune* (New Orleans), August 15, 1933; "Shots Fired at Pastor," *Morning Oregonian* (Portland), October 18, 1933; "Religion: Jonesboro Baptists," *Time*, January 15, 1934.

50. "Orthodoxy at Stake," *Dallas Morning News*, August 20, 1933.

51. "Baptist Laymen to Hear Talk by Dale Crowley," *Washington Post*, December 19, 1936; "Bible Theme of Talks by Four Congressmen," *Washington Post*, October 20, 1941; "Legislators to Take Part in Bible Quiz," *Washington Post*, June 2, 1951.

52. Ray Granade, "My Last Lecture: Hearing Voices, Seeing Visions," Oklahoma Baptist University, April 23, 2008.

53. "Pulpit and Pew," *Dallas Morning News*, March 25, 1944.

54. "Baptists to Launch Own Youth Crusade, Spurn Joint Effort," *Dallas Morning News*, September 4, 1945.

55. "Methodist Magazine Scores Youth Groups," *Dallas Morning News*, July 22, 1948.

56. "Three Meetings Slated by YCI," *Dallas Morning News*, December 6, 1947; "Youth for Christ Honors Cliff Barrows," Billy Graham Evangelistic Association, July 17, 2008, http://www.billygraham.org.

57. David M. Gardner, "Misrepresenting Baptists," *Baptist Standard* (September 21, 1950), 4.

58. "Baptist Hits Inactivity of New Members," *Dallas Morning News*, January 11, 1950.

59. "Eggs from Baptists Deluge Orphans Home," *Dallas Morning News*, March 3, 1951.

60. John P. Newport, "The Church Member," in *J. Howard Williams: Prophet of God and Friend of Man*, ed. H. C. Brown Jr. and Charles P. Johnson (San Antonio, TX: Naylor, 1963), 121–29, especially p. 125.

61. Graham's sermon in Dallas on July 4, 1953, was also made into a phonograph recording, "Let Freedom Ring," Billy Graham Evangelistic Association, Archive Collection, Billy Graham Library, Charlotte, NC.

62. Kevin D. Hendricks, "Billy Graham Switches Church Membership," *Billyspot* (December 31, 2008), online; Newport, "The Church Member," 125. Criswell had grown up in the Texas Panhandle, attended Baylor University in the late 1920s, and struggled through the Depression preaching at churches in Kentucky, Oklahoma, and Texas; described in W. A. Criswell, *Standing on the Promises: The Autobiography of W. A. Criswell* (Nashville, TN: Word Publishing Group, 1991).

63. Kenneth Dole, "Religious Roundup," *Washington Post*, March 28, 1953; Dole, "News of the Churches," *Washington Post*, June 13, 1953; Diana J. Kleiner, "H-E-B," *Handbook of Texas Online*, http://www.tshaonline.org.

64. Kristy Ozmun, "Butt, Howard Edward," *Handbook of Texas Online*, http://www .tshaonline.org; "H. E. Butt Grocery Company," http://www.heb.com.

65. Foundations for Laity Renewal, http://www.laityrenewal.org.

66. Bruce McIver, *Riding the Wind of God: A Personal History of the Youth Revival Movement* (Macon, GA: Smyth & Helwys, 2002), 18–20.

67. Ibid., 79–84.

68. Mary Knox, "Youth Revivalists Shaped a Generation," *Baptist Standard* (June 30, 1999), 1.

69. Dole, "Religious Roundup."

70. Southern Baptist Convention, *Annual of the Southern Baptist Convention* (Nashville, TN: Southern Baptist Convention, 1947), 294.

71. "Television," *Handbook of Texas Online*, http://www.tshaonline.org; U.S. Census Bureau, *Statistical Abstract* (Washington, DC: Government Printing Office, 1962), 514; *History of Television*, http://www.high-techproductions.com.

72. "Presbyterians Will Hear Baptist Billy Graham Talk," *Dallas Morning News*, January 7, 1951; "Evangelist Advocates Spiritual Boot Camp," *Dallas Morning News*, January 8, 1951.

73. Stuart M. Doss, "Dallas Ministers Praise TV as Means to Spread Gospel," *Dallas Morning News*, June 15, 1952.

74. "Shipments of TVs to Dealers by States, 1950–1953," http://www.tvhistory.tv.

75. U.S. Census Bureau, *Statistical Abstract* (Washington, DC: Government Printing Office, 1955), 515.

76. Belden Associates, *The Texas Poll* (Storrs, CT: Roper Center for Public Opinion, 1954), electronic data file; poll conducted face to face in November 1954 among 1,000 respondents representative of the adult residents of Texas: 788 white Anglos, 99 Hispanics, and 113 African Americans.

77. Darren Dochuk, "Moving Mountains: The Business of Evangelicalism and Extraction," in *What's Good for Business: Business and American Politics Since World War II*, ed. Kim Phillips-Fein and Julian E. Zelizer (New York: Oxford University Press, 2012), 72–90.

78. Rufus Jarman, "LeTourneau," *Life* (October 16, 1944), 49–59.

79. "LeTourneau Turns to Shell Making Using Equipment of His Own Design," *Wall Street Journal*, October 29, 1940.

80. LeTourneau Foundation, Internal Revenue Service 990 Form 2006, http://www .guidestar.org; "Gideons Warned on Perils Dormant in Class Hatreds," *Los Angeles Times*, July 27, 1940.

81. "Businessmen's Religious Body to Hear Rivers," *Atlanta Constitution*, August 11, 1940; Thomas M. Elliott, "LeTourneau Speaks Here to Ministers," *Atlanta Constitution*, March 4, 1941.

82. "Gideons Warned on Perils Dormant in Class Hatreds," *Los Angeles Times*, July 27, 1940; LeTourneau was a frequent speaker at conventions of Gideons, the men's organization that distributed Bibles to schools, hospitals, and hotels.

83. "Critics Change Minds about Industrialist's Christianity," *Los Angeles Times*, April 4, 1942.

84. Kenneth Foree, "Now He Argues Case for Lord," *Dallas Morning News*, April 30, 1950.

85. "History," LeTourneau University, http://www.letu.edu.

86. Harrietta Bishop, "LeTourneaus Put Money in Constructive Project," *Christian Science Monitor*, August 19, 1952; "C. W. Brannon, Evangelist, to Open Services," *Dallas Morning News*, October 15, 1951. *Now* magazine was published at the college from 1947 to 1955, when it was divided into separate college and company editions, and it has continued to be published in various formats since then; Archive Materials, LeTourneau University, http://www .letu.edu.

87. "LeTourneau Combined Religion, Business," *Dallas Morning News*, June 2, 1969; Tai Deckner Kreidler, "The Offshore Petroleum Industry: The Formative Years, 1945–1962" (PhD diss., Texas Tech University, 1997).

88. Frank X. Tolbert, "On Conquering Jungles for God," *Dallas Morning News*, April 4, 1955; "Industrialist Raps Plan for Booming Liberians," *Philadelphia Tribune*, August 14, 1951.

89. "With Bible and Bull-Dozer: Reclamation in Peru," *Manchester Guardian*, April 22, 1954.

90. "Two Unions Beaten in Longview Vote," *Dallas Morning News*, November 20, 1948. Frank Marshall Davis, "Youth for Christ Movement Called Front for Fascism," *Pittsburgh Courier*, January 12, 1946, quoted Chicago church leaders who criticized LeTourneau's support for Youth for Christ because the organization included only white youth and was said to encourage antilabor views and anti-Semitism; "Worthy of His Hire," *Christian Endeavor World*, August 1, 1949, as part of a young people's Bible study lesson advised that "happy relations between labor and management" require "true Christian hearts" and identified LeTourneau as one of the "Christian business men [whose] love for Christ is making their relations with their employees continually successful and peaceful."

91. LeTourneau's story was the focus of a Ripley radio broadcast on September 27, 1940; Sarah Ruth Hammond, " 'God's Business Men': Entrepreneurial Evangelicals in Depression

and War" (PhD diss., Yale University, 2010), 15; Erik Barnouw, *The Golden Web: A History of Broadcasting in the United States, 1933–1953* (New York: Oxford University Press, 1958), 58

92. LeTourneau, *Mover of Men and Mountains*, 3; although the book implied a relationship between faith and prosperity, that connection was more often made explicit by other writers; for example, Ralph W. Porter, "'Bootstrap' Career Airs Religious Ardor," *Christian Science Monitor*, June 16, 1960, observed in reviewing the book's first edition that the LeTourneau creed was simply "it pays to be in partnership with God."

93. "Hugh Roy Cullen, Philanthropist and Oil Operator, Dies," *Dallas Morning News*, July 5, 1957.

94. Carol V. R. George, *God's Salesman: Norman Vincent Peale and the Power of Positive Thinking* (New York: Oxford University Press, 1993).

95. Norman V. Peale, "Why Not Accept God as Partner?" *Dallas Morning News*, November 30, 1952, which featured the success story of Claud H. Foster of Cleveland, who earned a fortune selling shock absorbers for automobiles; among Southern Baptists, a similar example was Alabama timber magnate Gerald C. Coggin, Patsy Jo Faught, "Millionaire's Cue for Wealth Is God," *Dallas Morning News*, October 11, 1956.

96. Ed Townsend, "People at Work: Ministers in Industry," *Christian Science Monitor*, November 14, 1959, describes chaplaincy work at the LeTourneau plant in Longview and at the D-X Sunray Oil Company in Tulsa; James Tanner and Louis Kraar, "More Firms Retain Ministers to Advise, Comfort Employees," *Wall Street Journal*, March 3, 1959, mentions clergy paid to minister to employees or to assist with community relations at the John E. Mitchell automobile air conditioner plant in Dallas, the LeTourneau plant in Longview, and scattered other locations in plants owned by General Electric, Western Union, General Foods, Caterpillar, Westinghouse, Lone Star Steel, Reynolds Tobacco, and Fieldcrest Mills.

97. Gibson Winter, *The Suburban Captivity of the Churches: An Analysis of Protestant Responsibility in the Expanding Metropolis* (Garden City, NY: Doubleday, 1961).

98. "Methods of Worship Not Subject to Court," *Dallas Morning News*, March 27, 1945.

99. Hatcher Street Baptist pastor Carroll R. Greene as quoted in "Churches Meet Negro Problem," *Dallas Morning News*, March 8, 1952; additional church relocations are described in "Negro Expansion Causing Moves," *Dallas Morning News*, March 16, 1952; and "White Church Site Bought by Negroes," *Dallas Morning News*, June 26, 1952.

100. Stewart M. Doss, "AME Panel to Offer Rights Plea Support," *Dallas Morning News*, February 20, 1948.

101. Federal Council of the Churches of Christ in America, *Federal Council Bulletin* (New York: Religious Publicity Service, 1948).

102. Lynn W. Landrum, "Negro Housing," *Dallas Morning News*, November 13, 1947; Landrum, "Thinking Out Loud," *Dallas Morning News*, March 10, 1948.

103. "Study, Not Endorsement," *Dallas Morning News*, March 11, 1948.

104. "Did the 155 Really Represent 800,000?" *Dallas Morning News*, March 14, 1948.

105. Robert L. Ivy, "Can See No Reasons for Segregation," *Dallas Morning News*, March 7, 1948.

106. "Red Racial Equality Held Favoring Cause," *Dallas Morning News*, March 15, 1948.

107. "Shouting Pastor Ousted Bodily from Texas Baptist Convention," *Baltimore Sun*, November 13, 1947.

108. Stewart Doss, "Rights Stand by Churches under Attack," *Dallas Morning News*, April 8, 1948.

109. Stewart Doss, "High Baptist Doubts Rights Plan Success," *Dallas Morning News*, April 7, 1948.

110. Methodist Church General Conference, *Journal of the General Conference of the Methodist Church* (New York: Methodist Church General Conference, 1948), 739–40.

111. Southern Baptist Convention, *Annual of the Southern Baptist Convention* (Nashville, TN: Southern Baptist Convention, 1947), 47–48; Southern Baptist Convention, *Annual of the Southern Baptist Convention* (Nashville, TN: Southern Baptist Convention, 1948), 53; Stewart Doss, "Southern Baptists Thronging Memphis," *Dallas Morning News*, May 17, 1948; Doss, "J. Frank Norris Enrolled as Convention Messenger," *Dallas Morning News*, May 19, 1948.

112. Allen Duckworth, "Truman Predicts Texas to Stay True to Party," *Dallas Morning News*, September 28, 1948.

113. Kari Frederickson, *The Dixiecrat Revolt and the End of the Solid South, 1932–1968* (Chapel Hill: University of North Carolina Press, 2001), 116–17.

114. W. H. Lawrence, "Keep Powder Dry President Urges in Plea for Peace," *New York Times*, September 27, 1948; Harry S. Truman, "Informal Remarks in San Antonio, Texas," September 26, 1948, Harry S. Truman Library and Museum, http://www.trumanlibrary.org.

115. Results based on an analysis of county-level data from electronic data files for the 1948 general election and using 1950 census data for percentage African American, and 1952 religious bodies data as the closest year in which religious membership figures were available.

116. Warren Leslie, "Mounting Negro Population Hard Pressed for Housing," *Dallas Morning News*, March 9, 1949.

117. U.S. Census, 1950, electronic data files for Dallas and Harris counties, courtesy of Social Explorer, http://www.socialexplorer.com.

118. U.S. Census, 1940, electronic data files for Dallas and Harris Counties, courtesy of Social Explorer, http://www.socialexplorer.com; between 1940 and 1950 the total population of Dallas County increased 153,745, the white population increased 141,485, and the black population increased 12, 260; population density in tracts that were at least 50 percent black remained almost constant from 11,666 per square mile in 1940 to 11,318 in 1950, while population density in the remaining counties fell from 7,326 to 5,504; in Harris County the total population increased by 422,187, the white population increased by 356,593, the black population increased by 65,594, population density per square mile in predominantly black census tracts declined only from 10,727 to 9,322 compared to a decline in the remaining tracts from 7,911 to 4,266.

119. Clint Pace, "Negro Housing Permit Issued," *Dallas Morning News*, June 1, 1949.

120. "C. C. Group to Ask Jury Bomb Probe," *Dallas Morning News*, July 14, 1951; "New Negro Home Wrecked by Bomb," *Dallas Morning News*, July 12, 1951.

121. Linda Reed, *Simple Decency and Common Sense: The Southern Conference Movement, 1938–1963* (Bloomington: Indiana University Press, 1991), 75.

122. "Church Unit Backs Negro," *New York Times*, October 13, 1949.

123. "Texas Attorney General Slaps Church Brief," *Atlanta Daily World*, January 4, 1950.

124. "Order to Enroll Negro at UT Will Not Upset State System," *Big Spring Daily Herald*, June 6, 1950.

125. *Texas Poll*, 1954, electronic data file; the question asked, "As you know, the United States Supreme Court has ruled that all children, no matter what their race, have equal rights to go to the same schools. Now they have to figure out how to put this new law into effect all over the country. Suppose you were on the school board here, and they asked you to give your frank opinion. Which one of the dour statements on this card comes closest to the way you feel about it?" The responses I mention exclude those who had no opinion and for white respondents refer to the 740 respondents whose race was recorded as "Anglo," for black respondents refer to the 99 respondents whose race was coded as "Negro," and for Hispanic refer to the 93 respondents whose race was coded as "Latin."

126. "Robert M. Hayes, "Resentment Seen in Northeast Area," *Dallas Morning News*, October 9, 1952.

127. *Texas Poll*, 1954, electronic data file, 699 respondents who indicated how they had voted in 1952.

128. *Texas Poll*, 1954, electronic data file, responses for white Anglos who voted in 1952 among whom 294 were coded as being of average or above-average economic status and 77 were coded as being of low economic status; among the 163 respondents coded as "low plus" economic status, 55 percent voted for Eisenhower.

129. Numan V. Bartley and Hugh D. Graham, *Southern Primary and General Election Data, 1944–1972* (Ann Arbor, MI: Inter-University Consortium for Political and Social Research, 1977), electronic data file; the county data for Texas also show that Eisenhower received 54 percent of the vote in counties that included cities of 50,000 or more compared with 51 percent in less urbanized counties.

130. *Texas Poll*, 1954, electronic data file.

131. Dawson Duncan, "States' Righters Start Texas Blitz," *Dallas Morning News*, October 19, 1948.

132. The tidelands were an area submerged in shallow water off the Gulf of Mexico coast; with oil having been discovered there in 1938, the tidelands mushroomed in value, but in 1947 the U.S. Supreme Court ruled in a case against California that tidelands belonged to the federal government, thus posing the possibility that Texas would lose revenue and control over leasing rights; Eisenhower's promise to restore these rights was regarded as a reason for his victory in Texas in 1952; William K. Wyant, *Westward in Eden: The Public Lands and the Conservation Movement* (Berkeley: University of California Press, 1987).

133. Drew Pearson, "Ike Eisenhower and Texas Oil," *Dallas Morning News*, May 9, 1952.

134. "Cullen Raps Ike's Right on Amendment," *Dallas Morning News*, February 20, 1954.

135. Hugh Mulligan, "Church Integration Follows Same Pattern as Schools," *Corpus Christi Caller-Times*, March 4, 1956.

136. "Rights Evasion Decried," *New York Times*, January 8, 1955.

137. "Church Women of Texas Back Desegregation," *Chicago Defender*, March 12, 1956.

138. "Interposition Hit," *Seattle Times*, March 9, 1956; the council also advised church members against joining any organizations aiming to circumvent the Supreme Court's decision; Charles Lewis, "Prairie Scope," *Grand Prairie Texan*, April 3, 1956.

139. Robert F. Ford, "Integration in Texas Schools Swift in Many Parts of State," *Corpus Christi Caller-Times*, March 4, 1956.

140. Elias G. Rodriguez, "Segregation Wrong," *Dallas Morning News,* March 22, 1956; Rodriguez was an armed forces veteran who graduated in 1958, "Rodriguez Brothers to Graduate from Baptist Seminary July 18," *Kerrville Mountain Sun*, July 10, 1958.

141. "Integrating Churches," *Dallas Morning News*, January 2, 1956.

142. "God Made Negroes Inferior to Whites, Says Tex. Minister," *Philadelphia Tribune*, August 30, 1952.

143. Rev. Earl Anderson quoted in "Religion: Muted Trumpets in Dixie," *Time*, April 16, 1956; in a subsequent statement he declared, "If, indeed, we are looking for the biggest law to obey why not obey the highest law of all, the holy law of God which demands segregation," Earl Anderson, "Highest Law," *Dallas Morning News*, September 14, 1957.

144. "Baptist Pastor to Give 2nd Talk Opposing Integration," *Abilene Reporter News*, February 27, 1956.

145. Nels Hansen and Bill Coffey, "Criswell Rips Integration," *Dallas Morning News*, February 23, 1956.

146. Lynn Landrum, "Speaking Out," *Dallas Morning News*, February 24, 1956.

147. "Southern Church Leaders State Segregation Views," *Plaindealer* (Kansas City, KS), October 5, 1956.

148. "Integration Attack Stuns Texas Baptists," *Seattle Times*, February 23, 1956; the pastor who was "stunned" was Reverend Ernest C. Estell, pastor of St. John's Baptist Church, an African American congregation in Dallas.

149. "Segregation Blast Lifted from Text, Criswell Says," *Dallas Morning News*, March 16, 1956.

150. Bill Knott, " 'Dixie' Is Sweet," *Dallas Morning News*, March 22, 1956.

151. Ruth Davidson Smith, "Liberal Ministers," *Dallas Morning News*, March 22, 1956.

152. Respectively, Mrs. Homer A. Matthews, "Negroes in Churches"; Thomas N. Fisher, "Segregation in Church"; and S. A. Beaird, "Stand on Segregation," *Dallas Morning News*, February 27, 1956.

153. "Baptists Hear Bitter Attack on Integration," *Corpus Christi Caller-Times*, June 27, 1956.

154. "Baptist Group Will Discuss Segregation," *Dallas Morning News*, November 8, 1956.

155. Nels Hansen, "Dr. Warren Re-Elected Head of Southern Baptist Convention," *Dallas Morning News*, June 1, 1956.

156. Sue Connally, "Baptist Sees Segregated High School," *Dallas Morning News*, October 9, 1956; "Baptist Enemy of Integration Urges Church School," *Big Spring Daily Herald*, October 8, 1956.

157. Allen Duckworth, "Daniel's Pledge Sparks Rally," *Dallas Morning News*, August 19, 1956.

158. Allen Duckworth, "Daniel Asks Showdown on Politics," *Dallas Morning News*, June 20, 1956.

159. "Catholic Aspirants Stir Baptist Group," *New York Times*, November 6, 1959.

160. "163 Clerics Join Plea," *New York Times*, October 22, 1957; "Integration Suit Filed in Houston," *Afro-American* (Baltimore), January 12, 1957; "Houston School Board in Integration Test," *Cleveland Call and Post*, February 2, 1957.

161. "Texas Church Council Asks Integration Help," *Daily Defender* (Chicago), January 7, 1957.

162. Sue Connally, "Incumbents Win Posts in Record School Vote," *Dallas Morning News*, May 4, 1958.

163. Clarence Mitchell, "From the Work Bench: Everything Is Big in Texas?" *Afro-American*, March 8, 1958.

164. "Truman Preaches Good, Like Preacher Should," *Boston Globe*, October 25, 1959.

165. Ibid.

166. E. S. James, "Are Baptists Bigoted," *Baptist Standard* (December 10, 1958), 2.

167. U.S. Census, County Data, 1950 including 1952 churches and church membership, electronic data file.

168. Walter Winchell, "On Broadway," *Brownsville Herald*, March 13, 1951.

169. Robert Miller and Dorothea McGrath, "School Leaders Look to Austin," *Dallas Morning News*, May 18, 1954; the other leaders included Rabbi Levi A. Olan of Temple Emanu-El in Dallas, Episcopal bishop Avery Mason, John E. Anderson of Dallas's First Presbyterian Church, Arthur Swartz of the Dallas Central Christian Church, and Methodist bishop William C. Martin of Dallas, who was also president of the National Council of Churches; Wallace Bassett of Cliff Temple Baptist Church offered a mixed assessment, saying that the Court's decision was "not going to hurt."

170. "Parochial Schools Admit Negroes without Incident," *Dallas Morning News*, September 26, 1954.

171. "Diocesan Schools Drop Racial Bars with Ease," *Dallas Morning News*, February 5, 1955.

172. Blayne Salyer, "Parochial Schools Seen Receiving Negro Pupils," *Dallas Morning News*, September 4, 1954.

173. "Legislators Mum to Archbishop's Segregation Blast," *Dallas Morning News*, March 26, 1957; "Archbishop's Attack Ires Segregationists," *Dallas Morning News*, March 27, 1957.

174. "Mood of Texas: How It Feels on Integration," *Dallas Morning News*, October 6, 1957.

175. Ruth Schumm, "High Court Hears Discrimination Case," *Dallas Morning News*, January 12, 1954.

176. "Federal Court Hears Discrimination Suit," *Kerrville Daily Times*, October 31, 1956.

177. Interview conducted April 13, 2010, name withheld.

178. Ernesto Galarza, *Strangers in Our Fields* (Washington, DC: Joint United States–Mexico Trade Union Committee, 1956); quotation from Mary Hornaday, "Progress Reported in Aid to U.S. Migrant Workers," *Christian Science Monitor*, December 1, 1951.

179. Hector Garcia quoted in "GI Forum Presents Side," *Dallas Morning News*, July 20, 1957.

180. Joe Belden, "Resistance to Integration, Still Strong, Shows Drop," *Dallas Morning News*, July 28, 1957.

181. Dawson Duncan, "Lawmakers to Start Monday on Session's Showdown Week," *Dallas Morning News*, November 3, 1957.

182. Nels Hansen, "Baptists Shout 'No' on Debating Race," *Dallas Morning News*, June 1, 1957.

183. "Recall of Taylor Asked by Baptists," *Dallas Morning News*, September 9, 1948.

184. Stewart M. Doss, "Baptists Hear Charge Jonah Tale Discounted," *Dallas Morning News*, May 19, 1949.

185. "Strong Protests Greet Vatican Envoy Naming," *Dallas Morning News*, October 21, 1951.

186. The founders besides Louie Newton were Charles Clayton Morrison, former editor of *Christian Century*; Methodist Bromley Oxnam, who was also a leader in the World Council of Churches; Presbyterian John A. MacKay, president of Princeton Theological Seminary; and Edwin McNeill Poteat, president of Colgate-Rochester Divinity School; J. M. Dawson, *A Thousand Months to Remember* (Waco, TX: Baylor University Press, 1964), 201.

187. Luther C. Peak, "Pro-Red Church Activity," *Dallas Morning News*, January 16, 1948; Dawson, *A Thousand Months*, 194–95.

188. Lynn Landrum, "Parochial Schools," *Dallas Morning News*, January 13, 1948.

189. "Catholic Candidates Asked for Stands on Controversial Political Questions," *Galveston Daily News*, January 5, 1958.

190. Quoted in David Lawrence, "Kennedy Stand on Church, State Clear," *Galveston Daily News*, March 4, 1959.

191. *Texas Poll*, May 1960; electronic data file, face-to-face interviews among 1,000 adult residents of Texas, including 368 Baptists, 211 Methodists, and 170 Catholics; on the question pitting Kennedy against Nixon, Catholics favored Kennedy 58 percent to 19 percent, Baptists favored Nixon 44 percent to 37 percent, and Methodists favored Nixon 48 percent to 36 percent; when only white Baptists were considered, Nixon's margin over Kennedy was 46 percent to 36 percent; only 15 percent of white Baptists thought a Catholic candidate could win.

192. "S. Baxton Bryant Sitting Triumphantly Swathed in 2,670 Ft. of Bills Taped Together," *Life*, May 1, 1951, photo by George Silk; "Miles of Dollars Church," http://www.bellstexas.com.

193. "Dry Poll Canceled, Precinct 6 Revised," *Dallas Morning News*, August 19, 1952.

194. "Harry Puts Emphasis on Morals," *San Antonio Light*, October 19, 1959; "Truman in Pulpit Says U.S. Principles Rest on Bible," *New York Times*, October 19, 1959.

195. "Truman Sermon—How It Got from Tape to Globe," *Boston Globe*, October 25, 1959.

196. "Methodist Minister Raps Charges of Kennedy Bias," *Dallas Morning News*, July 21, 1960; Richard M. Morehead, "DOT Plans Crushed by LBJ Landslide," *Dallas Morning News*, June 15, 1960; Nina McCain, "Methodists Condemn Council's Attackers," *Dallas Morning News*, June 2, 1960.

197. Mike Quinn, "'Rally' for Nixon Angers 2 Clerics," *Dallas Morning News*, September 10, 1960.

198. John F. Kennedy, "Address to the Greater Houston Ministerial Association," September 12, 1960; video and transcript, John F. Kennedy Presidential Library and Museum, http://www.jfklibrary.org.

199. Gladwin Hill, "How Kennedy Is Being Received: The Texas and California Tours," *New York Times*, September 14, 1960; James Reston, "Powerful Texas Interests Aid Anti-Kennedy Drive," *Los Angeles Times*, September 14, 1960; Presnall H. Wood, "History of the Texas *Baptist Standard*, 1888–1959" (PhD diss., Southwestern Baptist Theological Seminary, 1964), 259.

200. Harry Hurt III, "Welcome, Mr. Kennedy, to Dallas," *Texas Monthly* (April 1981), 148–51, 236–52; John J. Lindsay, "Religion Still an Issue in Texas Politics," *Washington Post*, October 17, 1960; "Mailed Anti-Catholic Tracts before Convention, Hunt Says," *Washington Post*, October 29, 1960; Chandler Davidson, *Race and Class in Texas Politics* (Princeton, NJ: Princeton University Press, 1990), 213–14.

201. "Church Finds Opposition to Property Zone Change," *Dallas Morning News*, April 13, 1952.

202. "Braniff Says NCCJ Goal to Combat 'Hate' Groups," *Dallas Morning News*, February 21, 1952; see also Kevin M. Schultz, *Tri-Faith America: How Catholics and Jews Held Postwar America to Its Protestant Promise* (New York: Oxford University Press, 2011), 50–51.

203. Luther Holcomb quoted in "Brotherhood Is Topic of Panels," *Lubbock Morning Avalanche*, February 23, 1954.

204. Francis Raffetto, "NAACP Official Sees Bloc as Vote Factor," *Dallas Morning News*, January 9, 1956; Nels Hansen, "Minister to Reach Arctic on Mission," *Dallas Morning News*, September 30, 1956; "Dallas Minister Will Get Degree at Howard Payne," *Dallas Morning News*, May 31, 1957.

205. "Dr. Holcomb Gets Post in Church Unit," *Dallas Morning News*, January 19, 1958.

206. Wayne Phillips, "Clergy and Scholars Fight Religious Pleas to Voters," *New York Times*, September 12, 1960.

207. "Protests Continue on Name Use in Ad," *Dallas Morning News*, November 6, 1960.

208. Luther Holcomb, "Interview Conducted by Thomas Baker, July 8, 1969," Lyndon Baines Johnson Library, Austin, 1972.

209. "Kennedy Schedule Irks Rank and File," *Brownsville Herald*, November 19, 1963; Ronnie Dugger, "Squabbling in Democratic Party Clouds Kennedy Tour of Texas," *Washington Post*, November 20, 1963.

210. Dana Whitaker, "Recollections of Luther Holcomb," April 28, 2000, http://www.eeoc.gov.

CHAPTER 8
MEANEST, DIRTIEST, LOW-DOWN STUFF

1. Lyndon Johnson to Hubert Humphrey, White House Tapes, November 3, 1964, 5:57 p.m., ed. Robert DeRise; http://whitehousetapes.net.

2. Eric F. Goldman, *The Tragedy of Lyndon Johnson* (New York: Dell, 1969), 299; Robert Dallek, *Lyndon B. Johnson: Portrait of a President* (New York: Oxford University Press, 2004), 2–7; Dallek, *Lyndon Johnson and His Times, 1908–1960* (New York: Oxford University Press, 1991), 45–57.

3. Barry Goldwater, *The Conscience of a Conservative* (Princeton, NJ: Princeton University Press, 2007, originally published in 1960); Robert Alan Goldberg, *Barry Goldwater* (New Haven, CT: Yale University Press, 1995).

4. Robert Mann, *Daisy Petals and Mushroom Clouds: LBJ, Barry Goldwater, and the Ad That Changed American Politics* (Baton Rouge: Louisiana State University Press, 2011), 108.

5. From White House tapes, quoted in Michael R. Beschloss, *Reaching for Glory: Lyndon Johnson's Secret White House Tapes, 1964–1965* (New York: Simon and Schuster, 2001), 33.

6. Lyndon B. Johnson, "Remarks in Cadillac Square, Detroit," September 7, 1964, http://www.presidency.ucsb.edu; James Reston, "Democrats Change Roles from 'Lions' to 'Lambs,'" *Salt Lake Tribune*, September 9, 1964.

7. Lyndon B. Johnson, "Remarks in Salt Lake City at the Mormon Tabernacle," October 29, 1964, http://www.presidency.ucsb.edu.

8. Goldwater for President advertisements in the *Victoria Advocate*, October 30 and November 1, 1964.

9. Eric Sevareid, "Citizens Feel 'Something Is Wrong,'" *Dallas Morning News*, October 18, 1964.

10. Russell Freeburg, "Reveal FBI Told Jenkins Facts," *Chicago Tribune*, October 17, 1964.

11. David Wise, "LBJ Aide Jenkins Quits," *Boston Globe*, October 15, 1964.

12. Philip Dodd, "Texans Hear Barry Pound Moral Issue," *Chicago Tribune*, October 9, 1964.

13. "Nixon Demands LBJ Comment on Aide," *Dallas Morning News*, October 16, 1964.

14. "Goldwater or Johnson" and "White House Morality," *Pampa Daily News*, November 1, 1964.

15. "Church Council Raps Jenkins," *Victoria Advocate*, October 31, 1964.

16. "Baptists to Attend Convention," *Victoria Advocate*, October 31, 1964.

17. Billy Graham quoted in William Fripp, "Pleads for Morality," *Boston Globe*, September 25, 1964.

18. "Billy Graham Flooded by Back-Barry Wires," *Boston Globe*, November 3, 1964.

19. Billy Graham, White House Tapes, October 20, 1964, http://www.millercenter.org.

20. "Clergymen Condemn Use of Jenkins Morals Case in Political Campaign," *Dallas Morning News*, October 30, 1964.

21. The audio of Reagan's speech is available at http://www.americanrhetoric.com; and analyses of the speech are included in Jonathan M. Schoenwald, *A Time for Choosing: The Rise of Modern American Conservatism* (New York: Oxford University Press, 2001), 195; and James Berger, *After the End: Representations of Post-Apocalypse* (Minneapolis: University of Minnesota Press, 1999), 37.

22. Seymour Korman, "TV's Reagan Speaks Up Tonight for Barry," *Chicago Tribune*, October 27, 1964; William E. Pemberton, *Exit with Honor: The Life and Presidency of Ronald Reagan* (New York: M. E. Sharpe, 1998), 53–54, states that Reagan's speech was seen in 4.2 million homes and may have garnered as much as $8 million in contributions to the Republican National Committee.

23. Quoted from a transcript released to Drew Pearson, "Republicans Plot Secret Strategy on Crime," *Drew Pearson Merry-Go-Round*, October 20, 1964, http://dspace.wrlc.org; on

Citizens for Goldwater-Miller, see Rick Perlstein, *Before the Storm: Barry Goldwater and the Unmaking of the American Consensus* (New York: Hill and Wang, 2001), 480.

24. *Choice* [1964 Barry Goldwater Campaign Film], http://www.youtube.com; related information is included at http://conelrad.blogspot.com.

25. F. Clifton White, *Suite 3505: The Story of the Draft Goldwater Movement* (Ashland, OH: Ashbrook Press, 1992), 387; "Goldwater Repudiates Moral Film," *Dallas Morning News*, October 24, 1964; additional details about Goldwater's reaction to the film are given in Kathleen Hall Jamieson, *Packaging the Presidency: A History and Criticism of Presidential Campaign Advertising* (New York: Oxford University Press, 1992), 212–16; and Sean J. Savage, *JFK, LBJ, and the Democratic Party* (Albany: State University of New York Press, 2004), 239–40.

26. "Transcript of Informal Conference," September 22, 1964, Lyndon Baines Johnson Presidential Library and Museum, DNC Series 1, Box 325, folder: Goldwater, Barry: Mothers for Moral America Campaign, 1964.

27. Wayne Dehoney, "President's Address: Issues and Imperatives," *Annual of the Southern Baptist Convention* (June 1965), 94–95.

28. The total number of articles in the *Dallas Morning News* had increased 11 percent between 1950 and 1954 but was stable between 1955 and 1969; a comparison with two other large-circulation newspapers of record showed that mentions of moral, morals, or morality increased similarly in the *Chicago Tribune* but not in the *New York Times*.

29. Norman Vincent Peale, "Looseness in Morals," *Dallas Morning News*, May 31, 1964.

30. "Moral Transition," *Corpus Christi Caller-Times*, October 30, 1963.

31. James Hudnut-Beumler, *Looking for God in the Suburbs: The Religion of the American Dream and Its Critics* (New Brunswick, NJ: Rutgers University Press, 1994).

32. Reinhold Niebuhr quoted in "Noted Theologian Discusses Recent Reversal in U.S. Church Membership," *Corpus Christi Caller-Times*, April 7, 1963.

33. Michael W. Flamm, *Law and Order: Street Crime, Civil Unrest, and the Crisis of Liberalism in the 1960s* (New York: Columbia University Press, 2005), 44.

34. Department of Justice, Federal Bureau of Investigation, *Uniform Crime Reports for the United States* (Washington, DC: Government Printing Office, 1959 and 1963).

35. Willie Morris, "A Word in Defense of Texas," *New York Times*, April 5, 1964.

36. Examples are discussed in Sid Moody, "Psychiatrist Says World Full of Potential Oswalds," *Dallas Morning News*, June 7, 1964.

37. James T. Young, "Campus Carnage Toll," *Brownsville Herald*, August 2, 1966.

38. Quoted in "Massacre Brings Plea for Action on Arms Control," *Brownsville Herald*, August 2, 1966.

39. U.S. Census, 1950, 1960, and 1970, 1 percent Public Use Microsamples, electronic data files.

40. Norman Vincent Peale, "Morals of Youth," *Dallas Morning News*, May 24, 1964.

41. Will Durant, "On Morals: 'We Adults Are Senile Delinquents,'" *Dallas Morning News*, March 27, 1960.

42. "Boom Damaging Morals in U.S., Graham Says," *Dallas Morning News*, June 8, 1962; "Evangelist Calls Sex Magnified, Repulsive," *Dallas Morning News*, June 16, 1962.

43. Bethany Moreton, *To Serve God and Wal-Mart: The Making of Christian Free Enterprise* (Cambridge, MA: Harvard University Press, 2009), 176–180, notes that the state of Texas also took action by sponsoring some youth programs.

44. "Juvenile Delinquency," *La Marque Times*, April 16, 1964.

45. Lesbia Word Roberts, "Sid Williams Richardson," *Legacies: A History Journal for Dallas and North Central Texas* 11 (1999), 40–49; "Tycoons: Two-Man Parlay," *Time* (June 21, 1954), available at http://www.time.com; and Bryan Burrough, *The Big Rich: The Rise and Fall of the Greatest Texas Oil Fortunes* (New York: Penguin, 2009), 243, 280.

46. One investigation that received publicity among the general public was reported in Samuel Lubell, "U.S. Students Not as Rebellious, Radical as Pictured, Study Shows," *Dallas Morning News*, April 24, 1964.

47. Ray Shaw, "Birth Control Program Makes Early Gains in Heavily Catholic Area," *Wall Street Journal*, October 11, 1965.

48. "Communism Target of Indignant Women," *Dallas Morning News*, May 8, 1963.

49. Dallas County Democratic Party chair Lee Smith quoted in Mary Brinkerhoff, "Democratic Women Hear Party's Problems," *Dallas Morning News*, February 8, 1963.

50. Allen Duckworth, "Walker Preparing for Crusade," *Dallas Morning News*, February 17, 1963.

51. J. Claude Evans, "The Dallas Image Unveiled," *Christian Century* (November 20, 1963), 1438–40; "Pickets Protest Talks Given by Hargis, Walker," *Dallas Morning News*, March 28, 1963; "Ohioans Attack Right Wing Crusade," *Atlanta Daily World*, March 31, 1963; Ralph McGill, "Ike Likes Civil Rights," *Boston Globe*, August 25, 1963; Alistair Cooke, "Texans Go Madly for Adlai," *The Guardian*, October 26, 1963; "Walker Raps 2 Kennedys and U.N.," *Dallas Morning News*, October 27, 1963.

52. U.S. Supreme Court, *Engel et al. v. Vitale et al.*, 370 U.S. 421, June 25, 1962, http://www.nationalcenter.org. Daniel K. Williams, *God's Own Party: The Making of the Christian Right* (New York: Oxford University Press, 2011), 62–67, notes that the National Association of Evangelicals, *Christianity Today*, Carl McIntire, and Billy James Hargis accepted *Engel* but bitterly attacked the Supreme Court's 1963 decision in *Abington v. Schempp* banning Bible reading in public schools.

53. "Ministers Preach on Court's Prayer Ruling," *Del Rio News Herald*, July 2, 1962.

54. Jim Clark, "Devotionals to Continue in Amarillo," *Amarillo Globe Times*, June 26, 1962; "Schools Not Affected by High Court Ruling," *Brazosport Facts*, July 1, 1962.

55. "PTA Presidential Issue in Spotlight of State Session," *Brownwood Bulletin* (November 17, 1953); see also Michelle M. Nickerson, *Mothers of Conservatism: Women and the Postwar Right* (Princeton, NJ: Princeton University Press, 2012), 89.

56. "Parents Urged to Take Active Interest in Textbook Content," *Pampa Daily News* (May 19, 1963); see also Edward Jenkinson, *Censors in the Classroom: The Mind Benders* (Carbondale: Southern Illinois University Press, 1979), 111–16.

57. Stacey Sprague, "James Evetts Haley and the New Deal: Laying the Foundations for the Modern Republican Party in Texas" (Master's thesis, University of North Texas, 2004); "Haley for Governor," *Waco News Tribune*, March 22, 1956; "State's Rights Is Haley Platform,"

LaMarque Times, July 6, 1956; "Top Candidates Push Campaigns," *Corpus Christi Caller-Times*, July 17, 1956; "Governor Candidates Fire Final Blasts of Campaign," *Abilene Reporter News*, July 27, 1956; "Haley President of Texans for America," *Amarillo Globe Times*, April 17, 1957; "Mrs. Evetts Haley Dies, Rites Today," *Brownwood Bulletin*, December 21, 1958; "Ired Haley Slams High Court Ruling," *Victoria Advocate*, February 26, 1959; "Rancher, Historian Battle over Controversial Film," *Galveston Daily News*, April 29, 1961; "Witnesses See Red Plot in 'Obscene' Textbooks," *Dallas Morning News*, January 18, 1962; "Loan, Spending Pacts Reached," *Big Spring Daily Herald*, February 1, 1962; "Dobie Says Censors Bigots," *San Antonio Light*, February 1, 1962; "Baptist Minister Opposes Textbook Censorship; Cites Attempt to Clamp Down on Baylor University," *El Paso Herald Post*, February 6, 1962.

58. Hunt's anticommunist activities are discussed in Chandler Davidson, *Race and Class in Texas Politics* (Princeton, NJ: Princeton University Press, 1990), 205–12; Fred Koch was the father of David H. and Charles G. Koch, who became major donors to conservative and libertarian advocacy groups, including Americans for Prosperity and FreedomWorks.

59. Schwarz, an Australian physician and Baptist lay minister, lectured in Dallas on several occasions including ones in 1960, an appearance with singer Pat Boone in 1962, and another in 1963 to an audience of five hundred at the Hotel Adolphus at the invitation of the Dallas Freedom Forum; "Little Hope Seen in Red Division," *Dallas Morning News*, November 6, 1963; Frank Hildebrand, "Study to Contrast Freedom of U.S. and Communism," *Dallas Morning News*, December 7, 1960; Hildebrand, "White Declares Schools Alone to Map Study," *Dallas Morning News*, December 18, 1960; "Texts on Communism Await Further Study," *Dallas Morning News*, January 19, 1961. The Dallas Freedom Forum hosted numerous speakers in the early 1960s who spoke about moral decline, communism, and other threats to American freedom; the group hosted Ronald Reagan during a weeklong visit to Texas and considered him an attractive candidate for president at a meeting on February 27, 1962, and a number of its members supported Goldwater in 1964, "Rita Crocker Clements Personal Papers, 1932–2001: Republican Party Political Figures, Important Candidates, 1961–1980," Cushing Memorial Library and Archives, Texas A&M University Libraries, College Station.

60. An advertisement in the *El Paso Herald Post*, October 30, 1964, filled nearly a full page and focused on Russian and Chinese communists' efforts to encircle and conquer the United States.

61. Gerri von Frellick was located in Denver at the time but had worked in Dallas developing the Big Town Shopping Center prior to founding the Christian Citizen organization; Jack Castleman, "Protestants Asked to Join Political Unit," *Dallas Morning News*, February 2, 1962; Sara Diamond, *Roads to Dominion: Right-Wing Movements and Political Power in the United States* (New York: Guilford Press, 1995). According to Daniel K. Williams, *God's Own Party: The Making of the Christian Right* (New York: Oxford University Press, 2010), 61, von Frellick received encouragement from Campus Crusade for Christ founder Bill Bright to start the Christian Citizen groups, and by March 1962 the organization included two thousand members scattered across seventeen states. The cautionary statement by Jimmie R. Allen, director of the Baptist General Convention of Texas Christian Life Commission, as reported in Jack Castleman, "Baptists Reminded of Political Policy," *Dallas Morning News*, February 3,

1962, also noted that "no political movement or idea can ever be identified as thoroughly Christian," and "there is a risk of stirring anti-church sentiment and of damage to the spiritual purpose of the church."

62. Seymour Martin Lipset and Earl Raab, *The Politics of Unreason: Right Wing Extremism in America, 1790–1970* (New York: Harper and Row, 1973); Daniel Bell, ed., *The Radical Right* (New York: Doubleday, 1962); Richard Hofstadter, *The Paranoid Style in American Politics* (Cambridge, MA: Harvard University Press, 1964). Hunt struck up a personal friendship with McCarthy when the senator visited Dallas in 1952 and arranged for Smoot to introduce the senator; Murchison was said to be a supporter or McCarthy as well; Burrough, *The Big Rich*, 222–24.

63. Billy James Hargis quoted in "Hargis Compares Faith in God to Americanism," *Dallas Morning News*, December 8, 1962.

64. "Connally Quits Post to Run for Governor," *Mexia Daily News*, December 12, 1961.

65. "Liberalism Lambasted by Reagan," *Dallas Morning News*, February 28, 1962; "Stirring Address," *Dallas Morning News*, March 1, 1962.

66. J. Edgar Hoover, "The Red Menace," *Dallas Morning News*, January 7, 1961; Hoover's connections with Murchison and Richardson are described in Burrough, *The Big Rich*, 227–28; and in Jay Robert Nash, *Citizen Hoover: A Critical Study of the Life and Times of J. Edgar Hoover and His FBI* (Chicago: Nelson-Hall, 1972), 112–14.

67. National Archives, http://aad.archives.gov; U.S. Bureau of the Census, *Statistical Abstract of the United States: 1966* (Washington, DC: Government Printing Office, 1966), 255.

68. National Archives, http://aad.archives.gov; U.S. Bureau of the Census, *Statistical Abstract of the United States: 1970* (Washington, DC: Government Printing Office, 1970), 248, 251.

69. Gallup Polls, June 1965 and February 1968, courtesy of the Roper Center for Public Opinion Research.

70. Harris Survey, August 1968, courtesy of the Roper Center for Public Opinion Research.

71. Selznick and Steinberg, *The Tenacity of Prejudice*, 171; the survey was conducted by the National Opinion Research Center in October 1964 among 1,975 nationally representative respondents; the questions explored anti-Semitism in detail but included items about racial prejudice for comparison; the responses among northern whites and to additional questions are also reported.

72. National Opinion Research Center, *Anti-Semitism in the United States*, electronic data file; responses from 124 white southerners who reported their religious denomination as Southern Baptist and 73 white southerners who reported their religious denomination as Methodist.

73. Belden Associates, *The Texas Poll: Racial Relations, Civil Rights, State Government* (April 1968), conducted in face-to-face interviews among 1,079 residents of Texas age twenty-one and over, of whom 782 were white Anglos, 164 were Hispanics, and 133 were African Americans; electronic data file, courtesy of the Roper Center for Public Opinion Research.

74. *Statistical Abstract: 1966*, 27, 34.

75. U.S. Census, 1960, electronic data file for states and counties.

76. U.S. Census, 1 percent Public Use Microsample, electronic data file; Paul Barton, *Hispanic Methodists, Presbyterians, and Baptists in Texas* (Austin: University of Texas Press, 2006), 153.

77. U.S. Census, 1960, electronic data file for states and counties.

78. U.S. Census, 1 percent Public Use Microsample, electronic data file.

79. In the 1964 campaign Ralph Yarborough and John Connally sought support from competing African American groups led by black clergy; for example, "Connally, Negroes Huddle on Politics," *Dallas Morning News*, March 14, 1964.

80. Carl Harris, Panelists Wrestle with Church's Role," *Dallas Morning News*, May 15, 1964.

81. "Baptist Leader's Church Denies Negro Membership," *Dallas Morning News*, June 12, 1963; "Negro Is Rejected by Houston Church," *New York Times*, June 12, 1963; "White Attacks Liberalism as BGCT Convention Opens," *Dallas Morning News*, November 13, 1963.

82. "Third Negro Tries to Join Church of Baptist Chief," *Dallas Morning News*, July 2, 1963.

83. Carl Harris, "Many Texas Baptists Would Accept Negro," *Dallas Morning News*, September 19, 1963; Harris, "Baptist Churches in Dallas Vary on Negro Membership," *Dallas Morning News*, September 19, 1963.

84. "Segregation Called Natural," *San Antonio Express*, October 14, 1963; a wider inquiry showed similar patterns among Southern Baptists in other southern states but noted that in congregations permitting African American membership, few if any requests had been received; "Baptist Racial Line Tied to Geography," *Dallas Morning News*, November 5, 1963; "Baptists of South Exclude Negroes," *New York Times*, November 4, 1963.

85. Carl Harris, "Split Shows Up at Convention," *Dallas Morning News*, November 17, 1963.

86. Billy Graham quoted in an interview with Jack Castleman, "Doors Are Opening, Evangelist Believes," *Dallas Morning News*, February 3, 1963.

87. José Angel Gutiérrez at a rally on April 1, 1963, as quoted in Marc Simon Rodriguez, "A Movement Made of 'Young Mexican Americans Seeking Change': Critical Citizenship, Migration, and the Chicano Movement in Texas and Wisconsin, 1960–1975," *Western Historical Quarterly* 34 (Autumn 2003), 275–99, quotation on p. 275.

88. José Angel Gutiérrez, *The Making of a Civil Rights Leader* (Houston: Arte Público Press, 2005), 8; the role Gutiérrez played in pressing for school reform is included in Hank Resnik's half-hour film, *The Schools of Crystal City* (Stanford: Stanford Center for Research and Development in Teaching, Stanford University, 1976); and briefly described in Dennis J. Bixler-Marquez, "*The Schools of Crystal City*: A Chicano Experiment in Change," in *Recovering the Hispanic History of Texas*, ed. Monica Perales and Raúl A. Ramos (Houston: Arte Público Press, 2010), 92–110.

89. José Angel Gutiérrez, *The Making of a Chicano Militant: Lessons from Cristal* (Madison: University of Wisconsin Press, 1998), 24.

90. The Political Association of Spanish-Speaking Organizations and its relations with other groups in Crystal City are described in Rodolfo F. Acuña, *The Making of Chicana/o Studies: In the Trenches of Academe* (New Brunswick, NJ: Rutgers University Press, 2011),

22–25; farmworker mobilization in Crystal City is described in John Staples Shockley, *Chicano Revolt in a Texas Town* (South Bend, IN: University of Notre Dame Press, 1974); and Armando Navarro, *The Cristal Experiment: A Chicano Struggle for Community Control* (Madison: University of Wisconsin Press, 1998).

91. "Labor Backs Rio Grande Rights Move," *Dallas Morning News*, June 27, 1966.

92. "Parishioners March in Support of 4 Suspended Texas Priests," *New York Times*, May 1, 1967.

93. Louis Schneider and Louis Zurcher, "Toward Understanding the Catholic Crisis: Observations on Dissident Priests in Texas," *Journal for the Scientific Study of Religion* 9 (1970), 197–207; although the study focused on measuring psychotherapeutic orientations through a twenty-statements test, the contextual information included about the priests and their relationship to the archbishop is instructive.

94. The statistical results in these paragraphs are from county-level data for general and primary elections included in electronic data files, Numan V. Bartley, *Southern Primary and General Election Data, 1944–1972* (Ann Arbor, MI: Inter-University Consortium for Political and Social Research, 1973); and merged with data from the 1960 census; religion variables are interpolated for 1962 from the 1952 and 1971 county-level data files for *Churches and Church Membership in the United States*, courtesy of the Association of Religion Data Archives, http://www.thearda.com.

95. An indication of how voting patterns were different in 1964 from 1952 is given by the standardized regression coefficients for counties' percentage of votes cast for Goldwater with the percentage voting for Eisenhower in 1952 included in the model. The coefficient for the relationship of the Eisenhower vote to the Goldwater vote is 0.665; for percent black in 1960, 0.196; for percent Catholic in 1962, −0.277; for percent with family income of $10,000 or more in 1959, 0.244; for percent rural farm population in 1960, −0.170; and for oil revenue, 0.146 (all coefficients significant at or beyond the 0.001 level of probability; coefficients for Southern Baptists and Methodists as a percentage of Protestant members not significant). The relationship between higher incomes and Republican voting was also suggested by the results of a Texas Poll conducted in August 1962 in face-to-face interviews with 998 respondents, electronic data file, courtesy of the Roper Center for Public Opinion Research; among respondents who had decided between Connally and Cox, 36 percent of those with "above average" incomes opted for Cox compared with only 17 percent of those with "low" incomes; among only white Anglos, 36 percent in the above-average category and 19 percent in the low category favored Cox; only 14 percent of African Americans and 9 percent of Hispanics favored Cox.

96. Harry Hurt III, "Welcome, Mr. Kennedy, to Dallas," *Texas Monthly* (April 1981), 148–51, 237–52; "Backing Graham Denied by Hunt," *Baltimore Sun*, May 2, 1963; Jack Anderson, "Lonely H. L. Hunt," Transcript for Texas Papers, July 17, 1964, http://dspace.wrlc.org; "Texan Is Steering Republican Right," *Irish Times*, December 23, 1964.

97. George H. W. Bush, *Looking Forward* (New York: Bantam, 1988), 71–72; Bush, *All the Best: My Life in Letters and Other Writings* (New York: Scribner, 1999), 80.

98. "Dallas Glad, Regretful," *Baltimore Sun*, November 25, 1963; "Dallas to Name Park for Kennedy," *Los Angeles Times*, April 19, 1964; Dennis Hoover, " 'Pastor at Large' Takes on New

Task," *Dallas Morning News*, May 30, 1964; "Bronze Monument to JFK Unveiled in Dallas," *Boston Globe*, October 13, 1964; Doris Fleeson, "Discrimination Commission," *Boston Globe*, May 22, 1966; Dana Whitaker, "Recollections of Luther Holcomb," Equal Employment Opportunity Commission Transcript, April 28, 2000.

99. Interview with Zan Holmes, conducted by Natalie Searl, March 24, 1998; Carl Harris, "Dallas Negro Seems to Prefer His Church," *Dallas Morning News*, August 2, 1964; Carlos Conde, "Holmes Says Negroes Seek Equality Only," *Dallas Morning News*, June 17, 1964; "U.S. Attorney Will Address Negro Group," *Dallas Morning News*, December 16, 1964; "Group to Ask Negro Hiring," *Dallas Morning News*, March 20, 1966; Gene Ormsby, "Plans Viewed to Swell Council," *Dallas Morning News*, September 3, 1967; "Rev. Holmes Will Seek House Seat," *Dallas Morning News*, May 19, 1968; Stewart Davis, "House Extends Hours," *Dallas Morning News*, June 25, 1968.

100. Mike Quinn, " 'Rally' for Nixon Angers 2 Clerics," *Dallas Morning News*, September 10, 1960; James Reston, "Powerful Texas Interests Aid Anti-Kennedy Drive," *Los Angeles Times*, September 14, 1960; Larry Grove, "Loyalist Democrats Hail JFK Program," *Dallas Morning News*, May 30, 1961; "Bryant Gets Post with Treasury," *Dallas Morning News*, June 30, 1961; Tom Wicker, "Connally Faces Run-Off in Texas," *New York Times*, May 7, 1962; Ronnie Dugger, "Squabbling in Democratic Party Clouds Kennedy Tour of Texas," *Washington Post*, November 20, 1963; "Moral Issue, Bryant Says," *Dallas Morning News*, April 18, 1964; Paul Crume, "Big D," *Dallas Morning News*, June 30, 1965; Reverend William Barnes, "Interview," University of Florida Digital Collections, June 26, 2003, http://ufdc.ufl.edu; James Lawson, "Interview," Southern Oral History Program, October 24, 1983.

101. Letter from Will D. Campbell to Luther Holcomb, October 19, 1962, University of Southern Mississippi Libraries, Hattiesburg; Will D. Campbell, "Interview," *Journal of Southern Religion* (July 1, 2003), http://English.olemiss.edu; Michael K. Honey, *Going Down Jericho Road: The Memphis Strike, Martin Luther King's Last Campaign* (New York: Norton, 2007), 161; Southern Regional Council, *Special Report* (Atlanta, 1968), 18.

102. "Dallas Calls Rights Truce," *Chicago Daily Defender*, August 25, 1964; "Brown Defies Foe to Prove Claim," *Dallas Morning News*, October 9, 1964; "Topflight Speakers Slated," *New Pittsburgh Courier*, June 13, 1964.

103. "Texas Bapt. Cleric Sees Decade of Violence," *Philadelphia Tribune*, June 13, 1964; David K. Chrisman, "Religious Moderates and Race: The Texas Christian Life Commission and the Call for Racial Reconciliation, 1954–68," in *Seeking Inalienable Rights: Texans and Their Quests for Justice*, ed. Debra A. Reid (College Station: Texas A&M University Press, 2009), 97–121; "Houston's Schools Plan No Integration Speedup," *Dallas Morning News*, May 10, 1965; "Houston Conference Set on Integration Demands," *Dallas Morning News*, May 13, 1965; "Houston Negroes Press Campaign," *New York Times*, May 16, 1965; "Backlash Called Factor in Houston Bond Victory," *Dallas Morning News*, May 21, 1965; "Blond Coed Desegregates School in KKK Territory," *Afro-American* (Baltimore), May 22, 1965; "New Integration Plan Draws Fire at Houston," *Dallas Morning News*, June 17, 1965; "School Board Action Stirs Negroes' Ire," *Dallas Morning News*, June 23, 1965; Wylie Henry class of 1963 at Phillis Wheatley High School quoted in Michael Berryhill, "What's Wrong with Wheatley?" *Houston Press*, April 17, 1997.

104. "Texas Students Charged with Murder," *Bay State Banner* (Boston), August 3, 1967; O'Neil Hendrick, "Rights Drive Seen at Stage of War," *Washington Post*, May 21, 1967; Nicholas C. Chriss, "Texas Southern U. Riot Still Hangs Over Houston Like Cloud," *Los Angeles Times*, December 10, 1967; other eyewitness accounts and commentary are posted under "Infamous Riots in Our City," April 5, 2007, http://www.houstonarchitecture.com.

105. "Dr. King Announces Stars for Freedom Leadership," *Jet* (October 19, 1967), 52; "Texas Club to Hear Barbara Jordan Sunday," *Chicago Defender*, June 10, 1967; Monica Coleman, "Carolyn Scantlebury: New NAACP Houston Leader," *Defender Network*, February 1, 2010, http://www.defendernetwork.com; "Senator Jordan Will Speak," *Dallas Morning News*, April 14, 1968; Dorothie Erwin, "Texas Race Peace Held Conditional," *Dallas Morning News*, April 16, 1968; Barbara Jordan, *A Self-Portrait* (New York: Doubleday, 1979), 44; also discussed in Mary Beth Rogers, *Barbara Jordan: American Hero* (New York: Bantam, 1998), 37.

106. Rodney Stark, Charles Y. Glock, and Harold Quinley, "Sounds of Silence," *Psychology Today* (April 1970), 38–62; Harold E. Quinley, *The Prophetic Clergy: Social Activism among Protestant Ministers* (New York: Wiley, 1974).

107. Curtis W. Freeman, " 'Never Had I Been So Blind': W. A. Criswell's 'Change' on Racial Segregation," *Journal of Southern Religion* 10 (2007), 1–12; "Fields Urges Religious Editors to Fight Racism," *Baptist Press*, April 18, 1968.

CHAPTER 9
POWER TO THE PEOPLE

1. Terry Kliewer, "Standoff Ends Peacefully," *Dallas Morning News*, October 22, 1972; Marc Bernabo, "Daily Marches Endorsed," *Dallas Morning News*, October 22, 1972; Terry Kliewer and Robert Finklea, "Unforeseen Circumstances Hamper Both Sides," *Dallas Morning News*, October 22, 1972.

2. Tony Castro, "Shootings Unite Dallas Blacks," *Washington Post*, November 27, 1972; "Angry Dallas Residents Protest Police Slayings of 6 Blacks," *Atlanta Daily World*, November 17, 1972; Charles Bates, "Oak Cliff Man Shot in Car Theft," *Dallas Morning News*, October 30, 1972.

3. "Demonstrators Poised to Picket Cotton Bowl," *Big Spring Daily Herald*, January 1, 1970; "Dallas Marchers Protest Deaths," *Abilene Reporter News*, May 25, 1970; "Economic Boycott of Dallas Takes Shape," *Big Spring Daily Herald*, December 12, 1969; "Fast on City Hall Steps Receives Added Support," *Dallas Morning News*, March 20, 1971; Brian D. Behnken, *Fighting Their Own Battles: Mexican Americans, African Americans, and the Struggle for Civil Rights in Texas* (Chapel Hill: University of North Carolina Press, 2011), 144.

4. "Price, News Media Draw Fire over Jefferson Case," *Dallas Morning News*, November 13, 1969.

5. "Recall Group Looking for Enough Signatures," *Dallas Morning News*, March 27, 1970; "KKDA Obtains Court Injunction," *Dallas Morning News*, November 11, 1971; Terry Kliewer, "School Officials to Be Lenient," *Dallas Morning News*, November 17, 1972; "SCLC Leader, Worker Fined for Council Sit-In," *Dallas Morning News*, January 5, 1973; Tony Castro and Terry Kliewer, "Protesters See Split in Ranks," *Dallas Morning News*, November 20, 1972.

6. Quoted in Castro and Kliewer, "Protesters See Split in Ranks"; Dotty Griffith, "SCLC Unit Dying," *Dallas Morning News*, July 14, 1973.

7. Reverend S. M. Wright quoted in "Ministers Ask Study of Shootings," *Dallas Morning News*, October 15, 1972.

8. Virginia Hill quoted in Pulle, "Unfit to Print." On the Dallas Ministerial Alliance and Reverend Wright's support of various candidates and issues, "Negro Pastor Candidate for School Board Post," *Dallas Morning News*, March 11, 1959; Francis Raffetto, "Cabell Gets Backing of Negro Ministers," *Dallas Morning News*, February 28, 1963; "Negro Group Backs Cabell," *Dallas Morning News*, April 15, 1964; "Negro Groups at Odds on Political Candidates," *Dallas Morning News*, April 23, 1966; Forest Reece, "Gov. Connally to Assist Conservative Forces," *Dallas Morning News*, April 27, 1966.

9. Carolyn Barta, "Allen's Mail Shows Both Praise, Criticism," *Dallas Morning News*, September 6, 1970; "Allen Gets SCLC Support for Work as Mediator," *Dallas Morning News*, September 15, 1970; "Broadens Responsibility," *Dallas Morning News*, March 24, 1971; "Lakey Denies Move Was to Defuse Fast," *Dallas Morning News*, March 27, 1971; "Two Speakers Tear into Charter Group," *Dallas Morning News*, April 1, 1971; Carolyn Barta, "Wise Cuts into Vote," *Dallas Morning News*, April 8, 1971.

10. Parmley, "Leader Rises while SCLC Crumbling," "Natural Look Alikes," *Wichita Times*, August 31, 1972; Parmley, "U.S. Restructure Urged," *Dallas Morning News*, August 17, 1972; "Abernathy Urges Political Unity," *Dallas Morning News*, August 17, 1972; "Black Baptists at Two Conventions Indicate Opposition to Nixon," *New York Times*, September 10, 1972.

11. Norma Adams Wade, "Civil Rivalry in Dallas," *Black Enterprise* (April 1979), 19–20.

12. "A Hippie Doctor Is Buried as Many Mourners Stand in Rain," *Brazosport Facts*, July 19, 1970.

13. Mayor Winston F. Bott quoted in ibid.

14. Richard R. Bailey, "The Starr County Strike," *Red River Valley Historical Review* 4 (1979), 42–61.

15. "Farm Strikers Propose March Until Labor Day," *Big Spring Daily Herald*, July 5, 1966; Behnken, *Fighting Their Own Battles*, 107.

16. Quoted in Behnken, *Fighting Their Own Battles*, 108.

17. Helen Parmley, "New Archbishop of Boston Man of Action for Deprived," *Dallas Morning News*, September 9, 1970.

18. "Archbishop's Prestige on Line for Workers," *Abilene Reporter News*, June 30, 1966; "Bishop Backs Melon Strike," *Amarillo Globe Times*, June 28, 1966; "Farm Workers to Launch March on Austin Monday," *Brownwood Bulletin*, July 10, 1966.

19. David Montejano, *Quixote's Soldiers: A Local History of the Chicano Movement, 1966–1981* (Austin: University of Texas Press, 2010), 27.

20. Stan Steiner, *La Raza: The Mexican Americans* (New York: Harper and Row, 1970); "The Signs Mount," *San Antonio Express and News*, December 17, 1967; "Former Leading Carr Foe Jumps onto His Bandwagon," *Brownsville Herald*, April 11, 1968.

21. Robert Berrellez, "Mexican-Americans Beginning Own Civil Rights Organization," *Port Arthur News*, August 9, 1968.

22. "Latin Youths Are Told to Break with Gringos," *Corpus Christi Caller-Times*, April 20, 1969; "Truan Raps School Hate Mongers," *Corpus Christi Caller-Times*, April 20, 1969; Homer Bigart, "Mexican Americans Fight Mold, Are Stirring with New Militancy," *Corpus Christi Caller-Times*, April 20, 1969.

23. "Chicano School Boycott Trial to Be Held June 8," *Abilene Reporter News*, May 7, 1970.

24. "Chicano Protesters Go to Washington," *Abilene Reporter News*, December 19, 1969.

25. Richard Beene, "Raza Unida Party Suffers Setbacks," *Del Rio News Herald*, November 4, 1970.

26. "MAYO Speakers Take Stand at Political Rally," *Lubbock Avalanche Journal*, April 3, 1970.

27. "Solon Hits Texas on Segregation," *Victoria Advocate*, July 28, 1970.

28. Peggy Simpson, "Tragedy Brings Latins Together," *Abilene Reporter News*, September 3, 1970.

29. "Chavez Sees Texas 'Revolt,'" *Victoria Advocate*, February 7, 1971.

30. "Latins Claim Brutality, March Outside City Hall," *Big Spring Daily Herald*, July 30, 1971.

31. "ABCD Sets Two Lake Cleanups," *Dallas Morning News*, April 10, 1971; Tony Castro, "La Raza Unida Given Surprise SCLC Support," *Dallas Morning News*, August 18, 1972.

32. Marquis Childs, "Democratic Ethnic Splintering Could Increase in Future," *El Paso Herald Post*, November 22, 1972; Ashley P. Cheshire, "Two Parties Field 67 Candidates," *Denton Record Chronicle*, November 1, 1972.

33. Bob Ybarra, "Raza Unida Rejects Nixon and McGovern," *El Paso Herald Post*, September 4, 1972.

34. Ignacio M. Garcia, *United We Win: The Rise and Fall of La Raza Unida Party* (Tucson: University of Arizona Mexican American Studies Research Center, 1989); "Archbishop of Santa Fe Joins March," *Del Rio News Herald*, June 18, 1973; "Archbishop Furey Happy over Farah Accord," *San Antonio Light*, February 25, 1974; John Davidson, "A Simple Man," *Texas Monthly* (July 1981), 127.

35. U.S. Bureau of the Census, *Statistical Abstract of the United States: 1961* (Washington, DC: Government Printing Office, 1961), 126; and U.S. Bureau of the Census, *Statistical Abstract of the United States: 1972* (Washington, DC: Government Printing Office, 1972), 107.

36. Mario Marcel Salas, "Veteran of the Civil Rights Movement Turns 90 This Year," *African American*, September 13, 2006, http://www.aframnews.com; Reverend Claude William Black Jr., "The Civil Rights Movement in San Antonio," Oral History Interview Conducted by Cheri Wolfe, Institute of Texan Cultures, University of Texas at San Antonio, March 14, 1994.

37. Jimmy Banks, "Senate Panel OK's Curbs on Students," *Dallas Morning News*, March 4, 1969.

38. Stewart Davis, "The Happening at Winfrey Point: 5,000 March Chant Through Austin," *Dallas Morning News*, October 16, 1969; Henry Tatum, "1,500 Stay Orderly Here," *Dallas Morning News*, October 16, 1969; "Flareup Occurs at Denton," *Dallas Morning News*, October 16, 1969; Stewart Davis, "Antiwar Rally Staged at UT," *Dallas Morning News*, November 14, 1969; Rick Campbell, "M-Day 1969—Millions Gather in the Name of Peace," *Houston Chronicle*, November 19, 2009, http://blog.chron.com.

39. "Shutdowns, Vandalism Grip Nation's Campuses," *Dallas Morning News*, May 8, 1970; "Students Protest at Texas Colleges," *Dallas Morning News*, May 8, 1970; "Governor Says Texas Fortunate Student Unrest Has Not Gotten Out of Hand," *Dallas Morning News*, May 9, 1970.

40. "Activist, Peace Groups Holding Meet in Dallas," *Pampa Daily News*, November 26, 1971; "Coalition Meeting Slates Platform," *Abilene Reporter News*, November 26, 1971.

41. "Antiwar Rallies Attract Thousands Across U.S.," *Lubbock Avalanche Journal*, April 23, 1972; "Arrests, Injuries Rise in Anti-War Turbulence," *El Paso Herald Post*, April 21, 1972; "Riot Police Ready," *San Antonio Express and News*, April 23, 1972.

42. Judy Wiessler, "Moratorium Issue Going to Trustees," *Dallas Morning News*, October 22, 1969; see also Doug Rossinow, "'The Breakthrough to New Life': Christianity and the Emergence of the New Left in Austin, TX, 1956–1964," *American Quarterly* 46 (September 1994), 309–40; and Rossinow, *The Politics of Authenticity: Liberalism, Christianity, and the New Left in America* (New York: Columbia University Press, 1998).

43. "Holmes Says Churches Solve Ills," *Dallas Morning News*, March 13, 1969.

44. W. A. Criswell, "The Red Terror," Criswell Sermon Library, November 24, 1963, http://www.wacriswell.org; "'Arch-Liberals' Urged to Form Own Church," *Dallas Morning News*, November 12, 1969; Criswell, "Shepherding the Church of God," Criswell Sermon Library, October 19, 1969, http://www.wacriswell.org.

45. Jean Ann Jungman, "Service Offers Choice," *Denton Record Chronicle*, April 23, 1972.

46. "Your Kindness O Lord Endureth," *Galveston Daily News*, June 10, 1972; identical advertisements appeared in many other Texas newspapers; Criswell, "Shepherding the Church of God."

47. John G. Turner, *Bill Bright and Campus Crusade for Christ: The Renewal of Evangelicalism in Postwar America* (Chapel Hill: University of North Carolina Press, 2008), 138–46.

48. Betty Hicks at the Texas Tech Baptist Student Union as quoted in "Betty Hicks Is Employed at Tech's BSU," *Lubbock Avalanche Journal*, July 23, 1972; the survey of freshmen is summarized in David Poling, "Everybody Keeps an Eye on the Preacher's Kids," *Lubbock Avalanche Journal*, July 23, 1972; "Religious Emphasis Being Put on Individuals at Tech," *Lubbock Avalanche Journal*, September 3, 1972.

49. "Lawyer Heads Baptist Men," *Abilene Reporter News*, October 28, 1972.

50. Lester Kinsolving, "Rev. Humbard and His Cathedral of Tomorrow," *Abilene Reporter News*, July 15, 1972.

51. Quoted in George W. Cornell, "Don't Try to Convert Jews, Rabbi Requests," *Lubbock Avalanche Journal*, December 9, 1972; the Anti-Defamation League–funded study was Charles Y. Glock and Rodney Stark, *Christian Beliefs and Anti-Semitism* (New York: Harper and Row, 1966).

52. "Texas Democrats Irritated," *Dallas Morning News*, October 1, 1969; Robert E. Baskin, "Democrats Join Cause with Protest," *Dallas Morning News*, October 1, 1969; Baskin, "Tower Urges War Step Up," *Dallas Morning News*, October 2, 1969; "Republicans Urged to Fly Flag," *Dallas Morning News*, October 14, 1969; "Ralph Says He Backs Big Day," *Dallas Morning News*, October 14, 1969; "Texans Are Divided over Moratorium," *Dallas Morning News*, October 15, 1969.

53. Bill Towery, "Churches Move to Meet Needs of a Changing World," *Lubbock Avalanche Journal*, May 14, 1972; the rock concert was recalled in an essay by Ray Westbook, "1970 Southwest Peace Festival Brought Hippie Style to Town," *Lubbock Avalanche Journal*, August 8, 2010.

54. Gail Caldwell, *A Strong West Wind: A Memoir* (New York: Random House, 2006), 73.

55. The Honorable Eddie Bernice Johnson, "Special Tribute to Dr. S. M. Wright of Dallas, Texas," *Congressional Record* 140 (November 30, 1994), E.

CHAPTER 10
GOD CAN SAVE US

1. Sam Attlessey and Helen Parmley, "Reagan Vows He'll Reinstate Moral Values," *Dallas Morning News*, August 23, 1980; CBS News/The New York Times, *CBS News/New York Times Election Day Surveys* (Ann Arbor, MI: Inter-University Consortium for Political and Social Research, 1984), electronic data file; the survey was conducted as an exit poll on November 7, 1982, among 2,044 Texas voters who were asked who they voted for in the 1980 presidential election; the 84 percent who voted for Reagan refers to the responses given by 514 white voters who identified themselves as Protestants and conservatives; among all respondents, 53 percent said they voted for Reagan, closely resembling the actual vote; among all white Protestants, 64 percent voted for Reagan, as did 64 percent of white Catholics; among black Protestants, 13 percent voted for Reagan; and among Hispanic Catholics, 18 percent did.

2. Among the most useful discussions of the Religious Right are William Martin, *With God on Our Side: The Rise of the Religious Right in America* (New York: Broadway Books, 1996); and Daniel K. Williams, *God's Own Party: The Making of the Christian Right* (New York: Oxford University Press, 2010).

3. Pamela Colloff, "Remember the Christian Alamo," *Texas Monthly* (December 2001), http://www.tfn.org; one of the general accounts that mentions Roloff, although briefly, is Lew Daly, *God's Economy: Faith-Based Initiatives and the Caring State* (Chicago: University of Chicago Press, 2009), 121.

4. Frank X. Tolbert, "Deep in Pines a New College Is Shaping Up," *Dallas Morning News*, November 16, 1968; Maury Darst, "Radio Evangelist Entangled in Web of Controversy," *Galveston Daily News*, May 21, 1983.

5. Bill Kenyon, "Ambassador College Texas Branch Closing," *Dallas Morning News*, May 20, 1977; the Worldwide Church of God retained the campus until 2000, when it became the International ALERT Academy for Christian training in affiliation with the ministry of evangelical leader Bill Gothard.

6. "Christ Is the Answer," *Corpus Christi Caller-Times*, October 24, 1959; in the mid-1980s faith healers Gloria and David Farjardo acquired the building at 3401 South Alameda near the Driscol Children's Hospital as headquarters for their local ministry, Christian school, and international television broadcasts.

7. For example, as quoted in an advertisement for services at the Baptist Tabernacle in the *Danville Bee* (Danville, VA), September 19, 1970.

8. "Free Speech Challenged in Radio Court Decision," *Valley Morning Star* (Harlingen, TX), October 29, 1972.

9. "Rebekah Home Alumnae Throw Support to Roloff," *Dallas Morning News*, July 17, 1973.

10. "Lester Roloff Ordered Out of Jail," *Dallas Morning News*, February 13, 1974; Stewart Davis, "Water Plan Passed, but Child Home Bill Tabled," *Dallas Morning News*, April 18, 1975.

11. "Roloff Wants Candidate Mark White Defeated," *Paris News*, July 14, 1982.

12. George Kuempel, "Clements Sees Tax Reduction of $1 Billion," *Dallas Morning News*, November 23, 1978; Steve Blow, "Despite Lack of Funds, Roloff Wants to Buy East Texas Campus," *Dallas Morning News*, November 25, 1978; Christi Harlan, "Rebekah Rejects," *Dallas Morning News*, November 24, 1980.

13. Doug Swanson, "Brother Roloff Is Not Dead," *Dallas Morning News*, November 6, 1982; "God Will Punish Texas Because Boys Home Ordered Closed, Director Says," *Galveston Daily News*, May 22, 1986; "Grand Jury Looks into Alleged Abuse at Children's Home," *Kerrville Daily Times*, May 15, 2000; Colloff, "Remember the Christian Alamo"; Joanna Hannah, "Roloff Evangelist," http://www.baptist.org, January 17, 2011.

14. William Martin, "God's Angry Man," *Texas Monthly* (April 1981), 152–57, 223–35; Steve Blow, "East Texas Campus Given to Hurst Evangelist," *Dallas Morning News*, October 20, 1978. The anticipated donor was Virginia businessman F. William Menge, a Robison supporter who hoped to make the campus into a self-contained Christian city; however, the deal fell through; "Armstrong Church May Face Suit," *Dallas Morning News*, February 16, 1979.

15. Helen Parmley, "Youthful Evangelist Wins Souls to Christ," *Dallas Morning News*, September 13, 1970; "Noted Evangelist Will Appear Here in One-Night Rally," *Winnsboro News*, February 14, 1974.

16. W. A. Criswell quoted in Parmley, "Youthful Evangelist Wins Souls to Christ."

17. "Ex-Sinner T. Cullen Davis Now Part of Moral Majority," *Galveston Daily News*, November 23, 1980; Beth Pratt, "Cullen Davis Tells of Life Changes," *Lubbock Evening Journal*, September 12, 1983; "Cullen Davis Destroys $1 Million in Art Objects," *Paris News*, January 11, 1983.

18. "Evangelist's TV Show Reinstated by Channel 8 Following Statements," *Dallas Morning News*, May 28, 1977.

19. Perspectives on the Save Our Children campaign are included in Anita Bryant, *The Anita Bryant Story: The Survival of Our Nation's Families and the Threat of Militant Homosexuality* (New York: Revell, 1977); Dudley Clendinen and Adam Nagourney, *Out for Good: The Struggle to Build a Gay Rights Movement in America* (New York: Simon & Schuster, 1999); and Fred Fejes, *Gay Rights and Moral Panic: The Origins of America's Debate on Homosexuality* (New York: Palgrave MacMillan, 2008).

20. General Social Survey, 1976, conducted by the National Opinion Research Center, University of Chicago, electronic data file, with nationally representative results from 1,400 respondents, including 179 white southern evangelical Protestants.

21. "Evangelist's TV Show Reinstated."

22. Bill Kenyon, "Robison Mounts Media Blitz," *Dallas Morning News*, July 8, 1978.

23. Helen Parmley, "Homosexuality Remarks Kill TV Program," *Dallas Morning News*, March 3, 1979.

24. Robison quoted in ibid.

25. Helen Parmley, "Evangelist Considering Suit," *Dallas Morning News*, March 6, 1979.

26. Virginia Lucas Nick and Mary Wall, "Shocked at TV's Ban on Robison," *Dallas Morning News*, March 10, 1979.

27. Campbell B. Read, "Everyone Has to Obey Fairness Ruling," *Dallas Morning News*, March 15, 1979.

28. Helen Parmley, "Robison Case Gets Attention of Racehorse," *Dallas Morning News*, March 15, 1979.

29. Helen Parmley, "Flap Leaves Robison 'Scared,'" *Dallas Morning News*, April 1, 1979; "Lawyer Joins Team for Evangelist Robison," *Dallas Morning News*, April 18, 1979; "Tom Landry to Serve on Robison Funds Panel," *Dallas Morning News*, April 28, 1979; Helen Parmley, "Robison Says Miss Bryant to Miss Rally," *Dallas Morning News*, May 15, 1979.

30. "Plea for Freedom to Preach," *Dallas Morning News*, June 6, 1979.

31. James Robison, "Remembering Reagan," *James Robison Weekly Commentary*, June 8, 2004, http://archives.jamesrobison.net.

32. These results are drawn from analysis of county-level data for 1980 religious adherence by denomination and census data for median household income, urban population, and population change from 1970 to 1980.

33. Membership data and Sunday school enrollment figures are from the Annual Church Profile for Southern Baptist Convention Churches—Sunday School, 1980, electronic data file, courtesy of the Association of Religion Data Archives, University Park, PA, http://www.thearda.com.

34. Joel Gregory, *Too Great a Temptation: The Seductive Power of America's Super Church* (Fort Worth, TX: The Summit Group, 1994), 37.

35. W. A. Criswell, quoted in Blow, "Religion, Politics Mix in Criswell Philosophy."

36. "Baptists Form Group Defending Carter," *Big Spring Herald*, October 25, 1976; "'Vicious' Reaction Is Noted," *Brownsville Herald*, October 24, 1976.

37. Donald Shriver quoted in "Religion in Politics Stirs Critics of Race," *Corsicana Daily Sun*, May 28, 1976.

38. Baptist General Convention of Oklahoma executive director Joe L. Ingram as quoted in "Criswell Warns of Evil Forces Attacking U.S.," *Lubbock Avalanche Journal*, November 26, 1976.

39. Kathleen Carroll, "Criswell Dynasty at First Baptist in Dallas Is Legendary," *Paris News*, August 29, 1979.

40. D. Michael Lindsay, *Faith in the Halls of Power: How Evangelicals Joined the American Elite* (New York: Oxford University Press, 2007), 11–12; and D. Michael Lindsay, "Evangelicals in the Power Elite: Elite Cohesion Advancing a Movement," *American Sociological Review* 73 (2008), 60–82.

41. Charles Tilly, *Durable Inequality* (Berkeley: University of California Press, 1998), 10.

42. Helen Parmley, "Reagan Reaps Bible, Cap," *Dallas Morning News*, August 23, 1980; "'Here's Life' Receives $60.4 million in Pledges," *Dallas Morning News*, May 22, 1979; Dr. B. Clayton Bell and Highland Park Presbyterian Church are described in William Martin, "In the Beginning," *Texas Monthly* (May 1979), 193–96.

43. Nancy Tatom Ammerman, *Baptist Battles: Social Change and Religious Conflict in the Southern Baptist Convention* (New Brunswick, NJ: Rutgers University Press, 1990), 132–33; quote from an interview with Reverend Steve Dominy, First Baptist Church of Gatesville, conducted by Libby Smith, January 15, 2004.

44. Pressler quoted in Jeff Robinson, "Paul Pressler: Conservative Resurgence Was Grassroots Movement," *Baptist Press*, March 30, 2004, and further details discussed in Paul Pressler, *A Hill on Which to Die: One Southern Baptist's Journey* (Nashville: B&H, 2002).

45. Janet Warren, "Baptists Stand by Bible," *Dallas Morning* News, May 23, 1979; Helen Parmley, "Conservative Baptists Give Rogers Office," *Dallas Morning News*, June 13, 1979.

46. Michael Foust, "Adrian Rogers, Longtime Bellevue Pastor and Leader in Conservative Resurgence, Dies," *Baptist Press*, November 15, 2005; Helen Parmley, "Irregular Voting by SBC Revealed," *Dallas Morning News*, September 19, 1979.

47. Ammerman, *Baptist Battles*, 144, based on responses to a question that asked, "Admittedly, categories do not tell everything, but most of us think of ourselves more in some terms than in others. When you think about your theological position, which word best describes where you stand—fundamentalist, conservative, moderate, or liberal?"

48. Ibid., 136, from repercentaging the middle panel of table 5.2, which shows theological category by education rather than education by theological category.

49. Gregory, *Too Great a Temptation*, 47.

50. National Election Survey, 1980, electronic data file, courtesy of the Inter-University Consortium for Political and Social Research, University of Michigan, responses from 161 interviewees who indicated their religion as Southern Baptists; although 40 percent claimed some training beyond high school, only 9 percent had college degrees; in comparison, 34 percent of Presbyterians, 18 percent of Methodists, 14 percent of Catholics, and 32 percent of Jews had college degrees. Another way of identifying evangelicals in the survey was a question asking opinions of the Bible, showing that 9 percent of those who regarded the Bible as God's completely true word had college degrees compared with 23 percent of those who considered the Bible inspired but containing errors; in the 1964 National Election Survey, 5 percent of those giving the more conservative response had college degrees compared with 20 percent of those giving the more liberal response. Identifying evangelicals in a 1978 Gallup survey through a question about the Bible and two other questions, Hunter showed that 9 percent of evangelicals had college degrees compared with 14 percent of nonevangelical Protestants and 14 percent of Catholics; James Davison Hunter, *American Evangelicalism: Conservative Religion and the Quandary of Modernity* (New Brunswick, NJ: Rutgers University Press, 1983), 54. Other relationships between rising levels of education and religion in this period are discussed in Robert Wuthnow, *The Restructuring of American Religion: Society and Faith since World War II* (Princeton, NJ: Princeton University Press, 1988), 167–72.

51. Gregory, *Too Great a Temptation*, 218.

52. W. A. Criswell, *Why I Preach That the Bible Is Literally True* (Nashville, TN: Broadman Press, 1973).

53. U.S. Bureau of the Census, *Statistical Abstract of the United States: 1971* (Washington, DC: Government Printing Office, 1971), 104 and 212.

54. My analysis of Texas results from the 1970 U.S. Census, Public Use Microsample, electronic data file, courtesy of Steven Ruggles, J. Trent Alexander, Katie Genadek, Ronald Goeken, Matthew B. Schroeder, and Matthew Sobek, *Integrated Public Use Microdata Series: Version 5.0* (Minneapolis: University of Minnesota, 2010).

55. Sherilyn Brandenstein, "Texas Equal Rights Amendment," *Handbook of Texas Online*, 1983, http://www.tshaonline.org.

56. Mark Chaves, *Ordaining Women: Culture and Conflict in Religious Organizations* (Cambridge, MA: Harvard University Press, 1997), provides a valuable analysis of the relationships between questions about women's ordination and wider cultural controversies as well as references to many of the empirical studies.

57. Ammerman, *Baptist Battles*, 91–102; "Baptist Woman's Group President Endorses ERA," *Dallas Morning News*, October 20, 1976.

58. One of Criswell's most pointed statements on the topic was in a 1984 sermon in which he argued that feminism was undermining the family and urged women to stay in the home, where God intended them to be; W. A. Criswell, "Woman's Work in the Church," October 21, 1984, Criswell Sermon Library, http://www.wacriswell.org. Criswell's opposition to the ERA is discussed briefly in James McEnteer, *Deep in the Heart: The Texas Tendency in American Politics* (Westport, CT: Praeger, 2004), 162.

59. National Election Survey, 1976, conducted by the Center for Political Studies, University of Michigan, electronic data file, courtesy of the Inter-University Consortium for Political and Social Research, University of Michigan.

60. My results based on logistic regression analysis of the responses of women in the 1976 National Election Survey with approval of the ERA as the dependent variable and age (18 to 30 vs. older), college degree, working, Republican, South, black, weekly religious attendance, and feeling close to conservatives as the independent variables; similar results with somewhat stronger effects were evident in logistic regression analysis of responses to the question about women's liberation.

61. Abe Stroud quoted in Nancy Roberts, "Stroud Raps Equal Rights Amendment," *Corsicana Daily Sun,* April 11, 1975.

62. Lottie Beth Hobbs continued to be active in efforts to oppose the Equal Rights Movement and related gender-equality measures, including helping to convene events in 1979 related to the International Year of the Child and a Pro-Family Forum in Kansas City, Missouri, in 1984; Robert E. Hooper, *A Distinct People: A History of the Churches of Christ in the 20th Century* (West Monroe, LA: Howard, 1993), 250–51; excerpts from Hobbs's flyer and quotes from an interview are included in Judith N. McArthur and Harold L. Smith, *Texas through Women's Eyes: The Twentieth-Century Experience* (Austin: University of Texas Press, 2010), 246–50.

63. Sharon Cobler, "Anti-ERA Movement Goes National," *Dallas Morning News*, November 27, 1975.

64. Jane Ulrich, "Battle Lines on ERA Drawn," *Dallas Morning News*, December 6, 1974.

65. Andujar Glasgow, "In Memory of Bill Hilliard," *Senate Journal of Texas*, May 25, 1982.

66. Bonnie Pritchett, "Fort Worth Church Produced Baptist Leaders," *Southern Baptist Texan*, October 22, 2010.

67. Texas state representative Bill Hilliard quoted in Nene Foxhall, "ERA Opponents State March," *Dallas Morning News*, February 19, 1975.

68. David W. Brady and Kent I. Tedin, "Ladies in Pink: Religion and Political Ideology in the Anti-ERA Movement," *Social Science Quarterly* 56 (1976), 564–75; quotations on p. 569; the authors note that Baptists in the group were not classified as fundamentalists, although most were probably Southern Baptist and would likely have included some fundamentalists.

69. Richard Morehead, "Stop-ERA Faction: A Political Force," *Dallas Morning News*, April 20, 1975.

70. Phyllis Schlafly quoted in Nene Foxhall, "ERA Funding under Fire," *Dallas Morning News*, March 16, 1976.

71. Thomas E. Cavanagh, "Changes in American Voter Turnout, 1964–1976," *Political Science Quarterly* 96 (1981), 53–65; and related evidence on labor-force participation and women's interest in political issues in Kristi Andersen, "Working Women and Political Participation," *American Journal of Political Science* 19 (1975), 439–53.

72. My analysis of results in the 1976 National Election Survey, electronic data file, logistic regression analysis with having voted or not voted in the 1976 election as the dependent variable and age, college education, working, weekly church attendance, feeling close to conservatives, Republican, South, and black as the independent variables. Of course opposition to the ERA was not the only issue mobilizing conservatives, but when responses to the ERA were included in the analysis along with the conservatism and other variables, the odds of having voted in 1976 were still approximately 20 percent higher among opponents and among proponents of the ERA.

73. CBS Election Day Survey, conducted November 7, 1978, among 8,808 exiting voters, electronic data file, courtesy of the Roper Center for Public Opinion Research.

74. Donald T. Critchlow, *Phyllis Schlafly and Grassroots Conservatism: A Woman's Crusade* (Princeton, NJ: Princeton University Press, 2005), 70, 246–47; Schlafly quotation on pp. 247–48; sign about repentance quoted in "Thousands Protest Conference," *Victoria Advocate*, November 20, 1977.

75. Jane J. Mansbridge, *Why We Lost the ERA* (Chicago: University of Chicago Press, 1986).

76. Gladys R. Leff, "Opening Legal Doors for Women: Hermine Tobolowsky," in *Lone Stars of David: The Jews of Texas*, ed. Hollace Ava Weiner and Kenneth D. Roseman (Waltham, MA: Brandeis University Press, 2007), 233–38; "Hermine Tobolowsky: An Inventory of Her Papers, 1932–1995," Texas Archival Resources Online, http://www.lib.utexas.edu; Sarah Weddington, *A Question of Choice* (New York: Penguin, 1993), 18; Sharon Cobler, "Crusaders Never Kick the Habit," *Dallas Morning News*, July 13, 1975.

77. An example of arguments that the National Women's Year conference and ERA were not antifamily is Linda J. Westerlage, "It's Possible to Be Pro-Family and Pro-ERA," *Galveston Daily News*, December 2, 1977, with the political cartoon labeled "Help! (Glub) Help!" on the same page.

78. National Election Surveys, cumulative electronic data file, including results from 1976, 1978, and 1980.

79. "Commander Rejected in Court Plea," *Dallas Morning News*, May 17, 1964.

80. "Alger Says Morality in Office Sank," *Dallas Morning News*, October 24, 1964.

81. Harry McCormick, "Abortions Easy to Obtain, Law Hard to Enforce," *Dallas Morning News*, March 20, 1965.

82. The German measles epidemic of the early 1960s also played an important role, as argued in Leslie J. Reagan, *Dangerous Pregnancies: Mothers, Disabilities, and Abortion in Modern America* (Berkeley: University of California Press, 2010).

83. Francis Raffetto, "City Birth Control Eyed," *Dallas Morning News*, February 25, 1965.

84. Sue Connally, "Updating Urged for Abortion Law," *Dallas Morning News*, April 16, 1966.

85. Joseph Fletcher, *Situation Ethics: The New Morality* (Philadelphia: Westminster Press, 1966), became a widely discussed treatise in seminaries and divinity schools.

86. Reverend John A. Matzner quoted in "Editorial Raps Bill on Abortions," *Dallas Morning News*, January 14, 1967.

87. Quoted in George Dugan, "New York Catholics Urged to Fight Legalized Abortion," *Dallas Morning News*, February 13, 1967.

88. Sue Connally, "TMA Rules Abortion Bill Unacceptable," *Dallas Morning News*, May 6, 1967.

89. Stewart David, "Child, Parents Hold Rights, Court Rules," *Dallas Morning News,* October 5, 1967; the case involved suit for wrongful death of an infant born two or three months prematurely as the result of an automobile accident; the ruling overturned previous cases in which life for the purpose of establishing rights was generally considered to begin only after a child was born and established an independent existence through respiration and independent circulation.

90. These connections were clearly implied in an editorial titled "Illegitimacy," *Dallas Morning News*, October 1, 1968.

91. "Mail Hits Bill for Abortion," *Dallas Morning News*, February 18, 1969.

92. Marquita Moss, "Sponsor Concedes Abortion Bill Dead, Attacks Catholic Opposition," *Dallas Morning News*, March 20, 1969.

93. Marquita Moss, "Is Fetus Human? Is Abortion Murder?" *Dallas Morning News*, March 24, 1969.

94. James T. Towns III, M.D., "The Case for Legalized Abortion," *Dallas Morning News*, April 9, 1969.

95. "Baptists Endorse 1-Day Closing Law," *Dallas Morning News*, November 7, 1969.

96. Earl Golz, "Suits Challenge Abortion Laws," *Dallas Morning News*, March 4, 1970.

97. Jan Jarboe, "Catholic Reaction Strongest," *San Antonio Light*, February 22, 1974.

98. "Area Minister Hits Abortion," *Victoria Advocate*, March 15, 1974.

99. "Stand on Abortion Due Airing," *Big Spring Herald*, June 13, 1974.

100. John Falke, "Concerned," *El Paso Herald Post*, August 27, 1976.

101. "Delegates Push Reagan in El Paso," *El Paso Herald Post*, August 9, 1976.

102. General Social Survey, electronic data file, survey conducted among a representative national sample of adults in 1978.

103. An early poll in January 1980 showed Bush as 35 percent of registered voters' first choice for the Republican nomination, with Reagan coming in second at 32 percent. In a

face-off with Carter, though, the poll suggested that Bush would lose by 21 points and Reagan by 33 points. Survey conducted for *Time* magazine by Yankelovich, Skelly, and White, January 23 and 24, 1980, in telephone interviews among 1,227 registered voters; courtesy of the Roper Center Public Opinion Archives. The polls suggested, nevertheless, that Reagan had two advantages. When asked about Bush, a significant number of voters said they were unsure or not familiar enough with him to judge whether he would be acceptable as president or capable of winning against Carter. Reagan was better known. The other advantage was Reagan's personality. A poll in March 1980 showed that 56 percent of the public rated Reagan's personality as good or very good, while only 33 percent said that about Bush. Another poll showed that 56 percent of the public agreed that Reagan "has a highly attractive personality and would inspire confidence as president," compared to 43 percent who thought the same about Bush. In the Time/Yankelovich survey, 21 percent were unsure how they would vote in a race between Carter and Bush, compared with only 11 percent with Reagan against Carter; and when asked about Bush's acceptability as president, 34 percent said they were unsure or not familiar enough to have an opinion, whereas only 7 percent gave the same responses for Reagan; conducted shortly after the Iowa caucus, the poll also showed that when asked how the caucus had affected their opinions, 40 percent said they still had no opinion of Bush, while only 29 percent said that about Reagan. The questions about personality were asked in a Yankelovich, Skelly and White Poll conducted March 29 and 30, 1980, and in an ABC News Louis Harris and Associates Poll, conducted April 26 to 30, 1980. The other difference between Bush and Reagan was that only 11 percent of registered voters who thought Bush would be acceptable as president worried that he would be too conservative, while 34 percent thought that about Reagan. But in Republican primaries Reagan's perceived conservatism worked to his advantage, helping him both to cultivate stronger support among conservative Republicans than Bush and to differentiate himself more sharply from Carter. That advantage was evident in another poll that asked Republicans who supported Reagan over Bush their reasons for doing so. Besides saying they knew more about him, the top reason was that he was more conservative. Cambridge Reports Research International Survey, conducted in January 1980 through 1,500 personal interviews, 67 percent of whom said they were Republicans; courtesy of the Roper Center Public Opinion Archives.

104. Gilbert Garcia, *Reagan's Comeback: Four Weeks in Texas That Changed American Politics Forever* (San Antonio: Trinity University Press, 2012).

105. George H. W. Bush, "Presidential Announcement Statement of Ambassador George Bush," George Bush Presidential Library and Museum, May 1, 1979, http://www.4president.org.

106. Ronald Reagan, "Announcement for Presidential Candidacy," November 13, 1979, http://www.reagan.utexas.edu; video at http://millercenter.org.

107. Partial video of the debate is at http://www.ourcampaigns.com.

108. For these comparisons, I obtained the county-level Republican primary results from Rhodes Cook, *United States Presidential Primary Elections, 1968–1996: A Handbook of Election Statistics* (Washington, DC: CQ Press, 2000), and merged the electronic data files with 1980 county-level statistics on religion and the relevant census variables from electronic data files compiled by Social Explorer. The evangelical Protestant variable in the Social Explorer data is a standard code known in the sociology of religion literature as "reltrad," which

categorizes denominational membership by major denominational traditions. In these data for Texas, approximately two-thirds of the evangelical Protestants were Southern Baptists, and the remainder was members of smaller denominations such as Assemblies of God and independent Baptists. Calculating evangelicals as a percentage of Protestants is necessary to adjust for varying proportions of counties who essentially are not eligible to be conservative Protestants because of being Catholics or Jews. The percent of total population that was African American was included as a control variable to take into account the possibility that the white residents who made up nearly all of voters in the Republican primary may have been influenced by living in counties with larger black populations. The percentages that were Hispanic, below the poverty line, and urban were included as control variables for similar reasons, while the percentage of persons age twenty-five and older who had at least four years of college was included to see if the presence of more of these relatively well-educated, middle-class voters might result in elevated voting for Bush as the more moderate candidate. The standardized multiple regression coefficients for the effect of each variable on the percentage of total votes in counties cast for Reagan were 0.152 for percent of Protestant adherents that were evangelical (significant at the 0.02 level and an unstandardized coefficient of 0.179), −0.252 for percent of 1980 population that was black (significant at the 0.001 level), and −0.218 for percent of persons age twenty-five and over with at least four years of college (significant at the 0.01 level); the coefficients for percent Hispanic, percent urban, and percent below the poverty line were not significant. Alternative models in which the percent of Protestants who were Southern Baptists was included instead of the percent evangelical variable and in which median family income was included instead of the poverty variable produced nearly identical results (tests for multicollinearity showed that the poverty variable and median household income should not be included in the same models).

109. Douglas Harlan, "The Party's Over," *Texas Monthly* (January 1982), 114–19; Harlan's account also describes the more complicated relationships between Bush and Connally and Clements and Tower, which factored into the 1980 campaign; Sean P. Cunningham, *Cowboy Conservatism: Texas and the Rise of the Modern Right* (Lexington: University Press of Kentucky, 2010), 195–200.

110. "George W. Strake Jr.," http://www.muckety.com.

111. The names, dates, and amounts of donations as compiled by the Federal Election Commission are listed at http://www.city-data.com; in Houston more than 250 contributors donated $136,000 to Reagan's primary campaign.

112. "State GOP Takes in $1.3 Million at Big Ford-Reagan Fund-Raiser," *Paris News*, September 13, 1978; Carolyn Barta, "Reagan 'Anti-DC' Speech Electrifies 'Clements Convoy,'" *Dallas Morning News*, October 20, 1978.

113. My analysis of data from the CBS News/New York Times Election Survey conducted in November 1980 among 15,201 voters, electronic data file courtesy of the Inter-University Consortium for Political and Social Research at the University of Michigan, shows that the odds of voting for Reagan were 32.5 percent higher among self-identified "born-again" voters than among non-born-again voters, controlling for race, gender, age, education, and region; however, among only the 2,735 white southern voters, the coefficient for born again was not significant; a different conclusion emerges, though, from comparisons among these voters

with how they recalled voting in 1976; in that election, 47 percent of white southern born-again voters opted for Carter, while only 35 percent of white southern non-born-again voters did; the decline in votes for Carter in 1980 compared with 1976 was 9 points among born-again white southerners but only 2 points among white southern non-born-again voters.

114. In the 1980 CBS News/New York Times election survey, logistic regression analysis among southern voters of the odds of identifying as a conservative yielded odds ratios of 1.906 for white and 1.818 for born again, controlling for gender, age, and having any college education; among southern voters the odds of having voted for Reagan were nearly thirteen times greater among whites than among blacks, taking account of differences in age, education, and gender.

115. At least one African American state legislator was among the speakers at the Pro-Family conference in Houston, and African American pastor E. V. Hill from Los Angeles addressed the crowd at the National Affairs Briefing in Dallas.

CHAPTER 11
IN A COMPASSIONATE WAY

1. The Religious Right as a social movement was the perspective emphasized in the essays in Robert C. Liebman and Robert Wuthnow, eds., *The New Christian Right: Mobilization and Legitimation* (Hawthorne, NY: Aldine, 1983), and has been usefully employed in such studies as Mayer N. Zald and John D. McCarthy, "Religious Groups as Crucibles of Social Movements," in *Sacred Companies: Organizational Aspects of Religion and Religious Aspects of Organizations*, ed. N. J. Demerath III, Peter Dobkin Hall, Terry Schmitt, and Rhys H. Williams (New York: Oxford University Press, 1998), 24–49; Jeffrey K. Hadden, "Religious Broadcasting and the Mobilization of the New Christian Right," *Journal for the Scientific Study of Religion* 26 (1987), 1–24; and William Martin, *With God on Our Side: The Rise of the Religious Right in America* (New York: Random House, 1996).

2. Influential studies emphasizing public opinion include quantitative studies by Paul DiMaggio, John Evans, and Bethany Bryson, "Have Americans' Social Attitudes Become More Polarized?" *American Journal of Sociology* 102 (1996), 690–755; John H. Evans, "Have Americans' Attitudes Become More Polarized?—An Update," *Social Science Quarterly* 84 (2003), 71–90; and Morris Fiorina, *Culture War? The Myth of a Polarized America* (New York: Pearson Longman, 2005); and the qualitative studies of James D. Hunter, *Culture Wars* (New York: Basic Books, 1991); and Alan Wolfe, *One Nation, After All: What Americans Really Think about God, Country, Family, Racism, Welfare, Immigration, Homosexuality, Work, the Right, the Left and Each Other* (New York: Viking, 1998).

3. This reference is meant to be critical of the metaphor I used in some of my own work on the Religious Right, particularly in Robert Wuthnow, *The Struggle for America's Soul: Evangelicals, Liberals, and Secularism* (Grand Rapids, MI: Eerdmans, 1989).

4. The difference between religious conservatives and religious liberals on views of government spending for public welfare was statistically significant and strong, controlling for a number of other variables, in two national surveys that examined the issue; Robert Wuthnow,

"Restructuring of American Religion: Further Evidence," *Sociological Inquiry* 66 (1996), 303–29.

5. I elaborate on the theoretical argument briefly mentioned here in chapter 13. Work that valuably surveys the extensive literature about the Religious Right includes Clyde Wilcox and Carin Robinson, *Onward Christian Soldiers? The Religious Right in American Politics* (Boulder, CO: Westview Press, 2011); and Daniel K. Williams, *God's Own Party: The Making of the Christian Right* (New York: Oxford University Press, 2010).

6. George H. W. Bush, "Address Accepting the Presidential Nomination at the Republican National Convention in New Orleans," August 18, 1988, http://www.presidency.ucsb.edu; the reference to a shotgun house was to the kind of small, single-family dwelling in which doors connecting rooms opened in a line that would have made it possible to shoot a shotgun shell straight through the house from front door to back door; low-income families working in oil fields were often supplied with these houses as rentals by the oil companies.

7. Peggy Noonan, *What I Saw at the Revolution: A Political Life in the Reagan Era* (New York: Random House, 1990), 311–17, for Noonan's account of writing the speech and its reception at the convention. The Tocquevillean idea of mediating structures had been popularized among neoconservative social theorists in Peter L. Berger and Richard John Neuhaus, *To Empower People: The Role of Mediating Structures in Public Policy* (Washington, DC: American Enterprise Institute, 1977).

8. Noonan, *What I Saw at the Revolution*, 312; voluntary prayer in school was part of the speech.

9. The history of LULAC is given in Benjamin Marquez, *Constructing Identities in Mexican-American Political Organizations: Choosing Issues, Taking Sides* (Austin: University of Texas Press, 2003); and Cynthia E. Orozco, *No Mexicans, Women, or Dogs Allowed: The Rise of the Mexican American Civil Rights Movement* (Austin: University of Texas Press, 2009). Noonan's account mentions her familiarity with Knights of Columbus and Holy Name organizations growing up and her inclusion of the Order of AHEPA as a joke, but it does not discuss the reference to LULAC or Bible study groups.

10. Bush, "Address Accepting the Presidential Nomination."

11. Data on party representation in the Texas legislature from the Legislative Reference Library, Austin, Texas, as reported in Richard Murray and Sam Attlesey, "Texas: Republicans Gallop Ahead," in *Southern Politics in the 1990s*, ed. Alexander P. Lamis (Baton Rouge: Louisiana State University Press, 1999), 305–42.

12. "Poor Paying Larger Share of Texas Taxes," *New Braunfels Herald-Zeitung*, April 1, 1988.

13. Judith Zaffirini, "Reform Needed in State Welfare System," *Seguin Gazette Enterprise*, November 17, 1988.

14. Virgil Watson, "Welfare a Cancer on Society," *Kerrville Daily Times*, November 2, 1988.

15. Catherine S. Chilman, "Welfare Reform or Revision? The Family Support Act of 1988," *Social Service Review* 66 (1992), 349–77; "Clements to Appoint New Board," *Galveston Daily News*, December 11, 1988; "Governor Wants Welfare Reform," *Galveston Daily News*, April 27, 1988.

16. These figures are drawn from my analysis of estimates provided by 1990 U.S. Census, 1 percent Public Use Microsample, electronic data file, courtesy of Steven J. Ruggles, Trend Alexander, Katie Genadek, Ronald Goeken, Matthew B. Schroeder, and Matthew Sobeck, *Integrated Public Use Microdata Series, Version 5.0* (Minneapolis: University of Minnesota, 2010).

17. Campbell Gibson and Kay Jung, *Historical Census Statistics on Population Totals by Race, 1790 to 1990, and By Hispanic Origin, 1970 to 1990, for the United States, Regions, Divisions, and States* (Washington, DC: U. S. Census Bureau, 2002), table 58, "Texas Race and Hispanic Origin: 1850 to 1990," Internet release, September 13, 2002.

18. My analysis of the electronic data file of the CBS News, *CBS News Election Day Surveys, 1984* (Ann Arbor, MI: Inter-University Consortium for Political and Social Research, 1986), responses from 1,980 Texas voters.

19. Ibid.

20. My analysis of the electronic data file of the CBS News/New York Times, *CBS News/ New York Times Election Day Surveys, 1986* (Ann Arbor, MI: Inter-University Consortium for Political and Social Research, 1988), in which 1,478 Texas voters were included.

21. My analysis of the electronic data file of the ABC News/Washington Post, *ABC News/ Washington Post Exit Poll, 1986* (Ann Arbor, MI: Inter-University Consortium for Political and Social Research, 1987), including interviews with 20,844 voters nationally of whom 1,099 were in Texas.

22. Lee Atwater quoted in Alexander P. Lamis, "The Two-Party South: From the 1960s to the 1990s," in *Southern Politics in the 1990s*, ed. Alexander P. Lamis (Baton Rouge: Louisiana State University Press, 1999), 1–49, quotation on p. 8; reprinted in Bob Herbert, "Impossible, Ridiculous, Repugnant," *New York Times*, October 6, 2005.

23. "Poll: Racism Still Alive in America," *Galveston Daily News*, August 8, 1988.

24. Mike Barbee, "Klan Candidate Anti-White," *Sequin Gazette Enterprise*, January 17, 1986.

25. Survey by American Political Network and the Hotline, conducted by KRC Communications/Research, October 26–October 28, 1988, and based on 1,002 telephone interviews drawn from a national sample of registered voters; and survey by Times Mirror, conducted by Gallup Organization, October 23–October 26, 1988, and based on 2,006 telephone interviews drawn from a national sample of registered voters; Harris Poll, conducted by Louis Harris & Associates, October 28 to October 30, 1988, and based on 1,250 telephone interviews drawn from a national sample of likely voters; courtesy of the Roper Center for Public Opinion Research. Chandler Davidson, *Race and Class in Texas Politics* (Princeton, NJ: Princeton University Press, 1990), 268, notes the irony of Bush's Willie Horton advertisements given the fact that Texas had a prison furlough program that during the first term of Republican governor Clements furloughed nearly five thousand inmates, including more than five hundred murderers.

26. Robert R. Brischetto and Annette A. Aviña, "Trends in Ethnic Voting in Texas State Elections: 1978–1986," Southwest Voter Research Institute, presentation to the Leadership San Antonio Alumni Association, December 5, 1986, courtesy of Stanford Libraries, Stanford University.

27. Jennifer Dixon, "Justice Department Probes GOP Ads," *Kerrville Daily Times*, November 4, 1988; "Brooks Asks AG to Investigate Ads," *Galveston Daily News*, November 4, 1988.

28. My analysis of the electronic data file of the CBS News, *CBS News Texas Poll, July 1988* (Ann Arbor, MI: Inter-University Consortium for Political and Social Research, 2002), responses from 580 registered voters in Texas.

29. Ibid.

30. Lorena Adams, "One View of Liberal vs. Conservative," *Kerrville Daily Times*, October 30, 1988.

31. For example, see the statement by Galveston Right to Life Committee chair Robert G. B. Powell, "AP Gave Wrong View of Bentsen," *Galveston Daily News*, September 9, 1988.

32. Barry Hankins, *American Evangelicals: A Contemporary History of a Mainstream Religious Movement* (Lanham, MD: Rowman and Littlefield, 2008), 153; "Texas GOP Ponders Robertson," *Paris News*, April 3, 1988.

33. On the possibility of George W. Bush running for governor against liberal Democrats, see the insightful analysis in Bob Thaxton, "Trouble Seen in Party Future," *Seguin Gazette Enterprise*, November 27, 1988.

34. Roberto Suro, "Richards Promises a New Direction: Though Fiscally Conservative, She Is a Social Liberal Texan," *New York Times*, November 8, 1990.

35. Mike Cochran, *Claytie: The Roller-Coaster Life of a Texas Wildcatter* (College Station: Texas A&M University Press, 2007), 14–16.

36. Robin Toner, "Contest in Texas to Test Currents in U.S. Politics," *New York Times*, April 12, 1990.

37. Clayton Williams quoted in Brett Clanton, "Still the Same Old 'Claytie' at 79," *Houston Chronicle*, June 15, 2011.

38. "Remarks Put Baylor President, Baptist Fundamentalists at Odds," *Brazosport Facts*, May 21, 1988.

39. Dolph Tillotson, "Political View Liberal and Conservative," *Galveston Daily News*, February 28, 1988.

40. "Anti-Abortionists Blockade Clinics," *Brazosport Facts*, October 30, 1988.

41. "Activist Group May Have Fight on Hands to Keep Abortion Laws," *Kerrville Daily Times*, January 16, 1989.

42. Beverly Miller, "Ivins: Texas Politics Going from Gutter to the Sewer," *Galveston Daily News*, April 25, 1990.

43. David Maraniss, "The City Consumed by the Debate on Abortion: The Religious Right Takes Its Stand in Corpus Christi," *Washington Post*, October 8, 1990; "Black Clergyman Announced Anti-Abortion Group in Texas," *Philadelphia Tribune*, September 28, 1990; Lisa Belkin, "In Texas City, Newcomer Brings Abortion Turmoil," *New York Times*, July 7, 1990; Ari L. Goldman, "Bishop Excommunicates 2 in Texas for Abortion Stance," *New York Times*, June 30, 1990.

44. My analysis of electronic data file from Voter Research and Surveys, *Voter Research and Surveys: National Election Day Exit Poll, 1990*, courtesy of the Roper Center for Public Opinion Research, a survey conducted on November 6, 1990, among 19,888 voters nationally, of whom 1,018 voted in Texas.

45. "Compassion Fatigue, Political Uncertainty Slowing Donations," *Galveston Daily News*, December 4, 1992.

46. "Symposium Panelist Recalls Early History," *Seguin Gazette-Enterprise*, November 3, 1994; "War on Poverty Called War on God by UT Professor," *Orange Leader*, July 18, 1992.

47. Lynn Ray Ellison, "Black Philanthropy Ever a Tapestry of Compassion," *Texas City Sun*, November 20, 1994.

48. "Record Set Straight," *Paris News*, April 8, 1993.

49. Interview with Larry Allums, Dallas Institute of Humanities and Culture, conducted by Natalie Searl, March 25, 1997.

50. Terry Bozarth, "The Minister's Forum," *Lockhart Post Register*, April 14, 1994.

51. Jack Chambers, "Government Can't Provide All We Need," *Paris News*, April 8, 1993.

52. Molly Ivins, "Greed, Self-Interest Lead Health Reform Sweepstakes," *Galveston Daily News*, June 26, 1994; Dave Mann, "Honoring B Rapoport," *Texas Observer*, April 11, 2012.

53. Ann Richards, "Democratic Convention Keynote Address," July 19, 1988, http://www.americanrhetoric.com.

54. Voter News Service, *Voter News Service General Election Exit Polls, 1994: Texas* (Ann Arbor, MI: Inter-University Consortium for Political and Social Research, 2000), electronic data file; my analysis of the responses from 1,631 Texas voters.

55. The 1984, 1988, and 1992 figures are from my analysis of electronic data files; *CBS News Election Day Surveys, 1984: Texas*, courtesy of the Roper Center for Public Opinion Research; CBS News, *CBS News Texas Poll, July 1988* (Ann Arbor, MI: Inter-University Consortium for Political and Social Research, 2002); Voter Research and Surveys, *Voter Research and Surveys General Election Exit Polls, 1992: Texas* (Ann Arbor, MI: Inter-University Consortium for Political and Social Research, 1999).

56. William Raspberry, "Let Funds Directly Benefit Faith-Based Groups," *Washington Post*, December 14, 1995; Jeff Jacoby, " 'Compassion Tax Credit' Has Merit," *Orange Leader*, November 26, 1995; on the development of Charitable Choice and the role of religion, research studies include Mark Chaves, "Religious Congregations and Welfare Reform: Who Will Take Advantage of 'Charitable Choice'?" *American Sociological Review* 64 (1999), 836–46; and Robert Wuthnow, *Saving America? Faith-Based Services and the Future of Civil Society* (Princeton, NJ: Princeton University Press, 2004).

57. Virginia A. Hodgkinson, *From Belief to Commitment: The Community Service Activities and Finances of Religious Congregations in the United States* (Washington, DC: Independent Sector, 1993); and information about the practices of various religious organizations in Robert Wuthnow and Virginia A. Hodgkinson, editors, *Faith and Philanthropy in America: Exploring the Role of Religion in America's Voluntary Sector* (San Francisco: Jossey-Bass, 1990).

58. Robert Wuthnow, *Acts of Compassion: Caring for Others and Helping Ourselves* (Princeton, NJ: Princeton University Press, 1991), and on religion and government cooperation in international relief programs, Wuthnow, *Boundless Faith: The Global Outreach of American Churches* (Berkeley: University of California Press, 2009).

59. Oral history interview conducted by Sylvia Kundrats, January 20, 2011; name of interviewee withheld according to Princeton University Institutional Review Board rules governing the project.

60. Oral history interview conducted by Natalie Searl, February 25, 2000; name of interviewee withheld.

61. Interview conducted by Sylvia Kundrats, July 5, 2012; name of interviewee withheld.

62. Interview with Clara Hinojosa of the Mexican Cultural Center, conducted by Natalie Searl, February 7, 1998; interview conducted by Sylvia Kundrats, January 11, 2011; name of interviewee withheld.

63. Marc A. Musick, *Survey of Texas Adults, 2004* (Ann Arbor, MI: Inter-University Consortium for Political and Social Research, 2004), electronic data file; the data are analyzed in Marc A. Musick, *Volunteers: A Social Profile* (Bloomington: Indiana University Press, 2008).

64. Buckner Foundation, Consolidated Financial Statements for Fiscal Year Ending December 31, 2009; Internal Revenue Service Form 990, Buckner International, Dallas, Texas, 2010.

65. The Texas lead in preceding and implementing Charitable Choice faith-based initiatives is described in Rebecca Sager, *Faith, Politics, and Power: The Politics of Faith-Based Initiatives* (New York: Oxford University Press, 2011), 29–50.

66. "Task Force to Study Service Programs," *Texas City Sun*, May 3, 1996; Mary Madewell, "Welfare Plan to Use Churches May Bring Constitutional Battle," *Paris News*, January 27, 1997; "Bush Signs Bills Aimed at Involving Religious Groups," *Brazosport Facts*, June 14, 1997; Pamela Colloff, "Remember the Christian Alamo," *Texas Monthly*, December 2001, which includes details about the role played by Roloff's successor Wiley Cameron.

67. Chris Womack, "Taking Deregulation on Faith," *Texas Observer*, September 27, 2001.

68. Governor George W. Bush quoted in Roy Maynard and Marvin Olasky, "Governor Bush Backs Teen Challenge," *World Magazine*, July 29, 1995, and included in *The Texas Faith-Based Initiative at Five Years: Warning Signs as President Bush Expands Texas-Style Program at National Level* (Austin: Texas Freedom Network, 2002), 21.

69. According to "Texas Law Enforcement Agency Uniform Crime Reports, 1960 to 2010," http://www.disastercenter.com, violent crime increased from 111,889 in 1989 to 145,743 in 1991 before falling to 129,838 in 1994; the crime index fell from 1,346,866 in 1989 to 1,079,225 in 1994; the rate per 10,000 population declined from 7,926 in 1989 to 5,873 in 1994; "Texas Crime Report for 1999," Texas Department of Public Safety, http://www.dps.texas.gov.

70. Arlington Mayor Elzie Odom, quoted in "Bush Signs Bills Aimed at Involving Religious Groups."

71. Marvin Olasky, *Compassionate Conservatism: What It Is, What It Does, and How It Can Transform America* (New York: Free Press, 2000), Bush quoted on p. 55.

72. Ibid., xii.

73. My analysis of the electronic data file for the Campaign 2000 Typology Survey, conducted among 2,799 randomly selected nationally representative adults by the Pew Research Center, courtesy of the Association of Religion Data Archives.

74. Mimi Swartz, "Kirbyjon Caldwell," *Texas Monthly* (September 1996), 1–8; Karl Rove, *Courage and Consequence: My Life as a Conservative in the Fight* (New York: Simon and Schuster, 2010), 281; Gary Scott Smith, *Faith and the Presidency: From George Washington to George W. Bush* (New York: Oxford University Press, 2006), 384.

75. In 2005 Willett was appointed to the Texas Supreme Court; Rick Perry, "Don Willett Appointment," Office of the Governor, August 24, 2005, online text.

76. George W. Bush, *Rallying the Armies of Compassion* (Washington, DC: White House, 2001), quotation on p. ii, online at http://archives.hud.gov.

77. These figures are from my analysis of the electronic data file compiled by Stephen L. Klineberg, *Houston Area Survey, 1982–2010: Successive Representative Samples of Harris County Residents* (Ann Arbor, MI: Inter-University Consortium for Political and Social Research, 2011).

78. Helen Rose Ebaugh and Janet Saltzman Chafetz, eds., *Religion and the New Immigrants: Continuities and Adaptations in Immigrant Congregations* (Walnut Creek, CA: AltaMira Press, 2000).

79. U.S. Census 2000 decennial census, aggregated American Community Survey data for 2006 to 2010 and 2010 religion data for congregations with addresses and telephone numbers collected by the InfoGroup and tabulated and processed by Social Explorer, http://www.socialexplorer.com.

80. Bush, *Rallying the Armies of Compassion,* ii.

81. Grover G. Norquist, "Are Muslims Conservatives?" *Veritas* (January 2002), 8–11.

82. April Armstrong, " 'That's What Makes Me a Jew and Him a Baptist': Jews, Southern Baptists, and the American Public Square from the Reagan Revolution to the Dawn of the New Millennium" (PhD diss., Princeton University, 2012).

83. "Hindu Beliefs Include a God Who Is Ultimate But Unknowable," *Baptist Press,* November 12, 1999; Gustav Niebuhr, "Coalition of Jews Protests Southern Baptist Conversion Tactics," *New York Times*, November 9, 1999; interview conducted by Natalie Searl, February 7, 2000; name withheld.

84. Interview conducted by Natalie Searl, June 20, 2000; pseudonym used.

85. Interviews conducted by Natalie Searl, January 9 and March 21, 2001; further information from these interviews and the national survey in Wuthnow, *America and the Challenges of Religious Diversity.*

86. Former president Jimmy Carter quoted in Karen Hill, "Religious Groups Turn to Preventive Care," *Texas City Sun*, November 29, 1997.

87. Oral history interviews conducted by Natalie Searl, September 13, 2002, and January 21, 2003; names of interviewees withheld. A woman who attended a Catholic church in Columbus, Texas, put it this way when asked about Muslims and Hindus: "I guess they believe what they believe. It doesn't really matter to me. As long as somebody doesn't try to change my mind, I'm okay." Interview conducted by Libby Smith, October 8, 2002.

88. Susan Osborne, "Class Focuses on Moral Values," *Kerrville Daily Times*, January 19, 1995.

89. Greg Barr, "Let the Kids Pray," *Brazosport Facts* (Clute, TX), July 28, 1995.

90. "Souls," *Texas City Sun*, August 16, 1997.

91. Robert Wuthnow, *Sharing the Journey: Support Groups and America's New Quest for Community* (New York: Free Press, 1994).

92. Robert N. Bellah, Richard Madsen, William M. Sullivan, Ann Swidler, and Steven M. Tipton, *Habits of the Heart: Individualism and Commitment in American Life* (Berkeley: University of California Press, 1985), 221.

93. Oral history interview conducted by Natalie Searl, July 29, 2002; name of interviewee withheld.

94. Karma Lowe, "Faith Greatest Lesson," *Brazosport Facts*, March 8, 1998, italics added; Bellah et al., *Habits of the Heart*, 235.

95. George W. Bush, "Remarks at the Power Center in Houston Texas, September 12, 2003," *Public Papers of the Presidents of the United States: Administration of George W. Bush* (Washington, DC: Government Printing Office, 2003), 1151–56, quotation on p. 1153. How people adhered to their own beliefs while expressing tolerance toward other religions was nicely illustrated by a woman we talked to in a small town in South Texas who said her church was working hard to fulfill the Great Commission of spreading the gospel to everyone so that Jesus could come again, but who went on to say that she figured everyone would get to heaven no matter what their religion was.

96. *Texas Faith-Based Initiative at Five Years*; on the Branch Davidians, Nancy T. Ammerman, "Report to the Justice and Treasury Departments Regarding Law Enforcement Interaction with the Branch Davidians in Waco, Texas," Hartford Institute, September 3, 1993; John C. Danforth, *Interim Report to the Deputy Attorney General Concerning the 1993 Confrontation at the Mt. Carmel Complex* (Washington, DC: Office of the Attorney General, 2000).

97. Interview with a state senator in Austin, conducted by Natalie Searl, May 29, 2001; name of interviewee withheld.

98. Oral history interview conducted June 18, 2012, by Karen Myers;, name of interviewee withheld.

99. Oral history interview conducted March 23, 1998, by Natalie Searl, name of interviewee withheld.

100. Oral history interview with Leticia Paez, conducted December 11, 2001; by Natalie Searl.

101. My research in Pennsylvania and a review of other studies are presented in Wuthnow, *Saving America*; the critical assessment from an inside perspective was David Kuo, *Tempting Faith: An Inside Story of Political Seduction* (New York: Free Press, 2007).

102. Chaves, "Religious Congregations and Welfare Reform"; Wuthnow, *Saving America*; Winnifred F. Sullivan, *Prison Religion: Faith-Based Reform and the Constitution* (Princeton: Princeton University Press, 2009).

103. Results from the 2002 Religion and Public Life Survey, conducted by the Pew Research Center, based on my analysis of the data, as shown in Wuthnow, *Saving America*, 301.

104. From a 2001 national survey conducted by the Pew Research Center, discussed in Wuthnow, *Saving America*, 301.

105. These results are drawn from my analysis of the electronic data files for Voter News Service, *Voter News Service Primary Election Exit Polls, 2000, and Voter News Service General Election Exit Polls, 2000* (Ann Arbor, MI: Inter-University Consortium for Political and Social

Research, 2004), which included 1,353 voters in the Texas Republican primary and 830 voters in the Texas general election.

106. Results based on the Voter News Service General Election Exit Polls in which 13,259 voters participated nationally.

107. The 2000 data were collected by the Association of Statisticians of American Religious Bodies (ASARB) and include statistics for 149 religious groups, including number of churches and adherents. Dale E. Jones, Sherri Doty, Clifford Grammich, James E. Horsch, Richard Houseal, Mac Lynn, John P. Marcum, Kenneth M. Sanchagrin, and Richard H. Taylor supervised the collection. These data originally appeared in *Religious Congregations & Membership in the United States, 2000* (Cincinnati, OH: Glenmary Research Center, 2001), and are available at http://www.socialexplorer.com and the Association of Religion Data Archives. The 2004 study was Musick, *Survey of Texas Adults.*

108. Interview with Reverend Todd Bell, March 24, 1998, conducted by Natalie Searl.

109. Deborah Melanie Sharpe, "Denominationalism: What the Cynic Sees" (Senior thesis, Department of Sociology, Princeton University, 1985).

110. William Martin, "The Lord Giveth and the Lord Giveth," *Texas Monthly* (February 1982), 156–59; William Martin, "Prime Minister," *Texas Monthly* (August 2005), 106–10; John W. Storey, "Pagodas amid the Steeples: The Changing Religious Landscape," in *Twentieth-Century Texas: A Social and Cultural History,* ed. John W. Storey and Mary L. Kelley (Denton: University of North Texas Press, 2008), 135–63; Victoria Clark, *Allies for Armageddon: The Rise of Christian Zionism* (New Haven, CT: Yale University Press, 2007); Shayne Lee, *T. D. Jakes: America's New Preacher* (New York: New York University Press, 2005); Shayne Lee and Phillip Sinitiere, *Holy Mavericks: Evangelical Innovators and the Spiritual Marketplace* (New York: New York University Press, 2009).

111. Scott Thumma and Dave Travis, *Beyond Megachurch Myths: What We Can Learn from America's Largest Churches* (San Francisco: Jossey-Bass, 2007); online database of megachurches in the United States; and Omri Elisha, *Moral Ambition: Mobilization and Social Outreach in Evangelical Megachurches* (Berkeley: University of California Press, 2011); and on the relationship between church size and service ministries, Mark Chaves, *Congregations in America* (Cambridge, MA: Harvard University Press, 2004).

112. Interview with Reverend Steve Dominy, First Baptist Church, Gatesville, Texas, conducted by Libby Smith, January 15, 2004; additional information about First Contact is available at the organization's website, http://www.thewelcomeback.org.

113. These results are drawn from my analysis of the electronic data files for Texas and the United States from National Election Pool, Edison Media Research, and Mitosky International, *National Election Pool General Election Exit Polls, 2004* (Ann Arbor, MI: Inter-University Consortium for Political and Social Research, 2005).

114. Reverend Larry James, interviewed by Natalie Searl, March 23, 1998; Reverend James served for eight months in 1998 as executive director for the Greater Dallas Community of Churches after serving for fourteen years as senior minister of the Richardson East Church of Christ in Richardson and then devoted himself full-time to the CitySquare inner-city ministry in Dallas.

CHAPTER 12
AN INDEPENDENT LOT

1. On politics as a source of religious defection, Michael Hout and Claude S. Fischer, "Explaining the Rise of Americans with No Religious Preference: Generations and Politics," *American Sociological Review* 67 (2002), 165–90; and as a church member in Texas observed, "Pastor, go ahead and promote your preferences for voting, but how many members and lost people will part company with you?" Gilbert Thornton, "Political Churches," *Baptist Standard*, February 6, 2004, online. In several national studies, including the large surveys conducted in 2006 and 2008 and discussed later in this chapter, more than 50 percent of Texas adults said they attended religious services at least once or twice a month, whereas the proportion in California and New York was approximately 33 percent.

2. The best discussion of time in apocalyptic thinking is John R. Hall, *Apocalypse: From Antiquity to the Empire of Modernity* (Malden, MA: Polity Press, 2009).

3. Interview conducted by Peter Mundey, July 24, 2006; for research summarized in greater detail, Robert Wuthnow, *Be Very Afraid: The Cultural Response to Terror, Pandemics, Environmental Devastation, Nuclear Annihilation, and Other Threats* (New York: Oxford University Press, 2010); and Wuthnow, *The God Problem: Expressing Faith and Being Reasonable* (Berkeley: University of California Press, 2012).

4. Abortion figures for 2005 from "Facts on Induced Abortion in the United States," *Guttmacher Institute*, August 2011; "Anti-Abortion Activists Aim Expansion Drive at Urban Blacks and Hispanics," *Galveston Daily News*, August 23, 2006. Census data from the electronic data files for 1 percent estimates of the 2000 census, women age fifteen through forty-four.

5. Calculations based on figures for 2001 from the Texas Department of State Health Services.

6. Jim Vertuno, "State OKs Abortion Regulations," *Texas City Sun*, January 16, 2004.

7. "Lawmakers Chipping Away at Access for Abortions," *Texas City Sun*, February 15, 2004; April Castro, "Regulations Tentatively Approved," *Texas City Sun*, October 31, 2003.

8. The Justice Foundation, http://www.thejusticefoundation.org; Allan Parker, "State's Education Shows Troubling Pattern," *Paris News*, December 9, 1993; Selwyn Crawford and Gayle Reaves, "Abortion Foes Rally at Clinic," *Dallas Morning News*, January 22, 1995.

9. Wayne Slater, "Ministers' Group Plans to Oppose Conservatives in Austin," *Dallas Morning News*, June 19, 1996.

10. Sam Attlesey and Susan Feeney, "Candidates Court Texas Voters," *Dallas Morning News*, March 11, 1996.

11. Sam Attlesey and Wayne Slater, "GOP Delegates Heavily Anti-Abortion," *Dallas Morning News*, June 23, 1996

12. "Conservative Leaders Step Up to Defend Bush's Abortion Stand," *Dallas Morning News*, March 21, 1999.

13. Jack Eggers, "Former Abortion Clinic Worker Speaks at Kerrville Crisis Pregnancy Center Event," *Kerrville Daily Times*, November 19, 1999.

14. Weighted results from the electronic data file for 1,526 randomly selected adults included in Marc A. Musick, *Survey of Texas Adults, 2004* (Ann Arbor, MI: Inter-University Consortium for Political and Social Research, 2004).

15. David Crary, "Anti-Abortion Activists Prepare for Rallies," *Valley Morning Star* (Harlingen, TX), January 20, 2007.

16. "Explosives Left at Abortion Clinic," *New Braunfels Herald Zeitung*, April 27, 2007.

17. Internal Revenue Service Form 990 information for the organizations mentioned.

18. These results are from my analysis of the electronic data file for the 2007 Texas Lyceum Poll on church and state issues, conducted by the Texas Lyceum, May 2007, http://www.texaslyceum.org.

19. Reverend G. E. Patterson of the Churches of God in Christ, quoted in Woody Baird, "Black Pentecostals Not Part of 'Religious Right,'" *Baytown Sun*, November 20, 2004.

20. Allan Parker, "How Will the Church Respond to the Supreme Court's Call for Public Testimony?" Reformation Prayer Network, May 18, 2012, http://www.usrpn.org.

21. "Justice Foundation President Allan Parker Jr. Endorses Gov. Perry for Re-election," October 7, 2009, http://www.rickperry.org.

22. "Gov. Perry: Sonogram Legislation Helps Prevent the Tragedy of Abortion," Office of the Governor, May 24, 2011, http://governor.state.tx.us.

23. "South Texas Diocese Bars Sanchez, Sharp from Speaking," *Baytown Sun*, June 26, 2002.

24. "Bishop Raymundo J. Peña of Brownsville Retires; Successor Named," *West Texas Catholic*, December 20, 2009; Raymundo Peña, "Top 10 List for the New Year," *Rio Grande Valley Monitor*, January 11, 2008; Victor Castillo, "Valley Catholics Unite to Fight Abortion," *ValleyCentral.com*, February 11, 2009.

25. Joseph Pronechen, "Deep in the Heart of North Texas," *National Catholic Register*, June 16, 2007; "2011 Dallas March for Life," *Demotix News*, January 22, 2011, http://demotix.com; Bishop Kevin Farrell, "Letter to the Diocese of Dallas," January 26, 2012.

26. Pastor Stephen Broden quoted on the National Black Pro-Life Coalition website, http://www.blackprolifecoalition.org; Sarah Crawford, "Texas-Based Pro-Life Organization Gains National Recognition," *Life News*, April 7, 2011, http://www.texasrighttolife.com.

27. Holbrook's role is described in Tim McKeown, "Texas Pastor Paved Way for Southern Baptists in Sanctity of Life Battles," *Southern Baptist Texan*, May 28, 2004, http://texanonline.net. Richard Land's biography is from information provided by the Southern Baptist Convention's Ethics and Religious Liberty Commission, http://www.erlc.com. Hanna Rosin, "Beyond Belief," *The Atlantic*, January/February 2005, http://www.theatlantic.com.

28. Interviews conducted on July 13 and July 19, 2011, by Steve Myers and Karen Myers; interviewees identified with pseudonyms.

29. An assistant pastor at a large evangelical church in suburban Dallas was particularly candid about the appropriateness of preaching on political topics. "We preach scripture here," he explained, by which he meant taking a section of scripture and preaching through it. "And if that passage brought up political or things that address those issues, then out of faithfulness to the text and out of faithfulness to the authority of scripture and God almighty, he would preach those things to the best of his ability and to the best of his knowledge with a humble

heart, prayerfully asking the Holy Spirit to give him help and direction." Asked if that ever meant supporting conservative political candidates, he replied, "Like I said, we take a biblical stance, so our church is going to align with people who are anti-abortion and anti–gay marriage. Not that that would ever be preached from the pulpit, but there will definitely be a buzz in our congregation about people that do not agree that way." Interview conducted by Sylvia Kundrats, May 23, 2012; name withheld.

30. See discussion of the Jenkins case in chapter 8.

31. "Hester Repudiates Story of Reasons behind Slaying," *Valley Morning Star* (Harlingen, TX), May 3, 1949.

32. "Workman Asked False Testimony," *San Antonio Express*, February 22, 1958.

33. David K. Johnson, *The Lavender Scare: The Cold War Persecution of Gays and Lesbians in the Federal Government* (Chicago: University of Chicago Press, 2003).

34. Edward M. Pooley, "Congratulations, Policemen," *El Paso Herald-Post*, December 14, 1956.

35. Holmes Alexander, "No Good, Healthy Hi-Jinks?" *Big Spring Herald*, October 17, 1960.

36. Ele and Walt Dulaney, "Teens Ask for Advice on Homosexual Pals," *Brownsville Herald*, February 6, 1966.

37. General Social Survey conducted by the National Opinion Research Center at the University of Chicago, electronic data file courtesy of the Inter-University Consortium for Political and Social Research at the University of Michigan.

38. "Homosexual Teachers Facing Difficult Task in Texas," *Big Spring Herald*, October 9, 1977.

39. Merle Miller, "What It's Like to Be a Homosexual," *San Antonio Express*, January 24, 1971.

40. Jim Conley, "Abilene's Homosexual Community Not Viewed as Great Problem," *Abilene Reporter*, January 23, 1977; the survey result is mentioned here as well.

41. "Homosexual Behavior Is Sin," *Texas Baptists*, undated; http://texasbaptists.org.

42. "Election of Gay Layman to Methodist Board Causes Outpouring of Protests," *Galveston Daily News*, August 9, 1982.

43. "GLBT History of Denton," undated; http://ally.unt.edu.

44. Teri Crook, "Ministry at MCC Low-Key," *Galveston Daily News*, March 18, 1987; interview with Pastor Michael Piazza in Candace Chellew, "A Mega-Church to Call Our Own," *Whosoever*, undated, http://whosoever.org; Gustav Niebuhr, "Biggest Gay Church Finds a Home in Dallas," *New York Times*, October 30, 1994.

45. "Austin Will Vote on a City Housing Ordinance," *Paris News*, January 13, 1982.

46. B. Joe Cline, "Now Is the Time to Fight the Pro-Gay Agenda in Schools, Community," *Galveston Daily News*, April 4, 2005.

47. Interview with Richard Hamburger, conducted by Natalie Searl, March 24, 1998; Jimmy Fowler, "Wide Wing Span: Angels in America Author Tony Kushner Talks Politics," *Dallas Observer*, March 21, 1996. My examination of the relations between religious and arts organizations in Dallas, including interviews with Tony Kushner and Richard Hamburger, is found in Robert Wuthnow, "Arts Leaders and Religious Leaders: Mutual Perceptions," in

Crossroads: Art and Religion in American Life, ed. Alberta Arthurs and Glenn Wallach (New York: New Press, 2001), 31–70, and additional material from these interviews is included in Wuthnow, *Creative Spirituality: The Way of the Artist* (Berkeley: University of California Press, 2001). A community leader in Dallas who wished to remain unnamed recalled the response to *Angels in America* differently. "Dr. Criswell sat on a camp that launched missiles, hourly," he said, adding, "We're in a city where there's a lot of Brand X, far rights, the James Robisons and that group." Interview conducted by Natalie Searl, February 5, 1998.

48. Michie Akin of Cathedral Guadalupe, interviewed by Natalie Searl, March 25, 1998.

49. Steve Stockman, "Defense of Marriage Act a Necessary Step," *Texas City Sun*, June 9, 1996.

50. "*Daily News* Readers Speak Out on the Senate's Vote to Approve the Defense of Marriage Act," *Galveston Daily News*, September 15, 1996.

51. Ann Coulter, "Karl Rove's Campaign Strategy Kept Race Tight until End," *New Braunfels Herald Zeitung*, November 6, 2004.

52. Office of the Secretary of State, http://elections.sos.state.tx.us.

53. These results are from my analysis of the electronic data file for the 2006 Cooperative Congressional Election Survey, the principal investigator of which was Stephen Ansolabehere, release 3, August 2010.

54. Survey results from Texas Lyceum and University of Texas polls, texaspolitics.laits .utexas.edu; Diane Martinez, "Bible Not Only Moral Source," *Baytown Sun*, March 9, 2004; interviews conducted by Karen Myers, June 30 and September 23, 2011, names withheld.

55. Interview conducted by Karen Myers, June 6, 2012.

56. Interview conducted by Christi Martone, October 12, 2011.

57. Cheryl Berzanskis, "'Dude, You Have No Quran," *Amarillo Globe News*, September 14, 2010; Karen Smith Welch, "Controversial Pastor Endorses Grisham for Mayor," *Amarillo Globe News*, February 17, 2011; Rachel Tabachnick, "Repent Amarillo 'Executes' Santa, Continues Prayer Warfare against Other Congregations," *Talk to Action*, December 24, 2010.

58. The Religious Right's role in Texas textbook controversies is described in Richard V. Pierard and Charles McDaniel, "Reappropriating History for God and Country," *Journal of Church and State* 52 (2010), 193–202.

59. Ryan Valentine, deputy director of the Texas Freedom Network, interviewed by Karen Myers, July 20, 2012.

60. Barry Hankins quoted in Sandi Villarreal, "Social Justice Takes Back Seat to Hot-Button Political Issues," *Baptist Standard*, August 6, 2004.

61. Mary Lee Grant, "Illegal Immigrant Dies in Kenedy County Brush," *Corpus Christi Caller-Times*, June 9, 1998.

62. Don Graham, *Kings of Texas: The 150-Year Saga of an American Ranching Empire* (Hoboken, NJ: Wiley, 2003); Pamela Colloff, "The Desert of the Dead," *Texas Monthly* 34 (November 2006), 1–3; "Effectiveness of Operation Rio Grande Debated," *Brownsville Herald*, June 9, 1998.

63. Mary Lee Grant, "Heat Claims Another Illegal Immigrant," *Corpus Christi Caller-Times*, July 17, 1998; Grant, "Illegal Immigrant Dies in Kenedy County Brush," *Corpus Christi*

Caller-Times, August 11, 1998; Guy H. Lawrence, "10th Illegal Dies in Kenedy County Brush," *Corpus Christi Caller-Times*, August 20, 1998; untitled, *Associated Press*, October 13, 1998.

64. Jeremy Schwartz and Mary Lee Grant, "Border Patrol Banned from Kenedy Ranch," *Corpus Christi Caller-Times*, March 18, 2000; Robert Bezdek, "Brave Board Helps Protect Immigrants," *Corpus Christi Caller-Times*, January 19, 2001.

65. U.S. Censuses, 1980 and 2000, from http://www.socialexplorer.com.

66. U.S. Census, 2010, from ibid.

67. The figures here are from my analysis of Texas respondents in the electronic data file from Luis R. Fraga, John A. Garcia, Rodney Hero, Michael Jones-Correa, Valerie Martinez-Ebers, and Gary M. Segura, *Latino National Survey, 2006* (Ann Arbor, MI: Inter-University Consortium for Political and Social Research, 2006).

68. *National Election Pool General Election Exit Polls, 2006*; electronic data file for Texas voters.

69. Jeffrey S. Passel and D'Vera Cohn, *Unauthorized Immigrant Population: National and State Trends, 2010* (Washington, DC: Pew Hispanic Center, 2011); Ruth Ellen Wasem, *Unauthorized Aliens Residing in the United States: Estimates since 1986* (Washington, DC: Congressional Research Service, 2011).

70. Sarah Farris, "Pastor Helps Immigrants Gain Legal Status," *Baptist Standard*, January 21, 2005; Randena Hulstrand, "Church-Based Center Guides Immigrants," *Dallas Morning News*, November 25, 2007; Beth Pratt, "Catholic Family Services Is Dedicated to Helping with Immigration, Work Permits," *Lubbock Avalanche Journal*, February 25, 2006.

71. Guadalupe Silva, "Catholics Look for Reconciliation in the New Millennium," *El Paso Times*, January 14, 2000; Ken Camp, "Hispanic Convention Ratifies Mission Partnership to Start 400 Churches," *Baptist Standard*, July 11, 2003. Juhem Navarro-Rivera, Barry A. Kosmin and Ariela Keysar, *U.S. Latino Religious Identification 1990–2008: Growth, Diversity and Transformation* (Hartford, CT: Trinity College, 2008), 10, reported that the proportion of Texas Hispanics who were Catholic declined from 76 percent in 1990 to 64 percent in 2008, while the proportion "Christian Generic" increased from 4 percent to 8 percent, "Protestant sects" increased from 3 percent to 4 percent, "none" increased from 3 percent to 10 percent, and "don't know" increased from 0 to 5 percent.

72. Aaron Nelsen, "World Day of Migrants," *Brownsville Herald*, January 15, 2007; J. Michael Parker, "Archbishop May Defy Migrant Rules," *San Antonio Express*, April 14, 2006; Bishop Raymundo J. Peña, "Law of Love as Practiced in New Testament," *Valley Morning Star* (Harlingen, TX), January 13, 2007.

73. Mercedes Olivera, "Pro-Immigration Churches Led Latinos from Pews to Streets," *Dallas Morning News*, April 15, 2006; "Immigration," Dallas Area Interfaith, http://www .dallasareainterfaith.com.

74. Angela K. Brown, "Methodists Urge for Humane Treatment," *Rio Grande Valley Monitor*, April 25, 2008; Reverend Tyrone Gordon, "Immigration Rally," April 26, 2008, audio file, http://www.umc.org.

75. Allan Turner, "Cardinal Calls for Broad-Based Legalization Plan," *Houston Chronicle*, November 18, 2008.

76. Richard Ostling, "Immigration a Major Biblical Theme but One That Doesn't Settle Political Dispute," *Paris News*, June 9, 2006.

77. Roberta Combs quoted in Alexander Zaitchik, "Family Research Council Poll Shows Many Conservative Christians Hardlined against Illegal Immigration," *Southern Poverty Law Center Intelligence Report*, Winter 2006, http://www.splcenter.org.

78. Ramon Bracamontes, "Catholics Split on Church's Position on Immigration," *El Paso Times*, June 17, 2006.

79. These figures are from my analysis of the electronic data file results from Ansolabehere, *2006 Cooperative Congressional Election Survey*.

80. Father Armand Matthew, quoted in Laura Tillman, "Valley Perspective: The Catholic Dilemma," *Brownsville Herald*, November 12, 2008.

81. Data collected by the United States Census Bureau and compiled by http://www.usgovernmentspending.com.

82. Carl Davis, Kelly Davis, Matthew Gardner, Robert S. McIntyre, Jeff McLynch, and Alla Sapozhnikova, *Who Pays? A Distributional Analysis of the Tax Systems in All 50 States, 3rd Edition* (Washington, DC: Institute on Taxation and Economic Policy, 2009); Chandra Kring Villanueva, "Updated: Who Pays Texas Taxes?" *Center for Public Policy Priorities Policy Page*, March 24, 2011; additional information is included in Susan Combs, *Tax Exemptions and Tax Incidence: A Report to the Governor and the 82nd Texas Legislature* (Austin: Office of the Comptroller of Public Accounts, 2011).

83. Darren Dochuk, "Blessed by Oil, Cursed with Crude: God and Black Gold in the American Southwest," *Journal of American History* 99 (June 2012), 51–61.

84. U.S. Census Bureau, *Statistical Abstract of the United States: 2012* (Washington, DC: Government Printing Office, 2012), 468; figures for 2004 based on a sample of federal estate tax returns and using a multiplier technique to estimate the number of individuals with net worth of $1.5 million or more.

85. "The States with the Worst Income Inequality," *24/7 Wall St. Wire*, April 21, 2011, online.

86. Results from OLS regression analysis of the electronic data file for Stephen Ansolabehere, *2008 Congressional Election Survey* (Cambridge, MA: Harvard University, 2011); significant coefficients among Texas respondents included African American, Hispanic, female, unmarried, and not working full time (all negatively associated with a preference for spending cuts), while among all respondents nationally these variables and younger age, first-generation immigrant status, and union membership were negatively associated with a preference for spending cuts. Charles Varner assisted in developing the measure of tax regressivity, and Carol Ann MacGregor assisted with coding denominational membership and preparing the data for the regression analysis.

87. "Readers Get Feisty about Taxes, Tea and Texas Secession," *Waco Tribune-Herald*, April 18, 2009.

88. Mark Norris, "Slow Start for July 4th Tea Party," *Dallas Morning News*, July 5, 2009.

89. The figure includes those who said their views of the Tea Party movement were "very positive" or "somewhat positive," from the electronic data file for Stephen Ansolabehere, *2010 Cooperative Congressional Election Survey* (Cambridge, MA: Harvard University, 2012); the

study included responses from a nationally representative sample of more than 50,000 adults, including 3,113 respondents in Texas.

90. Texas Tribune Survey, October 19, 2010, electronic data file; the comparable national survey was CBS News, *CBS News Monthly Poll, September 2010* (Ann Arbor, MI: Inter-University Consortium for Political and Social Research, 2010), electronic data file; Geoff Folsom, "Crowd Gathers at City Hall to Protest Taxes, Bailouts," *Odessa American*, April 16, 2009.

91. Although Christian patriotism was certainly a factor; see Darren Dochuk, "Tea Party America and the Born-Again Politics of the Populist Right," *New Labor Forum* 21 (Winter 2012), 14–21.

92. Ordinary least squares regression analysis of the 2008 Cooperative Congressional Election data in which the previously mentioned variables were included as controls and in which conservative religion was measured by weekly church attendance, saying that one was born again, and holding membership in an evangelical Protestant denomination, and in which political party, opposition to abortion, and opposition to gay marriage were included. Among all respondents nationally, the coefficients for weekly attendance, born again, and evangelical membership remained significant but were reduced in strength by approximately two-thirds when party and the two social conservatism measures were included; among Texas respondents, the religion variables were initially strong and significant but became statistically insignificant when party and the social conservatism measures were included.

93. Interview conducted by Sylvia Kundrats, June 14, 2012; name of interviewee withheld.

94. These conclusions are drawn from my analysis of the 2010 Cooperative Congressional Election data in which binary logistic regression models were examined for positive attitudes toward the Tea Party with an item indicating that the respondent was born again as the main independent variable of interest and with male, married, family income under $30,000, black, Hispanic, and age fifty or more as control variables. The adjusted odds-ratio for the effect of born again on attitudes toward the Tea Party was 2.532, significant at the 0.001 level, and when opposition to abortion and gay marriage were included in the model, this coefficient fell to 1.371. Similar results were evident when only the Texas respondents were analyzed. Analysis of the 2010 data also replicated the results in the 2008 data for the relationships among these variables with attitudes toward fiscal conservatism.

95. Texas Tribune Survey, October 19, 2010.

96. National studies attempting to identify racial bias in the 2008 election have suggested that racial prejudice may have cost Obama at least 3 percent in the popular vote; Brian F. Schaffner, "Racial Salience and the Obama Vote," University of Massachusetts at Amherst, Department of Political Science, 2009; Alexandre Mas and Enrico Moretti, "Racial Bias in the 2008 Presidential Election," University of California at Berkeley, Department of Economics, 2008. In an innovative study comparing Google searches involving racist language in various media markets, similar results were obtained, and state comparisons in this study suggested that Texas was about the same as the national average; Seth Stephens-Davidowitz, "The Effects of Racial Animus on a Black Presidential Candidate: Using Google Search Data to Find What Surveys Miss," Harvard University, Department of Economics, 2012.

97. Interview conducted by Christi Martone, May 17, 2011; name withheld. Theda Skocpol and Vanessa Williamson, *The Tea Party and the Remaking of Republican Conservatism* (New

York: Oxford University Press, 2012), 35, note similar connections with conservative religion among the Tea Party adherents they interviewed and cite polls indicating this relationship as well.

98. Interviews conducted by Janice Derstine, Sylvia Kundrats, and Christi Martone, June 21, July 6, and July 13, 2011; names withheld.

99. Pastor Stephen Broden, "America's Awakening," speech at the 912 Project Fort Worth event, June 11, 2009, http://www.youtube.com; and at another event, "Grassroots America Meet in Tyler; Pastor Stephen Broden Speaks," KETK News [Tyler, TX], March 17, 2010, http://KETKnbc.com.

100. Similar Tea Party briefings for pastors in which Scarborough was involved are discussed in David Brody, *The Teavangelicals: The Inside Story of How the Evangelicals and the Tea Party Are Taking Back America* (Grand Rapids, MI: Zondervan, 2012), 165–68.

101. Richard Armey quoted in D. Michael Lindsay, *Faith in the Halls of Power: How Evangelicals Joined the American Elite* (New York: Oxford University Press, 2007), 65.

102. Dick Armey and Matt Kibbe, *Give Us Liberty: A Tea Party Manifesto* (New York: William Morrow, 2010); Dick Armey, "Christians and Big Government: Why Faith Requires Freedom," *FreedomWorks*, October 12, 2006.

103. Interview conducted by Karen Myers, June 15, 2012; pseudonym used.

104. Interviews conducted by Karen Myers, Sylvia Kundrats, and Steve Myers on January 11, 2011, February 2, 2012, and July 16, 2012; names withheld.

105. Interviews conducted by Karen Myers and Sylvia Kundrats on July 19, 2011, and September 2, 2011; names withheld.

106. Interview conducted by Christi Martone, July 21, 2011.

107. Manny Fernandez, "Perry Leads Prayer Rally for 'Nation in Crisis,'" *New York Times*, August 6, 2011.

108. "Rick Perry's Heavenly Host," Texans for Public Justice, August 2011, http://www.TPJ.org; Jay Root, "Perry to Conservatives: My Past Will Not Embarrass You," *Texas Tribune*, September 1, 2011; Tom Hamburger and Matea Gold, "Rick Perry's Furious Effort to Court Christian Leaders," *Los Angeles Times*, September 1, 2011; Richard Land, "Rick Perry Is No George W. Bush," *USA Today*, September 13, 2011. Leininger's relationship to Perry is described in Gail Collins, *As Texas Goes . . . : How the Lone Star State Hijacked the American Agenda* (New York: Liveright, 2012), 101–11; and Theresa Clift, "2 Texas Billionaires Give $20M to Super PACs," *San Antonio Express*, June 24, 2012.

109. Felicia Sonmez, "Santorum Wins Support of Evangelical Leaders at Texas Meeting," *Washington Post*, January 14, 2012; it was not widely publicized that the meeting was held at Pressler's ranch, nor was it much noted how endorsing a Catholic for president deviated from conservative Protestants' traditional views.

110. Tom Benning, "First Baptist Dallas Pastor Robert Jeffress—Quick to Call Mormonism a 'Cult'—Now Backs Mitt Romney," *Dallas Morning News*, April 17, 2012.

111. Laurie Goodstein, "Catholics File Suits on Contraceptive Coverage," *New York Times*, May 21, 2012; Molly Hennessy-Fiske, "Federal Judge Blocks Texas Funding Cuts to Planned Parenthood," *Los Angeles Times*, April 30, 2012; Kathleen McKinley, "My Interview with Ted Cruz," *Right Wing News*, February 20, 2012; Elizabeth Williamson, "Ted Cruz Interview: On Obama, GOP and Big Business," *Wall Street Journal*, May 29, 2012.

112. "Dr. Rick Scarborough Endorses David Dewhurst," May 22, 2012, Dewhurst for Senate campaign website; Vision America website.

113. "Ted Cruz '92 Believes in 'Compassionate Conservatism,'" *Princeton Alumni Weekly*, February 23, 2000; University of Texas/Texas Tribune, Texas Statewide Survey, May 7–13, 2012, Cruz was favored by 46 percent of Tea Party supporters and Dewhurst by 49 percent of other Republicans.

114. A pastor we talked to in a small country town in North Texas whose worship services seldom included more than a hundred people provided a remarkable illustration of such generosity in describing how several hundred Katrina refugees had come, bringing dogs and cats and even chickens, and spending four days at the church, sleeping on pews and being provided with food and blankets by the congregation.

115. The Southern Baptist Convention made history in 2012, electing its first African American president, Reverend Fred Luter Jr. of New Orleans. At the congregation level, research results about the effects of racial inclusion are mixed, with some encouraging findings from studies including congregations in Texas, especially Michael O. Emerson, *People of the Dream: Multiracial Congregations in the United States* (New York: Oxford University Press, 2006); and Gerardo Marti, *A Mosaic of Believers: Diversity and Innovation in a Multiethnic Church* (Bloomington: Indiana University Press, 2005); but Richard N. Pitt, "Fear of a Black Pulpit? Real Racial Transcendence versus Cultural Assimilation in Multiracial Churches," *Journal for the Scientific Study of Religion* 49 (2010), 218–23, suggests that racially inclusive attitudes may precede membership in multiracial churches rather than stem from it, and Paul Lichterman, *Elusive Togetherness: Church Groups Trying to Bridge America's Divisions* (Princeton: Princeton University Press, 2005), shows that multiracial efforts may be impeded by reticence to discuss the broader significance of racial differences.

CHAPTER 13
AFTERWORD

1. Mark Chaves, "Secularization as Declining Religious Authority," *Social Forces* 72 (1994), 749–74; David Martin, *A General Theory of Secularization* (New York: Harper & Row, 1978); Rudy Laermans, Bryan Wilson, and Jaak Billiet, eds. *Secularization and Social Integration* (Leuven, Belgium: Leuven University Press, 1998); Karel Dobbelaere, "The Meaning and Scope of Secularization," in *The Oxford Handbook of The Sociology of Religion*, ed. Peter B. Clarke (Oxford: Oxford University Press, 2009), 600–615.

2. Charles Y. Glock and Phillip E. Hammond, eds., *Beyond the Classics? Essays in the Scientific Study of Religion* (New York: Harper & Row, 1973); Roger O'Toole, *Religion: Classic Sociological Approaches* (Whitby, Ontario: McGraw-Hill Ryerson, 1984).

3. Christopher P. Scheitle, "Assessing the State of the Sociology of Religion," *Contemporary Sociology* 41 (2012), 155–57, quotation on p. 155. The rational choice approach can be traced most clearly to three somewhat separate strands of theorizing advanced in the late 1980s and early 1990s by economist Laurence R. Iannaccone, sociologists Rodney Stark and Roger Finke, and, with less emphasis on rational choice but comparable criticisms of

secularization theory, sociologist R. Stephen Warner. An overview is given in Malcolm Hamilton, "Rational Choice Theory: A Critique," in *The Oxford Handbook of the Sociology of Religion*, ed. Peter B. Clark (Oxford: Oxford University Press, 2009), 116–33; and see especially Laurence R. Iannaccone, "A Formal Model of Church and Sect," *American Journal of Sociology* 94 (1988), S241–S268; Laurence R. Iannaccone, "Voodoo Economics? Reviewing the Rational Choice Approach to Religion," *Journal for the Scientific Study of Religion* 34 (1995), 76–89; Rodney Stark and Laurence R. Iannaccone, "A Supply-Side Reinterpretation of the 'Secularization' of Europe," *Journal for the Scientific Study of Religion* 33 (1994), 230–52; Roger Finke and Rodney Stark, *The Churching of America, 1776–1990: Winners and Losers in Our Religious Economy* (New Brunswick, NJ: Rutgers University Press, 1992); R. Stephen Warner, "Work in Progress toward a New Paradigm for the Sociological Study of Religion in the United States," *American Journal of Sociology* 98 (1993), 1044–93; and Warner, *A Church of Our Own: Disestablishment and Diversity in American Religion* (New Brunswick, NJ: Rutgers University Press, 2005).

4. José Casanova, *Public Religions in the Modern World* (Chicago: University of Chicago Press, 1994); and with some useful extensions and criticisms in Chris Hann, "Problems with the (De)privatization of Religion," *Anthropology Today* 16 (2000), 14–20.

5. Steve Bruce, *Secularization: In Defense of an Unfashionable Theory* (New York: Oxford University Press, 2011), considers new religious movements, alternative spiritualities, and related beliefs in this light; see also Christian Smith, ed., *The Secular Revolution: Power, Interests, and Conflict in the Secularization of American Life* (Berkeley: University of California Press, 2003).

6. Courtney Bender, *The New Metaphysicals: Spirituality and the American Religious Imagination* (Chicago: University of Chicago Press, 2010), 44.

7. Pierre Bourdieu, *The Logic of Practice* (Stanford: Stanford University Press, 1990); Bourdieu, *Outline of a Theory of Practice* (Cambridge: Cambridge University Press, 1977); Jeffrey Stout, *Ethics After Babel* (Boston: Beacon Press, 1988); Alasdair MacIntyre, *After Virtue: A Study in Moral Theory* (Notre Dame, IN: University of Notre Dame Press, 1984); David D. Hall, ed., *Lived Religion in America: Toward a History of Practice* (Princeton, NJ: Princeton University Press, 1997).

8. Randall Collins, "On the Microfoundations of Macrosociology," *American Journal of Sociology* 86 (1981), 984–1014; Jeffrey C. Alexander and Bernhard Giesen, "From Reduction to Linkage: The Long View of the Micro-Macro Link," in *The Micro-Macro Link*, ed. Jeffrey C. Alexander, Bernhard Giesen, Richard Munch, and Neil J. Smelser (Berkeley: University of California Press, 1987), 1–44; Steve W. J. Kozlowski and Katherine J. Klein, eds., *Multilevel Theory, Research, and Methods in Organizations* (San Francisco: Jossey-Bass, 2000); Frederick P. Morgeson and David A. Hofmann, "The Structure and Function of Collective Constructs: Implications for Multilevel Research and Theory Development," *Academy of Management Review* 24 (1999), 249–65.

9. Alejandro Portes, "The Hidden Abode: Sociology as Analysis of the Unexpected: 1999 Presidential Address," *American Sociological Review* 65 (2000), 1–18, quotation on p. 15.

10. Charles Tilly, *Durable Inequality* (Berkeley: University of California Press, 1998).

11. Andreas Wimmer, "The Making and Unmaking of Ethnic Boundaries: A Multilevel Process Theory," *American Journal of Sociology* 113 (2008), 970–1022; Wimmer, "Elementary Strategies of Ethnic Boundary Making," *Ethnic and Racial Studies* 31 (2008), 1025–55.

12. These are examples of micro-macro connections that might be explored further in the important work on religious and spiritual practices in Robert Orsi, *The Madonna of 115th Street: Faith and Community in Italian Harlem* (New Haven, CT: Yale University Press, 1985); Elizabeth McAlister, "The Madonna of 115th Street Revisited: Vodou and Haitian Catholicism in the Age of Transnationalism," in *Gatherings in Daspora: Religious Communities and the New Immigration*, ed. R. Stephen Warner and Judith G. Wittner (Philadelphia: Temple University Press, 1998), 123–60; and Bender, *The New Metaphysicals*.

13. Michèle Lamont and Virag Molnár, "The Study of Boundaries in the Social Sciences," *Annual Review of Sociology* 28 (2002), 167–95; Paul DiMaggio, "Culture and Cognition," *Annual Review of Sociology* 23 (1997), 263–87; Susan T. Fiske and Shelly E. Taylor, *Social Cognition*, 2nd ed. (New York: McGraw-Hill, 1991); Douglas S. Massey, *Categorically Unequal: The American Stratification System* (New York: Russell Sage Foundation, 2007), 7–15. Elaine Howard Ecklund, *Korean American Evangelicals: New Models for Civic Life* (New York: Oxford University Press, 2006), is an illuminating account of the relationship between religious participation and Korean American versus Asian American ethnic categories; and G. Cristina Mora, "*De Muchos, Uno*: The Institutionalization of Latino Panethnicity, 1960–1990" (PhD diss., Princeton University, 2010), provides a rich analysis of the processes involved in the social construction of "Latino" as a panethnic category.

14. Among the more insightful discussions of the social processes involved in the formation of religious categories are Tomoko Masuzawa, *The Invention of World Religions: Or, How European Universalism Was Preserved in the Language of Pluralism* (Chicago: University of Chicago Press, 2005); Gauri Viswanathan, *Outside the Fold: Conversion, Modernity, and Belief* (Princeton, NJ: Princeton University Press, 1998); and Anna Sun, *Confucianism as a World Religion: Historical Concepts and Contemporary Realities* (Princeton, NJ: Princeton University Press, 2013).

15. Tilly, *Durable Inequality*, 121–36.

16. In "Cognition and Religion," *Sociology of Religion* 68 (2007), 341–60, and "Teach Us to Pray: The Cognitive Power of Domain Violations," *Poetics* 36 (2008), 493–506, I have developed these ideas in greater detail; Douglas's arguments are in Mary Douglas, *Purity and Danger: An Analysis of Concepts of Pollution and Taboo* (New York: Penguin, 1966).

17. Robert Wuthnow, *Communities of Discourse: Ideology and Social Structure in the Reformation, the Enlightenment, and European Socialism* (Cambridge, MA: Harvard University Press, 1989).

18. Roland Barthes, *Mythologies* (New York: Hill and Wang, 1972), 116.

19. Douglas, *Purity and Danger*.

20. Michel Foucault, *Discipline and Punish: The Birth of the Prison* (New York: Random House, 1977), 32.

21. Other insightful examples of multilevel theory in which narratives explaining rituals and symbolic boundaries are presented are in William H. Sewell Jr., "Ideologies and Social

Revolutions: Reflections on the French Case," *Journal of Modern History* 57 (1985), 57–85; and Sewell Jr., "A Theory of Structure: Duality, Agency and Transformation," *American Journal of Sociology* 98 (1992), 1–29.

22. E. P. Thompson, *The Making of the English Working Class* (New York: Knopf, 1963); Michael Hechter, *Internal Colonialism: The Celtic Fringe in British National Development, 1536–1966* (London: Routledge and Kegan Paul, 1975); Edward Page, "Michael Hechter's Internal Colonial Thesis: Some Theoretical and Methodological Problems," *European Journal of Political Research* 6 (1978), 295–317.

23. David Zaret, *The Heavenly Contract: Ideology and Organization in Pre-Revolutionary Puritanism* (Chicago: University of Chicago Press, 1985).

24. On related developments, Peter Dobkin Hall, "A Historical Overview of Philanthropy, Voluntary Associations, and Nonprofit Organizations in the United States, 1600–2000," in *The Nonprofit Sector: A Research Handbook—Second Edition*, ed. Walter W. Powell and Richard Steinberg (New Haven, CT: Yale University Press, 2006), 32–65.

25. Increasing possibilities for examining the relationships between religion and asset accumulation are evident in Lisa A. Keister, "Conservative Protestants and Wealth: How Religion Perpetuates Asset Poverty," *American Journal of Sociology* 113 (2008), 1237–71; and Keister, *Faith and Money: How Religious Belief Contributes to Wealth and Poverty* (New York: Cambridge University Press, 2012).

26. Weber of course was interested in variations among warrior heroes as refracted in different legends and through various religious traditions, and his writing is replete with references to other kinds of heroes and alternative ideas about fate; see especially Max Weber, *Economy and Society: An Outline of Interpretive Sociology*, ed. Guenther Roth and Claus Wittich (Berkeley: University of California Press, 1978), 472–76; Max Weber, *The Sociology of Religion*, trans. Ephraim Fischoff (Boston: Beacon Press, 1963), 85; H. H. Gerth and C. Wright Mills, *From Max Weber: Essays in Sociology* (New York: Oxford University Press, 1958), 279; Reinhard Bendix, *Max Weber: An Intellectual Portrait* (New York: Doubleday, 1960), 165–70; Peter Baehr, *Caesarism, Charisma and Fate: Historical Sources and Modern Resonances in the Work of Max Weber* (Piscataway, NJ: Transaction Publishers, 2008).

27. Two empirical studies that provide information about the moral criteria through which symbolic boundaries are defined are Michèle Lamont, *Money, Morals and Manners: The Culture of the French and the American Upper-Middle Class* (Chicago: University of Chicago Press, 1992); and Lamont, *The Dignity of Working Men: Morality and the Boundaries of Race, Class, and Immigration* (Cambridge, MA, and New York: Harvard University Press and Russell Sage Foundation, 2002).

28. Reinhard Bendix, *Nation-Building and Citizenship* (Berkeley: University of California Press, 1964), 66–112.

29. On state resources, economic development, and religion, Robert J. Barro and Rachel M. McCleary, "Religion and Economic Growth among Countries," *American Sociological Review* 68 (2003), 706–81; Rachel M. McCleary and Robert J. Barro, "Religion and Economy," *Journal of Economic Perspectives* 20 (2006), 49–72; and Cristobal Young, "Model Uncertainty in Sociological Research: An Application to Religion and Economic Growth," *American Sociological Review* 74 (2009), 380–97. See also Axel Schaefer, *Piety and Public Funding:*

Evangelicals and the State in Modern America (Philadelphia: University of Pennsylvania Press, 2012).

30. Michael Phillips, *White Metropolis: Race, Ethnicity and Religion in Dallas, 1841–2001* (Austin: University of Texas Press, 2006).

31. Robert Wuthnow, *America and the Challenges of Religious Diversity* (Princeton, NJ: Princeton University Press, 2005); Penny Edgell and Eric Tranby, "Shared Visions? Diversity and Cultural Membership in American Life," *Social Problems* 57 (2010), 175–204.

32. The value of insulation from congregational constraints was emphasized in Phillip E. Hammond, *The Campus Clergyman* (New York: Basic Books, 1966).

33. Robert Wuthnow, *The Restructuring of American Religion: Society and Faith since World War II* (Princeton, NJ: Princeton University Press, 1988).

34. Laurence R. Iannaccone, "Why Strict Churches Are Strong," *American Journal of Sociology* 99 (1994), 1180–1211; and further elaboration on the free-rider problem, Iannaccone, "Sacrifice and Community: Reducing Free-Riders in Cults, Communes and Other Collectivities," *Journal of Political Economy* 100 (1992), 271–92.

35. Gerald Marwell, "We Still Don't Know If Strict Churches Are Strong, Much Less Why: Comment on Iannaccone," *American Journal of Sociology* 101 (1996), 1097–1103.

36. Michael Hout, Andrew Greeley, and Melissa J. Wilde, "The Demographic Imperative in Religious Change in the United States," *American Journal of Sociology* 107 (2011), 468–500.

37. Christian Smith, *American Evangelicalism: Embattled and Thriving* (Chicago: University of Chicago Press, 1998).

38. James S. Coleman, *Foundations of Social Theory* (Cambridge, MA: Harvard University Press, 1990), 300–324.

39. Corwin Smidt, editor, *Religion as Social Capital: Producing the Common Good* (Waco, TX: Baylor University Press, 2003); Christian Smith, "Religious Participation and Network Closure Among American Adolescents," *Journal for the Scientific Study of Religion* 42 (2003), 259–67; Stephen Vaisey and Omar Lizardo, "Can Cultural Worldviews Influence Network Composition?" *Social Forces* 88 (2010), 1595–1618; Christopher P. Scheitle and Buster G. Smith, "A Note on the Frequency and Sources of Close Interreligious Ties," *Journal for the Scientific Study of Religion* 50 (2011), 410–21; Stephen M. Merino, "Neighbors Like Me? Religious Affiliation and Neighborhood Racial Preferences among Non-Hispanic Whites," *Religions* 2 (2011), 165–83.

40. Andreas Wimmer and Kevin Lewis, "Beyond and Below Racial Homophily: ERG Models of a Friendship Network Documented on Facebook," *American Journal of Sociology* 116 (2010), 583–642.

41. Robert D. Putnam and David E. Campbell, *American Grace: How Religion Divides and Unites Us* (New York: Simon and Schuster, 2010).

42. Delia Baldassarri, "Partisan Joiners: Associational Membership and Political Polarization in America (1974–2004)," *Social Science Quarterly* 92 (2011), 631–55; and Delia Baldassarri and Peter Bearman, "Dynamics of Political Polarization," *American Sociological Review* 72 (2007), 784–811.

43. Robert Wuthnow, *Red State Religion: Faith and Politics in America's Heartland* (Princeton, NJ: Princeton University Press, 2012).

SELECTED BIBLIOGRAPHY

Acheson, Sam Hanna. *Joe Bailey: The Last Democrat*. New York: Macmillan, 1932.

Acuña, Rodolfo F. *The Making of Chicana/o Studies: In the Trenches of Academe*. New Brunswick, NJ: Rutgers University Press, 2011.

Allen, Irene Taylor. *Saga of Anderson: The Proud Story of a Historic Texas Community*. New York: Greenwich, 1957.

Alexander, Jeffrey C., and Bernhard Giesen. "From Reduction to Linkage: The Long View of the Micro-Macro Link." In *The Micro-Macro Link*, edited by Jeffrey C. Alexander, Bernhard Giesen, Richard Munch, and Neil J. Smelser, 1–44. Berkeley: University of California Press, 1987.

Almonte, Juan N., and C. E. Castaneda. "Statistical Report on Texas [1835]." *Southwestern Historical Quarterly* 28 (1925), 177–222.

American Public Health Association. *Public Health Reports and Papers*. New York: Hurd and Houghton, 1875.

Ammerman, Nancy Tatom. *Baptist Battles: Social Change and Religious Conflict in the Southern Baptist Convention*. New Brunswick, NJ: Rutgers University Press, 1990.

Andersen, Kristi. "Working Women and Political Participation." *American Journal of Political Science* 19 (1975), 439–53.

Ansolabehere, Stephen. *2008 Congressional Election Survey*. Cambridge, MA: Harvard University, 2011.

———. *2010 Congressional Election Survey*. Cambridge, MA: Harvard University, 2012.

Armey, Dick, and Matt Kibbe. *Give Us Liberty: A Tea Party Manifesto*. New York: William Morrow, 2010.

Asbury, Herbert. "Is Protestantism Declining?" *Forum* 79 (February 1928), 181.

Attlesey, Sam. "Texas: Republicans Gallop Ahead." In *Southern Politics in the 1990s*, edited by Alexander P. Lamis, 305–42. Baton Rouge: Louisiana State University Press, 1999.

Baehr, Peter. *Caesarism, Charisma and Fate: Historical Sources and Modern Resonances in the Work of Max Weber*. Piscataway, NJ: Transaction Publishers, 2008.

Baggett, James Alex. "Origins of Early Texas Republican Party Leadership." *Journal of Southern History* 40 (1974), 441–54.

Bailey, Richard R. "The Starr County Strike." *Red River Valley Historical Review* 4 (1979), 42–61.

Baldassarri, Delia. "Partisan Joiners: Associational Membership and Political Polarization in America (1974–2004)." *Social Science Quarterly* 92 (2011), 631–55.

Baldassarri, Delia, and Peter Bearman. "Dynamics of Political Polarization." *American Sociological Review* 72 (2007), 784–811.

Banks, Melvin J. "The Pursuit of Equality: The Movement for First Class Citizenship among Negroes in Texas, 1920–1950." PhD diss., Syracuse University, 1962.

Barnouw, Erik. *The Golden Web: A History of Broadcasting in the United States, 1933–1953.* New York: Oxford University Press, 1958.

Barr, Alwyn. *Black Texans: A History of African Americans in Texas, 1828–1995.* Norman: University of Oklahoma Press, 1996.

———. "The Other Texas: Charities and Community in the Lone Star State." *Southwestern Historical Quarterly* 97 (1993), 1–10.

Barr, Amelia. *All the Days of My Life: An Autobiography.* New York: Appleton, 1913.

Barthes, Roland. *Mythologies.* New York: Hill and Wang, 1972.

Bartley, Numan V., and Hugh D. Graham. *Southern Primary and General Election Data, 1944–1972.* Ann Arbor, MI: Inter-University Consortium for Political and Social Research, 1977.

Barton, Arthur J. "The White Man's Task in the Uplift of the Negro." In *The Human Way: Addresses on Race Problems at the Southern Sociological Congress*, edited by James E. McCulloch, 118–36. Nashville: Southern Sociological Congress, 1913.

Barton, Paul. *Hispanic Methodists, Presbyterians, and Baptists in Texas.* Austin: University of Texas Press, 2006.

Bean, David. *Breaking the Trail: Hudson Stuck of Texas and Alaska.* Athens: Ohio University Press, 1988.

Beard, Richard. *Brief Biographical Sketches of Some of the Early Ministers of the Cumberland Presbyterian Church.* Nashville, TN: Cumberland Presbyterian Board of Publication, 1874.

Behnken, Brian D. *Fighting Their Own Battles: Mexican Americans, African Americans, and the Struggle for Civil Rights in Texas.* Chapel Hill: University of North Carolina Press, 2011.

Belden Associates. *The Texas Poll.* Storrs, CT: Roper Center for Public Opinion, 1954.

———. *The Texas Poll: Business/Presidential Election.* Storrs, CT: Roper Center for Public Opinion Research, 1960.

———. *The Texas Poll: Racial Relations, Civil Rights, State Government.* Storrs, CT: Roper Center for Public Opinion Research, 1968.

Bell, Daniel, ed. *The Radical Right.* New York: Doubleday, 1962.

Bellah, Robert N. *Beyond Belief: Essays on Religion in a Post-Traditional World.* New York: Harper & Row, 1970.

———. *The Broken Covenant: American Civil Religion in Time of Trial.* New York: Seabury Press, 1975.

Bellah, Robert N., Richard Madsen, William M. Sullivan, Ann Swidler, and Steven M. Tipton. *Habits of the Heart: Individualism and Commitment in American Life.* Berkeley: University of California Press, 1985.

Bender, Courtney. *The New Metaphysicals: Spirituality and the American Religious Imagination*. Chicago: University of Chicago Press, 2010.

Bendix, Reinhard. *Max Weber: An Intellectual Portrait*. New York: Doubleday, 1960.

———. *Nation-Building and Citizenship*. New York: John Wiley, 1964.

Bennett, Laura K. *Rural and Urban Boosterism in Texas, 1880s–1930s*. Master's Thesis, University of Texas, Arlington, 2008.

Berger, James. *After the End: Representations of Post-Apocalypse*. Minneapolis: University of Minnesota Press, 1999.

Berger, Peter L. "Some Second Thoughts on Substantive versus Functional Definitions of Religion." *Journal for the Scientific Study of Religion* 13 (1974), 125–33.

Berger, Peter L., and Richard John Neuhaus. *To Empower People: The Role of Mediating Structures in Public Policy*. Washington, DC: American Enterprise Institute, 1977.

Bernard, L. L. "Southern Sociological Congress." *American Journal of Sociology* 18 (1912), 258–59.

Bernstein, Patricia. *The First Waco Horror: The Lynching of Jesse Washington and the Rise of the NAACP*. College Station: Texas A&M University Press, 2005.

Beschloss, Michael R. *Reaching for Glory: Lyndon Johnson's Secret White House Tapes, 1964–1965*. New York: Simon and Schuster, 2001.

Biesele, Rudolph L. "Early Times in New Braunfels and Comal County." *Southwestern Historical Quarterly* 50 (1946), 75–92.

Bishop, Charles M. "The Causes, Consequences, and Cure of Mob Violence." In *Democracy in Earnest: Southern Sociological Congress, 1916–1918*, edited by James E. McCulloch, 191–200. Washington, DC: Southern Sociological Congress, 1918.

Bixler-Marquez, Dennis J. "*The Schools of Crystal City*: A Chicano Experiment in Change." In *Recovering the Hispanic History of Texas*, edited by Monica Perales and Raúl A. Ramos, 92–110. Houston: Arte Público Press, 2010.

Booth, Maud Ballington. *After Prison—What?* New York: Fleming H. Revell, 1903.

Bourdieu, Pierre. *The Logic of Practice*. Stanford, CA: Stanford University Press, 1990.

———. *Outline of a Theory of Practice*. Cambridge: Cambridge University Press, 1977.

Bourgeois, Christie L. "Stepping over Lines: Lyndon Johnson, Black Texans, and the National Youth Administration." *Southwestern Historical Quarterly* 91 (1987), 149–72.

Boyer, Paul S. *When Time Shall Be No More: Prophecy Belief in Modern American Culture*. Cambridge, MA: Harvard University Press, 1992.

Brady, David W., and Kent I. Tedin. "Ladies in Pink: Religion and Political Ideology in the Anti-ERA Movement." *Social Science Quarterly* 56 (1976), 564–75.

Brann, William Cowper. *The Complete Works of Brann, the Iconoclast*. New York: Brann, 1919.

Brewer, William M. "The Poll Tax and Poll Taxers." *Journal of Negro History* 29 (1944), 260–99.

Brooks, Elizabeth. *Prominent Women of Texas*. Akron, OH: Werner, 1896.

Brown, John Henry. *History of Dallas County, Texas: From 1837 to 1887*. Dallas: Milligan, Cornett & Farnham, 1887.

Brown, Norman D. *Hood, Bonnet, and Little Brown Jug: Texas Politics, 1921–1928*. College Station: Texas A&M University Press, 1984.

Bruce, Dickson D., Jr. *And They All Sang Hallelujah: Plain-Folk Camp-Meeting Religion, 1800–1845*. Knoxville: University of Tennessee Press, 1981.

Bruce, Steve. *Secularization: In Defense of an Unfashionable Theory*. New York: Oxford University Press, 2011.

Bryant, Anita. *The Anita Bryant Story: The Survival of Our Nation's Families and the Threat of Militant Homosexuality*. New York: Revell, 1977.

Bullock, Karen O'Dell. "The Life and Contributions of Robert Cooke Buckner: Progenitor of Organized Social Christianity among Texas Baptists, 1860–1919." PhD diss., Southwestern Baptist Theological Seminary, 1991.

Burrough, Bryan. *The Big Rich: The Rise and Fall of the Greatest Texas Oil Fortunes*. New York: Penguin, 2009.

Burton, Mae Knox. "Farmhouse Memories." In *Texas Millennium Book: The Way Things Used to Be*, edited by Jerry B. Lincecum and Peggy A. Redshaw, 83–90. Sherman, TX: Austin College, 1999.

Bush, George H. W. *Looking Forward*. New York: Bantam, 1988.

———. *All the Best: My Life in Letters and Other Writings*. New York: Scribner, 1999.

Bush, George W. *Rallying the Armies of Compassion*. Washington, DC: White House, 2001.

———. "Remarks at the Power Center in Houston Texas, September 12, 2003." In *Public Papers of the Presidents of the United States: Administration of George W. Bush*, edited by Office of the Federal Register, 1151–56. Washington, DC: Government Printing Office, 2008.

———. "Remarks in a Discussion in Cincinnati, Ohio, June 21, 2004." In *Public Papers of the Presidents of the United States, George W. Bush, 2004*, edited by Office of the Federal Register, 1099–1108. Washington, DC: Government Printing Office, 2004.

Butler, Anne M. *Daughters of Joy, Sisters of Misery: Prostitutes in the American West, 1865–90*. Urbana: University of Illinois Press, 1985.

Caldwell, Gail. *A Strong West Wind: A Memoir*. New York: Random House, 2006.

Campbell, Randolph B. "Carpetbagger Rule in Reconstruction Texas: An Enduring Myth." *Southwestern Historical Quarterly* 97 (1994), 587–96.

———. "Grass Roots Reconstruction: The Personnel of County Government in Texas, 1865–1876." *Journal of Southern History* 58 (1992), 99–116.

———. *Roots Reconstruction in Texas, 1865–1880*. Baton Rouge: Louisiana State University Press, 1998.

———. *A Southern Community in Crisis: Harrison County, Texas, 1850–1880*. Austin: Texas State Historical Association, 1983.

Cantrell, Gregg. "Racial Violence and Reconstruction Politics in Texas, 1867–1868." *Southwestern Historical Quarterly* 93 (1990), 333–55.

Carrigan, William D. *The Making of a Lynching Culture: Violence and Vigilantism in Central Texas, 1836–1916*. Urbana: University of Illinois Press, 2004.

Carroll, H. Bailey. "Texas Collection." *Southwestern Historical Quarterly* 50 (1946), 269–303.

Carroll, James Milton. *Texas Baptist Statistics, 1895*. Dallas: Baptist General Convention of Texas, Texas Baptist Historical Committee, 1985.

Casanova, José. *Public Religions in the Modern World*. Chicago: University of Chicago Press, 1994.

Castaneda, Carlos E. "Earliest Catholic Activities in Texas." *Catholic Historical Review* 17 (1931), 278–95.

Cavanagh, Thomas E. "Changes in American Voter Turnout, 1964–1976." *Political Science Quarterly* 96 (1981), 53–65.

Chalmers, David M. *Hooded Americanism: The History of the Ku Klux Klan.* Durham, NC: Duke University Press, 1981.

Chapman, David L. "Lynching in Texas." Master's thesis, Texas Tech University, 1973.

Chapman, Helen. *The News from Brownsville: Helen Chapman's Letters from the Texas Military Frontier, 1848–1852,* edited by Caleb Coker. Denton: Texas State Historical Association, 1992.

Chaves, Mark. *Congregations in America.* Cambridge, MA: Harvard University Press, 2004.

———. *Ordaining Women: Culture and Conflict in Religious Organizations.* Cambridge, MA: Harvard University Press, 1997.

———. "Religious Congregations and Welfare Reform: Who Will Take Advantage of 'Charitable Choice'?" *American Sociological Review* 64 (1999), 836–46.

———. "Secularization as Declining Religious Authority." *Social Forces* 72 (1994), 749–74.

Chilman, Catherine S. "Welfare Reform or Revision? The Family Support Act of 1988." *Social Service Review* 66 (1992), 349–77.

Chrisman, David K. "Religious Moderates and Race: The Texas Christian Life Commission and the Call for Racial Reconciliation, 1954–68." In *Seeking Inalienable Rights: Texans and Their Quests for Justice,* edited by Debra A. Reid, 97–121. College Station: Texas A&M University Press, 2009.

Clark, Victoria. *Allies for Armageddon: The Rise of Christian Zionism.* New Haven, CT: Yale University Press, 2007.

Clendinen, Dudley, and Adam Nagourney. *Out for Good: The Struggle to Build a Gay Rights Movement in America.* New York: Simon and Schuster, 1999.

Cochran, Mike. *Claytie: The Roller-Coaster Life of a Texas Wildcatter.* College Station: Texas A&M University Press, 2007.

Cocke, William A. *The Bailey Controversy in Texas with Lessons from the Political Life-Story of a Fallen Idol.* San Antonio: Cocke, 1908.

Cohen, Henry. "Introduction and Biography." In *Memorial Volume: Leo N. Levi,* edited by John Hay and Joseph Hirsh, 12–15. Chicago: Hamburger Printing, 1905.

Coke, Thomas, and Francis Asbury. *The Doctrines and Discipline of the Methodist Episcopal Church in America with Explanatory Notes.* Philadelphia: Henry Tuckness, 1798.

Colbenson, Elwyn Thomas. "Millennial Thought among Southern Evangelicals, 1830–1885." PhD diss., Georgia State University, 1980.

Cole, Stewart G. *The History of Fundamentalism.* Hamden, CT: Archon Books, 1931.

Coleman, James S. *Foundations of Social Theory.* Cambridge, MA: Harvard University Press, 1990.

Collins, Randall. *The Credential Society: A Historical Sociology of Education and Stratification.* New York: Academic Press, 1979.

———. "On the Microfoundations of Macrosociology." *American Journal of Sociology* 86 (1981), 984–1014.

Colloff, Pamela. "The Desert of the Dead." *Texas Monthly* 34 (November 2006), 1–3.

Combs, Susan. *Tax Exemptions and Tax Incidence: A Report to the Governor and the 82nd Texas Legislature.* Austin: Office of the Comptroller of Public Accounts, 2011.

Connally, Tom. *My Name Is Tom Connally.* New York: Crowell, 1954.

Cook, Lisa D. "Converging to a National Lynching Database: Recent Developments." Department of Economics Working Paper, Michigan State University, East Lansing, 2011.

Cook, Rhodes. *United States Presidential Primary Elections, 1968–1996: A Handbook of Election Statistics.* Washington, DC: CQ Press, 2000.

Cooper, Oscar H. *Sixth Biennial Report of the Superintendent of Public Instruction for the Scholastic Years Ending August 31, 1887, and July 1, 1888.* Austin: Texas Department of Education, 1888.

Crafts, Wilbur F. "The Potential Resources of the South for Leadership in Social Service." In *The Call of the New South: Addresses Delivered at the Southern Sociological Congress*, 311–21. Nashville: Southern Sociological Congress, 1913.

Cranfill, James Britton. *Dr. J. B. Cranfill's Chronicle: A Story of Life in Texas.* New York: Fleming H. Revell, 1916.

———. "An Interview with Dr. Harper." *Christian Observer* 84 (February 5, 1896), 16.

———. "The Lone Star State." *The Independent* 49 (July 15, 1897), 5.

———. "Religious Intelligence: New Things among Southern Baptists." *The Independent* 49 (December 16, 1897), 15.

Criswell, W. A. *Why I Preach that the Bible Is Literally True.* Nashville: Broadman Press, 1973.

Critchlow, Donald T. *Phyllis Schlafly and Grassroots Conservatism: A Woman's Crusade.* Princeton, NJ: Princeton University Press, 2005.

Crockett, David. *A Narrative of the Life of David Crockett of the State of Tennessee.* Philadelphia: Cary, Hart, 1834.

Crouch, Barry A. "'All the Vile Passions': The Texas Black Code of 1866." *Southwestern Historical Quarterly* 97 (1993), 12–34.

———. "A Spirit of Lawlessness: White Violence; Texas Blacks, 1865–1868." *Journal of Social History* 18 (1984), 217–32.

Crutchfield, Larry V. *The Origins of Dispensationalism: The Darby Factor.* Washington, DC: University Press of America, 1991.

Cunningham, Sean P. *Cowboy Conservatism: Texas and the Rise of the Modern Right.* Lexington: University Press of Kentucky, 2010.

Cutrer, Thomas J., ed. *Longstreet's Aide: The Civil War Letters of Major Thomas J. Goree.* Charlottesville: University Press of Virginia, 1995.

Dallek, Robert. *Lyndon Johnson and His Times, 1908–1960.* New York: Oxford University Press, 1991.

———. *Lyndon B. Johnson: Portrait of a President.* New York: Oxford University Press, 2004.

Daly, Lew. *God's Economy: Faith-Based Initiatives and the Caring State.* Chicago: University of Chicago Press, 2009.

Danforth, John C. *Interim Report to the Deputy Attorney General Concerning the 1993 Confrontation at the Mt. Carmel Complex.* Washington, DC: Office of the Attorney General, 2000.

Darwin, Charles. *On the Origin of Species by Means of Natural Selection, or the Preservation of Favoured Races in the Struggle for Life.* London: John Murray, 1859.

Davidson, John. "A Simple Man." *Texas Monthly* (July 1981), 127.

Davis, Carl, Kelly Davis, Matthew Gardner, Robert S. McIntyre, Jeff McLynch, and Alla Sapozhnikova. *Who Pays? A Distributional Analysis of the Tax Systems in All 50 States, 3rd Edition*. Washington, DC: Institute on Taxation and Economic Policy, 2009.

Davis, Cyclone. *Memoir*. Sherman: Courier Press, 1935.

Dawson, J. M. *A Century with Texas Baptists*. Nashville: Broadman Press, 1947.

———. *A Thousand Months to Remember: An Autobiography*. Waco, TX: Baylor University Press, 1964.

Deaf Smith Historical Society. *The Land and Its People, 1876–1981*. Deaf Smith County: Deaf Smith County Historical Society, 1982.

Dehoney, Wayne. "President's Address: Issues and Imperatives." *Annual of the Southern Baptist Convention* (June 1965), 94–95.

Diamond, Sara. *Roads to Dominion: Right-Wing Movements and Political Power in the United States*. New York: Guilford Press, 1995.

Dieffenbach, Albert C. "Religious Liberty—the Great American Illusion." *The Independent* 118 (January 8, 1927), 36.

DiMaggio, Paul. "Culture and Cognition." *Annual Review of Sociology* 23 (1997), 263–87.

DiMaggio, Paul, John Evans, and Bethany Bryson. "Have Americans' Social Attitudes Become More Polarized?" *American Journal of Sociology* 102 (1996), 690–755.

Dobbelaere, Karel. "The Meaning and Scope of Secularization." In *The Oxford Handbook of the Sociology of Religion*, edited by Peter B. Clarke, 600–615. Oxford: Oxford University Press, 2009.

Dollar, George W. *A History of Fundamentalism in America*. Greenville, SC: Bob Jones University Press, 1973.

Domenech, Abbé Emmanuel. *Missionary Adventures in Texas and Mexico: A Personal Narrative of Six Years' Sojourn in Those Regions*. London: Longman, 1858.

Doughty, Robin W. "Settlement and Environmental Change in Texas, 1820–1900." *Southwestern Historical Quarterly* 89 (1986), 423–42.

Douglas, Mary. *Purity and Danger: An Analysis of Concepts of Pollution and Taboo*. New York: Penguin, 1966.

DuBois, W. E. B. "The Waco Horror." *The Crisis* 12 (1916), 1–8.

———. *What the Negro Has Done for the United States and Texas*. Washington, DC: Government Printing Office, 1936.

Durkheim, Emile. *Elementary Forms of the Religious Life*. New York: Free Press, 1915.

Dyer, G. W. "The Purpose of Imprisonment." In *The Call of the New South: Addresses Delivered at the Southern Sociological Congress*, 87–91. Nashville: Southern Sociological Congress, 1913.

Dykes-Hoffmann, Judith Lynn. "On the Edge of the Balcones Escarpment: The Urban and Cultural Development of New Braunfels and San Marcos, Texas, 1845–1880." PhD diss., University of Texas at Austin, 2003.

Early, Joseph E. Jr. *A Texas Baptist History Sourcebook: A Companion to McBeth's Texas Baptists*. Denton: University of North Texas Press, 2004.

———. *A Texas Baptist Power Struggle: The Hayden Controversy*. Denton: University of North Texas Press, 2005.

Ebaugh, Helen Rose, and Janet Saltzman Chafetz, eds. *Religion and the New Immigrants: Continuities and Adaptations in Immigrant Congregations.* Walnut Creek, CA: AltaMira Press, 2000.

Eby, Frederick. *Education in Texas.* Austin: University of Texas Bulletin, 1918.

Edgell, Penny, and Eric Tranby. "Shared Visions? Diversity and Cultural Membership in American Life." *Social Problems* 57 (2010), 175–204.

Edwards, John N. *Biography, Memoirs, Reminiscences and Recollections.* Kansas City, MO: Jennie Edwards, 1889.

Enstam, Elizabeth York. *Women and the Creation of Urban Life: Dallas, Texas, 1843–1920.* College Station: Texas A&M University Press, 1998.

Evans, John H. "Have Americans' Attitudes Become More Polarized?—An Update." *Social Science Quarterly* 84 (2003), 71–90.

Fairchild, Louis. *The Lonesome Plains: Death and Revival on an American Frontier.* College Station: Texas A&M University Press, 2002.

Faust, Drew Gilpin. *Mothers of Invention: Women of the Slaveholding South in the American Civil War.* Chapel Hill: University of North Carolina Press, 1996.

Federal Council of the Churches of Christ in America. *Federal Council Bulletin.* New York: Religious Publicity Service, 1948.

Fejes, Fred. *Gay Rights and Moral Panic: The Origins of America's Debate on Homosexuality.* New York: Palgrave MacMillan, 2008.

Finke, Roger, and Rodney Stark. *The Churching of America, 1776–1990: Winners and Losers in Our Religious Economy.* New Brunswick, NJ: Rutgers University Press, 1992.

———. *The Churching of America, 1776–2005: Winners and Losers in Our Religious Economy.* New Brunswick, NJ: Rutgers University Press, 2005.

Fiorina, Morris. *Culture War? The Myth of a Polarized America.* New York: Pearson Longman, 2005.

First United Methodist Church. *Church at the Crossroads: A History of First United Methodist Church Dallas.* Dallas: UMR Communications, 1997.

Fiske, Susan T., and Shelly E. Taylor. *Social Cognition.* 2nd ed. New York: McGraw-Hill, 1991.

Fitts, LeRoy. *A History of Black Baptists.* Nashville, TN: Boardman Press.

Fletcher, Joseph. *Situation Ethics: The New Morality.* Philadelphia: Westminster Press, 1966.

Flynt, Wayne. "Religion and the Blues: Evangelicalism, Poor Whites, and the Great Depression." *Journal of Southern History* 71 (2005), 3–38.

Fogel, Robert W., and Stanley L. Engerman. *Mortality in the South, 1850.* Ann Arbor, MI: Inter-University Consortium for Political and Social Research, 1976.

Foley, Neil. *The White Scourge: Mexicans, Blacks, and Poor Whites in Texas Cotton Culture.* Berkeley: University of California Press, 1997.

Fortune, Alonzo W. "The Kentucky Campaign against the Teaching of Evolution." *Journal of Religion* 2 (1922), 225–35.

Foucault, Michel. *Discipline and Punish: The Birth of the Prison.* New York: Random House, 1977.

Fowler, Gene, and Bill Crawford. *Border Radio: Quacks, Yodelers, Pitchmen, Psychics, and Other Amazing Broadcasters of the American Airwaves.* Austin: University of Texas Press, 2002.

Fox, William F. *Regimental Losses in the American Civil War, 1861–1865.* New York: Albany Publishing Company, 1889.

Fraga, Luis R., John A. Garcia, Rodney Hero, Michael Jones-Correa, Valerie Martinez-Ebers, and Gary M. Segura. *Latino National Survey, 2006.* Ann Arbor, MI: Inter-University Consortium for Political and Social Research, 2006.

Frederickson, Kari. *The Dixiecrat Revolt and the End of the Solid South, 1932–1968.* Chapel Hill: University of North Carolina Press, 2001.

Freeman, A. C., ed. *The American Decisions Containing the Cases of General Value and Authority Decided in the Courts of the Several States,* vol. 83. San Francisco: Bancroft-Whitney, 1887.

Freeman, Curtis W. " 'Never Had I Been So Blind': W. A. Criswell's 'Change' on Racial Segregation." *Journal of Southern Religion* 10 (2007), 1–12.

Freidson, Eliot. *Professionalism: The Third Logic.* Chicago: University of Chicago Press, 2001.

Galarza, Ernesto. *Strangers in Our Fields.* Washington, DC: Joint United States–Mexico Trade Union Committee, 1956.

Gallagher, Gary W., and Alan T. Nolan, eds. *The Myth of the Lost Cause and Civil War History.* Bloomington: Indiana University Press, 2000.

Gallup Organization. *Gallup Poll 1962-0659: Politics/Religion/Stock.* Storrs, CT: Roper Center for Public Opinion Research, 1962.

Gambrell, J. B. "The Growing of a Great Religious Paper." *Baptist Standard* (April 25, 1907), 1.
———. "The Negro Problem." *Baptist Standard* (June 13, 1907), 4.

Garcia, Gilbert. *Reagan's Comeback: Four Weeks in Texas That Changed American Politics Forever.* San Antonio: Trinity University Press, 2012.

Garcia, Ignacio M. *United We Win: The Rise and Fall of La Raza Unida Party.* Tucson: University of Arizona Mexican American Studies Research Center, 1989.

Gardner, David M. "Misrepresenting Baptists." *Baptist Standard* (September 21, 1950), 4.

Geertz, Clifford. *The Interpretation of Cultures.* New York: Basic Books, 1973.

George, Carol V. R. *God's Salesman: Norman Vincent Peale and the Power of Positive Thinking.* New York: Oxford University Press, 1993.

Gerth, H. H., and C. Wright Mills. *From Max Weber: Essays in Sociology.* New York: Oxford University Press, 1958.

Gibson, Campbell, and Kay Jung. *Historical Census Statistics on Population Totals by Race, 1790 to 1990, and By Hispanic Origin, 1970 to 1990, for the United States, Regions, Divisions, and States.* Washington, DC: U.S. Census Bureau, 2002.

Giggie, John M. *After Redemption: Jim Crow and the Transformation of African American Religion in the Delta, 1875–1915.* New York: Oxford University Press, 2008.

Ginzburg, Ralph. *100 Years of Lynchings.* Baltimore: Black Classic Press, 1996.

Glock, Charles Y., and Phillip E. Hammond, eds. *Beyond the Classics? Essays in the Scientific Study of Religion.* New York: Harper & Row, 1973.

Glock, Charles Y., and Rodney Stark. *Christian Beliefs and Anti-Semitism.* New York: Harper & Row, 1966.

Godfrey, William Fike. "By the Grace of God." In *A History of Dickens County: Ranches and Rolling Plains,* edited by Fred Arrington, 344–51. Dickens, TX: Nortex Offset Publications, 1971.

Goldberg, Robert Alan. *Barry Goldwater.* New Haven, CT: Yale University Press, 1995.

Goldman, Eric F. *The Tragedy of Lyndon Johnson.* New York: Dell, 1969.

Goldwater, Barry. *The Conscience of a Conservative.* Princeton, NJ: Princeton University Press, 2007, originally published in 1960.

Goree, Langston James, V, ed. *The Thomas Jewett Goree Letters,* vol. 1: *The Civil War Correspondence.* Bryan, TX: Family History Foundation, 1981.

Gould, Lewis L. *Progressives and Prohibitionists: Texas Democrats in the Wilson Era.* Austin: University of Texas Press, 1973.

Graham, Don. *Kings of Texas: The 150-Year Saga of an American Ranching Empire.* Hoboken, NJ: Wiley, 2003.

Gregory, Joel. *Too Great a Temptation: The Seductive Power of America's Super Church.* Fort Worth, TX: Summit Group, 1994.

Griffith, R. Marie. *God's Daughters: Evangelical Women and the Power of Submission.* Berkeley: University of California Press, 1997.

Grubbs, Vincent W. *Practical Prohibition.* Greenville, TX: T. C. Johnson, 1887.

Gurasich, Marj. *Letters to Oma: A Young German Girl's Account of Her First Years in Texas, 1847.* Fort Worth: Texas Christian University Press, 1989.

Gurin, Gerald, Joseph Veroff, and Sheila Feld. *Americans View Their Mental Health.* Ann Arbor, MI: Inter-University Consortium for Political and Social Research, 1957.

Gutiérrez, José Angel. *The Making of a Chicano Militant: Lessons from Cristal.* Madison: University of Wisconsin Press, 1998.

———. *The Making of a Civil Rights Leader.* Houston: Arte Público Press, 2005.

Gutmann, Myron P. *Great Plains Population and Environment Data: Agricultural Data, 1870–1997.* Ann Arbor, MI: Inter-University Consortium for Political and Social Research, 2002.

Hadden, Jeffrey K. "Religious Broadcasting and the Mobilization of the New Christian Right." *Journal for the Scientific Study of Religion* 26 (1987), 1–24.

Hall, David D., ed. *Lived Religion in America: Toward a History of Practice.* Princeton, NJ: Princeton University Press, 1997.

Hall, Jacquelyn Dowd. *Revolt against Chivalry: Jessie Daniel Ames and the Women's Campaign against Lynching.* New York: Columbia University Press, 1979.

———. "Second Thoughts: On Writing a Feminist Biography," *Feminist Studies* 13 (1987), 19–37.

Hall, W. W. *Hall's Journal of Health.* New York: Russell Brothers, 1873.

Hamilton, Malcolm. "Rational Choice Theory: A Critique." In *The Oxford Handbook of the Sociology of Religion,* edited by Peter B. Clark, 116–33. Oxford: Oxford University Press, 2009.

Hammond, Sarah Ruth. " 'God's Business Men': Entrepreneurial Evangelicals in Depression and War." PhD diss., Yale University, 2010.

Hankins, Barry. *American Evangelicals: A Contemporary History of a Mainstream Religious Movement.* Lanham, MD: Rowman and Littlefield, 2008.

———. *God's Rascal: J. Frank Norris and the Beginnings of Southern Fundamentalism.* Lexington: University Press of Kentucky, 1996.

Hann, Chris. "Problems with the (De)privatization of Religion." *Anthropology Today* 16 (2000), 14–20.

Hannah, John D. *An Uncommon Union: Dallas Theological Seminary and American Evangelicalism.* Grand Rapids, MI: Zondervan, 2009.

Harlan, Douglas. "The Party's Over." *Texas Monthly* (January 1982), 114–19.

Harrison, Lowell H., and James C. Klotter. *A New History of Kentucky.* Lexington: University Press of Kentucky, 1997.

Hartpence, William Ross. *History of the Fifty-First Indiana Veteran Volunteer Infantry.* Cincinnati: Robert Clarke, 1894.

Harvey, Paul. "'Yankee Faith' and Southern Redemption: White Southern Baptist Ministers, 1850–1890." In *Religion and the American Civil War*, edited by Randall M. Miller, Harry S. Stout, and Charles Reagan Wilson, 167–86. New York: Oxford University Press, 1998.

Head, J. J., Lola Winters Head, and Lucy Alice Bruce Stewart. "The Black Jack Methodist Church, Cemetery, and School." In *Huntsville and Walker County, Texas: A Bicentennial History*, edited by D'Anne McAdams Crews, 435–38. Huntsville, TX: Sam Houston State University Press, 1976.

Heard, Alexander, and Donald S. Strong. *Southern Primary and General Election Data, 1920–1949.* Ann Arbor, MI: Inter-University Consortium for Political and Social Research, 1991.

Hechter, Michael. *Internal Colonialism: The Celtic Fringe in British National Development, 1536–1966.* London: Routledge and Kegan Paul, 1975.

Heintzelman, Samuel Peter. *Fifty Miles and a Fight: Major Samuel Peter Heintzelman's Journal of Texas and the Cortina War*, edited by Jerry Thompson. Denton: Texas State Historical Association, 1998.

Hill, Patricia Evridge. *Dallas: The Making of a Modern City.* Austin: University of Texas Press, 1996.

Hill-Aiello, Thomas A. "Dallas Cotton and the Transatlantic Economy, 1885–1956." PhD diss., University of Texas, Arlington.

Himes, Andrew. *The Sword of the Lord: The Roots of Fundamentalism in an American Family.* Seattle: Chiara Press, 2011.

Hodgkinson, Virginia A. *From Belief to Commitment: The Community Service Activities and Finances of Religious Congregations in the United States.* Washington, DC: Independent Sector, 1993.

Hoffman, Abraham. "Mexican Repatriation Statistics: Some Suggested Alternatives to Carey McWilliams." *Western Historical Quarterly* 3 (1972), 391–404.

Hofstadter, Richard. *The Paranoid Style in American Politics.* Cambridge, MA: Harvard University Press, 1964.

Holland, Richard A. "George W. Brackenridge, George W. Littlefield, and the Shadow of the Past." In *The Texas Book: Profiles, History, and Reminiscences of the University*, edited by Richard A. Holland, 85–104. Austin: University of Texas Press, 2006.

Holley, Helena. "What Woman Suffrage Will Do toward the Conservation of Public Health." In *The New Chivalry—Health*, edited by James E. McCulloch, 307–13. Washington, DC: Southern Sociological Congress, 1915.

Holmes, S. J. "Proposed Laws against the Teaching of Evolution." *Bulletin of the American Association of University Professors* 13 (1927), 549–54.

Honey, Michael K. *Going Down Jericho Road: The Memphis Strike, Martin Luther King's Last Campaign.* New York: Norton, 2007.

Hooper, Robert E. *A Distinct People: A History of the Churches of Christ in the 20th Century.* West Monroe, LA: Howard, 1993.

Hout, Michael, Andrew Greeley, and Melissa J. Wilde. "The Demographic Imperative in Religious Change in the United States." *American Journal of Sociology* 107 (2001), 468–500.

Horowitz, David A. "Introduction: Setting the Context." In *Inside the Klavern: The Secret History of a Ku Klux Klan of the 1920s,* edited by David A. Horowitz, 1–15. Carbondale: Southern Illinois University Press, 1999.

Horowitz, Irving Louis. *C. Wright Mills: An American Utopia.* New York: Free Press, 1983.

Houston, Sam. "Campaign of 1836 and Its Termination in the Battle of San Jacinto." *Texas Almanac* (1860), 18–35.

Hout, Michael, and Claude S. Fischer. "Explaining the Rise of Americans with No Religious Preference: Generations and Politics." *American Sociological Review* 67 (2002), 165–90.

Hout, Michael, Andrew Greeley, and Melissa J. Wilde. "The Demographic Imperative in Religious Change in the United States." *American Journal of Sociology* 107 (2001), 468–500.

Hume, F. Charles. "Walker County." *Texas Almanac* (1867), 169–70.

Humphrey, David C. "Prostitution and Public Policy in Austin, Texas, 1870–1915." *Southwestern Historical Quarterly* 86 (1983), 473–516.

Hunter, James Davison. *American Evangelicalism: Conservative Religion and the Quandary of Modernity.* New Brunswick, NJ: Rutgers University Press, 1983.

———. *Culture Wars.* New York: Basic Books, 1991.

Hurt, Harry III. "Welcome, Mr. Kennedy, to Dallas." *Texas Monthly* (April 1981), 148–51, 237–52.

Hutchinson County Historical Commission. *History of Hutchinson County, Texas: 104 Years, 1876–1980.* Dallas: Taylor, 1980.

Iannaccone, Laurence R. "A Formal Model of Church and Sect." *American Journal of Sociology* 94 (1988), S241–S268.

———. "Sacrifice and Community: Reducing Free-Riders in Cults, Communes and Other Collectivities." *Journal of Political Economy* 100 (1992), 271–92.

———. "Voodoo Economics? Reviewing the Rational Choice Approach to Religion." *Journal for the Scientific Study of Religion* 34 (1995), 76–89.

———. "Why Strict Churches Are Strong." *American Journal of Sociology* 99 (1994), 1180–1211.

Isaac, Paul E. "Municipal Reform in Beaumont, Texas, 1902–1909." *Southwestern Historical Quarterly* 78 (1975), 409–30.

Ivy, James D. " 'The Lone Star State Surrenders to a Lone Woman': Frances Willard's Forgotten 1882 Texas Temperance Tour." *Southwestern Historical Quarterly* 102 (1998), 44–61.

———. *No Saloon in the Valley: The Southern Strategy of Texas Prohibitionists in the 1880s.* Waco, TX: Baylor University Press, 2003.

Jackson, Samuel Macauley, ed. *The New Schaff-Herzog Encyclopedia of Religious Knowledge,* 13 vols. New York: Funk and Wagnalls, 1908–14.

Jacobs, J. R. "Orthodoxy and the 'Caldwell Case.'" *Christian Observer* 94 (February 7, 1906), 6.

James, Edward T., Janet Wilson James, and Paul S. Boyer. *Notable American Women: A Biographical Dictionary.* Cambridge, MA: Radcliffe College, 1971.

Jamieson, Kathleen Hall. *Packaging the Presidency: A History and Criticism of Presidential Campaign Advertising.* New York: Oxford University Press, 1992.

Jensen, Oliver. *The American Heritage History of Railroads in America.* New York: American Heritage, 1975.

Johnson, Charles P. "The Youth and Young Man." In *J. Howard Williams: Prophet of God and Friend of Man,* edited by H. C. Brown Jr. and Charles P. Johnson, 1–7. San Antonio: Naylor, 1963.

Johnson, Frank W. *A History of Texas and Texans,* 4 vols. Chicago: American Historical Society, 1914.

Jones, C. Allen. *Texas Roots: Agriculture and Rural Life before the Civil War.* College Station: Texas A&M University Press, 2005.

Jones, Dale E., Sherri Doty, Clifford Grammich, James E. Horsch, Richard Houseal, Mac Lynn, John P. Marcum, Kenneth M. Sanchagrin, and Richard H. Taylor. *Religious Congregations and Membership in the United States, 2000.* Cincinnati, OH: Glenmary Research Center, 2001.

Jones, R. L., and Andrew Davis. "Folk Life in Early Texas: The Autobiography of Andrew Davis." *Southwestern Historical Quarterly* 43 (1939), 158–75.

Jordan, Barbara. *A Self-Portrait.* New York: Doubleday, 1979.

Jordan, Dusty. "Baptists Bring War to Jonesboro." *Craighead County Historical Quarterly* 21 (1983), 1–9.

Josephy, Alvin M. *The Civil War in the American West.* New York: Knopf, 1991.

Kelton, Elmer. *Sandhills Boy: The Winding Trail of a Texas Writer.* New York: Tom Dougherty Associates, 2007.

Kerr, Homer L. "Migration into Texas, 1860–1880." *Southwestern Historical Quarterly* 70 (October 1966), 184–216.

Kessler, George. *A City Plan for Dallas.* Dallas: Report of Park Board, 1913.

Klineberg, Stephen L. *Houston Area Survey, 1982–2010: Successive Representative Samples of Harris County Residents.* Ann Arbor, MI: Inter-University Consortium for Political and Social Research, 2011.

Knight, Oliver. *Fort Worth: Outpost on the Trinity.* Fort Worth: Texas Christian University Press, 1990.

Knox, Mary. "Youth Revivalists Shaped a Generation." *Baptist Standard* (June 30, 1999), 1.

Koren, John. *Benevolent Institutions.* Washington, DC: Government Printing Office, 1904.

Kozlowski, Steve W. J., and Katherine J. Klein, eds. *Multilevel Theory, Research, and Methods in Organizations.* San Francisco: Jossey-Bass, 2000.

Kreidler, Tai Deckner. "The Offshore Petroleum Industry: The Formative Years, 1945–1962." PhD diss., Texas Tech University, 1997.

Laermans, Rudy, Bryan Wilson, and Jaak Billiet, eds. *Secularization and Social Integration.* Leuven, Belgium: Leuven University Press, 1998.

Lambing, A. A. "Scenes from the Texas Mission of Half a Century Ago." *American Catholic Historical Researches* 3 (1887), 2–12.

Lamis, Alexander P. "The Two-Party South: From the 1960s to the 1990s." In *Southern Politics in the 1990s*, edited by Alexander P. Lamis, 1–49. Baton Rouge: Louisiana State University Press.

Lamont, Michèle, and Virag Molnár. "The Study of Boundaries in the Social Sciences." *Annual Review of Sociology* 28 (2002), 167–95.

Lane, J. J. *History of Education in Texas.* Washington, DC: Government Printing Office, 1903.

Larson, Magali Sarfatti. *The Rise of Professionalism: A Sociological Analysis.* Berkeley: University of California Press, 1977.

Leavitt, Judith Walzer. *Brought to Bed: Childbearing in America, 1750–1950.* New York: Oxford University Press, 1986.

Ledbetter, Billy D. "White Texans' Attitudes toward the Political Equality of Negroes, 1865–1870." *Phylon* 40 (1979), 253–63.

Ledbetter, Patsy. "Defense of the Faith: J. Frank Norris and Texas Fundamentalism, 1920–1929." *Arizona and the West* 15 (1973), 45–62.

Lee, Blewett. "An Establishment of Religion." *Virginia Law Review* 14 (1927), 100–111.

Lee, Shayne. *T. D. Jakes: America's New Preacher.* New York: New York University Press, 2005.

Lee, Shayne, and Phillip Sinitiere. *Holy Mavericks: Evangelical Innovators and the Spiritual Marketplace.* New York: New York University, 2009.

Leff, Gladys R. "Opening Legal Doors for Women: Hermine Tobolowsky." In *Lone Stars of David: The Jews of Texas*, edited by Hollace Ava Weiner and Kenneth D. Roseman, 233–38. Waltham, MA: Brandeis University Press, 2007.

Lester, Charles Edwards. *Sam Houston and His Republic.* New York: Burgess, Stringer, 1846.

LeTourneau, R. G. *Mover of Men and Mountains.* New York: Prentice-Hall, 1960.

Levi, Leo N. "The Successful Life." *University of Texas Record* 1 (1899), 191–202.

Liebman, Robert C., and Robert Wuthnow, eds. *The New Christian Right: Mobilization and Legitimation.* Hawthorne, NY: Aldine, 1983.

Lindsay, D. Michael. "Evangelicals in the Power Elite: Elite Cohesion Advancing a Movement." *American Sociological Review* 73 (2008), 60–82.

———. *Faith in the Halls of Power: How Evangelicals Joined the American Elite.* New York: Oxford University Press, 2007.

Lipset, Seymour Martin, and Earl Raab. *The Politics of Unreason: Right Wing Extremism in America, 1790–1970.* New York: Harper & Row, 1973.

Logan, W. H. "Progress of Negro Churches in Houston since Emancipation or the Civil War." *Red Book of Houston: A Compendium of Social, Professional, Religious, Educational and Industrial Interests of Houston's Colored Population.* Houston: Sotex, 1915, 21–23.

Lohman, Arthur H. "Early Days in Two Rivers, Wisconsin, 1848–1900." *Manitowoc County Historical Society Occupational Monograph 50* (1983), 1–12.

Loveland, Anne C. "The 'Southern Work' of Reverend Joseph C. Hartzell, Pastor of Ames Church in New Orleans, 1870–1873." *Louisiana History* 16 (1975), 391–407.

MacIntyre, Alasdair. *After Virtue: A Study in Moral Theory.* Notre Dame, IN: University of Notre Dame Press, 1984.

Malone, Bill C. "'Sing Me Back Home': Growing Up in the South and Writing the History of Its Music." In *Shapers of Southern History: Autobiographical Reflections*, edited by John B. Boles, 91–113. Athens: University of Georgia Press, 2004.

Mann, Robert. *Daisy Petals and Mushroom Clouds: LBJ, Barry Goldwater, and the Ad That Changed American Politics*. Baton Rouge: Louisiana State University Press, 2011.

Mansbridge, Jane J. *Why We Lost the ERA*. Chicago: University of Chicago Press, 1986.

Marquez, Benjamin. *Constructing Identities in Mexican-American Political Organizations: Choosing Issues, Taking Sides*. Austin: University of Texas Press, 2003.

Marsden, George M. *Fundamentalism and American Culture: The Shaping of Twentieth-Century Evangelicalism, 1870-1925*. New York: Oxford University Press, 1980.

Martin, David. *A General Theory of Secularization*. New York: Harper & Row, 1978.

Martin, William. "God's Angry Man." *Texas Monthly* (April 1981), 152–57, 223–35.

——. "In the Beginning." *Texas Monthly* (May 1979), 193–96.

——. "Prime Minister." *Texas Monthly* (August 2005), 106–10.

——. *With God on Our Side: The Rise of the Religious Right in America*. New York: Broadway Books, 1996.

Marwell, Gerald. "We Still Don't Know If Strict Churches Are Strong, Much Less Why: Comment on Iannaccone." *American Journal of Sociology* 101 (1996), 1097–1103.

Mas, Alexandre, and Enrico Moretti. "Racial Bias in the 2008 Presidential Election." University of California at Berkeley, Department of Economics, 2008.

Massey, Douglas S. *Categorically Unequal: The American Stratification System*. New York: Russell Sage Foundation, 2007.

McArthur, Judith N., and Harold L. Smith. *Texas Through Women's Eyes: The Twentieth-Century Experience*. Austin: University of Texas Press, 2010.

McBeth, H. Leon. *The Baptist Heritage: Four Centuries of Baptist Witness*. Nashville, TN: Broadman Press, 1987.

McCarley, Howard. "Dust Bowl Days." In *Texas Millennium Book: The Way Things Used to Be*, edited by Jerry B. Lincecum and Peggy A. Redshaw, 133–35. Sherman, TX: Austin College, 1999.

McComb, David G. *Galveston: A History*. Austin: University of Texas Press, 1986.

——. *Spare Time in Texas: Recreation and History in the Lone Star State*. Austin: University of Texas Press, 2008.

——. *Texas: A Modern History*. Austin: University of Texas Press, 1989.

McCulloch, James E. *Distinguished Service Citizenship: Southern Sociological Congress, Knoxville, Tennessee, 1919*. Washington, DC: Southern Sociological Congress, 1919.

McDonnold, Benjamin Wilburn. *History of the Cumberland Presbyterian Church*. Nashville, TN: Board of Publication of Cumberland Presbyterian Church, 1888.

McEnteer, James. *Deep in the Heart: The Texas Tendency in American Politics*. Westport, CT: Praeger, 2004.

McIver, Bruce. *Riding the Wind of God: A Personal History of the Youth Revival Movement*. Macon, GA: Smyth & Helwys Publishing, 2002.

McMillen, Sally G. *Motherhood in the Old South: Pregnancy, Childbirth, and Infant Rearing*. Baton Rouge: Louisiana State University Press, 1990.

McNeill, Charles Chamberlain. "Young Men's Christian Association." *University of Texas Record* 9 (1909), 104–5.

McSwain, Larry. *Loving Beyond Your Theology: The Life and Ministry of Jimmy Raymond Allen.* Atlanta: Mercer University Press, 2010.

McWhirter, Cameron. *Red Summer: the Summer of 1919 and the Awakening of Black America.* New York: Henry Holt, 2011.

Merino, Stephen M. "Neighbors Like Me? Religious Affiliation and Neighborhood Racial Preferences among Non-Hispanic Whites." *Religions* 2 (2011), 165–83.

Methodist Church General Conference. *Journal of the General Conference of the Methodist Church.* New York: Methodist Church General Conference, 1948.

Meyer, John W. "The Effects of Education as an Institution." *American Journal of Sociology* 86 (1977), 340–63.

———. "Self and Life Course: Institutionalization and Its Effects." In *Institutional Structure: Constituting State, Society, and the Individual,* edited by George M. Thomas, John W. Meyer, Francisco O. Ramirez, and John Boli, 242–60. Newbury Park, CA: Sage, 1987.

Miller, Connie A., Sr. *Frederick Douglass: American Hero and International Icon of the Nineteenth Century.* New York: Xlibris, 2008.

Moneyhon, Carl H. *Republicanism in Reconstruction Texas.* Austin: University of Texas Press, 1980.

Monroe, Mary Catherine. "A Day in July: Hatton W. Sumners and the Court Reorganization Plan of 1937." Master's thesis, University of Texas, Arlington, 1973.

Montejano, David. *Quixote's Soldiers: A Local History of the Chicano Movement, 1966–1981.* Austin: University of Texas Press, 2010.

Moore, James Talmadge. *Acts of Faith: The Catholic Church in Texas, 1900–1950.* College Station: Texas A&M University Press, 2002.

———. *Through Fire and Flood: The Catholic Church in Frontier Texas, 1836–1900.* College Station: Texas A&M University Press, 1992.

Morgan, Edmund S. *Roger Williams: The Church and the State.* New York: Norton, 1967.

Morgenthaler, Jefferson. *The German Settlement of the Texas Hill Country.* Seattle: Mockingbird Books, 2011.

Morgeson, Frederick P., and David A. Hofmann. "The Structure and Function of Collective Constructs: Implications for Multilevel Research and Theory Development." *Academy of Management Review* 24 (1999), 249–65.

Morris, Willie. *North Toward Home.* New York: Vintage Books, 2000.

Morrow, Ralph E. *Northern Methodism and Reconstruction.* East Lansing: Michigan State University Press, 1956.

Munson, M. S. "Brazoria County." *Texas Almanac* (1867), 82–83.

Murphy, Dubose. "Early Days of the Protestant Episcopal Church in Texas." *Southwestern Historical Quarterly* 34 (1931), 293–316.

Murr, Erika L., ed. *A Rebel Wife in Texas: The Diary and Letters of Elizabeth Scott Neblett, 1852–1864.* Baton Rouge: Louisiana State University Press, 2001.

Murrah, David J. *C. C. Slaughter: Rancher, Banker, Baptist.* Austin: University of Texas Press, 1981.

Musick, Marc A. *Survey of Texas Adults, 2004*. Ann Arbor, MI: Inter-University Consortium for Political and Social Research, 2004.

———. *Volunteers: A Social Profile*. Bloomington: Indiana University Press, 2008.

Nash, Jay Robert. *Citizen Hoover: A Critical Study of the Life and Times of J. Edgar Hoover and His FBI*. Chicago: Nelson-Hall, 1972.

National Child Labor Committee. *Child Labor Facts*. New York: Herald-Nathan Press, 1938.

National Council of Churches. *Churches and Church Membership in the United States: An Enumeration and Analysis by Counties, States and Regions*. New York: National Council of Churches, 1956.

Navarro, Armando. *The Cristal Experiment: A Chicano Struggle for Community Control*. Madison: University of Wisconsin Press, 1998.

Newman, Katherine S., and Rourke L. O'Brien. *Taxing the Poor: Doing Damage to the Truly Disadvantaged*. Berkeley: University of California Press, 2011.

Newport, John P. "The Church Member." In *J. Howard Williams: Prophet of God and Friend of Man*, edited by H. C. Brown Jr. and Charles P. Johnson, 121–29. San Antonio: Naylor, 1963.

Nicholson, John. "San Augustine." *Texas Almanac* (1859), 181.

Noll, Mark A. *America's God: From Jonathan Edwards to Abraham Lincoln*. New York: Oxford University Press, 2002.

———. *The Old Religion in a New World: The History of North American Christianity*. Grand Rapids, MI: Eerdmans, 2002.

Noonan, Peggy. *What I Saw at the Revolution: A Political Life in the Reagan Era*. New York: Random House, 1990.

Noordberg, Henri Gerard. "The Yellow Fever Epidemic of 1867 at Huntsville." In *Huntsville and Walker County, Texas: A Bicentennial History*, edited by D'Anne McAdams Crews, 209–33. Huntsville, TX: Sam Houston State University Press, 1976.

Norvell, James R. "The Reconstruction Courts of Texas, 1867–1873." *Southwestern Historical Quarterly* 62 (1958), 141–63.

Nunn, William C. *Texas under the Carpetbaggers*. Austin: University of Texas Press, 1962.

Olasky, Marvin. *Compassionate Conservatism: What It Is, What It Does, and How It Can Transform America*. New York: Free Press, 2000.

———. *The Tragedy of American Compassion*. Wheaton, IL: Crossway Books, 1992.

Oliphint, Elizabeth. "Martha's Chapel Methodist Church." In *Huntsville and Walker County, Texas: A Bicentennial History*, edited by D'Anne McAdams Crews, 335–41. Huntsville, TX: Sam Houston State University Press, 1976.

Olmsted, Frederick Law. *A Journey through Texas, or a Saddle-Trip on the Southwestern Frontier*, introduction by Witold Rybczynski. Lincoln: University of Nebraska Press, 2004, originally published in 1857.

Orozco, Cynthia E. *No Mexicans, Women, or Dogs Allowed: The Rise of the Mexican American Civil Rights Movement*. Austin: University of Texas Press, 2009.

Orsi, Robert. "Everyday Miracles: The Study of Lived Religion." In *Lived Religion in America: Toward a History of Practice*, edited by David D. Hall, 3–21. Princeton, NJ: Princeton University Press, 1997.

Osterweis, Rollin Gustav. *The Myth of the Lost Cause, 1865–1900.* Hamden, CT: Archon Books, 1973.

O'Toole, Roger. *Religion: Classic Sociological Approaches.* Whitby, Ontario: McGraw-Hill Ryerson, 1984.

Paddock, B. B. *History and Biographical Record of North and West Texas,* vol. 1. Chicago: Lewis, 1906.

Page, Edward. "Michael Hechter's Internal Colonial Thesis: Some Theoretical and Methodological Problems." *European Journal of Political Research* 6 (1978), 295–317.

Parker, William B. *Notes Taken during the Expedition Commanded by Capt. R. B. Marcy, U.S.A., through Unexplored Texas, in the Summer and Fall of 1854.* Philadelphia: Hayes & Zell, 1856.

Parsons, Talcott. *The Social System.* New York: Free Press, 1951.

Passel, Jeffrey S., and D'Vera Cohn. *Unauthorized Immigrant Population: National and State Trends, 2010.* Washington, DC: Pew Hispanic Center, 2011.

Pearson, Mary Bowen, ed. *Evangelistic Sermons by the Rev. R. G. Pearson.* Richmond, VA: Richmond Press, 1915.

Pemberton, William E. *Exit with Honor: The Life and Presidency of Ronald Reagan.* New York: M. E. Sharpe, 1998.

Penton, M. James. *Apocalypse Delayed: The Story of Jehovah's Witnesses.* Toronto: University of Toronto Press, 1997.

Perlstein, Rick. *Before the Storm: Barry Goldwater and the Unmaking of the American Consensus.* New York: Hill and Wang, 2001.

Pettigrew, Thomas F. *The Sociology of Race Relations: Reflection and Reform.* New York: Simon and Schuster, 1980.

Phelan, Macum. *A History of the Expansion of Methodism in Texas, 1867 to 1902.* Dallas: Mathis, Van Nort, 1937.

Pilkington, Charles Kirk. "The Trials of Brotherhood: The Founding of the Commission on Interracial Cooperation." *Georgia Historical Quarterly* 69 (1985), 55–80.

Political Behavior Program, Survey Research Center. *American National Election Study, 1964.* Ann Arbor, MI: Inter-University Consortium for Political and Social Research, 1999.

Portes, Alejandro. "The Hidden Abode: Sociology as Analysis of the Unexpected: 1999 Presidential Address." *American Sociological Review* 65 (2000), 1–18.

Pressler, Paul. *A Hill on Which to Die: One Southern Baptist's Journey.* Nashville, TN: B&H, 2002.

Primer, Ben. *Protestants and American Business Methods.* Ann Arbor, MI: UMI Research Press, 1979.

Putnam, Robert D., and David E. Campbell. *American Grace: How Religion Divides and Unites Us.* New York: Simon and Schuster, 2010.

Quinley, Harold E. *The Prophetic Clergy: Social Activism among Protestant Ministers.* New York: Wiley, 1974.

Raines, C. W. "The Alamo Monument." *Quarterly of the Texas State Historical Association* 6 (1903), 300–10.

Rall, Harris Franklin. "Premillennialism and the Bible." *The Biblical World* 53 (1919), 459–69.

Randall, Henry S. "Summer and Winter Management of Sheep in Texas." *Texas Almanac* (1861), 152–66.

Rankin, George C. *The Story of My Life: More than a Half Century as I Have Lived It and Seen It Lived.* Dallas: Press of the Home and State, 1912.

Ranson, Edward. *The American Mid-Term Elections of 1922: An Unexpected Shift in Political Power.* New York: Edwin Mellen Press, 2007.

Rechy, John. "Jim Crow Wears a Sombrero." *The Nation* 10 (1950), 210–13.

Reed, Linda. *Simple Decency and Common Sense: The Southern Conference Movement, 1938– 1963.* Bloomington: Indiana University Press, 1991.

Reed, S. G. *A History of the Texas Railroads.* Houston: St. Clair, 1941.

Reichstein, Andreas V. *Rise of the Lone Star: The Making of Texas.* College Station: Texas A&M University Press, 1989.

Reid, Don Jr., "The Texas State Prison Has Been in Huntsville a Long Time." In *Huntsville and Walker County, Texas: A Bicentennial History*, edited by D'Anne McAdams Crews, 191– 97. Huntsville, TX: Sam Houston State University Press, 1976.

Resnik, Hank. *The Schools of Crystal City.* Stanford, CA: Stanford Center for Research and Development in Teaching, Stanford University, 1976.

Rich, Harold W. "Beyond Outpost: Fort Worth, 1880–1918." PhD. diss., Texas Christian University, 2006.

Riley, B. F. *History of the Baptists in Texas.* Dallas: B. F. Riley, 1907.

Roberts, Lesbia Word. "Sid Williams Richardson." *Legacies: A History Journal for Dallas and North Central Texas* 11 (1999), 40–49.

Robinson, Edward J. *Show Us How You Do It: Marshall Keeble and the Rise of Black Churches of Christ in the United States,1914–1968.* Tuscaloosa: University of Alabama Press, 2008.

Robinson, George. "Huntsville's Great Yellow Fever Epidemic of 1867." In *Huntsville and Walker County, Texas: A Bicentennial History*, edited by D'Anne McAdams Crews, 237– 47. Huntsville, TX: Sam Houston State University Press, 1976.

Rodriguez, Marc Simon. "A Movement Made of 'Young Mexican Americans Seeking Change': Critical Citizenship, Migration, and the Chicano Movement in Texas and Wisconsin, 1960–1975." *Western Historical Quarterly* 34 (Autumn 2003), 275–99.

Rogers, Mary Beth. *Barbara Jordan: American Hero.* New York: Bantam, 1998.

Roosevelt, Theodore. *Presidential Addresses and State Papers, November 15, 1907, to November 26, 1908.* New York: Review of Reviews, 1910.

Rousseau, Jean Jacques. *The Social Contract and Discourse on the Origin and Foundation of Inequality among Mankind*, edited by Lester G. Crocker. New York: Washington Square Press, 1967.

Rove, Karl. *Courage and Consequence: My Life as a Conservative in the Fight.* New York: Simon and Schuster, 2010.

Routh, Eugene Coke. "Baylor University and Pastor Norris." *Baptist Standard* (February 23, 1922), 1.

———. "Editorial: Concerning Evolution." *Baptist Standard* (January 5, 1922), 8.

———. *The Life Story of Dr. J. B. Gambrell.* Dallas: Baptist Book Store, 1929.

Rozek, Barbara J. *Come to Texas: Attracting Immigrants, 1865–1915.* College Station: Texas A&M University Press, 2003.

Ruggles, Steven J., Trend Alexander, Katie Genadek, Ronald Goeken, Matthew B. Schroeder, and Matthew Sobeck. *Integrated Public Use Microdata Series, Version 5.0.* Minneapolis: University of Minnesota, 2010.

Rusk, Jerold G. *A Statistical History of the American Electorate.* Washington, DC: Congressional Quarterly Press, 2001.

Ryrie, Charles C. *Dispensationalism.* Chicago: Moody Publishers, 2007.

Sager, Rebecca. *Faith, Politics, and Power: The Politics of Faith-Based Initiatives.* New York: Oxford University Press.

Samuel, Opal McAdams. "The Walker County Community of McAdams, Texas." In *Huntsville and Walker County, Texas: A Bicentennial History,* edited by D'Anne McAdams Crews, 391–92. Huntsville, TX: Sam Houston State University Press, 1976.

Sandeen, Ernest R. *The Roots of Fundamentalism.* Chicago: University of Chicago Press, 1970.

Savage, Sean J. *JFK, LBJ, and the Democratic Party.* Albany: State University of New York Press, 2004.

Schaffner, Brian F. "Racial Salience and the Obama Vote." University of Massachusetts at Amherst, Department of Political Science, 2009.

"Assessing the State of the Sociology of Religion." *Contemporary Sociology* 41 (2012), 155–57.

Scheitle, Christopher P., and Buster G. Smith. "A Note on the Frequency and Sources of Close Interreligious Ties." *Journal for the Scientific Study of Religion* 50 (2011), 410–21.

Schneider, Louis, and Louis Zurcher. "Toward Understanding the Catholic Crisis: Observations on Dissident Priests in Texas." *Journal for the Scientific Study of Religion* 9 (1970), 197–207.

Schoenwald, Jonathan M. *A Time for Choosing: The Rise of Modern American Conservatism.* New York: Oxford University Press, 2001.

Scott, Anne Firor. "After Suffrage: Southern Women in the Twenties." *Journal of Southern History* 30 (1964), 298–318.

Scroggs, William O. "Mob Violence—An Enemy of Both Races." In *Democracy in Earnest,* edited by James E. McCulloch, 185–90. Washington, DC: Southern Sociological Congress, 1918.

Selznick, Gertrude J., and Stephen Steinberg. *The Tenacity of Prejudice: Anti-Semitism in Contemporary America.* New York: Harper & Row, 1969.

Senter, E. G. "Remarks by Senator Senter on Bank Guaranty Bills." *Journal of the Senate of Texas: First Called Session of the Thirty-First Legislature,* 227–44. Austin: Von Boeckmann-Jones, 1909.

Sharpe, Deborah Melanie. "Denominationalism: What the Cynic Sees." Senior thesis, Department of Sociology, Princeton University, 1985.

Shockley, John Staples. *Chicano Revolt in a Texas Town.* South Bend, IN: University of Notre Dame Press, 1974.

Sibley, Marilyn M. *Lone Stars and State Gazettes: Texas Newspapers before the Civil War.* College Station: Texas A&M University Press, 1983.

Skocpol, Theda, and Vanessa Williamson. *The Tea Party and the Remaking of Republican Conservatism.* New York: Oxford University Press, 2012.

Smidt, Corwin, ed. *Religion as Social Capital: Producing the Common Good.* Waco, TX: Baylor University Press, 2003.

Smith, Christian. *American Evangelicalism: Embattled and Thriving.* Chicago: University of Chicago Press, 1998.

———. "Religious Participation and Network Closure among American Adolescents." *Journal for the Scientific Study of Religion* 42 (2003), 259–67.

Smith, Gary Scott. *Faith and the Presidency: From George Washington to George W. Bush.* New York: Oxford University Press, 2006.

Somerville, A. "Memoir of General Sidney Sherman." *Texas Almanac* (1858), 113–16.

Southern Baptist Convention. *Annual of the Southern Baptist Convention.* Nashville, TN: Southern Baptist Convention, 1932.

———. *Annual of the Southern Baptist Convention.* St. Louis, MO: Southern Baptist Convention, 1935.

———. *Annual of the Southern Baptist Convention.* St. Louis, MO: Southern Baptist Convention, 1936.

———. *Annual of the Southern Baptist Convention.* Nashville, TN: Southern Baptist Convention, 1940.

———. *Annual of the Southern Baptist Convention.* Nashville, TN: Southern Baptist Convention, 1947.

———. *Annual of the Southern Baptist Convention.* Nashville, TN: Southern Baptist Convention, 1948.

———. *Annual of the Southern Baptist Convention.* Nashville, TN: Southern Baptist Convention, 1953.

Sprague, Stacey. "James Evetts Haley and the New Deal: Laying the Foundations for the Modern Republican Party in Texas." Master's thesis, University of North Texas, 2004.

Stanley, Mark. "Booze, Boomtowns, and Burning Crosses: The Turbulent Governorship of Pat M. Neff of Texas, 1921–1925." Master's thesis, University of North Texas, 2005.

Stark, Rodney, Charles Y. Glock, and Harold Quinley. "Sounds of Silence." *Psychology Today* (April 1970), 38–62.

Stark, Rodney, and Laurence R. Iannaccone. "A Supply-Side Reinterpretation of the 'Secularization' of Europe." *Journal for the Scientific Study of Religion* 33 (1994), 230–52.

Stausberg, Michael, ed. *Contemporary Theories of Religion: A Critical Companion.* New York: Routledge, 2009.

Steeley, Guy. *The Modern Elocutionist or Popular Speaker: A Manual of Instruction on Cultivation of the Voice, Gesticulation, Expression, Posing, Etc.* Chicago: Thompson & Thomas, 1900.

Steelwater, Eliza. *The Hangman's Knot: Lynching, Legal Execution and America's Struggle with the Death Penalty.* Boulder, CO: Westview Press, 2003.

Stein, Bill. *Consider the Lily: The Ungilded History of Colorado County, Texas.* Columbus, TX: Nesbitt Memorial Library, 1999.

Steiner, Stan. *La Raza: The Mexican Americans.* New York: Harper & Row, 1970.

Stephens, A. Ray. "Letter from the Texas Secession Convention, 1861: Willard Richardson to George Ware Fulton." *Southwestern Historical Quarterly* 65 (1962), 394–96.

Stephens-Davidowitz, Seth. "The Effects of Racial Animus on a Black Presidential Candidate: Using Google Search Data to Find What Surveys Miss." Harvard University, Department of Economics, 2012.

Stockton, Jed. "Tin Wagon Keeps Depression Memories Alive." In *Telling Our Stories: Grayson County Reminiscences, the First 150 Years, 1846–1996,* edited by Jerry B. Lincecum, 92–95. Sherman, TX: Austin College, 1996.

Stokes, David R. *The Shooting Salvationist: J. Frank Norris and the Murder Trial That Captivated America.* New York: Steerforth Press, 2011.

Stone, William E., C. Calvin McAdams, and Johanna Kollert, "Early Prisoners of the Texas Department of Corrections." In *Huntsville and Walker County, Texas: A Bicentennial History,* edited by D'Anne McAdams Crews, 187–88. Huntsville, TX: Sam Houston State University Press, 1976.

Storey, John W. *Texas Baptist Leadership and Social Christianity, 1900–1980.* College Station: Texas A&M University Press, 2000.

Stout, Jeffrey. *Ethics after Babel.* Boston: Beacon Press, 1988.

Stout, Harry S. *Upon the Altar of the Nation: A Moral History of the Civil War.* New York: Penguin, 2006.

Strong, Donald S. "The Poll Tax: The Case of Texas." *American Political Science Review* 38 (1944), 693–709.

Sullivan, Winnifred F. *Prison Religion: Faith-Based Reform and the Constitution.* Princeton: Princeton University Press, 2009.

Sutton, William Seneca. "The Significance of Christian Education in the Twentieth Century." *University of Texas Record* 9 (1909), 263–76.

Swartz, Mimi. "Kirbyjon Caldwell." *Texas Monthly* (September 1996), 1–8.

Tallbert, Robert Harris. *Cowtown-Metropolis: Case Study of a City's Growth and Structure.* Fort Worth: Leo Potishman Foundation, Texas Christian University, Texas Christian University Special Collections, 1956.

Templin, E. H., and J. A. Kerr. *Soil Survey of Midland County, Texas.* Washington, DC: U.S. Department of Agriculture, Bureau of Chemistry and Soils, 1933.

Tennyson, Alfred Lord. *Poems.* Boston: W. D. Ticknor, 1842.

Texas Constitutional Convention. *Journal of the Constitutional Convention of the State of Texas.* Galveston, TX: News Office, 1875.

Thompson, E. P. *The Making of the English Working Class.* New York: Knopf, 1963.

Thrall, Homer S. "The Baptists of Texas and Other Religious Faiths." In *The People's Illustrated Almanac: Texas Hand-Book and Immigrant's Guide for 1880,* 79–82. St. Louis, MO: N. D. Thompson, 1880).

———. "Education in Texas." *Texas Almanac for 1870 and Emigrant's Guide to Texas* (1870), 83–87.

———. *History of Methodism in Texas.* Houston: E. H. Cushing, 1872.

———. "Yellow Fever Epidemics." P. 201 in *The People's Illustrated Almanac: Texas Hand-Book and Immigrant's Guide for 1880*. St. Louis, MO: N.D. Thompson, 1880.

Thumma, Scott, and Dave Travis. *Beyond Megachurch Myths: What We Can Learn from America's Largest Churches*. San Francisco: Jossey-Bass, 2007.

Tileston, Mary Wilder. *Hymns of Comfort*. Boston: Roberts Brothers, 1877.

Tilly, Charles. *Durable Inequality*. Berkeley: University of California Press, 1998.

Tocqueville, Alexis de. *Democracy in America*, edited by J. P. Mayer. New York: Harper & Row, 1966, originally published in 1838.

Tolnay, Stewart, and E. M. Beck. *A Festival of Violence: An Analysis of Southern Lynchings, 1882–1930*. Urbana: University of Illinois Press, 1995.

Tolnay, Stewart E., Glenn Deane, and E. M. Beck. "Vicarious Violence: Spatial Effects on Southern Lynchings, 1890–1919." *American Journal of Sociology* 102 (1996), 788–815.

Trevino, Roberto R. "Facing Jim Crow: Catholic Sisters and the 'Mexican Problem' in Texas." *Western Historical Quarterly* 34 (2003), 139–64.

Truesdell, Leon Edgar, and Timothy Francis Murphy. *Religious Bodies, 1926*. Washington, DC: Government Printing Office, 1929.

Trumbull, Charles G. *The Life Story of C. I. Scofield*. New York: Oxford University Press, 1920.

Turner, Helen Lee. "Fundamentalism in the Southern Baptist Convention: The Crystalliza-tion of a Millennialist Vision." PhD diss., University of Virginia, Charlottesville, 1990.

Tuttle, William M. Jr. *Race Riot: Chicago in the Red Summer of 1919*. Champaign: University of Illinois Press, 1970.

U.S. Bureau of Labor Statistics. *Handbook of Labor Statistics*. Washington, DC: Government Printing Office, 1936.

U.S. Bureau of the Census. *Mortality Statistics of the Seventh Census of the United States, 1850*. Washington, DC: A.O.P. Nicholson, 1855.

———. *Religious Bodies, 1916: Part I: Summary and General Tables*. Washington, DC: Govern-ment Printing Office, 1919.

———. *Religious Bodies, 1936*, vol. 1. Washington, DC: Government Printing Office, 1936.

———. *Religious Bodies, 1936*, vol. 2. Washington, DC: Government Printing Office, 1941.

———. *Statistical Abstract of the United States*. Washington, DC: Government Printing Office, 1931.

———. *Statistical Abstract of the United States*. Washington, DC: Government Printing Office, 1940.

———. *Statistical Abstract of the United States*. Washington, DC: Government Printing Office, 1952.

———. *Statistical Abstract of the United States*. Washington, DC: Government Printing Office, 1955.

———. *Statistical Abstract of the United States*. Washington, DC: Government Printing Office, 1961.

———. *Statistical Abstract of the United States*. Washington, DC: Government Printing Office, 1962.

———. *Statistical Abstract of the United States*. Washington, DC: Government Printing Office, 1966.

U.S. Bureau of the Census. *Statistical Abstract of the United States.* Washington, DC: Government Printing Office, 1970.

———. *Statistical Abstract of the United States.* Washington, DC: Government Printing Office, 1971.

———. *Statistical Abstract of the United States.* Washington, DC: Government Printing Office, 1972.

———. *Statistical Abstract of the United States.* Washington, DC: Government Printing Office, 2012.

U. S. Department of Agriculture. *Study of Consumer Purchases in the United States, 1935–36.* Ann Arbor, MI: Inter-University Consortium for Political and Social Research, 1999.

U.S. Department of Justice, Federal Bureau of Investigation. *Uniform Crime Reports for the United States.* Washington, DC: Government Printing Office, 1959, 1963.

U.S. House of Representatives. *The Ku Klux Klan: Hearings before the Committee on Rules.* Washington, DC: Government Printing Office, 1921.

Vaisey, Stephen, and Omar Lizardo. "Can Cultural Worldviews Influence Network Composition?" *Social Forces* 88 (2010), 1595–1618.

Villanueva, Chandra Kring. "Updated: Who Pays Texas Taxes?" *Center for Public Policy Priorities Policy Page,* March 24, 2011.

Vinson, Robert E. "Academic Freedom and Social Responsibility." In *Educational Problems in College and University,* edited by John Lewis Brumm, 93–102. Ann Arbor: University of Michigan, 1921.

———. "The Place of the Church in Education." *Union Seminary Review* 25 (1914), 178–92.

———. "The University Crosses the Bar." *Southwestern Historical Quarterly* 43 (1940), 281–94.

Voogd, Jan. *Race Riots and Resistance: The Red Summer of 1919.* New York: Peter Lang, 2008.

Wade, Norma Adams. "Civil Rivalry in Dallas." *Black Enterprise* (April 1979), 19–20.

Waldrep, B. Dwain. "Lewis Sperry Chafer and the Development of Interdenominational Fundamentalism in the South, 1900–1950." PhD diss., Auburn University, 2001.

Waldrep, Christopher. *African Americans Confront Lynching: Strategies of Resistance from the Civil War to the Civil Rights Era.* Lanham, MD: Rowman & Littlefield, 2009.

Wallace, Alfred Russel. *Social Environment and Moral Progress.* New York: Cassell, 1913.

Waller, Virginia R. "Girl in the Middle," in *Texas Millennium Book: The Way Things Used to Be,* edited by Jerry B. Lincecum and Peggy A. Redshaw, 141–45. Sherman, TX: Austin College, 1999.

War Department, Surgeon General's Office. *Report on Epidemic Cholera and Yellow Fever in the Army of the United States during the Year 1867.* Washington, DC: Government Printing Office, 1868.

Warner, R. Stephen. *A Church of Our Own: Disestablishment and Diversity in American Religion.* New Brunswick, NJ: Rutgers University Press, 2005.

Warren, William Fairfield. *Paradise Found: The Cradle of the Human Race at the North Pole.* Boston: Mifflin, 1885.

Wasem, Ruth Ellen. *Unauthorized Aliens Residing in the United States: Estimates since 1986.* Washington, DC: Congressional Research Service, 2011.

Waters, Andrew. *I was Born in Slavery: Personal Accounts of Slavery in Texas*. Winston-Salem, NC: John F. Blair, 2003.

Watson, Larry Jerome. "Evangelical Protestants and the Prohibition Movement in Texas, 1887–1919." PhD diss., Texas A&M University, 1993.

Weatherford, W. D. "How to Enlist the Welfare Agencies of the South for Improvement of Conditions among the Negroes." In *The Human Way: Addresses on Race Problems at the Southern Sociological Congress*, edited by James E. McCulloch, 8–18. Nashville, TN: Southern Sociological Congress, 1913.

Weber, Max. *Economy and Society: An Outline of Interpretive Sociology*, edited by Guenther Roth and Claus Wittich. Berkeley: University of California Press, 1978.

———. *The Sociology of Religion*, translated by Ephraim Fischoff. Boston: Beacon Press, 1963.

Weddington, Sarah. *A Question of Choice*. New York: Penguin, 1993.

Weiner, Hollace Ava. *Jewish Stars in Texas: Rabbis and Their Work*. College Station: Texas A&M University Press, 1999.

Wheelock, E. M. *Reports of Cases Argued and Decided in the Supreme Court of the State of Texas*, vol. 33. Austin: Tracy, Siemering, 1872.

Whisenhunt, Donald W. "The Bard in the Depression: Texas Style." *Journal of Popular Culture* 2 (1968), 370–86.

White, F. Clifton. *Suite 3505: The Story of the Draft Goldwater Movement*. Ashland, OH: Ashbrook Press, 1992.

White, Walter. *Rope and Faggot: A Biography of Judge Lynch*. Notre Dame, IN: University of Notre Dame Press, 2002.

Wilcox, Clyde, and Carin Robinson. *Onward Christian Soldiers? The Religious Right in American Politics*. Boulder, CO: Westview Press, 2011.

Wilensky-Lanford, Brook. *Paradise Lust: Searching for the Garden of Eden*. New York: Grove Press, 2011.

Wilkison, Kyle G. *Yeomen, Sharecroppers, and Socialists: Plain Folk Protest in Texas, 1870–1914*. College Station: Texas A&M University Press, 2008.

Williams, Daniel K. *God's Own Party: The Making of the Christian Right*. New York: Oxford University Press, 2010.

Williams, Frank B., Jr. "The Poll Tax as a Suffrage Requirement in the South, 1870–1901." *Journal of Southern History* 18 (1952), 469–96.

Williams, Franklin C. Jr. *Lone Star Bishops: The Roman Catholic Hierarchy in Texas*. Waco, TX: Texian Press, 1997.

Williams, Patrick G. "Of Rutabagas and Redeemers: Rethinking the Texas Constitution of 1876." *Southwestern Historical Quarterly* 106 (2002), 230–53.

Williams, Robert H. *With the Border Ruffians: Memories of the Far West, 1852–1868*, edited by E. W. Williams. London: John Murray, 1907.

Wilson, Edward O. *On Human Nature*. Cambridge, MA: Harvard University Press, 2004.

Wimmer, Andreas. "Elementary Strategies of Ethnic Boundary Making." *Ethnic and Racial Studies* 31 (2008), 1025–55.

———. "The Making and Unmaking of Ethnic Boundaries: A Multi-Level Process Theory." *American Journal of Sociology* 113 (2008), 970–1022.

Wimmer, Andreas, and Kevin Lewis. "Beyond and Below Racial Homophily: ERG Models of a Friendship Network Documented on Facebook." *American Journal of Sociology* 116 (2010), 583–642.

Winship, George Parker. *The Journey of Coronado, 1540–1542, from the City of Mexico to the Grand Canon of the Colorado and the Buffalo Plains of Texas, Kansas, and Nebraska.* New York: A. S. Barnes, 1904.

Winskill, P. T. *The Temperance Movement and Its Workers: A Record of Social, Moral, Religious, and Political Progress,* vol. 3. London: Blackie & Son, 1892.

Winston, George T. "The Education of Women in the University of Texas." *University of Texas Record* 1 (1898), 1–10.

Winter, Gibson. *The Suburban Captivity of the Churches: An Analysis of Protestant Responsibility in the Expanding Metropolis.* Garden City, NY: Doubleday, 1961.

Winters, John D. *The Civil War in Louisiana.* Baton Rouge: Louisiana State University Press, 1963.

Wintz, Cary D. "The Emergence of a Black Neighborhood: Houston's Fourth Ward, 1865–1915." In *Urban Texas: Politics and Development,* edited by Char Miller and Heywood T. Sanders, 97–100. College Station: Texas A&M University Press, 1990.

Wolfe, Alan. *One Nation, After All: What Americans Really Think about God, Country, Family, Racism, Welfare, Immigration, Homosexuality, Work, the Right, the Left and Each Other.* New York: Viking, 1998.

Wood, Presnall H. "History of the Texas *Baptist Standard,* 1888–1959." PhD diss., Southwestern Baptist Theological Seminary, 1964.

Woodson, C. G. "Negro Life and History in Our Schools." *Journal of Negro History* 4 (1919), 273–80.

Writers' Program of the Work Projects Administration in the City of Dallas. *The WPA Dallas Guide and History.* Dallas: Dallas Public Library and the University of North Texas Press, 1992.

Wuthnow, Robert. *Acts of Compassion: Caring for Others and Helping Ourselves.* Princeton, NJ: Princeton University Press, 1991.

———. *America and the Challenges of Religious Diversity.* Princeton, NJ: Princeton University Press, 2005.

———. "Arts Leaders and Religious Leaders: Mutual Perceptions." In *Crossroads: Art and Religion in American Life,* edited by Alberta Arthurs and Glenn Wallach, 31–70. New York: New Press, 2001.

———. *Boundless Faith: The Global Outreach of American Churches.* Berkeley: University of California Press, 2009.

———. "Cognition and Religion." *Sociology of Religion* 68 (2007), 341–60.

———. *Communities of Discourse: Ideology and Social Structure in the Reformation, the Enlightenment, and European Socialism.* Cambridge, MA: Harvard University Press, 1989.

———. *Creative Spirituality: The Way of the Artist.* Berkeley: University of California Press, 2001.

———. *Red State Religion: Faith and Politics in America's Heartland.* Princeton, NJ: Princeton University Press, 2012.

——. "Religion." In *Understanding America: The Anatomy of an Exceptional Nation*, edited by Peter H. Schuck and James Q. Wilson, 275–308. New York: Public Affairs, 2008.

——. *The Restructuring of American Religion: Society and Faith since World War II.* Princeton: Princeton University Press, 1988.

——. "Restructuring of American Religion: Further Evidence." *Sociological Inquiry* 66 (1996), 303–29.

——. *Saving America? Faith-Based Services and the Future of Civil Society.* Princeton, NJ: Princeton University Press, 2004.

——. *Sharing the Journey: Support Groups and America's New Quest for Community.* New York: Free Press, 1994.

——. *The Struggle for America's Soul: Evangelicals, Liberals, and Secularism.* Grand Rapids, MI: Eerdmans, 1989.

——. "Teach Us to Pray: The Cognitive Power of Domain Violations." *Poetics* 36 (2008), 493–506.

Wuthnow, Robert, and Virginia A. Hodgkinson, eds. *Faith and Philanthropy in America: Exploring the Role of Religion in America's Voluntary Sector.* San Francisco: Jossey-Bass, 1990.

Wyant, William K. *Westward in Eden: The Public Lands and the Conservation Movement.* Berkeley: University of California Press, 1987.

Zald, Mayer N., and John D. McCarthy. "Religious Groups as Crucibles of Social Movements." In *Sacred Companies: Organizational Aspects of Religion and Religious Aspects of Organizations*, edited by N. J. Demerath III, Peter Dobkin Hall, Terry Schmitt, and Rhys H. Williams, 24–49. New York: Oxford University Press, 1998.

Zaret, David. *The Heavenly Contract: Ideology and Organization in Pre-Revolutionary Puritanism.* Chicago: University of Chicago Press, 1985.

NEWS SOURCES

Abilene Daily Reporter
Afro American (Baltimore)
Amarillo Globe Times
Appleton's Journal of Literature, Science and Art
Assist News Service
Associated Press
Atkinson's Saturday Evening Post
Atlanta Constitution (GA)
Atlanta Daily World
Augusta Chronicle (GA)
Austin City Gazette
Austin Republican
Avalanche Journal (Lubbock)
Baltimore Sun

Baptist Standard

Bay State Banner

Beaumont Journal

Big Spring Daily Herald

Boston Daily Globe

Boston Evening Transcript

Boston Globe

Brazosport Facts

Brenham Banner

Broad Axe (Chicago)

Brookshire Times

Brownsville Herald

Brownwood Bulletin

Capital Plaindealer (Topeka)

Chicago Daily Tribune

Chicago Defender

Chicago Tribune

Christian Advocate

Christian Index

Christian Observer

Christian Science Monitor

Cincinnati Journal

Civilian and Galveston Gazette

Clarksville Standard

Clerburne Morning Review

Columbus Enquirer (GA)

Corpus Christi Caller-Times

Corsicana Daily Sun

Daily Alta California (San Francisco)

Daily Citizen and News (Lowell, MA)

Daily Enterprise (Beaumont)

Daily Inter Ocean (Chicago)

Daily National Intelligencer (Washington, DC)

Daily Picayune (New Orleans)

Dallas Herald

Dallas Morning News

Dallas Observer

Dallas Weekly Herald

Del Rio News Herald

Democratic Telegraph and Texas Register (Houston)

Denton Record Chronicle

Eclectic Review

El Heraldo de Brownsville

El Paso Herald Post
El Paso Times
Fincastle Mirror (VA)
Flake's Bulletin (Galveston)
Fort Worth Morning Register
Fort Worth Star Telegram
Galveston Daily News
Galveston Tri-Weekly News
Galveston Weekly News
Grand Prairie Texas
Houston Chronicle
Houston Daily Union
Houston Press
Houston Telegraph
Houston Times
Houston Transcript
Houston Union
Indianapolis Journal
Irish Times
Kalamazoo Gazette (MI)
Kerrville Daily Times
Kerrville Mountain Sun
La Marque Times
La Prensa (San Antonio)
Life
Literary Digest
Littell's Living Age
Lockhart Post Register
Los Angeles Times
Lubbock Evening Journal
Lubbock Morning Avalanche
Manchester Guardian
Mexia Weekly Herald
Middletown Constitution (CT)
Mississippi Free Trader (Natchez)
Montgomery Advertiser (AL)
Morning Oregonian (Portland)
National Catholic Register
Negro Star (Wichita)
New Braunfels Herald Zeitung
New Hampshire Gazette (Portsmouth)
New Orleans Picayune
New York Amsterdam News

New York Daily Times
New York Daily Tribune
New York Herald
New York Observer and Chronicle
New York Spectator
New York Times
New York Weekly Herald
Orange Leader
Oregonian (Portland)
Pall Mall Gazette (London)
Pampa Daily News
Paris News
Philadelphia Inquirer
Philadelphia Tribune
Pittsburgh Courier
Plain Dealer (Cleveland)
Plaindealer (Kansas City, KS)
Pomeroy's Democrat (Chicago)
Port Arthur News
Putnam's Monthly
Red Lander (San Augustine)
Rio Grande Valley Monitor
San Antonio Express
San Antonio Light
Saturday Evening Post
Savannah Tribune
Seattle Times
Seguin Gazette Enterprise
Semi-Weekly Telegraph (Salt Lake City)
Southern Baptist Texan
Springfield Republican (MA)
St. Louis Post Dispatch
St. Louis Republic
Telegraph and Texas Register (Austin)
Texas Almanac
Texas City Sun
Texas Monthly
Texas Observer
Texas Presbyterian
Texas State Gazette (Austin)
Texas Tribune
Texas Union (San Augustine)
Time

Times Picayune (New Orleans)
Trenton Sunday Times (NJ)
Tri-Weekly Republican (Austin)
University of Texas Record
USA Today
Valley Morning Star (Harlingen)
Victoria Advocate
Waco Advance
Waco News Tribune
Waco Times Herald
Waco Tribune Herald
Wall Street Journal
Washington Post
Weatherford Democrat
Wellington Leader
West Texas Catholic
Western Christian Advocate
Wichita Times (KS)
Wooster Republican (OH)
Wyandotte Echo (Kansas City, KS)

COLLECTIONS

Allen County Public Library, Fort Wayne, IN
Association of Religion Data Archives, Pennsylvania State University
Baylor University Institute for Oral History, Baylor University, Waco, TX
Billy Graham Evangelistic Association, Charlotte, NC
Cushing Memorial Library and Archives, Texas A&M University
Dallas Historical Society, Dallas, TX
Dallas Public Library, Dallas, TX
Deaf Smith County Historical Society, Hereford, TX
Dickens County Historical Society, Hereford, TX
Drew Pearson Archive, American University, Washington, DC
Eugene C. Barker Texas History Center, University of Texas at Austin
Harry S. Truman Library and Museum, Independence, MO
Hutchinson County Historical Commission, Borger, TX
Institute of Texas Cultures, University of Texas at San Antonio
Inter-University Consortium for Political and Social Research, University of Michigan,
    Ann Arbor
John F. Kennedy Presidential Library and Museum, Boston, MA

Kansas Memory Collection, Kansas State Historical Society, Topeka
LeTourneau University Archive, Longview, TX
Lyndon Baines Johnson Presidential Library and Museum, Austin, TX
Manitowoc County Historical Society, Manitowoc, WI
Mississippi Department of Archives and History, Jackson
Portal to Texas History, University of North Texas Libraries, Denton
Roper Center for Public Opinion Research, Storrs, CT
Sanborn Maps Collection, Firestone Library, Princeton University, Princeton, NJ
Southern Baptist Historical Library and Archive, Nashville, TN
Southern Oral History Program, University of North Carolina at Chapel Hill
Southwest Voter Research Institute, San Antonio, TX
Texas Department of State Health Services, Austin
Texas Historical Commission, Austin
Texas State Library and Archives Commission, Austin
University of Florida Digital Collections, University of Florida at Gainesville
University of Southern Mississippi Libraries, Hattiesburg
W. A. Criswell Sermon Library, Dallas, TX
Wisconsin Veterans Museum, Madison

ELECTRONIC DATA

ABC News/Washington Post Exit Poll, 1986
American Community Surveys, 2006 to 2010
American Political Network and Hotline Poll, 1988
Americans View Their Mental Health, 1957
Annual Church Profile for Southern Baptist Convention Churches, 1980
Anti-Semitism in the United States, 1964
Cambridge Reports Research International Survey, 1980
CBS News Election Day Surveys, 1980, 1984, 1986, 1988
CBS News Monthly Poll, 2010
Churches and Church Membership, 1952, 1972, 1980, 1990, 2000, 2010
Cooperative Congressional Election Surveys, 2006, 2008, 2010
Electoral Data for Counties in the United States, 1840–1990
Gallup Polls, 1937–1988
General Social Surveys, 1972–2010
Harris Surveys, 1968, 1988
Historical American Lynching Data, 1880–1930
Houston Area Surveys, 1982–2010
Latino National Survey, 2006
Mortality in the South, 1850

National Election Pool General Election Exit Polls, 2000, 2004, 2006

National Election Surveys, 1944–2006

Pew Research Center Campaign 2000 Typology Survey

Pew Research Center Religion and Public Life Survey, 2002

Religion and Politics Survey, 2000

Southern Primary and General Election Data, 1944–1972

State Legislative Returns in the United States, 1968–1993

Study of Consumer Purchases in the United States, 1935–36

Survey of Texas Adults, 2004

System for Catholic Research, Information, and Planning, 1940–1990

Texas Elections, Office of the Secretary of State, Texas

Texas Lyceum Polls, 2007, 2010

Texas Poll, 1954, 1960, 1968

Texas Tribune Survey, 2010

Time/Yankelovich Survey, 1980

Voter News Service General Election Exit Polls, 1994, 2000

Voter Research and Surveys National Election Day Exit Poll, 1990, 1992

U.S. Census, Decennial Censuses, County Data, 1850–2010

U.S. Census, Decennial Censuses, Incorporated Places, 1970–2010

U.S. Census, Public Use Micro Samples, 1960–2000

U.S. Census, Religious Bodies, 1870, 1890, 1906, 1916, 1926, 1936

U.S. Department of Agriculture County-Level Data, 1970–1940

U.S. Presidential Primary Elections, 1968–1996

INDEX

Note: Illustrations are indicated with italic page numbers.

700 Club (television program), 326

Abernathy, Ralph, 303–4, 305, 307–9, 314
Abilene: churches in, 150, 236; colleges and universities in, 73; fundamentalism in, 140, 150; gay rights issues in, 422; radio ministry in, 329; school boycott in, 312–13; segregation in, 257–58
Abilene Christian University, 73
abolition movement, 61
abortion, 1, 11, 21, 370; and African Americans, 413, 418–19; counseling requirements, 318–19, 361; federal funding for, 361; Hispanic Americans and, 386–87, 406, 413; income and rates of, 413; legalization, proposed legislation in Texas, 356–59; legislative restriction in Texas, 413–14; media reports on issue, 361; and mobilization of clergy, 322; parental consent requirements, 318; party affiliation and attitude toward, 361, 369, 386–87, 406, 407; as political campaign issue, 361, 378, 381, 385–87, 406, 407, 416; political scandals and, 356; religious affiliation and opinion on, 361; *Roe v. Wade* decision, 270, 356, 359–60, 384, 412, 414, 415; Roman Catholic Church and opposition to, 357–59, 361, 386, 418; sexual revolution and, 356–58; violence against abortion providers, 416; *Webster v. Reproductive Health Services,* 412
Adair, A. Garland, 144
advertising, political, 391; racial "code" in, 378; Willie Horton ads, 379, 572n25

African American Baptist churches, 43–44, 81, 230, 392–93; institution building, 168; membership and congregation statistics, 167–68; resources of, 168–70
African American churches: clergy and civil rights activism, 303–4; and faith-based programs, 400–402; during Great Depression, 202; institution building by, 168–69; membership and congregation statistics, 81, 167–68, 503n98; resources of, 168, 202, 392–93. *See also specific churches*
African American Methodist Church, 64, 80, 348
African Americans: abortion and, 413, 418–19; "Black Power" movement, 11, 303, 305, 315–16, 322, 463, 473; cooperation with Hispanic Americans, 314; and Democratic party, 322; farming and agricultural labor, 19, 206; and federal relief programs, 220; higher education and, 73; income statistics, 220, 227; Ku Klux Klan and attacks on, 174; literacy rates among, 179; population demographics, 252–53; relief programs and, 197–98; religion and (*see* African American churches); and vote suppression, 156, 161, 177–82, 269, 380; as voting constituency, 60–61, 161, 180, 322, 376–77, 386–87, 390, 403, 407; welfare programs and, 376. *See also* civil rights movement
African Methodist Episcopal Church, 46, 80, 167–68, 232, 248, 348
African Methodist Episcopal Zion Church, 167, 232

agriculture: Agricultural Adjustment Act, 205–6; agricultural subsidies, 205–6; cotton production, 16–17, 19, 27–28, 152, 157, 158, 161, *169,* 200, 216; drouth and, 10, 19, 152, 199–200, 209, 216; as economic and employment sector, 204–7, 227; during Great Depression, 10, 198–200, 204; mechanization of, 204–5; New Deal programs for, 205–6, 216–17; settlement and agricultural productivity, 18–19; sharecropping, 10, 17, 48, *72,* 152, 156, 206–7; slavery and, 8, 19, 161; tenant farming, 204–7

Ainsworth, William N., 176–77

the Alamo, 91–93, 112, 157, 462

alcohol. *See* prohibition

Alexander, Holmes, 421

alienation, 451

Allen, Asa A., 237

Allen, Jimmy, 201

Almonte, Juan, 27

Amarillo, 202, 426

Amazing Grace (Campbell and Putnam), 479

Ambassador College, 329, 332, 333

American Evangelicalism: Embattled and Thriving (Smith), 476–77

American Family Association (AFA), 438

Americanism, 173–76, 223, 336

Americans United, 262–63

Ames, Jessie Daniel, 186–92, *187,* 285

Ames, Roger Post, 186

Ammerman, Nancy Tatom, 343, 344–45, 349

Anderson, Earl, 150, 151, 192, 222, 257–58, 286

Anderson, John, 362

Anderson, Texas, 66

Anderson, William M., Jr., 150

Andrew Female College, 51–53

Angels in America (play, Kushner), 423, 581n47

annexation of Texas, 16, 27, 157

Ansley, Henry, 210–11

anti-Catholicism, 10, 117, 120, 176; Americanism and, 223; Baptists and, 115–16, 218, 260–66, 419; Ku Klux Klan and, 156, 176; and prohibition as political issue, 115–16

anti-government ideology: and fear of creeping socialism, 103, 216, 218, 339–40, 351, 389, 435, 438; federal government, 57, 432; and New Deal, 255; and opposition to ERA, 352; and perceived threat to conservative religion and values, 341, 378, 437–38; Reagan and, 12; Reconstruction and, 60, 197; regulations and, 103, 237, 330, 335–37; and separation of church and state, 218; states' rights and, 40, 55, 57, 194–95, 250, 286, 352, 363, 365, 432; Tea Party movement and, 435–38. *See also* "big government"

anti-intellectualism, 131

Antioch Missionary Baptist Church, 44

Anti-Saloon League, 107

anti-Semitism, 95, 190; and evangelism, 321; Ku Klux Klan and, 96

Archer, Glen L., 262

Armey, Dick, 278, 439–40

Armstrong, Garner Ted, 329

Armstrong, Herbert W., 329, 333

Assemblies of God, 207, 247, 321, 338, 475; membership and congregation statistics, 230, 477, 569n108

atheism, 96, 288

attendance, patterns of church, 36, 82–83, 249, 281, 423, 460; declines in, 280–81

Atwater, Lee, 378, 383

Auburn, Texas, 66

Austin: African Americans in, 220; antiwar movement in, 316; evolution debate in, 133; fundamentalism in, 144–45; gay rights in, 423; institution building in, 73; race relations in, 261; size of church congregations in, 65–66; Tea Party Activism in, 216

Austin, Stephen F., 29, 112

Ayer, William Ward, 238

Bacon, Sumner, 36

Bailey, Joseph W., 106, 178

Bakker, Jim and Tammy, 384

Baldassarri, Delia, 479

baptism, doctrinal controversies regarding, 115–16, 127–28, 234–35

Baptist churches. *See* African American Baptist churches; Northern Baptists; Southern Baptist Churches

Baptist General Convention of Texas, 63, 170

Baptist Missionary and Educational Convention of Texas, 167

Baptists for Life, 360, 419

Baptist Standard (newspaper), 114, 128, 130, 170, 234, 240, 261, 266, 267, 336

Baptist World Alliance, 154, 191, 221, 223, 231

Barkley, Allen W., 117

Barr family (Alexander, Amelia, Calvin, Lily, Mary, Robert), 17, 22

Barton, Arthur J., 110, 184
Bass, Perry, 12, 296
Bauch, Erich, 309–10
Bauer, Gary, 439
Baxter, W. R., 255
Baylor, R.E.B., 93–94
Baylor Female College, 73
Baylor Hospital, 507n41
Baylor University, 73, 99, 384; and evolution in
    the curriculum, 130, 138, 142–43; honorary
    degree award to Truman, 250, 328; intel-
    lectual freedom and biblical literalism con-
    troversies, 130, 134–35, 142–43, 196, 344,
    384; medical and dental schools, 158, 196;
    resources of, 234, 245, 296, 315; theological
    seminary at, 134–35
Baylor University, Medical and Dental Schools,
    Dallas, 158, 196
Behnken, Brian D., 310
Bell, B. Clayton, 342
Bellah, Robert N., 90
Bells, Texas, 264–65
Belton, 66, 131, 174
Bender, Courtney, 455
benevolent institutions, 87; criticisms of social
    welfare, 102–3; Great Depression and, 196;
    progressive era and support of, 102; and
    racial barriers, 87; resources of, 393. See also
    hospitals and medical centers
benevolent organizations, 198; churches and
    founding of, 74; racial segregation and, 468;
    statistics regarding, 75
Bennett, John C., 277
Bentsen, Lloyd, 313, 362, 374, 381
Bernice, Eddie, 350
Berrellez, Robert, 312
Beveridge, Albert, 106
Bible Belt, 5; Texas as part of, 8, 121, 123, 225
Bible Institutes, 149, 152, 320–21, 338, 343
Bible societies and Bible distribution, 35–36,
    100
biblical literalism, 136, 138–44, 152, 196, 343–
    46, 384, 440, 481
"big government," 365, 405–6; G. W. Bush and,
    195; as campaign issue, 12, 363, 373, 384,
    443; conservatism and opposition to, 383–
    84; Criswell and, 339–41; New Deal and,
    197; and opposition to ERA, 352; Reagan
    and, 363, 373, 384; Republican opposition
    to, 339–40, 395; as socialist, 339–40; Tea
    Party movement as reaction to, 435–40

Billy Graham Evangelistic Association, 240–
    41, 482
birth control, 223–24, 284, 360, 390, 415–16,
    418, 442–43; employer insurance mandate
    and, 443. See also abortion
Bishop, Charles M., 185
Black, Claude William, Jr., 315–16
Blow, Steve, 325
Blue Laws, 101–2, 106, 108
Blume, Louis J., 267
Bob Jones University, 239–40
bombings: abortion clinic as target, 416; and
    escalation of Vietnam War, 316–17; racially
    motivated, 220, 253
Booth, Maud Ballington, 102
boundaries. See symbolic boundaries
Boutler, Beau, 385
Bowie, Jim, 36, 90
boycotts: farmworkers and, 310, 315; labor
    activism and, 305–7, 310, 312; of Martin Lu-
    ther King, Jr., 307; student, 299–300, 312–13
Boy Scouts, 424
Bracamontes, Ramon, 431
Branch Davidian siege, 400
Braniff, Tom, 267
Brannon, Clifton, 243
Bravo, Felipe and Pablo, 427
Brenham, R. F., 91
bridging organizations, 2
Bright, Bill, 552n61
Brinkley, J. R., 237
broadcasting, religious, 5; AM *vs.* FM radio,
    237; and conservative political content, 287–
    88; early programs and stations in Texas,
    237; *Family Altar* (radio program), 328; FCC
    regulation of, 237, 330, 335–37; financial
    resources and, 237, 321, 330; homosexuality
    attacked via, 335–36; *Life Line* (radio pro-
    gram), 287–88, 330; Mexico as base for, 237;
    and national power and influence, 466–67;
    National Religious Broadcasters Associa-
    tion formed, 238; Norris's radio ministry,
    237, 257, 328–29; *Old-Fashioned Revival
    Hour* (radio program), 237, 330; and politi-
    cal mobilization, 326; Religious Right and
    Roloff's radio ministry, 328–33; Southern
    Baptist Convention and, 241–42; television
    ministries, 242, 326
Broden, Stephen, 418–19, 438–39
Brookes, James H., 147
Brooks, Samuel P., 143, 185

Brotherhood Week, 267

Brown, Charles, 303–4

Brown v. Board of Education of Topeka, 223, 254, 256, 261

Bryan, Phillip, 299

Bryan, William Jennings, 110–12, 117, 136, 152, 179

Bryant, Anita, 335, 337

Bryant, Baxton, 263, 265, 266–68, 298–99, 302, 331, 465

Buchanan, Pat, 370, 371

Buckner, Robert Cooke, 101, 126–28, 168, 393

Buckner Foundation, 393

Buckner Orphans' Home (Dallas), 101, *101,* 393

Buddhism, 396

Burma, John Harmon, 181

Burroughs, Nannie H., 206

Burton, Mae Burton, 198

Bush, George H. W., 11, 12, 270, 294, 295, 296–97, 313, 322, 338, 369, 567n103; as moderate Republican, 363; and Points of Light initiative, 373–74; race as campaign issue, 379; Reagan and, 338, 362–65; and religion as political issue, 262–63; religious idiom and, 399–400

Bush, George W., 11, 12, 324, 369; and faith-based programs, 391–96; as governor of Texas, 324, 372, 390; policies of, 372; religious constituencies and, 391, 396–97

Butt, Howard E., Jr., 240–41

Cabell, Earle, 308

Cahana, Moshe, 317

Caldwell, Gail, 323–24

Caldwell, Kirbyjon, 395, 400

Caldwell, William, 137

Callaway, Sara Isadore Sutherland, 502n91

Camacho, Alex, 429

campaign finances, 390

campaign issues: abortion, 361, 378, 381, 385, 386–87, 406, 407, 416; and appeal to religious conservatives, 144, 272–77, 325–26, 367–69, 377–79, 406; "big government," 12, 339, 352, 363, 373, 384, 443; birth control, 223; civil rights, 250–52, 270; crime, 379, 390–91, 394–95, 572n25; economic development, 380; education, 390, 391; Equal Rights Amendment, 346–47, 352–56; evolution, 144; fiscal conservatism, 12, 377, 382,

390–92, 391–92, 397, 407, 435–36, 585n94; healthcare reform, 218, 380, 389, 433, 435, 438–39, 443; immigration, 397, 429–32; "moral decay," 272–77; poverty, 308; racism and, 12, 119, 270, 278–79, 378–79, 572n25; religion of candidate, 90, 110–12, 114–15, 264–68; Vietnam War, 271, 288–89, 301, 304, 316, 322; welfare reform, 391–92

Campbell, David E., 479

Campbell, J., 496n137

Campbell. L. L., 170

Campbell, Will D., 298–99

Camp Logan riot, 187

camp meetings, 36, 38–39, 98, 492n93. *See also* revivals

Campus Crusade for Christ, 245, 320, 342, 482

Canyon, Texas, 285–86

Capers, William, 27

capitalism, 451

Capper, Arthur, 163

Carcano, Bishop Minerva, 430

Carlson, Frank, 244

Carmichael, Stokely, 308

Carmody, Edmond, 417

Carpenter, Liz, 352

Carr, Waggoner, 312

Carroll, B. H., 61, 127, 134–35, 138, 140

Carter, Jimmy, 270, 325–26, 337–38, 340–41, 363–64, 367, 398, 567n103; hostage crisis in Iran, 363; loss to Reagan, 326

cartoons: "Young Texas," 24

Casanova, José, 454

Cash, Johnny, 320, 334

cats, 18

censorship: book banning, 140–41, 286; of school textbooks, 122, 140–42, 151

Chacon, Alicia, 350

Chafer, Lewis Sperry, 150, 152

Chafetz, Janet Saltzman, 396

Chamberlain, Hiram, 36

"Charitable Choice," 391, 393, 402

charity. *See* benevolent institutions; relief

Chaves, Mark, 402

Chicano activism, 11, 310–15

Childers Classical Institute, 73

children: as civilizing force, 29–30; education as policing of, 58–59; mortality rates on the frontier, 20–21; religious values inculcated during childhood, 231

Chiles, Eddie, 336–37, 342, 365

Chinese Americans, 68, 190
Choice (short film), 278–79, 289
cholera, 20, 22
Christian Crusade Ministries, 287–88
Christian Endeavor Society, 102
Christian Scientists, 64, 222
church and state. *See* separation of church and state
church buildings: architecture of, 98–99, 155, 203, 247; construction of, 128, 236, 247–48; First Baptist Church of Dallas, *319*; as investments and assets, 64, 168, 202, 203, 216, 236; in Killeen, *81*; number of, 63–66, *64*, 81
Churches of Christ, 73
church membership: attendance rates, 25, 226, 280–81; and community acceptance, 66; community identity and, 66; fundamentalism and, 150; gender and, 80; moral improvement and, 67; number of churches and, 37–39; racial demographics, 168; rational choice theory and, 453, 470, 478; social benefits of, 66–67; social norms and, 78–79, 81–83; and volunteerism, 393. *See also under specific churches*
City Federations of Women's Clubs, Dallas, 102
civilization: civilizing missions of religion, 4–5; science and technical progress linked to, 55–56
civil religion, 90–97, 104, 157, 462
civil rights: activism (*see* Chicano activism; civil rights movement; Equal Rights Amendment); clergy and support of civil rights legislation, 248–49; Democratic Party and, 370; and liberty of conscience, 95; as moral issue, 289; as political issue, 270; sexual orientation and denial of, 420–24; voting rights, 32–33, 54, 60–61, 161, 181, 182, 186, 248
civil rights movement, 1, 5; "black power" movement and, 305; churches and participation in, 11, 303–4; cooperation between Hispanic and African Americans, 314; disagreements about strategies, 293–94, 305, 308–9, 314–16; political activism, 322; role of religion in, 303–4, 366
Civil War: Texas as member of the Confederacy, 7, 21, 40–41; Texas casualties during, 23. *See also* "lost cause" and southern identity

Clark, Addison, 73
Clark, Caesar, 73, 260, *307,* 307–8
Clark, James H., Jr., 358
Clark, Randolph, 358
class, social: racism and, 186; and social reform activism, 192–93 (*see also* income)
Clements, Bill, 332, 364–65, 367, 376, 378, 419
clergy: authority of, 3; avoidance of political engagement, 301–2, 446; desegregation and, 257; education and qualifications of, 100, 103, 403; endorsement of political candidates by, 115–20, 276–77, 308, 309, 339–41, 377–78; Great Depression and employment of, 201–2; heresy charges against, 134, 137, 144, 147, 342–43; and labor activism, 293; local responsibility of, 136; murder trials of, 208; as political candidates or office holders, 44–47, 296, 298; prohibition and political engagement of, 115–16; public roles of black clergy, 44; salaries of, 201–2; sexual orientation and, 422; social activism and, 61, 77, 193, 303–5; Tea Party movement, opinion of clergy on, 441–42; as Tea Party movement members, 440–41; as victims of violence, 36, 40, 46, 207. *See also specific individuals*
Cline, Joe, 423
Clinton, Bill, 12, 371, 389–90, 391, 399
clothing manufacturing, 216
coalition building, 304, 305–9, 317, 327
Cockrell, Lila, 350
Cold War, 244, 245, 257, 463
Cole, Anna Russell, 183
Coleman, James S., 477–78
Collins, Ernest, 162
Colquitt, Oscar Branch, 94
Colson, Charles "Chuck," 395, 439
Combs, Roberta, 431
Communism, 173–74, 181, 216, 249, 274, 286–89; anti-war activism equated with, 318; "big government" equated with, 339; Cold War, 244, 245, 257, 463; domino theory and threat of, 288, 318; Ku Klux Klan and anti-Bolshevism, 173–74, 181; McCarthyism, 122, 233, 237–38; Methodists accused of, 233; New Deal relief programs equated with, 218; racial integration and, 257–58; social reform linked to, 233
compassionate conservatism, 12, 373, 387–96, 400, 405, 407

Congregational Churches, 147; and antilynching activism, 183

congregations: cooperation between white and black, 167–68; enforcement of social norms by, 82–83; microlevel understanding of religion, 1–2

Conley, Jim, 422

Connally, John, 268, 288, 293, 294, 296, *307,* 308, 362

Connally, Tom, 163–64

conservatism, religious: political influence of, 226, 403; as symbolic boundary, 367–68. *See also* fundamentalism; Religious Right

Constitution of Texas, 15, 30, 48, 54, 57, 60

contraception. *See* birth control

convening power, 342

conversion, 95, 321, 397–98, 429, 576n87

Cooper, Oscar H., 71

Copeland, Kenneth, 404–5

Corpus Christi, 21, 237, 262, 284, 328–30, 436; anti-abortion activism in, 386, 414, 417–18; gay rights in, 423

Corpus Christi Caller-Times (newspaper), 280

Corsicana, Texas, 66, 78, 158, 162, 349–50

Costigan, Edward P., 163

Cotton, Leroy "Bud," 25

cotton industry, 16–17, 27–28, 152, 157, 158, 200, 216; mill, *98*; orphans harvesting, *169*; sharecroppers harvesting, *72*; slavery and, 8, 19, 161

Coy, Ed, 69–70

Crafts, Wilbur F., 184

Crane, Phil, 362

Cranfill, J. B., 61, 77, 96, 115–16, 141–42, 175, 499n38; as editor of *Baptist Standard,* 128, 138

Crawford, Thomas, 421

Crawford, William C., 93

creationism, 1, 426, 442. *See also* biblical literalism

crime: as campaign issue, 379, 390–91, 394–95; clergy as victims of violence, 36, 40, 46; faith-based programs and, 394–95; race and, 15; racial prejudice and, 176; rates, 280; during Reconstruction, 15, 16, 24–25, 41–44, 54; statistics, 281; as symptom of moral decay, 280, 282. *See also* lynching; murder

Criswell, W. A., 240, 242, 540n62; and anti-Catholicism, 266; anti-Communism and, 318; ERA and, 349; and FCC regulation of broadcast ministry, 336–37;

fundamentalism and, 344–46, 367, 482; homosexuality and, 370, 423; on humanism, 325; as opponent of "big government," 339–41; and opposition to desegregation, 258–60, 263–64, 302; political influence of, 339–42; Republican party affiliation and, 339–41, 362, 365; Robison and, 334; and sexual morality, 318, 320, 325, 423

Criswell College, 341, 343

Crockett, Davy, 90, 92, 96–97

The Cross and the Switchblade (Wilkerson), 330

Crowley, Dale, 238

Crowley, Mary, 341–42

Cruz, Ted, 443–44

Crystal City, 207, 310, 312–13

Culberson, Charles A., 136

Cullen, Hugh Roy, 245, 256

"culture wars," 271, 356, 370–73, 401, 440, 462–63

Cumberland Presbyterian Church, 35–36, 52, 111, 144, 167, 217; institutions founded by, 73, 75; membership and congregation statistics, 63, 64

Cunningham, Minnie Fisher, 84, 187, 199

Dallas, 10; abortion debate in, 356, 358–60, 385, 415, 418; anti-Communism in, 288; antiwar activism in, 315–17; broadcasting in, 242, 328–30; church construction in, 64, 236, 247; civil rights activism in, 298–99, 303–9, 314, 317; crime as concern in, 281; ERA debate in, 350–52; evolution debate in, 132–36, 140; First Baptist Church in, 126, *319,* 339, 367, 404; fundamentalism in, 123, 125, 137, 140, 151, 284–85; during Great Depression, 198–201, 212–15; growth and economic development in, 5, 99, 155, 157–58, 200–201, 216, 220, 227, 236, 247–48, 468; homosexuality or gay rights issues in, 335–37, 422–23, 581n47; institution building in, 28, 73, 101–2, 144, 149–50, 151, 158, 211–12, 247, 315; Kennedy assassination in, 225, 267; Ku Klux Klan in, 174–76; lynchings in, 68–69, 163, 170, 174, 186; megachurches in, 5; MegaMarch Immigration Rally in, 430, *431*; prohibition in, 104, 108, 117; race relations in, 220; racial demographics in, 113, 159, 252–53, 290, 340, 464; racial segregation in, 160–61, 191, 194, 247–48, 252–53, 257–60, 464; racial violence in, 220, 253, 464 (*see also* lynching *under this heading*); radio ministries in, 237; religious diversity in, 64, 90, 133; Religious Right in, 325–26; revival meetings in, 82, 240, 244; size of church congregations in, 5, 65–66, 153, 404–5; suburban development of, 247–48; Texas Centennial Exposition in, 154, 157–61, 194; and unemployment during Great Depression, 198, 200; W.W. I and antiwar activism, 221–22

Dallas Council of Churches, 298–99

Dallas Freedom Forum, 287, 288

Dallas Interdenominational Ministerial Alliance, 306–9

The Dallas Morning News (newspaper), 55, 78, 104–5, 134, 160, 215, 238, 245, 248, 257, 280, 358, 361

Dallas Spiritualist Society, 94

Dallas Theological Seminary, 149–50, 152, 239

dancing, 59

Daniel, Price, 254, 259–60

Davis, Addie, 348

Davis, Angela, 308–9

Davis, Archbishop James Peter, 315

Davis, Edmund J., 15, 54, 294

Davis, Fred, 440–41

Davis, James H. "Cyclone," 208

Davis, James Peter, 315

Davis, T. Cullen, 334–35, 342

Dawson, J. M., 66, 82, 128, 165–66, 263, 286

death penalty: and biblical commandment against murder, 190; electrocution as method of, 85, 86, 504n122; practice theory and, 456; public executions, 41–43, 47, 49–50, 85; racial dynamics of, 49–50, 85–86, 187, 208; reforms of justice system, 85–86; religion and sacralization of, 49–50, 85

Defense of Marriage Act, 423–24

deficit, federal, 363, 375, 380, 384, 406, 408, 435, 437–38. *See also* taxes

Democratic Party: and civil rights as signature issue, 370; Dixiecrats in the South, 250–52; and fiscal conservatism, 367, 383; freedom of religion and, 96; and healthcare reform as issue, 389, 435, 443; and immigration reform as issue, 432; and independent parties, 317; Methodists and support of, 265; National Convention in Houston (1928), 117; New Deal and, 197, 224; and poverty as issue, 11, 12, 308, 371, 375, 391; race and affiliation with, 322, 445; and racial equality as political issue, 119; religious affiliation and support of, 114–16; and Roman Catholic

Church, 322; voting constituencies of, 322, 376–77, 407, 428, 432

demonstrations: antiabortion protests, 385, 386, 418; campus unrest, 300, 304, 315–18; Chicano activism and, 310–13; civil rights marches, 305, 322; civil rights movement, 293, 299–301, 306, 322; clergy involvement in, 293, 301, 308, 322; against ERA, 359; fundamentalist concerns and, 384; MegaMarch Rally for immigration reform, 430, *431*; police brutality during, 300, 306; for prohibition, 108; Salvation Army and, 108; Tea Party rallies, *435,* 435–36; Vietnam War protests, 316–17; against W.W. I, 95. *See also* boycotts

Denny, Collins, 232

denominations, 2; differences among, 323; and financial support of churches, 39–40; intradenominational conflicts, 125–27; nondenominational congregations, 399, 404; nondenominational programs, 239; and party affiliation, 9–10, 251–52; symbolic boundaries and, 3. *See also specific denominations*

Denton, 73, 150

depression. *See* Great Depression

desegregation: churches and, 232, 248–49, 261, 268, 289, 291, 395; federal government and, 248–49, 255, 258–60, 289–90; interposition and efforts to block, 256; popular opinion and, 254–55, 262; and property values, 252–53; and racially-motivation violence, 220, 253–54; of religious organizations, 256–57; religious organizations and opposition to discrimination, 256–57; of schools, 223, 254–55, 259–63, 261, 289, 299–300, 544n125; of universities, 254; violent reaction to integration efforts, 220

Dewhurst, David, 443–44

Dickson, W. L., 168–69

Dickson Colored Orphanage, 168–69

Diehl, Grover L., 209

DiNardo, Daniel, 430

Disciples of Christ, 52, 64, 73, 95, 230; founding of Texas Christian University, 73; membership and congregation statistics, 230

diseases: AIDS, 393, 423; cholera, 20, 22; epidemics, 20, 21–22; as frontier hazard, 7–8, 17, 20–24; mortality rates from, 20, 487n27; venereal, 360; yellow fever, 21–23, 52, 186, 456, 496n3 dispensational theology, 10, 146–51, 192, 209, 238, 343, 411

Dixiecrats, 250–52

Dixon, A. C., 139–40

Dobson, James, 423, 439, 442

Dodge, William E., 60

Dole, Bob, 362, 415

Domenech, Abbé Emmanuel, 17, 35, 38–39

Doughty, Robin W., 23

drouth, 10, 19, 152, 199–200, 209, 216

DuBois, W.E.B., 154, 156, 166

Dukakis, Michael, 374–75, 379–81, 391

Durant, Will, 289

Durkheim, Émile, 449, 450, 451

dust bowl drouth, 199–200, 209

Dyer, G. W., 183–84

Dyer, Leonidas C., 163

Eagle, Joe H., 171–72

Eagle Forum, 352, 414

Ebaugh, Helen Rose, 396

economic development of Texas, 19, 124–25, 135, 226–28; church buildings and civic development, 247; and church resources, 124; government relief programs and, 190, 216; military spending and, 226–27, 243, 244, 288; and national political power, 226; oil industry and, 124, 202–3, 228, 235; post--W.W. II, 236; in rural areas, 227; transportation and, 19, 45, 55, 68, 86, 100, 128–29, 157, 186, 219, 487n18

Eddy, Sherwood, 248–49

education, 4–5, 9; African American schools, 188; bilingual, 313, 314, 380–81; *Brown v. Board of Education of Topeka,* 223, 254, 256, 261; as campaign issue, 390, 391; Catholic schools, 115, 261; churches and promotion of public, 30–31; as civilizing force, 30; civil rights activism and level of, 311; Common school laws and public, 30; denominational affiliation and level of, 234, 235; enrollment statistics, 30, 31, 33, 71, 73, 315, 490n68; *Everson v. Board of Education,* 262; evolution in school curriculum, 122, 123, 125, 130–36, 140–46, 426; for freed slaves, 45; fundamentalism and objections to curriculum in, 124, 285–86 (*see also* evolution *under this heading*); funding of schools, 71, 115, 218, 390; literacy, 179, 190; moral values instruction in schools, 58–59, 286–87; night schools, 102; prayer

in the schools, 1, 96, 115, 285, 360, 399, 414, 443; public funding for religious school, 262–63; racial discrimination unequal opportunities for, 71–73, 249, 292–93, 313; racial segregation of schools, 33, 254; racial uplift and, 172–73; religion in the public school curriculum, 78, 96; school desegregation and integration, 223, 254–55, 259–63, 261, 289, 299–300, 544n125; sex education controversies, 423; student boycotts and protests, 299–300; Texas as textbook market, 410; textbooks and controversial content, 140–41, 151, 158, 285–86, 399, 410, 426; voucher programs and school choice, 393, 414, 442; for women, 51–52. *See also* seminaries; universities and colleges

Edwards, C. D., 118

Edwards, John N., 62

Ehlers, Allen, 329

Eisendrath, Maurice, 321

Eisenhower, Dwight, 10, 223, 255–56

El Campo, lynchings in, 162–63

elections, gubernatorial:
 1869, Davis/Hamilton, 15;
 1910, Colquitt/Campbell, 179–81;
 1924, Ferguson/Butte, 182;
 1962, Cox/Connally, 294;
 1978, Clements/Hill, 332;
 1986, Clements/White, 378;
 1990, Richards/Williams, 372, 382, 386;
 1994 Bush/Richards, 372, 390–91

elections, presidential:
 1900, Bryan/McKinley, 178–79;
 1904, Roosevelt/Parker, 112, 178–79;
 1908, Taft/Bryan, 110–12, 510n76;
 1928, Hoover/Smith, 110–11, 181, 512n111;
 1940, Roosevelt/Willkie, 256;
 1948, Truman/Dewey, 250–52, 255;
 1952, Eisenhower/Stevenson, 10, 255, 294–96, 544n129;
 1956, Eisenhower/Stevenson, 10, 294;
 1960, Kennedy/Nixon, 10, 270, 294–96;
 1964, Johnson/Goldwater, 269–70, 294–96;
 1968, Nixon/Humphrey, 294–97;
 1976, Carter/Ford, 340–41, 346–47, 352–53, 367;
 1980, Reagan/Bush primary, 12, 338, 362–65;
 1980, Reagan/Carter, 270, 325–27, 337–38, 353, 375, 567n103;

1984, Reagan/Mondale, 377, 386;
1988, Bush/Dukakis, 369, 374–78, 380, 391;
1992, Clinton/Bush/Perot, 12, 391;
2000, Bush/Gore, 395, 402–3, 407, 424;
2004, Bush/Kerry, 406, 407, 419;
2008, Obama/Romney, 12, 416, 420, 428, 432, 435
elections, senatorial:
1922, Mayfield/Ferguson, 116, 174, 175;
1962 Tower/Yarborough, 294–96;
1964, Bush/Cox, George H. W., 294
electoral politics: clergy as political candidates, 44–47, 296, 298; endorsements of candidates by churches or clergy, 115–20, 276–77, 308, 309, 339–41, 377–78. *See also* campaign issues; elections; voting constituencies
Ellison, Lynn Ray, 388
El Paso: anti-abortion activism in, 414, 418; Catholic population in, 112, 261, 429; Chicano activism in, 313–14; civil rights activism in, 314; desegregation of schools in, 261–62; gay rights in, 421, 423; during Great Depression, 200–201, 216; immigration issues in, 429, 431; Mexican American population in, 290–91; race relations in, 180, 261, 262; racial demographics in, 113; segregation in, 262; student rights movement in, 313–15
employment: in agriculture, 204–7, 227; fair employment legislation, 248; illegal immigrants as scapegoats for unemployment, 379; migrant workers, 262; minimum wage and, 97, 188, 207, 262, 293, 310, 381, 411; New Deal jobs programs, 215–17; in professions, 83; Progressive-era legislation, 97; racial discrimination in, 305; religious discrimination in, 96; sexual orientation and discrimination in, 421–22; unemployment during Great Depression, 198, 200–201, 204–5, 210, 212, 215–17. *See also* labor
Engel v. Vitale, 285
Engerman, Stanley L., 20
Episcopal Churches, 35; black churches formed, 167–68; desegregation and, 261, 268; membership and congregation statistics, 230, 338; ordination of women, 348
Equal Rights Amendment, 346–56, 362, 364, 381, 382, 390, 411, 462, 466
Eskridge, Edgar, 208
Estell, E. C., Sr., 299, 306
Estes, Sol, 269

Evangelicalism, 35; and anti-Semitism, 321; Jimmy Carter and, 363–64, 367; National Association of Evangelicals, 244, 482; nondenominational organizations and, 245–46; organizational structure of ministries, 245–46; parachurch ministries and, 245–46; political engagement and, 270, 272, 326, 585n92; prosperity gospel messages and, 242, 244–45; religious broadcasting and, 270; and Republican affiliation, 13; Southern Baptist Churches and, 95, 397, 481–82; strictness as symbolic boundary, 476–77; Texas and, 10–11
Evangelical Theological College, 149–50
evangelism: conversion or proselytization and, 95, 321, 397–98, 429, 576n87; door-to-door, *213*; financial support of ministries, 245; Graham, 240–41, 482; independent churches and, 320–21; institution building, 245; missionaries and international, 244, 320; nondenominational organizations and, 245; organizational structure of ministries, 245–46; parachurch ministries and, 245–46; prosperity gospel messages and, 242, 244–45; religious broadcasting and, 270; support of foreign/international missionaries, 320; in Texas, 35. *See also* broadcasting, religious; missionaries; revival meetings
Everson v. Board of Education, 262, 263
evil: frontier and civilization as fight against, 8–9; and mobilization, 411; racialization of, 8–9, 13; religion and definition of, 4, 7
evolution, 10, 131; antievolution legislation proposed, 143–44; Free Thinkers and, 133; as heresy, 134, 137, 144, 147, 342–43; human progress, 56; legislative efforts to bar teaching of, 141–42; and liberty of conscience, 426; modernist / fundamentalist division on, 138–40; as political campaign issue, 144; in school curriculum, 122, 123, 125, 130–36, 140–46, 426; Scopes trial, 131, 144; Texas Freedom Network and, 426; in textbooks, 140, 151, 158, 285–86, 426

faith-based programs: and appeals to minority voters, 395, 398; Charitable Choice, 399–400; conservative organizations and, 402; cost effectiveness of, 401–2; government funding for, 400–402, 407; prison ministries, 394–95, 402; separation of church and state, violations of, 402; success rates of, 401

Falwell, Jerry, 11, 270, 325–26, 337, 343, 362, 366, 367, 370, 381

Family Altar (radio program), 328

Family Research Council, 431, 442–44

Farenthold, Frances Sissy, 352

Farrell, Bishop Kevin, 418

Farrow, Betty, 23

fascism, 541n90

Fatjo, Tom J., 365

Federal Communications Commission (FCC), 330, 335–37

federal government: antipathy toward, 443; desegregation efforts and the, 248–49, 255, 258–60, 289–90; as evil, 209; federal funding for abortion and birth control, 360; financial oversight of religious organizations, 341; Great Society welfare legislation, 11, 12, 308, 371, 375, 391; integration as imposition by, 284–85; and national political influence of Texas, 6, 11–12, 226, 372, 410, 444–45; New Deal and changing role of, 196–97, 255; regulation by, 106, 209, 219–20, 237, 330, 335–37, 380, 385; states' rights and, 40, 55, 57, 194–95, 250, 286, 352, 363, 365, 432; as threat to conservative religion and values, 341, 437–38. *See also* anti-government ideology; "big government"; fiscal conservatism; Supreme Court

federalism, 2

Ferguson, James E., 116, 174, 175, 186

Ferguson, Miriam A. "Ma," 182, 382

Ferrin, Minnie, 127

Feuerbach, Ludwig, 136

Finley, N. Webb, 136

First Baptist Church of Dallas, 126, *319*, 339, 367, 404

First Contact, 405–6

fiscal conservatism, 12; as campaign issue, 12, 377, 382, 390–92, 397, 407, 435–36, 585n94; deficit spending and, 363, 375, 380, 384, 406, 408, 435, 437–38; Democratic Party and, 367, 383; and faith-based initiatives, 407; religious conservatism and, 437, 445; Religious Right and, 12, 365, 367; Republican Party and, 363, 369–70, 372, 375, 377, 380, 384–84, 407, 442; Richards and, 382; social program spending and, 380, 384; and "southern strategy," 407; Tea Party movement and, 412–13, 435–40; as value in Texas, 12, 412–13

Flores, Archbishop Patrick Fernandez, 262

Focus on the Family, 442

Fogel, Robert W., 20–21

Foote, Billie and Winky, 334

Ford, Gerald, 340, 347, 364

foreign policy, U. S., 258, 363, 384

Forman, James, 308

Fort Sam Houston, 216, 421

Fortune, George, 127

Fort Worth: abortion protest in, 418; antiwar movement in, 316; Baptist churches in, 65–66, 128; broadcast ministries based in, 242; Catholic population in, 113; clergy and political engagement in, 118–19; economic development of, 128–29, 153, 155; fundamentalism in, 137–38, 141, 144; growth and economic development in, 98, 155, 227, 236; institution building in, 73, 75, 102–3, 129–30, 168, 236, 247; Ku Klux Klan in, 174–76; Presbyterian Churches in, 137; prohibition in, 108; race relations in, 113, 170, 247, 261; revivals in, 82, 240; size of church congregations in, 65–66, 153; Southwestern Baptist Theological Seminary, 73; suburban development of, 247–48; Tea Party activism in, 438–39

Fort Worth Star Telegram (newspaper), 389–90

Foundations of Social Theory (Coleman), 477

Fraser, William, 249

Freedman's Bureau, 45

freedmen: education of, 53; as political candidates, 47; voting rights, 32–33

freedom, intellectual, 130, 132–35, 142–43, 196, 322, 344, 384

freedom of religion, 1; as American value, 1, 95, 151, 266; coercion and, 37; fundamentalism and, 151; individualism and, 96–97; international recognition of, 263; minority religions and, 94–95; religious diversity and, 398–99; Roman Catholicism as threat to, 93, 96, 112, 114–15, 266; in Texas, 90–91, 103–4, 112. *See also* liberty of conscience; separation of church and state

freedom of speech: FCC regulation as violation of, 336–37; and intellectual freedom, 142–43; as moral danger, 142–43; student activism for, 271, 316, 322

FreedomWorks, 439–40

Freeman, Elisabeth, 166

Free Thinkers, 133

frontier: crime on, 23; death rates on, 21; disease on, 22–23; economic opportunity on,

28; and "evil" as racialized, 8–9, 13; frontier ministries, 35–41; frontier religion *vs.* "settler" religion, 323; lawlessness on, 23, 27; pioneers and settlement of, 17–18; and religion as nomizing, 7–9; as "rough country," 3–4, 7–8, 27; social order and civilization of, 25–26; Texas as, 6

Fuller, Charles E., 237, 330

fundamentalism: and antipathy toward federal government, 331–32; biblical literalism and, 136, 138–44, 152, 196, 343–46, 384, 440, 481; and conservative reforms, 192; Darwinian evolution and, 122, 130–36; dispensational theology and, 10, 123, 146–52, 192, 209, 238, 343, 411; higher criticism and, 136, 138, 139–41, 144, 147, 151–52; immigration and, 122; membership in fundamentalist churches, 150; modernism and, 122, 125–26, 136–40, 144–46, 152, 186, 231; origins of, 122; political influence of, 370, 391; and public school curriculum, 140–46; as religious identity, 367; respectability and, 367; revivals and, 58; shift to evangelicalism, 482; socioeconomics status and, 380; and strictness as symbolic boundary, 476–77; in Texas, 121–25. *See also* Evangelicalism

Fundamentalist (newspaper), 130

The Fundamentals (essay collections), 137

Furey, Archbishop Francis James, 315, 359

Gabler, Mel and Norma, 285

Gaines, Matthew, 47

Galveston: anti-abortion activism in, 414; Catholic population in, 261; crime in, 23; disease epidemics in, 20–22; gay rights in, 423; during Great Depression, 216; growth and economic development in, 98; institution building in, 73; natural disasters, 19–20, 22; prohibition in, 59–60; racial demographics in, 113; religious diversity in, 90, 94, 95–96

gambling, 106, 130, 210, 280, 284

Gambrell, J. H., 107, 128, 170

Garcia, Hector, 262

Gardner, David M., 240

gender, 271–72, 284, 326, 366; church engagement and, 80–82, 284, 456–57; discrimination in workplace, 346, 349; equality (*see* Equal Rights Amendment); feminist movement, 347; morality and gender roles, 80, 271–72; political campaigns and gender roles, 385–86; religion and definition of

gender roles, 347–48; traditional gender roles, 385. *See also* homosexuality; women

George, Robin, 443

Get Together (television program), 333–34

Gibbs, Barnett, 499n39

Gilbreath, Wes, 385

Gildersleeve, Fred, 165–66

Gildersleeve, Philip, 20

Gilmore, Texas, 168

Gingrich, Newt, 390

Give Us Liberty: A Tea Party Manifesto (Armey and Kibbe), 439

Godfrey, Bill, 199, 205

Goldenberg, Irwin, 317

Goldwater, Barry, 12, 269–70, 272–74, 278

Gonzales, Corky, 314

Gonzalez, Antonio, 310

Gonzalez, Henry, 262

Gordon, Tyrone, 430

Gore, Al, 395, 403

Goree, Eliza "Tommie" Nolley, 51, 53

Goree, Langston, 20–21, 83

Goree, Langston, III, 84

Goree, Melissa Hayes, 52

Goree, Robert, 21

Goree, Robert D., 52

Goree, Sarah Kittrell, 20–21

Goree, Thomas J., 53, 83–84

Gough, John B., 36

Gracida, Rene, 386

Graham, Billy, 225, 320, 357, 365, 420; and evangelistic "crusades," 240–41; racial integration and, 254, 258; and Youth for Christ, 240, 242, 244, 254, 258, 276–77, 283–84, 292, 296

Graham, Jack, 351

Grahmann, Bishop Charles, 418

Grapes of Wrath (Steinbeck), 198, 203, 210, 217, 286

Grassroots America, 438–39

Great Depression, 10; churches as relief providers during, 211–15; as context for social reform, 194–95; economic impacts on churches, 201–2; fundamentalism during, 151–52, 209–10; healing ministries during, 207; humor and, 210–11; Twenty-Third Psalm as rewritten during, 210; unemployment during, 198, 200–201, 204–5, 210, 212, 215–17. *See also* New Deal

Great Society, federal welfare legislation, 11, 12, 308, 371, 375, 391

Greeley, Andrew, 476–77
Gregory, Carl C., 118–19
Gregory, Joel, 339, 345
Griffin, Charles, 23
Grisham, David, Jr., 426
Groner, Frank S., 219
Groner, Orville, 219
Guerra, Carlos, 313
gun control, 282, 381, 390
Gurasich, Marj, 489n53
Gutiérrez, José Angel, 292–93, 314

H. E. Butt Foundation, 241
Habits of the Heart (Bellah, Madsen, Tipton, Sullivan, and Swindler), 399
Hagee, John, 404
Hale, Edward Everett, 32
Haley, J. Evetts, 285–86, 295
Hall, Jacquelyn Dowd, 194
Hallettsville, Texas, 86–87, 419
Hamburger, Richard, 423
Hamilton, Andrew Jackson, 16
Hammer, Buck, 329
Hance, Kent, 382
Hankins, Barry, 427
Hanks, R. T., 127, 140–42
Hanna, Sallie, 186, 190, 253, 419
Hanson, John, 397–98
Hardin-Simmons University (Abilene Baptist College), 73, 296, 343
Hardy, J. C., 188
Hardy, Lulu Daniel, 190
Hargis, Billy James, 285, 287–88, 321
Harper, William Rainey, 138, 186
Harris, James G., 341
Hartzell, Joseph C., 496n137
Harvey, Paul, 342
Hatfield, Mark, 244
Hayden, S. A., 127–28
Hayes, Melissa, 21
Haynes, Richard "Racehorse," 336–37
healing ministries, 207, 237
healthcare reform, 218, 380, 389, 433, 435, 438–39, 443
Hechter, Michael, 463–64
Hedrick, Wyatt C., 228
Heflin, James Thomas "Cotton Tom", 116–17
Heflin, R. T., 52
Heintzelman, Samuel, 36
Henry, Carl F. H., 244

Henry Holt Publishing., 288
Herbener, Mark, 305, 324
heresy, 134, 137, 142, 144, 238, 342–43
Heschel, Abraham, 277, 289
Hester, Arthur Clayton, 420
higher criticism, 131, 136, 138
Hill, John, 332
Hilliard, Bill, 351, 355
Hill's Chapel, 67
Hinduism, 396–98
Hispanic Americans: abortion and, 386–87, 406, 413; as Baptists, 290; Chicano activism, 310–15; cooperation with African Americans, 314; Democratic party affiliation, 322, 428; desegregation and, 255, 261–62, 290; discrimination against, 262; as ethic identity, 474; immigration and, 290–91, 474, 511n87; labor activism and organization by, 207, 262, 293, 305–7, 310, 312, 314; as political candidates, 314–15; relief programs and, 197–98; religion and ethnicity, 473–74; religiosity of, 428; Roman Catholicism and, 9–10, 290; and vote suppression, 379–80; as voting constituency, 313, 374, 376–77, 380, 386–87, 390, 403, 407, 432, 442; welfare programs and, 376. *See also* Mexican Americans
Hispanic Baptist Convention of Texas, 429
Hobbs, Lottie Beth, 350–53, 355, 565n62
Holbrook, Bob, 419
Holbrook, T. J., 216
Holcomb, Luther, 266–68, 298–99, 302, 305, 306, 465
Holland, George, 305–6
Holley, Helena, 186
Holmes, Oliver Wendell, 180
Holmes, Zan, 298, 317–18
homosexuality, 11, 276, 370, 420–27, 446; Anita Bryant and campaign against, 335; broadcast ministries and homophobia, 335–36; churches and antihomosexual activism, 335–36, 423–24, 581n47; civil rights violations against gays, 420–24; clergy and attitude toward, 422, 424–25; inclusion-oriented theologies and, 425; job discrimination, 420–21; Metropolitan Community Church and inclusion, 422–23; and mobilization of clergy, 322; and murder of John Lord, 420; as political issue, 407, 424–25; public opinion on, 424–25; same sex marriage, 1, 406, 424–26, 428, 437

Honey, Catherine (Cora Ella), 488n35
Honey, George W., 22, 44–47, *46*, 465, 494n132
Honey Grove, Texas: (1885), *62*
Hooper, Ben W., 183
Hoover, Herbert, 110–20, 118, 206, 215
Hoover, J. Edgar, 288, 318
Horton, Willie, Jr., 379, 572n25
Hoshizaki, Reiji, 241
hospitals and medical centers, 4–5; abortion services and, 360; religious organizations and founding of, 75; socialized medicine and government support of, 218
housing, 220; construction, post–W.W. II, 236; Dallas Housing Authority Board, 267; racial segregation and access to, 247, 252–53
Houston: anti-abortion activism in, 414; anti-war activism in, 316, 317; Camp Logan riot, 187; Catholic population in, 113, 261; Chicano activism in, 313; churches in, 5, 44, 64, 82, 105–6, 247, 393; conversion, objections to fundamentalist, 397–98; crime in, 23, 41–44, 85, 281, 464; Democratic National Convention in, 117; ERA and conventions in, 353; gay rights in, 423–26; during Great Depression, 198–201, 212, 216; growth and economic development in, 5, 10, 15, 98, 227, 236, 468; institution building in, 73, 168, 189, 254, 321; megachurches in, 5, 393, 404–5; prohibition in, 59–60, 104, 106; racial demographics in, 113, 252–53, 290–91; racial segregation in, 247, 252–53, 260, 291–92, 299–300, 464; religious diversity in, 64, 90, 396–98; republican primary debate in, 362–63; school integration in, 299–300; size of church congregations in, 65–66 (*see also* megachurches *under this heading*); suburban development of, 247–48, 253; television ministries in, 242; textbook controversies in, 286; yellow fever in, 21
Houston, Sam, 16, 38, 90, 92, 462, 464
Houston, Sam W., 159–60
Houston Infirmary Sanitarium, 75
Hout, Michael, 476–77
Howard, W. F., 241
Hubbard, Richard B., 84
Huckabee, Mike, 334–36
Huff, Thomas B., 196
Huie, Janice Riggle, 430
Humbard, Rex, 321, 330
Humphrey, Hubert, 269–70

hunger strikes, 305
Hunt, Elizabeth Bunker, 331
Hunt, Ellen Finley, 331
Hunt, H. L., 228, 266, 287–88, 296, 318, 331, 353
Hunt, J. W., 512n113
Hunt, Nelson Bunker, 331, 365
Huntsville, 51–54, 53–54, 86; town center (1870s), *55*
Huntsville Prison, 52, 85–86, 405, 504n108
hurricanes, 22, 281, 446

Iannaccone, Laurence R., 475–77
identity: church membership and community, 66; conservatism as symbolic boundary, 367–68; fundamentalists and religious, 367; and "other" as evil or inferior, 4, 355; religious idioms and narratives of, 2–3; self-made wealth and Texan, 382–83; symbolic boundaries and, 463; Texas as "Southern" state, 121, 123, 138–39, 290; us/them distinction and, 476–77
immigration: border patrol, 427–28; and change in religious demographics, 113–14, 396; churches and assistance to immigrants, 429; conservative opinion and, 430–31; fundamentalism and, 122; and growth of conservative denominations, 477; Hispanic population and, 377; as humanitarian issue, 427–28, 430; illegal, 427–28; immigrants as labor force, 200, 262, 379, 429; Islam and Muslim, 396–97, 458, 474–75; legislative reform efforts, 431–32; MegaMarch Immigration Rally in, 430, *431*; as political issue, 397, 429–32; population growth and, 97–98, 428, 477; reform and party preference, 432; religion and immigration rights advocacy, 432; and religious diversity, 396–97; and wage suppression, 262; xenophobia and, 281–82
income: and electoral politics, 255, 406–7; faith linked to worldly success, 329; and opposition to ERA, 351; and party preference, 372, 376–77, 380–81, 386, 390–91, 403, 406–7; prosperity, gospel of, 242; race and, 291; and tax burden in Texas, 375–76, 433–34
income inequality, 227; clergy and critiques of, 209; as moral issue, 208; and regressive taxes in Texas, 375–76, 433–34, 445; in Texas, 434. *See also* poverty

independent voters, 255, 390, 416

individualism, 9; entrepreneurs and, 469; in faith and spirituality, 399–400; morality and, 77, 84–87, 219; professionalism and, 84; religious freedom and, 96–97; social norms and, 84–87

institution building: churches and, 4, 74, 168–69 (*see also under specific denominations*); as competition between state and churches, 73–75; as defense against evil (crime), 70–71; and evangelicalism, 245; and nomizing role of religion, 7–9; philanthropy and, 468–69; progressivism and, 56–57; and racial integration, 468; religion and, 4–5, 48; religion and civic, 71; settlement of frontier and, 29; social order and, 25–26. *See also specific institutions*

intellectual freedom, 130, 132–35, 142–43, 196, 322, 344, 384

intelligent design, 1, 135–36, 426

interdenominational organizations, 102, 268

interfaith cooperation, 267, 277, 397, 400

interposition, 256

interracial cooperation, 156, 159–60, 183, 189–94, 247

Inter-Varsity Christian Fellowship, 245

Islam, 396–98, 400, 426, 441, 458, 474–75

Italy, Texas, 66

itinerant preachers, 35–36, 37

Ivins, Molly, 389–90

Ivy, Robert L., 248

Jackson, Jesse, 309

Jackson, Samuel Macauley, 148

Jake, T. D., 405

James, E. S., 266

James, Larry, 408

Japanese Americans, 173–74, 190

Jehovah's Witnesses, 132, 148

Jenkins, Walter, 269, 274–76, 274–77, 356

Jestor, Beauford, 250

Jews, 78–79, 95–96, 99, 129, 267, 391; abortion and, 358–59; anti-Semitism, 95, 96, 190, 321; conflicts with Southern Baptists, 397; desegregation and, 261; efforts to convert, 95, 321; ERA supported by, 355; population in Texas, 338; support of Chicano activism, 310; as voting constituency, 391

John Birch Society, 272, 286, 287

John Sealy Hospital, Galveston, 75

Johnson, Alexander, 174

Johnson, C. Oscar, 249

Johnson, Jake, 41–44

Johnson, Lady Bird, 267

Johnson, Lyndon Baines, 250, 269; civil rights and, 10–11; elected president, 270; Great Society legislation and war on poverty, 11, 12, 284, 308, 371, 375, 391; Kennedy assassination and, 225; as Kennedy's running mate, 264; and religious idiom, 272–74; as senatorial candidate, *252*

Johnson, Peter, 305

Johnson, Torrey, 239, 240

Johnson, Virginia, 211

Jones, Bob, 367

Jones, Bob, Jr., 332

Jones, Clifford, 224

Jones, Jesse Holman, 228

Jones, John T., 228

Jones, Sam, 82

Jonesboro church wars, 238

Jordan, Barbara, *300*, 300–302, 308, 316, 353

Judaism. *See* Jews

Juneteenth celebrations, 160, 161, 162, 173, 462

juvenile delinquency, 189, 243–44, 278, 283–85, 330–31, 332, 394, 470; faith-based programs and, 401; "wayward" girls, 168, 189

Kansas, 480–81

Kaufman, David S., 91–92

Keene (Bishop of Methodist Episcopal Church South), 131

Kelton, Elmer, 18

Kennedy, John F., 270; anti-Catholicism and, 266; assassination of, 225, 268, 281–82, 296; and Catholics as voting constituency, 264; clergy and support of, 267–68; and separation of church and state, 264–66

Kennedy, Robert F., 301

Kerrvill, 216

Khrushchev, Nikita, 278

Kibbe, Mark, 439

Kilgore, Presbyterian church in, 203–4

Killeen, Texas: Baptist Church in, *81*

King, Martin Luther, Jr., 277, 299–300, 301, 305, 307, 308

King, Rodney, 388

Kittrell, P. W., 52

Knickerbocker, Hubert D., 100–101, 116, 175

Koch, Fred, 287, 552n58

Kuba, Louis, 300

Ku Klux Klan, 25, 46, 122, 165, 378; anti-
    Bolshevism and, 173–74, 181; anti-
    Catholicism and, 156, 176; anti-Semitism
    and, 96; opposition to, 94, 175, 248; political
    influence of, 173–77, 174, 181, 182, 379;
    as prohibition advocates, 156; racism and
    appeal of, 156; religious mission of, 176; and
    violence, 174–75
Kulman, Katherine, 321
Kushner, Tony, 423

labor: African Americans and agricultural
    labor, 19, 206; boycotts, 305–7, 310, 312;
    collective bargaining organizations, 206–7,
    293, 310; Hispanics and labor activism,
    207, 262, 293, 305–7, 310, 312, 314; im-
    migrants as labor force, 200, 262, 379, 429;
    migrant labor, 200, 262, 310; prison labor,
    189
ladies auxiliaries, 70, 74, 81, 83, 168, 452
La Grange, Texas, 21
La Marque, Texas, 283
Land, Richard, 419, 430–31, 442
Landrum, Lynn, 225, 248, 258, 263–64
Landry, Tom, 336
land speculation, 26–27
language: abstract "code" in political cam-
    paigns, 378, 383, 407; and "anti-saloon"
    framing of prohibition, 107; bilingual
    education, 313, 314, 380–81; eloquence as
    ministerial skill, 100, 496n137; English as
    official, 380–81; and "faith" as inclusive term
    in, 398–99; gender inclusive, 348; Spanish-
    language church services, 429. See also
    religious idiom
The Last Temptation of Christ (film), 384
Latter-Day Saints, 218–19, 350
law, rule of, 9
lawlessness. See crime
Lawson, William, 299–300
League of United Latin American Citizens
    (LULAC), 313
Lee, Charles, 379
Lee, Sheila Jackson, 423
Leininger, James R., 442
LeTourneau, Evelyn, 246
LeTourneau, R. G., 225, 242–46, 246
Levi, Leo N., 78–79
liberation theology, 322
libertarianism, 12, 397
Liberty Institute, 439

liberty of conscience, 89–97, 331; and Baptist
    separation of church and state, 89, 114–15;
    and church involvement in prohibition,
    106–7; and civil rights of others, 95; and
    defense of minority faiths, 426–27; and
    engagement in politics, 410–11; and minor-
    ity churches, 94–95; and social reform, 103;
    and Texas civil religion, 90–97, 104, 157,
    462; theism as essential to, 96–97
Life Line (radio program), 287–88, 330
Lindsay, D. Michael, 439
Link, J. B., 126–27
literacy, 33, 374, 392
Lloyd, "Brother" (Sunday School teacher, Italy,
    Texas), 66
Lochman, John B., 25
Lockhart, Clinton B., 138
Logan, Fred, 309–10
Log Cabin Republicans, 424
Longview, Texas, 187, 203, 228, 235, 242, 243,
    258, 436
Lord, John, 420
"lost cause" and Southern identity, 138–39
Loveland, B. W., 14–15, 41–44
Lowber, James William, 100, 133
Lowrey, Joseph E., 303
Lubbock, 151, 199, 202, 214, 216, 227, 315,
    316, 323–24
Luce, Tom, 382
Lucey, Archbishop Robert E., 261, 262, 267,
    293, 311, 358
Luter, Fred, Jr., 587n115
Lutheran Churches, 360; gay rights issues
    and, 422; membership and congregation
    statistics, 338; Ohio Synod, 64; ordination of
    women, 348
lynching, 5, 10; antilynching legislation, 163,
    473; and biblical commandment against
    murder, 190; churches and antilynching
    advocacy, 182–94; clergy involved in, 208;
    demographics of victims, 164–66; first-hand
    accounts of, 165–66; frequency of incidents,
    163–65, 170, 182, 188; immolation as ele-
    ment of, 69, 165–66; interracial coopera-
    tion and opposition to, 156, 183, 189–90;
    Ku Klux Klan and, 25, 165, 174; "outrage"
    against white women as narrative, 68–69,
    162–63, 165, 170, 185, 194; practice theory
    and, 456; public opinion and decline in, 182;
    religion and, 165; women's mobilization
    against, 185–90, 473

Maddox, F. E., 147
Malone, Bill C., 205, 210
Mansbridge, Jane, 354
Manuel, Victor, 428
Marcy, Randolph B., 17
marginalization, social, 322, 367
marriage: civilization and institution of, 29, 50;
    Defense of Marriage Act, 423–24; gender
    equality as threat to, 355; interracial, 170,
    289, 461; prostitution and, 62–63; same-sex,
    1, 406, 411, 423–28, 437, 441
Marshall, Texas, 40, 66, 73, 174
Marshall, Thomas R., 117
Marshall, Thurgood, 256
Martin, Fred, 419
Martin, J. C., 111, 133
Martin, Matthew Thomas and Martinism,
    127, 133
Martin, William C., 233, 235, 267
Martinez, Thomas, 314
Masters of Deceit (Hoover), 288
Mathis, Texas, 309–10
Matteson, Glenn, 288
Mattox, Jim, 382
Matzner, John A., 357
Mayfield, Earle B., 116, 151, 174, 175, 518n149
McCain, John, 383, 420
McCarley, Howard, 199
McCarthyism, 122, 233, 237–38
McCorvey, Norma, 415, 418, 420, 481
McCotter, George, 340
McGovern, George, 309
McIntire, Carl, 276, 330
McKnight, H. L., 504n122
McNary, Charles L., 163
McPherson, J. Gordon, 171, 176, 177
Medeiros, Humberto, 293, 311–12
media: censorship of, 140–41, 286; FCC
    regulations and, 237, 330, 335–37; film
    used as political ad, 278–79, 289; and global
    ministries of Southern Baptist Church,
    241–42; "moral decay" and the, 282, 283;
    National Religious Broadcasters Association
    formed, 238; publishing, religious, 152, 168;
    religious newspapers, 59, 114, 126–28, 130,
    138, 170, 234, 239, 240, 261, 266, 267, 336,
    389; religious objections to content in, 384.
    See also broadcasting, religious
medicine: alcohol as medicinal, 60, 499n30;
    birth control, 223–24, 284, 360, 390, 415–16,

418, 442–43 (*see also* abortion); government
    and socialized, 218, 389; healing ministries,
    207, 237; healthcare reform, 389, 433, 435,
    438–39, 443; legal restrictions on birth
    control, 415–16; medical and dental schools,
    28, 158, 196. *See also* hospitals and medical
    centers
megachurches, 5, 246, 370, 393, 404–5, 405–5,
    481
Mencken, H. L., 121
Meredith, James, 298–99
Merton, Thomas, 277, 289
Methodist Churches: abortion and, 357, 361;
    anti-Catholicism and, 112–14, 116–20, 267;
    antilynching advocacy and, 176–77, 187–
    94; and antiwar activism, 317–18; Baptist
    Church as competition, 37, 63–66, 229–36,
    453, 475, 492n99; Chicano activism and,
    310; desegregation and, 232, 248–49, 261,
    268, 289, 291, 395; division between north-
    ern and southern branches, 40; education
    and membership in, 234; ERA supported
    by, 350, 355; evolution and, 131, 134–35,
    144–45, 148–49; and faith-based service
    initiatives, 395; fundamentalism and, 10,
    58, 139, 141, 144–45, 148–49, 152; gay
    rights issues and, 422, 423; and Hispanic
    Americans, 293, 310; immigration reform
    as issue, 430; institution building, 51–52,
    73–76, 158, 201; membership and congre-
    gation statistics, 35–36, 38, 63–66, 80, 114,
    129, 229–35, 338, 464, 491n84; merger of
    northern and southern branches, 231–36;
    ordination of women in, 348; organizational
    structure of, 193, 466; pacifism and, 221;
    political engagement of clergy, 44–47, 116,
    118, 120, 295; political influence of, 10,
    112, 119, 124–25, 264–65; prohibition as
    issue, 59–61, 104–10, 116; resources of, 40,
    100, 201, 216, 232, 233, 366, 464, 531n24;
    Roman Catholic Church as competition,
    480; and separation of church and state, 89–
    90, 106–7, 111, 217; and Youth for Christ,
    239. *See also* African Methodist Episcopal
    Church; African Methodist Episcopal Zion
    Church
Methodist Episcopal Church, 40, 125
Methodist Episcopal Church South, 63–64
Metropolitan Community Churches, 335, 422,
    423, 425

Mexican Americans, 474; agricultural labor and, 200, 207; Chicano activism, 11, 310–15; demographics of Texas residents, 113; Great Depression and impact on, 200, 207; and healing ministries, 207; income statistics, 227; Ku Klux Klan and attacks on, 174; labor activism and organization by, 207, 312, 314; racial prejudice against, 32

Mexican American Youth Organization (MAYO), 310–14; rally, *311*

Mexico: religious broadcasting from, 237; religious oppression in, 90–91, 93; War of Texan Independence against, 90–91, 113

Michau, M. M., 43

migrant labor, 200, 212–13, 262, 293, 310, 445

Miller, Keith, 365

Miller, William E., 275

Millican, Texas, 21–22

Mills, C. Wright, 122, 506n25

minimum wage, 97, 188, 207, 293, 310, 381, 411

missionaries, 58, 99–100, 128, 238; Baptist, 150, 167, 169–70, 193, 234, 320; and education, 45, 73; international evangelism and, 244, 320; itinerant preachers on the frontier, 35–36; Methodist, 193–94; overseas, 100, 168, 239, 243, 244, 246, 287, 320; Roman Catholic missions during colonial period, 112–13; social events as missionary work, 81–82; youth ministries, 239, 243

Mitchell, Bennie, 162

Mitchell, Jules, 41

Mitchell, Maggie, 25

moderate politics and politicians, 371, 381–82

Mondale, Walter, 313, 377

Moody, Dan, 121

Moody, Dwight L., 147

Moore, John W., 118, 135, 232, 235

morality: churches as responsible for, 63, 280–81; civil rights as moral issue, 289; Great Depression framed as moral failing, 209–10; individualism and, 77; Ku Klux Klan as enforcers of social norms, 174–75; legislation as moral instrument, 60–63, 249, 418; moral relativism and situational ethics, 279–80, 283, 370–71; moral strictness as symbolic boundary, 470–71, 475–77; newspapers and "moral decay" stories, 280; as political campaign issue, 208, 269, 272–86; public executions as moral instruction,

85–86; respectability and, 4, 83–84; schools as site of moral education, 58–59, 286–87; sex equality as immoral, 355–56; "sexual revolution" and changing, 280, 282–83, 318–20, 356–58, 366, 421; situational ethics and, 356–57, 370; social norms and church membership, 78–79, 81–83; symbolic boundaries and moral criteria, 470–71

Moral Majority, 326, 370, 382, 441

Moral Man and Immoral Society (Niebuhr), 277

Morehead, Richard, 352

Morris, Willie, 122

Moses, Rex, 386

Mothers for Moral America, 278–79

Mouzon, Edwin D., 116

Moyers, Bill, 272

multilevel theories, 455–59

Muñiz, Ramsey, 314

Murchison, Clinton Williams, 228, 283, 288, 296, 342

murder: of B. W. Loveland, 41–44; homophobia and, 420–21; Jake Johnson trial, 420; of Jesse Washington, 165–66; of John B. Lochman, 25; of John Lord, 420; as racially motivated, 25; as symptom of moral decay, 282; T. Cullen Davis trial, 334–35; of Thomas Crawford, 421. *See also* lynching

Muslims: as voting constituency, 396–97. *See also* Islam

Myers, Beverly, 350, 355

Nacogdoches, 26, 27, 28, 36, 175, 216, 439

Nation, Carry, 104

National Association for the Advancement of Colored People (NAACP), 180, 187–88, 220, 223, 254, 256, 261, 267, 306, 309

National Association of Evangelicals, 244, 482

National Baptist Convention, 309

National Conference of Christians and Jews (NCCJ), 267

National Religious Broadcasters Association formed, 238

natural disasters, 10, 19–20, 199–200, 446

Navarro, James, 310

Navasota, 21, 66, 84

Navigators, 245

Nazarene Churches, 230

Neblett, Lizzie Scott, 38, 48–49

Neblett, Will, 34

Neff, Pat, 250

neo-orthodox theology, 277

New Deal: agricultural subsidies, 205–6, 215–16; and changing role of government, 196–97, 255; construction projects, 216; and income equality, 228; long-term influence on Texas politics, 223; opposition to, 197, 216, 218, 255; racial equality and, 190

The New Metaphysicals (Bender), 455

newspapers: African American, 159–60; and narratives of moral decay, 280, 282; religious publishers, 59, 114, 126–28, 130, 138, 170, 234, 239, 240, 261, 266, 267, 336, 389. *See also specific newspapers*

Newton, Louie, 263

Niebuhr, Reinhold, 277, 281, 289, 341

Nixon, Richard, 10, 259, 264, 304, 313, 322

Nolley, Eliza "Tommie," 51, 53, 79

nomizing role of religion, 7–9

nonconformity, 80, 96–97

Noonan, Peggy, 373

Norquist, Grover G., 397

Norris, J. Frank, 128–30, 138–39, 142–46, 150–52, 158, 192, 202, 222, 249–51, *251*, 263, 411; arson trail of, 130; and *Fundamentalist* newspaper, 130; murder trial of, 145; racism and, 257; and radio broadcast ministry, 237, 328–29

Northern Baptists, 134, 159, 231, 249; evolution and, 143; factionalism and, 143, 145

nuclear weapons, 177–78, 272–73, 277–78, 288

Obama, Barack, 12, 418, 420, 428, 432, 437, 585n96; healthcare reform, 435, 443; opposition to, 435–36, 441–42

Ochoa, Bishop Armando, 429, 431

Odessa, 199, 315, 436

oil industry: and church resources, 202–3, 219, 236; and economic growth of Texas, 124, 202–3, 228, 235; and economic inequality, 434; employment in, 202–3; government regulation of, 106, 219–20, 228–29; and income inequality, 228; oil field (1930), *202*; and philanthropy, 468–69; political influence of, 226, 228–29, 256, 259; tax incentives for, 380, 434; tidelands oil leases, 554n132; wells owned by Presbyterian Church in Kilgore, *203*

Olasky, Marvin, 369, 388, 395, 396–97, 398, 401

Olazabál, Francisco, 207

Old-Fashioned Revival Hour (radio program), 237, 330

Olmstead, Frederick Law, 16–17, 32, 37

Olmstead, John Hull, 16–17, 37

Operation Rescue, 370, 386, 406, 414, 415

Orange, Texas, 208

orphanages, 4, 74–76, 87, 100, 101–2, 126, 168–69, 243–44; Buckner Orphans' Home, *101*, 393; orphans at work, *169*

Osteen, Joel, 404–5

Osteen, John, 404–5

Ostrom, Henry, 139

Otey, Armistead George, 51

Otey, James Hervey, 51

Otey, Lillian, 51

Otey, Martha Ann, 51–53, 79

the Other, 4, 281–82

Ovnand, Chester, 288

Owens, James, 305

pacifism, 221, 243

PADRES, 313

Palin, Sarah, 443–44

Pampa Daily News (newspaper), 275

parachurch ministries, 237–41, 245–46, 268, 469, 482

Parham, Charles, 465

Paris, Texas, 66, 68

Parker, A. C., 175

Parker, Allen, Jr., 414, 417

Parker, Alton, 112, 179

Parker, Sandy, 44, 465

Parkland Hospital, Dallas, 75

Parnell, Harvey, 238

partisan politics: ideological polarization and, 271, 304, 369–70, 371, 479; and liberal/conservative labels, 321–22, 383–85. *See also* Democratic Party; Republican Party; voting constituencies

Patterson, Paige, 342, 343–44, 397, 466

Patton, Francis L., 137

Paul, Ron, 278

Peale, Norman Vincent, 245, 280, 283, 365

Pearson, Drew, 256

Pearson, R. G., 82

Pease, Elisha Marshall, 496n137

Peña, Bishop Raymundo J., 418, 430, 432

Pentacostal churches: healing ministries, 207, 237; membership in, 230

Perkins, Tony, 442

Perot, H. Ross, 12

Perry, Rick, 6, 12, 409, 415, 417, 432–33, 435, 441–43

Personal Responsibility and Work Opportunity Act (1995), 391

Peterson, Alex, 199

Pew, J. Howard, 243

philanthropy: institution building and, 468–69; oil industry wealth and, 468–69; religiously oriented, 137, 234, 243–45, 365, 388, 393

Phillips, Bobby Joe, 315

Planned Parenthood, 294, 360, 414, 416, 443

Points of Light service initiative, 369, 373–74, 381–82, 385

polarization, 271, 304, 370–71, 479

police brutality, 303–4, 306, 309–10, 313, 315

political patronage, 84

poll taxes, 156, 161, 177–81, 248, 291, 295, 298, 445, 472

Pooley, Edward M., 421

population: birthrate statistics, 231; churches and number of families in area, 38–39; gender demographics on frontier, 29–30; and growth in congregations, 80–81; immigration and, 97–98, 113–14, 377, 396, 428, 477, 511n87; migration and, 290; mortality rates, 20, 487n27; number of clergy per resident, 500n48; postwar "baby boom," 229, 233–34, 236, 282–83, 477; racial demographics (see racial demographics); "white flight" to suburbs, 247–48

Populism, 139, 208, 272, 432

positive thinking, 245

Post, Don, 310

Potts. C. S., 183

poverty, 139, 375; abortion rates and, 413; faith-based programs to relieve, 388; hunger, 308, 468; hunger strike and campaign against hunger, 305; Johnson's Great Society legislation and war on, 11, 12, 284, 308, 371, 375, 391; as moral issue, 139, 208; New Deal relief programs, 190; as personal failing, 402–3; prosperity, gospel of, 242; racial minorities and, 227; rates in Texas, 434; welfare programs as socialist or communist threat, 216, 288, 389, 435

The Power of Positive Thinking (Peale), 243

practice theory, 455–57, 472

premillenialism, 10, 146–52, 329, 343, 411–12, 516n81

Presbyterian Church, 35, 40, 82, 99, 100, 203–4; abortion and, 358–59; African American congregations formed, 167; antilynching activism and, 166, 186–87; Billy Graham and, 240; birth control and, 223–24; and birth control as issue, 223; ERA supported by, 350, 355; and evolution, 131, 141, 144; fundamentalism and, 137, 141, 148–49; gay rights issues and, 422; Ku Klux Klan and, 178; membership in, 35, 37, 230–31; ordination of women, 348; political engagement of clergy, 47; and prohibition, 104, 107, 109, 118; racial segregation and, 248, 254, 261, 268; separation from Federal Council of Churches, 223–24. *See also* Cumberland Presbyterian Church

Presler, Charles W., 37

Pressler, Paul, 331, 343–44, 370, 442, 466

Priddy, Ashley, 365

prisoner-of-war camps in Texas, 226

Prison Fellowship{~?~thin#}/{~?~thin#}InnerChange, 395

prisons: faith-based programs and, 394–95, 401; reform efforts, 85–86, 97, 101, 102, 183, 188, 192, 390, 394–95, 471, 504n108; Texas State Penitentiary in Huntsville, 52, 85–86, 405, 504n108

progressivism, 55–56, 97–103; economic reforms and, 97; evolution and, 133; fundamentalist conservative reforms as response to, 192; social Darwinism and, 133–34

prohibition, 94, 274; and anti-Catholicism, 119–20; "blind pig" operations and, 60; churches and support of, 104–5; constitutional amendment of 1887, 61, 500n43; demographics and support of, 104–5; denominations and, 61; as federal law, 151; Ku Klux Klan support for, 156; local option laws, 60, 61, 103–4, 107–8, 110, 181, 323, 467, 508n48; medicinal sales of alcohol, 60, 499n30; as political issue, 103–20, 104–7, 110, 115–17, 499n39, 508n48, 509n69 (*see also* turnout *under this heading*); and race relations, 179–80; repeal of, 208, 217; Texas state-wide referendum (1910), 104–7, 110, 508n48; turnout rates in votes on, 105, 110, 508n48, 509n69, 525n116; women's suffrage and, 182

Promise Keepers, 399

proselytizing. *See* conversion

prosperity gospel collect, 242, 244–45

prostitution, 30, 62–63

Protestant Churches. *See specific denominations*

Protestants and Other Americans United for Separation of Church and State, 262–63

protests. *See* demonstrations

public executions, 85

public religion: Religious Right and, 366–68; and social order, 47–50

Public Religions in the Modern World (Casanova), 454

Putnam, Robert D., 479

Quakers, 35, 94

quarantines, 21, 23

Raatz, Gretchen, 350

race (as concept): "evil" as racialized, 8–9, 13; symbolic boundaries and, 3, 460; whiteness as racial construct, 474

race relations: and Asian Americans, 190; federal government and, 190, 284–85 (*see also* desegregation); interracial cooperation, 156, 159–60, 183, 189–94, 247; "living peaceably," 171–72; miscegenation laws, 170, 289, 461; racial inequality, 5, 33, 166–67, 184, 208, 289, 445–46; racial uplift, 166–73, 184, 191–92; religion and, 6, 167–68, 184, 445–46, 474; Texas Centennial Exposition, 154–63, 167, 191–92, 194; W.W. II and, 220–23. *See also* racism; segregation

racial demographics: of Dallas, 113, 159, 252–53, 290, 340, 464; of El Paso, 113; of Galveston, 113; of Houston, 113, 252–53, 290–91; immigration and, 511n87; migration and, 290; slavery as influence on, 31–32; of Texas, 8, 290, 473–74; of welfare recipients, 197–98, 376

racism: "code" in political campaigns, 378, 383, 407; conflated with anti-socialism, 173–74, 181; conservatism and racial exclusion, 367–68; fiscal conservatism and, 12; Hispanics as targets of, 91–92, 207, 292; Ku Klux Klan and racially motivated violence, 25, 67, 165, 174; in legal system, 41–44; and political campaign practices, 12, 270; in political campaigns, 12, 119, 270, 278–79, 378–79; during Reconstruction, 32–33; religion and perpetuation of, 389; religious rationales for, 171, 173, 257–58; revivalists and, 70; social Darwinism and, 57–58, 171–72; as social injustice, 188, 208; and "Southern strategy" of Republican party, 269–70; whites and

"reverse" discrimination, 379. *See also* segregation

radio ministries. *See* broadcasting, religious

railroads, 19, 45, 55, 68, 86, 128–29, 157, 186, 219, 427–28, 487n18

Rains, Jack, 382

Rankin, George C., 105–6

rape: as "outrage" against white women, 67–69, 162–63, 165, 170, 185, 194; statistics, 281

Rapoport, Bernard, 389

Raspberry, William, 391–92

rational choice theory, 449–50, 452–54, 458, 470, 472

rationalization, 451

Rayburn, Sam, 119, 226, 250

Raza Unida Party, 312–14, 317, 379

Reagan, Ronald, 11, 567n103; and "big government" as campaign issue, 363, 373, 384; as disappointment to conservatives, 384; fiscal conservatism and, 364–65; and Goldwater, 278; Reagan/Bush primary, 362–65; Religious Right and, 270, 325–26, 362, 367–69, 384

Reasoner, Calvin, 61

Reconstruction, 5; bitterness in Texas toward, 24; chaotic evil and violence during, 9; clergy as political candidates during, 44–45; partisan politics and, 34–35; race relations and, 8, 32–33, 54, 67–69; rape or "outrage" narratives, 67–69; and rise of African American churches, 167; and suspicion of federal government, 60, 197; violence during, 9, 15, 16, 24–25, 41–44, 54

Red Summer (1919), 187

referendums: ERA, 347; marriage amendment, 424; poll tax, 177; prohibition, 104–7, 110, 508n48, 509n69

regulation, government: and control of alcohol sales, 108; FCC regulations and, 237, 330, 335–37; progressive-era legislation and, 103; and progressive reforms, 97; and public/private social service partnerships, 394

relief: churches as providers of, 212–13, 214, 439–40, 446; concerns about dependency on, 212; government programs (*see* welfare, government programs); hunger assistance, 305, 308, 375, 376, 468; international humanitarian, 393; private charities and, 211–15, 429. *See also* New Deal; welfare

religious freedom. *See* freedom of religion; liberty of conscience

religious idiom, 2–3; comfort provided by, 210; and "morality" in political discourse, 272; in political discourse, 272–74, 278–79, 399–400; political discourse and deployment of, 272–74, 399–400; in public discourse, 48–49; and public school curriculum, 78; revival meetings and, 48; and sacrilization of death penalty, 49; and social reform, 193–94; in women's self-expression, 34–35

The Religious Messenger (newspaper), 126

religious prejudice: Americanism and Christianity, 174

religious prejudices, 398, 400, 426. *See also* anti-Catholicism; anti-Semitism

Religious Right: abortion and, 426; broadcast ministries and, 328–33, 335–37, 370, 381; Bush, G. W. and, 391, 402–3; "culture wars" and, 370–71; evolution and, 426; and faith-based service provision, 402; fiscal conservatism and, 12, 384, 437–38; Moral Majority and, 326, 370, 382; political influence of, 12–14, 269–70, 325–27, 370–71; as reaction to social changes, 270, 326–27, 370–71; Reagan and, 270, 325–26, 362, 367–69, 384; Republican Party and, 12–14, 269–70, 325–26, 337–38, 362–72, 371, 381, 402, 403, 406; and Robertson as presidential candidate, 381; Robison and, 333–37; Roloff and, 328–33; and separation of church and state, 403

Republican Party: African American voters and, 180; as anti-abortion, 361, 369; and "compassionate conservatism," 373; and conservatism, 361; and diversity of electorate, 374; financial resources of, 410; fiscal conservatism and, 363, 369–70, 372–73, 375, 377, 380, 384–85, 407, 437, 442; and gay marriage as political issue, 424; Hispanic American voters and, 313, 374, 386; and homophobia, 424; Log Cabin Republicans, 424; and racist political campaign practices, 12, 269–70; religious conservatives as voting constituency, 370, 386, 402–4, 446–47 (*see also* Religious Right *under this heading*); Religious Right and, 12–14, 269–70, 325–26, 337–38, 362–72, 381, 402, 406; "Southern strategy" and, 269–70, 407; Tea Party movement and, 441, 447

respect or respectability, 4, 8, 43, 83, 87, 368

Reston, James, 273

The Restructuring of American Religion (Wuthnow), 479

revival meetings, 38–39, 48, 50, 70, 89, 152; and competition between denominations, 37; demographics and, 82; described, 66; fundamentalism and, 122, 131, 139; prejudice and, 139; racial integration of, 320; religious idiom and, 48; Roman Catholicism and, 207; rural camp meetings, 98; temperance and, 38, 59; urban revivals, 82

"Revolution of 94," 391

Rice, John R., 152

Rice University, 73, 316

Richards, Ann, 372, 382, 384–87, 390–91, 394

Richardson, Bill, 380

Richardson, Sid W., 228–29, 255–56, 283–84, 296

Richardson, Thomas Hooker, 57–58

Richardson, Willard, 55–58, 87

Riedel, Anton, 1, 13

Riedel, Nicholas, 1, 13

right-minded individualism, 9

Riley, W. B., 139, 150

riots, 145, 179, 187, 279, 300, 303, 388

Roberts, Oral, 321, 384

Robertson, Pat, 11, 270, 326, 337–38, 370, 385, 406; as political candidate, 371, 381, 382

Robinson, Joseph Taylor, 117

Robinson, Mollie, 207

Robison, James, 333–37

Rocky Chapel, 67

Roger, Ollie Mae, 78

Rogers, Adrian, 344

Roman Catholic Church, 9–10; abortion opposed by, 357–59, 361, 386, 418; African American congregations, 167; anti-Catholicism, 10, 106, 110–17, 120, 176, 218, 223, 260–66, 419; birth control prohibitions, 284; Catholics as voting constituency, 264, 322, 391; Chicano activism and, 310–11, 315; civil rights movement and, 11; congregation and membership statistics, 63, 64, 80–81, 113–14, 261, 338; desegregation and, 261; early missionary activities and Spanish exploration, 112–13; electoral politics and anti-Catholic sentiment, 110–17; employer insurance mandate and birth control, 443; equated with political tyranny, 96; and

Roman Catholic Church (*cont'd*)
immigration issues, 429–30; liberation theology and social justice, 322; liberty of conscience and, 89–90; loyalty to papacy, 115, 118–19, 260–61; missions during colonial period, 112–13; political influence of, 263–64; and prohibition as political issue, 116–17; racial equality and, 261; racial integration and, 261; religious demographics of Texas, 113–14; and religious oppression, 90–91, 93, 112, 118–19; and separation of church and state, 260–61, 264; Vatican II and reforms in, 322
Romney, Mitt, 442–43
Roosevelt, Franklin D., 161, 190, 197; desegregation and, 161
Roosevelt, Theodore, 111, 179
Rope and Faggot: A Biography of Judge Lynch (White), 166
Roper, Harlin J., 239
"rough country," Texas as, 3–4, 17
Rousseau, Jean Jacques, 90
Routh, E. C., 130
Rove, Karl, 406
Rowan, Charles, 219
Royden, Maude, 221
rugged individualism, 9, 28
rural areas: population of, 204, 227; revival meetings and, 82; rural churches and relief efforts, 207; rural voters as constituency, 380–81
Rushbrooke, J. H., 221
Russell, Charles T., 132, 148
Russell Sage Foundation, 215
Rutersville, 21
Rutherford, Benjamin H., 26–27

St. Mary's Infirmary, Galveston, 75
St. Mary's University, San Antonio, 73, 310
St. Matthew's Home for Aged Women in Dallas, 75
Salazar, Gregory, 313
Salazar, Rubén, 313
salvation, 8–9, 469
Salvation Army, 108, 211, 214, 239, 330, 392
Samuel Houston College, 73
San Antonio: anti-abortion activism in, 414; antiwar movement in, 316; broadcasting in, 242; Catholic population in, 261; churches in, 64; civil rights activism in, 315;

fundamentalism in, 144; gay rights in, 423; during Great Depression, 200; growth and economic development in, 227, 236; Hispanic population in, 290–91; prohibition in, 59; race relations in, 261; religious diversity in, 64, 90; size of church congregations in, 65–66
San Augustine, 21, 27, 28, 35, 72
Sanger, Phillip, 96
San Jacinto, battle of, 8, 15–16, 91, 92, 96, 157, 162
Santa Rosa Infirmary, San Antonio, 75
Santorum, Rick, 383, 442, 443–44
Saunders, Landon, 329
Scales, James Ralph, 340
Scarborough, L. R., 142–43
Scarborough, Rick, 439
Schachtel, Hyman, 267
Schlafly, Phyllis, 352–53, 415
Schleiermacher, Friedrich, 136
Schlesinger, Arthur, 341
Schofield Bible, 147–48
schools. *See* education
Schwarz, Fred, 237, 287, 552n59
Scofield, C. I., 121, 147–50, 192
Scopes trial, 131, 144
Scott, Emmett J., 173
Scott, Lizzie, 34
Scroggins, Henry, 16
Seasholes, C. L., 132, 171
secession, 12, 15, 55, 57, 432–33, 436, 463
secularization theory, 449–52, 454, 458, 472
segregation: in Abilene, 257–58; benevolent organizations and racial, 468; churches as racially segregated, 5, 10, 39, 66, 167, 232–33, 247–48, 254, 260, 289, 291–93, 445; in Dallas, 160–61, 191, 194, 247–48, 252–53, 257–60, 464; in El Paso, 262; housing, 247, 252–54; in Houston, 247, 252–53, 260, 291–92, 299–300, 464; as legacy of slavery, 5; religious justification for, 292; of schools, 33, 254; slavery and, 5; of transportation, 160. *See also* desegregation
Seguin, Juan N., 91
Selecman, C. C., 217
Selvidge, W. R., 66
seminaries: and doctrinal consistency, 338–39, 344, 384, 440; establishment of, 87, 90, 100, 124, 144, 149–50, 167, 168, 320–21, 468; fundamentalist concern over curriculum

in, 125, 134–35, 140–42, 144, 151, 193, 231, 233, 342–44, 384; northern seminaries and liberal theology, 122, 135, 140–41, 231, 233, 263, 467; and spread of dispensational theology, 149–50

separation of church and state, 61; Baptist doctrine and liberty of conscience, 89, 114–15; and church involvement in prohibition, 106–7; as constitutional law, 451; constitution of Texas and, 93–94; and engagement of clergy in social activism, 61, 77, 303–5; and engagement of clergy with social issues, 11; faith-based programs as violation of, 400–401; and nonconformity, 96–97; and prayer in public schools, 285; and public/private social service partnerships, 393–94; and rational choice theory, 472; and relief programs, 217; and religion in public schools, 78; and religious diversity, 426–27; Religious Right and engagement in politics, 403; and roles in institution building, 4; Roman Catholic Church and, 260–61, 264; school curriculum and, 142; secularization theory and, 472; social reforms and issues of, 207; symbolic boundaries and, 472–73

Septian, Rafael, 342

settlement of Texas: economic potential and, 19; population demographics and, 8; promotion of, 39–40

Sevareid, Eric, 274

700 Club (television program), 326

Seven Storey Mountain (Merton), 277

Seventh Day Adventists, 64, 329

sex: birth control and, 284; homosexuality (*see* homosexuality); legislative prohibition of sexual acts, 423; "outrage" against white women as lynching narrative, 68–69, 162–63, 165, 170, 185, 194; and political scandals, 275–77; prohibition of interracial relationships, 170, 289, 461; racism and sexual threat, 45 (*see also* "outrage" *under this heading*); the sexual revolution, 280, 282–83, 318–20, 356–58, 366, 421. *See also* gender

Shackelford, Kelly, 439

sharecropping, 10, 17, 48, 152, 156, 206–7; cotton harvest, 72

Shillady, John, 187

Shriver, Donald, 341

the "silent majority," 301, 304, 322

Skelton, Donald, 329

Slaughter, C. C., 101

slavery: abolition movement, 61; agriculture and, 8, 19, 31–32; clergy and opposition to, 40; conflict with freedom as American value, 13; divisions within denominations regarding, 40; racially segregation and, 5; settler demographics and, 16; Southern Baptist Convention and, 1; Tocqueville on, 26; white supremacy and, 57–58

Smiley, Martha, 350, 355

Smith, Al, 90, 110, 114, 116–20, 181, 217, 331, 512n111

Smith, Bailey, 397, 472–73

Smith, Christian, 476–77

Smith, J. Frank, 137

Smith, Preston, 312

Smith, Sherrill, 310

Smith, W. L., 140–41

Smoot, Dan, 286

social capital, 342, 478. *See also* respect or respectability

social clubs: membership in, 236

social Darwinism, 133–34

Social Environment and Moral Progress (Wallace), 139

socialism, 142–43, 144, 389, 451; "big government" and, 339–40. *See also* Communism

social networks, 477–82

social reforms: and antilynching activism, 183–84; conservative, 191–92; Great Depression as context for, 194–95; and liberty of conscience, 103, 207; prison reform efforts, 85–86, 97, 101, 102, 183, 188, 192, 390, 394–95, 471, 504n108; progressive, 191–92; and race relations, 191; racial uplift as motive, 166–72; social Darwinism and, 171–73; Southern Sociological Congress and agenda of, 183–84

Social Security Act, 217, 219

social services: churches and provision of, 392, 405; government programs for (*see* New Deal; welfare, government programs); Great Depression and overwhelming need for, 211–15; public/private cooperation, 392–93 (*see also* faith-based programs); volunteer organizations and provision of, 387. *See also* welfare, government programs

sociological studies of religion, 448–52

Soliz, Olga, 350

Southeast Asia. *See* Vietnam War
Southern Baptist Churches: abortion as issue, 359, 360, 419; and African American Baptists, 168; anti-Catholicism and, 93, 113–18, 218, 260–66, 263, 419; anti-Communism and, 263; autonomy of clergy, 410; Billy Graham's relationship with, 240–41; and broadcast ministry, 241–42; civil rights legislation opposed by, 248–49; Civil War and, 40–41; Confession of Faith, 143–44; and conservative resurgence, 344–45; demographics of, 125; dispensational theology and, 150; education and membership in, 234; and education issues, 115, 262–64; evangelicalism and, 95, 397, 481–82; evolution rejected by, 125, 130–34, 138–40, 142–45; formation of Southern Baptist Convention, 1; fundamentalism and, 10, 58, 125, 138–40, 142–46, 150–52, 231, 249–50, 342–46, 372, 397–98, 481–82, 517n104; global ministries, 241–42; Hispanic American, 290, 429; homosexuality and, 422, 426; and immigration as issue, 430–31; institution building and, 64, 73, 99, 101, 168–69, 517n104; interdenominational cooperation and, 267; intradenominational conflicts, 125–28, 143–46, 231, 235, 342–46, 372, 410, 425, 481–82; Islam and, 426; in Killeen, Texas, *81*; Ku Klux Klan and, 175–76; lynching and, 163–64, 189–90; membership and congregation statistics, 5, 35–36, 39, 63–66, 80, 98, 99, 129, 167, 229–30, 231, 233–34, 235, 338, 396, 404, 477; Methodist Church as competition, 37–38, 63–66, 229–36, 453, 475, 492n99; and moral decay as issue, 209–10, 279–80; National Baptist Convention, 309; Northern Baptists and, 134, 159, 517n104; organizational structure of, 64, 167, 234, 410, 466; party affiliation and, 322, 342, 481–82; political influence of, 11–12, 112, 116, 119, 124–25, 234, 250–52, 268, 337, 342, 372; prohibition and, 104–5, 110, 116, 117–18; racial inclusion and, 425, 587n115; racial segregation and, 167, 256–59, 260, 289, 291–92, 302; racial uplift and, 167–70, 184, 191; religious tolerance and, 95–96; resources of, 64, 98–102, 201, 202, 219, 531n24; and separation of church and state, 11–12, 88–89, 218, 263, 351, 426; and Southern identity, 99; Texas as stronghold of, 5, 35–36, 234–35, 372; women as

ordained ministers in, 348–49; World War II mobilization supported by, 220–23; and Youth for Christ, 239–40
Southern Christian Leadership Conference (SCLC), 299, 305–8
Southern Interracial Commission, 189–90, 299
Southern Methodist University, 100–101, 158, 164, 189
Southern Sociological Congress, 183–86, 188, 193
Southern Tenant Farmers Union, 206–7
Southwest Advocate (newspaper), 239
Southwestern Theological Seminary, Fort Worth, 73, 95, 138, 142
Southwestern University, 185
Spiritualist churches, 64, 94, 133
Springer, "Ma," 198–99
Staff, Barbara, 365
states' rights, 40, 55, 57, 194–95, 250, 286, 352, 363, 365, 432
Sterling, Ross S., 228
Stevenson, Adlai, 255, 259
Stockman, Steve, 423–23
Strake, George W., 365
Straughn, James Henry, 232
Strong, A. H., 134
student activism, 313–22
Student Non-violent Coordinating Committee (SNCC), 315–16
student rights, 314
Students for a Democratic Society, 316
suburbs: churches and development of, 247–48
suffrage movement, 32–33, 60–61, 182, 186–88
Sumners, Hatton W., 163–64
Sunday, Billy, 141
Supreme Court, U.S.: and African American right to vote, 180; and Agricultural Adjustment Act, 205–6; *Brown v. Board of Education of Topeka*, 223, 254, 256, 261; *Engel v. Vitale* (school prayer), 285; *Everson v. Board of Education*, 262, 263; Hispanic-American civil rights cases, 262; objections to power of, 255–56, 285–86, 438; *Roe v. Wade* decision, 270, 356, 359–60, 384, 412, 414, 415; and segregated transportation as unconstitutional, 270; *Sweatt v. Painter, et al.,* 254; *Webster v. Reproductive Health Services,* 412
Sutton, William S., 188
Swaggart, Jimmy, 381–82, 384–85
Sweatt, Heman Marion, 254

Sweatt v. Painter, et al., 254
The Sword of the Lord (magazine), 152
symbolic boundaries, 3, 354, 449–50, 459–63, 466–67, 469–70; conservatism and racial exclusion, 367–68; languages and emergence of, 354; national border as, 474; realignment or redefinition of, 466; separation of church and state, 472–73; social networks and, 477–78; strictness as, 475–77; and us/them dichotomy, 354, 477–78

Taft, Howard, 110–12, 115
Tammany Hall, 118, 119, 181
Tappan, Arthur, 243
taxes: as campaign issue, 391; government funding of faith-based programs, 400–402; oil industry and tax incentives, 380; popular opinion on, 434–35; race and attitude toward, 434–35; and social services provided by state, 433; Tea Party and taxation as issue, 435–36; in Texas, 375–76, 433–34, 445
Taylor, Charles, 207
Tea Party movement, 12, 435–41, 443–44, 447; Austin rally (2009), *435*; groups affiliated with, 438–40; membership in, 436; and mobilization of conservative religious voters, 439; organizational structure of, 436; Perry and, 409, 413, 435, 441–42; religion and, 436–38, 440, 585n94; Republican Party and, 441, 447; social issues and, 437
Teen Challenge, 394
television: blamed for "moral decay," 282, 283; ministries, 242, 326
Temperance Family Visitor (newspaper), 59
temperance movement, 59–60
tenant farming, 204–7
terrorism, 411, 426. *See also* Ku Klux Klan; lynching
Texarkana, Texas: institution building in, 73, 315; Ku Klux Klan in, 174; lynching at, 69–70, 165
Texas, 13; economic development (*see* economic development of Texas); image and promotion of settlement in, 28–29; national political influence of, 6, 11–12, 226, 372, 410, 444–45; as part of Bible Belt, 8, 121, 123, 225, 325; as part of the Southwest, 123, 158–59; population demographics of, 16, 444–47; proposal to split into multiple states, 54, 464; settlement demographics of,

6–7; Southern identity of, 121, 123, 138–39, 290; and traditional values, 444; War of Independence, 90–91, 113 (*see also* the Alamo; San Jacinto, battle of)
Texas Almanac, 28–29
Texas A&M University, 73, 315
Texas Association of Christian Childcare Agencies (TACCA), 394
Texas Baptist Herald (newspaper), 126, 128
Texas Baptist (newspaper), 126–27
Texas Baptist Standard (newspaper), 138
Texas Blind Asylum, 75
Texas Centennial Exposition, 154–63, 191, 221, 224
Texas Christian University, Fort Worth (AdRan College), 73, 138
Texas Freedom Network (TFN), 426
Texas Holiness Association, 111
Texas Justice Foundation, 414, 415, 416, 417
Texas Observer (newspaper), 389
Texas School for the Deaf, 75
Texas Southern University, 299–300
Texas State Penitentiary, 52
Texas Tech University, 224
Texas Wesleyan University (Polytechnic College), 73
Texas Women's University, Denton, 73
textbooks: controversies over content of, 140–41, 151, 158, 285–86, 399, 410, 426; Texas as market for, 410
Theosophists, 133
Thompson, E. P., 463–64
Thrall, Homer S., 30–31, 33
Thrower, Bob, 329
Thurmond, J. Strom, 250–51, 255, 256
Tijerina, Reies Lopez, 314
Till (freedwoman), 16
Tillich, Paul, 277, 289
Tillotson, Dolph, 384
Tillotson Collegiate and Normal Institute, Austin, 73
Tilly, Charles, 342, 457
Tobolowsky, Hermine Dalkowitz, 350, 355
Tocqueville, Alexis de, 2, 9, 25–26
Toland Chapel, 67
tolerance, 62, 94–96, 238, 396–400, 478–79. *See also* liberty of conscience
Tönnies, Ferdinand, 451
Torrey, R. A., 141
Tower, John, 294–96, 312, 322

transportation: and economic development, 19, 45, 55, 68, 86, 100, 128–29, 157, 186, 219, 487n18; segregated, 160, 170, 186, 248, 254, 270

Travers, R. C., 133

Trinity University, Tehuacana, 73

Truan, Carlos, 312

Truett, George W., 88, 89, 102–3, 115, 128, 136, 154–55, 159, 191, 220–21, 237, 328

Truman, Harry S, 223

Tucker, W. Leon, 139

Turner, Mrs. J. S., 186

Tuscola, Texas, 236

Tyler, Texas, 104, 315, 436, 438

Union soldiers, 67

Unitarian Church, 133, 140–41, 426; gay rights issues and, 422; and religious freedom, 94–95

United Charities, 211–15

United Church Women of Texas, 256

Universalist Church, 64, 348, 426

universities and colleges: desegregation of, 254, 299–300; enrollment statistics, 73, 315; evangelical ministries and, 245–46; intellectual/academic freedom in, 130, 132–35, 142–43, 196, 322, 384; student activism and protests, 315–20; student activism on, 299–300. See also specific institutions

University of Chicago, 138

University of Mary Hardin-Baylor, 73

University of Texas, 73–74, 96, 186, 222, 313–14, 317; enrollments at, 315; evolution and intellectual freedom at, 132–34; mass shooting at, 282; racial integration at, 254

unwed mothers, 74, 75, 87, 355, 360, 468, 470

Valentine, Ryan, 426

Valenzuela, Juan, 329

values and party affiliation, 410–11

Vann, Bishop Kevin W., 418

Van Nuys, Frederick, 163

Velásquez, William C. "Willie," 310–12, 379–80

Vietnam War, 11, 282; anti-Communism and involvement in, 288; anti-war activism, 301–2, 304, 316; casualties in, 288–89; defense contracts and, 288; protests and anti-war activism, 322; public opinion on, 322–23

Viguerie, Richard, 384

Villa Acuña, Mexico, 237

Vinson, Robert E., 186, 188

violence: against abortion providers, 416; Branch Davidian siege, 400; clergy as victims of, 36, 40, 46; police brutality, 303–4, 306, 309–10, 313, 315; during protests, 316–17; Reconstruction as time of lawlessness and, 9, 15, 16, 24–25, 41–44, 54; riots, 145, 179, 187, 279, 300, 303, 388. See also lynching; murder

Vision America, 439

volunteerism, 74, 102

von Frellick, Gerri, 287, 552n61

voting: African Americans and right to vote, 54, 161, 182, 186 (see also vote suppression under this heading); changing population demographics, 376–77; growing diversity of electorate, 374; ideological affiliations, 405; legislation barring participation, 180; literacy rates and, 179; "Loyal League" and, 44; poll taxes and restrictions on, 156, 161, 177–78; religion as factor in, 380; and separation of church as state as issue, 110–11; voter turnout, 105, 110, 178–80, 179, 352–53, 424, 426, 508n48, 509n69, 525n116 (see also suppression under this heading); vote suppression, 23, 32–33, 156, 161, 177–82, 180, 269–70, 272, 379–80, 445; white primaries, 180–81; women's suffrage, 60–61, 182, 186. See also electoral politics; voting constituencies

voting constituencies: African Americans, 60–61, 161, 180, 322, 376–77, 386–87, 390, 403, 407; "Bubba" vote, 386, 407; Catholics, 264, 322, 391; denomination and party preference, 9–10; Hispanic Americans, 313, 374, 376–77, 380, 386–87, 390, 403, 407, 432, 442; income and party preferences, 296, 372, 376–77, 380–81, 386, 390–91, 403, 406–7; Muslims, 396–97; race and party preference, 380, 445, 446–47; religious conservatives, 10–11, 380, 386, 403–4 (see also Religious Right under this heading); Religious Right, 12–14, 269–70, 325–27, 337–38, 362–72, 381, 406; rural voters, 295–96, 380–81; whites, 377, 378, 386, 406, 407; women, 352–53, 354

Waco: Branch Davidian siege in, 400; evolution debate in, 133; gay rights in, 423, 425; growth and economic development in, 98; institution building in, 73, 98–99, 166; Ku

Klux Klan in, 175–76; lynching in, 165–66, 185, 522n55; number and size of church congregations in, 65–66, 98–99, 166; prohibition in, 61; sexual "outrages" reported in, 68–69
Wade, Henry, 359
Waggoner, Leslie, 132
Wagner, Robert F., 163
Walker, Edwin, 284, 286
Wallace, Alfred Russel, 139
Wallace, George, 270, 295, 296, 297
Walsh, G. T., 117
Wanamaker, John, 243
War of Independence, Texan, 90–91, 113. *See also* the Alamo; San Jacinto, battle of
Warren, Earl, 256
Washington, Booker T., 172
Washington, Jesse, 165–66, 522n55
Wayland Baptist University, 73
Wayne, John, 279
Weatherford, Texas, 150
Weatherford, W. D., 184
Weather Underground Organization, 316
Weber, Max, 451, 469
Webster v. Reproductive Health Services, 384, 412
Weddington, Sarah, 350, 355, 359, 382, 390
Weisberg, Alex, 96
Welch, Robert, Jr., 287
welfare, government programs: African Americans and, 220; benefit rates in Texas, 375–76; as "big government," 391; Clinton administration and reforms of, 371, 389–90; cuts in spending on, 434–35; dependency on, 212; faith-based alternatives to, 388; fiscal conservatism and, 369, 375, 380, 407; Great Society legislation, 11, 12, 284, 308, 371, 375, 391; number of Texans on rolls of, 216; private charities as alternatives to, 429; racial demographics of recipients, 197–98, 376; racism and opposition to, 388–89; as redistribution of wealth, 389; religious conservatives and opposition to, 402–3; Republican opposition to, 369; and separation of church and state, 197, 219; as socialist, 216, 288, 389, 435; Social Security Act, 217, 220; state supported, 376, 433; as threat to private institutions, 217. *See also* New Deal
Wells, Jane, 350, 352
Wharton, Turner Ashby, 100
Wheeler, Doc, 41

White, K. Owen, 291
White, Mark, 382
White, Walter, 166
whiteness: as racial construct, 474
white supremacy, 57, 173, 175–76, 248–49
Whitman, Charles J., 282
Why I Preach That the Bible Is Literally True (Criswell), 345
Wichita Falls: Ku Klux Klan, 174, 177; New Deal construction in, 216; prohibition in, 104–5; Tea Party Activism in, 216
Wilde, Melissa, 476–77
Wildmon, Donald E., 438
Wild Woman of Navidad, 18
Wiles, Soloman, 18
Wiley College, Marshall, 73
Wilkerson, David, 330, 394
Wilkins, Roy, 267
Willard, Francis, 61
Willet, Don R., 396, 443
William, Robert H., 30
Williams, Clayton, 372, 382–87, 403, 407
Williams, Dixon, 70, 82
Williams, J. Howard, 95, 240–41, 249
Williams, Lacey Kirk, 154–55, 191, 221
Williams, Roger, 88–89, 94, 113
Willkie, Wendell, 256
Wilson, Woodrow, 95
Winchester, A. B., 139
Winrod, Gerald, 237, 328
Winston, George T., 80
Winter, Gibson, 246
With No Fear of Failure (Fatjo and Miller), 365
Woman's Missionary Union, 169, 348
women: antilynching mobilization and, 185–90, 473; and birth control, 223–24; and church as social sphere, 38; church membership and gender, 80; education for, 84; Equal Rights Amendment, 346, 348–53, 351, 362, 364, 381, 382, 390, 411, 462, 466; feminism and gender equality, 284–85, 322; gender demographics on frontier, 29–30; gender equality, 11, 284–85, 322 (*see also* Equal Rights Amendment *under this heading*); gender roles and church activities, 81–82; as lynching victims, 166; moral education and role of, 79–80; mortality rates on the frontier, 20–21, 487n27; and opposition to racial discrimination, 256; ordination of, 322, 348–49, 477; "outrage" (rape) as justification for racial violence, 67–69, 162–63, 165, 170,

women (*cont'd*)
185, 194; Progressive-era legislation and women's rights, 97; religious idiom and self-expression, 34–35; roles within churches, 349 (*see also* ordination *under this heading*); suffrage and right to vote, 60–61, 182, 186; temperance movement and, 38, 59–60, 104, 118, 182, 186, 189, 190, 193
Women for Constitutional Government, 284–85
Women's Christian Temperance Union (WCTU), 118, 182, 186, 189, 190, 193
Workman, Lyle, 421
World War I, 95
World War II, 220–23
World Wide Church of God, 329
Wright, Clymer, 365
Wright, S. M., 306–8, *307*, 324
Wyrtzen, Jack, 239

xenophobia: and political influence of Ku Klux Klan, 173–77

Yarborough, Ralph W., 265, 282
yellow fever, 21–23, 52, 186, 456
Young Life, 245, 320–21, 342, 482, 552n61
youth: decline in religiosity among, 410; juvenile delinquency, 168, 189, 243–44, 278, 283–85, 330–31, 332, 394, 401, 470; ministries, 102, 201, 238–39, 330–31, 334; parachurch organizations, 238–41, 246; and political activism, 299–300, 304–5, 312–13, 315–18; and sexual promiscuity or premarital sex, 168, 189, 283, 284, 318–20, 421. *See also* juvenile delinquency
Youth for Christ, 239–44, 482

Zaret, David, 466
Ziglar, Zig, 345